The Longman Anthology of World Literature

VOLUME C

THE EARLY MODERN PERIOD

David Damrosch
COLUMBIA UNIVERSITY
The Ancient Near East; Mesoamerica

April Alliston
PRINCETON UNIVERSITY
The Age of the Enlightenment

Marshall Brown
UNIVERSITY OF WASHINGTON
The Nineteenth Century

Page duBois
UNIVERSITY OF CALIFORNIA, SAN DIEGO
Classical Greece

Sabry Hafez
UNIVERSITY OF LONDON
Arabic and Islamic Literatures

Ursula K. Heise
COLUMBIA UNIVERSITY
The Twentieth Century

Djelal Kadir
PENNSYLVANIA STATE UNIVERSITY
The Twentieth Century

David L. Pike
AMERICAN UNIVERSITY
Rome and the Roman Empire; Medieval Europe

Sheldon Pollock
UNIVERSITY OF CHICAGO
South Asia

Bruce Robbins
COLUMBIA UNIVERSITY
The Nineteenth Century

Haruo Shirane
COLUMBIA UNIVERSITY
Japan

Jane Tylus
NEW YORK UNIVERSITY
Early Modern Europe

Pauline Yu
AMERICAN COUNCIL OF LEARNED SOCIETIES
China

The Longman Anthology of World Literature

⊶ ❈ ⊷

David Damrosch

General Editor

VOLUME C

THE EARLY MODERN PERIOD

Jane Tylus

David Damrosch

with contributions by

Pauline Yu and Sheldon Pollock

PEARSON
Longman

New York   San Francisco   Boston
London   Toronto   Sydney   Tokyo   Singapore   Madrid
Mexico City   Munich   Paris   Cape Town   Hong Kong   Montreal

Vice President and Editor-in-Chief: *Joseph Terry*
Development Manager: *Janet Lanphier*
Development Editor: *Adam Beroud*
Senior Marketing Manager: *Melanie Craig*
Senior Supplements Editor: *Donna Campion*
Media Supplements Editor: *Nancy Garcia*
Production Manager: *Douglas Bell*
Project Coordination, Text Design, and Page Makeup: *Elm Street Publishing Services, Inc.*
Senior Design Manager/Cover Designer: *Nancy Danahy*
On the Cover: Detail from *The Geographer,* oil on canvas, by Johannes Vermeer
     (1632–1675). Copyright © The Granger Collection.
Photo Research: *Photosearch, Inc.*
Manufacturing Buyer: *Lucy Hebard*
Printer and Binder: *Quebecor-World/Taunton*
Cover Printer: *The Lehigh Press, Inc.*

Library of Congress Cataloging-in-Publication Data

The Longman anthology of world literature / David Damrosch, general editor.—1st ed.
     v.   cm.
   Includes bibliographical references and index.
   Contents: v. A. The ancient world—v. B. The medieval era—v. C. The early
modern period—v. D. The seventeenth and eighteenth centuries—v. E. The
nineteenth century—v. F. The twentieth century.
     ISBN 0-321-05533-0 (v. A).—ISBN 0-321-16978-6 (v. B).— 0-321-16979-4
(v. C).— 0-321-16980-8 (v. D).— 0-321-17306-6 (v. E).— 0-321-05536-5 (v. F).
     1. Literature—Collections.   2. Literature—History and criticism.
I. Damrosch, David.
PN6013.L66   2004
808.8—dc22
                                                          2003061890

Please visit us at http://www.ablongman.com/damrosch.

To place your order, please use the following ISBN numbers:

ISBN Volume One Package *The Ancient World to The Early Modern Period*
(includes Volumes A, B, and C): **0-321-20238-4**

ISBN Volume Two Package *The Seventeenth Century to The Twentieth Century*
(includes Volumes D, E, and F): **0-321-20237-6**

Or, to order individual volumes, please use the following ISBN numbers:

ISBN Volume A, *The Ancient World:* 0-321-05533-0
ISBN Volume B, *The Medieval Era:* 0-321-16978-6
ISBN Volume C, *The Early Modern Period:* 0-321-16979-4
ISBN Volume D, *The Seventeenth and Eighteenth Centuries:* 0-321-16980-8
ISBN Volume E, *The Nineteenth Century:* 0-321-17306-6
ISBN Volume F, *The Twentieth Century:* 0-321-05536-5

1 2 3 4 5 6 7 8 9 10—QWT—06 05 04 03

CONTENTS

Early Modern Europe   149

≔+ PERSPECTIVES +≔
Lyric Sequences and Self-Definition   226

LOPE FÉLIX DE VEGA CARPIO (1562–1635)   570

WILLIAM SHAKESPEARE (1564–1616)   610

JOHN DONNE (1572–1631)   675

Mesoamerica:
Before Columbus and After Cortés   761

⇒⇐ PERSPECTIVES ⇐⇒
The Conquest and Its Aftermath   810

LIST OF ILLUSTRATIONS

Maps

On the Cover

Detail from Johannes Vermeer, *The Geographer,* 1669. Holding a divider for measuring distances, a geographer looks up from his books and charts to plot the course of exploration in his mind's eye. Vermeer loved to paint intimate domestic spaces, into which the wider world subtly intrudes in the form of a visitor, or a letter, or a painting. Here, maps surround the geographer; a large vellum sea chart is rolled up beside him, more maps are scattered around the floor, and hanging on the wall (see the full image on the back cover) is a map of "all the seacoasts of Europe." The globe on the chest was made in 1618 by the Dutch geographer Jodocus Hondius (whose own portrait can be seen in the world map by his son Hendricus, on the inside front cover of this volume); Vermeer has positioned the globe to show the Indian Ocean. "The geographer" is probably the Dutch scientist Anton van Leeuwenhoek, who passed his examination as a surveyor in February of 1669, the year this painting was made. He shared Vermeer's fascination with optics and was a pioneer in the development of the microscope; he became the executor of Vermeer's estate after his death in 1675. This painting and a companion piece, *The Astronomer,* dramatize the excitement of the new sciences of exploration and discovery being developed during the early modern period.

PREFACE

Our world today is both expanding and growing smaller at the same time. Expanding, through a tremendous increase in the range of cultures that actively engage with each other; and yet growing smaller as well, as people and products surge across borders in the process known as globalization. This double movement creates remarkable opportunities for cross-cultural understanding, as well as new kinds of tensions, miscommunications, and uncertainties. Both the opportunities and the uncertainties are amply illustrated in the changing shape of world literature. A generation ago, when the term "world literature" was used in North America, it largely meant masterworks by European writers from Homer onward, together with a few favored North American writers, heirs to the Europeans. Today, however, it is generally recognized that Europe is only part of the story of the world's literatures, and only part of the story of North America's cultural heritage. An extraordinary range of exciting material is now in view, from the earliest Sumerian lyrics inscribed on clay tablets to the latest Kashmiri poetry circulated on the Internet. Many new worlds—and newly visible *older* worlds of classical traditions around the globe—await us today.

How can we best approach such varied materials from so many cultures? Can we deal with this embarrassment of riches without being overwhelmed by it, and without merely giving a glancing regard to less familiar traditions? This anthology has been designed to help readers successfully navigate "the sea of stories"—as Salman Rushdie has described the world's literary heritage. This preface will outline the ways we've gone about this challenging, fascinating task.

CONNECTING DISTINCTIVE TRADITIONS

Works of world literature engage in a double conversation: with their culture of origin and with the varied contexts into which they travel away from home. To look broadly at world literature is therefore to see patterns of difference as well as points of contact and commonality. The world's disparate traditions have developed very distinct kinds of literature, even very different ideas as to what should be called "literature" at all. This anthology uses a variety of means to showcase what is most distinctive and also what is commonly shared among the world's literatures. Throughout the anthology, we employ three kinds of grouping:

☞ CROSSCURRENTS: A major grouping at the beginning of each volume, bringing together literary responses to worldwide developments.

☞ PERSPECTIVES: Groupings that provide cultural context for major works, illuminating issues of broad importance.

☞ RESONANCES: Sources for a specific text or responses to it, often from a different time and place.

The "Crosscurrents" sections that open our six volumes highlight overarching issues or developments that many cultures have faced, often in conversation with neighboring cultures and more distant ones too. "Creation Myths and Social Realities" in antiquity, for example, brings together creation stories that circulated throughout the ancient Near East, westward to Greece, and eastward to India. "The Folk and Their Tales" in the nineteenth century shows the interplay of folk traditions between India and Europe, Africa and the Americas, Native Americans and Euro-Americans.

Regional divisions predominate in our Volumes A through C, reflecting the distinctive development of the world's major literary traditions over the centuries before the modern period. For each of these volumes, the Crosscurrents provide an initial, cross-cutting overview of a major issue, giving a reminder that there have been important contacts across cultures as far back as we know—and showing too how different cultures can independently address matters of common human concern. In our more globally organized later volumes D through F (mid-seventeenth century to the present), the Crosscurrents demonstrate the increasing interconnectedness of the world's literary traditions.

Throughout the anthology, our many "Perspectives" sections provide cultural context for the major works around them, giving insight into such issues as the representation of death and immortality (in the ancient Near East); the meeting of Christians, Muslims, and Jews in medieval Iberia; the idea of the national poet in the nineteenth century; and "modernist memory" in the twentieth. Perspectives sections also provide an opportunity for focused regional groupings within our globally structured later volumes, with "Other Americas" in the nineteenth century, for example, and "Modernism and Revolution in Russia" in the twentieth. Perspectives sections give a range of voices and views, strategies and styles, in highly readable textual groupings. The Perspectives groupings serve a major pedagogical as well as intellectual purpose in making these selections accessible and useful within the time constraints of a survey course.

Finally, our "Resonances" perform the crucial function of linking works across time as well as space. For Homer's *Iliad*, a Resonance shows oral composition as it is still practiced today north of Greece, while for the *Odyssey* we have Resonances giving modern responses to Homer by Franz Kafka, Derek Walcott, and the Greek poet George Seferis. Accompanying the traditional Navajo "Story of the Emergence" (Volume E) is an extended selection from *Black Elk Speaks* which shows how ancient imagery infused the dream visions of the Sioux healer and warrior Nicholas Black Elk, helping him deal with the crises of lost land and independence that his people were facing. Resonances for Conrad's *Heart of Darkness* (Volume F) give selections from Conrad's diary of his own journey upriver in the Congo, and a speech by Henry Morton Stanley, the explorer-journalist who was serving as publicist for King Leopold's exploitation of his colony in the years just before Conrad went there. Stanley's surreal speech—in which he calculates how much money the Manchester weavers can make providing wedding dresses and burial clothes for the Congolese—gives a vivid instance of the outlook, and the rhetoric, that Conrad grimly parodies in Mr. Kurtz and his associates.

PRINCIPLES OF SELECTION

Beyond our immediate groupings, our overall selections have been made with an eye to fostering connections across time and space: a Perspectives section on "Courtly Women" in medieval Japan (Volume B) introduces themes that can be followed up in

"Court Culture and Female Authorship" in Enlightenment-era Europe (Volume D), while the ancient Mediterranean and South Asian creation myths at the start of Volume A find echoes in later cosmic-creation narratives from Iceland (Volume B), Mesoamerica (Volume C), and indigenous peoples today (Volume E). Altogether, we have worked to create an exceptionally coherent and well-integrated presentation of an extraordinary variety of works from around the globe, from the dawn of writing to the present.

Recognizing that different sorts of works have counted as literature in differing times and places, we take an inclusive approach, centering on poems, plays, and fictional narratives but also including selections from rich historical, religious, and philosophical texts like Plato's *Republic* and the Qur'an that have been important for much later literary work, even though they weren't conceived as literature themselves. We present many complete masterworks, including *The Epic of Gilgamesh* (in a beautiful verse translation), Homer's *Odyssey,* Dante's *Inferno,* and Chinua Achebe's *Things Fall Apart,* and we have extensive, teachable selections from such long works as *The Tale of Genji, Don Quixote,* and both parts of Goethe's *Faust.*

Along with these major selections we present a great array of shorter works, some of which have been known only to specialists and only now are entering into world literature. It is our experience as readers and as teachers that the established classics themselves can best be understood when they're set in a varied literary landscape. Nothing is included here, though, simply to make a point: whether world-renowned or recently rediscovered, these are compelling works to read. Throughout our work on this book, we've tried to be highly inclusive in principle and yet carefully selective in practice, avoiding tokenism and also its inverse, the piling up of an unmanageable array of heterogeneous material. If we've succeeded as we hope, the result will be coherent as well as capacious, substantive as well as stimulating.

LITERATURE, ART, AND MUSIC

One important way to understand literary works in context is to read them in conjunction with the broader social and artistic culture in which they were created. Literature has often had a particularly close relation to visual art and to music. Different as the arts are in their specific resources and techniques, a culture's artistic expressions often share certain family resemblances, common traits that can be seen across different media—and that may even come out more clearly in visual or musical form than in translations of literature itself. This anthology includes dozens of black-and-white illustrations and a suite of color illustrations in each volume, chosen to work in close conjunction with our literary selections. Some of these images directly illustrate literary works, while others show important aspects of a culture's aesthetic sensibility. Often, writing actually appears on paintings and sculptures, with represented people and places sharing the space with beautifully rendered Mayan hieroglyphs, Arabic calligraphy, or Chinese brushstrokes.

Music too has been a close companion of literary creation and performance. Our very term "lyric" refers to the lyres or harps with which the Greeks accompanied poems as they were sung. In China, the first major literary work is the *Book of Songs.* In Europe too, until quite recent times poetry was often sung and even prose was usually read aloud. We have created two audio CDs to accompany the anthology, one for Volumes A through C and one for Volumes D through F. These CDs give a wealth of poetry and music from the cultures we feature in the anthology; they are both a valuable teaching resource and also a pure pleasure to listen to.

AIDS TO UNDERSTANDING

A major emphasis of our work has been to introduce each culture and each work to best effect. Each major period and section of the anthology, each grouping of works, and each individual author has an introduction by a member of our editorial team. Our goal has been to write introductions informed by deep knowledge worn lightly. Neither talking down to our readers nor overwhelming them with masses of unassimilable information, our introductions don't seek to "cover" the material but instead try to uncover it, to provide ways in and connections outward. Similarly, our footnotes and glosses are concise and informative, rather than massive or interpretive. Time lines for each volume, and maps and pronunciation guides throughout the anthology, all aim to foster an informed and pleasurable reading of the works.

GOING FURTHER

The Longman Anthology of World Literature makes connections beyond its covers as well as within them. Bibliographies at the end of each volume point the way to historical and critical readings for students wishing to go into greater depth for term papers. The Companion Website we've developed for the course (www.ablongman.com/worldlit) gives a wealth of links to excellent Web resources on all our major texts and many related historical and cultural movements and events. The Web site includes an audio version of our printed pronunciation guides: you can simply click on a name to hear it pronounced. Finally, the Web site includes readings of works in the original and in translation, with accompanying texts, giving extensive exposure to the aural dimension of many of the languages represented in the anthology.

For instructors, we have also created an extensive, two-volume instructor's manual, *Teaching World Literature*—written directly by the editors themselves, drawing on our years of experience in teaching these materials.

TRANSLATION ACROSS CULTURES

The circulation of world literature is always an exercise in cultural translation, and one way to define works of world literature is that they are the works that gain in translation. Some great texts remain so intimately tied to their point of origin that they never read well abroad; they may have an abiding importance at home, but don't play a role in the wider world. Other works, though, gain in resonance as they move out into new contexts, new conjunctions. Edgar Allan Poe found his first really serious readers in France, rather than in the United States. *The Thousand and One Nights,* long a marginal work in Arabic traditions oriented toward poetry rather than popular prose, gained new readers and new influence abroad, and Scheherazade's intricately nested tales now help us in turn to read the European tales of Boccaccio and Marguerite de Navarre with new attention and appreciation. A Perspectives section on *"The Thousand and One Nights* in the Twentieth Century" (Volume F) brings together a range of Arab, European, and American writers who have continued to plumb its riches to this day.

As important as cultural translation in general is the issue of actual translation from one language to another. We have sought out compelling translations for all our foreign-language works, and periodically we offer our readers the opportunity to think directly about the issue of translation. Sometimes we offer distinctively different translations of differing works from a single author or source: for the Bible, for example, we give Genesis 1–11 in Robert Alter's lively, oral-style translation, while we give selected psalms in the magnificent King James Version and the Joseph story in the lucid New International Version. Our selections from Homer's *Iliad* appear in Richmond Lattimore's stately older translation, while Homer's *Odyssey* is given in Robert Fagles's eloquent new version.

At other times, we give alternative translations of a single work. So we have Chinese lyrics translated by the modernist poet Ezra Pound and by a contemporary scholar; and we have Petrarch sonnets translated by the Renaissance English poet Thomas Wyatt and also by contemporary translators. These juxtapositions can show some of the varied ways in which translators over the centuries have sought to carry works over from one time and place to another—not so much by mirroring and reflecting an unchanged meaning, as by refracting it, in a prismatic process that can add new highlights and reveal new facets in a classic text. At times, when we haven't found a translation that really satisfies us, we've translated the work ourselves—an activity we recommend to all who wish to come to know a work from the inside.

We hope that the results of our years of work on this project will be as enjoyable to use as the book has been to create. We welcome you now inside our pages.

David Damrosch

ACKNOWLEDGMENTS

In the extended process of planning and preparing this anthology, the editors have been fortunate to have the support, advice, and assistance of many people. Our editor, Joe Terry, and our publisher, Roth Wilkofsky, have supported our project in every possible way and some seemingly impossible ones as well, helping us produce the best possible book despite all challenges to budgets and well-laid plans in a rapidly evolving field. Their associates Janet Lanphier and Melanie Craig have shown unwavering enthusiasm and constant creativity in developing the book and its related Web site and audio CDs and in introducing the results to the world. Our development editors, first Mark Getlein and then Adam Beroud, have shown a compelling blend of literary acuity and quiet diplomacy in guiding thirteen far-flung editors through the many stages of work. Peter Meyers brought great energy and creativity to work on our CDs. Donna Campion and Dianne Hall worked diligently to complete the instructor's manual. Celeste Parker-Bates cleared hundreds and hundreds of text permissions from publishers in many countries, and Sherri Zuckerman at Photosearch, Inc., cleared our many photo permissions.

Once the manuscript was complete, Doug Bell, the production manager, oversaw the simultaneous production of six massive books on a tight and shifting schedule. Valerie Zaborski, managing editor in production, also helped and, along the way, developed a taste for the good-humored fatalism of Icelandic literature. Our lead copyeditor, Stephanie Magean, and her associates Martha Beyerlein, Elizabeth Jahaske, and Marcia LaBrenz marvelously integrated everyone's writing, and then Amber Allen and her colleagues at Elm Street Publishing Services worked overtime to produce beautiful books accurate down to the last exotic accent.

We are specifically grateful for the guidance of the many reviewers who advised us on the creation of this book: Roberta Adams (Fitchburg State College); Adetutu Abatan (Floyd College); Magda al-Nowaihi (Columbia University); Nancy Applegate (Floyd College); Susan Atefat-Peckham (Georgia College and State University); Evan Balkan (CCBC-Catonsville); Michelle Barnett (University of Alabama, Birmingham); Colonel Bedell (Virginia Military Institute); Thomas Beebee (Pennsylvania State University); Paula Berggren (Baruch College); Mark Bernier (Blinn College); Ronald Bogue (University of Georgia); Terre Burton (Dixie State College); Patricia Cearley (South Plains College); Raj Chekuri (Laredo Community College); Sandra Clark (University of Wyoming); Thomas F. Connolly (Suffolk University); Vilashini Cooppan (Yale University); Bradford Crain (College of the Ozarks); Robert W. Croft (Gainesville College); Frank Day (Clemson University); Michael Delahoyde (Washington State University); Elizabeth Otten Delmonico (Truman State University); Jo Devine (University of Alaska Southeast); Gene Doty (University of Missouri—Rolla); James Earle (University of Oregon); R. Steve Eberly (Western Carolina University); Walter Evans (Augusta State University); Fidel Fajardo-Acosta (Creighton University); Mike Felker (South Plains College); Janice Gable (Valley Forge Christian College); Stanley Galloway (Bridgewater College); Doris Gardenshire (Trinity Valley Community College); Jonathan Glenn (University of Central Arkansas); Dean Hall (Kansas State University); Dorothy Hardman (Fort Valley State

University); Elissa Heil (University of the Ozarks); David Hesla (Emory University); Susan Hillabold (Purdue University North Central); Karen Hodges (Texas Wesleyan); David Hoegberg (Indiana University-Purdue University—Indianapolis); Sheri Hoem (Xavier University); Michael Hutcheson (Landmark College); Mary Anne Hutchinson (Utica College); Raymond Ide (Lancaster Bible College); James Ivory (Appalachian State University); Craig Kallendorf (Texas A & M University); Bridget Keegan (Creighton University); Steven Kellman (University of Texas—San Antonio); Roxanne Kent-Drury (Northern Kentucky University); Susan Kroeg (Eastern Kentucky University); Tamara Kuzmenkov (Tacoma Community College); Robert Lorenzi (Camden County College—Blackwood); Mark Mazzone (Tennessee State University); David McCracken (Coker College); George Mitrenski (Auburn University); James Nicholl (Western Carolina University); Roger Osterholm (Embry-Riddle University); Joe Pellegrino (Eastern Kentucky University); Linda Lang-Peralta (Metropolitan State College of Denver); Sandra Petree (University of Arkansas); David E. Phillips (Charleston Southern University); Terry Reilly (University of Alaska); Constance Relihan (Auburn University); Nelljean Rice (Coastal Carolina University); Colleen Richmond (George Fox University); Gretchen Ronnow (Wayne State University); John Rothfork (West Texas A & M University); Elise Salem-Manganaro (Fairleigh Dickinson University); Asha Sen (University of Wisconsin Eau Claire); Richard Sha (American University); Edward Shaw (University of Central Florida); Jack Shreve (Allegany College of Maryland); Jimmy Dean Smith (Union College); Floyd C. Stuart (Norwich University); Eleanor Sumpter-Latham (Central Oregon Community College); Ron Swigger (Albuquerque Technical Vocational Institute); Barry Tharaud (Mesa State College); Theresa Thompson (Valdosta State College); Teresa Thonney (Columbia Basin College); Charles Tita (Shaw University); Scott D. Vander Ploeg (Madisonville Community College); Marian Wernicke (Pensacola Junior College); Sallie Wolf (Arapahoe Community College); and Dede Yow (Kennesaw State University).

We also wish to express our gratitude to the reviewers who gave us additional advice on the book's companion Web site: Nancy Applegate (Floyd College); James Earl (University of Oregon); David McCracken (Coker College); Linda Lang-Peralta (Metropolitan State College of Denver); Asha Sen (University of Wisconsin—Eau Claire); Jimmy Dean Smith (Union College); Floyd Stuart (Norwich University); and Marian Wernicke (Pensacola Junior College).

The editors were assisted in tracking down texts and information by wonderfully able research assistants: Kerry Bystrom, Julie Lapiski, Katalin Lovasz, Joseph Ortiz, Laura B. Sayre, and Lauren Simonetti. April Alliston wishes to thank Brandon Lafving for his invaluable comments on her drafts and Gregory Maertz for his knowledge and support. Marshall Brown would like to thank his research assistant Françoise Belot for her help and Jane K. Brown for writing the Goethe introduction. Sheldon Pollock would like to thank Whitney Cox, Rajeev Kinra, Susanne Mrozik, and Guriqbal Sahota for their assistance and Haruo Shirane thanks Michael Brownstein for writing the introduction to Hozumi Ikan, and Akiko Takeuchi for writing the introductions to the Noh drama.

It has been a great pleasure to work with all these colleagues both at Longman and at schools around the country. This book exists for its readers, whose reactions and suggestions we warmly welcome, as *The Longman Anthology of World Literature* moves out into the world.

ABOUT THE EDITORS

David Damrosch (Columbia University). His books include *The Narrative Covenant: Transformations of Genre in the Growth of Biblical Literature* (1987), *Meetings of the Mind* (2000), and *What Is World Literature?* (2003). He has been president of the American Comparative Literature Association (2001–2003) and is general editor of *The Longman Anthology of British Literature* (1998; second edition, 2002).

April Alliston (Princeton University). Author of *Virtue's Faults: Correspondence in Eighteenth-Century British and French Women's Fiction* (1996), and editor of Sophia Lee's *The Recess* (2000). Her book on concepts of character, gender, and plausibility in Enlightenment historical narratives is forthcoming.

Marshall Brown (University of Washington). Author of *The Shape of German Romanticism* (1979), *Preromanticism* (1991), *Turning Points: Essays in the History of Cultural Expressions* (1997), and, forthcoming, *The Gothic Text*. Editor of *Modern Language Quarterly: A Journal of Literary History,* and the *Cambridge History of Literary Criticism,* Vol. 5: Romanticism.

Page duBois (University of California, San Diego). Her books include *Centaurs and Amazons* (1982), *Sowing the Body* (1988), *Torture and Truth* (1991), *Sappho Is Burning* (1995), *Trojan Horses* (2001), and *Slaves and Other Objects* (2003).

Sabry Hafez (University of London). Author and editor of twenty books in Arabic on poetry, drama, literary theory, the Arabic Novel, and the short story, including works on Naguib Mahfouz, Yusuf Idris, and Mahmoud Darwish. His books in English include *The Genesis of Arabic Narrative Discourse* (1993) and the edited volumes *A Reader of Modern Arabic Short Stories* and *Modern Arabic Criticism*. He is a member of the Modern Language Panel of the Arts and Humanity Research Board, the funding council for academic research in the arts and humanities in Britain.

Ursula K. Heise (Columbia University). Author of *Chronoschisms: Time, Narrative, and Postmodernism* (1997) and of the forthcoming *World Wide Webs: Global Ecology and the Cultural Imagination.*

Djelal Kadir (Pennsylvania State University). His books include *Columbus and the Ends of the Earth* (1992), *The Other Writing: Postcolonial Essays in Latin America's Writing Culture* (1993), and *Other Modernisms in an Age of Globalizations* (2002). He served in the 1990s as editor of *World Literature Today* and is coeditor of the *Comparative History of Latin America's Literary Cultures* (2004). He is the founding president of the International American Studies Association.

David L. Pike (American University). Author of *Passage Through Hell: Modernist Descents, Medieval Underworlds* (1997) and *Subterranean Cities: Subways, Sewers,*

Cemeteries and the Culture of Paris and London (forthcoming), and of articles on topics ranging from medieval otherworlds and underground Paris, London, and New York to Canadian cinema.

Sheldon Pollock (University of Chicago). His books include *The Ramayana of Valmiki* Volume 3 (1991) and *The Language of the Gods in the World of Men* (forthcoming). He recently edited *Literary Cultures in History: Reconstructions from South Asia* (2003), and (with Homi Bhabha et al.) *Cosmopolitanism* (2002).

Bruce Robbins (Columbia University). His books include *The Servant's Hand: English Fiction from Below* (1986), *Secular Vocations* (1993), *Feeling Global: Internationalism in Distress* (1999), and a forthcoming study of upward mobility narratives in the nineteenth and twentieth centuries. Edited volumes include *Cosmopolitics: Thinking and Feeling Beyond the Nation* (1998).

Haruo Shirane (Columbia University). Author of *The Bridge of Dreams: A Poetics of "The Tale of Genji"* (1987) and of *Traces of Dreams: Landscape, Cultural Memory, and the Poetry of Bashō* (1998). He is coeditor of *Inventing the Classics: Modernity, National Identity, and Japanese Literature* (2000) and has recently edited *Early Modern Japanese Literature: An Anthology 1600–1900*.

Jane Tylus (New York University). Author of *Writing and Vulnerability in the Late Renaissance* (1993), coeditor of *Epic Traditions in the Contemporary World* (1999), and editor and translator of Lucrezia Tornabuoni de' Medici's *Sacred Narratives* (2001). Her study on late medieval female spirituality and the origins of humanism is forthcoming.

Pauline Yu (American Council of Learned Societies). President of the American Council of Learned Societies, she is the author of *The Poetry of Wang Wei* (1980) and *The Reading of Imagery in the Chinese Poetic Tradition* (1987), the editor of *Voices of the Song Lyric in China* (1994), and coeditor of *Culture and State in Chinese History* (1997) and *Ways with Words: Writing about Reading Texts from Early China* (2000).

Don Cristobal Colon, Admiral of Ships Bound for the Indies. In Honorius Philoponus, *Nova typis transacta navigatio* (1621). In this image from a book by a German monk on missionary voyages, Columbus is poised at Europe's shore, the vast sea stretching away toward the Indies he can see in his mind's eye. The portrait combines eras as well as regions: Columbus is shown with a modern compass and ship, but he seems to bear the globe on his shoulder like the classical giant Atlas, while his feet rest on an ancient Christian symbol, the Anchor of Faith. While one hand gestures toward his charts, the other hand raises up toward God. The globe shows the major islands Columbus "discovered," Cuba and Hispaniola or "Spagnolla," but much more space is given to the lands Columbus himself never believed were there: not India at all but entirely separate continents. Brazil, Peru, Mexico, and North America beckon Honorius's reader to go beyond Columbus to new explorations, conquests and conversions in the still unmapped regions approaching the "Circumference of the Center of Gravity."

The Early Modern Period

In many regions of the world, the centuries between about 1400 and 1650 mark a time of transition from ancient, largely separate traditions to the rapidly evolving and inter-connected world of modernity: the term "early modern" is increasingly used to de-scribe this transitional era. The literatures presented in this volume reflect three great global movements: of worldwide exploration and conquest; of rational and scientific inquiry; and of the growing literary use of vernacular or common speech. These three developments are closely related. The world opened out dramatically after 1492, as the Eastern and Western Hemispheres came into direct contact, and even before then, contacts were intensifying as China's Ming dynasty extended its sway across the In-dian Ocean, the expanding Ottoman Empire linked vast territories from Mesopotamia to eastern Europe, and European navigators explored the coasts of Africa and India. Greatly increased contact between widely separated cultures stimulated reflection on religious doctrines, political structures, and cultural practices of all sorts. And as old traditions came newly into question, the ancient languages that had conveyed them, like Latin and Sanskrit, began to be supplemented and even replaced by modern ver-naculars, as writers sought modes of expression that would reflect the changing real-ity around them.

EMPIRES AND NATIONS

The early modern period was marked politically by two opposing forces: expansive imperial outreach by several major powers, and national consolidation and resistance to outside rule. At times, these forces could actually work together, as when the Castilian monarchs Ferdinand and Isabella conquered the Muslim kingdom of Grenada in southern Spain in 1492; beginning in that very year, the unified nation became a major launching-point for American exploration and imperial conquest. Yet unified nations could also gain new independence from outside control: the Protestant countries of Germany and Scandinavia broke free of papal authority and the related political sway of the Holy Roman Empire, and France, though remaining largely Catholic, asserted an increasingly unified cultural identity and political independence. An important aspect of political and cultural self definition became the establishment of national languages and literatures: French, German, English, and other national languages were increasingly used for serious literary work rather than Latin, and Italy itself was an early leader in "the vernacular revolution" as writers like Dante and Boc-caccio began to use Italian as well as Latin.

Local languages achieved new status in many parts of the world. Korea had long been in China's shadow both politically and culturally, but a new dynasty was estab-lished in 1392 by a general named Yi Song-gye. Under this dynasty, the Chosŏn—which lasted until 1910—specifically Korean arts and culture were cultivated. Like Japanese, Korean had always been written using Chinese characters, but the mid-1400s saw the establishment of a Korean alphabet. The first work written in the new

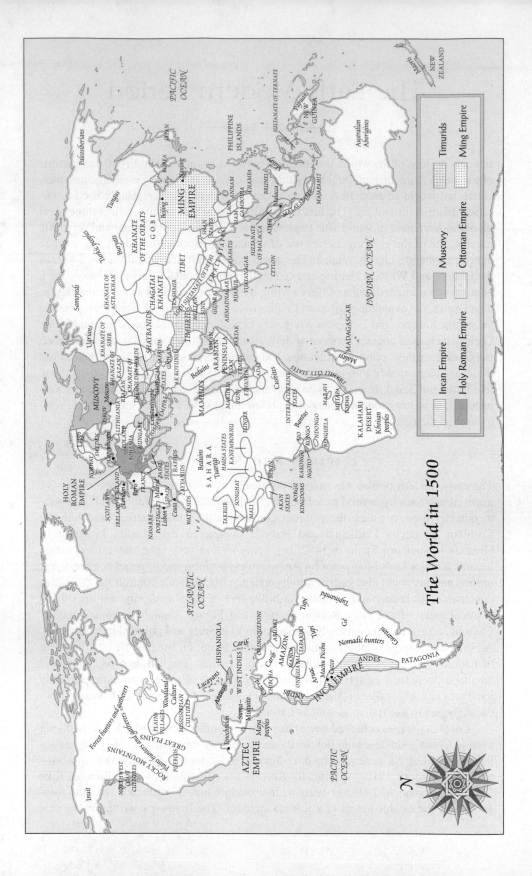

The World in 1500

Legend

Incan Empire	Muscovy
Holy Roman Empire	Ottoman Empire
Timurids	
Ming Empire	

PACIFIC OCEAN

ATLANTIC OCEAN

INDIAN OCEAN

PACIFIC OCEAN

Inuit

NORTHWEST COAST CULTURES

ROCKY MOUNTAINS

Plains hunters and farmers

GREAT PLAINS

PUEBLOS

Forest hunters and farmers

Woodland Culture

PLAINS VILLAGES

MISSISSIPPIAN CULTURE

Maya peoples

Tenochtitlán

AZTEC EMPIRE

Suma– Mixpuito

Lucayans

WEST INDIES

HISPANIOLA

Carib

Arawaks

ORINOQUEÑI

Carib

CHUCHA

CARANQUI

MANTA

ONGUAIMO

CARACO

Aruac

Cuzco

Machu Picchu

INCA EMPIRE

ANDES

ANDES

AMAZON

Tupi

Tupí

Gé

Tapanhona

Tupi

Guarani

Nomadic hunters

PATAGONIA

Palaeosiberians

Tungus

Buryats

Turkic/peoples

Samoyeds

Ugrians

MUSCOVY

Moscow

Pskov

Novgorod

SWEDEN

NORWAY

LAPPS

SCOTLAND

IRELAND ENGLAND

London

HOLY ROMAN EMPIRE

NAVARRE

PORTUGAL

Lisbon

SPAIN

Ceuta

Paris

FRANCE

Madrid

BOHEMIA

HUNGARY

POLAND

LITHUANIA

WATTASIDS

ZAYYANIDS

HAFSIDS

SAHARA

Beduins

Tuaregs

TAKRUR

MALI

SONGHAY

AKAN STATES

BORGU KINGDOMS

HAUSA STATES

KANEM-BORNU

BENIN

NUPE

KAKONGO

NGOYO

KONGO

OYO

KARAKO

NDONGO

BENGUELA

MATAMBA

MABAVI

LUBA

TORWA

KALAHARI DESERT

Khoisan peoples

Bantus

INTERLACUSTRINE STATES

Cushites

ETHIOPIA

FUN

MAKURIA

MAMLUKS

Beduins

Constantinople

OTTOMAN EMPIRE

GEORGIAN STATES

AK-KOYUNLU

Baghdad

GILAN

ARABIAN PENINSULA

YSAN

YEMEN

ADA

OMAN

HADRAMAUT

Swahili City States

Malays

MADAGASCAR

TIMURIDS

SAFAVIDS

SHAYBANIDS

KHANATE OF ASTRAKHAN

KHANATE OF SIBIR

KHANATE OF KAZAN

KHANATE OF THE GOLDEN HORDE

CHAGATAI KHANATE

SULTANATE OF DELHI

GUJARAT

SIND

MULTAN

KASHMIR

TIBET

AHMADNAGAR

BIJAPUR

GOLCONDA

VIJAYANAGAR

BERAR

KHANDESH

CEYLON

KHANATE OF THE OIRATS

GOBI

MING EMPIRE

Beijing

Nanjing

SHAN STATES

MALI STATES

LAOS

ANNAM

SIAM

CAMBODIA

CHAMPA

AVA

AUEH

SULTANATE OF MALACCA

Malacca

BRUNEI

MAJAPAHIT

SUMATRA

PHILIPPINE ISLANDS

SULTANATE OF TERNATE

KOREA

JAPAN

NEW GUINEA

Papuans

AUSTRALIA

Australian Aborigines

NEW ZEALAND

Maoris

N

alphabet was a long poem called "Songs of Flying Dragons" in praise of the memory of General Yi, presenting him as a model of national unity and resistance to outside influence:

> He opened the four borders,
> Island dwellers had no more fear of pirates.
> Southern barbarians beyond our waters,
> How could they not come to him?
>
> * * *
>
> If perverse theories of Western barbarians
> Threaten you with sin or allure with bliss,
> Remember, my Lord,
> His judgment and orthodoxy.

EXPLORATION AND CONQUEST

The Western barbarians were becoming increasingly visible around the world. Long-distance exploration began in earnest in the late 1400s, with Portuguese navigators exploring the coast of Africa in the 1480s and Vasco da Gama reaching as far as India in the 1490s. Columbus's epochal voyage of 1492 was followed by a flood of explorations westward and then the conquest of the Aztec and Incan empires in the early 1500s; Dutch, British, and French colonies followed Spanish settlements in North America in the early 1600s. Many regions were explored, and much literature was written about these explorations, both actual travel accounts and all sorts of poetic and fictional works derived from them, from Thomas More's philosophical fiction *Utopia* to Luis Vaz de Camões's *Lusiads* (1572) celebrating Vasco da Gama's exploits. Along with these works, this volume includes an extended section on Mesoamerica and its civilizations before, during, and after the region's conquest by a Spanish force under Hernán Cortés—a region for which we have an extraordinarily rich literary legacy of both native and European writing.

Several major empires were extending their reach in other parts of the world as well. In West Africa, the Songhai empire expanded during the 1500s from its base in Mali (see the *Epic of Son-Jara,* in Volume B). In China, the Ming dynasty, founded in 1368, ruled until 1644 at the close of the early modern period. Where previous dynasties had largely looked inward, or at most had been active in East Asia, Ming China extended its influence over an unprecedented region. The emperor Cheng Tsu (r. 1402–1424) sent a fleet of warships commanded by the enterprising eunuch admiral Cheng Ho to establish trading bases and exact tribute not only from Japan and Korea but from southern India and even the east coast of Africa. In the 1500s the Mughal Empire encompassed almost all of northern India and what is now Pakistan, while in the fifteenth through sixteenth centuries the Ottoman Empire expanded from Turkey to control Greece, the Balkans, Hungary, the Crimea, Mesopotamia, Syria, Palestine, Egypt, and the north coast of Africa all the way to Morocco at the western end of the Mediterranean. The Ottoman ruler Suleiman I, who reigned for almost half a century beginning in 1520, became known in Europe as "Suleiman the Magnificent" for the splendor of his court and his many victories.

SCIENTIFIC CONQUEST AND INQUIRY

The increasing interest in scientific inquiry and technological innovation also aided imperial outreach: modern armies and navies could now overwhelm much larger forces not equipped with rifles, cannon, and warships. The practitioners of science or "natural philosophy" could even think of themselves as conquering warriors. As the physician and alchemist Paracelsus explained in his *Great Surgery Book* in 1536, "Every experiment is like a weapon which must be used in a particular way—a spear to thrust, a club to strike. Experimenting requires a man who knows when to thrust and when to strike, each according to need and fashion." In these same years, the Polish astronomer Nicolas Copernicus was making the observations that would lead to his revolutionary assertion that the earth and other planets revolve around the sun, not the sun around the earth—a disorienting change of perspective that questioned both classical authority and Church doctrine. All phenomena and all traditions became subjects for probing, skeptical inquiry. In the 1570s Michel de Montaigne founded a new kind of writing, the essay or *essai*—French for "trial, experiment"—to convey his speculations on past and present events and on his own character. As he wrote in an inscription for his library, "I do not understand; I pause; I examine."

In Mughal India, the undogmatic ruler Akbar the Great (r. 1556–1605) organized discussions among a series of religious leaders—Zoroastrians, Christians, and Hindus, as well as Muslims. Though Akbar never abandoned Islam, the religion of his birth, he came to regard Muhammad as not necessarily the last or greatest of prophets, and he proclaimed tolerance for all religions in his realm. He reformed the judicial system in a similar spirit of inquiry, decreeing that judges "should not be satisfied with witnesses or oaths, but proceed by manifold inquiries, by the study of physiognomy, and the exercise of foresight." In Ming China, new emphasis was given to individual merit as demonstrated on civil service examinations. While established, wealthy families continued to have advantages in preparing their sons for these elaborate examinations, increasing numbers of people without marked wealth or connections were able to come into the government.

The importance given to the examinations stimulated the establishment of Chinese schools, both by the government and by private scholars; like the many new universities of Europe, these schools became centers of debate and of probing scholarship. The fifteenth and sixteenth centuries saw an outpouring of Chinese scholarship that assembled and assessed the classic works of the past. The most ambitious imperial anthology ran to no fewer than eleven thousand volumes. Textual scholars sought to establish correct texts, and one sixteenth-century scholar was so bold as to question the authenticity of portions of the classic *Book of Songs,* a text that had been a founding document for earlier Confucian orthodoxy.

The Ming scholars' interest in restoring and critically assessing their literary heritage went along with a heightened individualism and a new attention to colloquial prose fiction; Wu Cheng'en's comic novel *Journey to the West* (page 33) is even organized around a journey to India in search of accurate scriptural texts. A similar confluence can be seen in Europe as well, in the intensive reengagement with ancient texts and artworks that became known as "the Renaissance." As will be seen in many of the European works in this volume, writers and other artists engaged with new intensity with classic forms, creating modern epics, plays, poems, and fictions out of the materials of Greek and Latin tradition.

THE RISE OF PRINT CULTURE

A crucial development in the early modern period was the invention of printing, which enabled texts to be widely circulated in multiple copies and made ownership affordable to people not possessing extensive private means. The world's first movable type was developed in China by a printer named Pi Sheng in around 1000, using pottery rather than metal type, though the complexity of the thousands of Chinese characters meant that texts could still most readily be written by hand. Increasingly sophisticated methods of woodblock printing allowed for the printing of more and more texts, often to the displeasure of government officials unable to control private mass-production of texts.

In Europe, the invention of movable metal type in the 1450s revolutionized the production and circulation of texts. Among other consequences, the spread of print culture gave impetus to the protestant Reformation beginning in the early 1500s, which stressed individual reading and understanding of Scripture. Such individual reading was newly possible with the spread of printed copies of the Bible, increasingly published in vernacular languages that people could read without needing the expense and leisure required to learn Latin. Not only men but also women—rarely given classical educations—could take an active role in the writing and reading of vernacular texts, and all sorts of literary production were stimulated by the new possibilities of print and the new availability of the vernacular languages as resources for serious writing. This volume begins with examples of the developing vernacular writing in India, China, and Europe, as writers around the world began to explore the brave new worlds open to them.

THE EARLY MODERN PERIOD

YEAR	THE WORLD	LITERATURE
1300		
		1300s Aztecs begin producing painted screenfold books
1310		
1320		
	1325 Founding of Aztec capital, Tenochtitlán	1321 Dante dies
1330		
	1337–1453 Hundred Years' War between England and France	
1340		
	1348–1350 Black Death in Europe	
1350		
		1353–1354 Petrarch writing *Canzoniere* and Boccaccio, *Decameron*
1360		
	1363 Timur (Tamerlane) begins conquests in central Asia, Persia, Russia, and India	Early 1360s St. Catherine, *Letters*
	1368 Chinese overthrow Mongols; Ming dynasty replaces Yuan dynasty	
1370		
	1378 Pope Gregory XI leaves Avignon for Rome; beginning of Great Schism	
1380		
1390		
1400		
		1404 Christine de Pizan, *Book of the City of Ladies*
1410		
1420		
	1428–1440 Reign of Aztec emperor Itzcoatl; Aztecs become dominant regional power	
	1429 Joan of Arc leads siege at Orleans; burned at stake (1431)	
1430		
		1430s–1519 Elaboration of court poetry in service of the Aztec empire
	1434 Cosimo de'Medici becomes ruler of Florence	1430s Leon Battista Alberti, *On Painting*
1440		
	1440 Portuguese begin slave trade in Africa	
	1444 Mehmed II becomes sultan of Ottoman Empire	
1450		
	1450 Lorenzo Valla proves *Donation of Constantine* a forgery	1450s François Villon, poetic works
	1453 Gutenberg prints first Bible using movable metal type; Turks seize Constantinople; end of Byzantine Empire	

Plate 1 Albrecht Dürer, *Self-Portrait,* 1500. The art historian H. R. Janson called Dürer "the first artist to be fascinated by his own image." Whether or not this is the case, it is certainly striking to see the young German, here 29 years old, confronting us in Christlike solemnity, and to consider that the initials "AD" on the left side of the portrait not only mean *anno domini* (year of our Lord), but also signify Dürer's own initials. One of the first modern artists to benefit from the revolution in printing—Dürer launched his career as a woodcut designer in Basel and Strasbourg, urban centers with numerous publishing houses— he was largely responsible for bringing the influences of Italian Renaissance art to bear on the north. At the same time, as in this self-portrait, Dürer remained receptive to social and cultural developments in his own country, and he would enthusiastically embrace Martin Luther; one of his last major works, *The Four Apostles* from 1526, is a strong defense of the young Reformation and its most ardent spokesperson. *(Alte Pinakothek, Munich, Germany / SuperStock.)*

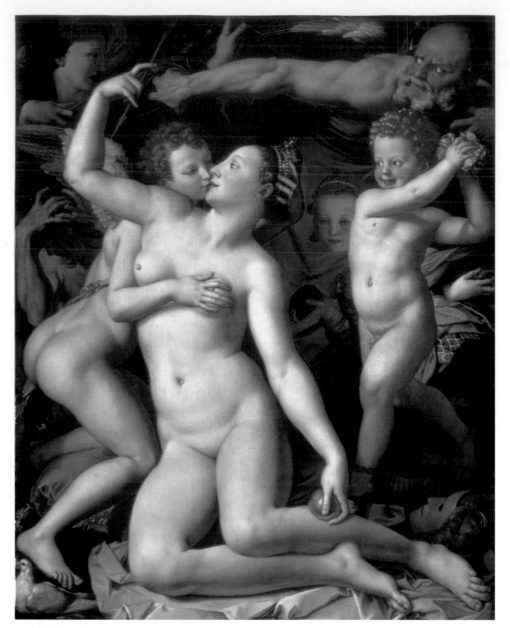

Plate 2 Agnolo Bronzino, *Allegory (Venus, Cupid, Folly and Time)*, c. 1545. Bronzino was for many years court painter to the Medici, producing stately portraits of Duke Cosimo and his Spanish wife, Eleonora. But Cosimo's taste did not run only to ducal settings, and in the mid-1540s he commissioned the painting variously known as "Allegory," "Exposure of Luxury," or most straightforwardly, "Venus, Cupid, Folly, and Time." The work foregrounds a shocking spectacle of incest. The young god of love fondles his mother's breast while she holds one of his poisonous arrows above her head and clutches the golden apple that created the discord leading to the Trojan War. Behind these two and a naked putto playfully tossing rose petals is a more sobering scene: an anguished Michelangelesque figure clutching her hair, elderly Time pulling back the curtain to "expose" the couple, and the chilling image of a girl whose body ends in a serpent's tail and whose supposedly benign offering to the spectator of a honeycomb can only be construed as suspicious. Painted on the eve of the Catholic Reformation and a period of increasing concern about sensuality and the influence of pagan art, Bronzino's work teases us with its explicit celebration of classically derived themes and with its brooding condemnation of its highly stylized perverseness. *(National Gallery, London / Bridgeman Art Library.)*

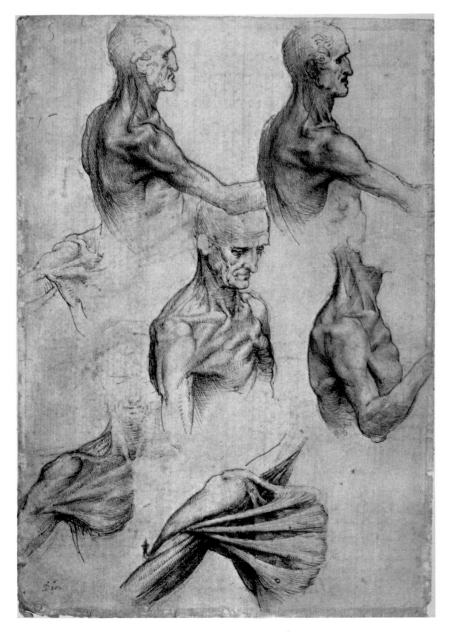

Plate 3 Leonardo da Vinci, *Muscles of the Neck and Shoulders,* early 1500s. A very different art of the body than Bronzino's *Allegory* can be seen in these anatomical sketches. Nothing escaped the attention of Leonardo da Vinci, who was as accomplished in anatomy and the science of warfare as he was in art. His indefatiguable curiosity has rightly earned him the title of the consummate Renaissance man, even as it spawned a restlessness that rarely allowed him to finish the massive projects he took up in the courts of Rome, Milan, and Paris. His scrawlings in notebooks allowed him both to indulge his creative powers and to cultivate independence from the demands of patrons, and over his long life he produced literally thousands of drawings. It is to da Vinci that we owe some of the finest botanical studies ever done, as well as designs for early flying machines (which when tested, actually flew). But perhaps his greatest achievement as an artist are his studies of the human body. His fascination with isolating tendons, bones, ligaments, and muscles allowed him to reveal the similarities between body and machine, tracing the organic in the inorganic. Yet as his *Mona Lisa* and many portraits of the Madonna attest, he was also gifted in depicting a female beauty at once aloof from its surroundings and immediate in its graceful physical presence. *(The Royal Library, Windsor Castle / SuperStock.)*

Plate 4 Sophonisba Anguissola, *The Chess Game,* 1555. Anguissola was the most prominent woman artist of the Italian Renaissance, painting in Cremona, Madrid, Genoa, and Palermo—where she was visited in her nineties by the Flemish painter Van Dyck. Like her five sisters, she was the beneficiary of an unusually sophisticated humanist education, and like them, she trained with artists in her native Cremona. Particularly skilled at portraits (and self-portraits; one of her more reflexive works paints the artist Bernardino Campi painting her), she made notable studies of King Phillip II of Spain and his wife Isabella. She was admired by both Michelangelo and his close friend Tommaso Cavalieri, who believed that she defied the general rule that women were inferior to men in artistic achievement. Her *Chess Game* features three of her sisters as well as a servant. The elaborate dress is exemplary of the nobility's garments of the time, but the subject matter is an uncommon one, as it turns the highly intellectual work of chess into a women's game, played not in the safe and intimate surroundings of domestic space but outdoors, with a view of what is probably Cremona below. *(Erich Lessing / Art Resource, New York.)*

Plate 5 Pieter Brueghel the Elder, *Landscape with the Fall of Icarus,* 1550s. W. H. Auden memorialized Brueghel's painting in his poem "Musée des Beaux Arts," where he contrasts the serene Flemish landscape and the odd, almost irrelevant detail of a boy's pale body plummeting into the water, having fallen from a place too near the sun: "Everything turns away / Quite leisurely from the disaster," such as the boat that "had somewhere to get to and sailed calmly on." Whether Brueghel too was concerned with man's casual indifference to man is another question. He and his sons dominated Antwerp's art scene in the mid 16th and 17th centuries, excelling in landscape painting and still life. Some of his most memorable works focus on peasant life and customs, while he also painted religious subjects such as the *Tower of Babel* and *The Parable of the Sower,* always with an eye to penetrating realistic detail in the manner of other northern European artists. Brueghel did not flinch from using his works as social commentaries, as attested by some of his satirical paintings on the troubled relationship between the Netherlands and Spain. The early *Fall of Icarus,* which exists in two versions, may well have been meant to convey the message of man's inhumanity. But just as easily it suggests the tragic necessity of death amidst life's overwhelming richness, or the final insignificance of those who, like Icarus, have foolishly ignored the warnings of their elders and flown too high. *(Musées Royaux des Beaux-Arts de Belgique, Brussels, Belgium / Giraudon-Bridgeman Art Library.)*

Plate 6 Frontispiece to the *Codex Fejérváry-Mayer,* Mexico, before 1521. This image painted by the Aztecs' Mixtec allies divides the world into its five sections: east (at the top), south, west, north, and center. The center represents the temple complex at the heart of the Aztec capital, Tenochtitlán, dominated by the sun and war god Huitzilopochtli. Radiating out from the center are the four quarters of the world, each with its own patron god, bird, tree, and color. The image maps time as well as space: it is the frontispiece to a divination book called a *tonalamatl,* "a book of days and destinies" used to chart people's lives and fortunes. Rows of hieroglyphs in each quadrant give two forms of day-count, one using a yearly cycle of 365 days, the other using a ritual calendar of 260 days. Each of the world's five divisions was associated with an age of the world; the Aztecs and their neighbors believed that they lived in the Fifth Age, named "4-Movement." *(Liverpool City Museum, Liverpool / Werner Forman / Art Resource, New York.)*

Plate 7   Malinche and Devil masks, Guerrero, Mexico, mid-20th century. Masks were an important part of ritual dances in pre-Conquest Mexico, helping the dancers identify with divinities and guardian animals, and they are still widely used in festivals now associated with Catholic feast days. The two masks shown here attest to the ongoing vitality of old traditions, now mixed with new elements—in these cases, with deliberate irony. The top mask shows Malinche, Cortés's Indian wife and interpreter, her pink skin symbolizing the passion that led her to aid Cortés against her own people. Usually Malinche masks have a native appearance, but this Malinche's blue eyes and slender features give a modern twist to the old theme of cultural betrayal. She takes on the imported beauty of a Hollywood starlet, uncannily offset by the horns protruding from her head, decorated with ribbons recalling the ancient colors of the four sacred directions. The second mask has a face inside an eagle helmet, formerly the mark of an Aztec warrior; but here, in place of a warrior, a devil leers out from his helmet. *(Private collection / photograph by David Damrosch.)*

Plate 8 Miguel Gabrera, Portrait of *Sor Juana Inés de la Cruz,* 1750. Painted half a century after Sor Juana's death from the plague, this portrait gives us the austere Mexican nun garbed in the signs of her profession: her black habit, her rosary beads, an enormous brooch depicting a prayerful female figure. But the books on the shelves behind her suggest Sor Juana's double life. We find not only a history of the papacy, but also the medical treatises of Galen and Hippocrates and Livy's *History of Rome,* among other classical and modern texts on thoroughly secular subjects. In her autobiographical account, *La respuesta,* Sor Juana wrote that in entering the convent, "I thought I was fleeing myself but—woe is me!—I brought myself with me, and brought my greatest enemy in my inclination to study, which I know not whether to take as a Heaven-sent favor or as a punishment." The serenity and self-command Gabrera here depicts seem to argue decisively for the former interpretation. *(The Art Archive / National History Museum, Mexico City / Dagli Orti.)*

YEAR	THE WORLD	LITERATURE
1460		
1470		
	1474 Isabella becomes Queen of Castile	**1470s** Lucrezia Tornabuoni de'Medici,
	1478 Spanish Inquisition begins	*Sacred Stories*
1480		
	1488 Bartolomeu Dias explores Cape of Good Hope	
1490		
	1492 Jews expelled from Spain; Columbus explores West Indies	**1493** Columbus writes first letters to Queen Isabella detailing his discoveries
		1494 Aldus Manutius establishes an important printing press in Venice
	1497 Leonardo da Vinci, *Last Supper*	
	1498 Vasco da Gama reaches India; Savonarola burned at stake in Florence	
	1499–1501 Amerigo Vespucci explores coast of Brazil	
1500		
	1500 Michelangelo, *David*	
	1502–1520 Reign of Moctezuma II in Mexico	**1509** Erasmus, *The Praise of Folly*
1510		
	1511 Cuba becomes Spanish colony	
	1514 Copernicus publishes work on heliocentric theory	**1513** Niccolò Machiavelli, *The Prince*
	1517 Luther writes 95 theses contesting Church's practice of granting indulgences	**1516** Thomas More, *Utopia*
	1519–1522 Magellan circumnavigates globe	**1519–1521** Cortés writes five long letters to Charles V on his exploits
	1519 Hernán Cortés invades Aztec empire, places Moctezuma under house arrest	
1520		
	1521 Three–month siege of Tenochtitlán ends in fall of Aztec empire. Cortés gains control over central and southern Mexico	**1522** Martin Luther translates New Testament
	1523 Pedro de Alvarado conquers Guatemala. Pope Clement VII sends a dozen missionaries to organize the conversion of the Mexican population	**1524** Aztec-Spanish dialogues on the merits of traditional religion versus Christianity
		1524–1525 Erasmus and Luther debate free will
	1525–1526 Peasants' rebellion in Germany; Thomas Muntzer executed	
	1527 Sack of Rome by Holy Roman Emperor Charles V	**1527** Baldassare Castiglione, *The Courtier*
	1529 Turks invade Austria; Bernardino de Sahagún arrives in Mexico	
1530		
	1532 Francisco Pizarro conquers Incan empire in Peru	**1530s** Lyrics of Michelangelo and Vittoria Colonna
	1533 Jean Calvin goes to Geneva	**1532** François Rabelais, *Pantagruel*
	1534 Henry VIII excommunicated	**1534** Rabelais, *Gargantua*
	1535 Thomas More beheaded	
	1539 First printing press in New World (Mexico)	
1540		
	1540 Jesuits approved by Pope as official order; Treatise signed between Turkey and Venice	**1540s** Clement Marot translates the Psalms; Marguerite de Navarre, *Heptameron*
		1540–1560s Wu Cheng'en, *Journey to the West*

YEAR	THE WORLD	LITERATURE
	1545–1562 Council of Trent reforms Catholic practices in response to Protestant challenges	**1547–1580s** Bernardino de Sahagún collects materials from native informants for his *General History of the Affairs of New Spain* and poetry collections
1550		
	1555 Calvinist mission to Brazil	**1555** Louise Labé, *Works*
	1557 Erasmus's works put on Index of Prohibited Books	
	1559 Elizabeth I becomes Queen of England	
1560		
	1562–1598 French Wars of Religion	**1560s** Bartolomé de las Casas, *Apolgetic History*
	1568–1648 War in Netherlands, ending with independence from Spain	**1564–1565** Bernal Díaz del Castillo, *True History of the Conquest of New Spain*
1570		
	1572 Battle of Lepanto, Spanish Catholic naval forces defeat Ottomans; St. Bartholomew's Day massacre	**1570s** Luis Vaz de Camões, *The Lusiads;* Jean de Léry, *History of a Voyage to Brazil*
	1578 King Sebastiaõ and Portuguese troops killed in northern Africa	**1577** Teresa of Avila, *Interior Castle*
1580		
	1582 Gregorian Calendar implemented	**1580s** Jan Kochanowski, *Laments;* Michel de Montaigne, *Essays*
	1580 Union of Portugal and Spain	
	1585 First English settlement in North America	
	1588 Spanish Armada defeated by England	
1590		
	1598 Restoration of shogunate in Japan	
1600		
	1609 Spain approaching bankruptcy; Moors expelled	
1610		
		1611 William Shakespeare, *The Tempest*
		1612 Miguel de Cervantes, *Don Quixote,* Part 1
		1614 Lope de Vega, *Fuenteovejuna*
	1618–1648 Thirty Years' War	**1616** Cervantes, *Don Quixote,* Part 2
1620		
	1620 Plymouth Colony founded in Massachusetts	
	1621 Philip IV becomes King of Spain	**1624** John Donne, *Devotions upon Emergent Occasions*
	1628 Recurrence of plague in Europe	**1629** Hernando Ruiz de Alarcón, *Treatise on the Superstitions of the Natives of This New Spain*
1630		
	1633 Galileo recants before the Inquisition	
1640		
	1640 Portuguese war of independence begins	
	1642–1649 English Civil War	**1641** René Descartes, *Meditations*
	1649 Charles I beheaded	
1650		
		1650 Anne Bradstreet, *The Tenth Muse Lately Sprung Up in America*
1660		
	1660 Restoration and return of Charles II to England	**1667** John Milton, *Paradise Lost*
		1667–1670 Sor Juana Inés de la Cruz writes first purely Mexican poems in Spanish

✠ CROSSCURRENTS ✠
The Vernacular Revolution

For a thousand years or more, from late antiquity until around 1200 C.E., almost all the world's literature was composed in elite languages, employing literary modes far removed from the speech of common people. Literacy was confined to a small number of people—almost always men—in court and temple circles, and writers usually strove to preserve and elaborate older literary traditions rather than to adapt their work to the changes of everyday language. Sanskrit in India, classical Chinese in Japan and in China itself, and Latin in Europe were for a millennium the dominant literary languages in their regions, even as people spoke ever more widely divergent dialects and languages in daily life.

This situation began to change between around 1000 and 1300 in many parts of the world. These changes took different forms in different cultures and occurred on varying timetables, yet collectively it is appropriate to speak of a worldwide "vernacular revolution" during these years and the centuries that followed. The works in this section show the varied purposes that common or vernacular language came to serve in several different cultures. In some cases, the older, elite literary language was still used as well, sometimes for privileged genres: thus in Japan, Chinese was often still used for poetry, even after prose writers like Murasaki Shikibu pioneered the use of Japanese for writing their prose romances. In China itself, the literary language and techniques perfected by the Tang dynasty poets of the seventh through ninth centuries continued to dominate upper-class poetry for another thousand years, but by the 1500s prose writers were coming to favor a "vernacular" style much closer to everyday speech. This shift in style went along with a shift in emphasis as well, toward more realistic portrayals in prose fiction of life in society, often with more attention to lower classes—"vernacular" itself comes from a Latin word, *verna*, meaning a household slave, and by extension "home-grown" or "native."

In India, Sanskrit began to give way to writing in many of the different languages spoken around the Indian subcontinent, such as Tamil and Telugu. Writers in these vernacular languages often came from artisan or merchant classes, and at times openly rejected the caste hierarchy that had put the Brahmins, and the Sanskrit language, above them. Sometimes these vernacular writings were secular in emphasis, with religious writing still favoring Sanskrit, but over time an increasing amount of religious and devotional writing came to be composed in the vernacular as well.

In Europe, German and Icelandic writers on the margins of the Latin tradition began to write in their local Germanic languages, and Anglo-Saxon, Irish, and Welsh literatures all flourished in the British Isles. By 1300, even in the strongholds of the Latin tradition, Dante in Italy and Provençal poets in France were using the vernacular to write great poetry. In a letter to his patron Can Grande della Scala, Dante defended writing his *Commedia* in Italian rather than Latin, saying that he wanted to reach as many of his countrymen—and women—as possible. The trade-off was that vernacular work would be less read abroad, and Dante and many others continued to use Latin when they wanted to reach an international audience directly. The great sixteenth-century scholar Erasmus of Rotterdam wrote and lectured in Latin all his life, communicating in this way with scholars across Europe as he worked in Holland, England, France, Italy, Belgium, Germany, and Switzerland.

As vernacular writing spread, translation began to play a prominent role in the circulation of literary texts, and Erasmus himself strongly promoted the translation of the Bible into vernacular languages. The Church had long favored the exclusive use of Latin for theological writing and for the Bible, so that all Christians could understand it in common and also so that Church authorities could control the text's form and the doctrines they derived from it. With the rise of Protestantism, however, reformers like Luther and Erasmus began to emphasize the individual's direct encounter with Scripture, and they sought to make the Bible accessible to all Christians, whatever their social class and whatever their language. As Erasmus declared—in Latin—in a preface to an edition of the Greek New Testament:

> Perhaps the state secrets of kings have to be concealed, but Christ wanted his mysteries to be disseminated as widely as possible. I should prefer that all women, even of the lowest rank, should read the evangelists and the epistles of Paul, and I wish these writings were translated into all the languages of the human race, so that they could be read and studied, not just by the Irish and the Scots, but by the Turks as well, and the Saracens. . . . I would hope that the farmer might chant a holy text at his plow, the spinner sing it as she sits at her wheel, the traveler ease the tedium of his journey with tales from Scripture.

In this passage, Erasmus allows that Latin, long the language of European diplomacy, may still have value for keeping "state secrets" out of general circulation; but the spread of the vernacular tended as well to lessen the control over information formerly held closely by royal courts. The rise of the different vernaculars also stimulated the consolidation of nation-states around a dominant language or dialect, and gave the means for a growing number of people in those states to express themselves and to seek direct participation in public life. Even as it opened up a greatly expanded and varied literary landscape, the vernacular revolution ultimately paved the way for the middle-class and then working-class revolutions that have shaped our modern world.

━┼━☰◆☰━┼━

Vernacular Writing in South Asia

For nearly a thousand years beginning in the last centuries B.C.E., the entire literary landscape of South Asia was occupied by Sanskrit (and to a far less extent, by the two languages related to Sanskrit—Prakrit and Apabhramsha—that had been used especially for literature meant to suggest the world of rural life in contrast to the court). We have no evidence that the regional languages of South Asia, with the important exception of Tamil, were ever used for the creation of written expressive texts during this period. But this situation changed dramatically near the end of the first millennium C.E., when writers in southern India first began to experiment with courtly registers of local dialects. Over the course of the next 500 years, local-language writing began to appear everywhere in South Asia. Scholars don't fully understand the conditions that made this vernacular revolution possible, and the fact that a remarkably similar transformation occurred in western Europe around the same period complicates explanation even more. But a revolution did occur, and it powerfully challenged the dominance of Sanskrit, and indeed other dimensions of Sanskrit culture and society as well.

In most regions of South Asia, the earliest vernacular writers were court poets who imitated Sanskrit literature in idiom, metrics, and themes. The religious dimension of their work, where present at all, was typically muted. However, this inaugural vernacular movement was followed by a second wave prominently marked by religious sentiment, especially by the idea of direct access to the divine sometimes termed *bhakti* (devotion). Unlike the vernacular transformation in Europe, which was hastened by translations of the Bible into regional languages (page 115), no attempt was ever made in South Asia before the modern period to translate Sanskrit scriptures. Instead, altogether new bodies of religious writing were created, some that would eventually attain canonical scriptural status. The devotional poets, often low-caste artisans or ascetics, rejected the high style of Sanskrit and the social values of caste hierarchy imputed (sometimes unjustly) to Sanskrit culture as a whole. In south India, the *Virashaivas*—Militant Devotees of the god Shiva—invented what they called the *vacana* (plain talking), an unversified, unadorned, and for the most part, it seems, unwritten form. In fact, this seems to have been meant as a kind of anti-literature, as radically anomalous in its aesthetic as was the Virashaivas' social critique, especially their rejection of the caste system and their denunciation of the wealthy and the grand temples that were the concrete manifestation of their power (and which low-caste people were prohibited from entering). Both men and women composed in the *vacana* form; among the latter, Mahadeviyakka produced *vacana*s that represent some of the earliest and most powerful expressions of erotic devotionalism in South Asia, and bear close comparison to the poems of Mahadevi's European contemporaries, Hildegard von Bingen and Mechthild von Magdeburg (see Volume B). Somewhat later in northern India, the weaver-poet Kabir (1400–1450) composed verses in Old Hindi whose idiom and style were as innovative as the criticism he expressed through them of Hindu and Muslim exclusivity. Like those of many of the vernacular devotional poets, the compositions of Kabir remain alive to this day on the lips of people across northern India.

Tukaram, who lived in western India in the early seventeenth century and wrote in the Marathi language, gave voice to the literary aspirations of many of these poets when he exclaimed, in one of his many confessional poems:

> I have no
> Personal skill.
> It is
> The Cosmic One
> Making me speak.

Yet the artistry and aesthetic long associated with Sanskrit did maintain themselves in many vernacular literary cultures. Especially instructive is the case of Telugu, the language of today's Andhra Pradesh in southeastern India. Court poets continued for centuries to write marvelously sophisticated literature in Telugu in the high style even as poets associated with one or another of the great temples in the region sought a simpler, more common idiom. But the division between the court and temple traditions is not always hard and fast; moreover, creative innovation continued in both spheres, in content as well as form. The songs (called *padam*) of the mid-seventeenth-century poet Kshetrayya illustrate these trends particularly well. Like many devotional poets before him, Kshetrayya adopts a female voice, of various kinds: that of the confused love-sick ingénue ("Those women, they deceived me"), for example, or the jilted mistress ("'Your body is my body'"), but most often the courtesan ("Pour gold as high as I stand"). He uses these different voices to evoke powerful, complex emotions of spiritual longing for the divine (called here Muvva Gopala, the name of Kshetrayya's village god), and all the feelings accompanying that longing: from despair at God's apparent indifference, to a readiness to negotiate with Him (as if he were a prostitute's customer), to the self-negating ecstasy of union. Although the language and form of these songs are simple and entirely local, the categories of eroticism and much of the imagery borrow creatively from the high tradition (as seen, for example, in "Love in a Courtly Language," Volume A). The wit and wisdom and passion, however, are Kshetrayya's alone, as is the transformation of the very subject matter itself. Sometimes it seems impossible to decide whether the vision of sex, with God as customer, is an expression of the ecstasy of religious union in the manner of the older mystical traditions mentioned above, or whether—in the new early-modern economy of southern India that was fluid, commercial, and dynamic and where old traditions were crumbling—the customer himself is viewed as God, and sex is nothing more, or less, than sex.

PRONUNCIATIONS:
bhakti: BHUK-tee
Virashaiva: VEER-uh-SHAI-vuh

Basavanna[1]

Like a monkey on a tree

Like a monkey on a tree
it leaps from branch to branch:
   how can I believe or trust
   this burning thing, this heart?
5 It will not let me go
   to my Father,
   my lord of the meeting rivers.[1]

You can make them talk

You can make them talk
if the serpent
has stung
them.

5 You can make them talk
   if they're struck
   by an evil planet.[1]

But you can't make them talk
if they're struck dumb
10 by riches.

   Yet when Poverty the magician
   enters, they'll speak
   at once,

      O lord of the meeting rivers.

The crookedness of the serpent

The crookedness of the serpent
   is straight enough for the snake-hole.

The crookedness of the river
   is straight enough for the sea.

5 And the crookedness of our Lord's men
   is straight enough for our Lord!

Before the grey reaches the cheek

Before
   the grey reaches the cheek,

---

1. Translated by A. K. Ramanujan. Basavanna (traditionally dated 1106–c. 1167) was a minister and treasurer of King Bijjala at Kalyana in Karnataka, against whom he is said to have led a coup. He is credited with founding the Virashaiva religious community.
1. After appearing in Basavanna's dreams, Shiva manifested himself at a temple in the village of Kudalasangama ("the river confluence at Kudala") and initiated him as the leader of the Virashaivas.
1. Some planets, such as Saturn, were believed to exert harmful influences.

the wrinkle the rounded chin
and the body becomes a cage of bones:

5   before
       with fallen teeth
       and bent back
       you are someone else's ward:

       before
10   you drop your hand to the knee
       and clutch a staff:

       before
       age corrodes
       your form:

15   before
       death touches you:

            worship
            our lord
            of the meeting rivers!

I don't know anything like time-beats and meter

I don't know anything like time-beats and meter
nor the arithmetic of strings and drums;
I don't know the count of iamb and dactyl.[1]

My lord of the meeting rivers,
5   as nothing will hurt you
I'll sing as I love.

The rich will make temples for Śiva

The rich
will make temples for Śiva.
What shall I,
a poor man,
5   do?

My legs are pillars,
the body the shrine,
the head a cupola
of gold.

10   Listen, O lord of the meeting rivers,
      things standing shall fall,
      but the moving ever shall stay.[1]

---

1. Iamb and dactyl are here used as loose English equivalents for Kannada *amritagana* and *devagana,* kinds of metrical unit [translator's note].
1. Virashaiva thought stresses the opposition between that which "stands" and that which "moves." What moves is synonymous with the dynamism of the wandering mendicant of the Virashaiva community, who has renounced the home and the world in devotion to Shiva. What stands still is representative of the rigid strictures of orthodox Hinduism and its temples.

RESONANCE

Palkuriki Somanatha: from *The Legend of Basavanna*[1]

One day, when these and the rest of the host of devotees were enjoying the pleasures of the empire of devotion, and flourishing with ancient glory, I fell prostrate like a stick before the glorious, innumerable *māheśvaras*.[2] I was anointed by the nectar of their compassionate devotion. And I submitted to the assembly, saying, "I want to narrate the incomparable *Basava Purāṇa*. Kindly tell me how to handle the thread of that story and make me fulfilled."

When I had submitted myself thus, praising them and desiring their help, the gathering of devotees was pleased. They looked at me affectionately, cast their kindly glances upon me, and said, "We have given you the ability to spread the *Basava Purāṇa*. Now you must compose it so that it pleases the steadfast devotees."

When they spoke, I accepted the command of the assembled devotees with great reverence. Therefore, I will now begin to compose this poem. * * *

In the sacred purāṇas, it is said that "Uma is our mother and Rudra is our father"; therefore, I am born of the Īśvara family.[3] I was born out of the womb-hand of the liṅga guru.[4] He is an embodiment of the *śaraṇas, the gaṇas,* and all the other attendants of Śiva.[5] The devotees have anointed me with their compassion. I am free of worldly bonds. I belong to the devotee *gotra*.[6] The brilliant Viṣṇurāmideva and the illustrious Śriyādevi love me as their son. I am dedicated to the heroic *māheśvara* tradition.[7] I am a honeybee on the lotus feet of Kaṭṭakūri Potidevara, the renowned devotee. I gained the power to compose poetry from Karasthali Viśvanātha, the compassionate devotee. I am a bosom friend of Cĕnna Rāma, the eminent student of Vadagāmu Rāmeśa. I avoid showing respect, holding conversation, or any other kind of association with *bhavis*.[8] My name is Pālkuriki Somanātha. I am a man of pure character.

Since beautiful, idiomatic Telugu is more commonly understood than heavy compositions of mixed prose and verse, I have chosen to compose this entirely in the *dvipada* meter. Let it not be said that these words are nothing but Telugu. Rather, look at them as equal to the Vedas. If you wonder how that can be, remember, if a *tūmu* is a standard of measure, so is *sola*. Is it not generally agreed that the stature of a poet derives from his ability to create great poetry from simple words?

The underlying strength of this work is my fixation on Basava. The collection of songs that are sung about the ancient devotees are in accordance with the Vedas and purāṇas. The songs are also acceptable to the esoteric theory of the liṅga. They will be

1. Translated by Velcheru Narayana Rao. Few works present so intense, and so eccentric and violent, an account of religious devotion as Somanatha's biography of Basavanna and the early leaders of the Militant Shaiva community. Written in the 13th century perhaps only a few generations after the death of Basava, Somanatha's work reveals in all its intensity the rage of the lower castes against the social and spiritual power of Brahmanism.
2. Devotees of Shiva.
3. *Puranas* are books of holy legend; Uma is the wife of Rudra, another name of Shiva; the Ishvara family signifies the family of Shiva.
4. A reference to a child's initiation into the Shaiva order on the part of the teacher. The *linga* is an abstract representation of Shiva.
5. The *sharanas* ("refuges") and the *ganas* ("troops") represent different types of Shaiva devotees.
6. A *gotra* is a lineage; to claim a "devotee *gotra*" is to reject one's natural family in favor of the new family of devotees of Shiva.
7. The tradition of the Virashaiva community.
8. Anyone not belonging to the Virashaiva community.

my original. I will compose this poem by using the story of Basava as a thread to string together the beads that are the stories of the ancient devotees. Do not say that it is wrong to get involved with describing Basava, whose body is actually the incomparable liṅga as a separate individual. Such a description is conductive to the development of devotion.

BASAVEŚVARA'S REFUSAL OF THE THREAD CEREMONY AND HIS ARGUMENT WITH HIS FATHER

In the eighth year after the child's conception, on an auspicious day, his father, being devoid of devotion, got enthusiastic about performing his thread ceremony.[9]

Then Basava spoke to his father: "Just what do you expect to gain by performing this thread ceremony? How can you possibly worship Śiva and still be such a fool? You already have the supreme soul as your guru; aren't you going to create a hell for yourself by worshiping evil human beings? Once a person has been purified in a previous birth, isn't it degrading to become a twice-born in this life? Isn't it a sin to go through a ritual rebirth when one is already the offspring of a compassionate guru? Isn't it a mistake to offer oblations of clarified butter in a fire once a person has worshiped his guru's feet? Isn't it a sin to learn other mantras once you know the mantra that is the soul of Śiva? Isn't it wrong to worship these thread-polluted brahmins with the same hands that worship the devotees of Śiva? Why should a person tie himself up again with cords of karma after severing the bonds of karma? Tell me, how is it possible to wear mean symbols again after once donning rudrākṣa, ashes, and the other distinguishing marks?[1]

"As for me, I am far beyond the fetters that bind. I have already taken the heroic māheśvara vow. And I have rooted out the two kinds of karma.[2] Is it right for you to try to drown me once again in this ocean of karma?

"You are blind! That is the only conceivable explanation for your desire to perform a thread ceremony for Basava. Basava has decapitated Brahma, and he has been born among pramathas;[3] how can you take him to be of the lineage of Brahma?

"Once a person has gone beyond caste and lineage, and once he has been born to a good guru, why should you again make him dependent upon caste and clan? How can you even decide on a caste for a devotee of Abhava,[4] who makes no distinction according to caste?

"No matter how you look at it, I should not go through with this thread ceremony! What is the point of talking about it any longer?"

THE STORY OF KAKKAYYA

"O Lord, there was a devotee of Three Eyes[5] named Kakkayya who was an enemy of the brahmins.

---

9. The sacred thread (running over the left shoulder and under the right) is worn continuously by Brahmans and other high-caste men from the time of their initiation into the Vedic community as boys.
1. Shaiva devotees often smear ash on the chest and forehead as a reminder of the transience of life. Rudrākṣa seeds were used as rosary beads.

2. Both good and bad deeds produce karma that keep one trapped in the cycle of rebirth.
3. Attendants of Shiva. Basavanna is equating himself with Shiva, who according to legend cut off one of Brahma's (originally) five heads.
4. "Birthless," a name of Shiva.
5. Shiva.

"A scholar sat at the city gate as a purāṇa reader, and, with all the *kāṭĕrukus*[6] listening in amazement, he sang purāṇas. He told the story of how Hara[7] used Brahma's skull as his begging bowl. But he would not narrate the story of how Hara killed Viṣṇu's commander with his spear and how he slew Viṣṇu himself. He sang about how Viṣṇu defeated Bali by growing very large, and how he lifted his foot in the Trivikrama form. But even then he would not tell about how Īśvara broke the spinal cord of that same Trivikrama.

"He told how Vyāsa raised up his hand, but he would not tell how that hand was broken by Śiva, and he would not point out the place where Keśava's head fell when Hara got angry and cut it off at the sacrifice. He told how Viṣṇu took the form of a man-lion and killed Hiraṇyākṣa, but he would not tell how Śiva took the form of a śarabha and destroyed the man-lion by tearing out its bowels.[8]

"He read the part that says that everything is permeated with Viṣṇu and explained it in detail, but he would not mention how Three Eyes destroyed Hari along with everything else. He explained that Hari is the creator of the world, but he would not mention that Īśvara is Hari's lord.[9] He mentioned that Hari also has the name Viśva, but he would not mention that Hara is Viśva's lord. He said that Hari is the supreme, but he would not say that Hara is the Supreme of the supreme. He said that Hari is the great Māyā,[1] but he would not say that Hara is the great god. Being ignorant of the real meaning of the word *harihara,* he claimed that Hari and Hara are one and the same. He would not say that Kāma Killer is called Harihara because he killed Hari.[2]

"He was a biased purāṇa reader who would not see things as they really are but simply cried out whatever he pleased.

"'Anyone who criticizes Śiva must be killed,' said Kakkayya. 'His book must be burned, and I am the one who has to do it!'

"Being enraged with the traitor to Śiva, Kakkayya ripped open his belly with a pruning hook, decapitated him, placed his head in his own belly, slew him, and was fully elated with what he had done.

"The purāṇa reader's body was torn completely to shreds and scattered around like a heap of worms."

THE STORY OF NIḌUMĀRA

"And then there was a king named Niḍumāra. In his realm he was the only individual who was not a Jain. When he got to thinking seriously about the matter, he could not imagine why there was not a single other individual who wore the three lines of ash on his forehead.[3] He had heard how a Kāma Killer devotee named Śivajñānasambandhi had gone to the Pāṇḍya king. He had also heard the story of his heroic māheśvara argument, and how he had impaled all the Jains of the rival religion on iron staves.

6. A forest tribe. It seems to be used in a derogatory sense to refer to the listeners, who are usually upper-caste people [translator's note].
7. Another name of Shiva. The references that follow are to various myths relating to the powers and relative status of Shiva and Vishnu. Vishnu's fifth incarnation was the dwarf Vamana, who subdued the demon-king Bali by growing to immeasurable proportions and occupying the whole universe in "three strides" (the meaning of "Trivikrama"). Ishvara is a name of Shiva.
8. A *sarabha* is a mythical creature with eight legs and

more strength than a lion. The demon-king Hiranyakashipu had received a boon that protected him from all harm from man or beast. Vishnu took on the combined form of the man-lion in order to slay him.
9. Hari is another name of Vishnu.
1. Cosmic illusion.
2. The common view of Harihara as a combined form of the two gods ("Hari and Hara") is here disputed (the "Hara, or Slayer, of Hari"). Shiva destroyed the god of love and hence is known as "Kama Killer."
3. A sign that one is a devotee of Shiva.

"When King Niḍumāra reflected on these stories that he had heard, he called the noted Jain teachers and all those who were expert in Jain mantras.

"'O you foolish followers of a senseless religion that has no basis in śruti![4] O you beastly animals who worship one who acts like an animal and know nothing of the lord of the beasts! O you sinners who wear no ashes and follow the evil doctrine of emptiness![5] O you untouchables who stray from the true path and employ illusory arguments based on nonduality and karma! O you enemies who have no interest in knowledge but instead set up yourselves as centers of ignorance! How have you managed to subject my people to your evil teachings for so long? Look what Piḷḷa Nāyanāru,[6] Abhava's devotee, has done. He has employed logic and miracles to establish Śiva as the author of everything. By doing so, he has wiped out the very names of Buddhism and Jainism from the Pāṇḍya country. He even impaled their sages on iron staves.

"'Therefore, you must worship Black Neck.[7] If you do not, I will impale you upside down on red-hot iron spears,' he said.

"With a sharp sword in his hand, the Śaiva devotee cut off their heads like animals and impaled them on staves. But when the Jains turned and became devotees of Śiva, he joyfully protected them, did he not?"

∽∞∾

⊷ ⚎◈⚎ ⊷

Mahadeviyakka[1]

Other men are thorn

Other men are thorn
under the smooth leaf.
I cannot touch them,
go near them, nor trust them,
5   nor speak to them confidences.

Mother,
because they all have thorns
in their chests,
I cannot take
10   any man in my arms but my lord

white as jasmine.[2]

4. The Vedas (literally, "the hearing" of sacred texts in recitation).

5. Followers of a school of Buddhist philosophy, who believed in the ultimate unreality of the world.

6. Another name of Jnanasambandhi.

7. Shiva, so called after swallowing the poison produced at the cosmic churning of the primeval milk ocean.

1. Translated by A. K. Ramanujan. A younger contemporary of Basavanna, Mahadeviyakka ("Elder sister Mahadevi," c. 1200) is said to have been initiated into Shiva worship at the age of ten. Pressured to marry a local chieftain, she abandoned him after enduring a violent relationship. In defiance of patriarchal custom she forsook clothing, wore matted hair, and wandered as a mendicant. Upon reaching Kalyana, the center of the Virashaiva community, she gained entry into the sect after much debate. She later wandered to the holy mountain Shri Shaila in Andhra Pradesh, with which she is still associated, and where she died, according to legend, into "oneness with Shiva" in her early twenties.

2. The form of Shiva in the temple of Mahadevi's native village was Cennamallikarjuna, here poetically translated as "lord white as jasmine."

Who cares

Who cares
   who strips a tree of leaf
   once the fruit is plucked?

Who cares
5   who lies with the woman
   you have left?

Who cares
   who ploughs the land
   you have abandoned?

10 After this body has known my lord
   who cares if it feeds
   a dog
   or soaks up water?

Better than meeting

Better than meeting
and mating all the time
is the pleasure of mating once
after being far apart.

5 When he's away
I cannot wait
to get a glimpse of him.

Friend, when will I have it
both ways,
10 be with Him
yet not with Him,
my lord white as jasmine?

—— 〓◆〓 ——

Kabir[1]

Saints, I see the world is mad[2]

Saints, I see the world is mad.
If I tell the truth they rush to beat me,

---

1. Translated by Linda Hess and Shukdev Sinha. Born probably at the beginning of the 15th century in the ancient north Indian city of Benares (Varanasi), Kabir belonged to a weaver community that had recently converted to Islam. As a young man he is thought to have become a disciple of the orthodox Hindu guru Ramananda. The confluence of these various strands of Islamic and Hindu thinking probably led him to adopt the form of devotion for which he is most famous, one directed toward an ecumenical and undifferentiated divine power (*nirguna*). Legend has it that at his death Hindu devotees claimed his corpse for cremation while Muslims claimed it for burial. As the two camps were about to resort to blows, the shroud was lifted, to revel nothing but a heap of flowers. *The Bijak* (which probably means "Account Book"), from which these poems are taken, is the preeminent among the several collections of Kabir's verse.

2. A number of Kabir's poems, which were likely performed before an audience representing all walks of life, are marked by an ambivalent form of address such as this, at once reverent and ironic.

if I lie they trust me.
I've seen the pious Hindus, rule-followers,
5   early morning bath-takers—
killing souls, they worship rocks.
They know nothing.
I've seen plenty of Muslim teachers, holy men
reading their holy books
10   and teaching their pupils techniques.
They know just as much.
And posturing yogis, hypocrites,
hearts crammed with pride,
15   praying to brass, to stones, reeling
with pride in their pilgrimage,
fixing their caps and their prayer-beads,
painting their brow-marks and arm-marks,
braying their hymns and their couplets,
20   reeling. They never heard of soul.
The Hindu says Ram is the Beloved,
the Turk says Rahim.[2]
Then they kill each other.
No one knows the secret.
25   They buzz their mantras from house to house,
puffed with pride.
The pupils drown along with their gurus.
In the end they're sorry.
Kabir says, listen saints:
30   they're all deluded!
Whatever I say, nobody gets it.
It's too simple.

Brother, where did your two gods come from?

Brother, where did your two gods come from?
Tell me, who made you mad?
Ram, Allah, Keshav, Karim, Hari, Hazrat—[1]

so many names.
5   So many ornaments, all one gold,
it has no double nature.[2]
For conversation we make two—
this *namaz,* that *puja,*
this Mahadev, that Muhammed,
10   this Brahma, that Adam,[3]
this a Hindu, that a Turk,

---

2. Ram or Rama was reckoned the seventh avatar of the Hindu god Vishnu. Rahim, "the Merciful," is an epithet for God in Islam.
1. Keshav and Hari are epithets of Vishnu. Karim, "the noble or magnificent one," and Hazrat are terms associated with God in Islam.
2. The idea of a singular underlying substance to the man-

ifold nature of the world is an idea stretching back to the Upanishads (see Volume A).
3. *Namaz* and *puja* are the Muslim and Hindu terms respectively for prayer. Mahadev, "the great god," is an epithet of Shiva, who along with Brahma and Vishnu is one of the preeminent gods of the Hindu pantheon. The biblical story of Adam and Eve also appears in the Qur'an.

but all belong to earth.
Vedas, Korans, all those books,
those Mullas and those Brahmins—
15   so many names, so many names,
but the pots are all one clay.
Kabir says, nobody can find Ram,
both sides are lost in schisms.
One slaughters goats, one slaughters cows,
20   they squander their birth in isms.

Pandit, look in your heart for knowledge

Pandit, look in your heart for knowledge.
Tell me where untouchability[1]
came from, since you believe in it.
Mix red juice, white juice and air—
5   a body bakes in a body.[2]
As soon as the eight lotuses
        are ready, it comes
        into the world. Then what's
        untouchable?
10   Eighty-four hundred thousand vessels
decay into dust, while the potter
keeps slapping clay
on the wheel, and with a touch
cuts each one off.
15   We eat by touching, we wash
by touching, from a touch
the world was born.
So who's untouched? asks Kabir.
Only he
20   who has no taint of Maya.[3]

When you die, what do you do with your body?

When you die, what do you do with your body?
Once the breath stops
you have to put it away.
There are several ways to deal
5   with spoiled flesh.
Some burn it, some bury it
in the ground.
Hindus prefer cremation,
Turks burial.
10   But in the end, one way or another,
both have to leave home.

---

1. The ritually polluting status of groups outside the four social orders into which Hindu society was theoretically divided.
2. *Ghat* can mean both "body" and "clay pot." Potters are considered untouchable in North India, and clay vessels are unclean, the cheap unbaked ones being thrown away after single use. The body is commonly referred to as a pot—one whose clay surrounds the eight lotuses or *chakras*, channels of spiritual energy [translator's note].
3. Cosmic illusion.

Death spreads the karmic net[1]
like a fisherman snaring fish.
What is a man without Ram?[2]
15   A dung beetle in the road.
Kabir says, you'll be sorry later
when you go from this house
to that one.

It's a heavy confusion

It's a heavy confusion.
Veda, Koran, holiness, hell, woman, man,
a clay pot shot with air and sperm . . .
When the pot falls apart, what do you call it?
5   Numskull! You've missed the point.
It's all one skin and bone, one piss and shit,
one blood, one meat.
From one drop, a universe.
Who's Brahman? Who's Shudra?[1]
10   Brahma *rajas,* Shiva *tamas,* Vishnu *sattva* . . .[2]
Kabir says, plunge into Ram!
There: No Hindu. No Turk.

The road the pandits took

The road the pandits° took,   *learned men*
crowds took.

Ram's pass is a high one.
Kabir keeps climbing.

+━━◆━━+

Tukaram[1]

I was only dreaming

I was only dreaming
Namdeo[2] and Vitthal
Stepped into my dream

"Your job is to make poems,"
5   said Namdeo.
"Stop fooling around."

1. The pattern of actions and attachments that keep people caught in the cycle of birth, death, and rebirth.
2. In Kabir's religious terminology, "Ram" can denote God in a universal unmanifest form expressed and experienced most effectively through chanting.
1. The lowest of the four ideal social orders of Hindu society.
2. According to ancient Indian thought, the three constituents of the material universe.
1. Translated by Dilup Chitre. Tukaram (traditionally 1608–1649), was born to a family of landed peasants in a village in what is now Maharashtra state in central India. Famine and plague took his parents and one of his two wives before he was 20, when he is said to have renounced the world. His highly individual poems are mostly written in honor of the form of Vishnu named Vitthal, worshipped in the village of Pandharpur in Maharashtra.
2. Namdeo (or Namdev, c. 14th century), a lower-caste cotton printer by profession, is revered as the composer of Marathi hymns to Vitthal, as well as other hymns in Hindi.

Vitthal gave me the measure
And slapped me gently
To arouse me
10   From my dream
Within a dream

"The grand total
Of the poems Namdeo vowed to write
Was one billion."
15   He said,
"All the unwritten ones, Tuka,
Are your dues."

If only you would

If only you would
Give me refuge O Lord
To stay at your feet
In a line of saints.

5   I've already left behind
The world I loved.
Don't stand still:
It's your move now.

My caste is low;
10   My origins humble.
A little help from you
Will go a long way.

Thanks to Namdeo
You visited me
15   In a dream that left me
Poetry.

Have I utterly lost my hold on reality

Have I utterly lost my hold on reality
To imagine myself writing poetry?
I am sure your illustrious devotees,
All famous poets, will laugh at me.

5   Today, I face the toughest test of life:
Whereof I have no experience,
Thereof I have been asked to sing.

I am the innocent one asked to sin,
Without any foretaste of what I must commit.
10   I am just a beginner, untutored in the art,
My Master Himself is unrevealed to me.

Illuminate, and inspire me, O Lord.
Says Tuka, my time is running out.

I scribble and cancel it again

I scribble and cancel it again,
O heavenly critic, to pass your test.

I choose a word, only to change it,
Hoping to find one you'd like the best.

5 I beg your pardon again; and again;
Lord, let not my words go waste.

Says Tuka, please, talk back at least
So that this poem will have something to say.

Where does one begin with you?

Where does one begin with you?
O Lord, you have no opening line.
It's so hard to get you started.

Everything I tried went wrong.
5 You've used up all my faculties.

What I just said vanished in the sky
And I've fallen to the ground again.

Says Tuka my mind is stunned:
I can't find a word to say.

Some of you may say

Some of you may say
I am the author
Of these poems.
But
5 Believe me
This voice
Is not my own.

I have no
Personal skill.
10 It is
The Cosmic One
Making me speak.

What does a poor fellow like me
Know of the subtleties of meaning?
15 I speak what Govind[1]
Makes me say.

He has appointed me
To measure it out.
The authority rests

---

1. Govind ("lord of cows") is an epithet of Krishna, a form of the creator god Vishnu.

20   With the Master;
      Not me.

      Says Tuka, I'm only the servant.
      See?
      All this bears
25   The seal of His Name.

To arrange words

      To arrange words
      In some order
      Is not the same thing
      As the inner poise
5   That's poetry.

      The truth of poetry
      Is the truth
      Of being.
      It's an experience
10   Of truth.

      No ornaments
      Survive
      A crucible.
      Fire reveals
15   Only molten
      Gold.

      Says Tuka
      We are here
      To reveal.
20   We do not waste
      Words.

When my father died

      When my father died
      I was too young to understand;
      I had not to worry
      About the family then.

5   Vithu,[1] this kingdom is Yours and mine.
      It's not the business of anyone else.

      My wife died:
      May she rest in peace.
      The Lord has removed
10   My attachment.

      My children died:
      So much the better.

1. A diminutive of Vitthal.

The Lord has removed
The last illusion.

15   My mother died
In front of my eyes.
My worries are all over
Says Tuka.

Born a Shudra, I have been a trader

Born a Shudra, I have been a trader,
This deity comes to me like a sacred heirloom.

I am unable to say any more, but O saints,
I shall honour my pledge to answer your question

5   I was extremely miserable as a householder
Ever since both my parents died.

Famine reduced me to penury, I lost my honour.
I had to watch one of my wives starve to death.

Ashamed of myself, I suffered great anguish
10   To find my business in ruins.

The shrine of my deity had fallen apart
And I felt like restoring it first.

In the beginning, I used to perform *keertan* there.[1]
On the day of *ekadashi,* in my untutored way.

15   I had learnt some sayings of the saints by rote
And I reproduced those with reverence and faith.

I would join the chorus that followed the lead singers,
I would sing the refrain with a pure heart.

20   I was never ashamed of following the saints.
The dust of their feet was sacred to me.

I worked hard so that my body could endure more.
I helped others as much as I could.

⤙ ⊷◆⊷ ⤚

Kshetrayya[1]

A Woman to Her Lover

"Your body is my body,"
you used to say,

1. Congregational singing in praise of Vitthal, performed
on the eleventh (*ekadashi*) day of the month.
1. Translated by A. K. Ramanujan, V. N. Rao, and David
Shulman. Kshetrayya is thought to have been active as a
court poet in southern India during the mid-17th century.

The village Muvvapuri and its deity Muvva Gopala figure
in his work, suggesting that he hailed from the village of
Movva in present-day Andhra Pradesh. His songs are still
sung by the Brahman males who take on female roles in
the *kucipudi* dance tradition.

and it has come true,
Muvva Gopāla.

5   Though I was with you
all these days,
I wasn't sure.

Some woman has scratched
nail marks on your chest,
10   but I'm the one who feels the hurt.

You go sleepless all night,
but it's my eyes
that turn red.

    "Your body is my body," you used to say

10   Ever since you fell for that woman,
it's my mind
that's in distress.

When I look at those charming love bites
she has left on your lips,
15   it's my lip that shakes.

    "Your body is my body," you used to say

Maybe you made love
to another woman,
for, O lord who rules me,
20   my desire is sated.

Forgive me, Gopāla,
but when you come back here,
I'm the one who feels small
with shame.

25   *"Your body is my body," you used to say*

A Young Woman to a Friend

Those women, they deceived me.
They told me he was a woman,
and now my heart is troubled
by what he did.

5   First I thought
she was my aunt and uncle's daughter,
so I bow to her, and she blesses me:
"You'll get married soon,
don't be bashful. I will bring you
10   the man of your heart."

"Those firm little breasts of yours
will soon
grow round and full," she says.

And she fondles them
15   and scratches them
with the edge of her nail.

"Come eat with me," she says,
as she holds me close
and feeds me as at a wedding.

20   *Those women, they told me he was a woman!*

Then she announces:
"My husband is not in town.
Come home with me."
So I go and sleep in her bed.

25   After a while she says,
"I'm bored. Let's play
a kissing game, shall we?
Too bad we're both women."

Then, as she sees me falling asleep,
30   off my guard,
she tries some
strange things on me.

        Those women, they told me he was a woman!

She says, "I can't sleep.
35   Let's do what men do."
Thinking "she" was a woman,
I get on top of him.

Then he doesn't let go:
he holds me so tight
40   he loses himself in me.
Wicked as ever, he declares:

"I am your Muvva Gopāla!"
And he touches me expertly
and makes love to me.

45   *Those women, they told me he was a woman!*

A Courtesan to Her Lover

Pour gold as high as I stand, I still won't sleep with you.
Why be stubborn, Muvva Gopāla? Why all these tricks?

You set women afloat on your words,
break into their secret places,
5   deceive them with affectionate lies,
excite them in love play,
get together the whole crowd one day,
and then you steal away like a spinach thief.

        Pour gold as high as I stand

10   You coax women's affections,
      make them amorous and faint,
      do things you shouldn't be doing,
      confuse them, lie in bed with them,
      and then you leave without a sound,
15   shaking your dust all over them.

   Pour gold as high as I stand

      You opportunist,
      you excite them from moment to moment,
      make mouths water,
20   show them love to make them surrender,
      drown them in a sea of passion,
      and by the time the morning star appears—
      you get up and vanish.

   Pour gold as high as I stand

A Married Woman Speaks to Her Lover

      I can't stay too long.
      I have to get home.
      There's no time for all the fun.
      Don't get me in trouble,
5   my clever man.

      I left my husband's embrace
      to come here
      just because you called.
      You want to leave your nail marks
10   on my breasts—
      I'm no prostitute!

      I have no quarrel with you.
      Satisfy your need
      and send me away.
15   Listen, lover:
      it's not good for your health
      to lose too much sleep.
      Why argue with me?

   Can't stay too long

20   You're biting my lips too hard.
      How can I hide the marks?
      Because sugarcane is sweet,
      you want to pull it up,
      root and all.
25   It's hard to bear.
      Just because I'm so taken with you,
      you trap me in your net of magic,
      you clever man.

Can't stay too long

30 You've made love to me often enough
for today.
Let go for now, Muvva Gopāla,
my lord.
Is it right to be stubborn now?
35 Is there a limit to greed?
The more you make love,
the more you want it.
This body of mine is your property.
I'll come whenever you want me.
40 Be good to me,
my clever man.

Can't stay too long

A Married Woman to Her Lover (1)

My old husband is better than you, and that's the truth.
You promise sweet things in private
and only now you show your face!

Where can I hide my desire,
5 to whom shall I give it now?
Enough, enough, go away.
Enough of this adventure at this ungodly hour!

My old husband is better than you!

Like a parrot waiting
10 for the fruit of the silk-cotton tree
I fell for your looks
and came to you.

My old husband is better than you!

Fighting off sleep all night
15 waiting for you, it was like pouring
into water what was meant for a fire.
It's late. I've got to go home, Muvva Gopāla.

My old husband is better than you!

A Married Woman to Her Lover (2)

Go find a root or something.
I have no girlfriends here I can trust.

When I swore at you, you didn't listen.
You said all my curses were blessings.
5 You grabbed me, you bastard,
and had me by force.
I've now missed my period
and my husband is not it.

> *Go find a root or something*

10   I have set myself up for blame.
What's the use of blaming you?
I've even lost my taste for food.
What can I do now?
Go to the midwives and get me a drug
15   before the women begin to talk.

> *Go find a root or something*

As if he fell from the ceiling,
my husband is suddenly home.
He made love to me last night.
20   Now I fear no scandal.
All my wishes, Muvva Gopāla,
have reached their end,
so, in your image,
I'll bear you a son.

25   *Go find a root or something*

[END OF VERNACULAR WRITING IN SOUTH ASIA]

————

Wu Cheng'en
c. 1500–1582

Journey to the West (Xi you ji) is one of four vernacular language novels produced during the Ming dynasty (1368–1644) that came to be identified by traditional critics as masterworks of Chinese fiction. Like the others, it is rooted in historical fact, in this case the expedition of a Tang dynasty monk named Xuanzang (596–664) to India to bring Buddhist scriptures back to China. It shares with other fictional works an indebtedness to the conventions of oral story-telling, evident in its reliance on sequences of events whose resolution is always suspended, with formulaic predictability, until the following chapter. Equally common to contemporary vernacular works is its use of both prose and verse to carry the narrative forward, a tradition established centuries before in didactic texts for popular consumption that elaborated imaginatively on stories about the lives of Buddhist saints. In *Journey to the West,* the passages of poetry are of higher quality and more central to the narrative than in other novels, but the most distinctive feature of the work is its development of the tradition's most captivating character, a wily, brash, and comic swashbuckler who happens to be a monkey.

Born into a family of high officials and schooled in the Confucian classics by his father, the historical Xuanzang renounced a political career and joined a Buddhist monastery at the age of thirteen. Inspired by lively doctrinal debates swirling about during the Tang dynasty, he determined that understanding and resolution would be impossible without resort to key scriptures currently unavailable in China. When the emperor refused to authorize an official journey to fetch them, Xuanzang embarked on his mission to India in secret with a merchant caravan, late in 627. He returned to the capital of Chang'an in early 645, laden with over 650 items and, equally important, an imperial pardon. Supported by the throne, he then spent the rest of his

life studying and translating the texts and also wrote an account of his harrowing travels to secure them.

By the early thirteenth century Xuanzang's pilgrimage had become rich material for legends, story cycles, and dramas about a band of increasingly colorful characters whose perils
and exploits across fantastic landscapes captured the popular imagination. These culminated in
the 100-chapter novel, *Journey to the West*, of which the earliest preserved edition dates to
1592. Its supposed author was a late Ming dynasty writer and official, Wu Cheng'en, who, after
passing the first level of the civil service examination, held minor government posts and traveled widely between the capital and the provinces. An accomplished poet, he circulated freely
in elite literary society. He was known both for his wit and his keen interest in the supernatural
and is said to have composed the novel toward the end of his life. Although the attribution of
authorship to Wu is relatively recent and based on rather scant evidence, none of its many chal-
lengers has offered a more compelling alternative.

A twelve-chapter prologue introduces Xuanzang's most fascinating and resourceful companion, Sun Wukong ("The Monkey Enlightened to Emptiness"), also called Pilgrim. The
monk's journey then consumes all but three chapters of *Journey to the West* and takes him
through a preordained series of eighty-one ordeals presented by assorted fiends, monsters, and
deities in disguise. The monk is usually referred to as Tripitaka—"Three Baskets," a name for
the body of Buddhist scriptures, thereby identifying the seeker and his goal. Scholars have
pointed to the formulaic nature of each adventure, in which the monk and his companions typically find their initially carefree travels disturbed, first by some natural discomfort (such as cold
or hunger) and then by some variety of demon, who usually succeeds in capturing Xuanzang.
Sun Wukong, who is generally not among the captives, almost always proves instrumental in
rescuing the monk from each trap, thanks to a formula or weapon or, sometimes, divine intervention; this dispels the thrall of the demon, who then reveals its true form. All the while the monkey's mischievous inclinations require constant discipline from his master as well. The remarkably hapless Xuanzang also relies on assistance from three other companions with supernatural
features: Zhu Bajie ("The Pig of Eight Prohibitions"), a Daoist deity banished from the pantheon
for drunkenness and transformed into a pig/human figure of grossly but amusingly sensual appetites; Sha Wujing ("Sand Awakened to Purity"), an erstwhile cannibalistic monster converted
to a morose but dutiful Buddhist; and a faithful white horse who was once a dragon prince.

Previous fictional and dramatic accounts of Xuanzang's trek had already introduced the
intriguing figure of a "monkey novice-monk" as guide and protector. He bears striking similarities to other tricksters, among them the character of Hanuman in the *Ramayana*, as can be seen
in the Resonance following the selections given here. Legends about Hanuman are known to
have reached China by way of the trade route known as the Silk Road. While no definitive connection has been established, some scholars have suggested that a common stock of motifs was
probably available to the author of *Journey to the West*. New to the novel, compared with earlier versions of the pilgrimage, is the elaborate history of the monkey's origins and magical
powers provided in the prologue, and his talents and exploits subsequently engendered an independent legacy of spin-offs in opera, puppet theater, film, and comic books. Another innovation is the novel's underlying framework of multiple allegories. Much discussed by traditional
commentators, these were discounted by influential modern Chinese scholars at the beginning
of the twentieth century in favor of a focus on its more popular and comic appeal, but they have
recently been reevaluated as an essential aspect of the text's meaning.

Direct references to Buddhism are surprisingly rare in the novel, despite the centrality to
the story of a search for its sacred texts. The pilgrims' interactions can best be understood,
however, within the religion's framework of karmic redemption. "Karma" is the Hindu and
Buddhist term for one's destiny as determined by the pattern of actions as one progresses
through a series of lives, deaths, and rebirth, ideally toward enlightenment and eventual liberation from the cycle of death and rebirth. Xuanzang would be helpless without the assistance of

Xuanzang with his disciples. Drawing by Chao Hung-pen and Chien Hsiao-tai in *Monkey Subdues the White-Bone Demon* (Beijing, 1973).

his unusual companions, but they in turn must provide it to him in order to atone for previous misdeeds and earn valuable merit on a karmic balance sheet. Moreover, scholars have noted that the pilgrims may be regarded not only as a group working collectively toward a shared goal, but also as the various components—mental, corporeal and spiritual—of a single character. And, as is often the case in pilgrimage narratives elsewhere, what takes place on other levels is as intriguing as the physical quest itself.

About the precise nature of those allegorical dimensions considerable scholarly ink has been spilled. Given the Buddhist framework, we might expect the story to represent a journey toward spiritual enlightenment. The repetitiveness of the episodes makes it difficult to discern any significant progress, but commentators have speculated that this reflects a commitment to Chan (Zen) Buddhist beliefs that enlightenment is always already there as a state to be realized once one's mind is properly illuminated. Repeated references to Sun Wukong as the "monkey of the mind" support such a reading, and Xuanzang's attainment of the scriptures at the end of the novel is almost anticlimactic in this context. Commentators have also discerned an overlay of Daoist alchemical metaphors for self-refinement and immortality in a process attuned to phases of cosmic change, as well as allusions to terms drawn from a Confucian vocabulary of self-cultivation. It is important to note that such syncretic or mixed views were very much at the heart of sixteenth-century intellectual debates in China, which argued for a unity of the three main philosophical and religious teachings. But it is probably even more important to remember that what has captivated generations of readers of *Journey to the West* are its fantasy, humor, and satire, conveyed most vividly in the figure of Sun Wukong.

PRONUNCIATIONS:

Boddhisattva: boh-dee-SAHT-vah
Hsüan-tsang / Xuanzang: shwen-dzahng
Pa-chieh / Bajie: bah GEE-eh
Sun Wu-k'ung / Wukong: swun wōō-kŏŏng
T'ai-tsung: tie-dzŏŏng
Wu Cheng'en: wōō CHENG-en

from Journey to the West[1]
from *Chapter 1*

The divine root being conceived, the origin emerges;
The moral nature once cultivated, the Great Tao is born.

Beyond the ocean there was a country named Ao-lai. It was near a great ocean, in the midst of which was located the famous Flower-Fruit Mountain. This mountain, which constituted the chief range of the Ten Islets and formed the origin of the Three Islands,[2] came into being after the creation of the world. As a testimonial to its magnificence, there is the following *fu* poem:

Its majesty commands the wide ocean;
Its splendor rules the jasper sea;
Its majesty commands the wide ocean
When, like silver mountains, the tide sweeps fishes into caves;
Its splendor rules the jasper sea
When snowlike billows send forth serpents from the deep.
Plateaus are tall on the southwest side;
Soaring peaks arise from the Sea of the East.
There are crimson ridges and portentous rocks,
Precipitous cliffs and prodigious peaks.
Atop the crimson ridges
Phoenixes sing in pairs;
Before precipitous cliffs
The unicorn singly rests.
At the summit is heard the cry of golden pheasants;
In and out of stony caves are seen the strides of dragons;
In the forest are long-lived deer and immortal foxes.
On the trees are divine fowls and black cranes.
Strange grass and flowers never wither;
Green pines and cypresses keep eternal their spring.
Immortal peaches are always fruit-bearing;
Lofty bamboos often detain the clouds.

---

1. Translated by Anthony C. Yu.   2. Regions where the immortals dwell.

> Within a single gorge the creeping vines are dense;
> The grass color of meadows all around is fresh.
> This is indeed the pillar of Heaven, where a hundred rivers meet—
> The Earth's great axis, in ten thousand kalpas[3] unchanged.

There was on top of that very mountain an immortal stone, which measured thirty-six feet and five inches in height and twenty-four feet in circumference. The height of thirty-six feet and five inches corresponded to the three hundred and sixty-five cyclical degrees, while the circumference of twenty-four feet corresponded to the twenty-four solar terms of the calendar. On the stone were also nine perforations and eight holes, which corresponded to the Palaces of the Nine Constellations and the Eight Trigrams. Though it lacked the shade of trees on all sides, it was set off by epidendrums on the left and right. Since the creation of the world, it had been nourished for a long period by the seeds of Heaven and Earth and by the essences of the sun and the moon, until, quickened by divine inspiration, it became pregnant with a divine embryo. One day, it split open, giving birth to a stone egg about the size of a playing ball. Exposed to the wind, it was transformed into a stone monkey endowed with fully developed features and limbs. Having learned at once to climb and run, this monkey also bowed to the four quarters, while two beams of golden light flashed from his eyes to reach even the Palace of the Polestar. The light disturbed the Great Benevolent Sage of Heaven, the Celestial Jade Emperor of the Most Venerable Deva, who, attended by his divine ministers, was sitting in the Cloud Palace of the Golden Arches, in the Treasure Hall of the Divine Mists. Upon seeing the glimmer of the golden beams, he ordered Thousand-Mile Eye and Fair-Wind Ear to open the South Heavenly Gate and to look out. At this command the two captains went out to the gate, and, having looked intently and listened clearly, they returned presently to report, "Your subjects, obeying your command to locate the beams, discovered that they came from the Flower-Fruit Mountain at the border of the small Ao-lai Country, which lies to the east of the East Pūrvavideha Continent. On this mountain is an immortal stone which has given birth to an egg. Exposed to the wind, it has been transformed into a monkey, who, when bowing to the four quarters, has flashed from his eyes those golden beams that reached the Palace of the Polestar. Now that he is taking some food and drink, the light is about to grow dim." With compassionate mercy the Jade Emperor declared, "These creatures from the world below are born of the essences of Heaven and Earth, and they need not surprise us."

That monkey in the mountain was able to walk, run, and leap about; he fed on grass and shrubs, drank from the brooks and streams, gathered mountain flowers, and searched out fruits from trees. He made his companions the tiger and the lizard, the wolf and the leopard; he befriended the civet and the deer, and he called the gibbon and the baboon his kin. At night he slept beneath stony ridges, and in the morning he sauntered about the caves and the peaks. Truly, "in the mountain there is no passing of time; the cold recedes, but one knows not the year." One very hot morning, he was playing with a group of monkeys under the shade of some pine trees to escape the heat. Look at them, each amusing himself in his own way by

> Swinging from branches to branches,
> Searching for flowers and fruits;
> They played two games or three

---

3. A kalpa is a vast cosmic era of 129,600 years.

> With pebbles and with pellets;
> They circled sandy pits;
> They built rare pagodas;
> They chased the dragon flies;
> They ran down small lizards;
> Bowing low to the sky,
> They worshiped Bodhisattvas;
> They pulled the creeping vines;
> They plaited mats with grass;
> They searched to catch the louse;
> They bit or crushed with their nails;
> They dressed their furry coats;
> They scraped their finger nails;
> Some leaned and leaned;
> Some rubbed and rubbed;
> Some pushed and pushed;
> Some pressed and pressed;
> Some pulled and pulled;
> Some tugged and tugged.
> Beneath the pine forest they played without a care,
> Washing themselves in the green-water stream.

So, after the monkeys had frolicked for a while, they went to bathe in the mountain stream and saw that its currents bounced and splashed like tumbling melons. As the old saying goes, "Fowls have their fowl speech, and beasts have their beast language." The monkeys said to each other, "We don't know where this water comes from. Since we have nothing to do today, let us follow the stream up to its source to have some fun." With a shriek of joy, they dragged along males and females, calling out to brothers and sisters, and scrambled up the mountain alongside the stream. Reaching its source, they found a great waterfall. What they saw was

> A column of rising white rainbows,
> A thousand fathoms of dancing waves—
> Which the sea wind buffets but cannot sever,
> On which the river moon shines and reposes.
> Its cold breath divides the green ranges;
> Its tributaries moisten the blue-green hillsides.
> This torrential body, its name a cascade,
> Appears truly like a hanging curtain.

All the monkeys clapped their hands in acclaim: "Marvelous water! Marvelous water! So this waterfall is distantly connected with the stream at the base of the mountain, and flows directly out, even to the Great Ocean." They said also, "If any of us had the ability to penetrate the curtain and find out where the water comes from without hurting himself, we would honor him as king." They gave the call three times, when suddenly the stone monkey leaped out from the crowd. He answered the challenge with a loud voice, "I'll go in! I'll go in!" What a monkey! For

> Today his fame will spread,
> His fortune arrives with the time;
> Fated to live in this place,
> He's sent as king to his palace.

Look at him! He closed his eyes, crouched low, and with one leap he jumped straight through the waterfall. Opening his eyes at once and raising his head to look around, he saw that there was neither water nor waves inside, only a gleaming, shining bridge. He paused to collect himself and looked more carefully again: it was a bridge made of sheet iron. The water beneath it surged through a hole in the rock to reach the outside, filling in all the space under the arch. With bent body he climbed on the bridge, looking about as he walked, and discovered a beautiful place that seemed to be some kind of residence. Then he saw

> Fresh mosses piling up indigo,
> White clouds like jade afloat,
> And luminous sheens of mist and smoke;
> Empty windows, quiet rooms,
> And carved flowers growing smoothly on benches;
> Stalactites suspended in milky caves;
> Rare blossoms voluminous over the ground.
> Pans and stoves near the wall show traces of fire;
> Bottles and cups on the table contain leftovers.
> The stone seats and beds were truly lovable;
> The stone pots and bowls were more praiseworthy.
> There were, furthermore, a stalk or two of tall bamboos,
> And three or five sprigs of plum flowers.
> With a few green pines always draped in rain,
> This whole place indeed resembled a home.

After staring at the place for a long time, he jumped across the middle of the bridge and looked left and right. There in the middle was a stone tablet on which was inscribed in regular, large letters: "The Blessed Land of Flower-Fruit Mountain, the Cave Heaven of Water-Curtain Cave." Beside himself with delight, the stone monkey quickly turned around to go back out and, closing his eyes and crouching again, leaped out of the water. "A great stroke of luck," he exclaimed with two loud guffaws, "a great stroke of luck." The other monkeys surrounded him and asked, "How is it inside? How deep is the water?" The stone monkey replied, "There isn't any water at all. There's a sheet iron bridge, and beyond it is a piece of heaven-sent property." "What do you mean that there's property in there?" asked the monkeys. Laughing, the stone monkey said, "This water splashes through a hole in the rock and fills the space under the bridge. Beside the bridge there is a stone mansion with trees and flowers. Inside are stone ovens and stoves, stone pots and pans, stone beds and benches. A stone tablet in the middle has the inscription, 'The Blessed Land of the Flower-Fruit Mountain, The Cave Heaven of the Water-Curtain Cave.'[4] This is truly the place for us to settle in. It is, moreover, very spacious inside and can hold thousands of the young and old. Let's all go live in there, and spare ourselves from being subject to the whims of Heaven. For we have in there

> A retreat from the wind,
> A shelter from the rain.
> You fear no frost or snow;
> You hear no thunderclap.
> Mist and smoke are brightened,

---

4. "Blessed Land" and "Cave Heaven" indicate dwellings of Daoists.

> Warmed by a holy light—
> The pines are ever green;
> Rare flowers, daily new."

When the monkeys heard that, they were delighted, saying. "You go in first and lead the way." The stone monkey closed his eyes again, crouched low, and jumped inside. "All of you," he cried, "Follow me in! Follow me in!" The braver of the monkeys leaped in at once, but the more timid ones stuck out their heads and then drew them back, scratched their ears, rubbed their jaws, and chattered noisily. After milling around for some time, they too bounded inside. Jumping across the bridge, they were all soon snatching dishes, clutching bowls, or fighting for stoves and beds—shoving and pushing things hither and thither. Befitting their stubbornly prankish nature, the monkeys could not keep still for a moment and stopped only when they were utterly exhausted. The stone monkey then solemnly took a seat above and spoke to them: "Gentlemen! 'If a man lacks trustworthiness, it is difficult to know what he can accomplish!'[5] You yourselves promised just now that whoever could get in here and leave again without hurting himself would be honored as king. Now that I have come in and gone out, gone out and come in, and have found for all of you this heavenly grotto in which you may reside securely and enjoy the privilege of raising a family, why don't you honor me as your king?" When the monkeys heard this, they all folded their hands on their breasts and obediently prostrated themselves. Each one of them then lined up according to rank and age, and, bowing reverently, they intoned, "Long live our great king!" From that moment, the stone monkey ascended the throne of kingship. He did away with the word "stone" in his name and assumed the title, Handsome Monkey King. There is a testimonial poem which says:

> When triple spring mated to produce all things,
> A divine stone was quickened by the sun and moon:
> The egg became a monkey and reached the Great Way.
> A name he had and in elixir success.
> His inward shape is concealed for it has no form,
> But his outward form is by his action plainly known,
> All mankind will be his subject in every age:
> He's called a king and a sage who rules over all.

The Handsome Monkey King thus led a flock of gibbons and baboons, some of whom were appointed by him as his officers and ministers. They toured the Flower-Fruit Mountain in the morning, and they lived in the Water-Curtain Cave by night. Living in concord and sympathy, they did not mingle with bird or beast but enjoyed their independence in perfect happiness. For such were their activities:

> In the spring they gathered flowers for food and drink.
> In the summer they went in quest of fruits for sustenance.
> In the autumn they collected taros and chestnuts to ward off time.
> In the winter they search for yellow-sperms[6] to live out the year.

The Handsome Monkey King had enjoyed this insouciant existence for three or four hundred years when one day, while feasting with the rest of the monkeys, he suddenly grew sad and shed a few tears. Alarmed, the monkeys surrounded him bowed down

---

5. From Confucius, *Analects*, 2.22.

6. A small plant whose roots were used for medicinal purposes.

and asked, "What is disturbing the Great King?" The Monkey King replied, "Though I am very happy at the moment, I am a little concerned about the future. Hence my vexation." The monkeys all laughed and said, "The Great King indeed does not know contentment! Here we daily have a banquet on an immortal mountain in a blessed land, in an ancient cave on a divine continent. We are not subject to the unicorn or the phoenix, nor are we governed by the rulers of mankind. Such independence and comfort are immeasurable blessings. Why, then, does he worry about the future?" The Monkey King said, "Though we are not subject to the laws of man today, nor need we be threatened by the rule of any bird or beast, old age and physical decay in the future will disclose the secret sovereignty of Yama, King of the Underworld. If we die, shall we not have lived in vain, not being able to rank forever among the heavenly beings?"

When the monkeys heard this, they all covered their faces and wept mournfully, each one troubled by his own impermanence. But look! From among the ranks a bareback monkey suddenly leaped forth and cried aloud, "If the Great King is so far-sighted, it may well indicate the sprouting of his religious inclination. There are, among the five major divisions of all living creatures,[7] only three species that are not subject to Yama, King of the Underworld." The Monkey King said, "Do you know who they are?" The monkey said, "They are the Buddhas, the immortals, and the holy sages; these three alone can avoid the Wheel of Transmigration as well as the process of birth and destruction, and live as long as Heaven and Earth, the mountains and the streams." "Where do they live?" asked the Monkey King. The monkey said, "They do not live beyond the world of the Jambūdvīpa, for they dwell within ancient caves on immortal mountains." When the Monkey King heard this, he was filled with delight, saying, "Tomorrow I shall take leave of you all and go down the mountain. Even if I have to wander with the clouds to the corners of the sea or journey to the distant edges of Heaven, I intend to find these three kinds of people. I will learn from them how to be young forever and escape the calamity inflicted by King Yama." Lo, this utterance at once led him to leap clear of the Web of Transmigration, and to turn him into the Great Sage, Equal to Heaven. All the monkeys clapped their hands in acclamation, saying, "Wonderful! Wonderful! Tomorrow we shall scour the mountain ranges to gather plenty of fruits, so that we may send the Great King off with a great banquet."

Next day the monkeys duly went to gather immortal peaches, to pick rare fruits, to dig out mountain herbs, and to chop yellow-sperms. They brought in an orderly manner every variety of orchids and epidendrums, exotic plants and strange flowers. They set out the stone chairs and stone tables, covering the tables with immortal wines and food, Look at the

> Golden balls and pearly pellets.
> Red ripeness and yellow plumpness.
> Golden balls and pearly pellets are the cherries,
> Their colors truly luscious.
> Red ripeness and yellow plumpness are the plums,
> Their taste—a fragrant tartness.
> Fresh lungans
> Of sweet pulps and thin skins.
> Fiery lychees
> Of small pits and red sacks.

7. Creatures with wings, or with hair, or with armor, or with scales, or naked creatures (humans).

Green fruits of the *Pyrus* are presented by the branches.
The loquats yellow with buds are held with their leaves.
Pears like rabbit heads and dates like chicken hearts
Dispel your thirst, your sorrow, and the effects of wine.
Fragrant peaches and soft almonds
Are sweet as the elixir of life;
Crisply fresh plums and strawberries
Are sour like cheese and buttermilk.
Red pulps and black seeds compose the ripe watermelons,
Four cloves of yellow rind enfold the big persimmons.
When the pomegranates are split wide,
Cinnabar grains glisten like specks of ruby;
When the chestnuts are cracked open,
Their tough brawns are hard like cornelian.
Walnut and silver almonds fare well with tea.
Coconuts and grapes may be pressed into wine,
Hazelnuts, yews, and crabapples overfill the dishes.
Kumquats, sugarcanes, tangerines, and oranges crowd the tables.
Sweet yams are baked,
Yellow-sperms overboiled,
The tubers minced with seeds of waterlily,
And soup in stone pots simmers on a gentle fire.
Mankind may boast its delicious dainties,
But what can best the pleasure of mountain monkeys?

The monkeys honored the Monkey King with the seat at the head of the table, while they sat below according to their age and rank. They drank for a whole day, each of the monkeys taking turn to go forward and present the Monkey King with wine, flowers, and fruits. Next day the Monkey King rose early and gave the instruction: "Little ones, cut me some pinewood and make me a raft. Then find me a bamboo for the pole, and gather some fruits and the like. I'm about to leave." When all was ready, he got onto the raft by himself. Pushing off with all his might, he drifted out toward the great ocean and, taking advantage of the wind, set sail for the border of South Jambūdvīpa Continent. Here is the consequence of this journey:

The heaven-born monkey, strong in magic might,
He left the mount, he rode the raft and caught the fair wind;
He drifted across the sea in search of immortals' way,
Determined in heart and mind to achieve great things
It is his cause—and his portion—to quit all earthly zeals;
He'll be enlightened without worries or cares.
He may be expected to meet some approving one
Who will reveal the origin and the dharma of all things.

It was indeed his fortune that, after he had boarded the wooden raft, a strong southeast wind which lasted for days sent him to the northwestern coast, the border of the South Jambūdvīpa Continent. He took the pole to test the water, and, finding it shallow one day, he abandoned the raft and jumped ashore. On the beach there were people fishing, hunting wild geese, digging clams, and draining salt. He approached them and, making a weird face and some strange antics, he scared them into dropping their baskets and nets and scattering in all directions. One of them could not run and was caught by the Monkey King, who stripped him of his clothes and put them on himself, aping the way humans wore them. With a swagger he walked through counties and prefectures, imitating human speech and human manners in the marketplaces. He rested by night and dined in the morning, but he was bent on finding the way of the Buddhas, immortals, and holy sages, on discovering the formula for eternal youth. He saw, however, that the people of the world were all seekers after profit and fame; there was not one who showed concern for his appointed end. This is their condition:

> The quest for fame and fortune, when will it end?
> This tyranny of early rising and retiring late!
> Riding on mules they long for noble steeds.
> Already prime ministers, they seek to be kings.
> For food and raiment they suffer stress and strain,
> Never fearful of Yama's call to reckoning.
> Searching for wealth and power to give to grandsons and sons,
> No one is ever willing to turn back.

The Monkey King searched diligently for the way of immortality, but he had no chance of meeting it. Going through big cities and visiting small towns, he unwittingly spent eight or nine years on the South Jambūdvīpa Continent before he suddenly came upon the Great Western Ocean. He thought that there would certainly be immortals living beyond the ocean; so, having built himself a raft like the previous one, he once again drifted across the Western Ocean until he reached the territory of the West Aparagodānīya Continent. After landing, he searched for a long time, when all at once he came upon a tall and beautiful mountain with thick forests at its base. ***

He turned around and suddenly perceived, at the top of the cliff, a stone slab approximately eight feet wide and over thirty feet tall. On it was written in large letters: "The Mountain of Heart and Mind; The Cave of Slanting Moon and Three Stars." Immensely pleased, the Handsome Monkey King said, "People here are truly honest. This mountain and this cave really do exist!" He stared at the place for a long time but dared not knock. Instead, he jumped onto the branch of a pine tree, picked a few pine seeds and ate them, and began to play.

After a moment he heard the door of the cave open with a squeak, and an immortal youth walked out. His bearing was exceedingly graceful; his features were highly refined. This was certainly no ordinary young mortal, for he had

> His hair bound with two cords of silk,
> A wide robe with two sleeves of wind.
> His body and face seemed most distinct,
> For visage and mind were both detached.
> Long a stranger to all worldly things
> He was the mountain's ageless boy.
> Untainted even with a speck of dust,
> He feared no havoc by the seasons wrought.

After coming through the door, the boy shouted, "Who is causing disturbance here?" With a bound the Monkey King leaped down from the tree, and went up to him bowing. "Immortal boy," he said, "I am a seeker of the way of immortality. I would never dare cause any disturbance." Laughing, the immortal youth asked, "Are you a seeker of Tao?" "I am indeed," answered the Monkey King. "My master at the house," the boy said, "has just left his couch to give a lecture on the platform. Before even announcing his theme, however, he told me to go out and open the door, saying, 'There is someone outside who wants to practice austerities. You may go and receive him.' It must be you, I suppose." The Monkey King said, laughing, "It is I, most assuredly!" "Follow me in then," said the boy. With solemnity the Monkey King set his clothes in order and followed the boy into the depths of the cave. They passed rows and rows of lofty towers and huge alcoves, of pearly chambers and carved arches. After walking through innumerable quiet chambers and empty studios, they finally reached the base of the green jade platform. Patriarch Subodhi was seen seated solemnly on the platform, with thirty lesser immortals standing below in rows. He was truly

> An immortal of great perception and purest mien,
> The Master Subodhi, whose wondrous form of the West
> Had no end or birth—such, the work of Double Three.[8]
> His whole appearance was with mercy suffused.
> Vacuous, spontaneous, and freely changing,
> His Buddha-nature could perform all things,
> His majestic body and Heaven's age were the same.
> Fully tried and enlightened was this grand priest.

As soon as the Handsome Monkey King saw him, he prostrated himself and kowtowed times without number, saying, "Master! Master! I, your pupil, pay you my sincere homage." The Patriarch said, "Where do you come from? Let's hear you state clearly your name and country before you kowtow again." The Monkey King said, "Your pupil came from the Water-Curtain Cave of the Flower-Fruit Mountain, in the Ao-lai Country of the East Pūrvavidcha Continent." "Chase him out of here!" the Patriarch shouted. "He is nothing but a liar and a fabricator of falsehood. How can he possibly be interested in attaining enlightenment?" The Monkey King hastened to kowtow unceasingly and to say, "Your pupil's word is an honest one, without any deceit." The Patriarch said, "If you arc telling the truth, how is it that you mention the East Pūrvavideha Continent? Separating that place and mine are two great oceans and the entire region of the South Jambūdvīpa Continent. How could you possibly get here?" Again kowtowing, the Monkey King said, "Your pupil drifted across the oceans and trudged through many regions for more than ten years before finding this place." The Patriarch said, "If you have come on a long journey in many stages, I'll let that pass. What is your *hsing*?[9] The Monkey King again replied, "I have no *hsing*.[9] If a man rebukes me, I am not offended; if he hits me, I am not angered. In fact, I simply repay him with a ceremonial greeting and that's all. My whole life's without ill temper." "I'm not speaking of your temper," the Patriarch said, "I'm asking after the name of your parents." "I have no parents either," said the Monkey King. The Patriarch said, "If you have no parents, you must have been born from a tree." "Not from a tree," said the Monkey King, "but from a rock. I recall that there used to be an immortal stone on the Flower-Fruit Mountain. I was born the year the stone split open."

When the Patriarch heard this, he was secretly pleased, and said, "Well, evidently you have been created by Heaven and Earth. Get up and show me how you walk." Snapping erect, the Monkey King scurried around a couple of times. The Patriarch laughed and said, "Though your features are not the most attractive, you do resemble a monkey (*hu-sun*) that feeds on pine seeds. This gives me the idea of deriving your surname from your appearance. I intended to call you by the name 'Hu.' Now, when

---

8. Advanced meditation, reflecting a doubling of the three standard practices.

9. Playing on the words "name" and "temper," both pronounced *hsing*.

the accompanying animal radical is dropped from this word, what's left is a compound made up of the two characters, *ku* and *yüeh*. *Ku* means aged and *yüeh* means female, but an aged female cannot reproduce. Therefore, it is better to give you the surname of 'Sun.' When the accompanying animal radical is dropped from this word, we have the compound of *tzŭ* and *hsi*. *Tzŭ* means a boy and *hsi* means a baby, so that the name exactly accords with the Doctrine of the Baby. So your surname will be 'Sun.'" When the Monkey King heard this, he was filled with delight. "Splendid! Splendid!" he cried, kowtowing. "At last I know my surname. May the Master be even more gracious! Since I have received the surname, let me be given also a personal name, so that it may facilitate your calling and commanding me." The Patriarch said, "Within my tradition are twelve characters which have been used to name the pupils according to their divisions. You are one who belongs to the tenth generation." "Which twelve characters are they?" asked the Monkey King. The Patriarch said, "They are: wide (*kuang*), great (*ta*), wise (*chih*), intelligence (*hui*), true (*chên*), conforming (*ju*), nature (*hsing*), sea (*hai*), sharp (*ying*), wake-to (*wu*), complete (*yüan*), and awakening (*chüeh*). Your rank falls precisely on the word 'wake-to' (*wu*). You will hence be given the religious name 'Wake-to-Vacuity' (*wu-k'ung*). All right?" "Splendid! Splendid!" said the Monkey King, laughing; "henceforth I shall be called Sun Wu-k'ung." So it was thus:

> When the world was first created, there was no name;
> To break the stubborn vacuity one needs to wake to vacuity.

We do not know what sort of Taoist cultivation he succeeded in practicing afterward and must await the explanation in the next chapter.

from *Chapter 2*

> The true wondrous doctrine of Bodhi thoroughly comprehended;
> The destruction of Māra and the return to origin unify the soul.[1]

Now we were speaking of the Handsome Monkey King, who, having received his name, jumped about joyfully and went forward to give Subhodhi his grateful salutation. The Patriarch then ordered the congregation to lead Sun Wu-k'ung outdoors and to teach him how to sprinkle water on the ground and dust, and how to speak and move with proper courtesy. The company of immortals obediently went outside with Wu-k'ung, who then bowed to his fellow students. They prepared thereafter a place in the corridor where he might sleep. Next morning he began to learn from his schoolmates the arts of language and etiquette. He discussed with them the scriptures and the doctrines; he practiced calligraphy and burned incense. Such was his daily routine. In more leisurely moments he would be sweeping the grounds or hoeing the garden, planting flowers or pruning trees, gathering firewood or lighting fires, fetching water or carrying drinks. He did not lack for whatever he needed, and thus he lived in the cave without realizing that six or seven years had slipped by. One day the Patriarch ascended the platform and took his high seat. Calling together all the immortals, he began to lecture on a great doctrine. He spoke

> With words so florid and eloquent
> That gold lotus sprang up from the ground.

---

1. Bodhi means enlightenment; Māra means the Destroyer or Evil One.

> The doctrine of three vehicles he subtly rehearsed,[2]
> Including even the laws' minutest tittle.
> The yak's-tail[3] waved slowly and spouted elegance;
> His thunderous voice moved e'en the Ninth Heaven.
> For a while he lectured on Tao.
> For a while he discoursed on Zen.
> To harmonize the three schools[4] was a natural thing.
> One word's elucidation in conformity to truth
> Would lead to a life birthless and knowledge most profound.

Wu-k'ung, who was standing there to listen, was so pleased with the talk that he scratched his ear and rubbed his jaw. Grinning from ear to ear, he could not refrain from dancing on all fours! Suddenly the Patriarch saw this and called out to him, "Why are you madly jumping and dancing in the ranks and not listening to my lecture?" Wu-k'ung said, "Your pupil was devoutly listening to the lecture. But when I heard such wonderful things from my reverend master, I couldn't contain myself for joy and started to leap and prance about quite unconsciously. May the master forgive my sins!" "Let me ask you," said the Patriarch, "if you comprehend these wonderful things, do you know how long you have been in this cave?" Wu-k'ung said, "Your pupil is basically feeble-minded and does not know the number of seasons. I only remember that whenever the fire burned out in the stove, I would go to the back of the mountain to gather firewood. Finding a mountainful of fine peach trees there, I have eaten my fill of peaches seven times." The Patriarch said, "That mountain is named the Ripe Peach Mountain. If you have eaten your fill seven times, I suppose it must have been seven years. What kind of Taoist art would you like to learn from me?" Wu-k'ung said, "I am dependent on the admonition of my honored teacher. Your pupil would gladly learn whatever has a smidgen of Taoist flavor." * * *

The Patriarch said, "How would it be if I taught you the practice of the Action division?" "What's it like in the Action division?" Wu-k'ung asked. "Plenty of activities," said the Patriarch, "such as gathering the yin to nourish the yang, bending the bow and treading the arrow, and rubbing the navel to pass breath. There are also experimentation with alchemical formulas, burning rushes and forging cauldrons, taking red mercury, making autumn stone,[5] and drinking bride's milk and the like." "Can such bring about long life?" asked Wu-k'ung. "To obtain immortality from such activities," said the Patriarch, "is also like scooping the moon from the water." "There you go again, Master!" cried Wu-k'ung. "What do you mean by scooping the moon from the water?" The Patriarch said, "When the moon is high in the sky, its reflection is in the water. Although it is visible therein, you cannot scoop it out or catch hold of it, for it is but an illusion." "I won't learn that either!" said Wu-k'ung.

When the Patriarch heard this, he uttered a cry and jumped down from the high platform. He pointed the ruler he held in his hands at Wu-k'ung and said to him: "What a mischievous monkey you are! You won't learn this and you won't learn that! Just what it is that you are waiting for?" Moving forward, he hit Wu-k'ung three times on the head. Then he folded his arms behind his back and walked inside, closing

---

2. The three vehicles carry living beings across mortality to the shores of *Nirvana* enlightenment.
3. Used as a fly-swatter or duster and associated with Daoist or Buddhist recluses as symbol of their purity and detachment.

4. Confucianism, Daoism, and Buddhism.
5. Red mercury is the name for a virgin's menstrual discharge, while autumn stone refers to the urine of a virgin boy. These are considered indispensable elements for the alchemical process.

the main doors behind him and leaving the congregation stranded outside. Those who were listening to the lecture were so terrified that everyone began to berate Wu-k'ung. "You reckless ape!" they cried, "you're utterly without manners! The master was prepared to teach you magic secrets. Why weren't you willing to learn? Why did you have to argue with him instead? Now you have offended him, and who knows when he'll come out again?" At that moment they all resented him and despised and ridiculed him. But Wu-k'ung was not angered in the least and only replied with a broad grin. For the Monkey King, in fact, had already solved secretly, as it were, the riddle in the pot; he therefore did not quarrel with the other people but patiently held his tongue. He reasoned that the master, by hitting him three times, was telling him to prepare himself for the third watch; and by folding his arms behind his back, walking inside, and closing the main doors, was telling him to enter by the back door so that he might receive instruction in secret.

Wu-k'ung spent the rest of the day happily with the other pupils in front of the Divine Cave of the Three Stars, eagerly waiting for the night. When evening arrived, he immediately retired with all the others, pretending to be asleep by closing his eyes, breathing evenly, and remaining completely still. Since there was no watchman in the mountain to beat the watch or call the hour, he could not tell what time it was. He could only rely on his own calculations by counting the breaths he inhaled and exhaled. Approximately at the hour of Tzŭ,[6] he arose very quietly and put on his clothes. Stealthily opening the front door, he slipped away from the crowd and walked outside. Lifting his head, he saw

> The bright moon and the cool, clear dew;
> In each corner was not a speck of dust.
> Secluded fowls rested deep in the woods;
> A brook flowed gently from its source.
> The glow of darting fireflies dispersed the gloom.
> Wild geese passed in calligraphic columns through the clouds.
> Precisely it was the third-watch hour—
> Time to seek the Truth, the Perfect Way.

You see him following the familiar path back to the rear entrance, where he discovered that the door was, indeed, ajar. Wu-k'ung said happily, "The reverend master truly intended to give me instruction. That's why the door was left open." He reached the door in a few large strides and entered sideways. Walking up to the Patriarch's bed, he found him asleep with his body curled up, facing the wall. Wu-k'ung dared not disturb him; instead, he knelt before his bed. After a little while, the Patriarch awoke. Stretching his legs, he recited to himself:

> Hard! Hard! Hard!
> The Way is most obscure!
> Deem not the gold elixir a common thing.[7]
> He who imparts dark mysteries not to a perfect man
> Is bound to make words empty, the mouth tired, and the tongue dry!

"Master," Wu-k'ung responded at once, "your pupil has been kneeling here and waiting on you for a long time." When the Patriarch heard Wu-k'ung's voice, he rose and put on his clothes. "You mischievous monkey!" he exclaimed, sitting down cross-

---

6. Around midnight.   7. In alchemy, the gold elixir brings immortality.

legged. "Why aren't you sleeping in front? What are you doing back here at my place?" Wu-k'ung replied, "Before the platform and the congregation yesterday, the master gave the order that your pupil, at the hour of the third watch, should come here through the rear entrance in order that he might be instructed. I was therefore bold enough to come directly to the master's bed." When the Patriarch heard this, he was terribly pleased, thinking to himself, "This fellow is indeed an offspring of Heaven and Earth. If not, how could he solve so readily the riddle in my pot!" "There is no one here save your pupil," Wu-k'ung said. "May the master be exceedingly merciful and impart to me the way of long life. I shall never forget this gracious favor." "Since you have solved the riddle in the pot," said the Patriarch, "it is an indication that you are destined to learn, and I am glad to teach you. Come closer and listen carefully. I will impart to you the wondrous way of long life." Wu-k'ung kowtowed to express his gratitude, washed his ears, and listened most attentively, kneeling before the bed. The Patriarch said:

> Know well this secret formula wondrous and true:
> Spare and nurse the vital forces, this and nothing else.
> All power resides in the semen, the breath, and the spirit;
> Guard these with care, securely, lest there be a leak.
> Lest there be a leak!
> Keep within the body!
> Hearken to my teaching and the Way itself will prosper.
> Remember the oral formulas so efficacious
> To purge concupiscence and lead to purity;
> To purity
> Where the light is bright.
> You may face the elixir platform and enjoy the moon.[8]
> The moon holds the jade rabbit, the sun hides the crow;
> See there also the snake and the tortoise tightly entwined.[9]
> Tightly entwined,
> The vital forces are strong.
> You can plant gold lotus e'en in the midst of flames.
> The Five Phases use together and in order reverse[1]—
> When that's attained, be a Buddha or immortal at will!

At that moment, the very origin was revealed to Wu-k'ung, whose mind became spiritualized as happiness came to him. He carefully committed to memory all the oral formulas. After kowtowing to thank the Patriarch, he left by the rear entrance. As he went out, he saw that the eastern sky was just beginning to pale with light, though golden beams were radiant from the Westward Way. Following the same path, he returned to the front door, pushed it open quietly, and went inside. He sat up in his sleeping place and purposely rustled the bed and the covers, crying "It's light! It's light! Get up!" All the other people were still sleeping and did not know that Wu-k'ung had received a good thing. He played the fool that day after getting up, but

8. In alchemy, the moon may be a symbol of perfection, the heart, and the brazier.
9. Daoist symbols of polar opposites.
1. In alchemical thought, there are five forces in the human body which correspond to the elements of water, fire, wood, metal, and earth. If the forces are allowed to follow their natural course, then the fluids become blood, and the blood becomes vital discharges (semen or vaginal fluids) which may flow out of the body. The teaching of reversing the five forces is aimed at retaining them within the body.

he persisted in what he had learned secretly by doing breathing exercises before the hour of Tzǔ and after the hour of Wu.[2]

Three years went by swiftly, and the Patriarch again mounted his throne to lecture to the multitude. He discussed the scholastic deliberations and parables, and he discoursed on the integument of external conduct. Suddenly he asked, "Where's Wu-k'ung?" Wu-k'ung drew near and knelt down. "Your pupil's here," he said. "What sort of art have you been practicing lately?" the Patriarch asked. "Recently," Wu-k'ung said, "your pupil has begun to apprehend the nature of all things and my foundational knowledge has become firmly established." "If you have penetrated to the dharma nature to apprehend the origin," said the Patriarch, "you have, in fact, entered into the divine substance. You need, however, to guard against the danger of three calamities." When Wu-k'ung heard this, he thought for a long time and said, "The words of the master must be erroneous. I have frequently heard that when one is learned in the Way and excels in virtue, he will enjoy the same age as Heaven; fire and water cannot harm him and every kind of disease will vanish. How can there be this danger of three calamities?" "What you have learned," said the Patriarch, "is no ordinary magic: you have stolen the creative powers of Heaven and Earth and invaded the dark mysteries of the sun and moon. Your success in mixing the elixir is something that the gods and the demons cannot countenance. Though your appearance will be preserved and your age lengthened, after five hundred years Heaven will send down the calamity of thunder to strike you. Hence you must be intelligent and wise enough to avoid it ahead of time. If you can escape it, your age will indeed equal that of Heaven; if not, your life will thus be finished. After another five hundred years Heaven will send down the calamity of fire to burn you. That fire is neither natural nor common fire; its name is the Fire of Yin, and it arises from within the soles of your feet to reach even the cavity of your heart, reducing your entrails to ashes and your limbs to utter ruin. The arduous labor of a millennium will then have been made completely superfluous. After another five hundred years the calamity of wind will be sent to blow at you. It is not the wind from the north, south, east, or west; nor is it one of the winds of four seasons; nor is it the wind of flowers, willows, pines, and bamboos. It is called the Mighty Wind, and it enters from the top of the skull into the body, passes through the midriff and penetrates the nine apertures.[3] The bones and the flesh will be dissolved and the body itself will disintegrate. You must therefore avoid all three calamities." When Wu-k'ung heard this, his hair stood on end, and, kowtowing reverently, he said, "I beg the master to be merciful and impart to me the method to avoid the three calamities. To the very end, I shall never forget your gracious favor." The Patriarch said, "It is not, in fact, difficult, except that I cannot teach you because you are somewhat different from other people." "I have a round head pointing to Heaven," said Wu-k'ung, "and square feet walking on Earth. Similarly, I have nine apertures and four limbs, entrails and cavities. In what way am I different from other people?" The Patriarch said, "Though you resemble a man, you have much less jowl." The monkey, you see, has an angular face with hollow cheeks and a pointed mouth. Stretching his hand to feel himself, Wu-k'ung laughed and said, "The master does not know how to balance matters! Though I have much less jowl than human beings, I have my pouch, which may certainly be considered a compensation." "Very well, then," said the Patriarch, "what method of escape would you like to learn? There is

---

2. Around noon.   3. Eyes, nostrils, ears, mouth, urethra, and anus.

the Art of the Heavenly Ladle, which numbers thirty-six transformations, and there is the Art of the Earthly Multitude, which numbers seventy-two transformations." Wu-k'ung said, "Your pupil is always eager to catch more fishes, so I'll learn the Art of the Earthly Multitude." "In that case," said the Patriarch, "come up here, and I'll pass on the oral formulas to you." He then whispered something into his ear, though we do not know what sort of wondrous secrets he spoke of. But this Monkey King was someone who, knowing one thing, could understand a hundred! He immediately learned the oral formulas and, after working at them and practicing them himself, he mastered all seventy-two transformations.

One day when the Patriarch and the various pupils were admiring the evening view in front of the Three Stars Cave, the master asked, "Wu-k'ung, has that matter been perfected?" Wu-k'ung said, "Thanks to the profound kindness of the master, your pupil has indeed attained perfection; I now can ascend like mist into the air and fly." The Patriarch said, "Let me see you try to fly." Wishing to display his ability, Wu-k'ung leaped fifty or sixty feet into the air, pulling himself up with a somersault. He trod on the clouds for about the time of a meal and traveled a distance of no more than three miles before dropping down again to stand before the Patriarch. "Master," he said, his hands folded in front of him, "this is flying by cloud-soaring." Laughing, the Patriarch said, "This can't be called cloud-soaring! It's more like cloud-crawling! The old saying goes, 'The immortal tours the North Sea in the morning and reaches Ts'ang-wu by night.' If it takes you half a day to go less than three miles, it can't even be considered cloud-crawling." "What do you mean," asked Wu-k'ung, "by saying, 'The immortal tours the North Sea in the morning and reaches Ts'ang-wu by night'?" The Patriarch said, "Those who are capable of cloud-soaring may start from the North Sea in the morning, journey through the East Sea, the West Sea, the South Sea, and return again to Ts'ang-wu. Ts'ang-wu refers to Ling-ling in the North Sea. It can be called true cloud-soaring only when you can traverse all four seas in one day." "That's truly difficult!" said Wu-k'ung, "truly difficult!" "Nothing in the world is difficult," said the Patriarch; "only the mind makes it so." When Wu-k'ung heard these words, he kowtowed reverently and implored the Patriarch, "Master, if you do perform a service for someone, you must do it thoroughly. May you be most merciful and impart to me also this technique of cloud-soaring. I would never dare forget your gracious favor." The Patriarch said, "When the various immortals want to soar on the clouds, they all rise by stamping their feet. But you're not like them. When I saw you leave just now, you had to pull yourself up by jumping. What I'll do now is to teach you the cloud-somersault in accordance with your form." Wu-k'ung again prostrated himself and pleaded with him, and the Patriarch gave him an oral formula, saying, "Make the magic sign, recite the spell, clench your fist tightly, shake your body, and when you jump up, one somersault will carry you a hundred and eight thousand miles." When the other people heard this, they all giggled and said, "Lucky Wu-k'ung! If he learns this little trick, he can become a dispatcher for someone to deliver documents or carry circulars. He'll be able to make a living anywhere!"

The sky now began to darken, and the master went back to the cave dwelling with his pupils. Throughout the night, however, Wu-k'ung practiced ardently and mastered the technique of cloud-somersault. From then on, he had complete freedom, blissfully enjoying his state of long life.

One day early in the summer, the disciples were gathered under the pine trees for fellowship and discussion. They said to him, "Wu-k'ung, what sort of merit did you accumulate in another incarnation that led the master to whisper in your ear, the other day, the method of avoiding the three calamities? Have you learned everything?" "I won't conceal this from my various elder brothers," Wu-k'ung said, laughing. "Owing to the master's instruction in the first place and my diligence day and night in the second, I have fully mastered the several matters!" "Let's take advantage of the moment," one of the pupils said. "You try to put on a performance and we'll watch." When Wu-k'ung heard this, his spirit was aroused and he was most eager to display his powers. "I invite the various elder brothers to give me a subject," he said. "What do you want me to change into?" "Why not a pine tree?" they said. Wu-k'ung made the magic sign and recited the spell; with one shake of his body he changed himself into a pine tree. Truly it was

> Thickly held in smoke through all four seasons;
> Its chaste fair form rose straight to the clouds,
> With not the least likeness to the impish monkey,
> But only frost-tried and snow-tested branches.

When the multitude saw this, they clapped their hands and roared with laughter, everyone crying, "Marvelous monkey! Marvelous monkey!" They did not realize that all this uproar had disturbed the Patriarch, who came running out of the door, dragging his staff. "Who is creating this bedlam here?" he demanded. At his voice the pupils immediately collected themselves, set their clothes in order, and came forward. Wu-k'ung also changed back into his true form, and, slipping into the crowd, he said, "For your information, Reverend Master, we are having fellowship and discussion here. There is no one from outside causing any disturbance." "You were all yelling and screaming," said the Patriarch angrily, "and were behaving in a manner totally unbecoming to those practicing the Great Art. Don't you know that those in the cultivation of Tao are wary of opening their mouths lest they dissipate their vital forces, or of moving their tongues lest they provoke arguments? Why are you all laughing noisily here?" "We dare not conceal this from the master," the crowd said. "Just now we were having fun with Wu-k'ung, who was giving us a performance of transformation. We told him to change into a pine tree, and he did indeed become a pine tree! Your pupils were all applauding him and our voices disturbed the reverend teacher. We beg his forgiveness." "Go away, all of you," the Patriarch said. "You, Wu-k'ung, come over here! I ask you what sort of exhibition were you putting on, changing into a pine tree? Did I give you spiritual ability just for showing off to people? Suppose you saw someone with this ability. Wouldn't you ask him at once how he acquired it? So when others see that you are in possession of it, they'll come begging. If you're afraid to refuse them, you will give away the secret; if you don't, they may hurt you. You are actually placing your life in grave jeopardy." "I beseech the master to forgive me," Wu-k'ung said kowtowing. "I won't condemn you," said the Patriarch, "but you must leave this place." When Wu-k'ung heard this, tears fell from his eyes. "Where am I to go, Teacher?" he asked. "From wherever you came," the Patriarch said, "you should go back there." "I came from the East Pūrvavideha Continent," Wu-k'ung said, his memory jolted by the Patriarch, "from the Water-Curtain Cave of the Flower-Fruit Mountain in the Ao-lai Country." "Go back there quickly and save your life," the Patriarch said. "You cannot possibly remain here!" "Allow me to inform my esteemed teacher," said Wu-k'ung, properly penitent, "I have been away from home for twenty years, and I certainly long to see my subjects and followers of bygone days again. But I keep thinking that my master's profound kindness to me has not yet been repaid: I therefore dare not leave." "There's nothing to be repaid," said the Patriarch. "See that you don't get into trouble and involve me; that's all I ask."

Seeing that there was no other alternative, Wu-k'ung had to bow to the Patriarch and take leave of the congregation. "Once you leave," the Patriarch said, "you're bound to end up evildoing. I don't care what kind of villainy and violence you engage in, but I forbid you ever to mention that you are my disciple. For if you but utter half the word, I'll know about it; you can be assured, wretched monkey, that you'll be skinned alive. I will break all your bones and banish your soul to the Place of Nine-fold Darkness, from which you will not be released even after ten thousand afflictions!" "I will never dare mention my master," said Wu-k'ung. "I'll say that I've learned this all by myself." Having thanked the Patriarch, Wu-k'ung turned away, made the magic sign, pulled himself up, and performed the cloud-somersault. He headed straight toward the East Pūrvavideha, and in less than an hour he could already see the Flower-Fruit Mountain and the Water-Curtain Cave. Rejoicing secretly, the Handsome Monkey King said to himself:

> Heavy with bones of mortal stock I left this place.
> But success in Tao has lighten'd both body and frame.
> 'Tis this world's pity that none is firmly resolved
> To learn the mystery, plain to all who seek.
> Hard was the advance in that hour of ocean crossing.
> How easy the journey of my homecoming today!
> Parting words of counsel still echo in my ears.
> Mine's not the hope to see so soon the eastern depths!

* * *

from *Chapter 7*

From the Brazier of Eight Trigrams the Great Sage escapes;
Beneath the Five Phases Mountain the Monkey of the Mind is stilled.

> Fame and fortune,
> All predestined;
> One must ever shun a guileful heart.
> Rectitude and truth,
> The fruits of virtue grow both long and deep.
> A little presumption brings on Heaven's wrath;
> Though yet unseen, it will surely come in time.
> If we ask the Lord of the East for reasons why
> Such pains and perils now appear,
> It's because pride has sought to scale the limits,
> Confounding the world's order and perverting the law.

We were telling you about the Great Sage, Equal to Heaven, who was taken by the celestial guardians to the monster execution block, where he was bound to the monster-subduing pillar. They then slashed him with a scimitar, hewed him with an ax, stabbed him with a spear, and hacked him with a sword, but they could not hurt his body in any way. Next, the Star Spirit of South Pole ordered the various deities of the Fire Department to burn him with fire, but that, too, had little effect. The gods of the Thunder Department were then ordered to strike him with thunderbolts, but not a single one of his hairs was destroyed. The demon king Mahābāli and the others therefore went back to report to the Throne, saying, "Your Majesty, we don't know where this Great Sage has acquired such power to protect his body. Your subjects slashed him with a scimitar and hewed him with an ax; we also struck him with thunder and burned him with fire. Not a single one of his hairs was destroyed. What shall we do?" * * *

At the time the various deities had the Great Sage surrounded, but they could not close in on him. All the hustle and bustle soon disturbed the Jade Emperor,[4] who at once sent the Wandering Minister of Inspection and the Immortal Master of Blessed Wings to go to the Western Region and invite the aged Buddha to come and subdue the monster.

The two sages received the decree and went straight to the Spirit Mountain. After they had greeted the Four Vajra-Buddhas and the Eight Bodhisattvas in front of the Treasure Temple of Thunderclap, they asked them to announce their arrival. The deities therefore went before the Treasure Lotus Platform and made their report. Tathāgata[5] at once invited them to appear before him, and the two sages made obeisance to the Buddha three times before standing in attendance beneath the platform. Tathāgata asked, "What causes the Jade Emperor to trouble the two sages to come here?"

The two sages explained as follows: "Some time ago there was born on the Flower-Fruit Mountain a monkey who exercised his magic powers and gathered to himself a troop of monkeys to disturb the world. The Jade Emperor threw down a decree of pacification and appointed him a pi-ma-wên,[6] but he despised the lowliness of that position and left in rebellion. Devarāja Li and Prince Naṭa were sent to capture him, but they were unsuccessful, and another proclamation of amnesty was given to him. He was then made the Great Sage, Equal to Heaven, a rank without compensation. After a while he was given the temporary job of looking after the Garden of Immortal Peaches, where almost immediately he stole the peaches. He also went to the Jasper Pool and made off with the food and wine, devastating the Grand Festival. Half-drunk, he went secretly into the Tushita Palace, stole the elixir of Lao Tzŭ,[7] and then left the Celestial Palace in revolt. Again the Jade Emperor sent a hundred thousand Heavenly soldiers, but he was not to be subdued. Thereafter Kuan-yin sent for the Immortal Master Erh-lang and his sworn brothers, who fought and pursued him. Even then he knew many tricks of transformation, and only after he was hit by Lao Tzu's diamond snare could Erh-lang finally capture him. Taken before the Throne, he was condemned to be executed; but, though slashed by a scimitar and hewn by an ax, burned by fire and struck by thunder, he was not hurt at all. After Lao Tzu had received royal permission to take him away, he was refined by fire, and the brazier was not opened until the forty-ninth day. Immediately he jumped out of the Brazier of Eight Trigrams and beat back the celestial guardians. He penetrated into the Hall of Perfect Light and was approaching the Hall of Divine Mists when Wang Ling-kuan, aide to the Immortal Master of Adjuvant Holiness, met and fought with him bitterly. Thirty-six thunder generals were ordered to encircle him completely, but they could never get near him. The situation is desperate, and for this reason, the Jade Emperor sent a special request for you to defend the Throne."

4. A supreme deity in the Daoist pantheon.
5. The Buddha, also known as Sakyamuni.
6. Guardian of the horses.

7. Laozi, supposed author of an important early Daoist classic.

When Tathāgata heard this, he said to the various bodhisattvas, "All of you remain steadfast here in the chief temple, and let no one relax his meditative posture. I have to go exorcise a demon and defend the Throne."

Tathāgata then called Ānanda and Kāśyapa, his two venerable disciples, to follow him. They left the Thunderclap Temple and arrived at the gate of the Hall of Divine Mists, where they were met by deafening shouts and yells. There the Great Sage was being beset by the thirty-six thunder deities. The Buddhist Patriarch gave the dharma-order: "Let the thunder deities lower their arms and break up their encirclement. Ask the Great Sage to come out here and let me ask him what sort of divine power he has." The various warriors retreated immediately, and the Great Sage also threw off his magical appearance. Changing back into his true form, he approached angrily and shouted with ill humor, "What region are you from, monk, that you dare stop the battle and question me?" Tathāgata laughed and said. "I am Śākyamuni, the Venerable One from the Western Region of Ultimate Bliss. I have heard just now about your audacity, your wildness, and your repeated acts of rebellion against Heaven. Where were you born? When did you learn the Great Art? Why are you so violent and unruly?"

> The Great Sage said, "I was
> Born of Earth and Heaven, immortal magically fused,
> An old monkey hailed from the Flower-Fruit Mount.
> I made my home in the Water-Curtain Cave;
> I sought friend and teacher to gain the Mystery Great.
> Perfected in the many arts of ageless life,
> I learned to change in ways boundless and vast.
> Too narrow the space I found on that mortal earth;
> I set my mind to live in the Green Jade Sky.
> In Divine Mists Hall none should long reside,
> For king may follow king in the reign of man
> It might is honor, let them yield to me.
> Only he is hero who dares to fight and win!"

When the Buddhist Patriarch heard these words, he laughed aloud in scorn. "A fellow like you," he said, "is only a monkey who happens to become a spirit. How dare you be so presumptuous as to want to seize the honored throne of the Exalted Jade Emperor? He began practicing religion when he was very young, and he has gone through the bitter experience of one thousand, seven hundred and fifty kalpas, with each kalpa lasting a hundred and twenty-nine thousand, six hundred years. Figure out yourself how many years it took him to rise to the enjoyment of his great and limitless position! You are merely a beast who has just attained human form in this incarnation. How dare you make such a boast? Blasphemy! This is sheer blasphemy, and it will surely shorten your allotted age. Repent while there's still time and cease your idle talk! Be wary that you don't encounter such peril that you will be cut down in an instant, and all your original gifts will be wasted."

"Even if the Jade Emperor has practiced religion from childhood," said the Great Sage, "he should not be allowed to remain here forever. The proverb says, 'Many are the turns of kingship, and next year the turn will be mine!' Tell him to move out at once and hand over the Celestial Palace to me. That'll be the end of the matter. If not, I shall continue to cause disturbances and there'll never be peace!" "Besides your immortality and your transformations," said the Buddhist Patriarch, "what other powers do you have that you dare to usurp this hallowed region of Heaven?" "I've plenty of them!" said the Great Sage. "Indeed, I know seventy-two transformations and a life that does not grow old through ten thousand kalpas. I know also how to cloud-somersault, and one leap will take me a hundred and eight thousand miles. Why can't I sit on the Heavenly throne?"

The Buddhist Patriarch said, "Let me make a wager with you. If you have the ability to somersault clear of this right palm of mine, I shall consider you the winner. You need not raise your weapon in battle then, for I shall ask the Jade Emperor to go live with me in the West and let you have the Celestial Palace. If you cannot somersault out of my hand, you can go back to the Region Below and be a monster. Work through a few more kalpas before you return to cause more trouble."

When the Great Sage heard this, he said to himself, snickering, "What a fool this Tathāgata is! A single somersault of mine can carry old Monkey a hundred and eight thousand miles, yet his palm is not even one foot across. How could I possibly not jump clear of it?" He asked quickly, "You're certain that your decision will stand?" "Certainly it will," said Tathāgata. He stretched out his right hand, which was about the size of a lotus leaf. Our Great Sage put away his compliant rod and, summoning his power, leaped up and stood right in the center of the Patriarch's hand. He said simply, "I'm off!" and he was gone—all but invisible like a streak of light in the clouds. Training the eye of wisdom on him, the Buddhist Patriarch saw that the Monkey King was hurtling along relentlessly like a whirligig.

As the Great Sage advanced, he suddenly saw five flesh-pink pillars supporting a mass of green air. "This must be the end of the road," he said. "When I go back presently, Tathāgata will be my witness and I shall certainly take up residence in the Palace of Divine Mists." But he thought to himself, "Wait a moment! I'd better leave some kind of memento if I'm going to negotiate with Tathāgata." He plucked a hair and blew a mouthful of magic breath onto it, crying, "Change!" It changed into a writing brush with extra thick hair soaked in heavy ink. On the middle pillar he then wrote in large letters the following line: "The Great Sage, Equal to Heaven, has made a tour of this place." When he had finished writing, he retrieved his hair, and with a total lack of respect he left a bubbling pool of monkey urine at the base of the first pillar. He reversed his cloud-somersault and went back to where he had started. Standing on Tathāgata's palm, he said, "I left, and now I'm back. Tell the Jade Emperor to give me the Celestial Palace." "You stinking, urinous ape!" scolded Tathāgata. "Since when did you ever leave the palm of my hand?" The Great Sage said, "You are just ignorant! I went to the edge of Heaven, and I found five flesh-pink pillars supporting a mass of green air. I left a memento there. Do you dare go with me to have a look at the place?" "No need to go there," said Tathāgata. "Just lower your head and take a look." When the Great Sage stared down with his fiery eyes and diamond pupils, he found written on the middle finger of the Buddhist Patriarch's right hand the sentence "The Great Sage, Equal to Heaven, has made a tour of this place." A pungent whiff of monkey urine came from the fork between the thumb and the first finger. Astonished, the Great Sage said, "Could this really happen? Could this really happen? I wrote those words on the pillars supporting the sky. How is it that they now appear on his finger? Could it be that he is exercising the magic power of foreknowledge without divination? I won't believe it! I won't believe it! Let me go there once more!"

Dear Great Sage! Quickly he crouched and was about to jump up again, when the Buddhist Patriarch flipped his hand over, and tossed the Monkey King out of the West Heavenly Gate. The five fingers were transformed into the Five Phases of metal, wood, water, fire, and earth. They became, in fact, five connected mountains, named Five-Phases Mountain, which pinned him down with just enough pressure to keep him there. The thunder deities, Ānanda, and Kāśyapa all folded their hands and cried in acclamation:

Wonderful! Wonderful!

> Taught to be manlike since hatching from an egg that year,
> He set his aim to learn and walk the Way of Truth.
> He lived in a lovely region by ten thousand kalpas unmoved.
> But one day he changed, dissipating vigor and strength.
> Craving high place, he flouted Heaven's dominion;
> Mocking sages, he stole pills and upset the great relations.
> Evil, full to the brim, now meets its retribution.
> We know not when he may hope to find release. * * *

from *Chapter 8*

> The Sovereign Buddha has made scriptures to impart ultimate bliss;
> Kuan-yin receives the decree to go up to Ch'ang-an.[8]

As the Buddhist Patriarch lived in the Treasure Monastery of the Thunderclap in the Spirit Mountain, he called together one day the various buddhas, arhats, guardians, bodhisattvas, diamond kings, mendicants, monks and nuns and said to them, "We do not know how much time has passed here since I subdued the wily monkey and pacified Heaven, but I suppose at least half a millennium has gone by on Earth. As this is the fifteenth day of the first month of autumn, I have prepared a treasure bowl filled with a hundred varieties of exotic flowers and a thousand kinds of rare fruit. I would like to share them with all of you in celebration of the Feast of the Ullambana Bowl.[9] How about it?" Every one of them folded his hands and paid obeisance to the Buddha three times to receive the festival. Tathāgata then ordered Ānanda to take the flowers and fruits from the treasure bowl, and Kāśyapa was asked to distribute them. All were thankful, and they presented poems to express their gratitude. The poem of blessing says:

> The star of blessing shines brightly before Lokajyeṣṭha,[1]
> Who enjoys blessing most enduring and immense.
> His boundless virtue and blessing last as long as Earth.
> His source of blessing is happily joined to the sky.
> His widely planted fields of blessing prosper year to year.
> His deep and vast sea of blessing is ever unchanged.
> His world's filled with blessing, thus all will be blessed.
> May his blessing increase, be boundless, and ever complete.

The poem of wealth says:

> His wealth's weighty as a mountain: so phoenixes sing.
> His wealth follows the seasons to extol his long life.
> He gains in wealth by ten thousand pecks as his body in health.
> He enjoys wealth of a thousand bushels as the world peace.

---

8. Capital of the Tang dynasty.
9. The feast of all dead souls, celebrated by both Daoists and Buddhists.

1. "The most venerable one of the world," or the Buddha.

> The range of his wealth, reaching to Heaven, is ever safe;
> The name of his wealth is like the sea—but purer.
> The grace of his wealth reaching afar is by many sought.
> The scope of his wealth is boundless, enriching countless lands.

The poem of longevity says:

> The Star of Longevity gave gifts to Tathāgata,
> From whom light radiates on this place of longevity.
> The fruits of longevity fill the bowl with hues divine.
> The blooms of longevity, newly plucked, deck the lotus seat.
> The poems of longevity, how elegant and finely wrought!
> The songs of longevity are scored by most gifted minds.
> The life of longevity lengthens to match the sun and moon.
> Longevity, like mountain and sea, is longer than both!

After the bodhisattvas had presented their poems, they invited Tathāgata to disclose the origin and elucidate the source. Tathāgata gently opened his benevolent mouth to expound the great dharma and to proclaim the truth. He lectured on the wondrous doctrines of the three vehicles, the five skandhas,[2] and the *Śūraṇgamā Sūtra*. As he did so, celestial dragons were seen circling above and flowers descended like rain in abundance. It was truly thus:

> The mind of Zen is bright as the moon of a thousand rivers.
> The true nature is pure and spacious as an unclouded sky.

When Tathāgata had finished his lecture, he said to the congregation, "I have watched the Four Great Continents, and the morality of their inhabitants varies from place to place. Those living on the East Pūrvavideha revere Heaven and Earth, and they are straightforward and peaceful. Those on the North Uttarakuru, though they love to destroy life, do so out of the necessity of making a livelihood. Moreover, they are rather dull of mind and lethargic in spirit, and they are not likely to do much harm. Those of our West Aparagodānīya are neither covetous nor prone to kill; they control their humor and temper their spirit. There is, to be sure, no illuminate of the first order, but everyone is certain to attain longevity. Those who reside in the South Jambūdvīpa, however, are prone to practice lechery and delight in evildoing, indulging in much slaughter and strife. Indeed, they are all caught in the treacherous field of tongue and mouth, in the wicked sea of slander and malice. However, I have three baskets of true scriptures which can persuade man to do good." When the various bodhisattvas heard these words, they folded their hands and bowed down. "What are the three baskets of authentic scriptures," they asked, "that Tathāgata possesses?" Tathāgata said, "I have one basket of vinaya, which speaks of Heaven; one basket of śāstras, which tells of the Earth; and one basket of sūtras, which redeems the damned. Altogether the three baskets of scriptures contain thirty-five divisions written in fifteen thousand, one hundred and forty-four scrolls. They are the scriptures for the cultivation of truth; they are the gate to ultimate goodness. I myself would like to send these to the Land of the East; but the creatures in that region are so stupid and so scornful of the truth that they ignore the weighty elements of our Law and mock the true sect of Yoga. Somehow we need a person with power to go to the Land of the East and find a virtuous believer. He will be asked to experience the bitter travail of passing through a thousand

2. The five components of an intelligent being: form, reception, thought, action, and cognition.

mountains and ten thousand waters to come here in quest of the authentic scriptures, so that they may be forever implanted in the east to enlighten the people. This will provide a source of blessings great as a mountain and deep as the sea. Which one of you is willing to make such a trip?" At that moment, the Bodhisattva Kuan-yin came near the lotus platform and paid obeisance three times to the Buddha, saying, "Though your disciple is untalented, she is willing to go to the Land of the East to find a scripture pilgrim." Lifting their heads to look, the various buddhas saw that the Bodhisattva had

> A mind perfected in the four virtues,[3]
> A golden body filled with wisdom,
> Fringes of dangling pearls and jade,
> Scented bracelets set with lustrous treasures,
> Dark hair piled smoothly in a coiled-dragon bun,
> And elegant sashes lightly fluttering as phoenix quills.
> Her green jade buttons
> And white silk robe
> Bathed in holy light;
> Her velvet skirt
> And golden cords
> Wrapped by hallowed air.
> With brows of new moon shape
> And eyes like two bright stars,
> Her jadelike face beams natural joy,
> And her ruddy lips seem a flash of red.
> Her immaculate vase overflows with nectar from year to year,
> Holding sprigs of weeping willow green from age to age.
> She disperses the eight woes;
> She redeems the multitude;
> She has great compassion;
> Thus she rules on the T'ai Mountain,
> And lives at the South Sea.
> She saves the poor, searching for their voices,
> Ever heedful and solicitous,
> Ever wise and efficacious,
> Her orchid heart delights in green bamboos;
> Her chaste nature loves the wistaria.
> She is the merciful ruler of the Potalaka Mountain,
> The Living Kuan-yin from the Cave of Tidal Sound.

When Tathāgata saw her, he was most delighted and said to her, "No other person is qualified to make this journey. It must be the Honorable Kuan-yin of mighty magic powers—she's the one to do it!" "As your disciple departs for the east," said the Bodhisattva, "do you have any instructions?" "As you travel," said Tathāgata, "you are to examine the way carefully. Do not journey high in the air, but remain at an altitude halfway between mist and cloud so that you can see the mountains and waters and remember the exact distance. You will then be able to give close instructions to the

3. For Confucianism, these are filial piety, brotherly deference, loyalty, and honesty. For Buddhism they are permanence, joy, selfhood, and purity. Kuan-yin, originally a male bodhisattva (someone who postpones his own enlightenment to assist others), was worshipped as the female Goddess of Mercy in China.

scripture pilgrim. Since he may still find the journey difficult, I shall also give you five talismans." He ordered Ānanda and Kāśyapa to bring out an embroidered cassock and a nine-ring priestly staff. He said to the Bodhisattva, "You may give this cassock and this staff to the scripture pilgrim. If he is firm in his intention to come here, he may put on the cassock and it will protect him from falling back into the wheel of transmigration. When he holds the staff, it will keep him from meeting poison or harm." The Bodhisattva bowed low to receive the gifts. Tathāgata then took out also three fillets and handed them to the Bodhisattva, saying, "These treasures are called the tightening fillets, and though they are all alike, their uses are not the same. I have a separate spell for each of them: the Golden, the Constrictive, and the Prohibitive Spell. If you encounter on the way any monster who possesses great magic powers, you must persuade him to learn to be good and to follow the scripture pilgrim as his disciple. If he is disobedient, this fillet may be put on his head, and it will strike root the moment it comes into contact with the flesh. Recite the particular spell which belongs to the fillet and it will cause the head to swell and ache so painfully that he will think his brains are bursting. That will persuade him to come within our fold."

After the Bodhisattva bowed to the Buddha and taken her leave, she called Disciple Hui-an to follow her. This Hui-an, you see, carried a huge iron rod which weighed a thousand pounds. He followed the Bodhisattva closely and served her as a powerful bodyguard. The Bodhisattva made the embroidered cassock into a bundle and placed it on his back; she hid the golden fillets, took up the priestly staff, and went down the Spirit Mountain. ⁕ ⁕ ⁕

As the mentor and her disciple journeyed, they suddenly came upon a large body of Weak Water, for this was the region of the Flowing Sand River.[4] "My disciple," said the Bodhisattva, "this place is difficult to cross. The scripture pilgrim will be of temporal bones and mortal stock. How will he be able to get across?" "Teacher," said Hui-an, "how wide do you suppose this river is?" ⁕ ⁕ ⁕ The Bodhisattva was looking over the river when suddenly a loud splash was heard, and from the midst of the waves leaped an ugly and ferocious monster. He appeared to have

> A green, though not too green,
> And black, though not too black,
> Face of gloomy complexion;
> A long, though not too long,
> And short, though not too short,
> Sinewy body with naked feet.
> His gleaming eyes
> Shone like two lights beneath the stove.
> His mouth, forked at the corners,
> Was like a butcher's bloody bowl.
> With teeth protruding like swords and knives,
> And red hair all disheveled,
> He bellowed once and it sounded like thunder,
> While his legs sprinted like whirling wind.

Holding in his hands a priestly staff, that fiendish creature ran up the bank and tried to seize the Bodhisattva. He was opposed, however, by Hui-an, who wielded his iron rod, crying, "Stop!" but the fiendish creature raised his staff to meet him. So the two

---

4. In northwestern China.

of them engaged in a fierce battle beside the Flowing Sand River which was truly terrifying.

> The iron rod of Moksa
> Displays its power to defend the Law;
> The monster-taming staff of the creature
> Labors to show its heroic might.
> Two silver pythons dance along the river's side.
> A pair of godlike monks charge each other on the shore.
> This one plies his talents as the forceful lord of Flowing Sand.
> That one protects Kuan-yin by strength to attain merit great.
> This one churns up foam and stirs up waves.
> That one belches fog and spits out wind.
> The stirred-up foams and waves darken Heaven and Earth.
> The spat-out fog and wind make dim both sun and moon.
> The monster-taming staff of this one
> Is like a white tiger emerging from the mountain;
> The iron rod of that one
> Is like a yellow dragon lying on the way.
> When used by one,
> This weapon spreads open the grass and finds the snake.
> When let loose by the other,
> That weapon knocks down the kite and splits the pine.
> They fight until the darkness thickens
> Save for the glittering stars,
> And the fog looms up
> To obscure both sky and land.
> This one, long a dweller in the Weak Water, is uniquely fierce.
> That one, newly leaving the Spirit Mountain, seeks his first triumph.

Back and forth along the river the two of them fought for twenty or thirty rounds without either prevailing, when the fiendish creature stilled the other's iron rod and asked, "What region do you come from, monk, that you dare oppose me?" "I'm the second son of the Pagoda Bearer Devarāja," said Moksa, "Moksa, Disciple Hui-an. I am serving as the guardian of my mentor, who is looking for a scripture pilgrim in the Land of the East. What kind of monster are you that you dare block our way?" "I remember," said the monster, suddenly recognizing his opponent, "that you used to follow the Kuan-yin of the South Sea and practice austerities there in the bamboo grove. How did you get to this place?" "Don't you realize," said Moksa, "that she is my mentor—the one over there on the shore?"

When the monster heard these words, he apologized repeatedly. Putting away his staff, he allowed Moksa to grasp him by the collar and lead him away. He lowered his head and bowed low to Kuan-yin, saying, "Bodhisattva, please forgive me and let me submit my explanation. I am no monster; I am rather the Curtain-Raising Marshal who waits upon the phoenix chariot of the Jade Emperor at the Divine Mists Hall. Because I carelessly broke a crystal cup at one of the Festivals of Immortal Peaches, the Jade Emperor gave me eight hundred lashes, banished me to the Region Below, and changed me into my present shape. Every seventh day he sends a flying sword to stab my breast and side more than a hundred times before it leaves me. Hence my present wretchedness! Moreover, the hunger and cold are unbearable, and I am driven every few days to come out of the waves and find a traveler for food. I certainly did not expect that my ignorance would today lead me to offend the great, merciful Bodhisattva."

"Because of your sin in Heaven," said the Bodhisattva, "you were banished. Yet the slaying of life in your present manner can surely be said to be adding sin to sin. By the decree of Buddha, I am on my way to the Land of the East to find a scripture pilgrim. Why don't you come into my fold, take refuge in good works, and follow the scripture pilgrim as his disciple when he goes to the Western Heaven to ask Buddha for the scriptures? I'll order the flying sword to stop piercing you. At the time when you achieve merit, your sin will be expiated and you will be restored to your former position. How do you feel about that?" "I'm willing," said the monster, "to seek refuge in right action." He said also, "Bodhisattva, I have devoured countless human beings at this place. There have even been a number of scripture pilgrims here, and I ate all of them. The heads of those I devoured I threw into the Flowing Sand, and they sank to the bottom, for such is the nature of this water that not even goose down can float on it. But the skulls of the nine pilgrims floated on the water and would not sink. Regarding them as something unusual, I chained them together with a rope and played with them at my leisure. If this becomes known, I fear that no other scripture pilgrim will want to come this way. Won't it jeopardize my future?"

"Not come this way? How absurd!" said the Bodhisattva. "You may take the skulls and hang them round your neck. When the scripture pilgrim arrives, there will be a use for them." "If that's the case," said the monster, "I'm now willing to receive your instructions." The Bodhisattva then touched the top of his head and gave him the commandments. The sand was taken to be a sign, and he was given the surname "Sha" and the religious name "Wu-ching," and that was how he entered the Gate of Sand.[5] After he had seen the Bodhisattva on her way, he washed his heart and purified himself; he never took life again but waited attentively for the arrival of the scripture pilgrim.

So the Bodhisattva parted with him and went with Mokṣa toward the Land of the East. They traveled for a long time and came upon a high mountain, which was covered by miasma so foul that they could not ascend it on foot. They were just about to mount the clouds and pass over it when a sudden blast of violent wind brought into view another monster of most ferocious appearance. Look at his

> Lips curled and twisted like dried lotus leaves;
> Ears like rush-leaf fans and hard, gleaming eyes;
> Gaping teeth as sharp as a fine steel file's;
> A long mouth wide open as a fire pot.
> A gold cap is fastened with bands by the cheek.
> Straps on his armor seem like scaleless snakes.
> He holds a rake—a dragon's out-stretched claws;
> From his waist hangs a bow of half-moon shape.
> His awesome presence and his prideful mien,
> Defy the deities and daunt the gods.

He rushed up toward the two travelers and, without regard for good or ill, lifted the rake and brought it down hard on the Bodhisattva. But he was met by Disciple Hui-an, who cried with a loud voice, "Reckless monster! Desist from such insolence!

---

5. *Sha* means "sand," a symbol of Buddhism, and *Wu-ching* means "he who awakes to purity." He is also referred to as Sha Monk in the novel.

Look out for my rod!" "This monk," said the monster, "doesn't know any better!
Look out for my rake!" The two of them clashed together at the foot of the mountain
to discover who was to be the victor. It was a magnificent battle!

> The monster is fierce.
> Hui-an is powerful.
> The iron rod jabs at the heart;
> The muckrake swipes at the face.
> Spraying mud and splattering dust darken Heaven and Earth;
> Flying sand and hurling rocks scare demons and gods.
> The nine-teeth rake,
> All burnished,
> Loudly jingles with double rings;
> The single rod,
> Black throughout,
> Leaps and flies in both hands,
> This one is the prince of a Devarāja;
> That one is the spirit of a grand marshal.
> This one defends the faith at Potalaka;
> That one lives in a cave as a monster.
> Meeting this time they rush to fight,
> Not knowing who shall lose and who shall win.

At the very height of their battle, Kuan-yin threw down some lotus flowers from
midair, separating the rod from the rake. Alarmed by what he saw, the fiendish creature asked, "What region are you from, monk, that you dare to play this 'flower-in-
the-eye' trick on me?" "Cursed beast of fleshly eyes and mortal stock!" said Mokṣa.
"I am the disciple of the Bodhisattva from South Sea, and these are lotus flowers
thrown down by my mentor. Don't you recognize them?" "The Bodhisattva from
South Sea?" asked the fiend. "Is she Kuan-yin who sweeps away the three calamities
and rescues us from the eight disasters?" "Who else," said Mokṣa, "if not she?" The
fiend threw away his muckrake, lowered his head, and bowed, saying, "Venerable
brother! Where is the Bodhisattva? Please be so good as to introduce me to her."
Mokṣa raised his head and pointed upward, saying, "Isn't she up there?" "Bodhisattva!" the fiend kowtowed toward her and cried with a loud voice, "Pardon my
sin! Pardon my sin!"

Kuan-yin lowered the direction of her cloud and came to ask him, "What region
are you from, wild boar who has become a spirit or old sow who has become a fiend,
that you dare bar my way?" "I am neither a wild boar," said the fiend, "nor am I an
old sow! I was originally the Marshal of the Heavenly Reeds[6] in the Heavenly River.
Because I got drunk and dallied with the Goddess of the Moon, the Jade Emperor had
me beaten with a mallet two thousand times and banished me to the world of dust. My
true spirit was seeking the proper home for my next incarnation when I lost my way,
passed through the womb of an old sow, and ended up with a shape like this! Having
bitten the sow to death and killed the rest of the litter, I took over this mountain ranch
and passed my days eating people. Little did I expect to run into the Bodhisattva. Save
me, I implore you! Save me!"

---

6. One of the four sages in the Daoist pantheon.

"What is the name of this mountain?" said the Bodhisattva. "It's called the Mountain of the Blessed Mound," said the fiendish creature, "and there is a cave in it by the name of Cloudy Paths. There was a Second Elder Sister Luan originally in the cave. She saw that I knew something of the martial art and therefore asked me to be the head of the family, following the so-called practice of 'standing backward in the door.'[7] After less than a year, she died, leaving me to enjoy the possession of her entire cave. I have spent many days and years at this place, but I know no means of supporting myself and I pass the time eating people. I implore the Bodhisattva to pardon my sin." The Bodhisattva said, "There is an old saying: 'If you desire to have a future, act with reverence for the future.' You have already transgressed in the Region Above, and yet you have not changed your violent ways but indulge in the taking of life. Don't you know that both crimes will be punished?" "The future! The future!" said the fiend. "If I listen to you, I might as well feed on the wind! The proverb says, 'If you follow the law of the court, you'll be beaten to death; if you follow the law of Buddha, you'll be starved to death!' Let me go! Let me go! I would much prefer catching a few travelers and munching on the plump and juicy lady of the family. Why should I care about two crimes, three crimes, a thousand crimes, or ten thousand crimes?" "There is a saying," said the Bodhisattva, "'Heaven helps those who have good intentions.' If you are willing to return to the fruits of truth, there will be means to sustain your body. There are five kinds of grain in this world and they all can relieve hunger. Why do you need to pass the time by feeding on human beings?"

When the fiend heard these words, he was like one who wakes from a dream, and he said to the Bodhisattva, "I would very much like to follow the truth. But 'since I have offended Heaven, even my prayers are of little avail.'" "I have received the decree from Buddha to go to the land of the east to find a scripture pilgrim," said the Bodhisattva. "You can follow him as his disciple and make a trip to the Western Heaven; your merit will cancel out your sins, and you will surely be delivered from your calamities." "I'm willing, I'm willing," promised the fiend with enthusiasm. The Bodhisattva then touched his head and gave him the instructions. Pointing to his body as a sign, she gave him the surname "Chu" and the religious name "Wu-nêng."[8] From that moment on, he accepted the commandment to return to the real. He fasted and ate only a vegetable diet, abstaining from the five forbidden viands and the three undesirable foods,[9] and waiting single-mindedly for the scripture pilgrim.

The Bodhisattva and Mokṣa took leave of Wu-nêng and proceeded again halfway between cloud and mist. As they were journeying, they saw in midair a young dragon calling for help. The Bodhisattva drew near and asked, "What dragon are you, and why are you suffering here?" The dragon said, "I am the son of Ao-jun, the Dragon King of the Western Ocean. Because I inadvertently set fire to the palace and burned some of the pearls in it, my father the king memorialized to the Heavenly Court and charged me with grave disobedience. The Jade Emperor hung me in the sky and gave me three hundred lashes, and I shall be executed in a few days. I beg the Bodhisattva to save me."

When Kuan-yin heard these words, she rushed with Mokṣa up to the South Heavenly Gate. She was received by Ch'iu and Chang, the two Divine Preceptors, who asked her, "Where are you going?" "This humble cleric needs to have an audience

---

7. Refers to a man's living in the wife's house after marriage.
8. *Chu* means "pig," and *Wu-neng* means "he who awakes to power." He is also referred to as Pa-chieh, "eight prohibitions."
9. Foods prohibited in Buddhist and Daoist teaching.

with the Jade Emperor," said the Bodhisattva. The two Divine Preceptors promptly made the report, and the Jade Emperor left the hall to receive her. After presenting her greetings, the Bodhisattva said, "This humble cleric is journeying by the decree of Buddha to the land of the East to find a scripture pilgrim. On the way I met a mischievous dragon hanging in the sky. I have come specially to beg you to spare his life and grant him to me. He can be a good means of transportation for the scripture pilgrim." When the Jade Emperor heard these words, he at once gave the decree of pardon, ordering the Heavenly sentinels to release the dragon to Bodhisattva. The Bodhisattva thanked the Emperor, while the young dragon also kowtowed to the Bodhisattva to thank her for saving his life and pledged obedience to her command. The Bodhisattva then sent him to live in a deep mountain stream with the instruction that when the scripture pilgrim should arrive, he was to change into a white horse and go to the Western Heaven. The young dragon obeyed the order and hid himself, and we shall speak no more of him for the moment.

The Bodhisattva then led Mokṣa past the mountain, and they headed again toward the Land of the East. They had not traveled long before they suddenly came upon ten thousand shafts of golden light and a thousand layers of radiant vapor. "Teacher," said Mokṣa, "that luminous place must be the Mountain of Five Phases. I can see the tag of Tathāgata imprinted on it." "So beneath this place," said the Bodhisattva, "is where the Great Sage, Equal to Heaven, who disturbed Heaven and the Festival of Immortal Peaches, is being imprisoned." "Yes, indeed," said Mokṣa. The mentor and her disciple ascended the mountain and looked at the tag, on which was inscribed the divine words of *Oṁ maṇi padme hūṁ*. When the Bodhisattva saw this, she could not help sighing, and composed the following poem:

> Rueful is the impish monkey who honored not the Law,
> Who rashly sought to be a hero in the years past.
> With mind puffed up he disrupted the Peach Banquet,
> And boldly plundered the Tushita Palace.
> He found no worthy rival in ten thousand troops;
> Through Heaven's nine spheres he spread his terror wide.
> Imprisoned now by Sovereign Tathāgata,
> When will he be free again to show his power?

As mentor and disciple were speaking, they disturbed the Great Sage, who called out loudly from the base of the mountain, "Who is up there on the mountain composing verses to reveal my short-comings?" When the Bodhisattva heard those words, she came down the mountain to take a look. There beneath the rocky ledges were the local spirit, the mountain god, and the Heavenly sentinels guarding the Great Sage. They all came and bowed to receive the Bodhisattva, leading her before the Great Sage. She looked and saw that he was pinned down in a kind of stone box: though he could speak, he could not move his body. "You whose name is Sun," said the Bodhisattva, "do you recognize me?" The Great Sage opened wide his fiery eyes and diamond pupils and nodded. "How could I not recognize you?" he cried loudly. "You are the Mighty Deliverer, the Great Compassionate Bodhisattva Kuan-yin from the Potalaka Mountain of the South Sea. Thank you, thank you for coming to see me! At this place every day is like a year, for not a single acquaintance has ever come to visit me. Where did you come from?" "I have received the decree from Buddha," said the Bodhisattva, "to go to the Land of the East to find a scripture pilgrim. Since I was passing through here. I rested my steps briefly to see you." "Tathāgata deceived me," said the

Great Sage, "and imprisoned me beneath this mountain. For over five hundred years already I have not been able to move. I implore the Bodhisattva to show a little mercy and rescue old Monkey!" "Great were your sinful works," said the Bodhisattva. "If I rescue you, I fear that you will again perpetrate violence, and that will be bad indeed." "Now I know the meaning of penitence," said the Great Sage. "So I entreat the Great Compassion to show me the proper path, for I am willing to practice religion." Truly it is that

> One wish born in the heart of man
> Is known throughout Heaven and Earth.
> If vice or virtue lacks reward,
> Unjust must be the universe.

When the Bodhisattva heard those words, she was filled with pleasure and said to the Great Sage, "The scripture says, 'When a good word is spoken, an answer will come from beyond a thousand miles; but when an evil word is spoken, there will be opposition from beyond a thousand miles.' If you have such a purpose, wait until I reach the Great T'ang Nation in the Land of the East and find the scripture pilgrim. He will be told to come and rescue you, and you can follow him as a disciple. You shall keep the teachings and hold the rosary to enter our gate of Buddha, so that you may again cultivate the fruits of righteousness. Will you do that?" "I'm willing, I'm willing," said the Great Sage repeatedly. "If you are indeed seeking the fruits of virtue," said the Bodhisattva, "let me give you a religious name." "I have one already," said the Great Sage, "and I'm called Sun Wu-k'ung." "There were two persons before you who came into our faith," said the delighted Bodhisattva, "and their names, too, are built on the word 'Wu.' Your name will agree with theirs perfectly, and that is splendid indeed. I need not give you any more instruction; I must be going." So our Great Sage, with enlightened mind and nature, returned to the Buddhist faith, while our Bodhisattva, with care and diligence, sought the divine monk.

She left the place with Mokṣa and proceeded straight to the east; in a few days they reached Ch'ang-an of the Great T'ang Nation. Forsaking the mist and abandoning the cloud, mentor and disciple changed themselves into two wandering monks covered with scabby sores[1] and went into the city. It was already dusk. As they walked through one of the main streets, they saw a temple of the local spirit. They both went straight in, alarming the spirit and the demon guards, who recognized the Bodhisattva. They kowtowed to receive her, and the local spirit then ran quickly to report to the city's guardian deity, the god of the soil, and the spirits of various temples of Ch'ang-an. When they learned that it was the Bodhisattva, they all came to pay homage, saying, "Bodhisattva, please pardon us for being tardy in our reception." "None of you," said the Bodhisattva, "should let a word of this leak out! I came here by the special decree of Buddha to look for a scripture pilgrim. I would like to stay just for a few days in one of your temples, and I shall depart when the true monk is found." The various deities went back to their own places, but they sent the local spirit off to the residence of the city's guardian deity so that the teacher and the disciple could remain incognito in the spirit's temple. We do not know what sort of scripture pilgrim was found, and so you must listen to the explanation in the next chapter.

* * *

---

1. In popular Chinese fiction, the wandering monk with scabby sores or leprosy is frequently a holy man in disguise.

from *Chapter 12*

The T'ang emperor, firm in sincerity, convenes the Grand Mass;
Kuan-yin, revealing herself, converts Gold Cicada.

We shall now tell you about the Bodhisattva Kuan-yin of the Potalaka Mountain in the South Sea, who, since receiving the command of Tathāgata, was searching in the city of Ch'ang-an for a worthy person to be the seeker of scriptures. For a long time, however, she did not encounter anyone truly virtuous. Then she learned that T'ai-tsung was extolling merit and virtue and selecting illustrious monks to hold the Grand Mass. When she discovered, moreover, that the chief priest and celebrant was the monk Child River Float, who was a child of Buddha born from paradise and who happened also to be the very elder whom she had sent to this incarnation, the Bodhisattva was exceedingly pleased. She immediately took the treasures bestowed by Buddha and carried them out with Mokṣa to sell them on the main streets of the city. "What were these treasures?" you ask. There were the embroidered cassock with rare jewels and the nine-ring priestly staff. But she kept hidden the Golden, the Constrictive, and the Prohibitive Fillets for use in a later time, putting up for sale only the cassock and the priestly staff. * * *

We tell you now about T'ai-tsung, who held a noon court and asked Wei Chêng[2] to summon Hsüan-tsang to an audience. That Master of the Law was just leading the monks in chanting sūtras and reciting geyas.[3] When he heard the emperor's decree, he left the platform immediately and followed Wei Chêng to come before the Throne. "We have greatly troubled our Master," said T'ai-tsung, "to render exemplary good works, for which we have hardly anything to offer you in thanks. This morning Hsiao Yü came upon two monks who were willing to present us with a brocaded cassock with rare treasures and a nine-ring priestly staff. We therefore call specially for you so that you may receive them for your enjoyment and use." Hsüan-tsang kowtowed to express his thanks. "If our Master of the Law is willing," said T'ai-tsung, "please put the garment on for us to have a look." The priest accordingly shook open the cassock and draped it on his body, holding the staff in his hands. As he stood before the steps, ruler and subjects were all delighted. Here was a true child of Tathāgata! Look at him:

> His looks imposing, how elegant and fine!
> This robe of Buddha fits him like a glove!
> Its splendor, most lustrous, spills over the world;
> Its radiant colors imbue the universe.
> Up and down are set rows of shining pearls.
> Back and front, layers of golden cords are threaded.
> Brocade gilds the robe's edges all around,
> With patterns embroidered most varied and rare.
> The frogs, thread-made, are shaped Eight Treasures like.
> A gold ring joins the collars with velvet loops.
> It shows on top and bottom Heaven's ranks,
> And stars, great and small, are placed left and right.
> Great is the fortune of Hsüan-tsang, the priest,
> Now most deserving of this precious thing.
> He seems a living arhat from the West,

2. T'ai-tsung was emperor of the Tang dynasty from 627 to 650, and Wei Cheng was his chief advisor.   3. A metered scripture.

> Or even better than its true elite.
> Holding his staff, with all its nine rings clanging;
> Benevolent in the Vairocana hat,
> He's a true child of Buddha, it's no idle tale!
> Nor is it false that he the Bodhi matched.

The various officials, both civil and military, stood before the steps and shouted "Bravo!" T'ai-tsung could not have been more pleased, and he told the Master of the Law to keep his cassock on and the staff in his hands. Two regiments of honor guards were ordered to accompany him along with many other officials. They left the gate of the court and proceeded on the main streets toward the temple, and the whole entourage gave the impression that a chuang-yüan[4] was making a tour of the city. The procession was a stirring sight indeed! The merchants and tradesmen in the city of Ch'ang-an, the princes and noblemen, the men of ink and letters, the grown men and the little girls—all vied to get a good view. Everyone exclaimed, "What a priest! He is truly a living arhat descended to Earth, a live bodhisattva coming to the world!" Hsüan-tsang went right to the temple where he was met by all the monks leaving their seats. The moment they saw him wearing that cassock and holding the staff, they all said that King Kṣitigarbha[5] had arrived! Everyone bowed to him and waited on him left and right. Going up to the main hall, Hsüan-tsang lighted incense to honor the Buddha after which he spoke of the emperor's favor to the multitude. * * *

Not one of the officials disagreed with the emperor, who then asked in the temple, "Who is willing to accept our commission to seek scriptures from Buddha in the Western Heaven?" Hardly had he finished speaking when the Master of the Law stepped from the side and saluted him, saying, "Though your poor monk has no talents, he is ready to perform the service of a dog and a horse. I shall seek these true scriptures on behalf of your Majesty, that the empire of our king may be firm and everlasting." The T'ang emperor was highly pleased. He went forward to raise up the monk with his royal hands, saying, "If the Master is willing to express his loyalty this way, undaunted by the great distance or by the journey over mountains and streams, we are willing to become bond brothers with you." Hsüan-tsang touched his forehead to the ground to express his gratitude. Being indeed a righteous man, the T'ang emperor went at once before Buddha's image in the temple and bowed to Hsüan-tsang four times, addressing him as "Our brother and holy monk." Deeply moved, Hsüan-tsang said, "Your Majesty, what ability and what virtue does your poor monk possess that he should merit such affection from your Heavenly Grace? I shall not spare myself in this journey, but I shall proceed with all diligence until I reach the Western Heaven. If I do not attain my goal, or the true scriptures, I shall not return to our land even if I have to die. I would rather fall into eternal perdition in Hell." He thereupon lifted the incense before Buddha and made that his vow. Highly pleased, the T'ang emperor ordered his carriage back to the palace to wait for the auspicious day and hour, when official documents could be issued for the journey to begin. And so the Throne withdrew as everyone dispersed.

Hsüan-tsang also went back to the Temple of Great Blessing. The many monks of that temple and his several disciples, who had heard about the quest for the scriptures, all came to see him. They asked, "Is it true that you have vowed to go to the

---

4. The top-scoring candidate in the most prestigious civil service examination.   5. A bodhisattva who assisted the ruler of the Underworld.

Western Heaven?" "It is," said Hsüan-tsang. "O Master," one of his disciples said, "I have heard people say that the way to the Western Heaven is long, filled with tigers, leopards, and all kinds of monsters. I fear that there will be departure but no return for you, as it will be difficult to safeguard your life." "I have already made a great vow and a profound promise," said Hsüan-tsang, "that if I do not acquire the true scriptures, I shall fall into eternal perdition in Hell. Since I have received such grace and favor from the king, I have no alternative but to serve my country to the utmost of my loyalty. It is true, of course, that I have no knowledge of how I shall fare on this journey or whether good or evil awaits me." He said to them again, "My disciples, after I leave, wait for two or three years, or six or seven years. If you see the branches of the pine trees within our gate pointing eastward, you will know that I am about to return. If not, I shall not be coming back." The disciples all committed his words firmly to memory.

The next morning T'ai-tsung held court and gathered all the officials together. They wrote up the formal rescript stating the intent to acquire scriptures and stamped it with the seal of free passage. The President of the Imperial Board of Astronomy then came with the report, "Today the positions of the planets are especially favorable for men to make a journey of great length." The T'ang emperor was most delighted. Thereafter the Custodian of the Yellow Gate also made a report, saying, "The Master of the Law awaits your pleasure outside the court." The emperor summoned him up to the treasure hall and said, "Royal Brother, today is an auspicious day for the journey, and your rescript for free passage is ready. We also present you with a bowl made of purple gold for you to collect alms on your way. Two attendants have been selected to accompany you, and a horse will be your means of travel. You may begin your journey at once." Highly pleased, Hsüan-tsang expressed his gratitude and received his gifts, not displaying the least desire to linger. The T'ang emperor called for his carriage and led many officials outside the city gate to see him off. The monks in the Temple of Great Blessing and the disciples were already waiting there with Hsüan-tsang's winter and summer clothing. When the emperor saw them, he ordered the bags to be packed on the horses first, and then asked an officer to bring a pitcher of wine. T'ai-tsung lifted his cup to toast the pilgrim saying, "What is the byname of our Royal Brother?" "Your poor monk," said Hsüan-tsang, "is a person who has left the family. He dares not assume a byname." "The Bodhisattva said earlier," said T'ai-tsung, "that there were three collections of scriptures in the Western Heaven. Our Brother can take that as a byname and call himself Tripitaka. How about it?" Thanking him, Hsüan-tsang accepted the wine and said, "Your Majesty, wine is the first prohibition of priesthood. Your poor monk has practiced abstinence since birth." "Today's journey," said T'ai-tsung, "is not to be compared with any ordinary event. Please drink one cup of this vegetarian wine, and accept our good wishes that go along with the toast." Hsüan-tsang dared not refuse; he took the wine and was about to drink, when he saw T'ai-tsung stoop down to scoop up a handful of dirt with his fingers and sprinkle it in the wine. Tripitaka had no idea what this gesture meant. "Dear Brother," said T'ai-tsung, laughing, "how long will it take you to come back from this trip to the Western Heaven?" "Probably in three years time," said Tripitaka, "I'll be returning to our noble nation." "The years are long and the journey is great," said T'ai-tsung. "Drink this, Royal Brother, and remember: Treasure a handful of dirt from your home, but love not ten thousand taels of foreign gold." Then Tripitaka understood the meaning of the handful of dirt sprinkled in his cup; he thanked the emperor once more and drained the cup. He went out of the gate and left, as the T'ang emperor returned in his carriage. We do not know what will happen to him on this journey, and you must listen to the explanation in the next chapter.

* * *

Chapter 53[6]

The Zen Master, taking food, was demonically conceived:
Yellow Hag brings water to dissolve the perverse pregnancy.

After traveling for a long time, it was again early spring and they heard

Purple swallows murmuring
And orioles warbling.
Purple swallows murmur, tiring their scented beaks;
Orioles warble, their artful notes persist.
The ground full of fallen petals like brocade spread out;
The whole mountain sprouting colors like cushion-piles.
On the peak green plums are budding;
By the cliff old cedars detain the clouds.
Faint, misty lights o'er the meadows;
Sandbars warmed by bright sunshine.
In several gardens flowers begin to bloom;
The sun comes back to Earth, willow sprouts anew.

As they walked along, they came upon a small river of cool, limpid currents. The elder T'ang reined in his horse to look around and saw in the distance several thatched huts beneath willows hanging jadelike. Pointing in that direction, Pilgrim said, "There must be someone running a ferryboat in those houses." "It's likely," said Tripitaka, "but since I haven't seen a boat, I don't dare open my mouth." Dropping down the luggage, Pa-chieh screamed: "Hey, ferryman! Punt your boat over here." He yelled several times and indeed, from beneath the shade of willows a boat emerged, creaking as it was punted. In a little while, it approached the shore while master and disciples stared at it. Truly,

As a paddle parts the foam,
A light boat floats on the waves,
With olive cabins brightly painted
And a deck made of flat, level boards.
On the bow, iron cords encircle;
At the stern, a shining rudder stem.
Though it may be a reed of a boat,
It will sail the lakes and the seas;
Though without fancy cables and tall masts,
It has, in fact, oars of cedar and pine.
It's unlike the divine ship of great distance,
But it can traverse a river's width.
It comes and goes only between two banks;
It moves only in and out of ancient fords.

6. In the intervening chapters, the monk Hsüan-tsang (Tripitaka) has acquired his three disciples, Sha Wu-ching, Chu Pa-chieh, and Sun Wu-k'ung (Pilgrim), as well as the assistance of the white horse. The pilgrims have already been subjected to numerous ordeals on their way to get the Buddhist scriptures in India.

In a moment, the boat touched the bank, and the person punting called out: "If you want to cross the river, come over here." Tripitaka urged his horse forward to take a look at the boatman and saw that the person had

> On the head a woolen wrap
> And on the feet, two black silk shoes.
> The body wore cotton coat and pants patched a hundred times;
> A thousand-stitched, dirty cloth-skirt hugged the waist.
> Though the wrists had coarse skin and the tendons, strength,
> The eyes were dim, the brows knitted, and the features aged.
> The voice was soft and coy like an oriole's,
> But a closer look disclosed a woman old.

Walking to the side of the boat, Pilgrim said, "You are the one ferrying the boat?" "Yes," said the woman. "Why is the ferryman not here?" asked Pilgrim. "Why is the ferrywoman punting the boat?" The woman smiled and did not reply; she pulled out the gangplank instead and set it up. Sha Monk then poled the luggage into the boat, followed by the master holding onto Pilgrim. Then they moved the boat sideways so that Pa-chieh could lead the horse to step into it. After the gangplank was put away, the woman punted the boat away from shore and, in a moment, rowed it across the river.

After they reached the western shore, the elder asked Sha Monk to untie one of the wraps and take out a few pennies for the woman. Without disputing the price, the woman tied the boat to a wooden pillar by the water and walked into one of the village huts nearby, giggling loudly all the time. When Tripitaka saw how clear the water was, he felt thirsty and told Pa-chieh: "Get the alms bowl and fetch some water for me to drink." "I was just about to drink some myself," said Idiot, who took out the alms bowl and bailed out a full bowl of water to hand over to the master. The master drank less than half of the water, and when Idiot took the bowl back, he drank the rest of it in one gulp before he helped his master to mount the horse once more.

After master and disciples found their way to the West they had hardly traveled half an hour when the elder began to groan as he rode. "Stomach-ache!" he said, and Pa-chieh behind him also said, "I have a stomach-ache, too." Sha Monk said, "It must be the cold water you drank." But before he even finished speaking, the elder cried out: "The pain's awful!" Pa-chieh also screamed: "The pain's awful!" As the two of them struggled with this unbearable pain, their bellies began to swell in size steadily. Inside their abdomens, there seemed to be a clot of blood or a lump of flesh, which could be felt clearly by the hand, kicking and jumping wildly about. Tripitaka was in great discomfort when they came upon a small village by the road; two bundles of hay were tied to some branches on a tall tree nearby. "Master, that's good!" said Pilgrim. "The house over there must be an inn. Let me go over there to beg some hot liquid for you. I'll ask them also whether there is an apothecary around, so that I can get some ointment for your stomach-ache."

Delighted by what he heard, Tripitaka whipped his white horse and soon arrived at the village. As he dismounted, he saw an old woman sitting on a grass mound outside the village gate and knitting hemp. Pilgrim went forward and bowed to her with palms pressed together saying. "*P'o-p'o,*[7] this poor monk has come from the Great T'ang in the Land of the East. My master is the royal brother of the T'ang court. Because he drank some water from the river back there after we crossed it, he is having a

---

7. Granny.

stomach-ache." Breaking into loud guffaws, the woman said, "You people drank some water from the river?" "Yes," replied Pilgrim. "we drank some of the clean river water east of here." Giggling loudly, the old woman said, "What fun! What fun! Come in, all of you. I'll tell you something."

Pilgrim went to take hold of T'ang monk while Sha Monk held up Pa-chieh; moaning with every step the two sick men walked into the thatched hut to take a seat, their stomachs protruding and their faces turning yellow from the pain. "*P'o-p'o*," Pilgrim kept saying, "please make some hot liquid for my master. We'll thank you." Instead of boiling water, however, the old woman dashed inside, laughing and yelling, "Come and look, all of you!"

With loud clip-clops, several middle-aged women ran out from within to stare at the T'ang monk, grinning stupidly all the time. Enraged, Pilgrim gave a yell and ground his teeth together, so frightening the whole crowd of them that they turned to flee, stumbling all over. Pilgrim darted forward and caught hold of the old woman, crying, "Boil some water quick and I'll spare you!" "O Father!" said the old woman, shaking violently, "boiling water is useless, because it won't cure their stomach-aches. Let me go, and I'll tell you." Pilgrim released her, and she said, "This is the Nation of Women of Western Liang. There are only women in our country, and not even a single male can be found here. That's why we were amused when we saw you. That water your master drank is not the best, for the river is called Child-and-Mother River. Outside our capital we also have a Male Reception Post-house, by the side of which there is also a Pregnancy Reflection Stream. Only after reaching her twentieth year would someone from this region dare go and drink that river's water, for she would feel the pain of conception soon after she took a drink. After three days, she would go to the Male Reception Post-house and look at her reflection in the stream. If a double reflection appears, it means that she will give birth to a child. Since your master drank some water from the Child-and-Mother River, he, too, has become pregnant and will give birth to a child. How could hot water cure him?"

When Tripitaka heard this, he paled with fright. "O disciple," he cried, "what shall we do?" "O father!" groaned Pa-chieh as he twisted to spread his legs further apart, "we are men, and we have to give birth to babies? Where can we find a birth canal? How could the fetus come out?" With a chuckle Pilgrim said, "According to the ancients, 'A ripe melon will fall by itself.' When the time comes, you may have a gaping hole at your armpit and the baby will crawl out."

When Pa-chieh heard this, he shook with fright, and that made the pain all the more unbearable. "Finished! Finished!" he cried. "I'm dead! I'm dead!" "Second Elder Brother," said Sha Monk, laughing, "stop writhing! Stop writhing! You may hurt the umbilical cord and end up with some sort of prenatal sickness." Our Idiot became more alarmed than ever. Tears welling up in his eyes, he tugged at Pilgrim and said, "Elder Brother, please ask the *P'o-p'o* to see if they have some midwives here who are not too heavy-handed. Let's find a few right away. The movement inside is becoming more frequent now. It must be labor pain. It's coming! It's coming!" Again Sha Monk said chuckling. "Second Elder Brother, if it's labor pain, you'd better sit still. I fear you may puncture the water bag."

"O *P'o-p'o*," said Tripitaka with a moan, "do you have a physician here? I'll ask my disciple to go there and ask for a prescription. We'll take the drug and have an abortion." "Even drugs are useless," said the old woman, "but due south of here there is a Male-Undoing Mountain. In it there is a Child Destruction Cave, and inside the cave there is an Abortion Stream. You must drink a mouthful of water from the stream before the pregnancy can be terminated. But nowadays, it's not easy to get that water. Last year, a Taoist by the name of True Immortal Compliant came on the scene and he changed the name of the Child Destruction Cave to the Shrine of Immortal Assembly. Claiming the water from the Abortion Stream as his possession, he refused to give it out freely. Anyone who wants the water must present monetary offerings together with meats, wines, and fruit baskets. After bowing to him in complete reverence, you will receive a tiny bowl of the water. But all of you are mendicants. Where could you find the kind of money you need to spend for something like this? You might as well suffer here and wait for the births." When Pilgrim heard this, he was filled with delight. "*P'o-p'o,*" he said, "how far is it from here to the Male-Undoing Mountain?" "About three thousand miles," replied the old woman. "Excellent! Excellent!" said Pilgrim. "Relax, Master! Let old Monkey go and fetch some of that water for you to drink."

Dear Great Sage! He gave this instruction to Sha Monk: "Take good care of Master. If this family ill behaves and tries to hurt him, bring out your old thuggery and scare them a little. Let me go fetch the water." Sha Monk obeyed. The old woman then took out a large porcelain bowl to hand over to Pilgrim, saying, "Take this bowl and try to get as much water as possible. We can save some for an emergency." Indeed Pilgrim took over the bowl, left that thatched hut, and mounted the cloud to leave. Only then did the old woman fall to her knees, bowing to the air, and cried, "O father! This monk knows how to ride the clouds!" She went inside and told the other women to come out to kowtow to the T'ang monk, all addressing him as arhat or bodhisattva. Then they began to boil water and prepare rice to present to the pilgrims, and we shall leave them for the moment. * * *

Dear Great Sage! He mounted the clouds and went straight back to the village hut, crying, "Sha Monk." Inside Tripitaka was moaning to endure the pain, while the groans of Pa-chieh were continuous. Delighted by the call, they said, "Sha Monk, Wu-k'ung's back." Sha Monk hurried out the door to ask, "Big Brother, have you brought water?" The Great Sage entered and gave a thorough account to the T'ang monk. Shedding tears, Tripitaka said, "O disciple! How is this going to end?" "I came back," said the Great Sage, "to ask Brother Sha to go with me. When we reach the shrine, old Monkey will fight with that fellow and Sha Monk can use the opportunity to get that water to save you." Tripitaka said, "Both of you who are healthy will be gone, leaving behind the two of us who are sick. Who will look after us?" The old woman waiting on them said, "Relax, old arhat. You don't need your disciples. We will serve you and take care of you. When you first arrived, we were already fond of you. Then we saw how this bodhisattva traveled by cloud and fog, and we knew that you had to be an arhat or bodhisattva. We'll never dare to harm you again."

"You are all women here," snapped Pilgrim. "Whom do you dare to harm?" "O dear father!" said the old woman, giggling. "You're lucky to have come to my house. If you had gone to another one, none of you would have remained whole." "What do you mean," said Pa-chieh, still groaning, "by not remaining whole?" The old woman replied: "The four or five of us in this family are all getting on in years. We have given up the activities of love. If you go to another family, there may be more youthful members than old ones. You think the young ones will let you go? They will want to have intercourse with you, and if you refuse, they will take your lives. Then they will cut you up to use your flesh to make fragrant bags." "In that case," said Pa-chieh, "I won't be hurt. They all smell nice, and they'll be good for fragrant bags. I'm a stinking hog, and even when I'm cut up, I still stink. That's why I can't be hurt."

"Don't be so talkative!" said Pilgrim, chuckling. "Save your strength, so you can give birth." The old woman said, "No need for delay. Go quickly to get the water." "Do you have a bucket in your house?" asked Pilgrim. "Please lend us one." The old woman went to the back to take out a bucket and rope to hand over to Sha Monk, who said, "Let's bring two ropes. We may need them if the well is deep."

After Sha Monk received the bucket and the ropes, he followed the Great Sage out of the village hut and they left together, mounting the clouds. In less than half an hour, they arrived at the Male-Undoing Mountain. As they lowered their clouds to go before the shrine, the Great Sage gave Sha Monk this instruction: "Take the bucket with the ropes and hide yourself. Old Monkey will go and provoke battle. When we are in the thick of fighting, you can use the opportunity to go inside, get the water, and leave." Sha Monk obeyed.

Wielding his iron rod, the Great Sage Sun approached the door and shouted: "Open the door! Open the door!" The Taoist who stood guard at the door hurried inside to report: "Master, that Sun Wu-k'ung is here again." Greatly angered, the master said, "This brazen ape is insolent indeed! I have always heard that he has considerable abilities, and today I know it's true. That rod of his is quite difficult to withstand." "Master," said the Taoist, "his abilities may be great, but yours are not inferior. You are, in fact, exactly his match." "But twice before," said the master, "I lost to him." "Only in a contest of sheer violence," said the Taoist. "Later, when he tried to bail water, your hook made him fall twice. Haven't you equalized the situation? He had little alternative but to leave at first, and now he's back. It must be that Tripitaka's pregnancy is so advanced and his body so heavy that his complaints have driven this monkey to return, against his better judgment. He must feel rather contemptuous toward his master, and I'm sure that you will win."

> When the True Immortal heard these words, he became
> Delighted and filled with elation;
> Full of smiles and brimming with power.

Holding straight his compliant hook, he walked out of the door and shouted, "Brazen simian! Why are you here again?" "Only to fetch water," answered the Great Sage. "That water," said the True Immortal, "happens to be in my well. Even if you are a king or a prime minister, you must come begging with offerings of meat and wines, and then I will only give you a little. You are my enemy no less, and you dare to ask for it with empty hands?" "You really refuse to give it to me?" asked the Great Sage, and the True Immortal replied, "Yes! Yes!" "You damned fool!" scolded the Great Sage. "If you don't give me the water, watch my rod!" He opened up at once and rushed at the True Immortal, bringing down the rod hard on his head. Stepping aside quickly to dodge the blow, the True Immortal met him with the hook and fought back. This time, it was even more ferocious a battle than last time. What a fight!

> Golden-hooped rod,
> Compliant hook,
> Two angry men so full of enmity.
> The cosmos darkens as sand and rocks fly up;
> Sun and moon sadden as dirt and dust soar high.
> The Great Sage seeks water to save his master,
> Denied by the fiend for his nephew's sake.
> The two exert their strength
> To wage a contest there,

Teeth are ground together
To strive for a victory,
More and more alert,
They arouse themselves.
They belch cloud and fog to sadden ghosts and gods.
Bing-bing and bang-bang clash both hook and rod,
Their cries, their shouts shake up the mountain range.
The fierce wind, howling, ravages the woods;
The violent airs surge past the dipper stars.
The Great Sage grows happier as he strives;
The True Immortal's gladder as he fights.
They do this battle with their whole hearts and minds;
They will not give up until someone dies.

The two of them began their fighting outside the shrine, and as they struggled and danced together, they gradually moved to the mountain slope below. We shall leave this bitter contest for a moment.

We tell you instead about our Sha Monk, who crashed inside the door, holding the bucket. He was met by the Taoist, who barred the way at the well and said, "Who are you that you dare come to get our water?" Dropping the bucket, Sha Monk took out his fiend-routing treasure staff and, without a word, brought it down on the Taoist's head. The Taoist was unable to dodge fast enough, and his left arm and shoulder were broken by this one blow. Falling to the ground, he lay there struggling for his life. "I wanted to slaughter you, cursed beast," scolded Sha Monk, "but you are, after all, a human being. I still have some pity for you, and I'll spare you. Let me bail out the water." Crying for Heaven and Earth to help him, the Taoist crawled slowly to the rear, while Sha Monk lowered the bucket into the well and filled it to the brim. He then walked out of the shrine and mounted the cloud and fog before he shouted to Pilgrim, "Big Brother, I have gotten the water and I'm leaving. Spare him! Spare him!"

When the Great Sage heard this, he stopped the hook with his iron rod and said, "I was about to exterminate you, but you have not committed a crime. Moreover, I still have regard for the feelings of your brother, the Bull Demon King. When I first came here, I was hooked by you twice and I didn't get my water. When I returned, I came with the trick of enticing the tiger to leave the mountain and deceived you into fighting me, so that my brother could go inside to get the water. If old Monkey is willing to use his real abilities to fight with you, don't say there is only one of you so called True Immortal Compliant; even if there are several of you, I would beat you all to death. But to kill is not as good as to let live, and so I'm going to spare you and permit you to have a few more years. From now on if anyone wishes to obtain the water, you must not blackmail the person."

Not knowing anything better, that bogus immortal brandished his hook and once more attempted to catch Pilgrim's legs. The Great Sage evaded the blade of his hook and then rushed forward, crying, "Don't run!" The bogus immortal was caught unprepared and he was pushed head over heels to the ground, unable to get up. Grabbing the compliant hook the Great Sage snapped it in two; then he bundled the pieces together and, with another bend, broke them into four segments. Throwing them on the ground, he said, "Brazen, cursed beast! Still dare to be unruly?" Trembling all over, the bogus immortal took the insult and dared not utter a word. Our Great Sage, in peals of laughter, mounted the cloud to rise into the air, and we have a testimonial poem.

The poem says:
For smelting true lead you need water true;
True water mixes well with mercury dried,
True mercury and lead have no maternal breath;
Divine drugs and cinnabar are elixir.
In vain there is the form of child conceived;
Earth Mother with ease has merit achieved.
Heresy pushed down, right faith held up,
The lord of the mind, all smiles, now returns.

Mounting the auspicious luminosity, the Great Sage caught up with Sha Monk. Having acquired the true water, they were filled with delight as they returned to where they belonged. After they lowered the clouds and went up to the village hut, they found Chu Pa-chieh leaning on the door post and groaning, his belly huge and protruding. Walking quietly up to him, Pilgrim said, "Idiot, when did you enter the delivery room?" Horrified, Idiot said, "Elder Brother, don't make fun of me. Did you bring the water?" Pilgrim was about to tease him some more when Sha Monk followed him in, laughing as he said, "Water's coming! Water's coming!" Enduring the pain, Tripitaka rose slightly and said, "O disciples, I've caused you a lot of trouble." That old woman, too, was most delighted, and all of her relatives came out to kowtow, crying, "O bodhisattva! This is our luck! This is our luck!" She took a goblet of flowered porcelain, filled it half full, and handed it to Tripitaka, saying, "Old master, drink it slowly. All you need is a mouthful and the pregnancy will dissolve." "I don't need any goblet," said Pa-chieh, "I'll just finish the bucket." "O venerable father, don't scare people to death!" said the old woman. "If you drink this bucket of water, your stomach and your intestines will all be dissolved." Idiot was so taken aback that he dared not misbehave; he drank only half a goblet.

In less than the time of a meal, the two of them experienced sharp pain and cramps in their bellies, and then their intestines growled four or five times. After that, Idiot could no longer contain himself: both waste and urine poured out of him. The T'ang monk, too, felt the urge to relieve himself and wanted to go to a quiet place. "Master," said Pilgrim, "you mustn't go out to a place where there is a draft. If you are exposed to the wind, I fear that you may catch some postnatal illness." At once the old woman brought to them two night pots so that the two of them could find relief. After several bowel movements, the pain stopped and the swelling of their bellies gradually subsided as the lump of blood and flesh dissolved. The relatives of the old woman also boiled some white rice congee and presented it to them to strengthen their postnatal weakness. "*P'o-p'o*," said Pa-chieh, "I have a healthy constitution, and I have no need to strengthen any postnatal weakness. You go and boil me some water, so that I can take a bath before I eat the congee." "Second Elder Brother," said Sha Monk, "you can't take a bath. If water gets inside someone within a month after birth, the person will be sick." Pa-chieh said, "But I have not given proper birth to anything; at most, I only have had a miscarriage. What's there to be afraid of? I must wash and clean up." Indeed, the old woman prepared some hot water for them to clean their hands and feet. The T'ang monk then ate about two bowls of congee, but Pa-chieh consumed over fifteen bowls and he still wanted more. "Coolie," chuckled Pilgrim, "don't eat so much. If you get a sand-bag belly, you'll look quite awful." "Don't worry, don't worry," replied Pa-chieh. "I'm no female hog. So, what's there to be afraid of?" The family members indeed went to prepare some more rice.

The old woman then said to the T'ang monk, "Old master, please bestow this water on me." Pilgrim said, "Idiot, you are not drinking the water anymore?" "My stomach-ache is gone," said Pa-chieh, "and the pregnancy, I suppose, must be dissolved. I'm quite fine now. Why should I drink any more water?" "Since the two of them have recovered," said Pilgrim, "we'll give this water to your family." After thanking Pilgrim, the old woman poured what was left of the water into a porcelain jar, which she buried in the rear garden. She said to the rest of the family, "This jar of water will take care of my funeral expenses." Everyone in that family, young and old, was delighted. A vegetarian meal was prepared and tables were set out to serve to the T'ang monk. He and his disciples had a leisurely dinner and then rested.

At dawn the next day, they thanked the old woman and her family before leaving the village. Tripitaka T'ang mounted up, Sha Monk toted the luggage, Chu Pa-chieh held the reins, and the Great Sage Sun led the way in front. So, this is how it should be:

> The mouth washed of its sins, the self is clean;
> Worldly conception dissolved, the body's fit.

We don't know what sort of affairs they must attend to when they reach the capital, and you must listen to the explanation in the next chapter.

* * *

from *Chapters 69–72*

> At night the Lord of the Mind prepares the medicines;
> At the banquet the king speaks of the perverse fiend.

We were telling you about the Great Sage Sun, who went with the palace attendant to the interior division of the royal palace.[8] He stood still only after he had reached the door of the royal bedchamber. Then he told the attendant to take the three golden threads inside along with the instruction: "Ask one of the palace ladies or eunuch to tie these three threads to the inch, the pass, and the foot sections of His Majesty's left hand where the radial pulse are felt.[9] Then pass the other ends of the threads out to me through the window shutters."

The attendant followed his instruction. The king was asked to sit up on the dragon bed, while the three sections of his pulse were tied by the golden threads, and their other ends were then passed out to Pilgrim. Using the thumb and the index finger of his right hand to pick up one of the threads, Pilgrim first examined the pulse of the inch section; next, he used his middle finger and his thumb to pick up the second thread and examine the pulse of the pass section; finally, he used the thumb and his fourth finger to pick up the third thread and examine the pulse of the foot section.

Thereafter Pilgrim made his own breathing regular[1] and proceeded to determine which of the Four Heteropathic *Ch'is,* the Five Stases, the Seven External Images of the Pulse, the Eight Internal Images of the Pulse, and the Nine Pulse Indications were present. His pressure on the threads went from light to medium to heavy; from heavy

8. Sun Wu-k'ung is on his own here, having been asked to look in on a king in great distress.

9. In traditional Chinese medicine, the human pulse is divided into three sections on the wrist: the one closest to the hand was called inch; the one further up the arm was called foot; and the one between these two pulses was

called pass [translator's note].

1. The physician uses the rhythm of his own breathing as a standard for measuring the patient's pulse. He then assesses the observable features of body temperature, circulation, etc.

to medium to light, until he could clearly perceive whether the condition of the patient was repletion or depletion of energy and its cause. Then he made the request that the threads be untied from the king's left wrist and be attached as before to the positions on his right wrist. Using now the fingers on his left hand, he then examined the pulse on the right wrist section by section. When he had completed his examination, he shook his body once and retrieved his hairs.

"Your Majesty," he cried in a loud voice, "on your left wrist the pulse of your inch section feels strong and tense, the pulse of your pass section feels rough and languid, and the pulse of your foot section feels hollow and sunken. On your right wrist the pulse of your inch section feels floating and smooth, the pulse of your pass section feels retarded and hesistant, and the pulse of your foot section feels accelerated and firm. Now, when the pulse of your left inch section feels strong and tense, it indicates an internal energetic depletion with pain in the cardiac system of functions. When the pulse of your left pass section feels rough and languid, it indicates sweating that has led to numbness in the flesh. When the pulse of your left foot section feels hollow and sunken, it indicates a pink tinge to your urine and blood in your stool. When the pulse of the inch section on your right wrist feels floating and smooth, it indicates a congestion blocking the *ch'i* circulation and leading to cessation of menses.[2] When the pulse of your right pass section feels retarded and hesitant, it indicates a stasis of alimentary matter in the stomach system with retention of fluids. When the pulse of your right foot section feels accelerated and firm, it indicates discomfort caused by sensations of stuffiness and chills caused by energetic depletion. To sum up, your illness has been caused by fear and anxiety, and it may be the manifestation type of an illness called the 'Paired Birds Separated from Company.'"

On hearing these words, the king was so delighted that he roused himself to answer loudly: "Your fingers have brought out the truth! Your fingers have brought out the truth! This is indeed our illness. Please go outside and prescribe us some medicines." * * *

Taking leave of the Master of the Law, the king took the Elixir of Black Gold and the sweet rain back to his palace. He swallowed first one pill with one flask of the rain; then he took another with the second flask. He went through this for a third time, swallowing all three pills and drinking all three flasks of the rain. In a little while, his stomach began to make a loud, rumbling noise, and he had to sit on the night pot and move his bowels four or five times. Thereafter, he took a little rice soup before he reclined on the dragon bed. Two palace ladies went to examine the pot; the filth and phlegm were indescribable, in the midst of which there was also a lump of glutinous rice. The ladies approached the dragon bed to report: "The root of the illness has been purged." * * *

After they drank and feasted for some time, the king again took up, a huge goblet to present to Pilgrim. "Your Majesty," said Pilgrim, "please be seated. Old Monkey will drink all the rounds. I'll never dare refuse you." "Your great kindness to me," said the king, "is as weighty as a mountain, and we can't begin to thank you enough. No matter what, please drink this huge goblet of wine first, and then we have something to tell you." "Please tell me first," said Pilgrim, "and old Monkey will be happy to drink this."

2. As it is impossible for a king to have menstrual periods, this is an obvious slip on the part of the author in his incorporation of medical materials for this episode of the narrative [translator's note].

"Our illness of several years," replied the king, "was caused by great anxiety. The single formula of efficacious elixir prescribed by the divine monk, however, broke through the cause and that's how I recovered." With a chuckle, Pilgrim said, "When old Monkey examined Your Majesty yesterday, I knew already that the illness had been caused by anxiety. But I don't know what you were anxious about."

The king said, "According to the ancients, 'The disgrace of a family should never be spread without.' But the divine monk, on the other hand, is our benefactor. If you do not laugh at us, we shall tell you." "How could I dare laugh at you?" said Pilgrim. "You need not hesitate to tell me." "As you journeyed from the East," said the king, "how many states have you passed through?" "About five or six," replied Pilgrim. "How do they address the consorts of the king?" he asked again. Pilgrim said, "The ranking wife of a king would be called the Central Palace, and those two consorts next in rank would be called the East Palace and the West Palace, respectively."

"The titles here are slightly different," said the king. "Our Central Palace bears the name of the Golden Sage Palace; the East Palace is called the Jade Sage Palace, and the West Palace has the title of Silver Sage Palace. At the moment, we have only the Jade and Silver consorts with us." "Why is the Golden Sage Palace absent?" asked Pilgrim.

As tears fell from his eyes, the king said, "She hasn't been with us for three years." "Where has she gone to?" asked Pilgrim again. The king said, "Three years ago, during the time of the Double Fifth Festival, our consorts and we were all gathered inside the Pomegranate Pavilion of our garden, cutting up rice cakes, affixing the artemisia plant to our garments, drinking wine made from the calamus and realgar,[3] and watching the dragon boat races. Suddenly a gust arose and a monster-spirit appeared in the air. Calling himself Jupiter's Rival, he claimed that he lived in the Cave of the Mythic Beast at the Unicorn Mountain. Because he did not have a wife, he made investigation and learned of the great beauty of our Golden Sage Palace. He demanded that we turn her out, and if we did not after his asking us three times, he would first eat us alive and then proceed to devour the various officials and the people of the entire capital. Burdened, therefore, by the care of the state and the people at the time, we had no alternative but to push Golden Sage Palace out of the Pomegranate Pavilion, where she was immediately abducted by the fiend with a single sound. That incident, of course, gave us a great fright, and the glutinous rice cakes we ate thus remained undigested in our body. Moreover, we were ridden with anxious thoughts night and day, which led to three long years of bitter illness. Now that we have the good fortune of taking the efficacious elixir of the divine monk, we have purged several times, and all that waste accumulated three years ago has been eliminated. That's why our frame has turned healthy and our body has lightened, and we feel as energetic as before. The life I regain today is entirely a gift of the divine monk. Even the weight of Mount T'ai cannot compare with the magnitude of your favor!"

When Pilgrim heard these words, he was filled with delight, so much so that he drank in two gulps that huge goblet of wine. Smiling broadly, he said to the king, "So, that was the cause of Your Majesty's fear and anxiety. Now you've met old Monkey, and you are lucky to be cured. But do you want the Golden Sage Palace returned to your kingdom?" Shedding tears again, the king replied, "There's not a day or a night that we do not yearn for her presence, but no one is able to arrest the monster-spirit

---

3. Aphrodisiac or alchemical ingredients.

for us. How could I not want her return?" "Let old Monkey go and bring that perverse fiend to submission," said Pilgrim. "How about it?" The king immediately went to his knees and said, "If you can rescue our queen, we are willing to lead all the residents of this palace and all my consorts out to the city to live as common people. We shall present our entire kingdom to you and let you be the ruler." * * *

"Let me ask your Majesty, did the Golden Sage Palace leave you any memento when she departed? If she did, give it to me." When the king heard him mention, the word, "memento," he felt as if a sword had run his heart through and he wept aloud, saying.

> When we toasted brightness and warmth that year,
> The vicious Jupiter uttered his cries.
> He took by force our queen to be his wife;
> We yielded her up for the people's sake.
> There were no words of greeting or farewell,
> No tender partings by the wayside stands.
> Mementos, scented purse—everything is gone,
> Except myself, all bitter and forlorn.

"Your Majesty," said Pilgrim, "your pain is near its end. Why torture yourself like that? If our lady did not leave you any memento, are there objects in the palace that she is most fond of? Give me one of these." "Why do you want them?" asked the king.

Pilgrim said, "That fiend king does have magic powers. When I saw the smoke, the fire, and the sand he released, I knew it would be difficult to bring him to submission. Even if I were to succeed, I fear that our lady would refuse to accompany me, a stranger, to return to the kingdom. She will trust me only if she sees me entrusted with some object most dear to her when she was in the palace. That's why I must take such an object along with me."

"In the dressing alcove," said the king, "at the Palace of the Bright Sun, there is a pair of gold bracelets, originally worn by our Golden Sage Palace. Because that day was the festival when she had to tie five colored threads to her arms, she took off the bracelets. As these were some of her favorite things, they are still kept in a jewel box. Because of the way we were separated, however, we could not bear the sight of these bracelets, for they reminded us so much of her lovely face. The moment we see them, we would be sicker than ever." "Let's not talk about illness anymore," said Pilgrim. "Bring me the bracelets. If you can part with them, give them to me. If not, I'll just take one of them."

The king asked the Jade Sage Palace to take them out. When the king saw the bracelets, he cried several times "Dearest, dearest Lady" before handing them over to Pilgrim. After Pilgrim took them, he put them on his arm.

Dear Great Sage! He refused the wine of merit and mounted the cloud-somersault instead. With a whistle he arrived once more at the Unicorn Mountain. Too preoccupied to enjoy the scenery, he at once began searching for the cave. As he walked along, he heard the raucous noise of people speaking. When he stood still to look more carefully, he found soldiers posted at the entrance of the Cave of Mythic Beast, some five hundred of them,

> All tightly lined up,
> And densely arrayed.
> Tightly lined up, they held spears and swords
> Which gleamed in the sun;

> Densely arrayed, they unfurled the banners
> Which fluttered in the wind.
> Tiger generals, bear captains, all able to change;
> Leopard warriors, striped-cat marshals, most spirited.
> Grey wolves, how savage!
> Brown elephants, still more potent!
> Sly hare, clever deer, wielding halberds and swords;
> Long snakes, huge serpents, hung with sabers and bows.
> The chimpanzee who understands human speech
> Leads the troops, secures the camp as one informed.

When Pilgrim saw them, he dared not proceed; instead, he turned and walked back out the way he came. Why did he turn back, you say. It was not because he was afraid of them. Actually, he returned to the spot where he had slain the little fiend and found again that brass gong and that yellow banner.

> Facing the wind, he made the magic sign;
> Thinking the image, he went into motion.

With one shake of his body, he changed himself into the form of that Going and Coming. Banging loud his gong, he stepped forward in great strides and marched right up to the Cave of the Mythic Beast. Just as he was looking over the cave, he heard the chimpanzee say, "Going and Coming, are you back?" Pilgrim had no alternative but to reply, "I'm back." "Get inside quickly!" said the chimpanzee. "The great king is waiting for your reply at the Skinning Pavilion." On hearing this, Pilgrim strode inside the front door, still beating his gong. Once inside, he saw hanging cliffs and precipitous walls, rock chambers and quiet rooms. There were exotic grasses and flowers on the left and right, and there were plenty of old cedars and aged pines front and back.

Soon he walked through the second-level door, where he saw an octagonal pavilion with eight translucent windows. In the middle of the pavilion was a gold inlaid armchair, on which was seated solemnly a demon king. Truly he had a savage appearance! You see

> Colored nimbus soaring up from his head
> And violent air bursting forth from his chest.
> Pointed teeth protrude like rows of sharp swords;
> His temple's tousled locks flare like red fume.
> Whiskers like arrows stick onto his lips;
> Hairs wrap his body like blanket layers.
> Mocking Jupiter are two copper-bell eyes;
> An iron club he holds looks tall as the sky.

Though Pilgrim saw him, he was bold enough to make light of the monster-spirit. Without in the least affecting good manners, Pilgrim turned his back on him and kept beating the gong. "Have you returned?" asked the fiend king, but Pilgrim did not answer him. "Going and Coming, have you returned?" he asked again, and still Pilgrim did not answer him. The fiend king walked up to him and tugged at Pilgrim, saying, "Why are you still beating the gong after you have come home? I ask you a question, and you don't answer me. Why?"

Dashing the gong to the ground, Pilgrim cried, "What's this Why, Why, Why? I told you I didn't want to go, and you insisted that I should. When I got there, I saw countless men and horses already arrayed in battle formations. The moment they saw me, they cried, 'Seize the monster-spirit! Seize the monster-spirit!' Pushing and shoving, they hauled me bodily into the city to see the king, who at once ordered me executed. It was fortunate that counselors from both rows of ministers invoked the old maxim that 'When two states are at war, the envoys are never executed.' They spared me and took away the declaration of war. Then they sent me out of the city, where before the entire army they caned me thirty times on my legs. I was released to tell you that they would be here soon to do battle with you."

"As you have put the matter," said the fiend king, "you have lucked out! No wonder you didn't answer me when I questioned you." Pilgrim said, "I was silent not because of anything. It's just that I was nursing my pain, and that's why I didn't reply."

"How many horses and men do they have?" asked the fiend king again. Pilgrim said, "I was scared silly, and I was further intimidated by their beatings. You think I would be able to account for the number of their horses and men? All I saw in thick rows were

> Bows, arrows, sabers, mail, and armor;
> Lances, swords, halberds, and tasseled banners;
> Poleaxes, crescent spades, and head-coverings;
> Huge axes, round shields, and iron caltrops;
> Long battle staffs;
> Short, fat cudgels;
> Steel tridents and petards and helmets, too.
> To be worn are tall boots, head gear, and quilted vests.
> Crops and whips, sleeve-pellets, and bronze mallets.

When the fiendish king heard this, he laughed and said, "That's nothing! That's nothing! A little fire and all such weapons will be wiped out. You should go now and tell our Lady Golden Sage not to worry. When she heard that I was growing angry and about to go into battle, she was already full of tears. Why don't you go now and tell her that the men and horses of her country are most fearsome and that they will certainly prevail against me. That ought to give her some relief for a while."

On hearing this, Pilgrim was very pleased, saying to himself, "Old Monkey can't ask for anything better!" Look at him! He seems to be especially familiar with the way! Rounding a small side door, he passed through halls and chambers. Deep inside the cave, you see, were all tall buildings and edifices, quite unlike what was in front. When he reached the rear palace where the Lady Golden Sage lived, he saw brilliantly colored doors. Walking through these to look around, he found two choirs of fiendish vixen and deer, all made up to appear as beautiful maidens standing on the left and right. In the middle was seated the lady, who held her chin in her hand as tears fell from her eyes. Indeed she had

> Soft, youthful features,
> Seductive good looks.
> Too lazy to do her hair,
> She left it piled up loosely;
> Fearful of make-up,
> She wore neither pins nor bracelets.
> Her face had no powder,
> She being scornful of rouge.
> Her hair had no oil,

For she kept unkempt her tresses.
Her cherry lips pouted
As she clenched her silvery teeth;
Her moth brows knitted
As tears drenched her starlike eyes.
All her heart
Yearned for the Scarlet-Purple ruler;
All her thoughts
Dwelled on fleeing at once this snare and net.
Truly it had been thus:
The fate of fair ladies was always harsh.
Weary and silent, she faced the east wind.

Walking up to her and bowing, Pilgrim said, "Greetings!" "This insolent imp!" said the lady. "How brash could he be! During the time when I shared the glory with the Scarlet-Purple ruler, those grand preceptors and prime ministers would prostrate themselves before me and dared not even raise their heads. How could this wild fiend just address me with a 'Greetings'? Where did this rustic boor come from?"

Some of the maids went forward and said, "Madam, please do not be angry. He is a trusted junior officer of Father Great King, and his name is Going and Coming. He was the one sent to deliver the declaration of war this morning." On hearing this, the lady suppressed her anger and said, "When you delivered the declaration, did you reach the Scarlet-Purple Kingdom?" "I took the declaration," replied Pilgrim, "straight into the capital, reaching, in fact, the Hall of the Golden Chimes. After I saw the king in person, I took his reply back here."

"When you saw the king," said the lady, "what did he have to say?" Pilgrim said, "He claimed he was ready to fight, and just now, I have already told the great king about how the enemy forces were being disposed. That ruler, however, also expressed great longing for Madam. He wanted to convey a few words of special interest to you, but there are too many people around and I can't speak here."

On hearing this, the lady shouted for the two rows of vixen and deer to leave. After he closed the palace door, Pilgrim gave his own face a wipe and changed back into his original form. He said to the lady, "Don't be afraid of me. I am a priest sent by the Great T'ang in the Land of the East to go seek scriptures from Buddha in the Thunderclap Monastery of India in the Great Western Heaven. My master is Tripitaka T'ang, the bond-brother of the T'ang emperor, and I am Sun Wu-k'ung, his eldest disciple. When we passed through your kingdom and had to have our travel rescript certified, we saw a royal proclamation issued for the recruitment of physicians. I exercised my great ability in the therapeutic arts, and I cured the king of his illness of ardent longing. During the banquet he gave to thank me, he told me while we were drinking about how you were abducted by the fiend. Since I have the knowledge of subduing dragons and taming tigers, he asked me specially to come arrest the fiend and rescue you back to the kingdom. It was I who defeated the vanguard, and it was I, too, who slew the little fiend. When I saw, however, how powerful the fiend was outside the gate, I changed myself into the form of Going and Coming in order to take the risk of contacting you here."

On hearing what he said, the lady fell silent. Whereupon Pilgrim took out the treasure bracelets and presented them with both hands, saying, "If you don't believe me, take a good look at these objects." The moment she saw them, the lady began to weep, as she left her seat to bow to Pilgrim, saying, "Elder, if you could indeed rescue me and take me back to the kingdom, I would never forget your great favor!"

"Let me ask you," said Pilgrim, "what sort of a treasure that is that releases fire, smoke, and sand?" "It's no treasure!" replied the lady. "They are actually three golden bells. When he gives the first bell one wave, he can release up to three thousand feet of fire to burn people. When he waves the second one, he can release three thousand feet of smoke to fumigate people. When he waves the third one, he can release three thousand feet of yellow sand to confound people. The smoke and the fire are not even as potent as the yellow sand, which is most poisonous. If it gets into someone's nostrils, the person will die." "Formidable! Formidable!" said Pilgrim. "I had the experience, all right, and even I had to sneeze a couple of times! Where, I wonder, does he put these bells?"

"You think he'd put them down!" said the lady. "He has them tied to his waist, and whether he is in or out of doors, whether he is up or lying down, they'll never leave his body." "If you still have some feelings for the Scarlet-Purple Kingdom," said Pilgrim, "if you want to see the king once more, you must banish for the moment all sorrow and melancholy. Put on your looks of pleasure and romance, and allow him to enjoy with you the sentiments of wedlock. Tell him to let you keep the bells for him. Then, when I have stolen them and brought this fiendish creature into submission, it will be simple to take you back to your dear mate so that both of you can enjoy peace and harmony once more." The lady agreed.

Our Pilgrim changed again into that trusted junior officer and opened the palace door to summon the various maids. Then the lady called out, "Going and Coming, go to the pavilion in front quickly and ask the great king to come here. I want to speak to him." Dear Pilgrim! He shouted his consent and dashed out to the Skinning Pavilion to say to the monster-spirit, "Great King, Lady Sage Palace desires your company." Delighted, the fiend king said, "Normally our lady has nothing but abuse for me. How is it that she desires my company today?" "Our lady," replied Pilgrim, "asked me about the ruler of the Scarlet-Purple Kingdom, and I told her, 'He doesn't want you anymore. He has chosen another queen from among his subjects.' When our lady heard this, she had to stop thinking about him, and that was why she asked for you." Exceedingly pleased, the fiend king said. "You are quite useful! When I have destroyed that kingdom, I'll appoint you a special court assistant."

Thanking him casually for his promised favor, Pilgrim walked quickly with the fiend king to the entrance of the rear palace, where the lady met them amiably and reached out with her hands to greet the monster. Backing off immediately and bowing, the fiend king said. "I'm honored! I'm honored! Thank you for your love, but I'm afraid of the pain in my hands, and I dare not touch you." "Please take a seat, Great King," said the lady, "for I want to speak to you." "Please do so without hesitation," replied the fiend king.

The lady said, "It has been three years since you first bestowed your love on me. Though we have not been able to share a bed together, it is still our foreordained affinity that we should become husband and wife. I think, however, that you must have some sentiments against me, and you are not treating me truly as your spouse. For I can recall the time when I was queen at the Scarlet-Purple Kingdom. Whenever the foreign nations presented their tributary treasures, the queen was asked to keep them after the king had inspected them. You have hardly any treasures here, of course; what you wear are furs, and what you eat are raw meats. I haven't seen any silks or damasks, any gold or pearls. All our coverings are only skins and furs. You may have some treasures, I suppose, but the distance you feel towards me prevents you from letting me see them or asking me to keep them for you. I have heard that you have some kind of bells or gongs—three of them, in fact—which, I suppose, must be treasures. Or else, why would you keep them with you when you are walking or when you are seated? You should let me keep them for you, and when you need them, I can take them out. After all, we *are* husband and wife, and you should at least show me some trust. If you don't, you must feel that I'm still an outsider!"

Breaking into loud guffaws as he bowed to her, the fiend king said, "Madam, your reprimands are just! Your reprimands are just! The treasures are right here. To-day, I turn them over to you for safe-keeping." He at once hitched up his clothes to take out the treasures. With unblinking eyes on one side, Pilgrim saw that after the fiend had hitched up two or three layers of clothing, he had tied to his body three small bells. These he took down and, having stuffed some cotton into the mouths of the bells, had them wrapped up in a piece of leopard skin before he handed them over to the lady. "Though these are lowly objects," he said, "you must guard them with care. Never shake or rattle them." Taking them over with her hands, the lady said, "I know. I'll put them right here on my dressing table. No one will shake them."

Then the lady said, "Little ones, prepare us some wine. I want to drink a few cups with the great king to celebrate our happiness and love." On hearing this, the servant girls at once spread out a table full of vegetables and fruits and laden with venison and rabbit meat. After they poured out some coconut wine, the lady put on her most se-ductive charms to deceive the monster-spirit.

On the side Pilgrim Sun also began his work; slipping slowly up to the dresser, he gently picked up those three golden bells before he inched his way out of the palace. When he arrived at an empty spot before the Skinning Pavilion, he opened up the leopard skin wrap to look at the contents. The middle bell was about the size of a tea mug, while the two on both ends were as big as fists. Not knowing how formidable these objects were, he yanked out the cotton. All he heard was a loud clang, and then the flame, the smoke, and the yellow sand poured out from the bells. He tried desper-ately to stuff the cotton back into the bells but to no avail. Instantly, flames leaped up and engulfed the pavilion. * * *

Suddenly a loud voice came from midair: "Sun Wu-k'ung, I've arrived!" As he turned his head upward quickly, Pilgrim saw that it was the Bodhisattva Kuan-yin; her left hand was supporting the immaculate vase, while her right hand was sprinkling sweet dew with her willow twig to put out the fire. Pilgrim was so startled that he quickly tucked the bells in his waist, folded his hands before his chest, and bowed low. After the Bodhisattva had sprinkled a few drops of the sweet dew, the smoke and fire all vanished in an instant and there was not a trace of the yellow sand. Kowtow-ing, Pilgrim said, "I did not know the Great Compassion had descended to Earth, and I have caused offense by not avoiding your sacred presence. May I ask where the Bodhisattva is going?" "I have come," replied the Bodhisattva, "especially to bring this fiend to submission."

"What was this fiend's origin," said Pilgrim, "that it should necessitate your golden form revealing itself in order to bring him to submission?" The Bodhisattva said, "He is actually the golden-haired wolf that I ride on. Because the lad who looks after him fell asleep, this cursed beast managed to bite through the iron chains and come here to dispel calamity for the king of the Scarlet-Purple Kingdom."

On hearing this, Pilgrim quickly bowed and said, "The Bodhisattva is twisting the truth! The fiend has mocked the ruler and cheated him of his queen here; he has corrupted the customs and violated the mores. He has, in fact, brought calamity to the ruler. How could you say that he has helped the king to dispel calamity?"

The Bodhisattva replied, "You have no idea that when the deceased king of the Scarlet-Purple Kingdom was still on the throne, the present king, then the crown-prince, was exceedingly fond of hunting when he was a youth. Leading men and horses, mounting hawks and hounds, he once came before the Phoenix-Down Slope, where two young birds, one male and another female, were perching. These happened to be the offspring of the Bodhisattva Great King Peacock. When the young prince stretched his bow, he wounded the male peacock, and the female one, too, returned to the West with an arrow stuck in her body. After the Buddha Mother had pardoned him, she decreed that he should be punished by being separated from his mate for three years and that his body should be inflicted with the illness of yearning. At the time, I was riding this wolf when I heard the sentence pronounced. Little did I realize that this cursed beast would remember it and come here to abduct the queen and dispel calamity for the king. It has been three years now, and his preordained chastisement has been fulfilled. You are to be thanked for arriving to heal the king, and I've come especially to bring the fiend to submission."

"Bodhisattva," said Pilgrim, "the story may go like this, but he has also defiled the queen, corrupted the customs, upset the relations, and perverted the law. He is worthy of death. Now that you have arrived in person, I shall spare his life but not his living punishment. Let me give him twenty strokes of my rod, and then you may take him away." "Wu-k'ung," said the Bodhisattva, "if you appreciate my epiphany, then you must, for my sake, grant him a plenary pardon. This will be considered entirely your merit, that of bringing the fiend to submission. If you raise your rod, he will be dead!" As he dared not disobey, Pilgrim had no choice but to bow and say, "After the Bodhisattva has taken him back to South Sea, he must not be permitted to return in secret to the human world again, for he can cause a lot of harm."

Only then did the Bodhisattva cry out: "Cursed beast! If you don't return to your origin now, when will you do so?" Rolling once on the ground, the fiend immediately appeared in his original form. As he shook out his furry coat, the Bodhisattva mounted his back, only to discover with one look that the three bells beneath his collar were nowhere to be seen. "Wu-k'ung," said the Bodhisattva, "return my bells." "Old Monkey doesn't know anything about bells!" replied Pilgrim.

"You thievish ape!" snapped the Bodhisattva. "If you hadn't succeeded in stealing the bells, even ten of you would not be able to approach him. Bring them out quickly!" "But really, I haven't seen them!" chuckled Pilgrim. "In that case," said the Bodhisattva, "allow me to recite the Tight-Fillet Spell a little."

At once alarmed, Pilgrim could only mutter. "Don't recite! Don't recite! The bells are here!" Thus it is that

> From the wolf's collar who'll untie the bells?
> The one untying asks the one who ties.

After the Bodhisattva had slipped the bells back onto the collar of the wolf, she mounted his back again. Look at him!

> Beneath his four legs lotus blossoms grow;
> O'er all his body thick golden threads glow.

The Great Compassion went back to South Sea, where we shall leave her.

We tell you instead about the Great Sage Sun, who, having tightened his skirt, wielded the iron rod to fight his way into the Cave of the Mythic Beast and slew all the rest of the fiends. Then he went into the palace to beckon the Lady Sage Palace to return to her country. The lady could not have been more grateful after Pilgrim gave her a thorough account of how the Bodhisattva had brought the fiend to submission and why she had to be separated from her mate. Then Pilgrim found some grass which he tied together to make a straw dragon. "Madam," he said, "climb on this and close your eyes. Don't be afraid. I'm taking you back to court to see your lord." The lady followed his instruction as Pilgrim began to exercise his magic power: all she heard was the sound of the wind.

In the period of half an hour they arrived at the capital. As they dropped from the clouds, he said, "Madam, please open your eyes." The queen opened her eyes and at once those dragon towers and phoenix bowers which she readily recognized gave her immense delight. She abandoned the straw dragon to ascend the treasure hall with Pilgrim. When the king saw her, he hurried down from the dragon couch. Taking the hand of the lady, he wanted to tell her how much he missed her when all of a sudden, he fell to the ground crying, "Oh my hand! It hurts! It hurts!"

Pa-chieh broke out in loud guffaws, saying, "O dear! You just don't have the luck to enjoy her. The moment you see her you are smitten to death!" "Idiot," said Pilgrim, "you dare give her a tug?" "What'll happen if I do?" asked Pa-chieh.

Pilgrim said, "The lady's body is covered with poisonous prickles, and her hands are full of vicious stings. Since she reached the Unicorn Mountain these three years, that fiend Jupiter's Rival has never claimed her body. For the moment he touched her, his body or his hands would be pained. On hearing this, the various officials exclaimed, "What shall we do?" So the officials outside the court became vexed, and the ladies of the palace, too, were alarmed. Meanwhile, Jade Sage and Silver Sage, the two other consorts, helped the ruler to his feet.

As they stood there in confusion, they heard someone calling out in midair: "Great Sage, I've arrived!" Pilgrim raised his head to look, and he heard

> Majestic crane cries in the sky,
> As someone drifted down to court.
> Auspicious radiance encircling;
> Creative auras tremulous.
> A coir and grass coat wrapped in cloud and mist.
> He trod straw sandals rarely seen.
> He held a fly-swat of rushes;
> A silk sash wound around his waist.
> Throughout the world he had formed human ties;
> Footloose, he roamed all the great earth.
> This was the Great Heaven's Immortal Purple Cloud,
> Bringing salvation this day to earth.

Going forward to meet him, Pilgrim said, "Chang Tzu-yang,[4] where are you going?" The Realized Immortal Tzu-yang went before the court and bowed, saying, "Great Sage, this humble immortal Chang Po-tuan raises my hand to salute you." Returning his bow, Pilgrim said, "Where have you come from?"

The realized immortal said, "Three years ago, I was on my way to a Buddha festival when I passed through this region. When I saw that the king was destined to be separated from his mate, I feared that the fiend might defile the queen and upset the human relation, so that afterwards it would be difficult for the king and queen to be reunited. I therefore changed an old coir coat of mine into a new shining robe, radiant

---

4. A famous 11th-century Daoist author of an important alchemical text.

in five colors, to present to the fiend king as an addition to the queen's wardrobe. The moment when she put it on, poisonous prickles sprouted on her body, but actually those prickles were the transformation of the coir coat. Now that I have learned of the Great Sage's success, I have come to bring deliverance."

"In that case," said Pilgrim, "we are indebted to you for coming from such a great distance. Please deliver her, quickly." The realized immortal walked forward and pointed at the lady with his finger; immediately, the coir coat came off and the lady's entire body was smooth as before. Shaking out the coat, the realized immortal draped it over himself and said to Pilgrim, "I beg your pardon, Great Sage, for this humble immortal must take leave of you." "Please wait for a moment," replied Pilgrim, "and allow the ruler to thank you." "No need, no need," said the immortal, laughing. He gave a long bow and rose into the air. The king, the queen, and all the officials were so astonished that they all bowed toward the sky.

Thereafter, the king gave the order for the Eastern Hall to be opened in order that the four priests might be thanked with a huge banquet. After the king led his subjects to kowtow to the pilgrims, he was reunited with his wife. As they drank merrily, Pilgrim said, "Master, take out that declaration of war." The elder took it out from his sleeve to hand over to Pilgrim, who passed it to the king and said, "This document was to be sent here by a junior officer of the fiend. The officer had been beaten to death by me at first, and I took him here to announce my merit. When I went back to the mountain afterwards, I changed into the form of the officer to get inside the cave. That was how I got to see the lady. After I succeeded in stealing the golden bells, I was almost caught by the fiend. Then I had to undergo transformation to steal the bells again. When he fought with me, it was my fortune that the Bodhisattva Kuan-yin arrived and brought him to submission. She also told me of the reason why you and your queen had to be separated." After he gave a thorough account of what had taken place, the king and all his subjects were full of gratitude and praise.

"It was the great good fortune of a worthy ruler in the first place," said the T'ang monk, "and it was also the merit of our humble disciple. This lavish banquet you have given us is perfection indeed! We must bow to take leave of you now. Do not delay this humble cleric's journey to the West." Having failed to persuade the priests to stay longer even with earnest pleading, the king had the rescript certified. Then he asked the T'ang monk to take a seat in the imperial chariot, while he and his consorts pushed it with their own hands to send the pilgrim out of the capital before they parted. Truly.

> With affinity, your anxious ailment's purged;
> With no thoughts or desires your mind's at peace.

As they go forth, we do not know what sort of good or evil will befall them, and you must listen to the explanation in the next chapter.

* * *

from *Chapter 98*

> Only when ape and horse are tamed will they cast their shells;
> When merit and work are perfected, they see the Real.

The Great Sage led the T'ang monk and his disciples slowly up the mountain.[5] They had not gone for more than five or six miles when they came upon a torrent of water,

---

5. The pilgrims have arrived at Spirit Mountain in India, home of the Buddha.

eight or nine miles wide. There was no trace of human activity all around. Alarmed by the sight, Tripitaka said, "Wu-k'ung, this must be the wrong way! Could the great immortal have made a mistake? Look how wide and swift this river is! Without a boat, how could we get across?"

"There's no mistake!" said Pilgrim, chuckling. "Look over there! Isn't that a large bridge? You have to walk across that bridge before you can perfect the right fruit." The elder walked up to the bridge and saw beside it a tablet, on which was the inscription. Cloud-Transcending Stream. The bridge was actually a single log. Truly

> Afar off, it's like a jade beam in the sky;
> Near, a dried stump that o'er the water lies.
> To bind up oceans it would easier seem.
> How could one walk a single log or beam,
> Shrouded by rainbows of ten thousand feet,
> By a thousand layers of silk-white sheet?
> Too slipp'ry and small for all to cross its spread
> Except those who on colored mists can tread.

Quivering all over, Tripitaka said, "Wu-k'ung, this bridge is not for human beings to cross. Let's find some other way."

"This *is* the way! This *is* the way!" said Pilgrim, laughing.

"If this is the way," said Pa-chieh, horrified, "who dares walk on it? The water's so wide and rough. There's only a single log here, and it's so narrow and slippery. How could I move my legs?"

"Stand still, all of you," said Pilgrim. "Let old Monkey take a walk for you to see." Dear Great Sage! In big strides he bounded on to the single-log bridge. Swaying from side to side, he ran across it in no time at all. On the other side he shouted: "Come across! Come across!"

The T'ang monk waved his hands, while Pa-chieh and Sha Monk bit their fingers, all crying, "Hard! Hard! Hard!"

Pilgrim dashed back from the other side and pulled at Pa-chieh, saying, "Idiot! Follow me! Follow me!" Lying flat on the ground, Pa-chieh said, "It's much too slippery! Much too slippery! Let me go, please! Let me mount the wind and fog to get over there."

Pushing him down, Pilgrim said, "What sort of a place do you think this is that you are permitted to mount wind and fog! Unless you walk across this bridge, you'll never become a Buddha."

"O Elder Brother!" said Pa-chieh. "It's okay with me if I don't become a Buddha. But I'm not going on that bridge!"

Right beside the bridge, the two of them started a tug-of-war. Only Sha Monk's admonitions managed to separate them. Tripitaka happened to turn his head, and he suddenly caught sight of someone punting a boat upstream and crying, "Ahoy! Ahoy!"

Highly pleased, the elder said, "Disciples, stop your frivolity! There's a boat coming." The three of them leaped up and stood still to stare at the boat. When it drew near, they found that it was a bottomless one. With his fiery eyes and diamond pupils, Pilgrim at once recognized that the ferryman was in fact the Conductor Buddha, also named the Light of Ratnadhvaja. Without revealing the Buddha's identity, however, Pilgrim simply said, "Over here! Punt it this way!"

Immediately the boatman punted it up to the shore. "Ahoy! Ahoy!" he cried. Terrified by what he saw, Tripitaka said, "How could this bottomless boat of yours carry anybody?" The Buddhist Patriarch said, "This boat of mine

> Since creation's dawn has achieved great fame;
> Punted by me, it has e'er been the same.
> Upon the wind and wave it's still secure;
> With no end or beginning its joy is sure.
> It can return to One, completely clean,
> Through ten thousand kalpas a sail serene.
> Though bottomless boats may ne'er cross the sea,
> This ferries all souls through eternity."

Pressing his palms together to thank him, the Great Sage Sun said, "I thank you for your great kindness in coming to receive and lead my master. Master, get on the boat. Though it is bottomless, it is safe. Even if there are wind and waves, it will not capsize."

The elder still hesitated, but Pilgrim took him by the shoulder and gave him a shove. With nothing to stand on, that master tumbled straight into the water, but the boatman swiftly pulled him out. As he stood on the side of the boat, the master kept shaking out his clothes and stamping his feet as he grumbled at Pilgrim. Pilgrim, however, helped Sha Monk and Pa-chieh to lead the horse and tote the luggage into the boat. As they all stood on the gunwale, the Buddhist Patriarch gently punted the vessel away from shore. All at once they saw a corpse floating down the upstream, the sight of which filled the elder with terror.

"Don't be afraid, Master," said Pilgrim, laughing. "It's actually you!"

"It's you! It's you!" said Pa-chieh also.

Clapping his hands, Sha Monk also said, "It's you! It's you!"

Adding his voice to the chorus, the boatman also said, "That's you! Congratulations! Congratulations!" Then the three disciples repeated this chanting in unison as the boat was punted across the water. In no time at all, they crossed the Divine Cloud-Transcending Stream all safe and sound. Only then did Tripitaka turn and skip lightly on to the other shore. We have here a testimonial poem, which says:

> Delivered from their mortal flesh and bone,
> A primal spirit of mutual love has grown.
> Their work done, they become Buddhas this day,
> Free of their former six-six senses'[6] sway.

Truly this is what is meant by the profound wisdom and the boundless Dharma which enable one to reach the other shore.

The moment the four pilgrims went ashore and turned around, the boatman and even the bottomless boat had disappeared. Only then did Pilgrim point out that it was the Conductor Buddha, and immediately Tripitaka awoke to the truth. Turning quickly, he thanked his three disciples instead.

Pilgrim said, "We two parties need not thank each other, for we are meant to support each other. We are indebted to our master for our liberation, through which we have found the gateway to the making of merit, and fortunately we have achieved the right fruit. Our master also has to rely on our protection so that he may be firm in keeping both law and faith to find the happy deliverance from this mortal stock. Master, look at this surpassing scenery of flowers and grass, pines and bamboos, phoenixes, cranes, and deer. Compared with those places of illusion manufactured by

6. The six impure qualities engendered by the objects and organs of sense: sight, sound, smell, taste, touch and idea [translator's note].

monsters and deviates, which ones do you think are pleasant and which ones bad? Which ones are good and which evil?" Tripitaka expressed his thanks repeatedly as every one of them with lightness and agility walked up the Spirit Mountain. Soon this was the aged Thunderclap Monastery which came into view:

> Its top touches the firmament;
> Its root joins the Sumeru range.
> Wondrous peaks in rows;
> Strange boulders rugged.
> Beneath the cliffs, jade-grass and jasper-flowers;
> By the path, purple agaric and scented orchid.
> Divine apes plucking fruits in the peach orchard
> Seem like fire-burnished gold;
> White cranes perching on the tips of pine branches
> Resemble mist-shrouded jade.
> Male phoenixes in pairs—
> Female phoenixes in twos—
> Male phoenixes in pairs
> Make one call facing the sun to bless the world;
> Female phoenixes in twos
> Whose radiant dance in the wind is rarely seen.
> You see too those mandarin duck tiles of lustrous gold,
> And luminous, patterned bricks cornelian-gilt.
> In the east
> And in the west
> Stand rows of scented halls and pearly arches;
> To the north
> And to the south,
> An endless sight of treasure lofts and precious towers.
> The Devarāja Hall emits lambent mists;
> The Dharma-guarding Hall sends forth purple flames.
> The stūpa's clear form;
> The Utpala's fragrance.
> Truly a fine place similar to Heaven
> With lazy clouds to make the day long.
> The causes cease, red dust can't come at all:
> Safe from all kalpas is this great Dharma Hall.

Footloose and carefree, master and disciples walked to the summit of Mount Spirit, where under a forest of green pines they saw a group of upāsikās and rows of worshipers in the midst of verdant cypresses. Immediately the elder bowed to them, so startling the upāsakas and upāsikās, the monks and the nuns, that they all pressed their palms together, saying, "Sage monk, you should not render us such homage. Wait till you see Śākyamuni, and then you may come to exchange greetings with us."

"He is *always* in such a hurry!" said Pilgrim, laughing. "Let's go to bow to those seated at the top!"

His arms and legs dancing with excitement, the elder followed Pilgrim straight up to the gate of the Thunderclap Monastery. There they were met by the Four Great Vajra Guardians, who said, "Has the sage monk arrived?"

Bending low, Tripitaka said, "Yes, your disciple Hsüan-tsang has arrived." No sooner had he given this reply than he wanted to go inside. "Please wait a moment,

Sage Monk," said the Vajra Guardians. "Allow us to announce your arrival first before you enter."

One of the Vajra Guardians was asked to report to the other Four Great Vajra Guardians stationed at the second gate, and one of those porters passed the news of the T'ang monk's arrival to the third gate. Those guarding the third gate happened to be divine monks who served at the great altar. When they heard the news, they quickly went to the Great Hero Hall to announce to Tathāgata, the Most Honored One, also named Buddha Śākyamuni, "The sage monk from the T'ang court has arrived in this treasure monastery. He has come to fetch the scriptures."

Highly pleased, Holy Father Buddha at once asked the Eight Bodhisattvas, the Four Vajra Guardians, the Five Hundred Arhats, the Three Thousand Guardians, the Eleven Great Orbs, and the Eighteen Guardians of Monasteries to form two rows for the reception. Then he issued the golden decree to summon in the T'ang monk. Again the word was passed from section to section, from gate to gate: "Let the sage monk enter." Meticulously observing the rules of etiquette, our T'ang monk walked through the monastery gate with Wu-k'ung, Wu-nêng, and Wu-ching, still leading the horse and toting the luggage. Thus it was that

> Commissioned that year, a resolve he made
> To leave with rescript the royal steps of jade.
> The hills he'd climb to face the morning dew
> Or rest on a boulder when the twilight fades.
> He totes his faith to ford three thousand streams,
> His staff trailing o'er endless palisades.
> His every thought's on seeking the right fruit.
> Homage to Buddha will this day be paid.

The four pilgrims, on reaching the Great Hero Treasure Hall, prostrated themselves before Tathāgata. Thereafter, they bowed to all the attendants of Buddha on the left and right. This they repeated three times before kneeling again before the Buddhist Patriarch to present their traveling rescript to him. After reading it carefully, Tathāgata handed it back to Tripitaka, who touched his head to the ground once more to say. "By the decree of the Great T'ang emperor in the Land of the East, your disciple Hsüan-tsang has come to this treasure monastery to beg you for the true scriptures for the redemption of the multitude. I implore the Buddhist Patriarch to vouchsafe his grace and grant me my wish, so that I may soon return to my country."

To express the compassion of his heart, Tathāgata opened his mouth of mercy and said to Tripitaka, "Your Land of the East belongs to the South Jambūdvīpa Continent. Because of your size and your fertile land, your prosperity and population, there is a great deal of greed and killing, lust and lying, oppression and deceit. People neither honor the teachings of Buddha nor cultivate virtuous karma; they neither revere the three lights nor respect the five grains. They are disloyal and unfilial, unrighteous and unkind, unscrupulous and selfdeceiving. Through all manners of injustice and taking of lives, they have committed boundless transgressions. The fullness of their iniquities therefore has brought on them the ordeal of hell and sent them into eternal darkness and perdition to suffer the pains of pounding and grinding and of being transformed into beasts. Many of them will assume the forms of creatures with fur and horns; in this manner they will repay their debts by having their flesh made for food for mankind. These are the reasons for their eternal perdition in Avīci without deliverance.

"Though Confucius had promoted his teachings of benevolence, righteousness, ritual, and wisdom, and though a succession of kings and emperors had established such penalties as transportation, banishment, hanging, and beheading, these institutions had little effect on the foolish and the blind, the reckless, and the antinomian.

"Now, I have here three baskets of scriptures which can deliver humanity from its afflictions and dispel its calamities. There is one basket of vinaya, which speak of Heaven; a basket of śastras, which tell of the Earth; and a basket of sūtras, which redeem the damned. Altogether these three baskets of scriptures contain thirty-five titles written in fifteen thousand one hundred and forty-four scrolls. They are truly the pathway to the realization of immortality and the gate to ultimate virtue. Every concern of astronomy, geography, biography, flora and fauna, utensils, and human affairs within the Four Great Continents of this world is recorded therein. Since all of you have traveled such a great distance to come here, I would have liked to give the entire set to you. Unfortunately, the people of your region are both stupid and headstrong. Mocking the true words, they refuse to recognize the profound significance of our teachings of Śramana."

Then Buddha turned to call out: "Ānanda and Kāśyapa, take the four of them to the space beneath the precious tower. Give them a vegetarian meal first. After the maigre, open our treasure loft for them and select a few scrolls from each of the thirty-five divisions of our three canons, so that they may take them back to the Land of the East as a perpetual token of grace."

The two Honored Ones obeyed and took the four pilgrims to the space beneath the tower, where countless rare dainties and exotic treasures were laid out in a seemingly endless spread. Those deities in charge of offerings and sacrifices began to serve a magnificent feast of divine food, tea, and fruit—viands of a hundred flavors completely different from those of the mortal world. After master and disciples had bowed to give thanks to Buddha, they abandoned themselves to enjoyment. In truth

> Treasure flames, gold beams on their eyes have shined;
> Strange fragrance and feed even more refined.
> Boundlessly fair the tow'r of gold appears,
> And immortal music that clears the ears.
> Such divine fare and flower humans rarely see;
> Long life's attained through strange food and fragrant tea.
> Long have they endured a thousand forms of pain.
> This day in glory the Tao they're glad to gain.

This time it was Pa-chieh who was in luck and Sha Monk who had the advantage, for what the Buddhist Patriarch had provided for their complete enjoyment was nothing less than such viands as could grant them longevity and health and enable them to transform their mortal substance into immortal flesh and bones.

When the four pilgrims had finished their meal, the two Honored Ones who had kept them company led them up to the treasure loft. The moment the door was opened, they found the room enveloped in a thousand layers of auspicious air and magic beams, in ten thousand folds of colored fog and hallowed clouds. On the sūtra cases and jeweled chests red labels were attached, on which the titles of the books were written in clerkly script. * * *

After Ānanda and Kāśyapa had shown all the titles to the T'ang monk, they said to him, "Sage Monk, having come all this distance from the Land of the East, what sort of small gifts have you brought for us? Take them out quickly! We'll be pleased to hand over the scriptures to you."

On hearing this, Tripitaka said, "Because of the great distance, your disciple, Hsüan-tsang, has not been able to make such preparation."

"How nice! How nice!" said the two Honored Ones, snickering. "If we imparted the scriptures to you gratis, our posterity would starve to death!"

When Pilgrim saw them fidgeting and fussing, refusing to hand over the scriptures, he could not refrain from yelling, "Master, let's go tell Tathāgata about this! Let's make him come himself and hand over the scriptures to old Monkey!"

"Stop shouting!" said Ānanda. "Where do you think you are that you dare indulge in such mischief and waggery? Get over here and receive the scriptures!" Controlling their annoyance, Pa-chieh and Sha Monk managed to restrain Pilgrim before they turned to receive the books. Scroll after scroll were wrapped and laid on the horse. Four additional luggage wraps were bundled up for Pa-chieh and Sha Monk to tote, after which the pilgrims went before the jeweled throne again to kowtow and thank Tathāgata. As they walked out the gates of the monastery, they bowed twice whenever they came upon a Buddhist Patriarch or a Bodhisattva. When they reached the main gate, they also bowed to take leave of the priests and nuns, the upāsakas and upāsikās, before descending the mountain. We shall now leave them for the moment.

We tell you now that there was up in the treasure loft the aged Dīpaṁkara, also named the Buddha of the Past, who overheard everything and understood immediately that Ānanda and Kāśyapa had handed over to the pilgrims scrolls of scriptures that were wordless. Chuckling to himself, he said, "Most of the priests in the Land of the East are so stupid and blind that they will not recognize the value of these wordless scriptures. When that happens, won't it have made this long trek of our sage monk completely worthless?" Then he asked, "Who is here beside my throne?"

The White Heroic Honored One at once stepped forth, and the aged Buddha gave him this instruction: "You must exercise your magic powers and catch up with the T'ang monk immediately. Take away those wordless scriptures from him, so that he will be forced to return for the true scriptures with words." Mounting a violent gust of wind, the White Heroic Honored One swept out of the gate of the Thunderclap Monastery. As he called up his vast magic powers, the wind was strong indeed! Truly

> A stalwart Servant of Buddha
> Is not like any common wind god;
> The wrathful cries of an immortal
> Far surpass a young girl's whistle!
> This mighty gust
> Causes fishes and dragons to lose their lairs
> And angry waves in the rivers and seas.
> Black apes find it hard to present their fruits;
> Yellow cranes turn around to seek their nests.
> The phoenix's pure cries have lost their songs;
> The pheasant's callings turn most boisterous.
> Green pine-branches snap;
> Blue lotus-blossoms soar.
> Stalk by stalk, verdant bamboos fall;
> Petal by petal, gold lotus quakes.
> Bell tones drift away to three thousand miles;
> The scripture chants o'er countless gorges fly,
> Beneath the cliff rare flowers' colors fade;
> Fresh, jadelike grasses lie down by the road.

> Phoenixes can't stretch their wings;
> White deer hide on the ledge.
> Vast waves of strange fragrance now fill the world
> As cool, clear breezes penetrate the heavens.

The elder T'ang was walking along when he encountered this churning fragrant wind. Thinking that this was only an auspicious portent sent by the Buddhist Patriarch, he was completely off guard when, with a loud crack in midair, a hand descended. The scriptures that were loaded on the horse were lifted away with no effort at all. The sight left Tripitaka yelling in terror and beating his breast, while Pa-chieh rolled off in pursuit on the ground and Sha Monk stood rigid to guard the empty pannier. Pilgrim Sun vaulted into the air. When that White Heroic Honored saw him closing in rapidly, he feared that Pilgrim's rod might strike out blindly without regard for good or ill to cause him injury. He therefore ripped the scriptures open and threw them toward the ground.

When Pilgrim saw that the scripture wrappers were torn and their contents scattered all over by the fragrant wind, he lowered the direction of his cloud to go after the books instead and stopped his pursuit. The White Heroic Honored One retrieved the wind and fog and returned to report to the Buddha of the Past.

As Pa-chieh sped along, he saw the holy books dropping down from the sky. Soon he was joined by Pilgrim, and the two of them gathered up the scrolls to go back to the T'ang monk. His eyes brimming with tears, the T'ang monk said, "O Disciples! We are bullied by vicious demons even in this land of ultimate bliss!"

When Sha Monk opened up a scroll of scripture which the other two disciples were clutching, his eyes perceived only snow-white paper without a trace of so much as half a letter on it. Hurriedly he presented it to Tripitaka, saying, "Master, this scroll is wordless!"

Pilgrim also opened a scroll and it, too, was wordless. Then Pa-chieh opened still another scroll, and it was also wordless. "Open all of them!" cried Tripitaka. Every scroll had only blank paper.

Heaving big sighs, the elder said, "Our people in the Land of the East simply have no luck! What good is it to take back a wordless, empty volume like this? How could I possibly face the T'ang emperor? The crime of mocking one's ruler is greater than one punishable by execution!"

Already perceiving the truth of the matter, Pilgrim said to the T'ang monk, "Master, there's no need for further talk. This has all come about because we had no gifts for these fellows, Ānanda and Kāśyapa. That's why we were given these wordless texts. Let's go back quickly to Tathāgata and charge them with fraud and solicitation for a bribe."

"Exactly! Exactly!" yelled Pa-chieh. "Let's go and charge them!" The four pilgrims turned and, with painful steps, once more ascended Thunderclap.

In a little while they reached the temple gates, where they were met by the multitude with hands folded in their sleeves. "Has the sage monk returned to ask for an exchange of scriptures?" they asked, laughing. Tripitaka nodded his affirmation, and the Vajra Guardians permitted them to go straight inside. When they arrived before the Great Hero Hall, Pilgrim shouted, "Tathāgata, we master and disciples had to experience ten thousand stings and a thousand demons in order to come bowing from the Land of the East. After you had specifically ordered the scriptures to be given to us, Ānanda and Kāśyapa sought a bribe from us; when they didn't succeed, they conspired

图 92   CROSSCURRENTS: The Vernacular Revolution

in fraud and deliberately handed over wordless texts to us. Even if we took them, what good would they do? Pardon me, Tathāgata, but you must deal with this matter!"

"Stop shouting!" said the Buddhist Patriarch with a chuckle. "I knew already that the two of them would ask you for a little present. After all, the holy scriptures are not to be given lightly, nor are they to be received gratis. Some time ago, in fact, a few of our sage priests went down the mountain and recited these scriptures in the house of one Elder Chao in the Kingdom of Śrāvastī, so that the living in his family would all be protected from harm and the deceased redeemed from perdition. For all that service they managed to charge him only three pecks and three pints of rice. I told them that they had made far too cheap a sale and that their posterity would have no money to spend. Since you people came with empty hands to acquire scriptures, blank texts were handed over to you. But these blank texts are actually true, wordless scriptures, and they are just as good as those with words. However, those creatures in your Land of the East are so foolish and unenlightened that I have no choice but to impart to you now the texts with words."

"Ānanda and Kāśyapa," he then called out, "quickly select for them a few scrolls from each of the titles of true scriptures with words, and then come back to me to report the total number."

The two Honored Ones again led the four pilgrims to the treasure loft, where they once more demanded a gift from the T'ang monk. Since he had virtually nothing to offer, Tripitaka told Sha Monk to take out the alms bowl of purple gold. With both hands he presented it to the Honored Ones, saying, "Your disciple in truth has not brought with him any gift, owing to the great distance and my own poverty. This alms bowl, however, was bestowed by the T'ang emperor in person, in order that I could use it to beg for my maigre throughout the journey. As the humblest token of my gratitude, I am presenting it to you now, and I beg the Honored Ones to accept it. When I return to the court and make my report to the T'ang emperor, a generous reward will certainly be forthcoming. Only grant us the true scriptures with words, so that His Majesty's goodwill will not be thwarted nor the labor of this lengthy journey be wasted." With a gentle smile, Ānanda took the alms bowl. All those vīra who guarded the precious towers, the kitchen helpers in charge of sacrifices and incense, and the Honored Ones who worked in the treasure loft began to clap one another on the back and tickle one another on the face. Snapping their fingers and curling their lips, every one of them said. "How shameless! How shameless! Asking the scripture seeker for a present!"

After a while, the two Honored Ones became rather embarrassed, though Ānanda continued to clutch firmly at the alms bowl. Kāśyapa, however, went into the loft to select the scrolls and handed them item by item to Tripitaka. "Disciples," said Tripitaka, "take a good look at these, and make sure that they are not like the earlier ones."

The three disciples examined each scroll as they received it, and this time all the scrolls had words written on them. Altogether they were given five thousand and forty-eight scrolls, making up the number of a single canon. After being properly packed, the scriptures were loaded onto the horse. An additional load was made for Pa-chieh to tote, while their own luggage was toted by Sha Monk. As Pilgrim led the horse, the T'ang monk took up his priestly staff and gave his Vairocana hat a press and his brocade cassock a shake. In delight they once more went before our Buddha Tathāgata. Thus it is that

> Sweet is the taste of the Great Piṭaka,
> Product most refined of Tathāgata.

Note how Hsüan-tsang has climbed the mount with pain,
Pity Ānanda who has but love of gain.
Their blindness removed by Buddha of the Past,
The truth now received peace they have at last—
Glad to bring scriptures back to the East.
Where all may partake of this gracious feast.

Ānanda and Kāśyapa led the T'ang monk before Tathāgata, who ascended the lofty lotus throne. He ordered Dragon-Tamer and Tiger-Subduer, the two arhats, to strike up the cloudy stone-chime to assemble all the divinities, including the three thousand Buddhas, the three thousand guardians, the Eight Vajra Guardians, the five hundred arhats, the eight hundred nuns and priests, the upāsakas and upāsikās, the Honored Ones from every Heaven and cave-dwelling, from every blessed land and spirit mountain. Those who ought to be seated were asked to ascend their treasure thrones, while those who should stand were told to make two columns on both sides. In a moment celestial music filled the air as layers of auspicious luminosity and hallowed mist loomed up in the sky. After all the Buddhas had assembled, they bowed to greet Tathāgata.

Then Tathāgata asked, "Ānanda and Kāśyapa, how many scrolls of scriptures have you passed on to him? * * *

"From the thirty-five titles of scriptures that are in the treasury, we have selected altogether five thousand and forty-eight scrolls for the sage monk to take back to the T'ang in the Land of the East. Most of these have been properly packed and loaded on the horse, and a few have also been arranged in a pannier. The pilgrims now wish to express their thanks to you."

Having tethered the horse and set down the poles, Tripitaka led his three disciples to bow to Buddha, each pressing his palms together in front of him. Tathāgata said to the T'ang monk, "The efficacy of these scriptures cannot be measured. Not only are they the mirror of our faith, but they are also the source of the Three Teachings. They must not be lightly handled, especially when you return to your South Jambūdvīpa Continent and display them to the multitude. No one should open a scroll without fasting and bathing first. Treasure them! Honor them! Therein will be found the mysteries of gaining immortality and comprehending the Tao, the wondrous formulas for the execution of the thousand transformations." Tripitaka kowtowed to thank him and to express his faith and obedience. As before, he prostrated himself in homage three times to the Buddhist Patriarch with all earnestness and sincerity before he took the scriptures and left. As he went through the three monastery gates, he again thanked each of the sages, and we shall speak no more of him for the moment.

After he had sent away the T'ang monk, Tathāgata dismissed the assembly for the transmission of scriptures. From one side stepped forth the Bodhisattva Kuan-shih-yin, who pressed her palms together to say to the Buddhist Patriarch, "This disciple received your golden decree that year to search for someone in the Land of the East to be a scripture seeker. Today he has succeeded. Altogether, his journey took fourteen years or five thousand and forty days. Eight more days and the perfect canonical number will be attained. Would you permit me to surrender in return your golden decree?"

Highly pleased, Tathāgata said, "What you said is most appropriate. You are certainly permitted to surrender my golden decree." He then gave this instruction to the Eight Vajra Guardians: "Quickly exercise your magic powers to lift the sage monk back to the East. As soon as he has imparted the true scriptures to the people there, bring him back here to the West. You must accomplish all this within eight days, so as to fulfill the perfect canonical number of five thousand and forty-eight. Do not delay." The Vajra Guardians at once caught up with the T'ang monk, crying, "Scripture seekers, follow us!" The T'ang monk and his companions, all with healthy frames and buoyant bodies, followed the Vajra Guardians to rise in the air astride the clouds. Truly

> Their minds enlightened, they bowed to Buddha;
> Merit perfected, they ascended on high.

We do not know how they will pass on the scriptures after they have returned to the Land of the East, and you must listen to the explanation in the next chapter.

from *Chapter 99*

> Nine times nine is the perfect number and *māra*'s extinguished;
> The work of Double Three[7] ended, the Tao returns to its root.

We shall not speak of the Eight Vajra Guardians escorting the T'ang monk back to his nation. We turn instead to those Guardians of the Five Quarters, the Four Sentinels, the Six Gods of Darkness and the Six Gods of Light, and the Guardians of Monasteries, who appeared before the triple gates and said to the Bodhisattva Kuan-yin, "Your disciples had received the Bodhisattva's dharma decree to give secret protection to the sage monk. Now that the work of the sage monk is completed, and the Bodhisattva has returned the Buddhist Patriarch's golden decree to him, we too request permission from the Bodhisattva to return your dharma decree to you."

Highly pleased also, the Bodhisattva said, "Yes, yes! You have my permission." Then she asked, "What was the disposition of the four pilgrims during their journey?"

"They showed genuine devotion and determination," replied the various deities, "which could hardly have escaped the penetrating observation of the Bodhisattva. The T'ang monk, after all, had endured unspeakable sufferings. Indeed, all the ordeals which he had to undergo throughout his journey have been recorded by your disciples. Here is the complete account." The Bodhisattva started to read the registry from its beginning, and this was the content:[8]

> The Guardians in obedience to your decree
> Record with care the T'ang monk's calamities.
> Gold Cicada banished is the first ordeal;
> Being almost killed after birth is the second ordeal;
> Being thrown in the river hardly a month old is the third ordeal;
> Seeking parents and their vengeance is the fourth ordeal;
> Meeting a tiger after leaving the city is the fifth ordeal;
> Falling into a pit and losing followers is the sixth ordeal;
> The Double-Fork Ridge is the seventh ordeal;
> The Mountain of Two Frontiers is the eighth ordeal;
> Changing horse at a steep brook is the ninth ordeal;
> Burning by fire at night is the tenth ordeal;
> Losing the cassock is the eleventh ordeal;
> Bringing Pa-chieh to submission is the twelfth ordeal;

---

7. Advanced meditation.   8. The following list summarizes the adventures of Chapters 8–98.

Being blocked by the Yellow Wind Fiend is the thirteenth ordeal;
Seeking aid with Ling-chi is the fourteenth ordeal;
Hard to cross Flowing-Sand is the fifteenth ordeal;
Taking in Sha Monk is the sixteenth ordeal;
The Four Sages' epiphany is the seventeenth ordeal;
The Five Villages Temple is the eighteenth ordeal;
The ginseng hard to revive is the nineteenth ordeal;
Banishing the Mind Monkey is the twentieth ordeal;
Getting lost at Black Pine Forest is the twenty-first ordeal;
Sending a letter to Precious Image Kingdom is the twenty-second ordeal;
Changing into a tiger at the Golden Chimes Hall is the twenty-third ordeal;
Meeting demons at Level-Top Mountain is the twenty-fourth ordeal;
Being hung high at Lotus-Flower Cave is the twenty-fifth ordeal;
Saving the ruler of Black Rooster Kingdom is the twenty-sixth ordeal;
Running into a demon's transformed body is the twenty-seventh ordeal;
Meeting a fiend in Roaring Mountain is the twenty-eighth ordeal;
The sage monk abducted by wind is the twenty-ninth ordeal;
The Mind Monkey being injured is the thirtieth ordeal;
Asking the sage to subdue monsters is the thirty-first ordeal;
Sinking in the Black River is the thirty-second ordeal;
Hauling at Cart Slow Kingdom is the thirty-third ordeal;
A mighty contest is the thirty-fourth ordeal;
Expelling Taoists to prosper Buddhists is the thirty-fifth ordeal;
Meeting a great water on the road is the thirty-sixth ordeal;
Falling into the Heaven-Reaching River is the thirty-seventh ordeal;
The Fish-Basket revealing her body is the thirty-eighth ordeal;
Meeting a fiend at Golden Helmet Mountain is the thirty-ninth ordeal;
Heaven's gods find it hard to win is the fortieth ordeal;
Asking the Buddha for the source is the forty-first ordeal,
Being poisoned after drinking water is the forty-second ordeal;
Detained for marriage at Western Liang Kingdom is the forty-third ordeal;
Suffering at the Cave of the Lute is the forty-fourth ordeal;
Banishing again the Mind Monkey is the forty-fifth ordeal;
The macaque hard to distinguish is the forty-sixth ordeal;
The road blocked at the Mountain of Flames is the forty-seventh ordeal;
Seeking the palm-leaf fan is the forty-eighth ordeal;
Binding the demon king is the forty-ninth ordeal;
Sweeping the pagoda at Sacrifice Kingdom is the fiftieth ordeal;
Recovering the treasure to save the monks is the fifty-first ordeal;[9]
Meeting disaster at Little Thunderclap is the fifty-third ordeal;
The celestial gods being imprisoned is the fifty-fourth ordeal;
Being blocked by filth at Pulpy Persimmon Alley is the fifty-fifth ordeal;
Applying medication at the Scarlet-Purple Kingdom is the fifty-sixth ordeal;
Healing fatigue and infirmity is the fifty-seventh ordeal;
Subduing monster to recover a queen is the fifty-eighth ordeal;
Delusion by the seven passions is the fifty-ninth ordeal;
Being wounded by Many Eyes is the sixtieth ordeal;
The way blocked at the Lion-Camel Kingdom is the sixty-first ordeal;

9. The 52nd ordeal is missing from this listing.

> The fiends divided into three colors is the sixty-second ordeal;
> Meeting calamity in the city is the sixty-third ordeal;
> Requesting Buddha to subdue the demons is the sixty-fourth ordeal;
> Rescuing the lads at Bhikṣu is the sixty-fifth ordeal;
> Distinguishing the true from the deviate is the sixty-sixth ordeal;
> Saving a fiend at a pine forest is the sixty-seventh ordeal;
> Falling sick in a priestly chamber is the sixty-eighth ordeal;
> Being imprisoned at the Bottomless Cave is the sixty-ninth ordeal;
> Problem of leaving Dharma-Destroying Kingdom is the seventieth ordeal;
> Meeting demons at Mist-Concealing Mountain is the seventy-first ordeal;
> Seeking rain at Phoenix-Immortal Prefecture is the seventy-second ordeal;
> Losing their weapons is the seventy-third ordeal;
> The festival of the rake is the seventy-fourth ordeal;
> Meeting disaster at Bamboo-Knot Mountain is the seventy-fifth ordeal;
> Suffering at Mysterious Flower Cave is the seventy-sixth ordeal;
> Capturing the rhinoceroses is the seventy-seventh ordeal;
> Being forced to marry at India is the seventy-eighth ordeal;
> Jailed at Bronze Terrace Prefecture is the seventy-ninth ordeal;
> Being freed of mortal bodies at Cloud-Transcending Stream is the eightieth ordeal;
> The journey: one hundred and eight thousand miles.
> The sage monk's ordeals are clearly on file.

After the Bodhisattva had read through the entire registry of ordeals she said hurriedly, "Within our order of Buddhism, nine times nine is the crucial means by which one returns to immortality. The sage monk has undergone eighty ordeals. Since one ordeal, therefore, is still still lacking, the sacred number is not yet complete."

At once she gave this order to one of the Guardians: "Catch up the Vajra Guardians and create one more ordeal." Having received this command, the Guardian soared toward the east astride the clouds. After a night and a day he caught up the Vajra Guardians and whispered in their ears, "Do this and this . . .! Don't fail to obey the dharma decree of the Bodhisattva." On hearing these words, the Eight Vajra Guardians immediately retrieved the wind that had borne aloft the four pilgrims, dropping them and the horse bearing the scriptures to the ground. Alas! Truly such is

> Nine times nine, hard task of immortality.
> Firmness of will yields the mysterious key.
> By bitter toil you must the demons spurn;
> Cultivation will the proper way return.
> Regard not the scriptures as easy things.
> So many are the sage monk's sufferings!
> Learn of the old, wondrous *Kinship of the Three:*[1]
> Elixir won't gel if there's slight errancy.

When his feet touched profane ground, Tripitaka became terribly frightened. Pachieh, however, roared with laughter, saying, "Fine! Fine! Fine! This is exactly a case of 'More haste, less speed!'"

"Fine! Fine! Fine!" said Sha Monk. "Because we've speeded up too much, they want us to take a little rest here." "Have no worry," said the Great Sage. "As the proverb says,

---

1. A 2nd-century book on alchemical theory, the earliest-known such text.

You sit on the beach for ten days
And shoot past nine in one day."

"Stop matching your wits, you three!" said Tripitaka. "Let's see if we can tell where we are." Looking all around, Sha Monk said, "I know the place! I know the place! Master, listen to the sound of water!"

Pilgrim said, "The sound of water, I suppose, reminds you of your ancestral home."

"Which is the Flowing-Sand River," said Pa-chieh.

"No! No!" said Sha Monk. "This happens to be the Heaven Reaching River." Tripitaka said, "O Disciples! Take a careful look and see which side of the river we're on."

Vaulting into the air, Pilgrim shielded his eyes with his hand and took a careful survey of the place before dropping down once more. "Master," he said, "this is the west bank of the Heaven-Reaching River."

"Now I remember," said Tripitaka. "There was a Ch'ên Village on the east bank. When we arrived here that year, you rescued their son and daughter. In their gratitude to us, they wanted to make a boat to take us across. Eventually we were fortunate enough to get across on the back of a white turtle. I recall, too, that there was no human habitation whatever on the west bank. What shall we do this time?"

"I thought that only profane people would practice this sort of fraud," said Pa-chieh. "Now I know that even the Vajra Guardians before the face of Buddha can practice fraud! Buddha commanded them to take us back east. How could they just abandon us in mid-journey? Now we're in quite a bind! How are we going to get across?"

"Stop grumbling, Second Elder Brother!" said Sha Monk. "Our master has already attained the Way, for he had already been delivered from his mortal frame previously at the Cloud-Transcending Stream. This time he can't possibly sink in water. Let's all of us exercise our magic of Displacement and take Master across."

"You can't take him over! You can't take him over!" said Pilgrim, chuckling to himself. Now, why did he say that? If he were willing to exercise his magic powers and reveal the mystery of flight, master and disciples could cross even a thousand rivers. He knew, however, that the T'ang monk had not yet perfected the sacred number of nine times nine. That one remaining ordeal made it necessary for them to be detained at the spot.

As master and disciples conversed and walked slowly up to the edge of the water, they suddenly heard someone calling, "T'ang Sage Monk! T'ang Sage Monk! Come this way! Come this way!" Startled, the four of them looked all around but could not see any sign of a human being or a boat. Then they caught sight of a huge, white, scabby headed turtle at the shoreline. "Old Master," he cried with outstretched neck, "I have waited for you for so many years! Have you returned only at this time?"

"Old Turtle," replied Pilgrim, smiling, "we troubled you in a year past, and today we meet again." Tripitaka, Pa-chieh, and Sha Monk could not have been more pleased.

"If indeed you want to serve us," said Pilgrim, "come up on the shore." The turtle crawled up the bank. Pilgrim told his companions to guide the horse onto the turtle's back. As before, Pa-chieh squatted at the rear of the horse, while the T'ang monk and Sha Monk took up positions to the left and to the right of the horse. With one foot on the turtle's head and another on his neck, Pilgrim said, "Old Turtle, go steadily."

His four legs outstretched, the old turtle moved through the water as if he were on dry level ground, carrying all five of them—master and disciples and the horse—straight toward the eastern shore. Thus it is that

In Advaya's gate[2] the dharma profound
Reveals Heav'n and Earth and demons confounds.
The original visage now they see;
Causes find perfection in one body.
Freely they move when Triyāna's won,
And when the elixir's nine turns are done.
The luggage and the staff there's no need to tote,
Glad to return on old turtle afloat.

Carrying the pilgrims on his back, the old turtle trod on the waves and proceeded for more than half a day. Late in the afternoon they were near the eastern shore when he suddenly asked this question: "Old Master, in that year when I took you across; I begged you to question Tathāgata, once you got to see him, when I would find my sought-after refuge and how much longer would I live. Did you do that?"

Now, that elder, since his arrival at the Western Heaven, had been preoccupied with bathing in the Yü-chên Temple, being renewed at Cloud-Transcending Stream, and bowing to the various sage monks, Bodhisattvas, and Buddhas. When he walked up the Spirit Mountain, he fixed his thought on the worship of Buddha and on the acquisition of scriptures, completely banishing from his mind all other concerns. He did not, of course, ask about the allotted age of the old turtle. Not daring to lie, however, he fell silent and did not answer the question for a long time. Perceiving that Tripitaka had not asked the Buddha for him, the old turtle shook his body once and dove with a splash into the depths. The four pilgrims, the horse, and the scriptures all fell into the water as well. Ah! It was fortunate that the T'ang monk had cast off his mortal frame and attained the Way. If he were like the person he had been before, he would have sunk straight to the bottom. The white horse, moreover, was originally a dragon, while Pa-chieh and Sha Monk both were quite at home in the water. Smiling broadly, Pilgrim made a great display of his magic powers by hauling the T'ang monk right out of the water and onto the eastern shore. But the scriptures, the clothing, and the saddle were completely soaked.

Master and disciples had just climbed up the riverbank when suddenly a violent gale arose; the sky darkened immediately and both thunder and lightning began as rocks and grit flew everywhere. What they felt was

One gust of wind
And the whole world teetered;
One clap of thunder
And both mountains and streams shuddered.
One flash of lightning
Shot flames through the clouds;
One sky of fog
Enveloped this great Earth.
The wind's mighty howl;
The thunder's violent roar;
The lightning's scarlet streaks;
The fog blanking moon and stars.
The wind hurtled dust and dirt at their faces;
The thunder sent tigers and leopards into hiding;

2. The entrance to the reality of the Buddha-nature.

The lightning raised among the fowl a ruckus;
The fog made the woods and trees disappear.
That wind caused waves in the Heaven-Reaching River to toss and churn;
That lightning lit up the Heaven-Reaching River down to its bottom;
That thunder terrified the Heaven-Reaching River's dragons and fishes;
That fog covered the shores of Heaven-Reaching River with a shroud of darkness.
Marvelous wind!
Mountains cracked as pines and bamboos toppled.
Marvelous thunder!
Its power stirred insects and injured humans.
Marvelous lightning!
Like a gold snake it brightened both land and sky.
Marvelous fog!

It surged through the air to screen the Ninefold Heaven. So terrified were the pilgrims that Tripitaka held firmly to the scripture wraps and Sha Monk threw himself on the poles. While Pa-chieh clung to the white horse, Pilgrim wielded his iron rod with both hands to give protection left and right. That wind, fog, thunder, and lightning, you see, had been a storm brought on by invisible demons, who wanted to snatch away the scriptures the pilgrims had acquired. The commotion lasted all night, and only by morning did the storm subside. Soaked from top to bottom and shaking all over, the elder said, "Wu-k'ung, how did this storm come about?"

"Master, you don't seem to understand," said Pilgrim, panting heavily, "that when we escorted you to acquire these scriptures, we had, in fact, robbed Heaven and Earth of their creative powers. For our success meant that we could share the age of the universe; like the light of the sun and moon, we would enjoy life everlasting for we had put on an incorruptible body. Our success, however, had also incurred the envy of Heaven and Earth, the jealousy of both demons and gods, who wanted to snatch away the scriptures from us. They could not do so only because the scriptures were thoroughly wet and because they had been shielded by your rectified dharma-body, which could not be harmed by thunder, lightning, or fog. Moreover, old Monkey was brandishing his iron rod to exercise the nature of pure yang and give you protection. Now that it is morning, the forces of yang are evermore in ascendancy, and the demons cannot prevail.

* * *

from *Chapter 100*

They return to the Land of the East;
The five sages attain immortality.

We tell you now instead about the Eight Vajra Guardians, who employed the second gust of fragrant wind to send the four pilgrims back to the Land of the East. In less than a day, the capital, Ch'ang-an, gradually came into view. That Emperor T'ai-tsung, you see, had escorted the T'ang monk out of the city three days before the full moon in the ninth month of the thirteenth year of the Chên-kuan reign period. By the sixteenth year, he had already asked the Bureau of Labor to erect a Scripture-Anticipation Tower outside the Hsi-an pass to receive the holy books. Each year T'ai-tsung would go personally to that place for a visit. It so happened that he had gone again to the tower that day when he caught sight of a skyful of auspicious mists drifting near from the West, and he noticed at the same time strong gusts of fragrant wind.

Halting in midair, the Vajra Guardians cried, "Sage monk, this is the city Ch'ang-an. It's not convenient for us to go down there, for the people of this region are quite intelligent, and our true identity may become known to them. Even the Great Sage Sun and his two companions needn't go; you yourself can go, hand over the scriptures, and return at once. We'll wait for you in the air so that we may all go back to report to Buddha."

"What the Honored Ones say may be most appropriate," said the Great Sage, "but how could my master tote all those scriptures? How could he lead the horse at the same time? We will have to escort him down there. May we trouble you to wait a while in the air? We dare not tarry."

"When the Bodhisattva Kuan-yin spoke to Tathāgata the other day," said the Vajra Guardians, "she assured him that the whole trip should take only eight days, so that the canonical number would be fulfilled. It's already more than four days now. We fear that Pa-chieh might become so enamored of the riches down below that we will not be able to meet our appointed schedule."

"When Master attains Buddhahood," said Pa-chieh, chuckling, "I, too, will attain Buddhahood. How could I become enamored of riches down below? Stupid old ruffians! Wait for me here, all of you! As soon as we have handed over the scriptures, I'll return with you and be canonized." Idiot took up the pole, Sha Monk led the horse, and Pilgrim supported the sage monk. Lowering their cloud, they dropped down beside the Scripture-Anticipation Tower.

When T'ai-tsung and his officials saw them, they all descended the tower to receive them. "Has the royal brother returned?" said the emperor. The T'ang monk immediately prostrated himself, but he was raised by the emperor's own hands. "Who are these three persons?" asked the emperor once more.

"They are my disciples made during our journey," replied the T'ang monk. Highly pleased, T'ai-tsung at once ordered his attendants, "Saddle one of our chariot horses for our royal brother to ride. We'll go back to the court together." The T'ang monk thanked him and mounted the horse, closely followed by the Great Sage wielding his golden-hooped rod and by Pa-chieh and Sha Monk toting the luggage and supporting the other horse. The entire entourage thus entered together the city of Ch'ang-an. Truly

A banquet of peace was held years ago.
When lords, civil and martial, made a grand show.
A priest preached the law in a great event;
From Golden Chimes the king his subject sent.
Tripitaka was given a royal rescript,
For Five Phases matched the cause of holy script.
Through bitter smelting all demons were purged.
Merit done, they now on the court converged.

The T'ang monk and his three disciples followed the Throne into the court, and soon there was not a single person in the city of Ch'ang-an who had not learned of the scripture seekers' return.

We tell you now about those priests, young and old, of the Temple of Great Blessing, which was also the old residence of the T'ang monk in Ch'ang-an. That day they suddenly discovered that the branches of a few pine trees within the temple gate were pointing eastward. Astonished, they cried, "Strange! Strange! There was no strong wind to speak of last night. Why are all the tops of these trees twisted in this manner?"

One of the former disciples of Tripitaka said, "Quickly, let's get our proper clerical garb. The old master who went away to acquire scriptures must have returned."

"How do you know that?" asked the other priests.

"At the time of his departure," the old disciple said, "he made the remark that he might be away for two or three years, or for six or seven years. Whenever we noticed that these pine-tree tops were pointing to the east, it would mean that he has returned. Since my master spoke the holy words of a true Buddha, I know that the truth has been confirmed this day."

They put on their clothing hurriedly and left; by the time they reached the street to the west, people were already saying that the scripture seeker had just arrived and been received into the city by His Majesty. When they heard the news, the various monks dashed forward and ran right into the imperial chariot. Not daring to approach the emperor, they followed the entourage instead to the gate of the court. The T'ang monk dismounted and entered the court with the emperor. The dragon horse, the scripture packs, Pilgrim, Pa-chieh, and Sha Monk were all placed beneath the steps of jade, while T'ai-tsung commanded the royal brother to ascend the hall and take a seat.

After thanking the emperor and taking his seat, the T'ang monk asked that the scripture scrolls be brought up. Pilgrim and his companions handed them over to the imperial attendants, who presented them in turn to the emperor for inspection. * * *

More delighted than ever, T'ai-tsung gave this command: "Let the Court of Imperial Entertainments prepare a banquet in the East Hall so that we may thank our royal brother." Then he happened to notice Tripitaka's three disciples standing beneath the steps, all with extra-ordinary looks, and he therefore asked. "Are your noble disciples foreigners?"

Prostrating himself, the elder said, "My eldest disciple has the surname of Sun, and his religious name is Wu-k'ung. Your subject also addresses him as Pilgrim Sun. He comes from the Water Curtain Cave of the Flower-Fruit Mountain, located in the Ao-lai Kingdom in the East Pūrvavideha Continent. Because he caused great disturbance in the Celestial Palace, he was imprisoned in a stone box by the Buddhist Patriarch and pressed beneath the Mountain of Two Frontiers in the region of the Western barbarians. Thanks to the admonitions of the Bodhisattva Kuan-yin, he was converted to Buddhism and became my disciple when I freed him. Throughout my journey I relied heavily on his protection.

"My second disciple has the surname of Chu, and his religious name is Wu-nêng. Your subject also addresses him as Chu Pa-chieh. He comes from the Cloudy Paths Cave of Fu-ling Mountain. He was playing the fiend at the Old Kao Village of Tibet when the admonitions of the Bodhisattva and the power of the Pilgrim caused him to become my disciple. He made his merit on our journey by toting the luggage and helping us to ford the waters.

"My third disciple has the surname of Sha, and his religious name is Wu-ching. Your subject also addresses him as Sha Monk. Originally he was a fiend at the Flowing-Sand River. Again the admonitions of the Bodhisattva persuaded him to take the vows of Buddhism. By the way, the horse is not the one my lord bestowed on me."

T'ai-tsung said. "The color and the coat seem all the same. Why isn't it the same horse?"

"When your subject reached the Eagle Grief Stream in the Serpent Coil Mountain and tried to cross it," replied Tripitaka, "the original horse was devoured by this horse. Pilgrim managed to learn from the Bodhisattva that this horse was originally the prince of the Dragon King of the Western Ocean. Convicted of a crime, he would have been executed had it not been for the intervention of the Bodhisattva, who ordered him to be the steed of your subject. It was then that he changed into a horse with exactly the same coat as that of my original mount. I am greatly indebted to him for taking me over mountains and summits and through the most treacherous passages. Whether it be carrying me on my way there or bearing the scriptures upon our return, we are much beholden to his strength."

On hearing these words, T'ai-tsung complimented him profusely before asking again, "This long trek to the Western Region, exactly how far is it?"

Tripitaka said, "I recall that the Bodhisattva told us that the distance was a hundred and eight thousand miles. I did not make a careful record on the way. All I know is that we have experienced fourteen seasons of heat and cold. We encountered mountains and ridges daily; the forests we came upon were not small, and the waters we met were wide and swift. We also went through many kingdoms, whose rulers had affixed their seals and signatures on our document." Then he called out: "Disciples, bring up the travel rescript and present it to our Lord."

It was handed over immediately. T'ai-tsung took a look and realized that the document had been issued on the third day before the full moon, in the ninth month of the thirteenth year during the Chên-kuan reign period. Smiling, T'ai-tsung said, "We have caused you the trouble of taking a long journey. This is now the twenty-seventh year of the Chên-kuan period!" The travel rescript bore the seals of the Precious Image Kingdom, the Black Rooster Kingdom, the Cart Slow Kingdom, the Kingdom of Women in Western Liang, the Sacrifice Kingdom, the Scarlet-Purple Kingdom, the Bhikṣu Kingdom, the Dharma-Destroying Kingdom. There were also the seals of the Phoenix-Immortal Prefecture, the Jade-Flower County, and the Gold-Level Prefecture. After reading through the document, T'ai-tsung put it away.

Soon the officer in attendance to the Throne arrived to invite them to the banquet. As the emperor took the hand of Tripitaka and walked down the steps of the hall, he asked once more, "Are your noble disciples familiar with the etiquette of the court?"

"My humble disciples," replied Tripitaka, "all began their careers as monsters deep in the wilds or a mountain village, and they have never been instructed in the etiquette of China's sage court. I beg my Lord to pardon them."

Smiling, T'ai-tsung said, "We won't blame them! We won't blame them! Let's all go to the feast set up in the East Hall." Tripitaka thanked him once more before calling for his three disciples to join them. Upon their arrival at the hall, they saw that the opulence of the great nation of China was indeed different from all ordinary kingdoms. You see

> The doorway o'erhung with brocade,
> The floor adorned with red carpets,
> The whirls of exotic incense,
> And fresh victuals most rare.
> The amber cups
> And crystal goblets
> Are gold-trimmed and jade-set;
> The gold platters
> And white-jade bowls
> Are patterned and silver-rimmed.
> The tubers thoroughly cooked.
> The taros sugar-coated;
> Sweet, lovely button mushrooms.

Unusual, pure seaweeds.
Bamboo shoots, ginger-spiced, are served a few times;
Malva leafs, honey-drenched, are mixed several ways.
Wheat-glutens fried with *hsiang-ch'un*[3] leaves;
Wood-ears cooked with bean-cured skins.
Rock ferns and fairy plants;
Chüeh flour and dried *Wei*.[4]
Radishes cooked with Szechwan peppercorns;
Melon strands stirred with mustard powder.
These few vegetarian dishes are so-so,
But the many rare fruits quite steal the show!
Walnuts and persimmons,
Lung-ans and lychees.
The chestnuts of I-chou and Shantung's dates;
The South's *ginko* fruits and hare-head pears.
Pine-seeds, lotus-seeds, and giant grapes;
Fei-nuts, melon seeds, and water chestnuts.
"Chinese olives" and wild apples;
P'in-p'os[5] and *sha-t'ung* pears;
Tz'ŭ-kus and young lotus roots;
Crisp plums and "Chinese strawberries."
Not one species is missing;
Not one kind is wanting.
There are, moreover, the steamed *mille-feuilles,* honeyed pastries, and fine viands;
And there are also the lovely wines, fragrant teas, and strange dainties.
An endless spread of a hundred flavors, true noble fare.
Western barbarians with great China can never compare!

Master and three disciples were grouped together with the officials, both civil and military, on both sides of the emperor T'ai-tsung, who took the seat in the middle. The dancing and the music proceeded in an orderly and solemn manner, and in this way they enjoyed themselves thoroughly for one whole day. Truly

The royal banquet rivals the sage kings';
True scriptures acquired excess blessings bring.
Forever these will prosper and remain,
As Buddha's light shines on the king's domain.

When it became late, the officials thanked the emperor; while T'ai-tsung withdrew into his palace, the various officials returned to their residences. The T'ang monk and his disciples, however, went to the Temple of Great Blessing, where they were met by the resident priests kowtowing. As they entered the temple gate, the priests said, "Master, the top of these trees were all suddenly pointing eastward this morning. We remembered your words and hurried out to the city to meet you. Indeed, you did arrive!" The elder could not have been more pleased as they were ushered into the abbot's quarters. By then, Pa-chieh was not clamoring at all for food or tea,

3. Aromatic greens.   5. A kind of crabapple.
4. Two kinds of ferns.

nor did he indulge in any mischief. Both Pilgrim and Sha Monk behaved most properly, for they had become naturally quiet and reserved since the Tao in them had come to fruition. They rested that night. * * *

We must tell you now about those Eight Great Vajra Guardians, who mounted the fragrant wind to lead the elder, his three disciples, and the white horse back to Spirit Mountain. The round trip was made precisely within a period of eight days. At that time the various divinities of Spirit Mountain were all assembled before Buddha to listen to his lecture. Ushering master and disciples before his presence, the Eight Vajra Guardians said, "Your disciples by your golden decree have escorted the sage monk and his companions back to the T'ang nation. The scriptures have been handed over. We now return to surrender your decree." The T'ang monk and his disciples were then told to approach the throne of Buddha to receive their appointments.

"Sage Monk," said Tathāgata, "in your previous incarnation you were originally my second disciple named Master Gold Cicada. Because you failed to listen to my exposition of the law and slighted my great teaching, your true spirit was banished to find another incarnation in the Land of the East. Happily you submitted and, by remaining faithful to our teaching, succeeded in acquiring the true scriptures. For such magnificent merit, you will receive a great promotion to become the Buddha of Candana Merit.

"Sun Wu-k'ung, when you caused great disturbance at the Celestial Palace, I had to exercise enormous dharma power to have you pressed beneath the Mountain of Five Phases. Fortunately your Heaven-sent calamity came to an end, and you embraced the teaching of Buddhism. I am pleased even more by the fact that you were devoted to the scourging of evil and the exaltation of good. Throughout your journey you made great merit by smelting the demons and defeating the fiends. For being faithful in the end as you were in the beginning, I hereby give you the grand promotion and appoint you the Buddha Victorious in Strife.

"Chu Wu-nêng, you were originally an aquatic deity of the Heavenly River, the Marshal of Heavenly Reeds. For getting drunk during the Festival of Immortal Peaches and insulting the divine maiden, you were banished to an incarnation in the Region Below which would give you the body of a beast. Fortunately you still cherished and loved the human form, so that even when you sinned at the Cloudy Paths Cave in Fu-ling Mountain, you eventually returned to our great teaching and embraced our vows. While you protected the sage monk on his way, you were still quite mischievous, for greed and lust were never wholly extinguished in you. For the merit of toting the luggage, however, I hereby grant you promotion and appoint you Janitor of the Altars."

"They have all become Buddhas!" shouted Pa-chieh. "Why am I alone made Janitor of the Altars?"

"Because you are still talkative and lazy," replied Tathāgata, "and you retain an enormous appetite. Within the four great continents of the world, there are many people who observe our teachings. Whenever there are Buddhist services, you will be asked to clear the altars. That's an appointment which offers you plenty of enjoyment. How could it be bad?

"Sha Wu-ching, you were originally the Great Curtain-Raising Captain. Because you broke a crystal chalice during the Festival of Immortal Peaches, you were banished to the Region Below, where at the River of Flowing-Sand you sinned by devouring humans. Fortunately you submitted to our teaching and remained firm in your faith. As you escorted the sage monk, you made merit by leading his horse over all those mountains. I hereby grant you promotion and appoint you the Golden-Bodied Arhat."

Then he said to the white horse, "You were originally the prince of Dragon King Kuang-chin of the Western Ocean. Because you disobeyed your father's command and committed the crime of unfiliality, you were to be executed. Fortunately you made submission to the Law and accepted our vows. Because you carried the sage monk daily on your back during his journey to the West and because you also took the holy scriptures back to the East, you too have made merit. I hereby grant you promotion and appoint you one of the dragons belonging to the Eight Classes of Supernatural Beings."

The elder, his three disciples, and the horse all kowtowed to thank the Buddha, who ordered some of the guardians to take the horse to the Dragon-Transforming Pool at the back of the Spirit Mountain. After being pushed into the pool, the horse stretched himself, and in a little while he shed his coat, horns began to grow on his head, golden scales appeared all over his body, and silver whiskers emerged on his cheeks. His whole body shrouded in auspicious air and his four paws wrapped in hallowed clouds, he soared out of the pool and circled inside the monastery gate, on top of one of the Pillars that Support Heaven.

As the various Buddhas gave praise to the great dharma of Tathāgata, Pilgrim Sun said also to the T'ang monk, "Master, I've become a Buddha now, just like you. It can't be that I still must wear a golden fillet! And you wouldn't want to clamp my head still by reciting that so-called Tight-Fillet Spell, would you? Recite the Loose-Fillet Spell quickly and get it off my head. I'm going to smash it to pieces, so that that so-called Bodhisattva can't use it anymore to play tricks on other people."

"Because you were difficult to control previously," said the T'ang monk, "this method had to be used to keep you in hand. Now that you have become a Buddha, naturally it will be gone. How could it be still on your head? Try touching your head and see." Pilgrim raised his hand and felt along his head, and indeed the fillet had vanished. So at that time, Buddha Candana, Buddha Victorious in Strife, Janitor of the Altars, and Golden-Bodied Arhat all assumed the position of their own rightful fruition. The Heavenly dragon-horse too returned to immortality, and we have a testimonial poem for them. The poem says:

> One reality fallen to the dusty plain
> Fuses with Four Signs and cultivates self again.
> In Five Phases terms, forms are but silent and void;
> The hundred fiends' false names one should all avoid.
> The great Bodhi's the right Candana fruition;
> Appointments complete their rise from perdition.
> When scriptures spread throughout the world the gracious light,
> Henceforth five sages live within Advaya's heights.

At the time when these five sages assumed their positions, the various Buddhist Patriarchs, Bodhisattvas, sage priests, arhats, guardians, bhikṣus, upāsakas and upāsikās, the immortals of various mountains and caves, the grand divinities, the Gods of Darkness and Light, the Sentinels, the Guardians of Monasteries, and all the immortals and preceptors who had attained the Way all came to listen to the proclamation before retiring to their proper stations. Look now at

Colored mists crowding the Spirit Vulture Peak,
And hallowed clouds gathered in the world of bliss.
Gold dragons safely sleeping,
Jade tigers resting in peace;
Black hares scampering freely,
Snakes and turtles circling at will.
Phoenixes, red and blue, gambol pleasantly;
Black apes and white deer saunter happily.
Strange flowers of eight periods,
Divine fruits of four seasons,
Hoary pines and old junipers,
Jade cypresses and aged bamboos.
Five-colored plums often blossoming and bearing fruit;
Millennial peaches frequently ripening and fresh.
A thousand flowers and fruits vying for beauty;
A whole sky full of auspicious mists.

Pressing their palms together to indicate their devotion, the holy congregation all chanted:

I submit to Dīpaṁkara, the Buddha of Antiquity.
I submit to Bhaiṣajya-vaiḍūrya-prabhāṣa, the Physician and Buddha of Crystal
    Lights.
I submit to the Buddha Śākyamuni.
I submit to the Buddha of the Past, Present, and Future.
I submit to the Buddha of Pure Joy.
I submit to the Buddha Vairocana.
I submit to the Buddha, King of the Precious Banner.
I submit to the Maitreya, the Honored Buddha.
I submit to the Buddha Amitābha.
I submit to Sukhāvatīvyūha, the Buddha of Infinite Life.
I submit to the Buddha who Receives and Leads to Immorality.
I submit to the Buddha of Diamond Indestructibility.
I submit to Sūrya, the Buddha of Precious Light.
I submit to Mañjuśrī, the Buddha of the Race of Honorable Dragon Kings.
I submit to the Buddha of Zealous Progress and Virtue.
I submit to Candraprabha, the Buddha of Precious Moonlight.
I submit to the Buddha of Presence without Ignorance.
I submit to Varuna, the Buddha of Sky and Water.
I submit to the Buddha Nārāyaṇa.
I submit to the Buddha of Radiant Meritorious Works.
I submit to the Buddha of Talented Meritorious Works.
I submit to Svāgata, the Buddha of the Well-Departed.
I submit to the Buddha of Candana Light.
I submit to the Buddha of Jeweled Banner.
I submit to the Buddha of the Light of Wisdom Torch.
I submit to the Buddha of the Light of Sea-Virtue.
I submit to the Buddha of Great Mercy Light.
I submit to the Buddha, King of Compassion-Power.
I submit to the Buddha, Leader of the Sages.
I submit to the Buddha of Vast Solemnity.

I submit to the Buddha of Golden Radiance.
I submit to the Buddha of Luminous Gifts.
I submit to the Buddha Victorious in Wisdom.
I submit to the Buddha Quiescent Light of the World.
I submit to the Buddha, Light of the Sun and Moon.
I submit to the Buddha, Light of the Sun-and-Moon Pearl.
I submit to the Buddha, King of the Victorious Banner.
I submit to the Buddha of Wondrous Tone and Sound.
I submit to the Buddha, Banner of Permanent Light.
I submit to the Buddha, Lamp that Scans the World.
I submit to the Buddha, King of Surpassing Dharma.
I submit to the Buddha of Sumeru Light.
I submit to the Buddha, King of Great Wisdom.
I submit to the Buddha of Golden Sea Light.
I submit to the Buddha of Great Perfect Light.
I submit to the Buddha of the Gift of Light.
I submit to the Buddha of Candana Merit.
I submit to the Buddha Victorious in Strife.
I submit to the Bodhisattva Kuan-shih-yin.
I submit to the Bodhisattva, Great Power-Coming.
I submit to the Bodhisattva Mañjuśrī.
I submit to the Bodhisattva Viśvabhadra and other Bodhisattvas.
I submit to the various Bodhisattvas of the Great Pure Ocean.
I submit to the Bodhisattva, the Buddha of Lotus Pool and Ocean Assembly.
I submit to the various Bodhisattvas in the Western Heaven of Ultimate Bliss.
I submit to the Great Bodhisattvas, the Three Thousand Guardians.
I submit to the Great Bodhisattvas, the Five Hundred Arhats.
I submit to the Bodhisattva, Bhikṣu íkṣaṇi.
I submit to the Bodhisattva of Boundless and Limitless Dharma.
I submit to the Bodhisattva, Diamond Great Scholar-Sage.
I submit to the Bodhisattva, Janitor of the Altars.
I submit to the Bodhisattva, Golden-Bodied Arhat of Eight Jewels.
I submit to the Bodhisattva of Vast Strength,
 the Heavenly Dragon of Eight Divisions of Supernatural Beings.
Such are these various Buddhas in all the worlds.
I wish to use these merits
To adorn Buddha's pure land—
To repay fourfold grace above
And save those on three paths below.
If there are those who see and hear,
Their minds will find enlightenment.
Their births with us in paradise
Will be this body's recompense.
All the Buddhas of past, present, future in all the world,
The various Honored Bodhisattvas and Mahāsattvas,
Mahā-prajñā-pāramitā![6]

Here ends *The Journey to the West.*

6. The Great Perfection of Wisdom.

⌘

RESONANCE

from *The Rāmāyana of Vālmīki*[1]

[HANUMAN SEARCHES FOR SITA]

Perched in that tree. Hanumān gazed all around him searching for Maithilī. He looked down to the ground and surveyed the entire grove.

With its trees and their clinging *santānaka* vines, it looked very beautiful. It was decorated everywhere and filled with heavenly essences and fragrances.

It was full of animals and birds and resembled the heavenly Nandana garden. It was crowded with mansions and palaces. It was filled with the songs of birds and the cry of the cuckoo arching above them all.

It was made beautiful by lotus ponds filled with red and blue lotuses fashioned of gold. It had many seats with costly coverings and numerous underground chambers.

It had lovely trees full of fruit that blossomed all year round. With the splendor of its blossoming *aśoka* trees, it had the radiance of the sunrise. * * *

Then he saw a woman clad in a soiled garment and surrounded by *rākṣasa* women. She was gaunt with fasting. She was dejected and she sighed repeatedly. She looked like the shining sliver of the waxing moon.

Her radiance was lovely; but with her beauty now only faintly discernible, she resembled a flame of fire occluded by thick smoke.

She was clad in a single, fine yellow garment, now much worn. Covered with dirt and lacking ornaments, she resembled a pond without lotuses.

Ashamed, tormented by grief, disconsolate, and suffering, she looked like the constellation Rohiṇī occluded by the planet Mars.

She was dejected, her face covered with tears. She was emaciated through fasting. She was depressed, given over to sorrow. Brooding constantly, she was consumed with her grief.

No longer seeing the people dear to her but only the hosts of *rākṣasa* women, she was like a doe cut off from her herd and surrounded by a pack of hounds.

She had a single braid—like a black serpent—falling down her back. Deserving only happiness and unaccustomed to calamity, she was consumed with sorrow.

Closely examining that wide-eyed woman so dirty and emaciated—he reasoned from these indicative signs. "She must be Sītā! "This woman looks exactly like the one I saw earlier being carried off by that *rākṣasa,* who can take on any form at will."

Sītā's face was like the full moon; her eyebrows were beautiful; her breasts were lovely and full. With her radiance that lady banished the darkness from all directions.

Her hair was jet black; her lips like *bimba* fruit. Her waist was lovely, and her posture was perfect. Her eyes were like lotus petals, and she looked like Rati, wife of Manmatha, god of love.

---

1. Translated by Robert P. Goldman and Sally J. Sutherland Goldman. The *Rāmāyāna* is one of the major ancient epics of India. Attributed to a poet named Vālmīki, it was written in Sanskrit in the sixth century B.C.E. The epic draws togther a wide range of legendary materials centering on a hero, Rāma, whose wife Sītā is abducted by a demon, Rāvaṇa, king of a race of evil demons called *rākṣasas.* An incarnation of the god Vishnu, Rāma comes to earth, wins the heart of Sītā, and sets about defeating the *rākṣasas.* In the fifth book of the epic, excerpted here, Rāma's ally the monkey-king Hanumān has gone in search of the abducted Sītā and finds her captive in a forest grove. The scenes that follow show many similarities to the Sun Wu-kong's rescue of Princess Golden Sage Palace in Chapter 69 of *Journey to the West* (page 73). For more on the *Rāmayāna,* see its principal listing in Volume A.

That lovely woman—as cherished by all living things as the radiance of the full moon—was seated on the ground like an ascetic woman practicing austerity.

Sighing constantly, that timorous woman resembled a daughter-in-law of a serpent lord. By virtue of the vast net of sorrow spread over her, her radiance was dimmed like that of a flame of fire obscured by a shroud of smoke. She was like a blurred memory or a fortune lost.

She was like faith lost or hope dashed, like success undermined by catastrophe or intellect dulled.

She was like a reputation lost through false rumors. She was distraught at being prevented from rejoining Rāma and anguished by her abduction by the *rākṣasa*.

That delicate, fawn-eyed woman was looking about here and there. Her sorrowful face with its black-tipped eyelashes was covered with a flood of tears. She sighed again and again.

Dejected, covered with dirt and grime, and devoid of ornaments—though she was worthy of them—she resembled the light of the moon, the king of stars, obscured by a black storm cloud.

As he examined Sītā closely. Hanumān's mind was once more afflicted with uncertainty; for she seemed barely discernible, like some vedic text once learned by heart but now nearly lost through lack of recitation.

It was only with great difficulty that Hanumān was able to recognize Sītā without her ornaments, just as one might make out the sense of a word whose meaning had been changed through want of proper usage.

Still, after closely examining the wide-eyed, blameless princess, he concluded that this was indeed Sītā, confirming his judgment through the telltale signs.

Then he noticed on Vaidehī's body—beautifying her limbs—the mass of jewelry that Rāma had described.

"Though blackened with long use, her beautifully formed earrings, her finely crafted 'dog's teeth,' and the handsome jewelry on her hands, variegated with gemstones and coral, are all in their proper places. I think they must be the very ones that Rāma described.

"I do not see the ones that fell back there, but those that have not fallen off are undoubtedly the very ones described by Rāma.

"Then, caught in a tree, where she had let it fall, the monkeys spied her splendid, yellow upper garment. It looked like a sheet of gold.

"On the ground they also found the large, jingling pieces of fine jewelry that she had thrown down.

"Although this garment of hers is exceedingly worn from long use, still, surely, it is the same splendid color as the other.

"This must be Rāma's beloved golden-hued queen, who, though she is lost to him, has not departed from his heart.

"This must be she on whose account Rāma has suffered fourfold misery: because of his compassion, because of his kindness, because of his grief, because of his love.

"His compassion has been aroused by the thought that a woman has been lost, his kindness by the thought that a supplicant has perished, his grief because his wife is gone, and his love because his beloved has been taken from him.

"The beauty of this black-eyed lady and the perfection of her every limb are just like Rāma's. She must therefore belong to him.

"This lady's thoughts are firmly fixed on him and his on her. It is for this reason alone that she and that righteous man have been able to survive even for a moment.

"Great-armed Rāma has accomplished the impossible in managing to survive even for a moment without this intoxicating lady, Sītā."

Having discovered Sītā in this fashion, the son of Pavana the wind god, in great delight, fixed his thoughts on Lord Rāma and praised him. * * *

As the monkey looked down upon that lady, who resembled a goddess in the Nandana gardens, several thoughts occurred to him.

"I have at last found her whom many thousands and tens of thousands of monkeys are seeking in all directions.

"I have also seen whatever was to be seen by a well-trained spy moving about covertly to determine an enemy's strength.

"I have now seen the relative strengths of the rākṣasas and their citadel, as well as the power of Rāvaṇa, their lord.

"It is now fitting for me to console the wife of him who is immeasurable and compassionate to all creatures, for she is longing to see her husband.

"I must comfort her whose face is like the full moon, for she who has never before experienced suffering can see no end to this suffering of hers. * * *

"Since I am so very tiny and a monkey to boot, I had best speak Sanskrit, the language of humans.

"On the other hand, if I were to speak Sanskrit like a Brahman, then Sītā would take me for Rāvaṇa and be frightened.

"Still, I must speak comprehensibly to her in the language of the people, for there is no other way for me to reassure this blameless woman.

"When she sees what I look like and hears how I speak, Jānakī, who has already been terrorized by the rākṣasas, may become terrified once again.

"And if the virtuous, wide-eyed lady should become terrified, she might cry out, taking me for Rāvaṇa, who can change his shape at will.

"And if Sītā should cry out, then that dreadful horde of rākṣasa women, like death itself, would rush here at once, armed with all manner of weapons.

"Then those hideous creatures would swarm all around me, trying their utmost to capture or kill me.

"If they should see me leaping among the trunks, limbs, and branches of these great trees, they would be filled with fear and apprehension.

"When they see my huge form as I race through this grove, the hideous rākṣasa women will be terrified.

"Those rākṣasa women would then summon the rākṣasas who are employed by the rākṣasa lord in his household.

"Those terrifying creatures will come rushing swiftly in turn to join the fray with spears, arrows, swords, and various other weapons in their hands.

"If I were to be surrounded by the army of the rākṣasas, I could, in the fury of battle, utterly destroy it. But then I might not be able to reach the farther shore of the mighty ocean.

"On the other hand, a large number of those swift creatures might pounce on me and capture me. Then she would not get my message, for I would be a prisoner.

"Or these creatures, who delight in violence, might kill the daughter of Janaka. Then the entire mission of Rāma and Sugrīva would come to nothing.

"Jānakī is now dwelling in this hidden and inaccessible country, which is surrounded by rākṣasas and completely isolated by the sea.

"If I were to be killed or taken in battle by the rākṣasas, I cannot think of anyone else who could help Rāma to accomplish his mission.

"Even upon reflection. I can think of no monkey who could leap over the great sea—a hundred leagues across—if I were slain.

"True, I am capable of annihilating thousands of *rākṣasas,* but then I would not be able to reach the far shore of the mighty ocean.

"Then again, battle is an uncertain business, and I do not like uncertainty. For what intelligent person would unreflectingly engage in an affair whose outcome is uncertain?

"Such is the great drawback in my speaking to Sītā. On the other hand, if I do not speak to her, Vaidehī may take her own life.

"If the place and time are not propitious or if the agent is injudicious, even well-conceived plans can come to nothing like darkness at sunrise.

"Even a firm decision as to what ought or ought not be done can come to nothing. For messengers who think they are clever can destroy an undertaking.

"How can the failure of the mission be avoided? How can I avoid making a blunder? How can I ensure that my leaping over the ocean will not prove to have been in vain?

"How might she hear what I have to say without becoming terrified?" When he had reflected in this fashion, wise Hanumān reached a decision.

"If I speak about her husband, Rāma, tireless in action, then I will not frighten her, for her mind will be absorbed in thoughts of him.

"If I speak words that are auspicious and in keeping with righteousness concerning celebrated Rāma, foremost of the Ikṣvākus, then in speaking these sweet words, I shall be able to get her to hear me out. I shall tell her everything in such a way that she believes me."

Thus demonstrating in many ways his concern for the wife of the lord of the universe, noble Hanumān—still hidden within the branches of the tree—began to speak sweetly and truthfully.

When he had deliberated in all these different ways, the great monkey spoke these sweet words within range of Vaidehī's hearing:

"There once was a king named Daśaratha, a master of chariots, elephants, and horses. He was pious in conduct, greatly renowned, honorable, and glorious. Born in a line of universal emperors, he was equal in strength to Indra, smasher of citadels.

"He was devoted to nonviolence, magnanimous, merciful, and truly valorous. He was the chief of the House of Ikṣvāku, and he was both prosperous and the increaser of prosperity.

"He was a bull among kings and very majestic. He was marked with all the signs of kingship. Happy and a giver of happiness, he was renowned throughout the four-cornered earth.

"His beloved eldest son—whose face was like the moon, the lord of stars—was named Rāma. He was learned and was the foremost among all bowmen.

"That scorcher of his enemies was the guardian of his own conduct and of his kinsmen. He was the guardian of all creatures and of righteousness itself.

"On the orders of his aged father, steadfast in truthfulness, that hero went into exile in the forest accompanied by his wife and his brother.

"There Jānakī was abducted by Rāvaṇa in his rage at hearing that Rāma, while out hunting in the deep forest, had killed Khara and Dūṣaṇa and effected a slaughter in Janasthāna.

"And now I have found her, for she is just as I heard Rāma describe her in respect to her beauty, her complexion, and her splendor."

When he had spoken these words, that bull among monkeys fell silent. But as for Jānakī, she was greatly astonished to hear them.

That timorous lady of the beautiful, curling tresses turned her face, framed by her flowing hair, upward and gazed at the *śiṃśapā* tree.

Looking sideways, up, and down, she spied at last the inconceivably wise son of the wind god and minister of the lord of the monkeys. He looked like the rising sun.

Her thoughts in a whirl, the lady spied a monkey hidden among the branches. He was soft-spoken and humble.

Seeing the splendid monkey standing humbly before her, lovely Maithilī thought, "This must be a dream!"

When she saw him, she completely lost consciousness and seemed almost as if dead. When, after a long time, she had regained consciousness, the wide-eyed lady thought:

"I have just now had a horrible dream! A monkey in a dream is held by all the *śāstras* to be inauspicious. May no evil befall Rāma, Lakṣmaṇa, or my father, King Janaka!

"But this cannot be a dream! For afflicted as I am with grief and sorrow, I cannot sleep. And there is no rest for me, so long as I am separated from him whose face is like the full moon.

"I am tormented by my love for him, my every thought is of him, and, from my incessant brooding upon him, I see and hear him constantly.

"I think this must be some hallucination, but then I reason with my mind, 'What is the basis for this? Such a thing has no substance.' But this creature who is addressing me has a clearly perceptible form.

"I pay homage to Bṛhaspati, lord of speech, along with Indra, wielder of the thunderbolt; to self-existent Brahmā, and to Agni, eater of oblations. Let what this forest creature has said in my presence prove true and not otherwise."

Placing his cupped hands to his head, mighty Hanumān, son of Māruta the wind god, then addressed Sītā in a sweet voice. * * *

"My lady, I am a messenger who has come to you at the bidding of Rāma. Rāma is well, Vaidehī, and inquires about your well-being. * * * It is he who has sent me as a messenger to your side. That is why I have come. Afflicted with misery in separation from you, he now inquires about your well being. That mighty man will soon kill Rāvaṇa in battle with arrows loosed in anger and blazing like fire.

"Great-armed Lakṣmaṇa, mighty enhancer of Sumitrā's joy, also respectfully salutes you and inquires after your welfare.

"Rāma also has an ally, my lady, the monkey Sugrīva, the king over all the monkey leaders. He too inquires after your welfare.

"Rāma thinks of you continually and so do Lakṣmaṇa and Sugrīva. You are lucky to be alive, Vaidehī, after falling into the clutches of the *rākṣasa* women!

"Very soon you will see Rāma, the great chariot warrior Lakṣmaṇa, and Sugrīva of immeasurable strength standing in the midst of tens of millions of monkeys.

"I am the monkey Hanumān, a minister of Sugrīva. I have leapt across the great ocean and entered Laṅkā.

"Relying on my own valor, I have come to see you and in so doing have placed my foot on the head of wicked Rāvaṇa.

"I am not what you think I am, my lady. Don't be afraid! You must believe me when I speak to you."

Hanumān, the immensely powerful son of Māruta the wind god, humbly addressed further words to Sītā in order to inspire her confidence:

"I am a monkey, virtuous woman, a messenger of wise Rāma. My lady, look at this ring marked with Rāma's name. Take heart, bless you, for your troubles will soon be at an end."

Taking her husband's ring and examining it, Jānakī was as joyous as if she had rejoined her husband.

Her lovely face—its long eyes all red and white—lit up with joy, like the moon, the lord of stars, when released from Rāhu, demon of the eclipse.

Then that shy young woman, delighted at the message from her husband and deeply gratified at hearing such good news, praised the great monkey:

"You must be valiant, capable, and wise, best of monkeys, since you have been able to breach the stronghold of the *rākṣasas* single-handedly.

"You are to be greatly praised for your valor, for in leaping you have crossed the mighty ocean, a hundred leagues in breadth, the lair of sea monsters, as easily as if it were a puddle in a cow's hoof-print.

"I do not think you are any ordinary monkey, bull among monkeys, since you have neither fear nor even the slightest agitation with regard to Rāvana.

"Since you have been sent by celebrated Rāma, you are worthy of conversing with me, best of monkeys. * * *

His desire now accomplished but his determination only heightened, the monkey gazed out over Laṅkā and considered what further action he might undertake.

"Now what else remains for me to do here whereby I may inflict still greater pain upon these *rākṣasas?*

"Thus far I have destroyed the grove, killed the most powerful *rākṣasas,* and wiped out part of the army. All that remains is the destruction of the citadel itself.

"Once the citadel is destroyed, my labors will have reached a favorable conclusion. By putting just a small additional effort into this task, my labors will be truly successful.

"It would be most fitting for me to gratify the fire god, bearer of oblations, who is blazing so brightly on my tail, with these splendid mansions."

Then the great monkey, his tail ablaze, moved about the rooftops of Laṅkā, like a storm cloud crossed by lightning.

Hanumān let loose a fire that was like the flames of the fire of Doom.

Fanned by the wind, the swift and powerful fire, eater of oblations, grew greater and blazed up like the fire of Doom.

The wind drove the blazing fire through the houses.

Thus the vast, bejeweled palaces with their fretwork of gold and their masses of pearls came crashing down.

They crashed to the ground, their lofty terraces shattered, just as the mansions of perfected beings might fall from the heavens once their merit was exhausted.

Hanumān saw streams of molten metal, flowing from a palace. Varied in hue, they were filled with diamonds, coral, lapis, pearls, and silver.

Just as fire is never sated with firewood and straw, so too Hanumān was not sated with killing the lords of the *rākṣasas.*

Overwhelmed by the power of Hanumān's wrath, the city of Laṅkā, engulfed in the flames of the fire, the eater of oblations, its heroes slain and its soldiers scattered, was devastated as if by a curse.

Wise Hanumān scanned Laṅkā. Marked everywhere by brightly blazing flames of fire, the eater of oblations, its *rākṣasas* in a state of terror, agitation, and despair, the city resembled the earth overwhelmed by the wrath of the self-existent Lord.

The Rise of the Vernacular in Europe

In 1200, Latin was still the undisputed language of the elite, and in most parts of Europe it was the only language for which there existed any sizable body of written texts. By 1600, virtually every country in what is now western Europe—and many in eastern Europe—not only had come close to standardizing a national written language, but had produced a major body of literary works in that vernacular. The enormous changes that took place in late medieval and Renaissance Europe included religious, political, artistic, and technological upheavals. Yet the first real revolution of early modernity was a linguistic one, and it undergirded all subsequent revolutions.

"Latin loosed the tongue of French," wrote the great scholar Ernst Robert Curtius. Not only does he call attention to the first modern European vernacular to assert itself, but he identifies the relationship between the new vernaculars and the monolithic language of the Roman empire as organic rather than antagonistic. Eventually, to be sure, there would be plenty of antagonism involved, particularly since Latin was also the language of the Catholic Church, target of the Protestant Reformation. Yet during the formative years of the late twelfth and thirteenth centuries, there was a new concern with studying the Latin language as a living, dynamic entity, an interest that became more emphatic with the growth of humanistic education. If Latin had developed over time, then surely the many oral dialects then flourishing in medieval Europe might also have their golden ages; as the Roman poet Horace had put it, "As the forests change their foliage in the headlong flight of years, as the first leaves fall, so does the old crop of words pass away, and the newly born, like men in the bloom of their youth, come then to the prime of their vigor." Simultaneously, a growing entrepreneurial middle class untrained in Latin was a demanding new audience for vernacular texts, while sophisticated courts such as those of Frederick II in Sicily and Alfonso X of Castile were providing fertile ground for poetic experimentation in Provençal, Galician, and other regional languages.

Yet the swift rise of vernacular literatures after 1300 often depended on charismatic figures bold enough to jettison Latin and forge a new idiom on which they would leave a highly personal stamp: Florence's Dante, Germany's Luther, Poland's Kochanowski. In Portugal, on the other hand, the powerful monarch King Denis (1279–1325) ordered that Arabic, Hebrew, and Latin texts be translated into Portuguese, which he designated as his country's new official language; two centuries later, King Christian III of Denmark commissioned a Danish translation of the Bible. Such individual efforts would be aided considerably by an invention that left its innovative creator broke and threatened with lawsuits: the movable-type printing press. Johann Gutenberg's groundbreaking invention in the early 1450s gave the highly oral world of late medieval Europe a degree of permanence and stability it had never enjoyed. What had once been the privilege of clerics and the elite—the ability to possess painstakingly made copies of precious manuscripts—was now within reach of the common man, and even woman, eager and able to buy, like the rustics in Shakespeare's *Winter's Tale,* things such as ballads "in print, a-life, for then we are sure they are true."

Colantonio, *St. Jerome in His Study* (1443). One of the early Fathers of the Church, Jerome was known during the Middle Ages chiefly as the inspired translator of the Hebrew and Greek Bible into Latin, as well as a staunch defender of celibacy. During the early Renaissnce, he acquired new importance for scholars who sought to emulate his encyclopedic knowledge of the classic works of pagan antiquity. Here he is seen in his cluttered study, his cardinal's hat draped over a table, as he calmly removes a thorn from the paw of the lion who was said to have been his companion during his years in the desert.

Biblical Translations

Who should be able to read the Bible—still the world's best-selling book today, as it was 500 years ago, when the printing press was still a new-fangled invention? The answer 500 years ago was far less clear than it is today. The industrious scholar Erasmus, the first to make available to the Western world the New Testament in the original Greek, argued passionately for translations on behalf of the masses. He was attacked for this by Church authorities who wished to maintain their control over Scripture and its interpretation. The irony of the attacks against Erasmus and others like him was that for over a thousand years the Bible had *always* been read in translation in the West: largely in the Vulgate, a Latin version of the original Hebrew, Greek, and Aramaic texts, produced by Saint Jerome in the late fourth century. Concern with the corrupt manuscripts of Jerome's text over the centuries led to efforts throughout the Middle Ages to produce a more "authentic" text, and as early as the thirteenth century, vernacular portions of the Old and New Testaments alike began appearing in translation. But with the dawn of the Reformation, a second, more immediate factor led to a burst of translations, especially in the north: the conviction that Christian faith was based on Scripture alone, particularly on one's own personal interpretation of Scripture, unencumbered by the weight of 1,500 years of church tradition.

To meet this need, precise versions of the original Greek and Hebrew texts had to be produced—thus demanding a different Bible from Jerome's corrupt Vulgate—and translations had to be made into the new European vernaculars that common people might read. Latin, moreover, was the hateful language of the Papacy, as well as of the clerical and intellectual elite. Translating Bibles into the vernacular was equivalent to shaking off a foreign tongue. Moreover, translating the Bible into the various languages of Renaissance Europe both accompanied and accelerated the rise of the vernacular, even—in the case of Luther's German and of Jan Kochanowski's patient biblical work in Polish—creating a literary vernacular that would help to propel the emergence of national literatures. Finally, for those who traveled to the far-off lands of the Americas, the translation of biblical materials into indigenous tongues such as Nahuatl and Natick-Algonquian, both represented here, was felt to be an absolute necessity so as to facilitate, as the early colonist John Eliot would have it, "this Good Work of Propagating Religion to these Natives."

Two biblical passages are reproduced here. The first is Psalm 23 ("The Lord is my Shepherd"), given in the Vulgate version and in several vernacular versions (French, Polish, American English), along with an English verse rendering for purposes of comparison. The second is Gabriel's address to Mary from the Gospel of Luke, as translated by an Italian poet, Martin Luther, and William Tyndale. Finally, the "New World Psalms" of Bernardino de Sahagún's *Psalmodia Christiana* are not literal—or even loose—translations of the psalms into the Nahuatl of Sahagún's Mexican converts. They are completely original poems that attempt to contextualize Christian feast days within Mexican culture, and hence to lure the people away from singing their own songs of pagan, "idolatrous" content.

COMPARATIVE VERSIONS OF PSALM 23 ("THE LORD IS MY SHEPHERD")[1]

from The Vulgate[2]

Psalmus David	*A Psalm of David*[3]
Dominus regit me, et nihil mihi deerit:	The Lord guideth me, and nothing is wanting to me,
In loco pascuae ibi me collocavit.	In the pasture He lets me rest.
Super aquam refectionis educavit me:	To refreshing waters He leadeth me;
Animam meam convertit.	He quickeneth my soul,
5 Deduxit me super semitas justitiae, propter nomen suum.	5 He guideth me on the right path for His name's sake.

1. The Book of Psalms has always occupied a special status in the Old Testament, in large part because its authorship has traditionally been credited to David, slayer of Goliath and second king of Israel. In medieval households, the Psalter was a common item, and the manuscripts were frequently adorned with decorations; many paintings of the Annunciation show Mary with a psalter in her lap. Above all, the psalms are poems, and in an era in which lyric poetry was becoming more diffuse, they were often turned to for inspiration. They were particularly in-

strumental in helping to shape the poetic vernacular: Petrarch, Queen Elizabeth I, Sir Philip Sidney, and many others tried their hand at translating the Psalms.
2. The Latin Bible was originally the work of Jerome, although efforts in medieval France to produce a streamlined version of the many flawed manuscripts then in circulation of Jerome's translation led to the production of what was called the Vulgate.
3. Translated by Patrick Boylan.

Nam, et si ambulavero in medio
umbrae mortis,
non timebo mala:
quoniam tu mecum es. Virga tua,
et baculus tuus:
10 ipsa me consolata sunt.

Parasti in conspectu meo mensam,
adversus eos, qui tribulant me.
Impinguasti in oleo caput meum:
et calix meus inebrians quam
praeclarus est!
Et misericordia tua subsequetur
me omnibus diebus vitae
meae:
Et ut inhabitem in domo Domini,
in longitudinem dierum.

For even if I walk in the midst of
the shadow of death,
I fear not misfortune:
Because Thou art with me; Thy
crook and Thy staff
10 Do strengthen me.

Thou preparest for me a banquet
In the sight of mine enemies.
Thou anointest my head with oil;
And the cup which refresheth
me—how goodly it is!

15 Thy kindness followeth me
All the days of my life,
So that I may dwell in the House
of the Lord
For ever and ever.

Clément Marot: *from* Psalms[1]

Psaume 23

Mon Dieu me paist sous sa puis-
sance haute:
C'est mon berger, de rien je
n'auray faute.
En tect bien seur, joignant les
beaux herbages,
Coucher me fait, me meine aux
clairs rivages,
5 Traite ma vie en douceur tres-
humaine,
Et pour son nom par droits sen-
tiers me meine.

Si seurement, que quand au val
viendroye
D'ombre de mort, rien de mal ne
craindroye.
Car avec moy tu es à chacune
heure:

Psalm 23[2]

Beneath his strong might my God
nourishes me,
He is my shepherd, there is nothing I will need.
Under a roof secure, alongside
lovely pastures
He makes me sleep, he leads me
to serene waters,
5 He fills my life with a sweetness
more than human,
And leads me in his name on
paths that are golden—

So surely, that when the valley
draws near
With its shadow of death, evil I
will not fear,
Because you are with me, at every
hour,

1. The French poet Clément Marot (1496–1544) began translating the psalms into verse at the request of Marguerite de Navarre, sister of the King of France and strong supporter of the reformist tendencies that periodically landed Marot in jail. A formative influence on French poetry, Marot completed his poetic paraphrases of the *Fifty Psalms of David, Composed in French Verse* in 1542, which was quickly condemned by the University of Paris. Nonetheless, the psalms enjoyed great popularity in the French court, where they were sung to music; as one sympathizer said, "the French people can now praise God with both their hearts and their voices." Protestants throughout Europe read them as well. For his work, Marot drew both on the translations of Calvin and on the Hebrew Bible. He translated Psalm 23 into three six-line stanzas of rhyming couplets.

2. Translated by Jane Tylus. The poem is prefaced by the brief summary statement: "He sings of the happiness and many good things that are his, and with marvellous trust promises himself that the God from whom all good has come will treat him the same way forever."

10   Puis ta houlette & conduite
     m'asseure.
   Tu enrichis de vivres
     necessaires
   Ma table, aux yeux de tous mes
     adversaires.

   Tu oings mon chef d'huiles &
     senteurs bonnes,
   Et jusqu'aux bords pleine tasse
     me donnes:
15   Voire & feras que ceste faveur
     tiene
   Tant que vivray compagnie me
     tiene:
   Si que tousjours de faire ay esper-
     ance
   En la maison du Seigneur demeu-
     rance.

10   Your staff and rod do so
     reassure.
   You enrich my table with all that
     is necessary
   To life, and in the eyes of my
     adversaries.

   You annoint my head with pleas-
     ant scents and oils,
   And you give me a cup so full it
     overflows.
15   See how it shall be: this kindness
     will I keep
   As long as you keep company
     with me,
   Such that I have hope of forever
     making
   The house of the Lord into my
     dwelling.

Jan Kochanowski: *from* Psalterz Dawidów[1]
23

23[2]

Mój wiekuisty pasterz mię
   pasie,
Nie zejdzie mi nic na żadnym
   wczasie;
Zawiódł mię w pasze
   niepospolite,
Nad zdroje żywej wody obfite.

5   Wrócił mię z dziwnych
     obtedliwości
   Na ścieżkę jawnej
     sprawiedliwości;
   Postanowił mię na drodze
     prawej,
   Z chęci ku studze swemu
     łaskawej.

   By dobrze stała śmierć tuż przede
     mną,
10   Bać się nie będę, bo Pan mój ze
     mną.
   Twój pręt, o Panie, i laska
     Twoja,

My everlasting shepherd tends to
   me,
No want or need shall e'er descend to me:
He hath taken me unto rare pastures,
To live waters springing ever after.

5   He turneth me from monstrous
     trespasses
   And showeth me the path of right-
     eousness:
   He hath set me upon the righteous
     way,
   Towards His servant He hath un-
     ending grace.

   I shall not fear though death's be-
     side me,
10   I shall ever trust the Lord to guide
     me.
   Thy blessed staff, yea, and thy
     holy rod,

1. Jan Kochanowski (1530–1584) was the most influential poet of the Polish Renaissance; he wrote extensively in both Latin and Polish. Probably his greatest work was his poetic paraphrase of the Psalms, *Psalterz Dawidów,* published in 1579; they were also set to music. Like Marot,

Kochanowski translated Psalm 23 using rhyming couplets. For the main entry on Kochanowski, see page 239.
2. Translated by Clare Cavanagh, with the assistance of Jan Miernowski.

W niebezpieczeństwie obrona
    moja.

Posadziłeś mię za stół
    kosztowny,
Skąd nieprzyjaciel boleje
    głowny;
15 Włos mój wszystek balsamem,
    płynie,
Czasza opływa w rozkosznem
    winie.

Ufam Twej łasce, że mię na
    wieki
Nie spuścisz, Panie, z swojej
    opieki;
I będę mieszkał w Twym świętym
    domu,
20 Nie ustępując laty nikomu.

Shall shield me from all peril,
    oh my God.

This bounteous table Thy good
    will bestows,
To the distress and sorrow of my
    foes:
15 My hair doth flow for me with
    balsam fine,
My cup brims over with delicious
    wine.

I trust unto Thy grace, that Thou
    shalt ne'er
Abandon me, Lord, from Thy lov-
    ing care:
And I will dwell within Thy holy
    home,
20 For countless years, longer than
    anyone.

The Bay Psalm Book[1]
A Psalme of David

The Lord to mee a shepheard is,
    want therefore shall not I.
Hee in the folds of tender-grasse,
    doth cause mee downe to lie:
5 To waters calme me gently leads.
    Restore my soule doth hee:
he doth in paths of righteousnes:
    for his names sake leade mee.
Yea though in valley of deaths shade
10   I walk, none ill I'le feare:
because thou art with mee, thy rod,
    and staffe my comfort are.
For mee a table thou hast spread,
    in presence of my foes:
15 thou dost annoynt my head with oyle,
    my cup it over-flowes.

1. The first book published in English in North America was the *Bay Psalm Book,* also known as the New American Psalter, in 1640. It is the work of three translators, one of whom was John Eliot, who also was the first to translate the Bible into a North American Indian language; see the translation of Psalm 23 in Natick-Algonquian, page 127. Like his two colleagues, Eliot had chosen to emigrate to colonial New England in 1631 because of his Puritan faith. The *Bay Psalm Book* was written in the "plain style" that the Puritans preferred in opposition to the fanciful baroque style they associated with Anglicanism (and the King James Bible); or as Richard Mather wrote in the preface to the translation, "God's altar needs not our polishing. We have respected rather a plain translation than to smooth our verses with the sweetness of any paraphrase; and so have attended conscience rather than elegance, fidelity rather than poetry." The editors nonetheless provided metrical versions of the psalms, which were sung by the congregations in the colony's Calvinist churches.

Goodnes & mercy surely shall
    all my dayes follow mee:
and in the Lords house I shall dwell
20   so long as dayes shall bee.

THE GOSPEL OF LUKE 1:26–39

Lucrezia Tornabuoni de' Medici:
from The Life of Saint John the Baptist[1]

In the sixth month God sent to Galilee,
to a town called Nazareth, Gabriel,
an angel of his kingdom;
he sent him to that virgin who was promised
5   to a man named Joseph,
of the worthy house of David,
and she was a virgin by the name of Mary.
Hear how the angel welcomed her:

"Greetings from God, you are full of grace,
10   and the Lord God is with you everywhere.
Blessed are you, luminous light;
you are the light and fire of all women."
Hearing him address to her this kind
of salutation disturbed her not a little.
15   "Mary, please, do not fear my words;
you have found great favor with God.

"Here in your womb you shall conceive,
and the mother of God will be you alone,
and in the fullness of time, you will give birth
20   to a son, and you shall call him Jesus.
Think how much gladness will be yours!
Unknown till now, nor shall it be known again;
this worthiest of children who is to be born
will be called the son of the Highest God,

25   "and to this glorious and worthy child,
God will give the seat of his father David,
and he will reign with true wisdom;
he will rule forever, with all his legions,
and his reign will have neither equal nor end."

---

1. Translated from the Italian by Jane Tylus. The Florentine aristocrat Lucrezia Tornabuoni (1426–1482) was the mother of Lorenzo de' Medici and like her son, a poet; during her lifetime she wrote no fewer than five lengthy *storie sacre* or "sacred histories" that paraphrase five books from the Old and New Testaments. Her verse translation of the passage in Luke is from her "Story of Saint John the Baptist," an account of the life of the precursor of Christ who was also Florence's patron saint. Never published in her lifetime, her *storie sacre* and shorter religious verses were probably written to enlighten and entertain her granddaughters; three of her biblical translations are based, in fact, on the lives of formidable Old Testament women, Judith, Esther, and the chaste Susanna. Tornabuoni's translation is drawn from the Vulgate, as well as from other vernacular treatments of the saint's life, recast from prose into eight-line stanzas. Given here are stanzas 20 through 25 from the poem.

30   Mary responded: "I am not able
      to be a mother. Now how can this be, since I
      have not yet desired to know any man?"

      "The Holy Spirit," the angel said,
      and the power of God will overshadow you,
35   and you will know great sweetness, rejoicing, and song
      on the day that the son of God is born.
      And Elizabeth, your cousin,
      who has been barren for so long,
      will in her old age give birth, an incredible birth;
40   know that nothing is impossible with God."

      As soon as she understood what he said,
      she answered him humbly, and with reverence:
      "I am his handmaiden"—so ready was she to speak—
      "let what you have just revealed
45   so clearly and so openly be done to me."
      The angel swiftly departed, and Mary went off too,
      setting out into the mountains,
      to the home of Zechariah.

Martin Luther: *from* The Bible[1]

And in the sixth month the angel Gabriel was sent by God to a city in Galilee, which is called Nazareth, to a virgin, who was engaged to a man by name of Joseph, from the house of David, and the virgin was called Maria. And the angel came inside to her and said, "Greetings be to you, gracious lady, the LORD is with you, you blessed lady among women."

But when she saw him, she was terrified by his words, and thought, "What kind of greeting is that?" And the angel said to her, "Do not be afraid, Maria, you have found favor with God; behold, you will become pregnant in your womb, and you will give birth to a son, whom you shall call Jesus by name. He will grow up and be named a son of the Highest. And God the LORD will give him the seat of his father David, and he will be king over the house of Jacob forever, and his kingdom will never end.

Then Maria said to the angel, "How is that supposed to happen, especially since I do not know of any man?" The angel answered and said to her, "The Holy Spirit will come over you, and the power of the Highest will overshadow you. For that reason the holy one, who will be born from you, will also be named the son of God. And, behold, Elizabeth, your relation, is also pregnant with a son, at her age, and is now in her sixth month, she, about whom it is said that she is barren. For

---

1. Translated by James A. Parente, Jr. Luther's translation of the Bible into German was not the first; soon after Gutenberg's printing press appeared on the scene, a German Bible appeared, and there were at least nine in print when Luther undertook his own project. But in 1522 and for the first time, a German New Testament appeared that was based directly on the Greek text, rather than the Vulgate, and Luther's goal—to make his translation a vehicle for the Reformation that was already in full swing—was far different from those of his fifteenth-century predecessors. Notable in his translation is his decision to make Mary a "gracious lady" rather than someone infused with God's grace, as well as his nomination of Jesus as "*a* son of the Highest."

nothing is impossible for God." Maria, however, said, "Behold: I am the hand-maiden of the LORD; let it happen to me as you have said." And the angel parted from her.

William Tyndale: *from* The New Testament[1]

And in the sixth month the angel Gabriel was sent by God unto a city in Galilee, named Nazareth, to a virgin spoused to a man whose name was Joseph, of the house of David, and the virgin's name was Mary. And the angel went in unto her, and said: Hail full of grace, the Lord is with thee: blessed art thou among women.

When she saw him, she was abashed at his saying: and cast in her mind what manner of salutation that should be. And the angel said unto her: fear not Mary: for thou hast found grace with God. Lo: thou shalt conceive in thy womb, and shalt bear a son, and shalt call his name Jesus. He shall be great, and shall be called the son of the highest. And the lord God shall give unto him the seat of his father David, and he shall reign over the house of Jacob for ever, and his kingdom shall be none end.

Then said Mary unto the angel: How shall this be, seeing I know not a man? And the angel answered and said unto her: The holy ghost shall come upon thee, and the power of the highest shall overshadow thee. Therefore also that holy thing which shall be born, shall be called the son of God. And behold thy cousin Elizabeth, she hath also conceived a son in her age. And this is her sixth month, though she be called barren: for with God can nothing be unpossible. And Mary said: behold the handmaiden of the lord, be it unto me even as thou hast said. And the angel departed from her.

NEW WORLD PSALMS

Bernardino de Sahagún: *from* Psalmodia Christiana[1]
To the Reader

Among the things of which the Indians of New Spain were very careful, one was the worship of their gods, who were many and to whom in various ways they paid honor and also sang praises extolling them in the temples and oratories day and night,

1. Translated by William Tyndale, while in exile in Antwerp, a port town across the Channel from his native England. He based his English translation not on the Vulgate, but on the newly available Greek text, as well as on Luther's German. His avoidance of Latinisms made his Bible an extremely readable one, while his translation of Greek terms such as *ekklesia* as "congregation" rather than "Church" inspired heated arguments when copies of the work poured into England, incurring the wrath of powerful figures such as Thomas More. "The Father of the English Bible" was betrayed by Catholic sympathizers on the Continent, and he was burned at the stake as a heretic in 1536. The tide in England, however, had ironically already turned, and even before Tyndale's death the English clergy was calling for an official translation, albeit one "by certain good and learned men, to be nominated by His Majesty, and [to] be delivered to the people for their instruction." The passage included here reflects the revisions Tyndale made to his 1526 translation in

what was to be his enormously popular 1534 edition.
1. Translated by Arthur J. O. Anderson. Serving native congregations in Mexico in the 1550s, the Spanish friar Bernardino de Sahagún became fascinated by native culture (see page 846 for selections from his encyclopedic *General History of the Affairs of New Spain*). Many missionaries simply tried to override pagan practices, but Sahagún felt that Christianity would more effectively take root if it could be expressed in the natives' own language and poetic style. He therefore had a collection of native songs compiled (see page 799 for examples), using them as a resource of techniques and images in order to compose a *Psalmodia Christiana* ("Christian Psalmody"), written in the native language of Nahuatl. It was published in 1583, and continued to be used until the 18th century, when it was denounced and banned by a bishop who felt that the poems tainted sacred history by expressing it in native terms—the very mixture that again makes these poems compelling reading today.

singing hymns and forming choruses and dances in their presence. When they did so they arrayed themselves variously in the many festivals, performed a number of varying dance movements, and sang a number of canticles in praise of the false gods whose festivals they were celebrating. Since the time they were baptized efforts have been made to force them to abandon those old canticles of praise to their false gods and to sing only in praise of God and His saints, and to do so in the daytime in the festival seasons, on Sundays, and on the saints' days of their churches. And for this purpose in many places they have been given canticles about God and His saints, so that they may abandon the other old canticles, and they have accepted and sung them, and still sing them in some places. But in other places—in most places— they persist in going back to singing their old canticles in their houses or their palaces (a circumstance that arouses a good deal of suspicion as to the sincerity of their Christian Faith); for in the old canticles mostly idolatrous things are sung in a style so obscure that none can understand them well except they themselves. And they use other canticles to persuade the population to do what they want, or about war or other matters that are not good; for they have canticles composed for these purposes that they refuse to abandon. In order easily to counteract this mischief, in this year, 1583, in this volume, called *Christian Psalmody*, these canticles have been printed in the Nahuatl language so that they will completely abandon the old canti- cles, a penalty being imposed applicable to any who go back to singing the old can- ticles. * * *

I humbly pray the lords in the most important areas of secular government to grant their consent and support that this work circulate among the Indians, and to or- der them (under heavy penalties) never again to sing the ancient canticles, but to sing only those of God and His saints, and to bring about the purpose here sought, that our Lord be praised by all His believers with Catholic, Christian praises, and that the praises of idols and idolatry be buried as they deserve.

PROLOGUE, FIRST PSALM

You children, you people of New Spain, know, understand that our Lord God has sent you light and glory. Honor them; weep for them: for exalted spiritual rank, the spiri- tual Kingdom are gifts made to you and to various people.

Understand and realize, you various people, that Christianity, unlike precious green stones, bracelets, emerald-green jade, even rubies smoking like quetzal plumes, is a heavenly thing, a marvelous miracle that the Lord God, that Jesus Himself, came here on earth to give us.

Beloved sons, people of New Spain, realize that your godly goods, your godly shields, your godly insignia and ornamentation do exist.

When the sun shone, when day broke, when the Word of God descended upon you, when you received the Sacrament—when you accepted the deep jade-green wa- ter of baptism—when God, God the King, adopted you all as His sons, you became spiritual children of the holy Church; your souls acquired godliness and in them was placed Christianity, which become your adornment, a gift for you, your lot.

God your Father and your mother holy Church have arranged for you, given you, presented you incomparable feathered bracelets and a variety of precious spiritual flowered vestments: the sign of the cross, and the Creed, and the Lord's Prayer, the Ave Maria, and the Salve Regina.

Your beloved Father, God, and your beloved mother, holy Church, give and bestow on you, present to you spiritual feathered bracelets, and golden bracelets with designs, valuable feathered bracelets. As what you deserve, as what is your lot, a gift for you, our Lord God gives you, bestows on you handfuls of various sweet, fragrant flowers, shields of flowers, tremendous, marvelous, precious—the sign of the cross, and the Creed, and the Lord's Prayer, the Ave Maria, and the Salve Regina.

THE NATIVITY OF OUR LORD JESUS CHRIST SECOND DAY, FOURTH PSALM

Let us pay honor to the Holy Gospel that Saint Luke wrote down, in which Jesus' birth is told.

Because of the emperor's command, Joseph went to Bethlehem. He took with him the virgin, Saint Mary.

When they had arrived in Bethlehem some days later, it was time for the Virgin to give birth.

She gave birth; she bore her beloved Babe, her firstborn Son.

When her beloved Babe was born, at once she wrapped Him in a cloth and laid Him in a manger, where deer ate.

And at the edge of Bethlehem the shepherds lived, caring for their sheep throughout the night.

And then an angel showed himself to them, and a brilliant light came down from Heaven.

The angel said to them: I have come to tell you of a great happiness, for now the Savior Jesus has been born in Bethlehem.

THIRD DAY, FIRST PSALM

In Heaven all kinds of precious troupials, trogons, rosy spoonbills came to make so memorable a din of precious rattle-bell-like sounds that angels also chanted.

The various birds, the precious birds, the birds of springtime, and the angels have come warbling as with the finest of jade flutes, have come to make a memorable sound of rattle-bells. Alleluia.

Goodly were the flowery troupial, chachalaca, emerald toucanet, and momotus birds. With goodly song the angels chanted: May God, God in Heaven, be praised. Alleluia, alleluia.

All the various precious little birds in Heaven flew like quetzal birds.[2] They said in song: May there be peace on earth. Alleluia.

SECOND PSALM

Their song came sparkling like a precious quetzal rattle-bell. They joyously came here with heavenly song. They said: May peace be with the people. Alleluia.

---

2. Among the many tropical American birds that Sahagún places in Palestine, the quetzal has special symbolic meaning: its long, turquoise feathers were highly prized, and it was associated with the major god Quetzalcoatl, "Quetzal-plumed serpent."

It all occurred in Bethlehem when our precious Savior Jesus Christ was born. Alleluia, alleluia.

The various flowers smelled sweet. Spread upon the ground lay scarlet tuberoses, bursting into flower. A golden quetzal-colored dew formed drops. The golden flowers are shedding petals; they are raining down. Alleluia.

Quaribeas, popcorn flowers, and scarlet philodendrons curve like quetzal-dew; they lie glistening like gold; they glow like precious jade. All kinds of precious stones, all brought together, are in Bethlehem. Alleluia.

Third Psalm

Magnolias, upright, spread their smell; quetzal rattle-bell flowers, red solandras are outspreading like the early light of dawn; they glow like gold. Alleluia, alleluia.

Castilian flowers[3] and frangipani are outspreading like the early light of dawn. Alleluia, alleluia.

Jade-like flowers are spreading, sparkling; scarlet tuberoses are extending far in masses. Alleluia, alleluia.

Grapevines have budded, have borne fruit in Engedi.[4] Alleluia, alleluia.

Fourth Psalm

Emerald-green jades, pearls, and amethysts flame, glisten where the air is clear. Alleluia, alleluia.

Let us marvel at the foamy quetzal-amber, at precious jades that scattered, that dispersed, that reached the ground in Bethlehem. Alleluia, alleluia.

Fine turquoises and rubies, fine green jades were wound about, were massed in Bethlehem when the Child, when the Baby Jesus was born. Alleluia, alleluia.

Fifth Psalm

The angel then appeared before the shepherds, called to them, and said: Alleluia, alleluia.

I come to give you news to make one very happy, friends of ours. Alleluia, alleluia.

Your Savior Jesus Christ has now been born. Alleluia, alleluia.

Go to Bethlehem; you will see Him there in David's City. Alleluia, alleluia.

Not just a few angels showed themselves and chanted in their song the wondrous news—alleluia—as they praised the Child, the newborn King. Alleluia, alleluia.

May our God in Heaven be most highly praised, and peace on earth be with those of good will.

Praise be to God

In Mexico

By permission. Pedro Ocharte, Printer, 1583

---

3. The Nahuatl term *castilan xochitl* or "Spanish flowers" referred to plants imported from Spain.

4. Region along the Dead Sea, south of Bethlehem.

John Eliot: *from* Up-Biblum God[1]
[THE HOLY BIBLE]

FROM DEDICATORY LETTER TO KING CHARLES II OF ENGLAND[2]

Most Dread Soveraign,

AS our former Presentation of the New-Testament was Graciously Accepted by Your Majesty; so with all Humble Thankfulness for that Royal Favour, and with the like hope, We are bold now to Present the *WHOLE BIBLE,* Translated into the Language of the Natives of this Country, by *A Pitiful Labourer in that Work,* and now *Printed* and *Finished,* by means of the Pious Beneficence of Your Majesties Subjects in *England:* which also by Your Special Favour hath been Convinced and Confirmed to the intended Use, and Advancement of so Great and Good a Work, as is the *Propagation of the Gospel to these poor Barbarians* in this (Ere-while) Unknown World.

Translations of Holy Scripture, *The Word of the King of Kings,* have ever been deemed not unworthy of the most Princely Dedications: Examples whereof are extant in divers Languages. But Your Majesty is the First that hath Received one in this Language, or from this *American World,* or from any Parts so Remote from *Europe* as these are, for ought that ever we heard of.

Publications also of these Sacred Writings to the Sons of Men (who here, and here onely, have the Mysteries of their Eternal Salvation revealed to them by the God of Heaven) is a Work that the Greatest Princes have Honoured themselves by.[3] But to Publish and Communicate the same to a Lost People, as remote from Knowledge and Civility, much more from Christianity, as they were from all Knowing, Civil and Christian Nations; a People without Law, without Letters, without Riches, or Means to procure any such thing; a People that *sate as deep in Darkness, and in the shadow of Death,*[4] as (we think) any since the Creation: This puts a Lustre upon it that is Superlative; and to have given Royal Patronage and Countenance to such a Publication, or to the Means thereof, will stand among the Marks of Lasting Honour in the eyes of all that are Considerate, even unto After-Generations.

And though there be in this Western World many Colonies of other European Nations, yet we humbly conceive, no Prince hath had a Return of such a Work as this; which may be some Token of the Success of Your Majesties Plantation of *New-England.* * * *

1. Known as "the Indian Apostle," John Eliot (1604–1690) was instrumental in translating the Bible into one of the regional dialects of the Massachusetts Indians, Natick-Algonquian. He also wrote a grammar of the language, "for the help of such as desire to learn the same, for the furtherance of the Gospel among the [Indians]." One of the main questions that confronted him as he undertook his mammoth translation was how to translate the Bible into a new language: use ready-made religious terms, or transpose the technical terms of the original into the new version? In the *Up-Biblum God* printed at the press of Harvard's first president, Henry Dunster, in 1663, he decided to render his psalms metrically, and liberally inserted Hebrew words such as "Jehovah" into Natick-Algonquian.

2. Despite the fact that Eliot along with many Puritans had chosen to leave England, he nonetheless dedicates his work to King Charles II, newly returned from exile in France during the period of Oliver Cromwell's Commonwealth. No doubt Eliot was concerned that the king might punish the Puritans in the British colonies for suspected sympathies with Cromwell, and the dedication may have served to underscore that Eliot and others chose to remain, as he says, "Subjects in England." As Eliot also notes, the New Testament had previously been published several years earlier, in London; the publication of the entire Bible in Boston—the first ever on the American continent—required approval by the king's commissioners.

3. Perhaps an allusion to the King James Bible, printed for Charles II's grandfather in 1611.

4. From Psalms 107:10, where the Psalmist refers to those afflicted ones, "such as sit in darkness and shadow," who call out to the Lord in their distress and are saved.

Psal. XXIII

UKKETOOH HOMÁONK DAVID

1. Iehovah *a* nullohkommœnukoowaeneum, wanne reag woh nukquenaahikoo.
2. Nusseepsum wahik ashkoskuhkontu nutassoowunuk ahtou pagodtut.
3. Wonk omohkinau nukketeahogkounoh nutussoowunuk wunnomwausseongane mayut newutche œweseonk.
4. Nux, pomusháon wutonkauhtómut œnáunkôŝe nuppœonk, *b* matta woh nukquehtamœ woskehittúonk: newutche kœweetomeh, kuppogkomunk, kah kutanwδhhou nœnenehukquog.
5. Koonechœhkah ut anaquabeh, anaquabhetrit nummatwomog: kullisséqunum nuppuhkuh nashpe pummee, nœtattámwáitch pomponeeupóh shau.
6. Wunnamuhkut conáyeuonk kah monaneteaonk pish nutásukkonkqínash tohsohkepomantam: kah pish nuttaih wcckit Jehovah⁵ micheme.

‡ ‡◊‡ ‡

Attacking and Defending the Vernacular Bible

The sixteenth century was unprecedented in its many "official" and unofficial translations of the Old and New Testaments, ranging from the famous Bibles of Tyndale and Luther, to translations in Czech, Danish, and Dutch, to an Arabic version printed in Rome in 1590. Bibles often had to be published outside Catholic countries where the Inquisition was especially forceful. A Portuguese New Testament appeared in Amsterdam, a Spanish Bible was printed in Basel. Translators suffered for daring to pursue their craft in Catholic countries. There the vernacular was often outlawed by authorities who saw translations as a challenge to the church's traditions and control of doctrine. Fra Luis de Léon, who translated the provocative Song of Songs into Spanish, spent considerable time in jail; Erasmus's Greek New Testament—and eventually all his published work—were put on the Index (the official list of banned books); Robert Estienne, a printer who worked for King Francis I, was censored by the Sorbonne and had to escape to Geneva.

Yet earnest scholars had been prevented from disseminating their work long before the Catholic Church began its campaign against Protestantism, and long before the Protestant Reformation officially began. John Wyclif, a teacher at Oxford, had been an outspoken critic of the church in England before his death in 1384. A translation of the New Testament Vulgate into English that was attributed to him and his circle provoked severe attacks by the Crown and the Church. Twenty years after his death, the so-called Constitutions of Oxford, issued by Archbishop Arundel, forbade future translations of Scripture into English: "We resolve therefore and ordain that no one henceforth on his own authority translate any text of Holy Scripture into the English or any other language. . . . and that no book, pamphlet or tract of this kind . . . be read in part or in whole, publicly or privately." Those who refused to comply were excommunicated. Over two centuries later, when the Protestant victory in England was a foregone conclusion, King James insisted on maintaining the spirit of Arundel's Constitutions by keeping a close eye on the process of translating and circulating a new English Bible: the Bible should "be set out and printed without any marginal notes and only to be used in all Churches of England in time of Divine Service." Despite royal supervision, the fifty-four scholars who

5. Note the repetition of "Jehovah" at the beginning and end of the psalm; otherwise, Eliot has found corresponding words in the Natick-Algonquian tongue, which he here transliterates. See page 116 for Psalm 23 in English.

assembled for two years to translate the Hebrew, Greek, and Aramaic texts into "the King's English" came up with a masterpiece, as well as an elegant account of their project. As they said in their prefatory letter to the readers, translation "it is that openeth the window, to let in the light; that breaketh the shell, that we may eat the kernel." This formulation might be compared with Martin Luther's guiding principle of his own frequently attacked translations. True to his mother tongue and hostile to the Church that would impose its interpretations from without, he claimed to always ask himself when sitting down to translate, "How does a German speak in such a case?"

Henry Knighton: *from* *Chronicle*[1]

This master John Wyclif translated the gospel, which Christ had entrusted to clerks and to the doctors of this church so that they might minister it conveniently to the laity and to meaner people according to the needs of the time and the requirement of the listeners in their hunger of mind; he translated it from Latin into the English, not the angelic, idiom [*in Anglicam linguam non angelicam*],[2] so that by this means that which was formerly familiar to learned clerks and to those of good understanding has become common and open to the laity, and even to those women who know how to read. As a result the pearls of the gospel are scattered and spread before swine,[3] and that which had been precious to religious and to lay persons has become a matter of sport to ordinary people of both.

Martin Luther: *from* On Translating: An Open Letter[1]
To the honorable and worthy N., my esteemed lord and friend.[2]

Grace and peace in Christ, honorable, worthy, and dear lord and friend. I have received your letter with the two questions, or inquiries, to which you ask my reply. First you ask why in translating the words of Paul in Romans 3[:28], *Arbitramur hominem justificari ex fide absque operibus,* I rendered them thus: "We hold that a man is justified without the works of the law, by faith alone."[3] You tell me, besides, that the papists[4] are making a tremendous fuss, because the word *sola* (alone) is not in Paul's text, and this addition of mine to the words of God is not to be tolerated. Second you ask whether the departed saints too intercede for us, since we read that angels indeed do intercede for us? With

---

1. Translated by Anne Hudson. Henry Knighton was an obscure 14th-century English chronicler who like many of his contemporaries had nothing but suspicion for the project announced by the radical John Wyclif: the first complete translation of the Latin Bible into the English vernacular. The early 1380s, when Wyclif's project was underway, were a time of great social unrest for England, marked by peasant rebellions and attacks on the Church by followers of Wyclif such as one Nicholas Hereford, who criticized clerical wealth and corruption. Whether Wycliff himself actually did the translation that began appearing in manuscript in the 1380s is unclear. The importance of his venture is that it promised to put into the hands of the laity the "tool" that it had been the clergy's alone to wield.
2. Knighton sarcastically revises a famous pun recorded by the medieval historian Bede, in which a visiting missionary marvels that the English (Angles) look like angels.
3. A reference to Matthew 7:6.
1. Translated by Charles Michael Jacobs, revised by

E. Theodore Bachmann. Martin Luther had followed his attack on the Church in 1517 with a number of treatises, as well as a German translation of the New Testament in 1522; he swiftly followed with a translation of the Old Testament, which would be published in installments. As his editor Wenceslas Link says in his preface to the letter, he hopes that now "the slander of the godless will be stopped and the scruples of the devout removed." For a fuller treatment of Luther's life, see page 307.
2. The identity of "N." is unknown; editors have suggested that Luther was using a literary device in order to have occasion to explore some issues related to his translation.
3. The Latin Vulgate text, the primary text for Catholics, is actually different, and there is, for example, no word for "alone." The reason for the dispute was the nature of "operibus" or "works," since Luther believed that nothing that man did could save him, while the Catholic Church insisted that man could perform deeds worthy of salvation.
4. Catholics.

reference to the first question, you may give your papists the following answer from me, if you like.

First if I, Dr. Luther, could have expected that all the papists taken together would be capable enough to translate a single chapter of the Scriptures correctly and well, I should certainly have mustered up enough humility to invite their aid and assistance in putting the New Testament into German. But because I knew—and still see with my own eyes—that none of them knows how to translate, or to speak German, I spared them and myself that trouble. It is evident, indeed, that from my German translation they are learning to speak and write German, and so are stealing from me my language, of which they had little knowledge before. They do not thank me for it, however, but prefer to use it against me. However I readily grant them this, for it tickles me that I have taught my ungrateful pupils, even my enemies, how to speak.

Second you may say that I translated the New Testament conscientiously and to the best of my ability. I have compelled no one to read it, but have left that open, doing the work only as a service to those who could not do it better. No one is forbidden to do a better piece of work. If anyone does not want to read it, he can let it alone. I neither ask anybody to read it nor praise anyone who does so. It is my Testament and my translation, and it shall continue to be mine.

* * *

Here, in Romans 2:28, I know very well that the word *solum* is not in the Greek or Latin text: the papists did not have to teach me that. It is a fact that these four letters *s o l a* are not there. And these blockheads stare at them like cows at a new gate. At the same time, they do not see that it conveys the sense of the text; it belongs there if the translation is to be clear and vigorous. I wanted to speak German, not Latin or Greek, since it was German I had undertaken to speak in the translation. But it is the nature of our German language that in speaking of two things, one of which is affirmed and the other denied, we use the word *solum (allein)*[5] along with the word *nicht* [not] or *kein* [no]. * * *

We do not have to inquire of the literal Latin, how we are to speak German, as these asses do. Rather we must inquire about this of the mother in the home, the children on the street, the common man in the marketplace. We must be guided by their language, the way they speak, and do our translating accordingly. That way they will understand it and recognize that we are speaking German to them.

For example, Christ says: *Ex abundantia cordis os loquitur* [Matt. 12:34, Luke 6:45]. If I am to follow these asses, they will lay the original before me literally and translate thus: "Out of the abundance of the heart the mouth speaks." Tell me, is that speaking German? What German could understand something like that? What is "the abundance of the heart"? No German can say that; unless, perhaps, he was trying to say that someone was altogether too magnanimous or too courageous, though even that would not yet be correct. For "abundance of the heart" is not German, any more than "abundance of the house," "abundance of the stove," or "abundance of the bench" is German. But the mother in the home and the common man say this, "What fills the heart overflows the mouth." That is speaking good German, the kind that I have tried for—and unfortunately not always reached or hit upon. For the literal Latin is a great hindrance to speaking good German. * * *

5. In English allein can be translated as either "alone" or "only."

Again, when the angel greets Mary, he says, "Hail Mary, full of grace, the Lord is with you!" [Luke 1:28]. Up to now that has simply been translated according to the literal Latin. Tell me whether that is also good German! When does a German speak like that, "You are full of grace"? What German understands what that is, to be "full of grace"? He would have to think of a keg "full of" beer or a purse "full of" money. Therefore I have translated it, "Thou gracious one," so that a German can at least think his way through to what the angel meant by this greeting.[6] Here, however, the papists are going wild about me, because I have corrupted the Angelic Salutation; though I have still not hit upon the best German rendering for it. Suppose I had taken the best German, and translated the salutation thus: "Hello there, Mary"—for that is what the angel wanted to say, and what he would have said, if he had wanted to greet her in German. Suppose I had done that! I believe that they would have hanged themselves out of tremendous fanaticism for the Virgin Mary, because I had thus destroyed the salutation.

But what do I care if they rage or rave? I shall not prevent them from translating as they please. However I shall translate too, not as they please but as I please. Whoever does not like it can just leave it alone and keep his criticism to himself, for I shall neither look at nor listen to it. They do not have to answer for my translation, nor bear any responsibility for it. Listen well to this! I shall say "gracious [*holdselige*] Mary," and "dear [*liebe*] Mary," and let them say "Mary full of grace [*volgnaden*]." Whoever knows German knows very well what a fine, expressive [*hertzlich*] word that word *liebe* is: the dear Mary, the dear God, the dear emperor, the dear prince, the dear man, the dear child. I do not know whether this word *liebe* can be said in Latin or other languages with such fulness of sentiment, so that it pierces and rings through the heart, through all the senses, as it does in our language. * * *

Therefore I must let the literal words go and try to learn how the German says that which the Hebrew expresses with *ish chamudoth*. I find then that the German says this, "You dear Daniel," "You dear Mary," or "You gracious maid," "You lovely maiden," "You gentle girl," and the like. For a translator must have a great store of words, so that he can have them on hand in the event that one word does not fit in every context.

And why should I talk so much about translating? If I were to point out the reasons and considerations back of all my words, I should need a year to write on it. I have learned by experience what an art and what a task translating is. * * *[7]

The King James Bible: *from* The Translators to the Reader[1]

Happie is the man that delighteth in the Scripture, and thrise happie that meditateth in it day and night.

But how shall men meditate in that, which they cannot understand? How shall they understand that which is kept close in an unknowen tongue? As it is written, *Except I know the power of voice, I shall be to him that speaketh, a Barbarian, and he that speaketh, shalbe a Barbarian to me.* The Apostle excepteth no tongue; not Hebrewe the ancientest, not Greeke the most copious, not Latine the finest.[2] Nature

6. See a translation of this passage from Luther's German on page 121. There is more to Luther's translation than good German, however; by denying Mary the "gratia" or grace visited upon her by God, he is also challenging the semi-divine status which Catholics would give her.
7. Luther ends in his usual vitriolic fashion, saying that "Scribblers and papal asses may blaspheme me, but real Christians—and Christ, their Lord—bless me!"
1. The 1611 Bible was prefaced with a long letter to the

"readers," written by Miles Smith, one of the 54 "learned men" who had been involved with the translation. From Oxford and a professed Calvinist, Smith saw the translation through from beginning to end, completing most of the final editing on his own. He became Bishop of Gloucester in 1616, probably as a reward for his work.
2. From the famous passage on love in 1 Corinthians 13; the "Apostle" is Paul.

thought a naturall man to confesse, that all of us in those tongues which wee doe not understand, are plainely deafe; wee may turne the deafe eare unto them. The *Scythian* counted the *Athenian,* whom he did not understand, barbarous; so the *Romane* did the *Syrian,* and the *Iew,* (even S. *Heirome*[3] himselfe calleth the Hebrew tongue barbarous, belike because it was strange to so many) so the Emperor of *Constantinople* calleth the *Latine* tongue, barbarous, though Pope *Nicolas* do storme at it: so the *Iewes* long before *Christ,* called all other nations, *Lognazim,* which is little better than barbarous. Therefore as one complaineth, that always in the Senate of *Rome,* there was one or other that called for an interpreter:[4] so lest the Church be driven to like exigent, it is necessary to have translations in a readinesse. Translation it is that openeth the window, to let in the light: that breaketh the shell, that we may eat the kernel; that putteth aside the curtaine, that we may looke into the most Holy place; that remooveth the cover of the well, that wee may come by the water, even as *Iacob* rolled away the stone from the mouth of the well, by which means the flockes of *Laban* were watered.[5] Indeede, without translation into the vulgar tongue, the unlearned are but like children at *Iacobs* well (which was deepe) without a bucket or something to draw with: or as that person mentioned by *Esay,* to whom when a sealed booke was delivered, with this motion, *Reade this, I pray thee,* hee was faine to make this answere, *I cannot, for it is sealed.*[6] * * *

Wee doe not deny, nay wee affirme and avow, that the very meanest translation of the Bible in English, set foorth by men of our profession (for wee have seene none of theirs of the whole Bible as yet) containeth the word of God, nay, is the word of God. As the Kings Speech which hee uttered in Parliament, being translated into *French, Dutch, Italian,* and *Latine,* is still the Kings Speech, though it be not interpreted by every Translator with the like grace, nor peradventure so fitly for phrase, nor so expressly for sence, every where. For it is confessed, that things are to take their denomination of the greater part; and a naturall man could say, *Verùm ubi multa nitent in carmine, non ego paucis offendor maculis, etc.*[7] A man may be counted a vertuous man, though hee have made many slips in his life, (els, there were none vertuous, *for in many things we offend all*)[8] also a comely man and lovely, though hee have some warts upon his hand, yes, not onely freakles upon his face, but also skarres. No cause therefore why the word translated should bee denied to be the word, or forbidden to be currant, notwithstanding that some imperfections and blemishes maybe noted in the setting foorth of it. For what ever was perfect under the Sunne, where Apostles or Apostolike men, that is, men indued with an extraordinary measure of Gods spirit, and priviledged with the priviledge of infallibilitie, had not their hand? The Romanistes therefore in refusing to heare, and daring to burne the Word translated,[9] did no lesse then despite the spirit of grace, from whom originally it proceeded, and whose sense and meaning, as well as mans weaknesse would enable, it did expresse. * * *

3. St. Jerome, 4th-century translator of the Hebrew and Aramaic Bible into Latin.

4. The "complainer" is Cicero, who writes of the request in his *De finibus,* ch. 5.

5. In Genesis 29:10, Jacob waters the flocks of Laban, his uncle, after he sees Laban's daughter Rachel, with whom he falls in love.

6. Isaiah 29:11, in a passage where the prophet is accusing the Hebrews of blindness; for them "the revelation of all this has become like the words of a sealed scroll."

7. From Horace's *Art of Poetry.* "But when the beauties of a poem are more in number, I shall not take offence at a few blots [which a careless hand has let drop, or human frailty has failed to avert]."

8. Epistle to James, 3:2.

9. A reference to the Roman Catholics; in the 1520s, Cardinal Wolsey had arranged for the burning of all "untrue translations" of the Bible in London. William Tyndale's Englished Bible, published in Worms in 1526, would have been caught in the conflagration.

We cannot follow a better patterne for elocution then God himselfe; therefore hee using divers words, in his holy writ, and indifferently for one thing in nature: we, if wee will not be superstitious, may use the same libertie in our English versions out of *Hebrew* and *Greeke*, for that copie or store that he hath given us. Lastly, wee have on the one side avoided the scrupulositie of the Puritanes, who leave the olde Ecclesiasti-call words, and betake them to other, as when they put *washing* for *Baptisme*, and *Congregation* in stead of *Church:* as also on the other side we have shunned the ob-scuritie of the Papists, in their *Azimes, Tunike, Rational, Holocausts, Præpuce, Pasche,* and a number of such like, whereof their late Translation is full, and that of purpose to darken the sense, that since they must needs translate the Bible, yet by the language thereof, it may bee kept from being understood.[1] But we desire that the Scripture may speake like it selfe, as in the language of *Canaan,* that it may bee un-derstood even of the very vulgar. * * *

It remaineth, that we commend thee to God, and to the Spirit of his grace, which is able to build further then we can aske or thinke. Hee removeth the scales from our eyes, the vaile from our hearts, opening our wits that wee may understand his word, enlarg-ing our hearts, yea correcting our affections, that we may love it above gold and silver, yea that we may love it to the end. Ye are brought unto fountaines of living water which yee digged not; doe not cast earth into them with the Philistines, neither preferre broken pits before them with the wicked Iewes.[2] Others have laboured, and you may enter into their labours; O receive not so great things in vaine, O despise not so great salvation!

+ + ⚓ + +

Women and the Vernacular

The phrase "mother tongue" is not an idle one. Children first hear language in the womb, in the cradle, and at the breast. In medieval and early modern Europe, that language was rarely (if ever) the Latin of clerics and the learned. When Dante's character reaches the final circle of Hell, he calls his Tuscan language the "the tongue that cries, 'mama,' 'daddy'"—one, in short, unsuited in its childlike innocence to describe the fearful punishments awaiting the world's worst sinners. While a few medieval women such as the abbess Hildegard of Bingen wrote ex-tensively in Latin, the vast majority of those who set pen on paper did so using the oral, vernac-ular languages with which they were familiar. In some cases, such as that of Hadewijch of Bra-bant, they were the first to use a given vernacular for writing, and so helped to launch the linguistic revolution that would shape the face of modern Europe.

It is notable that Hadewijch, a Beguine or religious woman unconstrained by strict con-vent rules, used her native Flemish to write letters and mystical poetry. Unlike most women of the thirteenth century, Hadewijch was versed in Latin. As one critic has suggested, the "mother tongue" is the language not only of childhood, but of intimacy, and Hadewijch chose Flemish to express her thoughts to those to whom she felt closest, namely God and other Beguines. The Renaissance as commonly understood—a profound engagement with the literature and philos-ophy of classical antiquity, and as a result of that engagement, an assertion of the secular indi-vidual—was somewhat peripheral to women writers like Hadewijch. Particularly in northern

1. Puritans in England read the Geneva Bible, published in 1560 by English exiles who were associated with John Calvin. An English translation of the New Testament by a group of Roman Catholic scholars who had been exiled from England during the reign of Elizabeth I was known as the Rheims-Douai Bible and was published in 1582;

the Old Testament would appear in 1609–1610.
2. A reference to the prophet Jeremiah's complaints about the Hebrews: "Two evils have my people done: they have forsaken me, the source of living waters; they have dug themselves cisterns, broken cisterns, that hold no water."

Italy in the fifteenth century, a number of women did benefit from an extraordinary education and were fluent in the Latin writings of antiquity. Laura Cereta (page 208) was an early advocate of women's education, and the accomplished Isotta Nogarola wrote a Latin disputation on Adam's and Eve's "equal or unequal sin." For the most part, however, women's writing before the fifteenth century centered on spiritual issues: Marguerite Porete's *Mirror for Simple Souls,* for which she was burned at the stake; Catherine of Siena's dialogue with God and almost 400 extant letters; the anchoress Julian of Norwich's *Showings.* The Reformation led to considerable soul-searching among women, in manuscript and in print. Marguerite de Navarre wrote a meditative treatise on her faith in addition to her far better-known imitation of Boccaccio, the *Heptameron* (page 189), and Queen Elizabeth I was as acclaimed for her paraphrases of the psalms as she was for her public orations. Many a militant woman during England's Puritan Revolution published her visions, such as Anna Trapnel, a radical Puritan who successfully defended herself against charges of witchcraft.

The feminist historian Joan Kelley has asked "Did women have a Renaissance?" With respect to women's cultural achievements, the answer is a definitive yes. Early modernity produced Teresa of Avila, the Countess of Pembroke, Elizabeth Carey, Veronica Franco, the painter Artemesia Gentileschi. The Ursulines, an order of nuns that chose to defy newly enforced rules of enclosure in the wake of the Counter-Reformation, took as their mission the creation of schools for girls in France, Italy, and the French settlements in Canada, and many noblewomen founded private girls' schools in their own homes. At the same time, women's Renaissances followed a path very different from that of most Renaissance men. As in the case of Marguerite, the emergence of women as secular writers was later than that of men (with the exception of the indefatigable Christine de Pizan, probably the first modern woman to make her living as a writer—of romances, compilations, and biographies of famous women, among other things—and the author of sayings as pungent as "Just as women's bodies are softer than men's, so their understanding is sharper"). A number of women contributed to the sixteenth-century vogue of the sonnet sequence, just as they would be formative in the rise of the modern, psychological novel.

Not surprisingly, however, as the rate of women's literacy gradually rose and mothers became increasingly central to their children's education, there was a backlash against their newfound talents. In one of his *Colloquies,* the open-minded humanist Erasmus finds himself forced to defend the intelligent middle-class "Lady" against an ignorant monk who complains that women surround themselves with too many books. Even as late as the close of the seventeenth century, Sor Juana Inés de la Cruz, probably the most erudite woman of colonial Mexico, would need to justify her considerable intellectual talents, relying on her cultivated Spanish prose and a wealth of Latin quotations to do so. Yet perhaps paradoxically, the very necessity of defense is what compelled Sor Juana and a number of her contemporaries to write at all. The excerpts below take us from Dante to Sor Juana, revealing the extent to which the "tongue that cries mama" was a tremendously enabling vehicle for women's entrance into the world of early modern letters.

Dante Alighieri: *from* Letter to Can Grande Della Scala[1]

The title of the work is, "Here begins the Comedy of Dante Alighieri, a Florentine by birth but not in character." To understand the title, it must be known that comedy is derived from *comos,* "a village," and from *oda,* "a song," so that a comedy is, so to speak, "a rustic song." Comedy, then, is a certain genre of poetic narrative differing from all others. For it differs from tragedy in its matter, in that tragedy is tranquil and

1. Translated by Robert S. Haller. The dedicatory letter to Can Grande della Scala, one of Dante's most generous patrons while he lived in exile from Florence, was written upon the completion of *Paradiso,* the third and final part of *The Divine Comedy.* Written in the Tuscan dialect, the

Comedy was one of the first major literary works of medieval Europe to be both composed in a vernacular and based on texts of classical antiquity; see Volume B for selections.

conducive to wonder at the beginning, but foul and conducive to horror at the end, or catastrophe, for which reason it is derived from *tragos,* meaning "goat," and *oda,* making it, as it were, a "goat song," that is, foul as a goat is foul. This is evident in Seneca's tragedies.[2] Comedy, on the other hand, introduces a situation of adversity, but ends its matter in prosperity, as is evident in Terence's comedies.[3] * * * And, as well, they differ in their manner of speaking. Tragedy uses an elevated and sublime style, while comedy uses an unstudied and low style. * * *

So from this it should be clear why the present work is called the *Comedy.* For, if we consider the matter, it is, at the beginning, that is, in Hell, foul and conducive to horror, but at the end, in Paradise, prosperous, conducive to pleasure, and welcome. And if we consider the manner of speaking, it is unstudied and low, since its speech is the vernacular, in which even women communicate.[4]

Desiderius Erasmus: *from* The Abbot and the Learned Lady[1]

ANTRONIUS: What furnishings do I see here?[2]

MAGDALIA: Elegant, aren't they?

ANTRONIUS: How elegant I don't know, but certainly unbecoming both to a young miss and a married woman.

MAGDALIA: Why?

ANTRONIUS: Because the whole place is full of books . . .

MAGDALIA: So you approve of those who live basely if only they have a good time?

ANTRONIUS: I believe those who have a good time are living well.

MAGDALIA: Where does this good time come from? From externals or from within?

ANTRONIUS: From externals.

MAGDALIA: Shrewd abbot but stupid philosopher! Tell me: how do you measure good times?

ANTRONIUS: By sleep, dinner parties, doing as one likes, money, honours.

MAGDALIA: But if to these things God added wisdom, you wouldn't enjoy yourself?

ANTRONIUS: What do you mean by wisdom?

MAGDALIA: This: understanding that a man is not happy without the goods of the mind; that wealth, honours, noble birth make him neither happier nor better.

ANTRONIUS: Away with that wisdom!

MAGDALIA: What if I enjoy reading a good author more than you do hunting, drinking, or playing dice? You won't think I'm having a good time?

2. The Roman philosopher and dramatist Seneca, who lived during the 1st century, wrote at least nine tragedies based on Greek subjects, and a tenth entitled *Octavia,* which took Roman history as its topic.

3. Terence was a Roman writer of comedies from the 2nd century B.C.E.

4. The "lowliness" of the vernacular hence makes it available to the uneducated, and there is ample evidence that the *Comedy* was read aloud to audiences. In his extensive treatise (in Latin) on the eloquence of the vernacular (*De vulgari eloquentia*), Dante defends the suppleness of Italian as a major literary language and defines the vernacular as follows: "that what we call the vernacular speech is that to which children are accustomed by those who are about them when they first begin to distinguish words; or to put it more shortly, we say that the vernacular speech is that which we acquire without any rule, by imitating our nurses."

1. Translated by Craig Thompson. Desiderius Erasmus (1469–1536), author of *Praise of Folly* and numerous other works, was also skilled in the art of writing dialogues or *Colloquies.* This one, first published in 1524, treats of an encounter between an ignorant Benedictine abbot and a "learned lady" who is probably modeled on Margaret Roper, the oldest daughter of Thomas More. In an earlier work, Erasmus had written that he had once thought women unfit for learning, but after meeting More's three daughters, educated by their father, he changed his mind. Margaret in fact translated into English Erasmus's popular Latin version of the Lord's prayer, *Precatio dominica;* it was published in 1524. For more on Erasmus, see the introduction to his *Praise of Folly,* page 293.

2. The setting for the encounter is obviously in the young woman's library.

ANTRONIUS: I wouldn't live like that.

MAGDALIA: I'm not asking what *you* would enjoy most, but what *ought* to be enjoyable.

ANTRONIUS: I wouldn't want my monks to spend their time on books.

MAGDALIA: Yet my husband heartily approves of my doing so. But exactly why do you disapprove of this in your monks?

ANTRONIUS: Because I find they're less tractable; they talk back by quoting from decrees and decretals, from Peter and Paul.[3]

MAGDALIA: So your rules conflict with those of Peter and Paul?

ANTRONIUS: What *they* may enjoin I don't know, but still I don't like a monk who talks back. And I don't want any of mine to know more than I do.

MAGDALIA: You could avoid that by endeavouring to know as much as possible.

ANTRONIUS: I haven't the leisure.

MAGDALIA: How come?

ANTRONIUS: Because I've no free time.

MAGDALIA: No free time to grow wise?

ANTRONIUS: No.

MAGDALIA: I won't say how you strike me. But why do these furnishings displease you?

ANTRONIUS: Because distaff and spindle are the proper equipment for women.

MAGDALIA: Isn't it a wife's business to manage the household and rear the children?

ANTRONIUS: It is.

MAGDALIA: Do you think she can manage so big a job without wisdom?

ANTRONIUS: I suppose not.

MAGDALIA: But books teach me this wisdom.

ANTRONIUS: Sixty-two monks I have in the monastery, yet you won't find a single book in my cell.

MAGDALIA: Those monks are well provided for!

ANTRONIUS: I could put up with books, but not Latin ones.

MAGDALIA: Why not?

ANTRONIUS: Because that language isn't fit for women.

MAGDALIA: I want to know why.

ANTRONIUS: Because it does little to protect their chastity.

MAGDALIA: Therefore French books, full of the most frivolous stories, do promote chastity?[4]

ANTRONIUS: There's another reason.

MAGDALIA: Tell me plainly, whatever it is.

ANTRONIUS: They're safer from priests if they don't know Latin.

MAGDALIA: Very little danger from you in that respect, since you take such pains not to know Latin!

ANTRONIUS: The public agrees with me, because it's a rare and exceptional thing for a woman to know Latin.

MAGDALIA: Why cite the public, the worst possible authority on conduct? Why tell me of custom, the mistress of every vice? Accustom yourself to the best; then the unusual will become habitual; the unpleasant enjoyable; the apparently unseemly, seemly.

ANTRONIUS: I hear you.

MAGDALIA: Is it fitting for a German woman to learn French?

3. Peter was one of the original disciples of Christ, often seen as founder of the Church; Paul was the 1st-century author of numerous epistles to Romans, Corinthians, and other groups he was active in converting to Christianity.
4. Probable reference to the many popular chivalric romances circulating at the time.

ANTRONIUS: Of course.

MAGDALIA: Why?

ANTRONIUS: To talk with those who know French.

MAGDALIA: And you think it unsuitable for me to know Latin in order to converse daily with authors so numerous, so eloquent, so learned, so wise; with counsellors so faithful?

ANTRONIUS: Books ruin women's wits—which are none too plentiful anyway.

MAGDALIA: How plentiful *yours* are, I don't know. Assuredly I prefer to spend mine, however slight, on profitable studies rather than on prayers said by rote, all-night parties, and heavy drinking.

ANTRONIUS: Bookishness drives people mad . . . I've often heard the common saying, "A wise woman is twice foolish."[5]

MAGDALIA: That's commonly said, yes, but by fools. A woman truly wise is not wise in her own conceit. On the other hand, one who thinks herself wise when she knows nothing is indeed twice foolish.

ANTRONIUS: I don't know how it is, but as pack-saddles don't fit an ox, so learning doesn't fit a woman.

MAGDALIA: But you can't deny that pack-saddles would fit an ox better than a mitre would fit an ass or a swine. What's your feeling about the Virgin Mother?

ANTRONIUS: I reverence her.

MAGDALIA: Didn't she read books?

ANTRONIUS: Yes, but not these.

MAGDALIA: What did she read, then?

ANTRONIUS: The canonical hours.[6]

MAGDALIA: According to which use?

ANTRONIUS: The Benedictine.

MAGDALIA: Very likely! What about Paula and Eustochium? Didn't they read the sacred Scriptures?[7]

ANTRONIUS: But that's rare nowadays.

MAGDALIA: So was an unlettered abbot a rare bird once upon a time! Nowadays nothing's more common. Once upon a time princes and emperors excelled as much in learning as in might. But even now this isn't so rare as you suppose. In Spain and Italy there are not a few women of the highest rank who can rival any man. In England there are the More daughters, in Germany the Pirckheimer and Blaurer ladies.[8] If you're not careful, the net result will be that we'll preside in the theological schools, preach in the churches, and wear your mitres.

ANTRONIUS: God forbid!

MAGDALIA: No, it will be up to *you* to forbid. But if you keep on as you've begun, geese may do the preaching sooner than put up with you tongue-tied pastors. The world's a stage that's topsy-turvy now, as you see. Everyone must play his part or—exit.

5. One of the many proverbs cited in the course of the dialogue that Erasmus would incorporate into his massive collection of common sayings, the *Adages.*

6. The times of day (and night) when the breviary or Book of Hours containing the Divine Office had to be read by those in religious orders.

7. Paula, heiress of a wealthy Roman family, and her daughter Eustochium were disciples of St. Jerome in the late 4th century; with him, they left Rome and settled in Bethlehem, where the two women presided over a convent. Some of Jerome's most stirring letters are to Paula; Letter 107, to Paula's daughter-in-law, instructs on "a girl's education" and suggests that she should "love the manuscripts of the Holy Scriptures."

8. Erasmus's friend Willibald Pirckheimer had eight sisters and five daughters, who were famed for their learning; Margarete Blaurer, sister of Ambrosius and Thomas, was known as a good Latinist.

Catherine of Siena: *from* a Letter to Raymond of Capua[1]

[God speaks to Catherine in a vision, which ends:]

"But in everything, in this as well as in every other thing,[2] my children, I will fulfill your desire, along with much suffering. My providence will be more or less near people in proportion to the measure of their confidence in me. And whatever I provide over and above what their measure holds, I do so to fulfill the desire of my servants who are praying to me for them. For I am not one to spurn those who humbly ask me, whether for themselves or for others. That is why I am inviting you to ask me for mercy for these and for the entire world. Conceive, my children, and give birth to this child, the human race, with hatred and sorrow for sin and with blazing and yearning love."

Oh dearest and sweetest father, when I saw and heard so much then from gentle First Truth, my heart felt as if it would break in two! I am dying and cannot die! Have compassion on your poor daughter, who is living in such torment because God is so offended, and who has no one to whom she can unburden herself—except that the Holy Spirit has provided for me interiorly by his mercy, and outwardly has provided me a diversion in writing.[3]

Let's all take heart in Christ gentle Jesus, and let suffering be our refreshment. And let's eagerly and without hesitation accept the sweet invitation, dear father. Rejoice, because you have been called so sweetly. Suffer with great joy and patience, without being crippled by pain, if you want to be a spouse of Truth and comforter of my soul. In no other way could you have grace, and that would deeply sadden me. That is why I said I long to see you a follower and lover of truth.

I'll say no more. Keep living in God's holy and tender love.

Bless Frate Matteo[4] in Christ gentle Jesus.

This letter and another I sent you I've written with my own hand on the Isola della Rocca, with so many sighs and tears that I couldn't see even when I was seeing.[5] But I was filled with wonder at myself and God's goodness when I thought of his mercy toward his human creatures and his overflowing providence toward me. He provided for my refreshment by giving me the ability to write—a consolation I've never known because of my ignorance—so that when I come down from the heights I might have a little something to vent my heart, lest it burst. Because he didn't want to take me yet from this dark life, he fixed it in my mind in a marvelous manner, the way

---

1. Translated by Susanne Noffke. St. Catherine of Siena (1347–1380), the twenty-fifth child of a Sienese dyer, became one of the most influential women of her time, thanks largely to the visits she made and the hundreds of letters she wrote to popes, kings and queens, and civic leaders throughout Italy. A member of the third order of Dominicans, she didn't live in a convent but devoted her short life to the assistance of others. In this particular letter to the Dominican Raymond of Capua, assigned as her confessor when the Dominican order suspected her of heresy, she recounts a lengthy vision that would become the basis for her famous *Dialogue*, a mystical treatise uttered to her by God. The letter is probably from late 1377.
2. The letter opened with Catherine's recounting a prayer she had uttered to God while attending Mass, and God's understanding response. At this point, God has just told

Catherine that people should "remove the cloud" of self-centeredness from their eyes, and then they will be able to "know the truth and love it."
3. At the end of the letter, Catherine will tell Raymond how she miraculously learned how to write. Always dependent on a group of scribes for her letters, she had no one near her when she experienced the vision she has just finished describing.
4. A Dominican who had accompanied Raymond to Rome.
5. The Isola della Rocca, or the "Island of the Fortress," refers to the fortified castle of the Salimbeni family, to the southwest of Siena. Catherine frequently visited Siena's warring families in their country residences in an effort to reconcile them.

a teacher does when he gives his pupil a model. Shortly after you left me, I began to learn in my sleep, with the glorious evangelist John and Thomas Aquinas.[6]

Forgive me for writing so much, but my hands and tongue run along with my heart. . . .

Sor Juana Inés de la Cruz: *from* Response to "Sor Filotea"[1]

In truth, I have written nothing except when compelled and constrained, and then only to give pleasure to others; not alone without pleasure of my own, but with absolute repugnance, for I have never deemed myself one who has any worth in letters or the wit necessity demands of one who would write; and thus my customary response to those who press me, above all in sacred matters, is, what capacity of reason have I? what application? what resources? what rudimentary knowledge of such matters beyond that of the most superficial scholarly degrees? Leave these matters to those who understand them; I wish no quarrel with the Holy Office,[2] for I am ignorant, and I tremble that I may express some proposition that will cause offense or twist the true meaning of some scripture. I do not study to write, even less to teach—which in one like myself were unseemly pride—but only to the end that if I study, I will be ignorant of less. This is my response, and these are my feelings.

I have never written of my own choice, but at the urging of others, to whom with reason I might say, *You have compelled me.*[3] But one truth I shall not deny (first, because it is well-known to all, and second, because although it has not worked in my favor, God has granted me the mercy of loving truth above all else), which is that from the moment I was first illuminated by the light of reason, my inclination[4] toward letters has been so vehement, so overpowering, that not even the admonitions of others—and I have suffered many—nor my own meditations—and they have not been few—have been sufficient to cause me to forswear this natural impulse that God placed in me: the Lord God knows why, and for what purpose. And He knows that I have prayed that He dim the light of my reason, leaving only that which is needed to keep His Law, for there are those who would say that all else is unwanted in a woman, and there are even those who would hold that such knowledge does injury.

6. The evangelist John was the writer of the last book of the New Testament, the Apocalypse; the Dominican Thomas Aquinas was the most important theologian in the medieval period, and his *Summa theologica* provided a synthesis between Christian and Aristotelian thought.
1. Translated by Margaret Sayers Peden. The colonial Mexican poet Sor Juana (1648–1695) became famous for her learning and for her sonnets while still a teenager. She then became a nun, continuing her studies despite growing opposition from church authorities. The "response," written in 1691, is a calm defense of women's rights to learn and write against one "Sor Filotea" or "Lover of God"—a pseudonym, as Sor Juana well knew, for the Bishop of Puebla. The Bishop had attacked Sor Juana's literary and scientific pursuits on the grounds that nuns should devote themselves to Christ: "It is a pity," he writes, "that so great a mind should stoop to lowly earthbound knowledge and not desire to probe into what transpires in heaven." Sor Juana had been an outspoken critic of a sermon by a famous Portuguese Jesuit, Antonio de Vieyra, and the Bishop himself had undertaken to publish Sor Juana's remarks. But most likely reacting to criticism from authorities above him, the Bishop then urged Sor

Juana in Sor Filotea's voice to give up her studies. At stake in the Bishop's letter is discomfort over Sor Juana's considerable use of Greek and Latin texts in her critique, and over her possibly heretical views regarding the meaning of Christ's love for humanity. The first few pages of Sor Juana's response stress her unworthiness and inability to write unless ordered to do so. For more on Sor Juana, see the introduction to her sonnets, page 241.
2. The Holy Office of the Inquisition attempted to enforce fidelity to Christian doctrine. In Latin America, those who were not European or who were ethnically mixed (as was Sor Juana, a *criolla* or Creole) did not come under the Holy Office's jurisdiction.
3. In 2 Corinthians 12:11, Paul says that the Corinthians have "compelled" him to boast about himself. Sor Juana quotes the Bible in Latin; all italicized phrases are in Latin in the original text.
4. In Spanish, *inclinación* can mean both a "gift" and a "temptation"; Sor Juana is clearly playing on both meanings. In his own letter to Sor Juana, the Bishop ("Sor Filotea") claims that he would call the intellectual blessings Sor Juana enjoys "punishments."

And my Holy Father knows too that as I have been unable to achieve this (my prayer has not been answered), I have sought to veil the light of my reason—along with my name—and to offer it up only to Him who bestowed it upon me, and He knows that none other was the cause for my entering into Religion, notwithstanding that the spiritual exercises and company of a community were repugnant to the freedom and quiet I desired for my studious endeavors.[5] And later, in that community, the Lord God knows—and, in the world, only the one who must know[6]—how diligently I sought to obscure my name, and how this was not permitted, saying it was temptation: and so it would have been. If it were in my power, lady, to repay you in some part what I owe you, it might be done by telling you this thing which has never before passed my lips, except to be spoken to the one who should hear it. It is my hope that by having opened wide to you the doors of my heart, by having made patent to you its most deeply-hidden secrets, you will deem my confidence not unworthy of the debt I owe to your most august person and to your most uncommon favors.

Continuing the narration of my inclinations, of which I wish to give you a thorough account, I will tell you that I was not yet three years old when my mother determined to send one of my elder sisters to learn to read at a school for girls we call the *Amigas*.[7] Affection, and mischief, caused me to follow her, and when I observed how she was being taught her lessons I was so inflamed with the desire to know how to read, that deceiving—for so I knew it to be—the mistress, I told her that my mother had meant for me to have lessons too. She did not believe it, as it was little to be believed, but, to humor me, she acceded. I continued to go there, and she continued to teach me, but now, as experience had disabused her, with all seriousness; and I learned so quickly that before my mother knew of it I could already read, for my teacher had kept it from her in order to reveal the surprise and reap the reward at one and the same time. And I, you may be sure, kept the secret, fearing that I would be whipped for having acted without permission. The woman who taught me, may God bless and keep her, is still alive and can bear witness to all I say.

I also remember that in those days, my tastes being those common to that age, I abstained from eating cheese because I had heard that it made one slow of wits, for in me the desire for learning was stronger than the desire for eating—as powerful as that is in children. When later, being six or seven, and having learned how to read and write, along with all the other skills of needle-work and household arts that girls learn, it came to my attention that in Mexico City there were Schools, and a University, in which one studied the sciences. The moment I heard this, I began to plague my mother with insistent and importunate pleas: she should dress me in boy's clothing and send me to Mexico City to live with relatives, to study and be tutored at the University. She would not permit it, and she was wise, but I assuaged my disappointment by reading the many and varied books belonging to my grandfather, and there were not enough punishments, nor reprimands, to prevent me from reading: so that when I came to the city many marveled, not so much at my natural wit, as at my memory, and at the amount of learning I had mastered at an age when many have scarcely learned to speak well.

---

5. Sor Juana had entered the Carmelite order in 1669; finding the reformed order of Santa Teresa of Avila too strict, she chose instead the laxer Convent of Santa Paula, part of the Hieronomite Order ("Sisters of Jerome").

6. Probably Sor Juana's confessor.

7. Friends; these were schools generally run by women in their private homes.

I began to study Latin grammar[8]—in all, I believe, I had no more than twenty lessons—and so intense was my concern that though among women (especially a woman in the flower of her youth) the natural adornment of one's hair is held in such high esteem, I cut off mine to the breadth of some four to six fingers, measuring the place it had reached, and imposing upon myself the condition that if by the time it had again grown to that length I had not learned such and such a thing I had set for myself to learn while my hair was growing, I would again cut it off as punishment for being so slow-witted. And it did happen that my hair grew out and still I had not learned what I had set for myself—because my hair grew quickly and I learned slowly—and in fact I did cut it in punishment for such stupidity: for there seemed to me no cause for a head to be adorned with hair and naked of learning—which was the more desired embellishment. And so I entered the religious order, knowing that life there entailed certain conditions (I refer to superficial, and not fundamental, regards) most repugnant to my nature; but given the total antipathy I felt for marriage, I deemed convent life the least unsuitable and the most honorable I could elect if I were to insure my salvation. Working against that end, first (as, finally, the most important) was the matter of all the trivial aspects of my nature that nourished my pride, such as wishing to live alone, and wishing to have no obligatory occupation that would inhibit the freedom of my studies, nor the sounds of a community that would intrude upon the peaceful silence of my books. These desires caused me to falter some while in my decision, until certain learned persons enlightened me, explaining that they were temptation, and, with divine favor, I overcame them, and took upon myself the state which now so unworthily I hold. I believed that I was fleeing from myself, but— wretch that I am!—I brought with me my worst enemy, my inclination, which I do not know whether to consider a gift or a punishment from Heaven, for once dimmed and encumbered by the many activities common to Religion, that inclination exploded in me like gunpowder, proving how *privation is the source of appetite.*

I turned again (which is badly put, for I never ceased), I continued, then, in my studious endeavour (which for me was respite during those moments not occupied by my duties) of reading and more reading, of study and more study, with no teachers but my books. Thus I learned how difficult it is to study those soulless letters, lacking a human voice or the explication of a teacher. But I suffered this labor happily for my love of learning. Oh, had it only been for love of God, which were proper, how worthwhile it would have been! I strove mightily to elevate these studies, to dedicate them to His service, as the goal to which I aspired was to study Theology—it seeming to me debilitating for a Catholic not to know everything in this life of the Divine Mysteries that can be learned through natural means—and, being a nun and not a layperson, it was seemly that I profess my vows to learning through ecclesiastical channels; and especially, being a daughter of a Saint Jerome and a Saint Paula,[9] it was essential that such erudite parents not be shamed by a witless daughter. This is the argument I proposed to myself, and it seemed to me well-reasoned. It was, however (and this cannot be denied) merely glorification and approbation of my inclination, and enjoyment of it offered as justification.

And so I continued, as I have said, directing the course of my studies toward the peak of Sacred Theology, it seeming necessary to me, in order to scale those heights,

---

8. An unusual thing for a girl. Latin was the language of universities in Mexico as in Europe.
9. An allusion to the order and convent Sor Juana has cho-sen for herself. The 4th-century Roman noblewoman Paula and her daughter were close friends of St. Jerome, with whom they traveled to Bethlehem.

to climb the steps of the human sciences and arts; for how could one undertake the study of the Queen of Sciences if first one had not come to know her servants?[1] How, without Logic, could I be apprised of the general and specific way in which the Holy Scripture is written? How, without Rhetoric, could I understand its figures, its tropes, its locutions? How, without Physics, so many innate questions concerning the nature of animals, their sacrifices, wherein exist so many symbols, many already declared, many still to be discovered? How should I know whether Saul's being refreshed by the sound of David's harp was due to the virtue and natural power of Music, or to a transcendent power God wished to place in David?[2] How, without Arithmetic, could one understand the computations of the years, days, months, hours, those mysterious weeks communicated by Gabriel to Daniel,[3] and others for whose understanding one must know the nature, concordance, and properties of numbers? How, without Geometry, could one measure the Holy Arc of the Covenant and the Holy City of Jerusalem, whose mysterious measures are foursquare in all their dimensions, as well as the miraculous proportions of all their parts? How, without Architecture, could one know the great Temple of Solomon, of which God Himself was the Author who conceived the disposition and the design, and the Wise King but the overseer who executed it, of which temple there was no foundation without mystery no column without symbolism, no cornice without allusion, no architrave without significance; and similarly others of its parts, of which the least fillet was never intended solely for the service and complement of Art, but as symbol of greater things? How, without great knowledge of the laws and parts of which History is comprised, could one understand historical Books? Or those recapitulations in which many times what happened first is seen in the narrated account to have happened later? How, without great learning in Canon and Civil Law, could one understand Legal Books? How, without great erudition, could one apprehend the secular histories of which the Holy Scripture makes mention, such as the many customs of the Gentiles, their many rites, their many ways of speaking? How without the abundant laws and lessons of the Holy Fathers could one understand the obscure lesson of the Prophets? And without being expert in Music, how could one understand the exquisite precision of the musical proportions that grace so many Scriptures, particularly those in which Abraham beseeches God in defense of the Cities,[4] asking whether He would spare the place were there but fifty just men therein; and then Abraham reduced that number to five less than fifty, forty-five, which is a ninth, and is as Mi to Re; then to forty, which is a tone, and is as Re to Mi; from forty to thirty, which is a diatessaron, the interval of the perfect fourth; from thirty to twenty, which is the perfect fifth, and from twenty to ten, which is the octave, the diapason; and as there are no further harmonic proportions, made no further reductions. How might one understand this without Music? And there in the Book of Job, God says to Job: *Shalt thou be able to join together the shining stars the Pleiades, or canst thou stop the turning about of Arcturus? Canst thou bring forth the day star in its time and make the evening star to rise upon the children of the earth?*[5] Which message, without knowledge of Astrology, would be impossible to apprehend. And not only these noble sciences; there is no applied art that is not mentioned. And,

---

1. Theology is the "queen" and her "servants" will be the numerous disciplines practiced in the 17th-century university.
2. David plays his harp for King Saul in 1 Kings 16: "and Saul was refreshed, and was better, for the evil spirit departed from him."
3. The angel Gabriel appears to Daniel in Daniel 9 to tell him that within 70 weeks the end of the world will come.
4. Sodom and Gomorrah (Genesis 18:23–32).
5. Job 38:31–32.

finally, in consideration of the Book that comprises all books,[6] and the Science in which all sciences are embraced,[7] and for whose comprehension all sciences serve, and even after knowing them all (which we now see is not easy, nor even possible), there is one condition that takes precedence over all the rest, which is uninterrupted prayer and purity of life, that one may entreat of God that purgation of spirit and illumination of mind necessary for the understanding of such elevated matters: and if that be lacking, none of the aforesaid will have been of any purpose.

Of the Angelic Doctor Saint Thomas the Church affirms: *When reading the most difficult passages of the Holy Scripture, he joined fast with prayer. And he was wont to say to his companion Brother Reginald that all he knew derived not so much from study or his own labor as from the grace of God.*[8] How then should I—so lacking in virtue and so poorly read—find courage to write? But as I had acquired the rudiments of learning, I continued to study ceaselessly divers subjects, having for none any particular inclination, but for all in general; and having studied some more than others was not owing to preference, but to the chance that more books on certain subjects had fallen into my hands, causing the election of them through no discretion of my own. And as I was not directed by preference, nor, forced by the need to fulfill certain scholarly requirements, constrained by time in the pursuit of any subject, I found myself free to study numerous topics at the same time, or to leave some for others; although in this scheme some order was observed, for some I deigned study and others diversion, and in the latter I found respite from the former. From which it follows that though I have studied many things I know nothing, as some have inhibited the learning of others. I speak specifically of the practical aspect of those arts that allow practice, because it is clear that when the pen moves the compass must lie idle, and while the harp is played the organ is stilled, *et sic de caeteris.*[9] And because much practice is required of one who would acquire facility, none who divides his interest among various exercises may reach perfection. Whereas in the formal and theoretical arts the contrary is true, and I would hope to persuade all with my experience, which is that one need not inhibit the other, but, in fact, each may illuminate and open the way to others, by nature of their variations and their hidden links, which were placed in this universal chain by the wisdom of their Author in such a way that they conform and are joined together with admirable unity and harmony. This is the very chain the ancients believed did issue from the mouth of Jupiter, from which were suspended all things linked one with another, as is demonstrated by the Reverend Father Athanasius Kircher in his curious book, *De Magnate.*[1] All things issue from God, Who is at once the center and the circumference from which and in which all lines begin and end.

I myself can affirm that what I have not understood in an author in one branch of knowledge I may understand in a second in a branch that seems remote from the first. And authors, in their elucidation, may suggest metaphorical examples in other arts: as when logicians say that to prove whether parts are equal, the mean is to the extremes as a determined measure to two equidistant bodies; or in stating how the argument of the logician moves, in the manner of a straight line, along the shortest

6. The Bible.
7. Theology.
8. The passage is from the Roman Breviary, which contains lessons or readings for the various feast days of the Catholic Church. The Dominican Thomas of Aquinas was the most important theologian of the late middle ages.
9. And so with all things (Latin).

1. A Jesuit and polymath, who wrote extensively on the natural world during the 17th century; his works, all in Latin, were much appreciated by Sor Juana, as is evident from the early 18th-century portrait of her in which several of his works appear on shelves in her study. *De Magnate* ("Of Magnets") probably refers to his *Magnet, Or On the Art of the Magnet* from 1641.

route, while that of the rhetorician moves, as a curve, by the longest, but that both finally arrive at the same point. And similarly, as it is when they say that the Exposi-
tors are like an open hand, and the Scholastics like a closed fist.[2] And thus it is no
apology, nor do I offer it as such, to say that I have studied many subjects, seeing
that each augments the other; but that I have not profited is the fault of my own ineptitude and the inadequacy of my intelligence, not the fault of the variety. But what
may be offered as exoneration is that I undertook this great task without benefit of
teacher, or fellow students with whom to confer and discuss, having for a master no
other than a mute book, and for a colleague, an insentient inkwell; and in the stead of
explication and exercise, many obstructions, not merely those of my religious obligations (for it is already known how useful and advantageous is the time employed in
them), rather, all the attendant details of living in a community: how I might be reading, and those in the adjoining cell would wish to play their instruments, and sing;
how I might be studying, and two servants who had quarreled would select me to
judge their dispute; or how I might be writing, and a friend come to visit me, doing
me no favor but with the best of will, at which time one must not only accept the inconvenience, but be grateful for the hurt. And such occurrences are the normal state
of affairs, for as the times I set apart for study are those remaining after the ordinary
duties of the community are fulfilled, they are the same moments available to my
sisters, in which they may come to interrupt my labor; and only those who have experience of such a community will know how true this is, and how it is only the
strength of my vocation that allows me happiness; that, and the great love existing
between me and my beloved sisters, for as love is union, it knows no extremes of
distance.

   With this I confess how interminable has been my labor; and how I am unable to
say what I have with envy heard others state—that they have not been plagued by the
thirst for knowledge: blessed are they. For me, not the knowing (for still I do not
know), merely the desiring to know, has been such torment that I can say, as has my
Father Saint Jerome (although not with his accomplishment) . . . *my conscience is
witness to what effort I have expended, what difficulties I have suffered, how many
times I have despaired, how often I have ceased my labors and turned to them again,
driven by the hunger for knowledge; my conscience is witness, and that of those who
have lived beside me.*[3] With the exception of the companions and witnesses (for I
have been denied even this consolation), I can attest to the truth of these words. And
to the fact that even so, my dark inclination has been so great that it has conquered
all else!

   It has been my fortune that, among other benefices, I owe to God a most tender
and affable nature, and because of it my sisters (who being good women do not take
note of my faults) hold me in great affection, and take pleasure in my company; and
knowing this, and moved by the great love I hold for them—having greater reason
than they—I enjoy even more *their* company. Thus I was wont in our rare idle moments to visit among them, offering them consolation and entertaining myself in their

2. Exposition here is analogous to interpretation, and possibly rhetorical training, said to be represented by the
open hand; scholasticism, or logic and disputation, was
the closed fist.
3. From St. Jerome's letter to Rusticus. Jerome was the
indefatiguable 4th-century translator of the Bible into
Latin and a professed admirer of pagan culture and philosophy. He is Sor Juana's "father" insofar as she is a
member of an order founded by him and the Roman matron Paula, but she also clearly sees his learnedness as a
guide and justification for her own.

conversation. I could not help but note, however, that in these times I was neglecting my study, and I made a vow not to enter any cell unless obliged by obedience or char-ity; for without such a compelling constraint—the constraint of mere intention not be-ing sufficient—my love would be more powerful than my will. I would (knowing well my frailty) make this vow for the period of a few weeks, or a month, and when that time had expired, I would allow myself a brief respite of a day or two before re-newing it, using that time not so much for rest (for *not* studying has never been restful for me) as to assure that I not be deemed cold, remote, or ungrateful in the little-de-served affection of my dearest sisters.

In this practice one may recognize the strength of my inclination. I give thanks to God, Who willed that such an ungovernable force be turned toward letters and not to some other vice. From this it may also be inferred how obdurately against the current my poor studies have sailed (more accurately, have foundered). For still to be related is the most arduous of my difficulties—those mentioned until now, either compulsory or fortuitous, being merely tangential—and still unreported the more-directly aimed slings and arrows that have acted to impede and prevent the exercise of my study. Who would have doubted, having witnessed such general approbation, that I sailed before the wind across calm seas, amid the laurels of widespread acclaim. But our Lord God knows that it has not been so; He knows how from amongst the blossoms of this very acclaim emerged such a number of aroused vipers, hissing their emulation and their persecution, that one could not count them. But the most noxious, those who most deeply wounded me, have not been those who persecuted me with open loathing and malice, but rather those who in loving me and desiring my well-being (and who are deserving of God's blessing for their good intent) have mortified and tormented me more than those others with their abhorrence.[4] "Such studies are not in conformity with sacred innocence; surely she will be lost; surely she will, by cause of her very perspicacity and acuity, grow heady at such exalted heights." How was I to endure? An uncommon sort of martyrdom in which I was both martyr and executioner.

And as for my (in me, twice hapless) facility in making verses, even though they be sacred verses, what sorrows have I not suffered? What sorrows not ceased to suf-fer? Be assured, lady, it is often that I have meditated on how one who distinguishes himself—or one on whom God chooses to confer distinction, for it is only He who may do so—is received as a common enemy, because it seems to some that he usurps the applause they deserve, or that he dams up the admiration to which they aspired, and so they persecute that person.

That politically barbaric law of Athens by which any person who excelled by cause of his natural gifts and virtues was exiled from his Republic in order that he not threaten the public freedom still endures, is still observed in our day, although not for the reasons held by the Athenians.[5] Those reasons have been replaced by another, no less efficient though not as well founded, seeming, rather, a maxim more appropriate to that impious Machiavelli[6]—which is to abhor one who excels, because he deprives others of regard. And thus it happens, and thus it has always happened.

* * *

4. Perhaps a reference to the Bishop himself.
5. Possible reference to one of the laws of Draco, Athen-ian legislator of the 6th century B.C.E. whose severity in-spired the epithet "draconian."

6. Niccolò Machiavelli was a Florentine whose early 16th-century works on the reality of political life earned for him (unjustly) the title of Satan; see selections from *The Prince,* page 247.

But how I have strayed, lady.[7] None of this pertains here, nor is it intended for your ears, but as I was discussing my accusers I remembered the words of one that recently have appeared, and, though my intent was to speak in general, my pen, unbidden, slipped, and began to respond in particular. And so, returning to our Arce,[8] he says that he knew in this city two nuns: one in the Convent of the Regina, who had so thoroughly committed the Breviary to memory that with the greatest promptitude and propriety she applied in her conversation its verses, psalms, and maxims of saintly homilies. The other, in the Convent of the Conception, was so accustomed to reading the Epistles of my Father Saint Jerome, and the Locutions of this Saint, that Arce says, *It seemed I was listening to Saint Jerome himself, speaking in Spanish.*[9] And of this latter woman he says that after her death he learned that she had translated these Epistles into the Spanish language. What a pity that such talents could not have been employed in major studies with scientific principles. He does not give the name of either, although he offers these women as confirmation of his opinion, which is that not only is it licit, but most useful and essential for women to study the Holy Word, and even more essential for nuns; and that study is the very thing to which your wisdom exhorts me, and in which so many arguments concur.

Then if I turn my eyes to the oft-chastised faculty of making verses—which is in me so natural that I must discipline myself that even this letter not be written in that form—I might cite those lines, *All I wished to express took the form of verse.*[1] And seeing that so many condemn and criticize this ability, I have conscientiously sought to find what harm may be in it, and I have not found it, but, rather, I see verse acclaimed in the mouths of the Sibyls, sanctified in the pens of the Prophets, especially King David, of whom the exalted Expositor my beloved Father says (explicating the measure of his metres): *in the manner of Horace and Pindar, now it hurries along in iambs, now it rings in alcaic, now swells in sapphic, then arrives in broken feet.*[2] The greater part of the Holy Books are in metre, as is the Book of Moses; and those of Job (as Saint Isidore states in his *Etymologiae*) are in heroic verse. Solomon wrote the Canticle of Canticles in verse; and Jeremiah, his *Lamentations*. And so, says Cassiodorus: *All poetic expression had as its source the Holy Scriptures.* For not only does our Catholic Church not disdain verse, it employs verse in its hymns, and recites the lines of Saint Ambrose, Saint Thomas, Saint Isidore, and others. Saint Bonaventure was so taken with verse that he writes scarcely a page where it does not appear. It is readily apparent that Saint Paul had studied verse, for he quotes and translates verses of Aratus: *For in him we live, and move, and are.* And he quotes also that verse of Parmenides: *The Cretans are always liars, evil beasts, slothful bellies.* Saint Gregory Nazianzen argues in elegant verses the questions of matrimony and virginity.

---

7. Sor Juana has spent the last several sections suggesting that like Christ, she has been unfairly persecuted, though for something she cannot control: her passion for learning, that makes her discover even in the kitchen "natural secrets," such as the marvelous properties of the egg. She then proceeds to list all of the women in the Bible who were learned, as well as more recent figures such as St. Teresa of Avila, turning statements by St. Paul typically interpreted as misogynistic—such as "Let women learn in silence"—to women's favor ("For this latter scripture works more to women's favor than their disfavor, as it commands them to learn").

8. Juan Díaz de Arce was a professor of philosophy in Mexico; he died in 1653.

9. The passage in Arce is unknown; Sor Juana is clearly invoking this influential philosopher and theologian in support of her argument that women should be learned.

1. A citation from the Roman poet Ovid, often regarded as scurrilous; the line is from his confessional poem *Tristia*.

2. The line is Jerome's. Horace was an accomplished 1st-century B.C.E. Roman poet, Pindar a Greek lyric poet active in the 5th century B.C.E.; both excelled in the writing of odes. Jerome's comparison of their writings to the Psalms of David, second King of Israel, provides an important defense to Sor Juana's love of classical scholarship. Sor Juana goes on to cite a range of biblical and theological works that contain poetry.

And, how should I tire? The Queen of Wisdom, Our Lady, with Her sacred lips, intoned the Canticle of the Magnificat;[3] and having brought forth this example, it would be offensive to add others that were profane, even those of the most serious and learned men, for this alone is more than sufficient confirmation; and even though Hebrew elegance could not be compressed into Latin measure, for which reason, although the sacred translator,[4] more attentive to the importance of the meaning, omitted the verse, the Psalms retain the number and divisions of verses, and what harm is to be found in them? For misuse is not the blame of art, but rather of the evil teacher who perverts the arts, making of them the snare of the devil; and this occurs in all the arts and sciences.

And if the evil is attributed to the fact that a woman employs them, we have seen how many have done so in praiseworthy fashion; what then is the evil in my being a woman? I confess openly my own baseness and meanness, but I judge that no couplet of mine has been deemed indecent. Furthermore, I have never written of my own will, but under the pleas and injunctions of others; . . .[5]

[END OF THE RISE OF THE VERNACULAR IN EUROPE]

⚑ END OF CROSSCURRENTS: THE VERNACULAR REVOLUTION ⚑

---

3. Mary's verses praising God when Gabriel announces to her that she will bear God's son (Luke 1:46–55).
4. Jerome.
5. Thus does Sor Juana return to the sentiment with which this selection opened. Despite her spirited defense, Sor

Juana closes her letter with the promise that any future "scribbling" will "always find its way to the haven of your holy feet and the certainty of your correction, for I have no other jewel with which to pay you." She ends asking the forgiveness of the "lady."

Francesco Traini, detail from *The Triumph of Death* (c. 1350, Campo Santo, Pisa). The noblemen and attendants recoil from the sight and putrid stench of rotting flesh, vividly enacting a scene that must have been frequent in times of plague. In various stages of decomposition, the dead are accompanied by the 4th-century St. Macarius, who points to the scroll as though to discover on it the names of the passersby themselves. Part of a large fresco that was considerably damaged during bombings in World War II, this detail is accompanied by others that show fasting monks and a group of well-dressed men and women talking and playing music, completely oblivious to the gruesome figure of Death who circles above them like a bat.

Early Modern Europe

In 1632, the aging astronomer Galileo Galilei declared before the Roman Inquisition that he had entertained "the false opinion that the Sun is the center of the world and immovable, and that the earth is not the center of the same and that it moves." "With God's help," he pledged to believe "all that is held, preached, and taught by the Holy Catholic and Apostolic Church." At stake was the received authority of Catholic doctrine and Aristotelian philosophy: two thousand years of venerable tradition attempting to hold its own against the evidence of things seen.

Galileo had published his heretical views in a dialogue about the revolutions of the earth, and his work exemplifies everything we tend to think of as "the Renaissance," a period in whose aftermath we still live. It was written in the commonsensical Tuscan language of his youth, rather than the academic Latin that would have kept his views from the "people" and therefore have made his ideas less dangerous; the Polish astronomer Copernicus had in fact written up his own mathematical theories about a heliocentric universe over a century earlier, but in Latin. The product of empirical observations through the lenses Galileo himself painstakingly polished, *Dialogue on the World Systems* showcased the scientist as both theorist and craftsman. And yet the bold, sometimes arrogant Galileo recanted toward the end of his life. A broken, elderly man, had he turned in his last years to orthodoxy, regretting the scientific excesses of his youth? Had he shrewdly resigned himself to the reigning politics of his time? Or was he haunted by thoughts of being burned at the stake like his compatriot, the intellectual Giordano Bruno?

Like most of his contemporaries, Galileo was a deeply religious man. He agonized over his inability to reconcile the "new science" he was helping develop with the Old Testament account of God stopping the sun so that Joshua could emerge victorious in battle. The young Cardinal Barberini, likewise interested in science, had befriended Galileo when the astronomer first came to Rome. As Pope Urban VIII, however, Barberini felt pressured to persecute the astronomer whose experiments had once intrigued him. Thus the true story behind Galileo's recantation is a combination of many factors, while the recantation itself raises questions about the very nature of the Renaissance: its definition, its dates, its lasting impact.

By some accounts, the Renaissance, at least in Italy, had ended a century earlier with the sack of Rome by imperial forces in 1527. The leading figures of the epoch—Petrarch, Luther, Leonardo da Vinci, Michelangelo, Monteverdi, Shakespeare, Cervantes—were already dead. (Milton, however, had not yet written about Galileo in *Paradise Lost,* where he compares Satan's shield to "the moon, whose orb / Through optic glass the Tuscan artist views / At evening from the top of Fesole, / Or in Valdarno, to descry new lands, / Rivers or mountains in her spotty globe.") Does the recantation of the "Tuscan artist" give the lie to one story of the Renaissance, the meteoric rise of the questing, self-conscious individual untrammeled by faith? Or does it suggest that the "Renaissance" was a brief moment, limited only to a certain privileged

Europe in 1590

SCOTLAND
Edinburgh
IRELAND
Dublin
York
ENGLAND
London
Canterbury
ATLANTIC
OCEAN
NORTH
SEA
DENMARK-NORWAY
SWEDEN
Stockholm
Copenhagen
BALTIC SEA
Königsberg
RUSSIA
Riga
COURLAND
PRUSSIA
Hamburg
NETHERLANDS
Utrecht
Brussels
Münster
Cologne
BRANDENBURG
Berlin
HOLY
ROMAN
EMPIRE
Wittenberg
SAXONY
Mühlberg
Schmalkalden
Prague
Warsaw
POLAND-LITHUANIA
Cracow
Crépy
Paris
Nemours
Orleans
Troyes
Worms
Speyer
Nuremberg
HUNGARY
MOLDAVIA
Nantes
FRANCE
Augsburg
BAVARIA
AUSTRIAN HABSBURG POSSESSIONS
Vienna
Buda
Debrecen
TRANSYLVANIA
Cognac
FRANCHE-
COMTÉ
Basle
Zurich
SWISS
CONFEDERATION
Trent
Gyulafehérvár
Bordeaux
NAVARRE
Bergerac
Lyon
Geneva
SAVOY
DUCHY
OF MILAN
Milan
Venice
VENETIAN REPUBLIC
Belgrade
WALLACHIA
Toulouse
Avignon
Parma
Genoa
MODENA
PAPAL STATES
Florence
FLORENCE
URBINO
MONTENEGRO
REPUBLIC
OF RAGUSA
BÉARN
REPUBLIC
OF GENOA
STATO
DEI PRESIDI
PAPAL
STATES
Rome
Salonica
OTTOMAN
EMPIRE
PORTUGAL
Madrid
Barcelona
Naples
NAPLES
Lisbon
Seville
SPAIN
SARDINIA
BALEARIC
ISLANDS
MEDITERRANEAN SEA

N

Spain   Denmark-Norway   Poland-Lithuania
French   Holy Roman Empire   Ottoman Empire

few, snuffed out where it had flowered by newly powerful institutions such as the Counter-Reformation church and the nation state?

The questions that arose about Galileo's investigations suggest that the era that extends roughly from 1350 to 1650 represents more than simply the unleashing of the imagination. It is also marked by constraints on this very "unleashing." Indeed, the tenacity of these constraints attests to the Renaissance's modernity. Long before the early seventeenth century, sovereigns, among them the pope, had seen themselves as absolute. But only during Galileo's lifetime did they actually come to possess the technological and bureaucratic means to realize their power. And the very fact that Galileo's inquiries and their publication in the vernacular were possible at all in the early 1600s, while they would have been inconceivable three hundred years earlier, argues that something revolutionary did happen in western Europe after the era in which Dante composed his *Divine Comedy*.

NEW KINGDOMS, NEW WORLDS, NEW CITIES

Galileo's insistence on a heliocentric universe was in many ways the last, most cosmic, of early modern challenges to views of the world that had held for hundreds of years. Dante knew of the existence of a single Christian religion. Yet even in his lifetime, the papacy Dante condemned as corrupt would move from Rome to Avignon, in southern France. When Catherine of Siena and others persuaded Pope Gregory XI to come back to Rome in 1377, the French cardinals responded by electing their own pope, resulting in the so-called Great Schism: a forty-year period in which western Christendom had two leaders rather than one. Such goings-on are a precursor to the far more violent splintering of the Catholic faith in the sixteenth century with the protests of Luther and the start of the Reformation. By Galileo's time, there were over twenty five versions of Christianity, ranging from Calvinism to Lutheranism to Anabaptism.

Dante's world, moreover, included only three continents, with Jerusalem, home to the world's three monotheistic religions, furnishing a pivotal center. By 1632, the year of Galileo's recantation, explorers had already traveled as far as the western coast of South America. The world's "center" was now reconfigured with mathematical precision as somewhere in the middle of the Atlantic Ocean. European political and religious expansion in turn quickly followed the initial explorations that a combination of classical and Arabic scientific methods had enabled. Five hundred years before Galileo, the Crusades had briefly united disparate European principalities to liberate Jerusalem from the infidel. But ongoing battles for territorial supremacy tore Europe apart for most of the sixteenth and seventeenth centuries, and kings of new nation-states sped their armies to far-off lands to compete for riches. In the wake of the religious divisiveness brought about by Protestants, Calvinists founded colonies off the coast of Brazil, Puritans defied the elements at Plymouth Rock, and Jesuits started schools in Ceylon (Sri Lanka) and China. Marco Polo's wanderings in the twelfth century had been an individual affair. These new wanderings were concerted efforts to win souls for Christ and to acquire gold, bread baskets, and new subjects for Europe's sovereign states.

These were countries, moreover, that Dante would not have recognized. While his native Italy failed to become the home of a revived Holy Roman Empire, as Dante had hoped, it did see a shift from a loose cluster of autonomous towns and courts to a number of duchies and extensions of foreign empire: Tuscany, the Marches, the Papal States, the Kingdom of Two Sicilies. Spain and France had become powerful states as former kingdoms and duchies were united under a single crown or, in the case of Spain, two crowns: the marriage of Ferdinand of Aragon and Isabella of Castile transformed the greater part of the Iberian peninsula into a powerful military presence. Likewise, England and Poland emerged in the fifteenth centuries as formidable monarchies. At the same time, in 1579 Europe experienced what one historian has called its "first modern war of national liberation" when the northern provinces of the Netherlands rose up against Spain. The English monarchy would soon face its own rebellion, culminating in the execution of Charles I in 1649. The economically thriving duchies of Germany, on the other hand, were the very heart of the Holy Roman Empire, revived in 1438 under the first representatives of what would be the long-lived Habsburg dynasty. Even if Holy Roman Emperor Charles V called Luther a heretic at a crucial confrontation in 1520, the German princes refused to go along with the accusation. As a result, much of what we now know as Germany embraced Luther's revolution, throwing off its fealty to the Catholic Church shortly after Charles V's proclamation. After a lifetime struggling against the German Protestants, Charles would abdicate his throne and retire to a monastery in Spain.

This redrawing of the earth's perimeters and its geopolitical makeup extended eastward as well. The Islamic presence in the Middle East and northwest Asia had grown steadily under the Sultan Osman, one of the early rulers of the Ottoman Empire. In 1453, Osman's armies captured the city of Constantinople, strategically situated on the edge of the Black Sea. Named for Constantine, the Roman emperor who had made Christianity the religion of his empire, Constantinople became Istanbul, and the great church of Santa Sophia became a mosque. The old spice route that had enabled enterprising merchants such as Marco Polo to pass through Turkey, Afghanistan, India, and even China was closed down, forcing other traders to find new routes to the Indies. Columbus's misguided pursuit of a new spice route to Asia led him instead to new worlds, while Vasco da Gama would reach the real India by boat in 1498. By 1521, Magellan would circumnavigate the globe.

The capture of Constantinople had other far-reaching effects. The Turks eventually advanced as far west as Vienna, and their threatening proximity polarized opposition to Islam, sparking talk of new Crusades. The "most holy Catholic kings" of Spain, Isabella and Ferdinand, overthrew the Arab kingdom of Granada in 1492, permanently banishing Muslims from a region that had once been the intellectual capital of southern Europe. Moreover, for a millennium Constantinople had served as the capital of the Byzantine Empire, home to a sophisticated civilization. As the Ottomans progressively conquered Athens, Damascus, Belgrade, and Rhodes, a large number of Greek-speaking scholars fled to western Europe, taking the quickest sea route to Venice. Among other things, their presence would enable the restoration of the Greek legacy of antiquity, dominated in the West for over a thousand years by Latinity. Plato, Homer, Sappho, the Greek tragedians, and eventually a freshly studied Aristotle became newly available to scholars and eventually, the general reader.

CONTINUITIES AND CHANGE

At the same time, the Renaissance was not the radical break with the past that it is commonly thought to be. There was much in Galileo's world that Dante would easily have recognized. One common feature was the ubiquity of war and civic strife, though on a newly global scale. The so-called Hundred Years' War between England and France, which featured such "heroes" as Joan of Arc, finally ended in 1453, the year of the Turks' victory at Istanbul, but only after it had devastated much of western Europe. The victorious French didn't find respite for long: a series of battles throughout the early sixteenth century with the Holy Roman Empire decimated their army, thanks largely to the Empire's savvy deployment of Spanish musketeers, marking the end of an era of knightly combat. The so-called Wars of Italy made the vulnerable peninsula a battleground for over sixty years, culminating with the absorption of Milan and Naples into the Spanish empire by 1559. A few years later, an angry mob tossed two of Emperor Ferdinand II's ministers from a window in Prague Castle; this "defenestration of Prague" set in motion the events that would ultimately lead to the Thirty Years' War (1618–1648), which engulfed most of central Europe.

Secondly, plague remained a constant blight on the landscape. The most severe epidemic ever to strike Europe was the Black Death of 1348–1350; Giovanni Boccaccio grimly recorded its devastating effects on Florence in the opening pages of his *Decameron*. Little had changed by the time of Galileo's recantation; the astronomer narrowly missed dying himself in the virulent plague that swept across southern Europe between 1627 and 1628. Largely because of the recurrence of disease, most of Europe's major cities would never attain during the Renaissance the populations they had in Dante's lifetime. The closest that early modern Florence ever got to its pre-1348 population of 100,000 was 75,000.

Finally, Dante probably would not have been surprised by the steady decline of the aristocracy and the rise of the merchant class, although he wouldn't have been particularly pleased. The cultural flowering of Dante's own era in the early fourteenth century was the product of vigorous social and economic changes that began in the small cities of northern Italy and Flanders, most of them situated on the rivers that constituted Europe's principal trade routes, or else on the highways pilgrims traveled to Rome. The increase of urbanization and commercial activity was further fueled by new markets opened up by the Crusades. A class of men was formed who had no ties to the farming that had sustained medieval feudalism, with its lords living off peasants' labor and its bishops controlling vast monasteries. They also tended to avoid professing loyalty to either of the two powers that dominated the medieval world, the emperor and the pope, and their civic charters proclaimed their cities to be fiercely independent. In many ways, the Renaissance reaped what the Middle Ages had sown, as energetic merchants and prosperous guild members challenged the ways in which a man's worth was valued: did it depend on bloodline and clerical privilege, or could honest labor and thrifty behavior play a major part? The Medici, who would rule Florence for centuries, began as merchants and became prominent bankers; the merchant-banker Jakob Fugger of Augsburg, in southern Germany, came from a family of weavers, and at his death had emperors in his debt. In Protestant countries, monasteries and convents were forcibly closed, and the path to religious perfection considerably widened for men and women alike.

Even as social relationships continued to be reconfigured throughout the Renaissance, however, the commercial growth and economic expansion that Dante's era had enjoyed came to an end with the Black Death of 1348. Depression and inflation characterized Europe until the sixteenth century, when the sagging economy was bolstered by the influx of gold and silver troves found in the New World—as well as in the mines of central Europe financed by Jakob Fugger and his contemporaries. As business recovered, the Holy Roman Empire did as well, invigorated by dynastic marriages that brought Spain within its orb. At the same time, the papacy, now firmly reestablished in Rome, sought to extend its political and temporal authority into a central Italy that had long avoided the sway of the "eternal city" to its south.

As a result, the small Italian towns that had provided the first impetus for change receded in importance, and courtly capitals tended to take their place. Rome is the best example of a city that was progressively rescued from ruin—thanks in no small part to the ambitious popes who ruled in the wake of the great schism. In the mid-fifteenth century when Nicholas V launched a major urban renovation, Rome was no more than a swamp dotted with half-buried ruins; two hundred years later it would witness the triumphant construction of Saint Peter's. King Francis I, inspired by trips to Italy, would refashion Paris in the 1530s and 1540s, a project continued by Catherine de' Medici and lavishly extended by Louis XIV. Lisbon flourished under the Henrys, Madrid under the Phillips, and the attractions of Elizabeth's and James's courts brought the European Renaissance fully to London. The presence of wealthy sovereigns busy setting up court was not only good for business. It was also good for culture, and the arts thrived in capital cities that sought to outdo each other in power and prestige.

At the same time, the new-world discoveries had made those countries bordering the Atlantic Ocean the maritime powers of the epoch, outpacing the cities that dotted the Mediterranean. Venice alone retained its importance as a major port city, largely because of the unique circumstances that enabled the republic to retain its independence from territorial rulers. England, the Netherlands and Spain were the beneficiaries of a somewhat belated Renaissance. The *siglo d'oro* or "golden century" celebrated by Spain was the century in which Shakespeare, Donne, Milton, Cervantes, Lope de Vega, Calderón, Tirso de Molina, Vermeer, Rembrandt, and many more artists and writers flourished.

Perhaps in this light it is better to speak of distinct national, even local "renaissances," and of the period as a whole as "early modern," insofar as the three hundred years from 1350 to 1650 anticipate modernity, yet differ from it significantly. Italy's renaissance heyday was over long before Spain's began; Poland, England, and France celebrated their renaissances in the sixteenth century. Yet while there is an undeniable relationship between economic prosperity and cultural creativity, it is far from constituting the entire story, and there were other sources of inspiration as well.

LOOKING BACKWARD

One of the most influential definitions of the Renaissance was proffered by the Swiss historian Jakob Burckhardt in the mid-nineteenth century, when he described it as "the revival of antiquity . . . [in] union with the genius of the Italian people." Although this revival wasn't the only driving force in the period, there is little question that the backward glance to antiquity provoked the "rebirth" implicit in the term "renaissance," resulting more often than not in profound competitiveness with the best the ancients had to offer. One of the greatest feats of modern engineering, the dome of Santa Maria del Fiore, still soars over Florence. Its creator, Filippo Brunelleschi, was praised by the architect and artist Leon Battista Alberti in the preface to his influential treatise on painting: "I had thought that nature, the teacher of all things, had become old and tired, and no longer produced those talented men in whom antiquity, during the young days of the earth, once revelled. But now . . . I see that first of all in you, Filippo . . . there is a talent of which antiquity could never have boasted, so supreme are you in all the arts."

Rebirth of the ancients, then, in the hopes of improving on the ancients. Botticelli's painting *Birth of Venus* portrays the rebirth of the Roman goddess of love, set within a framework inspired by two centuries of European love poetry and demonstrating the calm poise—if not the exact pose—of fifteenth-century Madonnas. Rabelais would look back to the training of Spartan athletes for his Renaissance prince and Machiavelli to the legendary figures of Moses, Romulus, and Cyrus for his, while the French poet Louise Labé modeled herself on the newly available legend of Sappho. But it was also to the style and intellectual building blocks of the ancients that early modern writers and artists turned in their desire both to emulate and improve upon the past. The Laocoön, grisly statue of a Roman priest and his sons being strangled by serpents, had lain submerged in the Tiber for centuries; it was hauled to the riverbank on one glorious day in 1506, prompting the period's greatest sculptors, Michelangelo among them, to emulate its sinuous curves and mannered features. And the learned Mexican nun Sor Juana Inés de la Cruz, writing in the late seventeenth century, would argue that to climb to the "peak of Sacred Theology," she had to ascend

> by the steps of the human sciences and arts; for how could one undertake the study of the Queen of Sciences if first one had not come to know her servants? How, without Logic, could I be apprised of the general and specific way in which the Holy Scripture is written? How, without Rhetoric, could I understand its figures, its tropes, its locutions? . . . How, without Architecture, could one know the great Temple of Solomon, of which God Himself was the Author?

Medieval Europe had also glanced backward: Dante and Augustine to Virgil, Thomas Aquinas to Aristotle. Yet decisively new in the backward glances of fifteenth- and sixteenth-century Europeans is the impulse to try to see the pagan ancients as they saw themselves, untouched by the blazing light of Christianity that had eclipsed them. Petrarch composed epistles to Horace and Virgil begging them to reveal themselves as they really were, uncontaminated by the barbarous readings that had characterized interpretation between the fall of the Roman empire and Petrarch's own time. The Dutch polymath Desiderius Erasmus notes in the *Adages,* his enormous collection of 4,251 proverbs, that his task is nothing less than "restoring the great works of ancient literature—of true literature," adding that such infinite labors can be performed only by a "real Hercules of the mind":

> This is the magnificent reward you are to earn with all your long vigils, your labour, your hardships. Sacrifice all the ordinary pleasures of human life, neglect your own affairs, be unsparing of your looks, your sleep, your health. Accept cheerfully the damage to your eyesight, bring on premature old age, shrug off the detriment to your own life.

Such labors went by the name of humanism: a manner of seeing the world which, as its name implies, placed man rather than God at the center. Initially, humanism can be said to have started out quietly enough. Petrarch desperately wanted to hear Virgil's genuine voice, to discover his true intentions rather than the ones visited upon him by Christian allegorists. "For this purpose," as the historian J. H. Hexter has written, "a most careful study of the language of the text is indispensable, so that philology and history replace dialectic and classification"—the hallmarks of the scholastic and analytical method practiced in the medieval universities—"as the instruments of investigation." The recovery of ancient thought and practice would not be limited, however, to pagan authors. In particular, humanists at newly created universities in northern Europe turned their attention to Scripture as well as writings of the early Church. Or supposed writings. Anticipating northern critics of the Church, the Italian Lorenzo Valla realized that the impoverished medieval Latin of the notorious letter in which the dying Emperor Constantine handed over land and temporal powers to the Pope in 337 was an eighth-century forgery, turning a thousand-year tradition of papal powers into a sham.

The look back, however, could be far less confident, and it wasn't always directed to a pristine Latin, Greek, or (less frequently) Hebrew unity of culture and thought. The medieval period was increasingly romanticized as unified, a simpler age than the one in which sixteenth-century Europe was immersed, torn as it was by religious and political wars waged with the latest technology, gunpowder. All this violence led to a number of poems focused on conflict: conflicts, however, that were placed in an era when solutions seemed more to hand. The medieval romances of Chrétien de Troye and the earlier *Chanson de Roland* provided the basis for new epic romances set in the days of Charlemagne or the First (and only successful) Crusade. Situating these poems in a period that predated Luther created the illusion of a united Europe, while they acknowledged the ongoing threat posed by the Turks. Luther might wryly observe that for good Protestants, the Turk was less of a threat than the Pope. But Islam posed an enormous threat after the fall of Constantinople, forcing the Holy Roman Empire to devote considerable military attention to the east when it would have preferred to concentrate on subduing France to the west or the Pope to the south. Making Islam the only enemy to European progress, as Luíz Vaz de Camões would do in the *Lusíads,* his epic of Portuguese eastern expansion, willfully ignored these complications of modern European statesbuilding. On the other hand, the sardonic Ludovico Ariosto used his fanciful epic-romance, the *Orlando furioso* (Mad Roland) to challenge the black-and-white oppositions of Christian versus Muslim by creating warriors who were virtually interchangeable—and by maintaining, in any case, that all poets are liars. In one of the poem's most memorable episodes, Saint John himself, author of the fourth gospel, tells a knight who has flown to the moon that "Aeneas was not as devoted, nor Achilles as strong, nor Hector as ferocious as their reputations suggest. . . . If you want to know what really happened, invert the story: Greece was vanquished, Troy triumphant, and Penelope a whore."

Milton's great epic, the last of its kind, also indulges in a profound backward look, even if it rejects the illusions offered by a unified medieval past: a look back to the origins of creation itself. Written in the wake of the failed Puritan republic in which Milton had played an active role, *Paradise Lost* is opposed to idealizations of any kind. Yet it seeks a new type of unity in the simple fact of all men's and women's distance from God. There is a looming sense in *Paradise Lost* as to the finality of that loss, long before Milton's time, while the last words of the poem are a move forward—albeit a hesitant, somewhat reluctant one—as Adam and Eve, exiled from Eden, go out into the great world:

> Some natural tears they dropped, but wiped them soon;
> The world was all before them, where to choose
> Their place of rest, and providence their guide:
> They hand in hand with wandering steps and slow,
> Through Eden took their solitary way.

Product of the classical traditions that had inspired Petrarch, as well as of the vernacular poetry that had earned England a Renaissance all its own, *Paradise Lost* was begun a decade after Galileo's death. As if in anticipation of the encyclopedias that would become a distinctive mark of the eighteenth century, Milton's poem is, like them, a thoughtful compilation of the best the ancients and the moderns had to offer.

LOOKING FORWARD

After their expulsion from Paradise, Adam and Eve do go forward, as they must; but what do they go forward to? The world that Milton knew was undoubtedly progressive with respect to advances in science, education, and society. For one thing, the brilliant new inventions like Galileo's telescopes made many things possible that were previously unthinkable. The widespread use of the quadrant by Portuguese navigators enabled ships to arrive in India and the New World. The invention of the printing press in Mainz, Germany, in the 1450s transformed the reading habits of Europeans and enabled them not only to publish but to own materials once restricted to clerics and the wealthy; over six million copies of books were printed in Europe by 1500. Advances in medicine were less forthcoming. The recurrence of plague has already been noted, and new diseases such as smallpox and syphilis, products of travels abroad, left their mark on Europe's landscape. But life expectancy did increase between 1300 and 1650. Economically, wealth was increasingly concentrated in cities such as London and Prague, while the feudal ties that had marked the medieval landscape continued to erode, changes that reflected the social mobility that characterized much of western Europe. The propertied classes in cities sought self-government and autonomy, and these benefits were occasionally sought by laborers as well, such as the Florentine wool-workers who initiated a tumultuous uprising in 1378. Peasants only recently released from serfdom, along with those who weren't, fomented a number of rebellions between 1350 and 1550. One of the bloodiest took place in southern Germany, and was incited by a charter that looked very similar to the charters of early modern towns. The *Twelve Articles of Peasantry,* written by a journeyman named Sebastian Lotzer, calls eloquently for social justice as it argues for peasants' rights to choose and elect their own priests, and against "the custom for us to be regarded as bondsmen, which is to be deplored, since Christ redeemed all of us with His precious blood, the shepherd as well as the man of highest station, without exception. Thus it is provided by the Scriptures that we are and shall be free."

As Lotzer's popular pamphlet attests, technological, educational, and social advances facilitated the emergence of a new phenomenon that could encompass a wide range of individuals, men as well as women: that of published authorship. Limited literacy in Latin had confined the technical act of writing mostly to clerics. Even highly cultured medieval monarchs such as Alfonso X of Castile were said to have relied exclusively on scribes. The need for a class of highly cultured individuals at Europe's courts and capitals would continue, however, even when the various European vernaculars began to rival Latin. The young Machiavelli worked as secretary for the city of Florence and the young Petrarch was secretary to a French pope; Milton's skill in languages led to his appointment as Secretary for the Foreign Tongues by Oliver Cromwell's Council of State. Many of these sophisticated centers were governed by newly made men (or women) whose claims to power were shaky: the Medici, Cromwell himself, and Elizabeth Tudor, who kept her chief rival to the English

Jost Amman, *The Peasant* (1568, Frankfurt), woodcut from *Das Ständebuch,* with rhymed verses by Hans Sachs. Sachs's book, published numerous times throughout the 16th century, engages in a genre beloved to the Germans, as it describes 114 of the professions, crafts, and trades, from "the highest to the lowest." While the peasants in the woodcut seem to be enjoying a moment of repose reminiscent of the peaceful- ness known to idealized shepherds, the verses accompanying the image tell a different story. The poetry supposedly uttered by the peasant both attests to his simple life and obedience to God—as did Adam, he lives on bread and water alone—and calls attention to the unjust social conditions under which he labored. Such conditions inspired a group of Swabian peasants to agree on 12 grievances or articles that a literate townsman wrote down and circulated in 1525. No fewer than 20 editions were printed within the first two months, and widespread peasant revolts followed.

throne, her cousin Mary Stuart, in the Tower for many years until having her be- headed on the eve of the Spanish Armada. They were eager for works acknowledging their legitimacy, and writers were quick to take up the challenge to provide stately po- ems to honor patrons or would-be patrons.

But if patronage provided one major catalyst for writing, there were others as well. The popular theaters in Spain and England gave Lope de Vega and Shakespeare possi- bilities for careers as both actors and playwrights, while later in the seventeenth century, Aphra Behn made respectable earnings from her poetry and plays. (Other attempts to live off one's writing were not as successful: Cervantes and Camões failed dismally to support themselves). Finally, for a growing number of people, writing was simply one aspect of one's daily activities. Many of them were women: Marguerite de Navarre, Sor Juana, and Vittoria Colonna all were able to compose their poetry and religious works in rooms of their own, thanks to associations with royalty, the relatively quiet rhythms of convent life, or a wealthy widowhood. François Rabelais, on the other hand, managed to find time when he wasn't practicing a physician's trade to write tales of giants.

Some of the most compelling characters to emerge from the pages of early modern literature take up the new, at times overwhelming possibilities that a seemingly unfettered age presented them. Yet it is striking that the most memorable of these characters hail from the period of greatest turmoil in early modern Europe, the sixteenth and early seventeenth centuries, as opposed to the relatively quiescent fifteenth, when the "Renaissance" had moved northward and westward from Italy. And one reason for their staying power must surely consist in their being forced to face the limitations of their newfound freedom. The great characters who best depict early modernity are not unequivocally free spirits at all, although they fiercely desire to be so: Don Juan, Faustus, Shakespeare's heroes and heroines, Milton's Satan. Even Don Quixote, who springs from the pages of that new literary form, the novel, experiences the tragicomic limits of reality's adaptability to his dreams of justice and glory. In this, he is much like the real-life figure of Christopher Columbus, praised by Columbus's Italian compatriot, the poet Torquato Tasso, as "the man of Liguria [who first] had the daring to set himself on the unknown course; and not the menacing howling of the wind, nor inhospitable seas, nor doubtful clime . . . could make the proud spirit content his lofty mind within the narrow proscriptions of the Mediterranean." Columbus's own optimism and self-confidence were constantly checked by the refusals of others to confirm his image of himself as the great admiral of the Indies. He died after his fourth and final voyage, a virtually impoverished man, still insisting that he hadn't discovered a "new world" at all, but only a new route to east Asia. Despite his many considerable accomplishments, Columbus's tale is finally that most memorable of Renaissance stories: one that attests to the limits of human inquiry and activity.

LOOKING INWARD

Fictional characters from the early modern period are increasingly articulate about these limitations, and their probing the limits of their own minds may signal early modernity's most dramatic innovation with respect to its medieval legacy. Characters more and more obey the laws of psychological realism, and their authors do as well, even if from behind cleverly-constructed personae. Although we may know Dante's biography with relative certainty, much of it is pieced together by inference from the dense allusions of the *Commedia* or *La Vita Nuova* from which we can extrapolate an individual voice. But it is a stylized voice, framed within the conventions of the *dolce stil nuovo* (sweet new style) and the epic tradition. Petrarch, Montaigne, Cervantes, Teresa of Avila, and Anne Bradstreet speak to us with a new directness and openness. These voices are stylized too, of course, but this stylization consists largely in the conviction that exposing one's most intimate life in its domestic and spiritual details is warranted by the occasion itself.

Part of this new accessibility has much to do with improved record-keeping on the part of cities, states, and religious organizations. The need to record, to scrutinize,

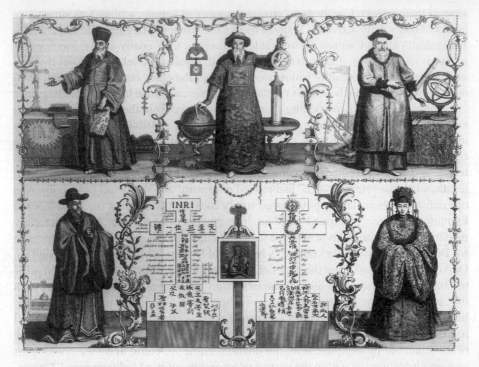

The Peking Mission. The Jesuit mission to China in the late 16th century was strictly speaking a failure, insofar as very few Chinese were converted by the small band of Italians, Spaniards, and Germans who lived among them for several decades. But the mission was about more than conversion. The top panel depicts three priests, Matteo Ricci, Adam Schaal, and Ferdinand Verbiest, representative less of their religious beliefs than of the recent innovations in Western science: the compass, the astrolabe, the quadrant. At the same time, science could be the path that led to conversion; Ricci would collaborate with one bureaucrat, Li Zhizao, on several mathematical works before Li became a Christian. Two such converts are shown in the lower panel, turned to face the cross which, the illustration says, "the Christians have now accustomed the Chinese to let themselves be buried with."

in order to find out "truths" amidst contingencies links Calvin's Geneva, the Inquisitorial trial of Galileo, and the arrival of Matteo Ricci, a Jesuit missionary, in the court of the emperor of China. Part of it also has to do with the fragmentation not only of a world, but of the literary genres that marked that world. Epic and tragedy, two classical imports much revised in the course of the early modern period, would find their share of practitioners. Other literary forms, some of them also salvaged from classical antiquity, were less monolithic and therefore perhaps less formidable. Those on the peripheries of elite culture found it easier to take up these lesser genres: the letter, the lyric, the essay, the autobiography, the short story and eventually the novel, in many ways a hodgepodge of all of the above. For most women, and for many men, entrance onto the literary scene began as simply the raising of a personal voice in reflection, in challenge, or in jest.

Given that early modern authors are so much more revealing about their lives, and given too that the invention of movable type and the centralizing of authority made the preserving of personal records easier than ever before, how much should our knowledge of an author's life influence our interpretation of a work? And how "personally" should early modern sonnets, essays, plays, and autobiographies be read? Should not perhaps the work stand apart, orphaned of its author, as does, of necessity, the *Iliad,* or *The Thousand and One Nights*? While a work's literary form can be a determining factor—Shakespeare is notoriously difficult to find in his plays, and no one will confuse Iago or Richard III, despite their many intimate asides, with the playwright—it is impossible to overlook the fact that a stance of humility, even anonymity, in regard to one's work, was soon overshadowed by a different, more assertive relationship. Nicola Pisano inscribed evidence of his authorship in the marble pulpit at Pisa, and Giotto, Dante's contemporary, became one of the first painters to cultivate a personally recognizable style. The great painter Albrecht Dürer would go so far as to identify his own self-portrait with Christ. If submission to the great creator had characterized an earlier artistic stance, in the period after Giotto the conviction grew that man had the freedom and authority to create in a world that was neither wholly secular nor wholly sacred. Such a recognition became part of the legacy that early modernity has passed down to us.

Still, the voices heard in the following pages attest to a volatile relationship between their words and the societies in which they lived. Not only was Galileo the victim of a judicial process, but Teresa of Avila, Catherine of Siena, and the unfortunate miller Domenico Scandella, alias Menocchio, were all sent before the Inquisition, the systematic inquiry (*inquisitio*) into heresy in the Catholic Church. All of Erasmus's works were placed on the Roman Index of Prohibited Books, along with writings by Rabelais, Boccaccio, and Petrarch. But Catholicism was not alone in persecuting potential heretics and subversives. Thomas More was decapitated for refusing to take the oath of allegiance to King Henry VIII after Henry repudiated the pope, and Martin Luther sanctioned the massacre of the peasants who rose up in support of Sebastian Lotzer's passionate words. In an era that played with the possibilities of alternate worlds and had the technological means to disseminate them ad infinitum, there were many who, having only recently attained authority or fighting desperately to keep others from attaining it, took "play" too seriously, and writers not infrequently paid the price. As a result, they often attempted to couch their radical arguments within deliberately distancing and sometimes disorienting frames. Erasmus's *Praise of Folly* is one example, Rabelais's *Gargantua* another. Others were careful to display a heightened sense of self-consciousness about the finally fictive status of their works, More's "Utopia" means "nowhere," while Shakespeare's Prospero reveals to Miranda and to us that the storm is only the result of a sleight-of-hand, and Vermeer's paintings, with their mirrors and drawing easels, constantly remind us of their own construction. The gleaning and publication of a supposedly self-evident truth, as Galileo learned, could be fraught with difficulties. And as in Galileo's case, such difficulties emerged from the perceived conflicts between profoundly held religious beliefs and the awareness of a new worldliness that militated against those very beliefs.

It is thus not surprising that early modern culture is marked throughout by reflections on its vulnerabilities. In many ways, this is a culture that emerges to protect a singular voice that at first boldly, and then perhaps more hesitatingly, called attention to the origins of art not in God or universals handed down for centuries, but in the thoughtful and creative self.

Giovanni Boccaccio

1313–1375

"These stories were told neither in a church, of whose affairs one must speak with a chaste mind and a pure tongue . . . nor in the schools of philosophers . . . [but] in a garden, in a place designed for pleasure, among people who, though young in years, were nonetheless fully mature and not to be led astray by stories." Thus does Giovanni Boccaccio defend his *Decameron* from its imagined detractors in the epilogue to his masterpiece. As its title indicates, the *Decameron* is the (fictional) record of ten days: days spent telling one hundred tales during one of the worst plagues ever to strike Europe. Centuries later, some readers were still blushing at the raciness of some of the stories told by ten young men and women who have fled plague-infested Florence; the tale of naive but insatiable Alibech, who exhausts an amorous hermit, was translated into English only in the late nineteenth century. Boccaccio himself had second thoughts in the wake of the visit of a monk to Florence a decade after the *Decameron* was finished, when Boccaccio had taken religious orders. Admonished to change his sinful ways, Boccaccio was moved by the conversation to wish to destroy his earlier "evil" writings. Only a timely letter from his good friend Francis Petrarch prevented the author from burning a work that has been hailed as the first European example of an immensely popular genre, the *novella* or short story.

Florence was a fertile place for the birth of such a collection. The same town that had exiled Dante in 1302 had become, by midcentury, a bustling commercial center, run by the city's merchant class rather than by its aristocrats. The stability of its banks and the success of its merchants, Boccaccio's father among them, produced the vibrant, wealthy city in which Boccaccio was born. This thriving city is not the plague-ridden town we see in the macabre preface, although it and other Tuscan cities like it reappear in all their local color in many tales told in the gardens to which Boccaccio's young conversationalists flee. The true birthplaces of the Renaissance in Italy, these towns were the first to witness the transition from a recognizably medieval era dominated by feudal relationships to a new age of which Boccaccio—occasionally thought of as "still" medieval—is representative in many ways. But if bustling Italian towns and their bourgeois inhabitants dominate many of the stories, they aren't the only hubs of activity. Boccaccio's eclectic storytellers take us from Babylon to the tangled pine forest outside Ravenna to the court of the king of Spain.

Boccaccio went to a wide range of sources for his tales, including Ovid's *Metamorphoses,* clerical manuals, French *lais,* and Arabic tales. Like Shakespeare, he was an avid borrower who transformed what he borrowed. The *Decameron* also reflects the courtly world which Boccaccio had known firsthand when he lived in Naples in the 1320s and 1330s. Here he spent some distasteful years first studying banking and law, then found Naples much more to his liking when he turned to poetry and joined the flourishing intellectual community of King Robert of Anjou. Boccaccio wrote his first works in Robert's court: his *Filostrato,* which would become the basis for Chaucer's *Troilus and Criseyde;* his epic *Filocolo,* about the misfortunes of the Muslim Biancifiore; and *Thesiad of the Marriage of Emilia.* All works in the vernacular, they look back to classical epic and culture while incorporating the meters and themes of medieval romance and contemporary Italian poetry. But this productive period in King Robert's court ended abruptly in 1341, when the Florentine bank for which Boccaccio's father worked met with disaster. Father and son regretfully returned to Florence where, in time, the young Boccaccio's house in Certaldo just south of the city would become the center of Florence's fledgling humanist movement.

The episode of the near book-burning might suggest that the *Decameron* represents the culmination of Boccaccio's youthful period, which includes one of the first psychological novels of European literature (*The Elegy of Madonna Fiammetta*) and the first modern pastoral (*Nymphs of Fiesole*). Such works, several of which feature men and women gathered in gardens to tell tales, were indeed good preparation for a collection of stories of knights, ladies, and magnanimous kings. At the same time, the *Decameron* is like nothing Boccaccio had written before, and like nothing Europe had seen before. Its encyclopedic scale looks ahead to Boccaccio's later Latin compendia, including his (unfinished) *Genealogy of the Pagan Gods* and *Lives of Famous Men,* begun under Petrarch's tutelage and carried out in the midst of Boccaccio's commitment to unraveling the obscurities of ancient texts (to the extent that he could boast of being one of the first Italians to have learned ancient Greek). Boccaccio's solicitude for women is visible in the *Decameron*'s preface when he suggests that his tales are for female readers who are forced to "spend most of their time cooped up within the narrow confines of their rooms." His attention to women is also evident in his collection of biographies of notable classical women, *De mulieribus claris,* dedicated, not incidentally, to a Florentine woman, Andrea Acciaiuoli. Finally, the Latinate style of Boccaccio's Italian is a testimony to his lifelong engagement with classical literature, while the fact that the *Decameron* is written in the vernacular may suggest the admiration Boccaccio had for his fellow Florentine Dante (whose daughter he visited in a nunnery to present her with ten gold florins from the Commune of Florence as partial restitution for her father's losses). He had to discontinue a series of public lectures on the *Inferno* because of illness in 1374, and shortly thereafter died.

Yet while the *Decameron* may adhere, like the *Divine Comedy,* to a careful structure, the sensibility of Boccaccio's work is markedly different from Dante's. Death in the *Decameron*'s introduction is portrayed as final, with no suggestion of a Dantesque afterlife, either infernal or redemptive. Rarely have the ravages of disease been so relentlessly described, and with them, the almost complete destruction of community and the bonds that hold it together. In this sense, the ten conversationalists' escape to the countryside is at once a strategy for survival (reminiscent of Scheherazade's witty tale-telling escapades in *The Thousand and One Nights*) and an attempt to restore what has been lost. But the world outside Florence cannot sustain them forever. The order created at the villa is only a tentative one. The songs they sing at the end of each day, the delicate feasts they enjoy, the beautiful Valley of the Ladies eloquently described on the seventh day, all point toward a kind of preciousness and fleeting beauty of their lives which are too fragile to last, but healing and of great comfort while they do.

The actual stories, on the other hand, largely reflect a different reality, far more durable and rugged. Only a very few transpire in places as pristine as the gardens in Fiesole, and the vast majority of them deal with the messy contingencies of everyday life: marriage to a husband who is impotent, or tyrannical, or adulterous; the lechery and greed of friars; the stupidity of one's neighbors and colleagues; the stinginess of a king. Yet for most of these problems the tales' protagonists find solutions. Many succeed through savvy and wit, as when Nathan the Wise confounds a Sultan who seeks to confound him. Some, particularly in the last day's stories, succeed through greatness of heart, as in the problematic tale of the patient wife Griselda. In some cases, though—particularly the tragedies of Day Four—there are no solutions to be found. Yet by taking into account the tragic along with the ribald, Chaucer's "gode Boccace" demonstrates how attentive he was to the vicissitudes of life and the narratives into which they can be placed, winning for the *Decameron* enthusiastic readers and imitators from every culture and every rung of the social ladder.

PRONUNCIATIONS:
Giovanni Boccaccio: jo-VAN-ni bo-KATCH-oh
Dioneo: dee-oh-NAY-oh

from DECAMERON[1]

from First Day

[INTRODUCTION]

Here begins the First Day of the Decameron, *wherein first of all the author explains the circumstances in which certain persons, who presently make their appearance, were induced to meet for the purpose of conversing together, after which, under the rule of* Pampinea, *each of them speaks on the subject they find most congenial.*

Whenever, fairest ladies,[2] I pause to consider how compassionate you all are by nature, I invariably become aware that the present work will seem to you to possess an irksome and ponderous opening. For it carries at its head the painful memory of the deadly havoc wrought by the recent plague,[3] which brought so much heartache and misery to those who witnessed, or had experience of it. But I do not want you to be deterred, for this reason, from reading any further, on the assumption that you are to be subjected, as you read, to an endless torrent of tears and sobbing. You will be affected no differently by this grim beginning than walkers confronted by a steep and rugged hill, beyond which there lies a beautiful and delectable plain. The degree of pleasure they derive from the latter will correspond directly to the difficulty of the climb and the descent. And just as the end of mirth is heaviness, so sorrows are dispersed by the advent of joy.

This brief unpleasantness (I call it brief, inasmuch as it is contained within few words) is quickly followed by the sweetness and the pleasure which I have already promised you, and which, unless you were told in advance, you would not perhaps be expecting to find after such a beginning as this. Believe me, if I could decently have taken you whither I desire by some other route, rather than along a path so difficult as this, I would gladly have done so. But since it is impossible without this memoir to show the origin of the events you will read about later, I really have no alternative but to address myself to its composition.

I say, then, that the sum of thirteen hundred and forty-eight years had elapsed since the fruitful Incarnation of the Son of God, when the noble city of Florence, which for its great beauty excels all others in Italy, was visited by the deadly pestilence. Some say that it descended upon the human race through the influence of the heavenly bodies, others that it was a punishment signifying God's righteous anger at our iniquitous way of life. But whatever its cause, it had originated some years earlier in the East, where it had claimed countless lives before it unhappily spread westward, growing in strength as it swept relentlessly on from one place to the next.

In the face of its onrush, all the wisdom and ingenuity of man were unavailing. Large quantities of refuse were cleared out of the city by officials specially appointed for the purpose, all sick persons were forbidden entry, and numerous instructions were issued for safeguarding the people's health, but all to no avail. Nor were the countless petitions humbly directed to God by the pious, whether by means of formal processions or in any other guise, any less ineffectual. For in the early spring of the

---

1. Translated from the Italian by G. H. McWilliam.
2. In his introduction to the *Decameron,* Boccaccio directly addresses women as his primary audience: "So in order that I may to some extent repair the omissions of Fortune, which (as we may see in the case of the more delicate sex) was always more sparing of support wher-

ever natural strength was more deficient, I intend to provide succour and diversion for the ladies, but only for those who are in love."
3. Written in the early 1350s, *The Decameron* looks back to the plague years of 1348–1349.

year we have mentioned, the plague began, in a terrifying and extraordinary manner, to make its disastrous effects apparent. It did not take the form it had assumed in the East, where if anyone bled from the nose it was an obvious portent of certain death. On the contrary, its earliest symptom, in men and women alike, was the appearance of certain swellings in the groin or the armpit, some of which were egg-shaped whilst others were roughly the size of the common apple. Sometimes the swellings were large, sometimes not so large, and they were referred to by the populace as *gavòccioli*.[4] From the two areas already mentioned, this deadly *gavòcciolo* would begin to spread, and within a short time it would appear at random all over the body. Later on, the symptoms of the disease changed, and many people began to find dark blotches and bruises on their arms, thighs, and other parts of the body, sometimes large and few in number, at other times tiny and closely spaced. These, to anyone unfortunate enough to contract them, were just as infallible a sign that he would die as the *gavòcciolo* had been earlier, and as indeed it still was.

Against these maladies, it seemed that all the advice of physicians and all the power of medicine were profitless and unavailing. Perhaps the nature of the illness was such that it allowed no remedy: or perhaps those people who were treating the illness (whose numbers had increased enormously because the ranks of the qualified were invaded by people, both men and women, who had never received any training in medicine), being ignorant of its causes, were not prescribing the appropriate cure. At all events, few of those who caught it ever recovered, and in most cases death occurred within three days from the appearance of the symptoms we have described, some people dying more rapidly than others, the majority without any fever or other complications.

But what made this pestilence even more severe was that whenever those suffering from it mixed with people who were still unaffected, it would rush upon these with the speed of a fire racing through dry or oily substances that happened to be placed within its reach. Nor was this the full extent of its evil, for not only did it infect healthy persons who conversed or had any dealings with the sick, making them ill or visiting an equally horrible death upon them, but it also seemed to transfer the sickness to anyone touching the clothes or other objects which had been handled or used by its victims.

It is a remarkable story that I have to relate. And were it not for the fact that I am one of many people who saw it with their own eyes, I would scarcely dare to believe it, let alone commit it to paper, even though I had heard it from a person whose word I could trust. The plague I have been describing was of so contagious a nature that very often it visibly did more than simply pass from one person to another. In other words, whenever an animal other than a human being touched anything belonging to a person who had been stricken or exterminated by the disease, it not only caught the sickness, but died from it almost at once. To all of this, as I have just said, my own eyes bore witness on more than one occasion. One day, for instance, the rags of a pauper who had died from the disease were thrown into the street, where they attracted the attention of two pigs. In their wonted fashion, the pigs first of all gave the rags a thorough mauling with their snouts after which they took them between their teeth and shook them against their cheeks. And within a short time they began to writhe as though they had been poisoned, then they both dropped dead to the ground, spreadeagled upon the rags that had brought about their undoing. * * *

4. Little goiters in local dialect.

In the face of so much affliction and misery, all respect for the laws of God and man had virtually broken down and been extinguished in our city. For like everybody else, those ministers and executors of the laws who were not either dead or ill were left with so few subordinates that they were unable to discharge any of their duties. Hence everyone was free to behave as he pleased. * * *

Some people, pursuing what was possibly the safer alternative, callously maintained that there was no better or more efficacious remedy against a plague than to run away from it. Swayed by this argument, and sparing no thought for anyone but themselves, large numbers of men and women abandoned their city, their homes, their relatives, their estates and their belongings, and headed for the countryside, either in Florentine territory or, better still, abroad. It was as though they imagined that the wrath of God would not unleash this plague against men for their iniquities irrespective of where they happened to be, but would only be aroused against those who found themselves within the city walls; or possibly they assumed that the whole of the population would be exterminated and that the city's last hour had come.

Of the people who held these various opinions, not all of them died. Nor, however, did they all survive. On the contrary, many of each different persuasion fell ill here, there, and everywhere, and having themselves, when they were fit and well, set an example to those who were as yet unaffected, they languished away with virtually no one to nurse them. It was not merely a question of one citizen avoiding another, and of people almost invariably neglecting their neighbours and rarely or never visiting their relatives, addressing them only from a distance; this scourge had implanted so great a terror in the hearts of men and women that brothers abandoned brothers, uncles their nephews, sisters their brothers, and in many cases wives deserted their husbands. But even worse, and almost incredible, was the fact that fathers and mothers refused to nurse and assist their own children, as though they did not belong to them. * * *

Whenever people died, their neighbours nearly always followed a single, set routine, prompted as much by their fear of being contaminated by the decaying corpse as by any charitable feelings they may have entertained towards the deceased. Either on their own, or with the assistance of bearers whenever these were to be had, they extracted the bodies of the dead from their houses and left them lying outside their front doors, where anyone going about the streets, especially in the early morning, could have observed countless numbers of them. Funeral biers would then be sent for, upon which the dead were taken away, though there were some who, for lack of biers, were carried off on plain boards. It was by no means rare for more than one of these biers to be seen with two or three bodies upon it at a time; on the contrary, many were seen to contain a husband and wife, two or three brothers and sisters, a father and son, or some other pair of close relatives. And times without number it happened that two priests would be on their way to bury someone, holding a cross before them, only to find that bearers carrying three or four additional biers would fall in behind them; so that whereas the priests had thought they had only one burial to attend to, they in fact had six or seven, and sometimes more. Even in these circumstances, however, there were no tears or candles or mourners to honour the dead; in fact, no more respect was accorded to dead people than would nowadays be shown towards dead goats. For it was quite apparent that the one thing which, in normal times, no wise man had ever learned to accept with patient resignation (even though it struck so seldom and unobtrusively), had now been brought home to the feeble-minded as well, but the scale of the calamity caused them to regard it with indifference.

Such was the multitude of corpses (of which further consignments were arriving every day and almost by the hour at each of the churches), that there was not sufficient consecrated ground for them to be buried in, especially if each was to have its own plot in accordance with long-established custom. So when all the graves were full, huge trenches were excavated in the churchyards, into which new arrivals were placed in their hundreds, stowed tier upon tier like ships' cargo, each layer of corpses being covered over with a thin layer of soil till the trench was filled to the top. * * *

What more remains to be said, except that the cruelty of heaven (and possibly, in some measure, also that of man) was so immense and so devastating that between March and July of the year in question, what with the fury of the pestilence and the fact that so many of the sick were inadequately cared for or abandoned in their hour of need because the healthy were too terrified to approach them, it is reliably thought that over a hundred thousand human lives were extinguished within the walls of the city of Florence? Yet before this lethal catastrophe fell upon the city, it is doubtful whether anyone would have guessed it contained so many inhabitants.[5]

Ah, how great a number of splendid palaces, fine houses, and noble dwellings, once filled with retainers, with lords and with ladies, were bereft of all who had lived there, down to the tiniest child! How numerous were the famous families, the vast estates, the notable fortunes, that were seen to be left without a rightful successor! How many gallant gentlemen, fair ladies, and sprightly youths, who would have been judged hale and hearty by Galen, Hippocrates and Aesculapius[6] (to say nothing of others), having breakfasted in the morning with their kinsfolk, acquaintances and friends, supped that same evening with their ancestors in the next world!

The more I reflect upon all this misery, the deeper my sense of personal sorrow; hence I shall refrain from describing those aspects which can suitably be omitted, and proceed to inform you that these were the conditions prevailing in our city, which was by now almost emptied of its inhabitants, when one Tuesday morning (or so I was told by a person whose word can be trusted) seven young ladies were to be found in the venerable church of Santa Maria Novella, which was otherwise almost deserted.[7] They had been attending divine service, and were dressed in mournful attire appropriate to the times. Each was a friend, a neighbour, or a relative of the other six, none was older than twenty-seven or younger than eighteen, and all were intelligent, gently bred, fair to look upon, graceful in bearing, and charmingly unaffected. I could tell you their actual names, but refrain from doing so for a good reason, namely that I would not want any of them to feel embarrassed, at any time in the future, on account of the ensuing stories, all of which they either listened to or narrated themselves. For nowadays, laws relating to pleasure are somewhat restrictive, whereas at that time, for the reasons indicated above, they were exceptionally lax, not only for ladies of their own age but also for much older women. Besides, I have no wish to supply envious tongues, ever ready to censure a laudable way of life, with a chance to besmirch the good name of these worthy ladies with their lewd and filthy gossip. And therefore, so that we may perceive distinctly what each of them had to say, I propose to refer to them by names which are either wholly or partially appropriate to the qualities of

5. The number is probably excessive. Before the plague, Florence is estimated as having had 100,000 citizens, making it one of the largest cities in Italy. As many as half of them died between 1348–1349.
6. Hippocrates and Galen were ancient Greek physicians;

Aesculapius was the Roman god of medicine.
7. The church was built by the Dominicans during the 13nth century on what were then the outskirts of Florence.

each. The first of them, who was also the eldest, we shall call Pampinea, the second Fiammetta, Filomena the third, and the fourth Emilia; then we shall name the fifth Lauretta, and the sixth Neifile, whilst to the last, not without reason, we shall give the name of Elissa.[8]

Without prior agreement but simply by chance, these seven ladies found themselves sitting, more or less in a circle, in one part of the church, reciting their paternosters.[9] Eventually, they left off and heaved a great many sighs, after which they began to talk among themselves on various different aspects of the times through which they were passing. But after a little while, they all fell silent except for Pampinea, who said:

"Dear ladies, you will often have heard it affirmed, as I have, that no man does injury to another in exercising his lawful rights. Every person born into this world has a natural right to sustain, preserve, and defend his own life to the best of his ability—a right so freely acknowledged that men have sometimes killed others in self-defence, and no blame whatever has attached to their actions. Now, if this is permitted by the laws, upon whose prompt application all mortal creatures depend for their well-being, how can it possibly be wrong, seeing that it harms no one, for us or anyone else to do all in our power to preserve our lives? If I pause to consider what we have been doing this morning, and what we have done on several mornings in the past, if I reflect on the nature and subject of our conversation, I realize, just as you also must realize, that each of us is apprehensive on her own account. This does not surprise me in the least, but what does greatly surprise me (seeing that each of us has the natural feelings of a woman) is that we do nothing to requite ourselves against the thing of which we are all so justly afraid.

"Here we linger for no other purpose, or so it seems to me, than to count the number of corpses being taken to burial, or to hear whether the friars of the church, very few of whom are left, chant their offices at the appropriate hours, or to exhibit the quality and quantity of our sorrows, by means of the clothes we are wearing, to all those whom we meet in this place. And if we go outside, we shall see the dead and the sick being carried hither and thither, or we shall see people, once condemned to exile by the courts for their misdeeds, careering wildly about the streets in open defiance of the law, well knowing that those appointed to enforce it are either dead or dying; or else we shall find ourselves at the mercy of the scum of our city who, having scented our blood, call themselves sextons and go prancing and bustling all over the place, singing bawdy songs that add insult to our injuries. Moreover, all we ever hear is 'So-and-so's dead' and 'So-and-so's dying'; and if there were anyone left to mourn, the whole place would be filled with sounds of wailing and weeping.

"And if we return to our homes, what happens? I know not whether your own experience is similar to mine, but my house was once full of servants, and now that there is no one left apart from my maid and myself, I am filled with foreboding and feel as if every hair of my head is standing on end. Wherever I go in the house, wherever I pause to rest, I seem to be haunted by the shades of the departed, whose faces no longer appear as I remember them but with strange and horribly twisted expressions that frighten me out of my senses.

"Accordingly, whether I am here in church or out in the streets or sitting at home, I always feel ill at ease, the more so because it seems to me that no one possessing pri-

---

8. The names carry varying mythological weight. Filom-ena means "nightingale," Laureta is associated with the laurel, and Elissa was another name for Dido, queen of Carthage in Virgil's *Aeneid*.
9. Our fathers, customary prayers.

vate means and a place to retreat to is left here apart from ourselves. But even if such people are still to be found, they draw no distinction, as I have frequently heard and seen for myself, between what is honest and what is dishonest; and provided only that they are prompted by their appetites, they will do whatever affords them the greatest pleasure, whether by day or by night, alone or in company. It is not only of lay people that I speak, but also of those enclosed in monasteries, who, having convinced themselves that such behaviour is suitable for them and is only unbecoming in others, have broken the rules of obedience and given themselves over to carnal pleasures, thereby thinking to escape, and have turned lascivious and dissolute.

"If this be so (and we plainly perceive that it is), what are we doing here? What are we waiting for? What are we dreaming about? Why do we lag so far behind all the rest of the citizens in providing for our safety? Do we rate ourselves lower than all other women? Or do we suppose that our own lives, unlike those of others, are bound to our bodies by such strong chains that we may ignore all those things which have the power to harm them? In that case we are deluded and mistaken. We have only to recall the names and the condition of the young men and women who have fallen victim to this cruel pestilence, in order to realize clearly the foolishness of such notions.

"And so, lest by pretending to be above such things or by becoming complacent we should succumb to that which we might possibly avoid if we so desired, I would think it an excellent idea (though I do not know whether you would agree with me) for us all to get away from this city, just as many others have done before us, and as indeed they are doing still. We could go and stay together on one of our various country estates, shunning at all costs the lewd practices of our fellow citizens and feasting and merrymaking as best we may without in any way overstepping the bounds of what is reasonable.

"There we shall hear the birds singing, we shall see fresh green hills and plains, fields of corn undulating like the sea, and trees of at least a thousand different species; and we shall have a clearer view of the heavens, which, troubled though they are, do not however deny us their eternal beauties, so much more fair to look upon than the desolate walls of our city. Moreover the country air is much more refreshing, the necessities of life in such a time as this are more abundant, and there are fewer obstacles to contend with. For although the farmworkers are dying there in the same way as the townspeople here in Florence, the spectacle is less harrowing inasmuch as the houses and people are more widely scattered. Besides, unless I am mistaken we shall not be abandoning anyone by going away from here; on the contrary, we may fairly claim that we are the ones who have been abandoned, for our kinsfolk are either dead or fled, and have left us to fend for ourselves in the midst of all this affliction, as though disowning us completely.

"Hence no one can reproach us for taking the course I have advocated, whereas if we do nothing we shall inevitably be confronted with distress and mourning, and possibly forfeit our lives into the bargain. Let us therefore do as I suggest, taking our maidservants with us and seeing to the dispatch of all the things we shall need. We can move from place to place, spending one day here and another there, pursuing whatever pleasures and entertainments the present times will afford. In this way of life we shall continue until such time as we discover (provided we are spared from early death) the end decreed by Heaven for these terrible events. You must remember, after all, that it is no more unseemly for us to go away and thus preserve our own honour than it is for most other women to remain here and forfeit theirs."

* * *

[THE WOMEN, ALONG WITH THREE YOUNG MEN ARRIVE IN FIESOLE.][1]

Scarcely had they travelled two miles from Florence before they reached the place at which they had agreed to stay.

The spot in question was some distance away from any road, on a small hill that was agreeable to behold for its abundance of shrubs and trees, all bedecked in green leaves. Perched on its summit was a palace, built round a fine, spacious courtyard, and containing loggias, halls, and sleeping apartments, which were not only excellently proportioned but richly embellished with paintings depicting scenes of gaiety. Delectable gardens and meadows lay all around, and there were wells of cool, refreshing water. The cellars were stocked with precious wines, more suited to the palates of connoisseurs than to sedate and respectable ladies. And on their arrival the company discovered, to their no small pleasure, that the place had been cleaned from top to bottom, the beds in the rooms were made up, the whole house was adorned with seasonable flowers of every description, and the floors had been carpeted with rushes.

Soon after reaching the palace, they all sat down, and Dioneo, a youth of matchless charm and readiness of wit, said:

"It is not our foresight, ladies, but rather your own good sense, that has led us to this spot. I know not what you intend to do with your troubles; my own I left inside the city gates when I departed thence a short while ago in your company. Hence you may either prepare to join with me in as much laughter, song and merriment as your sense of decorum will allow, or else you may give me leave to go back for my troubles and live in the afflicted city."

Pampinea, as though she too had driven away all her troubles, answered him in the same carefree vein.

"There is much sense in what you say, Dioneo," she replied. "A merry life should be our aim, since it was for no other reason that we were prompted to run away from the sorrows of the city. However, nothing will last for very long unless it possesses a definite form. And since it was I who led the discussions from which this fair company has come into being, I have given some thought to the continuance of our happiness, and consider it necessary for us to choose a leader, drawn from our own ranks, whom we would honour and obey as our superior, and whose sole concern will be that of devising the means whereby we may pass our time agreeably. But so that none of us will complain that he or she has had no opportunity to experience the burden of responsibility and the pleasure of command associated with sovereign power, I propose that the burden and the honour should be assigned to each of us in turn for a single day. It will be for all of us to decide who is to be our first ruler, after which it will be up to each ruler, when the hour of vespers approaches, to elect his or her successor from among the ladies and gentlemen present. The person chosen to govern will be at liberty to make whatever arrangements he likes for the period covered by his rule, and to prescribe the place and the manner in which we are to live."[2]

* * *

1. In the intervening pages, the seven women have met up with three men, who have joined them in the church: Pamphilo, Filostrato, and Dioneo (who is described as "more attractive and wittier than either of the other young men"). They agree that they can live virtuously together, and they leave the plague-ridden city together for Fiesole, a hill-town northeast of Florence.
2. Pampinea is elected queen for the first day, and following a siesta, suggests to her companions that they proceed to spend "this hotter part of the day" in telling stories, "an activity that may afford some amusement to the narrator and to the company at large. By the time each one of you has narrated a little tale of his own or her own, the sun will be setting, the heat will have abated and we shall be able to go and amuse ourselves wherever you choose." The company agrees to her suggestion, and she decrees that on the first day, "each of us should be free to speak upon whatever topic he prefers."

Third Story: [The Three Rings]

Melchizedek the Jew, with a story about three rings, avoids a most dangerous trap laid for him by Saladin.

Neifile's story was well received by all the company, and when she fell silent, Filomena began at the queen's behest to address them as follows:

The story told by Neifile reminds me of the parlous state in which a Jew once found himself. Now that we have heard such fine things said concerning God and the truth of our religion,[1] it will not seem inappropriate to descend at this juncture to the deeds and adventures of men. So I shall tell you a story which, when you have heard it, will possibly make you more cautious in answering questions addressed to you. It is a fact, my sweet companions, that just as folly often destroys men's happiness and casts them into deepest misery, so prudence extricates the wise from dreadful perils and guides them firmly to safety. So clearly may we perceive that folly leads men from contentment to misery, that we shall not even bother for the present to consider the matter further, since countless examples spring readily to mind. But that prudence may bring its reward, I shall, as I have promised, prove to you briefly by means of the following little tale:

Saladin, whose worth was so great that it raised him from humble beginnings to the sultanate of Egypt and brought him many victories over Saracen and Christian kings,[2] had expended the whole of his treasure in various wars and extraordinary acts of munificence, when a certain situation arose for which he required a vast sum of money. Not being able to see any way of obtaining what he needed at such short notice, he happened to recall a rich Jew, Melchizedek by name, who ran a money-lending business in Alexandria,[3] and would certainly, he thought, have enough for his purposes, if only he could be persuaded to part with it. But this Melchizedek was such a miserly fellow that he would never hand it over of his own free will, and the Sultan was not prepared to take it away from him by force. However, as his need became more pressing, having racked his brains to discover some way of compelling the Jew to assist him, he resolved to use force in the guise of reason. So he sent for the Jew, gave him a cordial reception, invited him to sit down beside him, and said:

"O man of excellent worth, many men have told me of your great wisdom and your superior knowledge of the ways of God. Hence I would be glad if you would tell me which of the three laws, whether the Jewish, the Saracen, or the Christian, you deem to be truly authentic."

The Jew, who was indeed a wise man, realized all too well that Saladin was aiming to trip him up with the intention of picking a quarrel with him, and that if he were to praise any of the three more than the others, the Sultan would achieve his object. He therefore had need of a reply that would save him from falling into the trap, and having sharpened his wits, in no time at all he was ready with his answer.

"My lord," he said, "your question is a very good one, and in order to explain my views on the subject, I must ask you to listen to the following little story:

---

1. The second story of the first day was about a Jew called Abraham who travels from Paris to Rome to see for himself how depraved the church hierarchy is. Yet he decides to convert to Christianity, seeing how the religion has "grown in popularity and become more splendid and illustrious" despite the church's corruption: "I can only conclude that, being a more holy and genuine religion than any of the others, it deservedly has the Holy Ghost as its foundation and support."

2. Salah-ed-din was sultan of Syria and Egypt in the 12th century. Under his rule the Muslims regained the city of Jerusalem from the Christians in 1187.

3. In Egypt.

"Unless I am mistaken, I recall having frequently heard that there was once a great and wealthy man who, apart from the other fine jewels contained in his treasury, possessed a most precious and beautiful ring. Because of its value and beauty, he wanted to do it the honour of leaving it in perpetuity to his descendants, and so he announced that he would bequeath the ring to one of his sons, and that whichever of them should be found to have it in his keeping, this man was to be looked upon as his heir, and the others were to honour and respect him as the head of the family.

"The man to whom he left the ring, having made a similar provision regarding his own descendants, followed the example set by his predecessor. To cut a long story short, the ring was handed down through many generations till it finally came to rest in the hands of a man who had three most splendid and virtuous sons who were very obedient to their father, and he loved all three of them equally. Each of the three young men, being aware of the tradition concerning the ring, was eager to take precedence over the others, and they all did their utmost to persuade the father, who was now an old man, to leave them the ring when he died.

"The good man, who loved all three and was unable to decide which of them should inherit the ring, resolved, having promised it to each, to try and please them all. So he secretly commissioned a master-craftsman to make two more rings, which were so like the first that even the man who had made them could barely distinguish them from the original. And when he was dying, he took each of his sons aside in turn, and gave one ring to each.

"After their father's death, they all desired to succeed to his title and estate, and each man denied the claims of the others, producing his ring to prove his case. But finding that the rings were so alike that it was impossible to tell them apart, the question of which of the sons was the true and rightful heir remained in abeyance, and has never been settled.

"And I say to you, my lord, that the same applies to the three laws which God the Father granted to His three peoples, and which formed the subject of your inquiry. Each of them considers itself the legitimate heir to His estate, each believes it possesses His one true law and observes His commandments. But as with the rings, the question as to which of them is right remains in abeyance."

Saladin perceived that the fellow had ingeniously side-stepped the trap he had set before him, and he therefore decided to make a clean breast of his needs, and see if the Jew would come to his assistance. This he did, freely admitting what he had intended to do, but for the fact that the Jew had answered him so discreetly.

Melchizedek gladly provided the Sultan with the money he required. The Sultan later paid him back in full, in addition to which he showered magnificent gifts upon him, made him his lifelong friend, and maintained him at his court in a state of importance and honour.

from Third Day[1]
Tenth Story: [Locking the Devil Up in Hell]

Alibech becomes a recluse, and after being taught by the monk, Rustico, to put the devil back in Hell, she is eventually taken away to become the wife of Neerbal.

---

1. The theme for the third day, under the rule of Neifile, is about people who achieved something they desired, or recovered something they lost. Dioneo, who by prior agreement always tells the final tale of each day, is also exempt from the rules regarding the theme.

Dioneo had been following the queen's story closely, and on perceiving that it was finished, knowing that he was the only speaker left, he smiled and began without waiting to be bidden:

Gracious ladies, you have possibly never heard how the devil is put back into Hell, and hence, without unduly straying from the theme of your discussions for to-day, I should like to tell you about it. By learning how it is done, there may yet be time perhaps for you to save our souls from perdition, and you will also discover that, even though Love is more inclined to take up his abode in a gay palace and a dainty bedchamber than in a wretched hovel, there is no denying that he sometimes makes his powers felt among pathless woods, on rugged mountains, and in desert caves; nor is this surprising, since all living things are subject to his sway.

Now, to come to the point, there once lived in the town of Gafsa, in Barbary,[2] a very rich man who had numerous children, among them a lovely and graceful young daughter called Alibech. She was not herself a Christian, but there were many Christians in the town, and one day, having on occasion heard them extol the Christian faith and the service of God, she asked one of them for his opinion on the best and easiest way for a person to "serve God," as they put it. He answered her by saying that the ones who served God best were those who put the greatest distance between themselves and earthly goods, as happened in the case of people who had gone to live in the remoter parts of the Sahara.[3]

She said no more about it to anyone, but next morning, being a very simple-natured creature of fourteen or thereabouts, Alibech set out all alone, in secret, and made her way towards the desert, prompted by nothing more logical than a strong adolescent impulse. A few days later, exhausted from fatigue and hunger, she arrived in the heart of the wilderness, where, catching sight of a small hut in the distance, she stumbled towards it, and in the doorway she found a holy man, who was astonished to see her in those parts and asked her what she was doing there. She told him that she had been inspired by God, and that she was trying, not only to serve Him, but also to find someone who could teach her how she should go about it.

On observing how young and exceedingly pretty she was, the good man was afraid to take her under his wing lest the devil should catch him unawares. So he praised her for her good intentions, and having given her a quantity of herb-roots, wild apples and dates to eat, and some water to drink, he said to her:

"My daughter, not very far from here there is a holy man who is much more capable than I of teaching you what you want to know. Go along to him." And he sent her upon her way.

When she came to this second man, she was told precisely the same thing, and so she went on until she arrived at the cell of a young hermit, a very devout and kindly fellow called Rustico, to whom she put the same inquiry as she had addressed to the others. Being anxious to prove to himself that he possessed a will of iron, he did not, like the others, send her away or direct her elsewhere, but kept her with him in his cell, in a corner of which, when night descended, he prepared a makeshift bed out of palm-leaves, upon which he invited her to lie down and rest.

2. Gafsa is a city in Tunisia; Barbary is the term used to describe northwest Africa, settled largely by Berbers.
3. More precisely, the deserts around Thebes, in ancient Egypt, where many monks and Christian anchorites retreated for lives of contemplation and penitence.

Once he had taken this step, very little time elapsed before temptation went to war against his willpower, and after the first few assaults, finding himself outmanoeuvred on all fronts, he laid down his arms and surrendered. Casting aside pious thoughts, prayers, and penitential exercises, he began to concentrate his mental faculties upon the youth and beauty of the girl, and to devise suitable ways and means for approaching her in such a fashion that she should not think it lewd of him to make the sort of proposal he had in mind. By putting certain questions to her, he soon discovered that she had never been intimate with the opposite sex and was every bit as innocent as she seemed; and he therefore thought of a possible way to persuade her, with the pretext of serving God, to gratify his desires. He began by delivering a long speech in which he showed her how powerful an enemy the devil was to the Lord God, and followed this up by impressing upon her that of all the ways of serving God, the one that He most appreciated consisted in putting the devil back in Hell, to which the Almighty had consigned him in the first place.

The girl asked him how this was done, and Rustico replied:

"You will soon find out, but just do whatever you see me doing for the present." And so saying, he began to divest himself of the few clothes he was wearing, leaving himself completely naked. The girl followed his example, and he sank to his knees as though he were about to pray, getting her to kneel directly opposite.

In this posture, the girl's beauty was displayed to Rustico in all its glory, and his longings blazed more fiercely than ever, bringing about the resurrection of the flesh.[4] Alibech stared at this in amazement, and said:

"Rustico, what is that thing I see sticking out in front of you, which I do not possess?"

"Oh, my daughter," said Rustico, "this is the devil I was telling you about. Do you see what he's doing? He's hurting me so much that I can hardly endure it."

"Oh, praise be to God," said the girl, "I can see that I am better off than you are, for I have no such devil to contend with."

"You're right there," said Rustico. "But you have something else instead, that I haven't."

"Oh?" said Alibech. "And what's that?"

"You have Hell," said Rustico. "And I honestly believe that God has sent you here for the salvation of my soul, because if this devil continues to plague the life out of me, and if you are prepared to take sufficient pity upon me to let me put him back into Hell, you will be giving me marvellous relief, as well as rendering incalculable service and pleasure to God, which is what you say you came here for to begin with."

"Oh, Father," replied the girl in all innocence, "if I really do have a Hell, let's do as you suggest just as soon as you are ready."

"God bless you, my daughter," said Rustico. "Let us go and put him back and then perhaps he'll leave me alone."

At which point he conveyed the girl to one of their beds, where he instructed her in the art of incarcerating that accursed fiend.

Never having put a single devil into Hell before, the girl found the first experience a little painful, and she said to Rustico:

"This devil must certainly be a bad lot, Father, and a true enemy of God, for as well as plaguing mankind, he even hurts Hell when he's driven back inside it."

---

4. A punning allusion to the Last Judgment.

"Daughter," said Rustico, "it will not always be like that." And in order to ensure that it wouldn't, before moving from the bed they put him back half a dozen times, curbing his arrogance to such good effect that he was positively glad to keep still for the rest of the day.

During the next few days, however, the devil's pride frequently reared its head again, and the girl, ever ready to obey the call to duty and bring him under control, happened to develop a taste for the sport, and began saying to Rustico:

"I can certainly see what those worthy men in Gafsa meant when they said that serving God was so agreeable. I don't honestly recall ever having done anything that gave me so much pleasure and satisfaction as I get from putting the devil back in Hell. To my way of thinking, anyone who devotes his energies to anything but the service of God is a complete blockhead."

She thus developed the habit of going to Rustico at frequent intervals, and saying to him:

"Father, I came here to serve God, not to idle away my time. Let's go and put the devil back in Hell."

And sometimes, in the middle of their labours, she would say:

"What puzzles me, Rustico, is that the devil should ever want to escape from Hell. Because if he liked being there as much as Hell enjoys receiving him and keeping him inside, he would never go away at all."

By inviting Rustico to play the game too often, continually urging him on in the service of God, the girl took so much stuffing out of him that he eventually began to turn cold where another man would have been bathed in sweat. So he told her that the devil should only be punished and put back in Hell when he reared his head with pride, adding that by the grace of Heaven, they had tamed him so effectively that he was pleading with God to be left in peace. In this way, he managed to keep the girl quiet for a while, but one day, having begun to notice that Rustico was no longer asking for the devil to be put back in Hell, she said:

"Look here, Rustico. Even though your devil has been punished and pesters you no longer, my Hell simply refuses to leave me alone. Now that I have helped you with my Hell to subdue the pride of your devil, the least you can do is to get your devil to help me tame the fury of my Hell."

Rustico, who was living on a diet of herb-roots and water, was quite incapable of supplying her requirements, and told her that the taming of her Hell would require an awful lot of devils, but promised to do what he could. Sometimes, therefore, he responded to the call, but this happened so infrequently that it was rather like chucking a bean into the mouth of a lion, with the result that the girl, who felt that she was not serving God as diligently as she would have liked, was found complaining more often than not.

But at the height of this dispute between Alibech's Hell and Rustico's devil, brought about by a surplus of desire on the one hand and a shortage of power on the other, a fire broke out in Gafsa, and Alibech's father was burnt to death in his own house along with all his children and every other member of his household, so that Alibech inherited the whole of his property. Because of this a young man called Neerbal who had spent the whole of his substance in sumptuous living, having heard that she was still alive, set out to look for her, and before the authorities were able to appropriate her late father's fortune on the grounds that there was no heir, he succeeded in tracing her whereabouts. To the great relief of Rustico, but against her own wishes, he took her back to Gafsa and married her, thus inheriting a half-share in her father's enormous fortune.

Before Neerbal had actually slept with her, she was questioned by the women of Gafsa about how she had served God in the desert, and she replied that she had served Him by putting the devil back in Hell, and that Neerbal had committed a terrible sin by stopping her from performing so worthy a service.

"How do you put the devil back in Hell?" asked the women.

Partly in words and partly through gestures, the girl showed them how it was done, whereupon the women laughed so much that they are laughing yet; and they said:

"Don't let it worry you, my dear. People do the job every bit as well here in Gafsa, and Neerbal will give you plenty of help in serving the Lord."

The story was repeated throughout the town, being passed from one woman to the next, and they coined a proverbial saying there to the effect that the most agreeable way of serving God was to put the devil back in Hell. The dictum later crossed the sea to Italy, where it survives to this day.

And so, young ladies, if you stand in need of God's grace, see that you learn to put the devil back in Hell, for it is greatly to His liking and pleasurable to the parties concerned, and a great deal of good can arise and flow in the process.

* * *

So aptly and cleverly worded did Dioneo's tale appear to the virtuous ladies, that they shook with mirth a thousand times or more. And when he had brought it to a close, the queen, acknowledging the end of her sovereignty, removed the laurel from her head and placed it very gracefully on Filostrato's, saying:

"Now we shall discover whether the wolf can fare any better at leading the sheep than the sheep have fared in leading the wolves."[5]

On hearing this, Filostrato laughed and said: "Had you listened to me, the wolves would have taught the sheep by now to put the devil back in Hell, no less skilfully than Rustico taught Alibech. But you have not exactly been behaving like sheep, and therefore you must not describe us as wolves. However, you have placed the kingdom in my hands, and I shall govern it as well as I am able." * * *

Seventh Day[1]
Fourth Story: [The Woman Who Locked Her Husband Out]

[THUS LAURETTA BEGAN HER TALE:]

O Love, how manifold and mighty are your powers! How wise your counsels, how keen your insights! What philosopher, what artist could ever have conjured up all the arguments, all the subterfuges, all the explanations that you offer spontaneously to those who nail their colours to your mast? Every other doctrine is assuredly behindhand in comparison with yours, as may clearly be seen from the cases already brought to our notice. And to these, fond ladies, I shall now add yet another, by telling you of the expedient adopted by a woman of no great intelligence, who to my way of thinking could only have been motivated by Love.

---

5. Filostrato will be the first man to lead the day's tale-telling.
1. Tales of the seventh day, over which Dioneo rules, are to be about "tricks which, either in the cause of love or for

motives of self-preservation, women have played upon their husbands, irrespecitve of whether or not they were found out."

In the city of Arezzo,[2] then, there once lived a man of means, Tofano[3] by name, who, having taken to wife a woman of very great beauty, called Monna Ghita, promptly grew jealous of her without any reason. On perceiving how jealous he was, the lady took offence and repeatedly asked him to explain the reason, but since he could only reply in vague and illogical terms, she resolved to make him suffer in good earnest from the ill which hitherto he had feared without cause.

Having observed that a certain young man, a very agreeable sort of fellow to her way of thinking, was casting amorous glances in her direction, she secretly began to cultivate his acquaintance. And when she and the young man had carried the affair to the point where it only remained to translate words into deeds, she once again took the initiative and devised a way of doing it. She had already discovered that one of her husband's bad habits was a fondness for drink, and so she began not only to commend him for it, but to encourage him deliberately whenever she had the chance. With a little practice, she quickly acquired the knack of persuading him to drink himself into a stupor, almost as often as she chose, and once she saw that he was blind drunk, she put him to bed and forgathered with her lover. This soon became a regular habit of theirs, and they met together in perfect safety. Indeed, the lady came to rely so completely on the fellow's talent for drinking himself unconscious that she made bold, not only to admit her lover to the premises, but on occasion to go and spend a goodly part of the night with him at his own house, which was no great distance away.

The amorous lady had been doing this for quite some time when her unfortunate husband happened to notice that although she encouraged him to drink, she herself never drank at all, which made him suspect (as was indeed the case) that his wife was making him drunk so that she could do as she pleased when he was asleep. In order to prove whether this was so, he returned home one evening, having refrained from drinking for the whole day, and pretended to be as drunk as a lord, scarcely able to speak or stand on his feet. Being taken in by all this, and concluding that he would sleep like a log without imbibing any more liquor, his wife quickly put him to bed, then left the house and made her way, as on previous occasions, to the house of her lover, where she stayed for half the night.

Hearing no sound from his wife, Tofano got up, went and bolted the door from the inside, and stationed himself at the window so that he would see her coming back and let her know that he had tumbled to her mischief; and there he remained until she returned. Great indeed was the woman's distress when she came home to find that she was locked out, and she began to apply all her strength in an effort to force the door open.

Tofano put up with this for a while, then he said:

"You're wasting your energies, woman. You can't possibly get in. Go back to wherever it is that you've been until this hour of the night, and rest assured that you won't return to this house till I've made an example of you in front of your kinsfolk and neighbours."

Then his wife began to plead with him for the love of God to let her in, saying that she had not been doing anything wrong, as he supposed, but simply keeping vigil with a neighbour of hers, who could neither sleep the whole night because it was too long, nor keep vigil in the house by herself.

---

2. A city in Tuscany, to the southeast of Florence.   3. From Cristoforo, or Christopher.

Her pleas were totally unavailing, for the silly ass was clearly determined that all the Aretines should learn about his dishonour, of which none of them had so far heard anything. And when she saw that it was no use pleading with him, the woman resorted to threats, and said:

"If you don't let me in, I shall make you the sorriest man on earth."

To which Tofano replied:

"And how are you going to do that?"

The lady had all her wits about her, for Love was her counsellor, and she replied:

"Rather than face the dishonour which in spite of my innocence you threaten me with, I shall hurl myself into this well, and when they find me dead inside it, they will all think that it was you who threw me into it when you were drunk; and so either you will have to run away, lose everything you possess, and live in exile, or you will have your head chopped off for murdering your wife, which in effect is what you will have done."

But having made up his stupid mind, Tofano was not affected in the slightest by these words, and so his wife said:

"Now look here, I won't let you torment me any longer; may God forgive you, I'll leave my distaff here, and you can put it back where it belongs."

The night was so dark that you could scarcely see your hand in front of your face, and having uttered these words, the woman groped her way towards the well, picked up an enormous stone that was lying beside it, and with a cry of "God forgive me!" she dropped it into the depths. The stone struck the water with a tremendous thump, and when Tofano heard this he was firmly convinced that she had thrown herself in. So he seized the pail and its rope, rushed head-long from the house, and ran to the well to assist her. His wife was lying in wait near the front door, and as soon as she saw him running to the well, she stepped inside the house, bolted the door, and went to the window, where she stood and shouted:

"You should water down your wine when you're drinking it, and not in the middle of the night."

When he heard her voice, Tofano saw that he had been outwitted and made his way back to the house. And on finding that he couldn't open the door, he ordered her to let him in.

Whereas previously she had addressed him in little more than a whisper, his wife now began to shout almost at the top of her voice, saying:

"By the cross of God, you loathsome sot, you're not going to come in here tonight. I will not tolerate this conduct of yours any longer. It's time I showed people the sort of man you are and the hours you keep."

Being very angry, Tofano too began to shout, pouring out a stream of abuse, so that the neighbours, men and women alike, hearing all this racket, got up out of bed and appeared at their windows, demanding to know what was going on.

The woman's eyes filled with tears, and she said: "It's this villain of a man, who returns home drunk of an evening, or else he falls asleep in some tavern or other and then comes back at this hour. I've put up with it for God knows how long and remonstrated with him until I was blue in the face. But I can't put up with it any longer, and so I've decided to take him down a peg or two by locking him out, to see whether he will mend his ways."

Tofano on the other hand, like the fool that he was, explained precisely what had happened, and came out with a whole lot of threats and abuse, whereupon his wife spoke up again, saying to the neighbours:

"You see the sort of man he is! What would you say if I were in the street and he was in the house, instead of the other way round? In God's faith I've no doubt you would believe what he was saying. So you can see what a crafty fellow he is. He accuses me of doing the very thing that he appears to have done himself. He thought he could frighten me by dropping something or other down the well; but I wish to God that he really had thrown himself in, and drowned himself at the same time, so that all the wine he's been drinking would have been well and truly diluted."

The neighbours, men and women alike, all began to scold Tofano, putting the blame on him alone and reviling him for slandering his poor wife; and in brief, they created such an uproar that it eventually reached the ears of the woman's kinsfolk.

Her kinsfolk hurried to the scene, and having listened to the accounts of several of the neighbours, they took hold of Tofano and hammered him till he was black and blue. They then went into the house, collected all the woman's belongings, and took her back with them, threatening Tofano with worse to follow.

Seeing what a sorry plight he had landed himself in on account of his jealousy, Tofano, since he was really very fond of his wife, persuaded certain friends of his to intercede on his behalf with the lady's kinsfolk, with whom he succeeded in making his peace and arranging for her to come back to him. And not only did he promise her that he would never be jealous again, but he gave her permission to amuse herself to her heart's content, provided she was sensible enough not to let him catch her out. So, like the stupid peasant, he first was mad and then was pleasant. Long live love, therefore, and a plague on all skinflints!

Tenth Day[1]
Tenth Story: [The Patient Griselda]

The Marquis of Saluzzo, obliged by the entreaties of his subjects to take a wife, follows his personal whims and marries the daughter of a peasant. She bears him two children, and he gives her the impression that he has put them to death. Later on, pretending that she has incurred his displeasure and that he has remarried, he arranges for his own daughter to return home and passes her off as his bride, having meanwhile turned his wife out of doors in no more than the shift she is wearing. But on finding that she endures it all with patience, he cherishes her all the more deeply, brings her back to his house, shows her their children, who have now grown up, and honours her as the Marchioness, causing others to honour her likewise.

Sweet and gentle ladies, [said Dioneo] this day has been devoted, so far as I can see, to the doings of kings and sultans and people of that sort; and therefore, so as not to place too great a distance between us, I want to tell you of a marquis, whose actions, even though things turned out well for him in the end, were remarkable not so much for their munificence as for their senseless brutality.[2] Nor do I advise anyone to follow his example, for it was a great pity that the fellow should have drawn any profit from his conduct.

---

1. For the final day, over which Panfilo presides, "the discussion turns upon those who have performed liberal or munificent deeds, whether in the cause of love or otherwise." As always, Dioneo goes last and is exempt from the thematic rule.
2. In Italian, "matta bestialitade" (mad bestiality), a phrase which echoes Dante's description of one of the "three dispositions/ that strike at Heaven's will: incontinence/ and malice and mad bestiality" (*Inferno* XI: 81-2); the phrase covers those found in the Seventh Circle, the violent against their neighbours, themselves, nature, and God.

A very long time ago, there succeeded to the marquisate of Saluzzo[3] a young man called Gualtieri, who, having neither wife nor children, spent the whole of his time hunting and hawking, and never even thought about marrying or raising a family, which says a great deal for his intelligence. His followers, however, disapproved of this, and repeatedly begged him to marry so that he should not be left without an heir nor they without a lord. Moreover, they offered to find him a wife whose parentage would be such as to strengthen their expectations and who would make him exceedingly happy.

So Gualtieri answered them as follows:

"My friends, you are pressing me to do something that I had always set my mind firmly against, seeing how difficult it is to find a person who will easily adapt to one's own way of living, how many thousands there are who will do precisely the opposite, and what a miserable life is in store for the man who stumbles upon a woman ill-suited to his own temperament. Moreover it is foolish of you to believe that you can judge the character of daughters from the ways of their fathers and mothers, hence claiming to provide me with a wife who will please me. For I cannot see how you are to know the fathers, or to discover the secrets of the mothers; and even if this were possible, daughters are very often different from either of their parents. Since, however, you are so determined to bind me in chains of this sort, I am ready to do as you ask; but so that I have only myself to blame if it should turn out badly, I must insist on marrying a wife of my own choosing. And I hereby declare that no matter who she may be, if you fail to honour her as your lady you will learn to your great cost how serious a matter it is for you to have urged me to marry against my will."

To this the gentlemen replied that if only he would bring himself to take a wife, they would be satisfied.

Now, for some little time, Gualtieri had been casting an appreciative eye on the manners of a poor girl from a neighbouring village, and thinking her very beautiful, he considered that a life with her would have much to commend it. So without looking further afield, he resolved to marry the girl; and having summoned her father, who was very poor indeed, he arranged with him that he should take her as his wife.

This done, Gualtieri brought together all his friends from the various parts of his domain, and said to them:

"My friends, since you still persist in wanting me to take a wife, I am prepared to do it, not because I have any desire to marry, but rather in order to gratify your wishes. You will recall the promise you gave me, that no matter whom I should choose, you would rest content and honour her as your lady. The time has now come when I want you to keep that promise, and for me to honour the promise I gave to you. I have found a girl after my own heart, in this very district, and a few days hence I intend to marry her and convey her to my house. See to it, therefore, that the wedding-feast lacks nothing in splendour, and consider how you may honourably receive her, so that all of us may call ourselves contented—I with you for keeping your promise, and you with me for keeping mine."

As of one voice, the good folk joyously gave him their blessing, and said that whoever she happened to be, they would accept her as their lady and honour her as such in all respects. Then they all prepared to celebrate the wedding in a suitably grand and sumptuous manner, and Gualtieri did the same. A rich and splendid nuptial feast

---

3. Saluzzo is in northwestern Italy, in the region of Piedmont.

was arranged, to which he invited many of his friends, his kinsfolk, great nobles and other people of the locality; moreover he caused a quantity of fine, rich robes to be tailored to fit a girl whose figure appeared to match that of the young woman he intended to marry; and lastly he laid in a number of rings and ornamental belts, along with a precious and beautiful crown, and everything else that a bride could possibly need.

Early on the morning of the day he had fixed for the nuptials, Gualtieri, his preparations now complete, mounted his horse together with all the people who had come to do him honour, and said:

"Gentlemen, it is time for us to go and fetch the bride."

He then set forth with the whole of the company in train, and eventually they came to the village and made their way to the house of the girl's father, where they met her as she was returning with water from the fountain, making great haste so that she could go with other women to see Gualtieri's bride arriving. As soon as Gualtieri caught sight of her, he called to her by her name, which was Griselda, and asked her where her father was, to which she blushingly replied:

"My lord, he is at home."

So Gualtieri dismounted, and having ordered everyone to wait for him outside, he went alone into the humble dwelling, where he found the girl's father, whose name was Giannùcole,[4] and said to him:

"I have come to marry Griselda, but first I want to ask her certain questions in your presence." He then asked her whether, if he were to marry her, she would always try to please him and never be upset by anything he said or did, whether she would obey him, and many other questions of this sort, to all of which she answered that she would.

Whereupon Gualtieri, having taken her by the hand, led her out of the house, and in the presence of his whole company and of all the other people there he caused her to be stripped naked. Then he called for the clothes and shoes which he had had specially made, and quickly got her to put them on, after which he caused a crown to be placed upon the dishevelled hair of her head. And just as everyone was wondering what this might signify, he said:

"Gentlemen, this is the woman I intend to marry, provided she will have me as her husband." Then, turning to Griselda, who was so embarrassed that she hardly knew where to look, he said: "Griselda, will you have me as your wedded husband?"

To which she replied:

"I will, my lord."

"And I will have you as my wedded wife," said Gualtieri, and he married her then and there before all the people present. He then helped her mount a palfrey, and led her back, honourably attended, to his house, where the nuptials were as splendid and as sumptuous, and the rejoicing as unrestrained, as if he had married the King of France's daughter.

Along with her new clothes, the young bride appeared to take on a new lease of life, and she seemed a different woman entirely. She was endowed, as we have said, with a fine figure and beautiful features, and lovely as she already was, she now acquired so confident, graceful and decorous a manner that she could have been taken for the daughter, not of the shepherd Giannùcole, but of some great nobleman, and consequently everyone who had known her before her marriage was filled with astonishment. But apart from this, she was so obedient to her husband,

4. "Little John."

and so compliant to his wishes, that he thought himself the happiest and most contented man on earth. At the same time she was so gracious and benign towards her husband's subjects, that each and every one of them was glad to honour her, and accorded her his unselfish devotion, praying for her happiness, prosperity, and greater glory. And whereas they had been wont to say that Gualtieri had shown some lack of discretion in taking this woman as his wife, they now regarded him as the wisest and most discerning man on earth. For no one apart from Gualtieri could ever have perceived the noble qualities that lay concealed beneath her ragged and rustic attire.

In short, she comported herself in such a manner that she quickly earned widespread acclaim for her virtuous deeds and excellent character not only in her husband's domain but also in the world at large; and those who had formerly censured Gualtieri for choosing to marry her were now compelled to reverse their opinion.

Not long after she had gone to live with Gualtieri she conceived a child, and in the fullness of time, to her husband's enormous joy, she bore him a daughter. But shortly thereafter Gualtieri was seized with the strange desire to test Griselda's patience, by subjecting her to constant provocation and making her life unbearable.

At first he lashed her with his tongue, feigning to be angry and claiming that his subjects were thoroughly disgruntled with her on account of her lowly condition, especially now that they saw her bearing children; and he said they were greatly distressed about this infant daughter of theirs, of whom they did nothing but grumble.

The lady betrayed no sign of bitterness on hearing these words, and without changing her expression she said to him:

"My lord, deal with me as you think best for your own good name and peace of mind, for I shall rest content whatever you decide, knowing myself to be their inferior and that I was unworthy of the honour which you so generously bestowed upon me."

This reply was much to Gualtieri's liking, for it showed him that she had not been puffed with pride by any honour that he or others had paid her.

A little while later, having told his wife in general terms that his subjects could not abide the daughter she had borne him, he gave certain instructions to one of his attendants, whom he sent to Griselda. The man looked very sorrowful, and said:

"My lady, if I do not wish to die, I must do as my lord commands me. He has ordered me to take this daughter of yours, and to . . ." And his voice trailed off into silence.

On hearing these words and perceiving the man's expression, Griselda, recalling what she had been told, concluded that he had been instructed to murder her child. So she quickly picked it up from its cradle, kissed it, gave it her blessing, and albeit she felt that her heart was about to break, placed the child in the arms of the servant without any trace of emotion, saying:

"There: do exactly as your lord, who is my lord too, has instructed you. But do not leave her to be devoured by the beasts and the birds, unless that is what he has ordered you to do."

The servant took away the little girl and reported Griselda's words to Gualtieri, who, marvelling at her constancy, sent him with the child to a kinswoman of his in Bologna, requesting her to rear and educate her carefully, but without ever making it known whose daughter she was.

Then it came about that his wife once more became pregnant, and in due course she gave birth to a son, which pleased Gualtieri enormously. But not being content with the mischief he had done already, he abused her more viciously than ever, and one day he glowered at her angrily and said:

"Woman, from the day you produced this infant son, the people have made my life a complete misery, so bitterly do they resent the thought of a grandson of Giannùcole succeeding me as their lord. So unless I want to be deposed, I'm afraid I shall be forced to do as I did before, and eventually to leave you and marry someone else."

His wife listened patiently, and all she replied was:

"My lord, look to your own comfort, see that you fulfil your wishes, and spare no thought for me, since nothing brings me pleasure unless it pleases you also."

Before many days had elapsed, Gualtieri sent for his son in the same way that he had sent for his daughter, and having likewise pretended to have had the child put to death, he sent him, like the little girl, to Bologna. To all of this his wife reacted no differently, either in her speech or in her looks, than she had on the previous occasion, much to the astonishment of Gualtieri, who told himself that no other woman could have remained so impassive. But for the fact that he had observed her doting upon the children for as long as he allowed her to do so, he would have assumed that she was glad to be rid of them, whereas he knew that she was too judicious to behave in any other way.

His subjects, thinking he had caused the children to be murdered, roundly condemned him and judged him a cruel tyrant, whilst his wife became the object of their deepest compassion. But to the women who offered her their sympathy in the loss of her children, all she ever said was that the decision of their father was good enough for her.

Many years after the birth of his daughter, Gualtieri decided that the time had come to put Griselda's patience to the final test. So he told a number of his men that in no circumstances could he put up with Griselda as his wife any longer, having now come to realize that his marriage was an aberration of his youth. He would therefore do everything in his power to obtain a dispensation from the Pope, enabling him to divorce Griselda and marry someone else. For this he was chided severely by many worthy men, but his only reply was that it had to be done.

On learning of her husband's intentions, from which it appeared she would have to return to her father's house, in order perhaps to look after the sheep as she had in the past, meanwhile seeing the man she adored being cherished by some other woman, Griselda was secretly filled with despair. But she prepared herself to endure this final blow as stoically as she had borne Fortune's earlier assaults.

Shortly thereafter, Gualtieri arranged for some counterfeit letters of his to arrive from Rome, and led his subjects to believe that in these, the Pope had granted him permission to abandon Griselda and remarry.

He accordingly sent for Griselda, and before a large number of people he said to her:

"Woman, I have had a dispensation from the Pope, allowing me to leave you and take another wife. Since my ancestors were great noblemen and rulers of these lands, whereas yours have always been peasants, I intend that you shall no longer be my wife, but return to Giannùcole's house with the dowry you brought me, after which I shall bring another lady here. I have already chosen her and she is far better suited to a man of my condition."

On hearing these words, the lady, with an effort beyond the power of any normal woman's nature, suppressed her tears and replied:

"My lord, I have always known that my lowly condition was totally at odds with your nobility, and that it is to God and to yourself that I owe whatever standing I possess. Nor have I ever regarded this as a gift that I might keep and cherish as my own, but rather as something I have borrowed; and now that you want me to return it, I must give it back to you with good grace. Here is the ring with which you married me: take it. As to your ordering me to take away the dowry that I brought, you will require no accountant, nor will I need a purse or a pack-horse, for this to be done. For it has not escaped my memory that you took me naked as on the day I was born. If you think it proper that the body in which I have borne your children should be seen by all the people, I shall go away naked. But in return for my virginity, which I brought to you and cannot retrieve, I trust you will at least allow me, in addition to my dowry, to take one shift away with me."

Gualtieri wanted above all else to burst into tears, but maintaining a stern expression he said:

"Very well, you may take a shift."

All the people present implored Gualtieri to let her have a dress, so that she who had been his wife for thirteen years and more would not have to suffer the indignity of leaving his house in a shift, like a pauper; but their pleas were unavailing. And so Griselda, wearing a shift, barefoot, and with nothing to cover her head, having bidden them farewell, set forth from Gualtieri's house and returned to her father amid the weeping and the wailing of all who set eyes upon her.

Giannùcole, who had never thought it possible that Gualtieri would keep his daughter as his wife, and was daily expecting this to happen, had preserved the clothes she discarded on the morning Gualtieri had married her. So he brought them to her, and Griselda, having put them on, applied herself as before to the menial chores in her father's house, bravely enduring the cruel assault of hostile Fortune.

No sooner did Gualtieri drive Griselda away, than he gave his subjects to understand that he was betrothed to a daughter of one of the Counts of Panago.[5] And having ordered that grandiose preparations were to be made for the nuptials, he sent for Griselda and said to her:

"I am about to fetch home this new bride of mine, and from the moment she sets foot inside the house, I intend to accord her an honourable welcome. As you know, I have no women here who can set the rooms in order for me, or attend to many of the things that a festive occasion of this sort requires. No one knows better than you how to handle these household affairs, so I want you to make all the necessary arrangements. Invite all the ladies you need, and receive them as though you were mistress of the house. And when the nuptials are over, you can go back home to your father."

Since Griselda was unable to lay aside her love for Gualtieri as readily as she had dispensed with her good fortune, his words pierced her heart like so many knives. But she replied.

"My lord, I am ready to do as you ask."

And so, in her coarse, thick, woollen garments, Griselda returned to the house she had quitted shortly before in her shift, and started to sweep and tidy the various chambers. On her instructions, the beds were draped with hangings, the benches in the halls were suitably adorned, the kitchen was made ready; and she set her hand, as though she were a petty serving wench, to every conceivable household task, never stopping to draw breath until she had everything prepared and arranged as befitted the occasion.

Having done all this, she caused invitations to be sent, in Gualtieri's name, to all the ladies living in those parts, and began to await the event. And when at last the

5. Panago, or Panico, is in the province of Emilio-Romagna, near Bologna.

nuptial day arrived, heedless of her beggarly attire, she bade a cheerful welcome to each of the lady guests, displaying all the warmth and courtesy of a lady of the manor.

Gualtieri's children having meanwhile been carefully reared by his kinswoman in Bologna, who had married into the family of the Counts of Panago, the girl was now twelve years old, the loveliest creature ever seen, whilst the boy had reached the age of six. Gualtieri had sent word to his kinswoman's husband, asking him to do him the kindness of bringing this daughter of his to Saluzzo along with her little brother, to see that she was nobly and honourably escorted, and to tell everyone he met that he was taking her to marry Gualtieri, without revealing who she really was to a living soul.

In accordance with the Marquis's request, the gentleman set forth with the girl and her brother and a noble company, and a few days later, shortly before the hour of breakfast, he arrived at Saluzzo, where he found that all the folk thereabouts, and numerous others from neighbouring parts, were waiting for Gualtieri's latest bride.

After being welcomed by the ladies, she made her way to the hall where the tables were set, and Griselda, just as we have described her, went cordially up to meet her, saying:

"My lady, you are welcome."

The ladies, who in vain had implored Gualtieri to see that Griselda remained in another room, or to lend her one of the dresses that had once been hers, so that she would not cut such a sorry figure in front of his guests, took their seats at table and addressed themselves to the meal. All eyes were fixed upon the girl, and everyone said that Gualtieri had made a good exchange. But Griselda praised her as warmly as any one present, speaking no less admiringly of her little brother.

Gualtieri felt that he had now seen all he wished to see of the patience of his lady, for he perceived that no event, however singular, produced the slightest change in her demeanour, and he was certain that this was not because of her obtuseness, as he knew her to be very intelligent. He therefore considered that the time had come for him to free her from the rancour that he judged her to be hiding beneath her tranquil outward expression. And having summoned her to his table, before all the people present he smiled at her and said:

"What do you think of our new bride?"

"My lord," replied Griselda, "I think very well of her. And if, as I believe, her wisdom matches her beauty, I have no doubt whatever that your life with her will bring you greater happiness than any gentleman on earth has ever known. But with all my heart I beg you not to inflict those same wounds upon her that you imposed upon her predecessor, for I doubt whether she could withstand them, not only because she is younger, but also because she has had a refined upbringing, whereas the other had to face continual hardship from her infancy."

On observing that Griselda was firmly convinced that the young lady was to be his wife, and that even so she allowed no hint of resentment to escape her lips, Gualtieri got her to sit down beside him, and said:

"Griselda, the time has come for you to reap the reward of your unfailing patience, and for those who considered me a cruel and bestial tyrant, to know that whatever I have done was done of set purpose, for I wished to show you how to be a wife, to teach these people how to choose and keep a wife, and to guarantee my own peace and quiet for as long as we were living beneath the same roof. When I came to take a wife, I was greatly afraid that this peace would be denied me, and in order to prove otherwise I tormented and provoked you in the ways you have seen. But as I have never known you to oppose my wishes, I now intend, being persuaded that you can offer me all the happiness I desired, to restore to you in a single instant that which I took from you little by little, and delectably assuage the pains I have inflicted upon you. Receive with gladsome heart, then, this girl whom you believe to be my bride, and also her brother. These are our children, whom you and many others have long supposed that I caused to be cruelly murdered; and I am your husband, who loves you above all else, for I think I can boast that there is no other man on earth whose contentment in his wife exceeds my own."

Having spoken these words, he embraced and kissed Griselda, who by now was weeping with joy; then they both got up from table and made their way to the place where their daughter sat listening in utter amazement to these tidings. And after they had fondly embraced the girl and her brother, the mystery was unravelled to her, as well as to many of the others who were present.

The ladies rose from table in transports of joy, and escorted Griselda to a chamber, where, with greater assurance of her future happiness, they divested her of her tattered garments and clothed her anew in one of her stately robes. And as their lady and their mistress, a rôle which even in her rags had seemed to be hers, they led her back to the hall, where she and Gualtieri rejoiced with the children in a manner marvellous to behold.

Everyone being delighted with the turn that events had taken, the feasting and the merrymaking were redoubled, and continued unabated for the next few days. Gualtieri was acknowledged to be very wise, though the trials to which he had subjected his lady were regarded as harsh and intolerable, whilst Griselda was accounted the wisest of all.

The Count of Panago returned a few days later to Bologna, and Gualtieri, having removed Giannùcole from his drudgery, set him up in a style befitting his father-in-law, so that he lived in great comfort and honour for the rest of his days. As for Gualtieri himself, having married off his daughter to a gentleman of renown, he lived long and contentedly with Griselda, never failing to honour her to the best of his ability.

What more needs to be said, except that celestial spirits may sometimes descend even into the houses of the poor, whilst there are those in royal palaces who would be better employed as swineherds than as rulers of men? Who else but Griselda could have endured so cheerfully the cruel and unheard of trials that Gualtieri imposed upon her without shedding a tear? For perhaps it would have served him right if he had chanced upon a wife, who, being driven from the house in her shift, had found some other man to shake her skin-coat for her,[6] earning herself a fine new dress in the process.

* * *

Dioneo's story had ended, and the ladies, some taking one side and some another, some finding fault with one of its details and some commending another, had talked about it at length, when the king,[7] having raised his eyes to observe that the sun had already sunk low in the evening sky, began, without getting up, to address them as follows:

"Graceful ladies, the wisdom of mortals consists, as I think you know, not only in remembering the past and apprehending the present, but in being able, through a

---

6. Dioneo often uses erotic metaphors of this kind.   7. Panfilo.

knowledge of each, to anticipate the future, which grave men regard as the acme of human intelligence.

"Tomorrow, as you know, a fortnight will have elapsed since the day we departed from Florence to provide for our relaxation, preserve our health and our lives, and escape from the sadness, the suffering and the anguish continuously to be found in our city since this plague first descended upon it. These aims we have achieved, in my judgement, without any loss of decorum. For as far as I have been able to observe, albeit the tales related here have been amusing, perhaps of a sort to stimulate carnal desire, and we have continually partaken of excellent food and drink, played music, and sung many songs, all of which things may encourage unseemly behaviour among those who are feeble of mind, neither in word nor in deed nor in any other respect have I known either you or ourselves to be worthy of censure. On the contrary, from what I have seen and heard, it seems to me that our proceedings have been marked by a constant sense of propriety, an unfailing spirit of harmony, and a continual feeling of brotherly and sisterly amity. All of which pleases me greatly, as it surely redounds to our communal honour and credit.

"Accordingly, lest aught conducive to tedium should arise from a custom too long established, and lest, by protracting our stay, we should cause evil tongues to start wagging, I now think it proper, since we have all in turn had our share of the honour still invested in me, that with your consent we should return from whence we came. If, moreover, you consider the matter carefully, our company being known to various others hereabouts, our numbers could increase in such a way as to destroy all our pleasure. And so, if my advice should command your approval, I shall retain the crown that was given me until our departure, which I propose should take effect tomorrow morning. But if you decide otherwise, I already have someone in mind upon whom to bestow the crown for the next day to follow."

The ladies and the young men, having debated the matter at considerable length, considered the king's advice, in the end, to be sensible and just, and decided to do as he had said. He therefore sent for the steward and conferred with him with regard to the following morning's arrangements, and having dismissed the company till supper-time, he rose to his feet.

The ladies and the other young men followed suit, and turned their attention to various pastimes as usual. When it was time for supper, they disposed of the meal with infinite relish, after which they turned to singing and music and dancing. * * *

Next morning they arose at the crack of dawn, by which time all their baggage had been sent on ahead by the steward, and with their wise king leading the way they returned to Florence. Having taken their leave of the seven young ladies in Santa Maria Novella, whence they had all set out together, the three young men went off in search of other diversions; and in due course the ladies returned to their homes.[8]

8. Thus ends the narrative part of the *Decameron*. Boccaccio follows with a brief epilogue, in which he anticipates the criticism that he has taken too many liberties with his stories. He defends himself by pointing out that the stories are told in a garden, not in a church; that only corrupt minds will find things to corrupt in his stories; and that after all, he "could only transcribe the stories as they were actually told, . . . But even if one could assume that I was the inventor as well as the scribe of these stories (which was not the case), I still insist that I would not feel ashamed if some fell short of perfection, for there is no craftsman other than God whose work is whole and faultless in every respect." He closes by reminding his reader that everything in the world is subject to constant change, including his own tongue. He then thanks God, and asks the "sweet ladies" whom he addressed in his introduction to remember him "if perchance these stories should bring you any profit."

‣ ⩩ ◆ ⩩ ‣

Marguerite de Navarre
1492–1549

Marguerite de Navarre was one of the most fascinating and influential women of the sixteenth century. Born into the nobility, she grew up in the court of Louis XII of France, where she was educated along with her brother François and learned a formidable number of languages, including German, Spanish, and Greek. François's surprising ascension to the monarchy in 1515 saved Marguerite from her loveless marriage to the probably illiterate Charles, Duke of Alençon. She spent virtually the rest of her life as adviser to her brother, traveling to Madrid after François was captured by Charles V of Spain and negotiating the Peace of Cambrai along with her mother and Margaret of Austria. Her appeal to Charles not only freed François but secured for Marguerite a marriage proposal when her husband died (a proposal politely but firmly refused). Marguerite did decide to remarry in 1527 when she accepted the offer of Henri of Navarre, the powerful king of the southernmost region of what is now France. Marguerite's well-honed diplomatic skills were not wasted in the brief periods spent in her husband's court, where she was able to ease the considerable tensions between Navarre and neighboring Spain. Nor was Marguerite merely a talented diplomat. A great lover of Italian culture, she and her brother introduced the fruits of the Italian Renaissance into the French court, luring, among others, the artists Benvenuto Cellini and Leonardo da Vinci to Paris, and cultivating talented French writers such as Clément Marot who were intrigued with Italy's considerable literary legacy.

It is in this climate of homage to Italy that the *Heptameron* was conceived. Marguerite's persona in the work, Parlamente, notes that "if Boccaccio could have heard how highly these illustrious people praised him, it would have been enough to raise him from the grave," and the *Heptameron,* so-called because it abruptly ends during the eighth day of tale-telling, shares many of the same qualities of the *Decameron.* As the prologue details, the ten *devisants* or "chatterers" are in flight from a variety of dangers (floods, bandits) and take temporary refuge in an abbey to devote themselves to the orderly sharing of stories. The differences from Boccaccio, however, are quite striking. The five men and five women are far more carefully delineated than those of the *Decameron,* and they discuss at length and often at cross-purposes the values and meaning of each tale that they narrate. Moreover, Parlamente suggests that while her companions should set out to do "the same as Boccaccio," they should differ in one thing: "they should not tell anything that was not a *véritable histoire*"—a true story. The result is a collection of seventy-two stories that are more limited in scope and chronology than Boccaccio's. At the same time, with notable exceptions (such as story seventy-one, in which a wife on her deathbed recovers her speech and her health while witnessing her husband frolicking with a maid), they tend to be less conclusive than those of the *Decameron.* This is the case in part because the stories are morally complex enough to pull our sympathies in different directions; in part because the world was no longer as straightforward as Boccaccio chose to represent it. Telling their tales in the context of France's social and religious upheavals in the wake of the Reformation, the pious Oisille, the rogue Saffredent, and the other characters debate such timely issues as the rights of wives within marriage, the legitimacy of rape, and the scandals perpetrated by Franciscan monks.

One of the most important influences on Marguerite's life was, in fact, the increasingly vocal and vulnerable band of intellectuals disaffected with the Roman Church and drawn, after 1520, to the reform movement. The climate in Paris in the years that followed was extremely tense. Marguerite's close friend Lefèvre d'Étaples was denounced as heretical; the Third Book of Rabelais's *Gargantua and Pantagruel,* dedicated to Marguerite, was condemned by the Sorbonne, as was Marguerite's own moving spiritual testament, *Mirror of the Sinful Soul,* written after the death of her only son. The vast majority of Marguerite's considerable body of writing is explicitly religious; she wrote a commentary on Paul's Epistle to the Romans, translated prayers, and wrote plays reminiscent of the medieval mysteries. At the same time, while the often bawdy world of the *Heptameron* mocks those who pervert their spiritual roles in society, it also counsels tolerance at large, particularly by people in positions of authority. Or in the words of Parlamente/Marguerite herself after we hear the story of the husband who avenged his wife's adultery by poisoning her: "If all those women who've had affairs with their domestics were obliged to eat salads like that one, then I know a few who wouldn't be quite so fond of their gardens as they are, but would pull up all their herbs to avoid the ones that restore the honour of families by taking the lives of wanton mothers!"

PRONUNCIATIONS:

   Bernage: bear-NAJ
   Dagoucin: da-goo-SEEN
   Geburon: jay-boo-RON
   Marguerite de Navarre: mar-gehr-EET de nah-VAR
   Oisille: wa-ZEEL
   Parlamente: par-la-MONT

from HEPTAMERON[1]

First Day, Story 5

[GEBURON TELLS THE STORY OF THE TWO FRIARS AND A SHREWD FERRYWOMAN][2]

At the port of Coulon near Niort,[3] there was once a woman whose job it was to ferry people night and day across the river. One day she found herself alone in her boat with two Franciscan friars from Niort. Now this is one of the longest crossings on any river in France, and the two friars took it into their heads that she would find it less boring if they made amorous proposals to her. But, as was only right and proper, she refused to listen. However, the two were not to be deterred. They had not exactly had their strength sapped by rowing, nor their ardours chilled by the chilly water nor, indeed, their consciences pricked by the woman's refusals. So they decided to rape her, both of them, and if she resisted, to throw her into the river. But she was as sensible and shrewd as they were vicious and stupid.

"I'm not as ungracious as you might think," she said to them, "and if you'll just grant me two little things, you'll see I'm just as keen to do what you want as you are."

The Cordeliers[4] swore by the good Saint Francis that they'd let her have anything she asked for, if she'd just let them have what they wanted.

"First of all, you must promise on your oath that neither of you will tell a soul about it," she said.

1. Translated by P. A. Chilton
2. The first day is dedicated to telling "of low tricks played by women on men and by men on women." Geburon's story responds to the disbelief of one interlocutor, Hircan, that a widowed princess had sufficient strength to overcome a would-be rapist: "I shall tell a story that I know to be true because I conducted an inquiry into it at the very place where it happened. As you'll

see, it isn't only princesses who've got good sense in their heads and virtue in their heart. And love and resourcefulness aren't always to be found where you'd expect them, either."
3. A major city in western France.
4. Franciscan friars so called because of the "cords" they belted around their brown cassock.

To this they readily agreed.

"Secondly, you must do what you want with me one at a time—I'd be too embarrassed to have both of you looking at me. So decide between you who's to have me first."

They thought this too was a very reasonable request, and the younger of the two offered to let the older man go first. As they sailed past a small island in the river, the ferrywoman said to the younger one: "Now my good father, jump ashore and say your prayers while I take your friend here to another island. If he's satisfied with me when he gets back, we'll drop him off here, and then you can come with me."

So he jumped out of the boat to wait on the island till his companion came back. The ferrywoman then took the other one to another island in the river, and while she pretended to be making the boat fast to a tree, told him to go and find a convenient spot.

He jumped out, and went off to look for a good place. No sooner was he on dry land than the ferrywoman shoved off with a kick against the tree, and sailed off down the river, leaving the two good friars stranded.

"You can wait till God sends an angel to console you, Messieurs!" she bawled at them. "You're not going to get anything out of me today!"

The poor friars saw they had been hoodwinked. They ran to the water's edge and pleaded on bended knees that she would take them to the port. They promised not to ask her for any more favours. But she went on rowing, and called back: "I'd be even more stupid to let myself get caught again, now I've escaped!"

As soon as she landed on the other side, she went into the village, fetched her husband and called out the officers of the law to go and round up these two ravenous wolves, from whose jaws she had just by the grace of God been delivered. They had plenty of willing helpers. There was no one in the village, great or small, who was not anxious to join in the hunt and have his share of the fun. When the two good brothers, each on his own island, saw this huge band coming after them, they did their best to hide—even as Adam hid from the presence of the Lord God, when he saw that he was naked. They were half dead for shame at this exposure of their sins, and trembled in terror at the thought of the punishment that surely awaited them. But there was nothing they could do. They were seized and bound, and led through the village to the shouts and jeers of every man and woman in the place. Some people said: "There they go, those good fathers who preach chastity to us yet want to take it from our wives!" Others said: "They are whited sepulchres, outwardly beautiful, but within full of dead men's bones and all uncleanness!" And someone else called out, "Every tree is known by his own fruit!"[5] In fact, they hurled at the two captives every text in the Gospels that condemns hypocrites. In the end their Father Superior came to the rescue. He lost no time in requesting their custody, reassuring the officers of the law that he would punish them more severely than secular law could. By way of reparation, they would, he promised, be made to say as many prayers and masses as might be required! [The Father Superior was a worthy man, so the judge granted his request and sent the two prisoners back to their convent, where they were brought before the full Chapter and severely reprimanded.][6] Never again did they take a ferry across a river, without making the sign of the cross and commending their souls to God!

5. Both quotations are from the Gospel of Matthew (23:27 and 12:33).

6. Bracketed passages here and elsewhere in the text reflect variants based on a manuscript from 1553.

"Now consider this story carefully, Ladies. We have here a humble ferrywoman who had the sense to frustrate the evil intentions of two vicious men. What then ought we to expect from women who all their lives have seen nothing but good examples, read of nothing but good examples and, in short, had examples of feminine virtue constantly paraded before them? If well-fed women are virtuous, is it not just as much a matter of custom as of virtue? But it's quite another matter if you're talking about women who have no education, who probably don't hear two decent sermons in a year, who have time for nothing but thinking how to make a meagre living, and who, in spite of all this, diligently resist all pressures in order to preserve their chastity. It is in the heart of such women as these that one finds pure virtue, for in the hearts of those we regard as inferior in body and mind the spirit of God performs his greatest works. Woe to those women who do not guard their treasure with the utmost care, for it is a treasure that brings them great honour if it is well guarded and great dishonour if it is squandered!"

"If you ask me, Geburon," observed Longarine, "there's nothing very virtuous in rejecting the advances of a friar. I don't know how anyone could possibly feel any affection at all for them."

"Longarine," he replied, "women who are not so used as you are to having refined gentlemen to serve them find friars far from unpleasant. They're often just as good-looking as we are, just as well-built and less worn out, because they've not been knocked about in battle. What is more, they talk like angels and are as persistent as devils. That's why I think that any woman who's seen nothing better than the coarse cloth of monks' habits should be considered extremely virtuous if she manages to escape their clutches."

"Good Heavens!" exclaimed Nomerfide loudly. "You may say what you like, but I'd rather be thrown in the river any day, than go to bed with a friar!"

"*So you're a strong swimmer, are you then!*" said Oisille, laughing.[7]

Nomerfide took this in bad part, thinking that Oisille did not give her as much credit as she would have liked, and said heatedly: "There *are* plenty of people who've refused better men than friars, without blowing their trumpets about it!"

"Yes, and they've been even more careful not to beat their drums about ones they've accepted and given in to!" retorted Oisille, amused to see that she was annoyed.

"I can see that Nomerfide would like to speak," Geburon intervened, "so I invite her to take over from me, in order that she may unburden herself by telling us a good story."

"I couldn't care less about people's remarks," she snapped, "they neither please nor annoy me. But since you ask me to speak, will you listen carefully, because I want to tell a story to show you that women can exercise their [cleverness] for bad purposes as well as for good ones. As we've sworn to tell the truth, I have no desire to conceal it. After all, just as the ferry-woman's virtue does not redound to the honour of other women unless they actually follow in her footsteps, so the vice of one woman does not bring dishonour on all other women. So, if you will listen . . ."[8]

7. Oisille is playing on the double sense of *nouer*: to swim and to tie together (with sexual connotations).
8. Namerfide, one of the younger and more spirited women of the group, whose name may mean "non perfide" (straightforward and loyal), turns to a tale in which an old man unsuccessfully tries to catch his wife with her lover.

Fourth Day, Story 32[1]

[THE WOMAN WHO DRANK FROM HER LOVER'S SKULL]

King Charles VIII sent to Germany a gentleman by the name of Bernage, Seigneur of Sivray, near Amboise.[2] This Bernage, seeking to expedite his mission, rested neither night nor day, and late one evening he came to a castle, where he asked for a night's lodging, which with great difficulty he was able to obtain. However, when the master of the house learned that he was in the service of so great a king, he went straight to him and begged him not to be annoyed at the discourtesy of his servants. The reason was that his wife's parents bore a grudge against him, and he was obliged to keep his house closed up. So Bernage told him the purpose of his mission, and the gentleman, offering to do everything in his power for his master the King, took him into the house, where he lodged and entertained him with due honour.

It was suppertime, and the gentleman led him into a beautiful room draped with magnificent tapestries. When the food was brought onto the table, he saw emerge from behind the tapestry the most beautiful woman it was possible ever to behold, though her hair was cropped and the rest of her body clad in black in the German style. After Bernage and the gentleman had washed together, the water was taken to the lady, who washed in her turn and went to sit at the end of the table without speaking to anyone and without anyone speaking to her. The Seigneur de Bernage looked at her closely. She seemed to him to be one of the most beautiful women he had ever seen, except that her face was very pale and her expression very sad. When she had eaten a little, she asked for something to drink, and a servant of the house brought her a most remarkable drinking-cup made of a skull, the [apertures] of which were filled in with silver. From this she took two or three draughts. When she had finished the meal and washed her hands, she curtseyed to the master of the house, and went back behind the tapestry without speaking. Bernage was taken aback at such a strange spectacle, and became quite melancholy and pensive. Seeing this, the gentleman said to him:

"I see you are surprised by what you've seen over this meal, but I perceive that you are an honourable man, and I do not want to hide the truth of the matter from you, lest you should think I am capable of such cruelty without good cause. The lady you saw is my wife, whom I have loved more than any man ever could, so much so that in order to marry her I left fear behind me and brought her here against her parents' wishes. She too showed me so many signs of affection that I would have risked ten thousand lives to bring her here and give her the happiness that was also my happiness. Indeed, for a long time we lived a quiet, contented life, and I considered myself the happiest gentleman in Christendom. But while I was away on a journey that for honour's sake I was obliged to undertake, she so forgot her conscience, her own honour and her love for me, that she became enamoured of a young gentleman whom I had brought up in this house. On my return I believed that I had detected their liaison, but I loved her so much that I could not bring myself to doubt her, until the moment when my eyes were opened and I saw for myself what I had feared more than

1. The fourth day is dedicated to tales about the "virtue and long-suffering of ladies in the winning over of their husbands, and of the prudence of men with respect to their wives for the preservation of the honour of their house and lineage." The story is told by Oisille.

2. Perhaps Claude Bernage, sent by King Louis XI of France to check on the fortifications of Reims. No known association between him and Charles VIII has been found.

death itself. So my love turned to fury and desperation. I kept a close watch on her, and one day, having told her I was going out, I hid in the room where she now lives. Not long after I had disappeared, she came into the room and sent word for the young man to join her there. I saw him come in with the kind of familiarity to which I alone have the right. But when I saw he was intending to climb on to the bed with her, I jumped out from my hiding-place, seized him while he was still in her arms and slew him. And since my wife's crime seemed to me to be so heinous that a similar death would hardly suffice, I imposed a punishment which I think she finds more painful than death. I decided to lock her up in the very room where she used to go to wallow in her pleasures, and keep her there in the company of the man she loved more than she had ever loved me. In a cupboard in the room I hung her lover's skeleton like some precious object in a private gallery. And so that she should never forget him even when eating and drinking, I made her sit [in front of me] at table and had her served from the man's skull instead of a cup, so that she would have before her both the living and the dead, both him whom through her sin she had transformed into a mortal enemy and [him whose love she had preferred to mine.] Thus when she takes dinner and supper she sees the two things that must distress her most, her living enemy and her dead lover, and all by her own sin. For the rest I treat her as myself, except that she has her hair shorn, for the crowning glory of woman no more becomes an adulteress than the veil becomes a harlot. So her head is shaved to show that she has lost her modesty and the honour of [chastity.] If you would care to see her, I'll take you to her."

Bernage gladly accepted. They went downstairs and found her in a beautiful room, seated in front of a fire. The gentleman drew a curtain in front of an alcove to reveal hanging there the skeleton of a dead man. Bernage wanted very much to talk to the lady, but dared not do so because of the husband. Realizing this, the gentleman said: "If you would like to say something to her, you'll see how graciously she speaks."

So Bernage said to her: "Madame, your resignation matches your suffering. I think you are the unhappiest woman in the world."

Tears came to the lady's eyes, and she spoke with the greatest possible grace and humility: "Monsieur, I confess that my sins are so great that all the suffering that is inflicted upon me by the lord of this house, whom I am not worthy to call my husband, is as nothing compared with the remorse I feel in having wronged him."

As she spoke she began to weep bitterly. The gentleman took Bernage by the arm, and drew him away. The next morning he left in order to carry out the mission entrusted to him by the King. But as he bade farewell to the gentleman he could not resist adding:

"Monsieur, the affection I bear you and the honours and kindness which you have shown me in your own house oblige me to say to you that as your poor wife's remorse is so deep, it is my belief that you should show some compassion towards her. Moreover, you are young and you have no children. It would be a great shame to let so fine a house as yours slip from your hands and permit it to be inherited by people who may be far from being your friends."

The gentleman, who had resolved never again to speak to his wife, thought for a long time about the things Bernage had said to him. Finally he realized that Bernage was right, and promised that if his wife continued to live in such humility, he would one day have pity on her. So Bernage went off to complete his mission. On his return to court he recounted the whole story to his master the King, who found upon inquiry that it was even as it had been told him. And having heard [tell] also of the lady's great beauty, he sent his painter, Jean de Paris,[3] to bring back her living likeness. This the painter did, with the approval of the husband, who, because of his desire to have children, and because of the compassion he felt for his wife in her humble submission to her penance, took her back, and subsequently had many fine children by her.

"Ladies, if all the women who behaved like this one were to drink from cups like hers, I fear that many a golden goblet would be replaced by a skull! From such things may God preserve us, for if His goodness did not restrain us, there is not one of us here who is not capable of doing things worse by far. But if we place our trust in Him, He will guard those women who confess that they cannot guard themselves. And women who trust in their own strength and virtue are in great danger of being tempted to the point where they have to confess their weakness. [I can assure you that there have been many whose pride has led to] their downfall in circumstances where [humility] saved women thought to be less virtuous. As the old proverb says, 'That which God guards is guarded well.'"

"I find the punishment extremely reasonable," said Parlamente. "For just as the crime was worse than death, so the punishment was worse than death."

"I don't agree," said Ennasuite, "I would far rather be shut up in my room with the bones of all my lovers for the rest of my days than die for them, since there's no sin one can't make amends for while one is alive, but after death there is no making amends."

"How could you make up for loss of honour?" said Longarine. "You know that nothing a woman can do after such a crime can ever restore her honour."

To which Ennasuite replied: "Tell me, I beg you, whether the Magdalene does or does not have more honour amongst men than her sister, who was a virgin?"[4]

"I admit," said Longarine, "that she is praised for her great love for Jesus Christ and for her great penitence, but even so she is still given the name of Sinner."

"I don't care," said Ennasuite, "what names men call me, only that God pardons me and my husband. There is no reason why I should wish to die."

"If the lady in the story had loved her husband as she should have done," said Dagoucin, "I am amazed she did not die of grief when she looked at the bones of the man whose death she had caused by her sin."

"What, Dagoucin," said Simontaut, "do you still have to learn that women possess neither love nor regrets?"

"Indeed, I have still to learn," said Dagoucin, "for I have never dared try out their love, for fear of finding less than I desired."

"So you live on faith and hope," said Nomerfide, "like a plover on the wind? You're easy to feed!"

"I am satisfied," he replied, "with the love I feel within me, and with the hope that in the hearts of ladies such love also resides. But if I knew for certain that it was even as I hoped, my joy would be too intense to bear, and I should die!"

"You should rather watch out for the plague," said Geburon, "because there's no need to worry about that sickness, I can assure you!"

* * *

---

3. A well-known painter with the court of Charles VIII in the late 15th century.

4. Mary Magdalene, devoted follower of Christ and repentant prostitute found in all four Gospels, was often confused with the Mary in the Gospel of Luke, Chapter 10, who sat by Jesus to listen to him speak while her sister Martha busied herself in the kitchen.

"Well, since it's my turn," said Ennasuite, "I shall spare neither men nor women, in order to make everything equal. And seeing that you can't bring yourselves to admit that men can be good and virtuous, I'll take up the thread of the last story,[5] and tell you one that is very similar."

Fourth Day, Story 36

[THE HUSBAND WHO PUNISHED HIS FAITHLESS WIFE BY MEANS OF A SALAD]

It is about a man who was president of the Parlement of Grenoble—a man whose name I can't reveal, although I can tell you he wasn't a Frenchman. He was married to a very beautiful woman, and they lived a happy and harmonious life together. However, the President was getting on in years, and the wife began an affair with a young clerk who was called Nicolas. Every morning, when her husband went off to the Palais de Justice, Nicolas would go to her bedroom to take his place. This was noticed by one of the President's servants, a man who had been in his household for thirty years, and who, being loyal to his master, could not do otherwise than tell him. The President was a prudent man, and was not prepared to believe the story without further evidence. He said that the servant was merely trying to sow discord between his wife and himself. If it was true, he said, then he ought to be able to show him the living proof. If he could not do so, then he would conclude that the man had been lying in order to destroy the love which he and his wife had for one another. The servant assured him that he should see with his own eyes what he had described.

One morning, as soon as the President had left for the courts and Nicolas had gone into the bedroom, the servant sent one of his fellow-servants to tell the master to come, while he stayed by the door to make sure Nicolas did not leave. When the President saw the servant give him the signal, he pretended he was feeling unwell, left the court, and hurried back home, where he found his other faithful old servant by the bedroom door assuring him that Nicolas was inside and that he had indeed only just gone in.

"Do not move from here," said the President. "As you know, there is no way in or out except through the small private room to which I alone have the key."

In went the President and found his wife and Nicolas in bed together. Nicolas, who had nothing on but his shirt, threw himself at the President's feet, begging forgiveness, while the wife started to weep.

"Your misdemeanour is a serious one, as you well know," said the President to his wife. "However, I do not wish to see my household dishonoured or the daughters I have had by you disadvantaged. Therefore, I order you to cry no more and to listen to what I mean to do. And you, Nicolas, hide in my private room and make no noise."

Then he opened the door, called his old servant, and said:

"Did you not tell me that you would show me Nicolas and my wife in bed together? I came here on the strength of your word and might have killed my poor wife. I have found nothing to bear out what you have told me. I have looked all over the room and there is no one here, as I now desire to demonstrate to you."

So saying, he made the servant look under the beds and everywhere else in the room. When he found nothing, the old man was amazed, and said to his master: "The

---

5. The previous story concerns a husband who successfully wins his wife away from her attentiveness to a friar.

Devil must have carried him off! I saw him come in, and he didn't come out through the door—yet I can see that he is not here!"

Then his master replied: "You are a miserable servant to try to sow discord between my wife and myself. Therefore I give you leave to depart. For the services that you have rendered I shall pay what I owe you and more. But leave quickly and take care not to be found in this town when twenty-four hours have passed!"

The President gave him five or six years' wages in advance, and knowing how loyal he was, said that he hoped to reward him further. So the servant went off in tears, and the President brought Nicolas out of his hiding-place. After telling his wife and her lover what he thought of their wicked behaviour, he forbade them to give any hint of it to anyone. He then instructed his wife to dress more elegantly than usual and to take part in all the social gatherings, dances and festivities. He ordered Nicolas too to make merry more than before, but added that the moment he whispered in his ear the words "Leave this place!" he should take care to be out of town within three hours. So saying, he returned to the Palais de Justice without the slightest hint that anything had happened.

For the next fortnight he set about entertaining his friends and neighbours—something he had not at all been in the habit of doing. After the banquets which he gave, there were musicians with drums for the ladies to dance to. On one occasion he noticed that his wife wasn't dancing, and told Nicolas to be her partner. Nicolas, thinking the President had forgotten what had happened, danced with her quite gaily. But after the dance was over, the President, on the pretext of giving him some instructions about domestic duties, whispered into Nicolas's ear: "Leave this place and never return!"

Now Nicolas was sorry indeed to leave his lady, but nonetheless glad to escape with his life. The President impressed upon all his relatives, friends and neighbours how much he loved his wife. Then, one fine day in the month of May, he went into his garden and picked some herbs for a salad. After eating it, his wife did not live more than twenty-four hours, and the grief that the President showed was so great that nobody suspected that he was the agent of her death. And so he avenged himself on his enemy and saved the honour of his house.

"It is not my wish, Ladies, to praise the President's conscience, but rather to portray a woman's laxity, and the great patience and prudence of a man. And do not take offence, Ladies, I beg you, because the truth sometimes speaks just as much against you as against men. Both men and women have their share of vice as well as of virtue."

"If all those women who've had affairs with their domestics," said Parlamente, "were obliged to eat salads like that one, then I know a few who wouldn't be quite so fond of their gardens as they are, but would pull up [all] their herbs to avoid the ones that restore the honour of families by taking the lives of wanton mothers!"

Eighth Day, Prologue[1]

When morning came they inquired how work on their bridge was progressing, and learned that it might be completed within two or three days.[2] Some of them were rather sorry to hear this, for they would have liked it to take longer, so that they might

1. The final day will be devoted to stories that are "the most foolish and the most true" tales that the speakers can think of.
2. As the introductory pages to the *Heptameron* relate, the ten conversationalists have been stranded at the abbey because of severe flooding of the Gave de Pau and the collapse of the bridges over it. They convince some workmen to construct a new foot-bridge, but the travelers are told that the work would take 10 or 12 days. As Marguerite notes, "To this day there are planks at this point for the use of foot-travelers coming from Oléron who do not want to use the ford."

continue to enjoy the happy life they were leading. But, recognizing that there were only two or three days left, they made up their minds to make the most of them. Oisille was asked to administer her spiritual nourishment, as was her wont, and this she did, though she kept them longer than usual, being anxious that they should reach the end of the canonical epistles of Saint John before leaving.[3] So well did she deliver the reading that the Holy Spirit, full of sweetness and love, seemed to be speaking through her mouth. Inflamed with this fire they went off to hear high mass. After that they dined together, still talking about the previous day's story-telling and challenging one another to make the new day its equal. And to ensure that it should be so, they each withdrew for a while to their rooms in order to prepare their stories. At the appointed hour, they came to present their accounts in the meadow, where the grass stretched out like green baize across a table top. The monks had already arrived and taken their places. When everyone was seated, they asked who should begin.

"You have done me the honour," said Saffredent, "of letting me begin two days. I think it would be unfair to the ladies if one of them also did not begin two days."

"In that case," replied Oisille, "we must either stay here longer, or else one of you and one of us must go without starting a second day."

"As far as I'm concerned," said Dagoucin, "I would have given my place to Saffredent, had I been chosen."

"And as for me," said Nomerfide, "I would have given mine to Parlamente, for accustomed as I am to serve, I could not command."

With this everyone agreed, and Parlamente began to speak.[4]

"Ladies, every day so far has been taken up with so many wise tales that I would like to propose that today should be taken up with stories which are the most foolish and the most true we can think of. So, to start you going, I shall begin."

Eighth Day, Story 71

[THE WIFE WHO CAME BACK FROM THE DEAD]

In the town of Amboise there was once a saddler by the name of Brimbaudier. He was saddle-maker to the Queen of Navarre,[5] and as for his character, you could tell from the colour of his face that he was a servant of Bacchus, rather than a servant of the priests of Diana. He had married a good woman, who managed his home [and children] very capably, and he was very contented. One day word was brought to him that his wife was dangerously ill. He was greatly afflicted at this, and set off as fast as he could to see what he could do for her. But he found the poor woman so far gone that a confessor rather than a doctor was what was required. His distress was piteous to behold. To report it really truthfully, I ought to put on a throaty voice like his, and it'd be even better if I could imitate the expression on his face. When he had done for her everything he possibly could, she asked to be given a cross, and he had one brought for her. This spectacle was too much for the poor fellow. He threw himself in desperation on to a bed, bellowing away in his funny thick voice: "Woe is me! I'm going to lose my wife! What'll I do? Woe is me!" and the like. Eventually he looked up and realized there was no one else in the room, apart from a little chambermaid—a pretty

---

3. Each day, Oisille, an older woman who may have been modeled on one of Marguerite's ladies-in-waiting, reads to the group from Scripture, after which they attend Mass at the abbey.

4. Parlamente is generally agreed to be Marguerite herself.
5. A reference either to Catherine, Marguerite's mother-in-law, or to Marguerite herself.

lass, and shapely too. He called her across to him and said, "My dear, I'm going to die, no, it's worse than if I was already dead and gone, seeing your mistress dying like that. I don't know what to do, I don't know what to say, except I need you to help me. Take the keys I've got hanging at my side. Look after the house and children for me. Do the housekeeping, because I can't manage any more!"

The poor girl felt sorry for him. She pleaded with him not to despair, and not to make her lose her kind master as well as her mistress. He replied: "My dear, it cannot be. I'm dying. Look how cold my face is. Come a bit nearer with your cheeks and warm me up a bit!" So saying, he thrust his hand into her bosom! She did get a little bit difficult, but he told her not to be alarmed. They must get to know one another a bit better, he said. At this point he grabbed her in his arms and threw her on to the bed. The wife had been left on her own with the cross and a drop of holy water. She had not spoken a word for two whole days. But now she started to shout as loud as her feeble voice allowed her to.

"Aaah! I'm not dead yet! I'm not dead yet!" she cried shaking her fist at the pair. "Swine! Brute! I'm not dead yet!"

The husband and the serving girl jumped up. The wife was so enraged that her anger burnt up the catarrhal humours that had prevented her speaking, and she was able to hurl at them all the abuse she could devise. Indeed, from that moment on she began to get better, and for ever after nagged her husband for not loving her enough!

"There you are, Ladies. That just shows what hypocrites men are. It doesn't take much to console them when they're mourning the loss of their wives, does it?"

"How do you know he hadn't heard that that was the best way to cure his wife?" asked Hircan. "He'd been treating her very considerately, and that didn't cure her, so he thought he'd see if the opposite would work any better. And he discovered it worked very well. I'm surprised you women have so frankly admitted your true colours. It's not feminine sweetness, it's feminine rancour that cures them!"

"Without a doubt, that sort of thing would make me jump up from the grave, let alone from a sick-bed!" said Longarine.

"What was he doing wrong, though," asked Saffredent, "in seeking consolation, when he thought she was dead? Everyone knows that marriage is only supposed to be binding for life, and that afterwards one is set free."

"Yes," replied Oisille, "free from your vows and obligations, but anyone with a true heart is never released from the ties of love. It didn't take *him* long to recover from his grief, for he could not even wait till his wife had breathed her last!"

"What I find most strange," said Nomerfide, "is the fact that even with the spectacle of death and the cross in front of his nose he wasn't deterred from offending the Lord."

"That's a fine argument!" exclaimed Simontaut. "Do you mean to say you're not shocked by such goings-on, provided that they don't take place anywhere near a church or a graveyard?"

"You can make fun of me as much as you like," replied Nomerfide, "but all the same, meditating on death is enough to chill the heart of anyone, however young."

"I'd agree with you wholeheartedly," said Dagoucin, "if it weren't for the fact that a certain princess once told me that the contrary is the case." * * * [6]

---

6. Dagoucin relates a story about a scandalous monk, after which the *Heptameron* breaks off, unfinished.

Francis Petrarch
1304–1374

Francis Petrarch is one of the crucial figures who launched the modern era, an era that embodied the very contradictions that characterized Petrarch himself. For most of his life, he fervently upheld the superiority of Latin, but he spent forty years working on his collection of lyric poetry in Italian. He cultivated the persona of the independent scholar, but attached himself to powerful, at times repugnant patrons—such as the Visconti—who could fund his personal library, which became the largest manuscript collection in Europe. He took his own religious profession lightly, but lambasted popes for not returning to Rome and advocated a Crusade. While the image that has come down to us of Petrarch is of a modernist—perhaps our first— he looks backward as much as forward. To a modern eye his least satisfying works are his attempts to write in the ancient genres of the epic and the eclogue, as well as his allegorical poems in Italian. But his look back across the long Middle Ages to what was for him the Golden Age of Rome also revealed to him the great ancients—Cicero, Virgil, Augustine—as familiar figures rather than unapproachable icons, writers from whom he might learn what it is to be human and whose words he might plunder. As he wrote in one of his letters: "the skillful juxtaposition of others' words and concepts often makes them ours." In juxtaposing "others' words" in order to articulate what, indeed, was "his," Petrarch launched the cult of the personality, and few personalities are as complex or as fascinating as that of Petrarch.

Born in 1304 to a father who, like Dante, had been exiled from Florence for his political sympathies, Petrarch spent his earliest years in Italy, near Arezzo. When he was only eight, his father took his family to Avignon in southern France where he would continue his profession as notary for the French Pope, Clement V. Although Petrarch was sent to Bologna to pursue legal studies, it quickly became clear that the law was not his passion. He returned to Avignon in 1326 after his father's death and began pursuing what *was* his passion: the study of classical antiquity through the collecting and transcribing of ancient manuscripts. With its enormous library and its large number of scholars connected to the papal court, Avignon offered the young Franciscus Petracchi—he would change his name only later to the more Latin-sounding Petrarca—the opportunity to begin honing his scholarly skills. The late 1320s saw his pioneering edition of the Roman historian Livy, the first venture to organize the scattered manuscripts of the *History of Rome* into a coherent whole. He also mingled with like-minded men who would become his companions and in some cases, his patrons for life, including the monk Dionigi da Borgo San Sepolcro, who gave Petrarch the small copy of Augustine's *Confessions* that he carried with him until his death. Southern France also offered him the restful climes of Vaucluse, a village on the Sorgue River where he bought a house and escaped from Avignon to write his first literary works in the 1330s and early 1340s: his (incomplete) epic, *Africa,* based on the heroic events of the Roman general Scipio Africanus; his collection of lives of famous men, *De viris illustribus;* and the first of his poems in Italian about a woman whom he had supposedly first glimpsed in a church in Avignon on April 6, 1327: the unattainable "Laura," whose identity remains unknown. Having decided to embrace the life of a man of the church—a decision which didn't prevent him from fathering two children—Petrarch was awarded with a canonry in the nearby cathedral of Lombez, an appointment that carried few responsibilities but sufficient income to pursue his writing.

One significant measure of Petrarch's widespread fame by the time he was thirty-six was an invitation, in 1340, to be crowned poet-laureate by the University of Paris—an invitation that was matched, supposedly only hours later, by the Roman Senate. Petrarch accepted the honor from Rome, and was crowned on the Capitoline Hill the following year. The next decade would see the writing of the *Secretum,* a dialogue between Petrarch and Augustine, who up-braids him for his passion for Laura, and the undertaking of a carefully organized collection of letters to both living and dead figures, inspired by Petrarch's discovery in Verona of Cicero's epistles. But the 1340s saw a number of changes in Petrarch's life that would considerably in-fluence his future writing. He enthusiastically supported a short-lived attempt of the nobleman Cola di Rienzo to unite Italy's reigning principates, but the venture ended in disaster and even-tually Cola's death at the stake as a heretic. Petrarch's brother Gherardo decided in 1343 to be-come a monk, depriving Petrarch of one of his most constant companions; his letter on Mount Ventoux, probably composed after Gherardo's withdrawal from the world, looks back to the happier days of the 1320s when the two were virtually inseparable. And the Black Death recorded so gruesomely by Boccaccio in the opening pages of his *Decameron* took as its vic-tims a number of Petrarch's close friends, among them his most steadfast patron, Giacomo Colonna, and his beloved "Laura." Such devastation inspired the *Triumph of Death,* an allegor-ical pageant that unfolds before a stunned and saddened Petrarch, and the one hundred final po-ems of the *Canzoniere* that mourn the loss of the poet's lady.

But other circumstances would alter Petrarch's life as well. After Colonna's death, Pe-trarch was in need of a patron, and he left Avignon and Vaucluse for good in 1353. He settled first in Milan under the patronage of the autocratic Visconti, and then lived for a while in Venice; finally in 1368 he was given land in Arquà near Padova. He continued his assiduous transcription of ancient manuscripts, taking up Greek for a while, which he confessed to have learned badly; he went on compiling his own collections of letters; he labored on revisions of his *Rime Sparsi* ("Scattered Rhymes"). Particularly important to Petrarch in these years was his friendship with Giovanni Boccaccio, whom he had met during his first visit to Florence in 1350. Under Petrarch's guidance, Boccaccio would begin his *Genealogy of the Pagan Gods,* and one of Petrarch's last literary undertakings was his translation of the final novella of the *Decameron*—the story of patient Griselda—into Latin. A flurry of diplomatic missions marked Petrarch's final years, but he died in his home in Arquà in July 1374, a copy of Virgil opened on the desk before him.

While we know almost the exact date on which Petrarch began a project, we rarely know when, or even if, he completed one. The work he considered his major Latin contribution, the *Africa,* was left in draft; his ambitious collections of letters are probably unfinished; the order in which we have his *Canzoniere* might well have changed had he lived longer. Restless, ener-getic, supremely egoistic, he refused both the cloying university culture of cities such as Bologna and the chaotic republican life of the Italian communes—he turned down an offer of Florentine citizenship on the grounds that he preferred to be a citizen of the world. Instead he fashioned a life within other kinds of communities, some of them tyrannies, to be sure, but also the imaginary ones generated by the written word. Books, as he often put it, were his friends. They were the medium through which he was able to evoke the voices of their authors, thus bringing the dead back to life and making the absent present. But it is the powerful and self-as-sured voice of Petrarch himself that allowed for this renaissance of the dead and bequeathed to us a literary heritage that includes the distinctively modern genres of the letters to familiar friends, the soul-searching dialogue, and the sonnet sequence.

LETTERS ON FAMILIAR MATTERS   Petrarch's letters reveal to us his voice at its most inti-mate, even as they were obviously written for an audience beyond their immediate reader. At times, the purported reader of a letter isn't even alive: the last book of the *Rerum libri,* Book 24, consists primarily of letters to the luminaries of Roman antiquity written in prose and verse, as well as a letter to Homer. The epistle to Dionigi da Borgo San Sepolcro about Petrarch's climb and descent of Mount Ventoux, probably the most famous of his letters, was written after Dionigi's death; Petrarch nonetheless chose to generate for us the aura of immediacy, as he shows himself wrestling firsthand with an errant nature that contrasts strikingly with the spiritual focus of his brother Gherardo. Here as in his poems we see the meticulous crafting of a personality that comes alive only in its exchanges with others, even, and perhaps especially, when his voice is thrown not just across the Apennines—as in his lively exchanges with Boccaccio—but across the chasm of the centuries.

from LETTERS ON FAMILIAR MATTERS
To Dionigi da Borgo San Sepolcro
[ON CLIMBING MT. VENTOUX][1]

Today, led solely by a desire to view the great height of it, I climbed the highest mountain of this region which is appropriately called Windy Mountain.[2] The idea for this trip had been in my mind for many years. As you know, my destiny has been to live here since childhood. This mountain visible from any direction has always been in my sight. The drive to do what I did today finally overcame me, especially after having re-read some days ago in Livy's history of Rome how Philip, King of Macedonia—the one who waged the war against the Roman people—ascended Mount Hemo in Thessaly from the summit of which he believed two seas were visible, the Adriatic and the Black.[3] Whether his belief is true or false I have been unable to ascertain, both because the mountain is far removed from our land and because the disagreement among the authorities makes it a doubtful matter. To mention but a few, Pomponius Mela, the cosmographer, asserts without hesitation that it is true; Titus Livy considers it false;[4] as for me, if I could climb that mountain as readily as I can this, I would quickly clear up the uncertainty. But putting this matter aside, I shall return to my mountain, and tell you that it appeared excusable for an ordinary young man to do something considered appropriate for an old king. Yet in thinking about a companion to accompany me, I found no one, alas, who seemed to qualify for the undertaking, so rare even among dearest friends is that perfect harmony of inclination and of custom. One seemed too slow, another too careful; one too deliberate, another too rash; one too gloomy, another too joyful; finally one too foolish and one, whom I wished to have come along, appeared too prudent. The silence of this one, the impudence of that one, the size and weight of another one, and the thinness and feebleness of still another terrified me. The cool incuriosity of this one and the burning concern of another dissuaded me. Although they are serious, such faults may be endured at home—for charity supports all things and friendship rejects no burden. But on a journey the same faults become very serious. Therefore my delicate mind, seeking honorable delight, carefully considered each quality individually without detriment to any friendship, and it quietly foresaw and rejected whatever seemed to be troublesome for the proposed trip. What do you think? I finally turned to a strictly domestic assistance, and I disclosed my plan to my only brother who was younger than I and whom you know well. He was delighted at the news and rejoiced that he was considered both a brother and a friend by me.

1. Book 4, Letter 1. The letters are translated from the Latin by Aldo S. Bernardo. Francesco Dionigi de' Roberti was an Augustinian monk and professor in Paris; Petrarch probably came to know him in Avignon around 1333. Dionigi had given him a tiny copy of Augustine's *Confessions,* which Petrarch would keep with him his entire life.
2. A translation of the Latin "Ventosus" (in French, Ven-

toux). Mt. Ventoux is in southern France near Avignon, where Petrarch grew up and resided when in service to the pope.
3. Mt. Haemus, one of the tallest mountains in the Balkans, is actually in Thrace, not Thessaly.
4. A contemporary of Augustus Caesar, Livy wrote a classic history of Rome; the Spanish Pomponius Mela was a first-century Roman geographer.

On the determined day we left home and came to Malaucène in the evening, a place at the foot of the mountain, looking north. We lingered there for a day and finally the next day with our individual servants we climbed the mountain after considerable difficulty. It is a steep mountain with rocky and almost inaccessible cliffs. It was well said by the poet, however: "Persistent toil overcomes all things."[5] The day was long, the air was mild, and the determination of our minds, the firmness and readiness of our bodies and other circumstances were favorable to the climbers. The only obstacle was the nature of the place. We came across an elderly shepherd on a slope of the mountain who made every effort with many words to keep us from continuing our climb, saying that fifty years earlier, driven by a like youthful motivation, he had climbed to the very top and had brought back from there nothing but repentance, weariness, and his body and clothing torn by stones and bushes, and that no one had been known before or since to dare undertake a similar climb. As he shouted all these things, we, like all young people who refuse to heed warnings, felt our desire increase as a result of the prohibition. When the old man observed that he was arguing in vain, he accompanied us a short way among the cliffs and pointed out the steep path, giving and repeating many warnings as we turned our backs to him. Leaving behind with him our extra garments and whatever else might have been a hindrance, we made ready to start the climb alone, and began to do so cheerfully, but, as usually happens, weariness swiftly followed our extraordinary effort.

Not long after our start, therefore, we stopped on a cliff. From there we once again began our climb but more slowly; and I, in particular, pursued a more modestly inclined mountainous path. My brother proceeded to the heights by shortcuts over the ridges of the mountain, but I, being weaker, turned toward the lower reaches. To my brother, who would call me back and indicate the most direct path, I would answer that I hoped to find an easier passage on the other side of the mountain and that I would not be afraid of a longer road if I could advance more easily. Having offered this excuse for my laziness, I was still wandering through the valleys without finding a more gentle access anywhere by the time the others had reached the summit. The road got longer and my burden grew heavy. Meanwhile, exhausted with weariness and troubled by the confused straying I was determined to seek the heights. Finally after I had reached, tired and distressed, my industrious brother who had refreshed himself with a long rest, we climbed along for some time side by side. We had scarcely left that hill, however, when I, forgetful of my former wandering, pursued the easy length of the paths and headed down hill to end once again in the valleys. Thus as before, I encountered serious trouble. I had tried to put off the annoyance of having to climb, but the nature of things does not depend on human wishes, and it is impossible for a body to arrive at a summit by descending. What more need I say? This happened to me three or more times within a few hours, not without my annoyance or my brother's laughter. Having been thus frequently deluded, I sat in one of the valleys and there proceeding from the physical to the metaphysical in mental flights I reproached myself with these or similar words:

"What you have experienced so often today in trying to climb this mountain you should know happens to you and to many others as they approach the blessed life. This is not easily realized by men, however, because although the movements of the body are visible, the movements of the mind are invisible and concealed. The life we

---

5. From the *Georgics,* Virgil's poem about labor and agriculture.

call blessed is certainly located on high, and, as it is said, a very narrow road leads to it.[6] Many hills also intervene and one must proceed from virtue to virtue with very deliberate steps. At the summit lies the end of all things and the limit of the path to which our traveling is directed. There everyone aspires, but, as Naso says, 'To wish is not enough; you must long for something so that you may succeed in anything.'[7] You yourself certainly—unless as with many other matters, you are deceived in this too—not only wish but long for it. What detains you? Certainly nothing except the more level and, as it looks at first confrontation, less impeded road of earthly and base pleasures. Nevertheless, after you have wandered widely, you must ascend to the summit of that blessed life burdened by labor ill-deferred or you will sink slowly into the pitfalls of your sins. And if—God forbid—the darkness and shadows of death should find you there, you would lose the eternal light in perpetual torments." Incredibly such meditation brought new strength to my mind and to my body and made me willing to face whatever remained. How I wish that I could complete with my mind that journey for which I sigh day and night as I overcame all the difficulties of today's journey with my physical body! And I wonder why what may be done through an active and immortal mind without any physical action in the blinking of an eye should be far easier than something done over a period of time at the indulgence of a mortal and perishable body and under the cumbersome weight of heavy limbs.

The highest slope of the mountain is one which the inhabitants call "Sonny." Why I do not know, except that I suppose it is said by way of antonymy,[8] as in some other cases, for indeed it seems to be the father of all neighboring mountains. On its summit there is a small plain. There finally we paused in a state of exhaustion. Since you have heard what thoughts ascended into my mind in the ascent, hear, father, the rest, and please grant one hour of yours to the reading of what happened to me in one day. First of all, moved by a certain unaccustomed quality of the air and by the unrestricted spectacle, I stood there as in a trance. I looked back. Clouds were beneath me. And suddenly what I had heard and read about Athos and Olympus[9] became less incredible to me when I looked out from this mountain of lesser fame. I then directed my sight toward Italy where my heart always inclines. The Alps themselves, frozen and snow-covered, through which that wild enemy of the Roman people once crossed and, if we believe the story, broke through the rocks with vinegar, seemed very close to me although separated by a great distance.[1] I confess that I heaved a deep sigh toward the sky of Italy which was visible to my mind rather than to my eyes, and I was overcome by an overwhelming desire to see once again my friend and my homeland. However, the way this happened led me to feel shame for my as yet unmanly desire for both these things, even though I did not lack either an excuse or the aid of scores of great examples for wanting both. My mind thus was overcome by a new thought and was transferred from those places to these times. And I began saying to myself: "Today completes the tenth year since you departed from Bologna after completion of your youthful studies."[2] Oh, immortal God, oh immutable wisdom, how extensive

6. Alluding to the Sermon on the Mount: "How narrow the gate and close the way that leads to life! And few there are who find it" (Matthew 7:14).
7. From Ovid's *Letters from Sea*, four books of elegiac poetry written by the Roman poet when he was in exile.
8. Using a word in a way contrary to its meaning. Here Petrarch is misinterpreting a Provençal word, *fibolo*, which may derive from a phrase for a water conduit.
9. Mt. Olympus, on the boundary of Thessaly and Greece,
was the legendary residence of the gods in Greek myth; Athos was a mountain sacred to Zeus.
1. Hannibal crossed the Alps in 218 B.C.E. en route to Rome; Livy records the occasionally gruesome details of his winter crossing in his history of Rome.
2. With his brother Gherardo, Petrarch studied civil law at the University of Bologna on and off between 1320 and 1326, when he was called back to Avignon.

and how many changes within me during this interim! I shall skip an infinitude of them since not yet being in port I cannot recall in security the storms through which I have passed. The time will perhaps come when I shall enumerate all of these storms that beset my life in their appropriate order, prefacing it with those words of your Augustine: "I wish to recall all my past foulness and the carnal corruption of my soul not because I love them but so that I might love you, my God."[3] As for me, there still remains indeed a great deal that is uncertain and troublesome. What I used to love I no longer love. I am wrong, I do love it but too little. There, I am wrong again. I love it but I am too ashamed of it and too sad over it. Now indeed I have said it right. For that is the way it is; I love, but something I would like not to love, and would like to hate. Nevertheless I love, but unwillingly, constrainedly, sorrowfully and mournfully. And in myself I miserably experience the meaning of that very famous verse, "I shall hate if I can; if not I shall love unwillingly."[4] The third year has not yet passed since that perverse and worthless inclination, which held sway over me and ruled over my heart without opponent, began to be replaced by another inclination which was rebellious and reluctant.[5] Between these inclinations a very insistent and uncertain battle for control of my two selves has been going on for a long time in my mind. Thus I pondered the decade just past. Then I began to project my troubles into the future and asked myself the following: "If it chanced that this transitory life would be extended another ten years for you, and you were to approach as far toward virtue as during the past two years—through your new inclination doing battle with your old—you retreated from your former obstinacy, could you not then, although not certainly but at least hopefully, go to meet death in your fortieth year or disregard calmly the remainder of a life which is vanishing into old age?"

These and similar thoughts were running through my mind, dear father. I was rejoicing in whatever success I had enjoyed, I was weeping for my imperfections and I was bewailing the general mutability of human actions. And I seemed somehow forgetful of the place to which I had come and why, until, after laying aside my cares as more suitable to another place, I looked around and saw what I had come to see. Having been reminded and almost awakened to the fact that the time for departure was at hand because the sun was already setting and the shadow of the mountain was growing, I turned to look behind me toward the West. The boundary between Gaul and Spain, the Pyrenees, cannot be seen from there not because anything intervenes as far as I know, but because the human sight is too weak. However, the mountains of the province of Lyons could be seen very clearly to the right, and to the left the sea at Marseilles and at the distance of several days the one that beats upon Aigues-Mortes. The Rhone itself was beneath my eyes. While I was admiring such things, at times thinking about earthly things and at times, following the example of my body, raising my mind to loftier things, it occurred to me to look into the *Book of Confessions* of St. Augustine, a gift of your kindness, which I shall always keep on hand in memory of the author and of the donor, a handy little work very small but of infinite sweetness. I opened it and started to read at random, for what can emerge from it except pious and devout things? By chance it was the tenth book of that work to which I opened. My brother stood by attentively to hear me read something from Augustine. May God be my witness, and my very brother, that my eyes happened to light where

3. From *Confessions* 2.1.
4. Ovid's *Amores* 3.2.
5. The "perverse and worthless inclination" is Petrarch's

love for Laura, which began in 1327 when he saw her in a church in Avignon. The other inclination seems to be his desire for spiritual progress and perfection.

it was written: "And they go to admire the summits of mountains and the vast billows of the sea and the broadest rivers and the expanses of the ocean and the revolutions of the stars and they overlook themselves."[6] I confess that I was astonished, and hearing my eager brother asking for more I asked him not to annoy me and I closed the book enraged with myself because I was even then admiring earthly things after having been long taught by pagan philosophers that I ought to consider nothing wonderful except the human mind compared to whose greatness nothing is great.

Then indeed having seen enough of the mountain I turned my inner eyes within, and from that moment there was no one who heard me speak until we arrived back at the foot of the mountain. The passage had tormented my silence, nor could I believe that it happened by chance but rather thought that whatever I had read there had been directed to me and to no one else. I recalled how Augustine had supposed the same thing had happened to him when in his reading of the book of the Apostle, as he himself relates, he first came across these words: "Not in banquets nor in drunkenness, in beds or in rudeness, in strife or in envy, but put on the Lord Jesus Christ and do not provide nourishment for the flesh in your lusts."[7] Something similar had already happened earlier to Antonius when he heard these words written in the gospel: "If you wish to be perfect, go and sell whatever you own and give to the poor, and come and follow me and you will have your treasures in heaven."[8] And believing that these words of Scripture had been read particularly for him, as his biographer Athanasius says, he gained the Lord's kingdom for himself. Just as Antonius upon hearing these words sought nothing more, and like Augustine, who having read went no further, so did I find in the few words which I have given the main point of the entire reading, and silently considered the extent to which true judgment was lacking to mortals who in overlooking the most noble part of themselves scatter their interests in various directions and become lost in vain speculations. What could be found within they go seeking without. I admired the nobility of the mind except as it had voluntarily deteriorated and wandered from its first beginnings and had converted into disgrace what the Lord had given to it for its honor. How often, do you think, upon returning home that day, when I turned back to look at the summit of the mountain, it seemed to me scarcely a cubit high in comparison with the loftiness of human meditation if only it were not plunged into the mire of earthly filthiness. This thought also occurred to me at every step: if I had willingly undergone so much perspiration and toil to take my body a little closer to heaven, what cross, what prison, what torture rack should frighten the mind drawing nearer to God and willing to conquer the extremes of insolence and mortal destiny? And this thought also occurred to me: how many are there who will not divert the mind from this normal path either from fear of hardships or through desire for pleasures? Too happy man!—if there is any such person anywhere, I would think it is about him that the poet gave his verdict: "Happy is he who could know the causes of things and submitted his fears to an inexorable fate and the rumblings of greedy Acheron to his scorn!"[9] Oh with how great zeal one must toil, not to achieve a more lofty place on earth, but to trample underfoot our appetites which are exalted by earthly impulses!

6. *Confessions* 10.8, in which Augustine is meditating on the force of memory that allows him to speak of "mountains and the vast billows of the sea."

7. At the turning point of his spiritual journey, Augustine hears a child's voice calling to him, "Take up and read." He then opens his Bible at random and finds this passage (from Paul's Letter to the Romans 13:13–4).

8. Saint Anthony had been converted to Christianity by hearing this passage from Matthew 19:21. Petrarch thus inserts himself in a distinguished line of dramatic converts to Christianity.

9. From Virgil's *Georgics,* Book 2, in a passage referring to *On the Nature of Things* by the Roman poet Lucretius, who expounds the origins and meaning of the universe.

Among these movements of my searching heart and without any sense of the stony pathway, I returned late at night to that little rustic inn from which I had set out before daylight, the full moon offering a welcome service to the way-farers. And meanwhile, therefore, while the duties of preparing the meal occupy the servants, I have gone alone to a hidden portion of the inn in order to write this to you hastily and extemporaneously lest with delay my determination to write might subside with the change of place or of our feelings. See, therefore, beloved father, how I wish that nothing of me be hidden from your eyes, having carefully opened not only my entire life to you but even my simple thoughts. I beg you to pray for them so that having been rambling and unstable for so long, they may sometimes find rest, and having been tossed about hither and yon, they may be directed to the one, the good, the true, the certain and the stable. Farewell.

Malaucène, 26 April [1336]

from To Boccaccio

[ON IMITATION][1]

There is one thing that I thought must not be kept from you or excluded from this letter, something that was unknown to me until today, and still is unbelievable and astonishing. Whenever we write something new, we often err in what is most familiar to us, for it deceives us in the very act of writing; whatever we have slowly learned we know better. You will ask: "What are you saying? Isn't this a contradiction? It is impossible for opposites to be both true; how can you write that what we know better we know less, and what we absorbed more slowly we know more firmly? What Sphinx or enigma is this?" I shall explain. Something similar happens in other areas, as, for example, when something hidden more carefully by the head of a household is less readily available, or when something buried more deeply is uncovered with greater difficulty; but these apply to material things, with which I am not dealing. So as not to keep you in suspense with circumlocutions, here is an example. Only once have I read Ennius, Plautus, Felix Capella, and Apuleius,[2] and then it was done hastily and quickly, brooking no delay except as one would in unknown territory. Proceeding in this fashion, I saw many things, culled a few, retained even fewer, and these I laid aside as common property in an open place, in the very atrium, so to speak, of my memory. Consequently, whenever I happen either to hear or use them, I quickly recognize that they are not mine, and recall whose they are; these really belong to others, and I have them in my possession with the awareness that they are not my own. I have read Virgil, Flaccus, Severinus, Tullius not once but countless times,[3] nor was my reading rushed but leisurely, pondering them as I went with all the powers of my intellect; I ate in the morning what I would digest in the evening, I swallowed as a boy what I would ruminate upon as an older man. I have thoroughly absorbed these writ-

---

1. Book 21, Letter 15. Petrarch met the Florentine writer Boccaccio after the younger man sent him a Latin poem sometime around 1350. A number of letters to Boccaccio are included in Petrarch's two collections of letters, the *Letters on Familiar Matters,* from which this one is taken, and *Seniles,* or *Letters Written in Old Age.*
2. Petrarch's least favorite Latin writers. Ennius is known as the father of Latin literature, and his works include tragedies, a history of Rome, and humorous poetry. Plautus's comedies were widely read in medieval and Renais-

sance Europe. The 2nd-century Apuleius wrote the romance *The Golden Ass.* Felix Capella is Martianus Capella, author of a learned allegory, *The Marriage of Mercury and Philology.*
3. Petrarch cites his personal favorites by nickname: Virgil, author of the *Aeneid;* Horace, or Quintus Horatius Flaccus, who wrote many odes and lyric poems and to whom Petrarch devotes one of his letters; Livy (Severinus), the Roman historian; and Marcus Tullius Cicero, the Roman orator of the 1st century B.C.E.

ings, implanting them not only in my memory but in my marrow, and they have so become one with my mind that were I never to read them for the remainder of my life, they would cling to me, having taken root in the innermost recesses of my mind. But sometimes I may forget the author, since through long usage and continual possession I may adopt them and for some time regard them as my own; and besieged by the mass of such writings, I may forget whose they are and whether they are mine or others'. This then is what I meant about more familiar things deceiving us more than others; if at times out of habit they return to the memory, it often happens that to the preoccupied mind, deeply intent on something else, they seem not only to be yours but to your surprise, new and original. Why do I say you would be surprised? Surely, you too will readily admit to having experienced something similar. I have really spent a great deal of time trying to identify my sources; I call to witness our Apollo, the only son of the heavenly Jove and true God of wisdom, Christ, that I have not been eager to plunder, that I have refrained from intellectual as well as from material thefts. If anything contrary to this is found in my works, it results from an intellectual kinship in the case of authors whom I have not read (as I wrote you in my previous letter) or, in the case of others, from the type of error or forgetfulness that we are now discussing. I grant that I like to embellish my life with sayings and admonitions from others, but not my writings unless I acknowledge the author or make some significant change in arriving at my own concept from many and varied sources in imitation of the bees.[4] Otherwise, I much prefer that my style be my own, uncultivated and rude, but made to fit, as a garment, to the measure of my mind, rather than to someone else's, which may be more elegant, ambitious, and adorned, but deriving from a greater genius, one that continually slips off, unfitted to the humble proportions of my intellect. Every garment befits the actor but not every style the writer; each must develop and keep his own lest either by dressing grotesquely in others' clothes or by being plucked of our feathers by birds flocking to reclaim their own, we may be ridiculed like the crow. Surely each of us naturally possesses something individual and personal in his voice and speech as well as in his looks and gestures that is easier, more useful, and more rewarding to cultivate and correct than to change. Someone may comment, "And what do you think of yourself?" Not you, my dear friend, who know me well, but one of those who observe others, being totally secure in their silence and safe from critics, have learned to direct stinging barbs against our every word. Let them carefully listen since they bluster only on the basis of what they hear. I do not resemble Juvenal's description, "A distinguished prophet not of public vein, who usually repeats nothing that has been said, nor strikes a poem with common and ordinary coin," whom the writer himself did not wish to identify but simply to imagine. Nor am I like Horace: "I was the first to plant free footsteps along an untrodden path," or "I first revealed Parian iambics to Latium"; nor am I like Lucretius: "Alone do I wander over the remote pathways of the Muses, previously trodden by no man"; nor like Virgil: "I love to climb gentle slopes to the heights where never had earlier footsteps gone to the Castalian fount "[5] And so? I am one who intends to follow our forebears' path but not always others' tracks; I am one who wishes upon occasion to make use of others' writings, not secretly but with their leave, and whenever possible

---

4. A frequent metaphor for the poet in Renaissance letters, originating with Lucretius at the opening of *The Nature of Things* ("From your pages, as bees in flowery glades sip every blossom, so I crop all your golden sayings").
5. Petrarch contrasts his own supposed lack of ambition with the daring vaunts of the major Latin poets: Juvenal, the Roman satirist; Horace (Petrarch quotes two lines from his Epistle to his patron Maecenas [1.19]); Lucretius (from Book 4 of *On the Nature of Things*); and of course, Virgil (from Book 3 of the *Georgics*).

I prefer my own; I am one who delights in imitation and not in sameness, in a resemblance that is not servile, where the imitator's genius shines forth rather than his blindness or his ineptitude; I am one who much prefers not having a guide than being compelled to follow one slavishly. I do want a guide who leads me, not one who binds me to him, one who leaves me free use of my own sight, judgment, and freedom; I do not want him to forbid me to step where I wish, to go beyond him in some things, to attempt the inaccessible, to follow a shorter or, if I wish, an easier path, and to hasten or stop or even to part ways and to return.

⁓

RESONANCE

Laura Cereta: To Sister Deodata di Leno[1]

The subtlety of your question has opened my mind to more important roads to understanding. But I am not the person to defend the argument at hand, since empty air does not support wings that have no feathers. I have no desire to enter into an academic wrestling match with you since I have acquired only a shadow of learning, and this outside the academy and without any study of the fine points of logic. You asked about our departure point and the sequence of places on our itinerary. The story would be plain enough, but the difficulty lies wholly in our destinations, for you tacitly impugn pleasure when you attack our delight in Epicurus.[2] Still, I would not so easily attribute pleasure to vice, since the philosopher locates this pleasure not in the delights of the senses but in the sating of the mind. But more on this later. Now to what you ask.

Our journey began at the town of Cereto. We arrived at Lake Iseo at dawn with a company of men on horseback.[3] Marco, who was waiting there, brought us in no time up to the citadel, which is completely protected by a natural formation of rock. When we had had a pleasant meal there, a crowd of friends suddenly converged on us. After a short time they went off in different directions, and we withdrew to bed to rest, since the sun had set and the stars were already beginning to shine.

As soon as Aurora's rays shone, we boarded a boat from which merchants were already hurrying up to the outskirts of the town. We left the harbor and set sail, for light winds were gusting from the east. And so, the sailors plowed the long furrows of the Sabine lake with a happy oar, trailing their nets and songs. When we reached the other shore, messengers who had come from the next village approached us. With these people showing us the road through the adjacent mountains, we arrived at a set-

1. Translated from the Latin by Diana Robin. Cereta (1469–1499) was a precocious woman humanist from Brescia, who wrote the majority of her surviving letters, all in Latin, in the brief period between the death of her husband when she was 16 and the death of her father when she was 19. Her wide-ranging epistles engage a number of issues central to humanist thought, such as the active versus contemplative life, the role of passion and the emotions, and above all, the education of women. Uncompromising in her enlightened views of women, she took on scholars in Brescia and portrayed herself in her letters as Italy's leading woman scholar. The letter to her sister, a nun who resided in a convent near her home, was written in 1487. It is clearly meant to imitate Petrarch's letter on Mt. Ventoux, although it departs signifi-

cantly from Petrarch's narrative, particularly in its vivid description of the mountain setting and the postponing of Cereta's reflections to the end of her journey.
2. The letter obviously picks up from a previous argument over Epicurus, the 3rd-century Athenian philosopher who identified pleasure not with sensuality but with a tranquility that results in the harmony of mind and body, brought together through the pursuit of virtue. In Cereta's sympathetic rendition, Epicureanism is not unlike the spiritual delights of Christianity. The subtitle of the letter in its manuscript version is in fact "A Topography and Defense of Epicurus."
3. Lake Iseo is outside Cereto, a village in northern Italy. Unlike Petrarch, Cereta doesn't identify who else was in her party.

tlement of farm houses where the peak of the first hill could be seen rising up from its very roots. The entire populace was out waiting for us there with great bustling and excitement; the people's faces were full of friendship and yet kindly deference as well. At this level, the deep vales echoed with the resonant lowings of cattle; and from the highest crags, the pipes of shepherds could be heard, so that I might have thought Diana and Sylvanus inhabited these woods.[4]

Thus the ascent was easy, but the path was rugged. We sat, caught our breath, and pushed on, peacefully picking strawberries and flowers in the lush meadow. We were led to other small gardens where climbing vines with knotty tendrils and trees heavy-laden with apples provided shade. Here freedom from care—and this is what helped us seize grapes by the handful and gobble them down, since hunger was definitely the architect of our tour—gave us the strength to continue, and laughingly we put aside all thought of turning back. We returned to the path, and embarked upon the alpine slopes. Uncertain of our way, we wandered about, arriving at deserted places without a path and mountain ridges steep and overgrown with brambles.

Finally, taking diverse routes, once we had reached the mountaintop and the highest point of its summit, we launched a cascade of rocks which rolled headlong down into the depths of the valley. Then, roused by the racket, rabbits flew down the slopes ahead of us. Dogs, keen-scented and well-trained for the hunt, accompanied us. Next, right in front of our eyes, a small, trembling goat began to grow agitated at the sound of their yelping, and while the dogs followed his scent and trail with aggressive intent, he, with the violent dogs at his heels, chose flight by leaping down from the jutting ridges.

Then seeking the way home again, we withdrew, since our path was obstructed, to the place where the dense forest rose to its highest level. Here we thirstily drank down great flagons of milk, for our cabins in the inn where we were staying were a long way away. Within sight of this side of the promontory was a lookout point with a prospect of the most charming farmhouses below us. After sliding down the breast of the mountain, we traversed narrow crags that faced one another, taking the unavoidable pass that lay between them. A roaring, rushing sound accompanied us as we walked, a sound which was met by an echo, and after this we sang about Pallas and the Muses, one after another in turn, under a rocky cave carved out within the promontory.

Then finally, walking on our tiptoes since we could scarcely put the soles of our feet on the ground, so severely had the fires of the hot sun burned them, we took hidden paths down to the river, slowly and unsteadily, where no traveler appeared to have gone previously. We washed, rubbed ourselves down, and, having spread out leaves beneath a sheltering tree, we decided to lie down where the land is watered by a winding stream. Soon, with the sound of falling water, a peaceful sleep easily stole over us, for the rushing creek and its curving banks foamed from the rapid current, while a skylark perched above us gently filled the air with song.

But Fortune, the mocker of us all, sent a cuckoo down to tease us repeatedly, waking us from our sleep. We laughed and threatened the bird with birdlime and snares. And then the greedy bird fell into the tumbling, jutting rocks and the stream which inundated him in the roaring torrent from the cataract pounding down from above, and afterwards he was hidden and his path could not be seen. Not long after he

---

4. Diana is the goddess of chastity and hunting; Sylvanus is a woodland deity.

disappeared, he met his end, whereupon, in a shallow part of the stream, he belched out a pebble.

After this episode, we dispersed to head for home, where we were greeted with heavy-laden tables set out in a narrow passageway that provided a supper worthy of Xenocrates.[5] The first course consisted of chestnuts, turnips, and polenta—a delicious snack for us. On a second table, individual loaves of barley bread were set out, and on a table in the middle stood one small jug of wine to be passed around. As for delicacies, hazelnuts and fruits were offered to us diners, and our hunger was adequately requited.

The sage is content with plain foods: he asks for that which nourishes rather than that which delights. For his frugal lifestyle and his moderation brought Socrates more glory than the enjoyment of luxury brought to Sardanapalus.[6] For one can compare the frugality in one's life to the life of the belly. While frugality and prudence raise up the contemplation of the mind to the heavens through the fire of love, the indulgence of the belly causes human life to resemble that of a greedy wolf. Magnanimity of the soul and the enslavement to pleasure cannot be contained in one and the same body; only the wretched flee from adversity and trial.

Let us awaken our souls from sleep, dear sister. Let those of us who are reclining and who are cowardly rise to greater illuminations of the faith. Let us put away the cares of this age from the threshold of anxiety and let us tear the slender threads of arrogance from falsehood and deception. Enjoyment has to be considered the least important of human things and pleasures ignorant of constancy must be severed from the governance of the unreliable emotions. What does the serenity which comes from looking down on the fields from the tops of mountains do for the happiness of mind and soul? What has the quiet exuberance of a heart becalmed given us, although it allowed us to survey the far-flung mountains without noise or any mishap of fate? What help has this refuge, this prodigious and extended flight across steep crags and hilltops been, far from which the quickly passing year has now fled the most troublesome spaces of our days? Long enough have we wandered in all directions in an attempt to change places. But can this wandering through various pastures, this exchange of one forest for another, touch in any way the mind of one for whom the whole world is a hometown that feels too confining and small. Surely what I thought was as follows, contrary to the precepts of the philosophers: I believed that I was crossing a threshold to greater tranquility by this running to and fro of mine.[7]

Virtue alone finds the road to true peace of mind. False, sister, are the painted enticements that Epicurus was accustomed to scorn as ephemeral and transitory pleasures. For he, since he was a man of great moderation and temperance, spurned these casual diversions among the quieting forms of relaxation, and not rashly so. For just as the inclination of our emotions draws us toward those things which appear shining and beautiful on the surface, so the appetite becomes sated to the point of nausea once our desires have been requited. Epicurus thought that the pleasure which is born in us is constantly reborn in a more vigorous form through the agency of the freedom that comes from a pure heart and mind. For the mind that emulates the gods in its pursuit of happiness is full and contented. All other joys, because they grow old, torment us cruelly, with a sense of burning.

---

5. An Athenian philosopher said to have laid out a plentiful table for Alexander the Great when he visited unexpectedly.

6. The famously dissolute last king of the Assyrians.

7. A clear echo of Petrarch.

The great blessedness of virtue ought to be admired. Thus that man Epicurus, full of moral fiber and wisdom, believed that all short-lived sweetness, all imaginary petty devices, all erroneous efforts to achieve true serenity would be punished. We, whom this foolish satiety in sweet things rightfully exhausts, should satisfy our hearts more delightfully with God's love and we should chart a course for a virtue unviolated in this fleeting life, with the sail of our hearts pulled taut.

In the meantime, let society women, whose counterfeit finery exposes their notorious lack of modesty, pet themselves and bask, to the extent that they can, in their own vanity. But we women, since we are the objects of contempt, should be conscious with the humility of our chastity that these fragile, small bodies of ours are chaff for fire and filth. And although I am not yet called Laura in the place where you dwell, sister—that would be to put a skylark[8] next to a phoenix—still, out of the kindness of your heart, you will not cast me out of the purview of your love. For the magpie did not think the nightingale unworthy of her; nor did the peacock always show disdain for the hoopoe. You will come up with a fair plan, I do not doubt, if you reflect how anxiety-ridden this time of ours is, for it draws all things born in this world, in an irrevocable course, to one end.

This end, however, has but one object for our soul: the one God; and he, so that we might enter Paradise, has placed us, since we are sojourners, in the exile of our fragile flesh. Let us devote ourselves, therefore, wholly to virtue and to the innocent and celibate life of our Savior and let our sinful life revert to him also. Let us imitate the many illustrious men in the Church who, detached from all desires, have yearned with full hearts for eternal life. Nature has taught us always to incline our hearts freely and deliberately towards the good, so that it will finally come about for us that God will win us over as heavenly beings for all eternity.

This living of ours is so uncertain and aimless that time, speeding onward, tightly binds the day of our birth to that of our death. And so, no day should slip, for the sake of leisure, through our hands. Let us reclaim the nights with our speeches; let ordered thoughts alone give our minds respite. Let us believe each day that this is our last on earth; let us ponder that this life is a turbid well of grief, and that death is the parent of worms and decay. Look, the iniquity of raging Fortune carries us and all other things away, and all grounds for arrogance fly upwards when the spirit has fled the body. But surely our mind is too often bereft of judgment, clouded by blind hope and the false promise of flimsy pleasure.

To sum up, let us sweep away the seeds of the question here and now. A pleasure that lives and endures is a thing not generally known; for disdaining that which belongs to this world, it purchases that which is immortal with the currency of virtue. This pleasure delights and cares for our minds in its nurturing bosom; it inhabits the fortress of respected religion. And it is protected, free from care, and blessed, even amid the Syrtes[9] and the most difficult terrain of our life. This one pleasure represents the highest fulfillment of the contented mind, the most tranquil satiety of our solace, by which we are led by the safe path of faith to God. For the right-thinking mind is the companion of the gods; and in this mind neither idleness, nor darkness, nor ghosts, nor any emotion shall hold dominion. All other murky allurements have been sucked into that ocean of evils which cause the voyaging human mind, whenever it is caught up in sudden storms, to drown in softness and false and empty consolation.

---

8. *Lauda* in Latin, thus punning on "Laura." Cereta had refused to enter the religious life after her husband's death in 1486.   9. Treacherous sandbanks in northern Africa.

Write often, if you think of anything. Write even if you don't. Afterwards it will not be permitted to me to see you in that solitude of yours. Your letters raise my spirits so much that the wonderful memory of you brings you back to me as though you were here. Farewell. December 12, 1487.

CANZONIERE Petrarch spent many years writing, revising, and ordering and reordering the 366-poem sequence known as the *Canzoniere* or *Rime sparse* ("Scattered rhymes"). The chronology he carefully constructs from these "fragments" allows us to participate in the unfolding not simply of an unrequited passion, but of a life. That this life speaks to us with such directness, despite the formality of the metrical and verse constraints within which Petrarch worked, is one of the paradoxes of the sequence, and one that poets after him struggled to repeat with varying degrees of success.

While Petrarch wrote in a variety of metrical forms, including the flexible *canzone* and the sestina, the one that he employed most is the sonnet, perfecting the form to the extent that fourteen-line poems with a clear break between their eighth and ninth lines are simply referred to as "Petrarchan sonnets." For the most part, the four stanzas that comprise the sonnet are syntactically compact units: the octet is broken into two stanzas of four lines each, with an *a-b-b-a* rhyme scheme; the sestet is composed of two stanzas of three lines each, with a *c-d-c* rhyme. Such compactness allows for suggestive but brief sketches of Laura's beauty and the speaker's unrequited love; the discreteness of the stanza (a word that means "room") dictates that connections among them depend more on comparison and allusion than syntactical complexity. At the same time, the continuity of rhyme and Petrarch's frequent use of assonance and alliteration— plays with language and sound that the Italian language encourages, with its fluidity and inherent musicality—create a subtle, often sensuous impression of unity.

Italian though the *Canzoniere* may be, it represents in many ways a continued dialogue with classical culture such as we find in the letters. Mythological allusions abound, particularly to myths retold by Ovid: Apollo and Daphne (Sonnet 30), Diana and Actaeon (52), Pygmalion (78) and the aging Tithonus, who watches his eternally-young lover Aurora depart each morning to herald the new day (291). The Virgilian legacy is also strongly marked, as in the echo of Aeneas's frustrated glimpse of Venus (90) and the extended meditation on the poignant nightingale simile from the tale of Orpheus in Virgil's fourth *Georgic* (311, 353, 365). Such classical references aren't included simply for the sake of displaying intellectual wares. They help to situate Petrarch's often unanchored persona and give form to the elusive Laura: from the transformed laurel tree, to the threatening Diana who forbids Actaeon's speech, to the graceful Aurora who, in death, leaves an aging Petrarch behind on earth.

Yet Petrarch models his sequence equally on modern innovations. The sonnet, for one thing, derived from the formal experimentations of both the French Provençal school and the late thirteenth-century practitioners of the *dolce stil nuovo* ("sweet new style") to which Petrarch pays homage in his seventieth poem. Petrarch quotes lines from Arnaut Daniel, Guido Cavalcanti, and the great Dante himself, only to move beyond them in a final stanza where he tellingly quotes—who else?—himself. The idea of a poetry "book" looks back to the Roman poets Catullus and Propertius (whose manuscripts Petrarch had discovered and transcribed) but Petrarch gives his sequence a Christian focus, starting with his confessional lament and closing with a recantation addressed not to Laura but to the "Virgin mother," Mary.

Petrarch uses devotional imagery to describe Laura, first glimpsed in a church on Good Friday. Yet there is something potentially idolatrous about this earthly passion. Petrarch's supposed inability to choose between Christian salvation and his idolatrous love is poignantly foreshadowed in the *Canzoniere,* especially in those sonnets where he mourns the fact that life is swiftly overtaking him and that he has nothing to show for his gray locks but a handful of poems. Unlike the supremely divine Beatrice of Dante's own poetry book, the *Vita nuova* (see Volume B), Laura finally cannot function as the medium for the poet's salvation.

Often castigated for his preciousness, as well as for a misogynistic treatment of Laura, Petrarch reveals himself as fully aware of the choices he has made and their implications. The real Laura, the Petrarchan narrator knows all too well, is nowhere to be found in his poems. One of the many conflicts of the *Canzoniere,* in fact, is the tension between the poet's fiction and the world beyond it. From time to time, Petrarch directly addresses political events as well as the patrons who generously supported him. Though his lyrics are primarily about his interior life, Petrarch also speaks to the contexts that privilege such a life.

CANZONIERE

DURING THE LIFE OF MY LADY LAURA[1]

1

O you[2] who hear within these scattered verses
the sound of sighs with which I fed my heart
in my first errant youthful days when I
in part was not the man I am today;

5   for all the ways in which I weep and speak
between vain hopes, between vain suffering,
in anyone who knows love through its trials,
in them, may I find pity and forgiveness.

But now I see how I've become the talk
10   so long a time of people all around
(it often makes me feel so full of shame),

and from my vanities there comes shame's fruit,
and my repentance, and the clear awareness
that worldly joy is just a fleeting dream.

3

It was the day the sun's ray had turned pale
with pity for the suffering of his Maker
when I was caught (and I put up no fight),[3]
my lady, for your lovely eyes had bound me.

5   It seemed no time to be on guard against
Love's blows; therefore, I went my way
secure and fearless—so, all my misfortunes
began in midst of universal woe.

Love found me all disarmed and saw the way
10   was clear to reach my heart down through the eyes,
which have become the halls and doors of tears.

It seems to me it did him little honor

---

1. Translated from the Italian by Mark Musa.
2. Petrarch uses *Voi* to address his reader, which can be read as the plural form of "you" or as the formal address

to a single reader, as contrasted with the more informal *tu.*
3. The day Petrarch was "taken" by his Lady is Good Friday, or 6 April 1327.

to wound me with his arrow in my state
and to you, armed, not show his bow at all.

16

The old man takes his leave, white-haired and pale,
of the sweet place where he filled out his age
and leaves his little family, bewildered
to see its own dear father disappear;

5   from there, dragging along his ancient limbs
throughout the very last days of his life,
helping himself with good will all he can,
broken by years, and wearied by the road,

he comes to Rome, pursuing his desire,
10   to look upon the likeness of the One
that he still hopes to see up there in Heaven.[4]

Just so, alas, sometimes I go, my lady,
searching, as much as possible, in others
for your true, your desirable form.

35

Alone and deep in thought I measure out
the most deserted fields, with slow, late steps,
with eyes intent to flee whatever sign
of human footprint left within the sand.

5   I find no other shield for my protection
against the knowing glances of mankind,
for in my bearing all bereft of joy
one sees from outside how I burn within.

So now, I think, only the plains and mountains,
10   the rivers and the forests know the kind
of life I lead, the one concealed from all.

And still, I never seem to find a path
too harsh, too wild for Love to always join
me and to speak to me, and I to him!

52

Diana never pleased her lover more,
when just by chance all of her naked body
he saw bathing within the chilly waters,[5]

---

4. The allusion is to the veil with which Veronica is said
to have wiped Christ's face while he was carrying the
cross; Christ's image was preserved on the cloth, which
was kept in St. Peter's and attracted large numbers of pilgrims to see it. Petrarch is drawing on a simile from
Dante's *Paradiso*, Canto 31, in which a pilgrim from
Croatia who comes to see the "Veronica" is compared to
Dante himself.

5. The goddess of chastity who lives among her nymphs
in the woods, Diana was surprised by the hunter Actaeon
while she was bathing. For his transgression, she turned
him into a stag; and he was torn apart by his own dogs.
Throughout the *Canzoniere*, Petrarch often refers to himself through a series of metamorphosed figures.

than did the simple mountain shepherdess
5   please me, the while she bathed the pretty veil
that holds her lovely blonde hair in the breeze.[6]

So that even now in hot sunlight she makes me
tremble all over with the chill of love.

90

She'd let her gold hair flow free in the breeze
that whirled it into thousands of sweet knots,
and lovely light would burn beyond all measure
in those fair eyes whose light is dimmer now.

5   Her face would turn the color pity wears,
a pity true or false I did not know,
and I with all Love's tinder in my breast—
it's no surprise I quickly caught on fire.

The way she walked was not the way of mortals
10   but of angelic forms, and when she spoke
more than an earthly voice it was that sang:[7]

a godly spirit and a living sun
was what I saw, and if she is not now,
my wound still bleeds, although the bow's unbent.

126

Clear, cool, sweet, running waters
where she, for me the only
woman, would rest her lovely body;
kind branch on which it pleased her
5   (I sigh to think of it)
to make a column for her lovely side;
and grass and flowers which her gown,
richly flowing, covered
with its angelic folds;
10   sacred air serene
where Love with those fair eyes opened my heart:
listen all of you together
to these my mournful, my last words.[8]

If it, indeed, must be my fate,
15   and Heaven works its ways,
that Love close up these eyes while they still weep,
let grace see my poor body

---

6. "From the breeze" is *a l'aura* in Italian—one of
Petrarch's many wordplays on Laura's name.
7. In the forests of Carthage in *Aeneid* 1 the goddess
Venus appears to Aeneas disguised as a young maiden,
speaking to him with a more than human voice.
8. This depiction of the *locus amoenus* or beautiful place

is drawn from Vaucluse, on the south bank of the Sorgue
River, where Petrarch bought a house in the mid 1330s,
finding there the serenity and peace he couldn't have in
Avignon. The "clear, cool, sweet waters" are those of the
Sorgue.

be buried there among you
and let my soul return to its home naked;
20   then death would be less harsh
if I could bear this hope
unto that fearful crossing,
because the weary soul
could never in a more secluded port,
25   in a more tranquil grave,
flee from my poor belabored flesh and bones.

And there will come a time, perhaps,
that to the well-known place
the lovely animal returns,[9] and tamed,
30   and there where she first saw me
that day which now is blessed,
she turns her eyes with hope and happiness
in search of me, and—ah, the pity—
to see me there as dust
35   among the stones, Love will
inspire her and she will sigh
so sweetly she will win for me some mercy
and force open the heavens
drying her eyes there with her lovely veil.

40   Falling from gracious boughs,
I sweetly call to mind,
were flowers in a rain upon her bosom,
and she was sitting there
humble in such glory
45   now covered in a shower of love's blooms:
a flower falling on her lap,
some fell on her blond curls,
like pearls set into gold
they seemed to me that day;
50   some fell to rest on ground, some on the water,
and some in lovelike wandering
were circling down and saying, "Here Love reigns."

How often I would say
at that time, full of awe:
55   "For certain she was born up there in Heaven!"[1]
And her divine behavior,
her face and words and her sweet smile
so filled me with forgetfulness
and so divided me
60   from the true image
that I would sigh and say:

---

9. Laura herself.
1. The imagery in the preceding stanza recalls Dante's description of the Garden of Eden, from *Purgatory* 30, and

Laura is here modeled on Dante's Beatrice who appears "within a cloud of flowers."

"Just how and when did I come here?"
thinking I was in Heaven, not where I was;
and since then I have loved
65   this bank of grass and find peace nowhere else.

If you had all the beauty you desired,
you could with boldness leave
the wood and make your way among mankind.[2]

195

From day to day my face and hair are changing,
but I still bite the sweetly baited hook
and hold tight to the green and enlimed branches
of the tree that has no care of cold or heat.[3]

5   The sea will lose its water, sky its stars
before I fear no longer and desire
her lovely shade, and I not love and hate
the deep and loving wound I hide so badly.

I do not hope to ever rest my labors
10   until I am deboned, defleshed, demuscled,
or till my enemy shows me her pity.

All things that cannot be will be before
another or she or Death will heal the wound
that Love with her fair eyes made in my heart.

AFTER THE DEATH OF MY LADY LAURA
267[4]

O God! that lovely face, that gentle look,
O God! that charming way of hers, so proud!
O God! those words that any wild, harsh heart
could tame and cowards turn to courageous men!

5   And, O God, that sweet smile whence came the arrow
of death, the only good I hope for now!
Royal soul, the worthiest of all to rule,
if only you had not joined us so late:

it is for you I burn, in you I breathe
10   for I am yours alone; deprived of you,
I suffer less for all my other pains;

with hope you filled me once and with desire
the time I left that highest charm alive,
but all those words were scattered in the wind.

---

2. The last stanza, referred to as the *congedo* or leave-taking, is addressed to the poem itself.
3. The tree is the evergreen laurel, another play on Laura's name.

4. With this poem, the poet is confronted with Laura's death by plague, which occurred on 6 April 1348. In the manuscript, there is a space between poems 266 and 267.

277

If Love does not give me some new advice,
I shall be forced to change my life with death,
such fear and grief afflict my saddened soul
because desire lives and hope is dead,

5   and so bewildered, unconsoled my life
is totally, that night and day it weeps,
weary without a helm in stormy seas
and on a dubious course with no true guide.

An imaginary guide is driving it,
10   the true one's underground—no, she's in Heaven
whence she shines even brighter through my heart,

not through my eyes, because a veil of sorrow
forbids them to behold the longed-for light
and turns my hair to grey before it's time.

291

When I see coming down the sky Aurora
with roses on her brow and gold in hair,
Love seizes me and losing all my color
I sigh as I say, "Laura is there now.[5]

5   "O glad Tithonus,[6] you know when it's time
to hold your precious treasure once again;
but I, what can I do with my sweet laurel?
To see her once again I have to die.

"Your partings aren't so difficult to take—
10   at least at nighttime she returns to you,
and she does not despise your head of white;

"my nights she saddens and my days she darkens,
the one who carried off my thoughts with her
and left me of herself only her name."

311

That nightingale so tenderly lamenting
perhaps his children or his cherished mate,
in sweetness fills the sky and countryside
with many notes of grief skillfully played,

5   and all night long he stays with me it seems,
reminding me of my harsh destiny;
I have no one to blame except myself

5. "Ivi è Laura ora," playing on "Dawn" (*l'Aurora*).
6. A mortal who fell in love with Dawn; at her request, the gods granted him eternal life, but since she hadn't asked that he stay young forever, he became eternally an aged man.

for thinking Death could not rule such a goddess.[7]

How easy to deceive one who is sure!
10   Those two lights, lovely, brighter than the sun,
whoever thought would turn the earth so dark?

And now I know what this fierce fate of mine
would have me learn as I live on in tears:
that nothing here can please and also last.

⌘

RESONANCE

Virgil: from *Fourth Georgic*
[*Orpheus Likened to a Bereaved Nightingale*][1]

septem illum totos perhibent ex ordine mensis
rupe sub aëria deserti ad Strymonis undam
flevisse, et gelidis haec evolvisse sub antris,
mulcentem tigris et agentem carmine quercus;
qualis populea maerens philomela sub umbra
amissos queritur fetus, quos durus arator
observans nido implumis detraxit; at illa
flet noctem, ramoque sedens miserabile carmen
integrat, et maestis late loca questibus implet.

Month in, month out, seven whole months, men say beneath a skyey cliff by lonely Strymon's wave, he wept, and, deep in icy caverns, unfolded this his tale, charming the tigers, and making the oaks attend his strain; even as the nightingale, mourning beneath the poplar's shade, bewails the loss of her brood, that a churlish ploughman hath espied and torn unfledged from the nest: but she weeps all night long, and, perched on a spray, renews her piteous strain, filling the region round with sad laments.[2]

⌘

353[1]

O lovely little bird singing away
in tones of grief for all the time gone by,
you see the night and winter at your side,
the day and all those happy months behind;

---

7. The first half of the poem is drawn from Virgil's extended nightingale simile in the fourth *Georgic*: see the Resonance below.

1. Translated by H. R. Fairclough. Virgil compares the mourning nightingale to the musician and poet Orpheus, whose daring trip to Hades to rescue his bride, Eurydice, from the realm of the dead, resulted in failure. The larger context of the *Georgics* is clearly important for Petrarch who also saw himself as the consummate poet, trying to use his verses to restore Laura from death.

2. Petrarch echos and revises various features in the Latin text, two of which are especially worthy of note. First, his nightingale is male, and one who "perhaps" is mourning

either his cherished mate (like Orpheus) or his children (like Virgil's nightingale). Second, in speaking of the "churlish ploughman," Virgil uses the Latin word *durus,* or harsh. Petrarch uses the Italian *dura* twice in his sonnet, playing on two different meanings: when he laments his "harsh fate" (*dura sorte*) in the second stanza, and when in the final line he observes that his "fierce fate" has taught him that "nothing here can please and also last" (*come nulla qua giù diletta et dura*).

1. Originally, Petrarch had made this sonnet the next to last poem (365) in the collection; it shows his ongoing fascination with the weeping bird as an analogy for himself as singer.

5   aware as you are of your grievous troubles
       could you be so of my plight as your own,
       you would fly straight to the bosom of this wretch
       to share with him some of his painful grief.

       I cannot say our portions would be equal,
10   since she you weep for may still have her life
       with which Heaven and Death for me are stingy;

       but the forbidding season and the hour,
       the memory of sweet years and bitter ones,
       invites me to discuss with you my pity.

365

I go my way lamenting those past times
I spent in loving something which was mortal
instead of soaring high, since I had wings
that might have taken me to higher levels.

5   You who see all my shameful, wicked errors,
       King of all Heaven, invisible, immortal,
       help this frail soul of mine for she has strayed,
       and all her emptiness fill up with grace,

       so that, having once lived in storms, at war,
10   I may now die in peace, in port; and if my stay
       was vain, at least let my departure count.

       Over the little life that still remains to me,
       and at my death, deign that your hand be present:
       You know You are the only hope I have.

from 366[2]

Virgin, so lovely, clothed in the sun's light
and crowned with stars, so pleased the highest Sun
that inside you He chose to hide his light:
love urges me to speak of you in verse,
5   but I cannot begin without your help
       and His who loving placed himself in you.
       I call upon the one who always answered
       whoever called with faith.
       Virgin, if toward mercy
10   for extreme misery of worldly things
       you ever turned, then bend now to my prayer,
       and help me in my war,
       though I am dust and you are queen of Heaven.

---

2. The final poem in the collection is a lengthy canzone dedicated not to Laura, but to the Virgin Mary. To depict Mary, Petrarch borrows from the language of the final book in the Bible, the Apocalypse, as well as from the prayer *Ave Maria* and the final canto of Dante's *Paradiso,* which opens with an invocation to Mary by St. Bernard.

Virgin so wise, one of the lovely number
15 of all the blessèd, prudent virgins—rather,
the first of them and with the brightest light,[3]
O sturdy shield for all who are afflicted
against the blows that Death and Fortune wield
beneath which they're triumphant, more than saved,
20 O refuge from blind ardor that is raging
in foolish mortals here.
Virgin, those lovely eyes
that saw in sorrow those pitiless wounds
upon the sweet limbs of your cherished son,
turn to my dangerous state,
25 who come imprudent to you for your help.

w w A

Virgin, how many tears I've shed already,
80 how many flattering words and prayers in vain
for nothing but my pain and grievous loss!
Since I was born upon the Arno's banks,[4]
then wandering from one place to another,
my life has always been nothing but trouble.
85 Mortal beauty, actions, and words are what
have burdened all my soul.
Virgin holy, bountiful,
do not delay, this could be my last year;
my days more swift than arrows have sped off
90 through wretchedness and sin,
and there is only Death awaiting me.

Virgin, that one is dust and holds in grief
my heart, who while alive kept it in tears
and of my thousand sufferings knew not one;
95 and even had she known them then, what happened
would still have happened—had she wished otherwise,
it would have meant my death and her dishonor.
Now you, Lady of Heaven, you our Goddess,
(if such a term be fitting),
100 Virgin of superb senses,
you can see all, and what could not be done
by others is no match for your great power:
end now my suffering
and bring honor to you, to me salvation.

105 Virgin, in whom I place all of my hope
you can and will help me in my great need:
do not abandon me at the last pass,
not for my sake but His who made me man,

3. An allusion to the parable in Matthew 25 about ten virgins who go forth to meet a bridegroom and his bride: the
five wise ones take oil in their vessels, the five foolish ones
do not. The ones with oil are invited to the wedding feast.
4. Petrarch was born in Arezzo, on the banks of the Arno
River.

let not my own worth but His own high likeness
110   in me move you to care for one so low.
Medusa and my sin turned me to stone
dripping useless moisture.[5]
Virgin, now with repentant
and holy tears fill up my weary heart;
115   at least let my last weeping be devout,
without the mud of earth,
as was the first and insane vow of mine.

Virgin so kind, the enemy of pride,
let love of our same origin move you,
120   have pity on a sorry, humble heart;
for if a bit of mortal, fleeting dust
can make me love with faith so marvelous,
how then will I love you, a noble thing?
If from my state so wretched and so vile
125   I rise up at your hands,
Virgin, then in your name
I cleanse and give my thoughts and wit and style,
my tongue and heart, my tears and sighs to you.
Show me a better crossing
130   and please look kindly on my changed desires.

The day draws near, it cannot be far off;
time runs and flies so fast,
Virgin, the one and only one,
and death and conscience now stab at my heart;
135   commend me to your Son who is the true
man and the truth of God,
that He accept my final breath in peace.

◇◇◇

RESONANCES

PETRARCH AND HIS TRANSLATORS[1]

Petrarch: "Canzoniere" 190 (Italian)

Una candida cerva sopra l'erba
verde[2] m'apparve con duo corna d'oro,
fra due riviere all'ombra d'un alloro,
levando 'l sole a la stagione acerba.

---

5. Medusa is the mythological gorgon whose gaze turns men to stone. Laura's stony gaze had been a frequent theme in the earlier rhymes.

1. Petrarch's sonnets were widely imitated and translated throughout the 15th and 16th centuries. *Canzoniere* 190, "Una candida cerva" ("A white doe"), enjoyed notable popularity, particularly in its connection between the beloved and the beautiful, untouchable deer. The poem is printed here in both Italian and English. Translated by Robert Durling.

2. Note the internal rhymes of *-er: cerva, l'erba, verde,* which help to offset the more formal rhyme structure of *a-b-b-a* and create a sense of fluidity between lines. Other internal rhyming is provided with *farmi / parve* in line 11, *sol / volto* in line 12, etc.

5   Era sua vista sì dolce superba
       ch' i' lasciai per seguirla ogni lavoro,
       come l'avaro che 'n cercar tesoro
       con diletto l'affanno disacerba.

       "Nessun mi tocchi," al bel collo d'intorno[3]
10   scritto avea di diamanti et di topazi.
       "Libera farmi al mio Cesare parve."

       Et era 'l sol già vòlto al mezzo giorno,
       gli occhi miei stanchi di mirar, non sazi,
       quand' io caddi ne l'acqua et ella sparve.

"Canzoniere" 190 (English)

A white doe on the green grass appeared to me, with two golden horns, between two rivers, in the shade of a laurel,[4] when the sun was rising in the unripe season.

Her look was so sweet and proud that to follow her I left every task, like the miser who as he seeks treasure sweetens his trouble with delight.

"Let no one touch me,"[5] she bore written with diamonds and topazes around her lovely neck. "It has pleased my Caesar to make me free."[6]

And the sun had already turned at midday; my eyes were tired by looking but not sated, when I fell into the water,[7] and she disappeared.

Thomas Wyatt: Whoso List to Hunt[1]

       Whoso list° to hunt, I know where is an hind,°   *wishes / doe*
       But as for me, helas, I may no more:
       The vain travail hath wearied me so sore.
       I am of them that farthest cometh behind.
5   Yet may I by no means my wearied mind
       Draw from° the deer:° but as she fleeth afore,   *forget / also, dear*
       Fainting I follow. I leave off therefore,
       Since in a net I seek to hold the wind.

3. With the sestet, or final six lines, the rhyme scheme changes to *a-b-c, a-b-c.*
4. While Laura does not technically appear in the poem, the *alloro* or laurel creates a suggestive allusion to her presence.
5. Translation of the Latin *Noli mi tangere,* the words with which Christ greets Mary Magdalene after his resurrection (John 20:17).
6. Christ's saying to Mary may well have had its origins in the collars found on the necks of white stags, inscribed with the saying: *Noli me tangere, Caesaris sum* ("Do not touch me, I belong to Caesar"). The 3rd-century historian Solinus records the ongoing tradition in the Roman empire.
7. Possible allusion to the fate of Narcissus, who falls into the water at the height of noon after staring hopelessly at his reflection; see Ovid, Volume A.

1. Thomas Wyatt was accomplished both in the world of politics—he was a tireless diplomat for Henry VIII, dying while on a mission for him in 1542 when he was only thirty-nine—and poetry; in many ways, he can be said to have been responsible for bringing Petrarch to England and helping to spark the poetic renaissance that would claim as its practitioners Edmund Spenser, Sir Philip Sidney, and Shakespeare. Much of his poetry was in the sonnet form, adapted to English meter and style; his sestets follow *c-d-d-c-d-d* rhyme schemes, and the final couplet tends to represent a culminating moment to, sometimes an ironic or surprising departure from, the main body of the text. The poem was published in 1557 after Wyatt's death, in an anthology called *Songs and Sonnets;* not a literal translation of *Canzoniere* 190, it is a free reworking of its themes.

Who list her hunt I put him out of doubt,
10   As well as I may spend his time in vain:
And, graven with diamonds, in letters plain
There is written her fair neck round about:

Noli me tangere, for Caesar's I am,
And wild for to hold though I seem tame.[2]

Petrarch: "Canzoniere" 209 (Italian)

I dolci colli ov' io lasciai me stesso,
partendo onde partir giamai non posso,
mi vanno innanzi, et emmi ogni or a dosso
quel caro peso ch' Amor m'à commesso.

5   Meco di me mi meraviglio spesso
ch' i' pur vo sempre, et non son ancor mosso
dal bel giogo più volte indarno scosso,
ma com' più me n'allungo et più m'appresso.

Et qual cervo ferito di saetta
10   col ferro avelenato dentr' al fianco
fugge et più duolsi quanto più s'affretta,

tal io, con quello stral dal lato manco
che mi consuma et parte mi diletta,
di duol mi struggo et di fuggir mi stanco.

"Canzoniere" 209 (English)[1]

The sweet hills where I left myself, when I departed from the place I can never depart from, are before me as I go, and still behind me is that sweet burden Love has entrusted to me.

Within myself I am often amazed at myself, for I still go and yet have not moved from the sweet yoke that I have shaken off in vain many times, but the farther I go from it the closer I come.

As a hart struck by an arrow,[2] with the poisoned steel within its side, flees and feels more pain the faster it runs,

so I, with that arrow in my left side which destroys me and at the same time delights me, am tormented by sorrow and weary myself with fleeing.

2. Critics have speculated that the "hind" is Anne Boleyn, and "Caesar" King Henry VIII. Wyatt was close to Boleyn, who was the king's mistress and, following his divorce to Catherine of Aragon, his second wife. "Wild" can mean dangerous, as well as undomesticated.
1. Translated by Robert Durling.

2. A hind or doe. One of the most famous earlier images in literature of a wounded deer was in the *Aeneid* 4 in which Virgil compares Dido to a "a heedless hind" wounded by the "poison" of Cupid's arrow; Petrarch inverts the gendered roles as he becomes the hart.

Chiara Matraini: *Fera son io di questo ombroso loco*

Fera son io di questo ombroso loco,
   Che vo con la saetta in mezzo al core,
   Fuggendo, lassa, il fin del mio dolore,
   E cerco chi mi strugge a poco a poco.

5   E com'augel che fra le penne il foco
   Si sente acceso, onde volando fuore
   Dal dolce nido suo, mentre l'ardore
   Fugge, con l'ale più raccendo il foco.

Tal io fra queste fronde a l'aura estiva
10   Con l'ali del desio volando in alto,
   Cerco il foco fuggir che meco porto.

Ma quando vado più di riva in riva
   Per fuggir 'l mio mal, con fiero assalto
   Lunga morte procaccio al viver corto.

Chiara Matraini: *I am a wild deer in this shady wood*[1]

I am a wild deer in this shady wood
With a sharp arrow driven through my heart.
I flee, alas, that which would end my pain
And seek him who destroys me bit by bit;

5   And like a bird that feels among her feathers
A lighted fire, which makes her fly away
From her belovèd nest: the heat goes with her
And all the time her wing-beats fan the flame.

So I, among these leaves in summer air,
10   Flying on high with wings of strong desire,
Attempt to quench the flame I carry with me.

But howsoever much from bank to bank
I go to flee my ill, with fierce assault
I gain a long death for my little life.

1. Translated by Laura Anna Stortoni and Mary Prentic Lillie. Chiara Matraini was one of the most gifted Italian poets of the 16th century. Born in 1514 in Lucca, she was widowed at a comparatively young age when her husband was murdered. She devoted herself to poetry and philosophy, and published a number of her poems and prose pieces in an edition of 1555. She also wrote a number of religious works, among them a life of the Virgin Mary and "Reflections on the Seven Penitential Psalms"; she died in 1604.

═══ PERSPECTIVES ═══

Lyric Sequences and Self-Definition

Petrarch's poems were enormously popular in early modern Europe. Editions, commentaries, and imitations of the *Canzoniere* vastly exceeded those of *The Divine Comedy*. Petrarch's probing lyrics set the tone for an elaborate inquiry into the speaker's identity in its cultural, religious, and gendered manifestations, all through the delicate and always dynamic relationship between that speaker and a distant, at times deceased, "other." As an Arabic paraphrase on Aristotle's *Poetics* put it, all lyric originates in praise and blame. Between praising Laura for her unmatched beauty and condemning her for her indifference to Petrarch's agony lay a wide gulf of poetic attitudes concerning the true source of power in the poems. In the lover, whose voice is the only one that we ever really hear? Or in the beloved who, in life as well as death, exerts such force over the lover that he is reduced to "fire and ice"?

Over the course of the sixteenth and seventeenth centuries, the scope of the poetic sequence widened considerably to include poems by women about men (Vittoria Colonna, Louise Labé) and by men about other men (Michelangelo, Shakespeare). Similarly, the sonnet, the metrical form most widely used, would undergo revisions, particularly in England. The typical Italian sonnet was divided into an eight-line opening (the octet) and a six-line conclusion (the sestet), but English poets came to prefer three four-line stanzas with a dramatic closing couplet. The poems, moreover, were not always about erotic attraction. The Polish poet Jan Kochanowski wrote a very different kind of sequence with his laments for his deceased daughter, only some of which are sonnets. Some of Petrarch's longer poems spell out the political malaise of fourteenth-century Italy. And Labé and other women used their poetry "books" as an explicit defense of their right to *write,* and publish.

In the sixteenth and seventeenth centuries there were two forms of "publication"—the circulation of manuscripts among a coterie of acquaintances, and the far more widespread circulation of printed texts among unknown readers. To what extent can the voice that speaks to us so immediately in the lyric sequence be considered a "private one," and how many of its revelations can be assumed to be truthful? To a large extent, the poetic sequence seemed to offer a place where the narrative voice might speak untramelled by social constraints, thereby attracting both women writers and unconventional topics. Yet their narrators meditate everywhere on those constraints, and most, like Louise Labé, are highly conscious of the contemporaries who would read and possibly reproach them. Shakespeare, who apparently had no hand in the publication of his sonnets, comments explicitly on the ability of his poems to memorialize the mysterious young man and dark lady alike, as well as the sordid relationship between them. Indeed, the ambiguous role that autobiography plays in the sequences is yet another reason for their fascination. Where does the "life" end and the work of art begin, the art so carefully crafted and compressed within rhyming and metrically balanced fragments? While the sonnet could decline into a stale and thoroughly predictable form in the hands of lesser writers, it also managed to attract the best of Europe's poets, challenging them to games of disclosure, concealment, and self-reflection that could be as serious as they were playful.

Louise Labé
c. 1520–1566

"I can do nothing but beseech virtuous ladies to elevate their minds a little above their distaffs and spindles." So does Louise Labé, known as "La Belle Cordière"—the beautiful rope-maker—urge her bourgeoise counterparts in France to read her poems. In the lively commercial center of Lyon in the 1530s and 1540s, Labé received an unusually solid classical education thanks to her well-to-do parents (ropemakers themselves) and put that education to excellent use. Her *Oeuvres,* published in 1555, is full of allusions to Petrarch and the Latin poets Catullus and Ovid. No pious imitation of either classical or contemporary traditions, her dialogue, three long elegies, and twenty-four sonnets take up directly the transgressive issue of female desire. It is one thing for the male Catullus to instruct Lesbia to kiss him a thousand times. It is quite another for the married Labé to ask the poet Olivier de Magny to return her affections and to insist in her prefatory letter that men take stock of the damage they have done to women by depriving them of learning. From this bold dedicatory preface to the wealthy landowner Madame Clémence de Bourges, to her closing request that her women readers "not reproach her," Labé shows an uncanny awareness of her problematic reception as the "Lyonnais Sappho," as one of the accompanying verses to the volume addresses her (in Greek). Indeed, the Catholic Labé was condemned as scandalous by the Protestant theologian Jean Calvin and suspected of poisoning her husband. Her adroit remaking of Petrarch's dynamics as her own not only opened the door to assertions that her life mirrored her art, but also made her acclaimed as one of Renaissance France's greatest poets.

PRONUNCIATION:
   Louis Labé: lou-EASE lah-BAY

When I behold you[1]

When I behold you, your blond tresses crowned
With laurel green, and hear you play the lute
Till rocks and trees are plucked up by the root
To follow its complaints,[2] see you renowned

5   Of all, while many thousand virtues ring you,
And I see you, ahead of all, attain the peak,
And hear how all your praises loudest speak—
Then must my heart, by passion driven, sing you:

These countless virtues, making you so loved
10   By everyone, these things that make you praised—
Could they not make you just as well a lover?
Thus higher yet your honor would be raised,
Were you by pity so to love me moved,
And for my sweet love an answering flame discover.

Lute, companion of my wretched state[3]

Lute, companion of my wretched state,
True witness of my never-ceasing sighs,
Faithful scribe of all my grieving cries,

---

1. Translated from the French by Frank Warnke. The 24 sonnets from which the poems here are taken comprised the final section of the volume of Labé's *Evvres* ("Oeuvres" or "Works"), published in 1555. The first sonnet of the section, written in Italian, suggests in its opening line that "neither Ulysses nor the greatest sage" could have predicted the suffering Labé has known for her beloved. "When I behold you" is the tenth sonnet in the sequence.
2. Labé associates her musician with Orpheus, the mythi-

cal musician praised in Ovid's *Metamorphoses* as having the power to make the trees follow him. The "laurel green" was used to crown poets. The beloved in question may be Olivier de Magny, a well-known poet and translator, who spent time in Lyon while he was traveling to Rome.
3. Sonnet 12, in which the lute now becomes Labé's "companion."

In lamentation you have been my mate;

5   My piteous sighs have caused you such distress
That often you've been forced to change your strains,
Replacing your delectable refrains
With notes that my tormented mood express.

And if I would compel your former measure,[4]
10   Your strings growing slack, you force me to be still;
But when you see me tenderly complain,
You give approval to my grieving pleasure,
And I'm obliged to yield unto your will,
Still hoping for sweet outcome from sweet pain.

Kiss me again[5]

Kiss me again, again, kiss me again!
Give me one of the luscious ones you have,
Give me one of the loving ones I crave:
Four hotter than burning coals I shall return.
5   What, are you moaning? Let me soothe the pain,
Giving you now ten kisses more, but sweetly;
Thus, our happy kisses joining meetly,
Let us enjoy each other to our gain.

A double life for each of us ensues.[6]
10   Each in the self and in the lover lives.
Allow me, Love, to feign a pleasing folly:
Living as one, I'm always ill at ease,
And sweet content within me never thrives
Unless outside myself I sometimes sally.

Alas, what boots it[7]

Alas, what boots it that not long ago
You praised with such finesse my golden hair,
And the beauty of my eyes chose to compare
To double Suns, whence Love allowed to grow
5   Those features which are cause of all your woe?
Where are you, tears of short duration? Where
The Death that should give evidence most rare
Of your constant love confirmed by solemn vow?

Did this your malice have no other goal
10   Than to enslave me, feigning to be my slave?
Forgive me, Darling, I'm half out of my mind,

---

4. Force you to play more pleasing songs.
5. Sonnet 18. The title alludes to a line from the famous verse of the 1st-century B.C.E Roman poet Catullus that begins "Let us live, my Lesbea, and love," and asks for "a thousand kisses, then a hundred, a thousand more."
6. Labé shifts to a more philosophical register, invoking the concept of the "double life" as the true union of souls

found in Plato's *Symposium* and made popular in the Renaissance by the Italian philosopher Marsilio Ficino. Such union can only be found through the "folly" of being transported outside of oneself—the folly to which Labé refers in the last two tercets.
7. Sonnet 23. "What boots it": what good does it do.

With bitter pain and anger in my soul:
But I tell myself, wherever you may rove,
You feel an anguish of the selfsame kind.

Do not reproach me, Ladies[8]

Do not reproach me, Ladies, if I've loved:
If I have felt a thousand burning arrows,
A thousand pains, a thousand biting sorrows,
If I to constant weeping have been moved,
5   Alas, let not your judgment scorn my name.
If I have erred, the punishments I feel;
Don't sharpen any more their pointed steel,
But judge that Love can do to you the same;

Not needing Vulcan to excuse your passion,
10   Nor the beauty of Adonis its strange fashion,[9]
Love can, when he wishes, make you fall in love;
With less good reason for your fall than mine,
To a stronger, stranger passion you'll incline.
Beware lest greater misery you prove.

Michelangelo Buonarroti
1475–1564

Still derided in the twentieth century as full of "disagreeable improprieties, obscurities, contortions, and difficulty," as one critic put it, Michelangelo's poetry has never enjoyed the universal praise of his sculpture or painting. Yet the boldness and originality of the *David* or the magnificent frescoes of the Sistine Chapel find their way into Michelangelo's considerable body of verse as well, much of which is an anguished meditation on the turmoils of his long life as artist and deeply spiritual thinker often at odds with the strict mores of Counter-Reformation Italy. Equally original, and no doubt unsettling for his contemporaries, were the poems that elevated the male body of which Michelangelo was such an accomplished sculptor into a paragon of beauty. Along with the requisite Petrarchan sonnets to an unattainable lady—the widowed Vittoria Colonna with whom Michelangelo enjoyed a close friendship—are more than fifty poems to the Roman gentleman Tommaso de'Cavalieri, charged with a physical intensity lacking in Michelangelo's verse for the austere and deeply religious Colonna. These poems to Cavalieri represent some of the most sustained homoerotic meditations in literature, even as the elderly Michelangelo acknowledges the unrequited nature of his love.

Written over a period of fifty-five years and never published in Michelangelo's lifetime he withdrew plans for publication in 1546, perhaps because of the intensely personal nature of his poetry—many of the 302 sonnets, madrigals, and *canzoni* and forty-two fragments survive only on the backs of drawings, apparently scribbled in haste. Others were the focus of intense revisions, some of the most interesting of which involve changes in gendered pronouns. And like some of his greatest sculptures—the so-called *Prisoners,* or his final *Pietà*—a number of

---

8. Sonnet 24, the final poem in the collection. The Ladies Labé addresses are the women of Lyon.
9. Women can fall in love even if their husbands aren't as

ugly as Vulcan, the misshapen god to whom Venus was married, or if their lovers aren't as beautiful as Adonis, the gorgeous youth who was the beloved of Venus.

Michelangelo, Tomb of Giuliano de' Medici, 1520–1534, Church of San Lorenzo, Florence. Much of Michelangelo's work reflects both the artist's preoccupation with death—his own as well as others— and the increasing importance of commemorating the dead in monumental fashion in early modern Europe. Michelangelo devoted an entire cycle of epitaphs to Cecchino Bracci, the 15-year-old nephew of one of Michelangelo's patrons, and he spent innumerable years designing and executing the tomb of Pope Julius II, a project destined to remain unfinished. The tombs for two young Medici princes, Giuliano and Lorenzo, were likewise left incomplete when the artist departed for Rome in 1534, but enough had been done to suggest that the artist conceived the project as a melancholy meditation on time's passing. Dressed in Roman armor, Giuliano sits above the figures of Night and Day, barely able to lift his head to gaze at the statue of his brother across the sacristy. While Night and Day seem similarly locked in anguished reflection, Michelangelo imagined them at one point in dialogue: "Night and Day are speaking and saying, 'We have with our swift course brought to death the Duke Giuliano.'"

his poems are left unfinished, testimony, perhaps, to Michelangelo's unwillingness to transmit to paper the depth of his erotic and religious feelings, or symptomatic of a restless spirit more fascinated by the process of creativity than the final product.

This comes of dangling from the ceiling[1]

This comes of dangling from the ceiling—
I'm goitered like a Lombard cat[2]
(or wherever else their throats grow fat)—
it's my belly that's beyond concealing,
5   it hangs beneath my chin like peeling.
My beard points skyward, I seem a bat
upon its back, I've breasts and splat!
On my face the paint's congealing

Loins concertina'd in my gut,
10   I drop an arse as counterweight
and move without the help of eyes.
Like a skinned martyr I abut
on air, and, wrinkled, show my fate.
Bow-like, I strain towards the skies.

15   No wonder then I size
things crookedly; I'm on all fours.
Bent blowpipes send their darts off-course.
Defend my labour's cause,
good Giovanni,[3] from all strictures:
20   I live in hell and paint its pictures.[4]

My Lord, in your most gracious face[5]

My Lord, in your most gracious face I see
what here on earth may never be portrayed:
my soul, which mortal flesh and blood pervade,
climbs Godward with it[6] to eternity.
5   And should the mob with its stupidity
foist on to others feelings which degrade,[7]
no less intense is my sweet longing made,
my love, my trust, my honest amity.
So from the sacred fount whence all men come
10   each earthly beauty takes its attributes
and we are told that these from God are sent;

1. Translated from the Italian by Peter Porter and George Bull. The "ceiling" is that of the Sistine Chapel, on which Michelangelo worked for roughly four years, between 1508 and 1512. There is a sketch on the manuscript of the poem in which Michelangelo depicts himself standing on his scaffold painting a fresco directly above him.
2. Goiter produces swelling of the thyroid, in the throat. The "Lombard cats" may be slang for peasants.
3. Probably Giovanni di Benedetto from Pistoia, a humanist to whom Michelangelo addressed several other poems.
4. The poem in Italian ends literally "Defend my dead painting, Giovanni, and my honor, since I'm neither in a good place nor a painter"—an attack on Pope Julius II who had commissioned Michelangelo's work for the chapel.
5. The "Signore" or Lord of this sonnet is the young Roman aristocrat Tommaso Cavalieri; the poem was probably written in 1534, roughly a year after Michelangelo and Cavalieri met.
6. That is, with Cavalieri's face.
7. An attack on the crowd that seems to be gossiping about Michelangelo and Cavalieri.

And for its image there's no other home,
for heaven on earth, or for our worldly fruits.
Thus loving you makes death beneficent.

I wish to want, Lord[8]

I wish to want, Lord, what eludes my will:
between your passion and my heart a block
of ice deflects your fire, and makes a mock
of everything I write with perjured quill.
5   I love you with my lips, then groan that still
your love can't reach my heart, nor will it knock
and force the door, that joys of all kinds flock
about my heart, your purpose to fulfil.
Dissolve that block, my lord, tear down the wall
10   whose thickness keeps me from the piercing light
of your sweet presence, no longer seen on earth.
Be like a bridegroom, let your brightness fall
upon a yearning soul which at your sight
is warmed at heart, having from you its birth.

No block of marble[9]

No block of marble but it does not hide
the concept living in the artist's mind—
pursuing it inside that form, he'll guide
his hand to shape what reason has defined.
5   The ill I flee, the good I hope to find
in you, exalted lady of true pride,
are also circumscribed; and yet I'm lied
to by my art which to my will is blind.
Love's not to blame, nor your severity,
10   disdainful beauty, nor what fortune shows,
or destiny: I fixed my own ill course.
Though death and mercy side by side I see
lodged in your heart, my passion only knows
how to carve death: this is my skill's poor force.

How chances it, my Lady[1]

How chances it, my Lady, that we must
from long experience learn that what endures
in stone is but the image it immures°   confines, imprisons
though he who liberates it turn to dust?

---

8. Another sonnet from the Cavalieri period, although
here "Signore" most likely refers to God. The first line
echoes the dilemma expressed by Saint Paul in his Epistle
to the Romans ("I do not understand what I do, for it is
not what I wish that I do, but what I hate, that I do . . . I do
not the good that I wish, but the evil that I do not wish"
[7:15–19]), while the next two lines from the first stanza

introduce the contrasting imagery of Petrarch's sonnets.
9. One of Michelangelo's most famous sonnets, this was
dedicated to the poet Vittoria Colonna. Michelangelo
presents the sculptor as removing excess stone to reveal
the ideal form within it, which the artist has perceived in
advance.
1. Another sonnet for Colonna.

5   This cause to its effect will so adjust
       that our fine work defeat of time ensures.
       I know this true and prove it in my sculptures:
       art lives forever, death forfeits its trust.
       Therefore, long life in colours or with stone,
10   in either form, I give to you and me
       and our own two resemblances devise,
       and for a thousand years when we have gone
       posterity will find my woe, your beauty
       matched, and know my loving you was wise.

Vittoria Colonna
1492–1547

A member of the noble Roman family that patronized Petrarch, Vittoria Colonna was at the center of the prominent intellectual and religious circles of early sixteenth-century Italy, counting among her friends Baldessar Castiglione (whom she angered by circulating copies of his unfinished *Courtier*), the epic poet Ludovico Ariosto, and Michelangelo. Colonna is best known for the sonnets she wrote in honor of her husband, who was killed at the battle of Pavia in 1525 fighting alongside the Emperor Charles V and against Marguerite de Navarre's brother, King Francis I. These idealizing sonnets memorialized the Marquis of Pescara, earning Colonna the tribute from Ariosto that she "rescued her triumphant spouse from the dark shore of the Styx." In a very different vein, Colonna wrote a number of strident lyrics about the need for ecclesiastical reform, and Michelangelo refers to her "sacred ink" from which he sought help in understanding divine things. She finally refused, however, to stray too far in the direction of the Reformers, particularly as the circle of the Inquisition threatened to close around her. Colonna went into semi-seclusion in various convents in Rome and Orvieto after the Marquis's death, leaving behind a legacy of more than 400 poems.

Between harsh rocks and violent wind[1]

       Between harsh rocks and violent wind I feel
       The waves of life striking my fragile bark
       Which I have neither wit nor art to steer;
       All help will come too late to save me now.
5   In one brief moment bitter death extinguished
       The lodestar of my life, my constant guide;
       I have no help against the turbulent sea
       And threatening clouds. Now ever more I fear,
       Not the sweet singing of the cruel sirens,[2]
10   Nor shipwreck here between these lofty cliffs,
       Nor sinking helplessly in shifting sands,
       But to sail on forever in rough waters,

---

1. Translated from the Italian by Laura Anna Stortoni and Mary Prentic Lillie.
2. Colonna compares herself to Odysseus, who in Book 9 of the *Odyssey* sailed by the reef where sirens tried to lure him to his death. Petrarch too compared his journey to that of being in a "fragile bark."

Cutting my furrow with no gleam of hope;
For death conceals from me my sheltering port.

Whatever life I once had

Whatever life I once had in my senses
Bitter death seized on one day, with my sun,
Delivering him of care and me of error;
I live no more; his better part heaven holds.
For me, I feel the fruits of earth as grass—
My soul could never gather even leaves—
And when she[3] recollects his former thoughts
She keeps herself enclosed within their bounds.
Because he made himself alive by dying,[4]
He made me dead, alive, and still from heaven
Keeps me from self,[5] content only with him.
And, while he sees my life withdrawn and fearful,
Holding a bridle on my mortal flesh,
I feel his spirit still desires my love.

5

—•—✠—•—

William Shakespeare
1564–1616

During a period of enforced absence from the stage—a combination of recurrent plague and
bans against actors for unruly behavior—William Shakespeare, fresh from his first tragedy (the
bloody *Titus Andronicus*) and his comedy *The Taming of the Shrew,* turned to poetry. This at
least is one theory for the genesis of Shakespeare's 154 sonnets. While they were remarked
upon as early as 1598, they weren't published until 1609, toward the end of the playwright's
career, and well after the vogue for sonnet-making in England had passed. But as many readers
have realized, there is something timeless in these sonnets—and the theme of art's timelessness
is one on which Shakespeare's complex, cunning narrator himself insists as he tells his beloved
that in his "war with Time for love of you / As he takes from you, I ingraft you new." Like
Petrarch, Shakespeare is forced to settle for fame rather than reciprocity in love. But he does so
by staging a series of intricate, emotional dramas that broaden the sonnet sequence's domain
while unsettling the Petrarchan exaltation of chastity and love.

The focus of attention for the first 126 sonnets is a young man, probably an aristocrat
whose social station, like that of Michelangelo's beloved, is higher than the narrator's. The relationship of the narrator to the young man is, however, far more complicated than that found in
Michelangelo. The volume opens with the so-called "procreation poems," eighteen sonnets in
which Shakespeare urges the young man to have a child so that the world will not lose him forever when he dies; the final sonnets in this sequence then suggest that only poetry can truly
"give life to thee." Many of the subsequent poems to the young man are taken up with the
"pow'rful rime" of both the poet and, increasingly, rival poets who threaten to write about the
young man as well. But these poems also illustrate the torment of the jealous lover whose faith
in his supposedly chaste young man, as in his literary medium, is considerably shaken. The

3. The soul, which is feminine in Italian.   5. From self-absorption.
4. By going to heaven.

poem in which the poet bids his lover "Farewell: thou art too dear for my possessing" represents one low point of the collection, while the arrival of the "dark lady" onto the sonnets' stage with sonnet 127 shatters once and for all the delicate equilibrium attained earlier. Sonnet 147 closes, "I have sworn thee fair, and thought thee bright, / Who art as black as hell, as dark as night"; once mistress only to the narrator, this unsettling female presence is now actively pursuing the young man as well.

The order of the sonnets in the 1609 volume is contested, since there is no evidence that Shakespeare ever authorized his poems' publication. Still, it is possible to argue that the sequence may initially develop a Petrarchan quest for poetic glory, only to undo that quest and all it stands for. On the other hand, the narrator's stance is so changeable, as he himself admits, and Shakespeare's understanding of the dynamics of Petrarchism so penetrating, that perhaps the sonnets are never serious about their mission of preserving the "timeless" reputation of their author or of the young man who occupies center stage.

For more on Shakespeare, see his principal listing, page 610.

from THE SONNETS[1]

1

From fairest creatures we desire increase,
That thereby beauty's rose might never die,
But as the riper should by time decease,
His tender heir might bear his memory;
5 But thou, contracted° to thine own bright eyes,   *betrothed*
Feed'st thy light's flame with self-substantial° fuel,   *of your own making*
Making a famine where abundance lies,
Thyself thy foe, to thy sweet self too cruel.
Thou that art now the world's fresh ornament
10 And only herald to the gaudy° spring,   *bright*
Within thine own bud buriest thy content
And, tender churl, mak'st waste in niggarding.°   *hoarding*
   Pity the world, or else this glutton be,
   To eat the world's due, by the grave and thee.[2]

3

Look in thy glass, and tell the face thou viewest
Now is the time that face should form another,
Whose fresh repair° if now thou not renewest,   *condition*
Thou dost beguile the world, unbless some mother.[3]
5 For where is she so fair whose uneared womb
Disdains the tillage of thy husbandry?[4]
Or who is he so fond° will be the tomb   *foolish*
Of his self-love, to stop posterity?
Thou art thy mother's glass, and she in thee
10 Calls back the lovely April of her prime;

---

1. The 1609 edition of the *Sonnets*, published by Thomas Thorpe, was prefaced with this dedication, followed by Thorpe's initials: "To the Only Begetter of these ensuing sonnets Mr. W. H. All happiness and that eternity promised by our ever-living poet wisheth the well-wishing adventurer in setting forth."

2. The last line gives the cannibalistic image of the "tender chorl" eating "the world's due," i.e., his offspring, by refusing to procreate.
3. Prevent a woman from enjoying the blessings of motherhood.
4. Cultivation, but with a play on "husband."

So thou through windows of thine age shalt see,
Despite of wrinkles, this thy golden time.[5]
    But if thou live rememb'red not to be,
    Die single, and thine image dies with thee.

17

Who will believe my verse in time to come
If it were filled with your most high deserts?
Though yet, heaven knows, it is but as a tomb
Which hides your life and shows not half your parts.
5   If I could write the beauty of your eyes
And in fresh numbers number all your graces,
The age to come would say, "This poet lies
Such heavenly touches ne'er touched earthly faces.'
So should my papers, yellowed with their age,
10   Be scorned, like old men of less truth than tongue,
And your true rights be termed a poet's rage
And stretchèd metre° of an antique song.   *exaggerations*
    But were some child of yours alive that time,
    You should live twice—in it and in my rime.[6]

55

Not marble nor the gilded monuments
Of princes shall outlive this pow'rful rime,
But you shall shine more bright in these contents
Than° unswept stone, besmeared with sluttish° time.   *than in / lazy*
5   When wasteful war shall statues overturn,
And broils° root out the work of masonry,   *tumults*
Nor° Mars his sword nor war's quick fire shall burn   *Neither*
The living record of your memory.
'Gainst death and all oblivious enmity°   *oblivion*
10   Shall you pace forth; your praise shall still find room
Even in the eyes of all posterity
That wear this world out to the ending doom.
    So, till the judgment° that° yourself arise,   *Judgment Day / when*
    You live in this, and dwell in lovers' eyes.

73

That time of year thou mayst in me behold
When yellow leaves, or none, or few, do hang
Upon those boughs which shake against the cold,
Bare ruined choirs where late the sweet birds sang.
5   In me thou seest the twilight of such day
As after sunset fadeth in the west,

---

5. Just as he furnishes his mother a "glass" through which she might see her youth, so would his children afford him a "window" in his old age to his "golden time."

6. This sonnet concludes the so-called "procreation sonnets" in which the narrator is encouraging the young man to "increase."

Which by and by black night doth take away,
Death's second self that seals up all in rest.
In me thou seest the glowing of such fire
10 That° on the ashes of his youth doth lie,   *As*
As the death bed whereon it must expire,
Consumed with that which it was nourished by.
   This thou perceiv'st, which makes thy love more strong,
   To love that well which thou must leave ere long.

87

Farewell: thou art too dear° for my possessing,   *costly*
And like enough thou know'st thy estimate.°   *value*
The charter of thy worth gives thee releasing;[7]
My bonds° in thee are all determinate.°   *claims / expired*
5 For how do I hold thee but by thy granting,
And for that riches where is my deserving?
The cause of this fair gift in me is wanting,
And so my patent° back again is swerving.   *deed or title*
Thyself thou gav'st, thy own worth then not knowing,
10 Or me, to whom thou gav'st it, else mistaking;
So thy great gift, upon misprision growing,°   *originating in error*
Comes home again, on better judgment making.
   Thus have I had thee as a dream doth flatter,
   In sleep a king, but waking no such matter.°   *substance*

116

Let me not to the marriage of true minds
Admit impediments;[8] love is not love
Which alters when it alteration finds
Or bends with the remover to remove.
5 O, no, it is an ever-fixèd mark°   *landmark*
That looks on tempests and is never shaken;
It is the star to every wand'ring bark,
Whose worth's unknown, although his height be taken.[9]
Love's not Time's fool, though rosy lips and cheeks
10 Within his bending sickle's compass° come;   *range*
Love alters not with his brief hours and weeks,
But bears it out even to the edge of doom.°   *the last day*
   If this be error, and upon° me proved,   *against*
   I never writ, nor no man ever loved.

126

O thou, my lovely boy, who in thy power
Dost hold Time's fickle glass,° his sickle hour;°   *mirror / hourglass*

---

7. You are worth so much that you have the privilege of being able to "release" yourself from all obligations to me.
8. The marriage service directs the congregation, "If any of you know cause or just impediment why these persons should not be joined together. . . ."
9. Both "worth" and "height" (altitude) apply to the star.

Who hast by waning grown, and therein show'st
Thy lovers withering as thy sweet self grow'st;
5   If Nature, sovereign mistress over wrack,°   *ruin*
As thou goest onwards, still will pluck thee back,
She keeps thee to this purpose, that her skill
May Time disgrace and wretched minutes kill.
Yet fear her, O thou minion of her pleasure!
10   She may detain, but not still° keep, her treasure;   *always*
Her audit,° though delayed, answered must be,   *final reckoning*
And her quietus° is to render° thee.[1]   *settlement / surrender*

127

In the old age black was not counted fair,[2]
Or, if it were, it bore not beauty's name;
But now is black beauty's successive heir,
And beauty slandered with a bastard shame;[3]
5   For since each hand hath put on nature's power,
Fairing the foul with art's false borrowed face,
Sweet beauty hath no name, no holy bower,
But is profaned, if not lives in disgrace.
Therefore my mistress' brows are raven black,
10   Her eyes so suited,° and they mourners seem   *dressed in black*
At such° who, not born fair, no beauty lack,   *For*
Sland'ring creation with a false esteem:
    Yet so they mourn, becoming° of their woe,   *gracing*
    That every tongue says beauty should look so.

130

My mistress' eyes are nothing like the sun;
Coral is far more red than her lips' red;
If snow be white, why then her breasts are dun;°   *dark*
If hairs be wires, black wires grow on her head.
5   I have seen roses damasked,° red and white,   *mingled*
But no such roses see I in her cheeks;
And in some perfumes is there more delight
Than in the breath that from my mistress reeks.
I love to hear her speak; yet well I know
10   That music hath a far more pleasing sound:
I grant I never saw a goddess go;
My mistress, when she walks, treads on the ground.[4]
    And yet, by heaven, I think my love as rare
    As any she° belied with false compare.°   *any woman / comparison*

---

1. This is the only poem in the series that lacks the final two lines, perhaps suggesting the dramatic "rendering" of the young man. This is also the final sonnet addressed directly to the young man; with 127, the "dark lady" sonnets begin.
2. "Fair" as in both "beautiful" and "blonde."
3. "Fair" beauty is rendered illegitimate, as women turn increasingly to cosmetics.
4. Perhaps an allusion to *Aeneid* 1, in which Aeneas watches his mother Venus part from him: "her gown was long and to the ground; even her walk was sign enough she was a goddess"; the moment is later echoed in Petrarch and others.

╺┄ ⋝◈⋜ ┄╸

Jan Kochanowski
1530–1584

The greatest poet of the Polish Renaissance, Jan Kochanowski made his mother tongue the vehicle for a national literature. A consummate humanist, he was as steeped in the three venerable
traditions of antiquity—Latin, Greek, and Hebrew—as he was in the folk culture and customs
of his native country. While serving as secretary at the lively court of King Sigismund II Augustus, he turned from the Latin language in which he had made an international reputation and
shifted to Polish, writing lyrics, epigrams, a verse tragedy, and a famous autobiographical
poem called "The Muse." After Sigismund's death in 1572, he settled into life as a farmer,
translating the Psalms and working on an edition of his poems.

The publication of the *Treny* or *Laments* in 1580 was a novelty: nineteen poems written
for his young child, who had died at two and a half—an all too common fate in early modern
society. The young Ursula's death provided Kochanowski with a very real occasion for expressing the powerful portrait of a man in creative, religious, and emotional turmoil. The poems
range from serious meditations on the parallels between Ursula and mythological women who
died tragically young—Persephone, Eurydice—to pleas that God pity his despair and uphold
his flagging religious faith, to wrenching statements such as the opening of the eighth lament:

> "Thou hast made all the house an empty thing,
> Dear Ursula, by this thy vanishing.
> Though we are here, 'tis yet a vacant place—
> One little soul had filled so great a space."

PRONUNCIATION:
  Jan Kochanowski: YAN co-chan-OFF-ski

from LAMENTS[1]
Lament 1

Come, Heraclitus and Simonides,[2]
Come with your weeping and sad elegies:
Ye griefs and sorrows, come from all the lands
Wherein ye sigh and wail and wring your hands:
5   Gather ye here within my house today
And help me mourn my sweet, whom in her May[3]
Ungodly Death hath ta'en to his estate,
Leaving me on a sudden desolate.
'Tis so a serpent glides on some shy nest
10   And, of the tiny nightingales possessed,
Doth glut its throat, though, frenzied with her fear,
The mother bird doth beat and twitter near
And strike the monster, till it turns and gapes

---

1. Translated by D. P. Radin, M. B. Peacock, R. E. Mer-
rill, H. H. Havermale, and G. R. Noyes. The subtitle of
the *Laments* is "To Ursula Kochanowski: A charming, delightful, gifted child, who, after showing great promise of
all maidenly virtues and talents suddenly, prematurely, in
her unripe years, to the great and unbearable grief of her
parents, departed hence."

2. Heraclitus was known as the "melancholy philosopher"
given his pessimism and severely aristocratic views;
Simonides was a 5th-century Greek lyric poet who wrote
a number of elegies, including one on the warriors killed
during the Persian Wars.
3. Her springtime—i.e., in her youth.

To swallow her, and she but just escapes.
15   "'Tis vain to weep," my friends perchance will say.
Dear God, is aught in life not vain, then? Nay,
Seek to lie soft, yet thorns will prickly be:
The life of man is naught but vanity.[4]
Ah, which were better, then—to seek relief
20   In tears, or sternly strive to conquer grief?

Lament 6

Dear little Slavic Sappho,[5] we had thought,
Hearing thy songs so sweetly, deftly wrought,
That thou shouldst have an heritage one day
Beyond thy father's lands: his lute to play.
5   For not an hour of daylight's joyous round
But thou didst fill it full of lovely sound,
Just as the nightingale doth scatter pleasure
Upon the dark, in glad unstinted measure.
Then Death came stalking near thee, timid thing,
10   And thou in sudden terror tookest wing.
Ah, that delight, it was not overlong,
And I pay dear with sorrow for brief song.
Thou still wert singing when thou cam'st to die;
Kissing thy mother, thus thou saidst goodbye:
15   "My mother, I shall serve thee now no more
Nor sit about thy table's charming store;
I must lay down my keys to go from here,
To leave the mansion of my parents dear."
    This and what sorrow now will let me tell
20   No longer, were my darling's last farewell.
Ah, strong her mother's heart, to feel the pain
Of those last words and not to burst in twain!

Lament 10

My dear delight, my Ursula, and where
Art thou departed, to what land, what sphere?
High o'er the heavens wert thou borne, to stand
One little cherub midst the cherub band?
5   Or dost thou laugh in Paradise, or now
Upon the Islands of the Blest art thou?[6]
Or in his ferry o'er the gloomy water
Doth Charon bear thee onward, little daughter?[7]
And having drunken of forgetfulness
10   Art thou unwitting of my sore distress?

---

4. An echo of Ecclesiastes 1:1–2: "Vanity of vanities, says the preacher, vanity of vanities! All things are vanity!"
5. The 7th-century lyric poet from Lesbos, most famous classical woman writer.
6. In Greek myth, islands in the far west where the "blessed" dead were said to live again in eternal bliss.
7. Charon is the elderly ferryman in Virgil's and Dante's underworlds who takes newly perished souls across the Styx; Kochanowski refers to him as the "grim-faced boatman" in Lament 14.

Or, casting off thy human, maiden veil,
Art thou enfeathered in some nightingale?[8]
Or in grim Purgatory must thou stay
Until some tiniest stain be washed away?
15 Or hast returned again to where thou wert
Ere thou wast born to bring me heavy hurt?
Where'er thou art, ah! pity, comfort me;
And if not in thine own entirety,
Yet come before mine eyes a moment's space
20 In some sweet dream that shadoweth thy grace!

Lament 14

Where are those gates through which so long ago
Orpheus descended to the realms below
To seek his lost one?[9] Little daughter, I
Would find that path and pass that ford whereby
5 The grim-faced boatman ferries pallid shades
And drives them forth to joyless cypress glades.
But do thou not desert me, lovely lute!
Be thou the furtherance of my mournful suit
Before dread Pluto, till he shall give ear
10 To our complaints and render up my dear.
To his dim dwelling all men must repair,
And so must she, her father's joy and heir;
But let him grant the fruit now scarce in flower
To fill and ripen till the harvest hour!
15 Yet if that god doth bear a heart within
So hard that one in grief can nothing win,
What can I but renounce this upper air
And lose my soul, but also lose my care?[1]

+→ ⌇◈⌇ →+

Sor Juana Inés de la Cruz
1651–1695

Like Anne Bradstreet, her English counterpart to the north, Sor Juana Inés de la Cruz was hailed in Europe as a "tenth muse" whose poems sprang forth miraculously in an uncultivated New World. But unlike Bradstreet, Juana Ramírez de Asbaje was born in the New World. She

---

8. A possible allusion to Plato's *Republic,* Book 10, in which the musician and poet Thamyras asks to be transformed into a nightingale in his next incarnation.
9. The musician Orpheus descended into Hades to try to bring back his bride, Eurydice, from the realm of the dead. As Virgil recounts in his fourth *Georgic* and Ovid in the *Metamorphoses,* Orpheus's singing so enchanted Hades' king, Pluto, that he was granted permission to bring her to earth, with one condition: that he not turn around to gaze at Eurydice while they ascended from Hades. He couldn't resist a look, and she returned to Hades forever. See Volume A for Ovid.

1. Unable to be a second Orpheus, Kochanowski will turn in the final laments to embrace a renewed trust in God. The last lament—the longest, at more than 150 lines—is a consoling nocturnal vision of Ursula in the arms of the poet's mother, who tells him "Though dust returns to dust, the spirit, given / A life eternal, must go back to heaven, / And little Ursula hath not gone out / Forever like a torch . . . / Still she offers up her prayers for you / As here on earth, when yet no words she knew." But the consolation of the vision is thrown into question by the closing lines, when the poet wakes, "and know not if to deem / This truth itself, or but a passing dream."

was attuned to the literary legacy Spaniards had carried with them to Mexico, but was also receptive to the indigenous language and traditions of her native land. Even if her sonnets rigorously follow the Italianate form, they openly contest old world poetics, particularly the passive place that Spanish poets had assigned women.

Composed for the most part after 1669 when she entered the convent of Santa Paula in Mexico City, Sor Juana's enormous poetic output looks back to her lively decade at the court of the vice-regent, where she dazzled audiences as a brilliant conversationalist and autodidact. Her terse epigrams, lengthy "philosophical satire," and especially her sonnets offer us an unflinching consideration of the stupidities caused by love and women's vanity, as well as of her own anomalous situation in both the convent and the court. Illegitimate daughter of a Basque adventurer and a mother of Mexican descent, Juana was an apparently beautiful woman who discounted her beauty as vanity and regarded her intellect as her greatest asset (see her portrait, Color Plate 8). Yet her intellect endangered her in colonial Latin America—particularly since she could rarely suppress it. Or as Doña Leonor says of herself in Sor Juana's comedy, *Trials of a Noble House,* "if [I am] silent, none will know / the truth of me. . . ." But after engaging in a battle with Mexico's most prominent clergymen and forcefully defending her right to her immense learning in the *Response to Sor Filotea,* Sor Juana was indeed silenced: first, apparently, of her own accord (the 1691 *Response* is the last work she wrote) and, four years later, by the plague, to which she succumbed while she was nursing her sisters.

For more on Sor Juana, see her "Response to Sor Filotea" (page 138) and her *Loa for the Auto Sacramental of the Divine Narcissus* (page 880).

PRONUNCIATION:

Sor Juana Inés de la Cruz: soar WA-nah ee-NEZ day la CROOZ

She disavows the flattery visible in a portrait of herself, which she calls bias[1]

These lying pigments facing you,
with every charm brush can supply
set up false premises of color
to lead astray the unwary eye.
5   Here, against ghastly tolls of time,
bland flattery has staked a claim,
defying the power of passing years
to wipe out memory and name.
    And here, in this hollow artifice[2]—
10   frail blossom hanging on the wind,
vain pleading in a foolish cause,
    poor shield against what fate has wrought—
all efforts fail and in the end
a body goes to dust, to shade, to nought.

---

1. Translated by Alan S. Trueblood. Color Plate 8 is one of several early portraits of Sor Juana, although all of them were painted after her death.
2. The painting.

She complains of her lot, suggesting her aversion to vice and justifying her resort to the Muses[3]

World, in hounding me, what do you gain?
How can it harm you if I choose, astutely,
rather to stock my mind with things of beauty,
than waste its stock on every beauty's claim?
Costliness and wealth bring me no pleasure;
the only happiness I care to find
derives from setting treasure in my mind,
and not from mind that's set on winning treasure.
I prize no comeliness. All fair things pay
to time, the victor, their appointed fee
and treasure cheats even the practiced eye.
Mine is the better and the truer way:
to leave the vanities of life aside,
not throw my life away on vanity.

She shows distress at being abused for the applause her talent brings[4]

Fate, was my crime of such enormity
that, to chastise me or torment me more,
beyond that torture which the mind foresees,
you whisper you have yet more harm in store?
Pursuing me with such severity,
you make your heartlessness only too plain:
when you bestowed this gift of mind on me,
you only sought to aggravate my pain.
Bringing me applause, you stirred up envy's ire.
Raising me up, you knew how hard I'd fall.
No doubt it was your treachery saddled me
with troubles far beyond misfortune's call,
that, seeing the store you gave me of your blessings,
no one would guess the cost of each and all.

In which she visits moral censure on a rose, and in it, on fellow humans[5]

Rose, celestial flower finely bred,
you offer in your scented subtlety
crimson instruction in everything that's fair,
snow-white sermons to all beauty.
Semblance of our human shapeliness,
portent of proud breeding's doom,

---

3. Translated by Alan S. Trueblood. The Muses, daughters of Mnemosyne (memory), are the goddesses of the arts.

4. Translated by Alan S. Trueblood.

5. Translated by Alan S. Trueblood. The rose appears often in the poetry of Sor Juana and other baroque writers, typically seen as emblematic of haughtiness and show.

in whose being Nature chose to link
a joyous cradle and a joyless tomb.
      How haughtily you broadcast in your prime
10   your scorn of all suggestion you must die!
Yet how soon as you wilt and waste away,
      your withering brings mortality's reply.
Wherefore with thoughtless life and thoughtful death,
in dying you speak true, in life you lie.

She answers suspicions in the rhetoric of tears[6]

      My love, this evening when I spoke with you,
and in your face and actions I could read
that arguments of words you would not heed,
my heart I longed to open to your view.
5   In this intention, Love my wishes knew
and, though they seemed impossible, achieved:
pouring in tears that sorrow had conceived,
with every beat my heart dissolved anew.
      Enough of suffering, my love, enough:
10   let jealousy's vile tyranny be banned,
let no suspicious thought your calm corrupt
      with foolish gloom by futile doubt enhanced,
for now, this afternoon, you saw and touched
my heart, dissolved and liquid in your hands.

On the death of that most excellent lady, the Marquise de Mancera[7]

      Let them die with you, Laura, now you are dead,
these longings that go out to you in vain,
these eyes on whom you once bestowed
a lovely light never to gleam again.
5   Let this unfortunate lyre that echoes still
to sounds you woke, perish calling your name,
and may these clumsy scribblings represent
black tears my pen has shed to ease its pain.
      Let Death himself feel pity, and regret
10   that, bound by his own law, he could not spare you,
and Love lament the bitter circumstance
      that if once, in his desire for pleasure,
he wished for eyes that they might feast on you,[8]
now weeping is all those eyes could ever do.

 END OF PERSPECTIVES: LYRIC SEQUENCES AND SELF-DEFINITION ≒

---

6. Translated by Margaret Sayers Peden.
7. Translated by Alan S. Trueblood. The Marquise de Mancera, called "Laura" by Sor Juana, was the poet's

powerful patroness; Sor Juana wrote three funerary sonnets for her when she died.
8. Love was typically represented as blind.

Niccolò Machiavelli
1469–1527

Few thinkers have been as maligned as Machiavelli, whose very name has become a term for amoral scheming. Yet much of his work follows from a distinctively Renaissance impulse: to fit everything to the measure of man. Machiavelli's model "man" was cunning, shrewd, and surrounded by fools—which shouldn't particularly surprise, given the conditions under which Machiavelli wrote his major works. Literally overnight, Machiavelli went from being a prominent official in Florence to suffering imprisonment and torture when the Medici family ousted his party and returned to power. Consigned to permanent exile from the political world in which he had thrived as a diplomat and envoy for fourteen years, Machiavelli wrote the works which are at once bids for attention and sobering meditations on the present and future state of Italian cities: his *Discourses on the First Ten Books of Livy,* his Florentine history, *The Art of War,* three trenchant comedies, and above all, *The Prince.*

Machiavelli's own life reveals a constant pragmatist at work. Born to a family with little money, the young Machiavelli trained himself in Latin and the ancients, as well as in Dante and contemporary vernacular literature. Little is known of his activities before 1498, the year that the Dominican Girolamo Savonarola, who had tried to turn Florence into a city of God, was burned at the stake. Machiavelli began his political career thereafter in the new secular republican regime led by Piero Soderini. Appointed secretary and second Chancellor, Machiavelli was soon traveling regularly on major diplomatic missions to the papal courts, Paris, and the Romagna in central Italy, where he witnessed firsthand the tactics of Pope Alexander VI's bastard son, Cesare Borgia—which included, among other things, the display of the mysteriously decapitated body of one of his former henchmen in a public square. Increasingly a valued advisor to Soderini, Machiavelli was responsible for the controversial and difficult task of mobilizing a militia of Florentine men for the successful reconquest of Pisa in 1509, a feat that convinced Machiavelli of the necessity of volunteer armies for the survival of republics. During this period, Machiavelli first dabbled in writing. His *Portraits* of 1508–1515 feature sketches of political figures whom he had encountered in his travels, while the first *Decennale* is an account, in verse, of ten years of Florentine history, from 1494 to 1504.

Machiavelli's political career came to an abrupt end when his troops failed to prevent Spain's invasion of nearby Prato in July 1512. The Medici family returned a month later, bringing an end to the republic, dismantling its militia, and imprisoning Machiavelli for his suspected involvement in a plot to overthrow the new government. Released from prison, Machiavelli was barred from entering Florence as well as from leaving the city's territories. As he says in the preface to *The Prince,* he turned to writing of the things that he had learned, "over so many years and with so much affliction and peril." First drafted in 1513 and published only in 1532, *The Prince* was only the first of Machiavelli's masterpieces. His *Discourses on Livy* (around 1517) is an extended commentary on the famous Roman historian; its primary focus is republics rather than principalities, social institutions rather than powerful individuals. Three comedies followed. Two of them are based on plays of the Roman playwrights Terence and Plautus; the third, *Mandragola* or *Mandrake Root,* an original and vibrant work, is riotously funny, but its picture of human society is so bleak that it is hard to say whether it is a comedy at all. By the early 1520s, Machiavelli had succeeded in winning the Medici's confidence; he was commissioned to write the *Florentine Histories,* which—paradoxically, perhaps, given its patron—focuses on the demise of the Florentine republic. He also enjoyed a brief return to a political appointment when he was asked in

1526 by a Medici pope, Clement VII, to advise him on fortifications and the military. It is an irony of history that when the Medici were chased again out of Florence and a republic was temporarily restored, Machiavelli had become too closely associated with the ruling family to be acknowledged as a republican sympathizer. He died several months later, in June of 1527.

Of Machiavelli's works, *The Prince* has achieved the greatest fame, not least because of its bold separation of politics from ethics. Dedicated first to Giuliano de'Medici, and after Giuliano's death, to his nephew Lorenzo, the book is divided into roughly three sections. Machiavelli opens with an anatomy of principalities, bringing in examples from both antiquity and present-day Italy; he then passes to three chapters on a topic near and dear to his heart, military organization and the disastrous consequences of hiring mercenary troops. In his final section, beginning in Chapter 15, he turns his attention to "how a prince must govern his conduct toward his subjects or his friends," and here his tone becomes more intimate and his advice more pointed. And, it would seem, for good reason. Machiavelli's prince is an isolated figure, cut off from a social world he must nonetheless know how to control if he is to seize and maintain power. Machiavelli's ideal princes from the past are all brazen usurpers: Theseus, Romulus, Moses. Too few men in the present have shown such brazeness, with the exception of Pope Julius II, whose impetuousity enabled him to capture Fortune and—as Machiavelli crudely puts it in Chapter 25—beat her.

Machiavelli substitutes for this absent world nothing less than himself: the advisor on whom the prince must depend for his knowledge of the people he needs to deceive. The public sphere shrinks to the private relationship between counselor and prince, in which the counselor proffers a policy grounded in deception. Contemporary evidence, Machiavelli suggests, "shows that princes who have achieved great things have been those who have given their word lightly, who have known how to trick men with cunning, and who, in the end, have overcome those abiding by honest principles." Placing this cunning advice at the very center of his political treatise, the exiled Machiavelli seeks to create for himself a role in which he might once again be politically efficacious. It is telling that the ever-vigilant Machiavelli includes a chapter informing a prince how to choose advisors, another warning him to avoid flatterers.

But *The Prince* is also motivated by the very real tragedy of the times—an Italy at war with itself and oppressed by foreign powers—and by Machiavelli's desire to put his own considerable experience of worldly affairs to use for the health of Florence. Ultimately, he looks toward a unified Italy of which he and his countrymen could only dream for another 350 years. Such a dream explains the desperate cry of the last chapter of *The Prince,* addressed to the Medici as Moses-like saviors of Italy's people, if we are indeed to read that cry as sincere. How might this chapter be of a piece with a book that has steadfastly undermined the very principles of ethics, as well as the utility of ancient examples for contemporary life? To what extent did Machiavelli genuinely believe in the ability of the Medici, who by 1516 controlled not only Florence and much of Tuscany but the papacy as well, to put an end to the factiousness that dominated the peninsula? These questions must remain to some extent unanswered; at the same time, their very existence suggests a dimension to the treatise, and to Machiavelli himself, that cannot easily be reduced to the cold political "Machiavellian" calculation for which he is best known. At the heart of Machiavelli's *realpolitik* is fierce Florentine patriotism—the same, perhaps, that had led Dante, another exile from his native city, to save Florence by casting its most profligate and corrupt citizens into hell.

PRONUNCIATIONS:
Cesare Borgia: CHAY-ze-ray BOR-zhah
Niccolò Machiavelli: nee-ko-LO mah-kee-ah-VEL-li

from THE PRINCE[1]
Dedicatory Letter
Niccolò Machiavelli to the Magnificent Lorenzo de' Medici[2]

It is customary, in most cases, for those who desire to win the favor of a Prince to present themselves to him with those things they cherish most or which they know please him most; hence, we often see Princes presented with horses, arms, gold vestments, precious stones and similar adornments worthy of their greatness. Desiring, then, to offer myself to Your Magnificence with some proof of my devotion to you, I have not found among my possessions anything that I cherish more or value so much as my knowledge of the accomplishments of great men, which I learned through long experience in contemporary affairs and continuous study of antiquity; having very diligently and for a long time thought about and analyzed these accomplishments, and now having condensed them into a little book, I am sending them to Your Magnificence.

And although I regard this work unworthy of your consideration, I am nevertheless quite confident that your kindness will convince you to accept it, for I could not make you a greater gift than to give you the means to be able in very short time to understand all that which I, over many years and with many difficulties and dangers, came to know and understand.[3] I have neither adorned nor filled this book with polished sentences, with rich and magnificent words, or with any other kind of rhetorical or superfluous ornamentation, the likes of which many writers are accustomed to using in describing and embellishing their material; for it was my desire that nothing distinguish my book or make it pleasing other than the unusualness of its material and the importance of its contents exclusively. I hope it will not be thought presumptuous if a man of low and inferior station dare to debate and regulate the government of princes; for, just as those persons who sketch landscapes place themselves in a low position on the plain in order to study the nature of the mountains and highlands, and in order to study the lowlands place themselves high on top of mountains, in like fashion, in order to know well the nature of the people one must be a prince, and to know well the nature of princes one must be a common citizen.[4]

Accept then, Your Magnificence, this little gift in the spirit that I send it; and if you deign to consider and read it with care, you will discover in it my utmost desire that you may reach that greatness which fortune and your own capacities predict for you. And if Your Magnificence from the summit of his high position will at some time move his eyes toward those lowlands, he will know to what extent I unjustly endure the great and continuous maleficence of fortune.[5]

---

1. Translated by Mark Musa.
2. Lorenzo de' Medici, Duke of Urbino, was the grandson of the better-known "Lorenzo the Magnificent," and became ruler of Florence shortly after the Medici returned from exile in 1512—a return that resulted in Machiavelli's imprisonment. His uncle Giuliano had been the original dedicatee of *The Prince;* after Giuliano's death in 1516, Machiavelli redirected the dedication to Lorenzo, who died in 1519. Lorenzo is commemorated, along with Giuliano, in Michelangelo's (unfinished) tomb in the new sacristy in Florence's San Lorenzo; see page 230.

3. Machiavelli's years of service for the Florence republic numbered 14.
4. With this play of perspectives, Machiavelli uses a well-known classical trope, perhaps most familiar from the opening of Seneca's *Oedipus:* "As lofty peaks to ever catch the winds, and as the cliff, which with its jutting rocks cleaves the vast deep, is beaten by the waves of even a quiet sea, so does exalted empire lie exposed to fate."
5. The last word sets up one of the major themes of *The Prince,* to be treated most fully in Chapter 25.

Chapter 6
On New Principalities Acquired by Means
of One's Own Arms and Ingenuity[1]

No one should be surprised if, in my discussion of principalities that are completely new in respect to their prince and composition, I make use of the most outstanding examples;[2] since men almost always walk the path made by others and conduct their affairs through imitation, although they are not altogether able to stay on the path of others nor arrive at the ingenuity of those they imitate, a prudent man should always take the path trodden by great men and imitate those who have been most outstanding; so that, if his own ingenuity does not come up to theirs, at least it will have the smell of it; and he should act like those prudent archers, who, when the target they are aiming at seems too far off, aware of the capacity of their bow, set their sight a good deal higher than the desired target, not to reach such a height with their arrow but rather to be able, with the help of aiming high, to reach their target.

I say, then, that in entirely new principalities, where there is a new prince, one will find more or less difficulty in maintaining them according to the greater or lesser ingenuity of the one who acquires them. And since this event of transition from ordinary citizen to prince presupposes either ingenuity or fortune, it would seem that either the one or the other of these two things should, to some extent, mitigate many of the difficulties; nevertheless, he who has trusted less in fortune has held on to his position best. Things are made easier also by the fact that the prince, having no other state to rule, is forced to come and live there in person. But to come to those who, by means of their own ingenuity and not by fortune, have become princes, let me say that the most outstanding are Moses, Cyrus, Romulus, Theseus and the like. And although one should not discuss Moses, for he was a mere executor of the things God had commanded, he still should be admired if only for that grace which made him worthy of speaking with God.[3] But let us consider Cyrus[4] and the others who acquired or founded kingdoms: you will find them all admirable; and if their particular actions and institutions are examined, they do not appear to differ from those of Moses, who had so great a preceptor. And examining their actions and lives, we see that from fortune they received nothing but the occasion; which in turn offered them the material they could then shape into whatever form they pleased; and without that occasion their very ingenuity would have been extinguished, and without that ingenuity the occasion would have come in vain.

Therefore it was necessary for Moses to find the people of Israel in Egypt slaves and oppressed by the Egyptians, so that they, in order to escape this servitude, might be disposed to following him. It was imperative that Romulus not remain in Alba and for him to be exposed at birth, so that he might become king of Rome and

---

1. The first three chapters of *The Prince* focus on various kinds of principalities; Machiavelli then discusses the problems princes face when they take over former kingdoms.
2. Machiavelli follows his humanist education by proffering *grandissimi esempli* both from antiquity and the recent past.
3. In Exodus, God approaches Moses by means of a burn-

ing bush; despite Moses' protests that he doesn't possess the qualities of a leader, he nonetheless becomes the liberator of the Hebrews out of Egypt.
4. Cyrus the Great, who died in 529, founded the Persian empire. He first captured the throne of Media, and then soon overthrew the king of Lydia, captured Babylon, and took over the Greek city-states.

founder of that nation.[5] It was requisite that Cyrus find the Persians dissatisfied with the empire of the Medes and the Medes soft and effeminate through years of peace. Theseus could not have displayed his ingenuity if he had not found the Athenians dispersed.[6] These occasions, then, made these men successful, and their outstanding ingenuity made that occasion known to them; whereby their nations were made renowned and they became prosperous.

Those who, like these men, become princes by means of ingenuity, acquire their principality with difficulty, but hold on to it with ease; and the difficulties they encounter in acquiring the principality arise, in part, from the new institutions and methods they are forced to introduce in order to establish their state and their security. And it should be kept in mind that there is nothing more difficult to carry out nor more doubtful of success nor more dangerous to manage than to introduce a new system of things; for the introducer has as his enemies all those who benefit from the old system, and lukewarm defenders in all those who would benefit from by the new system. This lukewarmness originates partly from fear of their adversaries, who have the law on their side, and partly from the incredulousness of men in general, who do not really believe something new unless they actually have had experience with it; therefore it happens that, whenever those who are enemies have the occasion to attack, they do so with the fervor of partisans, and those others come to the defense lukewarmly, so that both the prince and his friends are in danger.

It is necessary, however, if we wish to discuss this matter thoroughly, to observe whether these innovators stand on their own or are dependent on others; that is, if in order to carry out their work, they are obliged to beg, or are able to use force. In the first case, they always come to a bad end and never achieve anything; but when they depend on themselves and are able to use force, then very seldom will they find themselves in danger. From this comes the fact that the armed prophets conquered and the unarmed came to ruin. Besides what has been said, people in general are unstable; and it is easy to persuade them of something but difficult to hold them to that persuasion; and therefore things should be arranged so that, when people no longer believe, they can be made to believe by force. Had Moses, Cyrus, Theseus and Romulus been unarmed they would not have had their institutions respected by the people for very long; just as in our own times it happened to Brother Girolamo Savonarola, who was defeated by his new institutions when the multitude began not to believe in him; and he had no means of holding firm those who had believed nor of making the disbelievers believe.[7] Therefore men such as these have great difficulty in getting ahead, and they encounter all their dangers as they advance, and they must overcome them by means of their ingenuity, but once they have overcome them and have begun to be held in veneration, and once they have done away with those who were envious of their abilities, they remain powerful, secure, honored, [and] prosperous. * * *

5. Legendary founder of Rome, Romulus was thrown with his brother into the Tiber by the last Alban king. The twins were rescued by a she-wolf, and many years later built a city where they had been washed ashore.
6. Son of Aegeus, legendary king of Athens, Theseus became king after a series of remarkable adventures to, among other places, Crete. While he is no doubt a mythical character, the Athenians believed that he had brought together the disparate Attic communities into a single state.
7. A Dominican friar, Savonarola ruled Florence from 1494 to 1498 as a "holy republic"; after incurring the wrath of the pope and supporters of the exiled Medici, he was burned at the stake for heresy. Following his death, Florence was ruled by Machiavelli's supporter and close friend Soderini.

Chapter 18
How a Prince Should Keep His Word[1]

How praiseworthy it is for a prince to keep his word and live by honesty and not deceit, everyone knows; nevertheless we see, by what goes on in our own times, that
those princes who have accomplished great things are the ones who had cared little for
keeping promises and who knew how to manipulate the minds of men with shrewd-
ness; and in the end they won out over those who founded themselves on loyalty.

You should know, then, that there are two ways of fighting: one with the law, the
other with force: the first way is peculiar to man, the other to beasts; but since the first
in many instances is not enough, it becomes necessary to resort to the second. Therefore, a prince must know how to make good use of the beast and the man. This role
was taught to princes indirectly by the ancient writers, who wrote how Achilles and
many other ancient princes were given to Chiron the Centaur to be brought up and
trained under his direction.[2] This can only mean, having as a teacher a half-beast and
half-man, that a prince ought to know how to make use of both natures; and the one
without the other cannot endure.

Since a prince must know how to make good use of the beast, he should choose
then the fox and the lion; for the lion has no protection from traps, and the fox is de-
fenseless against the wolves. It is necessary, therefore, to be a fox in order to know
the traps, and a lion to frighten the wolves. Those who live by the lion alone do not
understand matters. And so, a wise ruler cannot, nor should he, keep his word when
doing so would be to his disadvantage and when the reasons that led him to make
promises no longer exist. And if all men were good, this principle would not be good;
but since men are a contemptible lot, and would not keep their promises to you, you
too need not keep yours to them. To a prince legitimate reasons to break promises are
never lacking. Of this an infinite number of present-day examples could be noted, indicating how many peace treaties, how many promises have been made null and void
by the unfaithfulness of princes: and he who has known best how to use the fox has
come to a better end. But one must know how to disguise this nature well, and how to
be a fine liar and hypocrite; and men are so simple-minded and so dominated by their
present needs that one who deceives will always find one who will allow himself to
be deceived.

There is one of these recent examples I do not wish to be silent about. Alexander VI did nothing else, he thought about nothing else, except to deceive men, and
he always found the occasion to do it.[3] And never was there a man more forceful in
his assertions, and who affirmed a thing with more promises who kept his word less;
nevertheless, the deceits he planned were always successful, because he was well acquainted with this facet of life.

It is not necessary, then, for a prince to have all of the qualities mentioned above,
but it is certainly necessary that he appear to have them. In fact, I would go so far as
to say this, that having them and observing them at all times, they are harmful; and
appearing to have them, they are useful; for example, appearing to be compassionate,
faithful, humane, upright, religious, and being so; but his mind should be disposed in

---

1. With Chapter 16, Machiavelli has begun to discuss the
qualities that a strong prince should have.
2. Son of Cronus, the centaur Chiron, half-horse and half-
man, was celebrated for his knowledge, and was said to
have taught Jason, Achilles, and other Greek heroes.

3. Alexander VI had been pope from 1492–1503; he was
known for his nepotism and political scheming. His illegitimate son was Cesare Borgia, featured on numerous
occasions in the book as the exemplary—that is, ruthless—prince.

such a way that should it become necessary not to be so, he will be able and know how to change to the contrary. And it must be understood that a prince, and in particular a new prince, cannot observe all those things by which men are considered good, for it is often necessary, in order to maintain the state, to act against your word, against charity, against kindness, against religion. And so, he must have a mind ready to turn itself according as the winds of fortune and the fluctuation of things command him, and, as I said above, he must not separate himself from the good, if he is able, but he must know how to take up evil, should it become necessary.

A prince, therefore, should take great care never to say a single thing that is not infused with the five qualities mentioned above; he should appear, when seen and heard, to be all compassion, all faithfulness, all integrity, all kindness, all religion. And nothing is more essential than to appear to have this last quality. And men, in general, judge more according to their eyes than their hands; since everyone is in a position to observe, just a few to touch. Everyone sees what you appear to be, few touch what you are; and those few do not dare oppose the opinions of the many who have the majesty of the state defending them; and with regard to the actions of all men, and especially with princes where there is no court of appeal, we must look at the final result. Let a prince, then, conquer and maintain the state; his methods will always be judged honorable and they will be praised by all; because the ordinary people are always taken by the appearance and the outcome of a thing; and in the world there is nothing but ordinary people; and there is no room for the few while the many have a place to lean on. A certain prince[4] in our own time, whose name is better left unmentioned, preaches nothing but peace and good faith, and he is exceedingly hostile to both of them; and if he had put both of them into practice on more than one occasion they would have lost him either his reputation or his state.

* * *

Chapter 25
How Much Fortune Can Do in Human Affairs and How to Contend with It[1]

I am not unaware that many have been and still are of the opinion that worldly affairs are in a way governed by fortune and by God, that men with their wisdom are not able to control them, indeed, that men can do nothing about them; and for this reason they would conclude that there is no point in sweating much over these things, instead let them be governed by chance. This opinion has been held more in our own day, because of the great changes in things that have been observed and are being observed every day that are beyond human imagination. When I think about this sometimes, I am to some extent inclined toward their opinion. Nevertheless, so that our free choice may not be obliterated, I hold that it could be true that fortune is the arbiter of half our actions, but that she still leaves the other half, or close to it, to be governed by us. And she resembles one of those violent rivers that, when they become enraged, flood the plains, tear down trees and buildings, lift up the earth from

---

4. King Ferdinand II of Spain (1452–1516), called "the most Catholic King."

1. The intervening chapters have discussed counselors, flatterers, and "why the princes of Italy have lost their states." Machiavelli accuses those who have lost their principalities out of laziness: "because, never having thought during peaceful times that conditions could change . . . when adverse times then came, they thought about running away instead of defending themselves."

one side and deposit it on the other; everyone flees before them, everybody yields to their impact, unable to oppose them in any way. And although they are this way, it does not mean therefore that men, when times are quiet, cannot take precautions with floodgates and embankments, so that, when they swell up again, either they would move along through a canal, or their rush would not be so unchecked or so harmful. The same happens with fortune, who displays her force where there is no prepared resource to resist her; and she directs her impact there where she knows that floodgates and banks have not been constructed to contain her. And if you consider Italy, which is the seat of these changes and the one that put them into motion, you will see that she is a country without embankments and without any floodgates: for if she had been protected with suitable resources, like Germany, Spain and France, either this flood would not have caused the great changes it has, or it would not have come about at all.[2] And let what I have just said suffice as a general discussion on opposing fortune.

But confining myself more to particulars, let me say that we may see a prince prosper today, and tomorrow come to ruin, without having seen a change in his character or in anything else. This I believe stems, first, from the causes discussed at length earlier; that is, that a prince who relies entirely on fortune will come to ruin as soon as she changes. I believe, furthermore, that he will prosper who adapts his course of action to conditions of the present time, and similarly that he will not prosper who with his course of action conflicts with the times. For men can be seen, in the things which lead them to the goal that each has before him, namely, glory and wealth, to proceed in different ways: one with cautiousness, another with impetuousness; one by violence, another with strategy; one by patience, another by way of its contrary; and each one by these diverse methods can arrive at his goal. Moreover, in the case of two cautious men, we can see one carry out his plan, the other not; and likewise two men prospering equally well by means of two different methods, one being cautious and the other impetuous: which stems from nothing else if not from the conditions of the times that do or do not conform to their course of action. From this arises what I have said, that two men, working in different ways, can produce the same effect; and two men working in the same way, one achieves his goal, and the other does not. From this depends also the mutability of what is good; for, if a man governs himself with caution and patience, and the times and circumstances are in accord so that his course of procedure is good, he will go along prospering; but, if times and circumstances change, he is ruined, because he does not change his course of action. Nor does one find a man wise enough to know how to adapt himself to this; not only because he cannot deviate from that to which he is naturally inclined, but also because, having always prospered while following along one path, he cannot be persuaded to leave it. And therefore the cautious man, when it is time for him to act with impetuousness, does not know how; and so he is ruined; for, if he were to change his nature with the times and the circumstances, his fortune would not change.

Pope Julius II in all his dealings acted impetuously;[3] and he found the times and the circumstances very much in accord with his course of action, which always produced favorable results. Consider the first battle he waged, against Bologna, while

---

2. The "flood" is primarily the invasion of the Holy Roman Emperor, Charles V, in 1494; many Italian cities also chose to defend themselves with mercenaries, a practice Machiavelli criticized.

3. Pope from 1503 to 1513, called by Erasmus and others "the warrior pope" for his frequent military ventures.

Messer Giovanni Bentivogli was still alive.[4] The Venetians were not happy about it, and neither was the king of Spain; he was negotiating with France over the enterprise; and nonetheless, with his fierceness and impetuousness, he personally put that campaign into motion. Such a motion kept Spain and the Venetians in check and in place, the latter out of fear, and the other by the desire to regain all the kingdom of Naples; at the same time he drew the king of France into it, because the king, having seen him make this move, and desiring to make him a friend in order to defeat the Venetians, decided he could not deny him his troops without obviously offending him. And so Julius accomplished, with his impetuous move, what no other pontiff, possessing all human wisdom, could accomplish; for, if he had waited to leave Rome until the agreements were established and everything was settled, as any other pontiff would have done, he would never have succeeded; because the king of France would have found a thousand excuses, and the others would have instilled in him a thousand fears. I want to leave aside his other deeds, for all of them were similar, and all of them turned out well. And the brevity of life did not allow him to experience the opposite; because, if such times had come that might have required him to act with caution, his ruin would have followed from it: for never would he have deviated from those methods to which nature inclined him.

I conclude, then, that fortune varying, and men remaining fixed in their ways, while the two are in accordance with each other men are prosperous, and when they are in discord, unprosperous. I am certainly convinced of this: that it is better to be impetuous than cautious, because fortune is a woman, and it is necessary, if one wishes to hold her down, to beat her and fight with her. And we see that she allows herself to be taken over more by these men than by those who make cold advances; and then, being a woman, she is always the young man's friend, because they are less cautious, more reckless and with greater audacity command her.

Chapter 26
Exhortation to Take Hold of Italy and Liberate Her from the Barbarians

So, having deliberated on all the things discussed above, and meditating over whether the time is right in Italy, at present, to honor a new prince, and if there is the material that might afford one who is wise and ingenious the occasion to give it a form that would bring honor to him and good to all the people of Italy, it seems to me that so many things are concurring to favor a new prince that I know of no other time more appropriate than this. And if, as I have said, it was necessary in order to see the capability of Moses that the people of Israel be slaves in Egypt, and to know the great courage of Cyrus that the Persians be oppressed by the Medes, and to know the excellence of Theseus that the Athenians be scattered; likewise, at the present time, in order to recognize the capability of an Italian spirit, it was necessary that Italy be reduced to the condition she is in at present, and that she be more of a slave than the Hebrews, more servile than the Persians, more scattered than the Athenians; without a leader, without order; beaten, despoiled, torn apart, overrun; and it was necessary for her to have put up with all kinds of desolation.

---

4. The Bentivoglio family had dominated Bologna until 1506, when Julius personally led an expedition to the city. France joined Julius along with the Holy Roman Emperor in order to wrest other lands in the Romagna away from Venice. Julius later won the support of Venice and Spain to try to expel French forces from Italy.

And even though before now some glimmer of light may have shown itself in the person of a certain man, such that made it possible to believe that he was ordained by God for her redemption, nevertheless it was seen afterward how, at the culminating point of his career, he was rejected by fortune.[1] So now she exists without life, she awaits that one who might heal her wounds and put an end to the sacking of Lombardy,[2] to the extortions in the Kingdom and in Tuscany, and cure those sores of hers which for so long a time have been festering. Look how she prays God that He may send someone to redeem her from these barbarous cruelties and outrages; look at her ever ready and willing to follow a banner, if only there were some person to raise it. There is no one in sight, at present, in whom she can have more hope than in your illustrious house, that with its fortune and ingenuity, favored by God and by the Church, of which it is now prince, could make itself head of this redemption.[3] To do this would not be very difficult, if you keep before you the actions and lives of those named above. And although those men are exceptional and phenomenal, they were nonetheless men, and each of them had less opportunity than the present; for their undertaking was not more just than this, nor simpler, nor was God more a friend to them than to you. There is much justice in this: "only those wars that are necessary are just, and those arms are holy without which there would be no hope."[4] There is a great willingness at present; and where there is great willingness there cannot be great difficulty, if you hold to the methods of those I have set up as targets. Besides this, at present we have witnessed extraordinary happenings without precedent brought about by God: the sea has opened; a cloud has cleared your path; the rock has poured water; it has rained manna here; everything has run in favor of your greatness.[5] The rest you must do yourself. God does not want to do everything, so as not to take from us our free will and a part of that glory that belongs to us.

And it is no wonder if some of the Italians mentioned previously were not able to do what is hoped may be done by your illustrious house; and if, during the numerous revolutions in Italy and during the numerous manoeuvres of war, it always seems that her military strength is extinguished; this arises from the fact that her old methods were not good, and that there was no one who knew how to invent new ones; and nothing brings as much honor to a newly rising man as do the new laws and new methods invented by him. These things, when they are well-established and carry with them the idea of greatness, will make him worthy of reverence and admiration. And in Italy there is no lack of material to be given form; and at present there is great strength in her members, were it not for her lack of heads. Consider how in duels and clashes involving just a few the Italians are superior in force, dexterity and inventiveness; but when it comes to armies, they do not compare. And it all stems from the weakness of the heads; because those who know are not obeyed, and with everyone seeming to know, there has not been up to the present anyone who has known how to distinguish himself, by ingenuity and fortune, to the extent of making the others yield to him. As a result, during so much time, during the many wars waged over the past

---

1. Most likely a reference to Cesare Borgia, who died in 1507; the death of his father, Pope Alexander VI, in 1503, had put an end to his hopes to conquer central Italy.
2. Lombardy fell to the French in 1509.
3. "Your illustrious house" is the Medici, who with the election of Giovanni de' Medici to the papacy in 1513 as Leo X controlled both substantial portions of Tuscany and Rome.
4. From Livy's history of Rome (bk 9, ch.10).
5. Machiavelli may be referring here to Leo X's election; the imagery is biblical, largely taken from Exodus and the story of the Hebrews' emergence out of slavery.

twenty years, whenever there was an entirely Italian army, it always made a bad showing. As proof of this there is first Taro, then Alexandria, Capua, Genoa, Vailà, Bologna, Mestri.[6]

Therefore, if your illustrious house wishes to follow those outstanding men who redeemed their lands, you should, above all other things, and as a true foundation for every enterprise, provide yourself with native troops; for you could not have more faithful nor more loyal nor better soldiers. And while each one of them alone is valiant, when all of them are united they will become even more valiant, having experienced the command of their prince and been honored and well treated by him. It is necessary, therefore, to provide yourself with troops such as these, so that with Italian strength you will be able to defend yourself from outsiders. And while the Swiss and Spanish infantries may be considered formidable, nevertheless both of them have defects so that a third army could not only oppose them but be confident of overcoming them. For the Spanish cannot withstand men on horseback, and the Swiss will be frightened by foot soldiers they meet in battle who are as bold as themselves. So it has been seen and experience will show, the Spanish cannot withstand a French cavalry, and the Swiss are defeated by a Spanish infantry. And although this last case has not been entirely confirmed, nonetheless there was an indication of it at the battle of Ravenna, when the Spanish infantry confronted the German battalions, which follow the same methods as the Swiss; and the Spanish, with their agile bodies and aided by their spiked shields, got under and through their pikes and into a position to attack them safely without the Germans being able to do a thing about it; and if it had not been for the cavalry that charged them, they would have killed all of them.[7] Therefore, once the defects of both these kinds of troops are known, a new kind can be organized, which can resist horsemen and not be afraid of foot soldiers: this will be accomplished by creating new armies and changing battle formations. And these are among those things that, newly introduced, give prestige and greatness to a new prince.

This opportunity, then, must not be allowed to pass by, in order that Italy, after so long a time, may behold its redeemer. I cannot express with what love he will be greeted in all those provinces that have suffered through these foreign inundations; with what thirst for vengeance, with what firm loyalty, with what devotion, with what tears. What doors would be closed to him? what people would deny him obedience? what envy could oppose him? what Italian would not pay homage to him? This barbarian domination stinks to everyone! May then your illustrious house take up this mission with that courage and with that hope in which just enterprises are taken up; so that, under your banner, this country may be ennobled and, under your auspices, those words of Petrarch may come true.

> Ingenuity against rage
> Will take up arms and make the battle short.
> For the ancient valor
> In Italian hearts is not yet dead.[8]

6. All Italian towns that, between 1495 and 1513, fell into the control of the French or Spanish; Machiavelli lists the cities in the order of their defeat.
7. The French defeated the Spanish at Ravenna, on the eastern coast of Italy, in 1512.

8. From one of Petrarch's most famous *canzoni* (128), which opens "Italia mia"; addressed to the princes of Italy at a time of considerable civic unrest in the 1340s, the poem is a plea for unity and, as the last words stress, "peace, peace, peace."

RESONANCE

Baldesar Castiglione: from *The Book of the Courtier*[1]

[THE ART OF CONCEALING ART]

[I.25] Said Count Ludovico da Canossa,[2] "Just so I, perhaps, shall be able to tell you what a perfect Courtier should be, but not to teach you what you must do to become one. Still, in order to answer your question in so far as I can (although it is almost proverbial that grace is not learned), I say that if anyone is to acquire grace in bodily exercises (granting first of all that he is not by nature incapable), he must begin early and learn the principles from the best of teachers. And how important this seemed to King Philip of Macedon can be seen by the fact that he wished Aristotle, the famous philosopher and perhaps the greatest the world has ever known, to be the one who should teach his son Alexander the first elements of letters. And among men whom we know today, consider how well and gracefully signor Galeazzo Sanseverino, Grand Equerry of France, performs all bodily exercises; and this because, besides the natural aptitude of person that he possesses, he has taken the greatest care to study with good masters and to have about him men who excel, taking from each the best of what they know. For just as in wrestling, vaulting, and in the handling of many kinds of weapons, he took our messer Pietro Monte as his guide, who is (as you know) the only true master of every kind of acquired strength and agility—so in riding, jousting, and the rest he has ever had before his eyes those men who are known to be most perfect in these matters.[3]

[26] "Therefore, whoever would be a good pupil must not only do things well, but must always make every effort to resemble and, if that be possible, to transform himself into his master. And when he feels that he has made some progress, it is very profitable to observe different men of that profession; and, conducting himself with that good judgment which must always be his guide, go about choosing now this thing from one and that from another. And even as in green meadows the bee flits about among the grasses robbing the flowers, so our Courtier must steal this grace from those who seem to him to have it, taking from each the part that seems most worthy of praise;[4] not doing as a friend of ours whom you all know, who thought he

---

1. Translated by Charles S. Singleton. Castiglione (1478–1529) had a prominent career as a courtier and diplomat for the Italian courts of Mantua and Urbino; after the death of his wife in 1520, he took minor orders, and was appointed papal ambassador to the court of Charles V in Spain. *The Courtier,* Castiglione's major work, is the product of his close association with Guidobaldo da Montefeltro, Duke of Urbino until 1508. Written in stages between 1513 and 1524, *The Courtier* professes to immortalize a series of conversations held in Urbino's sophisticated court in 1506 about the making of the "perfect courtier." The conversationalists are from among the best and the brightest of Italy's courtiers, leaders, and religious figures, including Duke Giuliano de' Medici, Cardinal Bernardo Dovizi da Bibbiena, one of the first to write an Italian comedy inspired by the comedies of Latin antiquity, and the Duchess of Urbino, Elisabetta Gonzaga, who in the absence of her ailing husband Guidobaldo, presides over the lively discussions that characterize the four days.

A melancholy tone hangs over the work, since Castiglione notes in his prefatory letter, written shortly before the book was published in 1528, that he is seized "by no little sadness" as he realizes that "the greater part of those persons who are introduced in the conversations were already dead." This includes the Duchess, who "was worth more than the others," and to whom he "was much more bound than to all the rest. Therefore, in order not to delay paying what I owe to the memory of so excellent a lady, and to that of the others who are no more . . . I have had [my book] printed and published in such form as the brevity of time permitted."

2. Ambassador to England and France for Pope Leo X.

3. Galeazzo Severino was a French military captain; Pietro Monte taught military exercises at the court of Urbino and elsewhere.

4. The classic metaphor of the bee as a figure of the accomplished poet had already been used by Petrarch (see his letter to Boccaccio, page 206); Castiglione here invokes it as a model for the courtier as well.

greatly resembled King Ferdinand the Younger of Aragon, but had not tried to imitate him in anything save in the way he had of raising his head and twisting one side of his mouth, which manner the King had contracted through some malady. And there are many such, who think they are doing a great thing if only they can resemble some great man in something; and often they seize upon that which is his only bad point.

"But, having thought many times already about how this grace is acquired (leaving aside those who have it from the stars), I have found quite a universal rule which in this matter seems to me valid above all others, and in all human affairs whether in word or deed: and that is to avoid affectation in every way possible as though it were some very rough and dangerous reef; and (to pronounce a new word perhaps) to practice in all things a certain *sprezzatura,*[5] so as to conceal all art and make whatever is done or said appear to be without effort and almost without any thought about it. And I believe much grace comes of this: because everyone knows the difficulty of things that are rare and well done; wherefore facility in such things causes the greatest wonder; whereas, on the other hand, to labor and, as we say, drag forth by the hair of the head, shows an extreme want of grace, and causes everything, no matter how great it may be, to be held in little account.

"Therefore we may call that art true art which does not seem to be art; nor must one be more careful of anything than of concealing it, because if it is discovered, this robs a man of all credit and causes him to be held in slight esteem. And I remember having read of certain most excellent orators in ancient times who, among the other things they did, tried to make everyone believe that they had no knowledge whatever of letters; and, dissembling their knowledge, they made their orations appear to be composed in the simplest manner and according to the dictates of nature and truth rather than of effort and art; which fact, had it been known, would have inspired in the minds of the people the fear that they could be duped by it.

"So you see how art, or any intent effort, if it is disclosed, deprives everything of grace. Who among you fails to laugh when our messer Pierpaolo dances after his own fashion, with those capers of his, his legs stiff on tiptoe, never moving his head, as if he were a stick of wood, and all this so studied that he really seems to be counting his steps? What eye is so blind as not to see in this the ungainliness of affectation; and not to see the grace of that cool *disinvoltura* [ease] (for when it is a matter of bodily movements many call it that) in many of the men and women here present, who seem in words, in laughter, in posture not to care; or seem to be thinking more of everything than of that, so as to cause all who are watching them to believe that they are almost incapable of making a mistake?"

* * *

[WOMEN EXEMPLIFY GRACE]

[I.40] "Madam," replied the Count, "I think the thread is broken.[6] Still, if I am not mistaken, I believe we were saying that the bane of affectation always produces extreme gracelessness in all things and that, on the other hand, the greatest grace is produced by simplicity and nonchalance: in praise of which, and in blame of affectation, many other things could be said; but I wish to add only one thing more. All women

5. Nonchalance. A word coined by Castiglione, *sprezzatura* derives from the Italian verb "sprezzare," to scorn or hold in disdain.
6. The intervening chapters have constituted what one speaker, Signora Emilia Pia, deemed a digression: a discussion on the merits of the Tuscan language, at the time the principal literary language in Italy. The Count now attempts to return to the earlier discussion regarding the need of the courtier to resist affectation.

have a great desire to be—and when they cannot be, at least to seem—beautiful. Therefore, wherever nature has failed in this regard, they try to remedy it with artifice: whence that embellishing of the face with so much care and sometimes with pain, that plucking of the eye-brows and the forehead, and the use of all those methods and the enduring of those nuisances which you ladies think, are hidden to men, but which are well known."

Here madam Costanza Fregosa[7] laughed and said: "It would be much more courteous of you to go on with your discussion, and tell us what the source of grace is, and speak of Courtiership, instead of trying to uncover the defects of women, which is not to the purpose."

"On the contrary, it is much to the purpose," replied the Count, "for the defects that I am speaking of deprive you ladies of grace, since they are caused by nothing but affectation, through which you openly let everyone know your inordinate desire to be beautiful. Do you not see how much more grace a woman has who paints (if at all) so sparingly and so little that whoever sees her is uncertain whether she is painted or not; than another woman so plastered with it that she seems to have put a mask on her face and dares not laugh so as not to cause it to crack, and never changes color except in the morning when she dresses; and, then, for the rest of the entire day remains motionless like a wooden statue and shows herself only by torchlight, like wily merchants who display their cloth in a dark place. And how much more attractive than all the others is one (not ugly, I mean) who is plainly seen to have nothing on her face, it being neither too white nor too red, but has her own natural color, a bit pale, and tinged at times with an open blush from shame or other cause, with her hair artlessly unadorned and in disarray, with gestures simple and natural, without showing effort or care to be beautiful. Such is that careless purity which is so pleasing to the eyes and minds of men who are ever fearful of being deceived by art.

"Beautiful teeth are very attractive in a woman, for since they do not show as openly as the face, not being visible most of the time, we may believe that less care has been taken to make them beautiful than with the face: and yet whoever laughs without cause and solely to display the teeth would betray his art, and, no matter how beautiful they are, would seem most ungraceful to all, like Catullus' Egnatius.[8] The same is true of the hands which, if they are delicate and beautiful, and are uncovered at the proper time, when there is need to use them and not merely to make a show of their beauty, leave one with a great desire to see them more and especially when they are covered with gloves again; for whoever covers them seems to have little care or concern whether they are seen or not, and to have beautiful hands more by nature than by any effort or design.

"Have you ever noticed when a woman, in passing along the street to church or elsewhere, unwittingly happens (in play or through whatever cause) to raise just enough of her dress to show her foot and often a little of her leg? Does this not strike you as something full of grace, if she is seen in that moment, charmingly feminine, dressed in velvet shoes and dainty stockings. Certainly to me it is a pleasing sight, as I believe it is to all of you, because everyone thinks that such elegance of dress, when it is where it would be hidden and rarely seen, must be natural and instinctive

---

7. Sister to Federico Fregoso, archbishop of Salerno and well-known patron of the arts, and Ottaviano Fregoso, both of whom participate in the discussions at Urbino. Like Emilia Pia, Costanza was a close companion of the Duchess.

8. The Roman poet Catullus speaks of Egnatius in one of his poems (39): "Because Egnatius has white teeth, he smiles wherever he goes."

with the lady rather than calculated, and that she has no thought of gaining any praise thereby.

[41] "In such a way one avoids or hides affectation, and you may now see how opposed the latter is to grace, how it deprives of grace every act of the body and the soul; of which so far we have spoken but little, and yet this is not to be neglected; for, as the soul is far more worthy than the body, it deserves to be more cultivated and adorned. And as to what ought to be done in the case of our Courtier, we will lay aside the precepts of the many wise philosophers who have written on this subject to define the virtues of the soul and who discuss their worth with such subtlety; and, holding to our purpose, we will declare in a few words that it suffices if he is, as we say, a man of honor and integrity: for included in this are prudence, goodness, forti- tude, and temperance of soul, and all the other qualities proper to such an honored name. And I maintain that he alone is a true moral philosopher who wishes to be good; and for this he has need of few precepts beyond that wish. Socrates was right, therefore, in saying that all his teachings seemed to him to bear good fruit when any- one was incited by them to wish to know and understand virtue:[9] for those persons who have reached the point of desiring nothing more ardently than to be good manage easily to learn all that is needed for that. Hence, we will discuss this no further."

[QUEEN ISABELLA OF SPAIN][1]

[III. 51] Messer Cesare had ceased speaking and signor Gasparo was about to reply, when signor Ottaviano said, laughing: "In Heaven's name, grant him the victory, for I know that you have little to gain in this; and, as I see it, you will make not only all these ladies your enemies, but the greater part of the men as well."[2]

Signor Gasparo laughed and said: "Nay, the ladies have very good reason to thank me; because, if I had not contradicted signor Magnifico and messer Cesare, we should not have heard all the praises they have given to women."

Then messer Cesare said: "The praises that the Magnifico and I have given to women, and many others besides, are very well known and thus have been superflu- ous. Who does not know that without women we can take no pleasure or satisfaction in this life of ours, which, but for them, would be uncouth and devoid of all sweet- ness, and wilder than that of wild beasts? Who does not know that women alone take from our hearts all vile and base thoughts, woes, miseries, and those troubled humors that so often attend such things? And if we will carefully consider the truth, we shall see also that in our understanding of great matters women do not distract but rather awaken our minds, and in war they make men fearless and daring beyond measure. Certainly it is impossible that cowardice should ever again prevail in a man's heart where once the flame of love has entered; for one who loves always desires to make himself as lovable as possible, and always fears that he may incur some disgrace that will cause him to fall low in the estimation of the one by whom he desires to be highly esteemed. Nor does he hesitate to risk his life a thousand times a day to prove himself worthy of her love; hence, if one could assemble an army of lovers that would fight in the presence of the ladies they love, that army would conquer the whole world, unless

---

9. In Plato's *Theatetus,* Socrates suggests that he is like a midwife, except for the fact that he looks after souls, not bodies, "and the triumph of my art is in thoroughly exam- ining whether the thought which the mind of the young man brings forth is a false idol or a noble and true birth."
1. The courtiers are now in their third day of conversa-

tions, which they have decided to dedicate to the making of the perfect court lady, or *donna di palazzo.*
2. Messer Cesare Gonzaga, related to the Duchess and to Castiglione himself, has just defended women from charges of lasciviousness brought against them by the misogynist of the group, Gasparo Pallavicino.

similarly another army of lovers were to oppose it. And be sure that the ten years' stand of Troy against all Greece came from nothing if not the fact that a few lovers, when they made ready to go forth to battle, armed themselves in the presence of their women; and these women often gave a hand and, as they left, spoke to them some word that inflamed them and made them more than men. Then in battle they knew that their women were watching them from the walls and towers; wherefore it seemed to them that every act of courage, every proof they gave, won them their women's praise, which was the greatest reward they could have in the world.[3]

"There are many who believe that the victory of King Ferdinand and Queen Isabella of Spain against the King of Granada was due in large measure to women; for most of the times when the Spanish army went out to meet the enemy, Queen Isabella also went out with all her maids of honor, and in the army there were many noble cavaliers in love.[4] The latter would go along talking with their ladies until they reached the place where the enemy was seen, then each would take leave of his own lady; and, with the ladies looking on, they would go forth to meet the enemy with the fierce spirit that love gave them, and with the desire to show their ladies that they were served by men of valor; hence, a very small band of Spanish cavaliers was often seen to put a host of Moors to flight and death, thanks to the gentle and beloved ladies. So, signor Gasparo, I do not see what perversity of judgment brings you to censure women."

[III. 51] Messer Cesare had discussed something and signor Gasparo was about to reply, when signor Ottaviano said, laughing: "In Heaven's name, grant him the victory, for I know you would gain little."

[THE ENDS OF COURTIERSHIP][5]

[IV.4] "So," said Signor Ottaviano, "to continue the reasoning of these gentlemen, which I wholly approve and confirm, I say that, among the things which we call good, there are some which, simply and in themselves, are always good, such as temperance, fortitude, health, and all the virtues that bring tranquillity of mind; others, which are good in various respects and for the end to which they are directed, such as law, liberality, riches, and other like things. Therefore I think that the perfect Courtier, such as Count Ludovico and messer Federico have described him, may indeed be good and worthy of praise, not, however, simply and in himself, but in regard to the end to which he is directed. For indeed if by being of noble birth, graceful, charming, and expert in so many exercises, the Courtier were to bring forth no other fruit than to be what he is, I should not judge it right for a man to devote so much study and labor to acquiring this perfection of Courtiership as anyone must do who wishes to acquire it. Nay, I should say that many of those accomplishments that have been attributed to him (such as dancing, merrymaking, singing, and playing) were frivolities and vanities and, in a man of any rank, deserving of blame rather than of praise; for these elegances of dress, devices, mottoes, and other such things as pertain to women and love (although many will think the contrary), often serve merely to make spirits effeminate, to corrupt youth, and to lead it to a dissolute life; whence it comes about that the Italian name is reduced to op-

esteemed. Nor does he hesitate to risk his life as though a thousand times a day to prove himself worthy of this love; hence, if one could assemble an army of lovers that would fight in

3. In Homer's *Iliad*, the Trojan hero Hektor arms himself with his wife's help, and women watch from the walls of Troy as their husbands defend the city.
4. Queen of Castile, Isabella (1451–1501) ruled jointly with Ferdinand of Aragon, whom she married in 1469. A strong proponent of holy war, Isabella supported repeated campaigns against Granada, the last vestige of Muslim power on the Iberian peninsula, which was finally overtaken by Spain in 1492.
5. From Book 4, describing a fourth and final day of dis-

cussions, and added by Castiglione almost a decade after the first three books were complete. This book turns on the role of the courtier vis-à-vis his prince; or, as Ottaviano says in Chapter 4, on "the end to which he is directed." The tone of Book 4 reveals some anxiety that the courtier's training in horsemanship, arts and letters, and military prowess has no political value; Ottaviano and Gasparo Pallavacino will attempt to correct this perception in the closing day's conversation.

probrium, and there are but few who dare, I will not say to die, but even to risk any danger. And certainly there are countless other things, which, if effort and study were put into them, would prove much more useful, both in peace and in war, than this kind of Courtiership taken in and for itself. But if the activities of the Courtier are directed to the good end to which they ought to be directed, and which I have in mind, I feel certain that they are not only not harmful or vain, but most useful and deserving of infinite praise.

[5] "Therefore, I think that the aim of the perfect Courtier, which we have not spoken of up to now, is so to win for himself, by means of the accomplishments ascribed to him by these gentlemen, the favor and mind of the prince whom he serves that he may be able to tell him, and always will tell him, the truth about everything he needs to know, without fear or risk of displeasing him; and that when he sees the mind of his prince inclined to a wrong action, he may dare to oppose him and in a gentle manner avail himself of the favor acquired by his good accomplishments, so as to dissuade him of every evil intent and bring him to the path of virtue. And thus, having in himself the goodness which these gentlemen attributed to him, together with readiness of wit, charm, prudence, knowledge of letters and of many other things—the Courtier will in every instance be able adroitly to show the prince how much honor and profit will come to him and to his from justice, liberality, magnanimity, gentleness, and the other virtues that befit a good prince; and, on the other hand, how much infamy and harm result from the vices opposed to these virtues. Hence, I think that even as music, festivals, games, and the other pleasant accomplishments are, as it were, the flower; so to bring or help one's prince toward what is right and to frighten him away from what is wrong are the true fruit of Courtiership. And because the real merit of good deeds consists chiefly in two things, one of which is to know how to find means timely and fitting to attain that good end—it is certain that a man aims at the best end when he sees to it that his prince is deceived by no one, listens to no flatterers or slanderers or liars, and distinguishes good from evil, loving the one and hating the other."[6]

Sir Thomas More
1478–1535

In 1516, the year that Thomas More published his magnificent *Utopia,* everything seemed possible for this "Citizen and Sheriff of the Famous City of London," as his title page proudly announces. More was closely associated with the group of Christian humanists who were changing the intellectual face of Europe. Erasmus had written *Praise of Folly* while a guest in his

6. The discussion as to the appropriate goals of the courtier will continue until chapter 50, when Pietro Bembo, an important Venetian humanist and literary stylist, and eventually a cardinal, will reintroduce the topic of love as a motivating force for the perfect courtier. The book virtually ends with Bembo's neo-Platonic hymn to love as not merely the key to good courtiership, but the path to the divine. In one of the book's gently comic moments, when Bembo is finally silent, Emilia Pia "plucked him by the hem of his robe and, shaking him a little, said, 'Take care, messer Pietro, that with these thoughts your soul, too, does not forsake your body.'" Seeing that it is already dawn, the group retires, and *The Courtier* is brought to a close, but not without the promise, made by Emilia, that the misogynistic Gasparo should be made to "stand trial" for his hostility to women.

household, and Peter Giles, the editor of Greek and Latin texts who appears in *Utopia*'s first book, was More's close friend. An advocate for women's education, More no doubt took pride in his own children's intellectual accomplishments; his eldest daughter Margaret wrote Latin letters to Erasmus and was the likely model for the erudite female conversationalist in his colloquy, "The Abbot and the Learned Lady." Most importantly, his public life was moving forward at breathtaking pace. More's earlier education at Oxford and London's Inns of Court had prepared him well for the career of the intellectual in public service. His *History of Richard III* is an exemplary work of historiography in its portrait of the ruthless, Machiavellian king. In 1517 he became a member of Henry VIII's inner sanctum, the King's Council, and in 1521 he was knighted and elevated to the office of under-Treasurer. Eight years later, Henry gave him the most important job in England, that of Lord Chancellor.

The author of *Utopia* cannot possibly have foreseen all of these honors; nor, of course, could he have predicted his death at the hands of the king who would bestow them on him. And neither could he have envisioned what in a short time would become the most severe crisis that Catholicism had ever faced, one that would cost him his life. More's fervent defense of the church throughout the 1520s against emergent Protestantism is in part ironic, given the freewheeling nature of his critique in *Utopia* of the trappings of organized religion; like Erasmus, he was dedicated to serious reforms of the sixteenth-century church. But he is equally if not more committed to reforms of the state; and while he professes to be ignorant of Utopia's whereabouts (indeed, the word in Greek means "nowhere"), its fifty-four city-states, the name of its capital (Amaurotum or "Darkling City," an appropriate name for foggy London), its extensive agricultural holdings, and its physical and metaphorical insularity make it an uncanny double for More's England: an England into which he would infuse the "primitive" practices of early radical Christianity—equality and the abolition of private property.

These were issues that Plato had addressed in his portrait of an ideal society, the *Republic* (see Volume A); and like other humanists of his era, More was greatly inspired by the Greeks (the Utopians are Greek in origin, although their language is based on Persian and their chief God takes a Persian name). The period encouraged the kinds of thought-experiments of which More's work is exemplary, as writers such as Castiglione and Erasmus tried to imagine the possibility of perfection on earth rather than only in Augustine's celestial Jerusalem (Machiavelli too would fashion a paradigm of perfection in his *Prince,* though untouched by the ethical considerations dominating the others' works). The Dominican and erstwhile landowner Bartolomeo de las Casas would seek to bring into being a perfect society in Cuba and Hispaniola based in part on Plato's vision. And the Utopian nation described by the sunburnt traveller Hythlodaeus whom "More" spots in deep conversation with his friend Peter Giles is nothing if not perfect. In Hythlodaeus's engaging, anthropological account, there is no monarchy; the fifty-four states are capably governed by mayors who are elected by an assembly. Agricultural and intellectual labors are shared by all so as to prevent the corrosive effects of boredom and drudgery, as well as class distinction.

Poverty is nonexistent thanks to the careful accumulation and distribution of resources. The Utopians' relative isolation and peace-loving ways protect them from most international conflicts and when they are reluctantly drawn into war, they hire mercenaries from their substantial treasury (they have no personal use for gold, which they relegate to the lowest of metals, but find it useful when dealing with other countries). The workday permits generous doses of leisure time and communal activities, as well as siestas. And all children—girls and boys—are introduced to literature, learning the "various branches of knowledge in their native tongue": music, dialectic, arithmetic, geometry, and astronomy, disciplines which the Utopians have developed on their own without the aid of classical texts. The priests of Utopia traffic not in obfuscating ritual and superstition but in reason and natural philosophy, and Utopia is remarkably tolerant of a variety of religions. When Hythlodaeus, one of the few foreigners who has had the good fortune to dwell with this remote people, introduces them to Christ, they willingly embrace him, so similar are their egalitarian practices and Christ's original message of charity.

Such emphatic contrasts with English and contemporary European customs suggest that More used Utopia to criticize the world he knew well, much as Montaigne would later contrast the "barbarians'" customs with those of Europeans, and find the latter wanting (see page 409). At the same time, while *Utopia*'s author holds out great hopes for the conversion of the peoples beyond the sea to Christianity, he is generally pessimistic about the human condition, anticipating Hobbes's dispiriting view of human appetite and brutality more than the optimism of Locke. For all its liberating habits of thought, Utopia is excessively, alarmingly rule-bound. Slaves dragged down with golden chains are everywhere, given all the infractions punishable by enslavement—adultery, escaping from one's city-state without permission, theft—not to mention those prisoners of war and "hard-working and poverty-stricken drudge[s]" of other countries who make their way to Utopia and voluntarily choose slavery. Privacy was increasingly valued in an early modern society that was fashioning both architectural and mental spaces privileging solitude, but it is nonexistent in Utopia: everyone is watched, always, in every waking hour.

The culture of shame produced by such relentless scrutiny is said to encourage upright behavior, and certainly it would have alleviated the pangs of inner guilt which were as much a feature of the period's Catholicism—More reputedly wore a hairshirt and practiced flagellation—as of the Lutheranism on the horizon. Someone of More's powerful sensitivites would no doubt have been relieved to escape the tribulations of doubt and inner anguish (he would also have appreciated living in a country from which lawyers have been banished; while Utopia has many rules, it has "very few laws because very few are needed for persons so educated"). At the same time, life in Utopia would deny More a great deal that was essential to his own sense of who he was. It was only after More wrote Hythlodaeus's monologue on Utopia that he wrote the dialogue about Utopia's utility, or lack thereof, for modern Europe, and decided to put it first. We are thus introduced to the insular republic only through the lively exchange among educated men that constitutes Book I, men who delight in argument and persuasion and taking on the world as it is: namely, Peter Giles and More himself.

Only Raphael Hythlodaeus, whose last name translates roughly as "wise in nonsense" and whose first name is that of the Biblical angel who guided Tobias to the recovery of his father's riches and a wife in strange lands, resists the rough and tumble of the *vita activa* or active life. He protests that the independence of spirit and thought which he has cultivated as a traveller with Amerigo Vespucci would never be welcomed by tyrants who wish to hear only what pleases them: "If I proposed beneficial measures to some king and tried to uproot from his soul the seeds of evil and corruption, do you not suppose that I should be forthwith banished or treated with ridicule?" To which "More" responds: "if you cannot cure according to your heart's desire vices of long standing, yet you must not on that account desert the commonwealth. . . . [nor] must you force upon people new and strange ideas which you realize will carry no weight with persons of opposite conviction." He rather counsels the "indirect approach": "what you cannot turn to good you must at least make as little bad as you can For it is impossible that all should be well unless all men were good, a situation which I do not expect for a great many years to come!"

In real life, More would do his best in this indirect fashion. He published his work—which cries out passionately at one point, "what is to be done with England?"—in Latin, and served as Henry's trusted counselor until 1532. But like Hythlodaeus, he didn't always mince his words. He was relentless in his attacks on Erasmus's enemies, and he refused to compromise his deepest principles, which were increasingly tied to the tenets and traditions of a Roman Catholic church assailed by a vocal band of Englishmen, including Henry VIII himself. More continued in office after his monarch unceremoniously dispatched his first wife, who had failed to produce a male heir, to marry his mistress. But he refused to take the Oath of Allegiance to his king as supreme head of the church of England after Henry was predictably excommunicated by Pope Clement VII. Sentenced to the Tower of London, More calmly wrote his last work, the deeply moving *Dialogue of Comfort Against Tribulation*. On July 1, 1535, he was accused and convicted of treason, and beheaded five days later on Tower Hill. The Catholic Church canonized him four centuries after his death.

from Utopia[1]
The Best State of a Commonwealth
and the New Island of Utopia

A Truly Golden Handbook,
No Less Beneficial Than Entertaining,
by the Distinguished and Eloquent Author
THOMAS MORE
Citizen and Sheriff of the Famous City
of London

Thomas More to Peter Giles,[2]
Greetings.

I am almost ashamed, my dear Peter Giles, to send you this little book about the state of Utopia after almost a year, when I am sure you looked for it within a month and a half. Certainly you know that I was relieved of all the labor of gathering materials for the work and that I had to give no thought at all to their arrangement. I had only to repeat what in your company I heard Raphael[3] relate. Hence there was no reason for me to take trouble about the style of the narrative, seeing that his language could not be polished. It was, first of all, hurried and impromptu and, secondly, the product of a person who, as you know, was not so well acquainted with Latin as with Greek. Therefore the nearer my style came to his careless simplicity the closer it would be to the truth, for which alone I am bound to care under the circumstances and actually do care.

I confess, my dear Peter, that all these preparations relieved me of so much trouble that scarcely anything remained for me to do. Otherwise the gathering or the arrangement of the materials could have required a good deal of both time and application even from a talent neither the meanest nor the most ignorant. If it had been required that the matter be written down not only accurately but eloquently, I could not have performed the task with any amount of time or application. But, as it was, those cares over which I should have had to perspire so hard had been removed. Since it remained for me only to write out simply what I had heard, there was no difficulty about it.

Yet even to carry through this trifling task, my other tasks left me practically no leisure at all. I am constantly engaged in legal business, either pleading or hearing, either giving an award as arbiter or deciding a case as judge. I pay a visit of courtesy to one man and go on business to another. I devote almost the whole day in public to other men's affairs and the remainder to my own. I leave to myself, that is to learning, nothing at all.

When I have returned home, I must talk with my wife, chat with my children, and confer with my servants. All this activity I count as business when it must be done—and it must be unless you want to be a stranger in your own home. Besides, one must take care to be as agreeable as possible to those whom nature has supplied, or chance

---

1. Translated by C. G. Richards, rev. Edward Surtz, S.J.
2. More was made undersheriff of London in 1510, sitting as judge and representing the sheriff's cases in the city court. His friend Peter Giles (c. 1486–1533) was a classi-

cal scholar, a member of Erasmus's circle, and city clerk of Antwerp, where he oversaw commercial business.
3. Raphael Hythlodaeus, the fictional traveler who tells the character Sir Thomas More about Utopia.

has made, or you yourself have chosen, to be the companions of your life, provided you do not spoil them by kindness, or through indulgence make masters out of your servants.

Amid these occupations that I have named, the day, the month, the year slip away. When, then, can we find time to write? Nor have I spoken a word about sleep, nor even of food, which for many people takes up as much time as sleep—and sleep takes up almost half a man's life! So I get for myself only the time I filch from sleep and food. Slowly, therefore, because this time is but little, yet finally, because this time *is* something, I have finished *Utopia* and sent it to you, my dear Peter, to read— and to remind me of anything that has escaped me.

In this respect I do not entirely distrust myself. (I only wish I were as good in intelligence and learning as I am not altogether deficient in memory!) Nevertheless, I am not so confident as to believe that I have forgotten nothing. As you know, John Clement,[4] my pupil-servant, was also present at the conversation. Indeed I do not allow him to absent himself from any talk which can be somewhat profitable, for from this young plant, seeing that it has begun to put forth green shoots in Greek and Latin literature, I expect no mean harvest some day. He has caused me to feel very doubtful on one point.

According to my own recollection, Hythlodaeus[5] declared that the bridge which spans the river Anydrus at Amaurotum is five hundred paces in length. But my John says that two hundred must be taken off, for the river there is not more than three hundred paces in breadth. Please recall the matter to mind. If you agree with him, I shall adopt the same view and think myself mistaken. If you do not remember, I shall put down, as I have actually done, what I myself seem to remember. Just as I shall take great pains to have nothing incorrect in the book, so, if there is doubt about anything, I shall rather tell an objective falsehood than an intentional lie—or I would rather be honest than wise.

Nevertheless, it would be easy for you to remedy this defect if you ask Raphael himself by word of mouth or by letter. You must do so on account of another doubt which has cropped up, whether more through my fault or through yours or Raphael's I do not know. We forgot to ask, and he forgot to say, in what part of the new world Utopia lies. I am sorry that point was omitted, and I would be willing to pay a considerable sum to purchase that information, partly because I am rather ashamed to be ignorant in what sea lies the island of which I am saying so much, partly because there are several among us, and one in particular, a devout man and a theologian by profession, burning with an extraordinary desire to visit Utopia. He does so not from an idle and curious lust for sight seeing in new places but for the purpose of fostering and promoting our religion, begun there so felicitously.

To carry out his plan properly, he has made up his mind to arrange to be sent by the pope and, what is more, to be named bishop for the Utopians. He is in no way deterred by any scruple that he must sue for this prelacy, for he considers it a holy suit which proceeds not from any consideration of honor or gain but from motives of piety.

---

4. John Clement (d. 1572), who tutored More's children, was also a distinguished humanist: a Reader at Oxford; coeditor of the first Greek edition of Galen (c. 130–200), a celebrated physician whose works on medicine remained authoritative through the early modern period; and physician to Henry VIII.

5. This reference introduces the play on Greek words that will characterize the description of Utopia in Book 2. Hythlodaeus means "learned in nonsense"; the river Anydrus means "waterless" and the city Amaurotum means "made dark or dim."

Therefore I beg you, my dear Peter, either by word of mouth if you conveniently can or by letter if he has gone, to reach Hythlodaeus and to make sure that my work includes nothing false and omits nothing true. I am inclined to think that it would be better to show him the book itself. No one else is so well able to correct any mistake, nor can he do this favor at all unless he reads through what I have written. In addition, in this way you will find out whether he accepts with pleasure or suffers with annoyance the fact that I have composed this work. If he himself has decided to put down in writing his own adventures, perhaps he may not want me to do so. By making known the commonwealth of Utopia, I should certainly dislike to forestall him and to rob his narrative of the flower and charm of novelty. * * *

The Best State of a Commonwealth,
The Discourse of the Extraordinary
Character, Raphael Hythlodaeus, as
Reported by the Renowned Figure,
THOMAS MORE,
Citizen and Sheriff
of the Famous City of
Great Britain,
London

BOOK 1

The most invincible King of England, Henry, the eighth of that name, who is distinguished by all the accomplishments of a model monarch, had certain weighty matters[6] recently in dispute with His Serene Highness, Charles, Prince of Castile.[7] With a view to their discussion and settlement, he sent me as a commissioner to Flanders—as a companion and associate of the peerless Cuthbert Tunstal, whom he has just created Master of the Rolls[8] to everyone's immense satisfaction. Of the latter's praises I shall say nothing, not because I fear that the testimony of a friend should be given little credit but because his integrity and learning are too great for it to be possible, and too well-known for it to be necessary, for me to extol them—less I should wish to give the impression, as the proverb goes, of displaying the sun with a lamp!

We were met at Bruges, according to previous arrangement, by those men put in charge of the affair by the Prince—all outstanding persons. Their leader and head was the Burgomaster[9] of Bruges, a figure of magnificence, but their chief speaker and guiding spirit was Georges de Themsecke,[1] Provost of Cassel, a man not only trained in eloquence but a natural orator—most learned, too, in the law and consummately skillful in diplomacy by native ability as well as by long experience. When after one or two meetings there were certain points on which we could not agree sufficiently, they bade farewell to us for some days and left for Brussels to seek an official pronouncement from the Prince.

---

6. The "weighty matters" that took More to Flanders concerned the payment of tolls to Flemish ports by the English merchant fleet.
7. The future Charles I of Spain and Charles V, Holy Roman emperor; he ruled the Spanish kingdoms, Spanish America, Naples, Sicily, the Low Countries, and parts of Austria.
8. The principal clerk of the Chancery Court, a court of appeals from decisions by the common-law courts.
9. Mayor.
1. A Flemish diplomat, employed on numerous missions, who died in 1536.

Meanwhile, as my business led me, I made my way to Antwerp. While I stayed there, among my other visitors, but of all of them the most welcome, was Peter Giles, a native of Antwerp, an honorable man of high position in his home town yet worthy of the very highest position, being a young man distinguished equally by learning and character; for he is most virtuous and most cultured, to all most courteous, but to his friends so open-hearted, affectionate, loyal, and sincere that you can hardly find one or two anywhere to compare with him as the perfect friend on every score. His modesty is uncommon; no one is less given to deceit, and none has a wiser simplicity of nature. Besides, in conversation he is so polished and so witty without offense that his delightful society and charming discourse largely took away my nostalgia and made me less conscious than before of the separation from my home, wife, and children to whom I was exceedingly anxious to get back, for I had then been more than four months away.

One day I had been at divine service in Notre Dame, the finest church in the city and the most crowded with worshippers. Mass being over, I was about to return to my lodging when I happened to see him in conversation with a stranger, a man of advanced years, with sunburnt countenance and long beard and cloak hanging carelessly from his shoulder, while his appearance and dress seemed to me to be those of a ship's captain.

When Peter had espied me, he came up and greeted me. As I tried to return his salutation, he drew me a little aside and, pointing to the man I had seen him talking with, said:

"Do you see this fellow? I was on the point of taking him straight to you."

"He would have been very welcome," said I, "for your sake."

"No," said he, "for his own, if you knew him. There is no mortal alive today who can give you such an account of unknown peoples and lands, a subject about which I know you are always most greedy to hear."

"Well, then," said I, "my guess was not a bad one. The moment I saw him, I was sure he was a ship's captain."

"But you are quite mistaken," said he, "for his sailing has not been like that of Palinurus but that of Ulysses or, rather, of Plato.[2] Now this Raphael—for such is his personal name, with Hythlodaeus as his family name—is no bad Latin scholar, and most learned in Greek. He had studied that language more than Latin because he had devoted himself unreservedly to philosophy, and in that subject he found that there is nothing valuable in Latin except certain treatises of Seneca and Cicero.[3] He left his patrimony at home—he is a Portuguese—to his brothers, and, being eager to see the world, joined Amerigo Vespucci[4] and was his constant companion in the last three of those four voyages which are now universally read of, but on the final voyage he did not return with him. He importuned and even wrested from Amerigo permission to be one of the twenty-four who at the farthest point of the last voyage were left behind in the fort. And so he was left behind that he might have his way, being more anxious for travel than about the grave. These two sayings are constantly on his lips: 'He who

2. Palinurus: the pilot of the ship sailed by Aeneas from Troy to Italy in Virgil's *Aeneid;* he fell overboard while sleeping at the helm. Ulysses: the Latin name for Odysseus, the hero of Homer's epic poem, the *Odyssey,* who returns to his kingdom, Ithaka, after years of wandering. Plato: the Greek philosopher who is said to have trav-

eled throughout the Mediterranean world.
3. Two Roman writers who composed works on moral and political philosophy.
4. Florentine merchant adventurer (1451–1512), whose accounts of his voyages to the New World were reprinted in many editions; the Americas are named for him.

has no grave is covered by the sky,' and 'From all places it is the same distance to heaven.' This attitude of his, but for the favor of God, would have cost him dear.[5] However, when after Vespucci's departure he had traveled through many countries with five companions from the fort, by strange chance he was carried to Ceylon, whence he reached Calicut.[6] There he conveniently found some Portuguese ships, and at length arrived home again, beyond all expectation."

When Peter had rendered this account, I thanked him for his kindness in taking such pains that I might have a talk with one whose conversation he hoped would give me pleasure; then I turned to Raphael. After we had greeted each other and exchanged the civilities which commonly pass at the first meeting of strangers, we went off to my house. There in the garden, on a bench covered with turfs of grass, we sat down to talk together.

He recounted how, after the departure of Vespucci, he and his friends who had stayed behind in the fort began by degrees through continued meetings and civilities to ingratiate themselves with the natives till they not only stood in no danger from them but were actually on friendly terms and, moreover, were in good repute and favor with a ruler (whose name and country I have forgotten). Through the latter's generosity, he and his five companions were supplied with ample provision and travel resources and, moreover, with a trusty guide on their journey (which was partly by water on rafts and partly over land by wagon) to take them to other rulers with careful recommendations to their favor. For, after traveling many days, he said, they found towns and cities and very populous commonwealths with excellent institutions.

To be sure, under the equator and on both sides of the line nearly as far as the sun's orbit extends, there lie waste deserts scorched with continual heat. A gloomy and dismal region looms in all directions without cultivation or attractiveness, inhabited by wild beasts and snakes or, indeed, men no less savage and harmful than are the beasts. But when you have gone a little farther, the country gradually assumes a milder aspect, the climate is less fierce, the ground is covered with a pleasant green herbage, and the nature of living creatures becomes less wild. At length you reach peoples, cities, and towns which maintain a continual traffic by sea and land not only with each other and their neighbors but also with far-off countries.

Then they had opportunity of visiting many countries in all directions, for every ship which was got ready for any voyage made him and his companions welcome as passengers. The ships they saw in the parts first traveled were flat-bottomed and moved under sails made of papyrus or osiers[7] stitched together and sometimes under sails made of leather. Afterwards they found ships with pointed keels and canvas sails, in fact, like our own in all respects.

Their mariners were skilled in adapting themselves to sea and weather. But he reported that he won their extraordinary favor by showing them the use of the magnetic needle[8] of which they had hitherto been quite ignorant so that they had hesitated to trust themselves to the sea and had boldly done so in the summer only. Now, trusting to the magnet, they do not fear wintry weather, being dangerously confident. Thus,

5. More's paraphrases of two classical authors indicate his humanist training. From Lucan's epic *Pharsalia* he takes: "Mother Earth has room for all her children, and he who lacks an urn has the sky to cover him" (8.819); and from Cicero's *Tusculan Disputations* he takes: "There is a fine remark of Anaxagoras. He was dying at Lampasacus, and his friends asked if he wanted to be taken home.... 'There's no need,' he said, 'it's the same distance from anywhere to the underworld'" (1.43.104).
6. Seaport on the west coast of India.
7. Papyrus: reed paper; osiers: willow twigs.
8. Compass.

there is a risk that what was thought likely to be a great benefit to them may, through their imprudence, cause them great mischief.

What he said he saw in each place would be a long tale to unfold and is not the purpose of this work. Perhaps on another occasion we shall tell his story, particularly whatever facts would be useful to readers, above all, those wise and prudent provisions which he noticed anywhere among nations living together in a civilized way. For on these subjects we eagerly inquired of him, and he no less readily discoursed; but about stale travelers' wonders we were not curious. Scyllas and greedy Celaenos and folk-devouring Laestrygones[9] and similar frightful monsters are common enough, but well and wisely trained citizens are not everywhere to be found.

To be sure, just as he called attention to many ill-advised customs among these new nations, so he rehearsed not a few points from which our own cities, nations, races, and kingdoms may take example for the correction of their errors. These instances, as I said, I must mention on another occasion. Now I intend to relate merely what he told us of the manners and customs of the Utopians, first, however, giving the talk which drew and led him on to mention that commonwealth.

Raphael had touched with much wisdom on faults in this hemisphere and that, of which he found very many in both, and had compared the wiser measures which had been taken among us as well as among them; for he remembered the manners and customs of each nation as if he had lived all his life in places which he had only visited. * * *

"To be sure, my dear Raphael," I commented, "you have given me great pleasure, for everything you have said has been both wise and witty. Besides, while listening to you, I felt not only as if I were at home in my native land but as if I were become a boy again, by being pleasantly reminded of the very Cardinal in whose court I was brought up as a lad.[1] Since you are strongly devoted to his memory, you cannot believe how much more attached I feel to you on that account, attached exceedingly as I have been to you already. Even now, nevertheless, I cannot change my mind but must needs think that, if you could persuade yourself not to shun the courts of kings, you could do the greatest good to the common weal by your advice. The latter is the most important part of your duty as it is the duty of every good man. Your favorite author, Plato, is of opinion that commonwealths will finally be happy only if either philosophers become kings or kings turn to philosophy.[2] What a distant prospect of happiness there will be if philosophers will not condescend even to impart their counsel to kings!"

"They are not so ungracious," he rejoined, "that they would not gladly do it—in fact, many have already done it in published books—if the rulers would be ready to take good advice. But, doubtless, Plato was right in foreseeing that if kings themselves did not turn to philosophy, they would never approve of the advice of real philosophers because they have been from their youth saturated and infected with wrong ideas. This truth he found from his own experience with Dionysius.[3] If I proposed beneficial measures to some king and tried to uproot from his soul the seeds of

9. Fabulous monsters from the *Odyssey* and the *Aeneid*: Scylla is a six-headed sea monster; Celaeno, a harpy, is a bird with a woman's face; the Lestrygonians were gigantic cannibals.
1. More served for two years as a page in the household of Cardinal Morton (1420–1500).
2. *Republic*, 5.473d.
3. Having tried to instruct Dionysius II, King of Syracuse, in the art of ruling as a philosopher, Plato became a virtual prisoner of the court.

evil and corruption, do you not suppose that I should be forthwith banished or treated with ridicule?

"Come now, suppose I were at the court of the French king and sitting in his privy council. In a most secret meeting, a circle of his most astute councilors over which he personally presides is setting its wits to work to consider by what crafty machinations he may keep his hold on Milan and bring back into his power the Naples which has been eluding his grasp; then overwhelm Venice and subjugate the whole of Italy; next bring under his sway Flanders, Brabant, and finally, the whole of Burgundy—and other nations, too, whose territory he has already conceived the idea of usurping.

"At this meeting, one advises that a treaty should be made with the Venetians to last just as long as the king will find it convenient, that he should communicate his intentions to them, and that he should even deposit in their keeping part of the booty, which, when all has gone according to his mind, he may reclaim. Another recommends the hiring of German *Landsknechte* [infantry], and another the mollification of the Swiss with money, and another the propitiation of the offended majesty of the emperor with gold as an acceptable offering. Another thinks that a settlement should be made with the King of Aragon and that, as a guarantee of peace, someone else's kingdom of Navarre should be ceded him! Another proposes that the Prince of Castile be caught by the prospect of a marriage alliance and that some nobles of his court be drawn to the French side by a fixed pension.

"Meanwhile the most perplexing question of all comes up: what is to be done with England? They agree that negotiations for peace should be undertaken, that an alliance always weak at best should be strengthened with the strongest bonds, and that the English should be called friends but suspected as enemies. The Scots therefore must be posted in readiness, prepared for any opportunity to be let loose on the English if they make the slightest movement. Moreover, some exiled noble must be fostered secretly—for treaties prevent it being done openly—to maintain a claim to the throne, that by this handle France may keep in check a king in whom it has no confidence.

"In such a meeting, I say, when such efforts are being made, when so many distinguished persons are vying with each other in proposals of a warlike nature, what if an insignificant fellow like myself were to get up and advise going on another tack? Suppose I expressed the opinion that Italy should be left alone. Suppose I argued that we should stay at home because the single kingdom of France by itself was almost too large to be governed well by a single man so that the king should not dream of adding other dominions under his sway. Suppose, then, I put before them the decisions made by the people called the Achorians[4] who live on the mainland to the south-southeast of the island of Utopia.

"Once upon a time they had gone to war to win for their king another kingdom to which he claimed to be the rightful heir by virtue of an old tie by marriage. After they had secured it, they saw they would have no less trouble in keeping it than they had suffered in obtaining it. The seeds of rebellion from within or of invasion from without were always springing up in the people thus acquired. They realized they would have to fight constantly for them or against them and to keep an army in continual readiness. In the meantime they were being plundered, their money was being taken

---

4. A people "without place, region, or district."

out of the country, they were shedding their blood for the little glory of someone else, peace was no more secure than before, their morals at home were being corrupted by war, the lust for robbery was becoming second nature, criminal recklessness was emboldened by killings in war, and the laws were held in contempt—all because the king, being distracted with the charge of two kingdoms, could not properly attend to either.

"At length, seeing that in no other way would there be any end to all this mischief, they took counsel together and most courteously offered their king his choice of retaining whichever of the two kingdoms he preferred. He could not keep both because there were too many of them to be ruled by half a king, just as no one would care to engage even a muleteer whom he had to share with someone else. The worthy king was obliged to be content with his own realm and to turn over the new one to one of his friends, who was driven out soon afterwards.

"Furthermore, suppose I proved that all this war-mongering, by which so many nations were kept in a turmoil on the French king's account, would, after draining his resources and destroying his people, at length by some mischance end in naught and that therefore he had better look after his ancestral kingdom and make it as prosperous and flourishing as possible, love his subjects and be loved by them, live with them and rule them gently, and have no designs upon other kingdoms since what he already possessed was more than enough for him. What reception from my listeners, my dear More, do you think this speech of mine would find?"

"To be sure, not a very favorable one," I granted.

"Well, then, let us proceed," he continued. "Picture the councilors of some king or other debating with him and devising by what schemes they may heap up treasure for him. One advises crying up the value of money when he has to pay any and crying down its value below the just rate when he has to receive any—with the double result that he may discharge a large debt with a small sum and, when only a small sum is due to him, may receive a large one. Another suggests a make-believe war under pretext of which he would raise money and then, when he saw fit, make peace with solemn ceremonies to throw dust in his simple people's eyes because their loving monarch in compassion would fain avoid human bloodshed.

"Another councilor reminds him of certain old and moth-eaten laws, annulled by long non-enforcement, which no one remembers being made and therefore everyone has transgressed. The king should exact fines for their transgression, there being no richer source of profit nor any more honorable than such as has an outward mask of justice! Another recommends that under heavy penalties he prohibit many things and especially such as it is to the people's advantage not to allow. Afterwards for money he should give a dispensation to those with whose interests the prohibition has interfered. Thus favor is won with the people and a double profit is made: first, by exacting fines from those whose greed of gain has entangled them in the snare and, second, by selling privileges to others—and, to be sure, the higher the price the better the king, since he hates to give any private citizen a privilege which is contrary to the public welfare and will not do so except at a great price!

"Another persuades him that he must bind to himself the judges, who will in every case decide in favor of the king's side. In addition, he must summon them to the palace and invite them to debate his affairs in his presence. There will be no cause of his so patently unjust in which one of them will not, either from a desire to contradict or from shame at repeating another's view or to curry favor, find some loophole whereby the law can be perverted. When through the opposite opinions of the judges a thing in itself as clear as daylight has been made a subject of debate, and when truth has become a matter of doubt, the king is opportunely furnished a handle to interpret the law in his own interest. Everyone else will acquiesce from shame or from fear. Afterwards the decision is boldly pronounced from the Bench. Then, too, a pretext can never be wanting for deciding on the king's side. For such a judge it is enough that either equity be on his side or the letter of the law or the twisted meaning of the written word or, what finally outweighs all law with conscientious judges, the indisputable royal prerogative![5]

"All the councilors agree and consent to the famous statement of Crassus:[6] no amount of gold is enough for the ruler who has to keep an army. Further, the king, however much he wishes, can do no wrong; for all that all men possess is his, as they themselves are, and so much is a man's own as the king's kindness has not taken away from him. It is much to the king's interest that the latter be as little as possible, seeing that his safeguard lies in the fact that the people do not grow insolent with wealth and freedom. These things make them less patient to endure harsh and unjust commands, while, on the other hand, poverty and need blunt their spirits, make them patient, and take away from the oppressed the lofty spirit of rebellion.

"At this point, suppose I were again to rise and maintain that these counsels are both dishonorable and dangerous for the king, whose very safety, not merely his honor, rests on the people's resources rather than his own. Suppose I should show that they choose a king for their own sake and not for his—to be plain, that by his labor and effort they may live well and safe from injustice and wrong. For this very reason, it belongs to the king to take more care for the welfare of his people than for his own, just as it is the duty of a shepherd, insofar as he is a shepherd, to feed his sheep rather than himself.[7]

"The blunt facts reveal that they are completely wrong in thinking that the poverty of the people is the safeguard of peace. Where will you find more quarreling than among beggars? Who is more eager for revolution than he who is discontented with his present state of life? Who is more reckless in the endeavor to upset everything, in the hope of getting profit from some source or other, than he who has nothing to lose? Now if there were any king who was either so despicable or so hateful to his subjects that he could not keep them in subjection otherwise than by ill usage, plundering, and confiscation and by reducing them to beggary, it would surely be better for him to resign his throne than to keep it by such means—means by which, though he retain the name of authority, he loses its majesty. It is not consistent with the dignity of a king to exercise authority over beggars but over prosperous and happy subjects. This was certainly the sentiment of that noble and lofty spirit, Fabricius,[8] who replied that he would rather be a ruler of rich people than be rich himself.

"To be sure, to have a single person enjoy a life of pleasure and self-indulgence amid the groans and lamentations of all around him is to be the keeper, not of a kingdom, but of a jail. In fine, as he is an incompetent physician who cannot cure one dis-

---

5. Conditions in which the principle of equity is subverted: the law is bent or twisted to suit the interest of a particular party. In England the courts of equity were often devoted to matters of state and were susceptible to corruption in the interest of promoting royal business. The prerogative was the absolute power of the monarch only in special categories of activity (e.g., the import and export trade), and it was exempt from any legal restrictions.
6. Marcus Licinius Crassus (d. 53 B.C.E.), a man of great

wealth who, together with Julius Caesar and Pompey, formed a coalition known as the first triumvirate.
7. A king who did not care for the welfare of his people was usually identified as a tyrant. As Aristotle stated, a tyranny is a perversion of a monarchy and it is characterized by "irresponsible rule over subjects . . . with a view to its own private interest and not in the interest of the persons ruled" (*Politics*, 4.8.3).
8. Roman commander of the republican period.

ease except by creating another, so he who cannot reform the lives of citizens in any other way than by depriving them of the good things of life must admit that he does not know how to rule free men.

"Yea, the king had better amend his own indolence or arrogance, for these two vices generally cause his people either to despise him or to hate him. Let him live harmlessly on what is his own. Let him adjust his expenses to his revenues. Let him check mischief and crime, and, by training his subjects rightly, let him prevent rather than allow the spread of activities which he will have to punish afterwards. Let him not be hasty in enforcing laws fallen into disuse, especially those which, long given up, have never been missed. Let him never take in compensation for violation anything that a private person would be forbidden in court to appropriate for the reason that such would be an act of crooked craftiness.

"What if then I were to put before them the law of the Macarians,[9] a people not very far distant from Utopia? Their king, on the day he first enters into office, is bound by an oath at solemn sacrifices that he will never have at one time in his coffer more than a thousand pounds of gold or its equivalent in silver. They report that this law was instituted by a very good king, who cared more for his country's interest than his own wealth, to be a barrier against hoarding so much money as would cause a lack of it among his people. He saw that this treasure would be sufficient for the king to put down rebellion and for his kingdom to meet hostile invasions. It was not large enough, however, to tempt him to encroach on the possessions of others. The prevention of the latter was the primary purpose of his legislation. His secondary consideration was that provision was thus made to forestall any shortage of the money needed in the daily business transactions of the citizens. He felt, too, that since the king had to pay out whatever came into his treasury beyond the limit prescribed by law, he would not seek occasion to commit injustice. Such a king will be both a terror to the evil and beloved by the good To sum it all up, if I tried to obtrude these and like ideas on men strongly inclined to the opposite way of thinking, to what deaf ears should I tell the tale!"

"Deaf indeed, without doubt," I agreed, "and, by heaven, I am not surprised. Neither, to tell the truth, do I think that such ideas should be thrust on people, or such advice given, as you are positive will never be listened to. What good could such novel ideas do, or how could they enter the minds of individuals who are already taken up and possessed by the opposite conviction? In the private conversation of close friends this academic philosophy is not without its charm, but in the councils of kings, where great matters are debated with great authority, there is no room for these notions."

"That is just what I meant," he rejoined, "by saying there is no room for philosophy with rulers."

"Right," I declared, "that is true—not for this academic philosophy which thinks that everything is suitable to every place. But there is another philosophy, more practical for statesmen, which knows its stage, adapts itself to the play in hand, and performs its role neatly and appropriately. This is the philosophy which you must employ. Otherwise we have the situation in which a comedy of Plautus is being performed and the household slaves are making trivial jokes at one another and then you come on the stage in a philosopher's attire and recite the passage from the

9. "Happy Ones."

Octavia where Seneca is disputing with Nero.[1] Would it not have been preferable to take a part without words than by reciting something inappropriate to make a hodge-podge of comedy and tragedy? You would have spoiled and upset the actual play by bringing in irrelevant matter—even if your contribution would have been superior in itself. Whatever play is being performed, perform it as best you can, and do not upset it all simply because you think of another which has more interest.

"So it is in the commonwealth. So it is in the deliberations of monarchs. If you cannot pluck up wrongheaded opinions by the root, if you cannot cure according to your heart's desire vices of long standing, yet you must not on that account desert the commonwealth. You must not abandon the ship in a storm because you cannot control the winds.

"On the other hand, you must not force upon people new and strange ideas which you realize will carry no weight with persons of opposite conviction. On the contrary, by the indirect approach you must seek and strive to the best of your power to handle matters tactfully. What you cannot turn to good you must at least make as little bad as you can. For it is impossible that all should be well unless all men were good, a situation which I do not expect for a great many years to come!"

"By this approach," he commented, "I should accomplish nothing else than to share the madness of others as I tried to cure their lunacy. If I would stick to the truth, I must needs speak in the manner I have described. To speak falsehoods, for all I know, may be the part of a philosopher, but it is certainly not for me. Although that speech of mine might perhaps be unwelcome and disagreeable to those councilors, yet I cannot see why it should seem odd even to the point of folly. What if I told them the kind of things which Plato creates in his republic or which the Utopians actually put in practice in theirs? Though such institutions were superior (as, to be sure, they are), yet they might appear odd because here individuals have the right of private property, there all things are common.

"To persons who had made up their minds to go headlong by the opposite road, the man who beckons them back and points out dangers ahead can hardly be welcome. But, apart from this aspect, what did my speech contain that would not be appropriate or obligatory to have propounded everywhere? Truly, if all the things which by the perverse morals of men have come to seem odd are to be dropped as unusual and absurd, we must dissemble among Christians almost all the doctrines of Christ. Yet He forbade us to dissemble them to the extent that what He had whispered in the ears of His disciples He commanded to be preached openly from the housetops.[2] The greater part of His teaching is far more different from the morals of mankind than was my discourse. But preachers, crafty men that they are, finding that men grievously disliked to have their morals adjusted to the rule of Christ and following I suppose your advice, accommodated His teaching to men's morals as if it were a rule of soft lead[3] that at least in some way or other the two might be made to correspond. By this method I cannot see what they have gained, except that men may be bad in greater comfort.

---

1. More's character "More" illustrates the poor social skills of the philosopher by imagining a situation in which the philosopher quotes lines from Seneca's tragedy while everyone else is enjoying a comedy by Plautus. "More" asks not only that the philosopher observe conditions of time and place, but also that he not give up his civic obligations and go into retirement when people ignore his advice.

2. Hythlodaeus paraphrases Matthew 10:27 and Luke 12:3; he proposes that the practical and accommodating flexibility that "More" advocates finds its limits in the absolute moral doctrine preached by Jesus Christ and therefore to be followed by Christians.

3. A bendable yardstick, used by Aristotle to illustrate the concept of flexible legal interpretation.

"And certainly I should make as little progress in the councils of princes. For I should hold either a different opinion, which would amount to having none at all, or else the same, and then I should, as Mitio says in Terence, help their madness.[4] As to that indirect approach of yours, I cannot see its relevancy; I mean your advice to use my endeavors, if all things cannot be made good, at least to handle them tactfully and, as far as one may, to make them as little bad as possible. At court there is no room for dissembling, nor may one shut one's eyes to things. One must openly approve the worst counsels and subscribe to the most ruinous decrees. He would be counted a spy and almost a traitor, who gives only faint praise to evil counsels.

"Moreover, there is no chance for you to do any good because you are brought among colleagues who would easily corrupt even the best of men before being re-formed themselves. By their evil companionship, either you will be seduced yourself or, keeping your own integrity and innocence, you will be made a screen for the wickedness and folly of others. Thus you are far from being able to make anything better by that indirect approach of yours.

"For this reason, Plato by a very fine comparison shows why philosophers are right in abstaining from administration of the commonwealth. They observe the people rushing out into the streets and being soaked by constant showers and cannot induce them to go indoors and escape the rain. They know that, if they go out, they can do no good but will only get wet with the rest. Therefore, being content if they themselves at least are safe, they keep at home, since they cannot remedy the folly of others.[5]

"Yet surely, my dear More, to tell you candidly my heart's sentiments, it appears to me that wherever you have private property and all men measure all things by cash values, there it is scarcely possible for a commonwealth to have justice or prosperity—unless you think justice exists where all the best things flow into the hands of the worst citizens or prosperity prevails where all is divided among very few—and even they are not altogether well off, while the rest are downright wretched.

"As a result, when in my heart I ponder on the extremely wise and holy institutions of the Utopians, among whom, with very few laws, affairs are ordered so aptly that virtue has its reward, and yet, with equality of distribution, all men have abundance of all things, and then when I contrast with their policies the many nations elsewhere ever making ordinances and yet never one of them achieving good order—nations where whatever a man has acquired he calls his own private property, but where all these laws daily framed are not enough for a man to secure or to defend or even to distinguish from someone else's the goods which each in turn calls his own, a predicament readily attested by the numberless and ever new and interminable lawsuits—when I consider, I repeat, all these facts, I become more partial to Plato and less surprised at his refusal to make laws for those who rejected that legislation which gave to all an equal share in all goods.

"This wise sage, to be sure, easily foresaw that the one and only road to the general welfare lies in the maintenance of equality in all respects. I have my doubts that the latter could ever be preserved where the individual's possessions are his private

---

4. Hythlodaeus insists that for a philosopher to cross a person in authority will only make the philosopher appear nonsensical and therefore render the ruler less reasonable than he was at first; that is, both philosopher and ruler will appear to be madmen. He cites Mitio, a character in Terence's play *The Brothers,* who declares: "Still, if I inflamed or even fell in with his passionate temper, I should surely give him another madman for company" (1.145–147).

5. Cf. *Republic* 6.496d: "he keeps quiet and minds his own business—as a man in a storm . . . stands aside under a little wall. Seeing others filled with lawlessness, he is content if somehow he himself can live his life here pure of injustice and unholy deeds."

property. When every man aims at absolute ownership of all the property he can get, be there never so great abundance of goods, it is all shared by a handful who leave the rest in poverty. It generally happens that the one class preeminently deserves the lot of the other, for the rich are greedy, unscrupulous, and useless, while the poor are well-behaved, simple, and by their daily industry more beneficial to the common-wealth than to themselves. I am fully persuaded that no just and even distribution of goods can be made and that no happiness can be found in human affairs unless private property is utterly abolished.[6] While it lasts, there will always remain a heavy and in-escapable burden of poverty and misfortunes for by far the greatest and by far the best part of mankind. * * *

"But," I ventured, "I am of the contrary opinion. Life cannot be satisfactory where all things are common. How can there be a sufficient supply of goods when each withdraws himself from the labor of production? For the individual does not have the motive of personal gain and he is rendered slothful by trusting to the industry of others. Moreover, when people are goaded by want and yet the individual cannot legally keep as his own what he has gained, must there not be trouble from continual bloodshed and riot? This holds true especially since the authority of magistrates and respect for their office have been eliminated, for how there can be any place for these among men who are all on the same level I cannot even conceive."

"I do not wonder," he rejoined, "that it looks this way to you, being a person who has no picture at all, or else a false one, of the situation I mean. But you should have been with me in Utopia and personally seen their manners and customs as I did, for I lived there more than five years and would never have wished to leave except to make known that new world. In that case you unabashedly would admit that you had never seen a well-ordered people anywhere but there."

"Yet surely," objected Peter Giles, "it would be hard for you to convince me that a better-ordered people is to be found in that new world than in the one known to us. In the latter I imagine there are equally excellent minds, as well as commonwealths which are older than those in the new world. In these commonwealths long experi-ence has come upon very many advantages for human life—not to mention also the chance discoveries made among us, which no human mind could have devised."

"As for the antiquity of commonwealths," he countered, "you could give a sounder opinion if you had read the historical accounts of that world. If we must believe them, there were cities among them before there were men among us. Fur-thermore, whatever either brains have invented or chance has discovered hitherto could have happened equally in both places. But I hold for certain that, even though we may surpass them in brains, we are far inferior to them in application and industry.

"According to their chronicles, up to the time of our landing they had never heard anything about our activities (they call us the Ultra-equinoctials) except that twelve hundred years ago a ship driven by a tempest was wrecked on the island of Utopia. Some Romans and Egyptians were cast on shore and remained on the island without ever leaving it. Now mark what good advantage their industry took of this one oppor-

6. It was thought that early humans didn't understand that property could be private and belong to one party only. As tribes formed, however, private property was established by markers: boundary lines, signs and emblems, and distinctive styles of manufacture. This moment also saw the institution of a civil society characterized by religion and law. By advocating a state in which there is no private property, Hythlodaeus posits a political and economic situation that his contemporaries would have recognized in limited societies such as monasteries.

tunity. The Roman empire possessed no art capable of any use which they did not either learn from the shipwrecked strangers or discover for themselves after receiving the hints for investigation—so great a gain was it to them that on a single occasion some persons were carried to their shores from ours.

"But if any like fortune has ever driven anyone from their shores to ours, the event is as completely forgotten as future generations will perhaps forget that I had once been there. And, just as they immediately at one meeting appropriated to themselves every good discovery of ours, so I suppose it will be long before we adopt anything that is better arranged with them than with us. This trait, I judge, is the chief reason why, though we are inferior to them neither in brains nor in resources, their commonwealth is more wisely governed and more happily flourishing than ours."

"If so, my dear Raphael," said I, "I beg and beseech you, give us a description of the island. Do not be brief, but set forth in order the terrain, the rivers, the cities, the inhabitants, the traditions, the customs, the laws, and, in fact, everything which you think we should like to know. And you must think we wish to know everything of which we are still ignorant."

"There is nothing," he declared, "I shall be more pleased to do, for I have the facts ready to hand. But the description will take time."

"In that case," I suggested, "let us go in to dine. Afterwards we shall take up as much time as we like."

"Agreed," he replied.

So we went in and dined. We then returned to the same place, sat down on the same bench, and gave orders to the servants that we should not be interrupted. Peter Giles and I urged Raphael to fulfill his promise. As for him, when he saw us intent and eager to listen, after sitting in silent thought for a time, he began his tale as follows.

THE END OF BOOK 1

BOOK 2

The island of the Utopians extends in the center (where it is broadest) for two hundred miles and is not much narrower for the greater part of the island, but toward both ends it begins gradually to taper. These ends form a circle five hundred miles in circumference and so make the island look like a new moon, the horns of which are divided by straits about eleven miles across. The straits then unfold into a wide expanse. As the winds are kept off by the land which everywhere surrounds it, the bay is like a huge lake, smooth rather than rough, and thus converts almost the whole center of the country into a harbor which lets ships cross in every direction to the great convenience of the inhabitants.

The mouth of this bay is rendered perilous here by shallows and there by reefs. Almost in the center of the gap stands one great crag which, being visible, is not dangerous. A tower built on it is occupied by a garrison. The other rocks are hidden and therefore treacherous. The channels are known only to the natives, and so it does not easily happen that any foreigner enters the bay except with a Utopian pilot. In fact, the entrance is hardly safe even for themselves, unless they guide themselves by landmarks on the shore. If these were removed to other positions, they could easily lure an enemy's fleet, however numerous, to destruction.

On the outer side of the island, harbors are many. Everywhere, however, the landing is so well defended by nature or by engineering that a few defenders can prevent strong forces from coming ashore.

As the report goes and as the appearance of the ground shows, the island once was not surrounded by sea. But Utopus, who as conqueror gave the island its name (up to then it had been called Abraxa[7]) and who brought the rude and rustic people to such a perfection of culture and humanity as makes them now superior to almost all other mortals, gained a victory at his very first landing. He then ordered the excavation of fifteen miles on the side where the land was connected with the continent and caused the sea to flow around the land. He set to the task not only the natives but, to prevent them from thinking the labor a disgrace, his own soldiers also. With the work divided among so many hands, the enterprise was finished with incredible speed and struck the neighboring peoples, who at first had derided the project as vain, with wonder and terror at its success.

The island contains fifty-four city-states,[8] all spacious and magnificent, identical in language, traditions, customs, and laws. They are similar also in layout and everywhere, as far as the nature of the ground permits, similar even in appearance. None of them is separated by less than twenty-four miles from the nearest, but none is so isolated that a person cannot go from it to another in a day's journey on foot. From each city three old and experienced citizens meet to discuss the affairs of common interest to the island once a year at Amaurotum, for this city, being in the very center of the country, is situated most conveniently for the representatives of all sections. It is considered the chief as well as the capital city. * * *

THE OFFICIALS

Every thirty families choose annually an official whom in their ancient language they call a syphogrant[9] but in their newer a phylarch. Over ten syphogrants with their families is set a person once called a tranibor but now a protophylarch.[1] The whole body of syphogrants, in number two hundred, having sworn to choose the man whom they judge most useful, by secret balloting appoint a governor, specifically one of the four candidates named to them by the people, for one is selected out of each of the four quarters of the city to be commended to the senate.

The governor holds office for life, unless ousted on suspicion of aiming at a tyranny. The tranibors are elected annually but are not changed without good reason. The other officials all hold their posts for one year.

The tranibors enter into consultation with the governor every other day and sometimes, if need arises, oftener. They take counsel about the commonwealth. If there are any disputes between private persons—there are very few—they settle them without loss of time. They always admit to the senate chamber two syphogrants, and different ones every day. It is provided that nothing concerning the commonwealth be ratified if it has not been discussed in the senate three days before the passing of the decree. To take counsel on matters of common interest outside the senate or the popular assembly is considered a capital offense. The object of these measures, they say, is to prevent it from being easy, by a conspiracy between the governor and the tranibors and by tyrannous oppression of the people, to change the order of the commonwealth. Therefore whatever is considered important is laid before the assembly of the syphogrants who, after informing their groups of families, take counsel together and

---

7. The name for the highest of 365 heavens, according to the Gnostic philosopher Basilides.
8. When More wrote *Utopia,* England consisted of 53

counties and the City of London, its principal urban center.
9. Wise old man.
1. Tranibor: glutton; protophylarch: principal chief.

report their decision to the senate. Sometimes the matter is laid before the council of the whole island.

In addition, the senate has the custom of debating nothing on the same day on which it is first proposed but of putting it off till the next meeting. This is their rule lest anyone, after hastily blurting out the first thought that popped into his head, should afterwards give more thought to defending his opinion than to supporting what is for the good of the commonwealth, and should prefer to jeopardize the public welfare rather than to risk his reputation through a wrongheaded and misplaced shame, fearing he might be thought to have shown too little foresight at the first—though he should have been enough foresighted at the first to speak with prudence rather than with haste!

OCCUPATIONS

Agriculture is the one pursuit which is common to all, both men and women, without exception. They are all instructed in it from childhood, partly by principles taught in school, partly by field trips to the farms closer to the city as if for recreation. Here they do not merely look on, but, as opportunity arises for bodily exercise, they do the actual work.

Besides agriculture (which is, as I said, common to all), each is taught one particular craft as his own. This is generally either wool-working or linen-making or masonry or metal-working or carpentry. There is no other pursuit which occupies any number worth mentioning. As for clothes, these are of one and the same pattern throughout the island and down the centuries, though there is a distinction between the sexes and between the single and married. The garments are comely to the eye, convenient for bodily movement, and fit for wear in heat and cold. Each family, I say, does its own tailoring.

Of the other crafts, one is learned by each person, and not the men only, but the women too. The latter as the weaker sex have the lighter occupations and generally work wool and flax. To the men are committed the remaining more laborious crafts. For the most part, each is brought up in his father's craft, for which most have a natural inclination. But if anyone is attracted to another occupation, he is transferred by adoption to a family pursuing that craft for which he has a liking. Care is taken not only by his father but by the authorities, too, that he will be assigned to a grave and honorable householder. Moreover, if anyone after being thoroughly taught one craft desires another also, the same permission is given. Having acquired both, he practices his choice unless the city has more need of the one than of the other.

The chief and almost the only function of the syphogrants is to manage and provide that no one sit idle, but that each apply himself industriously to his trade, and yet that he be not wearied like a beast of burden with constant toil from early morning till late at night. Such wretchedness is worse than the lot of slaves, and yet it is almost everywhere the life of workingmen—except for the Utopians. The latter divide the day and night into twenty-four equal hours and assign only six to work. There are three before noon, after which they go to dinner. After dinner, when they have rested for two hours in the afternoon, they again give three to work and finish up with supper. Counting one o'clock as the first hour after noon, they go to bed about eight o'clock, and sleep claims eight hours.

The intervals between the hours of work, sleep, and food are left to every man's discretion, not to waste in revelry or idleness, but to devote the time free from work to some other occupation according to taste. These periods are commonly devoted to intellectual pursuits. For it is their custom that public lectures are daily delivered in the hours before daybreak. Attendance is compulsory only for those who have been specially chosen to devote themselves to learning. A great number of all classes, however, both males and females, flock to hear the lectures, some to one and some to another, according to their natural inclination. But if anyone should prefer to devote this time to his trade, as is the case with many minds which do not reach the level for any of the higher intellectual disciplines, he is not hindered; in fact, he is even praised as useful to the commonwealth.

After supper they spend one hour in recreation, in summer in the gardens, in winter in the common halls in which they have their meals. There they either play music or entertain themselves with conversation. Dice and that kind of foolish and ruinous game they are not acquainted with. They do play two games not unlike chess. The first is a battle of numbers in which one number plunders another. The second is a game in which the vices fight a pitched battle with the virtues. In the latter is exhibited very cleverly, to begin with, both the strife of the vices with one another and their concerted opposition to the virtues; then, what vices are opposed to what virtues, by what forces they assail them openly, by what stratagems they attack them indirectly, by what safeguards the virtues check the power of the vices, by what arts they frustrate their designs; and, finally, by what means the one side gains the victory.

But here, lest you be mistaken, there is one point you must examine more closely. Since they devote but six hours to work, you might possibly think the consequence to be some scarcity of necessities. But so far is this from being the case that the aforesaid time is not only enough but more than enough for a supply of all that is requisite for either the necessity or the convenience of living. This phenomenon you too will understand if you consider how large a part of the population in other countries exists without working. First, there are almost all the women, who constitute half the whole; or, where the women are busy, there as a rule the men are snoring in their stead. Besides, how great and how lazy is the crowd of priests and so-called religious! Add to them all the rich, especially the masters of estates, who are commonly termed gentlemen and noblemen. Reckon with them their retainers—I mean, that whole rabble of good-for-nothing swashbucklers. Finally, join in the lusty and sturdy beggars who make some disease an excuse for idleness. You will certainly find far less numerous than you had supposed those whose labor produces all the articles that mortals require for daily use.

Now estimate how few of those who do work are occupied in essential trades. For, in a society where we make money the standard of everything, it is necessary to practice many crafts which are quite vain and superfluous, ministering only to luxury and licentiousness. Suppose the host of those who now toil were distributed over only as few crafts as natural needs and conveniences require. In the great abundance of commodities which must then arise, the prices set on them would be too low for the craftsmen to earn their livelihood by their work. But suppose all those fellows who are now busied with unprofitable crafts, as well as all the lazy and idle throng, any one of whom now consumes as much of the fruits of other men's labors as any two of the workingmen, were all set to work and indeed to useful work. You can easily see how small an allowance of time would be enough and to spare for the production of all that is required by necessity or comfort (or even pleasure, provided it be genuine and natural).

The very experience of Utopia makes the latter clear. In the whole city and its neighborhood, exemption from work is granted to hardly five hundred of the total of men and women whose age and strength make them fit for work. Among them the syphogrants, though legally exempted from work, yet take no advantage of this privilege so that by their example they may the more readily attract the others to work. The same exemption is enjoyed by those whom the people, persuaded by the recommendation of the priests, have given perpetual freedom from labor through the secret vote of the syphogrants so that they may learn thoroughly the various branches of knowledge. But if any of these scholars falsifies the hopes entertained of him, he is reduced to the rank of workingman. On the other hand, not seldom does it happen that a craftsman so industriously employs his spare hours on learning and makes such progress by his diligence that he is relieved of his manual labor and advanced into the class of men of learning. It is out of this company of scholars that they choose ambassadors, priests, tranibors, and finally the governor himself, whom they call in their ancient tongue Barzanes but in their more modern language Ademus.[2]

Nearly all the remaining populace being neither idle nor busied with useless occupations, it is easy to calculate how much good work can be produced in a very few hours. Besides the points mentioned, there is this further convenience that in most of the necessary crafts they do not require as much work as other nations. In the first place the erection or repair of buildings requires the constant labor of so many men elsewhere because what a father has built, his extravagant heir allows gradually to fall into ruin. As a result, what might have been kept up at small cost, his successor is obliged to erect anew at great expense. Further, often even when a house has cost one man a large sum, another is so fastidious that he thinks little of it. When it is neglected and therefore soon becomes dilapidated, he builds a second elsewhere at no less cost. But in the land of the Utopians, now that everything has been settled and the commonwealth established, a new home on a new site is a rare event, for not only do they promptly repair any damage, but they even take care to prevent damage. What is the result? With the minimum of labor, buildings last very long, and masons and carpenters sometimes have scarcely anything to do, except that they are set to hew out timber at home and to square and prepare stone meantime so that, if any work be required, a building may the sooner be erected.

In the matter of clothing, too, see how little toil and labor is needed. First, while at work, they are dressed unpretentiously in leather or hide, which lasts for seven years. When they go out in public, they put on a cape to hide their comparatively rough working clothes. This garment is of one color throughout the island and that the natural color. Consequently not only is much less woolen cloth needed than elsewhere, but what they have is much less expensive. On the other hand, since linen cloth is made with less labor, it is more used. In linen cloth only whiteness, in woolen cloth only cleanliness, is considered. No value is set on fineness of thread. So it comes about that, whereas elsewhere one man is not satisfied with four or five woolen coats of different colors and as many silk shirts, and the more fastidious not even with ten, in Utopia a man is content with a single cape, lasting generally for two years. There is no reason, of course, why he should desire more, for if he had them he would not be better fortified against the cold nor appear better dressed in the least.

Wherefore, seeing that they are all busied with useful trades and are satisfied with fewer products from them, it even happens that when there is an abundance of all

2. Barzanes: "son of Zeus"; Ademus, "peopleless." These names indicate that the governor of Utopia is so impartial in his efforts to rule that he seems to belong to no family, region, or people.

commodities, they sometimes take out a countless number of people to repair whatever public roads are in bad order. Often, too, when there is nothing even of this kind of work to be done, they announce publicly that there will be fewer hours of work. For the authorities do not keep the citizens against their will at superfluous labor since the constitution of their commonwealth looks in the first place to this sole object: that for all the citizens, as far as the public needs permit, as much time as possible should be withdrawn from the service of the body and devoted to the freedom and culture of the mind. It is in the latter that they deem the happiness of life to consist.

SOCIAL RELATIONS

But now, it seems, I must explain the behavior of the citizens toward one another, the nature of their social relations, and the method of distribution of goods. Since the city consists of households, households as a rule are made up of those related by blood. Girls, upon reaching womanhood and upon being settled in marriage, go to their husbands' domiciles. On the other hand, male children and then grandchildren remain in the family and are subject to the oldest parent, unless he has become a dotard with old age. In the latter case the next oldest is put in his place.

But that the city neither be depopulated nor grow beyond measure, provision is made that no household shall have fewer than ten or more than sixteen adults; there are six thousand such households in each city, apart from its surrounding territory. Of children under age, of course, no number can be fixed.[3] This limit is easily observed by transferring those who exceed the number in larger families into those that are under the prescribed number. Whenever all the families of a city reach their full quota, the extra persons help to make up the deficient population of other cities.

And if the population throughout the island should happen to swell above the fixed quotas, they enroll citizens out of every city and, on the mainland nearest them, wherever the natives have much unoccupied and uncultivated land, they found a colony under their own laws. They join with themselves the natives if they are willing to dwell with them. When such a union takes place, the two parties gradually and easily merge and together absorb the same way of life and the same customs, much to the great advantage of both peoples. By their procedures they make the land sufficient for both, which previously seemed poor and barren to the natives. The inhabitants who refuse to live according to their laws, they drive from the territory which they carve out for themselves. If they resist, they wage war against them. They consider it a most just cause for war when a people which does not use its soil but keeps it idle and waste nevertheless forbids the use and possession of it to others who by the rule of nature ought to be maintained by it.

If ever any misfortune so diminishes the number in any of their cities that it cannot be made up out of other parts of the island without bringing other cities below their proper strength (this has happened, they say, only twice in all the ages on account of the raging of a fierce pestilence), they are filled up by citizens returning from colonial territory. They would rather that the colonies should perish than that any of the cities of the island should be enfeebled.

But to return to the dealings of the citizens. The oldest, as I have said, rules the household. Wives wait on their husbands, children on their parents, and generally the younger on their elders.

---

3. In England, women came of age at 18, men at 22.

Every city is divided into four equal districts. In the middle of each quarter is a market of all kinds of commodities. To designated market buildings the products of each family are conveyed. Each kind of goods is arranged separately in storehouses. From the latter any head of a household seeks what he and his require and, without money or any kind of compensation, carries off what he seeks. Why should anything be refused? First, there is a plentiful supply of all things and, secondly, there is no underlying fear that anyone will demand more than he needs. Why should there be any suspicion that someone may demand an excessive amount when he is certain of never being in want? No doubt about it, avarice and greed are aroused in every kind of living creature by the fear of want, but only in man are they motivated by pride alone— pride which counts it a personal glory to excel others by superfluous display of possessions. The latter vice can have no place at all in the Utopian scheme of things. * * *

[UTOPIAN TRAVEL, ETC.]

What opposite ideas and feelings are created by customs so different from those of other people came home to me never more clearly than in the case of the Anemolian ambassadors. They arrived in Amaurotum during my stay there. Because they came to treat of important matters, the three representatives of each city had assembled before their appearance. Now all the ambassadors of neighboring nations, who had previously visited the land, were well acquainted with the manners of the Utopians and knew that they paid no respect to costly clothes but looked with contempt on silk and regarded gold as a badge of disgrace. These persons usually came in the simplest possible dress. But the Anemolians, living farther off and having had fewer dealings with them, since they heard that in Utopia all were dressed alike, and in a homespun fashion at that, felt sure that they did not possess what they made no use of. Being more proud than wise, they determined by the grandeur of their apparel to represent the gods themselves and by their splendid adornment to dazzle the eyes of the poor Utopians.

Consequently the three ambassadors made a grand entry with a suite of a hundred followers, all in parti-colored clothes and most in silk. The ambassadors themselves, being noblemen at home, were arrayed in cloth of gold, with heavy gold necklaces and earrings, with gold rings on their fingers, and with strings of gleaming pearls and gems upon their caps; in fact, they were decked out with all those articles which in Utopia are used to punish slaves, to stigmatize evil-doers, or to amuse children. It was a sight worth seeing to behold their cockiness when they compared their grand clothing with that of the Utopians, who had poured out into the street to see them pass. On the other hand, it was no less delightful to notice how much they were mistaken in their sanguine[4] expectations and how far they were from obtaining the consideration which they had hoped to get. To the eyes of all the Utopians, with the exception of the very few who for a good reason had visited foreign countries, all this gay show appeared disgraceful. They therefore bowed to the lowest of the party as to the masters but took the ambassadors themselves to be slaves because they were wearing gold chains, and passed them over without any deference whatever.

Why, you might have seen also the children who had themselves discarded gems and pearls, when they saw them attached to the caps of the ambassadors, poke and nudge their mothers and say to them:

4. Optimistic.

"Look, mother, that big rascal is still wearing pearls and jewels as if he were yet a little boy!"

But the mother, also in earnest, would say:

"Hush, son, I think it is one of the ambassadors' fools."

Others found fault with the golden chains as useless, being so slender that a slave could easily break them or, again, so loose that at his pleasure he could throw them off and escape anywhere scot-free.

After spending one or more days there, the ambassadors saw an immense quantity of gold held as cheaply and in as great contempt there as in honor among themselves. They saw, too, that more gold and silver were amassed to make the chains and fetters of one runaway slave than had made up the whole array of the three of them. They then were crestfallen and for shame put away all the finery with which they had made themselves haughtily conspicuous, especially when, after familiar talk with the Utopians, they had learned their ways and opinions.

The Utopians wonder that any mortal takes pleasure in the uncertain sparkle of a tiny jewel or precious stone when he can look at a star or even the sun itself. They wonder that anyone can be so mad as to think himself more noble on account of the texture of a finer wool, since, however fine the texture is, a sheep once wore the wool and yet all the time was nothing more than a sheep.

They wonder, too, that gold, which by its very nature is so useless, is now everywhere in the world valued so highly that man himself, through whose agency and for whose use it got this value, is priced much cheaper than gold itself. This is true to such an extent that a blockhead who has no more intelligence than a log and who is as dishonest as he is foolish keeps in bondage many wise men and good men merely for the reason that a great heap of gold coins happens to be his. Yet if some chance or some legal trick (which is as apt as chance to confound high and low) transfers it from this master to the lowest rascal in his entire household, he will surely very soon pass into the service of his former servant—as if he were a mere appendage of and addition to the coins! But much more do they wonder at and abominate the madness of persons who pay almost divine honors to the rich, to whom they neither owe anything nor are obligated in any other respect than that they are rich. Yet they know them to be so mean and miserly that they are more than sure that of all that great pile of cash, as long as the rich men live, not a single penny will ever come their way. * * *

SLAVERY, [ETC.]

Prisoners of war are not enslaved unless captured in wars fought by the Utopians themselves; nor are the sons of slaves,[5] nor anyone who was in slavery when acquired of slaves, nor anyone whom they could acquire from slavery in other countries. Their slaves are either such or such as have been condemned to death elsewhere for some offense. The greater number are of this latter kind. They carry away many of them; sometimes they buy them cheaply; but often they ask for them and get them for nothing. These classes of slaves they keep not only continually at work but also in chains. Their own countrymen are dealt with more harshly, since their conduct is regarded as all the more regrettable and deserving a more severe punishment as an object lesson

---

5. More uses the Latin word *servus*, which means servant, slave, and serf. Most commonly captives in war, slaves were also persons punished for crime, as in Utopia. Voluntary slavery, aside from indentured servitude (for a set term), was rare except in theory; presumably such persons chose to work as slaves in exchange for a subsistence living.

because, having had an excellent rearing to a virtuous life, they still could not be restrained from crime.

There is yet another class of slaves, for sometimes a hard-working and poverty-stricken drudge of another country voluntarily chooses slavery in Utopia. These individuals are well treated and, except that they have a little more work assigned to them as being used to it, are dealt with almost as leniently as citizens. If anyone wishes to depart, which seldom happens, they do not detain him against his will nor send him away empty-handed.

The sick, as I said, are very lovingly cared for, nothing being omitted which may restore them to health, whether in the way of medicine or diet. They console the incurable diseased by sitting and conversing with them and by applying all possible alleviations. But if a disease is not only incurable but also distressing and agonizing without any cessation, then the priests and the public officials exhort the man, since he is now unequal to all life's duties, a burden to himself, and a trouble to others, and is living beyond the time of his death, to make up his mind not to foster the pest and plague any longer nor to hesitate to die now that life is torture to him but, relying on good hope, to free himself from this bitter life as from prison and the rack, or else voluntarily to permit others to free him.[6] In this course he will act wisely, since by death he will put an end not to enjoyment but to torture. Because in doing so he will be obeying the counsels of the priests, who are God's interpreters, it will be a pious and holy action.

Those who have been persuaded by these arguments either starve themselves to death or, being put to sleep, are set free without the sensation of dying. But they do not make away with anyone against his will, nor in such a case do they relax in the least their attendance upon him. They do believe that death counseled by authority is honorific. But if anyone commits suicide without having obtained the approval of priests and senate, they deem him unworthy of either fire or earth and cast his body ignominiously into a marsh without proper burial.

Women do not marry till eighteen, men not till they are four years older. If before marriage a man or woman is convicted of secret intercourse, he or she is severely punished, and they are forbidden to marry altogether unless the governor's pardon remits their guilt. In addition, both father and mother of the family in whose house the offense was committed incur great disgrace as having been neglectful in doing their duties. The reason why they punish this offence so severely is their foreknowledge that, unless persons are carefully restrained from promiscuous intercourse, few will contract the tie of marriage, in which a whole life must be spent with one companion and all the troubles incidental to it must be patiently borne.

In choosing mates, they seriously and strictly espouse a custom which seemed to us very foolish and extremely ridiculous. The woman, whether maiden or widow, is shown naked to the suitor by a worthy and respectable matron, and similarly the suitor is presented naked before the maiden by a discreet man. We laughed at this custom and condemned it as foolish. They, on the other hand, marvelled at the remarkable folly of all other nations. In buying a colt, where there is question of only a little money, persons are so cautious that though it is almost bare they will not buy until they have taken off the saddle and removed all the trappings for fear some sore lies

---

6. Neither suicide nor euthanasia was considered immoral in Greek and Roman society.

concealed under these coverings. Yet in the choice of a wife, an action which will cause either pleasure or disgust to follow them the rest of their lives, they are so careless that, while the rest of her body is covered with clothes, they estimate the value of the whole woman from hardly a single handbreadth of her, only the face being visible, and clasp her to themselves not without great danger of their agreeing ill together if something afterwards gives them offense.

All are not so wise as to regard only the character of the spouse, and even in the marriages of the wise, bodily attractions also are no small enhancement to the virtues of the mind. Certainly such foul deformity may be hidden beneath these coverings that it may quite alienate a man's mind from his wife when bodily separation is no longer lawful. If such a deformity arises by chance after the marriage has been contracted, each person must bear his own fate, but beforehand the laws ought to protect him from being entrapped by guile.

This provision was the more necessary because the Utopians are the only people in those parts of the world who are satisfied with one spouse and because matrimony there is seldom broken except by death, unless it be for adultery or for intolerable offensiveness of character. When husband or wife is thus offended, leave is granted by the senate to take another mate.[7] The other party perpetually lives a life of disgrace as well as of celibacy. But they cannot endure the repudiation of an unwilling wife, who is in no way to blame, because some bodily calamity has befallen her. They judge it cruel that a person should be abandoned when most in need of comfort and that old age, since it both entails disease and is a disease itself, should have only an unreliable and weak fidelity.

It sometimes happens, however, that when a married couple agree insufficiently in their dispositions and both find others with whom they hope to live more agreeably, they separate by mutual consent and contract fresh unions, but not without the sanction of the senate. The latter allows of no divorce until its members and their wives have carefully gone into the case. Even then they do not readily give consent because they know that it is a very great drawback to cementing the affection between husband and wife if they have before them the easy hope of a fresh union.

Violators of the conjugal tie are punished by the strictest form of slavery. If both parties are married, the injured parties, provided they consent, are divorced from their adulterous mates and couple together, or else are allowed to marry whom they like. But if one of the injured parties continues to feel affection for so undeserving a mate, it is not forbidden to have the marriage continue in force on condition that the party is willing to accompany and share the labor of the other who has been condemned to slavery. Now and then it happens that the penance of the one and the dutiful assiduity of the other move the compassion of the governor and win back their liberty. Relapse into the same offense, however, involves the penalty of death.

For all other crimes there is no law prescribing any fixed penalty, but the punishment is assigned by the senate according to the atrocity, or veniality, of the individual crime. Husbands correct their wives, and parents their children, unless the offense is so serious that it is to the advantage of public morality to have it punished openly. Generally the worst offenses are punished by the sentence of slavery since this prospect, they think, is no less formidable to the criminal and more advantageous to

---

7. In England, divorce was granted only on the grounds of adultery. By contrast, the Utopians grant divorce for incompatibility and extend the privilege to the wife as well as the husband. Adultery, however, is punished with slavery.

the state than if they make haste to put the offenders to death and get them out of the way at once. Their labor is more profitable than their death, and their example lasts longer to deter others from like crimes. But if they rebel and kick against this treatment, they are thereupon put to death like untameable beasts that cannot be restrained by prison or chain. If they are patient, however, they are not entirely deprived of all hope. When tamed by long and hard punishment, if they show such repentance as testifies that they are more sorry for their sin than for their punishment, then sometimes by the prerogative of the governor and sometimes by the vote of the people their slavery is either lightened or remitted altogether.

To tempt another to an impure act is no less punishable than the commission of that impure act. In every crime the deliberate and avowed attempt is counted equal to the deed, for they think that failure ought not to benefit one who did everything in his power not to fail.

They are very fond of fools.[8] It is a great disgrace to treat them with insult, but there is no prohibition against deriving pleasure from their foolery. The latter, they think, is of the greatest benefit to the fools themselves. If anyone is so stern and morose that he is not amused with anything they either do or say, they do not entrust him with the care of a fool. They fear that he may not treat him with sufficient indulgence since he would find in him neither use nor even amusement, which is his sole faculty.

To deride a man for a disfigurement or the loss of a limb is counted as base and disfiguring, not to the man who is laughed at but to him who laughs, for foolishly upbraiding a man with something as if it were a fault which he was powerless to avoid. While they consider it a sign of a sluggish and feeble mind not to preserve natural beauty, it is, in their judgment, disgraceful affectation to help it out by cosmetics. Experience itself shows them how no elegance of outward form recommends wives to husbands as much as probity and reverence. Some men are attracted only by a handsome shape, but no man's love is kept permanently except by virtue and obedience.

Not merely do they discourage crime by punishment but they offer honors to invite men to virtue. Hence, to great men who have done conspicuous service to their country they set up in the market place statues to stand as a record of noble exploits and, at the same time, to have the glory of forefathers serve their descendants as a spur and stimulus to virtue.

The man who solicits votes to obtain any office is deprived completely of the hope of holding any office at all. They live together in affection and good will. No official is haughty or formidable. They are called fathers and show that character. Honor is paid them willingly, as it should be, and is not exacted from the reluctant. The governor himself is distinguished from citizens not by a robe or a crown but by the carrying of a handful of grain, just as the mark of the high priest is a wax candle borne before him.

They have very few laws because very few are needed for persons so educated. The chief fault they find with other peoples is that almost innumerable books of laws and commentaries are not sufficient. They themselves think it most unfair that any group of men should be bound by laws which are either too numerous to be read through or too obscure to be understood by anyone.

---

8. In early modern Europe, a "fool" could be a professional jester; usually, he was employed at a royal or noble court and had special license to amuse and even criticize his master.

Moreover, they absolutely banish from their country all lawyers, who cleverly manipulate cases and cunningly argue legal points. They consider it a good thing that every man should plead his own cause and say the same to the judge as he would tell his counsel. Thus there is less ambiguity and the truth is more easily elicited when a man, uncoached in deception by a lawyer, conducts his own case and the judge skillfully weighs each statement and helps untutored minds to defeat the false accusations of the crafty. To secure these advantages in other countries is difficult, owing to the immense mass of extremely complicated laws. But with the Utopians each man is expert in law. First, they have, as I said, very few laws and, secondly, they regard the most obvious interpretation of the law as the most fair interpretation.

* * *

Now I have described to you, as exactly as I could, the structure of that commonwealth which I judge not merely the best but the only one which can rightly claim the name of a commonwealth. Outside Utopia, to be sure, men talk freely of the public welfare—but look after their private interests only. In Utopia, where nothing is private, they seriously concern themselves with public affairs. Assuredly in both cases they act reasonably. For, outside Utopia, how many are there who do not realize that, unless they make some separate provision for themselves, however flourishing the commonwealth, they will themselves starve? For this reason, necessity compels them to hold that they must take account of themselves rather than of the people, that is, of others.

On the other hand, in Utopia, where everything belongs to everybody, no one doubts, provided only that the public granaries are well filled, that the individual will lack nothing for his private use. The reason is that the distribution of goods is not niggardly. In Utopia there is no poor man and no beggar. Though no man has anything, yet all are rich.

For what can be greater riches for a man than to live with a joyful and peaceful mind, free of all worries—not troubled about his food or harassed by the querulous demands of his wife or fearing poverty for his son or worrying about his daughter's dowry, but feeling secure about the livelihood and happiness of himself and his family: wife, sons, grandsons, great-grandsons, great-great-grandsons, and all the long line of their descendants that gentlefolk anticipate? Then take into account the fact that there is no less provision for those who are now helpless but once worked than for those who are still working.

At this point I should like anyone to be so bold as to compare this fairness with the so-called justice prevalent in other nations, among which, upon my soul, I cannot discover the slightest trace of justice and fairness. What brand of justice is it that any nobleman whatsoever or goldsmith-banker or moneylender or, in fact, anyone else from among those who either do no work at all or whose work is of a kind not very essential to the commonwealth, should attain a life of luxury and grandeur on the basis of his idleness or his nonessential work? In the meantime, the common laborer, the carter, the carpenter, and the farmer perform work so hard and continuous that beasts of burden could scarcely endure it and work so essential that no commonwealth could last even one year without it. Yet they earn such scanty fare and lead such a miserable life that the condition of beasts of burden might seem far preferable. The latter do not have to work so incessantly nor is their food much worse (in fact, sweeter to their taste) nor do they entertain any fear for the future. The workmen, on the other hand, not only have to toil and suffer without return or profit in the present but agonize over the thought of an indigent old age. Their daily wage is too scanty to suffice even for the day: much less is there an excess and surplus that daily can be laid by for their needs in old age.

Now is not this an unjust and ungrateful commonwealth? It lavishes great rewards on so-called gentlefolk and banking goldsmiths and the rest of that kind, who are either idle or mere parasites and purveyors of empty pleasures. On the contrary, it makes no benevolent provision for farmers, colliers, common laborers, carters, and carpenters without whom there would be no commonwealth at all. After it has misused the labor of their prime and after they are weighed down with age and disease and are in utter want, it forgets all their sleepless nights and all the great benefits received at their hands and most ungratefully requites them with a most miserable death.

What is worse, the rich every day extort a part of their daily allowance from the poor not only by private fraud but by public law. Even before they did so it seemed unjust that persons deserving best of the commonwealth should have the worst return. Now they have further distorted and debased the right and, finally, by making laws, have palmed it off as justice. Consequently, when I consider and turn over in my mind the state of all commonwealths flourishing anywhere today, so help me God, I can see nothing else than a kind of conspiracy of the rich, who are aiming at their own interests under the name and title of the commonwealth.[9] They invent and devise all ways and means by which, first, they may keep without fear of loss all that they have amassed by evil practices and, secondly, they may then purchase as cheaply as possible and abuse the toil and labor of all the poor. These devices become law as soon as the rich have once decreed their observance in the name of the public—that is, of the poor also!

Yet when these evil men with insatiable greed have divided up among themselves all the goods which would have been enough for all the people, how far they are from the happiness of the Utopian commonwealth! In Utopia all greed for money was entirely removed with the use of money. What a mass of troubles was then cut away! What a crop of crimes was then pulled up by the roots! Who does not know that fraud, theft, rapine, quarrels, disorders, brawls, seditions, murders, treasons, poisonings, which are avenged rather than restrained by daily executions, die out with the destruction of money? Who does not know that fear, anxiety, worries, toils, and sleepless nights will also perish at the same time as money? What is more, poverty, which alone money seemed to make poor, forthwith would itself dwindle and disappear if money were entirely done away with everywhere.

To make this assertion clearer, consider in your thoughts some barren and unfruitful year in which many thousands of men have been carried off by famine. I emphatically contend that at the end of that scarcity, if rich men's granaries had been searched, as much grain could have been found as, if it had been divided among the people killed off by starvation and disease, would have prevented anyone from feeling that meager return from soil and climate. So easily might men get the necessities of life if that blessed money, supposedly a grand invention to ease access to those necessities, was not in fact the only barrier to our getting what we need.

9. Hythlodaeus condemns practices associated with the accumulation of wealth as capital and the corresponding exploitation of workers in the interest of increasing capital. This goal is promoted by various legal "devices," particularly involving estates, that preserve capital within the upper ranks of society. But capital cannot be accumulated in a barter economy, where goods are exchanged for goods rather than for money. Hence Hythlodaeus eliminates money as a way of preventing the formation of capital.

Even the rich, I doubt not, have such feelings. They are not unaware that it would be a much better state of affairs to lack no necessity than to have abundance of superfluities—to be snatched from such numerous troubles rather than to be hemmed in by great riches. Nor does it occur to me to doubt that a man's regard for his own interests or the authority of Christ our Savior—who in His wisdom could not fail to know what was best and who in His goodness would not fail to counsel what He knew to be best—would long ago have brought the whole world to adopt the laws of the Utopian commonwealth, had not one single monster, the chief and progenitor of all plagues, striven against it—I mean, Pride.

Pride measures prosperity not by her own advantages but by others' disadvantages. Pride would not consent to be made even a goddess if no poor wretches were left for her to domineer over and scoff at, if her good fortune might not dazzle by comparison with their miseries, if the display of her riches did not torment and intensify their poverty. This serpent from hell entwines itself around the hearts of men and acts like the suckfish in preventing and hindering them from entering on a better way of life.

Pride is too deeply fixed in men to be easily plucked out. For this reason, the fact that this form of a commonwealth—which I should gladly desire for all—has been the good fortune of the Utopians at least, fills me with joy. They have adopted such institutions of life as have laid the foundations of the commonwealth not only most happily, but also to last forever, as far as human prescience can forecast. At home they have extirpated the roots of ambition and factionalism, along with all the other vices. Hence there is no danger of trouble from domestic discord, which has been the only cause of ruin to the well-established prosperity of many cities. As long as harmony is preserved at home and its institutions are in a healthy state, not all the envy of neighboring rulers, though it has rather often attempted it and has always been repelled, can avail to shatter or to shake that nation.

When Raphael had finished his story, many things came to my mind which seemed very absurdly established in the customs and laws of the people described—not only in their method of waging war, their ceremonies and religion, as well as their other institutions, but most of all in that feature which is the principal foundation of their whole structure. I mean their common life and subsistence—without any exchange of money. This latter alone utterly overthrows all the nobility, magnificence, splendor, and majesty which are, in the estimation of the common people, the true glories and ornaments of the commonwealth.

I knew, however, that he was wearied with his tale, and I was not quite certain that he could brook any opposition to his views, particularly when I recalled his censure of others on account of their fear that they might not appear to be wise enough, unless they found some fault to criticize in other men's discoveries. I therefore praised their way of life and his speech and, taking him by the hand, led him in to supper. I first said, nevertheless, that there would be another chance to think about these matters more deeply and to talk them over with him more fully. If only this were some day possible!

Meanwhile, though in other respects he is a man of the most undoubted learning as well as of the greatest knowledge of human affairs, I cannot agree with all that he said. But I readily admit that there are very many features in the Utopian commonwealth which it is easier for me to wish for in our countries than to have any hope of seeing realized.

END OF BOOK 2

══╪ PERSPECTIVES ╪══
Literature of Religious Crisis

Religion defined the early modern world as sharply as it had defined the medieval one, with one enormous difference: Western Europeans could no longer speak of subscribing to the same faith. Despite the schism that had produced two popes for several decades after 1377, those European peoples that were not under the sway of the patriarch of Constantinople called themselves Roman Catholic. But at the very moment that Catholic Europe was trying to purify itself of Jews—England and Spain had expelled their Jewish communities by the late fifteenth century, and the first ghetto was created in Venice in 1516—the outrage of a German monk was tearing a supposedly unified Christianity apart. When Pope Leo X decided to finance the new basilica of Saint Peter's by selling a record number of indulgences (the absolution of sins for a price), Martin Luther objected strenuously and publicly, opening the door not only to his own excommunication but to the once-unimaginable break between Rome and thousands of disaffected Catholics. Attracted by Luther's insistence on liberating the common man (and to a lesser extent, woman) from the trappings of Catholic dogma, hierarchy, and ritual, hordes of people left the Church, literally overnight.

Clearly hostility to papal corruption and control had been festering for decades, even centuries. And concerned individuals within the Church, such as Erasmus, had been working and would continue to work for reform. But fueled by nationalist sentiment and readily available printing presses, Protestantism gained footholds from Scotland to Bohemia, cutting across social classes, and prompting reassessments of traditional gender roles. The Catholic hierarchy, initially too stunned to act, set in official motion a Counter-Reformation—or more generously, a Catholic Reformation—to try to establish a common ground for reconciliation. But it was too late for compromise. Protestantism was hardly a single, monolithic enemy. Already by 1545, when the first Council of Trent met, numerous sects of Anabaptists ("rebaptizers"), far more radical than Luther, had sprung up in Amsterdam and northern Germany, while John Calvin had set up a theocracy in Geneva. Blood in the name of religious difference had already been shed in Paris; Catholics under Edward of England and Protestants under Mary would soon lose their lives. The Church did its part by reopening the Roman Inquisition, dormant since the beginning of the century, to try potential heretics against the faith. Ignatius Loyola, a knight inspired by chivalric texts such as *Amadis de Gaul* (a book that would later inspire Don Quixote), founded the new religious order of the Jesuits to carry Catholicism across the ocean, as well as to educate priests and students against the heresies of Protestantism at home. Ironically, as Islam was gaining renewed force under the Ottoman emperor Suleyman I, the universal Christian empire was falling apart—as the emperor Charles V recognized when, in 1556, he abdicated his crown to retire to a quiet end near a monastery in Spain.

For all their disputatious variety, almost all of the reformers had one thing in common: they availed themselves of the pen. Their reliance on writing is testimony to both the rise of literacy in early modern Europe and the lasting force of a Renaissance with which the Reformation is often said to have been in conflict. So it was, to an extent, particularly as regards the elitism and secular character with which the Renaissance is often associated. Yet the reformers shared the Renaissance humanists' faith in the power of the word. John Calvin was trained in rhetoric, Milton in classical epic; the Jesuits incorporated theater into their education, and Johann Reuchlin's Hebrew grammar was important for Luther's commentaries. All attest to a firm belief in the power of the word to effect what the consummate Renaissance man Erasmus said of Scripture: "it desires nothing but conversion, ardor, and improvement." Without the Renaissance's embrace of antiquity, including the early centuries of Christianity, and its corresponding elevation of the individual, inquiring mind, the Reformation probably could not have happened. But with the Reformation, the Renaissance was undeniably altered. By the end of the bloody Thirty Years War in 1648—fundamentally a war of religion, and one which dragged into battle virtually every country in western and central Europe—the map of the world had changed in ways which Petrarch, three centuries earlier, could scarcely have imagined.

The texts that follow demonstrate the manifold dimensions of the Reformation in both its Catholic and Protestant variants, suggesting the need to go beyond simple black-and-white distinctions such as associating Catholicism with a retrograde medievalism and Protestantism with introspective forward-thinking. For one thing, the genial and committed Catholic Desiderius Erasmus was one of the most outspoken advocates of reform in the early sixteenth century; "Erasmus laid the egg that Luther hatched" went a popular saying. For another, as Thomas Müntzer's vociferous debate with Luther from the 1520s shows, there was more than a single version of Protestantism, even in its earliest years. Catholicism too had many faces which the at times overly reactive Church couldn't suppress, despite sporadic attempts of the Inquisition to crush suspected heresies. The poor miller Menocchio died at the stake, but Saint John of the Cross's disquieting poetry and Saint Teresa of Avila's passionate mysticism and pleas for change within the religious orders circumvented institutional wariness. As their names reveal, these two Spanish writers were eventually canonized by an institution that in the course of missions overseas and humanist education at home showed itself to be capable of surprising capaciousness.

✦ ✠ ✦

Desiderius Erasmus
c. 1466–1536

Few writers were as central to the turbulences of early modern Europe as Erasmus. Scholar, erstwhile monk, polemicist, and gadfly, this illegitimate child of a Dutch priest had a publishing agenda surpassing that of all his contemporaries, though this was an age when many men rushed everything into print. Nothing escaped his attention: neither the most homespun proverb, such as "Twice-cooked cabbage is death" (he compiled a mammoth edition of adages) nor the most sublime prose (he lovingly translated and extensively commented on the New Testament). Equally critical of the Catholic Church and the burgeoning Protestant Reformation, Erasmus nonetheless hoped that the religious crises of his time could be healed. He worked to create an international society of learned and charitable men (despite his affection for Thomas More's highly learned daughters, he saw no real public role for women), but he eventually became disillusioned with the reform he had helped set in motion. As he wrote late in life, "now the evil is beyond remedy, and meanwhile the rulers of the world make endless war on each other."

Erasmus composed his dialogue *Praise of Folly* or *Encomium Moriae* in Latin 1509, a "little diversion" while Erasmus was recovering from a kidney ailment at More's country home. As its Latin title punningly suggests, it is both a praise of folly ("moria" in Greek) and an encomium of Thomas More—like Erasmus, a "wise fool," witty, ironic, immensely learned in pagan antiquity and the early Church Fathers. Both More's masterpiece, *Utopia,* and *Praise of Folly* admirably display their authors' deep learning, and they are equally infused with an understanding of human foibles and the wisdom of accommodating, even learning to love, those foibles in a true Christian community. The presence of unreliable narrators—the eccentric traveler Hythlodaeus in More, the scatter-brained Folly in Erasmus—makes both works intriguing puzzles, their authors hidden cunningly behind contradictions and ambiguities.

Erasmus's playfulness couldn't fully mask his incisive critique of a corrupt Roman church he had visited earlier in the decade, nor his impatience with the dry scholastic learning he had been subjected to at the University of Louvain. Those who failed to see in Folly a refreshing portrait of "the madness of fools for Christ" vociferously attacked Erasmus. He replied in kind, as with his elegant but biting reproach to one narrow-minded Martin Dorp of the Sorbonne: "You can see that everywhere I've always been careful to avoid anything which could be at all offensive. But those whose ears are open only to propositions, conclusions and corollaries pay no heed to that." Erasmus claimed that he profoundly disliked assertions—this in response to the always-assertive Luther—and he profoundly objected to Dorp's quickness to condemn rather than engage in animated dialogue over the world's problems. In many ways, it was precisely such intolerance, on the sides of Catholics and Protestants alike, that led to the demise of the vibrant Christian humanism Erasmus spent his life championing—and the death of the wise fool More.

from Praise of Folly[1]

[FOLLY IS RESPONSIBLE FOR CIVILIZATION][2]

If you look at history you'll find that no state has been so plagued by its rulers as when power has fallen into the hands of some dabbler in philosophy or literary addict. The two Catos are sufficient proof of this, I think, when one of them was a disturber of the peace of the republic with his crazy denunciations, and the other showed his wisdom by defending the liberty of the Roman people, but in doing so completely destroyed it. Then there are the families of Brutus and Cassius, the Gracchi brothers and even Cicero himself, who was just as much a scourge to the republic of Rome as Demosthenes was to Athens.[3] As for Marcus Aurelius, we have to admit that he was a good emperor, but I could still deny him this distinction on the grounds that he was unpopular and disliked amongst his subjects for the very reason that he was so much of a philosopher. And even admitted that he was good, he undoubtedly did more harm to Rome by leaving such a son as his than he ever benefited it by his administration. In fact this type of man who is devoted to the study of wisdom is always most unlucky in everything, and particularly when it comes to procreating children; I imagine this is because Nature wants to ensure that the evil of wisdom shall not spread further throughout mankind. So it's well known that Cicero had a degenerate son, and the children of the great sage Socrates himself took after their mother rather than their father, as someone put it rather well: meaning, they were fools.[4]

One could put up with it somehow if these folk would play 'the ass with the lyre'[5] only in public affairs, and not be so utterly incompetent in every single thing in life. Ask a wise man to dinner and he'll upset everyone by his gloomy silence or tiresome questions. Invite him to a dance and you'll have a camel prancing about. Haul him off to a public entertainment and his face will be enough to spoil the people's enjoyment. He'll have to leave the theatre like Cato the Wise when he couldn't lay aside his scowl.[6] If he joins in a conversation, all of a sudden there's the wolf in the fable. If

1. Translated from the Latin by Betty Radice.
2. *Praise of Folly* opens with the garrulous Folly justifying herself as "the true bestower of 'good things,'" and she launches into a discussion of her birthplace, a list of her followers, and the distinct advantages she offers both to gods and to men, concluding that nothing is more important than self-love. She then proceeds to an attack on philosophers, of which the first excerpt is a part.
3. The two Catos, Cato the Censor and Cato of Utica, were Romans who bitterly denounced, respectively, the loose morals of republican Rome and the rise of Julius Caesar. Brutus, Cassius, and Cicero were likewise enemies of Caesar, while the Gracchi were tribunes in Rome in the 2nd century B.C.E. who tried to push through major

administrative reforms to aid the poor and extend Roman citizenship to Italians. Marcus Aurelius was emperor from 161–180 C.E., whose intimate notebooks, the *Meditations,* are much influenced by Stoic philosophy.
4. Historians agree that Marcus Aurelius's only mistake was passing his kingdom on to his son, Commodus, who restricted many of the Senate's powers and spent much of his time both watching and fighting gladiators. Cicero's son had a reputation as a profligate.
5. As Erasmus says in his collection of *Adages:* "An ass [listening] to the lyre" refers to "people who lack judgment through their ignorance."
6. Cato the Wise, or Cato the Censor, was known for his frowning.

there's anything to be bought or an arrangement to be made, in fact if any one of those things has to be done without which our daily life can't be carried on, you'll call your wise man a blockhead, not a man. It's quite impossible for him to be of any use to himself, his country or his family because he's ignorant of ordinary matters and far removed from any normal way of thinking and current practice. And so inevitably he is also disliked, doubtless because of the vast discrepancy between ordinary life and minds like his. For nothing happens in this world which isn't full of folly, performed by fools amongst fools. If any individual wants to make a stand against the rest, I'd recommend him to take his lead from Timon and move off to some wilderness where he can enjoy his own wisdom in solitude.[7]

But to return to my subject. Take those wild men sprung from rocks and trees— what power brought them together into a civilized society if not flattery? This is all that's meant by the lyre of Amphion and Orpheus.[8] Who was it which recalled the Roman mob to harmony in the state when it was plotting violence—a philosopher's speech? Not a bit of it. It was a silly, childish fable made up about the belly and the other parts of the body. A similar sort of story told by Themistocles about a fox and a hedgehog had the same effect.[9] No sage's speech could ever have achieved so much as that fictitious white hind of Sertorius or the ridiculous anecdote invented about the famous Spartan with his two dogs, and the one about pulling the hairs out of a horse's tail, to say nothing of Minos and Numa who both ruled the foolish mob by means of fantastic trumped-up tales.[1] It's absurdities like these that sway the mighty, powerful monster which is the common people.

But what society ever took its laws from Plato or Aristotle or the teachings of Socrates? Again, what made the house of Decius choose to dedicate their lives to the gods of the underworld and brought Quintus Curtius to the abyss if not the vain hope of fame, the sweetest of all sirens, though damned by your wise men to a remarkable degree?[2] Nothing is so foolish, they say, as for a man to stand for office and woo the crowd to win its vote, buy its support with presents, court the applause of all those fools and feel self-satisfied when they cry their approval, and then in his hour of triumph to be carried round like an effigy for the public to stare at, and end up cast in bronze to stand in the market-place. Then there are changes of names and surnames, divine honours awarded to a nobody, official ceremonies devised, to raise even the most criminal of tyrants to the level of the gods. All this is utterly foolish, and more than one Democritus is needed for these absurdities, everyone agrees.[3] Yet from this source spring the deeds of valiant heroes to be lauded to the skies in the writings of so many eloquent men. This same folly creates societies and maintains empires, official-

---

7. Timon of Athens was the original misanthrope, who left his city to live in a cave.

8. The legendary musician Amphion is said to have built the walls of Thebes with the power of his lyre; Orpheus civilized beasts with his music.

9. The fable of the belly is told by Menenius Agrippa to calm the Roman mobs in the 5th century B.C.E.; the story is in Livy's *History of Rome*. Themistocles is said by Plutarch to have dissuaded the Athenians from refusing to pay taxes with the story of a fox and a hedgehog.

1. Folly alludes to a series of myths of divine inspiration told by rulers trying to calm restless subjects. Minos of Crete and Numa, King of Rome after Romulus, boasted divine inspiration, while Sertorious, in charge of organizing an army to march against Rome in the 1st century

B.C.E., claimed that the white hind was the symbol of his powers.

2. The Roman "house of Decius" had at least three generations of military men, all of whom died in Rome's service. The allusion to the underworld concerns the original Publius Decius, said to have committed himself and his enemy forces to the Underworld by riding at breakneck speed into the ranks of the Latins. Livy tells of a Quintus Curtius who sought fame by throwing himself and his horse into an "abyss" that opened up in the midst of Rome's forum.

3. Democritus of Thrace was known as the "laughing philosopher" because of his belief that the true goal of life was happiness.

dom, religion, law courts and councils—in fact the whole of human life is nothing but a sport of folly.

Now let us turn to the arts. What else has fired men's natural talents to devise and hand on to posterity so many disciplines which they think remarkable if not their thirst for fame? With all their toil and sweat and sleepless nights men have thought to gain some sort of reputation, emptiest of acquisitions, and thereby showed themselves complete fools. Meanwhile it's Folly to whom you owe so many of life's major blessings, and the nicest thing of all is that you have someone else's madness to thank for your enjoyment.

Well, now I've proved that I must be given credit for courage and industry, shall I go on to lay claim to prudence?[4] You might as well mix fire and water, I can hear someone say. But here again I believe I can succeed, if you'll continue to give me your ears and attention as before. First of all, if prudence develops through experience, does the honour of possessing a claim to it rightly belong to the wise man who attempts nothing, partly through his sense of propriety, partly through his natural timidity, or to the fool who isn't deterred from anything either by the propriety which he hasn't got or the dangers which he doesn't think about? The wise man seeks refuge in his books of antiquity and learns from them the pure subtleties of what the ancients say. The fool tries everything, meets his dangers at first hand, and thereby acquires what I'm sure is genuine prudence. That is something Homer appears to have seen, despite his blindness, when he says 'even the fool is wise after the event'.[5] For the two main obstacles to learning by experience are a sense of propriety which clouds the judgement and fear which advises against an undertaking once danger is apparent. Folly offers a splendid liberation from both of them. Few mortals realize how many other advantages follow from being free from scruples and ready to venture anything.

But if people prefer the sort of prudence which comes from forming opinions on life, please hear how far those who pride themselves on that account really are from having it. In the first place, it's well known that all human affairs are like the figures of Silenus described by Alcibiades and have two completely opposite faces, so that what is death at first sight, as they say, is life if you look within, and vice versa, life is death.[6] The same applies to beauty and ugliness, riches and poverty, obscurity and fame, learning and ignorance, strength and weakness, the noble and the base-born, happy and sad, good and bad fortune, friend and foe, healthy and harmful—in fact you'll find everything suddenly reversed if you open the Silenus. Maybe some of you will think I've expressed this too philosophically; well, I'll speak bluntly, as the saying goes, to make myself clear. We all agree a king is rich and powerful, but if he lacks all spiritual goods and can never be satisfied, then he's surely the poorest of men. And if he's addicted to a large number of vices he's no more than a cheap slave. We could philosophize about others in the same way, but one example will suffice.

What's the point of this, someone will say. Hear how we'll develop the argument. If anyone tries to take the masks off the actors when they're playing a scene on the stage and show their true natural faces to the audience, he'll certainly spoil the whole play and deserve to be stoned and thrown out of the theatre for a maniac.[7] For a

---

4. Prudence was one of the virtues most valued by Erasmus and other humanists. She was often represented as a woman with two faces, one to look ahead, the other behind.
5. From the *Iliad* 17.32, said by Menelaos to a Trojan who dares him to fight.

6. In Plato's *Symposium*, Alcibiades compares the ugly Socrates to a Silenus, a small distorted image that could be opened up to reveal its inner divinity and beauty.
7. Such an event will actually happen in Book 2 of *Don Quixote* [page 532].

new situation will suddenly arise in which a woman on the stage turns into a man, a youth is now old, and the king of a moment ago is suddenly Dama, the slave, while a god is shown up as a common little man. To destroy the illusion is to ruin the whole play, for it's really the illusion and make-up which hold the audience's eye. Now, what else is the whole life of man but a sort of play? Actors come on wearing their different masks and all play their parts until the producer orders them off the stage, and he can often tell the same man to appear in different costume, so that now he plays a king in purple and now a humble slave in rags. It's all a sort of pretence, but it's the only way to act out this farce.

At this point let us suppose some wise man dropped from heaven confronts me and insists that the man whom all look up to as god and master is not even human, as he is ruled by his passions, like an animal, and is no more than the lowest slave for serving so many evil masters of his own accord. Or again, he might tell someone else who is mourning his father to laugh because the dead man is only just beginning to live, seeing that this life of ours is nothing but a sort of death. Another man who boasts of his ancestry he might call low-born and bastard because he is so far removed from virtue, which is the sole source of nobility. If he had the same sort of thing to say about everyone else, what would happen? We should all think him a crazy madman. Nothing is so foolish as mistimed wisdom, and nothing less sensible than misplaced sense. A man's conduct is misplaced if he doesn't adapt himself to things as they are, has no eye for the main chance, won't even remember that convivial maxim 'Drink or depart,' and asks for the play to stop being a play. On the other hand, it's a true sign of prudence not to want wisdom which extends beyond your share as an ordinary mortal, to be willing to overlook things along with the rest of the world and wear your illusions with a good grace. People say that this is really a sign of folly, and I'm not setting out to deny it—so long as they'll admit on their side that this is the way to play the comedy of life.

* * *

[FOLLY AND SELF-LOVE][8]

By far the most enjoyable form of insanity is that which makes many people boast about any talent in their household as if it were their own. An example of this is the doubly-fortunate rich man in Seneca. He kept servants at hand to whisper the names whenever he had a tale to tell, and though he was so frail he was hardly alive, he was quite ready to take up a challenge of fisticuffs, secure in the knowledge that he had plenty of stout fellows at home.[9] As for those who teach and practise the arts—what shall I say about them? They all have their special form of Self-love, and you're more likely to find one who'll give up his family plot of land than one who'll yield an inch where his ability is in question. This is especially true of actors, singers, orators and poets; the more ignorant one of them is, the more immoderate his self-satisfaction, boastfulness and conceit. They can always find like to meet their like, in fact anything

8. In the intervening pages, Folly has argued against the "philosophers" who insist that "it can only be misery to live in folly, illusion, deception, and ignorance. But it isn't—it's human." She goes on to prove how happy fools really are since they readily acknowledge what is, after all, "the common lot of mankind." The last group of fools she identifies before proceeding to this section are those Christians whose ordinary life "everywhere abounds" in

"varieties of silliness"; her cataloguing of Catholics who believe in the power of relics and buy indulgences both expresses Erasmus's severe criticisms of church practices and anticipates his later argument that the truest fools are those who are fools for Christ.
9. Seneca discusses the foolish rich man in his *Letters* 27.5.

wins more admiration the sillier it is. The worst always pleases the most people, since the majority of men, as I said before, are prone to folly. Besides, if an artist is all the more pleased with himself and the more generally admired the less skilled he is, why should he choose to undergo a proper course of instruction? It'll cost him a lot in the first place, then make him more nervous and self-conscious, and he'll end up pleasing far fewer people.

Now, just as Nature has implanted his personal self-love in each individual person, I can see she has put a sort of communal variety in every nation and city. Consequently the British think they have a monopoly, amongst other things, of good looks, musical talent and fine food. The Scots pride themselves on their nobility and the distinction of their royal connexions as much as on their subtlety in dialectic. The French lay claim to polite manners, the Parisians demand special recognition for their theological acumen which they think exceeds nearly everyone else's.[1] The Italians usurp culture and eloquence, and hence they're all happy congratulating themselves on being the only civilized race of men. In this kind of happiness the Romans take first place, still blissfully dreaming of the past glories of Rome, while the Venetians have their own opinion of their noble descent to keep them happy. Meanwhile the Greeks, as originators of the arts, imagine they should still share the honours of the illustrious heroes of their past; while the Turks and all the real barbarian riff-raff actually demand recognition for their religion and pour scorn on Christians for their superstition. The Jews go even further, still faithfully awaiting their Messiah and clinging fast to their Moses to this very day. The Spaniards admit no rival in the glories of war, while the Germans boast of their height and their knowledge of the magic arts.

I'm sure you can see without my going into further details how much pleasure Self-love brings to men, both individual and collective, and her sister Flattery does almost as much. Philautia is only flattery of yourself, and if you do the same to someone else it becomes 'Kolakia.'[2] Fawning on people has fallen into disrepute today, but only amongst those who are less concerned with facts than the names applied to them. They think it's incompatible with sincerity, but examples from dumb animals could prove them quite wrong. No animal fawns so much as a dog, and none is so faithful. Nothing has such winning ways as a squirrel, and where could you find a greater friend to man? Unless perhaps you think savage lions, fierce tigers or dangerous leopards contribute more to the life of man. There *is* a kind of flattery which is wholly noxious, and a good many treacherous persons use it in mockery in order to destroy their unfortunate victims. But the form I use stems from a sort of ingenuous goodness of heart and is far nearer being a virtue than the critical asperity which is its opposite: what Horace calls a harsh and disagreeable surliness.[3] Mine raises downcast spirits, comforts the sad, rouses the apathetic, stirs up the stolid, cheers the sick, restrains the headstrong, brings lovers together and keeps them united. It attracts children to pursue the study of letters, makes old men happy, and offers advice and counsel to princes in the form of praise which doesn't give offence. In short, it makes everyone

---

1. This cataloguing of the foibles of national identity was a common theme in works of the period. Erasmus gets a special dig in at Paris because of the stature of its universities, at one time the avant-garde of European intellectual life, but by the 16th century known for their stubborn resistance to reform and the humanistic principles that exemplified Erasmus's own scholarly life.
2. Philautia means "self-love," or as Erasmus explains in the *Adages,* "Horace paraphrases it neatly: 'Blind love of self.'" Earlier in *Praise of Folly,* Erasmus personifies "Kolakia" (Flattery) as "the one clapping her hands with laughter in her eyes."
3. From Horace's *Epistles* 1.18, in which he is urging his friend Lollius to seek virtue as a mean "between vices, remote from both extremes."

more agreeable and likeable to himself, and this is the main ingredient in happiness. What shows such willingness to please as the way mules scratch each other? For the moment I'll say nothing about the large part flattery plays in your celebrated eloquence, a larger one in medicine and its largest in poetry, but will sum up by saying that it is what sweetens and gives savour to every human relationship.

But it's sad, people say, to be deceived. Not at all, it's far sadder *not* to be deceived. They're quite wrong if they think man's happiness depends on actual facts; it depends on his opinions. For human affairs are so complex and obscure that nothing can be known of them for certain, as has been rightly stated by my Academicians, the least assuming of the philosophers.[4] Alternatively, if anything can be known, more often than not it is something which interferes with the pleasure of life. Finally, man's mind is so formed that it is far more susceptible to falsehood than to truth. If anyone wants an immediate clear example of this he has only to go to church at sermon time, where everyone is asleep or yawning or feeling queasy whenever some serious argument is expounded, but if the preacher starts to rant (I beg your pardon, I mean orate) on some old wives' tale as they often do, his audience sits up and takes notice, openmouthed. And again, if there's some legendary saint somewhat celebrated in fable (you can put George or Christopher or Barbara in that category if you need an example)[5] you'll see that he receives far more devout attention than Peter or Paul or even Christ himself. But this is not the point for the moment.

Now this gain in happiness costs very little, whereas real facts often take a lot of trouble to acquire, even when they are quite unimportant, like grammar. An opinion, on the other hand, is very easily formed, and it is equally conducive to happiness, or even more so. Just suppose that a man is eating rotten salt fish, and they taste like ambrosia to him though another man can't stand the stink; does that affect his happiness? Whereas if the taste of sturgeon makes someone sick, what can it add to the blessings of life? If anyone has a particularly ugly wife who has the power to rival Venus in her husband's eyes, isn't it just the same as if she were genuinely beautiful? The possessor of a dreadful daub in red and yellow paint who gazes at it in admiration, convinced that it is a painting by Apelles or Zeuxis,[6] would surely be happier than someone who has paid a high price for a genuine work by one of these artists but perhaps gets less pleasure from looking at it. I know someone of my name who made his new bride a present of some jewels which were copies, and as he had a ready tongue for a joke, persuaded her that they were not only real and genuine but also of unique and incalculable value.[7] Now, if the young woman was just as happy feasting her eyes and thoughts on coloured glass, what did it matter to her that she was keeping such trinkets hidden carefully away in her room as if they were some rare treasure? Meanwhile her husband saved expense, enjoyed his wife's illusion, and kept her as closely bound in gratitude to him as if he'd given her something which had cost him a fortune.

What difference is there, do you think, between those in Plato's cave who can only marvel at the shadows and images of various objects, provided they are content and don't know what they miss, and the philosopher who has emerged from the cave

---

4. The Academicians are the Skeptics, who argue that the real world cannot be known.
5. Saint Christopher was said to have carried the Christ child across a river (hence his name, Christ-bearer); St. George slew a dragon, and St. Barbara's father was struck by lightning when he denounced her as a Christian.

Erasmus is attacking the authenticity of these legendary figures.
6. The greatest painters of antiquity.
7. Folly's name in Greek is "Moria"; no doubt this is a reference to Erasmus's good friend, Thomas More.

and sees the real things?[8] If Mycillus in Lucian had been allowed to go on dreaming that golden dream of riches forevermore, he'd have had no reason to desire any other state of happiness.[9] And so there's nothing to choose between the two conditions, or if there is, the fools are better off, first because their happiness costs them so little, in fact only a grain of persuasion, secondly because they share their enjoyment of it with the majority of men.

Indeed, no benefit gives pleasure unless it is enjoyed in company. Yet we all know how few sages there are, always supposing there's one at all. Out of all those centuries the Greeks can count seven sages at the most, and if anyone looks at them more closely I swear he'll not find so much as a half-wise man or even a third of a wise man among them. Next, among the many things to Bacchus's credit must be counted what is his chief claim to fame—his ability to free our minds from care. Of course the effect lasts only a short time, for as soon as you've slept off your drink your troubles come racing back in triumph, as the saying goes.

Isn't the blessing I confer much more generous and effective? I fill the mind with a kind of perpetual intoxication, with transports of rejoicing and delight, all without any effort, and I don't leave a single mortal without a share in my bounty, though the gifts of the other deities are unevenly bestowed. Not every region produces the mellow wine of good quality which can banish care and flow with rich hopes. Few have a lovely face, the gift of Venus, and still fewer the eloquence which Mercury grants. Not many owe their wealth to Hercules, and Homer's Jupiter doesn't allow authority to all comers. Often enough Mars remains neutral in battle, and a lot of people return disconsolate from Apollo's oracle. Saturn's son can flash lightning and Phoebus shoot plague with his arrows, while Neptune destroys more lives than he spares. As for those underworld Jupiters, Plutos, Discords, Punishments, Fevers and all that lot, I don't call them gods, but murderers. I, Folly, am the only one who extends my ever-ready generosity to all alike.

I don't expect prayers, and I don't lose my temper and demand expiation for some detail of ceremony which has been overlooked. Nor do I confound heaven and earth if someone has sent invitations to all the other gods and left me out, so that I'm not admitted to a sniff of the steaming victims.[1] The rest of the gods are so particular about these matters that you'd almost find it better and even safer to leave them alone instead of worshipping them. There are several men who are just the same, so hard to please and easily offended that it's wiser to have nothing at all to do with them than treat them as friends.

But no one offers sacrifice to Folly, people say, or sets up a temple. Well, I'm quite surprised myself, as I said before, at such ingratitude, but I'm easy-going and take it all in good part. Besides, I can't say this is really what I want. Why should I need a whiff of incense, a sacrificial meal, a goat or a pig? Mortals all over the world worship me in a manner which is highly approved, even by the theologians. Ought I to envy Diana because she was propitiated by human blood?[2] I hold the view that I'm

8. A reference to Plato's famous image in Book 7 of the *Republic* in which men are depicted as fools satisfied with the shadows on cave walls and unwilling to explore the real world beyond.
9. Lucian was the 2nd-century writer of a number of satirical dialogues, among them *The Cock,* which features the impoverished Micyllos whose rooster (a reincarnation of the philosopher Pythagoras) awakens him each night from his dreams of wealth.

1. An allusion to the story of Eris, which underlies the origins of the Homeric poems: when she wasn't invited to the wedding of Peleus and Thetis, the future parents of Achilles, Eris set conflicts in motion that led to the Trojan war.
2. The goddess Diana (Artemis in Greek) was notoriously vengeful when she was not observed; when King Oeneus of Calydon neglected her, Artemis sent a wild boar to attack the city.

worshipped with truest devotion when all men everywhere take me to their hearts, express me in their habits, and reflect me in their way of life—as in fact they do. This form of worship even of the saints and among Christian believers is quite rare. Think of the many who set up a candle to the Virgin, Mother of God, and at midday too, when it isn't needed, and of the few who care about emulating her chastity of life, her modesty and love of heavenly things. Yet that is surely the true way to worship and by far the most acceptable to heaven. Besides, what should I want with a temple? The entire world is my temple, and a very fine one too, if I'm not mistaken, and I'll never lack priests to serve it as long as there are men. And I'm not yet so foolish as to demand statues carved in stone and coloured with paint which can often do harm to the cult of us gods, when the stupid and thick-headed give their devotion to images instead of to the divinities they represent, and we suffer the fate of being supplanted by our substitutes. I fancy I can count as many statues set up to me as there are men who wear my living image in their faces, whether willingly or not. And so I've no reason to be envious of the other gods because they're each worshipped in their own corner of the earth on fixed days, like Apollo, for example, in Rhodes, Venus in Cyprus, Juno at Argos, Minerva at Athens, Jupiter at Olympus, Neptune at Tarentum, and Priapus at Lampsacus. To me the whole world offers far more precious victims, without ceasing and with one accord.

In case anyone thinks I'm presuming too far and not speaking the truth, let's take a brief look at the way men live, and it will then become clear how much they owe me and how they appreciate me, whether great men or humble. We won't go into every kind of life, it would take too long, but will pick out some outstanding examples from which it will be easy to judge the rest, and there's no point in mentioning the vulgar crowd and humble folk who all belong to me without question. They abound in so many forms of folly and devise so many new ones every day that a thousand Democrituses wouldn't be enough to laugh at them, and we'd always have to call in one Democritus more. It's hardly believable how much laughter, sport and fun you poor mortals can provide the gods every day. For they allocate their sober morning hours to settling altercations and listening to prayers, but once the nectar is flowing freely they want a change from serious business, and that is when they settle down on some promontary of heaven and lean over to watch the goings-on of mankind, a show they enjoy more than anything.

Heavens, what a farce it is, what a motley crowd of fools! I often join them myself and sit amongst the poets' gods. Here's a man who has lost his heart to a young woman, the more hopelessly in love the less he's loved in return. Another marries a dowry, not a wife, and while one man prostitutes his bride, another is watching his as jealous-eyed as Argus.[3] Here's one in mourning, and dear me, what foolish things he says and does, hiring mourners like actors to play a comedy of grief. There's another shedding tears at his step-mother's tomb. This one gives everything he can scrape together to his belly, but soon he'll go hungry again, and that one finds his happiness in idleness and sleep. There are men who spend their time bustling about on other people's affairs to the neglect of their own. One thinks himself rich on loans and credit though he'll soon be bankrupt, and another enjoys nothing so much as living like a pauper in order to enrich his heir. This one scours the seas for a meager and uncertain profit, entrusting to wind and wave his life which no money can replace, while that

---

3. The herdsman Argus had a hundred eyes, and was instructed by Hera to watch over Io, a princess turned into a heifer by her paramour Zeus.

one prefers to seek his fortune in war to living in peace and safety at home. Others fancy they've found an easy road to wealth by cultivating childless old men, and there are plenty of people too who court the affections of rich old women with the same end in view. Both groups provide special entertainment to the audience of gods when they end by being duped by the guile of the very people they set out to ensnare. Most foolish of all, the meanest, is the whole tribe of merchants, for they handle the meanest sort of business by the meanest methods, and although their lies, perjury, thefts, frauds and deceptions are everywhere to be found, they still reckon themselves a cut above everyone else simply because their fingers sport gold rings. There are plenty of sycophantic friars too who will sing their praises and publicly address them as honourable, doubtless hoping that a morsel of these ill-gotten gains will come their way.

* * *

To sum up, if you could look down from the moon, as Menippus once did, on the countless hordes of mortals, you'd think you saw a swarm of flies or gnats quarrelling amongst themselves, fighting, plotting, stealing, playing, making love, being born, growing old and dying.[4] It's hard to believe how much trouble and tragedy this tiny little creature can stir up, shortlived as he is, for sometimes a brief war or an outbreak of plague can carry off and destroy many thousands at once.[5]

* * *

[FOOLS FOR CHRIST'S SAKE][6]

Now let me get back to Paul. "You suffer fools gladly," he says, speaking of himself. And again, "Receive me as a fool," and "I do not speak according to God but as if I were foolish";[7] and elsewhere too he says, "We are fools for Christ's sake." This is high tribute to folly from a great authority. Moreover, he is an open advocate of folly as a prime necessity and a great benefit: "Whoever among you thinks himself wise must become a fool to be truly wise."[8] And according to Luke, Jesus addressed the two disciples whom he joined on the road to Emmaus as fools.[9] Should we be surprised at this, seeing that St Paul attributes some folly even to God? "God's foolishness," he says, "is wiser than men."[1] Origen subsequently objected in his commentary that we cannot really explain this folly by reference to the views held by men, as we can in the passage "The doctrine of the cross is folly to those that are perishing."[2]

4. Another of Lucian's dialogues, the *Icaromenippus*, features the Cynic philosopher Menippus who visits heaven on the back of an eagle so that he can hear the gods attack all philosophers; en route he is treated to a view of the earth while he stops at the moon.
5. Some of the most biting pages of *Praise of Folly* follow, as Folly attacks the foolishness not only of self-interested merchants and the friars who flattered them, but of philosophers, theologians "who interpret hidden mysteries to suit themselves," members of the religious orders, who "aren't interested in being like Christ but in being unlike each other," princes and courtiers who seek only the lap of luxury, and cardinals, bishops, and popes. Erasmus's hostility to Pope Julius II is especially evident in the final chapter of this section, when he has Folly take credit for the pope's ability to "live so comfortably" with few cares: "they believe they do quite enough for Christ if they play their part as overseer by means of every kind of ritual, near-theatrical ceremonial and display, benedictions and anathemas, and all their titles of your Beatitude, Reverence, and Holiness. For them it's out-of-date and

outmoded to perform miracles; teaching the people is too much like hard work, interpreting the holy scriptures is for schoolmen, and praying is a waste of time."
6. In this last excerpted section from *Praise of Folly*, Folly turns to a new, and for Erasmus, most genuine kind of Folly: that exemplified by Saint Paul when he called himself and his followers "fools for Christ's sake" (1 Corinthians 4:10).
7. References to Christian folly abound in Paul's two letters to the Corinthians; these quotations are from 2 Corinthians 11:16–19.
8. 1 Corinthians 3:18.
9. Luke 24:25; after Jesus is resurrected, he encounters two of his disciples on the road to Emmaus, who fail to recognize him, prompting him to berate them: "O foolish ones and slow of heart to believe in all that the prophets have spoken!"
1. 1 Corinthians 1:25.
2. 1 Corinthians 1:18. Origen was a Church Father of the 3rd century, and a great scholar in Greek; he was influential for Erasmus and other humanists.

But there is no need for me to worry about producing all this evidence to prove my point when Christ openly says to his Father in the sacred Psalms "Thou knowest my foolishness."[3]

It is also significant that fools have always given great pleasure to God, and this, I fancy, is the reason. Great princes eye men who are too clever with hostility and suspicion, as Julius Caesar did Brutus and Cassius, though he had no fear of drunken Antony, and as Nero did Seneca and Dionysius did Plato, though they both delight in men of duller and simpler wits.[4] In the same way, Christ always loathes and condemns those 'wiseacres' who put their trust in their own intelligence; as Paul bears witness in no uncertain words when he says "God has chosen the foolish things of the world," and again "God chose to save the world through folly," since it could not be redeemed by wisdom.[5] God himself makes this clear enough when he proclaims through the mouth of the prophet "I will destroy the wisdom of the wise and reject the intelligence of the intelligent."[6] So does Christ, when he gives thanks because the mystery of salvation had been hidden from the wise but revealed to little children, that is, to fools. (The Greek word for a child means foolish, and is the opposite of sophos, wise.)[7] There are also some relevant passages in the gospel where Christ attacks Pharisees and scribes and teachers of the Law while giving his unfailing protection to the ignorant multitude. What else can "Woe unto you, Scribes and Pharisees" mean but "Woe unto you who are wise"?[8] But Christ seems to have taken special delight in little children, women and fishermen, while the dumb animals who gave him the greatest pleasure were those furthest removed from cleverness and cunning. So he preferred to ride a donkey, though had he chosen he could safely have been mounted on a lion; and the holy spirit descended in the form of a dove, not of an eagle or a hawk, while throughout the scriptures there is frequent mention of harts, young mules and lambs. Moreover, he calls those who are destined for eternal life his sheep though there is no animal so stupid: witness the proverbial expression in Aristotle, "sheeplike character", which is derived from the slow-wittedness of the animal and is commonly used as a taunt against dull and stupid men. Yet Christ declares himself the shepherd of this flock, and even takes pleasure himself in the name of Lamb, as when John reveals him in the words "Behold the Lamb of God." The same expression often appears in the Apocalypse.[9]

All this surely points to the same thing; that all mortals are fools, even the pious. Christ too, though he is the wisdom of the Father, was made something of a fool himself in order to help the folly of mankind, when he assumed the nature of man and was seen in man's form; just as he was made sin so that he could redeem sinners. Nor did he wish them to be redeemed in any other way save by the folly of the cross and through his simple, ignorant apostles, to whom he unfailingly preached folly. He

---

3. Psalm 69 is a lamentation not, of course, of Christ's, but of the psalmist David.

4. Plutarch talks about Caesar's fear of Brutus and Cassius in his *Life of Caesar;* the dissolute tyrant Nero mistrusted the reputable Stoic philosopher Seneca, who for a time had managed to influence Nero's behavior for the better but was eventually condemned to death on charges of conspiracy. Plato was sent out of Syracuse by its tyrant, Dionysius I, who (story has it) sold the philosopher to slaveowners.

5. Once again, Folly quotes from 1 Corinthians (1:26 and 1:21).

6. Isaiah 29:14.

7. Jesus makes many statements privileging the role of children in his kingdom; see, for example, Matthew 18: 3, when he tells his disciples, "Unless you turn and become like little children, you will not enter into the kingdom of heaven."

8. From Jesus' attack on the Scribes and Pharisees in Matthew 23.

9. Erasmus included Aristotle's expression in the *Adages.* In the first chapter of the Gospel of John, John the Baptist refers several times to Jesus as the "lamb of God," and the Lamb sacrificed for its people appears in Chapter 5 of the Apocalypse or Book of Revelation.

taught them to shun wisdom, and made his appeal through the example of children, lilies, mustard-seed and humble sparrows, all foolish, senseless things, which live their lives by natural instinct alone, free from care or purpose.[1] And then when he forbade his disciples to worry about how they should answer the charges of the governors and told them not to seek to know times and seasons, it was surely because he wanted them not to rely on their own intelligence but be wholly dependent on him. This is also the explanation of why God the creator of the world forbade man to eat of the tree of knowledge, as if knowledge was poisonous to happiness. So Paul openly condemns knowledge for building up conceit and doing harm, and I believe St Bernard had him in mind when he interpreted the mountain on which Lucifer set up his seat as the mount of knowledge.[2]

Then perhaps we shouldn't overlook the argument that folly finds favour in heaven because she alone is granted forgiveness of sins, whereas the wise man receives no pardon. So when men pray for forgiveness, though they may have sinned in full awareness, they make folly their excuse and defence. If I remember rightly, that is how Aaron in the Book of Numbers intercedes against the punishment of his sister: "I beseech you, master, do not charge us with this sin, which we committed foolishly." Saul uses the same words in praying David to forgive his fault: "for it is clear that I acted foolishly." And again, David himself tries to placate the Lord by saying, "I beseech thee, O Lord, take away the iniquity of thy servant, for I have acted foolishly," as if he could only win forgiveness by pleading folly and ignorance.[3] Still more forceful is the argument that when Christ prayed on the cross for his enemies, "Father, forgive them" he made no other excuse for them but their ignorance: "for they know not what they do."[4] Paul writes to Timothy in the same vein, "But I was granted God's mercy because I acted ignorantly, in unbelief."[5] What else is acting ignorantly but acting foolishly, with no evil intent? And when Paul speaks of being granted mercy, he clearly implies that he would not have been granted it had he not had folly to plead in his defence. The sacred psalmist whom I forgot to quote in his proper place, also speaks for us all when he says, "Remember not the sins of my youth and my ignorances," and you will have marked that his two excuses are youth, which finds in me a constant companion, and ignorances, which are numbered as plural so that we may appreciate the full power of folly.[6]

To sum up (or I shall be pursuing the infinite), it is quite clear that the Christian religion has a kind of kinship with folly in some form, though it has none at all with wisdom. If you want proofs of this, first consider the fact that the very young and the very old, women and simpletons, are the people who take the greatest delight in sacred and holy things, and are therefore always found nearest the altars, led there doubtless solely by their natural instinct. Secondly, you can see how the first great

---

1. Erasmus refers here to a number of parables Jesus shared with his apostles, taken mostly from the Gospel of Matthew: the lilies-of-the-field are from 6:28, the mustard seed from 13:31, and the sparrows from 10:29 ("Are not two sparrows sold for a farthing? and yet not one of them will fall to the ground without your Father's leave.").
2. In 1 Corinthians 8:1 Paul contrasts knowledge and charity; the first "puffs up," the second "edifies." St. Bernard wrote a commentary on the Book of Isaiah in which he notes of Isaiah 14:12 ("How have you fallen from the heavens, O morning star, son of the dawn!") that the angel Lucifer's pursuit of knowledge led to his death.
3. Erasmus cites three examples of repentance from the Old Testament: Mariam, the sister of Aaron, was turned into a leper when she and Aaron spoke against Moses out of jealousy (Numbers 12:1–11); Saul asks forgiveness for seeking the death of David (1 Kings 26:21); David himself acts pridefully when he has a census taken of his people (2 Kings 24:10).
4. Luke 23:34.
5. In the first letter to Timothy, Paul speaks of himself as a former "blasphemer, a persecutor, and a bitter adversary"; God forgave him because he had acted in ignorance and unbelief (1:13).
6. The sacred psalmist is traditionally seen as David; the Psalm is 25.

founders of the faith were great lovers of simplicity and bitter enemies of learning. Finally, the biggest fools of all appear to be those who have once been wholly possessed by zeal for Christian piety. They squander their possessions, ignore insults, submit to being cheated, make no distinction between friends and enemies, shun pleasure, sustain themselves on fasting, vigils, tears, toil and humiliations, scorn life and desire only death—in short, they seem to be dead to any normal feelings, as if their spirit dwelt elsewhere than in their body. What else can that be but madness? And so we should not be surprised if the apostles were thought to be drunk on new wine, and Festus judged Paul to be mad.[7]

But now that I have donned "the lionskin," let me tell you another thing.[8] The happiness which Christians seek with so many labours is nothing other than a certain kind of madness and folly. Don't be put off by the words, but consider the reality. In the first place, Christians come very near to agreeing with the Platonists that the soul is stifled and bound down by the fetters of the body which by its gross matter prevents the soul from being able to contemplate and enjoy things as they truly are. Next, Plato defines philosophy as a preparation for death because it leads the mind from visible and bodily things, just as death does.[9] And so as long as the mind makes proper use of the organs of the body it is called sane and healthy, but once it begins to break its bonds and tries to win freedom, as if it were planning an escape from prison men call it insane. If this happens through disease or some organic defect, by general consent it is called insanity. Even so, we see this type of person foretelling the future, showing a knowledge of languages and literature they had never previously learned, and giving clear indication of something divine. Undoubtedly this happens because the mind is beginning to free itself from contamination by the body and exercise its true natural power. I think this also explains why those who are struggling at the hour of death often experience something similar, so that they speak wonders as if inspired. Again, if this happens through pious fervour, it may not be quite the same kind of insanity, but is so like it that most people make no distinction, especially as the number of humble folk who differ in their whole way of life from the general run of mankind is very small.

And so we have a situation which I think is not unlike that in the myth in Plato, where those who were chained in a cave marvelled at shadows, whereas the man who had escaped and then returned to the cavern told them that he had seen real things and they were much mistaken in their belief that nothing existed but their wretched shadows. This man who has gained understanding pities his companions and deplores their insanity which confines them to such an illusion, but they in their turn laugh at him as if he were crazy and turn him out. In the same way, the common herd of men feels admiration only for the things of the body and believes that these alone exist, whereas the pious scorn whatever concerns the body and are wholly uplifted towards

7. The Book of Acts discusses the community's reactions to the first apostles. When the Holy Spirit descends and gives them the gift of speaking in tongues, some people say in mockery, "They are full of new wine" (Acts 2:13). After Paul tells King Agrippa, son of Herod, of his conversion, one Festus proclaims him mad (Acts 26:24).

8. "You are dressing me up in the lionskin" is another proverb Erasmus discusses in his *Adages*, used to describe someone who undertakes a work beyond his means. Erasmus speculates that the term refers to Hercules, who wore a lionskin and carried a club when he made his famous descent to Hades.

9. In the *Phaedo*—a report from Socrates' disciple, Phaedo, on Socrates' preparations for death by hemlock—Socrates says that "as the true philosophers are ever studying death, to them, of all men, death is the least terrible." Cicero also famously says in his Tusculan Orations (I.30) that "to philosophize is to learn to die." Folly will continue the paragraph using the imagery of neo-Platonism, in which the soul is said to leave the body so that it might have communion with the divine. Plato's allegory of the cave from the *Republic,* referred to in the next paragraph, was a source for much neo-Platonic doctrine of the Renaissance.

the contemplation of invisible things. The ordinary man gives first place to wealth, the second to bodily comforts, and leaves the last to the soul—which anyway most people believe doesn't exist because it is invisible to the eye. By contrast, the pious direct their entire endeavour towards God, who is absolute purity, and after him towards what is closest to him, the soul. They have no thought for the body, despise wealth and avoid it like trash, and if they are obliged to deal with such matters they do so with reluctance and distaste, having as if they did not have, possessing as if they did not possess.

There are moreover in each of these things widely differing degrees. To begin with, though all the senses have some kinship with the body, some of them are grosser, such as touch, hearing, sight, smell and taste, while other faculties are less physical, for instance, memory, intellect and will. The power of the soul depends on its inclinations. Since, then, all the power of the pious soul is directed towards what is furthest removed from the grosser senses, these become blunted and benumbed. The vulgar crowd of course does the opposite, develops them very much and more spiritual faculties very little. That explains what we have heard happened to several saints, who drank oil by mistake for wine.[1] Again, take the affections of the soul. Some have more traffic with the grossness of the body, such as lust, desire for food and sleep, anger, pride and envy, and on these the pious wage unceasing war, while the crowd thinks life impossible without them. Then there are what we could call intermediate affections which are quasi-natural to all, like love for one's country, and affection for children, parents and friends. The crowd sets great store by these, yet the pious strive to root them too from their soul, or at least sublimate them to the highest region of the soul. They wish to love their father not as a father, for he begot nothing but the body, and this too is owed to God the father, but as a good man and one in whom is reflected the image of the supreme mind which alone they call the *summum bonum* and beyond which they declare nothing is to be loved or sought. This is the rule whereby they regulate all the remainder of life's duties, so that anything visible, if it is not wholly to be despised, is still valued far less than what cannot be seen.

They[2] also say that even in the sacraments and the actual observances of their religion, both body and spirit are involved. For example, they think little of fasting if it means no more than abstaining from meat and a meal—which for the common man is the essential of a fast. It must at the same time reduce the passions, permitting less anger or pride than usual, so that the spirit can feel less burdened by the matter of the body and can aim at tasting and enjoying the blessings of heaven. It is the same with the Eucharist: the ritual with which it is celebrated should not be rejected, they say, but it serves no useful purpose or can be positively harmful if it lacks the spiritual element represented by those visible symbols. It represents the death of Christ, which men must express through the mastery and extinction of their bodily passions, laying them in the tomb, as it were, in order to rise again to a new life wherein they can be united with him and with each other. This then is how the pious man acts, and this is his purpose. The crowd, on the other hand, thinks the sacrifice of the mass means no more than crowding as close as possible to the altars, hearing the sound of the words, and watching the ritual down to the smallest detail. I quote this only as one example;

---

1. St. Bernard was said to have been so engrossed in meditating on scripture that he drank oil without noticing that it wasn't water.

2. The "pious" mentioned in the preceding paragraph, continuing Folly's differentiation between those few who are attuned to spiritual goods, and the general crowd who are not.

in fact the pious man throughout his whole life withdraws from the things of the body and is drawn towards what is eternal, invisible and spiritual. Consequently, there is total disagreement between the two parties, on every point, and each thinks the other mad; though in my view, the epithet is more properly applied to the pious, not the common man.

This will be clearer if I do as I promised, and show briefly how the supreme reward for man is no other than a kind of madness. First consider how Plato imagined something of this sort when he wrote that the madness of lovers is the highest form of happiness.[3] For anyone who loves intensely lives not in himself but in the object of his love, and the further he can move out of himself into his love, the happier he is. Now, when the soul is planning to leave the body and ceases to make proper use of its organs, it is thought to be mad, and doubtless with good reason. This, surely, is what is meant by the popular expressions "he is beside himself," "come to" and "he is himself again." Moreover, the more perfect the love, the greater the madness—and the happier. What, then, will life in heaven be like to which all pious minds so eagerly aspire? The spirit will be the stronger, and will conquer and absorb the body, and this it will do the more easily for having previously in life purged and weakened the body in preparation for this transformation. Then the spirit will itself be absorbed by the supreme Mind, which is more powerful than its infinite parts. And so when the whole man will be outside himself, and be happy for no reason except that he is so outside himself, he will enjoy some ineffable share in the supreme good which draws everything into itself. Although this perfect happiness can only be experienced when the soul has recovered its former body and been granted immortality, since the life of the pious is no more than a contemplation and foreshadowing of that other life, at times they are able to feel some foretaste and savour of the reward to come. It is only the tiniest drop in comparison with the fount of eternal bliss, yet it far exceeds all pleasures of the body, even if all mortal delights were rolled into one, so much does the spiritual surpass the physical, the invisible the visible. This is surely what the prophet promises: "Eye has not seen nor ear heard, nor have there entered into the heart of man the things which God has prepared for those that love him."[4] And this is the part of Folly which is not taken away by the transformation of life but is made perfect.

So those who are granted a foretaste of this—and very few have the good fortune—experience something which is very like madness. They speak incoherently and unnaturally, utter sound without sense, and their faces suddenly change expression. One moment they are excited, the next depressed, they weep and laugh and sigh by turns; in fact they truly are quite beside themselves. Then when they come to, they say they don't know where they have been, in the body or outside it, awake or asleep. They cannot remember what they have heard or seen or said or done, except in a mist, like a dream.[5] All they know is that they were happiest when they were out of their senses in this way, and they lament their return to reason, for all they want is to be mad for ever with this kind of madness. And this is only the merest taste of the happiness to come.

---

3. In the *Phaedrus,* where Plato specifies that the noblest madness is love of the beautiful.

4. 1 Corinthians 2:9.

5. This description echoes Paul's ecstatic journey to heaven described in 2 Corinthians 12:2: "I know a man in Christ [Paul himself] who fourteen years ago—whether in the body I do not know, or out of the body I do not know, God knows—such a one was caught up to the third heaven. And I know such a man . . . that he was caught up into paradise and heard secret words that man may not repeat."

But I've long been forgetting who I am, and I've "overshot the mark."[6] If anything I've said seems rather imprudent or garrulous, you must remember it's Folly and a woman who's been speaking. At the same time, don't forget the Greek proverb "Often a foolish man speaks a word in season," though of course you may think this doesn't apply to women. I can see you're all waiting for a peroration, but it's silly of you to suppose I can remember what I've said when I've been spouting such a hotchpotch of words. There's an old saying, "I hate a fellow-drinker with a memory," and here's a new one to put alongside it: "I hate an audience which won't forget."

And so I'll say Goodbye. Clap your hands, live well and drink, distinguished initiates of FOLLY.

━━┅═◆═┅━━

Martin Luther
1483–1546

"What is more miserable than uncertainty?" Martin Luther asked in a telling moment in a treatise called *The Enslaved Will.* Exasperated by the eloquent but (he felt) empty arguments of Erasmus in *On Free Will,* Luther, a self-proclaimed "barbarian occupied with the barbarous," wrote a treatise three times as long as that of Erasmus. He had nothing to lose. Excommunicated from "unhappy, hopeless, blasphemous Rome," declared an outlaw by the Holy Roman Emperor Charles V, this former monk had already burned his bridges with his past—as well as with the last fifteen hundred years of Christianity. The new center of Christendom, if Luther had his way, would no longer be Rome, but Germany, the country that had been enslaved for so long by the papacy.

From this new center, Luther launched his entreaties to all who would listen: the German nobility whom he begged in his *Open Letter* to take up arms against Rome; the German people for whom he translated the Bible. He appealed to strong nationalist sentiments, to the anti-elitism of growing urban populations that were neither illiterate nor versed in humanist subtleties, and to the general disaffection with a church that he argued encouraged dependence and superstition. He found many sympathetic ears, while he protested when others took his appeals too far afield. Even though he was proud to be the son and grandson of peasants, he refused to subscribe to the platforms of the peasant rebellion, articulated most eloquently in *The Twelve Articles of Peasantry* by Sebastian Lotzer: "If God deigns to hear the peasants, who is to blame the will of God?"

Luther was the sixteenth century's best-selling author, and it isn't difficult to see why. He writes with gusto, directness and often with vitriol. These qualities are readily apparent in his *The Enslaved Will,* addressed to the "infidel" Erasmus. Among other things, Erasmus had suggested that the Bible is rife with ambiguities that can only be clarified by recourse to the long history of biblical interpretation sanctioned by the Church. Outraged by the suggestion that the common man was ill-equipped to grasp the simple truths of Scripture, Luther mockingly scrapes and bows before Erasmus's intellectual prowess, while making it perfectly clear that God's grace alone "favors us unworthy creatures who deserve damnation rather than anything else." And only of God's grace can one be certain in life. "If I lived and worked to all eternity, my conscience would never reach comfortable certainty as to how much it must do to satisfy God": a testament that both opposes the practices of the money-grubbing Church, and expresses Luther's endless anxieties concerning his own spiritual health.

---

6. The proverbs cited in this paragraph are all mentioned in the *Adages.* Folly's final words constitute a playful recantation in which Erasmus defends against the trenchant satire of so much of his work by asking us to remember that his interlocutor is only "a woman who's been speaking."

from To the Christian Nobility of the German Nation[1]

Dedicatory Letter [Luther as fool]

To the Esteemed and Reverend Master, Nicholas von Amsdorf, Licentiate of Holy Scripture, and Canon of Wittenberg, my special and kind friend, from Doctor Martin Luther.[2]

The grace and peace of God be with you, esteemed, reverend, and dear sir and friend.

The time for silence is past, and the time to speak has come, as Ecclesiastes says [3:7]. I am carrying out our intention to put together a few points on the matter of the reform of the Christian estate, to be laid before the Christian nobility of the German nation, in the hope that God may help his Church through the laity, since the clergy, to whom this task more properly belongs, have grown quite indifferent. I am sending the whole thing to you, reverend sir, [that you may give] an opinion on it and, where necessary, improve it.

I know full well that I shall not escape the charge of presumption because I, a despised, inferior person, venture to address such high and great estates on such weighty matters, as if there were nobody else in the world except Doctor Luther to take up the cause of the Christian estate and give advice to such high-ranking people. I make no apologies no matter who demands them. Perhaps I owe my God and the world another work of folly.[3] I intend to pay my debt honestly. And if I succeed, I shall for the time being become a court jester. And if I fail, I still have one advantage—no one need buy me a cap or put scissors to my head. It is a question of who will put the bells on whom.[4] I must fulfill the proverb, "Whatever the world does, a monk must be in the picture, even if he has to be painted in." More than once a fool has spoken wisely, and wise men have often been arrant fools. Paul says, "He who wishes to be wise must become a fool" [I Cor. 3:18]. Moreover, since I am not only a fool, but also a sworn doctor of Holy Scripture,[5] I am glad for the opportunity to fulfill my doctor's oath, even in the guise of a fool.

I beg you, give my apologies to those who are moderately intelligent, for I do not know how to earn the grace and favor of the superintelligent. I have often sought to do so with the greatest pains, but from now on I neither desire nor value their favor. God help us to seek not our own glory but his alone. Amen.

At Wittenberg, in the monastery of the Augustinians,
on the eve of St. John Baptist [June 23]
in the year fifteen hundred and twenty.

from The Enslaved Will[1]

To begin with, I would like to review some parts of your Preface in which you[2] attempt to disparage our case and to embellish your own.

---

1. Translated from the German by C. M. Jacobs and revised by James Ackerman.
2. The prefatory letter, given here, is addressed to Nicholas von Amsdorf, with whom Luther had studied when he was at Wittenberg. The lengthy treatise that follows is addressed to the Holy Roman Emperor, Charles V, and the German nobility.
3. Luther no doubt alludes to Erasmus's *Praise of Folly*, published a decade earlier.
4. Court fools were known for their traditional caps and

bells; monks wore a cowl and were tonsured. Thus Luther's transformation from Augustinian monk to jester would be a relatively simple one.
5. As a "Doctor," Luther had the obligation to teach Scripture.
1. Translated from the Latin by Ernst F. Winter. The section given here from Luther's *De servo arbitrio* focuses on his response to the preface of Erasmus's earlier treatise, *De libero arbitrio*, "Of Free Will."
2. Erasmus.

First, I notice that, as in your other works, you censure me for obstinacy of assertion. Here in this book you say your "dislike of assertions is so great that you prefer the views of the sceptics wherever the inviolable authority of Scripture and the decisions of the Church permit; though you gladly submit your opinion whether you comprehend what she prescribes or not." Such outlook appeals to you. I assume (in courtesy bound) that you say these things from your charitable mind and love of peace. If, however, another had said it, I should, perhaps, have attacked him in my usual way. And even you, well-meaning as you are, I ought not to allow to err in this matter. Not to delight in assertions is not the mark of a Christian heart. Indeed, one must delight in assertions to be a Christian at all! To avoid misunderstandings, let me define *assertion.* I mean a constant adhering to and affirming of your position, avowing and defending it, and invincibly persevering in it. . . . Far be it from us Christians to be sceptics and academics![3]

Let there be men who assert twice as determined as the very Stoics themselves! I pray you, how often does the Apostle Paul require that assurance of faith, that is, a most certain and firm assertion of conscience. In Romans 10:10 he calls it confession, "and with the mouth profession of faith is made unto salvation." And Christ says, "Therefore, everyone who acknowledges me before men, I also will acknowledge him before my Father in heaven" (Matthew 10:32). Peter commands us to give a reason of the hope that is in us.[4]

But what's the need for so many proofs? Nothing is more known and characteristic among Christians than assertions. Take away assertions and you take away Christianity. Indeed, the Holy Spirit is given to Christians from heaven, so that He may in them glorify Christ and confess Him even unto death. And to die for what you confess and assert is not an assertion? What a clown I would hold a man to be who does not really believe, nor unwaveringly assert the things he is reproving others with! Why, I would send him to Anticyra![5]

But I am the biggest fool, losing words and time on something clearer than the sun. What Christian can bear that assertions should be deprecated? That would be to deny at once all piety and religion, like asserting that piety, religion and all dogmas are nothing at all. Why do *you assert* your "dislike of assertions" and your preferring an open mind?

But you remind me, and rightly so, that you were not referring to confessing Christ and His doctrines. And in courtesy to you, I give up the right of which I normally avail myself and refrain from judging your heart. I leave this for another time, or to other writers. In the meantime, I admonish you to correct your tongue and your pen, and to refrain henceforth from using such expressions. However upright and honest your heart may be, your words, which are the index of the heart, they say, are not so.

* * *

What a Proteus[6] is the man talking about "inviolable authority of Scriptures and the decisions of the Church"!—as if you had the greatest respect for the Scriptures and the Church, when in the same breath you explain that you wish you had the liberty to be a sceptic! What Christian could talk like this? * * * A Christian will rather

---

3. "Skeptics" for Luther were those who professed the inability to know with certainty; "academicians" those who belonged to members of the Platonic academy.
4. 1 Peter 3:15: "Be ready always with an answer to everyone who asks a reason for the hope that is in you."

5. Health resort in ancient Greece where hellebore, which supposedly cured madness, grew in abundance.
6. Mythological shape-changer possessed of prophetic powers that mortals could put to their use if they could succeed in preventing his metamorphoses.

say this: I am so against the sentiments of sceptics that, so far as the weakness of the flesh permits, I shall not only steadfastly adhere to the sacred writings everywhere, and in all parts of them, and assert them, but also I wish to be as positive as possible on nonessentials that lie outside Scriptures, because what is more miserable, than uncertainty. * * * In short, your words amount to this, that it matters little to you what anyone believes anywhere, as long as the peace of the world is undisturbed. * * * You seem to look upon the Christian doctrines as nothing better than the opinions of philosophers and men. Of course, it is stupid to wrangle and quarrel over these, as nothing results but contention and disturbance of the public peace. * * * So you wish to end *our* fighting as an intermediate peacemaker. * * * Allow *us* to be assertors. You go ahead and favor your sceptics and academics, till Christ calls you too! The Holy Spirit is no sceptic, and what He has written into our hearts are no doubts or opinions, but assertions, more certain and more firm than all human experience and life itself.

* * * I hope you credit Luther with some acquaintance with and judgment in the sacred writings. If not, beware and I'll wring the admission from you! This is the distinction which I make (for I too am going to act a little the rhetorician and logician): God and the Scriptures are two things, just like God and creation are two things. Nobody doubts that in God many things are hidden of which we know nothing. * * * But that there are in Scriptures some things abstruse and not quite plain, was spread by the godless Sophists,[7] whom you echo, Erasmus. They have never yet produced one article to prove this their madness. Satan has frightened men from reading the sacred writings, and has rendered Holy Scriptures contemptible, so as to ensure his poisonous philosophy to prevail in the church. I admit that many passages in Scriptures are obscure and abstruse. But that is due to our ignorance of certain terms and grammatical particulars, and not to the majesty of the subject. This ignorance does not in any way prevent our knowing all the contents of Scriptures. What things can Scriptures still be concealing, now that the seals are broken, the stone rolled from the door of the sepulchre, and that greatest of all mysteries brought to light: Christ became man; God is Trinity and Unity; Christ suffered for us and will reign forever? Are not these things known and proclaimed even in our streets? Take Christ out of Scriptures and what will you find remaining in them? All the things contained in the Scriptures, therefore, are made manifest (even though some passages containing unknown words are yet obscure). But it is absurd and impious to say that things are obscure, because of a few obscure words, when you know the contents of Scriptures being set in the clearest light. And if the words are obscure in one place, yet they are clear in another.

* * *

You draft for us a list of those things which you consider sufficient for Christian piety. Any Jew or Gentile utterly ignorant of Christ could easily draw up the same, because you do not mention Christ in a single letter. As though you thought that Christian piety is possible without Christ, if God be but worshipped with one's whole heart as being a "naturally most benign God." What shall I say here, Erasmus? You ooze Lucian from every pore; you swill Epicurus by the gallons.[8] If you consider this

---

7. Luther calls the Scholastics sophists. Scholasticism had been the dominant philosophy taught in medieval universities, and had featured disputation and learned dispute. Luther derides scholastics by calling them sophists—or as Aristotle would say of them in his dialogue "On

Sophists," those who appear to be wise without being so.
8. Writer of satirical dialogues during the 2nd century, Lucian was a great favorite of Erasmus; Epicurus was a Greek philosopher who held that the greatest good is pleasure.

subject not necessary to Christians, I ask you to withdraw from the debate. We have no common ground. I consider it vital.

If, as you say, it be irreligious, curious, superfluous to know whether God's fore-knowledge is contingent; whether our will can contribute anything pertinent to our eternal salvation, or whether it simply endures operative grace; whether everything we do, good or evil, is done out of mere necessity, or whether we are rather enduring, what then, I ask, is religious, serious and useful knowledge? This is weak stuff, Erasmus. *Das ist zu viel!*[9]

It is difficult to attribute this to your ignorance, because you are now old, you have lived among Christians and you have long been studying the sacred writings.[1] You leave me no room for excusing or thinking well of you. And yet the Papists[2] pardon and put up with these outrageous statements, because you are writing against Luther. Without a Luther in the case, they would tear you apart. Here I must speak like Aristotle when arguing with his master Plato: Plato is my friend, but truth must be honored above all.[3] Granted you have but little understanding of Scripture and Christian piety, surely even an enemy of Christians ought to know what Christians do, consider useful and necessary. But you, a theologian and teacher of Christianity, wanting to write an outline guide for Christianity, forget your own sceptical way. Otherwise you would vacillate as to what is profitable and necessary for Christians. In fact, you defy your own principles and make an unheard of assertion that here is something nonessential. If it is really unessential, and not surely known, then neither God, Christ, the gospel, faith nor anything else even of Judaism, let alone Christianity, is left. In the name of the immortal God, Erasmus, how wide a window, how big a field are you opening up for attack against you.

* * * The essence of Christianity which you describe * * * is without Christ, without the Spirit, and chillier than ice. * * * You plainly assert that the will is effective in things pertaining to eternal salvation, when you speak of its striving. And again you assert that it is passive, when saying that without the mercy of God it is ineffective. But you fail to define the limits within which we should think of the will as acting and as being acted upon. Thus you keep us in ignorance as to how far the mercy of God extends, and how far our own will extends; what man's will and God's mercy really *do* effect. That prudence of yours carries you along. You side with neither party and escape safely through Scylla and Charybdis,[4] in order that coming into open sea, overwhelmed and confounded by the waves, you can then assert all that you now deny, and deny all that you now assert!

* * * It is not irreligious, curious or superfluous, but extremely wholesome and necessary for a Christian to know whether or not his will has anything to do in matters pertaining to salvation. This, let me tell you, is the very hinge upon which our disputation turns. It is the crucial issue between you and me. It is our aim to inquire what free will can do, in what it is passive, and how it is related to the grace of God. If we know nothing of these things, we shall know nothing whatsoever of Christianity, and shall be worse off than all the heathens. Whoever does not understand this, let him confess that he is not a Christian. But he who derides and ridicules it, should know

---

9. Luther's temper forces him to write in his native German, not Latin. "That's too much!"
1. In 1524 when Erasmus wrote his treatise on the free will, he would have been 58.
2. Roman Catholics—those who follow the Pope.
3. Aristotle's works often take issue with those of Plato;

among other things, he contested the existence of ideal Forms in which Plato believed, preferring to focus on the material world.
4. Two monsters between whom Odysseus must navigate his boat; the phrase is used proverbially to indicate the difficulties of getting through an encounter.

that he is the greatest foe of Christians. * * * It is necessary to distinguish most clearly between the power of God and our own, between God's works and ours, if we are to live a godly life.

* * * In this book, therefore, I shall harry you and all the Sophists until you shall define for me the power of free will. And I hope so to harry you (Christ helping me) as to make you heartily repent ever having published your Diatribe. It is then essentially necessary and wholesome for Christians to know that God foreknows nothing contingently, but that he foresees, purposes and does all things according to His immutable, eternal and infallible will. This thunderbolt throws free will flat and utterly dashes it to pieces. Those who want to assert it must either deny this thunderbolt or pretend not to see it.

Thomas Müntzer
c. 1489–1525

"I speak of God's word and all its manifold treasures," says the supremely confident Thomas Müntzer in the same letter in which he christens Martin Luther "Dr. Liar" and accuses him of treachery, cunning, and worse: "You are asinine flesh, you would take a long time to cook and would be a tough dish for your mealy-mouthed friends." Müntzer neither minced words nor wasted time, for time was the one thing he didn't have, convinced as he was that the final days were at hand and Christ was demanding that Germany's corrupt social order be overturned so that the apocalypse could come.

To this end, Müntzer preached to princes, peasants, and miners ("Arise! arise! it is time. The scoundrels are disheartened, let them be hunted down like dogs!"). Müntzer studied at Wittenberg from 1517 to 1519, where he met Luther and embraced his ideas for reform. But he was always more of an activist than Luther, firmly believing that changes in religion should be accompanied by changes in the political order, and the insurrections he fomented in Saxony led to his expulsion to Prague. Increasingly disheartened with Luther's conservatism, he broke off with his erstwhile mentor. Back in Germany he sought to establish in Mülhausen a utopian society in which property was shared and municipal leaders expelled. His biggest following was the peasantry, in whose plight Müntzer saw nothing short of unjust enslavement, and in early 1525 he joined forces with leaders of the peasant rebellion that Luther had condemned as satanic. The rebellion—like Müntzer's apocalyptic reforms—was doomed to failure; five thousand peasants died in an attack by the Saxon lords on the city of Frankenhausen which Müntzer had made his base, and Müntzer himself was captured and beheaded. After his death, his pamphlets attracted the attention of Protestants such as John Knox, who advocated the overthrow of England's Catholic queen, Mary Tudor.

Müntzer's confidence came from Scripture and his belief in himself as a spiritualist: someone inspired by the Holy Ghost to deliver God's word to unbelievers and believers alike. One of the most active proponents of what has been called the radical Reformation, Müntzer was prepared to sunder absolutely the division Luther wanted to maintain between church and state. His speech from 1523, excerpted here, to Saxony's princes—Duke John of Allstedt, nominally sympathetic to Müntzer's views, and his son who was far less so—tested the propensity of Germany's elect to be "misled by hypocritical parsons" and "constrained by false consideration and indulgence. . . . The poor laity and the peasants see it much more clearly than you." This combination of challenge, insult and threat, characteristic of Müntzer's oratorical style, not surprisingly failed to win him much support among the princes. Following the sermon he was ordered to appear at Weimar for a hearing and was told in no uncertain terms to cease his agitations.

from Sermon to the Princes[1]

In the chapter of Daniel being discussed (Chap. 2), it is shown that the king was not inclined to believe the cunning soothsayers and sorcerers when he said, "Tell me my dream, then give your interpretation of it, otherwise you will tell me nothing but trickery and lies." What was that dream? They were unable to tell him and said, "Your Majesty, no one on earth can tell you the dream, only the gods, and they do not maintain communication with humans."[2] To the extent of their understanding they spoke quite reasonably. But they had no belief in God, being godless hypocrites and sycophants, saying what their rulers wanted to hear, just like the pedantic divines in our times,[3] who love tasty morsels at court. But they are refuted by what is written in Jeremiah 5, also in Chapter 8. Here the text says that there would be people who had communication with heaven. Oh, that's a bitter pill for the cunning ones to swallow! Yet St. Paul says it to be so too (Phil. 3). Such learned scribes still claimed to interpret the mysteries of God. Oh, the world now has a great number of such rogues who publicly arrogate that function to themselves. Of these Isaiah speaks (Chap. 58), saying, "They delight to know my ways, as a people that did righteousness." Such learned scribes are the soothsayers who publicly deny God's revelation, but interfere with the work of the Holy Spirit and yet would instruct the whole world.[4] That which is beyond the feeble power of their poor intellect must come straight from the Devil. Yet they have no assurance of their own salvation, which should be of utmost concern (Rom. 8). They babble nicely about faith and brew a drunken faith for poor confused consciences. All this is caused by the uninformed judgment and terrible abomination they have from the hateful trickery of those accursed and venomous monks' dreams by means of which the Devil puts his pet schemes into operation and has, in fact, irreparably deceived many of the pious elect, because, lacking all discernment, they have straightway granted credulity to those visions and dreams. Thus their rules and frivolous hocus-pocus are prescribed by the revelation of the Devil, against which the Colossians are so urgently warned by St. Paul (Col. 2). But the accursed monk dream-mongers have not known how to draw upon the power of God, and for that reason are now obdurately headed in the wrong direction and are a matter of sin and shame to everybody, as much as are indolent good-for-nothings. They are still blind in their folly. Nothing else has led them astray, and is leading them still further astray in these times, but false belief. For without any experience of the arrival of the Holy Spirit, the Master of the fear of God, they cannot distinguish good from evil, since they spurn divine wisdom. God cries out against the likes of them through Isaiah (Chap. 5), "Woe unto them that call evil good, and good evil." Therefore it is not in the nature of decent people to spurn good for evil. For St. Paul says to the Thessalonians (Chap. 5), "Despise not prophesyings; prove all things; hold fast that which is good," etc. * * *

1. Translated by Robert A. Fowkes. The sermon was delivered on 13 July 1524 in Allstedt, before Duke John, his son, and numerous officials. Its full title is "Exposition of the Second Chapter of Daniel the prophet, preached at the Castle of Allstedt before the active and amiable Dukes and Administrators of Saxony by Thomas Müntzer, minister of the Word of God."

2. Daniel was a young Israelite who lived in Babylon during the period of exile there. The second chapter of the Book of Daniel tells of a dream of the Babylonian king, Nebuchadnezzar, about a statue whose feet were made of iron and clay. A stone strikes the feet, breaking them into pieces, and forcing the statue to crumble away, while the stone itself "became a great mountain and filled the whole earth." The king narrates the dream to his wise men, who fail to explain it. Inspired by God, Daniel interprets the dream for the king, prophesying the triumph of the Hebrew God over the Babylonian idols. For his abilities he was made ruler of the whole province of Babylon and prefect over Babylon's wise men.

3. I.e., the Lutherans.

4. Müntzer believed that he was a prophet, inspired by the Holy Spirit.

Therefore, beloved fathers of Saxony, you must dare this for the sake of the Gospel.[5] But God will chasten you lightly, as His most beloved sons (Deut. 1). Since He is exceedingly slow to wrath, blessed are all who rely upon God. Speak freely in the spirit of Christ, saying, "I will not be afraid of a hundred thousand if they besiege me." I suppose that our learned men will point out the graciousness of Christ, which they distort in their hypocrisy. But they should, on the other hand, have regard for the wrath of Christ (Jn. 2, Ps. 69), when he destroyed the roots of idolatry, as Paul says in the first chapter of his Epistle to the Colossians that, for the same reason, the wrath of God cannot be taken away from the congregation. If He has now humbled those who are slight in our estimation, He would doubtless not have spared the idols and images, had they been there. He himself commanded through Moses (Deut. 2), saying, "You are a holy people, you shall have no mercy for the idolatrous, but shall destroy their altars and smash their images and burn them, so that I may not be angry with you."

Christ has not abrogated those words but will rather help us fulfill them (Mt. 5). Figures of speech have all been interpreted by the prophets, but there are plain, clear words which will always endure (Is. 40). God cannot say yes today and no tomorrow. He is unchangeable in His word (Mal. 3, 1 Kgs. 15, Num. 22). To the fact that the Apostles did not destroy the idols I respond thus: St. Peter was a timorous man who fawned hypocritically in the presence of the heathens (Jn. 21); he was, though, at the end, intensely afraid of death, and there is no reason to accept him as a norm in this. But St. Paul spoke out most severely against idolatry (Acts 17), and if he had been able to put his teaching into full effect among the Athenians, he would without doubt have entirely eliminated idolatry, as God had commanded through Moses, and was later done by the martyrs in well-attested accounts.[6] Therefore, the failings or short-comings of the saints do not give us any reason to allow the godless to persist in their ways. Since they have acknowledged God's name with us, they shall choose one of two things: either to renounce the Christian religion completely, or to put away their idols (Mt. 18). But for our learned hypocrites to come forward and say with Daniel, in their godless and warped way, that the Antichrist should be abolished without violence, is going too far. He is already discouraged, as were the elect when they were about to enter the Promised Land. Joshua writes, "He did not spare them the sword." See Ps. 44 and 1 Chron. 14; you'll find the solution there. They did not conquer the land with the sword but by the power of God, though the sword was the means of annihilating the godless (Rom. 13), as eating and drinking are the means of living. In order that the same thing may now happen in fit and proper manner, our beloved fathers, the princes who profess Christ with us, should act. If, however, they fail to do so, the sword will be taken away from them (Dan. 7), for they profess Him with their words but deny Him in their acts (Tim. 1). Therefore, if they make peace with the enemies, if they claim to be spiritual yet still do not take into account the power of God, they shall be done away with (1 Cor. 5). But what I ask for them, with righteous Daniel, is, if they are not against the revelation of God but act contrary to it, that they shall be strangled without mercy, the way Hezekiah, Josiah, Cyrus, Daniel, and Elijah destroyed the priests of Baal (1 Kgs. 18). Otherwise the Christian Church cannot return to its pure pristine state. The weeds must be eradicated from God's vineyard at the time of harvest. Then the fine red wheat will take permanent root and will rightly

5. Müntzer is challenging the princes of Saxony to engage in revolution.
6. Peter, the "timorous man" who refused to destroy the idols of the pagans, became the "rock" of the Catholic Church, while Paul, who did not fear incurring others' hostility, was a model for the true Protestant.

thrive (Mt. 13). The angels who sharpen their sickles for that purpose are the sincere servants of God who complete the zeal of divine wisdom (Mal. 3).

Nebuchadnezzar perceived the divine wisdom in Daniel and fell down before him after the powerful truth had overcome him, but he was moved like a reed by the wind, as Chapter 3 proves.[7] Similarly, there are now great numbers of people who accept the Gospel with great joy as long as all goes smoothly (Lk. 8); but when God puts such people to the test of the crucible or the fire (1 Pet. 1), they, alas, take offense at the slightest word, as Christ proclaimed (Mk. 4). By the same token, many inexperienced people will no doubt be annoyed by this pamphlet, since I say, with Christ (Lk. 19, Mt. 18) and with Paul (1 Cor. 5), as well as with the instruction of the whole law of God, that godless leaders, especially priests and monks, who call the Gospel heresy, while simultaneously claiming to be the best of Christians, should be put to death. Hypocritically feigned piety becomes tremendously enraged and bitter and will defend the godless, saying that Christ never killed anyone, etc. It will shamefully toss the friends of God to the winds. In this, the prophesy of Paul (2 Tim. 3) is fulfilled: In the last days lovers of pleasure having a form of godliness will deny its power. Nothing on earth has a better semblance and guise than sham holiness; therefore all corners are full of vain hypocrites, among whom none is bold enough to tell the real truth. Thus, in order that truth may be brought to light, you rulers (God grant it, whether you do it willingly or not) must conduct yourselves according to the conclusion of this chapter of Daniel, namely: Nebuchadnezzar made the holy man Daniel a high official, so that he might render righteous verdicts, as the Holy Spirit says (Ps. 58); for the godless have no right to live except that which the elect may grant them, as is written in Ex. 23. Rejoice, you true friends of God, that the hearts of the enemies of the cross have been broken; they must do what is right, though they have not even dreamt of it. If we fear God, why should we be afraid of good-for-nothing, worthless men? (Num. 14, Josh. 11).

Just be brave. He to whom all power is given in heaven and on earth will wield the authority Himself (Mt. 28). May He preserve you beloved ones forever. Amen.

— ≠◊≡ —

Saint Teresa of Avila
1515–1582

The strong-minded Teresa de Cepeda Ahumada grew up in Spain in a family of *conversos* or converted Jews, disappointing her father's hopes for a worthy marriage when she decided to enter a Carmelite convent in her early twenties. The informal environment of the convent proved too relaxed for the young Teresa, who would eventually advocate a return to the original, stern simplicity of the Carmelite rule. She opened the first house of the "discalced" or barefoot Carmelites in 1562, and until her death in 1582, Teresa trudged throughout Spain, often with Carmelite friars such as John of the Cross at her side, to found a total of seventeen new communities in the face of vigorous opposition. Despite such relentless activity the future saint and Doctor of the Church found time not only for periods of extended contemplation but for a significant amount of writing: her intensely personal *Life,* in which she describes being pierced by an angelic spear (an event memorialized, and eroticized, by the sculptor Bernini in the

---

7. In Daniel 3, Nebuchadnezzar capitulates to his wise men and has three of David's companions thrown into a fiery furnace. God protects them by sending an angel, and the amazed King releases them with the promise never to harm them or the Israelites again.

church of Santa Maria della Vittoria in Rome); her *Way of Perfection,* a manual of instruction for nuns; and *Las Moradas* [The Mansions] or *Interior Castle,* with its poetic image of the soul as a castle "made of a single diamond or of very clear crystal, in which there are many rooms, just as in Heaven there are many mansions."

The *Interior Castle* was written between June and November of 1577 at the behest of her friend Fray Diego de Yepes for the nuns of the convents of "Our Lady of Carmel" in order to "solve their difficulties concerning prayer"—for women, she notes, "best understand each other's language." Teresa's book takes her female reader on a discerning, often lyrical voyage through the Castle. Teresa's sisters begin in the "Mansions of Humility," and thanks to the author's gentle prodding, eventually arrive at the final Mansion, the dwelling-place of the "King," where they experience the bliss of holy matrimony. Invoking such homely images as the hedgehog and tortoise, Teresa reveals her kinship with the evocative visual imagery of her fellow Spaniard Ignatius Loyola, founder of the Jesuit order, as well as the gentle language of John of the Cross.

But such gentleness should not deceive. This was, after all, a woman who faced down inquisitors and hostile critics, and who convinced suspicious confessors of the veracity of her visions (one confessor, she reports in the sixth mansion, accused her of diabolical influences). As the seventeenth-century Catholic English poet Richard Crashaw writes, she was both "eagle and dove."

PRONUNCIATION:
Teresa de Avila: tay-RAY-sah day AH-vee-la

from The Interior Castle[1]

[PREFACE: WOMEN BEST UNDERSTAND EACH OTHER'S LANGUAGE]

I write as mechanically as birds taught to speak, which, knowing nothing but what is taught them and what they hear, repeat the same things again and again. If the Lord wishes me to say anything new, His Majesty will teach it me or be pleased to recall to my memory what I have said on former occasions; and I should be quite satisfied with this, for my memory is so bad that I should be delighted if I could manage to write down a few of the things which people have considered well said, so that they should not be lost. If the Lord should not grant me as much as this, I shall still be the better for having tried, even if this writing under obedience tires me and makes my head worse, and if no one finds what I say of any profit.

And so I begin to fulfil my obligation on this Day of the Holy Trinity, in the year MDLXXVII, in this convent of St. Joseph of Carmel in Toledo, where I am at the present, submitting myself as regards all that I say to the judgment of those who have commanded me to write, and who are persons of great learning.[2] If I should say anything that is not in conformity with what is held by the Holy Roman Catholic Church, it will be through ignorance and not through malice. This may be taken as certain, and also that, through God's goodness, I am, and shall always be, as I always have been, subject to her. May He be for ever blessed and glorified. Amen.

1. Translated from the Spanish by E. Allison Peers.
2. The Day of the Holy Trinity is 2 June 1577, when Teresa was 62 and suffering from various illnesses. The person who "commanded" Teresa to write was Jerónimo Gracián, Teresa's confessor since 1575. Gracián himself would come under suspicion by the Inquisition, and was ultimately expelled from his position as the first head of the order of Discalced Carmelites in 1592. Along with

Teresa and the Dominican theologian Diego de Yanguas, Gracián painstakingly revised the manuscript after Teresa wrote it—quickly—between June and November 1577, shortly after Teresa herself had been questioned, and cleared, by the Inquisition. Nonetheless, Teresa's works, including *Interior Castle,* were sequestered by the Inquisition and were only published after her death.

I was told by the person who commanded me to write that, as the nuns of these convents of Our Lady of Carmel[3] need someone to solve their difficulties concerning prayer, and as (or so it seemed to him) women best understand each other's language, and also in view of their love for me, anything I might say would be particularly useful to them. For this reason he thought that it would be rather important if I could explain things clearly to them and for this reason it is they whom I shall be addressing in what I write—and also because it seems ridiculous to think that I can be of any use to anyone else. Our Lord will be granting me a great favour if a single one of these nuns should find that my words help her to praise Him ever so little better. His Majesty well knows that I have no hope of doing more, and, if I am successful in anything that I may say, they will of course understand that it does not come from me. Their only excuse for crediting me with it could be their having as little understanding as I have ability in these matters if the Lord of His mercy does not grant it me.

* * *

[FOURTH MANSION; CHAPTER 3: ABOUT ENTERING THE CASTLE][4]

It is sometimes said that the soul enters within itself and sometimes that it rises above itself;[5] but I cannot explain things in that kind of language, for I have no skill in it. However, I believe you will understand what I am able to tell you, though I may perhaps be intelligible only to myself. Let us suppose that these senses and faculties (the inhabitants, as I have said, of this castle, which is the figure that I have taken to explain my meaning) have gone out of the castle, and, for days and years, have been consorting with strangers, to whom all the good things in the castle are abhorrent. Then, realizing how much they have lost, they come back to it, though they do not actually re-enter it, because the habits they have formed are hard to conquer. But they are no longer traitors and they now walk about in the vicinity of the castle. The great King, Who dwells in the Mansion within this castle, perceives their good will, and in His great mercy desires to bring them back to Him. So, like a good Shepherd, with a call so gentle that even they can hardly recognize it, He teaches them to know His voice and not to go away and get lost but to return to their Mansion; and so powerful is this Shepherd's call that they give up the things outside the castle which had led them astray, and once again enter it.[6]

I do not think I have ever explained this before as clearly as here. When we are seeking God within ourselves (where He is found more effectively and more profitably than in the creatures, to quote Saint Augustine, who, after having sought Him in many places, found Him within)[7] it is a great help if God grants us this favour. Do not

---

3. The convent of St. Joseph of Carmel was founded by Teresa in 1569. She spent much of her time traveling from one convent to another in the hopes of encouraging her nuns to observe the strict reforms she had ushered in for the order of the Discalced Carmelites.

4. Previously Teresa has explored the terrain around the castle, seen as a metaphor for the soul in which God dwells, as well as the walls that surround it. In this fourth "mansion" she begins to explore the ways in which one can begin to enter the castle, and the present chapter (Chapter 3) opens with the effects of what Teresa calls the "Prayer of Recollection."

5. A likely allusion to the spiritual work by one of the first Spanish mystics, Francisco de Osuna (1492–1540), the *Third Spiritual Alphabet*. This book had a profound influence on Teresa's life; Osuna's work is particularly rele-

vant here, since it is largely focused on the mystical technique of recollection and prayer that is the subject of the fourth mansion.

6. The Shepherd, also described as King, is God. Jesus refers to himself as a shepherd in numerous passages from the Gospels, such as John 10:14: "I am the good shepherd, and I know mine and mine know me. . . . and they shall hear my voice, and there shall be one fold and one shepherd."

7. In *Confessions* 10.27 Augustine laments that he came "too late" to love God: "And behold, you were within me, and I out of myself, where I searched for you: I rushed headlong upon those beautiful things you have made." This verse inspired Teresa on numerous occasions, as references to it in her *Life* and *Way of Perfection* attest.

suppose that the understanding can attain to Him, merely by trying to think of Him as within the soul, or the imagination, by picturing Him as there. This is a good habit and an excellent kind of meditation, for it is founded upon a truth—namely, that God is within us. But it is not the kind of prayer that I have in mind, for anyone (with the help of the Lord, you understand) can practise it for himself. What I am describing is quite different. These people are sometimes in the castle before they have begun to think about God at all. I cannot say where they entered it or how they heard their Shepherd's call: it was certainly not with their ears, for outwardly such a call is not audible. They become markedly conscious that they are gradually retiring within themselves; anyone who experiences this will discover what I mean: I cannot explain it better. I think I have read that they are like a hedgehog or a tortoise withdrawing into itself; and whoever wrote that must have understood it well.[8] These creatures, however, enter within themselves whenever they like; whereas with us it is not a question of our will—it happens only when God is pleased to grant us this favour. For my own part, I believe that, when His Majesty grants it, He does so to people who are already leaving the things of the world. I do not mean that people who are married must actually leave the world—they can do so only in desire: His call to them is a special one and aims at making them intent upon interior things. I believe, however, that if we wish to give His Majesty free course, He will grant more than this to those whom He is beginning to call still higher.

Anyone who is conscious that this is happening within himself should give God great praise, for he will be very right to recognize what a favour it is; and the thanksgiving which he makes for it will prepare him for greater favours. One preparation for listening to Him, as certain books tell us, is that we should contrive, not to use our reasoning powers, but to be intent upon discovering what the Lord is working in the soul; for, if His Majesty has not begun to grant us absorption, I cannot understand how we can cease thinking in any way which will not bring us more harm than profit, although this has been a matter of continual discussion among spiritual persons. For my own part, I confess my lack of humility, but their arguments have never seemed to me good enough to lead me to accept what they say. One person told me of a certain book by the saintly Fray Peter of Alcántara (for a saint I believe he is), which would certainly have convinced me, for I know how much he knew about such things;[9] but we read it together, and found that he says exactly what I say, although not in the same words; it is quite clear from what he says that love must already be awake. It is possible that I am mistaken, but I base my position on the following reasons.

First, in such spiritual activity as this, the person who does most is he who thinks least and desires to do least: what we have to do is to beg like poor and needy persons coming before a great and rich Emperor and then cast down our eyes in humble expectation. When from the secret signs He gives us we seem to realize that He is hearing us, it is well for us to keep silence, since He has permitted us to be near Him and there will be no harm in our striving not to labour with the understanding—provided, I mean, that we are able to do so. But if we are not quite sure that the King has heard us, or sees us, we must not stay where we are like ninnies, for there still remains a great deal for the soul to do when it has stilled the understanding; if it did nothing more it would experience much greater aridity and the imagination would grow more restless because of the effort caused it by cessation from thought. The Lord wishes us

---

8. Teresa probably found the hedgehog analogy in Osuna (Book 6).

9. Peter of Alcántara wrote the *Treatise of Prayer and Meditation* to which Teresa is probably referring.

rather to make requests of Him and to remember that we are in His presence, for He knows what is fitting for us. I cannot believe in the efficacy of human activity in matters where His Majesty appears to have set a limit to it and to have been pleased to reserve action to Himself. There are many other things in which He has not so reserved it, such as penances, works of charity[1] and prayers; these, with His aid, we can practise for ourselves, as far as our miserable nature is capable of them.

The second reason is that all these interior activities are gentle and peaceful, and to do anything painful brings us harm rather than help. By "anything painful" I mean anything that we try to force ourselves to do; it would be painful, for example, to hold our breath. The soul must just leave itself in the hands of God, and do what He wills it to do, completely disregarding its own advantage and resigning itself as much as it possibly can to the will of God. The third reason is that the very effort which the soul makes in order to cease from thought will perhaps awaken thought and cause it to think a great deal. The fourth reason is that the most important and pleasing thing in God's eyes is our remembering His honour and glory and forgetting ourselves and our own profit and ease and pleasure. And how can a person be forgetful of himself when he is taking such great care about his actions that he dare not even stir, or allow his understanding and desires to stir, even for the purpose of desiring the greater glory of God or of rejoicing in the glory which is His? When His Majesty wishes the working of the understanding to cease, He employs it in another manner, and illumines the soul's knowledge to so much higher a degree than any we can ourselves attain that He leads it into a state of absorption, in which, without knowing how, it is much better instructed than it could ever be as a result of its own efforts, which would only spoil everything. God gave us our faculties to work with, and everything will have its due reward; there is no reason, then, for trying to cast a spell over them—they must be allowed to perform their office until God gives them a better one.

As I understand it, the soul whom the Lord has been pleased to lead into this Mansion will do best to act as I have said. Let it try, without forcing itself or causing any turmoil, to put a stop to all discursive reasoning, yet not to suspend the understanding, nor to cease from all thought, though it is well for it to remember that it is in God's presence and Who this God is. If feeling this should lead it into a state of absorption, well and good; but it should not try to understand what this state is, because that is a gift bestowed upon the will. The will, then, should be left to enjoy it, and should not labour except for uttering a few loving words, for although in such a case one may not be striving to cease from thought, such cessation often comes, though for a very short time.

I have explained elsewhere the reason why this occurs in this kind of prayer (I am referring to the kind which I began to explain in this Mansion).[2] With it I have included this Prayer of Recollection which ought to have been described first, for it comes far below the consolations of God already mentioned, and is indeed the first step towards attaining them. For in the Prayer of Recollection it is unnecessary to abandon meditation and the activities of the understanding. When, instead of coming

---

1. A reference to the seven acts of mercy or misericordia, which included assisting the sick, burying the dead, and giving alms to the poor. While her focus in this book is on mystical practice, Teresa believed that contemplative life alone did not lead to perfection. As she says in Ways of Perfection, an earlier work also addressed to nuns in which she discusses the more practical aspects of prayer, "Mary and Martha"—representatives of the contemplative and active lives in Luke 10—"must go together."

2. Teresa had discussed this suspension of the will in her Ways of Perfection (see Chapter 31). Much of the fourth mansion is about the necessity of beginning to yield one's will and discursive reasoning in order to more fully enjoy what God offers and hence to begin to "enter" the castle.

through conduits, the water springs directly from its source, the understanding checks its activity, or rather the activity is checked for it when it finds it cannot understand what it desires, and thus it roams about all over the place, like a demented creature, and can settle down to nothing. The will is fixed so firmly upon its God that this disturbed condition of the understanding causes it great distress; but it must not take any notice of this, for if it does so it will lose a great part of what it is enjoying; it must forget about it, and abandon itself into the arms of love, and His Majesty will teach it what to do next; almost its whole work is to realize its unworthiness to receive such great good and to occupy itself in thanksgiving.

In order to discuss the Prayer of Recollection I passed over the effects or signs to be observed in souls to whom this prayer is granted by God Our Lord. It is clear that a dilation or enlargement of the soul takes place, as if the water proceeding from the spring had no means of running away, but the fountain had a device ensuring that, the more freely the water flowed, the larger became the basin. So it is in this kind of prayer; and God works many more wonders in the soul, thus fitting and gradually disposing it to retain all that He gives it. So this gentle movement and this interior dilation cause the soul to be less constrained in matters relating to the service of God than it was before and give it much more freedom.

* * *

There is one peril of which I want to warn you, though I have spoken of it elsewhere; I have seen persons given to prayer fall into it, and especially women, for, as we are weaker than men, we run more risk of what I am going to describe. It is this: some women, because of prayers, vigils and severe penances, and also for other reasons, have poor health. When they experience any spiritual consolation, therefore, their physical nature is too much for them; and as soon as they feel any interior joy there comes over them a physical weakness and languor, and they fall into a sleep, which they call "spiritual," and which is a little more marked than the condition that has been described. Thinking the one state to be the same as the other, they abandon themselves to this absorption; and the more they relax, the more complete becomes this absorption, because their physical nature continues to grow weaker. So they get it into their heads that it is *arrobamiento,* or rapture. But I call it *abobamiento,* foolishness; for they are doing nothing but wasting their time at it and ruining their health.

One person was in this state for eight hours; she was not unconscious, nor was she conscious of anything concerning God. She was cured by being told to take more food and sleep and to do less penance; for, though she had misled both her confessor and other people and, quite involuntarily, deceived herself, there was one person who understood her. I believe the devil would go to any pains to gain such people as that and he was beginning to make good progress with this one.[3]

It must be understood that although, when this state is something that really comes from God, there may be languor, both interior and exterior, there will be none in the soul, which, when it finds itself near God, is moved with great joy. The experience does not last long, but only for a little while. Although the soul may become absorbed again, yet this kind of prayer, as I have said, except in cases of physical weakness, does not go so far as to overcome the body or to produce in it any exterior sensation. Be advised, then, and, if you experience anything of this kind, tell your superior, and relax as much as you can. The superior should give such persons fewer

---

3. The "person" of whom Teresa speaks here may be Teresa herself.

hours of prayer—very few, indeed—and should see that they sleep and eat well, until their physical strength, if it has become exhausted, comes back again. If their constitution is so weak that this does not suffice, they can be certain that God is not calling them to anything beyond the active life. There is room in convents for people of all kinds; let anyone of this type, then, be kept busy with duties, and let care be taken that she is not left alone very much, or her health will be completely ruined. This sort of life will be a great mortification to her, but it is here that the Lord wishes to test her love for Him by seeing how she bears His absence and after a while He may well be pleased to restore her strength; if He is not, her vocal prayer and her obedience will bring her as much benefit and merit as she would have obtained in other ways, and perhaps more.

There may also be some who are so weak in intellect and imagination—I have known such—that they believe they actually see all they imagine. This is highly dangerous and perhaps we shall treat of it later, but no more shall be said here; for I have written at great length of this Mansion, as it is the one which the greatest number of souls enter. As the natural is united with the supernatural in it, it is here that the devil can do most harm; for in the Mansions of which I have not yet spoken the Lord gives him fewer opportunities. May He be for ever praised. Amen.

* * *

[SIXTH MANSION; CHAPTER 9: IMAGINARY VISIONS; WOMEN AND THEIR CONFESSORS][1]

Let us now come to imaginary visions, in which the devil is said to interfere more frequently than in those already described.[2] This may well be the case; but when they come from Our Lord they seem to me in some ways more profitable because they are in closer conformity with our nature, except for those which the Lord bestows in the final Mansion, and with which no others can compare.

Let us now imagine, as I said in the last chapter, that this Lord is here. It is as if in a gold reliquary there were hidden a precious stone of the highest value and the choicest virtues: although we have never seen the stone, we know for certain that it is there and if we carry it about with us we can have the benefit of its virtues. We do not prize it any the less for not having seen it, because we have found by experience that it has cured us of certain illnesses for which it is a sovereign remedy. But we dare not look at it, or open the reliquary in which it is contained, nor are we able to do so; for only the owner of the jewel knows how to open it, and though he has lent it to us so that we may benefit by it, he has kept the key and so it is still his own. He will open it when he wants to show it to us and he will take it back when he sees fit to do so. And that is what God does, too.

And now let us suppose that on some occasion the owner of the reliquary suddenly wants to open it, for the benefit of the person to whom he has lent it. Obviously this person will get much greater pleasure from it if he can recall the wonderful brilliance of the stone, and it will remain the more deeply engraven upon his memory.

---

1. With this mansion, the soul has begun to communicate in special ways with God, and God with the soul. Teresa has just ended the previous chapter with the warning that while God is capable of addressing himself to the soul through visions, the sisters who have these experiences should not think they "are better than the rest": "The saintliest will be she who serves Our Lord with the greatest mortification and humility and purity of conscience."

2. One of Teresa's concerns in this chapter and elsewhere is the ambiguous origin of visions, which can as easily come from the devil as from God. Her term "imaginary visions" (las visiones imaginarias) does not necessarily have a derogatory meaning. As becomes clear in the following pages, confessors sometimes play a role, and not always a supportive one, in questioning the veracity of a nun's vision.

This is what happens here. When Our Lord is pleased to bestow greater consolations upon this soul, He grants it, in whatever way He thinks best, a clear revelation of His sacred Humanity, either as He was when He lived in the world, or as He was after His resurrection; and although He does this so quickly that we might liken the action to a flash of lightning, this most glorious image is so deeply engraven upon the imagination that I do not believe it can possibly disappear until it is where it can be enjoyed to all eternity.

I speak of an "image," but it must not be supposed that one looks at it as at a painting; it is really alive, and sometimes even speaks to the soul and shows it things both great and secret. But you must realize that, although the soul sees this for a certain length of time, it can no more be gazing at it all the time than it could keep gazing at the sun. So the vision passes very quickly; though this is not because its brilliance hurts the interior sight—that is, the medium by which all such things are seen—as the brilliance of the sun hurts the eyes.[3] When it is a question of exterior sight, I can say nothing about it, for the person I have mentioned, and of whom I can best speak, had not experienced this; and reason can testify only inadequately to things of which it has no experience. The brilliance of this vision is like that of infused light or of a sun covered with some material of the transparency of a diamond, if such a thing could be woven. This raiment looks like the finest cambric. Almost invariably the soul on which God bestows this favour remains in rapture, because its unworthiness cannot endure so terrible a sight.

I say "terrible," because, though the sight is the loveliest and most delightful imaginable, even by a person who lived and strove to imagine it for a thousand years, because it so far exceeds all that our imagination and understanding can compass, its presence is of such exceeding majesty that it fills the soul with a great terror. It is unnecessary to ask here how, without being told, the soul knows Who it is, for He reveals Himself quite clearly as the Lord of Heaven and earth. This the kings of the earth never do: indeed, they would be thought very little of for what they are, but that they are accompanied by their suites, or heralds proclaim them. * * *

I can tell you truly that, wicked as I am, I have never feared the torments of hell, for they seem nothing by comparison with the thought of the wrath which the damned will see in the Lord's eyes—those eyes so lovely and tender and benign. I do not think my heart could bear to see that; and I have felt like this all my life. How much more will anyone fear this to whom He has thus revealed Himself, and given such a consciousness of His presence as will produce unconsciousness! It must be for this reason that the soul remains in suspension; the Lord helps it in its weakness so that this may be united with His greatness in this sublime communion with God.

When the soul is able to remain for a long time looking upon the Lord, I do not think it can be a vision at all. It must rather be that some striking idea creates a picture in the imagination: but this will be a dead image by comparison with the other.

Some persons—and I know this is the truth, for they have discussed it with me; and not just three or four of them, but a great many—find that their imagination is so weak, or their understanding is so nimble, or for some other reason their imagination becomes so absorbed, that they think they can actually see everything that is in their mind. If they had ever seen a true vision they would realize their error beyond the possibility of doubt. Little by little they build up the picture which they see with their

---

3. At the end of *Paradiso* Dante has a similar reference to the blinding light of the sun, which for him is also God; see Volume B.

imagination, but this produces no effect upon them and they remain cold—much more so than they are after seeing a sacred image. No attention, of course, should be paid to such a thing, which will be forgotten much more quickly than a dream.

The experience we are discussing here is quite different. The soul is very far from expecting to see anything and the thought of such a thing has never even passed through its mind. All of a sudden the whole vision is revealed to it and all its faculties and senses are thrown into the direst fear and confusion, and then sink into that blessed state of peace. It is just as when Saint Paul was thrown to the ground and there came that storm and tumult in the sky;[4] just so, in this interior world, there is a great commotion; and then all at once, as I have said, everything grows calm, and the soul, completely instructed in such great truths, has no need of another master. True wisdom, without any effort on its own part, has overcome its stupidity; and for a certain space of time it enjoys the complete certainty that this favour comes from God. However often it may be told that this is not so it cannot be induced to fear that it may have been mistaken. Later, when the confessor insinuates this fear, God allows the soul to begin to hesitate as to whether He could possibly grant this favour to such a sinner.[5] But that is all; for, as I have said in these other cases, in speaking of temptations in matters of faith, the devil can disturb the soul, but he cannot shake the firmness of its belief. On the contrary, the more fiercely he attacks it, the more certain it becomes that he could never endow it with so many blessings—which is actually true, for over the interior of the soul he wields less power. He may be able to reveal something to it, but not with the same truth and majesty, nor can he produce the same results.

As confessors cannot see all this for themselves, and a soul to whom God has granted such a favour may be unable to describe it, they have misgivings about it, and quite justifiably. So they have to proceed cautiously, and even to wait for some time to see what results these apparitions produce, and to observe gradually how much humility they leave in the soul and to what extent it is strengthened in virtue; if they come from the devil there will soon be signs of the fact, for he will be caught out in a thousand lies. If the confessor is experienced, and has himself been granted such visions, it will not be long before he is able to form a judgment, for the account which the soul gives will at once show him whether they proceed from God or from the imagination or from the devil, especially if His Majesty has granted him the gift of discerning spirits.[6] If he has this and is a learned man, he will be able to form an opinion perfectly well, even though he may be without experience.

The really essential thing, sisters, is that you should speak to your confessor very plainly and candidly—I do not mean here in confessing your sins, for of course you will do so then, but in describing your experiences in prayer. For unless you do this, I cannot assure you that you are proceeding as you should or that it is God Who is teaching you. God is very anxious for us to speak candidly and clearly to those who are in His place, and to desire them to be acquainted with all our thoughts, and still more with our actions, however trivial these may be. If you do this, you need not be disturbed, or worried, for, even if these things be not of God, they will do you no

---

4. Paul's dramatic conversion experience is recounted in Acts 9: as he traveled to Damascus, "a light from heaven shone round about him; and falling to the ground, he heard a voice. . . ."

5. Typically each convent had a confessor or priest assigned to it to hear nuns' confessions on a regular basis.

6. A number of treatises were written for confessors with the purpose of instructing them how to identify "good" spirits from "bad"; perhaps the most famous work was *On Distinguishing True from False Revelations* by the French theologian Jean Gerson, who in his last work argued that there was no reason to think that the visions of his contemporary, Joan of Arc, were diabolical.

harm if you are humble and have a good conscience. His Majesty is able to bring good out of evil and you will gain by following the road by which the devil hoped to bring you to destruction. For, as you will suppose that it is God Who is granting you these great favours, you will strive to please Him better and keep His image ever in your mind. A very learned man used to say that the devil is a skilful painter, and that, if he were to show him an absolutely lifelike image of the Lord, it would not worry him, because it would quicken his devotion, and so he would be using the devil's own wicked weapons to make war on him. However evil the painter be, one cannot fail to reverence the picture that he paints, if it is of Him Who is our only Good.

This learned man thought that the counsel, given by some people, to treat any vision of this kind with scorn, was very wrong: we must reverence a painting of our King, he said, wherever we see it. I think he is right; even on a worldly plane we should feel that. If a person who had a great friend knew that insulting things were being said about his portrait he would not be pleased. How much more incumbent upon us is it, then, always to be respectful when we see a crucifix or any kind of portrait of our Emperor!

Although I have written this elsewhere, I have been glad to set it down here, for I knew someone who was in great distress because she had been ordered to adopt this derisive remedy.[7] I do not know who can have invented such advice, for, if it came from her confessor, it would have been a torture to her: she would be bound to obey him, and would have thought herself a lost soul unless she had done so. My own advice is that, if you are given such counsel, you should not accept it and should with all humility put forward this argument that I have given you. I was extremely struck by the good reasons against the practice alleged by the person who advised me in this case.

The soul derives great profit from this favour bestowed by the Lord, for thinking upon Him or upon His life and Passion recalls His most meek and lovely face, which is the greatest comfort, just as in the earthly sphere we get much more comfort from seeing a person who is a great help to us than if we had never known him. * * *

Let us place ourselves in His hands so that His will may be done in us; if we cling firmly to this maxim and our wills are resolute we cannot possibly go astray. And you must note that you will merit no more glory for having received many of these favours; on the contrary, the fact that you are receiving more imposes on you greater obligations to serve. The Lord does not deprive us of anything which adds to our merit, for this remains in our own power. There are many saintly people who have never known what it is to receive a favour of this kind, and there are others who receive a favour of this kind, and there are others who received such favours, although they are not saintly. Do not suppose, again, that they occur continually. Each occasion on which the Lord grants them brings with it a great many trials; and thus the soul does not think about receiving more, but only about how to put those it receives to a good use.[8]

Saint John of the Cross
1542–1591

Nowhere do the imaginative writings of the Arabic world and those of the European Renaissance come together more suggestively than in the poetry and prose of Juan de Yepes, best

7. Teresa is most likely this "someone"; she had already written in her *Life* about occasionally severe misunderstandings with confessors.

8. The book will end in the seventh mansion, where the soul experiences "the greatest happiness in finding repose and in living with Christ."

known as Saint John of the Cross. Nor are there more acute examples of the perils of Europe's intolerance during the late sixteenth century. Written in a toilet stall in Toledo where John was imprisoned by his fellow Carmelite monks for nine months, John's most famous poem, "The Dark Night" (*Noche Oscura*), vividly depicts the soul's desperate and solitary journey to an unknowable God. Persuaded by Teresa of Avila to work with her to reform the Carmelite order rather than to remain a solitary monk, he lived a life of extremes. On the one hand, he was active as rector and prior in the new Discalced Carmelite order. On the other his recalcitrant brothers banished him to posts of punishing isolation (such as Úbeda, where he died).

This productive vacillation paradoxically enabled him to write the haunting poetic meditations of which his fellow friars, and the Spanish Inquisition, were so suspicious. Among John's most problematic works in his relatively small corpus are his queries on the names of God, reminiscent of the Arab Sufi poets, and his commentaries on his own poetry, particularly the lengthy "Spiritual Canticle." They are works that dared to paraphrase, and creatively interpret, passages from the Vulgate Bible in Spanish at a time when vernacular translations were prohibited, and in a manner that makes the mystical journey as sensuous as it is cerebral.

"The Dark Night"[1]
Songs

of the soul, which rejoices at having reached
that lofty state of perfection:
union with God by the way
5   of spiritual negation.[2]

      Once in the dark of night
when love burned bright with yearning, I arose
      (O windfall of delight!)
      and how I left none knows—
10   dead to the world my house in deep repose;

      in the dark, where all goes right,
thanks to a secret ladder, other clothes,
      (O windfall of delight!)
      in the dark, enwrapped in those—
15   dead to the world my house in deep repose.

      There in the lucky dark,
none to observe me, darkness far and wide;
      no sign for me to mark,
      no other light, no guide
20   except for my heart—the fire, the fire inside!

      That led me on
true as the very noon is—truer too!—
      to where there waited one
      I knew—how well I knew!—
25   in a place where no one was in view.

      O dark of night, my guide!
night dearer than anything all your dawns discover!

---

1. Translated by John Frederick Nims. In Spanish the title is simply "Noche oscura," without the article.

2. In most editions of the poem, this first stanza is given as a prose introduction.

O night drawing side to side
the loved and lover—
30   she that the lover loves, lost in the lover![3]

Upon my flowering breast,
kept for his pleasure garden, his alone,
the lover was sunk in rest;
I cherished him—my own!—
35   there in air from plumes of the cedar blown.

In air from the castle wall
as my hand in his hair moved lovingly at play,
he let cool fingers fall
—and the fire there where they lay!—
40   all senses in oblivion drift away.

I stayed, not minding me;
my forehead on the lover I reclined.
Earth ending, I went free,
left all my care behind
45   among the lilies falling and out of mind.

—•— ≍◆≍ —•—

Domenico Scandella
1532–1599

Hundreds of people were sentenced as heretics and executed in the years following the vigorous Catholic reaction to the Protestant Reformation. Domenico Scandella, a semiliterate miller from a tiny town in northern Italy, had the misfortune to be one of them. Better known by his nickname Menocchio, Scandella allegedly promoted a number of misguided beliefs while he sold grain at his mill (along with the tavern and church, one of the centers of the town's activities) or played music in neighboring villages. Among these heresies was the conviction that in the beginning, the universal chaos congealed as cheese. The cheese then made worms, and worms became the first angels—one of whom was God. Brought to trial for these statements, Scandella was convicted on the testimony of his neighbors and imprisoned. On his release in 1586, he was consigned to wear the yellow cross as a sign of infamy, and ordered "never to speak of or mention his wrongheaded opinions, except detesting them and reproaching himself for his frivolity and vacuity." But the unfortunate miller didn't hold his tongue for long. In July 1599, the sixty-seven-year-old was again denounced. Brought for a second time before the Inquisition, his backsliding was quickly established, and he was sent to local authorities for the only possible punishment: death by fire.

The trials of Menocchio were meticulously documented by authorities of the Inquisition in Udine, and hundreds of pages of testimony by thirteen witnesses against Menocchio and by Menocchio himself survive. Excerpted here is a section from the original trials against Menocchio, his confession, and the letter that led to his second denouncement in 1599.

---

3. In the Spanish, the difference between *lover* and *loved* is less distinct; both are referred to with the term *amado* (beloved), although one is masculine, the other feminine (*amada*). Much of the linguistic play on the relationship between lover and beloved, as well as on the imagery of the garden, is drawn from the biblical Song of Songs.

PRONUNCIATION:
Menocchio: meh-NO-kyo

from His Trials Before the Inquisition[1]

from *The First Trial, Tuesday, 7 February 1584*[2]

The guard led out the prisoner, who was wearing a certain vestment, and over it a cloak and cap and other pieces of clothing all of white wool. He was asked to take an oath to tell the truth about himself and his companions, and then asked by the reverend vicar: "Who are you?" He replied: "I have the name of Domenego Scandella, called Menocchio."

And asked if he knew why he was standing there in the presence of monsignor the vicar, he replied: "The father inquisitor had me summoned in Montereale and asked me who I am, and I replied that I was Domenego Scandella. His lordship informed me that I had been denounced to the Holy Office. Then under penalty of a hundred ducats I had to show up at Maniago, where that father had me arrested and led handcuffed to Concordia."

Asked where he was born, he replied: "I am from Montereale, in the diocese of Concordia. My father was called Zuane and my mother Menega and I have lived in Montereale most of my life, except for two years when I was banished, of which I spent one in Arba and one in Cargna, and I was banished for being in a brawl."

Questioned, he replied: "My trades are that of miller, carpenter, sawyer, builder of walls and other things."

Questioned, he replied: "Yes sir, I do know how to read, write and do figures."

Asked if he knows how to say the Credo, as every faithful Christian is obliged to do, which is called the symbol of the apostles, and that other Credo which the holy Roman Church still uses and is recited on Sunday at Mass and on certain holy days, he replied: "I know how to recite the Credo and also the one said in the Mass; I have heard it spoken and have helped to sing it in the church of Montereale."

Asked: "Since you know the Credo, what do you say about that article 'et in Iesum Christum, filium eius, unicum Dominum nostrum, qui conceptus est de Spiritu Sancto, natus ex Maria virgine?'[3] What did you say and believe about it in the past, and what do you believe now?" And when asked, do you understand the words: 'qui conceptus est de Spiritu Santo, natus ex Maria virgine?' he replied: 'Yes sir, I understand.' And he added: Since I made confession many times with a priest of Barcis, I told him: 'Can it be that Jesus Christ was conceived by the Holy Spirit and born from the Virgin Mary?' But I would add that I believed it, but that sometimes the Devil tempted me about this, and he replied yes, that I should believe it firmly, and this happened two or three years ago. This idea of mine was based on the fact that so many men are born in the world and none are born from a virgin woman, and since I had read that the glorious Virgin was married to St. Joseph, I believed that our Lord Jesus

---

1. Translated from the Italian by John and Anne C. Tedeschi.

2. The trial against Menocchio had begun the previous October, and was held in the episcopal court of Concordia, the diocese in which Menocchio's village of Montereale was located. Thirteen witnesses had already been questioned and Menocchio's house thoroughly searched for "suspected or prohibited books" (none were found) by the time Menocchio himself was called to the inquisitor's stand.

3. A line from the Creed, recited during Mass: "and [I believe] in Jesus Christ, his son, our only Lord, conceived by the Holy Spirit and born of the Virgin Mary."

Anonymous, *Death of Savonarola*, 1498, in the Piazza della Signoria, Florence (16th century). As in Brueghel's painting of the death of Icarus (Color Plate 5), Savonarola's execution for heresy is ignored by many of the figures in Florence's central piazza; they too seem to have "somewhere to get to" and casually turn away from the spectacle of the friar's death. Along with two of his fellow friars, Savonarola, who for four years capably governed the city of Florence so lovingly portrayed here, is escorted to the fire. According to the historian Guicciardini, some of his followers expected a miracle to happen and their beloved leader to emerge unscathed. In the absence of such miracles, Guicciardini goes on, Savonarola died, "suffering his death with a constant heart, and without uttering any words that would acknowledge either his crime or his innocence." As the later execution of the miller Menocchio suggests, public executions were not limited to the famous; over two thousand would die in Europe while the Inquisition was in full swing, with Spain claiming the majority of lives.

Christ was the son of St. Joseph, because I read in some stories that St. Joseph called our Lord Jesus Christ son. I read this in a book called *The Little Flower of the Bible*."[4]

Asked whether he had said these words in the form of preaching or exhortation in front of people, he replied: "It is true that I spoke these words to different people, but not to make them believe them. On the contrary, I exhorted many people, saying: 'Do you want me to teach you the true way? Do good and walk in the path of our predecessors and do as holy mother Church commands.' But those words above I spoke because I had been tempted and not because I believed them or wanted to teach them to

4. A popular Italian compilation of religious texts, including the Bible and several orthodox biblical commentaries.

others. It was the evil spirit who made me believe those things, and he also instigated me to say them to others." * * *

Asked about what he believes and said concerning that article of the faith which states: 'passus sub Pontio Pilato, crucifixus, mortuus et sepultus,'[5] and if he ever said these or similar words: that it showed little wisdom on the part of Our Savior Jesus Christ, since he is omnipotent, as it is preached, to let himself be killed on the cross, he replied: "I said that if Jesus Christ was eternal God, he should not have let himself be caught and crucified. And I was not certain on this point, but had my doubts, as I said, because it seemed an important thing that a Lord should let himself be taken like this. And so I wondered whether, since he had been crucified, he was not God, but some prophet, some great man sent by God to preach in this world. I discussed this too with that Francesco Fasseta."[6]

Asked what he had said about God and what he had believed and believes that God is, because he has been heard to say that God is only air, earth, etc., he replied: "I believe that the whole world, that is air, earth and all the beautiful things of this world are God, and that the sun is a creature of God, because we say that man is made in the image and likeness of God[7] and in man there is air, fire, earth and water and from this it follows that air, earth, fire and water are God."

Asked if he had ever said that in the beginning this world was nothing and that the water of the sea was beaten into a foam, which coagulated like a cheese, from which a great multitude of worms was born, and these worms became men, of which the most powerful was God, to whom the others rendered obedience; and that there was one evil one with his legions, Satan, who tried to oppose God and was conquered, and this God, similar to a great captain, sent his son as an ambassador to men in this world, who let himself be hung up like a beast, he replied: "I have said that, in my opinion, all was chaos, that is, earth, air, water, and fire were mixed together; and out of that bulk a mass formed—just as cheese is made out of milk—and worms appeared in it, and these were the angels. The most holy majesty decreed that these should be God and the angels, and among that number of angels, there was also God, he too having been created out of that mass at the same time, and he was made lord, with four captains, Lucifer, Michael, Gabriel, and Raphael. That Lucifer sought to make himself lord equal to the king, who was the majesty of God, and for this arrogance God ordered him driven out of heaven with all his host and his company; and this God later created Adam and Eve and people in great number to take the place of the angels who had been expelled. And as this multitude did not follow God's commandments, he sent his son, whom the Jews seized, and he was crucified." He added: "I never said that he allowed himself to be hung up like a beast. Indeed, I really said that he let himself be crucified, and he who was crucified was one of the children of God, because we are all God's children, and of the same nature as the one who was crucified and he was a man like the rest of us, but with more dignity just as the pope is a man like us, but of greater rank, because he has power, and he who was crucified was born of St. Joseph and Mary, the Virgin."

5. Another line from the Creed: Christ "suffered under Pontius Pilate, was crucified, died, and was buried."
6. The first witness to testify, Fasseta was related to Menocchio. According to his testimony, Menocchio "did say that if he had been God he would not have allowed himself to be crucified, and he did not believe that Our Savior Jesus Christ was crucified. And he spoke these words to me alone in the precincts of Montereale, I do not remember when, but in the more than twenty years that I have known him, he said them more than once."
7. Quoting Genesis 1:26: "God said, 'Let us make mankind in our image and likeness.'"

Questioned, he replied: "I said this to Francesco Fasseta and I said Mary, the Virgin, because she was called virgin having been in the temple of the virgins. There was a temple where twelve virgins were kept, and as they grew up they were married off. And I read this in a book called *Rosary of the Glorious Virgin*[8] which was loaned to me when I was in Arba."

Asked if he had ever said, speaking of the most holy sacrament of the Eucharist: "This is a piece of dough and not God, and I do not believe in a God you cannot see," he replied: "I have said that the wafer is a piece of dough, but that the Holy Spirit comes down from heaven in it, and this I really believe."

Asked what he thinks the Holy Spirit is, he replied: "I believe he is God."

Asked if he knows how many are the persons in the Holy Trinity, he replied: "Yes sir, I do, the Father, Son and Holy Spirit."

Questioned: "In which of these three persons do you think the Eucharist is converted?" he replied: "Into the Holy Spirit."

Asked again which person precisely of the holy Trinity is in that host, he replied: "I believe that it is the Holy Spirit."

Questioned, he replied: "I did not say that I do not believe in a God I cannot see."

Questioned: "When your parish priest preached on the most holy sacrament, what did he say was in that most holy host?" he replied: "He said that it was the body of Christ, nonetheless I thought it was the Holy Spirit, and that is because I believe that the Holy Spirit is greater than Christ, who was a man, and the Holy Spirit came from the hand of God. . . ."

Cautioned to consider the truth more carefully, the reverend and most excellent lord vicar had him led back under close guard to his cell. After the foregoing testimony was read back to Ser Domenico, he ratified and signed it.

And I Domenego Scandella of Montereale ratify what I have testified to above.

At this point the aforesaid Domenico added: "Sir, that which I have said either out of the inspiration of God or of the Devil; I do not confirm it is either the truth or a lie, but I ask for mercy and I will do whatever is taught me."

A short time later the jailer attested that he had conducted the aforesaid Domenico to his cell and had left him under close guard.

* * *

19 January 1586[9]

There appeared Ser Domenico Scandella before the same persons as above, who as soon as he was conducted before the most reverend and most illustrious bishop, and the most reverend inquisitor general, and the reverend and most excellent vicar, prostrating himself on the ground tearfully beseeched pardon for his errors with humble words and supplications. And when he was questioned by the reverend inquisitor, he replied: "My son presented that petition, about which you ask me, in my name, and again with my own voice I beseech you for what it contains, resigning myself always to God's mercy and to the mercy of this Holy Office."

Questioned, he replied: "I am deeply repentant that I have offended my Lord God, and I wish now that I had not said the foolish things that I said, into which I stupidly fell blinded by the Devil and not understanding myself what he was telling me."

---

8. Another vernacular devotional book from 1575 by the Dominican Fra Alberto da Castello.

9. Almost two years have elapsed since Menocchio's arrest.

Questioned, he replied: "Not only have I not regretted doing the penance that was imposed on me and being in that prison, but I felt such a great happiness, and God comforted me always while I was praying to his divine majesty, that I felt I was in heaven."

And when he was asked: "If it should please the Holy Office that you continue to make your penance in prison, would you stay willingly?" he replied: "I would do whatever was pleasing to our most holy majesty." And these were his actual words: "If I did not have a wife and children, whose love pulls at me, since I, if I remain in this place, will be their ruin, I would willingly stay as long as I live to do penance for my offenses to the Lord Jesus Christ." And he said this clasping his hands and raising them from his eyes to heaven.

Questioned, he replied: "If I should be granted this grace, if I am worthy of it, of returning home to my little family, I will not hesitate to stick firm to this resolution to be a Catholic and a true Christian and to perform all those penances that this reverend tribunal will impose on me."

Questioned, he replied: "Two years have passed and I now begin a third year in prison."

Questioned, he replied: "I am fifty-three years old, going on fifty-four and have seven children, boys and girls, and my oldest son has a wife and children, and my wife is about fifty years old. As for my possessions, I am very poor and only have two rented mills and two fields which I lease and with these I supported and support my poor family."

Questioned, he replied: "The prison in which I am confined is harsh, earthen, dark and humid, so that I was very sick this winter and lay four months without getting out of bed. And this year I had swollen legs, and I also swelled up in the face, as you can see, and I almost lost my hearing, and became weak and almost beside myself." And truly while he was saying this he was very pale in appearance, and an invalid in his body, and in a poor way. This testimony having been received, he was dismissed, etc.[1]

from *The Second Trial*[2]

LETTER FROM LEONARDO SIMON TO FRA GIOVANNI BATTISTA ANGELUCCI, 7 MARCH 1596

Most magnificent and reverend, my highly esteemed lord. Having heard the bull concerning heresy, I cannot fail but to write these few words for the sake of my soul and also to wash away these sins. I found myself in Udine one day and conversing with a person called Menocchio, a miller of Montereale, he spoke these words to me, since he had heard that I wanted to become a monk: "I hear that you want to go and become a monk." And I said to him: "What do you think, wouldn't it be a good thing?" And he replied: "No, because it is a beggarly business, and those who die for love of God, we do not even know if they go to heaven or hell. It is true that God is master and can make and unmake." And then I told him that even Jews and Lutherans believe that he

---

1. Menocchio was assigned to his village of Montereale, "which he was to consider as his prison and never attempt to leave without the permission of the Holy Office." He was also obliged to give 200 ducats as security against his escape from the village, to dispense alms every Friday, confess his sins six times yearly, and "never to speak or mention his wrongheaded opinions" again.

2. Ten years after the first trial, Menocchio is again spreading "wrongheaded opinions," as attested by this letter from one Leonardo Simon, who had played violin with Menocchio during holiday celebrations.

can make and unmake, but they do not believe that he was born from the Virgin Mary, and he replied that this is something we cannot know. And then I told him that we should not be probing what is hidden by God, because the Gospel says: "Blessed are those who have not seen and yet believe," and he retorted: "Who do you think made these Gospels? No one else but monks, who have nothing better to do and write what they please." And I told him: "So, then, you do not believe in the Gospel?" and he replied, "No, I do not believe in it."

I should have written many days ago, perhaps a month ago, but I did not know him well, and many cares interfered so that I did not write. But now a Jubilee has come and I want to absolve myself with God's help. Nothing more. I kiss the hand of your most reverend lordship.

Porcia, 1596, 7 March
Of your most reverend lordship, Lunardo Simon.[3]

━━◈ END OF PERSPECTIVES: LITERATURE OF RELIGIOUS CRISIS ◈━━

━━◈◈◈━━

François Rabelais
c. 1495–1553

François Rabelais' giants are larger than life, and so, it seems, was Rabelais himself. A Franciscan friar who left the cloister to become first a Benedictine and then a doctor and secular priest, at odds with both the Catholic hierarchy of his day and the Calvinist Reformation that was tearing France apart, Rabelais revelled in parodying everything from the excesses of scholastic education to the newfangled explorations overseas. As restless in his intellectual life as he was in his daily life, he is one of the most eclectic and problematic of early modern writers. Irreverent and giddy at one moment, as in the prologue of *Gargantua* when he derides his readers as "dunderheads"; serious, even dogmatic at another, as in Gargantua's letter to his son Pantagruel, the Rabelaisian narrator leaves us without secure footholds in the five-volume "chronicle" of his giants and their friends.

These are volumes that Rabelais wrote over twenty years, beginning in 1532 with *The Terrible and Frightening Deeds and Acts of Prowess of the Very Renowned Pantagruel, King of the Dipsodes,* supposedly written by one Alcofribas Nasier (an anagram of "François Rabelais"). *Pantagruel* was followed two years later by its prequel, *Gargantua,* which tells of the fantastic birth, youth, and exploits of Pantagruel's father. Commonly regarded as Rabelais's masterpiece, *Gargantua* was published shortly after Rabelais returned from Rome, where he had served as Bishop Jean du Bellay's personal physician. The book got him into serious trouble with the Sorbonne, the Parisian university whose scholars had become arbiters of orthodoxy and good taste; they criticized Rabelais so heatedly that du Bellay had to whisk him back to Italy. An expurgated edition of both books appeared in 1542 (*Pantagruel* had been condemned for obscenity). The omission of some of the more audacious moments won Rabelais no friends at the stern

---

3. Following the receipt of Simon's letter, Menocchio was examined again, declared a heretic, and on 8 August 1599, consigned by the Holy Office to civil officials. By August 16 he had been executed in the manner dictated by Venetian law: "The punishment of the heretic . . . is fire, as prescribed in divine, canon, civil, and common law, so that the body while still living should be burned up and be reduced to ashes."

Sorbonne, since the publisher had simultaneously printed a new edition of the original books without Rabelais's consent. On the surface, the *Third Book of the Heroic Deeds and Sayings of the Good Pantagruel* (1546) waxes far less satirical of university and ecclesiastical authorities. It rather contributes, tongue-in-cheek, to the ongoing *Querelle des femmes* or "Quarrel about the ladies," as it focuses misogynistically on the attempts of Pantagruel's friend Panurge to ascertain through means both supernatural and pedestrian whether he will be cuckolded or cheated on when he marries. Yet it met with no better fate, even though Rabelais dedicated it to Marguerite de Navarre, sister of the king. The *Fourth Book* is a rambling account of Pantagruel's and Panurge's voyage by sea to visit the Oracle of the Holy Bacbuc, a mission that is never completed, and indeed, at times seems almost forgotten. It was published (and predictably condemned) in 1552, a year before Rabelais's death; the unfinished *Fifth Book,* which returns to search for the Oracle, is of dubious authenticity and appeared posthumously.

The string of condemnations, provoking in turn a pattern of hiding, exile, return, and rewriting, was in part brought on by moments like the following, from the end of the *Fourth Book.* Having just soiled himself from fear, Panurge tries to redirect the mockery of his companions with a verbal harangue: "But ho! What the devil's this? Do you call it shit, turds, crots, ordure, deposit, fecal matter, excrement, droppings, fumets, motion, dung, stronts, sycbale, or spyrathe? It's saffron from Ireland, that's what I think it is." This passage demonstrates one of Rabelais's leading qualities: his revelry in language's plenitude, in its capacity to become as earthy and as tangible as the material world it so amply describes. The words also exemplify the character of Panurge himself; Rabelais is one of the first modern writers to make language an expression of man— a particular man. Always ready to call a turd a turd, Rabelais had no patience for the abstractions of theologians or the meaningless rhetoric of the medieval educators of Paris's universities. Hence the ridicule that greets Master Janotus de Bragmardo, who opens his appeal to Gargantua to return bells he had taken from the cathedral of Notre Dame by saying that the people of Bordeaux "wanted to buy them for the substantific quality of the elementary complexion which is inherent in the terrestiality of their quidditive nature." This ridicule was another reason for the theologians to attack Rabelais. He challenged their modes of argumentation and authority through Gargantua's tutor Ponocrates, who educates his student's body as well as his mind, assigning him not theological study, but horsemanship, the study of music, the empirical observation of natural phenomena, and the spontaneous praise of the divine. "Without health, life is not life," Dr. Rabelais tells us in his preface to the *Fourth Book,* and Ponocrates ensures that his student will have the requisite vigor to become a true renaissance man.

Such an education is humanist in spirit, a humanism with which Rabelais was familiar thanks to his occasional sojourns in Lyon, France's most active intellectual center and the hub of its publishing business, as well as through his association with François I's court and his friendship with figures like Erasmus. Rabelais's medical studies at Montpellier, from which he received his license in 1532 and his doctorate in 1537, sharpened his interest in natural observations and personal experience, exemplified by study of the human body: Gargantua tells his son that "by frequent dissections you will gain a perfect knowledge of that other world which is man." Humanist studies were endangered, however, once Luther began challenging the Church, using Erasmus's Greek New Testament to do so. Although Rabelais would go on to translate and lecture on Hippocrates and Galen, while still a monk he had his Greek books confiscated. The giants' extolling of humanist education was thus also a key factor in the condemnation of Rabelais's work, no matter how carefully he disguised his critiques as a continuation of a medieval chronicle of giants, as a work addressed only to "noble boozers," as a scatalogical account of the origins of the Seine river, as a work that celebrated "Pantagruelism"—what Rabelais defines in the prologue to the *Fourth Book* as "a certain lightness of spirit compounded of contempt for the chances of fate."

Such "lightness of spirit" finally triumphs in a corpus more celebratory than shrill. The typograhical layout alone is a testament to new-found pleasures of technological innovation; Rabelais particularly enjoys extravagant lists, such as the catalogue of materials Pantagruel finds in the Library of St. Victor's and the 212 games of Chapter 22 of *Gargantua* (which include Pinch without Laughing, The Salvo of Farts, and *St. Cosmo, I come to adore you*). And the births of Gargantua and Pantagruel are mythical in scope, as Gargantua emerges through his mother's ear and Pantagruel is born on a day that the earth "was so heated that it burst into a great sweat." *Gargantua* features the energetic Friar John, who may mangle his Psalms but who brilliantly attacks the forces of the odious Picrochole; he is awarded for his vigor with the Abbey of Thélème, where there is only one rule: "Do what you will." Panurge, who first appears in *Pantagruel* and dominates the *Third Book,* is an odyssean figure whose verbal excesseses are matched only by those of his giant friend. Finally, both Pantagruel and Gargantua are models of wise statesmen who exemplify the virtues of good governance, clemency toward the vanquished, and effective rhetorical skills (this despite their battle-hungry ways—reflecting, perhaps, the constant presence of war in sixteenth-century Europe). Both also value the importance of friendship, as with Pantagruel's unconditional affection for the shifty Panurge.

How far the reader is to try to find a deeper meaning in Rabelais's text is the subject of the preface to *Gargantua.* But if Rabelais stages for us, again and again, our own uncertainties with regard to the purposes of his work, we occasionally glimpse the author's unease with the politically and religiously charged climate that gave his books a poorer reception than he had hoped for. In the prologue to the *Third Book,* Rabelais tells a story of the Egyptian king Ptolemy, who, returned from conquests in the East, "presented the Egyptians with a completely black Bactrian camel, and a slave parti-coloured in such a way that one portion of his body was black and the other white." "Such phenomena," the author goes on,

> had never yet been seen in Egypt, and Ptolemy hoped that by offering the people these rarities he would increase their love for himself. But what was the result? At the appearance of the camel they were all frightened and indignant; at the sight of the parti-coloured man, some mocked and others were shocked by what they considered a loathsome monster, created by an error of Nature. In short, his hopes of pleasing his Egyptians . . . slipped through his fingers. He discovered that they took more pleasure and delight in the handsome, the elegant, and the perfect than in ridiculous and monstrous objects.

Ever slippery, Rabelais doesn't allow us easily to equate Ptolemy and himself: "After this, [Ptolemy] had a very poor opinion of the slave and the camel; so poor indeed that soon afterwards, owing to neglect and lack of common sustenance, they exchanged life for death." Rabelais will never let his own monsters "die," although his giants may seem to decrease in size as the ship of the *Fourth Book* makes its way through uncharted seas and its travelers encounter beings far more marvelous than Pantagruel. But in this tale as in many of the narratives that burst without apparent order or design from Rabelais's texts, we find a self-reflectiveness that makes the chronicles of Gargantua and his son far more than the fantastic adventures of giants.

PRONUNCIATIONS:
François Rabelais: fran-SWAH ra-BLAY
Gargantua: gar-GAN-tyu-ah
Pantagruel: pan-TAH-gru-el
Panurge: pa-NOORJ
Picrochole: PEE-cro-shol
Thélème: tay-LEM

from GARGANTUA AND PANTAGRUEL[1]

from Gargantua[2]

ADVICE TO READERS

> *Good friends who come to read this book,*
> *Strip yourselves first of affectation;*
> *Do not assume a pained, shocked look,*
> *For it contains no foul infection,*
> *Yet teaches you no great perfection,*
> *But lessons in the mirthful art,*
> *The only subject for my heart.*
> *When I see grief consume and rot*
> *You, mirth's my theme and tears are not,*
> *For laughter is man's proper lot.*[3]

The Author's Prologue

Most noble boozers, and you my very esteemed and poxy friends—for to you and you alone are my writings dedicated—when Alcibiades, in that dialogue of Plato's entitled *The Symposium,* praises his master Socrates, beyond all doubt the prince of philosophers, he compares him, amongst other things, to a Silenus.[4] Now a Silenus, in ancient days, was a little box, of the kind we see today in apothecaries' shops, painted on the outside with such gay, comical figures as harpies, satyrs, bridled geese, horned hares, saddled ducks, flying goats, stags in harness, and other devices of that sort, light-heartedly invented for the purpose of mirth, as was Silenus himself, the master of good old Bacchus. But inside these boxes were kept rare drugs, such as balm, ambergris, cardamum, musk, civet, mineral essences, and other precious things.

Just such an object, according to Plato, was Socrates. For to view him from the outside and judge by his external appearance, no one would have given a shred of an onion for him, so ugly was his body and so absurd his appearance, with his pointed nose, his bovine expression, and his idiotic face. Moreover his manners were plain and his clothes boorish; he was blessed with little wealth, was unlucky in his wives, and unfit for any public office. What is more, he was always laughing, always drinking glass for glass with everybody, always playing the fool, and always concealing his divine wisdom. But had you opened that box, you would have found inside a heavenly and priceless drug: a superhuman understanding, miraculous virtue, invincible courage, unrivalled sobriety, unfailing contentment, perfect confidence, and an incredible contempt for all those things men so watch for, pursue, work for, sail after, and struggle for.

Now what do you think is the purpose of this preamble, of this preliminary flourish? It is that you, my good disciples and other leisured fools, in reading the pleasant titles of certain books of our invention, such as *Gargantua, Pantagruel, Toss-pint, On*

---

1. Translated by J. M. Cohen.
2. Book 1, which treats of Gargantua, was actually written and published in 1534, two years after Book 2, the story of Gargantua's son, Pantagruel. Neither of the first two books was published with Rabelais's name on the title page; he used a pseudonym, Master Alcofribras.
3. A sentiment exemplified by the 5th-century philoso-

pher Democritus, known as the "laughing philosopher" because of his views of human happiness as the ultimate pursuit of mankind.
4. Erasmus and other Renaissance writers took the figure of a Silenus as an analogue not only for Socrates, as introduced by Plato in the *Symposium,* but for Christ. Here, Silenus becomes a figure for Rabelais' own book.

the Dignity of Codpieces, Of Peas and Bacon, cum commento,[5] &c, may not too easily conclude that they treat of nothing but mockery, fooling, and pleasant fictions; seeing that their outward signs—their titles, that is—are commonly greeted, without further investigation, with smiles of derision. It is wrong, however, to set such small store by the works of men. For, as you yourselves say, the habit does not make the monk; some wear a monkish cloak who are the very reverse of monkish inside, and some sport a Spanish cape who are far from Spanish in their courage. That is the reason why you must open this book, and carefully weigh up its contents. You will discover then that the drug within is far more valuable than the box promised; that is to say, that the subjects here treated are not so foolish as the title on the cover suggested.

But even suppose that in the literal meanings you find jolly enough nonsense, in perfect keeping with the title, you must still not be deterred, as by the Sirens' song, but must interpret in a more sublime sense what you may possibly have thought, at first, was uttered in mere light-heartedness. Have you ever picked a lock to steal a bottle? Good for you! Call to mind your expression at the time. Or did you ever see a dog—which is, as Plato says, in the second book of his *Republic,* the most philosophical creature in the world—discover a marrow-bone? If ever you did, you will have noticed how devotedly he eyes it, how carefully he guards it, how fervently he holds it, how circumspectly he begins to gnaw it, how lovingly he breaks it, and how diligently he licks it. What induces him to do all this? What hope is there in his labour? What benefit does he expect? Nothing more than a little marrow. It is true that this little is more delicious than great quantities of any other meat; for, as Galen says in his third Book, *On the Natural Faculties,* and in his eleventh, *On the Parts of the Body and their Functions,* marrow is the perfect food concocted by Nature.[6]

Now you must follow this dog's example, and be wise in smelling out, sampling, and relishing these fine and most juicy books, which are easy to run down but hard to bring to bay. Then, by diligent reading and frequent meditation, you must break the bone and lick out the substantial marrow—that is to say the meaning which I intend to convey by these Pythagorean symbols[7]—in the hope and assurance of becoming both wiser and more courageous by such reading. For here you will find an individual savour and abstruse teaching which will initiate you into certain very high sacraments and dread mysteries, concerning not only our religion, but also our public and private life.

But do you faithfully believe that Homer, in writing his *Iliad* and *Odyssey,* ever had in mind the allegories squeezed out of him by Plutarch, Heraclides Ponticus, Eustathius, and Phornutus, and which Politian afterwards stole from them in his turn?[8] If you do, you are not within a hand's or a foot's length of my opinion. For I believe them to have been as little dreamed of by Homer as the Gospel mysteries were by Ovid in his *Metamorphoses;* a case which a certain Friar Lubin,[9] a true bacon-picker, has actually tried to prove, in the hope that he may meet others as crazy as himself and—as the proverb says—a lid to fit his kettle.

---

5. Rabelais alludes to the previously published *Pantagruel,* along with several imaginary titles he cited in that work's prologue. The *Chronicles of Gargantua* were a popular collection of tales about giants who wander in and out of the stories of Arthurian romance; Rabelais positions his works as a kind of sequel.
6. Galen was a 2nd-century Greek physician who wrote extensively on medicine; as a doctor, Rabelais was especially interested in his works.
7. Supposedly inspired by the Delphic oracle, Pythagoras was a Greek philosopher and mathematician whose simple teachings were believed to have had profound allegorical meanings.
8. With the exception of Plutarch, all writers who had written extensive commentaries on Homer's poetry.
9. Name commonly used for a simple-minded monk.

If you do not believe those arguments, what reason is there that you should not treat these new and jolly chronicles of mine with the same reserve, seeing that as I dictated them I gave no more thought to the matter than you, who were probably drinking at the time, as I was? For I never spent—or wasted—any more—or other—time in the composing of this lordly book, than that fixed for the taking of my bodily refreshment, that is to say for eating and drinking. Indeed, this is the proper time for writing of such high matters and abstruse sciences; as Homer, who was the paragon of all philologers, very well knew, and Ennius, the father of the Latin poets too, as Horace testifies, although a certain imbecile declared that his verses smack rather of wine than of oil.[1]

There is an upstart who says as much of my books. But a turd for him! How much more appetizing, alluring, and enticing, how much more heavenly and delicious is the smell of wine than the smell of oil! I shall be as proud when men say of me that I spent more on wine than on oil as was Demosthenes, when he was told that he spent more on oil than on wine. To be called a good companion and fellow-boozer is to me pure honour and glory. For with that reputation I am welcome in all choice companies of Pantagruelists. It was said against Demosthenes by some envious wretch that his *Orations* smelt like the rag stopper of some foul and filthy oil-lamp.[2] Interpret all my deeds and words, therefore, in the most perfect sense, show deep respect for the cheeselike brain that feeds you on these delicate maggots, and do your best to keep me always merry. Now be cheerful, my dear boys, and read joyfully on for your bodily comfort and to the profit of your digestions. But listen to me, you dunderheads—God rot you!—do not forget to drink my health for the favour, and I'll return you the toast, post-haste.

* * *

Chapter 3. How Gargantua Was Carried Eleven Months in His Mother's Belly[3]

Grandgousier was a good jester in his time, with as great a love of tossing off a glass as any man then in the world. He had also quite a liking for salt meat. For this reason he generally kept a good store of Mayence and Bayonne hams, plenty of smoked ox-tongues, an abundance of chitterlings in their season and beef pickled in mustard, a supply of botargos, and a provision of sausages; though not of Bologna sausages, for he feared Lombard concoctions—but of those from Bigorre, Longaulnay, La Brenne, and Le Rouergue. In the prime of his years he married Gargamelle, daughter of the king of the Butterflies, a fine, good-looking piece, and the pair of them often played the two-backed beast, joyfully rubbing their bacon together, to such effect that she became pregnant of a fine boy and carried him into the eleventh month. For so long and even longer women can carry a child, especially when he is some masterpiece of nature, a personage destined in his time to perform great deeds. As witness Homer, who tells us that the child which Neptune begot upon the nymph was born at the end of a full year, that is to say in the twelfth month. For, as Aulus Gellius says in his third

---

1. Horace mentions both the epic poet Ennius and Homer in his famous *Epistle* to his patron Maecenas, 1.19: "Homer, by his praises of wine, is convicted as a winelover; even father Ennius never sprang forth to tell of arms save after much drinking."

2. Demosthenes (383–322 B.C.E.) was probably the great-

est orator of ancient Athens.

3. The first two chapters of *Gargantua* invite the reader to peruse the book that follows, suggesting that it was written on elm-bark and found in a meadow by men digging a ditch.

book, this long period befitted the majesty of Neptune, since it took that time for the child to be perfectly shaped. For a similar reason Jupiter made the night he slept with Alcmena last forty-eight hours; for in a shorter time he could not have forged Hercules, who cleansed the world of monsters and tyrants.[4]

My masters, the Pantagruelists of old, have confirmed what I say, and have declared the birth of a child born of a woman eleven months after her husband's death not only to be possible but also legitimate. See Hippocrates, *lib. De Alimento,* Pliny, *lib. vii, cap. v,* Plautus, *in Cistellaria,* Marcus Varro, in his satire headed the *Testament,* in which he claims Aristotle's authority on the subject, Censorinus, *lib. De die natali,* Aristotle, *lib. vii, cap. iii et iv, De Nat. animalium,* Gellius, *lib. iii, cap. xvi,* Servius *on the Eclogues* in explaining the line of Virgil, *Matri longa decem.* &c,[5] and a thousand other madmen, the number of whom has been increased by the lawyers, *f. De suis, et legit. 1. Intestato, paragrapho fin,* and *in Authent. De Restitut. et ea quae parit in xi mense.* What is more they have scrawled it into their Bacon-pinching law, *Gallus, ff. De lib. et posthu., et 1. septimo ff. De Stat. homi.,* and into certain others which at the moment I dare not name; on the strength of which laws widows may freely play at the close-buttock game with all their might and at every free moment, for two months after their husbands' decease. So I beg of you, all my fine lechers, if you find any of these same widows worth the trouble of untying your codpiece, mount them and bring them to me. For if they conceive in the third month, their issue will be the dead man's legal heir; and once the pregnancy is public they may push boldly on, full sail ahead, since the hold is full, after the example of Julia, daughter of the Emperor Octavian, who never gave herself up to her belly-drummers unless she knew that she was pregnant, after the manner of a ship, which does not take on her pilot until she is caulked and loaded. And if anyone reproaches them for allowing themselves to be thus sported with in their pregnancy, seeing that animals never allow the covering male near them once they are big, they will answer that beasts are beasts, but that they are women and fully understand the grand and jolly little rights of superfetation; as Populia answered of old, according to Macrobius's account, in the second book of his *Saturnalia.*[6]

If the deuce doesn't want their bellies to swell, he must twist the spigot and close the hole.

Chapter 4. How Gargamelle, When Great with Gargantua, Ate Great Quantities of Tripe

This was the manner in which Gargamelle was brought to bed—and if you don't believe it, may your fundament fall out! Her fundament fell out one afternoon, on the third of February, after she had overeaten herself on *godebillios. Godebillios* are the fat tripes of *coiros. Coiros* are oxen fattened at the stall and in *guimo* meadows, and *guimo* meadows are those that carry two grass crops a year. They had killed three hundred and sixty-seven thousand and fourteen of these fat oxen to be salted down on

4. The nymph who is Neptune's lover in Homer was Tyro, who gave birth to sons. Aulus Gellius wrote a series of essays called *Attic Nights* in the 2nd century C.E., and Jupiter's long night with Alcmena is the subject of Plautus's comedy, *Amphitryon.*
5. The complete line in Virgil's fourth *Eclogue* (verse 61) translates as "to your mother, 10 months have brought the weariness of travail." The pedantic compilation of classical sources in the passage, all of them authentic, is obviously done for comic effect.
6. A veritable encyclopedia of Roman life and lore written during the empire's declining years, in the late 5th century.

Shrove Tuesday, so that in the spring they should have plenty of beef in season, with which to make a short *commemoration* at the beginning of meals, for the better enjoyment of their wine. The tripes were plentiful, as you will understand, and so appetizing that everyone licked his fingers. But the devil and all of it was that they could not possibly be kept any longer, for they were tainted, which seemed most improper. So it was resolved that they should be consumed without more ado. For this purpose there were invited all the citizens of Cinais, of Seuilly, of La Roche-Clermault, and of Vaugaudry, not to forget those of Le Coudray-Montpensier and the Gué de Vède,[7] and other neighbours: all strong drinkers, jovial companions, and good skittle-players.

Now, the good man Grandgousier took very great pleasure in this feast and ordered that all should be served full ladles. Nevertheless he told his wife to eat more modestly, seeing that her time was near and that this tripe was not very commendable meat. "Anyone who eats the bag," he said, "might just as well be chewing dung." Despite his warning, however, she ate sixteen quarters, two bushels, and six pecks. Oh, what fine fecal matter to swell up inside her!

After dinner they all rushed headlong to the Willow-grove; and there on the luxuriant grass they danced to the gay sound of the flutes and the sweet music of the bagpipes, so skittishly that it was a heavenly sport to see them thus frolicking.

* * *

Chapter 6. The Very Strange Manner of Gargantua's Birth

Whilst they were pleasantly tattling on the subject of drinking, Gargamelle began to feel disturbed in her lower parts. Whereupon Grandgousier got up from the grass, and comforted her kindly, thinking that these were birth-pangs and telling her that since she had been resting under the willows she would soon be in a good state. She ought to take new heart, he said, at the coming of her new baby. For although the pains would be somewhat severe, they would nevertheless be quickly over, and the joy which would follow after would banish all her pain, so that only the memory of it would be left.

"Have a sheep's courage," he said. "Bring this boy into the world, and we'll soon make another."

"Ah," she answered. "It's easy for you men to talk. Well, I swear to God I'll do my best, since you ask it of me. But I wish to heaven you had cut it off!"

"What?" asked Grandgousier.

"Ha," she said. "Just like a man! You know what I mean well enough."

"My member?" he said. "By the blood of all the goats, send for a knife if that's what you want."

"Oh," she said. "God forbid! God forgive me, I didn't really mean it. Don't do anything to it on account of anything I say. But I shall have trouble enough today, unless God helps me, all on account of your member, and just because I wanted to please you."

"Take heart," he said. "Don't you worry, but let the four leading oxen do the work. I'll go and take another swig. If any pain comes on you in the meantime I shan't be far off. Give me a shout and I'll be with you."

---

7. All villages in the area called Chinonais, a particularly fertile area in northwestern France near Tours. Rabelais had property in the vicinity, in a town called La Devinière.

A little while later she began to groan and wail and shout. Then suddenly swarms of midwives came up from every side, and feeling her underneath found some rather ill-smelling excrescences, which they thought were the child; but it was her fundament slipping out, because of the softening of her right intestine—which you call the bum-gut—owing to her having eaten too much tripe, as has been stated above.

At this point a dirty old hag of the company, who had the reputation of being a good she-doctor and had come from Brizepaille, near Saint Genou, sixty years before, made her an astringent, so horrible that all her sphincter muscles were stopped and constricted. Indeed you could hardly have relaxed them with your teeth—which is a most horrible thought—even if you had copied the method of the devil at the Mass of St Martin, when he wrote down the chatter of two local girls and stretched his parchment by tugging with his teeth.[8]

By this misfortune the cotyledons of the matrix were loosened at the top, and the child leapt up through them to enter the hollow vein. Then, climbing through the diaphragm to a point above the shoulders where this vein divides in two, he took the left fork and came out by the left ear.

As soon as he was born he cried out, not like other children: "Mies! Mies!" but "Drink! Drink! Drink!," as if inviting the whole world to drink, and so loud that he was heard through all the lands of Booze and Bibulous.[9]

I doubt whether you will truly believe in this strange nativity. I don't care if you don't. But an honest man, a man of good sense, always believes what he is told and what he finds written down. Is this a violation of our law or our faith? Is it against reason or against Holy Scripture? For my part I find nothing written in the Holy Bible which contradicts it. If this had been the will of God, would you say that he could not have performed it? For goodness' sake do not obfuscate your brains with such an idle thought. For I say to you that to God nothing is impossible. If it had been His will women would have produced their children in that way, by the ear, for ever afterwards.

Was not Bacchus begotten by Jupiter's thigh? Was not Rocquetaillade born from his mother's heel, and Crocquemouche from his nurse's slipper? Was not Minerva born from Jupiter's brain by way of his ear, and Adonis from the bark of a myrrh-tree, and Castor and Pollux from the shell of an egg laid and hatched by Leda?[1] But you would be even more flabbergasted if I were now to expound to you the whole chapter of Pliny in which he speaks of strange and unnatural births; and, anyhow, I am not such a barefaced liar as he was. Read Chapter three of the seventh book of his *Natural History,* and don't tease my brain any more on the subject.[2]

Chapter 7. How Gargantua Received His Name, and How He Gulped His Liquor

While that good man Grandgousier was drinking and joking with the others he heard the horrible cry made by his son as he entered the world, and bawled out for "Drink! Drink! Drink!" Whereupon he said, "Que grand tu as."—What a big one you've

8. The devil ends up falling when the parchment rips, as recounted in a legend about the life of St. Martin.

9. Beusse and Bibaroys, two neighboring regions whose names evoke thoughts of drink.

1. Among several examples of marvelous births from Greek mythology, Rabelais includes the made-up French

figures of Rocquetaillade ("Mongrel-cut") and Crocque-mouche ("Glutton-fly").

2. Pliny's *Natural History,* written during the 1st century, is an enormous compilation of scientific observations and mythological and historical lore. The seventh book is on human physiology.

got!—(the gullet being understood); and when they heard this the company said that the child ought properly to be called Gargantua—after the example of the ancient Hebrew custom—since that had been the first word pronounced by his father at his birth.[3] The father graciously agreed to their suggestion; it was most pleasing to the mother as well; and to quiet the child they gave him enough drink to break his larynx. Then he was carried to the font and there baptized, as is the habit of all good Christians.

And they ordered for him seventeen thousand nine hundred and thirteen cows from Pontille and Bréhémont for his every-day supplies of milk. For it was impossible to find a nurse to satisfy him anywhere in the country, considering the great quantity of nourishment that he required. Certain Scotist doctors have nevertheless affirmed that his mother suckled him, and that she could draw from her breasts fourteen hundred and two pipes and nine pails of milk at a time.[4] But this is improbable, and the proposition has been declared mammalianly scandalous, offensive to pious ears, and distantly redolent of heresy.

In this state he lived till he was a year and ten months old, at which time, by the advice of physicians, they began to take him out, and a fine ox-wagon was made for him, to the design of Jean Denyau. In this he travelled around most merrily to one place and another; and they made a great show of him. For he had a fine face and almost eighteen chins; and he cried very seldom. But he shat himself every hour. For he was amazingly phlegmatic in his actions, partly from natural character and partly for accidental reasons connected with over-indulgence in the new wines of September. But he never drank a drop without reason. For if by chance he was vexed, angry, displeased, or peeved, if he stamped, if he wept or if he screamed, they always brought him drink to restore his temper, and immediately he became quiet and happy.

One of his governesses told me, on her Bible oath, that he was so accustomed to this treatment, that at the mere sound of pint-pots and flagons he would fall into an ecstasy, as if tasting the joys of paradise. Taking this divine disposition of his into account, therefore, in order to cheer him up in the mornings they would have glasses chinked for him with a knife, or flagons tapped with their stoppers; and at this sound he would become merry, leap up, and rock himself in his cradle, nodding his head, playing scales with his fingers, and beating slow time with his bottom.

* * *

Chapter 11. Concerning Gargantua's Childhood

From his third to his fifth year Gargantua was brought up and disciplined in all necessary ways, such being his father's orders; and he spent that time in the same manner as the other little children of that country: that is to say in drinking, eating, and sleeping: in eating, sleeping, and drinking; in sleeping, drinking, and eating.

He was always rolling in the mud, dirtying his nose, scratching his face, and treading down his shoes; and often he gaped after flies, or ran joyfully after the butterflies of whom his father was the ruler. He pissed in his shoes, shat in his shirt, wiped his nose on his sleeve, snivelled into his soup, paddled about everywhere, drank out of his slipper, and usually rubbed his belly on a basket. He sharpened his teeth on a shoe, washed his hands in soup, combed his hair with a wine-bowl, sat between two stools with his arse on the ground, covered himself with a wet sack, drank while eating his soup, ate his biscuit without bread, bit as he laughed and laughed as

3. Like Grandgousier, Gargantua is named for his "big throat."

4. Rabelais is poking fun at Duns Scotus, a theologian of the 13th-century.

he bit, often spat in the dish, blew a fat fart, pissed against the sun, ducked under water to avoid the rain, struck the iron while it was cold, had empty thoughts, put on airs, threw up his food or, as they said, flayed the fox, mumbled his prayers like a monkey, returned to his muttons, and turned the sows out to hay.[5] He would beat the dog in front of the lion, put the cart before the oxen, scratch where he did not itch, draw the worms from his nose, grip so hard that he caught nothing, eat his white bread first, shoe the grasshoppers, and tickle himself to make himself laugh. He was a good guzzler in the kitchen, offered the gods straw for grain, sang *Magnificat* at matins and thought this the right time, ate cabbages and shat beet, could find the flies in his milk and pulled the legs off them, scrawled on paper, blotted parchment, got away by his heels, played ducks and drakes with his purse, reckoned without his host, beat the bushes and missed the birds, and took the clouds for brass frying-pans and bladders for lanterns. He would draw two loads from one sack, play the donkey to get the bran, use his fist for a mallet, take cranes at the first leap, think a coat of mail was made link by link, always look a gift horse in the mouth, ramble from cock to bull, put one ripe fruit between two green, make the best of a bad job, protect the moon from the wolves, hope to catch larks if the heavens fell, take a slice of whatever bread he was offered, care as little for the bald as for the shaven, and flay the fox every morning. His father's little dogs ate out of his dish, and he ate with them. He bit their ears and they scratched his nose; he blew at their rumps and they licked his lips.

And d'you know what, my boys? May the drink fly to your heads! That little lecher was always feeling his governesses, upside down, back-to-front, and get along with you there! And he was already beginning to exercise his codpiece, which his governesses decorated every day with fine garlands, lovely ribbons, pretty flowers, and gay silken tufts. And they amused themselves by rubbing it between their hands like a roll of pastry, and then burst out laughing when it raised its ears, as if the game pleased them. One of them called it my pillicock, another my ninepin, another my coral-branch, another my stopper, my cork, my quiverer, my driving-pin, my auger, my dingle-dangle, my rough-go stiff-and-low, my crimping iron, my little red sausage, my sweet little cocky.

"It's mine," one would say.

"It belongs to me," said another.

"What about me?" cried a third. "Don't I get a share in it? Gracious me, I shall cut it off, then."

"What," said another. "Cut it off. Why, that would hurt him, Madam. Is it your way to cut off children's *things?* Why, then he'd be Master Short."

And so that he should amuse himself like the small children of the country, they made him a pretty weathercock from the sails of a Mirebalais windmill.

* * *

Chapter 16. How Gargantua Was Sent to Paris, of the Huge Mare That Carried Him, and How She Destroyed the Ox-flies of La Beauce[6]

Fayoles, fourth king of Numidia, sent to Grandgousier from the land of Africa the greatest and most enormous mare that ever was seen; and she was the most monstrous

---

5. Here and in the rest of the paragraph Rabelais cites a dizzying number of proverbial warnings which Gargantua manages to utterly ignore in his adolescent naiveté.
6. In the intervening chapters, Gargantua has been subject to an abysmal education at the hands of various sophists.

When Grandgousier hears a young page named Eudemon deliver a fine speech in Latin, he assigns Ponocrates, the page's tutor, to the role of Gargantua's teacher, and they decide to go to Paris "to learn what the young men of France were studying at that time."

too, since you know very well that Africa is always producing some new monstrosity. She was as big as six elephants, she had her hoofs divided into toes, like Julius Caesar's horse, and pendent ears, like the goats of Languedoc, and a little horn on her rump. For the rest, her coat was of a burnt sorrel with dapple-grey spots and, what is more, she had the most fearsome tail. For it was as large, more or less, as the pillar of Saint Mars, near Langès, and as square;[7] and its tufts were as spiky, in every respect, as blades of wheat.

If this description astounds you, you will be even more astounded by what I tell you about the tail of the Scythian ram, which weighed more than thirty pounds, or about that of the Syrian sheep, to whose rump (if Thenaud speaks true)[8] they have to fix a little cart to carry it, it is so long and heavy. You clods from the flat lands possess nothing to compare with that. This mare was brought by sea in three caracks and a brigantine, to the port of Olonne in the Talmont country; and when Grandgousier saw her he said: "Here is just the beast to carry my son to Paris. Now I swear to God, all will go well. He will be a great scholar in times to come. If it weren't for the beasts we should all live like scholars."[9]

The next day—after drinking, as you will understand—they started on their way, Gargantua, his tutor Ponocrates, and his servants, together with the young page Eudemon; and as the weather was calm and temperate Grandgousier had dun-coloured boots made for his son; Babin calls them buskins.

So they passed joyfully along the highway, always in high spirits, till they came above Orléans, at which place there was a great forest a hundred and five miles long and fifty-one miles wide, or thereabouts. This forest was horribly abundant and copiously swarming with ox-flies and hornets, so that it was an absolute brigands' lair for the poor mares, asses, and horses. But Gargantua's mare handsomely avenged all the outrages ever perpetrated there on the beasts of her kind, by a trick of which they had not the slightest inkling beforehand. As soon as they had entered this forest and the hornets had opened their attack she threw out her tail, and at her first skirmish swatted them so completely that she swept down the whole wood. Crossways and lengthways, here and there, this way and that, to front and to side, over and under, she swept down the trees as a mower does the grass, so that since that time there has been neither wood nor hornets, and the whole country has been reduced to a plain.

At the sight of this Gargantua felt very great delight. But the only boast he made was to say to his people: "I find this fine" (*Je trouve beau ce*); from which saying the country has ever afterwards been called La Beauce. But all they got for breakfast was empty air; in memory of which to this day the gentlemen of La Beauce break their fast on yawns, do very well by it, and spit the better for it.[1]

At last they arrived in Paris, in which town Gargantua refreshed himself for two or three days, making merry with his people, and inquiring what learned men there were in the place just then, also what wine was drunk there.

Chapter 17. How Gargantua Repaid the Parisians for Their Welcome, and How He Took the Great Bells from the Church of Notre-Dame

Some days after they had finished their refreshment, Gargantua went to see the sights of the town, and everyone stared at him in great wonder. For the Parisians are such

---

7. A tower near Chinon.
8. Jean Thenaud was a theologian who had written a travel journal.

9. Reversing the proverb "if it weren't for the scholars, we should all live like beasts."
1. The inhabitants of La Beauce were notoriously poor.

simpletons, such gapers, and such feckless idiots that a buffoon, a pedlar of indulgences, a mule with bells on its collar, or a fiddler at a crossroad will draw a greater crowd than a good preacher of the Gospel.

The people so pestered him, in fact, that he was compelled to take a rest on the towers of Notre-Dame; and when from there he saw so many, pressing all around him, he said in a clear voice:

"I think these clodhoppers want me to pay for my kind reception and offer them a *solatium*.[2] They are quite justified, and I am going to give them some wine, to buy my welcome. But only in sport, *par ris*."

Then, with a smile, he undid his magnificent codpiece and, bringing out his johnthomas, pissed on them so fiercely that he drowned two hundred and sixty thousand, four hundred and eighteen persons, not counting the women and small children.

A number of them, however, were quick enough on their feet to escape this pissflood; and when they reached the top of the hill above the University, sweating, coughing, spitting, and out of breath, they began to swear and curse, some in a fury and others in sport (*par ris*). "Carymary, Carymara! My holy tart, we've been drenched in sport! We've been drenched *par ris*."

Hence it was that the city was ever afterwards called Paris. Formerly it had been named *Leucetia*, as Strabo tells us in his fourth book; which in Greek signifies *white place*.[3] This was on account of the white thighs of the ladies of that city. And since at this re-christening all the spectators swore, each by the saints of his own parish, the Parisians, who are made up of all nations and all sorts, have proved by nature both good swearers and good men of law, also somewhat overbearing. For which reason Joaninus de Baranco in *libro de copiositate reverentiarum*, considers that they derive their name of Parrhesians from the Greek, in which language the word signifies bold of speech.[4]

After this exploit Gargantua examined the great bells that hung in those towers, and played a harmonious peal on them. As he did so it struck him that they would serve very well for cow-bells to hang on the collar of his mare, which he had decided to send back to his father, loaded with Brie cheese and fresh herrings. So he took them straight off to his lodgings.

There passed in the meantime a Master-mendicant of the Order of St Anthony, on his begging quest for pig-meat; and he tried to sneak the bells, so that in future he might be heard from afar off, and the very hams tremble in the salting-pans. But he left them out of sheer honesty, not because they were too hot, but because they were a little too heavy for him to carry. This was not the Master at Bourg, who is too good a friend of mine for that.

The whole population was in an uproar, a state of things to which, as you know, Parisians are so prone that foreigners marvel at the patience of France's kings in not suppressing them, as in strict justice they might, considering the troubles that daily arise from their turbulence. I wish to God I knew the den in which these factions and plots are concocted, and I would report them to the guilds of my parish! You may be sure that the place where the people assembled, all befooled and alarmed, was the Hôtel de Nesle, at that time the seat of Lutetia's oracle, which it is no longer;[5] and before

---

2. Small gift of welcome given to bishops when they arrived in their diocese.
3. The 4th-century Roman emperor Julian actually named the city.
4. The names of the author and book ("On the Copiousness of Reverences") are as fanciful as the etymology.
5. King Francis I had established at the Hôtel de Nesle a judge to hear trials related to university matters. The allusion to the oracle of Lutetia is obscure.

that court the case of the stolen bells was pleaded, and the inconvenience of their loss deplored.

After a thorough argument *pro et contra,* it was decided by a simple syllogism that the oldest and most authoritative member of the faculty should be sent to Gargantua to point out to him the terrible inconvenience caused by the loss of those bells; and despite the objections of certain faculty members who claimed that this task could more fitly be performed by an orator than by a sophist, our Master, Janotus de Bragmardo, was chosen to carry it out.[6]

* * *

Chapter 21. Gargantua's Studies According to the Directions of His Tutors, the Sophists

The first days having been spent in this way and the bells restored to their place, the citizens of Paris, in acknowledgment of this courtesy, offered to maintain and feed Gargantua's mare for as long as he wished—an offer which he gladly accepted. So they sent her to graze in the Forest of Bière. I believe that she is no longer there.

After this Gargantua was anxious to put himself at Ponocrates' disposal in the matter of his studies. But for a beginning, his tutor ordered him to go on in his usual way, so that he might find out how it was that his former instructors had spent so long in making him so foolish, simple, and ignorant.

So Gargantua arranged his time in such a way that he generally woke between eight and nine, whether it was light or not; for these had been the orders of his former governors, who had cited the words of David: *Vanum est vobis ante lucem surgere.*[7] Then he turned and stretched and wallowed in his bed for some time, the better to rouse his animal spirits, and dressed according to the season. What he liked to wear was a great long gown of coarse frieze furred with foxskins. After this he combed his hair in the handsome fashion, that is to say with four fingers and a thumb. For his tutors said that to comb or wash or clean oneself in any other way was to lose time in this world.

Then he shat, pissed, spewed, belched, farted, yawned, spat, coughed, hiccuped, sneezed, blew his nose like an archdeacon, and breakfasted, to protect himself from the dew and the bad air, on fine fried tripes, good rashers grilled on the coals, delicate hams, tasty goat stews, and plenty of early morning soup.

Ponocrates protested that he ought not to eat so soon after getting out of bed without having first taken some exercise. But Gargantua replied: "What, haven't I taken enough exercise? I rolled myself over seven or eight times before I got up. Isn't that enough? Pope Alexander adopted that habit on the advice of his Jewish physician, and lived till his dying day in despite of his enemies.[8] My first masters have accustomed me to it. They said that breakfast is good for the memory; therefore they took their first drink then. I find that it does me a lot of good, and makes me enjoy my dinner better. Master Tubal told me—and he took first place as Licentiate in Paris—that all the advantage doesn't lie in running fast, but in starting early. So the total health of the human race consists in not gulping it down like ducks, but rather in drinking early. *Unde versus*—hence you find:

6. Predictably, Janotus delivers a nonsensical oration, and the case is adjourned by the court ("it is," Rabelais informs us, "before them still").
7. "It is vain for you to get up before the dawn" (Psalm 127:2.)—leaving out the moral point of the verse, "unless the Lord watches over the city."
8. Pope Alexander I (1492–1503) had a Jewish physician, Bonnet de Lotes, who converted to Christianity and wrote a treatise on astrology—a topic Rabelais scorned.

> Early to rise brings little wealth;
> But early drinking's good for the health.

After having taken a thorough breakfast, he went to church, and they carried in for him, in a great basket, a huge slippered breviary weighing, what with grease, clasps, and parchment, eleven hundred and six pounds. There he heard twenty-six or thirty Masses. In the meantime his orison-reader would arrive, muffled in his cloak like a hoopoe, and with his breath well disinfected by copious vine-syrup. With him Gargantua mumbled all the litanies, and fingered them over so carefully that not a single grain fell to the ground.

As he left church they brought him on an ox-wagon a heap of rosaries from Saint-Claude, each bead as big as a hatblock, and as he walked through the cloisters, galleries, or garden he told more of them than sixteen hermits.

Then he studied for a miserable half-hour, his eyes fixed on his book, but—as the comic poet says—his soul was in the kitchen.[9] So, after pissing a good pot-full, he next sat down to table; and, being of a phlegmatic nature, began his meal with some dozens of hams, smoked ox-tongues, botargos, sausages, and other advance-couriers of wine. Meanwhile his servants threw into his mouth, one after another, full bucketfuls of mustard, without stopping. Then he drank a monstrous gulp of white wine to relieve his kidneys; and after that ate, according to the season, meats agreeable to his appetite. He left off eating when his belly was tight.

For drinking he had neither end nor rule. For he said that the ends and limits of drinking were when the cork-sole of the drinker's shoe swelled up half a foot as he drank.

* * *

Chapter 23. How Gargantua Was So Disciplined by Ponocrates That He Did Not Waste an Hour of the Day

When Ponocrates saw Gargantua's vicious manner of living, he decided to educate him differently. But for the first days he bore with him, knowing that Nature cannot without great violence endure sudden changes. Therefore, to make a better beginning of his task, he entreated a learned physician of that time, Master Theodore by name, to consider if it would be possible to set Gargantua on a better road. Theodore purged the youth in due form with black hellebore, and with this drug cured his brain of its corrupt and perverse habits. By this means also Ponocrates made him forget all that he had learnt from his old tutors, as Timotheus did for his pupils who had been trained under other musicians.[1] The better to do this, Ponocrates introduced him into the society of the learned men of the region, in emulation of whom his wit increased, as did his desire to change his form of study and to show his worth; and after that the tutor subjected his pupil to such a discipline that he did not waste an hour of the day, but spent his entire time on literature and sound learning.

Gargantua now woke about four o'clock in the morning and, whilst he was being rubbed down, had some chapter of Holy Writ read to him loudly and clearly, with a pronunciation befitting the matter; and this was the business of a young page called Anagnostes,[2] a native of Basché. Moved by the subject and argument of that lesson, he often gave himself up to worship and adoration, to prayers and entreaties, ad-

---

9. The comic poet is Terence, the play *The Eunuch*.   2. Greek for "reader."
1. As Quintilian reports in his *Institutes of the Orator*.

dressed to the good God whose majesty and marvellous wisdom had been exemplified in that reading. Then he went into some private place to make excretion of his natural waste-products, and there his tutor repeated what had been read, explaining to him the more obscure and difficult points. On their way back they considered the face of the sky, whether it was as they had observed it the night before, and into what sign the sun, and also the moon, were entering for that day.

This done, Gargantua was dressed, combed, curled, trimmed, and perfumed, and meanwhile the previous day's lessons were repeated to him. Next, he himself said them by heart, and upon them grounded some practical examples touching the state of man. This they sometimes continued for as long as two or three hours, but generally stopped as soon as he was fully dressed. Then for three full hours he was read to.

When this was done they went out, still discussing the subjects of the reading, and walked over to the sign of the Hound or to the meadows, where they played ball or tennis or the triangle game, gaily exercising their bodies as they had previously exercised their minds. Their sports were entirely unconstrained. For they gave up the game whenever they pleased, and usually stopped when their whole bodies were sweating, or when they were otherwise tired. Then they were well dried and rubbed down, changed their shirts, and sauntered off to see if dinner was ready; and whilst they were waiting there they clearly and eloquently recited some sentences remembered from their lesson. In the meantime my lord Appetite came in, and when the happy moment arrived they sat down at table.

At the beginning of the meal there was a reading of some pleasant tale of the great deeds of old, which lasted till Gargantua had taken his wine. Then, if it seemed good, the reading was continued. Otherwise, they began to converse gaily together, speaking in the first place of the virtues, properties, efficacy, and nature of whatever was served to them at table: of the bread, the wine, the water, the salt, the meats, fish, fruit, herbs, and roots, and of their dressing. From this talk Gargantua learned in a very short time all the relevant passages in Pliny, Athenaeus, Dioscorides, Julius Pollux, Galen, Porphyrius, Oppian, Polybius, Heliodorus, Aristotle, Aelian, and others.[3] As they held these conversations they often had the afore-mentioned books brought to table, to make sure of their quotations; and so well and completely did Gargantua retain in his memory what had been said that there was not a physician then living who knew half as much of this as he.

Afterwards they discussed the lessons read in the morning; and as they concluded their meal with a confection of quinces, he picked his teeth with a mastic branch, and washed his hands and eyes with good fresh water. Then they gave thanks to God by reciting some lovely canticles, composed in praise of the Divine bounty and munificence. After this cards were brought in, not to play with, but so that he might learn a thousand little tricks and new inventions, all based on arithmetic. In this way he came to love this science of numbers, and every day, after dinner and supper, whiled away the time with it as pleasantly as formerly he had done with dice and cards; and so he came to know the theory and practice of arithmetic so well that Tunstal, the Englishman who had written so copiously on the subject,[4] confessed that really, in comparison with Gargantua, all that he knew of it was so much nonsense. And Gargantua did not only become skilled in that branch, but also in such other mathematical sciences

3. A list of ancient physicians and writers of natural history.
4. A well-known bishop of Durham (England) and writer   of an arithmetical treatise printed in Paris shortly before Rabelais published *Pantagruel*.

as geometry, astronomy, and music. For while they waited for his meal to be prepared and digested they made a thousand pretty instruments and geometrical figures, and also practised the astronomical canons.

After this they amused themselves by singing music in four or five parts or on a set theme, to their throats' content. With regard to musical instruments, he learnt to play the lute, the spinet, the harp, the German flute, the nine-holed flute, the viol, and the trombone. After spending an hour in this way, his digestion being complete, he got rid of his natural excrements, and then returned to his principal study for three hours or more, during which time he repeated the morning's reading, went on with the book in hand, and also practised writing, drawing, and shaping the Gothic and Roman letters.

This done, they left their lodging in the company of a young gentleman of Touraine, named Squire Gymnaste, who taught Gargantua the art of horsemanship; and after changing his clothes, the pupil mounted in turn a charger, a cob, a jennet, a barb, and a light horse, and made each run a hundred courses, clear the ditch, leap over the barrier, and turn sharp round to the right and to the left. He did not break his lance. For it is the greatest nonsense in the world to say: "I broke ten lances at tilt or in battle"—a carpenter could do it easily—but "it is a glorious and praiseworthy thing with one lance to have broken ten of your enemies." So with his lance steel-tipped, tough, and strong, he would break down a door, pierce a harness, root up a tree, spike a ring, or carry off a knight's saddle, coat of mail, and gauntlets; and all this he did armed from head to foot.

As for riding to the sound of trumpets and chirruping to encourage his horse, he had no master; the vaulter of Ferrara was a mere ape by comparison.[5] He was singularly skilled also at leaping rapidly from one horse to another without touching the ground—these horses were called *desultories*—at getting up from either side, lance in hand and without stirrups, and at guiding his horse wherever he would without a bridle. For such feats are helpful to military discipline.

Another day he practised with the battle-axe, which he wielded so well, so lustily repeating his cutting strokes, so dexterously swinging it round his head, that he was passed as a knight-at-arms in the field and at all trials. Then he brandished the pike, played with the two-handed sword, the thrusting sword, the Spanish rapier, the dagger, and the poniard, in armour or without, with a buckler, a rolled cape, or a handguard.

He would hunt the stag, the roebuck, the bear, the boar, the hare, the partridge, the pheasant, and the bustard. He would play with the great ball, and make it fly into the air either with his foot or his fist. He wrestled, ran, and jumped, not at three steps and a leap, not with a hop or with the German action—for, as Gymnaste said, such leaps are useless and serve no purpose in war—but with one bound he would clear a ditch, sail over a hedge, or get six foot up a wall, and in this way climb into a window a lance-length high.

He would swim in deep water on his belly, on his back, on his side, with his whole body, or only with his legs, or with one hand in the air holding a book. Indeed, he would cross the whole breadth of the Seine without wetting that book, dragging his cloak in his teeth, as Julius Caesar did.[6] Then with one hand he would powerfully lift himself into a boat, from there dive head foremost back into the water, sound the depths, explore the hollows of the rocks, and plunge into the gulfs and abysses. Then

---

5. Rabelais alludes to a celebrated jockey, Cesare Fiaschi.   6. Reported by Plutarch in his life of Julius Caesar.

he would turn the boat, steer it, row it quickly, slowly, with the stream, against the current, check it in full course, guide it with one hand while flourishing a great oar with the other, hoist the sail, climb the mast by the shrouds, run along the spars, fix the compass, pull the bowlines to catch the wind, and wrench at the helm.

Coming out of the water, he sturdily scaled the mountain-side and came down as easily; he climbed trees like a cat, jumped from one to another like a squirrel, and tore down great branches like another Milo.[7] With two stout poniards, as sharp as tried bodkins, he would run up the wall of a house like a rat, and then drop down from the top to the bottom with his limbs in such a posture that he suffered no hurt from the fall. He threw the dart, the bar, the stone, the javelin, the boar-spear, and the halbert; drew a bow to the full, bent by main force great rack-bent cross-bows, lifted an arquebus to his eye to aim it, planted the cannon, shot at the butts, at the popinjay, riding uphill, riding downhill, frontways, sideways, and behind him, like the Parthians. They tied a cable for him to the top of some high tower, with the end hanging to the ground, up which he climbed hand over hand, and then came down so firmly and sturdily that no one could have done better on a level plain. They put up a great pole for him, supported by two trees; and from this he would hang by his hands, moving up and down along it without touching anything with his feet, so fast that you could not catch up with him if you ran at full speed. And to exercise his chest and lungs, he would shout like all the devils. I heard him once calling Eudemon from the Porte St Victor to Montmartre; never had Stentor such a voice at the battle of Troy.[8]

Then, for the strengthening of his sinews, they made him two great sows of lead, each weighing eight hundred and seventy tons, which he called his dumb-bells. These he lifted in either hand, and raised in the air above his head, where he held them without moving for three-quarters of an hour and more, an inimitable feat of strength. He fought at the barriers with the strongest, and when the tussle came, his foot-hold was so firm that he would let the toughest of them try to move him, as Milo did of old; and in imitation of that champion he would hold a pomegranate in his hand and give it to whoever could get it from him.

After these pastimes and after being rubbed, washed, and refreshed by a change of clothes, he returned quietly; and as they walked through the meadows, or other grassy places, they examined the trees and the plants, comparing them with the descriptions in the books of such ancients as Dioscorides, Marinus, Pliny, Nicander, Macer, and Galen;[9] and they brought back whole handfuls to the house. These were in charge of a young page called Rhizotome,[1] who also looked after the mattocks, picks, grubbing-hooks, spades, pruning-knives, and other necessary implements for efficient gardening.

Once back at the house, while supper was being prepared, they repeated some passages from what had been read, before sitting down to table. And notice here that Gargantua's dinner was sober and frugal, for he only ate enough to stay the gnawings of his stomach. But his supper was copious and large, for then he took all that he needed to stay and nourish himself. This is the proper regimen prescribed by the art of good, sound medicine, although a rabble of foolish physicians, worn out by the wrangling of the sophists, advise the contrary. During this meal the dinner-time lesson was

7. Milo of Croton, a famous athlete from the 6th century B.C.E., who won many wrestling matches at Olympia.
8. The Porte St. Victor was in the university quarter, far from the hill of Montmartre. Stentor is said in the *Iliad*

(Book 5) to shout as loud as 50 men.
9. All authors of treatises on botany; Marinus is unknown.
1. Greek for "root-cutter."

continued for as long as seemed right, the rest of the time being spent in good, learned, and profitable conversation. After grace had been said, they began to sing melodiously, to play on tuneful instruments, or to indulge in those pleasant games played with cards, dice, or cups; and there they stayed, making good cheer and amusing themselves sometimes till bedtime. But sometimes they went to seek the society of scholars or of men who had visited foreign lands.

When it was quite dark, they went before retiring to the most open side of the house, to view the face of the sky, and there took note of the comets, if there were any, also of the figures, situations, aspects, oppositions, and conjunctions of the stars. After which Gargantua briefly ran over with his tutor, in the manner of the Pythagoreans,[2] all that he had read, seen, learnt, done, and heard in the course of the whole day. And so they prayed to God the Creator, worshipping Him, reaffirming their faith in Him, glorifying Him for His immense goodness, rendering thanks to Him for all the past, and recommending themselves to His divine clemency for all the future. This done, they went to their rest.

* * *

Chapter 25. How a Great Quarrel Arose Between the Cake-bakers of Lerné and the People of Grandgousier's Country, Which Led to Great Wars

At that time, which was the vintage season at the beginning of autumn, the shepherds of the country were employed in guarding the vines to prevent the starlings from eating the grapes; and they were thus occupied at a moment when the bakers of Lerné were passing the great crossroad, taking ten or twelve loads of cakes to the town.[3] Now the said shepherds courteously requested the bakers to sell them some of their cakes for cash at the market price. For note that grapes and fresh cake for breakfast is a dish for the gods, especially pineau-grapes, fig-grapes, muscatels, great black grapes, and purgative grapes for those whose bowels are constipated. For these make them squirt the length of a hunting-spear; and often when a man means to fart he shits himself; from which these grapes get the name of *wet-farters*.

The cake-bakers, however, were not at all inclined to accede to this request and, what is worse, they heaped insults on the shepherds, calling them babblers, snaggle-teeth, crazy carrot-heads, scabs, shit-a-beds, boors, sly cheats, lazy louts, fancy fellows, drunkards, braggarts, good-for-nothings, dunderheads, nut-shellers, beggars, sneak-thieves, mincing milksops, apers of their betters, idlers, half-wits, gapers, hovel-dwellers, poor fish, cacklers, conceited monkeys, teeth-clatterers, dung-drovers, shitten shepherds, and other such abusive epithets. They added that these dainty cakes were not for their eating, and that they must be satisfied with black bread and wholemeal loaves.

To which insults one of the shepherds, Forgier by name, a distinguished young man of very respectable appearance, replied quietly:

"Since when have you sprouted horns that you've grown so fresh? Bless my soul, you used to let us have them willingly enough, and now—if you please—you refuse. That's not the behaviour of honest neighbours. We never treat you like this when you come to buy our good corn, to make your cakes and scones with. What is more, we should have given you some of our grapes into the bargain. But, by God, you may

---

2. Cicero mentions this practice in his work, *Of Old Age.*
3. Lerné is a village in the canton of Chinon, roughly one kilometer from La Devinière. Its cakes were known throughout the region, and still are today.

come to be sorry for this one day, when there is something you want from us. Then we'll serve you as you serve us, and you'll remember this."

Then Marquet, the grand mace-bearer of the cake-bakers' guild, replied: "Your crest's very high this morning, my fine cock. You must have eaten too much millet last night. But come here, just come here, and I'll give you some of my cakes!"

Then in all simplicity Forgier went over to him, taking a shilling from his leather purse and thinking that Marquet was really going to hand him over some cakes. But the mace-bearer slashed him across the legs with his whip so hard that the weals showed, and began to run away. At this Forgier shouted "Murder! Help!" at the top of his voice, and threw a great cudgel at him, which he carried under his arm. This struck Marquet on the coronal suture of his head, over the temporal artery on the right side; and he dropped from his mare, to all appearances more dead than alive.

Meanwhile the small farmers, who were shelling nuts near by, rushed up with their long poles and thrashed these cake-bakers like so much green rye. The shepherds and shepherdesses too, hearing Forgier shout, came up with their slings and sticks, and pursued them with great volleys of stones, which fell as thick as hail. Finally they caught the bakers up and took from them about four or five dozen cakes, for which they paid them the usual price, however, giving them a hundred walnuts and three baskets of white grapes into the bargain. Then the bakers helped Marquet, who had a nasty wound, on to his mare, and they returned to Lemé, turning off the Parilly road, with fierce and ugly threats against the drovers, shepherds, and small farmers of Seuilly and Cinais.

When they had gone, the shepherds and shepherdesses made a good feast of the cakes and fine grapes, and sported gaily to the pleasant sound of the bagpipe, scoffing at those grand, vainglorious cake-bakers, who had struck bad luck that morning, through not crossing themselves with the right hand when they got up. And they neatly dressed Forgier's legs with big common grapes, so that they soon healed.

Chapter 26. How the Inhabitants of Lerné, at the Command of Their King Picrochole, Made an Unexpected Attack on Grandgousier's Shepherds

On their return to Lerné the cake-bakers neither ate nor drank, but went straight to the Capitol, and there made their complaint before their King Picrochole, the third of that name,[4] displaying their broken bread-baskets, their crumpled caps, their torn coats, their cakeless bags and, worse than that, the sorely wounded Marquet. All this damage, they declared, had been done by Grandgousier's shepherds and small-farmers, near the great highway beyond Seuilly.

The King promptly flew into a furious rage and, without any further question of why or how, called out his vassals great and small, commanding every one, under pain of the halter, to assemble armed in the great square in front of the castle at the hour of midday; and for the furtherance of this design he had the drum beaten all round the town. He himself, while his dinner was being prepared, went to see his artillery limbered up, his ensign and standard displayed, and his wagons loaded with store of ammunition both for the field and the belly. While he dined he made out the commissions; and by his edict Lord Hairychest was appointed to the vanguard, in which were numbered sixteen thousand and fourteen arquebusiers and thirty-five

4. "Picrochole" means bitter or black bile; tradition has it that Rabelais caricatures the lord of Lerné, a doctor by name of Gaucher de Sainte-Marthe.

thousand and eleven free-booting volunteers. The artillery was put in charge of Blow-trumpet, the Grand Master of the Horse; and it was made up of nine hundred and four-teen great bronze pieces, including cannon, double-cannon, basilisks, serpentines, culverins, bombards, falcons, passevolans, spiroles, and other pieces. The rearguard was put in charge of Duke Rakepenny, and in the main body rode the King and the princes of his realm.

When they were thus hastily equipped but before setting out on the road, they sent forward three hundred light horsemen under the command of Captain Swillwind to reconnoitre the territory and see if there was any ambush in the countryside. But after a diligent search they found all the land around peaceful and quiet, and no gathering of people anywhere; upon the receipt of which news Picrochole ordered everyone to advance speedily under his colours.

Thereupon in rash and disorderly fashion they took to the fields pell-mell, wasting and destroying wherever they passed, sparing neither poor nor rich, sacred place nor profane. They drove off oxen, cows, bulls, calves, heifers, ewes, rams, she-goats, hens, capons, chickens, goslings, ganders, geese, hogs, sows, and little pigs; knocking down the nuts, stripping the vines, carrying off the vine-stocks, and shaking down all the fruit from the trees. The destruction they did was unparalleled, and they encountered no resistance. Everyone begged for mercy, and implored to be treated with more humanity, considering the fact that they had always been good and friendly neighbours, and that they had never committed any excess or outrage against the people of Lerné, to deserve this sudden harshness, for which, indeed, God would punish the perpetrators. But the only reply that the men of Lerné made to these remonstrances was that they would teach them to eat cakes.

Chapter 27. How a Monk of Seuilly Saved the Abbey-close from Being Sacked by the Enemy

So they went on, wasting, pillaging, and stealing till they arrived at Seuilly,[5] where they robbed men and women alike and took everything they could; nothing was too hot or too heavy for them. Although there was plague in almost every house, they broke into all of them and plundered everything inside; and none of them caught any infection, which is a most wonderful thing. For the priests, curates, preachers, physicians, surgeons, and apothecaries who went to visit, dress, heal, preach to, and admonish the sick had all died of the infection. Yet these robbing and murdering devils never took any harm. What is the reason for that, gentlemen? Consider the problem, I beg of you.

When the town was thus pillaged they went to the abbey in a horrible tumult, but they found it well bolted and barred. So the main body of their army marched on towards the ford of Vède, except for seven companies of foot and two hundred knights with their retainers, who remained there and broke down the walls of the close in order to ravage the vineyard. The poor devils of monks did not know which of their saints to turn to. Whatever the risk, they had the bell tolled for a meeting of the chapter, at which it was decided to march in a stately procession, rendered more effective by grand chants and litanies *contra hostium insidias,* and fine responses *pro pace.*[6]

---

5. A village due east of Lerné; the abbey is just outside its walls.

6. Litanies "against the snares of the enemy"; responses "for peace."

There was in the abbey at that time a cloister monk, named Friar John of the Hashes,[7] a young, gallant, sprightly, jovial, resourceful, bold, adventurous, resolute, tall, and thin fellow with a great gaping mouth and a fine outstanding nose. He was grand mumbler of matins, dispatcher of masses, and polisher off of vigils, and, to put it briefly, a true monk if ever there has been one since the monking world monked its first monkery; and moreover in the matter of his breviary he was a clerk to his very teeth.

Now when this monk heard the noise that the enemy were making in the close of their vineyard, he came out to see what they were doing; and finding them to be picking the grapes of their close, on which their provision for the whole year depended, he returned to the choir of the church, where the rest of the monks, gaping like so many stuffed pigs, were singing: *Ini nim, pe, ne, ne, ne, ne, ne, ne, num, num, ini, i, mi, i, mi, co, o, ne, no, ne, no no, no, rum, ne, num, num.*[8]

"That's shitten well sung!" he cried when he saw them. "But, for God's sake, why don't you sing: 'Baskets farewell; the harvest's done'? The devil take me if they aren't in our close, and so thoroughly cutting both vines and grapes that, God's body, there'll be nothing but gleanings there for the next four years. Tell me, by St. James's belly, what shall we drink in all that time? What'll there be for us poor devils? Lord God, *da mihi potum.*"[9]

Then said the Prior of the convent: "What does this drunkard want here? Let him be taken to the punishment cell for disturbing the divine service!"

"But," said the monk, "what about the wine service? Let's see that isn't disturbed. For you yourself, my lord Prior, like to drink of the best, and so does every decent fellow. Indeed, no man of honour hates a good wine; which is a monkish saying. But these responses you're singing here are very much out of season, by God. Now tell me, why are our services short at the harvest-tide and the vintage, and during Advent too, and all the winter? The late Friar Mace Pelosse, of blessed memory, a true zealot for our faith—devil take me if he wasn't—told me the reason, as I remember. It was that we might press and make the wine properly at the vintage, and in winter drink it down. So listen to me, all you who love wine; and follow me too, in God's name. For I tell you boldly, may St. Anthony's fire burn me if anyone tastes the grape who hasn't fought for the vine. Church property it is, by God, and hands off it! Devil take it, St. Thomas of Canterbury was willing to die for the Church's goods, and if I were to die for them, shouldn't I be a Saint as well?[1] But I shan't die, for all that. It's I that will be the death of others."

As he said this he threw off his heavy monk's cloak and seized the staff of his cross, which was made of the heart of a sorb-apple tree. It was as long as a lance, a full hand's grip round, and decorated in places with lily flowers, which were almost all rubbed away. Thus he went out in a fine cassock, with his frock slung over his shoulder, and rushed so lustily on the enemy, who were gathering grapes in the vineyard without order or ensign, trumpet or drum. For the standard-bearers and ensigns had put down their standards and ensigns beside the walls, the drummers had knocked

7. In French, "Frère Jean des Entommeures," or Friar John of minced meat (or hash). The verb *entamer* means to make a first cut or incision, and as the following chapters will show, Friar John is appropriately named.

8. Put all together, the syllables spell out *impetum inimicorum ne timueritis,* or "you shall not fear the attack of the enemy."

9. "Give me to drink."

1. Archbishop of Canterbury, St. Thomas Becket was killed in his church in 1170 by King Henry II for having defended the clergy's privileges against royal authority.

in one side of their drums to fill them with grapes, the trumpeters were loaded with the fruit, and everyone was in disorder. He rushed, as I said, so fiercely on them, without a word of warning, that he bowled them over like hogs, striking right and left in the old fencing fashion.

He beat out the brains of some, broke the arms and legs of others, disjointed the neck-bones, demolished the kidneys, slit the noses, blackened the eyes, smashed the jaws, knocked the teeth down the throats, shattered the shoulder-blades, crushed the shins, dislocated the thigh-bones, and cracked the fore-arms of yet others. If one of them tried to hide among the thickest vines, he bruised the whole ridge of his back and broke the base of his spine like a dog's. If one of them tried to save himself by flight, he knocked his head into pieces along the lambdoidal suture. If one of them climbed into a tree, thinking he would be safe there, Friar John impaled him up the arse with his staff. If any one of his old acquaintance cried out: "Ha, Friar John, my friend, Friar John, I surrender!" he replied: "You can't help it. But you'll surrender your soul to all the devils as well." And he gave the fellow a sudden thumping.

If any man was seized with such a spirit of rashness as to try to face up to him, then he showed his muscular strength by running him through the chest by way of the mediastine to the heart. In the case of others, thrusting under the hollow of their short ribs, he turned their stomachs over, so that they died immediately. Others he smote so fiercely through the navel that he made their bowels gush out. Others he struck on the ballocks and pierced their bum-gut. It was, believe me, the most hideous spectacle that ever was seen.

Some invoked St. Barbara, others St. George, others St. Hands-off, others Our Lady of Cunault, of Loretto, of Good Tidings, of Lenou, of Rivière.[2] Some called on St. James, others on the Holy Shroud of Chambéry—but it was burnt three months later so completely that they could not save a single thread[3]—others on the Shroud of Cadouin, others on St. John of Angély, others on St. Eutropius of Saintes, St. Maximus of Chinon, St. Martin of Candes, St. Cloud of Cinais, the relics of Javarzay, and a thousand other pleasant little saints.[4]

Some died without a word, others spoke without dying; some died as they spoke, others spoke as they died, and others cried aloud: "Confession! Confession! Confiteor! Miserere! In manus!"[5]

Such was the shouting of the wounded that the Prior of the abbey came out with all his monks; and when they saw these poor creatures tumbled there among the vines and mortally wounded, they confessed some of them. But whilst the priests amused themselves by taking confessions, the little monklings ran to the place where Friar John stood, and asked him how they could help him.

His reply was that they should slit the throats of those lying on the ground. So, leaving their great cloaks on the nearest fence, they began to cut the throats of those whom he had already battered, and to dispatch them. Can you guess with what instruments? With fine *whittles*, which are the little jack-knives with which the small children of our country shell walnuts.

2. St. Barbara is the patron saint of artillerymen, George the patron saint of horsemen. Rabelais then lists several shrines to the Virgin Mary, all in France except for that of Loreto, where Mary's house was believed to have been carried. The final one, Our Lady of Rivière, was near Chinon.
3. The reliquary burned on 4 December 1532; the relic it-self, however, was spared.
4. All authentic saints, at least two of them with local cults (the confessor St. Maximus was buried in Chinon; St. Martin, Bishop of Tours, died at Candes, near Chinon, where many of his relics are preserved).
5. "I confess. Have mercy on me. Into your hands."

Meanwhile, still wielding the staff of his cross, Friar John reached the breach which the enemy had made, while some of the little monks carried off the ensigns and standards to their cells, to cut them into garters. But when those who had made their confession tried to get out through this breach, the monk rained blows upon them, crying: "These men are shriven and repentant, and have earned their pardons. They'll go right to paradise, as straight as a sickle or the road to Faye."

Thus, by his prowess, all that part of the army that had got into the close was discomfited, to the number of thirteen thousand, six hundred and twenty-two, not counting the women and small children—as is always understood. For never did Maugis the Hermit[6]—of whom it is written in the Deeds of the Four Sons of Aymon—wield his pilgrim's staff so valiantly against the Saracens as this monk swung the staff of his cross in his encounter with the enemy.

* * *

Chapter 38. How Gargantua Ate Six Pilgrims in a Salad

The story requires us to relate the adventures of six pilgrims, on their way from Saint-Sebastien, near Nantes.[7] To find themselves shelter for that night, they had hidden themselves, out of fear of the enemy, among the pea-straw in the garden, between the cabbages and the lettuces. Now Gargantua found himself rather thirsty, and asked if there were any lettuces to be had to make a salad; and hearing that some of the finest and largest in the country grew there, as big as plum or walnut trees, he decided to go to the garden himself, and brought away as many as he fancied in his hand. With them he picked up the six pilgrims, who were so terrified that they had not the courage to speak or cough.

As Gargantua was giving his lettuces a preliminary washing at the fountain, the pilgrims said to one another in a whisper: "What's to be done? We shall drown here among the lettuces. Shall we speak? But if we speak he will kill us as spies." And as they were thus deliberating, Gargantua put them with his lettuces into a dish belonging to the house, which was as large as the tun of Cîteaux,[8] and ate them with oil, vinegar, and salt as an appetizer before his supper, stuffing into his mouth at the same time five of the pilgrims.

The sixth was in the dish, hidden under a lettuce except for his pilgrim's staff, which was sticking out, and which Grandgousier saw. Whereupon he exclaimed: "That's a snail's horn, I think. Don't eat it."

"Why?" asked Gargantua. "They're good all this month," And pulling at the staff, he picked up the pilgrim with it, making a good meal of him. Then he took a huge gulp of strong white wine, and they waited for the supper to be brought in.

The pilgrims, thus devoured, kept themselves out of the way of his molars as best they could, and felt as if they had been put into the lowest dungeon of some prison. When Gargantua took his great gulp, indeed, they expected to drown in his mouth. The torrent of wine almost carried them down into the abyss of his stomach. However, leaping on their staffs, like pilgrims to St. Michael's Mount, they got into shelter behind his teeth. But unfortunately one of them, testing the ground with his staff to

---

6. Legendary character and cousin of the four brothers Aymon, who accompanied him to the Crusades.
7. Pilgrimages were made to Saint-Sebastien to find cures from serpent bites. Picrochole has continued to spread violence, forcing a reluctant Grandgousier to send an emis-

sary to him to find out the reason for all the unpleasantness, and to bring Gargantua back from Paris so he can help defend Grandgousier's lands.
8. A wooden tun or cask from the grounds of the abbey of Cîteaux in Bourgogne, founded by St. Bernard.

see whether they were in safety, struck roughly into the hole of a decayed tooth, hitting the mandibular nerve. This gave Gargantua very great pain, and he began to cry out in sudden rage. Then, to ease his pain, he sent for his toothpick, and probing towards the young walnut-tree, dislodged the noble pilgrims from their nest.

He caught one by the legs, another by the shoulders, another by the pouch, another by the scarf, and the poor wretch who had probed him with his staff he hooked up by the codpiece; which was, however, a great stroke of luck for him, for it broke an ulcerous lump which had been torturing him ever since they had passed Ancenis.

So the dislodged pilgrims fled across the plantation at a lively trot, and Gargantua's pain died down, just at the moment when he was called by Eudemon to supper, for everything was ready.

"I'll go and piss away my misfortune, then," he answered.

So copiously did he piss indeed that his urine cut the pilgrims' road, and they were compelled to cross the great canal. Passing from there by the bank of La Touche along the open road, they all fell, except Fournillier, into a trap that had been laid for catching wolves in a net, from which they escaped by the resourcefulness of the said Fournillier, who cut all the meshes and ropes. When they had escaped from there, they lay for the rest of the night in a lodging near Le Couldray, and there they were comforted for their misfortunes by the good words of one of their company named Wearybones, who pointed out to them that this adventure had been predicted by David in the Psalms. "*Cum exurgerent homines in nos, forte vivos deglutissent nos,* when we were eaten in a salad with a grain of salt; *cum irascerefur furor eorum in nos, forsitan aqua absorbuisset nos,* when he drank down the great gulp; *torrentem pertransivit anima nostra,* when we crossed the great canal; *forsitan pertransisset anima nostra aquam intolerabilem,* with his urine, with which he cut our road. *Benedictus Dominus, qui non dedit nos in captionem dentibus eorum. Anima nostra, sicut passer, erepta est de laqueo venantium,* when we fell into the trap; *laqueus contritus est* by Fournillier, *et nos liberati sumus. Adjutorium nostrum,* &c."[9]

from Chapter 39. How the Monk Was Feasted by Gargantua, and of the Fine Discourse He Delivered During Supper

When Gargantua was at table, and the first part of the good things had been consumed, Grandgousier began to recount the origins and cause of the war being waged between him and Picrochole; and when he came to the point of narrating how Friar John of the Hashes had triumphed at the defence of the abbey-close, he commended his prowess as above that of Camillus, Scipio, Pompey, Caesar, and Themistocles.[1]

Then Gargantua desired that the friar should be sent for at once, so that he might be consulted on what was next to be done. At their request the major-domo went to fetch him, and brought him back merrily with the staff of his cross on Grandgousier's mule; and when he arrived he was greeted with a thousand caresses, a thousand embraces, a thousand good-days:

9. A passage illustrating Rabelais's mockery of the pilgrims' superstition and the tendency to use biblical verses to illuminate mundane aspects of daily life. The Psalm cited is 124, minus its first verse, which Wearybones largely follows: "When men rose up against us, then would they have swallowed us alive [when we were eaten in a salad with a grain of salt]. When their fury was inflamed against us, then would the waters have overwhelmed us [when he drank down the great gulp]. The torrent would have swept over us [when we crossed the great canal]; over us then would have swept the raging waters [with his urine, with which he cut our road]. Blessed be the Lord, who did not leave us a prey to their teeth. We were rescued like a bird from the fowlers' snare [when we fell into the trap]. Broken was the snare [by Fournillier], and we were freed. Our help, etc." [Revised Standard Version].

1. All great ancient generals.

"Ha, Friar John, my friend, Friar John, my fine cousin, Friar John, devil take you! Let me hug you round the neck, my friend."

"Let me take you in my arms!"

"Come let me grip you, my ballocky boy, till I break your back."

And what a joker Friar John was! Never was a man so charming or so gracious.

"Come, come," said Gargantua, "take a stool here beside me, at this end."

"Most willingly," said the monk, "since it is your pleasure. Page, some water! Pour it out, my boy, pour it out. It will refresh my liver. Give it here, and let me gargle."

"*Deposita cappa,*" said Gymnaste, "off with this habit."

"Ho, by God," said the monk, "my dear sir, there's a chapter *in statutis Ordinis*— in the Statutes of my Order—that would object to that."[2]

"A turd!" said Gymnaste. "A turd for your chapter. That frock weighs down both your shoulders. Take it off."

"My friend," said the monk, "let me wear it. For, by God, it only makes me drink the better. It jollifies my whole body. If I take it off, my friends the pages will cut it up into garters, which was what happened to me once at Coulaines. And I shall have no appetite into the bargain. But if I sit down to table in this habit I shall drink, by God I shall, both to you and to your horse—with all my heart. God save the company! I had supped; but I shan't eat any the less for that. I have a paved stomach as hollow as St. Benedict's tun, and always gaping like a lawyer's purse. Of every fish except the tench[3]—take the wing of a partridge or a nun's thigh. Isn't it a jolly death, to die with a stiff john-thomas? Our Prior's very fond of white capon meat."

"In that," said Gymnaste, "he's unlike a fox. They never eat the white meat of the hens, pullets, and capons they carry off."

"Why?" asked the monk.

"Because," said Gymnaste, "they have no cooks to cook it, and if it isn't properly cooked it stays red and not white. The redness of meat is a sign that it is not properly cooked, except for lobsters and crayfish, which are cardinalized in the cooking." * * *

Chapter 40. Why Monks Are Shunned by the World, and Why Some Have Bigger Noses Than Others

"By my faith as a Christian," said Eudemon, "this monk's an astoundingly good fellow. He's an entertainment to every one of us. Now tell me why men won't allow monks in any good company? Why are they called spoil-sports and driven off, much as bees drive the drones from around their hives?—'*Ignavum fucos pecus a presepibus arcent,*' as Virgil puts it."[4]

To which Gargantua replied: It's the absolute truth that the frock and the cowl draw on themselves the opprobrium, insults, and curses of the world, just as the wind called Caecias attracts the clouds. The conclusive reason is that they eat the world's excrement, that is to say, sins; and as eaters of excrement they are cast into their privies—their convents and abbeys that is—which are cut off from all civil intercourse, as are the privies of a house. If you can understand why a monkey is always teased and mocked by the family, then you will realize why monks are rejected by all, old and young alike. A monkey doesn't guard a house, like a dog; he doesn't draw the plough,

---

2. Rabelais may be alluding to his decision to leave his religious order without requesting proper authorization.
3. Friar John cites only the beginning of a proverb, "For every fish except the Tench, take the back and leave the belly"; he truncates it in the interest of turning a lewd phrase.
4. A quote about bees from Virgil's *Georgics:* "The cowardly swarm drive the drones from the hives."

like an ox; he produces no milk or wool, like a sheep; he doesn't carry burdens, like a horse. All that he does is to beshit and ruin everything, which is the reason why he gets mockery and beatings from everyone. Similarly a monk—I mean one of these lazy monks—doesn't till the fields like a peasant, nor guard the country like a soldier, nor cure the sick like a physician, nor preach and instruct the world like a good gospeller and preceptor, nor carry commodities and things that the public need like a merchant. That is the reason why everyone hoots at them and abhors them."

"Yes," said Grandgousier, "but they pray to God for us."

"Nothing of the sort," replied Gargantua. "The fact is that they disturb their whole neighbourhood with the clanking of their bells."

"Yes indeed," said the monk. "A Mass, a Matins, or a Vespers well rung is half sung."

"They mumble through ever so many miracle stories and psalms which they don't in the least understand. They count over a number of Paternosters interlarded with long Ave-Marias, without understanding them or giving them so much as a thought; and that I call not prayer, but mockery of God. Still, may the Lord come to their aid if they do pray for us, and not through fear of losing their fresh bread and fat soups. All true Christians, of all degrees, in all places and at all times, pray to God, and the Holy Spirit prays and intercedes for them, and God receives them into his grace. Now our good Friar John is a true good Christian. Therefore everyone desires his company. He's no bigot, he's no wastrel; he is honest, gay, and resolute, and a good companion; he works, he labours, he defends the oppressed, he comforts the afflicted, he aids the suffering, and he saves the close of his abbey."

"I do a great deal more than that," said the monk. "For whilst we're dispatching our Matins and Masses for the dead in the choir I make cross-bow strings, I polish bolts and quarrels, I manufacture snares and nets to catch rabbits. I'm never idle. But ho, ho there! Drink! Bring us some drink! Bring in the fruit. These are chestnuts from the wood of Estrocs. With good fresh wine they'll set you farting. You're not frisked up here yet. By God, I drink at every ford, like a proctor's horse."

"Friar John," said Gymnaste, "wipe off that drip that's hanging on your nose."

"Ha, ha!" said the monk, "am I not in danger of drowning, seeing that I'm in water up to the nose? No, no, *quare? Quia.*[5]

It goes not in as water, though as water it may come out,
For it's properly corrected with grape-juice antidote.

O my friend, anyone who had winter boots of such leather could boldly preach to the oysters, for they would never let water."

"Why is it," asked Gargantua, "that Friar John has such a handsome nose?"

"Because," replied Grandgousier, "God wished it so, and he makes us in such shape and to such end as pleases his divine will, even as a potter fashions his pots."[6]

"Because," said Ponocrates, "he was one of the first at Nose-fair. He chose one of the finest and biggest."

"Stuff and nonsense," said the monk. "According to true monastic reasoning it was because my nurse had soft breasts: when she suckled me my nose sank in, as if into butter, and there it swelled and grew like dough in the kneading-trough. Hard

---

5. "Why? Because."

6. Reminiscent of a passage from Paul's letter to the Romans.

breasts in nurses make children snub-nosed. But come, come! *Ad formam nasi cognoscitur, ad te levavi.*[7] I never eat sweets. . . . Page, some drink, and bring some more toast!"

Chapter 41. How the Monk Made Gargantua Sleep, and of His Hours and Breviaries

Supper over, they discussed the business in hand, and it was decided that about midnight they should go out skirmishing to discover what precautions and watch the enemy kept; and that in the meantime they should rest a little, in order to be the fresher for their foray. But Gargantua could not sleep whichever way he turned. Whereupon the monk said to him: "I never sleep really comfortably, except when I am at a sermon, or at my prayers. Let's begin, I beg of you, you and I, the seven penitential psalms, and see if you won't soon be asleep."

The idea greatly pleased Gargantua and, beginning with the first psalm, when they came to the *Beati quorum*[8] they both fell asleep. But the monk never failed to wake up before midnight, so used was he to the hour of claustral Matins;[9] and when he woke up he roused all the rest by loudly singing the song:

> Ho, Regnault, wake, awake!
> O, Regnault, wake![1]

When they were all awake he said: "Gentlemen, they say that Matins generally begin with a cough, and supper with drinking. Let us act the other way round. Let's begin our Matins now with a drink, and this evening, when supper comes in, we'll cough as hard as we can."

"To drink so soon after sleeping," said Gargantua at this, "is to behave contrary to the rules of medicine. We ought first to clear the stomach of superfluities and excrements."

"The prescription's good," replied the monk. "A hundred devils leap on my body if there aren't more old drunkards than old physicians. I have come to an agreement with my appetite to this effect, that it always goes to bed when I do, and in return I always take good care of it during the day; also it gets up with me. You take as much trouble with your droppings as you like, I'm going to attend to my purge."

"What purge do you mean?" asked Gargantua.

"My breviary," said the monk. "For just as falconers, before they feed their hawks, make them seize on a hen's leg to purge their brains of vapours, and give them an appetite, so by taking up this jolly breviary of mine in the mornings, I scour my lungs through, and here I am ready to drink."

"According to what rite do you recite this fine Book of Hours of yours?" asked Gargantua.

"According to the rite of When-and-where: with three psalms and three lessons, or with nothing at all for those who want nothing. I never subject myself to hours;

---

7. "By the shape of his nose is he known, to you I have lifted [it]", parodying the opening of Psalm 123, "to you I have lifted my eyes."
8. "Blessed are they"; beginning of Psalm 32.
9. Recited at midnight, matins were one of the canonical hours of the breviary or Book of Hours, the book contain-

ing the "Divine Office" for each day, which those in religious orders were bound to read. The Office consisted of psalms, collects, and lessons, or readings from Scripture and saints' lives.
1. The refrain from a popular medieval song.

hours were made for man, and not man for hours. Therefore I make mine in the fashion of stirrup-leathers. I shorten them or lengthen them when I see fit; *brevis oratio penetrat celos, longa potatio evacuat cyphos.*[2] Where is that written?"

"By my faith," said Ponocrates, "I don't know, my pillicock, but you're worth more than gold."

"In that," said the monk, "I resemble you. But *venite, apotemus.*"[3]

Then they cooked an abundance of rashers on the coals and some early morning soup, and the monk drank as he would, some keeping him company and some leaving the stuff alone. After that each began to arm and equip himself, and they forced the monk to do the same, although he wanted no other protection but his habit over his stomach and the staff of his cross in his hand. Nevertheless at their wish he was encased in armour from head to foot and mounted on a fine Neapolitan charger, with a stout short-sword at his side. With him rode Gargantua, Ponocrates, Gymnaste, Eudemon, and twenty-five of the most adventurous of Grandgousier's house, all armed at proof, with lances in their hands, and mounted like St. George, each with an arquebusier following him.

Chapter 42. How the Monk Encouraged His Companions, and How He Hanged on a Tree

Thus the noble champions set out on their adventure, resolutely seeking what enterprise they should pursue and what guard against when the day of the great and terrible battle should come.

And the monk encouraged them, saying: "My children, have neither fear nor doubts. I will conduct you safely. May God and St. Benedict be with us! If I had strength equal to my courage, by God I'd pluck 'em for you like a duck! I'm afraid of nothing except artillery. Yet I know a prayer, taught me by the sub-sacristan of our abbey, which safeguards a man against all fiery mouths. But it will do me no good because I have no faith in it. Nevertheless the staff of my cross will play Old Harry with them. And if one of you does a bolt, the devil may take me if I don't make him a monk instead of me, and tie my frock round his neck, by God. It carries a cure for cowardice in men. Have you never heard of my lord of Meurles' greyhound, which was no good in the field? My lord put a frock round his neck and, by the living God, not a hare or a fox ever escaped him and, what's more, he covered all the bitches in the country, though up to then he'd been weak in the back and *de frigidis et maleficiatis.*"[4]

As he spoke these heated words, the monk passed beneath a walnut-tree, on the way to the Willow-wood, and spitted the vizor of his helmet on the broken end of a great bough. Nothwithstanding this, he spurred his horse fiercely. The beast, being skittish under the spur, made a bound forward, and the monk, trying to disengage his vizor from the hook, let go the reins and hung on to the branch with his hand, while his horse slipped from under him. In this way he was left suspended in the walnut tree, crying "Help!" and "Murder!," and swearing also that there was treason afoot.

Eudemon was the first to perceive him, and he called out to Gargantua: "Sire, come and see Absalom hanging!"[5] But when Gargantua rode up, he looked closely at

---

2. A short prayer pierces the heavens, a long drink empties out the hump.

3. "Come, let us drink": which rhymes with the Latin *venite adoremus,* or "come let us adore him."

4. "Of the cold and impotent."

5. In 2 Kings 18, Absalom, rebellious son of King David, is fleeing when his head is stuck in the branches of an oak tree; he is then viciously killed by Joab, one of David's generals.

the monk's countenance and at the way he was hanging. Then he said to Eudemon: "You're a bit out when you compare him to Absalom. Absalom hung by the hair. But the monk, being cropped, is hanging by the ears."

"Help me," cried the monk, "in the name of the devil! Do you think this is the moment for chatter? You remind me of the Decretalist preachers, who say that if anyone sees his neighbour in peril of death he must, under pain of three-pronged excommunication, admonish him to make confession and put himself in a state of grace, before coming to his aid. When I see anyone in future, who has fallen into the river and is just going to drown, instead of going after him and lending him a hand, I'll read him a fine, long sermon *de contemptu mundi et fuga seculi*,[6] and when he's stark dead I'll go and fish him out."

"Don't you stir, my dear fellow," said Gymnaste. "I'll come and help you, for you're a pretty little *monachus*.

> Monachus in claustro
> Non valet ova duo;
> Sed, quando est extra,
> Bene valet triginta.[7]

I've seen more than five hundred hanged men, but I never saw one who hung more gracefully. If I hung as gracefully I'd willingly stay there for the whole of my life."

"Will you soon have finished preaching?" asked the monk. "Help me in God's name, since you won't for the other Power's sake. But by the habit I wear you'll repent of this, *tempore et loco prelibatis*."[8]

Then Gymnaste dismounted and, climbing the tree, lifted the monk up by the armpits with one hand, while with the other he unhooked his vizor from the broken branch. Then he dropped him to the ground and himself followed after.

Once on the ground, the monk took off all his armour and, picking up the staff of his cross, remounted his horse, which Eudemon had stopped from running away. And so they went merrily on, keeping to the road to the Willow-wood.

* * *

[*The battle won, Gargantua rewards the victors, ending with Friar John.*]

Chapter 52. How Gargantua Had the Abbey of Thélème Built for the Monk

There only remained the monk to be provided for, and Gargantua wanted to make him abbot of Seuilly, but he refused the post. He next proposed to give him the abbey of Bourgueil or of Saint-Florant, whichever would suit him better, or both, if he fancied them.[9] But the monk answered categorically that he wanted neither charge nor government of monks.

"For how should I be able to govern others," he said, "when I don't know how to govern myself? If it seems to you that I have done you, and may in the future do you welcome service, give me leave to found an abbey after my own devices."

---

6. "On the disdain of the world and flight from all secular things."
7. "A monk in his cell isn't worth two eggs. But when he has left it, he's worth at least thirty."
8. "Assuming the time and place are right."
9. Two of the wealthiest abbeys in France in Rabelais's time.

This request pleased Gargantua, and he offered him all his land of Thélème,[1] beside the River Loire, to within six miles of the great forest of Port-Huault. The monk then requested Gargantua to institute his religious order in an exactly contrary way to all others.

"First of all, then," said Gargantua, "you mustn't build walls round it. For all other abbeys have lofty walls (murs)."

"Yes," said the monk, "and not without reason. Where there's a *mur* before and a *mur* behind, there are plenty of murmurs, envy, and mutual conspiracy."

Moreover, seeing that in certain monasteries in this world it is the custom that if any woman enters—I speak of chaste and honest women—they wash the place where she trod, it was ordained that if any monk or nun happened to enter here, the spot where he or she had stood should be scrupulously washed likewise. And because in the religious foundations of this world everything is encompassed, limited, and regulated by hours, it was decreed that there should be no clock or dial at all, but that affairs should be conducted according to chance and opportunity. For Gargantua said that the greatest waste of time he knew was the counting of hours—what good does it do?—and the greatest nonsense in the world was to regulate one's life by the sound of a bell, instead of by the promptings of reason and good sense. Item, because at that time they put no women into religious houses unless they were one-eyed, lame, hunchbacked, ugly, malformed, lunatic, half-witted, bewitched, and blemished, or men that were not sickly, low-born, stupid, or a burden on their family.

"By the way," said the monk, "if a woman is neither fair nor good, what can you do with her?"

"Make her a nun," said Gargantua.

"Yes," said the monk, "and a sempstress of shirts."

It was decreed that here no women should be admitted unless they were beautiful, well-built, and sweet-natured, nor any men who were not handsome, well-built, and of pleasant nature also.

Item, because men never entered nunneries except secretly and by stealth, it was decreed that here there should be no women when there were no men, and no men when there were no women.

Item, because both men and women, once accepted into a monastic order, after their novitiate year, were compelled and bound to remain for ever, so long as they lived, it was decreed that both men and women, once accepted, could depart from there whenever they pleased, without let or hindrance.

Item, because ordinarily monks and nuns made three vows, that is of chastity, poverty, and obedience, it was decreed that there anyone could be regularly married, could become rich, and could live at liberty.

With regard to the lawful age of entry, women were to be received at from ten to fifteen, and men at from twelve to eighteen.

from *Chapter 53. How the Thélèmites' Abbey Was Built and Endowed*

For the building and furnishing of the abbey Gargantua had counted out in ready money two million seven hundred thousand, eight hundred and thirty-one fine gold

---

1. "Thélème" is Greek for "will," appropriate for an abbey the motto of which is *Fay ce que vouldras,* "do what you will." The abbey will be situated in the Indre, in the same general area of Chinon where Montaigne had his property.

Agnus Dei crowns; and for every year until the work was completed he assigned out of his income from the River Dive, one million, six hundred and sixty-nine thousand Sun crowns, and an equal number stamped with the sign of Pleiades.[2] While for its foundation and upkeep he granted in perpetuity two million three hundred and sixty-nine thousand rose nobles as a freehold endowment, exempt from all burdens and services, and payable every year at the abbey gate; and this he confirmed in due letters-patent. * * *

Chapter 57. The Rules According to Which the Thélèmites Lived

All their life was regulated not by laws, statutes, or rules, but according to their free will and pleasure. They rose from bed when they pleased, and drank, ate, worked, and slept when the fancy seized them. Nobody woke them; nobody compelled them either to eat or to drink, or to do anything else whatever. So it was that Gargantua had established it. In their rules there was only one clause:

DO WHAT YOU WILL

because people who are free, well-born, well-bred, and easy in honest company have a natural spur and instinct which drives them to virtuous deeds and deflects them from vice; and this they called honour. When these same men are depressed and enslaved by vile constraint and subjection, they use this noble quality which once impelled them freely towards virtue, to throw off and break this yoke of slavery. For we always strive after things forbidden and covet what is denied us.

Making use of this liberty, they most laudably rivalled one another in all of them doing what they saw pleased one. If some man or woman said, "Let us drink," they all drank; if he or she said, "Let us play," they all played; if it was "Let us go and amuse ourselves in the fields," everyone went there. If it were for hawking or hunting, the ladies, mounted on fine mares, with their grand palfreys following, each carried on their daintily gloved wrists a sparrow-hawk, a lanneret, or a merlin, the men carrying the other birds.

So nobly were they instructed that there was not a man or woman among them who could not read, write, sing, play musical instruments, speak five or six languages, and compose in them both verse and prose. Never were seen such worthy knights, so valiant, so nimble both on foot and horse; knights more vigorous, more agile, handier with all weapons than they were. Never were seen ladies so good-looking, so dainty, less tiresome, more skilled with the fingers and the needle, and in every free and honest womanly pursuit than they were.[3]

For that reason, when the time came that anyone in that abbey, either at his parents' request or for any other reason, wished to leave it, he took with him one of the ladies, the one who had accepted him as her admirer, and they were married to one another; and if at Thélème they had lived in devotion and friendship, they lived in still greater devotion and friendship when they were married. Indeed, they loved one another to the end of their days as much as they had done on their wedding day.[4]

---

2. An imaginary currency; the Pleiades were seven sisters, turned into a constellation when they were chased by the hunter Orion.

3. Rabelais was not the only one of his era to imagine a perfect courtly society; see the excerpts from Castiglione's *Courtier* (page 256), published shortly before *Gargantua and Pantagruel*.

4. The first book will end with the text of a riddle, found in the abbey's foundations. The protagonists puzzle over its meaning, with Gargantua arguing that it reveals profound Christian truths, and Friar John having the final word: "I don't think there is any other sense concealed in it than the description of a game of tennis wrapped up in strange language."

from Pantagruel [The Second Book]

Chapter 8. How Pantagruel, When at Paris, Received a Letter from His Father Gargantua, Together with a Copy of the Same[1]

As you may well suppose, Pantagruel studied very hard. For he had a double-sized intelligence and a memory equal in capacity to the measure of twelve skins and twelve casks of oil. But while he was staying in Paris, he one day received a letter from his father which read as follows:

Most dear Son,

Among the gifts, graces, and prerogatives with which the Sovereign Creator, God Almighty, endowed and embellished human nature in the beginning, one seems to me to stand alone, and to excel all others; that is the one by which we can, in this mortal state, acquire a kind of immortality and, in the course of this transitory life, perpetuate our name and seed; which we do by lineage sprung from us in lawful marriage. By this means there is in some sort restored to us what was taken from us by the sin of our first parents, who were told that, because they had not been obedient to the commandment of God the Creator, they would die, and that by death would be brought to nothing that magnificent form in which man has been created.

But by this method of seminal propagation, there remains in the children what has perished in the parents, and in the grandchildren what has perished in the children, and so on in succession till the hour of the Last Judgement, when Jesus Christ shall peacefully have rendered up to God His Kingdom, released from all danger and contamination of sin. Then all generations and corruptions shall cease, and the elements shall be free from their continuous transformations, since peace, so long desired, will then be perfect and complete, and all things will be brought to their end and period.

Not without just and equitable cause, therefore, do I offer thanks to God, my Preserver, for permitting me to see my grey-haired age blossom afresh in your youth. When, at the will of Him who rules and governs all things, my soul shall leave this mortal habitation, I shall not now account myself to be absolutely dying, but to be passing from one place to another, since in you, and by you, I shall remain in visible form here in this world, visiting and conversing with men of honour and my friends as I used to do. Which conversation of mine has been, thanks to God's aid and grace, although not free from sin, I confess—for we all sin, and continually pray to God to wipe out our sins—at least without evil intention.

If the qualities of my soul did not abide in you as does my visible form, men would not consider you the guardian and treasure-house of the immortality of our name; in which case my pleasure would be small, considering that the lesser part of me, which is my body, would persist, and the better part, which is the soul, and by which our name continues to be blessed among men, would be bastardized and degenerate. This I say not out of any distrust of your virtue, which I have already tried and approved, but in order to encourage you more strongly to proceed from good to better. For what I write to you at present is not so much in order that you may live in this virtuous manner as that you may rejoice in so living and in so having lived, and may strengthen yourself in the like resolution for the future, for the furtherance and perfection of these ends I have, as you will easily remember,

---

1. Pantagruel is the son of Gargantua and the giantess Badebec, who dies in childbirth because of the enormous size of her child. The name his father gives him, as Rabelais explains in Chapter 2, means "all thirsty," "by this meaning to infer that at the hour of the child's nativity the world was all thirsty, and also seeing, in a spirit of prophecy, that one day his son would be ruler over the thirsty." Like his father, Pantagruel is sent to Paris to study.

spared no expense. Indeed, I have helped you towards them as if I treasured nothing else in this world but to see you, in my lifetime, a perfect model of virtue, honour, and valour, and a paragon of liberal and high-minded learning. I might seem to have desired nothing but to leave you, after my death, as a mirror representing the person of me your father, and if not as excellent and in every way as I wish you, at least desirous of being so.

But although my late father Grandgousier, of blessed memory, devoted all his endeavours to my advancement in all perfection and political knowledge, and although my labour and study were proportionate to—no, even surpassed—his desire; still, as you may well understand, the times were not as fit and favourable for learning as they are today, and I had no supply of tutors such as you have. Indeed the times were still dark, and mankind was perpetually reminded of the miseries and disasters wrought by those Goths who had destroyed all sound scholarship.[2] But, thanks be to God, learning has been restored in my age to its former dignity and enlightenment. Indeed I see such improvements that nowadays I should have difficulty in getting a place among little schoolboys, in the lowest class, I who in my youth was reputed, with some justification, to be the most learned man of the century. Which I do not say out of vain boastfulness, although I might commendably do so in writing to you,—for which you have the authority of Marcus Tullius[3] in his work on Old Age, and Plutarch's statement in his book entitled: *How a Man may praise himself without Reproach*—but in order to inspire you to aim still higher.

Now every method of teaching has been restored, and the study of languages has been revived: of Greek, without which it is disgraceful for a man to call himself a scholar, and of Hebrew, Chaldean, and Latin. The elegant and accurate art of printing, which is now in use, was invented in my time, by divine inspiration; as, by contrast, artillery was inspired by diabolical suggestion. The whole world is full of learned men, of very erudite tutors, and of most extensive libraries, and it is my opinion that neither in the time of Plato, of Cicero, nor of Papinian were there such facilities for study as one finds today.[4] No one, in future, will risk appearing in public or in any company, who is not well polished in Minerva's workshop. I find robbers, hangmen, free-booters, and grooms nowadays more learned than the doctors and preachers were in my time.

Why, the very women and girls aspire to the glory and reach out for the celestial manna of sound learning. So much so that at my present age I have been compelled to learn Greek, which I had not despised like Cato,[5] but which I had not the leisure to learn in my youth. Indeed I find great delight in reading the Morals of Plutarch, Plato's magnificent *Dialogues,* the *Monuments* of Pausanias, and the *Antiquities* of Athenaeus,[6] while I wait for the hour when it will please God, my Creator, to call me and bid me leave this earth.

Therefore, my son, I beg you to devote your youth to the firm pursuit of your studies and to the attainment of virtue. You are in Paris. There you will find many praiseworthy examples to follow. You have Epistemon for your tutor, and he can give you living instruction by word of mouth. It is my earnest wish that you shall become a perfect master of languages. First of Greek, as Quintilian advises; secondly, of Latin; and then of Hebrew, on account of the Holy Scriptures; also of Chaldean and Arabic, for the same reason; and I would have you model your Greek style on Plato's and your Latin on that of Cicero. Keep your memory well stocked with every tale from history, and here you will find help in the Cosmographes of the historians. Of the liberal arts, geometry, arithmetic, and

---

2. A reflection on the emergence of the Renaissance from the "dark" or gothic ages. The letter is often cited in the context of setting forth the education for the perfect "Renaissance man," as well as exemplifying the style and admirable pithiness of that man himself.

3. Cicero.

4. Plato lived during the height of Athens' golden age, Cicero during the last days of Rome's republic. Papinian

was a Roman jurist who worked under the enlightened emperor Marcus Aurelius.

5. Cato was said by Plutarch to have refused to learn Greek.

6. All significant texts in Greek; Pausanius wrote a descriptive guidebook to Greece, and the 2nd-century writer Athenaeus composed *Banquet of the Sophists,* a compilation of Greek literature and anecdotes.

music, I gave you some smattering when you were still small, at the age of five or six. Go on and learn the rest, also the rules of astronomy. But leave divinatory astrology and Lully's art alone, I beg of you, for they are frauds and vanities.[7] Of Civil Law I would have you learn the best texts by heart, and relate them to the art of philosophy. And as for the knowledge of Nature's works, I should like you to give careful attention to that too; so that there may be no sea, river, or spring of which you do not know the fish. All the birds of the air, all the trees, shrubs, and bushes of the forest, all the herbs of the field, all the metals deep in the bowels of the earth, the precious stones of the whole East and the South—let none of them be unknown to you.

Then scrupulously peruse the books of the Greek, Arabian, and Latin doctors once more, not omitting the Talmudists and Cabalists, and by frequent dissections[8] gain a perfect knowledge of that other world which is man. At some hours of the day also, begin to examine the Holy Scriptures. First the New Testament and the Epistles of the Apostles in Greek; and then the Old Testament, in Hebrew. In short, let me find you a veritable abyss of knowledge. For, later, when you have grown into a man, you will have to leave this quiet and repose of study, to learn chivalry and warfare, to defend my house, and to help our friends in every emergency against the attacks of evildoers.[9]

Furthermore, I wish you shortly to show how much you have profited by your studies, which you cannot do better than by publicly defending a thesis in every art against all persons whatsoever, and by keeping the company of learned men, who are as common in Paris as elsewhere.

But because, according to the wise Solomon, Wisdom enters not into the malicious heart,[1] and knowledge without conscience is but the ruin of the soul, it befits you to serve, love, and fear God, to put all your thoughts and hopes in Him, and by faith grounded in charity to be so conjoined with Him that you may never be severed from Him by sin. Be suspicious of the world's deceits and set not your heart on vanity; for this life is transitory, but the word of God remains eternal. Be helpful to all your neighbours, and love them as yourself. Respect your tutors, avoid the company of those whom you would not care to resemble, and do not omit to make use of those graces which God has bestowed on you. Then, when you see that you have acquired all the knowledge to be gained in those parts, return to me, so that I may see you and give you my blessing before I die.

My son, the peace and grace of Our Lord be with you, Amen.
From Utopia,[2] this seventeenth day of the month of March,

Your father, GARGANTUA

After receiving and reading this letter, Pantagruel took fresh courage and was inspired to make greater advances than ever. Indeed, if you had seen him studying and measured the progress he made, you would have said that his spirit among the books was like fire among the heather, so indefatigable and ardent was it.

Chapter 9. How Pantagruel Found Panurge, Whom He Loved All His Life

One day when Pantagruel was walking outside the city towards the Abbey of Saint-Antoine, arguing and philosophizing with his people and some other students, he met a man of handsome build, elegant in all his features, but pitifully wounded in various

7. The Spaniard Raymond Lull wrote treatises on alchemy in the 13th century.
8. Rabelais was known for performing dissections, still a fairly unusual practice in his day and often criticized as an unholy prying into God's mysteries.
9. Distinguishing between the "contemplative" and "ac-

tive" lives.
1. The Book of Wisdom 1:4 (attributed to Solomon): "into a soul that plots evil, wisdom enters not, nor dwells she in a body under debt of sin."
2. Thomas More coined the term from the Greek, which means "nowhere" (see page 261).

places, and in so sorry a state that he looked as if he had escaped from the dogs, or to be more accurate, like some apple-picker from the Perche country.[3]

When he caught sight of this fellow from the distance, Pantagruel said to his companions: "Do you see that man coming along the road from the Charenton bridge? On my faith, he is only poor in fortune. His physiognomy tells me for certain that he comes of some rich and noble stock. It must be the misfortunes which always befall the adventurous that have reduced him to his present ragged and penurious state." Then, when the fellow had come right up to them, Pantagruel asked him: "My friend, stay here a little, I beg you, and be so kind as to answer certain questions that I shall ask you. You will not repent it, I assure you. For I have a very great desire to give you all the aid in my power in the calamity in which I find you. In fact, I feel great pity for you. Therefore, my friend, tell me who you are, where you come from, where you are going, what you are looking for, and what is your name."

The fellow answered him in the German tongue:[4]

"Junker, Gott geb euch Glück unnd hail. Zuvor, lieber juncker, ich las euch wissen, das da ihr mich von fragt, ist ein arm unnd erbarmglich ding, unnd wer vil darvon zu sagen, welches euch verdruslich zu hæren, unnd mir zu erzelen wer, vievol, die Poeten unnd Orators vorzeiten haben gesagt in iren Sprüchen und Sententzen, das die Gedechtnus des Ellends unnd Azmuot vorlangst erlitten ist ain grosser Lust."[5]

To this Pantagruel replied: "My friend, I don't understand a word of this gibberish. If you want to be understood you must speak another language."

Upon which the fellow replied:

"Al barildim gotfano dech min brin alabo dordin falbroth ringuam albaras. Nin porth zadilkin almucathim milko prim al elmin enthoth dal heben ensouim: kuth im al dim alkatim nim broth dechoth porth min michas im endoth, pruch dal maisoulum hol moth dansririm lupaldas im voldemoth. Nin hur diavolth mnarbothim, dal gousch pal frupin duch im scoth pruch galeth dal chinon, min foulthrich al conin butathen doth dal prim."[6]

"Do you understand any of that?" Pantagruel asked the company; and Epistemon[7] replied: "I think that it is the language of the Antipodes. The devil himself couldn't get his teeth into it."

Then said Pantagruel: "My friend, I don't know whether the walls can understand you. But not one of us can make out a syllable."

Then said the fellow:

"Signor mio, voi vedete per essempio che la cornamusa non suona mai s'ela non a il ventre pieno; cosi io parimente non vi saprei contare le mie fortune, se prima il tribulato ventre non a la solita refectione, al quale è avviso che le mani et il dent habbiano perso il loro ordine naturale et del tuto annichillati."[8]

---

3. A proverbial comparison; Perche is known for its apples, and the apple-pickers often had holes in their clothes where they were torn by branches.

4. Thus begins a series of exchanges with the stranger which demonstrate the realities of a world in which there is no universal language. The original editions of *Pantagruel* would not have contained any translations.

5. "Young sir, may God give you fortune and prosperity. My dear young sir, let me tell you first, that the story you ask me to tell you is a sad and pitiable one. It is a subject on which there would be much to say that would be tiresome for you to hear and for me to relate, although the poets and orators of the old times affirmed in their sayings and their maxims that the memory of pain and poverty is a great joy" [translator's note].

6. This passage is in no known language.

7. Pantagruel's tutor; from the Greek verb for understanding.

8. (Italian) "Example will show you that the bagpipe can never sound except with a full paunch. In the same way, I cannot tell you my adventures unless my rumbling belly receives its customary nourishment, for lack of which my hands and teeth have lost their usual function and are totally annihilated" [translator's note].

To which Epistemon replied: "No better than the last."

Then said Panurge in English: Lord, if you be so vertuous of intelligence, as you be naturally releaved to the body, you should have pity of me: for nature hath made us equal, but fortune hath some exalted, and others depreit: non ye less is vertue often deprived, and the vertuous man despised: for before the last end iss none good.

"Obscurer than ever," replied Pantagruel. * * *

"Really, my friend, I haven't the least doubt that you can talk several languages. But tell us what you want in some language that we can understand."

Then the fellow said:

"Myn Herre, endog, jeg med inghen tunge ta lede, lygeson boen, ocg uskuulig creatner! Myne Kleebon och my ne legoms magerhed udviser alligue klalig huuad tyng meg meest behoff girered somder sandeligh mad och drycke; hvuarpor forbarme teg omsyder offuer-meg; oc befarlat gyffuc meg nogueth; aff hvylket ieg kand styre myne groeendes magher lygeruff son man Cerbero en soppe forsetthr. Soa shal tuloeffue lenge och lycksaligth."[9]

"I believe that the Goths spoke like that," said Eusthenes, "and if God wished us to speak through our backsides we should speak like that too."

Then said the fellow:

"Adoni, scholom lecha: im ischar harob hal habdeca, bemeherah thithen il kikar lehem, chancatbub: Laah al Adonia chonenral."[1]

To which Epistemon replied: "This time I did understand him. That was the Hebrew language most beautifully pronounced."

Then said the fellow:

"Despota tinyn panagathe, diati sy mi uc arto dotis? horas gar limo analiscomenon eme athlios. Ce en to metaxy eme uc cleis udanios, zetis de par emu ha u chre, ce homos philologi pantes homologusi tote logus te kerhemata peritta hyparchin, opote pragma asto pasi delon esti. Entha gar anankei monon logi isin, hina pragmata (hon peri amphisbetumen) me phosphoros epiphenete."[2]

"Why!" exclaimed Pantagruel's lackey Carpalim. "It's Greek, I understood him. But how is that? Have you lived in Greece?"

And the fellow replied:

"Agonou dont oussys vou denaguez algarou, nou den farou zamist vou mariston ulbrou, fousquez vou brol tam bredaguezmoupreton den goul houst, daguez daguez nou croupys fost bardou noflist nou grou. Agou paston tol nalprissys hourtou los ecbatonous, prou dhouquys brol panygou den bascrou nou dous cagnous goulfren goul oust troppassou."[3]

"I seem to understand," said Pantagruel. "For either it is the language of my native Utopia, or else it has a very similar sound."

---

9. (Danish) "Sir, even supposing that, like some small child or a wild animal, I did not speak any language, my clothes and the thinness of my body would show you clearly what I need, that is to say food and drink. Take pity on me, therefore, and get them to give me something to tame my crying stomach, as men throw a sop to Cerberus, so you will live happily and long" [translator's note]. Cerberus was the three-headed dog who guards the entrance to the underworld in classical mythology.

1. (Hebrew) "Sir, peace be with you. If you wish to do your servant a favour, give me a crumb of bread immedi-

ately. For it is written: He that hath pity on the poor lendeth to the Lord" [translator's note].

2. (Greek) "Excellent master, why do you not give me some bread? You see me miserably perishing from hunger, and yet you have no pity on me, and ask me improper questions. All lovers of learning are agreed, however, that speeches and words are superfluous when the facts are evident to all. Speeches are only necessary when the facts under discussion are not completely clear" [translator's note].

3. Again, the words are nonsense.

But just as he was going to begin some observations the fellow said:

"Jam toties vos, per sacra, perque deos deasque omnis, obtestatus sum, ut, si qua vos pietas permovet, egestatem meam solaremini, nec hilum proficio clamans et ejulans. Sinite, quaeso, sinite, viri, impii, quo me fata vocant abire, nec ultra vanis vestris interpellationibus obtundatis, memores veteris illius adagii, quo venter famelicus auriculis carere dicitur."[4]

"Really, my friend," asked Pantagruel, "don't you know how to speak French?"

"Yes, very well, my lord," replied the fellow. "Heaven be praised, it's my natural mother-tongue. For I was born and brought up as a child in Touraine, which is the garden of France."

"Then," said Pantagruel, "tell us what your name is and where you come from. I've taken such a liking to it, I swear, that if I have my way you'll never stir from my side. Indeed you and I will make such another pair of friends as Aeneas and Achates."[5]

"My lord," said the fellow, "my true and proper baptismal name is Panurge, and just now I have come from Turkey, where I was taken prisoner during the ill-fated attack on Mytilene.[6] I'll gladly tell you my story. For I have had adventures more marvellous than Ulysses. But since it is your wish to keep me with you—and I gladly accept your offer, and swear that I'll never leave you even if you go down to the devils in hell—we shall have leisure enough to speak of them at some more convenient time. For at this present moment I feel an urgent necessity to feed. Whetted teeth, empty belly, dry throat, clamorous appetite, all are bent on it. If you will only set me to work it'll be a treat for you to see me stuff myself. In Heaven's name, order me some food."

Then Pantagruel commanded that Panurge should be taken to his lodging, and that plenty of victuals should be put before him, which was done; and the fellow ate heartily that evening.

The Fourth Book[1]
Chapter 55. Pantagruel, on the High Seas, Hears Various Words That Have Been Thawed

As we[2] were banqueting, far out at sea, feasting and speechifying and telling nice little stories, Pantagruel suddenly jumped to his feet, and took a look all round him. "Can you hear something, comrades?" he asked. "I seem to hear people talking in the air. But I can't see anything. Listen."

We all obeyed his command, and listened attentively, sucking in the air in great earfuls, like good oysters in the shell, to hear if any voice or other snatches of sound could be picked up; and so as to miss nothing, some of us cupped the palms of our

---

4. (Latin) "I have implored you so often, by all that is sacred, by every god and goddess, that if you are susceptible to pity, you may relieve my extreme want, but all my crying and imploring does not benefit me a jot. Let me, I beg of you—let me go, most pitiless of men, where the fates call me, and bother me no more with your vain questions. Only remember the old adage that an empty stomach has no ears" [translator's note].
5. Achates is Aeneas's constant companion during his travels from Troy to Italy.
6. "Panurge" is Greek for a swindler or cheat. The Chris-

tians were defeated by the Turks in Mytilene, a city on the island of Lesbos, in 1502.
1. While *Pantagruel* contains the various, often random adventures of Pantagruel and Panurge, *The Third Book* has a singularly focused plot, as Panurge tries to find a definitive answer to the question as to whether he should marry. Unable to do so, the companions voyage in *The Fourth Book* to consult the distant Oracle of the holy Bacbuc.
2. The narrator is a shadowy presence on the journey.

hands to the backs of our ears, after the manner of the Emperor Antoninus.[3] But, notwithstanding, we protested that we could hear no voice whatever. Pantagruel, however, continued to affirm that he could hear several voices on the air, both male and female; and then we decided that either we could hear them too, or else there was a ringing in our ears. Indeed, the more keenly we listened, the more clearly we made out voices, till in the end we could hear whole words. This greatly frightened us, and not unnaturally, since we could see no one, yet could hear voices and different sorts of sounds of men, women, children, and horses.

It was all so clear that Panurge cried out: "God's my life, is this a trick? We are lost. Let's get away. We've fallen into an ambush. Brother John, are you there, my friend? Keep close to me, I beg of you. Have you got your cutlass? Make sure it doesn't stick in the scabbard. You never scour it half enough. We're lost. Listen. My God, those are cannon-shots. Let's run away, I won't say with our feet and hands as Brutus did at the battle of Pharsalia,[4] but with sail and oar. Let's get away. I've no courage on the sea. In a cellar or elsewhere I've more than enough. Let's run away. Let's save ourselves. I don't say this because I'm afraid, for I fear nothing except danger. That's what I always say, and so did the free-archer of Baignolet. So let's take no risks, and we'll get no slaps. Let's flee, and about turn! Turn the helm, you son of a whore! I would to God I were at Les Quinquenais at this moment, even if it meant never marrying! Let's fly. We're no match for them. They outnumber us by ten to one, I'm sure of it. Besides, they're on their own dunghills, and we don't know the country. Let's run away. It'll be no disgrace. Demosthenes said that he who flies lives to fight another day. At least let's retire. Starboard, larboard, to the foresails, to the topsails! We're dead men. In the name of all the devils, let's get away!"

On hearing Panurge make all this uproar, Pantagruel asked: "Who is that coward down there? Let's see first what people they are. They may happen to be our friends. But still I can't catch sight of anyone, though I can see a hundred miles all round. But let's listen. I have heard that a certain philosopher called Petron believed that there are several worlds touching one another as at the points of an equilateral triangle. The inner area of this triangle, he said, was the abode of truth and there lived the names and forms, the ideas and images of all things past and future. Outside this lies the Age—our secular world.[5] In certain years, however, at long intervals, some part of these falls on humankind like distillations, or as the dew fell on Gideon's fleece,[6] to remain there laid up for the future, awaiting the consummation of the Age. I remember, too, that Aristotle maintains Homer's words to be bounding, flying, and moving, and consequently alive. Antiphanes, also, said that Plato's teaching was like words that congeal and freeze on the air, when uttered in the depths of winter in some distant country. That is why they are not heard. He said as well that Plato's lessons to young children were hardly understood by them till they were old.[7]

"Now it would be worth arguing and investigating whether this may not be the very place where such words thaw out. Shouldn't we be greatly startled if it proved to be the head and the lyre of Orpheus? After the Thracian women had torn him to

3. Emperor Antoninus Caracalla, reputed to have been always surrounded by secret police.
4. At the battle of Philippi (not Pharsalia), Brutus was said to have announced that he had to flee with his hands—through the act of suicide.
5. Petron was a Pythagorean philosopher, who thought the universe had the form of an equilateral triangle.
6. In the Book of Judges, Gideon asks God for a promise:

if he is to save Israel, the morning dew will gather only on the woolen fleece on the threshing floor. The event comes to pass, and Gideon spends the next morning wringing the dew from the fleece.
7. These fascinating remarks on Homer's poetry—which we now know to have been part of an oral repertoire for several centuries—are from Aristotle's fragments (151) and Plutarch's *De profectibus in virtute,* Chapter 7.

pieces, they threw his head and lyre into the river Hebrus, down which they floated to the Black Sea, and from there to the island of Lesbos, still riding together on the waters. And all the time there issued from the head a melancholy song, as if in mourning for Orpheus's death, while the lyre, as the moving winds strummed it, played a harmonious accompaniment to this lament.[8] Let's look if we can see them hereabouts."

Chapter 56. Pantagruel Hears Some Gay Words Among Those That Are Thawed

It was the captain that answered: "My lord, don't be afraid. This is the edge of the frozen sea, and at the beginning of last winter there was a great and bloody battle here between the Arimaspians and the Cloud-riders. The shouts of the men, the cries of the women, the slashing of the battle-axes, the clashing of the armour and harnesses, the neighing of the horses and all the other frightful noises of battle became frozen on the air. But just now, the rigours of winter being over and the good season coming on with its calm and mild weather, these noises are melting, and so you can hear them."

"By God," cried Panurge. "I believe you. But could we see just one of them? I remember reading that, as they stood around the edges of the mountain on which Moses received the Laws of the Jews, the people palpably saw the voices."[9]

"Here, here," exclaimed Pantagruel, "here are some that are not yet thawed."

Then he threw on the deck before us whole handfuls of frozen words, which looked like crystallized sweets of different colours. We saw some words gules, or gay quips, some vert, some azure, some sable, and some or. When we warmed them a little between our hands, they melted like snow, and we actually heard them, though we did not understand them, for they were in a barbarous language. There was one exception, however, a fairly big one. This, when Friar John picked it up, made a noise like a chestnut that has been thrown on the embers without being pricked. It was an explosion, and made us all start with fear. "That," said Friar John, "was a cannon shot in its day."

Panurge asked Pantagruel to give him some more. But Pantagruel answered that only lovers gave their words.

"Sell me some, then," said Panurge.

"That's a lawyer's business," replied Pantagruel, "selling words. I'd rather sell you silence, though I should ask a higher price for it, as Demosthenes did once, when bribed to have a quinsy."

Nevertheless he threw three or four handfuls on the deck, and I saw some very sharp words among them: bloody words which, as the Captain told us, sometimes return to the place from which they come but with their throats cut; some terrifying words, and others rather unpleasant to look at. When they had all melted together, we heard: Hin, hin, hin, hin, his, tick, tock, crack, brededin, brededac, frr, frrr, frrrr, bou, bou, bou, bou, bou, bou, bou, tracc, tracc, trr, trrr, trrrr, trrrrr, trrrrrr, on, on, on, on, on, ououououon, Gog, Magog, and goodness knows what other barbarous sounds. The Captain said that these were the battle-cries, and the neighings of the chargers as they clashed together. Then we heard other great noises going off as they melted, some like drums and fifes, others like clarions and trumpets. Believe me, we were

8. The reference is to two accounts of Orpheus's gruesome death at the hands of the Thracian women, one in the fourth book of Virgil's *Georgics,* the other in the eleventh book of Ovid's *Metamorphoses.*

9. In Exodus 20, the people are said to "witness the thunder and lightning" that accompanies God's giving to Moses the ten commandments.

greatly amused. I wanted to preserve a few of the gay quips in oil, the way you keep snow and ice, and then to wrap them up in clean straw. But Pantagruel refused, saying that it was folly to store up things which one is never short of, and which are always plentiful, as gay quips are among good and jovial Pantagruelists.

Here Panurge somewhat annoyed Friar John, and put him in a huff. For he took him at his word at a moment when he least expected it, and threatened to make him as sorry for this, as Guillaume Jousseaulme was for having sold the noble Patelin cloth on credit.[1] If ever Panurge married, said the Friar, he'd seize him by the horns like a calf, since Panurge had deceived him like a man. Panurge, in derision, made an ugly face at him, and cried out: "Would to God that I could have the oracle of the Holy Bottle, without travelling any further!"[2]

✦ ⧓ ✦

Luís Vaz de Camões
c. 1524–1580

When Luís Vaz de Camões wrote about the "exiled gaze" of Vasco da Gama's mariners as they set sail from Lisbon for unknown lands, he knew of what he wrote. His own travels began in violence. In 1550, Camões was arrested and jailed in Lisbon after a brawl during a Corpus Christi procession; he was released only on the condition that he set forth for India. Three years later, he did just that, in a convoy of four ships; only the one he was on managed to reach India, on the outskirts of Portugal's vast colonial empire. This distant relative of Vasco da Gama proceeded to spend seventeen years in Portuguese outposts as soldier, colonial administrator, and occasional playwright, traveling as far as Cambodia and Macao (off the coast of China). His intimate familiarity with the route da Gama had taken a half century before him and his deep reading in antiquity from his days at the University of Coimbra produced Portugal's most beloved work of poetry, The Lusíads.

"Os Lusíadas" literally means "The sons of Lusus," otherwise known as the Portuguese. The ten cantos which Camões supposedly clutched in the Mekong River after a shipwreck could not be more accurately named; in many ways, Os Lusíadas is the modern era's first nationalist poem. While the poem principally celebrates da Gama, it takes equal care to praise all "the heroes who, leaving their native Portugal behind them, opened a way to Ceylon and farther, across seas no man had ever sailed before," as Camões says in his preface. And it is also a story "of a line of kings who kept ever advancing the boundaries of faith and empire," kings whose progeny included Dom Henrique, better known as Prince Henry the Navigator, who founded an influential school of navigation in 1416 and explored the west African coast in his own caravels. Henry's scientific interests were in the service of religious conviction, which centered on arresting Muslim expansion in southern Europe and the Persian Gulf, and gaining control over the Holy Sepulchre in Jerusalem. Along with visions of a booming empire of trade, these unfulfilled dreams preoccupied Henry's successors, who in the next century lined the African, Indian, and Chinese coastlines with settlements, and sailed westward to Brazil as well.

Camões wrote not of Brazilian ventures but of the area of the world he knew best, the fickle oceans of the Eastern Hemisphere. His maritime poem looked quite naturally to the two great poems of classical antiquity that featured extensive contact with the sea: Homer's Odyssey and Virgil's Aeneid. Like these epics, The Lusíads has a band of sailors who encounter

1. Allusion to a popular French farce.
2. The voyage is doomed to remain incomplete in Book 4. The trip to the Oracle continues in Book 5, and the friends succeed in meeting Babuc, from whom they receive three leather bottles. The authenticity of the fifth book, published after Rabelais's death, is much debated.

disaster and shipwreck. Vasco da Gama spends Cantos 3 through 5 describing for the Sultan of Malindi his travels, much as Aeneas relates to Dido the story of his exile and Odysseus recounts his watery passage to the Phaiakians. *The Lusíads* also features numerous prophecies of great things to come, as well as a panoply of pagan deities who either help the heroes—Jove and his ravishing daughter Venus—or deter them—Bacchus, ever protective of his Muslims. But unlike the earlier epics based on shadowy legend and myth, *The Lusíads* has the virtue that its principal events are true, a truthfulness enhanced by Camões's intimate knowledge of the flora and fauna of Africa, of India's advanced Hindu civilization, and of the frustrating encounters among peoples who are stymied by the multiplicity of languages after the Tower of Babel. Camões in fact makes the poem's historical veracity the index of its superiority over the ancients: "My own tale in its naked purity / Outdoes all boasting and hyperbole."

Camões's boasting here reflects the daring nature of both da Gama's journey and his own poetic one. As da Gama's boat rounds the Cape of Good Hope, "that vast, secret promontory" which the Portuguese called "the Cape of Storms," the Titan Adamastor, turned by vengeful gods into stone, curses the voyagers who make such "audacious passage" and "breach what is forbidden," as did the Ulysses of Dante's *Divine Comedy.* Unlike Ulysses, da Gama succeeds, finding his pains rewarded at epic's end with arrival in India and the delights of the floating Isle of Love which Venus wafts toward him and his men (populated with coy nymphs who only pretend to resist their pursuers' amorous designs). Camões likewise succeeds in championing Portugal's imperial claims, as he forges not only a national poem but a national language in *The Lusíads* and his considerable body of lyric and elegiac poems, bringing Latinisms and Castilian Spanish to bear on the vernacular in order to make it a supple vehicle for literary works. *The Lusíads* was snapped up by the boy king Dom Sebastião when Camões returned to Portugal in 1570—the ecclesiastical censors were kinder to Camões's unruly deities than they might have been, dismissing them as simple "ornaments"—and it had an electifying effect on later readers, becoming a rallying point for the Portuguese in 1640 to unburden themselves of Spanish rule.

But there is much in Camões's poem that works against a facile nationalism, even if his portrait of Islam is likely to strike the contemporary reader as offensive (the Sultan of Malindi laments that he's not European, and Muslims throughout are seen, like Sinon the Greek, as liars). For one thing, when the poem was published in 1572, Portugal was already finding itself unable to manage its vast empire. The emotional words of the old man at Lisbon's port as da Gama's sailors are departing—"O pride of power! O futile lust / For that vanity known as fame!"—both evoke a pastoral nostalgia for simplicity and suggest that late sixteenth-century Portugal could no longer sustain the heroism of da Gama's age. Moreover, given Camões's constant struggles simply to survive—he was frequently jailed for debt and made little money from his literary efforts—it is no surprise that the poem often meditates on the insignificance of man's life and work. The end of Canto 1 finds da Gama's men about to be betrayed by their Muslim host, and the narrator musing,

> Where may frail humanity shelter
> Briefly, in some secure port,
> Where the bright heavens cease to vent their rage
> On such insects on so small a stage?

Struck by the plague that infested Lisbon in 1580, Camões died among the kindly friars of São Domingos, having failed to receive the riches he expected from Vasco da Gama's family. It has been said that Camões died in despair as well as penury; two years earlier, King Dom Sebastião had vanished along with sixteen thousand soldiers on an ill-fated venture to Morocco. A religious fanatic who was swayed by ruthless military advisors, he intended to conquer Morocco from the Moors. His disastrous failure put an end to Portugal's hopes of expansion and autonomy from Spain. His death at the hands of the Moors was the subject of one of Camões's final sonnets as well as a poem by one Diego Bernardes, chosen to accompany the king on his last mission. Finding himself captive rather than victor, Bernardes opens his

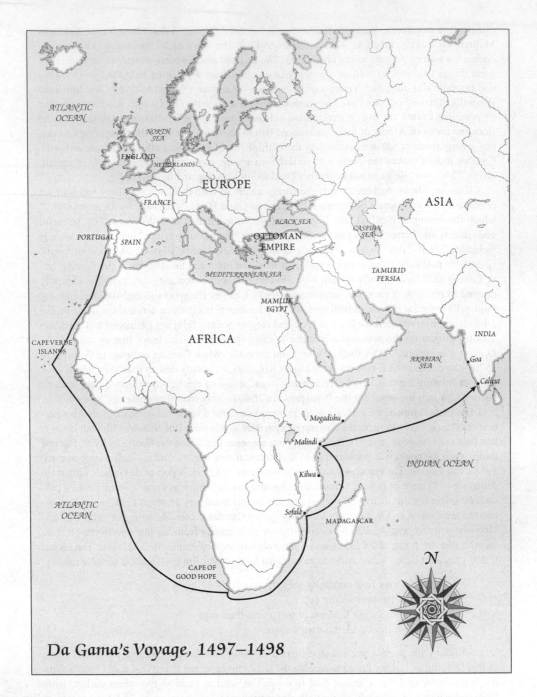

Da Gama's Voyage, 1497–1498

elegy with "I, who free, sang to the sound of the waters of the lovely, gentle, and clear Lima . . . now to the sounds of the chain which wounds my uncovered foot, a captive, weep where weeping avails not, and where love is valueless." Arguably the poem marks the definitive eclipse of Portugal's days of glory and a turn toward its imminent takeover by Spain. Yet Camões's complex vision of the struggle for empire occupies pride of place in Portugal's literary tradition.

PRONUNCIATIONS:
Coelho: koo-WEYL-yo
João: joo-AHNG
Luis Vaz de Camões: loo-EESH vaz de ka-MOINSH
Lusíads: loo-SEE-ads (rhymes with *Aeneid*)
Sebastião: se-bas-tee-AHNG

from THE LUSÍADS[1]
from Canto 1
[INVOCATION]

1

Arms are my theme, and those matchless heroes[2]
Who from Portugal's far western shores
By oceans where none had ventured
Voyaged to Taprobana° and beyond,   Ceylon
5   Enduring hazards and assaults
Such as drew on more than human prowess
Among far distant peoples, to proclaim
A New Age and win undying fame;

2

Kings likewise of glorious memory
10   Who magnified Christ and Empire,
Bringing ruin on the degenerate
Lands of Africa and Asia;[3]
And others whose immortal deeds
Have conquered death's oblivion
15   —These words will go wherever there are men
If art and invention steer my pen.

3

Boast no more about the subtle Greek°   Odysseus
Or the long odyssey of Trojan Aeneas;
Enough of the oriental conquests
20   Of great Alexander and of Trajan;
I sing of the famous Portuguese
To whom both Mars and Neptune bowed.
Abandon all the ancient Muse revered,
A loftier code of honour has appeared.

4

25   And you, nymphs of the Tagus,[4] who
First suckled my infant genius,
If ever in my rustic verses
I celebrated your companionable river,
Return me now a loftier tone,

---

1. Translated by Landeg White.
2. The opening line paraphrases the first line of Virgil's *Aeneid*, "I sing of arms and a man."
3. Many Portuguese kings had fought the Moors in North Africa, and Henry of Bourgogne fought in the Holy Land.
4. Camões invokes as his native muse the nymphs of the river Tagus (Tajo), which runs through central Portugal to empty out in the port city of Lisbon.

30   *A style both grand and contemporary;*
            Be to me Helicon.[5] Let Apollo choose
            Your waters as the fountain of my muse.

                       5

            Fire me now with mighty cadences,
            Not a goatherd's querulous piping
35   *But the shouts of a battle trumpet,*
            Stirring the heart, steeling the countenance;
            Give me a poem worthy of the exploits
            Of those heroes so inspired by Mars,
            To propagate their deeds through space and time
40   *If poetry can rise to the sublime.*

                       6

            And you, my boy King,[6] guarantor
            Of Portugal's ancient freedoms,
            And equal surety for the expansion
            Of Christendom's small empire;
45   *You, who have the Moors trembling,*
            The marvel prophesied for our times,
            Given to the world, in God's eternal reign,
            To win for God much of the world again.

                       7

            You, tender and green sapling
50   *Of that tree more precious to Christ*
            Than any other Western lineage,
            Whether in the French or Roman line[7]
            (Witness your scutcheon, visibly
            Stamped with the victory at Ourique,
55   *When Christ bestowed, as emblems to emboss,*
            The five wounds he suffered on the cross);[8]

                       8

            You, mighty King, on whose India
            The new-born sun directs his first beam,
            Shines on your palace in mid-hemisphere,
60   *And casts his last ray on the Brazils;*
            You, to whom we look to yoke and humble
            Arabia's wild horseman, infidel
            Turks, and India's sons and daughters
            Who yet drink the Ganges' sacred waters:[9]

                       9

65   *Descend a little from such majesty,*
            For I see on your youthful countenance

---

5. Helicon was the spring sacred to Apollo.
6. Sebastião (1554–1578), who was proclaimed king when he was only three.
7. Either the line of Charlemagne or that of the Holy Roman Empire.
8. An allusion to Portugal's coat-of-arms. The victory of Afonso, Portugal's first king, over the Moors at Ourique in 1139 is celebrated on the coat-of-arms with five shields, said to symbolize the five wounds of the crucified Christ. Legend has it that Christ spoke to Afonso during the battle at Ourique to pledge his support for Portugal's independence from the Moors.
9. With Portugal's empire expanding, Camões hopes that Sebastião will help convert the heathen Muslims and Hindus.

Already inscribed that maturity
You will bear to eternity's temple;
Bend those royal and benign eyes
70   *Earthwards, and behold this loving tribute;*
The most valiant deeds of modern times
Given to the world in sure, well-cadenced rhymes.

10

You will witness a love of country, not
Driven by greed but true and enduring,
75   *For it is no unworthy reward to be famed*
Writing in praise of my native land.
Observe: you will see names exalted
Of those of whom you are supreme lord,
And you can judge which is the better case,
80   *King of the world or king of such a race.*

11

Observe, it is not for counterfeit
Exploits, fantasies such as muses
Elsewhere have dreamed or invented,
That you will hear your people acclaimed.
85   *Historic deeds such as theirs*
Transcend fables, and would eclipse
Boiado's Orlando, and Ariosto's too,
Even if all they wrote of him were true.[1]

12

Instead, I give you Nuno Álvares
90   *Who showed country and king such service;*[2]
It would take Homer's lyre to commend
Sufficiently Egas Moniz and Fuas Roupinho;
For France's twelve peers, I give you
The twelve of England led by Magriço,
95   *And likewise Vasco da Gama, whose genius*
Snatched renown from wandering Aeneas.[3]

13

If you are looking for stature equal
To Charlemagne or Julius Caesar,
Consider Afonso the first whose lance
100   *Eclipsed all foreign reputations,*
Or João the first whose reign bequeathed us
The security of his great victory;
Or the second João, honourably spurred,
Or the fourth or fifth Afonso, or the third.

14

105   *Nor will my lines leave uncommemorated*

---

1. The Italian poets Matteo Boiardo and Ludovico Ariosto had both written long epic-romance poems about Charlemagne's knight Orlando.
2. Here and in the next stanza Camões celebrates Portugal's kings and generals who were crucial in wrenching territory and power from their two traditional enemies: Spain and the Moors, going from the reign from Afonso I through João II (1481–1495).
3. Vasco da Gama's real-life voyage to India in 1497–1498 has gone far beyond the legendary wanderings of Virgil's hero Aeneas from Troy to Italy.

Those who in the lands of the Dawn
Bore their arms with such excellence
Your standard was always victorious:
Matchless Pacheco, and the fearsome
110 Almeidas, whom the Tagus still laments,
Albuquerque the fierce, Castro the brave,
And others whose exploits have survived the grave.[4]

15

While I celebrate these I say nothing
Of you, great King, not presuming so far;
115 Take up the reins of your kingdom
To furnish matter for another epic.
Let the world tremble as it senses
All you are about to accomplish,
Africa's land and Oriental seas
120 The promised theatre of your victories.

16

On you, the fearful Moor has his eyes
Fixed, knowing his fate prefigured;
At a glimpse of you, the unbroken
Indian offers his neck to the yoke;
125 Tethys, Neptune's bride, has prepared
The world's green oceans as a dowry,
Holding your youth and beauty in such awe
She hopes to win you for her son-in-law.

17

There gaze down from Mount Olympus
130 Your two grandsires,[5] famous in their day,
—One for the golden peace of his reign,
The other for his bloody battles.
Both look to see resurrected in you
Their times and heroic works, keeping
135 In earnest of their true paternity,
Your place in the temple of eternity.

18

But while your long reign passes slowly
Matching your people's dearest wish,
Look kindly on my boldness so
140 This epic may become your own.
You will watch, cutting the salt seas
Portuguese Argonauts,[6] who will see in turn
They are watched over by you. Be ready

---

4. These more recent figures extended empire to the East in the wake of da Gama's exploits. Francisco de Almeida was the first Viceroy of India, while Afonso de Albuquerque seized Goa in 1510 and was its capable first governor.
5. João III and Emperor of the Holy Roman Empire, Charles V.
6. The mythic Greek hero Jason and his crew aboard the Argo sailed from Greece to seize the Golden Fleece from the desolate land of Colchis, passing through one of the ends of the Greek world—the Bosporus, the channel that connects the Mediterranean to the Black Sea.

To hear your name invoked in jeopardy.

* * *

from Canto 4

[KING MANUEL'S DREAM; VASCO DA GAMA AND HIS MEN EMBARK FOR INDIA][1]

66

It appears that bright heaven preserved
For King Manuel,[2] with all his merits,
This arduous venture which stirred him
To such illustrious, exalted deeds;
Manuel, who succeeded João
Both to the kingdom and his exalted quest,
Was just as eager in his devotion
To exploring and mastering the ocean.

67

The noble vision of his unique
Inheritance, from forbears whose constant
Passion was to enlarge the kingdom,
Never ceased for an instant
To dominate his thoughts until once
Upon a time, when the clear daylight
Faded, and the glimmering stars began to shine,
Beckoning to slumber at their first decline,

68

Being stretched out on his golden bed
Where imaginings can be so vivid,
His thoughts returning continuously
To his office and descent and duty,
His heavy eyelids drooped without
His heart becoming vacant, for as
Sleep descended quietly to restore him
Morpheus, in various guises, rose before him.

69

First, he dreamed he had been spirited
Up to touch the first sphere, and could
See beneath him various nations
With many strange and wild peoples;[3]
But there, close to where the sun rises,
Straining his eyes in the distance,

5

10

15

20

25

30

1. The story has begun with Vasco da Gama's ships off
the coast of East Africa in the channel of Mozambique.
The god Bacchus, who wants to protect Muslim India
from the arrival of Europeans, has aroused against them
considerable hostility from the Moors in Mozambique
and neighboring Mombassa. At the end of Canto 2,
guided by the friendly Mercury, they arrive in Malindi, a
Swahili city on the east coast of Africa that will prove to
be the only welcoming port (the *Journal of the First Voyage of Vasco da Gama* praises the people of Malindi for
their hospitality; see page 407). Da Gama is greeted
warmly by the Sultan, to whom he tells his adventures
thus far. The following section opens with da Gama's account of his mission and the ships' departure from Lisbon.
2. King Manuel I, who ruled between 1495 and 1521, followed in the footsteps of his predecessor, João II, encouraging Portuguese trade and exploration to the east.
3. In the Ptolemaic universe which Camões rigorously
obeys, the first sphere above the stationary earth is that of
the moon.

From a range of mountains, ancient and vast,
He saw two noble rivers tumble past.[4]

                              70

Wild birds and savage beasts were
All that lived in that towering jungle;
35   Thick undergrowth and ancient trees
Barred human passage and influence.
Those hard, inhospitable crags
Were visibly a region where,
Since Adam's sin down to the present day,
40   No human foot had ever found a way.

                              71

From the rivers, he seemed to see emerge
Two ancients, bending towards him
With slow paces like countrymen,
And of venerable appearance;
45   Water dripped from their uncombed locks
Making their whole bodies glisten;
Their skin was leathery and cinnamon,
Their shaggy beards dishevelled and undone.

                              72

The foreheads of both were crowned
50   With chaplets of grass and nameless fronds.
One seemed more deliberate in his gait
As if he had tramped the further;
And his river with its slower current
Seemed to have come from elsewhere,
55   Like Alpheus flowing to meet his Arethuse
Underground from Arcadia to Syracuse.[5]

                              73

And having the graver bearing of the two,
He spoke up to Manuel from afar:
—"You, to whose crown and kingdom
60   So much of the world is reserved:
We others, also known to fame
Whose necks were never before yoked,
Counsel you now, the moment is at hand
To accept the tribute flowing from our land.

                              74

65   "I am the famous Ganges whose waters
Have their source in the earthly paradise;
This other is the Indus, which springs
In this mountain which you behold.
We shall cost you unremitting war,
70   But persevering, you will become

---

4. The Ganges and the Indus.
5. In this myth made famous by Virgil, the river-god Alpheus pursues the nymph Arethusa from Arcadia to

Syracuse in Sicily, where she is turned into a fountain and his waters are mingled with hers.

Peerless in victory, knowing no defeat,
Conquering as many peoples as you meet."

75

75
The famous, sacred river said no more
And both disappeared on the instant.
Manuel awoke with the thrill of discovery
And a new direction to his thoughts.
Now Phoebus stretched his mantle
Over the dark, sleeping hemisphere,
And dawn emerged, dipping in her pallet
80
Of multi-coloured flowers for rose and scarlet.

76

The king summoned the lords to council
To tell of the figures of his dream;
The words spoken by the venerable saint
Were a great wonder to them all.
85
They resolved at once to equip
A fleet and an intrepid crew,
Commissioned to plough the remotest seas,
To explore new regions, make discoveries.

77

For myself,° though not knowing the outcome   *Vasco da Gama*
90
If what I wanted should ever happen,
My heart had always whispered to me
Of some great enterprise of this kind;
Nor do I know for what intimation,
Or what confidence he placed in me,
95
Manuel the Fortunate laid in these very hands
The key to this pursuit of unknown lands.

78

And with entreaties and affectionate words
Which with kings are the more binding,
He said: 'The price of heroic deeds
100
Is great effort and endurance;
To risk life to the point of losing it
Is the guarantee of glory;
The man who is not cowed by abject fears,
Though life be short, his fame survives the years.

79

105
"I have chosen you from among all others
For this enterprise which you well deserve,
And I know for mine and glory's sake
You will bear the hazards and hardships."
I could bear no more, but: "Small as it
110
Is to endure iron, fire, and snow,
The more it grieves me, O most noble king
My life should be so poor an offering.

80

"Command me to such vast labours

As Eurystheus devised for Hercules:[6]
115 The Cleonaean lion, the Stymphalian harpies,
The Erymanthian boar, and the Hydra,
Or to descend to the dark and empty shades
Where the Styx flows through Pluto's fields;
The greater danger, the greater daring;
120 Spirit in this, and flesh, will be unsparing."

81

The king thanked me with signal favours
And complimented my good will,
For virtue rewarded is redoubled,
And praise encourages great deeds.
125 On the instant, compelled by love
And comradeship as by desire for glory,
There offered to sail with me none other
Than Paulo da Gama, my dear brother.[7]

82

Nicolau Coelho[8] also joined me,
130 A man to endure any labour,
And like my brother, valiant and wise
And a fierce and tested warrior.
I equipped myself with young people
All driven by a thirst for glory;
135 All spirited and, in fact, so appearing
Simply by the act of volunteering.

83

King Manuel rewarded them generously,
Giving greater zeal to their preparations,
And inspired them with noble words
140 For whatever hardships might come.[9]
It was as when the Argonauts assembled
To battle for the Golden Fleece
In that prophetic ship, the first to be
Launched by man on the Black (or any) Sea.

84

145 So at last in Ulysses' famous harbour[1]
With noble bustle and resolve
(Where the Tagus mingles its fresh water
And white sands with the salt sea),
The ships lay ready; and no misgivings
150 Subdued the youthful spirits

---

6. The sadistic king Eurystheus forced Hercules to perform 12 labors, five of which are mentioned here, and the most difficult of which was the trip to the underworld to rescue Theseus.

7. Paulo da Gama accompanied his younger brother on the historic trip to India as commander of one of the fleet's four vessels. He died on the return journey home.

8. Commander of another of the four ships.

9. Apparently King Manuel chose not to leave his summer vacation spot in the mountains of Monfurado to see Vasco da Gama and his men off in the sweltering capital of Lisbon in July, 1497.

1. According to legend, the city of Lisbon ("Ulysippo") was founded by Ulysses.

For the mariners' and soldiers' one desire
Was to follow me through tempest and fire.

85

The soldiers came along the margin
Clad in various colours and fashions,
155 And furnished equally in spirit
To explore new regions of the globe.
The powerful ships signalled quietly,
Their flags rippling in the gentle wind,
As if confident their tale would never die,
160 But live on like *Argo* in the night sky.[2]

86

Having done everything practical
To make ready for so long a voyage,
We prepared our souls to meet death
Which is always on a sailor's horizon.
165 To God on high who alone sustains
The heavens with his loved presence,
We asked His favour that He should endorse
Our every enterprise and steer our course.

87

The holy chapel from which we parted
170 Is built there on the very beach,
And takes its name, Belém, from the town
Where God was given to the world as flesh.[3]
O King, I tell you, when I reflect
On how I parted from that shore,
175 Tormented by so many doubts and fears,
Even now it is hard to restrain my tears.

88

That day, a vast throng from the city
(As friends, as family, others
Only to watch), crowded the shore,
180 Their faces anxious and dismayed
Looking on, as in the holy company
Of a thousand zealous monks,
With heartfelt intercessions on our lips
We marched in solemn file towards the ships.

89

185 The people considered us already lost
On so long and uncertain a journey,
The women with piteous wailing,
The men with agonizing sighs;
Mothers, sweethearts, and sisters, made
190 Fretful by their love, heightened

---

2. In the best-known account of Jason and the Argonauts, Valerius Flaccus's *Argonauticon,* the travelers' ship is miraculously made into a constellation.

3. Vasco da Gama and his other captains spent the night before their departure in prayer at the chapel of Our Lady of Belém (Bethlehem), near Lisbon.

The desolation and the arctic fear
We should not return for many a long year.

90

One such was saying: "O my dear son,
My only comfort and sweet support
195   In this my tottering old age, now
Doomed to end in grief and pain,
Why do you leave me wretched and indigent?
Why do you travel so far away,
To be lost at sea as your memorial,
200   And bloated fish your only burial?"[4]

91

Or one bareheaded: "O dearest husband,
But for whose love I could not exist,
Why do you risk on the angry seas
That which belongs to me, not you?
205   Why, for so dubious a voyage, do you
Forget our so sweet affection?
Is our passion, our happiness so frail
As to scatter in the wind swelling the sail?"

92

As these piteous, loving speeches
210   Poured from gentle, human hearts,
The old and the children took them up
In the different manner of their years.
The nearest mountains echoed them,
As if stirred by deepest sympathy,
215   While tears as many as the grains of sand
Rained without ceasing on the white strand.

93

As for us, we dared not lift our faces
To our mothers and our wives, fearing
To be harrowed, or discouraged
220   From the enterprise so firmly begun,
And I decided we should all embark
Without the customary farewells,
For, though they may be love's proper course,
They make the pain of separation worse.

94

225   But an old man of venerable appearance
Standing among the crowd on the shore,
Fixed his eyes on us, disapproving,
And wagged his head three times,
Then raising a little his infirm voice
230   So we heard him clearly from the sea,

---

4. The mother's plaintive lament evokes those of other parents bidding their sons farewell; the best-known is the plaint in *Aeneid* 9 by the mother of Euryalus, who will die in battle against the Latins.

With a wisdom only experience could impart,
He uttered these words from a much-tried heart:

95

—"O pride of power! O futile lust
For that vanity known as fame!
That hollow conceit which puffs itself up
And which popular cant calls honour!
What punishment, what poetic justice,
You exact on souls that pursue you!
To what deaths, what miseries you condemn
Your heroes! What pains you inflict on them!

96

"You wreck all peace of soul and body,
You promote separation and adultery;
Subtly, manifestly, you consume
The wealth of kingdoms and empires!
They call distinction, they call honour
What deserves ridicule and contempt;
They talk of glory and eternal fame,
And men are driven frantic by a name!

97

"To what new catastrophes do you plan
To drag this kingdom and these people?
What perils, what deaths have you in store
Under what magniloquent title?
What visions of kingdoms and gold-mines
Will you guide them to infallibly?
What fame do you promise them? What stories?
What conquests and processions? What glories?

98

"And as for you, heirs of that madcap
Adam, whose sin and disobedience
Not only drove us from paradise
Into this exile and sad absence,
But deprived us for ever of the divine
State of simple tranquillity,
That golden age of innocence, before
This age of iron experience and war.[5]

99

"Already in this vainglorious business
Delusions are possessing you,
Already, ferocity and brute force
Are labelled strength and valour,

235

240

245

250

255

260

265

5. This famous speech by the old man of Belém contains numerous conventions familiar to readers of classical literature; in particular, his lament about the end of the age of innocence echoes similar sentiments in Virgil's *Fourth Eclogue* and Ovid's *Metamorphoses.* But he is not simply a literary fiction. Opposition in Portugal to the overseas ventures was real, and there were many isolationists in Vasco da Gama's time.

The heresy "Long live Death!" is already
270 Current among you, when life should always
Be cherished, as Christ in times gone by
Who gave us life was yet afraid to die.

100

"Is not the Ishmaelite close at hand,
With whom you have waged countless wars?[6]
275 If a fresh crusade is your purpose,
Does he not bow to the faith of Arabia?
If it is land and riches you desire,
Does he not own a thousand cities?
Or if it's fresh battle honours you covet,
280 Is he not still a formidable target?

101

"You ignore the enemy at the gate
In the search for another so far away,
Unpeopling the ancient kingdom,
Leaving it vulnerable and bereft!
285 You are lured by the dangers of the unknown,
So history will flatter you, as
'Seigneurs' (or titles yet more copious),
India's, Persia's, Arabia's, Ethiopia's!

102

"The devil take the man who first put
290 Dry wood on the waves with a sail!
Hell's fires are too good for him
If the laws I live by are righteous!
And may no solemn chronicler,
No sweet harpist nor eloquent poet
295 Commend your deeds or celebrate your fame,
But let your folly vanish with your name!

103

"Prometheus stole the fire from heaven
Which rages in every human heart,
Setting the world ablaze with arms,
300 With death and dishonour, and all for nothing!
How much better for us, Prometheus,
How much less harmful for the world,
Had you not breathed into your famous statue
The restlessness that goads mankind to match you![7]

104

305 "Unhappy Phaethon would not have crashed
Apollo's car, nor craftsman Daedalus

---

6. Ishmaelites are the Arabs, reputed descendants of Ishmael, the son of Abraham and his mistress Hagar (Genesis 16).

7. In Greek myth, Prometheus breathed life into clay statues, making them men; he later stole fire from the heavens to give his new creation warmth and protection from savage beasts.

Dropped from the sky with his son, naming
The latter a sea, the former a river.[8]
In what great or infamous undertaking,
310   Through fire, sword, water, heat, or cold,
Was Man's ambition not the driving feature?
Wretched circumstance! Outlandish creature!"

from Canto 5

1

As the honourable old man was uttering
These words, we spread our wings
To the serene and tranquil breezes
And departed from the loved harbour;
5   And, as is now the custom at sea,
The sails unfurled, we bellowed:
"God speed!," and the north winds as usual
Heard and responded, shifting the great hull.

2

The sun was in Leo, the ferocious
10   Beast of Nemea, slain by Hercules,
And the world was in the sixth age
Of its decline since Christ's birth,
Having witnessed, as custom has it,
Fourteen hundred journeys of the sun
15   Plus ninety-seven, the last still in motion
When our small armada turned to face the ocean.[1]

3

Little by little our gaze was exiled
From the native hills we left behind;
There remained the dear Tagus and green
20   Sintra,[2] and on those our sight long dwelt;
Our hearts, too, stayed behind us,
Lodged with their griefs in the loved land;
And when at last all faded from the eye,
Nothing was visible but sea and sky.

4

25   We were navigating waters only
Portuguese had sailed before us,
Seeing the islands and latitudes
Plotted by Henry, our noble prince;[3]
Off to our left were the mountains

---

8. The old man follows with more stories of transgression, both recounted in detail in Ovid's *Metamorphoses* (see Volume A). Phaethon lost control of Apollo's cart and crashed into the earth, the sun in tow. Icaraus, the son of Daedalus, flew too close to the sun with the wax wings his father had fashioned for him, and he plummeted to earth as the wax melted. The Po River in northern Italy is named for Phaethon, the Icarian Sea is named for Icarus.
1. Camões puts the exact date for da Gama's departure at 8 July 1497.
2. A town on the extreme edge of the Portuguese coast.
3. Henry "the Navigator," much interested in the islands off the coast of Portugal and the west African coast.

30   And towns of Mauretania, once home
       Of giant Antaeus,[4] while on the right hand
       All was unknown, though rumour spoke of land.

                          * * *

                  [THE CURSE OF ADAMASTOR]

                              37
       Five more suns had risen and set
       Since we embarked from that beach,[5]
       Cutting seas no other nation had braved,
       With the winds gusting favourably,
5   When that night as we kept watch
       At the sharp prow and at our ease,
       A cloud above the mast loomed huge and high
       Blackening out completely the night sky.

                              38
       So fearful it looked, so overpowering,
10   It put great terror in our hearts;
       The dark, invisible waters roared
       As if frustrated, pounding on some reef.
       "Oh Omnipotent and Sublime," I cried,
       "What demon does this region hold,
15   Rising before us in this dreadful form
       For it seems something mightier than a storm?"

                              39
       Even as I spoke, an immense shape
       Materialized in the night air,
       Grotesque and of enormous stature,
20   With heavy jowls, and an unkempt beard,
       Scowling from shrunken, hollow eyes,
       Its complexion earthy and pale,
       Its hair grizzled and matted with clay,
       Its mouth coal black, teeth yellow with decay.

                              40
25   So towered its thick limbs, I swear
       You could believe it a second
       Colossus of Rhodes, that giant
       Of the ancient world's seven wonders.[6]
       It spoke with a coarse, gravelly voice
30   Booming from the ocean's depths;
       Our hair was on end, our flesh shuddering,
       Mine and everyone's, to hear and behold the thing.

                              41
       It addressed us: "O reckless people,

---

4. A giant defeated by Hercules.
5. The Portuguese make swift progress as they sail down the African coast; the beach referred to here is St. Helena Bay, north of Cape Town. At this point the sailors have been gone for five months.

6. The Colossus was an enormous statue dedicated to Apollo, situated in the harbor on the island of Rhodes. Along with the Egyptian pyramids and the hanging gardens of Babylon, it was one of the seven wonders of the ancient world.

Bolder than any the world has known,
35   As stubborn in your countless,
Cruel wars as in vainglorious quests;
Because you have breached what is forbidden,
Daring to cross such remote seas,
Where I alone for so long have prevailed
40   And no ship, large or small, has ever sailed,

                42
"Because you have desecrated nature's
Secrets and the mysteries of the deep,
Where no human, however noble
Or immortal his worth, should trespass,
45   Hear from me now what retribution
Fate prescribes for your insolence,
Whether ocean-borne, or along the shores
You will subjugate with your dreadful wars;

                43
"No matter how many vessels attempt
50   The audacious passage you are plotting,
My cape will be implacably hostile
With gales beyond any you have encountered;[7]
On the next fleet which broaches
These turbulent waters, I shall impose
55   Such retribution and exact such debts
The destruction will be far worse than my threats.

                44
"Here, in my reckoning, I'll take sweet revenge
On Dias who betrayed me to the world,[8]
Nor is he the only Portuguese
60   Who will pay for your foolish persistence;
If what I imagine comes to pass,
Year by year your fleets will meet
Shipwreck, with calamities so combined
That death alone will bring you peace of mind.

                45
65   "As for your first viceroy,[9] whose fame
Fortune will beacon to the heavens,
Here will be his far-flung tomb
By God's inscrutable judgement,
Here he will surrender the opulent
70   Trophies wrung from the Turkish fleet,
And atone for his bloody crimes, the massacre
Of Kilwa, the levelling of Mombasa.

---

7. The "immense shape" that surges before the mariners is
the Cape of Good Hope at the tip of South Africa, personified as a giant like the Cyclops in the *Odyssey,* utterer of
a curse that will haunt Odysseus ever after.
8. Bartolomeu Dias first rounded the Cape in 1488 and

hence was the first to report it "to the world," naming it
the "Cape of Storms." He would indeed drown off the
Cape on a voyage to India in 1500.
9. Francisco de Almeida, a renowned warrior who would
die in a storm off the Cape in 1510.

46

"Another will come, a man of honour,
Noble, generous, and a lover
75   Bringing with him a beautiful lady,
Love's due reward for his virtues;
Vindictive fate will deliver them,
To these harsh, implacable shores;
They will have time to contemplate my curse,
80   Weathering shipwreck to endure far worse.[1]

47

"They will watch their dear children,
Fruits of such love, perish of hunger;
They will see harsh, grasping people
Tear her clothes from the lovely lady,
85   And her body of such crystal beauty
Exposed to frost and the scorching winds,
After marching so far in the terrible heat,
Tramping the rough sand with her delicate feet.

48

"Those who avoid their dreadful fate
90   Must witness further sufferings,
Two hapless lovers falling victim
To the parched, relentless bush;
After softening the very rocks
With tears distilled from grief and pain,
95   They lie embraced, their souls already flown
Their wretched gaol of exquisite flesh and bone."

49

The fearsome creature was in full spate
Chanting our destiny when, rising
I demanded; "Who are you, whose
100   Outlandish shape utterly dumbfounds me?"
His mouth and black eyes grimaced
Giving vent to an awesome roar,
Then answered bitterly, with the heavy voice
Of one who speaks compelled and not by choice:

50

105   —"I am that vast, secret promontory
You Portuguese call the Cape of Storms,
Which neither Ptolemy, Pompey, Strabo,
Pliny, nor any authors knew of.[2]
Here Africa ends. Here its coast
110   Concludes in this, my vast inviolate
Plateau, extending southwards to the Pole
And, by your daring, struck to my very soul.

1. Manuel de Sousa de Sepúlveda and his wife and children died, apparently at the hands of natives, after suffering shipwreck in 1552, a year before Camões himself set sail for India for the first time.

2. Thanks to the daring of Portuguese sailors, the modern world knows far more than did the geographers of antiquity.

51

"I was one of those rugged Titans
With Enceladus, Aegeon, and Briareus;
115   I am called Adamastor, and we fought
With the Shaker of Vulcan's thunderbolts.[3]
No, I could not hurl mountain on mountain
But choosing to fight on the waters,
I was Lord of the sea. Whatever tactic
120   Neptune attempted, I was on his track.

52

"Desire for Peleus" immortal wife[4]
Entangled me hopelessly in this affair;
I spurned all heaven's goddesses
For love of the princess of the ocean.
125   My whole being became enslaved
When I saw her with the daughters
Of Nereus, advancing naked up the shore
And to this day there is nothing I want more.

53

"But knowing I could never win her
130   With an ugly, swollen face like mine,
I resolved to seize her by force
Telling Doris, her mother, of my plans;
In her fear, the goddess spoke to Tethys,
But she, practical in her beauty,
135   Laughed, "What loves could any nymph devise
To satisfy a monster of such size?

54

"'Yet to keep the oceans secure from war
I will do what's unavoidable
Though preserving my honour intact.'
140   This was my go-between's reply;
I could not tumble to any deceit
(For who is so blind as a lover?)
But believed myself blessed and set apart,
Such hopes and longings quickened in my heart.

55

145   "Like a poor fool, I abandoned the war,
And one night, as Doris had sworn
Tethys approached, with her glorious
Face and her naked, matchless body;
Like a madman I ran, with arms
150   Outstretched, to her who was my
Soul's life, heart's joy, body's prayer
Kissing her lovely eyes, her cheeks, her hair.

3. The Titans who challenged Jupiter and the other
Olympians and were subsequently buried by the king of
the gods.

4. Peleus, a human, married the immortal Thetis, daughter
of the sea-gods Nereus and Doris; their son was the almost invincible Achilles.

56

"But, oh, what words for my chagrin!
Convinced my beloved was in my arms,
155   I found myself hugging a hillside
Of undergrowth and rough bush;
I was cheek to cheek with a boulder
I had seized as her angelic face,
Unmanned utterly, dumb and numb with shock,
160   A rock on an escarpment, kissing rock!

57

"O nymph, loveliest of all the ocean,
Though my existence gave you no joy,
What did it cost you to beguile me
With mountain, cloud, dream, or void?
165   I stormed off, all but insane
With hurt and my humiliation
To find some world where she would not resort
Who turned my grief into such splendid sport.

58

"By this time, my Titan brothers
170   Had been conquered and expelled,
Pinned beneath various mountains
So the Gods could live in peace;
No hand can prevail against the heaven,
And I, tormented by my tears,
175   Slowly began to feel what heavy state
Was planned for my audacity by Fate.

59

"My flesh was moulded to hard clay,
My bones compressed to rock;
These limbs you see, and this trunk
180   Were stretched out over the waters;
The gods moulded my great bulk
Into this remote promontory;
And of all tortures, the most agonizing
Is that Tethys surrounds me, tantalizing."

60

185   So he finished, and sighing dreadfully
Vanished suddenly from our sight;
The black clouds dispersed and a resonant
Moaning echoed over the sea.
Raising my hands to the sacred chorus
190   Of angels, who had long watched over us,
I prayed to God that He should turn aside
The evils Adamastor prophesied.

61

By now Apollo's team of four
Were bringing back the sun's chariot
195   And Table Mountain was revealed to us

To which the giant was transformed.
At long last, hugging this coast,
Our prows were pointing eastwards;
I followed it some miles, and once again
200   Turned for the shore and landed with my men.[5]

62

The people who owned the country here,
Though they were likewise Ethiopians,
Were cordial and humane, unlike
Those others who proved so treacherous;[6]
205   They came towards us on the sandy beach
With dancing and an air of festival,
Their wives along with them, and they were driving
Humped cattle which looked sleek and thriving.

63

Their wives, black as polished ebony,
210   Were perched on gently lumbering oxen,
Beasts which, of all their cattle
Are the ones they prize the most.
They sang pastoral songs in their own
Tongue, sweetly and in harmony,
215   Whether rhymed, or in prose, we could not gauge
But like the pipes of Virgil's golden age.[7]

64

These, as their smiling faces promised,
Dealt with us as fellow humans,
Bringing sheep and poultry to barter
220   For the goods we had on board;
But as for news of what we sought,
For all our desire to converse with them,
Neither with words nor signs could we prevail,
So we once again raised anchor and set sail.

65

225   By now we had made a complete circuit
Of black Africa's coast, pointing
Our prows towards the equator,
Leaving the Antarctic in our wake.
We passed Santa Cruz where Dias,
230   Having rounded the Cape of Storms,
And planted a memorial column,
Not knowing of his triumph, turned for home.

66

From here we sailed on many days
Into both fair and wretched weather,

---

5. It is thought that the sailors landed at São Bras, north of Cape Town on the eastern coast.
6. Earlier in Canto 5, the Portuguese were turned back from landing by hostile inhabitants: "Countless arrows and stones rained / On the rest of us in a thick cloud . . ." (5:33).
7. Referring to Virgil's fourth *Eclogue* with its images of pastoral nostalgia and the simplicity and innocence of the golden age.

235   Charting a new course on the ocean,
       Swept along only by our hopes,
       At times fighting the sea itself
       As, changing its moods wilfully,
       It conjured up a current of such force
240   Our ships could make no headway in their course.

                        67

       So overbearing was its pressure
       It drove us backward in our tracks,
       The whole sea running against us
       Though the breeze was in our favour;
245   But at this, the south and south-west
       Winds, as though whipped to anger by
       The sea's challenge, unleashed a furious gale,
       So what dragged the hull was conquered by the sail.

                        68

       The sun dawned on that holy day
250   On which three kings from the Orient
       Came in search of a King, newly born,
       Who is One, and yet Three in One;[8]
       We made landfall once again, among
       Equally gentle people, at the mouth
255   Of a river to which we gave the name
       Epiphany, to match the day we came.

                        69

       Once more, we were offered without stint
       Fresh food, and water from the river,
       But no sign of India, for with them
260   It was again as if we were dumb.
       Consider, O King, how far we had voyaged
       Encountering only pastoral people,
       Without any precise news, nor the least
       Rumour of what we searched for in the East!

                        70

265   Reflect how close by now we were,
       To defeat, emaciated by hunger,
       Exhausted by storms, by climates
       And seas beyond all our experience,
       So weary of promises dashed, so
270   Often driven to despair beneath
       Heavens with scarcely one familiar star
       And hostile to the kind of men we are!

                        71

       Our provisions were thoroughly rancid;
       To consume them made our bodies worse,
275   While nothing brought any comfort

---

8. The Feast of the Epiphany (January 6) celebrates the arrival of the three kings from the Orient at the manger in Bethlehem, where they presented Jesus with their gifts.

In pursuing such fleeting hopes!
Would you believe that had our company
Of soldiers not been Portuguese,
They would have remained so long obedient
280 To their king and to me, their king's agent?

72

Do you imagine if I, their captain,
Opposed them, they would not have mutinied,
Driven to become pirates out of sheer
Rage and desperation and hunger?
285 Truly, their metal has been tested;
There is no trial so great could turn
Such soldiers from their natural qualities
Of discipline, of being Portuguese.

73

So we left that haven of sweet water
290 To resume ploughing the salt seas;
We stood off a little from the coast,
Heading out of sight of land
For the cool, southern breezes
Might have becalmed us in that bay
295 Where the coast turns eastwards to a famous town,
Ancient Sofala, where the gold comes down.⁹

74

Once past, however, we swung the helm,
With a fervent prayer to St Nicholas,¹
Pointing our prow with the other ships
300 To where breakers roared on the coast.
Our hearts were torn with fear and desire,
Aware of the feeble planks beneath us
And of hopes thwarted. Then, approaching shore,
We saw a sight to make our spirits soar.

75

305 It happened that, being close to land
So that bays and beaches were visible,
On a river flowing to the open sea
Boats with sails were coming and going.
Our rejoicing knew no bounds, for
310 Surely, coming upon a people skilled
In the art of navigation, we thought
They must know of the India we sought.

76

These, too, were Ethiopians, but seemed
More in touch with the larger world;
315 Some Arabic words were mingled

---

9. South of Mozambique, the area of Sofala boasted gold mines; the king who owned the mines was said to be the richest man in that part of the world.
1. Patron saint of sailors.

With the language they were speaking;[2]
They covered their heads with turbans
Of fine cotton-weave fabric,
And round their privy parts, as a further clue,
320   They wore a length of cotton coloured blue.

77

In the little Arabic they could manage
And which Fernão Martins spoke fluently,
They said their sea was crossed and recrossed
By ships equalling ours in size;
325   They appeared from where the sun rises,
Sailing south to where the coast bulges,
Then back towards the sun where (as they say)
Live people like us "the colour of the day."

78

So overjoyed were we at meeting
330   These people, and even more by their news,
From the omens we encountered there,
We named that river the Good Signs,
And we raised up a stone column
(We carried a number to mark
335   Such places), naming it for St Raphael,
Tobias's gracious guide to Gabael.[3]

79

Here we careened the ships, scraping
The hulls clean of six months' sludge,
And barnacles and limpets, harmful
340   Parasites of an ocean voyage;
From the friendly people nearby we had,
In that glad time, every kindness,
Furnishing our food, and generously,
Without a hint of guile or treachery.

80

345   But for all the joy and fervent hope
That harbour gave us, pleasure was not
Unsullied, for Fortune, to compensate,
Struck us with further hardship.
So serene heaven dispenses;
350   We are born with this onerous
Condition—that suffering is persistent
While joy, by its nature, is transient.

81

From a disease more cruel and loathsome
Than I ever before witnessed, many

2. Most likely Swahili, spoken in much of southeastern Africa at the time.
3. In the biblical Book of Tobias, God sends the angel Raphael to escort the young Tobias on a difficult journey to reclaim money once lent by his father to a relative, Gabael. Raphael becomes the patron of merchants and travelers.

355   Slipped from life, and in an alien land
        Their bones are forever sepulchred.
        Would any credit without seeing it?
        It attacked the mouth. The gums
        Swelled horribly, and the flesh alongside
360   Turned tumid and soon after putrefied.⁴

                        82

        Putrefied with a fetid stench
        Which poisoned the surrounding air.
        We had no learned doctor with us,
        Still less an experienced surgeon;
365   But some, with some little knowledge
        Of this art, cut away the rotting meat
        As if they were corpses, for as we said,
        If it remained they were as good as dead.

                        83

        And so in that unmapped wilderness,
370   We left, for all eternity, comrades
        Who, in all our trials and misfortunes,
        Had always risked all at our side.
        How simple it is to bury a man!
        Any wave of the sea, any foreign
375   Mound, as with our friends, will accommodate
        Flesh, no matter how lowly or how great.

                        84

        So we departed from that estuary
        With great hope and greater grief,
        And hugging the coast we cut the sea
380   In search of more certain news;
        We came at length to Mozambique
        Of whose treachery and bad faith
        You, O King, are already a connoisseur,
        Likewise of inhospitable Mombasa.⁵

                        85

385   At long last, to this safe anchorage,
        This welcoming harbour which gives health
        To the living and life to the dead,
        God in his mercy piloted us.
        Here, O King, rest after labour,
390   Sweet solace and peace of mind
        You provided. Now I lay down my task,
        Having answered everything I heard you ask.

4. The disease was scurvy, which killed dozens of Vasco da Gama's men in early 1498.
5. The king whom da Gama is addressing is the sultan of Malindi. He has obviously had his own difficulties with his neighbors, as his question to da Gama in Canto 2 suggests: he asks that the Portuguese "tell us, too, of the long circuit / You have made across the angry oceans, / What outlandish customs you have seen / In this uncivil Africa of ours" (110).

86

Did you think, O King, the world contained
Men who would tackle such a journey?
395 Do you imagine that Aeneas and subtle
Ulysses ever ventured so far?
Did either of them dare to embark on
Actual oceans? For all the poetry
Written about them, did they see a fraction
400 Of what I know through strategy and action?

87

Homer so drank of the Aonian spring,°   *Mt. Helicon*
That Rhodes, Smyrna, Ios, and Athens,
Colophon, Arcos, and Salamis claim
The honour of being his birthplace;
405 Virgil brought fame to all Italy;
Hearing his exalted voice,
In pastoral mode, his native Mincius[6] sighed,
While his epic made the Tiber swell with pride;

88

Let them sing on, piling praises
410 On their more-than-human heroes,
Inventing Circe and Polyphemus,
Sirens who make men sleep with song;[7]
Let them sail under canvas and oar
To the Cicones, leaving their
415 Shipmates in that lotus-befuddled realm,
Losing even their pilot at the helm;

89

Let them fantasize, of winds leaping
From wine-skins, and of amorous Calypsos;
Harpies who foul their own banquets;
420 Pilgrimages to the underworld;
However they polish and decorate
With metaphor such empty fables,
My own tale in its naked purity
Outdoes all boasting and hyperbole.

90

425 All the Malindians were spellbound
By the eloquent captain's words,
As he brought to an end his long account
Of exalted and heroic deeds.
The king spoke of the high courage
430 Of the kings made famous by such wars;
Of the people he praised their fealty,
Their strength of spirit and nobility.

---

6. A stream near Mantua in northern Italy, Virgil's
birthplace.
7. This stanza and the next compress the story contained

in *Odyssey* 9–12 of Odysseus's wanderings and his encounters with figures such as the Cyclops (Polyphemus),
the Sirens, and Calypso.

91

As they went their ways, they recounted
The episodes each was most struck by;
435   None could take his eyes from the heroes
Who had rounded such horizons.
But now Apollo guided the reins,
Once steered so recklessly by Phaethon,
To rest in the lovely arms of Tethys,
440   And the king's barge returned him to his palace.

92

How sweet is the praise and the glory
Of our exploits, when it rings true!
True nobility strives to leave
A name surpassing the ancients.
445   So often it happens that greatness
Springs from emulation of the great;
What brave man, committed to what cause
Will not be given fresh impulse by applause?

93

It was not Achilles' glorious deeds
450   Alexander held in such high regard
But great Homer's harmonious numbers;°   *verses*
It was these he praised and coveted.
The fame of Miltiades at Marathon
Roused Themistocles only to envy;
455   Nothing, he said, could give him any pleasure
Till his own deeds were praised in equal measure.[8]

94

Vasco da Gama laboured to prove
Those odysseys the world acclaims
Did not merit as much fame and glory
460   As his own, which shook heaven and earth.
True. Yet only as Emperor Augustus
Esteemed, honoured, and recompensed
The Mantuan,° could Aeneas' story   *Virgil*
Give resonance and wings to Rome's glory. * * *

99

465   Let da Gama be grateful to the muses
That they love his country as they do,
Being constrained to honour in poetry
His title, fame, and exploits in war;
For in truth, neither he nor his lineage
470   Condescend to be Calliope's° friend,   *the muse of epic poetry*
Nor encourage the nymphs of Tagus to trim
Their cloths of gold and sing instead of him.[9]

---

8. Alexander the Great was said to envy Achilles' feats less than the fact that Achilles had a poet as splendid as Homer to record them. Similarly, the Athenian general Themistocles envied the fame of Militiades, who was cru-cial in the victory of the Athenians over the Persians at Marathon.
9. A dig at da Gama's family, which was unforthcoming in its financial support of Camões.

100

Sheer sisterly love and the pure desire
To honour with due and measured praise
475 The achievements of the Portuguese
Are what move the Tagus nymphs;
So let no one with great deeds
In his heart cease to persevere,
Or neglect to keep some lofty goal in view,
480 Lest he fail to reap the honour that's his due.

from Canto 6

1

The Muslim king was at his wits' end
How to entertain the brave mariners,
To gain the Christian king's alliance
And the friendship of such strong people.
5 He spoke of his grief he was lodged so far
From the abundant lands of Europe,
Lamenting fortune had not placed his villas
Much nearer Hercules' illustrious pillars.[1]

2

With games, dances, and other pleasures
10 Very Malindian in their fashion,
And with pleasant fishing excursions
As when the Egyptian beguiled Antony,[2]
Every day the distinguished Sultan
Feasted his Lusitanian° guests,   *Portuguese*
15 With banquets of game and fowl and fish,
Strange fruits, and many an unknown dish.

3

But the captain, aware he was lingering
Too long, with the fresh winds urging
Departure, and being supplied with pilots
20 And fresh provisions from the land,
Resolved to stay no longer, having
Much of the silver ocean to travel.
He took his leave of the kindly, generous Moor
Who urged that this new friendship should endure.

4

25 The Sultan begged further, that his port
Should always be honoured by their ships,
That he wished no less than to offer
Such heroes his throne and his kingdom,

1. One of Hercules' labors was to open up the Straits of Gibraltar, using two pillars to mark the narrow channel between the southernmost tip of Spain and Ceuta in Morocco. 2. The Egyptian is Cleopatra; the allusion suggests that da Gama should depart unless he wishes, like Antony, to become enslaved to the "Muslim king." Yet the Sultan has only da Gama's best interests at heart, and even offers him a pilot to help steer his course across the Indian Ocean.

And that while his soul ruled his body,
30   He would be ready to sacrifice
His country and his life at any time
To a king so good, a people so sublime.

* * *

[THE STORM; THE VOYAGERS REACH INDIA]

76

By now,[3] furious Neptune's waves
Were piling up to the clouds, then
Yawning as if to the innermost
Entrails of the deepest depths;
5   Winds from all quarters sought
To smash the very fabric of the world;
Blue lightning crackled in the pitch-black night,
And the whole heavens were ablaze with light.

77

All along the storm-swept coast
10   The Halcyon birds raised their lament,
Recalling those tears so long ago
Provoked by the raging waters.[4]
The lovesick dolphins, all this while,
Hid in their underwater caves,
15   Fleeing the breakers and relentless gale,
Yet even there they trembled and grew pale.

78

Never was such lightning forged
Against the overweening Titans
By the muscular, sooty blacksmith
20   Who wrought Aeneas' shining armour;
Not even Jove himself hurled
Such thunderbolts in that deluge
When survived only Pyrrha and Deucalion
Who cast stones to fashion women and men.[5]

79

25   How many mountains were toppled that day
By the frantic lashing of the waves!
How many ancient trees uprooted
By the wind's unremitting fury!
Those buttress roots never foresaw
30   One day they would stare at the sky,

---

3. At this point in Canto 6, the Portuguese are veering away from the African coast in order to cross the Indian Ocean. Bacchus, enemy to the Portuguese, realizes that "heaven was fully resolved / To make of Lisbon a second Rome," and in order to prevent their arrival in India, he calls on Neptune to unleash his winds and provoke a great storm to drive the sailors off course.
4. The "tears" are those of Alcyone, who drowned herself when she learned that her husband was drowned at sea;

the couple were changed into kingfishers. Camões is invoking the storm that tosses Aeneas's boats onto the shores of Africa in *Aeneid* 1.
5. The stanza alludes to the war between Jupiter and the Titans (Jupiter's lightning bolts were forged by Vulcan, maker among other things of Aeneas's armor), as well as to the flood described in Ovid's *Metamorphoses* in which only the elderly Pyrrha and Deucalion survived.

Nor the sands of the deep that oceans might
Swirl their sediments to such a height.

80

Vasco da Gama, realizing that close
To his goal he was about to drown,
35   Watching the seas, now gaping to hell,
Now mounting in fury to the heavens,
Confused by fears, unsure of life
Where no human help could avail,
Cried out to Him, from the depths of despair,
40   To whom all things are possible, this prayer:

81

—"Divine guardian, merciful providence,
Who art Lord of earth, sea, and heaven;
You, who guided the children of Israel
Through the waters of the Red Sea;
45   You, who delivered St Paul in safety
From the quicksands of Syrtes;[6]
Who saved Noah with his sons, and bade him
Be to the drowned world a second Adam;

82

"Must I endure another Scylla
50   And Charybdis like those we have passed,
More gulfs like Syrtes with its quicksands,
More rocks like the Acroceraunia?[7]
At the climax of so many travails,
Why, O God, do you now forsake us?
55   Where is the offence? How are we to blame
For this service undertaken in Thy name?

83

"Blessed are those who met their death
At the point of an African lance,
Upholding the sacred law of Christ
60   In the deserts of Mauretania![8]
Whose illustrious deeds are exalted,
Whose memories are still fresh,
Who became immortal through the lives they gave,
For Death is sweet when Honour shares the grave."

84

65   As he uttered this prayer the winds howled,
Butting like a herd of wild bulls,
Lashing the storm to greater fury,
And screaming through the shrouds;

6. St. Paul voyaged near the sandbanks of Syrtes, in northern Africa, as recounted in the Book of Acts.
7. A rocky cap in Greece. Odysseus was forced to navigate between the monsters Scylla and Charybdis during his travels, losing several of his sailors in the process.

8. Echoing Aeneas's resigned plea to the gods when he fears he will die in the tempest in the *Aeneid* book 1. Mauritania, in northwest Africa, had been the site of Portuguese battles against the Moors.

70
The fork-lightning never paused;
Thunder hammered as if bent on
Demolishing the seven firmaments
As battle raged between the elements.

85

But now the amorous star, morning's
Messenger dawned on the horizon,
75
Heralding the sun, and surveying
Land and sea with her bright face.
Venus, whose star it is, making
Orion with his sword turn tail,
Gazed below at the fleet she held so dear
80
And was seized at once by anger mixed with fear.

86

—"This is, for certain, Bacchus' work,
But it will do him no good," she vowed,
"Now, as will always happen,
I know exactly what harm he intends."
85
So saying, she sped in an instant,
Down from the sky to the broad ocean,
Instructing her ardent nymphs to wear
Chaplets of sweet rosebuds in their hair.

87

Chaplets, she advised, in varied colours
90
Contending with their golden hair;
Who could tell the flowers were not springing
Naturally from the gold Love braided?
Her plan was to appease through love
The horrid regiment of the winds,
95
By displaying her dear Nereids, who are
Unmatched for radiance by any star.

88

So it proved, for as soon as the gales
Glimpsed them, the virulence
Of their combat dwindled, and they
100
Surrendered like a beaten army;
Their hands and feet seemed entangled
By that hair which outshone the sun.
The lovely Orithyia played her part
With Boreas,[9] for whom she yearned at heart;

89

105
—"Do not assume, fierce Boreas, I am
Seduced by your oaths of constancy;
Tenderness is love's surest sign
And fury does not rhyme with fidelity;
If you cannot rein in your madness,

---

9. Boreas is one of the winds unleashed against the Portuguese; Notus, encountered shortly, is another.

110   From this day forward, do not expect
       To take me as your lover any longer
       For my fear of you will always be stronger."

                        90
       So, too, the beautiful Galateia
       Admonished fierce Notus, for she knew
115   How long he had been watching her
       And that she could tempt him to anything.
       The wild one could not believe his luck,
       His heart thumping in his breast,
       And keen to know what was the lady's game,
120   Cared not a scrap how pliable he became.

                        91
       In the same manner, the other nymphs
       Swiftly tamed the remaining lovers;
       Soon they had surrendered to lovely Venus
       All their anger and their tumult;
125   She promised, seeing them so fond,
       Her eternal favour in their amours,
       Receiving in her lovely hands their homage,
       And their promise of a prosperous voyage.

                        92
       At this, bright dawn broke in those heights
130   Where the River Ganges has its source,
       As the sailors, aloft at the mast head,
       Saw mountains glimmering before the prow.
       Now, after the storm and the long,
       Pioneer voyage, their fears subsided.
135   Then cheerfully said their Malindian pilot,
       —"That land ahead is surely Calicut![1]

                        93
       "This is the land you have been seeking,
       This is India rising before you;
       Unless you desire yet more of the world,
140   Your long task is accomplished."
       Rejoicing to see he knew the country,
       Da Gama contained himself no longer
       But knelt on deck, arms raised towards the sky,
       And gave his heartfelt thanks to God on high.

                        94
145   He gave thanks to God, as well he should,
       Not only for guiding him to the coast
       He had voyaged to with so many fears
       And through such enduring travails,
       But more that, in the face of death

---

1. Seaport in southwest India.

150   Devised by the winds and the cruel
        Waves, God had been so prompt to redeem
        Them, like awakening from some dreadful dream.

                        95
        For indeed, it is through such perils,
        Such wearisome and fearful labours,
155   That those for whom fame is the spur
        Achieve honour and lasting esteem;
        Not by depending on an ancient name
        Or a long lineage of ancestors,
        Nor sprawling on gold beds made comfortable
160   By furs of the finest Russian sable,

                        96
        Nor with new and exquisite recipes,
        Nor relaxing, local excursions,
        Nor society's teeming pleasures
        Which emasculate noble hearts;
165   Nor by surrendering to his appetites,
        Nor by allowing his sweet fortune
        So to pamper him that a man never
        Embarks upon some virtuous endeavour;

                        97
        But by seeking out, with a strong arm,
170   Honours he can make truly his own,
        Vigilant, clothed in forged steel,
        Exposed to gales and tempestuous seas,
        Conquering the numbing cold
        Of the deep, inhospitable south,
175   Eating corrupt rations day after day,
        Seasoned only by the hardships of the way;

                        98
        And by instructing the face, white with shock,
        To look resolute and cheerful
        As the hot cannon-ball whistles
180   And takes the arm or leg of a comrade.
        So the heart develops a callous
        Honourable contempt for titles
        And wealth, rank, and money, which Destiny
        Counterfeits, but is never Virtue's way.

                        99
185   So one's judgement grows enlightened,
        And experience brings serenity,
        Studying, as from a great height
        Mankind's pettiness and confusion;
        Such a person, if order and justice
190   Prevail, and not self-interest,
        Will rise (as he must) to great position,
        But reluctantly, and not through ambition.

from Canto 7

1

At long last, they were nearing the land
So many others before had longed for,
Spread out between the River Indus
And the Ganges which rises in Eden.[1]
5 Courage, heroes! You have aspired
So long to bear the victor's palm,
You have arrived! The land of your pleasure
Extends before you, with all its treasure!

2

To you, heirs of Lusus, I have this to say:
10 *Your share of the earth is a small one,*
And small, too, your portion of Christ's
Fold, shepherded from Heaven;
You, whom no forms of danger
Prevented from conquering the infidel,
15 *Nor greed, nor reluctance in sacrifice*
To the Holy Mother of God in paradise;

3

You, Portuguese, as few as you are valiant,
Make light of your slender forces;
Through martyrdom, in its manifold forms,
20 *You spread the message of eternal life;*
Heaven has made it your destiny
To do many and mighty deeds
For Christendom, despite being few and weak,
For thus, O Christ, do you exalt the meek![2]

---

1. The river Ganges was believed to have its source in the garden of Eden.
2. The "meek" Portuguese will eventually disembark in Calicut, but they won't be safe there. Bacchus continues to cause trouble, stirring up the Muslims in Calicut against da Gama, and da Gama is forced to flee the people who have become his captors. Venus, believing that her Portuguese need to be rewarded for their many labors, creates an island in the midst of the Indian Ocean on which the sailors can rest. Venus's Nereids let themselves be captured and seduced by da Gama's men, while the captain learns from Tethys about the future of his people: after describing to him such lands as Sumatra, Cambodia, Laos, and Ceylon, Tethys concludes "Such are the new regions of the East / You Portuguese are adding to the world, / Opening the gates to that vast ocean / Which you navigate with such courage" (10:138). The poem ends with the easy return of the Portuguese to Lisbon and the poet appealing to the young king to pay him heed even as he despairs over Portugal's decline since the days of Vasco da Gama: "No more, Muse, no more, my lyre / Is out of tune and my throat hoarse, / Not from singing but from wasting song / On a deaf and coarsened people" (10:145).

RESONANCE

from *The Journal of the First Voyage of Vasco da Gama (1497–1499)*[1]

[ROUNDING THE CAPE][2]

At daybreak of Thursday the 16th of November [1497], having careened our ships and taken in wood, we set sail. At that time we did not know how far we might be abaft the Cape of Good Hope. Pero d'Alenquer thought the distance about thirty leagues, but he was not certain, for on his return voyage [when with B. Dias] he had left the Cape in the morning and had gone past this bay with the wind astern, whilst on the outward voyage he had kept at sea, and was therefore unable to identify the locality where we now were. We therefore stood out towards the S.S.W. and late on Saturday [November 18] we beheld the Cape. On that same day we again stood out to sea, returning to the land in the course of the night. On Sunday morning, November 19, we once more made for the Cape, but were again unable to round it, for the wind blew from the S.S.W., whilst the Cape juts out towards the S.W. We then again stood out to sea, returning to the land on Monday night. At last, on Wednesday [November 22], at noon, having the wind astern, we succeeded in doubling the Cape, and then ran along the coast.

To the south of this Cape of Good Hope, and close to it, a vast bay, six leagues broad at its mouth, enters about six leagues into the land.

* * *

[ARRIVAL IN MALINDI][3]

On Thursday, [19 April 1498] the captain-major and Nicolau Coelho rowed along the front of the town, bombards having been placed in the poops of their long-boats. Many people were along the shore, and among them two horsemen, who appeared to take much delight in a sham-fight. The king was carried in a palanquin from the stone steps of his palace to the side of the captain-major's boats. He again begged the captain to come ashore, as he had a helpless father who wanted to see him, and that he and his sons would go on board the ships as hostages. The captain, however, excused himself.

We found here four vessels belonging to Indian Christians.[4] When they came for the first time on board Paulo da Gama's ship, the captain-major being there at the time, they were shown an altar-piece representing Our Lady at the foot of the cross, with Jesus Christ in her arms and the apostles around her. When the Indians saw this

---

1. Translated by E. G. Ravenstein. Vasco da Gama (1460–1524) succeeded where Columbus failed. Outfitted by King Manuel of Portugal, he found a trade route to the east by sea, 45 years after land access had been definitively blocked with the fall of Constantinople to the Arabs. Long experienced in matters of the sea—in 1492, he had seized French ships in the harbor of Algarve as vengeance against pirates—da Gama went farther than navigators before him, pressing around the Cape of Good Hope to navigate his way safely to Calicut in southwest India. Packed into four seaworthy vessels were approximately 160 men, including pilots, clerks, interpreters skilled in Arabic (at least one of them a slave), priests, and convicts; fewer than half of them would survive the trip and return to Portugal. Da Gama's efforts bore fruit, and quickly. By the middle of the 16th century, the Portuguese trade empire extended from Brazil to China. The excerpts here are from a journal kept by a member of da Gama's crew, probably a clerk or soldier, during the epoch-making journey from Lisbon to India between 1497 and 1499.

2. The first entry from the journal is a more understated treatment of the rounding of the Cape of Good Hope than that found in *The Lusíads;* difficulties there were, but not as earth-shattering as Camões made them.

3. The next three entries take us from the boats' arrival in Malindi (where Camões puts us in Canto 2), to the heavy storms encountered in the Arabian sea (detailed in Canto 6) to the astonishment at hearing Portuguese spoken upon arrival in Calicut.

4. The identities of these "Indian Christians" are in doubt. They may have been merchants or natives from Banya—and may not have been Christians at all.

picture they prostrated themselves, and as long as we were there they came to say their prayers in front of it, bringing offerings of cloves, pepper, and other things.

These Indians are tawny men; they wear but little clothing and have long beards and long hair, which they braid. They told us that they ate no beef. Their language differs from that of the Arabs, but some of them know a little of it, as they hold much intercourse with them.

On the day on which the captain-major went up to the town in the boats, these Christian Indians fired off many bombards from their vessels, and when they saw him pass they raised their hands and shouted lustily *Christt! Christ!*[5]

That same night they asked the king's permission to give us a night-fête. And when night came they fired off many bombards, sent up rockets, and raised loud shouts.

These Indians warned the captain-major against going on shore, and told him not to trust to their "fanfares," as they neither came from their hearts nor from their good will.

On the following Sunday, the 22nd of April, the king's *zavra*[6] brought on board one of his confidential servants, and as two days had passed without any visitors, the captain-major had this man seized, and sent word to the king that he required the pilots whom he had promised. The king, when he received this message, sent a Christian pilot, and the captain-major allowed the gentleman, whom he had retained in his vessel, to go away.

We were much pleased with the Christian pilot whom the king had sent us. We learnt from him that the island of which we heard at Moçambique as being inhabited by Christians was in reality an island subject to this same King of Moçambique; that half of it belonged to the Moors and the other half to the Christians; that many pearls were to be found there, and that it was called Quyluee. This is the island the Moorish pilots wanted to take us to, and we also wished to go there, for we believed that what they said was true.

The town of Malindi lies in a bay and extends along the shore. It may be likened to Alcouchette.[7] Its houses are lofty and well white-washed, and have many windows; on the landside are palm-groves, and all around it maize and vegetables are being cultivated.

We remained in front of this town during nine days, and all this time we had fêtes, sham-fights, and musical performances ("fanfares").

[ACROSS THE GULF—THE ARABIAN SEA]

We left Malindi on Tuesday, the 24th of the month [of April] for a city called Qualecut [Calicut], with the pilot whom the king had given us. The coast there runs north and south, and the land encloses a huge bay with a strait. In this bay, we were told, were to be found many large cities of Christians and Moors, including one called Quambay [Cambay], as also six-hundred known islands, and within it the Red Sea and the "house" [Kaabah] of Mecca.

On the following Sunday [April 29] we once more saw the North Star, which we had not seen for a long time.

On Friday, the 18th of May, after having seen no land for twenty-three days, we sighted lofty mountains, and having all this time sailed before the wind we could not have made less than 600 leagues.[8] The land, when first sighted, was at a distance of eight leagues, and our lead reached bottom at forty-five fathoms. That same night we

5. One editor suggests that what the Portuguese heard as "Christ" was really "Krishna," one of the incarnations of Vishnu, suggesting that the peoples encountered were not, in fact, Christian.
6. A native vessel used on the Arabian sea, generally with a single mast.
7. A town in Portugal on the Tagus, near Lisbon.
8. The mountain spotted by da Gama and his crew is Mt. Eli in India, more than 2,000 miles from Malindi from which the Portuguese had set sail 23 days earlier.

took a course to the S.S.W., so as to get away from the coast. On the following day [May 19] we again approached the land, but owing to the heavy rain and a thunderstorm, which prevailed whilst we were sailing along the coast, our pilot was unable to identify the exact locality. On Sunday [May 20] we found ourselves close to some mountains, and when we were near enough for the pilot to recognise them he told us that they were above Calicut, and that this was the country we desired to go to.

[CALICUT]

[*Arrival.*] That night [May 20] we anchored two leagues from the city of Calicut, and we did so because our pilot mistook *Capua,* a town at that place, for Calicut. Still further there is another town called *Pandarani.* We anchored about a league and a half from the shore. After we were at anchor, four boats (*almadias*) approached us from the land, who asked of what nation we were. We told them, and they then pointed out Calicut to us. On the following day [May 21] these same boats came again alongside, when the captain-major sent one of the convicts to Calicut, and those with whom he went took him to two Moors from Tunis, who could speak Castilian and Genoese.[9] The first greeting that he received was in these words: "May the Devil take thee! What brought you hither?" They asked what he sought so far away from home, and he told them that we came in search of Christians and of spices. They said: "Why does not the King of Castile, the King of France, or the Signoria of Venice send hither?" He said that the King of Portugal would not consent to their doing so, and they said he did the right thing. After this conversation they took him to their lodgings and gave him wheaten bread and honey. When he had eaten he returned to the ships, accompanied by one of the Moors, who was no sooner on board, than he said these words: "A lucky venture, a lucky venture! Plenty of rubies, plenty of emeralds! You owe great thanks to God, for having brought you to a country holding such riches!" We were greatly astonished to hear his talk, for we never expected to hear our language spoken so far away from Portugal.[1]

Michel de Montaigne
1533–1592

Michel de Montaigne introduces his longest essay, "Apology for Raymond Sebond," with a vivid portrait of the household in which he grew up. "Inflamed with that new ardor with which

9. An indication of the varied nature of the crew with which da Gama traveled.

1. The journal goes on to describe the entry of da Gama himself into Calicut. He tours the city's temples, identified by the journal writer as "churches" that contain images (probably of Krishna and his mother Devaki) imagined to be Mary and Jesus, as well as numerous saints "painted variously, with teeth protruding an inch from the mouth, and four or five arms." But hostilities arise between da Gama and the King of Calicut, as the king becomes increasingly suspicious of the Portuguese's motives. After three difficult months, "On Wednesday, the

29th [of August 1498], the captain-major [Vasco da Gama] and the other captains agreed that, inasmuch that we had discovered the country we had come in search of, as also spices and precious stones, and it appeared impossible to establish cordial relations with the people, it would be as well to take our departure." The Portuguese do so, with five hostages on board, who, "it was resolved . . . might be useful to us in establishing friendly relations. We therefore set sail and left for Portugal, greatly rejoicing at our good fortune in having made so great a discovery."

King Francis I embraced letters, [my father] sought with great diligence and expense the acquaintance of learned men, receiving them at his house like holy persons having some particular inspiration of divine wisdom." According to the essayist, his father, Eyquem de Montaigne, a prosperous merchant who had received little formal education, treated scholars with "reverence and religion" only because he was wholly unqualified to judge them. "Myself," Montaigne continues, "I like them well enough, but I do not worship them."

This attack on his father's naive enthusiasm for "learned men" may also seem to be an indictment of the time and considerable expense Eyquem spent on his son's education. Brought up with a German tutor who taught him Latin as his mother tongue, the future author of some of the finest and most spirited works in the French language—the incomparable *Essays*—was sent to the prestigious Collège de Guienne in Bordeaux, trained in law, and went on to become a magistrate in the Parliament of Bordeaux. But at the age of thirty-seven, Montaigne abruptly chose to retire from Parliament and retreat to the family home that had become his (and from which he took his last name). Here he had the beams in his library carved with his favorite quotations from classical authors, and in a medallion he had made for himself in 1576, he inscribed the question, *Que sçay-je?*—"what do I know?" The answer, one pondered throughout a lifetime in his *Essays,* was *Rien* (or "nothing")—nothing, that is, save himself. "I would rather be an authority on myself than on Cicero," he remarks in his final essay, "Of Experience," and it is clear from the sum total of the *Essays* that any claim to be an authority on Cicero would be instantly suspect.

And yet to a certain extent, such a query represents the very fruit of Renaissance learning. Two hundred years earlier, Petrarch had posed the same question, framed as an attack on the pedantic nature of scholastic learning that had dominated the medieval universities: "What good is it to know the nature of the beasts and the birds, the fish and the snakes, if we ignore and don't bother to learn the nature of man: why we are born, from whence we come, where are we going?" Montaigne's compatriot Rabelais had challenged the dry university education that produced unthinking parrots; far better the humanist training that addressed the whole man. Moreover, like Erasmus, Montaigne turned for his most valued model to the one ancient figure who didn't presume on his own considerable knowledge, who believed that there is nothing "so ridiculous as that this miserable and puny creature, who is not even master of himself . . . should call himself master and emperor of the universe": the Greek philosopher Socrates. Or as Montaigne describes him: "Socrates was a man, and wanted neither to be nor to seem anything else" ("On some verses of Virgil"). But unlike Rabelais or Erasmus—or even Socrates, for that matter—Montaigne deploys in his 107 essays an intensely personal voice that became more frankly autobiographical as the years went on. Thanks to the meticulous care that Montaigne devoted to his writings, we are able to see how his thinking developed over a period of twenty years.

The *Essays* began as a "commonplace book," a collection of pithy quotations with selective commentary on topics as diverse as "smells," "sleep," "war horses," and "liars." Perhaps, as Montaigne suggests in one of his shortest essays, "Of Idleness," he began writing in order to harness the "idle thoughts" that plagued him in the years immediately after his retirement. But his book eventually grew to voluminous size, as Montaigne created a new and flexible narrative form which he christened with the French word *essais*—trials or attempts, on which he puns in "Of repentance": "If my mind could gain a firm footing, I would not make essays, I would make decisions; but it is always in apprenticeship and on trial." And these "trials" increasingly revolved around none other than Montaigne himself, revealed in all his foibles. His memory is so poor that he has often picked up a book believing it to be the first time, only to find his extensive notes scribbled in the margins; he has only modest strengths (there are few friends more loyal than he), and he has suffered from a variety of physical ailments, ranging from a concussion he suffered when he fell from his horse, to the maladies which increase as he ages, such as the painful bouts with kidney stones that sent him to Italy and Germany in 1580 in search of spas that could grant him relief. (His lively *Travel Journal* is the product of his trip, which was interrupted when he was summoned to return to Bordeaux to preside for two terms as mayor.) Although there is plenty of engagement with Virgil, Lucretius, Sextus Empiricus, and countless other classical writers (occasionally quoted inaccurately, thereby verifying what Montaigne says about his poor memory), Montaigne uses these borrowings to take us from the potentially abstract realms of philosophy and Roman history to the most immediate of concerns: his health, his love affairs, his inability to stay at the table after he has finished eating a meal, and his—and our—impending death.

Some have criticized Montaigne for this egoistic turn inward, reflective, perhaps, of the new bourgeois consciousness that privileged the private space over the public and civic space. The seventeenth-century philosopher and mathematician Blaise Pascal, who was greatly influenced by the *Essays,* was nonetheless one of many who chastised his predecessor for his obsessive self-preoccupation and his vacillation over the burning issues of his day. Yet Montaigne, writing at the height of France's religious wars, had seen enough blood and incivility to know that fanatical partisanship on disputed questions was not the answer to the ills plaguing post-Reformation Europe. The fact that he was called in to negotiate between the Catholic Henri de Guise and the Protestant Henry of Navarre suggests that others prized his ability to refrain from too quickly taking sides and to weigh all possible options before coming—if coming—to decisions. It also suggests that Montaigne deliberately underplayed the important political role he did have, both before and after his "retirement." In the same way, the ventures into the New World didn't prove to Montaigne the superiority of European culture. They demonstrated something quite to the contrary: the barbaric nature of European practices, as Montaigne wittily suggests in his classic essay "Of Cannibals." At the same time, he knew that he couldn't simply deny the culture that had created him. As he mentions in his preface to the *Essays,* since he had not been born "among those nations which are said to live still in the sweet freedom of nature's first laws," he was unable to portray himself "entire and wholly naked." Stepping outside oneself to become another was an impossibility, in the same way that placing oneself at the universe's center was the highest folly.

This brings us to what may be called the paradox of Montaigne's massive project: why did he write, and, more significantly, publish his *Essays*? They began, Montaigne suggests, not merely as a cure for idleness but as consolation for a friendship that had ended tragically in 1563 when Montaigne's "soulmate" from school, Étienne de la Boétie, died of the plague. It is telling in this light that Marie de Gornay, a young woman whom Montaigne befriended and made his adoptive daughter and literary executrix, lovingly attended to the *Essays* after Montaigne's death in 1592, transcribing his marginalia and overseeing the publication of the posthumous version in 1595. Particularly in his later essays, Montaigne tries to create a familiar, even intimate, relationship with his readers, anxious to convey simply himself, rather than to pass on profound wisdom; "it should not be held against me if I publish what I write," he says in "Of practice." "What is useful to me may also by accident be useful to another. Moreover, I am not spoiling anything, I am using only what is mine." The "accident" of the essays' utility thereby becomes a convenient aftermath of what Montaigne imagines to be the essays' real purpose, the portrayal of himself in all his dimensions. Another accidental aftermath might also have been this: to find a true friend who might understand him, and, perhaps, be understood in turn. Mademoiselle de Gornay is said to have claimed that she knew Montaigne long before she met him. No doubt many since then have also felt well-acquainted with the man who seemed to have taken the sincerest pleasure in being among the first to expose himself, almost if not completely naked, to generations of avid readers.

The *Essays* went through numerous publications, beginning in 1580 with a publication of the first two (of three) books, in Bordeaux, where Montaigne would soon be mayor. Several editions with numerous additions and modifications followed. The 1588 edition, published in Paris, was the first to contain the third book of essays. Between 1588 and 1592, the year of his death, Montaigne continued to reflect on and augment his literary creation; the posthumous 1595 edition incorporates the many changes he made in the margins to his 1588 text. While the various strata of the essays will not generally be noted below, it is important to recognize that the essays changed significantly over time.

PRONUNCIATION:
Michel de Montaigne: mee-SHELL duh mon-TEN

from ESSAYS
Of Idleness[1]

Just as we see that fallow land, if rich and fertile, teems with a hundred thousand kinds of wild and useless weeds, and that to set it to work we must subject it and sow it with certain seeds for our service; and as we see that women, all alone, produce mere shapeless masses and lumps of flesh, but that to create a good and natural offspring they must be made fertile with a different kind of seed; so it is with minds. Unless you keep them busy with some definite subject that will bridle and control them, they throw themselves in disorder hither and yon in the vague field of imagination.

> Thus, in a brazen urn, the water's light
> Trembling reflects the sun's and moon's bright rays,
> And, darting here and there in aimless flight,
> Rises aloft, and on the ceiling plays.
>   VIRGIL[2]

And there is no mad or idle fancy that they do not bring forth in this agitation:

> Like a sick man's dreams,
> They form vain visions.
>   HORACE

The soul that has no fixed goal loses itself; for as they say, to be everywhere is to be nowhere:

> He who dwells everywhere, Maximus, nowhere dwells.
>   MARTIAL

Lately when I retired to my home, determined so far as possible to bother about nothing except spending the little life I have left in rest and seclusion, it seemed to me I could do my mind no greater favor than to let it entertain itself in full idleness and stay and settle in itself, which I hoped it might do more easily now, having become weightier and riper with time. But I find—

> Ever idle hours breed wandering thoughts
>   LUCAN

—that, on the contrary, like a runaway horse, it gives itself a hundred times more trouble than it took for others, and gives birth to so many chimeras and fantastic mon-

---

1. Translated by Donald Frame. Book I, Chapter 8, of the *Essays.*
2. The citation is from Virgil's *Aeneid,* Book 8. Like the passage from Martial, it was added by Montaigne to his revised edition of the *Essays* published in 1588. Mon-

taigne constantly weaves quotations from classical writers into his prose, often to express his meaning succinctly, and to give a general resonance to his own experience. The most notable of these references will be footnoted.

sters, one after another, without order or purpose, that in order to contemplate their ineptitude and strangeness at my pleasure, I have begun to put them in writing, hoping in time to make my mind ashamed of itself.

Of the Power of the Imagination[1]

A strong imagination creates the event, say the scholars. I am one of those who are very much influenced by the imagination. Everyone feels its impact, but some are overthrown by it.[2] Its impression on me is piercing. And my art is to escape it, not to resist it. I would live solely in the presence of gay, healthy people. The sight of other people's anguish causes very real anguish to me, and my feelings have often usurped the feelings of others. A continual cougher irritates my lungs and throat. I visit less willingly the sick toward whom duty directs me than those toward whom I am less attentive and concerned. I catch the disease that I study, and lodge it in me. I do not find it strange that imagination brings fevers and death to those who give it a free hand and encourage it.

Simon Thomas was a great doctor in his time. I remember that one day, when he met me at the house of a rich old consumptive with whom he was discussing ways to cure his illness, he told him that one of these would be to give me occasion to enjoy his company; and that by fixing his eyes on the freshness of my face and his thoughts on the blitheness and overflowing vigor of my youth, and filling all his senses with my flourishing condition, he might improve his constitution. But he forgot to say that mine might get worse at the same time.

Gallus Vibius strained his mind so hard to understand the essence and impulses of insanity that he dragged his judgment off its seat and never could get it back again; and he could boast of having become mad through wisdom.[3] There are some who through fear anticipate the hand of the executioner. And one man who was being unbound to have his pardon read him dropped stone dead on the scaffold, struck down by his mere imagination. We drip with sweat, we tremble, we turn pale and turn red at the blows of our imagination; reclining in our feather beds we feel our bodies agitated by their impact, sometimes to the point of expiring. And boiling youth, fast asleep, grows so hot in the harness that in dreams it satisfies its amorous desires:

> So that as though it were an actual affair,
> They pour out mighty streams, and stain the clothes they wear.
> LUCRETIUS

And although it is nothing new to see horns grow overnight on someone who did not have them when he went to bed, nevertheless what happened to Cippus, king of Italy, is memorable; having been in the daytime a very excited spectator at a bullfight and having all night in his dreams had horns on his head, he grew actual horns on his forehead by the power of his imagination. Passion gave the son of Croesus the voice that nature had refused him. And Antiochus took fever from the beauty of Stratonice too vividly imprinted in his soul. Pliny says he saw Lucius Cossitius changed from a

1. Book 1, Chapter 21.
2. The remainder of this paragraph and the next are from post-1588 publications of the *Essays,* and reflects the increasingly intimate reflections of the late editions.
3. Cited in the Roman philosopher Seneca's *Controversies;* Gallus was a declaimer who apparently went mad.

woman into a man on his wedding day. Pontanus and others report similar metamorphoses as having happened in Italy in these later ages. And through his and his mother's vehement desire,

> Iphis the man fulfilled vows made when he was a girl.[4]
>
> OVID

Passing through Vitry-le-François, I might have seen a man whom the bishop of Soissons had named Germain at confirmation, but whom all the inhabitants of that place had seen and known as a girl named Marie until the age of twenty-two. He was now heavily bearded, and old, and not married. Straining himself in some way in jumping, he says, his masculine organs came forth; and among the girls there a song is still current by which they warn each other not to take big strides for fear of becoming boys, like Marie Germain. It is not so great a marvel that this sort of accident is frequently met with. For if the imagination has power in such things, it is so continually and vigorously fixed on this subject that in order not to have to relapse so often into the same thought and sharpness of desire, it is better off if once and for all it incorporates this masculine member in girls.

Some attribute to the power of imagination the scars of King Dagobert and of Saint Francis.[5] It is said that thereby bodies are sometimes removed from their places. And Celsus tells of a priest who used to fly with his soul into such ecstasy that his body would remain a long time without breath and without sensation. Saint Augustine names another who whenever he heard lamentable and plaintive cries would suddenly go into a trance and get so carried away that it was no use to shake him and shout at him, to pinch him and burn him, until he had come to; then he would say that he had heard voices, but as if coming from afar, and he would notice his burns and bruises. And that this was no feigned resistance to his senses was shown by the fact that while in this state he had neither pulse nor breath.

It is probable that the principal credit of miracles, visions, enchantments, and such extraordinary occurrences comes from the power of imagination, acting principally upon the minds of the common people, which are softer. Their belief has been so strongly seized that they think they see what they do not see.

I am still of this opinion, that those comical inhibitions by which our society is so fettered that people talk of nothing else are for the most part the effects of apprehension and fear. For I know by experience that one man, whom I can answer for as for myself, on whom there could fall no suspicion whatever of impotence and just as little of being enchanted, having heard a friend of his tell the story of an extraordinary impotence into which he had fallen at the moment when he needed it least, and finding himself in a similar situation, was all at once so struck in his imagination by the horror of this story that he incurred the same fate. And from then on he was subject to relapse, for the ugly memory of his mishap checked him and tyrannized him. He found some remedy for this fancy by another fancy: which was that by admitting this weakness and speaking about it in advance, he relieved the tension of his soul, for when the

---

4. After noting a number of supposedly historical metamorphoses—the account of Cippus, for example, is taken from Pliny's *Natural History,* the story of Croesus, who spoke in a man's voice for the first time only when he saw his father on his deathbed, is from Herodotus—Montaigne turns to Ovid's *Metamorphoses* for the story of Iphis. A girl raised as a boy, she falls in love with the bride she is given to marry, and the goddess Isis transforms her into a young man.

5. Dagobert had been covered by scars provoked by his fear of gangrene. St. Francis of Assisi was said to bear the stigmata, the wounds made on Christ's body by the nails of the cross.

trouble had been presented as one to be expected, his sense of responsibility diminished and weighed upon him less. When he had a chance of his own choosing, with his mind unembroiled and relaxed and his body in good shape, to have his bodily powers first tested, then seized and taken by surprise, with the other party's full knowledge of his problem, he was completely cured in this respect. A man is never after incapable, unless from genuine impotence, with a woman with whom he has once been capable.

This mishap is to be feared only in enterprises where our soul is immoderately tense with desire and respect, and especially if the opportunity is unexpected and pressing; there is no way of recovering from this trouble. I know one man who found it helpful to bring to it a body that had already begun to be sated elsewhere, so as to lull his frenzied ardor, and who with age finds himself less impotent through being less potent. And I know another who was helped when a friend assured him that he was supplied with a counterbattery of enchantments that were certain to save him. I had better tell how this happened.

A count, a member of a very distinguished family, with whom I was quite intimate,[6] upon getting married to a beautiful lady who had been courted by a man who was present at the wedding feast, had his friends very worried and especially an old lady, a relative of his, who was presiding at the wedding and holding it at her house. She was fearful of these sorceries, and gave me to understand this. I asked her to rely on me. I had by chance in my coffers a certain little flat piece of gold on which were engraved some celestial figures, to protect against sunstroke and take away a headache by placing it precisely on the suture of the skull; and, to keep it there, it was sewed to a ribbon intended to be tied under the chin: a kindred fancy to the one we are speaking of. Jacques Peletier had given me this singular present. I thought of making some use of it, and said to the count that he might incur the same fate as others, there being men present who would like to bring this about; but that he should boldly go to bed and I would do him a friendly turn and would not, if he needed it, spare a miracle which was in my power, provided that he promised me on his honor to keep it most faithfully secret; he was only to make a given signal to me, when they came to bring him the midnight meal, if things had gone badly with him. He had had his soul and his ears so battered that he did find himself fettered by the trouble of his imagination, and gave me his signal. I told him then that he should get up on the pretext of chasing us out, and playfully take the bathrobe that I had on (we were very close in height) and put it on him until he had carried out my prescription, which was this: when we had left, he should withdraw to pass water, say certain prayers three times and go through certain motions; each of these three times he should tie the ribbon I was putting in his hand around him and very carefully lay the medal that was attached to it on his kidneys, with the figure in such and such a position; this done, having tied this ribbon firmly so that it could neither come untied nor slip from its place, he should return to his business with complete assurance and not forget to spread my robe over his bed so that it should cover them both. These monkey tricks are the main part of the business, our mind being unable to get free of the idea that such strange means must come from some abstruse science. Their inanity gives them weight and reverence. All in all, it is certain that the characters on my medal proved themselves more venereal than solar,

6. Montaigne is probably referring to the count of Gurson, Louis de Foix, who married his relative, Diane de Foix de Candale, in 1579. Montaigne was very close to the family, and dedicated one of his best-known essays, "Of the Education of Children" (1:26), to Diane de Foix.

more useful for action than for prevention. It was a sudden and curious whim that led me to do such a thing, which was alien to my nature. I am an enemy of subtle and dissimulated acts and hate trickery in myself, not only for sport but also for someone's profit. If the action is not vicious, the road to it is.

Amasis, king of Egypt, married Laodice, a very beautiful Greek girl; and he, who showed himself a gay companion everywhere else, fell short when it came to enjoying her, and threatened to kill her, thinking it was some sort of sorcery. As is usual in matters of fancy, she referred him to religion; and having made his vows and promises to Venus, he found himself divinely restored from the first night after his oblations and sacrifices.[7]

Now women are wrong to greet us with those threatening, quarrelsome, and coy countenances, which put out our fires even as they light them. The daughter-in-law of Pythagoras used to say that the woman who goes to bed with a man should put off her modesty with her skirt and put it on again with her petticoat. The soul of the assailant, when troubled with many various alarms, is easily discouraged; and when imagination has once made a man suffer this shame—and it does so only at the first encounters, inasmuch as these are more boiling and violent, and also because in this first intimacy a man is much more afraid of failing—having begun badly, he gets from this accident a feverishness and vexation which lasts into subsequent occasions.

Married people, whose time is all their own, should neither press their undertaking nor even attempt it if they are not ready; it is better to fail unbecomingly to handsel the nuptial couch, which is full of agitation and feverishness, and wait for some other more private and less tense opportunity, than to fall into perpetual misery for having been stunned and made desperate by a first refusal. Before taking possession, the patient should try himself out and offer himself, lightly, by sallies at different times, without priding himself and obstinately insisting on convincing himself definitively. Those who know that their members are naturally obedient, let them take care only to counteract the tricks of their fancies.

People are right to notice the unruly liberty of this member, obtruding so importunately when we have no use for it, and failing so importunately when we have the most use for it, and struggling for mastery so imperiously with our will, refusing with so much pride and obstinacy our solicitations, both mental and manual.

If, however, in the matter of his rebellion being blamed and used as proof to condemn him, he had paid me to plead his cause, I should perhaps place our other members, his fellows, under suspicion of having framed this trumped-up charge out of sheer envy of the importance and pleasure of the use of him, and of having armed everyone against him by a conspiracy, malignantly charging him alone with their common fault.[8] For I ask you to think whether there is a single one of the parts of our body that does not often refuse its function to our will and exercise it against our will. They each have passions of their own which rouse them and put them to sleep without our leave. How many times do the forced movements of our face bear witness to the

7. The story is told in Herodotus's *History*, Book 2, Chapter 181. The vow to Aphrodite (Venus) was made, however, by poor Laodice herself, who promised to present a statue to Aphrodite's temple in Cyrene should her husband have intercourse with her. Montaigne not infrequently misremembers or misquotes his sources.

8. Although Montaigne is unique in coming to the defense of the penis, the "trial" of body parts has a long history in ancient literature. The fable of the belly and the limbs has its origin in Livy's Roman history, Book 2, in which Menenius Agrippa tells a Roman mob of the importance of the stomach in the commonwealth and is able to prevent them from violence. Shakespeare's *Coriolanus* opens with this scene as Menenius tells the "mutinous Citizens" of "a time when all the body's members / Rebell'd against the belly" (1.1.97–98).

thoughts that we were holding secret, and betray us to those present. The same cause that animates this member also animates, without our knowledge, the heart, the lungs, and the pulse; the sight of a pleasing object spreading in us imperceptibly the flame of a feverish emotion. Are there only these muscles and these veins that stand up and lie down without the consent, not only of our will, but even of our thoughts? We do not command our hair to stand on end or our skin to shiver with desire or fear. The hand often moves itself to where we do not send it. The tongue is paralyzed, and the voice congealed, at their own time. Even when, having nothing to put in to fry, we should like to forbid it, the appetite for eating and drinking does not fail to stir the parts that are subject to it, no more nor less than that other appetite; and it likewise abandons us inopportunely when it sees fit. The organs that serve to discharge the stomach have their own dilatations and compressions, beyond and against our plans, just like those that are destined to discharge the kidneys. To vindicate the omnipotence of our will, Saint Augustine alleges that he knew a man who commanded his behind to produce as many farts as he wanted, and his commentator Vives goes him one better with another example of his own time, of farts arranged to suit the tone of verses pronounced to their accompaniment; but all this does not really argue any pure obedience in this organ; for is there any that is ordinarily more indiscreet or tumultuous? Besides, I know one so turbulent and unruly, that for forty years it has kept its master farting with a constant and unremitting wind and compulsion, and is thus taking him to his death.[9]

But as for our will, on behalf of whose rights we set forth this complaint, how much more plausibly may we charge it with rebellion and sedition for its disorderliness and disobedience! Does it always will what we would will it to will? Doesn't it often will what we forbid it to will, and that to our evident disadvantage? Is it any more amenable than our other parts to the decisions of our reason?

To conclude, I would say this in defense of the honorable member whom I represent: May it please the court to take into consideration that in this matter, although my client's case is inseparably and indistinguishably linked with that of an accessory, nevertheless he alone has been brought to trial; and that the arguments and charges against him are such as cannot—in view of the status of the parties—be in any manner pertinent or relevant to the aforesaid accessory. Whereby is revealed his accusers' manifest animosity and disrespect for law. However that may be, Nature will meanwhile go her way, protesting that the lawyers and judges quarrel and pass sentence in vain. Indeed, she would have done no more than is right if she had endowed with some particular privilege this member, author of the sole immortal work of mortals. Wherefore to Socrates generation is a divine act; and love, a desire for immortality and itself an immortal daemon.

Perhaps it is by this effect of the imagination that one man here gets rid of the scrofula which his companion carries back to Spain.[1] This effect is the reason why, in such matters, it is customary to demand that the mind be prepared. Why do the doctors work on the credulity of their patient beforehand with so many false promises of a cure, if not so that the effect of the imagination may make up for the imposture of their decoction? They know that one of the masters of the trade left them this in writing, that there have been men for whom the mere sight of medicine did the job.

9. Augustine's *City of God* 14.24 refers to such a man in the context of a chapter entitled "That if men had remained innocent and obedient in Paradise, the generative organs should have been in subjection to the will as the other members are." Juan Luis Vives, a Spanish humanist, wrote commentaries and treatises on education. The "turbulent and unruly" organ is probably Montaigne's.
1. The king of France had the reputation of having the "royal touch" that cured scrofula, a disease of the lymph glands in the neck.

And this whole caprice has just come to hand apropos of the story that an apothe-cary, a servant of my late father, used to tell me, a simple man and Swiss, of a nation little addicted to vanity and lying. He had long known a merchant at Toulouse, sickly and subject to the stone, who often needed enemas, and ordered various kinds from his doctors according to the circumstances of his illness. Once they were brought to him, nothing was omitted of the accustomed formalities; often he tested them by hand to make sure they were not too hot. There he was, lying on his stomach, and all the motions were gone through—except that no injection was made. After this ceremony, the apothecary having retired and the patient being accommodated as if he had really taken the enema, he felt the same effect from it as those who do take them. And if the doctor did not find its operation sufficient, he would give him two or three more, of the same sort. My witness swears that when to save the expense (for he paid for them as if he had taken them) this sick man's wife sometimes tried to have just warm water used, the effect revealed the fraud; and having found that kind useless, they were obliged to return to the first method.

A woman, thinking she had swallowed a pin with her bread, was screaming in agony as though she had an unbearable pain in her throat, where she thought she felt it stuck; but because externally there was neither swelling nor alteration, a smart man, judging that it was only a fancy and notion derived from some bit of bread that had scratched her as it went down, made her vomit, and, on the sly, tossed a crooked pin into what she threw up. The woman, thinking she had thrown it up, felt herself sud-denly relieved of her pain. I know that one gentleman, having entertained a goodly company at his house, three or four days later boasted, as a sort of joke (for there was nothing in it), that he had made them eat cat in a pie; at which one lady in the party was so horrified that she fell into a violent stomach disorder and fever, and it was im-possible to save her. Even animals are subject like ourselves to the power of imagina-tion. Witness dogs, who let themselves die out of grief for the loss of their masters. We also see them yap and twitch in their dreams, and horses whinny and writhe.

But all this may be attributed to the narrow seam between the soul and body, through which the experience of the one is communicated to the other. Sometimes, however, one's imagination acts not only against one's own body, but against some-one else's. And just as a body passes on its sickness to its neighbor, as is seen in the plague, the pox, and soreness of the eyes, which are transmitted from one body to the other—

> By looking at sore eyes, eyes become sore:
> From body into body ills pass o'er
>
> OVID

—likewise the imagination, when vehemently stirred, launches darts that can injure an external object. The ancients maintained that certain women of Scythia, when ani-mated and enraged against anyone, would kill him with their mere glance. Tortoises and ostriches hatch their eggs just by looking at them, a sign that their sight has some ejaculative virtue. And as for sorcerers, they are said to have baleful and harmful eyes:

> Some evil eye bewitched my tender lambs.
> VIRGIL

To me, magicians are poor authorities. Nevertheless, we know by experience that women transmit marks of their fancies to the bodies of the children they carry in their womb; witness the one who gave birth to the Moor. And there was presented to

Charles, king of Bohemia and Emperor, a girl from near Pisa, all hairy and bristly, who her mother said had been thus conceived because of a picture of Saint John the Baptist hanging by her bed.[2]

With animals it is the same: witness Jacob's sheep,[3] and the partridges and hares that the snow turns white in the mountains. Recently at my house a cat was seen watching a bird on a treetop, and, after they had locked gazes for some time, the bird let itself fall as if dead between the cat's paws, either intoxicated by its own imagination or drawn by some attracting power of the cat. Those who like falconry have heard the story of the falconer who, setting his gaze obstinately upon a kite in the air, wagered that by the sole power of his gaze he would bring it down, and did. At least, so they say—for I refer the stories that I borrow to the conscience of those from whom I take them.[4] The reflections are my own, and depend on the proofs of reason, not of experience; everyone can add his own examples to them; and he who has none, let him not fail to believe that there are plenty, in view of the number and variety of occurrences. If I do not apply them well, let another apply them for me.

So in the study that I am making of our behavior and motives, fabulous testimonies, provided they are possible, serve like true ones. Whether they have happened or no, in Paris or Rome, to John or Peter, they exemplify, at all events, some human potentiality, and thus their telling imparts useful information to me. I see it and profit from it just as well in shadow as in substance. And of the different readings that histories often give, I take for my use the one that is most rare and memorable. There are authors whose end is to tell what has happened. Mine, if I could attain it, would be to talk about what can happen. The schools are justly permitted to suppose similitudes when they have none at hand. I do not do so, however, and in that respect I surpass all historical fidelity, being scrupulous to the point of superstition. In the examples that I bring in here of what I have heard, done, or said, I have forbidden myself to dare to alter even the slightest and most inconsequential circumstances. My conscience does not falsify one iota; my knowledge, I don't know.

In this connection, I sometimes fall to thinking whether it befits a theologian, a philosopher, and such people of exquisite and exact conscience and prudence, to write history. How can they stake their fidelity on the fidelity of an ordinary person? How be responsible for the thoughts of persons unknown and give their conjectures as coin of the realm? Of complicated actions that happen in their presence they would refuse to give testimony if placed under oath by a judge; and they know no man so intimately that they would undertake to answer fully for his intentions. I consider it less hazardous to write of things past than present, inasmuch as the writer has only to give an account of a borrowed truth.

Some urge me to write the events of my time, believing that I see them with a view less distorted by passion than another man's, and from closer, because of the access that fortune has given me to the heads of different parties.[5] What they forget is that even for all the glory of Sallust, I would not take the trouble, being a sworn enemy of obligation, assiduity, perseverance; and that there is nothing so contrary to my

---

2. There are many accounts in ancient and medieval literature of an infant who bears no resemblance to its parents but to an image or painting on which a mother had been looking while she was pregnant or when she conceived. Some of these involve a black child born to white parents.
3. In Genesis 30, Jacob has goats mate in front of boughs from which he has peeled back the bark. The lambs are born with patterns on their wool resembling those on the branches, either speckled or spotted.
4. The original essay, first published in 1580, ended here; Montaigne added the remainder of the essay after 1588.
5. One of the rare references Montaigne makes to his public activities as mayor and diplomat.

style as an extended narration. I cut myself off so often for lack of breath; I have neither composition nor development that is worth anything; I am more ignorant than a child of the phrases and terms that serve for the commonest things. And so I have chosen to say what I know how to say, accommodating the matter to my power. If I took a subject that would lead me along, I might not be able to measure up to it; and with my freedom being so very free, I might publish judgments which, even according to my own opinion and to reason, would be illegitimate and punishable. Plutarch might well say to us, concerning his accomplishments in this line, that the credit belongs to others if his examples are wholly and everywhere true; but that their being useful to posterity, and presented with a luster which lights our way to virtue, that is his work.[6] There is no danger—as there is in a medicinal drug—in an old story being this way or that.

Of Cannibals[1]

When King Pyrrhus passed over into Italy, after he had reconnoitered the formation of the army that the Romans were sending to meet him, he said: "I do not know what barbarians these are" (for so the Greeks called all foreign nations), "but the formation of this army that I see is not at all barbarous." The Greeks said as much of the army that Flamininus brought into their country, and so did Philip, seeing from a knoll the order and distribution of the Roman camp, in his kingdom, under Publius Sulpicius Galba.[2] Thus we should beware of clinging to vulgar opinions, and judge things by reason's way, not by popular say.

I had with me for a long time a man who had lived for ten or twelve years in that other world which has been discovered in our century, in the place where Villegaignon landed, and which he called Antarctic France.[3] This discovery of a boundless country seems worthy of consideration. I don't know if I can guarantee that some other such discovery will not be made in the future, so many personages greater than ourselves having been mistaken about this one. I am afraid we have eyes bigger than our stomachs, and more curiosity than capacity. We embrace everything, but we clasp only wind.

Plato brings in Solon, telling how he had learned from the priests of the city of Saïs in Egypt that in days of old, before the Flood, there was a great island named Atlantis, right at the mouth of the Strait of Gibraltar, which contained more land than Africa and Asia put together, and that the kings of that country, who not only possessed that island but had stretched out so far on the mainland that they held the breadth of Africa as far as Egypt, and the length of Europe as far as Tuscany, undertook to step over into Asia and subjugate all the nations that border on the Mediterranean, as far as the Black Sea; and for this purpose crossed the Spains, Gaul, Italy, as far as Greece, where the Athenians checked them; but that some time after, both the Athenians and themselves and their island were swallowed up by the Flood.[4]

---

6. The great Greek biographer Plutarch (1st century C.E.), cited often by Montaigne, wrote 50 *Lives* of prominent Greek and Roman figures such as Julius Caesar, Cicero, and Pericles.

1. Book 1, Chapter 31.

2. Plutarch recounts the first two stories, of Pyrrhus's and the Greeks' comments on the Romans. The account of Philip, King of Macedon—another Greek unimpressed by a Roman army—is found in Livy.

3. Brazil, where Nicolas Durand de Villegaignon led an

expedition in 1555–156, with the hope of gaining some military clout. Among those who traveled with him were a group of Calvinist sympathizers, including the Calvinist Jean de Léry (see page 429), as well as a Franciscan friar named André Thevet. Both Thevet and Léry published extensive writings of their travels, from which Montaigne borrowed freely.

4. The legendary lost island of Atlantis is mentioned by Plato in the *Timaeus*.

It is quite likely that that extreme devastation of waters made amazing changes in the habitations of the earth, as people maintain that the sea cut off Sicily from Italy—

> 'Tis said an earthquake once asunder tore
> These lands with dreadful havoc, which before
> Formed but one land, one coast
>
> VIRGIL

—Cyprus from Syria, the island of Euboea from the mainland of Boeotia; and elsewhere joined lands that were divided, filling the channels between them with sand and mud:

> A sterile marsh, long fit for rowing, now
> Feeds neighbor towns, and feels the heavy plow.
>
> HORACE

But there is no great likelihood that that island was the new world which we have just discovered; for it almost touched Spain, and it would be an incredible result of a flood to have forced it away as far as it is, more than twelve hundred leagues; besides, the travels of the moderns have already almost revealed that it is not an island, but a mainland connected with the East Indies on one side, and elsewhere with the lands under the two poles; or, if it is separated from them, it is by so narrow a strait and interval that it docs not deserve to be called an island on that account.

It seems that there are movements, some natural, others feverish, in these great bodies, just as in our own. When I consider the inroads that my river, the Dordogne, is making in my lifetime into the right bank in its descent, and that in twenty years it has gained so much ground and stolen away the foundations of several buildings, I clearly see that this is an extraordinary disturbance; for if it had always gone at this rate, or was to do so in the future, the face of the world would be turned topsy-turvy. But rivers are subject to changes: now they overflow in one direction, now in another, now they keep to their course. I am not speaking of the sudden inundations whose causes are manifest. In Médoc, along the seashore, my brother, the sieur d'Arsac,[5] can see an estate of his buried under the sands that the sea spews forth; the tops of some buildings are still visible; his farms and domains have changed into very thin pasturage. The inhabitants say that for some time the sea has been pushing toward them so hard that they have lost four leagues of land. These sands are its harbingers; and we see great dunes of moving sand that march half a league ahead of it and keep conquering land.

The other testimony of antiquity with which some would connect this discovery is in Aristotle, at least if that little book Of Unheard-of Wonders is by him. He there relates that certain Carthaginians, after setting out upon the Atlantic Ocean from the Strait of Gibraltar and sailing a long time, at last discovered a great fertile island, all clothed in woods and watered by great deep rivers, far remote from any mainland; and that they, and others since, attracted by the goodness and fertility of the soil, went there with their wives and children, and began to settle there. The lords of Carthage, seeing that their country was gradually becoming depopulated, expressly forbade anyone to go there any more, on pain of death, and drove out these new inhabitants, fearing, it is said, that in course of time they might come to multiply so greatly as to

---

5. Montaigne had five brothers; the "sieur of Arsac" was younger than he.

supplant their former masters and ruin their state. This story of Aristotle does not fit our new lands any better than the other.

This man I had was a simple, crude fellow—a character fit to bear true witness; for clever people observe more things and more curiously, but they interpret them; and to lend weight and conviction to their interpretation, they cannot help altering history a little. They never show you things as they are, but bend and disguise them according to the way they have seen them; and to give credence to their judgment and attract you to it, they are prone to add something to their matter, to stretch it out and amplify it. We need a man either very honest, or so simple that he has not the stuff to build up false inventions and give them plausibility; and wedded to no theory. Such was my man; and besides this, he at various times brought sailors and merchants, whom he had known on that trip, to see me. So I content myself with his information, without inquiring what the cosmographers say about it.

We ought to have topographers who would give us an exact account of the places where they have been. But because they have over us the advantage of having seen Palestine, they want to enjoy the privilege of telling us news about all the rest of the world. I would like everyone to write what he knows, and as much as he knows, not only in this, but in all other subjects; for a man may have some special knowledge and experience of the nature of a river or a fountain, who in other matters knows only what everybody knows. However, to circulate this little scrap of knowledge, he will undertake to write the whole of physics. From this vice spring many great abuses.

Now, to return to my subject, I think there is nothing barbarous and savage in that nation, from what I have been told, except that each man calls barbarism whatever is not his own practice; for indeed it seems we have no other test of truth and reason than the example and pattern of the opinions and customs of the country we live in. *There is always the perfect religion, the perfect government, the perfect and accomplished manners in all things.* Those people are wild, just as we call wild the fruits that Nature has produced by herself and in her normal course; whereas really it is those that we have changed artificially and led astray from the common order, that we should rather call wild. The former retain alive and vigorous their genuine, their most useful and natural, virtues and properties, which we have debased in the latter in adapting them to gratify our corrupted taste. And yet for all that, the savor and delicacy of some uncultivated fruits of those countries is quite as excellent, even to our taste, as that of our own. It is not reasonable that art should win the place of honor over our great and powerful mother Nature. We have so overloaded the beauty and richness of her works by our inventions that we have quite smothered her. Yet wherever her purity shines forth, she wonderfully puts to shame our vain and frivolous attempts:

> Ivy comes readier without our care;
> In lonely caves the arbutus grows more fair;
> No art with artless bird song can compare.
>   PROPERTIUS

All our efforts cannot even succeed in reproducing the nest of the tiniest little bird, its contexture, its beauty and convenience; or even the web of the puny spider. All things, says Plato, are produced by nature, by fortune, or by art; the greatest and most beautiful by one or the other of the first two, the least and most imperfect by the last.

These nations, then, seem to me barbarous in this sense, that they have been fashioned very little by the human mind, and are still very close to their original naturalness. The laws of nature still rule them, very little corrupted by ours; and they are in such a state of purity that I am sometimes vexed that they were unknown earlier, in the days when there were men able to judge them better than we. I am sorry that Lycurgus and Plato did not know of them;[6] for it seems to me that what we actually see in these nations surpasses not only all the pictures in which poets have idealized the golden age and all their inventions in imagining a happy state of man, but also the conceptions and the very desire of philosophy. They could not imagine a naturalness so pure and simple as we see by experience; nor could they believe that our society could be maintained with so little artifice and human solder. This is a nation, I should say to Plato, in which there is no sort of traffic, no knowledge of letters, no science of numbers, no name for a magistrate or for political superiority, no custom of servitude, no riches or poverty, no contracts, no successions, no partitions, no occupations but leisure ones, no care for any but common kinship, no clothes, no agriculture, no metal, no use of wine or wheat. The very words that signify lying, treachery, dissimulation, avarice, envy, belittling, pardon —unheard of.[7] How far from this perfection would he find the republic that he imagined: *Men fresh sprung from the gods* [Seneca].

> These manners nature first ordained.
> VIRGIL

For the rest, they live in a country with a very pleasant and temperate climate, so that according to my witnesses it is rare to see a sick man there; and they have assured me that they never saw one palsied, bleary-eyed, toothless, or bent with age. They are settled along the sea and shut in on the land side by great high mountains, with a stretch about a hundred leagues wide in between. They have a great abundance of fish and flesh which bear no resemblance to ours, and they eat them with no other artifice than cooking. The first man who rode a horse there, though he had had dealings with them on several other trips, so horrified them in this posture that they shot him dead with arrows before they could recognize him.

Their buildings are very long, with a capacity of two or three hundred souls; they are covered with the bark of great trees, the strips reaching to the ground at one end and supporting and leaning on one another at the top, in the manner of some of our barns, whose covering hangs down to the ground and acts as a side. They have wood so hard that they cut with it and make of it their swords and grills to cook their food. Their beds are of a cotton weave, hung from the roof like those in our ships, each man having his own; for the wives sleep apart from their husbands.

They get up with the sun, and eat immediately upon rising, to last them through the day; for they take no other meal than that one. Like some other Eastern peoples, of whom Suidas[9] tells us, who drank apart from meals, they do not drink then; but they drink several times a day, and to capacity. Their drink is made of some root, and is of the color of our claret wines. They drink it only lukewarm. This beverage keeps only two or three days; it has a slightly sharp taste, is not at all heady, is good for the stomach, and has a laxative effect upon those who are not used to it; it is a very pleasant drink for anyone who is accustomed to it. In place of bread they use a certain white substance like preserved coriander. I have tried it; it tastes sweet and a little flat.

---

6. Lycurgus was a legendary Spartan legislator who radically reformed his city's laws. Among Plato's many treatises was the *Republic,* where he talks about the ideal society.
7. Gonzalo's irritating speech to Sebastian in *The Tem-*

pest (see page 613) borrows from these two lines as translated by Montaigne's earliest English translator, John Florio.
8. The Suidas was the name given to a great Greek encyclopedia, compiled around the 10th century C.E.

The whole day is spent in dancing. The younger men go to hunt animals with bows. Some of the women busy themselves meanwhile with warming their drink, which is their chief duty. Some one of the old men, in the morning before they begin to eat, preaches to the whole barnful in common, walking from one end to the other, and repeating one single sentence several times until he has completed the circuit (for the buildings are fully a hundred paces long). He recommends to them only two things: valor against the enemy and love for their wives. And they never fail to point out this obligation, as their refrain, that it is their wives who keep their drink warm and seasoned.

There may be seen in several places, including my own house, specimens of their beds, of their ropes, of their wooden swords and the bracelets with which they cover their wrists in combats, and of the big canes, open at one end, by whose sound they keep time in their dances. They are close shaven all over, and shave themselves much more cleanly than we, with nothing but a wooden or stone razor. They believe that souls are immortal, and that those who have deserved well of the gods are lodged in that part of heaven where the sun rises, and the damned in the west.

They have some sort of priests and prophets, but they rarely appear before the people, having their home in the mountains. On their arrival there is a great feast and solemn assembly of several villages—each barn, as I have described it, makes up a village, and they are about one French league from each other. The prophet speaks to them in public, exhorting them to virtue and their duty; but their whole ethical science contains only these two articles: resoluteness in war and affection for their wives. He prophesies to them things to come and the results they are to expect from their under-takings, and urges them to war or holds them back from it; but this is on the condition that when he fails to prophesy correctly, and if things turn out otherwise than he has predicted, he is cut into a thousand pieces if they catch him, and condemned as a false prophet. For this reason, the prophet who has once been mistaken is never seen again.

Divination is a gift of God; that is why its abuse should be punished as imposture. Among the Scythians, when the soothsayers failed to hit the mark, they were laid, chained hand and foot, on carts full of heather and drawn by oxen, on which they were burned.[9] Those who handle matters subject to the control of human capacity are excusable if they do the best they can. But these others, who come and trick us with assurances of an extraordinary faculty that is beyond our ken, should they not be pun-ished for not making good their promise, and for the temerity of their imposture?

They have their wars with the nations beyond the mountains, further inland, to which they go quite naked, with no other arms than bows or wooden swords ending in a sharp point, in the manner of the tongues of our boar spears. It is astonishing what firmness they show in their combats, which never end but in slaughter and bloodshed; for as to routs and terror, they know nothing of either.

Each man brings back as his trophy the head of the enemy he has killed, and sets it up at the entrance to his dwelling. After they have treated their prisoners well for a long time with all the hospitality they can think of, each man who has a prisoner calls a great assembly of his acquaintances. He ties a rope to one of the prisoner's arms, by the end of which he holds him, a few steps away, for fear of being hurt, and gives his dearest friend the other arm to hold in the same way; and these two, in the presence of the whole assembly, kill him with their swords. This done, they roast him and eat him

9. The story is from Herodotus; the term "Scythians" was used to describe the peoples from the north, who supposedly practiced a number of barbaric customs such as scalping and flaying their enemy.

in common and send some pieces to their absent friends. This is not, as people think, for nourishment, as of old the Scythians used to do; it is to betoken an extreme revenge. And the proof of this came when they saw the Portuguese, who had joined forces with their adversaries, inflict a different kind of death on them when they took them prisoner, which was to bury them up to the waist, shoot the rest of their body full of arrows, and afterward hang them.[1] They thought that these people from the other world, being men who had sown the knowledge of many vices among their neighbors and were much greater masters than themselves in every sort of wickedness, did not adopt this sort of vengeance without some reason, and that it must be more painful than their own; so they began to give up their old method and to follow this one.

I am not sorry that we notice the barbarous horror of such acts, but I am heartily sorry that, judging their faults rightly, we should be so blind to our own. I think there is more barbarity in eating a man alive than in eating him dead; and in tearing by tortures and the rack a body still full of feeling, in roasting a man bit by bit, in having him bitten and mangled by dogs and swine (as we have not only read but seen within fresh memory, not among ancient enemies, but among neighbors and fellow citizens, and what is worse, on the pretext of piety and religion),[2] than in roasting and eating him after he is dead. Indeed, Chrysippus and Zeno, heads of the Stoic sect, thought there was nothing wrong in using our carcasses for any purpose in case of need, and getting nourishment from them; just as our ancestors, when besieged by Caesar in the city of Alésia, resolved to relieve their famine by eating old men, women, and other people useless for fighting.[3]

> The Gascons once, 'tis said, their life renewed
> By eating of such food.
>
> JUVENAL

And physicians do not fear to use human flesh in all sorts of ways for our health, applying it either inwardly or outwardly. But there never was any opinion so disordered as to excuse treachery, disloyalty, tyranny, and cruelty, which are our ordinary vices.

So we may well call these people barbarians, in respect to the rules of reason, but not in respect to ourselves, who surpass them in every kind of barbarity.

Their warfare is wholly noble and generous, and as excusable and beautiful as this human disease can be; its only basis among them is their rivalry in valor. They are not fighting for the conquest of new lands, for they still enjoy that natural abundance that provides them without toil and trouble with all necessary things in such profusion that they have no wish to enlarge their boundaries. They are still in that happy state of desiring only as much as their natural needs demand; anything beyond that is superfluous to them.[4]

They generally call those of the same age, brothers; those who are younger, children; and the old men are fathers to all the others. These leave to their heirs in common the full possession of their property, without division or any other title at all than just the one that Nature gives to her creatures in bringing them into the world.

---

1. The Portuguese had settled in Brazil long before the French.
2. A reference to the wars of religion that had divided France since the early 1570s.
3. "Our ancestors" are the Galls, referred to by Caesar himself in his *Gallic Wars*. The quote by Juvenal that follows also refers to the Gascons or Galls.
4. Much of this description of the native Brazilians (the Tupinamba Indians) is drawn from Jean de Léry's account; see the Resonance on page 429.

If their neighbors cross the mountains to attack them and win a victory, the gain of the victor is glory, and the advantage of having proved the master in valor and virtue; for apart from this they have no use for the goods of the vanquished, and they return to their own country, where they lack neither anything necessary nor that great thing, the knowledge of how to enjoy their condition happily and be content with it. These men of ours do the same in their turn. They demand of their prisoners no other ransom than that they confess and acknowledge their defeat. But there is not one in a whole century who does not choose to die rather than to relax a single bit, by word or look, from the grandeur of an invincible courage; not one who would not rather be killed and eaten than so much as ask not to be. They treat them very freely, so that life may be all the dearer to them, and usually entertain them with threats of their coming death, of the torments they will have to suffer, the preparations that are being made for that purpose, the cutting up of their limbs, and the feast that will be made at their expense. All this is done for the sole purpose of extorting from their lips some weak or base word, or making them want to flee, so as to gain the advantage of having terrified them and broken down their firmness. For indeed, if you take it the right way, it is in this point alone that true victory lies:

> It is no victory
> Unless the vanquished foe admits your mastery.
>   CLAUDIAN

The Hungarians, very bellicose fighters, did not in olden times pursue their advantage beyond putting the enemy at their mercy. For having wrung a confession from him to this effect, they let him go unharmed and unransomed, except, at most, for exacting his promise never again to take up arms against them.

We win enough advantages over our enemies that are borrowed advantages, not really our own. It is the quality of a porter, not of valor, to have sturdier arms and legs; agility is a dead and corporeal quality; it is a stroke of luck to make our enemy stumble, or dazzle his eyes by the sunlight; it is a trick of art and technique, which may be found in a worthless coward, to be an able fencer. The worth and value of a man is in his heart and his will; there lies his real honor. Valor is the strength, not of legs and arms, but of heart and soul; it consists not in the worth of our horse or our weapons, but in our own. He who falls obstinate in his courage, *if he has fallen, he fights on his knees* [Seneca]. He who relaxes none of his assurance, no matter how great the danger of imminent death; who, giving up his soul, still looks firmly and scornfully at his enemy—he is beaten not by us, but by fortune; he is killed, not conquered.

The most valiant are sometimes the most unfortunate. Thus there are triumphant defeats that rival victories. Nor did those four sister victories, the fairest that the sun ever set eyes on—Salamis, Plataea, Mycale, and Sicily—ever dare match all their combined glory against the glory of the annihilation of King Leonidas and his men at the pass of Thermopylae.[5]

Who ever hastened with more glorious and ambitious desire to win a battle than Captain Ischolas to lose one? Who ever secured his safety more ingeniously and painstakingly than he did his destruction? He was charged to defend a certain pass in

---

5. The first three victories were triumphs by the Greeks over the Persians in 479–480 B.C.E.; simultaneously the Greeks halted Carthaginian expansion in Sicily with a stunning victory at Himera. With a slender army, Leonidas held back the Persians for several days at the pass of Thermopylae, inflicting heavy casualities; when a native showed the Persians a mountain path that would enable them to attack the Greeks from the rear, Leonidas was killed and his army defeated.

the Peloponnesus against the Arcadians. Finding himself wholly incapable of doing this, in view of the nature of the place and the inequality of the forces, he made up his mind that all who confronted the enemy would necessarily have to remain on the field. On the other hand, deeming it unworthy both of his own virtue and magnanimity and of the Lacedaemonian name to fail in his charge, he took a middle course between these two extremes, in this way. The youngest and fittest of his band he preserved for the defense and service of their country, and sent them home; and with those whose loss was less important, he determined to hold this pass, and by their death to make the enemy buy their entry as dearly as he could. And so it turned out. For he was presently surrounded on all sides by the Arcadians, and after slaughtering a large number of them, he and his men were all put to the sword. Is there a trophy dedicated to victors that would not be more due to these vanquished? The role of true victory is in fighting, not in coming off safely; and the honor of valor consists in combating, not in beating.

To return to our story. These prisoners are so far from giving in, in spite of all that is done to them, that on the contrary, during the two or three months that they are kept, they wear a gay expression; they urge their captors to hurry and put them to the test; they defy them, insult them, reproach them with their cowardice and the number of battles they have lost to the prisoners' own people.

I have a song composed by a prisoner which contains this challenge, that they should all come boldly and gather to dine off him, for they will be eating at the same time their own fathers and grandfathers, who have served to feed and nourish his body. "These muscles," he says, "this flesh and these veins are your own, poor fools that you are. You do not recognize that the substance of your ancestors' limbs is still contained in them. Savor them well; you will find in them the taste of your own flesh." An idea that certainly does not smack of barbarity. Those that paint these people dying, and who show the execution, portray the prisoner spitting in the face of his slayers and scowling at them. Indeed, to the last gasp they never stop braving and defying their enemies by word and look. Truly here are real savages by our standards; for either they must be thoroughly so, or we must be; there is an amazing distance between their character and ours.

The men there have several wives, and the higher their reputation for valor the more wives they have. It is a remarkably beautiful thing about their marriages that the same jealousy our wives have to keep us from the affection and kindness of other women, theirs have to win this for them. Being more concerned for their husbands' honor than for anything else, they strive and scheme to have as many companions as they can, since that is a sign of their husbands' valor.

Our wives will cry "Miracle!" but it is no miracle. It is a properly matrimonial virtue, but one of the highest order. In the Bible, Leah, Rachel, Sarah, and Jacob's wives gave their beautiful handmaids to their husbands; and Livia seconded the appetites of Augustus, to her own disadvantage; and Stratonice, the wife of King Deiotarus, not only lent her husband for his use a very beautiful young chambermaid in her service, but carefully brought up her children, and backed them up to succeed to their father's estates.[6]

And lest it be thought that all this is done through a simple and servile bondage to usage and through the pressure of the authority of their ancient customs, without reasoning or judgment, and because their minds are so stupid that they cannot take any

6. Leah and Rachel are Jacob's wives; Sarah is the wife of Abraham, who sent her Egyptian maid Hagar to her husband that he might have an heir. Livia bore Augustus no children; King Deiotarus and Stratonice, allies of Rome during the first century B.C.E., are written of in Plutarch's *Bravery of Women*.

other course, I must cite some examples of their capacity. Besides the warlike song I have just quoted, I have another, a love song, which begins in this vein: "Adder, stay; stay, adder, that from the pattern of your coloring my sister may draw the fashion and the workmanship of a rich girdle that I may give to my love; so may your beauty and your pattern be forever preferred to all other serpents." This first couplet is the refrain of the song. Now I am familiar enough with poetry to be a judge of this: not only is there nothing barbarous in this fancy, but it is altogether Anacreontic.[7] Their language, moreover, is a soft language, with an agreeable sound, somewhat like Greek in its endings.

Three of these men, ignorant of the price they will pay some day, in loss of repose and happiness, for gaining knowledge of the corruptions of this side of the ocean; ignorant also of the fact that of this intercourse will come their ruin (which I suppose is already well advanced: poor wretches, to let themselves be tricked by the desire for new things, and to have left the serenity of their own sky to come and see ours!)—three of these men were at Rouen, at the time the late King Charles IX was there.[8] The king talked to them for a long time; they were shown our ways, our splendor, the aspect of a fine city. After that, someone asked their opinion, and wanted to know what they had found most amazing. They mentioned three things, of which I have forgotten the third, and I am very sorry for it; but I still remember two of them. They said that in the first place they thought it very strange that so many grown men, bearded, strong, and armed, who were around the king (it is likely that they were talking about the Swiss of his guard) should submit to obey a child, and that one of them was not chosen to command instead. Second (they have a way in their language of speaking of men as halves of one another), they had noticed that there were among us men full and gorged with all sorts of good things, and that their other halves were beggars at their doors, emaciated with hunger and poverty; and they thought it strange that these needy halves could endure such an injustice, and did not take the others by the throat, or set fire to their houses.

I had a very long talk with one of them; but I had an interpreter who followed my meaning so badly, and who was so hindered by his stupidity in taking in my ideas, that I could get hardly any satisfaction from the man. When I asked him what profit he gained from his superior position among his people (for he was a captain, and our sailors called him king), he told me that it was to march foremost in war. How many men followed him? He pointed to a piece of ground, to signify as many as such a space could hold; it might have been four or five thousand men. Did all his authority expire with the war? He said that this much remained, that when he visited the villages dependent on him, they made paths for him through the underbrush by which he might pass quite comfortably.

All this is not too bad—but what's the use? They don't wear breeches.

---

7. Anacreon was a 6th century B.C.E. Greek lyric poet.
8. The occasion dates to 1562. Charles IX, who succeeded to the throne in 1560, would have been only 12 at the time, which explains the men's comment that they thought it odd "that so many grown men . . . should submit to obey a child."

⚮

RESONANCE

Jean de Léry: from *History of a Voyage to the Land of Brazil, Otherwise Called America*[1]

WHAT ONE MIGHT CALL RELIGION AMONG THE SAVAGE AMERICANS: OF THE ERRORS IN
WHICH CERTAIN CHARLATANS CALLED *CARAÏBES*[2] HOLD THEM IN THRALL; AND OF THE
GREAT IGNORANCE OF GOD IN WHICH THEY ARE PLUNGED

Although the adage of Cicero is held by all as an indubitable maxim—that there is no
people so brutish, nor any nation so barbarous and savage, as to have no feeling that
there is a divinity[3]—nonetheless when I consider closely our Tupinamba of America,
I find myself somewhat at a loss in applying it to them. Not only are they utterly ignorant of the sole and true God; what is more, in contrast to the custom of all the ancient
pagans, who had many gods (as do the idolaters of today, even the Indians of Peru—a
land adjacent to theirs and about five hundred leagues beyond it—who sacrifice to the
sun and moon),[4] they neither confess nor worship any gods, either of heaven or of
earth. Consequently, having no rites nor any designated place of assembly for holding
any ordinary service, they do not pray by any religious form to anything whatsoever,
either in public or in private. Likewise, being ignorant of the creation of the world,
they do not distinguish the days by names, nor do they give one day preference over
another, any more than they count weeks, months or years; they only number and retain time by moons.

They know nothing of writing, either sacred or secular; indeed, they have no kind
of characters that signify anything at all. When I was first in their country, in order to
learn their language I wrote a number of sentences which I then read aloud to them.
Thinking that this was some kind of witchcraft, they said to each other, "Is it not a
marvel that this fellow, who yesterday could not have said a single word in our language, can now be understood by us, by virtue of that paper that he is holding and
which makes him speak thus?"

And this is the same idea that the savages of Hispaniola had of the Spaniards who
were first there: for he who wrote its history[5] said that the Indians, knowing that the
Spaniards understood each other without seeing or speaking to each other but only
by sending letters from place to place, believed either that they had the spirit of
prophecy, or that the missives spoke. The savages, he said, fearing that they would be

---

1. Translated by Janet Whatley. In 1556, a crew of
Calvinists torn by mutiny arrived dissheveled on the coast
of Brazil. Like the Pilgrims half a century later, these
Protestants were fleeing persecution in their native land
and hoped to find a beacon in the wild; unlike the Pilgrims, they were unable to create a cohesive community,
and the survivors would eventually return to Europe. In
the meantime, however, they had a series of encounters
with the Tupi: indigenous groups of people who lived in
southern Brazil, engaged in cannibalistic sacrifices, and
inscribed their bodies with remarkable tatoos.

One of the French settlers, Jean de Léry, recorded his
observations of the Tupi with a mixture of revulsion and
fascination. When it was published in 1578, his *History of
a Voyage to the Land of Brazil* would find an avid reader
in Montaigne and others intrigued by the foreignness of

New World civilizations. He also revealed himself a
fledgling grammarian: one of the last chapters is a language lesson, as the Frenchman struggles with a patient
informant to learn how to say "I have a fever" and
"Everything that we have is at our Prince's command."
After returning to Europe, Léry went on to Geneva to become a Calvinist minister; he died in Switzerland in 1613.

2. A shaman or someone who claimed to have prophetic
powers; a charlatan is a trickster.

3. From Cicero's *De Legibus*; the sentiment is also found
in Jean Calvin's *Institutes of the Christian Religion*, published in 1536.

4. The Incas were the dominant peoples in Peru.

5. A reference to the Spanish writer Francisco López de
Gómara, author of *General History of the Indies*.

Mourning Tupi, from Jean de Léry, *History of a Voyage to the Land of Brazil, Otherwise Called America* (1580). Léry's adventure-filled voyage to the coast of Brazil in 1556 constituted one of the first Protestant missions to the Americas, but it also created the occasion for Léry's astute ethnography of the Tupinamba Indians. In the chapter entitled "How the Savages Treat Each Other in their Illnesses Together with their Burials and Funeral Ceremonies and the Great Lamentations They Make Over Their Dead," the author writes of the "drinking, singing, and dancing" that take place around the hammock of an invalid; but "if it happens that he should die, and especially if he is a respected head of a household, all the singing is suddenly turned to tears, and they lament so loudly that if we were in a village where someone had recently died, either we didn't try to find a bed there, or we didn't expect to sleep that night. Above all, it is amazing to hear the cries of the women, as loud as the howling of dogs and wolves, wailing these lamentations and responses"—not unlike, Léry is quick to note, the laments of some Frenchwomen who in the midst of their weeping will remember the deceased with phrases such as *Yere, yher, O le bet renegadou, ô le bet jougadou qu'here* ("'Alas, alas, what a grand swearer, what a fine gambler he was!'").

caught red-handed, were by this means so firmly held to their duty that they no longer dared to lie to the Spaniards or steal from them.

Here is a fine subject for anyone who would like to enlarge upon it: both to praise and to exalt the art of writing, and to show how the nations that inhabit these three parts of the world—Europe, Asia, and Africa—have reason to praise God more than do the savages of that fourth part, called "America." For while they can communicate nothing except by the spoken word, we, on the other hand, have this advantage, that without budging from our place, by means of writing and the letters that we send, we can declare our secrets to whomever we choose, even to the ends of the earth. So even aside from the learning that we acquire from books, of which the savages seem likewise completely destitute, this invention of writing, which we possess and of which they are just as utterly deprived, must be ranked among the singular gifts which men over here have received from God.

To return to our Tupinamba. In our conversations with them, when it seemed the right moment, we would say to them that we believed in a sole and sovereign God, Creator of the World, who, as He made heaven and earth with all the things contained therein, also now governs and disposes of the whole as it pleases Him to do. Hearing us hold forth on this subject, they would look at each other, saying "Teh!"—their customary interjection of astonishment—and be struck with amazement. As I will recount at more length, when they hear thunder, which they call *Toupan*, they are much afraid. Adapting ourselves to their crudeness, we would seize the occasion to say to them that this was the very God of whom we were speaking, who to show his grandeur and power made heavens and earth tremble; their resolution and response was that since he frightened them in that way, he was good for nothing.

And that, sad to say, is where these poor people are now. "What!" someone will now say, "can it be that, like brute beasts, these Americans live without any religion at all?" Indeed they do, or with almost none; I think that there is no nation on earth that is further from it. Still, let me begin by declaring what light I perceived that they do, nevertheless, possess in the midst of the dense shadows of ignorance where they lie in bondage: in the first place, not only do they believe in the immortality of souls, but they also firmly maintain that after the death of bodies, the souls of those who have lived virtuously (that is, according to them, those who have properly avenged themselves and have eaten many of their enemies)[6] go off behind the high mountains where they dance in beautiful gardens with the souls of their forebears (these are the Elysian Fields of the poets);[7] while on the contrary, the souls of the effeminate and worthless, who have neglected the defense of their fatherland, go with Aygnan (for so they call the devil in their language), by whom, they say, these unworthy ones are incessantly tormented.

And here it must be noted that these poor people are so afflicted throughout their lives with this evil spirit (whom they also call *Kaagerre*)[8] that when the torment comes upon them, they cry out suddenly as if in a fit of madness—as I have seen them do several times even while they were speaking to us, saying, "Alas, defend us from Aygnan, who is beating us." In fact, they would say that they actually saw him,

---

6. Léry had devoted the preceding chapter, "The Ceremonies for Killing and Eating Prisoners," to the Tupi practice of cannibalism. While he spares us no detail in telling us "the way the American savages cook the flesh of their prisoners of war," like Montaigne, he is also anxious to insist on the cannibalism of the French, who have engaged in "execrable butchery" in the name of religious difference.
7. Gardens of the blessed dead.
8. "Demon of the bush."

sometimes in the guise of a beast or bird or in some other strange form. They marveled to see that we were not assaulted by him. When we told them that such exemption came from the God of whom we spoke so often and who, being incomparably stronger than Aygnan, kept him from molesting or harming us, it sometimes happened that, feeling hard-pressed, they would promise to believe in Him as we did. But, as the proverb says, "When danger is past we mock the saint," so as soon as they were delivered, they no longer remembered their promises. Nevertheless, to show that what they endure is no child's play: I have often seen them so apprehensive of this hellish fury that when they remembered what they had suffered in the past, they would strike their thighs with their hands, the sweat of anguish beading their brow, and lament to me or to another of our company, saying, "*Mair Atouassap, acequeiey Aygnan Atoupavé,*" that is, "Frenchman, my friend—my perfect ally—, I fear the devil (or the evil spirit) more than any other thing." On the other hand, if the one they addressed said to them, "*Nacequeiey Aygnan,*" that is, "I do not fear him," then, bewailing their state, they would answer, "Alas, how happy we would be if we were saved as you are!" "You would have to believe and trust, as we do, in Him who is stronger and mightier," we would reply. But although at times, as they saw the evil approaching or already present, they declared they would do so, afterwards it all vanished from their brain.

Before going on, I will add something more to the remark I have made, that our American Brazilians consider the soul immortal. The historian of the West Indies said that the savages of Cuzco, the principal city of Peru, and those of that region, likewise confess the immortality of the soul.[9] What is more (despite the maxim, which has always been commonly held by theologians, that all the philosophers, pagans, and other Gentiles and barbarians had been ignorant of and denied the resurrection of the flesh), they even believe in the resurrection of the body. And here is the example he offers: The Indians, upon seeing that the Spaniards who were opening the sepulchres to get at the gold and riches were scattering the bones of the dead all about, entreated them not to disperse them that way, lest it prevent them from being brought back to life; for they (the savages of that country) believe in the resurrection of the body and the immortality of the soul. * * *

Now since I promised earlier, when I spoke of the dancing at their drinking bouts and *caouinages,*[1] that I would also tell of their other way of dancing, the more fully to represent them, I will describe the solemn poses and gestures that they used here. They stood close to each other, without holding hands or stirring from their place, but arranged in a circle, bending forward, keeping their bodies slightly stiff, moving only the right leg and foot, with the right hand placed on the buttocks, and the left hand and arm hanging: in that posture they sang and danced.

Because there were so many of them, there were three circles, and in the middle of each circle there were three or four of these *caraïbes,* richly decked in robes, headdresses, and bracelets made of beautiful natural feathers of various colors, holding in each hand a *maraca* or rattle made of a fruit bigger than an ostrich-egg (of which I have spoken elsewhere). So that (as they said) the spirit might thereafter speak through these rattles, to dedicate them to this use they made them sound incessantly. And you could find no better comparison than to the bell-ringers that accompany

9. Gómara, *History,* Book 4, Chapter 124.
1. "Caouin" was described earlier as a cloudy, fermented liquid like beer that comes from the roots of native plants.

Léry adds a French word ending to denote a drinking feast; elsewhere he will make of it an infinitive (*caouiner*).

those impostors who, exploiting the credulity of our simple folk over here, carry from place to place the reliquaries of Saint Anthony or Saint Bernard,[2] and other such instruments of idolatry. In addition to this description, I have tried to illustrate all this for you by the accompanying figure of a dancer and a *maraca*-player.

Moreover, these *caraïbes*, advancing and leaping forward, then drawing back, did not always stay in one place as the others did. I noticed that they would frequently take a wooden cane four or five feet long, at the end of which was burning some of the dried herb *petun* (which I have mentioned elsewhere); turning and blowing the smoke in all directions on the other savages, they would say to them, "So that you may overcome your enemies, receive all of you the spirit of strength." And thus these master *caraïbes* did several times.

These ceremonies went on for nearly two hours, with the five or six hundred men dancing and singing incessantly; such was their melody that—although they do not know what music is—those who have not heard them would never believe that they could make such harmony. At the beginning of this witches' sabbath,[3] when I was in the women's house, I had been somewhat afraid; now I received in recompense such joy, hearing the measured harmonies of such a multitude, and especially in the cadence and refrain of the song, when at every verse all of them would let their voices trail, saying *Heu, heuaure, heura, heuraure, heura, heura, oueh*—I stood there transported with delight. Whenever I remember it, my heart trembles, and it seems their voices are still in my ears. When they decided to finish, each of them struck his right foot against the earth more vehemently than before, and spat in front of him; then all of them with one voice uttered hoarsely two or three times the words *He, hua, hua, hua*, and then ceased.

Since I did not understand their language perfectly at that time, they had said several things that I had not been able to comprehend, and I asked the interpreter to explain them to me. He told me that at the beginning of the songs they had uttered long laments for their dead ancestors, who were so valiant, but in the end, they had taken comfort in the assurance that after their death they would go join them behind the high mountains, where they would dance and rejoice with them. Likewise, they had pronounced violent threats against the Ouetaca[4] (a nation of enemy savages, who, as I have said elsewhere, are so warlike that they have never been able to subdue them), to capture and eat them, as their *caraïbes* had promised. Moreover, mingled in their songs there was mention of waters that had once swelled so high above their bounds that all the earth was covered, and all the people in the world were drowned, except for their ancestors, who took refuge in the highest trees. This last point, which is the closest they come to the Holy Scriptures, I have heard them reiterate several times since. And, indeed, it is likely that from father to son they have heard something of the universal flood that occurred in the time of Noah.[5] In keeping with the habit of men, which is always to corrupt the truth and turn it into falsehood, together with what we have already seen—that, being altogether deprived of writing, it is hard for them to retain things in their purity—they have added this fable (as did the poets), that their ancestors took refuge in the trees.

2. Supposedly Catholics have tried to convert the Tupi using the supposed relics of saints.

3. A term Léry uses specifically to compare Brazilian sorcerers with European witches, who similarly take Satan as their master.

4. Léry discusses the Ouetaca (Waitaca) in Chapter 5, calling them "the most barbarous, cruel, and dreaded nations that can be found in all the West Indies and the land of Brazil" since they eat raw flesh, speak a language no one else can understand, and wage "open and continual war against all their neighbors as well as against strangers in general."

5. Other early anthropologists would remark on the Tupi story of the flood as well. There was a belief that Noah's three sons had peopled the earth after the flood; hence the assumption that the tale has been passed down orally from father to son over generations.

To return to our *caraïbes*. They were cordially received that day by all the other savages, who entertained them magnificently with the best food they could find, not forgetting to make them drink and *caouiner*, according to their custom. My two French companions and I, who as I said had found ourselves unexpectedly present at this bacchanalia, were also well feasted by our *moussacats* (that is, by the generous householders who give food to people who are passing through). In addition to all this, after these solemn days have passed (during which, every three or four years, all the mummery you have heard about takes place again among our Tupinamba), and even sometimes before, the *caraïbes* go from one village to another, and have each family adorn three or four of these big rattles that they call *maracas*, using the finest plumes they can find. When the *maracas* are thus decked out, they stick the long end of the rod that runs through them into the earth, and arrange them along the middles of the houses; they then demand that the *maracas* be given food and drink. So these impostors make those poor simpletons believe that these fruits and gourds, hollowed out, adorned, and consecrated, will then eat and drink at night. Since each head of a household credits this, he never fails to put out beside his *maracas* not only flour with meat and fish, but also some of their *caouin*. They usually leave them planted in the earth for two or three weeks, always attended to in the same way; and they have a strange belief concerning these *maracas* (which they almost always have in hand): attributing a certain sanctity to them once this bewitchment has been accomplished, they say that whenever they make them sound, a spirit speaks.

As we passed through their longhouses, if we saw some fine morsels presented to these *maracas* and took and ate them (as we often did), our Americans, duped as they were, and judging that such a deed would bring some misfortune down upon us, were no less offended than those superstitious ones, successors of the priests of Baal, at seeing someone take the offerings brought to their puppets—on which offerings, however, to the dishonor of God, they themselves feed gluttonously and idly with their whores and bastards.[6] If, when we seized the occasion to point out their errors, we told them that the *caraïbes,* who gave it out that the *maracas* ate and drank, were deceiving them; and also, that it was not the *caraïbes* (as they falsely boasted) who caused their fruits and their big roots to grow, but rather the God in whom we believe and whom we were making known to them—well, that had about as much effect as speaking against the Pope over here, or saying in Paris that the reliquary of St. Geneviève doesn't make it rain.[7] Therefore these *caraïbe* charlatans hated us no less than the false prophets of Israel (fearing to lose their fat morsels) hated Elijah, the true servant of God, who similarly revealed their abuses;[8] they began to hide from us, fearing even to approach or to sleep in the villages where they knew we were lodging.

Pursuing what I said at the beginning of this chapter: our Tupinamba (all their ceremonies notwithstanding) do not worship either their *caraïbes* or their *maracas* or any creatures whatsoever by kneeling or by any other external gesture; much less do they pray to them or invoke them. Nonetheless, I will cite another example of what I have perceived in them concerning religion. I was with some compatriots in a village named *Ocarentin,* two leagues from Cotiva. As we were having our dinner in an open

---

6. The "successors of the priests of Baal" are presumably Roman Catholics. Baal was a name given to a variety of ancient Canaanite deities, some of whom were worshipped by the Israelites themselves. The "puppets" are probably statues of the saints.

7. "Here" is Europe; St. Geneviève, who protected Paris

from Attila the Hun in the 5th century, was patron saint of the city.

8. In 1 Kings 18, Elijah chastises the Hebrew king Ahab for backsliding and praying to Baal and his consort Asherah as a source of rain; Elijah demonstrates that only prayer to God brings rain.

area, the savages of that place assembled—not to eat with us but to view us. For if they want to do honor to a personage they do not take their meal while he does (not even the old men, who were proud to see us in their village, and showed us all possible signs of friendship). Each one had in his hand the nosebone of a certain fish, two or three feet long and saw-shaped. Rather like our footmen archers, they stood around us to chase away the children, saying to them in their language: "Get out of here, you little rascals! The likes of you are not to come near these people."

After this whole crowd had let us dine in peace without interrupting a single word of our conversation, an old man who had observed that we had prayed to God at the beginning and end of our meal asked us, "What does this mean, this way of doing things, taking off your hat twice, and remaining silent except for one speaker? To whom was all that addressed, those things he was saying? Is it to you who are here, or to others who are absent?" Seizing the occasion that he offered us to speak of the true religion, and considering that this village of Ocarentin is one of the biggest and most populated of that country, and that the savages seemed more attentive than usual and more ready to listen to us, I enlisted our interpreter to help me make them understand what I was about to say.

I first answered the old man's question by telling him that it was to God that we had addressed our prayers, and that although He was not visible, nonetheless He not only heard us but He knew what we were thinking and what was in our hearts. I then began to speak to them about the creation of the world. Above all, I insisted on their understanding that if God had made man excellent above all other creatures, it was so that he might all the more glorify his Creator. I added that, because we served Him, He preserved us as we crossed the sea, even as we lived on that sea continually for four or five months without putting foot to ground, just so that we might seek them out. We did not fear, as they did, being tormented by Aygnan, neither in this life nor in the other: so, I said, if they were willing to turn away from the errors in which their lying and deceiving *caraïbes* held them captive, and leave their barbarity and no longer eat the flesh of their enemies, they would receive the same grace whose effects they had seen in us. In short, so that we might prepare them to receive Jesus Christ, having told them of man's perdition, we spent more than two hours on the matter of the Creation, constantly making comparisons with things that were known to them (on which, however, for the sake of brevity, I will speak no further).

All of them, lending ear, listened attentively and with great wonder. Amazed at what they had heard, another old man spoke up: "Certainly you have told us of marvels that we had never heard of. Still, your discourse has recalled to me something we often heard our grandfathers tell of: a long time ago, so many moons ago that we cannot count them, a *Mair* (that is, a Frenchman or a stranger) dressed and bearded like some of you, came into this country, and, thinking to bring them to an obedience to your God, spoke to them in the same manner that you have just done. But, as we have also heard from father to son, they refused to believe. And so there came another who, as a sign of a curse, left them the sword with which we have been killing each other ever since. And we have entered so far into our possession of it that if we were to desist and abandon our custom, all neighboring nations would mock us." We replied vehemently that, far from concerning themselves with the jibes of others, they had only to worship and serve the sole and true God of heaven and earth, whom we were making known to them; then if their enemies came and attacked them, they would overcome and vanquish them all. In short, by the efficacy that God gave to our words, our Tupinamba were so stirred that several of them promised to live as we had taught them, and even to leave off eating the human flesh of their enemies. After this colloquy (which, as I have said, lasted a long time), they got down on their knees with us, and one of our company, giving thanks to God, offered aloud in the midst of this people a prayer, which was then explained by the interpreter. Then they bedded us down in their style, in cotton beds suspended in the air.[9] But before we fell asleep, we heard them singing together, that in order to avenge themselves on their enemies, they must capture and eat more of them than they ever had before.

And there you have the inconstancy of this poor people, a fine example of the corrupt nature of man.[1] Still, I am of the opinion that if Villegagnon had not revolted from the Reformed Religion, and if we had stayed longer in that country, we would have drawn and won some of them to Jesus Christ.[2]

❧

Of Repentance[1]

Others form man; I tell of him, and portray a particular one, very ill-formed, whom I should really make very different from what he is if I had to fashion him over again. But now it is done.

Now the lines of my painting do not go astray, though they change and vary. The world is but a perennial movement. All things in it are in constant motion—the earth, the rocks of the Caucasus, the pyramids of Egypt—both with the common motion and with their own. Stability itself is nothing but a more languid motion.

I cannot keep my subject still. It goes along befuddled and staggering, with a natural drunkenness. I take it in this condition, just as it is at the moment I give my attention to it. I do not portray being: I portray passing. Not the passing from one age to another, or, as the people say, from seven years to seven years, but from day to day, from minute to minute. My history needs to be adapted to the moment. I may presently change, not only by chance, but also by intention. This is a record of various and changeable occurrences, and of irresolute and, when it so befalls, contradictory ideas: whether I am different myself, or whether I take hold of my subjects in different circumstances and aspects. So, all in all, I may indeed contradict myself now and then; but truth, as Demades said, I do not contradict. If my mind could gain a firm footing, I would not make essays,[2] I would make decisions; but it is always in apprenticeship and on trial.

I set forth a humble and inglorious life; that does not matter. You can tie up all moral philosophy with a common and private life just as well as with a life of richer stuff. Each man bears the entire form of man's estate.

Authors communicate with the people by some special extrinsic mark; I am the first to do so by my entire being, as Michel de Montaigne, not as a grammarian or a

---

9. "Hammocks"; the word is an Indian one.
1. Subsequently, however, Léry will spend Chapter 18 talking about his experiences of Tupi hospitality and speak fondly of their appreciation of his name: "Since by a lucky chance my surname, 'Léry,' means 'oyster' in their language, I told them that my name was 'Léry-oussou,' that is, a big oyster. This pleased them greatly; with their 'Teh!' of admiration, they began to laugh. . . . And indeed, I can say with assurance that never did Circe metamorphose a man into such a fine oyster, nor into one who could converse so well with Ulysses, as since then I have been able to do with our savages."

2. Nicolas Durand de Villegagnon was supposedly asked by Calvin himself to lead the expedition to Brazil, although he had also secured funding from Catholics. In Léry's telling, Villegagnon betrayed the Calvinist group that accompanied him, eventually putting three of their party to death. By 1560, there was no one from the original group left in Brazil, and the Portuguese, already extensively involved as traders and owners of sugercane factories along the coast, would take over the colony.
1. Book III, chapter 2.
2. Montaigne plays here in the French with the meanings of the word *essayer,* "to try," "to prove."

poet or a jurist. If the world complains that I speak too much of myself, I complain that it does not even think of itself.[3]

But is it reasonable that I, so fond of privacy in actual life, should aspire to publicity in the knowledge of me? Is it reasonable too that I should set forth to the world, where fashioning and art have so much credit and authority, some crude and simple products of nature, and of a very feeble nature at that? Is it not making a wall without stone, or something like that, to construct books without knowledge and without art? Musical fancies are guided by art, mine by chance.

At least I have one thing according to the rules: that no man ever treated a subject he knew and understood better than I do the subject I have undertaken; and that in this I am the most learned man alive. Secondly, that no man ever penetrated more deeply into his material, or plucked its limbs and consequences cleaner, or reached more accurately and fully the goal he had set for his work. To accomplish it, I need only bring it to fidelity; and that is in it, as sincere and pure as can be found. I speak the truth, not my fill of it, but as much as I dare speak; and I dare to do so a little more as I grow old, for it seems that custom allows old age more freedom to prate and more indiscretion in talking about oneself. It cannot happen here as I see it happening often, that the craftsman and his work contradict each other: "Has a man whose conversation is so good written such a stupid book?" or "Have such learned writings come from a man whose conversation is so feeble?"

If a man is commonplace in conversation and rare in writing, that means that his capacity is in the place from which he borrows it, and not in himself. A learned man is not learned in all matters; but the capable man is capable in all matters, even in ignorance.

In this case we go hand in hand and at the same pace, my book and I. In other cases one may commend or blame the work apart from the workman; not so here; he who touches the one, touches the other. He who judges it without knowing it will injure himself more than me; he who has known it will completely satisfy me. Happy beyond my deserts if I have just this share of public approval, that I make men of understanding feel that I was capable of profiting by knowledge, if I had had any, and that I deserved better assistance from my memory.

Let me here excuse what I often say, that I rarely repent and that my conscience is content with itself—not as the conscience of an angel or a horse, but as the conscience of a man; always adding this refrain, not perfunctorily but in sincere and complete submission: that I speak as an ignorant inquirer, referring the decision purely and simply to the common and authorized beliefs. I do not teach, I tell.

There is no vice truly a vice which is not offensive, and which a sound judgment does not condemn; for its ugliness and painfulness is so apparent that perhaps the people are right who say it is chiefly produced by stupidity and ignorance. So hard it is to imagine anyone knowing it without hating it.

Malice sucks up the greater part of its own venom, and poisons itself with it. Vice leaves repentance in the soul, like an ulcer in the flesh, which is always scratching itself and drawing blood. For reason effaces other griefs and sorrows; but it engenders that of repentance, which is all the more grievous because it springs from within, as the cold and heat of fevers is sharper than that which comes from outside. I consider as vices (but each one according to its measure) not only those that reason and nature condemn, but also those that man's opinion has created, even false and erroneous opinion, if it is authorized by laws and customs.

---

3. This bold claim is a late one, added after the 1588 publication of the essays.

There is likewise no good deed that does not rejoice a wellborn nature. Indeed there is a sort of gratification in doing good which makes us rejoice in ourselves, and a generous pride that accompanies a good conscience. A boldly vicious soul may perhaps arm itself with security, but with this complacency and satisfaction it cannot provide itself. It is no slight pleasure to feel oneself preserved from the contagion of so depraved an age, and to say to oneself: "If anyone should see right into my soul, still he would not find me guilty either of anyone's affliction or ruin, or of vengeance or envy, or of public offense against the laws, or of innovation and disturbance, or of failing in my word; and in spite of what the license of the times allows and teaches each man, still I have not put my hand either upon the property or into the purse of any Frenchman, and have lived only on my own, both in war and in peace; nor have I used any man's work without paying his wages." These testimonies of conscience give us pleasure; and this natural rejoicing is a great boon to us, and the only payment that never fails us.

To found the reward for virtuous actions on the approval of others is to choose too uncertain and shaky a foundation. Especially in an age as corrupt and ignorant as this, the good opinion of the people is a dishonor. Whom can you trust to see what is praiseworthy? God keep me from being a worthy man according to the descriptions I see people every day giving of themselves in their own honor. *What were vices now are moral acts* [Seneca].

Certain of my friends have sometimes undertaken to call me on the carpet and lecture me unreservedly, either of their own accord or at my invitation, as a service which, to a well-formed soul, surpasses all the services of friendship, not only in usefulness, but also in pleasantness. I have always welcomed it with the wide-open arms of courtesy and gratitude. But to speak of it now in all conscience, I have often found in their reproach or praise such false measure that I would hardly have erred to err rather than to do good in their fashion.

Those of us especially who live a private life that is on display only to ourselves must have a pattern established within us by which to test our actions, and, according to this pattern, now pat ourselves on the back, now punish ourselves. I have my own laws and court to judge me, and I address myself to them more than anywhere else. To be sure, I restrain my actions according to others, but I extend them only according to myself. There is no one but yourself who knows whether you are cowardly and cruel, or loyal and devout. Others do not see you, they guess at you by uncertain conjectures; they see not so much your nature as your art. Therefore do not cling to their judgment; cling to your own. *You must use your own judgment. . . . With regard to virtues and vices, your own conscience has great weight: take that away, and everything falls* [Cicero].

But the saying that repentance follows close upon sin does not seem to consider the sin that is in robes of state, that dwells in us as in its own home. We can disown and retract the vices that take us by surprise, and toward which we are swept by passion; but those which by long habit are rooted and anchored in a strong and vigorous will cannot be denied. Repentance is nothing but a disavowal of our will and an opposition to our fancies, which leads us about in all directions. It makes this man disown his past virtue and his continence:

> Why had I not in youth the mind I have today?
> Or why, with old desires, have red cheeks flown away?
> HORACE

It is a rare life that remains well ordered even in private. Any man can play his part in the side show and represent a worthy man on the boards; but to be disciplined within, in his own bosom, where all is permissible, where all is concealed—that's the point. The next step to that is to be so in our own house, in our ordinary actions, for which we need render account to no one, where nothing is studied or artificial. And therefore Bias, depicting an excellent state of family life, says it is one in which the master is the same within, by his own volition, as he is outside for fear of the law and of what people will say. And it was a worthy remark of Julius Drusus to the workmen who offered, for three thousand crowns, to arrange his house so that his neighbors would no longer be able to look into it as they could before. "I will give you six thousand," he said; "make it so that everyone can see in from all sides." The practice of Agesilaus is noted with honor, of taking lodging in the churches when traveling, so that the people and the gods themselves might see into his private actions.[4] Men have seemed miraculous to the world, in whom their wives and valets have never seen anything even worth noticing. Few men have been admired by their own households.

No man has been a prophet, not merely in his own house, but in his own country,[5] says the experience of history. Likewise in things of no importance. And in this humble example you may see an image of greater ones. In my region of Gascony they think it a joke to see me in print. The farther from my lair the knowledge of me spreads, the more I am valued. I buy printers in Guienne,[6] elsewhere they buy me. On this phenomenon those people base their hopes who hide themselves while alive and present, to gain favor when dead and gone. I would rather have less of it. And I cast myself on the world only for the share of favor I get now. When I leave it, I shall hold it quits.

The people escort this man back to his door, with awe, from a public function. He drops his part with his gown; the higher he has hoisted himself, the lower he falls back; inside, in his home, everything is tumultuous and vile. Even if there is order there, it takes a keen and select judgment to perceive it in these humble private actions. Besides, order is a dull and somber virtue. To win through a breach, to conduct an embassy, to govern a people, these are dazzling actions. To scold, to laugh, to sell, to pay, to love, to hate, and to deal pleasantly and justly with our household and ourselves, not to let ourselves go, not to be false to ourselves, that is a rarer matter, more difficult and less noticeable.

Therefore retired lives, whatever people may say, accomplish duties as harsh and strenuous as other lives, or more so. And private persons, says Aristotle, render higher and more difficult service to virtue than those who are in authority. We prepare ourselves for eminent occasions more for glory than for conscience. The shortest way to attain glory would be to do for conscience what we do for glory. And Alexander's virtue seems to me to represent much less vigor in his theater than does that of Socrates in his lowly and obscure activity. I can easily imagine Socrates in Alexander's place; Alexander in that of Socrates, I cannot.[7] If you ask the former what he knows how to do, he will answer, "Subdue the world"; if you ask the latter, he will

---

4. The three references to Bias, Julius Drusus, and Agesilaus are all drawn from various works of Plutarch.
5. Jesus remarks that "No man is accepted as a prophet in his own country" when the people of Nazareth resist his teachings (Luke 4:24).

6. A city near Montaigne's home, in southwest France.
7. Montaigne alludes to Alexander the Great (356–323 B.C.E.), student of Aristotle and master of the Hellenic empire that would be extended under his sway into Syria, Egypt, and India.

say, "Lead the life of man in conformity with its natural condition"; a knowledge much more general, more weighty, and more legitimate.

The value of the soul consists not in flying high, but in an orderly pace. Its greatness is exercised not in greatness, but in mediocrity. As those who judge and touch us inwardly make little account of the brilliance of our public acts, and see that these are only thin streams and jets of water spurting from a bottom otherwise muddy and thick; so likewise those who judge us by this brave outward appearance draw similar conclusions about our inner constitution, and cannot associate common faculties, just like their own, with these other faculties that astonish them and are so far beyond their scope. So we give demons wild shapes. And who does not give Tamerlane raised eyebrows, open nostrils, a dreadful face, and immense size, like the size of the imaginary picture of him we have formed from the renown of his name?[8] If I had been able to see Erasmus in other days, it would have been hard for me not to take for adages and apophthegms everything he said to his valet and his hostess.[9] We imagine much more appropriately an artisan on the toilet seat or on his wife than a great president, venerable by his demeanor and his ability. It seems to us that they do not stoop from their lofty thrones even to live.

As vicious souls are often incited to do good by some extraneous impulse, so are virtuous souls to do evil. Thus we must judge them by their settled state, when they are at home, if ever they are; or at least when they are closest to repose and their natural position.

Natural inclinations gain assistance and strength from education; but they are scarcely to be changed and overcome. A thousand natures, in my time, have escaped toward virtue or toward vice through the lines of a contrary training:

> As when wild beasts grow tame, shut in a cage,
> Forget the woods, and lose their look of rage,
> And learn to suffer man; but if they taste
> Hot blood, their rage and fury is replaced,
> Their reminiscent jaws distend, they burn,
> And for their trembling keeper's blood they yearn.
>
> LUCAN

We do not root out these original qualities, we cover them up, we conceal them. Latin is like a native tongue to me; I understand it better than French; but for forty years I have not used it at all for speaking or writing.[1] Yet in sudden and extreme emotions, into which I have fallen two or three times in my life—one of them when I saw my father, in perfect health, fall back into my arms in a faint—I have always poured out my first words from the depths of my entrails in Latin; Nature surging forth and expressing herself by force, in the face of long habit. And this experience is told of many others.

Those who in my time have tried[2] to correct the world's morals by new ideas, reform the superficial vices; the essential ones they leave as they were, if they do not increase them; and increase is to be feared. People are likely to rest from all other well-

---

8. Tamerlane, or Tamburlaine, was Timur Khan, who conquered the Mongols early in his military career and went to advance as far west as Turkey and Arabia. He died in 1405.
9. The industrious Dutch scholar and humanist Desiderius Erasmus spent his lifetime compiling the *Adagia,* a collection of adages or proverbs. ("Apophthegms" are witty sayings.)

1. Montaigne says in *Essays* I:26 that his father hired a tutor when he was born to teach him Latin as his first language: "I was over six before I understood any more French or Perigordian than Arabic."
2. Once again, Montaigne plays with the verb "essayer" as he talks about those who have tried ("ceux qui ont essaié") to change the world's morals.

doing on the strength of these external, arbitrary reforms, which cost us less and bring greater acclaim; and thereby they satisfy at little expense the other natural, consubstantial, and internal vices.

Just consider the evidence of this in our own experience. There is no one who, if he listens to himself, does not discover in himself a pattern all his own, a ruling pattern, which struggles against education and against the tempest of the passions that oppose it. For my part, I do not feel much sudden agitation; I am nearly always in place, like heavy and inert bodies. If I am not at home, I am always very near it. My excesses do not carry me very far away. There is nothing extreme or strange about them. And besides I have periods of vigorous and healthy reaction.

The real condemnation, which applies to the common run of men of today, is that even their retirement is full of corruption and filth; their idea of reformation, blurred; their penitence, diseased and guilty, almost as much as their sin. Some, either from being glued to vice by a natural attachment, or from long habit, no longer recognize its ugliness. On others (in whose regiment I belong) vice weighs heavily, but they counterbalance it with pleasure or some other consideration, and endure it and lend themselves to it for a certain price; viciously, however, and basely. Yet it might be possible to imagine a disproportion so extreme that the pleasure might justly excuse the sin, as we say utility does; not only if the pleasure was incidental and not a part of the sin, as in theft, but if it was in the very exercise of the sin, as in intercourse with women, where the impulse is violent, and, they say, sometimes invincible.

The other day when I was at Armagnac, on the estate of a kinsman of mine, I saw a country fellow whom everyone nicknames the Thief. He gave this account of his life: that born a beggar, and finding that by earning his bread by the toil of his hands he would never protect himself enough against want, he had decided to become a thief; and he had spent all his youth at this trade in security, by virtue of his bodily strength. For he reaped his harvest and vintage from other people's lands, but so far away and in such great loads that it was inconceivable that one man could have carried off so much on his shoulders in one night. And he was careful besides to equalize and spread out the damage he did, so that the loss was less insupportable for each individual. He is now, in his old age, rich for a man in his station, thanks to this traffic, which he openly confesses. And to make his peace with God for his acquisitions, he says that he spends his days compensating, by good deeds, the successors of the people he robbed; and that if he does not finish this task (for he cannot do it all at once), he will charge his heirs with it, according to the knowledge, which he alone has, of the amount of wrong he did to each. Judging by this description, whether it is true or false, this man regards theft as a dishonorable action and hates it, but hates it less than poverty; he indeed repents of it in itself, but in so far as it was thus counterbalanced and compensated, he does not repent of it. This is not that habit that incorporates us with vice and brings even our understanding into conformity with it; nor is it that impetuous wind that comes in gusts to confuse and blind our soul, and hurls us for the moment headlong, judgment and all, into the power of vice.

I customarily do wholeheartedly whatever I do, and go my way all in one piece. I scarcely make a motion that is hidden and out of sight of my reason, and that is not guided by the consent of nearly all parts of me, without division, without internal sedition. My judgment takes all the blame or all the praise for it; and the blame it once takes, it always keeps, for virtually since its birth it has been one; the same inclination, the same road, the same strength. And in the matter of general opinions, in childhood I established myself in the position where I was to remain.

There are some impetuous, prompt, and sudden sins: let us leave them aside. But as for these other sins so many times repeated, planned, and premeditated, constitutional sins, or even professional or vocational sins, I cannot imagine that they can be implanted so long in one and the same heart, without the reason and conscience of their possessor constantly willing and intending it to be so. And the repentance which he claims comes to him at a certain prescribed moment is a little hard for me to imagine and conceive.

I do not follow the belief of the sect of Pythagoras, that men take on a new soul when they approach the images of the gods to receive their oracles.[3] Unless he meant just this, that the soul must indeed be foreign, new, and loaned for the occasion, since their own showed so little sign of any purification and cleanness worthy of this office.

They do just the opposite of the Stoic precepts, which indeed order us to correct the imperfections and vices that we recognize in us, but forbid us to be repentant and glum about them. These men make us believe that they feel great regret and remorse within; but of amendment and correction, or interruption, they show us no sign. Yet it is no cure if the disease is not thrown off. If repentance were weighing in the scale of the balance, it would outweigh the sin. I know of no quality so easy to counterfeit as piety, if conduct and life are not made to conform with it. Its essence is abstruse and occult; its semblance, easy and showy.

As for me, I may desire in a general way to be different; I may condemn and dislike my nature as a whole, and implore God to reform me completely and to pardon my natural weakness. But this I ought not to call repentance, it seems to me, any more than my displeasure at being neither an angel nor Cato.[4] My actions are in order and conformity with what I am and with my condition. I can do no better. And repentance does not properly apply to the things that are not in our power; rather does regret. I imagine numberless natures loftier and better regulated than mine, but for all that, I do not amend my faculties; just as neither my arm nor my mind becomes more vigorous by imagining another that is so. If imagining and desiring a nobler conduct than ours produced repentance of our own, we should have to repent of our most innocent actions, inasmuch as we rightly judge that in a more excellent nature they would have been performed with greater perfection and dignity, and we should wish to do likewise.

When I consider the behavior of my youth in comparison with that of my old age, I find that I have generally conducted myself in orderly fashion, according to my lights; that is all my resistance can accomplish. I do not flatter myself; in similar circumstances I should always be the same. It is not a spot, it is rather a tincture with which I am stained all over. I know no superficial, halfway, and perfunctory repentance. It must affect me in every part before I will call it so, and must grip me by the vitals and afflict them as deeply and as completely as God sees into me.

In business matters, several good opportunities have escaped me for want of successful management. However, my counsels have been good, according to the circumstances they were faced with; their way is always to take the easiest and surest course. I find that in my past deliberations, according to my rule, I have proceeded wisely, considering the state of the matter proposed to me, and I should do the same a thousand years from now in similar situations. I am not considering what it is at this moment, but what it was when I was deliberating about it.

3. Seneca discusses this particular doctrine in his letters.
4. Marcus Cato (to whom Montaigne probably refers) was known as the "conscience of Rome" in his staunch opposition to Caesar and empire. Dante makes him guardian to the mountain of Purgatory.

The soundness of any plan depends on the time; circumstances and things roll about and change incessantly. I have fallen into some serious and important mistakes in my life, not for lack of good counsel but for lack of good luck. There are secret parts in the matters we handle which cannot be guessed, especially in human nature—mute factors that do not show, factors sometimes unknown to their possessor himself, which are brought forth and aroused by unexpected occasions. If my prudence has been unable to see into them and predict them, I bear it no ill will; its responsibility is restricted within its limitations. It is the outcome that beats me; and if it favors the course I have refused, there is no help for it; I do not blame myself; I accuse my luck, not my work. That is not to be called repentance.

Phocion had given the Athenians some advice that was not followed. When however the affair came out prosperously against his opinion, someone said to him: "Well, Phocion, are you glad that the thing is going so well?" "Indeed I am glad," he said, "that it has turned out this way, but I do not repent of having advised that way."[5]

When my friends apply to me for advice, I give it freely and clearly, and without hesitating as nearly everyone else does because, the affair being hazardous, it may come out contrary to my expectations, wherefore they may have cause to reproach me for my advice; that does not worry me. For they will be wrong, and I should not have refused them this service.

I have scarcely any occasion to blame my mistakes or mishaps on anyone but myself. For in practice I rarely ask other people's advice, unless as a compliment and out of politeness, except when I need scientific information or knowledge of the facts. But in things where I have only my judgment to employ, other people's reasons can serve to support me, but seldom to change my course. I listen to them all favorably and decently; but so far as I can remember, I have never up to this moment followed any but my own. If you ask me, they are nothing but flies and atoms that distract my will. I set little value on my own opinions, but I set just as little on those of others. Fortune pays me properly. If I do not take advice, I give still less. Mine is seldom asked, but it is followed even less; and I know of no public or private enterprise that my advice restored to its feet and to the right path. Even the people whom fortune has made somewhat dependent on it have let themselves be managed more readily by anyone else's brains. Being a man who is quite as jealous of the rights of my repose as of the rights of my authority, I prefer it so; by leaving me alone, they treat me according to my professed principle, which is to be wholly contained and established within myself. To me it is a pleasure not to be concerned in other people's affairs and to be free of responsibility for them.

In all affairs, when they are past, however they have turned out, I have little regret. For this idea takes away the pain: that they were bound to happen thus, and now they are in the great stream of the universe and in the chain of Stoical causes. Your fancy, by wish or imagination, cannot change a single point without overturning the whole order of things, and the past and the future.

For the rest, I hate that accidental repentance that age brings. The man who said of old that he was obliged to the years for having rid him of sensuality had a different viewpoint from mine;[6] I shall never be grateful to impotence for any good it may do me. *Nor will Providence ever be so hostile to her own work that debility should be ranked among the best things* [Quintilian]. Our appetites are few in old age; a pro-

---

5. Recounted in Plutarch; Phocion, a soldier, advised the Athenians against a war that they ended up winning.

6. The "man" is Sophocles, reported by Cicero in his *On Aging*.

found satiety seizes us after the act. In that I see nothing of conscience; sourness and weakness imprint on us a sluggish and rheumatic virtue. We must not let ourselves be so carried away by natural changes as to let our judgment degenerate. Youth and pleasure in other days did not make me fail to recognize the face of vice in voluptuousness; nor does the distaste that the years bring me make me fail to recognize the face of voluptuousness in vice. Now that I am no longer in that state, I judge it as though I were in it.

I who shake up my reason sharply and attentively, find that it is the very same I had in my more licentious years, except perhaps in so far as it has grown weaker and worse as it has grown old. And I find that even if it refuses, out of consideration for the interests of my bodily health, to put me in the furnace of this pleasure, it would not refuse to do so, any more than formerly, for my spiritual health. I do not consider it any more valiant for seeing it *hors de combat*. My temptations are so broken and mortified that they are not worth its opposition. By merely stretching out my hands to them, I exorcise them. If my reason were confronted with my former lust, I fear that it would have less strength to resist than it used to have. I do not see that of itself it judges anything differently than it did then, nor that it has gained any new light. Wherefore, if there is any convalescence, it is a deformed convalescence.

Miserable sort of remedy, to owe our health to disease! It is not for our misfortune to do us this service, it is for the good fortune of our judgment. You cannot make me do anything by ills and afflictions except curse them. They are for people who are only awakened by whipping. My reason runs a much freer course in prosperity. It is much more distracted and busy digesting pains than pleasures. I see much more clearly in fair weather. Health admonishes me more cheerfully and so more usefully than sickness. I advanced as far as I could toward reform and a regulated life when I had health to enjoy. I should be ashamed and resentful if the misery and misfortune of my decrepitude were to be thought better than my good, healthy, lively, vigorous years, and if people were to esteem me not for what I have been, but for ceasing to be that.

In my opinion it is living happily, not, as Antisthenes said, dying happily, that constitutes human felicity.[7] I have made no effort to attach, monstrously, the tail of a philosopher to the head and body of a dissipated man; or that this sickly remainder of my life should disavow and belie its fairest, longest, and most complete part. I want to present and show myself uniformly throughout. If I had to live over again, I would live as I have lived. I have neither tears for the past nor fears for the future. And unless I am fooling myself, it has gone about the same way within me as without. It is one of the chief obligations I have to my fortune that my bodily state has run its course with each thing in due season. I have seen the grass, the flower, and the fruit; now I see the dryness—happily, since it is naturally. I bear the ills I have much more easily because they are properly timed, and also because they make me remember more pleasantly the long felicity of my past life.

Likewise my wisdom may well have been of the same proportions in one age as in the other; but it was much more potent and graceful when green, gay, and natural, than it is now, being broken down, peevish, and labored. Therefore I renounce these casual and painful reformations.

God must touch our hearts. Our conscience must reform by itself through the strengthening of our reason, not through the weakening of our appetites. Sensual plea-

7. The fourth-century Athenian Antisthenes was a Cynic, who saw freedom from the passions as the only key to happiness.

sure is neither pale nor colorless in itself for being seen through dim and bleary eyes. We should love temperance for itself and out of reverence toward God, who has commanded it, and also chastity; what catarrh lends us, and what I owe to the favor of my colic, is neither chastity nor temperance. We cannot boast of despising and fighting sensual pleasure, if we do not see or know it, and its charms, its powers, and its most alluring beauty.

I know them both; I have a right to speak; but it seems to me that in old age our souls are subject to more troublesome ailments and imperfections than in our youth. I used to say so when I was young; then they taunted me with my beardless chin. I still say so now that my gray hair gives me authority to speak. We call "wisdom" the difficulty of our humors, our distaste for present things. But in truth we do not so much abandon our vices as change them, and, in my opinion, for the worse. Besides a silly and decrepit pride, a tedious prattle, prickly and unsociable humors, superstition, and a ridiculous concern for riches when we have lost the use of them, I find there more envy, injustice, and malice. Old age puts more wrinkles in our minds than on our faces; and we never, or rarely, see a soul that in growing old does not come to smell sour and musty. Man grows and dwindles in his entirety.

Seeing the wisdom of Socrates and several circumstances of his condemnation, I should venture to believe that he lent himself to it to some extent, purposely, by prevarication, being seventy, and having so soon to suffer an increasing torpor of the rich activity of his mind, and the dimming of its accustomed brightness.[8]

What metamorphoses I see old age producing every day in many of my acquaintances! It is a powerful malady, and it creeps up on us naturally and imperceptibly. We need a great provision of study, and great precaution, to avoid the imperfections it loads upon us, or at least to slow up their progress. I feel that, notwithstanding all my retrenchments, it gains on me foot by foot. I stand fast as well as I can. But I do not know where it will lead even me in the end. In any event, I am glad to have people know whence I shall have fallen.

+—⟨◇⟩—+

Miguel de Cervantes Saavedra
1547–1616

"There's one thing I can say to you in passing, that there's nothing so pleasant in the world for an honest man as to be squire to a knight errant, that seeks adventures." So says Sancho Panza to his wife at the end of the first part of the book that bears the knight errant's name. Indeed, this most beloved of novels is a novel of and about the road. Neither epic nor chivalric poem, neither pastoral romance nor picaresque, *Don Quixote* maintains a guarded and ironic distance from all these readily identifiable genres, even as its prologue beckons its *desoccupado lector* or idle reader to travel with Alonso Quixano, alias Don Quixote, and his endlessly talkative squire.

In *Don Quixote,* these are travels in the world of early seventeenth-century Spain: a world from which Jews and then Moors had been banished, where the forces of the Inquisition were ubiquitous and the importance of *limpieza de sangre*—purity of blood—was paramount. This was a world in which Miguel de Cervantes, like his knight errant, may not have been always at

8. Socrates was sentenced to death in 399 B.C.E. on the charge of having corrupted the youth of Athens. As recounted by Plato in the *Apology,* he responded ambiguously to the charges against him rather than pleading for his life as expected.

home. Son of an impoverished doctor, he departed for Italy following a fight when he was twenty-one to serve in the household of a cardinal in Rome. Ten years after his return, he petitioned to work in colonial Latin America (he was told in no uncertain terms to look for something in Spain). Beginning in the early 1580s, Cervantes tried to make a go of the profession of writing, succeeding only with the publication of *Don Quixote* when he was fifty-eight, considerably older than the *hidalgo* who made his fortune. Yet Cervantes and his creation are no direct mirrors for one another. Don Quixote never leaves Spain and can only dream of meaningful military action. Cervantes joined the Spanish army shortly after arriving in Italy, fighting in 1571 in the major battle of Lepanto that annihilated the Turkish fleet and restored Catholic Europe's faith in its military superiority over the Muslims. Five years later, the boat he was taking back to Spain was captured by pirates, and he was sold to a Greek in Algiers, where he remained for several years. Such episodes lie behind "The Captive's Tale" from the first part of the novel, while Cervantes' later experience in Spanish jails no doubt informs the lively chapter on the galley slaves. Nor was Cervantes a gentleman—a member of the lesser nobility that with the accession of Philip III to the throne found itself with less and less to do. One of the most powerful monarchies in Europe, even after the British defeated its naval Armada, the Spanish crown, whimsical enough to move its quarters from Madrid to Valladolid and back again in the space of five years, was also one of the most centralized.

Along with his family and innumerable courtiers, Cervantes moved back and forth with Phillip as well, no doubt hoping to win courtly approval for a government position—he had tried his hand at tax collecting for a number of years—or an occasional commission for a patriotic work, such as his play *The Seige of Numantia.* But it was only with the publication of *Don Quixote* in 1605 that Cervantes came to the attention of his fellow Spaniards and probably his king. The success of Book I was so great (as Cervantes has one fictional enthusiast put it, "Children finger it; young people read it; grown men know it by heart, and old men praise it") that pirated editions of the work began to appear almost immediately, and one Alonso Fernández de Avellaneda was motivated in 1613 to write a sequel. An ailing Cervantes completed a second part that attacks Avellaneda in its preface and has Sancho and Don Quixote laughing at the "inaccurate" sequel. But the jabs at Avellaneda are merely one aspect of the work's self-consciousness regarding its place in a world of "idle readers." In Book 2, published in 1615, just a year before the author's death, Cervantes acknowledges that his character has acquired a history and reputation all his own, and Don Quixote is constantly running into people who have already read about him and who expect him to live up to his reputation. Initially a product of the many books of chivalry he had wasted his patrimony on, Don Quixote becomes, in Book 2, the product of another book: his own. Throughout Book 2, he is forced to confront his own fictionality in a world of "real" people.

Like Jorge Luis Borges and other modernist writers he inspired, Cervantes is fascinated with the madness that ensues when the real and the fictive are confused. *Don Quixote* offers a genealogy of the knight's madness, and in a certain sense provides a requiem to a Renaissance man who thrived on folly. On the one hand, Don Quixote comes from a long line of mad heroes, from Chrètien de Troye's Ivain to the "mad Roland" (*Orlando furioso*) of Ludovico Ariosto's sixteenth-century poem, who goes beserk when he discovers that his beloved Angelica yielded her virginity to a Moorish footsoldier—a drama that Don Quixote sadly realizes he cannot imitate: "For I dare swear that my Dulcinea del Toboso has never seen a real Moor in his real Moorish dress in all her life." But on the other hand, the romances of chivalry, and the chivalric code behind them, had long had a tenuous relationship to reality; as the historian Gerhart Ladner has noted, the knight's only choices are to transcend the world or be destroyed by it. The knight in shining armor from Arthurian legend would find his life's work in pledging eternal fealty to a woman he would never possess and performing great deeds in her name—a model of ideal behavior that few could or would ever want to attain, an idealism marked both by profound Christian faith and by a fiercely sublimated eroticism. While manuals of chivalric behavior were legion after Ramon Lull's best-selling *Book of the Order of Chivalry,* by the seventeenth century, there was little inclination to find in the vestiges of medieval chivalry anything other than entertainment.

For a time, the missionary zeal inspired by the discovery of the Americas, especially among followers of the Spanish Jesuit Loyola, and the new wars with the Turk which Cervantes experienced firsthand had renewed the fervor for the chivalric glories of the past. But this fervor had diminished by the time Cervantes sat down to write his novel. In large part, it is the absence of a community that takes chivalry seriously that renders Cervantes' hero so marginal (a marginality exacerbated, as Borges has wryly remarked, by the name of Don Quixote's village: "Don Quixote de la Mancha, that now has the sound of nobility in Spanish, was intended to sound then as Don Quixote of Kansas City.") At every turn, the knight encounters greed, self-interest, and cold-blooded calculation that are the antitheses of a knight errantry meant "to redress wrongs, aid widows and protect maidens." In his first adventure, in an inn he imagines to be a castle, he finds not a castellan and ladies-in-waiting but a greedy owner, prostitutes, and a laborer who showers Don Quixote with stones. When Don Quixote later seeks solace among shepherds, he launches into a long speech about the pastoral origins of a golden age when men were considerate of their fellow human beings, a speech the goatherds listen to "in fascination and bewilderment." But the knight and his squire will end their sojourn in the supposedly idyllic countryside when they are beaten and bruised by a band of angry rustics defending their mares from the amorous advances of Don Quixote's horse, Rocinante. Shortly thereafter Don Quixote will wade into a flock of sheep and do battle with them thinking they are two powerful armies, and his "tilting at windmills" mistaken for giants has become proverbial for foolish enthusiasm.

Cervantes nonetheless complicates this repeated juxtaposition of Don Quixote's version of events and the way they "really" are, particularly in regard to the characters with whom the knight has most sustained contact. On occasion, Don Quixote's madness brings out the good in others, as he evokes their sympathy and enables them to express a compassion to which they are unaccustomed. The innkeeper doesn't demand payment from the injured knight, and the laborer who takes Don Quixote back to La Mancha after his first round of adventures "waits till it was rather darker [to ride into the village], so that no one should see the battered gentleman on so shameful a mount." Far more than sympathy is exacted from Sancho Panza, who initially rides off with Don Quixote for purely mercenary motives—he wants to govern the island promised him as reward for his patient services—but who becomes seduced by the profound pleasures of the life of knight-errantry: it is clearly a life more exciting, more meaningful, than his sedentary life in the village. Between him and Don Quixote grows a bond fashioned from sharing intimate moments, ranging from their lengthy discourses in the lonely Sierra Morena, to their vomiting over one another after the episode of the sheep.

At the same time, Sancho Panza becomes adept at learning Don Quixote's language and at exploiting it, as when he claims that a peasant girl he met on the road was an enchanted Dulcinea. Yet there are far more subtle ways in which Don Quixote's companions are influenced by his vision of the world—a world where "every man is the child of his works" and one has faith in things not seen. While Don Quixote's madness is surely ridiculous, and his naive belief in the old chivalric stories is condemned, the reader is often led to the same query posed by two gentlemen with whom Don Quixote dines late in Book 2: "One moment they thought him a man of sense, and the next he slipped into craziness; nor could they decide what degree to assign him between wisdom and folly."

Where Cervantes himself stands in relationship to his hero is a puzzle. This is in part because of the playful distance he placed between himself and Don Quixote's story. The story after Chapter 10 comes to us from a Moorish enchanter named Cide Hamete Benengeli and is translated by a Moor the author meets in the marketplace. But since "men of that [Arabic] nation [are] ready liars," neither the history itself nor the translation can be trusted. Moreover,

Gustave Doré, engraving for Cervantes' *Don Quixote*. Doré was a prominent sculptor and painter in mid-nineteenth-century France, but he is best remembered for his illustrations for literary masterpieces such as Rabelais's works, *Paradise Lost* and Dante's *Inferno* (with many a gruesome punishment vividly displayed for the reader's entertainment). *Don Quixote* attracted Doré's attention as well, and in 1862—two years before publishing an illustrated Bible—the artist gave the world arresting images such as this one, showing Don Quixote's collision with a windmill, while a frantic Sancho Panza yells from afar.

as Cervantes matures as a writer, Don Quixote tends to slip from our sight. He is very much the focus of Book 1, save for the story of "The Captive's Tale." But in Book 2, other characters take center stage for extended periods of time, as the university student Sansón Carrasco and a seemingly sadistic duke and duchess increasingly manipulate the book's events. Perhaps the novel must inevitably prepare for the moment when the world which Don Quixote had made so colorful must go on without him: Alonxo Quixano may be unable to survive the destruction of his fantasy, but others must continue in its absence.

Cervantes himself, though, did not live long after the publication of Book 2. A flurry of literary activity in his last few years had led him to write his *Exemplary Novels* (1613), a collection of short stories that subverts the genre of the picaresque, and he then wrote an ambitious romance, *Persiles and Sigismunda,* published posthumously. But Cide Hamete's observation at the close of his manuscript, "For me alone Don Quixote was born and I for him," may be true for Cervantes himself. Perhaps the great irony of this work by one of the master ironists of all time is that Don Quixote is a victim of the fictions he has read; yet it is he who, along with his faithful servant, is the most compelling and immediate of the novel's characters. He is the one most likely to pull us as readers—and perhaps Cervantes as author—into the dangerous new world of the novel, as refracted through the endearingly mad habitations of his mind.

PRONUNCIATIONS:
> *Cide Hamete Benengeli:* SEE-day ha-MEE-tay ben-en-HEL-lee
> *Don Jerónimo:* DON hay-RO-nee-mo
> *Don Quixote:* DON kee-HO-tay
> *Dulcinea:* dole-see-NAY-ah
> *Gines de Pasamonte:* he-NACE day pahs-ah-MON-tay
> *Rocinante:* ro-see-NAN-tay
> *Roque Guinart:* RO-kay gee-NAR
> *Quejana:* kay-HAN-na
> *Quesada:* kay-SAH-da

DON QUIXOTE[1]
Book 1
Chapter 1

CONCERNING THE FAMOUS HIDALGO[2] DON QUIXOTE DE LA MANCHA'S POSITION, CHARACTER AND WAY OF LIFE

In a village in La Mancha, the name of which I cannot quite recall,[3] there lived not long ago one of those country gentlemen or hidalgos who keep a lance in a rack, an ancient leather shield, a scrawny hack and a greyhound for coursing. A midday stew with rather more shin of beef than leg of lamb, the leftovers for supper most nights, lardy eggs on Saturdays, lentil broth on Fridays and an occasional pigeon as a Sunday treat ate up three-quarters of his income. The rest went on a cape of black broadcloth, with breeches of velvet and slippers to match for holy days, and on weekdays he walked proudly in the finest homespun. He maintained a housekeeper the wrong side of forty, a niece the right side of twenty and a jack of all trades who was as good at saddling the nag as at plying the pruning shears. Our hidalgo himself was nearly fifty; he had a robust constitution, dried-up flesh and a withered face, and he was an early riser and a keen huntsman. His surname's said to have been Quixada, or Quesada (as if he were a jawbone, or a cheesecake):[4] concerning this detail there's some discrepancy among the authors who have written on the subject, although a credible conjecture does suggest he might have been a plaintive Quexana. But this doesn't matter much, as far as our story's concerned, provided that the narrator doesn't stray one inch from the truth.

Now you must understand that during his idle moments (which accounted for most of the year) this hidalgo took to reading books of chivalry with such relish and enthusiasm that he almost forgot about his hunting and even running his property, and his foolish curiosity reached such extremes that he sold acres of arable land to buy these books of chivalry, and took home as many of them as he could find; he liked none of them so much as those by the famous Feliciano de Silva,[5] because the brilliance of the prose and all that intricate language seemed a treasure to him, never

---

1. Translated by John Rutherford.
2. *Hidalgo* literally means a person "of some distinction," a member of the lowest rung of the nobility who would have been exempt from taxation. Don Quixote is neither a *don* nor a knight or *caballero*, who would have had jurisdiction over land.
3. La Mancha is an arid region of Castile in south-central

Spain, not far from the major cities of Toledo and Madrid.
4. A *quixote* is a piece of armor, a far cry from the comic images suggested by the variants of his name (a *quijado* is a jawbone; *queso* is cheese).
5. A 16th-century writer of the chivalric romances that had been vastly popular in Spain.

more so than when he was reading those amorous compliments and challenges delivered by letter, in which he often found: "The reason for the unreason to which my reason is subjected, so weakens my reason that I have reason to complain of your beauty." And also when he read: " . . . the lofty heavens which with their stars divinely fortify you in your divinity, and make you meritorious of the merits merited by your greatness." Such subtleties used to drive the poor gentleman to distraction, and he would rack his brains trying to understand it all and unravel its meaning, something that Aristotle himself wouldn't have been capable of doing even if he'd come back to life for this purpose alone. He wasn't very happy about the wounds that Sir Belianis kept on inflicting and receiving, because he imagined that, however skilful the doctors who treated him, his face and body must have been covered with gashes and scars. But, in spite of all that, he commended the author for ending his book with that promise of endless adventure, and often felt the urge to take up his quill and bring the story to a proper conclusion, as is promised there; and no doubt he'd have done so, and with success too, if other more important and insistent preoccupations hadn't prevented him. He had frequent arguments with the village priest (a learned man—a Sigüenza graduate no less) about which had been the better knight errant, Palmerin of England or Amadis of Gaul;[6] but Master Nicolás, the village barber, argued that neither of them could hold a candle to the Knight of Phoebus, and that if anyone at all could be compared to him it was Don Galaor, Amadis of Gaul's brother, because there was no emergency he couldn't cope with: he wasn't one of your pernickety knights, nor was he such a blubberer as his brother, and he was every bit his equal as far as courage was concerned.

In short, our hidalgo was soon so absorbed in these books that his nights were spent reading from dusk till dawn, and his days from dawn till dusk, until the lack of sleep and the excess of reading withered his brain, and he went mad. Everything he read in his books took possession of his imagination: enchantments, fights, battles, challenges, wounds, sweet nothings, love affairs, storms and impossible absurdities. The idea that this whole fabric of famous fabrications was real so established itself in his mind that no history in the world was truer for him. He would declare that El Cid, Ruy Díaz, had been an excellent knight, but that he couldn't be compared to the Knight of the Burning Sword,[7] who with just one back-stroke had split two fierce and enormous giants clean down the middle. He felt happier about Bernardo del Carpio, because he'd slain Roland the Enchanted at Roncesvalles, by the same method used by Hercules when he suffocated Antaeus, the son of Earth—with a bear-hug.[8] He was full of praise for the giant Morgante[9] because, despite belonging to a proud and insolent breed, he alone was affable and well-mannered. But his greatest favourite was Reynald of Montalban, most of all when he saw him sallying forth from his castle and plundering all those he met, and when in foreign parts he stole that image of Muham-

---

6. A third-rate university was to be found at Sigüenza, a town northwest of Madrid. Palmerin of England was the protagonist of a Portuguese chivalric romance, Amadis of Gaul that of Spain's most famous romance, *Amadís de Gaula*, written by Garci Rodríguez de Montalvo in 1508. Montalvo combined battle scenes with those of courtly love, and ended his work with the rather unusual flourish of a marriage.

7. The Cid was the hero of the first epic poem written in Spain, noted for his deeds against the Moors; see *The Poem of the Cid*, Volume B. The Knight of the Burning Sword is a character in one of Feliciano de Silva's romances, *The Ninth Book of Amadis of Gaul* (1530).

8. The Castilian warrior Bernardo del Carpio appears in mid–16th-century Spanish works as the defeater of Roland, Charlemagne's most powerful knight. He quickly attained the status of Spain's national hero. Antaeus derived his strength from his contact with "mother" Earth; Hercules lifted him up until he became weak, then killed him.

9. The genial giant of Luigi Pulci's late 15th-century mock-epic poem, *Morgante Maggiore*.

mad made of solid gold, as his history records.[1] He'd have given his housekeeper, and even his niece into the bargain, to trample the traitor Ganelon in the dust.[2]

And so, by now quite insane, he conceived the strangest notion that ever took shape in a madman's head, considering it desirable and necessary, both for the increase of his honour and for the common good, to become a knight errant, and to travel about the world with his armour and his arms and his horse in search of adventures, and to practise all those activities that he knew from his books were practised by knights errant, redressing all kinds of grievances, and exposing himself to perils and dangers that he would overcome and thus gain eternal fame and renown. The poor man could already see himself being crowned Emperor of Trebizond,[3] at the very least, through the might of his arm; and so, possessed by these delightful thoughts and carried away by the strange pleasure that he derived from them, he hastened to put into practice what he so desired.

His first step was to clean a suit of armour that had belonged to his forefathers and that, covered in rust and mould, had been standing forgotten in a corner for centuries. He scoured and mended it as best he could; yet he realized that it had one important defect, which was that the headpiece was not a complete helmet but just a simple steel cap; he was ingenious enough, however, to overcome this problem, constructing out of cardboard something resembling a visor and face-guard which, once inserted into the steel cap, gave it the appearance of a full helmet. It's true that, to test its strength and find out whether it could safely be exposed to attack, he drew his sword and dealt it two blows, with the first of which he destroyed in a second what it had taken him a week to create. He couldn't help being concerned about the ease with which he'd shattered it, and to guard against this danger he reconstructed it, fixing some iron bars on the inside, which reassured him about its strength; and, preferring not to carry out any further tests, he deemed and pronounced it a most excellent visored helmet.

Then he went to visit his nag, and although it had more corns than a barleyfield and more wrong with it than Gonella's horse, which *tantum pellis et ossa fuit,* it seemed to him that neither Alexander's Bucephalus nor the Cid's Babieca was its equal.[4] He spent four days considering what name to give the nag; for (he told himself) it wasn't fitting that the horse of such a famous knight errant, and such a fine horse in its own right, too, shouldn't have some name of eminence; and so he tried to find one that would express both what it had been before it became a knight's horse and what it was now, for it was appropriate that, since its master had changed his rank, it too should change its name, and acquire a famous and much-trumpeted one, as suited the new order and new way of life he professed. And so, after a long succession of names that he invented, eliminated and struck out, added, deleted and remade in his mind and in his imagination, he finally decided to call it *Rocinante,* that is, *Hackafore,* a name which, in his opinion, was lofty and sonorous and expressed what the creature had been when it was a humble hack, before it became what it was now— the first and foremost of all the hacks in the world.

---

1. Reynald (Rinaldo) appears in the two major chivalric romances of the Italian Renaissance, Boiardo's *Orlando Innamorato* (Orlando [Roland] in love) and Ludovico Ariosto's *Orlando furioso* (Mad Orlando).
2. In the original *Song of Roland,* the jealous Ganelon betrays Charlemagne and Roland to the Moors and causes the army's defeat at Roncesvalles.

3. A region of the Byzantine empire; the name was used broadly for Asiatic Turkey.
4. Pietro Gonella was a famous jester in Ferrara. The Latin phrase means "all skin and bone." The wild horse Bucephalus was tamed by the young Alexander, who then rode him during his conquests of India and the East, while Babieca was the Cid's famous steed.

Having given his horse a name, and one so much to his liking, he decided to give himself a name as well, and this problem kept him busy for another eight days, at the end of which he decided to call himself *Don Quixote,* that is, *Sir Thighpiece,* from which, as has already been observed, the authors of this most true history concluded that his surname must have been Quixada, and not Quesada as others had affirmed. Yet remembering that brave Amadis hadn't been content to call himself Amadis alone, but had added the name of his kingdom and homeland, to make it famous, and had styled himself Amadis of Gaul, so Don Quixote, as a worthy knight, decided to add his own country to his name and call himself *Don Quixote de la Mancha,* by doing which, in his opinion, he declared in a most vivid manner both his lineage and his homeland, and honoured the latter by taking it as his surname.

Having, then, cleaned his armour, turned his steel cap into a visored helmet, baptized his nag and confirmed himself, he realized that the only remaining task was to find a lady of whom he could be enamoured; for a knight errant without a lady-love is a tree without leaves or fruit, a body without a soul. He said to himself:

"If, for my wicked sins or my good fortune, I encounter some giant, as knights errant usually do, and I dash him down in single combat, or cleave him asunder, or, in short, defeat and vanquish him, will it not be proper to have someone to whom I can send him as a tribute, so that he can come before my sweet lady and fall to his knees and say in humble tones of submission: 'I, my lady, am the giant Caraculiambro, the Lord of the Isle of Malindrania,[5] vanquished in single combat by the never sufficiently praised knight Don Quixote de la Mancha, who has commanded me to present myself before Your Highness so that Your Highness may dispose of me as you will'"?

Oh my, how our worthy knight rejoiced once he'd spoken these words—even more, once he'd found someone he could call his lady! The fact was—or so it is generally believed—that in a nearby village there lived a good-looking peasant girl, with whom he'd once been in love (although it appears that she was never aware of this love, about which he never told her). She was called Aldonza Lorenzo, and this was the woman upon whom it seemed appropriate to confer the title of the lady of his thoughts; and seeking a name with some affinity with his own, which would also suggest the name of a princess and a fine lady, he decided to call her *Dulcinea del Toboso,* because she was a native of El Toboso: a name that, in his opinion, was musical and magical and meaningful, like all the other names he'd bestowed upon himself and his possessions.

Chapter 2

CONCERNING THE INGENIOUS DON QUIXOTE'S FIRST SALLY

Once he'd made these preparations he decided not to wait any longer before putting his plans into action, encouraged by the need that he believed his delay was creating in the world: so great was his determination to redress grievances, right wrongs, correct injustices, rectify abuses and fulfil obligations. And so, without telling anyone about his plans or being seen by anyone, one morning, before dawn because it was going to be one of those sweltering July days, he donned his armour, mounted Rocinante, with his ill-devised visor in place, took up his leather shield, seized his lance

5. An imaginary island; the giant's name translates roughly as "face of an ass."

and rode out into the fields through the side-door in a yard wall, in raptures of joy on seeing how easy it had been to embark upon his noble enterprise. But no sooner was he outside the door than he was assailed by a terrible thought, which almost made him abandon his undertaking: he remembered that he hadn't been knighted and by the laws of chivalry shouldn't and indeed couldn't take up arms against any knight; and that even if he had been knighted, he would, as a novice, have been obliged to bear white arms, that is to say a shield without any insignia on it, until he'd won them by his own prowess. These thoughts made him waver in his plans; but, since his madness prevailed over all other considerations, he decided to have himself knighted by the first person he chanced upon, in imitation of many others who'd done the same, as he'd read in the books that had reduced him to this state. As for the white arms, he resolved to give his lance and his armour such a scouring, as soon as an opportunity arose, as to make them cleaner and whiter than ermine; and thus he calmed down and continued on his chosen way, which in reality was none other than the way his horse chose to follow, for he believed that in this consisted the essence of adventure.

As our fledgling adventurer rode along, he said to himself:

"Who can doubt but that in future times, when the true history of my famous deeds sees the light, the sage who chronicles them will, when he recounts this my first sally, so early in the morning, write in this manner: 'Scarce had ruddy Apollo spread over the face of the wide and spacious earth the golden tresses of his beauteous hair, and scarce had the speckled little birds with their harmonious tongues hailed in musical and mellifluous melody the approach of rosy Aurora who, rising from her jealous husband's soft couch, disclosed herself to mortals in the portals and balconies of La Mancha's horizon, when the famous knight Don Quixote de la Mancha, quitting the slothful feathers of his bed, mounted his famous steed Rocinante and began to ride over the ancient and far-famed Plain of Montiel'"?[1]

And it was true that this was where he was riding. And he added:

"Happy will be the age, the century will be happy, which brings to light my famous exploits, worthy to be engraved on sheets of bronze, carved on slabs of marble and painted on boards of wood as a monument for all posterity. O sage enchanter, whomsoever you may be, to whom it falls to be the chronicler of this singular history, I beg you not to overlook my good Rocinante, my eternal companion in all my travels and wanderings."

Then he turned and said, as if he really were in love:

"O Princess Dulcinea, mistress of this hapless heart! Great injury have you done me in reproaching and dismissing me, with the cruel command not to appear in the presence of your wondrous beauty. Vouchsafe, my lady, to be mindful of this your subject heart, which suffers such sorrow for love of you."

He strung these absurdities together with many others, all in the style of those that he'd learned from his books. This made his progress so slow, and the sun was rising so fast and becoming so hot, that his brains would have melted, if he'd had any.

He rode on almost throughout that day and nothing happened worth mentioning, which reduced him to despair because he was longing for an early encounter with someone on whom he could test the worth of his mighty arm. Some authors say that the first adventure that befell him was that of the Pass of Lápice, others claim that it was that of the windmills, but what I've been able to discover about this matter, and

1. Site of a major battle in 1369.

indeed what I've found recorded in the annals of La Mancha, is that he rode on throughout that day, and that at nightfall both he and his nag were exhausted and half dead from starvation; and that, looking all around to see if he could spot some castle or shepherds' hut where they might retire and find some remedy for their great hunger and dire want, he caught sight of an inn not far from the road along which he was travelling, which was as if he had seen a star leading him not just to the portals but to the very palace of his redemption. He quickened his pace, and he reached the inn as night was falling.

Sitting by the inn door there happened to be two young women, of the sort known as ladies of easy virtue, on their way to Seville with some muleteers who'd chanced to break their journey that night at the inn. And since whatever our adventurer thought, saw or imagined seemed to him to be as it was in the books he'd read, as soon as he saw the inn he took it for a castle with its four towers and their spires of shining silver, complete with its drawbridge and its deep moat and all the other accessories that such castles commonly boast. He approached the inn that he took for a castle, and at a short distance from it he drew rein, waiting for some dwarf to appear upon the battlements and announce with a trumpet-blast the arrival of a knight. But finding that there was some delay, and that Rocinante was impatient to get to the stable, he rode on towards the inn door and saw the two dissolute wenches sitting there, and thought that they were two beautiful maidens or fine ladies taking their ease at the castle gate. At this point a swineherd who was gathering together some pigs (begging nobody's pardon, because that's what they're called) from a stubble field happened to sound his horn to round them up, and Don Quixote thought that his wish had been fulfilled and that a dwarf was announcing his arrival; so it was with unusual satisfaction that he reached the inn and the ladies, who, on observing the approach of a man dressed like that in armour and clutching a lance and a leather shield, started to run in terror back into the inn. But Don Quixote, conjecturing their fear from their flight, and raising his card-board visor to reveal his dry and dusty face, addressed them with courteous demeanour and tranquil voice:

"Flee not, nor fear the least affront; for in the order of knighthood which I profess it neither belongs nor behoves to offer any such, much less to high-born maidens, as your presence testifies you to be."

The girls had been peering at him and trying to make out his face, hidden behind the ill-made visor; but when they heard themselves called maidens, a term so much at odds with their profession, they couldn't contain their laughter, which was so hearty that Don Quixote flared up and exclaimed:

"Moderation befits the fair; furthermore, laughter which springs from a petty cause is a great folly; but I say this unto you not to grieve you nor yet to sour your disposition; for mine is none other than to serve you."

This language, which the ladies didn't understand, together with the sorry figure cut by the knight, only redoubled their laughter and his wrath, and things would have come to a pretty pass if it hadn't been for the appearance at that moment of the innkeeper, a man who, being very fat, was very peaceable, and who on seeing such an ungainly figure, with such ill-matched equipment as the long stirrups, the lance, the leather shield and the infantryman's body-armour, was more than willing to join the maidens in their merry-making. But he was also intimidated by all these paraphernalia and, deciding to address the knight in a civil manner, he said:

"If, sir caballero, you're looking for somewhere to stay the night, you'll find plenty of everything you need here—all except a bed that is, we haven't got any of those."

Don Quixote, observing the humility of the governor of the castle, for they were what he took the innkeeper and the inn to be, replied:

"For me, sir castellano,[2] anything will suffice, because
My arms are my bed-hangings,
And my rest's the bloody fray."[3]

The host thought that Don Quixote had called him castellano because he'd taken him for one of the Castilian conmen, whereas in reality he was an Andalusian, a prime picaroon from the Playa district of Sanlúcar, no less a thief than Cacus,[4] and no less an evildoer than any experienced page-boy, and he replied:
"In that case,

Your bed must be the hard, hard rock,
And your sleep to watch till day

—and that being so, you go ahead and dismount in the certainty of finding in this humble abode plenty of opportunities not to sleep for a whole year, let alone one night."

And with these words he went and held Don Quixote's stirrup, and the knight dismounted with the greatest difficulty, not having broken his fast all day long.

He then instructed the innkeeper to take great care of his horse, for a finer steed had never eaten barley. The innkeeper looked at the animal, which didn't seem half as good as Don Quixote had claimed, and, after housing it in the stable, went back to receive orders from his guest, whom the maidens, now reconciled, were helping out of his armour. Although they'd taken off his breast and back plates, they couldn't fathom how to disengage his gorget or remove his imitation visor, tied on with green ribbons that would have to be cut, since it was impossible to undo the knots; but he would by no means consent to this, and kept his helmet on all night, making the funniest and strangest figure imaginable. As these trollops unarmed him, he, thinking they were illustrious ladies of the castle, wittily declaimed:

"And never sure was any knight
So served by damsel or by dame
As Quixote was, one happy night
When from his village first he came:
Maids waited on that man of might,
Princesses on his steed, whose name . . .

is Rocinante, good ladies, and mine is Don Quixote de la Mancha; for although I had intended not to discover myself until the deeds done for your benefit and service should have made me known, yet the necessity to accommodate this ancient ballad of Sir Lancelot[5] to our present purpose has been the occasion of your knowing my name ere it were meet; but a time will come when you will command and I shall obey, and when the might of this arm will manifest the desire I have to serve you."

The girls, who weren't used to such rhetorical flourishes, didn't answer, but just asked if he'd like a bite to eat.

"I would fain eat anything," replied Don Quixote, "for, by my troth, much good would it do me."

2. Governor or constable of a castle.
3. The lines are from a well-known Spanish ballad.
4. The Playa district was an area of thieves and swindlers, while in Roman legend the brigand Cacus is said to have stolen the cattle of Hercules.
5. One of King Arthur's knights; Don Quixote has just altered the words to a popular ballad about him.

It happened to be a Friday, so there was no food in the inn except a few helpings of what is known in Castile as *abadejo,* in Andalusia as *bacallao* and in other parts of Spain as *curadillo*—in other words the humble salt cod; but in these parts it was strangely called *truchuela.* They asked him if he'd like some of this troutling, because that was all the fish there was.

"If you have a goodly number of troutlings," replied Don Quixote, "they will serve me as well as a trout, because it makes no difference to me whether I am given eight separate reals or a single piece of eight. What is more, it might even be that these troutlings are like veal, which is better than beef, or like kid, which is better than goat. But whatever this fish is, let it be served; for the travails and the burden of arms cannot be borne on an empty stomach."

A table was set at the door of the inn, where it was cooler, and the innkeeper brought a dish of inadequately soaked and worse cooked salt cod, and a loaf of bread as black and mouldy as the hidalgo's armour; and it was a source of great mirth to watch him eat because, since he was wearing his helmet and holding up the visor, he couldn't put any food into his mouth with his own hands, and somebody else had to do so for him, a task performed by one of the ladies. But when they tried to give him some drink, they found this an impossible task, and he wouldn't have drunk a drop if the innkeeper hadn't bored a hole through a length of cane and put one end into his mouth and poured the wine into the other; and Don Quixote suffered it all with great patience, so as not to allow his helmet-ribbons to be cut. In the midst of these activities a sow-gelder happened to arrive at the inn, and as he did so he sounded his pan-pipes four or five times, which convinced Don Quixote that he was indeed in some famous castle, and that he was being served to the accompaniment of music, and that the salt cod was trout, the bread baked from the whitest wheat-flour, the prostitutes fine ladies and the innkeeper the lord of the castle; and it all confirmed that his decision to sally forth had been a wise one. Yet what most bothered him was that he hadn't yet been knighted, because he knew that he couldn't lawfully embark on any adventure without first having been admitted to the order of chivalry.

Chapter 3

WHICH RELATES THE AMUSING WAY IN WHICH DON QUIXOTE HAD HIMSELF KNIGHTED

And so, troubled by this thought, Don Quixote made short work of his meagre lodging-house supper, and then called for the innkeeper and, shutting himself up with him in the stable, fell upon his knees before him and said:

"I shall ne'er, O valorous knight, arise from where I kneel, until your courtesy vouchsafes me a boon which I desire to beg of you and which will redound to your own praise and to the benefit of humankind."

The innkeeper, seeing his guest at his feet and hearing such pleadings, gazed down at him in perplexity, not knowing what to do or say, and kept telling him to stand up; but he kept refusing, and the innkeeper had to promise to grant his request.

"No less did I expect from your munificence, sir," replied Don Quixote. "Know therefore that the boon which I have begged and which your liberality has vouchsafed me is that tomorrow you shall knight me; and tonight, in the chapel of this your castle, I will keep the vigil of arms; and tomorrow, as I have said, what I so desire shall be accomplished, so that I can legitimately roam through the four corners of the world in quest of adventures for the relief of the needy, as is the duty of chivalry and of knights errant such as I, whose desire towards such exploits is inclined."

The innkeeper, who, as I've said, was something of a wag, and had already suspected that his guest wasn't in his right mind, found his suspicion confirmed when he heard these words and, to have something to laugh at that night, decided to humour him; so he said that he was quite right to pursue these objectives, and that such desires were natural and fitting in such a knight as he seemed to be and as his gallant presence testified; and that he himself in his younger days had followed the same honourable profession, roaming through different parts of the world in search of adventure, without omitting to visit such districts as Percheles and Islas de Riarán in Malaga, Compás in Seville, Azoguejo in Segovia, Olivera in Valencia, Rondilla in Granada, Playa in Sanlúcar, Potro in Cordova and Ventillas in Toledo,[1] and many other places where he'd exercised the dexterity of his hands and the nimbleness of his heels, doing many injuries, wooing many widows, ruining a few maidens and swindling a few orphans, and, in short, making himself known in most of the law courts and tribunals in Spain; and that he'd finally retired to his castle, where he lived on his own means and on those of others, accommodating all knights errant, whatever their status or position, solely because of the great affection he felt for them and so that they could share their wealth with him, to repay him for his kindness.

He also told Don Quixote that in his castle there wasn't any chapel where he could keep the vigil of arms, because it had been demolished to build a new one, but he knew that in case of need vigil might be kept anywhere, and Don Quixote could do so that night in a courtyard within the castle; and in the morning, God willing, the proper ceremonies would be performed to make him into a knight, so very thoroughly that no knight in the whole wide world could be more of a knight than he.

He asked Don Quixote if he had any money on him; Don Quixote replied that he did not have so much as a single real,[2] because he had never read in histories of knights errant that any of them had ever carried money. To this the innkeeper retorted that he was deluding himself—even if it wasn't written in the histories, because their authors had considered that there wasn't any need to record something as obviously necessary as money or clean shirts, that wasn't any reason to believe that they'd travelled without supplies of both; so he could take it as true and proven that all knights errant, of which so many books are full to overflowing, kept their purses well lined in readiness for any eventuality, and that they also carried shirts and small chests full of ointments for curing the wounds they received; because there wasn't always someone available to treat them in every field or desert where they engaged in combat and were injured, unless they had some wise enchanter for a friend, and he came to their aid, summoning through the air, on some cloud, a damsel or a dwarf with a flask of water of such magical properties that, on tasting just one drop, they were instantly cured of their wounds and injuries, as if they'd never been hurt. But, just in case this didn't happen, the knights of old had considered it wise to see that their squires were provided with money and other necessities such as lint and ointments to dress their wounds; and if any such knight happened not to have a squire (a most unusual occurrence), he himself would carry all these supplies in small saddle-bags that were scarcely visible, on the crupper of his steed, as if they were something else of much

1. All notorious lowlife districts in some of Spain's major cities.   2. A coin worth about five cents.

greater importance because, except in such circumstances, carrying saddle-bags was rather frowned upon among knights errant; and the innkeeper therefore advised Don Quixote—although he could, if he wished, command him as the godson that he was about to become—never again to travel without money and all the other supplies just mentioned, and he'd discover when he least expected it how useful they could be.

Don Quixote promised to do exactly as he'd been told, and then he was given orders to keep the vigil of arms in a large yard on one side of the inn; and he gathered his armour together and placed it on a water-trough next to a well, and, taking up his leather shield and seizing his lance, he began with stately bearing to pace back and forth in front of the trough; and as his pacing began, night was beginning to fall.

The innkeeper told everyone in the hostelry about his guest's insanity, his vigil and the knighting that he awaited. They wondered at such a strange kind of madness and went to watch him from a distance, and saw that, with a composed air, he sometimes paced to and fro and, at other times, leaning on his lance, gazed at his armour without looking away for some while. Night fell, but the moon was so bright that it competed with the source of its brightness, and every action of the novice knight could be clearly observed by all. And now one of the muleteers staying at the inn decided to water his animals, and to do so he had to remove from the trough the armour placed there by Don Quixote, who, on seeing him approach, cried out:

"O rash knight, whomsoever you may be, coming to lay hands on the armour of the most valiant knight errant who ever girded sword! Take care what you do, and touch it not, unless you wish to pay with your life for your temerity."

The muleteer wouldn't toe the line (it would have been better for the rest of his anatomy if he had); instead, grasping the armour by its straps, he hurled it to one side. When Don Quixote saw this, he raised his eyes to heaven and, fixing his thoughts, as it seemed, on his lady Dulcinea, he said:

"Assist me, dear lady, in this first affront suffered by this breast that is enthralled to you; let not your favour and your succour abandon me in this first moment of peril."

And with these and other similar words he dropped his leather shield, raised his lance with both hands, and dealt the muleteer so powerful a blow to the head that he fell on the ground in such a sorry state that had it been followed by another blow he wouldn't have needed a doctor to treat him. Then Don Quixote replaced his armour and continued pacing to and fro with the same composure as before. After a while another muleteer, not knowing what had happened (because the first one still lay stunned), also came to water his animals and, as he went to remove the armour from the trough, Don Quixote, without uttering a word or asking anybody for her favour, again dropped his leather shield and raised his lance, and didn't break it over the second muleteer's head but rather broke the head, into more than three pieces, because he criss-crossed it with two blows. All the people in the hostelry came running at the noise, the innkeeper among them. When Don Quixote saw them, he took up his leather shield and, with one hand on his sword, declared:

"O beauteous lady, strength and vigour of my enfeebled heart! Now is the time for you to turn the eyes of your greatness towards this your hapless knight, on the brink of so mighty an adventure."

With this he felt so inspirited that if all the muleteers in the world had attacked him he wouldn't have retreated one inch. The wounded men's companions, seeing them in such a state, began to rain stones on Don Quixote, who fended them off with his leather shield as best he could, unwilling to move away from the water-trough and leave his armour unprotected. The innkeeper was yelling at them to let him be—he'd already told them he was a madman, and as such would go scot-free even if he killed the lot of them. Don Quixote was shouting too, even louder, calling them perfidious traitors and the lord of the castle a poltroon and a base-born knight, who allowed knights errant to be treated in such a way and who, if he had been admitted to the order of chivalry, would have been made to regret his treachery:

"But to you, vile and base rabble, I pay no heed; stone me, come, draw near, assail me as best you can, for you will soon see how you are made to pay for your folly and your insolence."

He spoke with such vehemence and spirit that he struck fear into his assailants; and this, together with the innkeeper's arguments, persuaded them to stop, and he allowed them to remove the wounded, and continued keeping the vigil of arms, with the same composure as before.

The innkeeper wasn't amused by his guest's capers, and decided to put an end to them by giving him his wretched order of chivalry before any further calamities occurred. And so he approached him and apologized for the insolent behaviour of that rabble, about which he'd known nothing; but they had been properly punished for their impudence. He said that, as he'd mentioned before, there wasn't any chapel in the castle, and in any case there wasn't any need of one for what was left to be done; because the essence of being knighted lay in the cuff on the neck and the touch on the shoulder, according to his information about the ceremonial of the order, and all of that could be done in the middle of a field if necessary, and his guest had already fulfilled the bit about keeping the vigil of arms, because two hours of it were quite enough, and he'd been at it for over four. Don Quixote believed every word; he was there ready to obey him, and could he please expedite the process as much as possible, for if he were to be attacked again, after having been knighted, he did not intend to leave a single soul alive in the castle except those whom its lord commanded be spared and whom, out of respect for him, he would not harm.

The castellan, thus forewarned and now even more concerned, hurried away to fetch a ledger in which he kept the muleteers' accounts for straw and barley and, accompanied by a lad carrying a candle-end and by the two maidens, he came back to Don Quixote and ordered him to kneel; and, after reading for a while from his ledger, as if reciting some devout prayer, he raised his hand and cuffed him on the neck and then, with Don Quixote's own sword, gave him a handsome thwack on the shoulder, all the while muttering as if praying. And then he commanded one of the maidens to gird on the novice knight's sword, a task performed with much grace and discretion, with which she needed to be well provided so as not to burst out laughing at each stage of the ceremony; but the exploits that they'd watched him perform kept their laughter in check. As the good lady girded on his sword, she said:

"May God make you a most fortunate knight and give you good fortune in your battles."

Don Quixote asked what was her name, so that he should thenceforth know to whom he was indebted for the favour received, because he intended to bestow upon her a share of the honour he was to win by the might of his arm. She humbly replied that her name was La Tolosa, and that she was the daughter of a cobbler from Toledo who lived near the Sancho Bienaya market stalls, and that wherever she was she'd serve him and regard him as her lord. Don Quixote replied that, for his sake and as a favour to him, she should thenceforth take the title of a lady, and call herself Doña Tolosa. She promised to do so, and the other maiden buckled on his spurs; there ensued almost exactly the same dialogue as with the lady of the sword. He asked what was her name, she said it was La Molinera, because she was the daughter of an honourable miller from Antoquera, and Don Quixote also asked her to take a title, and call herself Doña Molinera, and offered her further services and favours.

Now that these unprecedented ceremonies had been performed, at top speed, Don Quixote couldn't wait to be on horseback sallying forth in search of adventures, and he saddled and mounted Rocinante and, having embraced his host, made such extraordinary statements as he thanked him for the favour of dubbing him knight that it would be impossible to do them justice in writing. The innkeeper, concerned only to be rid of his guest, replied to his rhetoric in no less high-flown although somewhat briefer terms, and was so delighted to see the back of the man that he didn't demand any payment for his stay at the inn.

Chapter 4

ABOUT WHAT HAPPENED TO OUR KNIGHT WHEN HE LEFT THE INN

It must have been about daybreak when Don Quixote left the inn, so happy, so gallant, so delighted at being a properly dubbed knight that the very girths of his horse were bursting with his joy. But remembering his host's advice about the essential supplies that he should take with him, and in particular money and shirts, he decided to return home and equip himself with them and with a squire, resolving to take into his service a neighbour, a poor farmer who had a large family but was well suited to the squirely office. With this in mind he turned Rocinante towards his home village, and the nag, half sensing its old haunts, began to trot with such zest that its hooves seemed not to touch the ground.

He hadn't gone far when he thought he could hear, coming from a dense wood on his right, faint sounds as of someone moaning, and he said:

"I thank heaven for the favour it now grants me, providing me with such an early opportunity to fulfil the duties of my profession and gather the fruit of my honourable intentions. These cries come, no doubt, from some man or woman in distress, who stands in need of my protection and assistance."

He turned right and rode over to where he thought the sounds were coming from. A few steps into the wood he saw a mare tied by the reins to an evergreen oak, and tied to another a lad of about fifteen, naked from the waist up, and this was the one who was crying out, not without reason, because a burly farmer was flogging him with a leather belt, accompanying each blow with a word of reproof and advice:

"Keep your mouth shut and your eyes open."

And the lad replied:

"I won't do it again, sir, by Christ who died on the Cross I swear I won't, I promise that from now on I'll take more care of the flock."

When Don Quixote saw what was happening, he fired up and said:

"Discourteous knight: it ill becomes you to assault one who cannot defend himself; mount your steed and take up your lance," (for the man also had a lance leaning up against the oak to which his mare was tethered) "and I shall force you to recognize that your actions are those of a coward."

The farmer, seeing such a figure bearing down on him, encased in armour and brandishing a lance under his nose, gave himself up for dead and meekly replied:

"This lad I'm punishing, sir knight, is one of my servants, and his job is to look after a flock of sheep for me, but he's so careless that every day one of them goes missing; and although what I'm punishing is his carelessness, or his wickedness, he says I'm doing it because I'm a skinflint, so as not to pay him his wages—but I swear by God and by my eternal soul that he's lying."

"You dare to use that word in my presence, you villainous wretch?"[1] said Don Quixote. "I swear by the sun that shines down on us that I am minded to run you through with this lance. Pay him immediately, and do not answer back; otherwise, by God who rules us, I shall exterminate and annihilate you this very instant. Untie him."

The farmer bowed his head and, without uttering a word, untied his servant, whom Don Quixote asked how much his master owed him. The reply was nine months at seven reals a month. Don Quixote worked it out and found that it came to seventy-three reals, which he told the farmer to hand over there and then, if he didn't want to die. The fearful countryman swore by the tight corner he was in and by the oath he'd already sworn (he hadn't sworn any oath at all), that it wasn't as much as all that, because an allowance and deduction had to be made for three pairs of shoes he'd given the lad, and one real paid for two blood-lettings when he'd been ill.

"That is all very well," replied Don Quixote, "but the shoes and the blood-lettings will be set against the flogging you have given him without due cause: for if he has done some damage to the hide of the shoes that you bought him, you have damaged his own hide, and if the barber bled him when he was ill, you have done the same to him in good health; so that on this account he owes you nothing."

"The problem is, sir knight, I haven't got any money on me; if Andrés would like to come home with me, I'll pay him every single real I owe him."

"Me, go with him, ever again?" said the lad. "No fear! No sir, I wouldn't even dream of it—so that as soon as we're alone again he can flay me like St Bartholomew?"[2]

"He shall do no such thing," replied Don Quixote. "My command will be sufficient to ensure his obedience; and provided that he gives me his oath by the laws of the order of chivalry into which he has been admitted, I shall allow him to go free, and personally guarantee the payment."

"Think what you're saying, sir," said the lad. "My master here isn't a knight at all, and he's never been admitted into any order of chivalry—he's just Juan Haldudo, the rich farmer from Quintanar."

"That is of little consequence," replied Don Quixote, "there is no reason why someone with a plebeian name should not be a knight, for every man is the child of his own deeds."

"That's as may be," said Andrés, "but this master of mine, what deeds is he the child of, seeing as how he refuses to pay me any wages for my sweat and toil?"

"I'm not refusing you anything at all, my dear Andrés," replied the farmer. "Please do be so kind as to come with me—I swear by all the orders of chivalry in the world to pay you, as I said, every single real I owe you, and with brass knobs on too."

"You may dispense with the brass knobs," said Don Quixote. "Pay him in silver reals, and that will satisfy me; and take good care to do exactly as you have sworn to do, for otherwise, by that same oath, I swear that I will come back to punish you, and that I will find you, even if you hide yourself away like a lizard. And if you wish to know who is issuing these commands, so as to be the more obliged to obey them,

---

1. The word in question is "lying"; Don Quixote takes the farmer's words as a personal assault, since he has chosen to defend the young boy.

2. A martyr who was flayed alive.

know that I am the valiant Don Quixote de la Mancha, the righter of wrongs and in-justices; and God be with you, and do not forget for one moment what you have promised and sworn, under pain of the penalties prescribed."

And as he said this he spurred Rocinante, and before very long he had got under way. The farmer followed him with his gaze, and as soon as he was certain that he'd ridden out of the wood and was out of sight, he turned to his servant Andrés and said:

"Come here, my son, I want to pay you what I owe you, just as that righter of wrongs has ordered."

"I swear you will, too," said Andrés, "and you'll do well to obey that good knight's commands, God bless him, because he's such a brave man and such a good judge, by all that's holy, that if you don't pay me he'll come back and do what he said he'd do."

"And I swear I will, too," said the farmer, "but, since I'm so very fond of you, I think I'll increase the debt first, just so as to increase the repayment."

And seizing him by the arm, he tied him back to the evergreen oak and flogged him half dead.

"And now, Señor Andrés," said the farmer, "you can call upon your righter of wrongs. As you'll see, he isn't going to right this particular wrong in a hurry. But I don't think I've done with the wronging quite yet, because I'm feeling the urge to skin you alive, just as you feared I would."

But at length he untied him and told him he could go off in search of his judge so that this gentleman could carry out the sentence he'd pronounced. Andrés crept sullenly away, swearing that he was going in search of the brave Don Quixote de la Mancha to tell him exactly what had happened, and that the farmer would pay for it sevenfold. But, for all that, Andrés departed in tears and his master was left laughing.

This was how the valiant Don Quixote redressed that wrong; and delighted with what had happened, and considering that he had made a most happy and glorious beginning to his knight-errantry, he rode towards his village full of satisfaction, and murmuring:

"Well may you call yourself fortunate above all women who dwell on this earth, O Dulcinea del Toboso, fairest of the fair, for it has befallen your lot to hold subjected and enslaved to your every wish and desire a knight as valiant and far-famed as is and shall be Don Quixote de la Mancha, who (as all the world knows) was but yesterday admitted to the order of chivalry and today has righted the greatest injury and wrong ever devised by unreason and perpetrated by cruelty: today he has wrested the scourge from the hand of that pitiless enemy who was so unjustly flogging that delicate child."

As he was saying this he came to a crossroads, and this brought to his mind those other crossroads where knights errant would pause to consider which way to go; and, to imitate them, he remained motionless for a while; but after careful thought he let go of the reins, surrendering his will to that of his nag, which followed its original inclination—to head for its stable. After a couple of miles, Don Quixote spotted a throng of people who, as it afterwards transpired, were merchants from Toledo on their way to Murcia to buy silk.[3] There were six of them, each beneath his sunshade, accompanied by four servants on horseback and three footmen. As soon as Don Quixote saw them, he imagined that here was the opportunity for a new adventure; and, wishing to imitate in every way he believed he could the passages of arms he'd read about in his

---

3. Murcia is on the southwest coast of Spain.

books, he decided that one he had in mind was perfect for this situation. And so, with a gallant bearing and a resolute air, he steadied himself in his stirrups, clutched his lance, lifted his leather shield to his chest and, taking up his position in the middle of the highway, awaited the arrival of these knights errant, for this was what he judged them to be; and when they came within sight and earshot, Don Quixote raised his voice and, striking a haughty posture, declared:

"You will none of you advance one step further unless all of you confess that in all the world there is no maiden more beauteous than the Empress of La Mancha, the peerless Dulcinea del Toboso."

The merchants halted when they heard these words and saw the strange figure uttering them, and from the figure and the words they realized that the man was mad; but they had a mind to stay and see what would be the outcome of the required confession and one of them, waggish and sharp-witted, said:

"Sir knight, we don't know who this worthy lady is; do let us see her, because if she's as beautiful as you claim she is, we'll most freely and willingly confess that what you say is true."

"If I were to let you see her," retorted Don Quixote, "what merit would there be in confessing so manifest a truth? The whole point is that, without seeing her, you must believe, confess, affirm, swear and uphold it; if not, monstrous and arrogant wretches, you shall face me in battle forthwith. For whether you present yourselves one by one, as the order of chivalry requires, or all together, as is the custom and wicked practice of those of your ilk, here I stand and wait for you, confident in the justice of my cause."

"Sir knight," replied the merchant, "I beg you, in the name of all us princes gathered here, that—so as not to burden our consciences by confessing something never seen or heard by any of us, particularly since it is so detrimental to the Empresses and Queens of La Alcarria and Extremadura[4]—you be pleased to show us a portrait of that lady, even if no bigger than a grain of wheat; because the skein can be judged by the thread, as they say, and this will leave us satisfied and reassured, and leave you pleased and contented; indeed I believe we are already so far inclined in her favour that, even if her portrait shows that one of her eyes has gone skew-whiff and that sulphur and cinnabar ooze out of the other one, we will, just to please you, say in her favour whatever you want us to say."

"It does not ooze, you infamous knaves," replied Don Quixote, burning with anger. "It does not ooze, I repeat, with what you say, but with ambergris and civet kept in finest cotton; and she is not skew-whiff or hunch-backed, but straighter than a Guadarrama spindle.[5] And you shall pay for the great blasphemy you have uttered against such beauty as that of my lady!"

And so saying he charged with lowered lance at the blasphemer in such fury that, if good fortune hadn't made Rocinante trip and fall on the way, things would have gone badly for the reckless merchant. But Rocinante did fall, and his master rolled over the ground for some distance, and he tried to get up, but he couldn't, so encumbered was he by his lance, his leather shield, his spurs and his helmet, together with the burden of all the rest of his ancient armour. And as he struggled in vain to rise he cried:

---

4. La Alcarria, known for its production of honey, and Extremadura, on the border of Portugal, are relatively underdeveloped regions in Spain; the designation is thus vaguely insulting.

5. Guadarrama is a mountainous area outside of Madrid well-known for its cloth production.

"Flee not, you paltry cowards; you wretches, bide your time. 'Tis my horse's fault and not my own that I am lying here."

One of the footmen—not, it seems, a very well-intentioned one—on hearing all this bluster from the poor fallen fellow, couldn't resist giving him an answer on his ribs. And coming up to him he grabbed his lance and, breaking it into pieces, took one of them and began to give our Don Quixote such a pounding that, in spite of all his armour, he ended up as well threshed as the finest chaff. The muleteer's masters were shouting to him not to hit so hard, and to stop, but the lad was by now so caught up in his game that he wouldn't leave it until he'd played all the cards of his fury, and, picking up the other pieces of the lance, he shattered them, too, on the poor fallen man who, in the face of the storm of blows raining down, never stopped shouting as he threatened heaven and earth and those brigands, as he imagined them to be.

The lad grew tired, and the merchants continued their journey, supplied with enough to talk about throughout it on the subject of the poor pounded knight. Once he found himself alone, he again tried to get up; but if he hadn't been able to do so when fit and well, how was he going to manage it now that he was pummelled to pieces? Even so he considered himself lucky, in the belief that this was a fitting misfortune for knights errant, and he blamed his horse for it all; and it was impossible to get up, so very bruised and battered was his body.

Chapter 5

IN WHICH THE STORY OF OUR KNIGHT'S MISFORTUNE IS CONTINUED

Finding, then, that he couldn't move, it occurred to him to resort to his usual remedy, which was to think about some passage from his books; and his madness brought to his memory the episode from the story of Baldwin and the Marquis of Mantua in which Carloto leaves Baldwin wounded in the forest, a tale known to every little boy, not unfamiliar to youths, celebrated and even believed by old men, yet with no more truth in it than the miracles of Muhammad.[1] It was perfect for the predicament in which he found himself; and so, with many manifestations of extreme suffering, he began to writhe about on the ground and to say in the faintest of voices what the wounded knight of the forest is said to have said:

> Where are you, mistress of my heart?
> Are you not pained by my distress?
> Maybe you know not of my plight,
> Maybe you're false and pitiless.

And on he went reciting the ballad right up to the lines that go:

> O noble Marquis, gentle sire,
> My uncle and my lord by blood . . .

Fortune decreed that at this point a farmer from his own village, one of his neighbours, happened to be returning home after taking a hundredweight of wheat to the mill. Seeing a man lying there the farmer came up and asked him who he was and what was the matter with him, moaning away like that. No doubt Don Quixote

---

1. Don Quixote is thinking of a ballad about the son of Charlemagne (Carloto), who wounds the nephew of the Marquis of Mantua; the Marquis in turn will seek perpetual revenge. The anti-Islamic sentiment is not unusual in the period.

thought that this was the Marquis of Mantua, his uncle, and so his only response was to continue reciting his ballad, informing the man of his misfortune and of the love that the Emperor's son felt for his wife, exactly as the ballad relates.

The farmer was astonished to hear all this nonsense; and, removing the man's visor, which had been battered to pieces, he wiped his face, which was covered in dust. And once he'd done wiping he recognized him and said:

"Señor Quixana," (for this must have been his name when he was sane and hadn't yet turned from a placid hidalgo into a knight errant) "who's done this to you?"

But he continued to reply with his ballad to everything he was asked. Sizing up the situation, the farmer took his back and breast plates off as best he could, to see if he was wounded, but couldn't see any blood or signs of any hurt. He managed to lift him up, and with great difficulty hoisted him on to the donkey, since this seemed the more tranquil animal. He picked up the armour and arms, including the fragments of the lance, and tied them on to Rocinante, which he took by the reins, and taking his donkey by the halter he set off in the direction of his village, deep in thought as he heard the nonsense being spoken by Don Quixote, who was no less pensive and so badly bruised that he couldn't keep his seat on the donkey, and every so often breathed sighs loud enough to reach heaven; so that the farmer again felt he should ask what was wrong, and it must have been the devil himself who made Don Quixote recall tales to fit the events, because at that moment, forgetting all about Baldwin, he remembered Abindarráez the Moor being captured and taken as a prisoner to his castle by the Governor of Antequera, Rodrigo de Narváez. So that when the farmer asked him again how he felt and what was the matter with him, he replied with the very same words and arguments used by the captive Moor to reply to Rodrigo de Narváez, as he'd read the story in Jorge de Montemayor's *Diana*,[2] making such appropriate use of it that the farmer wished himself to the devil for having to listen to such a pack of absurdities. He realized his neighbour was mad, and hurried on to the village so as not to have to put up with Don Quixote's interminable harangue more than necessary. It concluded like this:

"You must know, Señor Don Rodrigo de Narváez, that this fair Jarifa I have mentioned is now the beauteous Dulcinea del Toboso, for whom I have performed, do perform and shall perform the most famous deeds of chivalry that have been witnessed, are witnessed and shall be witnessed in this world."

The farmer replied:

"Look here sir, as I'm a sinner I'm not Don Rodrigo de Narváez, nor the Marquis of Mantua, but Pedro Alonso, your neighbour; and you aren't Baldwin, nor Abindarráez, but the honourable hidalgo Señor Quixana."

"I know who I am," retorted Don Quixote, "and I know that I can be not only all those whom I have mentioned, but every one of the Twelve Peers of France, and every one of the Nine Worthies as well, because all the deeds performed by them both singly and together will be exceeded by mine."[3]

2. A popular pastoral romance; begun by Gil Polo, its second part was written by Jorge de Montemayor in the mid-16th century. The episode about Abindarráez, the captive Moor, is from the novel.
3. The 12 peers were the warriors of Charlemagne's court in late 8th-century France. The nine worthies consisted of three groups of Christians, Jews, and Gentiles; Charle-

magne, David, and Alexander are among them. Along with the Knights of the Round Table, a band of worthies assembled by the legendary King Arthur of England, these three groups of warriors provide constant (even interchangeable) points of comparison for the deluded Quixote.

With these exchanges and other similar ones they approached the village at nightfall, but the farmer waited until it was darker so that nobody could see the battered hidalgo so wretchedly mounted. When he thought the time had come he entered the village and went straight to Don Quixote's house, which was in an uproar: the priest and the barber, great friends of Don Quixote's, were there, and his housekeeper was shouting:

"And what's your opinion, Father Pero Pérez sir," (for this was the priest's name) "about my master's misfortune? Three days it's been now without a trace of him, his nag, his leather shield, his lance or his armour. A fine pickle I'm in! It's my belief, as sure as I was born to die, that his brain's been turned by those damned chivalry books of his he reads all the time—I remember often hearing him say to himself that he wanted to be a knight errant and go off in search of adventures. The devil take all those books, and Barabbas[4] take them too, for scrambling the finest mind in all La Mancha!"

The niece said much the same and even more:

"And let me tell you this, Master Nicolás," (for this was the barber's name). "My uncle would often be reading those evil books of misadventure for two whole days and nights on end, and then he'd throw his book down, grab his sword and slash the walls of his room, and once he was exhausted he'd say that he'd killed four giants as big as four towers, and that the sweat pouring from him was blood from the wounds received in battle, and then he'd drink a pitcher of cold water and feel calm and well again, claiming that the water was a most precious draught brought by the famous sage Squiffy, a great enchanter and friend of his.[5] But I'm the one to blame for it all, not telling you gentlemen about my uncle's madness so you could have done something about it and burned those unchristian books of his before it came to all this; he's got lots and lots of them, and they do deserve to be put to the flames, like heretics."

"I agree with that," said the priest, "and I swear that before another day has passed they'll be put on public trial and condemned to the flames so that they can't make anyone reading them do what my friend must have done."

All this was overheard by Don Quixote and the farmer, who could no longer have any doubts about his neighbour's illness, and so he began to shout:

"Open up to Sir Baldwin and the Marquis of Mantua, who's sore wounded here, and to the Moor Abindarráez, brought captive by the valiant Rodrigo de Narváez, the Governor of Antequera."

These shouts brought all four running into the porch, and as the men recognized their friend, and the women their master and uncle, who hadn't dismounted from the donkey because he couldn't, they ran to embrace him. He said:

"Stop, all of you, for I am sore wounded through the fault of my steed. Carry me to my bed and, if you are able, summon the wise Urganda[6] to heed and tend my wounds."

"Just look at him, in the name of the devil!" cried the housekeeper. "Didn't I know in the marrow of my bones what was wrong with the master? Up you go, sir, up you go to bed, we'll cure you well enough without any need for that there Ugandan woman. Damn those chivalry books, damn the lot of them, getting you into such a state!"

---

4. The thief whom Pilate released to the Jews when they requested that he be freed rather than Jesus.

5. An enchanter (Alquife) from *Amadis of Gaul*.
6. Alquife's wife.

They took him to his bed and, examining him for wounds, couldn't find any; he told them that it had been a general, overall battering sustained when he and his steed Rocinante suffered a terrible fall as he was doing battle with ten giants, the most lawless and reckless giants to be found almost anywhere on the face of the earth.

"I see, I see!" said the priest. "So there are giants in the game as well, are there? I swear by this Holy Cross that I'll burn them tomorrow, before the day is over."

They asked Don Quixote a thousand questions, and his only reply was to request food and to be allowed to sleep, for this was his greatest need. And then the priest asked the farmer to tell him exactly how he'd found Don Quixote. The farmer told him the whole story, including the nonsense that on being discovered and transported the knight had uttered, which made the priest even more anxious to do what the very next day he did do: call on his friend the barber Master Nicolás, with whom he walked to Don Quixote's house.

from *Chapter 6*

ABOUT THE AMUSING AND EXHAUSTIVE SCRUTINY THAT THE PRIEST AND
THE BARBER MADE IN THE LIBRARY OF OUR INGENIOUS HIDALGO

Who was still asleep. The priest asked the niece for the keys of the room where the books, the authors of the mischief, were kept, and she was happy to hand them over. They went in, the housekeeper too, and found more than a hundred large volumes, finely bound, and some small ones; and as soon as the housekeeper saw them, she ran out of the room and back again clutching a bowl of holy water and some hyssop, and said:

"Here you are, reverend father, you take this and sprinkle the room with it, just in case there's one of those hordes of enchanters from those books in here, and he puts a spell on us as a punishment for the torments they'll undergo once we've wiped them off the face of the earth."

The priest laughed at the housekeeper's simple-mindedness, and told the barber to hand him the books one by one so that he could see what was in them, since he might find some that didn't deserve to be committed to the flames.[1]

"No," said the niece, "there's no reason to let any of them off, they're all to blame. Better throw the whole lot of them out of the windows into the courtyard, and make a pile of them, and set fire to them, or take them to the backyard and make the bonfire there, where the smoke won't be such a nuisance."

The housekeeper said much the same, so anxious were both women to see those innocents massacred, but the priest wouldn't agree without at least reading the titles. The first one that Master Nicolás put into his hands was *The Four Books of Amadis of Gaul,* and the priest said:

"This is a strange coincidence: I've heard that this was the very first chivalry romance to be printed in Spain, and that all the others have their origin and beginning in it; so it seems to me that, as the prophet of such a pernicious sect, it should be condemned to the flames without delay."

---

1. The auto-de-fé which the priest is orchestrating—a public exhibition of those convicted of heresy—would have been a familiar sight in the days of the Inquisition; at times such an exhibition culminated in the death by fire of the heretic. There were calls to burn chivalric books as well in the mid-16th century when the fashion of chivalric romances was at its height.

"No, no," said the barber. "I've also heard that it's the very best of all the books of this kind that have ever been written; and so, being unique in its artistry, it ought to be pardoned."

"You're right," said the priest, "so its life is spared for the time being. Let's see that one next to it."

"This," said the barber, "is *The Exploits of Esplandian,* Amadis of Gaul's legitimate son."[2]

"Well, to be sure," said the priest, "the excellence of the father isn't going to be of any avail to the son. Here you are, ma'am, open that window and throw it into the yard, the first faggot on the bonfire we're going to make."

The housekeeper was delighted to do so, and the good Esplandian flew out into the courtyard, where he patiently awaited the flames with which he was threatened.

"Let's see the next one," said the priest.

"This," said the barber, "is *Amadis of Greece,* and all the books on this side, I think, are members of that same family."[3]

"Then out into the yard with the lot of them," said the priest. "Just to be able to burn Queen Pintiquiniestra, and the shepherd Darinel, and his eclogues, and his author's devilish, contorted language, I'll burn the father that begot me, too, if I catch him going about as a knight errant."

"I agree," said the barber.

"So do I," added the niece.

"That being so," said the housekeeper, "let's have them here, and out into the courtyard they all go."

They gave them to her, and since there were so many of them she spared herself the stairs again and flung them out of the window. . . .

And not wanting to weary himself any more reading chivalry romances, the priest ordered the housekeeper to take all the big books and throw them out into the yard. His command didn't fall on deaf ears, because she'd rather have been burning those books than weaving the finest and largest piece of fabric in the world, and, seizing about eight of them, she heaved them out of the window. But because she took up so many of them together, one fell at the barber's feet and, curious to know what it was, he saw: *History of the Famous Knight Tirante the White.*[4]

"Good heavens!" cried the priest. "Fancy Tirante the White being here! Give it to me, my friend: I reckon I've found in this book a treasure of delight and a mine of entertainment. In it you'll discover Don Quirieleisón de Montalbán, a most courageous knight, and his brother Tomás de Montalbán, and the knight Fonseca, together with the fight that the brave Tirante had with the mastiff, and the witticisms of the maiden Placerdemivida, and the amours and the trickery of the widow Reposada, and the lady empress in love with her squire Hipólito. Let me tell you this, my friend; as far as its style is concerned this is the best book in the world. In it knights eat and sleep and die in their beds and make wills before they die, and other such things that are usually omitted from books of this sort. But in spite of all this I do have to say that the man who wrote it deserved to be sent to the galleys for life, for not knowing what he was doing when he was writing such nonsense. Take it home and read it, and you'll see that what I say is true."

"That I'll do," replied the barber, "but what about these other little books here?"

2. Written by the author of *Amadis of Gaul* and published two years later.

3. The Amadis story provoked a number of imitations.
4. A late 15th-century Catalan chivalric romance.

"They can't be books of chivalry," said the priest, "but books of poetry."

And, opening one of them he saw that it was Jorge de Montemayor's *Diana* and, convinced that they were all of the same sort, he said:

"These don't deserve to be burned with the others, because they aren't and never will be as damaging as those books of chivalry have been—these are books for the intellect, and do nobody any harm."

"Oh sir," cried the niece, "please have them burned like the rest, because it could well happen that once my uncle gets over his chivalry illness he starts reading all these other books and takes it into his head to become a shepherd and wander about the forests and meadows singing and playing music and, what would be even worse than that, turn into a poet, which they say is a catching and incurable disease."

"The girl's right," said the priest, "and it'll be a good idea to remove this dangerous stumbling-block from our friend's way."

* * *

Chapter 7

About our worthy knight Don Quixote de la Mancha's second sally

And now Don Quixote began to bellow:

"Come, come, you valiant knights; 'tis now you must display the worth of your mighty arms, for the courtiers are getting the better of the tourney."

They ran to see what the commotion was all about, and this put a stop to the scrutiny of the remaining books; as a result it's believed that *Carolea* and *The Lion of Spain,* together with *The Exploits of the Emperor* by Luis de Avila,[1] went to the flames without any trial at all, because they must have been among the remainder; and perhaps if the priest had examined them they wouldn't have received such a severe sentence.

By the time they reached Don Quixote's room he was out of bed, shouting and raving, laying about him with his sword in all directions with slashes and backstrokes, as wide awake as if he'd never slept. They wrestled him back to bed, and once he'd calmed down a little, he turned to the priest and said:

"Indeed, my Lord Archbishop Turpin, it is a disgrace for us, who call ourselves the Twelve Peers, so meekly to allow those knights courtiers to carry off the victory in this tournament, after we knights adventurers had won all the honours on the previous three days."[2]

"Hush, my friend," said the priest, "God will grant a change of fortune so that what is lost today is won tomorrow, and for the moment you should look to your health—you seem to be overtired, if not sore wounded."

"Wounded I am not," said Don Quixote, "but weak and exhausted I am indeed, for the bastard Roland has been pounding me with the trunk of an evergreen oak, and all out of envy, because he can see that I am the only man who opposes his bravado. But my name would not be Reynald of Montalbán if, as soon as I rise from this bed, I did not make him pay for it, in spite of all his magic spells.[3] For the present, however,

1. *La Carolea* and *The Lion of Spain* were heroic poems about Charles V (1500–1558), who was both Holy Roman Emperor and king of Spain; *The Exploits of the Emperor* chronicled Charles V's deeds in prose.
2. Turpin was archbishop at Charlemagne's court and the fabled author of the *Song of Roland.*
3. Reynald (Rinaldo) was Roland's cousin; Roland (Orlando) is conceived as virtually invulnerable to injury in the Italian romance tradition.

bring me victuals, for they, I know, will be more to my purpose, and leave it to me to seek my revenge."

And that's what they did: they gave him some food, and he fell asleep again, and they fell to marvelling at his madness.

That night the housekeeper burned to ashes all the books in the courtyard and the house, and some must have perished that deserved to be treasured in perpetual archives; but fate, and the scrutineer's laziness, wouldn't permit it, and in them was fulfilled the proverb which says that the just sometimes pay for sinners.

One of the remedies that the priest and the barber had prescribed at that time for their friend's malady was to have his library walled up and sealed off, so that he couldn't find his books when he got up—maybe if the cause was removed the effect might cease—and to tell him that an enchanter had carried them off, with the library and all; and this was done without delay. Two days later Don Quixote did get up, and his first action was to go and look at his books; and, since he couldn't find the room in which he'd left them, he wandered all over the house searching for it. He kept going up to the place where the door used to be, and feeling for it with his hands, and running his eyes backwards and forwards over the walls without uttering a word; and after some time doing this he asked his housekeeper where his library was. Well trained in her answer, she said:

"And what library do you think you're looking for? There's no library and no books left in this house, because the devil himself took them away."

"No it wasn't the devil," replied the niece, "it was an enchanter who came one night on a cloud, after you'd gone away, and he climbed off a serpent he was riding and he went into the library and I don't know what he got up to in there, because a bit later he flew away over the roof and left the house full of smoke; and when we made up our minds to go and see what he'd done, we couldn't find any books or any library. All we remember is that as that wicked old man flew away he shouted that because of a secret grudge he bore the owner of the books and the library, he'd done the house the damage that we were about to discover. He also said that he was called the sage Munaton."

"Frestón is what he must have said," said Don Quixote.

"I don't know," said the housekeeper, "whether he was called Frestón or Piston or whatever, all I know is his name ended in ton."[4]

"That is indeed his name," said Don Quixote, "and he is a wise enchanter, a great enemy of mine, who bears me much malice, because he knows by his arts and his learning that the time will come when I shall engage in single combat a knight who is a favourite of his, and defeat him, without his being able to do anything to prevent it, and for this reason he tries to make as much mischief for me as he can; but I can promise him that he is powerless to gainsay or avert what heaven has decreed."

"Who can doubt that?" said the niece. "But uncle, why do you have to go and get involved in these arguments? Wouldn't it be better to stay quietly at home instead of looking for better bread than what's made from wheat, and forgetting that many a man's gone out shearing and come back shorn?"

"My dear niece!" replied Don Quixote. "How wrong you are! Before anyone shears me I will pluck the beards off the chins of all those who even contemplate touching a single hair of mine!"

4. Probably Frestón, an enchanter in the chivalric romance *Don Belianís de Grecia*.

Neither woman answered him back, because they could see that he was grow-ing heated.

And yet he did stay quietly at home for a whole fortnight without showing any signs of wanting to re-enact his former follies, and during this time he talked all kinds of amusing bunkum with his friends the priest and the barber, as he declared that what the world most needed was knights errant and a rebirth of knight-errantry. Sometimes the priest contradicted him and sometimes he gave in to him, because if he didn't make use of this tactic it would be impossible to restore his sanity.

During this fortnight Don Quixote set to work on a farmer who was a neighbour of his, an honourable man (if a poor man can be called honourable) but a little short of salt in the brain-pan. To be brief, Don Quixote told him, reasoned with him and promised him so much that the poor villager decided to go away with him and serve him as squire. Don Quixote told the man, among other things, that he ought to be de-lighted to go, because at some time or other he could well have an adventure in which he won an island in the twinkling of an eye and installed his squire as governor. These and other similar promises persuaded Sancho Panza, for this was the farmer's name, to leave his wife and children and go into service as his neighbour's squire.

Don Quixote immediately set about raising money, and by selling one posses-sion, pawning another, and always making a bad bargain, he scraped together a rea-sonable sum. He also found himself a little round infantryman's shield, borrowed from a friend, and, patching up his shattered helmet as best he could, he told his squire Sancho the day and time he intended to set out, so that he too could obtain whatever he considered most necessary. Don Quixote was particularly insistent on saddle-bags, and Sancho said that indeed he would bring some, and he'd bring a very fine donkey of his too, because he wasn't all that much given to going very far on foot. At this Don Quixote hesitated, racking his brains to try and remember if any knight errant had ever been escorted by a donkey-mounted squire, but none came to mind; yet for all that he decided that Sancho should ride his donkey, proposing to pro-vide him with a more honourable mount at the earliest opportunity, by unhorsing the first discourteous knight he came across. Don Quixote stocked up with shirts and everything else he could, following the advice that the innkeeper had given him; and once all these preparations had been made, without Panza saying goodbye to his wife and children, or Don Quixote to his housekeeper and niece, they left the village un-seen one night, and by daybreak they'd ridden so far they felt certain no one would be able to find them however hard he looked.

Sancho Panza rode his ass like a patriarch, complete with saddle bags and leather bottle, longing to be the governor of the island his master had promised him. Don Quixote happened to take the same road he'd followed on his first sally, across the plain of Montiel, with less discomfort than before, because it was early morning and the sun, being low, didn't bother them. Sancho Panza said to his master:

"You'll be sure, won't you, sir knight, not to forget what you promised me about the island. I'll be up to governing it all right, however big it is."

To which Don Quixote replied:

"I would have you know, my good friend Sancho Panza, that it was a custom much in use among the knights errant of old to make their squires the governors of the islands or kingdoms that they conquered, and I have determined that such an ancient usage shall not lapse through my fault. Quite on the contrary, I intend to improve upon it: for those knights would sometimes—more often than not, perhaps—wait until their squires were old men and, once they were tired of serving and of suffering bad days and worse nights, give them some title, such as count or at the most marquis of some valley or paltry province; but if your life and mine are spared, it could well be that within six days I shall conquer a kingdom with others annexed, any one of which would be perfect for you to be crowned king of it. And you must not think that there would be anything extraordinary about that: incidents and accidents befall us knights in such unprecedented and unimagined ways that I might easily be able to give you even more than I have promised."

"And so," said Sancho Panza, "if by one of those miracles you've just said I became king, then Juana Gutiérrez, my old woman, would be queen no less, and the kids would be princes and princesses."

"Who can doubt it?" replied Don Quixote.

"I can," retorted Sancho Panza. "To my mind, even if God rained kingdoms down on this earth none of them would sit well on my Mari Gutiérrez's head. Look here, sir, she wouldn't be worth two brass farthings as a queen—countess would suit her better, and even that'd be hard going for her."

"Commend the matter to God, Sancho," replied Don Quixote, "and he will give her what is best for her; but you must not be so daunted that you agree to content yourself with anything less than being a provincial governor."

"I shan't do that, sir," replied Sancho, "not with such a fine master as you, who'll be able to give me everything that's good for me and I can cope with."

Chapter 8

ABOUT THE BRAVE DON QUIXOTE'S SUCCESS IN THE DREADFUL AND UNIMAGINABLE ADVENTURE OF THE WINDMILLS, TOGETHER WITH OTHER EVENTS WORTHY OF HAPPY MEMORY

As he was saying this, they caught sight of thirty or forty windmills standing on the plain, and as soon as Don Quixote saw them he said to his squire:

"Fortune is directing our affairs even better than we could have wished: for you can see over there, good friend Sancho Panza, a place where stand thirty or more monstrous giants with whom I intend to fight a battle and whose lives I intend to take; and with the booty we shall begin to prosper. For this is a just war, and it is a great service to God to wipe such a wicked breed from the face of the earth."

"What giants?" said Sancho Panza.

"Those giants that you can see over there," replied his master, "with long arms: there are giants with arms almost six miles long."

"Look you here," Sancho retorted, "those over there aren't giants, they're windmills, and what look to you like arms are sails—when the wind turns them they make the millstones go round."

"It is perfectly clear," replied Don Quixote, "that you are but a raw novice in this matter of adventures. They are giants; and if you are frightened, you can take yourself away and say your prayers while I engage them in fierce and arduous combat."

And so saying he set spurs to his steed Rocinante, not paying any attention to his squire Sancho Panza, who was shouting that what he was charging were definitely windmills not giants. But Don Quixote was so convinced that they were giants that he neither heard his squire Sancho's shouts nor saw what stood in front of him, even though he was by now upon them; instead he cried:

"Flee not, O vile and cowardly creatures, for it is but one solitary knight who attacks you."

A gust of wind arose, the great sails began to move, and Don Quixote yelled:

"Though you flourish more arms than the giant Briareus,[1] I will make you pay for it."

So saying, and commending himself with all his heart to his lady Dulcinea, begging her to succour him in his plight, well protected by his little round infantry-man's shield, and with his lance couched, he advanced at Rocinante's top speed and charged at the windmill nearest him. As he thrust his lance into its sail the wind turned it with such violence that it smashed the lance into pieces and dragged the horse and his rider with it, and Don Quixote went rolling over the plain in a very sore predicament. Sancho Panza rushed to help his master at his donkey's fastest trot and found that he couldn't stir, such was the toss that Rocinante had given him.

"For God's sake!" said Sancho. "Didn't I tell you to be careful what you were do-ing, didn't I tell you they were only windmills? And only someone with windmills on the brain could have failed to see that!"

"Not at all, friend Sancho," replied Don Quixote. "Affairs of war, even more than others, are subject to continual change. All the more so as I believe, indeed I am cer-tain, that the same sage Frestón who stole my library and my books has just turned these giants into windmills, to deprive me of the glory of my victory, such is the en-mity he feels for me; but in the end his evil arts will avail him little against the might of my sword."

"God's will be done," replied Sancho Panza.

He helped his master to his feet, and his master remounted Rocinante, whose shoulder was half dislocated. And talking about this adventure they followed the road towards the Pass of Lápice, because Don Quixote said they couldn't fail to encounter plentiful and varied adventures there, as it was a much frequented spot. But he was dejected by the destruction of his lance, and he told his squire so, and added:

"I remember reading that a Spanish knight called Diego Pérez de Vargas, having broken his sword in battle, tore a weighty bough or trunk from an evergreen oak, and did such deeds with it that day, and thrashed so many Moors, that he was nicknamed Machuca, that is to say, the thrasher; and from that day onwards his surname and that of his descendants was changed to Vargas y Machuca.[2] I have told you this because from the first oak tree that comes before me I intend to tear off another such trunk, as good as the one I have in mind, and with it I intend to do such deeds as to make you consider yourself most fortunate to be deemed worthy to behold them, and to witness that which can hardly be believed."

"God's will be done," said Sancho. "I believe every word you say. But do sit up straighter, you're riding all lopsided, it must be that hammering you got when you fell off your horse."

"That is indeed the case," replied Don Quixote, "and if I do not utter any com-plaint about the pain it is because knights errant are not permitted to complain about wounds, even if their entrails are spilling out of them."

"If that's so there's nothing more for me to say," replied Sancho, "but God knows I'd like you to complain if anything hurts. As for me, I can tell you I'm going to moan like anything about the slightest little pain, unless that stuff about not com-plaining goes for knight errants' squires as well."

1. One of the mythological Titans, Briareus had 100 arms.   2. "Machuca" was the subject of ballads; he was instru-mental at the 13th-century battle of Jerez.

Don Quixote couldn't help laughing at his squire's simple-mindedness, and declared that he could moan as and when he pleased, whether he felt any pain or not, for he had not yet read anything to the contrary in the order of chivalry. Sancho pointed out that it was time to eat. His master replied that he didn't need any food yet, but that Sancho could eat whenever he liked. So Sancho settled himself down as best he could on his donkey and, taking out of his saddle-bags what he'd put into them, he jogged along and munched away behind his master, and every so often he'd take a swig from his leather bottle with such relish that the most self-indulgent innkeeper in Malaga[3] would have envied him. And as Sancho trotted on, drinking his fill, he didn't remember any of the promises his master had made him, and reckoned that going in search of adventures, however dangerous they might be, was more like good fun than hard work.

To cut a long story short, they spent that night under some trees, and from one of them Don Quixote tore a dead branch that might almost serve as a lance, and fastened on to it the iron head that he'd taken off the broken one. He didn't sleep in all the night, thinking about his lady Dulcinea, to conform with what he'd read in his books, where knights errant spent many sleepless nights in glades and deserts, engrossed in the recollection of their ladies. Not so Sancho Panza who, with his stomach full, and not of chicory water either, slept right through until morning; and, if his master hadn't called him, neither the rays of the sun, falling full on his face, nor the songs of the birds that, in great throngs and with expansive joy, greeted the coming of the new day, would have been capable of awaking him. He got up, had his breakfast swig and found his leather bottle rather slimmer than the evening before; and his heart sank, because it didn't look as if this lack was going to be remedied as soon as he'd have liked. Don Quixote refused breakfast because, as we know, he had decided to subsist on savoury recollections. They continued along the road to the Pass of Lápice, and at about three o'clock in the afternoon they sighted it.

"Over there, brother Sancho Panza," said Don Quixote when he saw it, "we can dip our arms right up to our elbows in what people call adventures. But take note that, even if you see me in the greatest peril imaginable, you must not seize your sword to defend me, unless you should see that those who attack me are rabble and common people, in which case you can most certainly come to my aid; but should they be knights and gentlemen, it is on no account licit or permitted by the laws of chivalry for you to assist me, until you yourself be knighted."

"You can be sure, sir," replied Sancho, "of being fully obeyed there, specially since I'm a peaceful man by nature and don't like getting involved in rows and brawls. Though I do have to say that when it comes to defending myself I'm not going to take much notice of those there laws of yours, because divine and human justice both let anyone defend himself against attack."

"I do not disagree in the slightest," replied Don Quixote, "but as regards assisting me against knights, you must keep your natural impetuosity under control."

"I'll do that all right," replied Sancho. "I'll keep that particular promise as strictly as the Sabbath."

As they talked away like this, two friars of the order of St Benedict appeared on the road, each seated upon a dromedary: their mules were no less tall than that. They came complete with their riding masks and their sunshades. Behind them was a coach

---

3. A port-town on the southern coast of Spain.

with four or five horsemen escorting it, and two footmen walking. In the coach, as was later discovered, there was a Basque lady on her way to Seville to join her husband, who was going to America to take up an important post. The friars weren't travelling with her, they just happened to be on the same road; but as soon as Don Quixote caught sight of them he said to his squire:

"Either I am much mistaken or this will be the most famous adventure ever witnessed; for those black figures over there must be and no doubt are enchanters abducting a princess in that coach, and I must redress this wrong to the utmost of my power."

"This'll be worse than the windmills," said Sancho. "Look here, sir, those there are Benedictine friars, and the coach must just be taking some travellers on their way. Look, look, do take care what you're doing, this could be one of the devil's own tricks."

"I have already told you, Sancho," replied Don Quixote, "that you know next to nothing on the subject of adventures. What I say is true, as you will soon see."

So saying, he rode forward and planted himself in the middle of the road down which the friars were plodding and, when he thought they were near enough to hear him, he cried:

"Diabolical and monstrous wretches, release this very moment the noble princesses whom you are abducting in that coach, or prepare to be killed this instant as a just punishment for your wicked works."

The friars reined in their mules and sat there in astonishment at the figure cut by Don Quixote and at the words he'd spoken, to which they replied:

"Sir knight, we aren't diabolical or monstrous at all, we're just two Benedictine friars going about our business, and we haven't the faintest idea whether there are any abducted princesses in this coach."

"Soft words will not work with me, for I know you only too well, perfidious knaves!" said Don Quixote.

And without awaiting any more replies he spurred Rocinante and charged with levelled lance at the friar in front with such determination and fury that, if the friar hadn't thrown himself from his mule, the knight would have brought him to the ground sore vexed and indeed sore wounded, if not stone dead. The other friar, seeing how his companion was being treated, dug his heels into his castle of a mule and made off across the plain faster than the wind.

Sancho Panza, seeing the friar sprawling on the ground, slipped off his donkey, ran over to him and began to strip him of his habits. And now two of the friars' servants came up and asked what he thought he was doing stripping their master like that. Sancho replied that the clothes were rightly his, the spoils of the battle his master Don Quixote had won. The servant-lads, who lacked a sense of humour and knew nothing about spoils and battles, seeing that Don Quixote had gone off to talk to the ladies in the coach, fell upon Sancho, knocked him to the ground, gave his beard a thorough plucking and his body a merciless kicking, and left him lying there breathless and senseless. Without pausing for an instant the friar remounted, terrified and trembling and drained of all colour, and spurred his mule in the direction of his companion, who was waiting a good distance away to see what would be the outcome of this nightmare; and not wanting to stop for the conclusion of the incident they continued on their way, making more signs of the cross than if they had the very devil at their backs.

Don Quixote, as has been said, was talking to the lady in the coach, and saying:

"You may now, in your ineffable loveliness, my lady, dispose of your person as best pleases you, for the pride of your ravishers lies on the ground, o'erthrown by this mighty arm of mine; and that you may not pine to know the name of your deliverer, be informed that I am Don Quixote de la Mancha, knight adventurer and errant, and captive to the peerless and beauteous Doña Dulcinea del Toboso; and in requital of the benefit you have received from me, all I desire is that you turn back to El Toboso and on my behalf present yourself before that lady and inform her of what I have accomplished for your deliverance."

Everything that Don Quixote said was overheard by one of the squires escorting the coach, a Basque; who, seeing that the man didn't want to let the coach continue on its way, but was saying that it must turn back at once to El Toboso, rode up to Don Quixote and, seizing him by the lance, said in bad Castilian and worse Basque:[4]

"Go on way, knight, and go with devil. By God made me, if not leaving coach, you as killed by Basque as stand there."

Don Quixote understood him perfectly, and with great composure he replied:

"If you were a knight and a gentleman, which you are not, I should already have punished your folly and audacity, you wretched creature."

To which the Basque replied:

"Me not gentleman? I swear God you lie as me Christian. If leaving lance and taking sword, soon see you monkey making! Basque on land, gentleman on sea, gentleman for devil, and see lie if other saying."

"'Now you shall see,' quoth Agrages,"[5] quoted Don Quixote.

And throwing his lance to the ground, he drew his sword, took up his little round shield and set upon the Basque, intending to kill him. The Basque, seeing the knight advance, would have preferred to dismount from his mule, which was a hired one and therefore a bad one and not to be trusted, but all he had time to do was to draw his sword; and it was lucky for him that he happened to be next to the coach, from which he was able to snatch a cushion to serve as a shield; and then the two men went for each other as if they were mortal enemies. The rest of the party would have made peace between them but they couldn't, because the Basque was saying in his topsy-turvy tongue that if they didn't let him finish his battle he'd kill his mistress and anyone else who got in his way. The lady in the coach, astonished and terrified at this sight, made the coachman drive a safe distance off, and then settled down to watch the desperate struggle, in the course of which the Basque dealt Don Quixote such a mighty blow on the shoulder, over the top of his shield, that if he hadn't been wearing armour he'd have been split down the middle. When Don Quixote felt the impact of the terrible stroke he cried:

"O lady of my soul, Dulcinea, flower of all beauty, succour this your knight who, through his desire to satisfy your great goodness, finds himself in this dire peril!"

Uttering these words, gripping his sword, raising his shield and launching himself at the Basque was the work of a moment, as Don Quixote resolved to venture everything on the fortune of a single blow. The Basque, seeing Don Quixote advance, could see from his spirited bearing what a brave man he was, and decided to follow his example; so he stood his ground, well protected by his cushion but unable to turn the mule one way or the other because by now, exhausted and unaccustomed to such pranks, it couldn't budge a single step.

---

4. The Basque region is in northern Spain. Basques were renowned for their fighting abilities, and their traditional limberness also made them good dancers. Their language is unrelated to Spanish. Castilian is another word for what has become the Spanish language.

5. A warrior from the *Amadis de Gaul* who typically says this phrase at the start of a fight.

So Don Quixote was advancing, as described, on the well-shielded Basque, with his sword aloft, determined to split him in half, and the Basque was awaiting him with his sword also aloft, and upholstered in his protective cushion, and all the bystanders were terrified and wondering what was going to be the outcome of the prodigious blows with which the two men were threatening each other; and the lady in the coach and her maids were making a thousand vows and offerings to all the images and holy places in Spain for God to deliver their squire and themselves from this great peril. But the trouble is that at this very point the author of this history leaves the battle unfinished, excusing himself on the ground that he hasn't found anything more written about these exploits of Don Quixote than what he has narrated. It is true, though, that the second author of this work refused to believe that such a fascinating history had been abandoned to the laws of oblivion, or that the chroniclers of La Mancha had been so lacking in curiosity that they hadn't kept papers relating to this famous knight in their archives or their desks; and so, with this in mind, he didn't despair of finding the end of this delectable history, which indeed, with heaven's help, he did find in the way that will be narrated in the second part.

SECOND PART OF THE INGENIOUS HIDALGO
DON QUIXOTE DE LA MANCHA

Chapter 9

IN WHICH THE STUPENDOUS BATTLE BETWEEN THE GALLANT BASQUE AND
THE VALIANT MAN FROM LA MANCHA IS BROUGHT TO A CONCLUSION

In the first part of this history we left the valiant Basque and the famous Don Quixote with naked swords aloft, about to deliver two such devastating downstrokes that if their aim was true they would at the very least split each other from top to bottom and cut each other open like pomegranates; and at this critical point the delightful history stopped short and was left truncated, without any indication from its author about where the missing section might be found.

This worried me, because the pleasure afforded by the little I had read turned to displeasure as I considered what an uphill task awaited me if I wanted to find the great bulk of material that, as I imagined, was missing from this delectable tale. It seemed impossible and contrary to all good practice that such an excellent knight shouldn't have had some sage who'd have made it his job to record his unprecedented deeds, something never lacked by any of those knights errant

Who go, as people say,
Adventuring their way,[1]

because every one of them had one or two sages, made to measure for him, who not only recorded his exploits but also depicted his least thoughts and most trivial actions, however hidden from the public gaze they were; and such an excellent knight couldn't have been so unfortunate as to be totally lacking in what Platir and the like had more than enough of.[2] So I couldn't bring myself to believe that such a superb history had been left maimed and mutilated, and I laid the blame on malicious time,

1. Likely to be a refrain from a contemporary ballad, one repeated several times in the novel.

2. A knight whose deeds were supposedly recorded.

the devourer and demolisher of all things, which had either hidden or destroyed what was missing.

It also struck me that, since modern books like *The Undeceptions of Jealousy* and *The Nymphs and Shepherds of Henares* had been found in his library, his history must also be a recent one, and that, even if it hadn't been put into writing, it must live on in the memory of the people of his village and others near by. All these thoughts left me feeling puzzled and eager for exact and authentic knowledge of the complete life and works of our famous Spaniard Don Quixote de la Mancha, the light and mirror of the chivalry of that land, and the first man in our times, in these calamitous times of ours, to devote himself to the toils and exercise of knight-errantry, and to the redressing of wrongs, the succouring of widows and the protecting of maidens, those maidens who used to ride about, up hill and down dale, with their whips and their palfreys, carrying their maidenhead with them; for unless raped by some blackguard, or by some peasant with his hatchet and his iron skullcap, or by some monstrous giant, there were maidens in those times gone by who, at the age of eighty and not having slept a single night under a roof, went to their graves with their maidenheads as intact as the mothers who'd borne them. I say, then, that for these and many other reasons our gallant Don Quixote is worthy of continuous and memorable praise—which shouldn't be denied me, either, for all the hard work and diligence I devoted to searching out the conclusion to this agreeable history; although I'm well aware that if heaven, chance and fortune hadn't helped me, the world would have been left without the pleasurable entertainment that an attentive reader of this work can enjoy for nearly two hours. And this is how I found the missing part:

One day when I was in the main shopping street in Toledo, a lad appeared, on his way to sell some old notebooks and loose sheets of paper to a silk merchant; and since I'll read anything, even scraps of paper lying in the gutter, this leaning of mine led me to pick up one of the notebooks that the lad had for sale, and I saw it was written in characters that I recognized as Arabic. Although I knew that much, I couldn't read them, and so I looked around to see if there was some Spanish-speaking Moor in the street, and it wasn't very hard to find one, because even if I'd been looking for a translator from another better and older language,[3] I should have found him, too. In short, chance provided me with a man who, when I told him what I wanted and put the book in his hands, opened it in the middle and after reading a little began to laugh. I asked him why, and he replied that he was laughing at something written in the margin of the book by way of annotation. I told him to tell me what it was and, still laughing, he replied:

"As I said, this is written here in the margin: 'This woman Dulcinea del Toboso, so often mentioned in this book, is said to have been a dabber hand at salting pork than any other woman in La Mancha.'"

When I heard "Dulcinea del Toboso" I was dumbfounded, because it immediately suggested that the notebooks contained the history of Don Quixote. So I told him to read me the title-page that very instant and he did so, making an extempore translation from the Arabic, and it said: *History of Don Quixote de la Mancha, written by Cide Hamete Benengeli, an Arab historian.*[4] I had to draw on all the discretion I

---

3. Hebrew. Despite the supposed banishing of both Moors and Jews from Spain in the late 15th and early 16th centuries, quite a few remained; many had become converts or *conversos*.

4. "Cide" (as in El Cid) means "Lord" in Arabic, and "Hamete" means "He who praises." "Benengeli," on the other hand, derives from the Spanish word for eggplant.

possess not to reveal how happy I felt when I heard the title of the book; and, getting in ahead of the silk merchant, I bought all the papers and notebooks from the lad for half a real; and if the lad himself had had any discretion and had noticed how much I wanted them, he could well have expected and indeed exacted more than six reals. Then I went off with the Moor to the cathedral cloister and asked him to translate the notebooks, or at least all those that had to do with Don Quixote, into Castilian, without adding or omitting a single word, and I offered to pay him whatever he asked. He was satisfied with fifty pounds of raisins and two bushels of wheat, and promised to make a good, faithful translation, and to be quick about it, too. But to ensure the smooth working of our agreement, and not to let such a find out of my sight, I brought the Moor home with me, and in little more than a month and a half he translated the whole text just as it is set down here.

In the first notebook there was a realistic picture of Don Quixote's battle with the Basque, with both of them in the positions described in the history, their swords aloft, one protected by his little round infantry man's shield and the other by his cushion, and the Basque's mule so lifelike that you could tell from a mile off that it was a hired one. At the Basque's feet were written the words *Don Sancho de Azpetia,* which must have been his name; and at Rocinante's feet were these other words: *Don Quixote.* Rocinante was depicted in such wonderful detail—as long as a wet week and as lean as a lath, with a jutting spine and far gone in consumption— that it was easy to see how appropriately he had been named Rocinante. Next to him stood Sancho Panza, holding his ass by the halter, and at his feet were the words *Sancho Zancas;* and he must, to judge from the picture, have had a short body, a plump paunch and long shanks, these last two features being expressed in the words Panza and Zancas[5] respectively, because he's given both these surnames at different points in this history. Other details could be observed, but none of them is important, or relevant to the truthful narration of this history—and no history is bad so long as it is truthful.

If there is any objection to be made about the truthfulness of this history, it can only be that its author was an Arab, and it's a well-known feature of Arabs that they're all liars; but since they're such enemies of ours, it's to be supposed that he fell short of the truth rather than exaggerating it. And this is, indeed, what I suspect he did, because where he could and should have launched into the praises of such an excellent knight, he seems to have been careful to pass them over in silence, which is something he shouldn't have done or even thought of doing, because historians should and must be precise, truthful and unprejudiced, without allowing self-interest or fear, hostility or affection, to turn them away from the path of truth, whose mother is history: the imitator of time, the storehouse of actions and the witness to the past, an example and a lesson to the present and a warning to the future. In this history I know that everything anyone could want to find in the most delectable history is to be found; and if anything worthwhile is missing from it, it's my belief that it's the dog of an author who wrote it that's to blame, rather than any defect in the subject. At all events the second part began like this, according to the translation:

The keen-edged swords of the two valiant and enraged combatants, thus raised aloft, seemed to be threatening the very heavens, earth and watery abysses, such was the determination displayed by both men. The first to deliver his blow was the wrathful Basque, and he did so with such force and fury that, if his sword had not twisted in

---

5. "Panza" means belly or paunch; "zancas" means legs.

the course of its descent, that stroke alone would have been enough to put an end to the fearful fight and to all our knight's adventures; but fortune, which had better things in store for him, turned his opponent's blade aside so that, although it struck his left shoulder, all the damage it did was to disarm him on that side, carrying with it a large part of his helmet together with half his ear, all of which tumbled to the ground in hideous ruin, leaving him in a sorry state indeed.

By God, who could describe the rage that took possession of the heart of the man of La Mancha on seeing himself treated in this way? All that can be said is that it was so great that he rose at last in his stirrups and, gripping his sword with both hands, brought it down with such fury full on the Basque's cushion and head that his admirable protection was of no avail and, as if a mountain had fallen on top of him, blood began to trickle from his nose, and from his mouth, and from his ears, and he started to slide off his mule, from which he would no doubt have fallen had he not clung to its neck; but even so he lost his stirrups and dropped his reins, and the animal, terrified by the awful blow, began to gallop this way and that, and soon bucked its rider off.

Don Quixote was calmly watching this scene, and when he saw the Basque fall he jumped from his horse, ran up to him and, putting the tip of his sword between his eyes, told him to surrender or he would cut off his head. The Basque was so stunned that he could not reply, and his fate would have been sealed, so blind with rage was Don Quixote, if the ladies in the coach, who had been watching the fight in consternation, had not hastened to where he stood and pleaded with him to do them the great kindness and favour of sparing their squire's life. To which Don Quixote, haughty and grave, replied:

"To be sure, fair ladies, I am well content to do as you request; but I insist on one condition to which you must agree, which is that this knight promise me to repair to the village of El Toboso and present himself on my behalf before the peerless Doña Dulcinea, that she may dispose of him according to her pleasure."

The fearful, disconsolate ladies, without stopping to think about what Don Quixote was demanding or even asking who Dulcinea was, promised that the squire would do whatever was required of him.

"Since you have given me your word, I shall do him no further harm, even though he richly merits it."

Chapter 10

About what happened next between Don Quixote and the Basque, and the peril with which he was threatened by a mob of men from Yanguas

By this time Sancho Panza had struggled to his feet, somewhat mauled by the friars' servants, and had stood watching Don Quixote's battle, as in his heart he prayed to God to be so kind as to give his master the victory and let him win some island of which he could make his squire the governor, as promised. So once Sancho saw that the fight was over and that his master was about to remount Rocinante, he went over to hold his stirrup and, before he started climbing, knelt down before him and, grasping his hand, kissed it and said:

"Don Quixote sir, please make me the governor of the island you've just won in this dreadful battle. However big it is, I'm sure I'll be strong enough to govern it as well as anyone who ever governed islands anywhere in the world."

To which Don Quixote replied:

"I would have you know, brother Sancho, that this adventure and others like it are not island adventures but roadside adventures, in which there is nothing to be won but a broken head and a missing ear. Be patient, for there will be adventures that will enable me to make you not only a governor but something greater still."

Sancho thanked him profusely and, again kissing his hand, and the skirts of his armour too, helped him on to Rocinante, and himself mounted his donkey and set out after his master, who, without a word of farewell to the ladies in the coach, rode off at a brisk pace into a nearby wood. Sancho followed as fast as his donkey could trot, but Rocinante's speed was such that Sancho fell further and further behind and had to call out to his master to wait for him. Don Quixote did so, reining Rocinante in until his weary squire caught up with him, and said:

"What I'm thinking, sir, is that it'd be a good idea to go and take refuge in some church somewhere, because that man you fought is in a really bad way, and it would-n't surprise me if we were reported to the Holy Brotherhood and they came to arrest us.[1] And by God, if they do that, we'll sweat blood before we get out of prison."

"Not at all, Sancho," said Don Quixote. "Where have you ever seen or read of a knight errant standing trial, whatever outrages he is accused of?"

"I don't know anything about getting out of rages, I've never been in one in my life—all I do know is that people who go fighting in the fields are dealt with by the Holy Brotherhood, and I'm not going to poke my nose into that other thing you said."

"Do not worry, my friend," replied Don Quixote, "for I shall rescue you from the Chaldeans themselves if need be,[2] let alone the Holy Brotherhood. But tell me, pray: have you ever seen a knight more valiant than I on all the face of the earth? Have you ever read in histories of any knight who is or has been more spirited in the attack, more persevering in the pursuit, more dexterous in the wounding or more skilful in the unhorsing?"

"To tell you the honest truth," replied Sancho, "I haven't ever read a history, be-cause I can't read or write, but what I will dare bet is that in all the days of my born life I've never served a braver master than you—and I pray God these braveries of yours aren't paid for where I just said. And what I pray you to do is to see to that ear of yours, you're losing a lot of blood from it. Here in my saddle-bags I've got some lint and white ointment."

"All this would have been quite unnecessary," replied Don Quixote, "if I had re-membered to make a flask of the Balsam of Fierabras: for but one drop of it would have saved us both time and medicine."[3]

"What flask and what balsam is that?" said Sancho Panza.

"It is," said Don Quixote, "a balsam the recipe for which I carry in my memory, and if provided with it one need not fear death or contemplate dying from any kind of wound. And so, once I make some and give it to you, all you have to do when you see that in some battle I have been cut in two (as often happens) is to take the part of my body that has fallen to the ground and, before the blood congeals, neatly and carefully place it on top of the part remaining in the saddle, being quite sure to make it fit exactly. Then you will have me drink just two mouthfuls of the balsam, and I shall be as sound as a bell."

---

1. Created during Ferdinand's and Isabella's reign, the Holy Brotherhood dealt largely with rural criminals and highway robbers.
2. The Chaldeans were a group of tribes who became dominant in Babylonia and were regarded as enemies of the Israelites.

3. The balsam in which Christ's body was embalmed, supposedly possessed of miraculous powers of healing. Fierabras is a giant who steals the balsam from the Chris-tians in the legends surrounding the history of Charle-magne; Charlemagne himself eventually retrieves it.

"If that's so," said Sancho, "I here and now renounce being governor of the island you've promised me, and all I want in payment for my many good services is for you to let me have the recipe for that wonderful potion—to my mind it'll fetch more than two reals an ounce anywhere, so it's all I need to live an honourable and easy life. But first I'd better know if it costs a lot to make."

"For less than three reals you can make twelve pints of it," replied Don Quixote.

"Strike me blind!" replied Sancho. "What are you waiting for, why not make some here and now and show me how?"

"Enough of that, my friend," replied Don Quixote. "I intend in due course to show you even greater secrets and do you even greater favours. But now let us see to this ear of mine, for it is hurting more than I should like."

Sancho took lint and ointment out of his saddle-bags. But when Don Quixote saw his broken helmet he was on the point of going berserk, and, placing his hand on his sword and raising his eyes to heaven, he said:

"I swear by the Creator of all things, and by the four evangelists and all their holy writings, that I will lead the life led by the great Marquis of Mantua when he swore to avenge his nephew Baldwin's death, and until then 'ne'er at table to eat bread nor with his wife to lie,' and other such things that, although I cannot remember them now, can be taken as spoken, until I have exacted full vengeance on the perpetrator of this outrage."

When Sancho heard this he said:

"I'd just like to point out, Don Quixote sir, that if that knight has done as he was told and has gone to present himself before my lady Dulcinea del Toboso, then he's done his duty and doesn't deserve another punishment unless he commits another crime."

"You have spoken well and to the purpose," replied Don Quixote, "and so I hereby annul my oath as regards exacting fresh vengeance on him; but I swear anew and confirm that I will lead the life I have just described until I wrest from some knight another helmet at least as fine as this. And do not imagine, Sancho, that I am doing this without a solid basis, for I have a clear model to follow: exactly the same thing happened, down to the very last detail, with Mambrino's helmet, which cost Sacripante so dear."[4]

"You just send all those oaths of yours to the devil, sir," retorted Sancho, "they're bad for your health and worse for your conscience. Or else tell me this—supposing days and days go by and we don't come across anyone in a helmet, what then? Have we got to honour the oath, regardless of all the inconvenience and discomfort, always sleeping in our clothes, never under a roof, and those hundreds of other penances in the mad old Marquis of Mantua's vow, that you're so set on reviving? Just think about it, sir—it isn't men in armour you'll find on these here roads but carters and muleteers, who not only don't wear helmets but have probably never even heard of them."

"You are mistaken about that," said Don Quixote, "because before we have been riding along these highways and byways for two hours we shall see more men in arms than fell upon Albracca to carry off the fair Angelica."[5]

---

4. Rinaldo, elsewhere cited as Reynaldo of Montelban, steals the enchanted helmet of the Moorish king Sacripante in Book 1 of Boiardo's *Orlando Innamorato*.

5. Daughter of a Moorish king who dwells in the castle of Albracca; in Boiardo's poem, the castle is besieged by Agricane and his men.

"All right, then, so be it," said Sancho, "and please God we come well out of all this and the time soon arrives to conquer this island that's going to cost me so dear— and then I can die happy."

"I have already told you, Sancho, not to worry about all that; for if finding an island presents any problems, there is always the kingdom of Denmark or the kingdom of Soliadisa,[6] which would fit you like a glove, and still more so being as it is on terra firma, which should make you even happier. But let us leave these matters until it is time to deal with them; and now see if you have anything to eat in your saddle-bags, so that we can go without delay in search of some castle where we can stay for the night and make the balsam about which I have told you; for I swear to God that my ear is very painful."

"There's an onion here, and a bit of cheese, and a few scraps of bread," said Sancho, "but that isn't food for a valiant knight like you."

"How mistaken you are!" replied Don Quixote. "I would have you know, Sancho, that it is an honour for knights errant not to eat for a whole month, and if they do eat, it must be what they find readiest to hand, and you would know this well enough if you had read as many histories as I have; for in all those very very many that I have read, I have not found any mention of knights errant eating, except when it happened that some sumptuous banquet was held for them, but otherwise they used to live on next to nothing. And although it is evident that they could not have gone without eating and satisfying all the other needs of nature, because, after all, they were men like us, it is also evident that since they spent most of their time wandering in woods and wildernesses, without cooks, their everyday food must have been country fare, like that which you are offering me now. And so, friend Sancho, do not be afflicted by what pleases me; do not seek to build the world anew, or to turn knight-errantry on its head."

"I'm sorry I'm sure," said Sancho. "Not knowing how to read or write, as I said before, I haven't been able to find out about all those rules of knighthood. From now on I'll put all sorts of nuts and raisins into the saddle-bags for you, being as you are a knight, and for me, not being one, I'll put in feathered provisions of greater substance."

"I am not saying, Sancho," replied Don Quixote, "that it is obligatory for knights errant not to eat anything other than those nuts to which you refer; but that they must have been their usual sustenance, together with certain herbs, known to them and to me, which they found in the fields."

"It's a good idea," said Sancho, "to know about those there herbs. I fancy we're going to need that knowledge one fine day."

Then he took out what he'd said he'd brought, and the two men ate together in peace and good fellowship. But anxious to find somewhere to stay that night they didn't linger over their dry and frugal meal. They remounted and hurried on, to try and reach a village before nightfall, but both the day and their hopes of doing so came to an end as they were passing some goatherds' huts, and they decided to spend the night there. Sancho's sorrow at not reaching a village was matched by his master's delight at sleeping in the open air, because he considered that each time he did so he performed an act of possession that provided fresh proof of his chivalry.

---

6. Perhaps Cervantes (or Quixote) is confusing names here; Soliadisa is a princess, not a kingdom, in a 16th-century romance.

from *Chapter 11*

ABOUT WHAT HAPPENED TO DON QUIXOTE WITH SOME GOATHERDS

He received a hearty welcome from the goatherds. Once Sancho had accommodated Rocinante and the donkey as best he could, he set off on the trail of the smell being given out by some chunks of goat meat that were boiling in a pot over the fire; and, although he'd have liked to find out there and then if they were ready to be transferred from the pot to the stomach, this wasn't possible, because the goatherds took them off the fire and, spreading some sheepskins on the ground, made haste to lay their rustic table and, showing great goodwill, invited them to share their meal. There were six goatherds using that fold and they all sat down around the skins, after begging Don Quixote, with rough ceremony, to sit on an upside-down bowl that they placed there for him. Don Quixote did so, and Sancho stayed standing to serve him the drinking horn. When Don Quixote saw his squire on his feet, he said:

"So that you may see, Sancho, what great good there is in knight-errantry, and how close those exercising any of its ministries always are to being honoured and esteemed by the world, it is my wish that you should come and sit by my side in the company of these excellent people, and be one with me, your natural lord and master—that you should eat from my very own plate and drink from my very own cup: for of knight-errantry may be said what is said of love, that it makes all things equal."

"What a great honour!" said Sancho. "But just let me tell you one thing, sir—if I had plenty to eat, I'd eat it as well or even better standing up and by myself as sitting down next to an emperor. The truth is that what I eat in my own little corner without any fuss or bother, even if it is only bread and onions, tastes much better to me than all the fine turkeys on other tables where I'd have to chew slowly, drink hardly a drop, wipe my mouth all the time, never sneeze or cough if I felt like it, or do all those other things that being by yourself and free and easy lets you do. So, sir, as for these honours that you want to confer on me for being a follower and servant of knight-errantry, which is what I am as your squire, I'd rather you turned them into something more practical and useful, and I renounce all your honours from here to eternity—though I'm very grateful to you I'm sure."

"You shall sit down all the same; for he that humbleth himself shall be exalted."

And seizing Sancho by the arm he forced him to squat by his side.

The goatherds couldn't make head or tail of this gibberish about squires and knights errant, and they just sat there eating in silence and staring at their guests who, with great elegance and even greater appetite, were stowing away chunks of meat as big as their fists. Once the meat course was finished, a quantity of sweet acorns was spread on the sheepskins together with half a cheese, harder than if it had been made of mortar. Meanwhile the drinking horn was being kept busy, circulating so often (now full, now empty, like a bucket on a water wheel) that it soon exhausted one of the two wineskins hanging near by. * * *

Chapter 12

ABOUT WHAT A GOATHERD TOLD DON QUIXOTE AND THE OTHERS

And now one of the lads who brought provisions from the village appeared and said:

"Hey, do you know what's happened down in the village?"

"How are we supposed to know that?" replied one of them.

"Well, it's like this," the lad continued. "That famous student-shepherd Grisóstomo died this morning, and it's rumoured he died of love for that fiendish Marcela,
rich Guillermo's daughter, that girl who wanders about all those God-forsaken places
dressed up as a shepherdess."

"Marcela you said?" asked one of them.

"Marcela I said," the lad replied. "And the best part is he's left in his will that he
wants to be buried out in the wilds, like some Moor, at the foot of the rock by the
cork-oak spring, because rumour has it that's where he first saw her, and they say he
said so himself. And he's left other things to be done, too, but the village priests say
they won't be done, and that it wouldn't be right to do them, because they're more
like what pagans get up to. To all this, that great friend of his, Ambrosio—you know,
that student who dressed up as a shepherd with him—replies that it'll all be done just
as Grisóstomo ordered, and the village is in an uproar about it, but, to judge from
what everyone's saying, they're going to end up doing what Ambrosio and all his
shepherd friends want, and tomorrow they're coming to bury him with great pomp
and ceremony where I said. And it's my belief it's going to be well worth seeing—at
least I'm not going to miss it, not even if it means that I can't get back to the village
tomorrow."

"That's what we'll all do," added the goatherds, "and we'll draw lots to see
who'll stay behind to look after the goats."

"A good idea, Pedro," said one, "but there won't be any need for that, I'll stay behind with everybody's goats. And don't put it down to virtue or lack of curiosity on
my part, but to me not being able to walk, because of that broken branch that went
through my foot the other day."

"Thanks all the same," replied Pedro.

Don Quixote asked this Pedro to tell him about the dead man and the shepherdess, to which Pedro replied that all he knew was that the dead man was a rich hidalgo who lived in a village in the sierra and who'd been a student at Salamanca University for many years, after which he'd come back to the village with a reputation for
being wise and well-read.[1]

"In particular, people said he knew all about the science of the stars, and what the
sun and the moon do up there in the sky, because he used to tell us exactly when the
clips were going to come."

"*Eclipse* is the word, my friend, not *clips*, for the obscuration of the two great luminaries," said Don Quixote.

But Pedro, not troubling himself with trifles, went on with his story:

"And he also used to predict whether a year was going to be fruitful or hysterical."

"You mean *sterile*, my friend," said Don Quixote.

"Sterile or hysterical," replied Pedro, "it all boils down to the same thing. As I
was saying, with all this predicting his father and his friends grew very rich, because
they believed him and did as he advised when he said: 'Sow barley this year, not
wheat; this year you'd better sow chick-peas, not barley; next year there's going to be
a bumper crop of olives, but the following three there won't be any at all.'"

---

1. A sierra is a mountain range. Don Quixote will shortly wander into the Sierra Morena, a name given to the southcentral
stretch of Spain that encompasses parts of the provinces of Cordoba and Sevilla and separates La Mancha from Andalucia.
Salamanca University was respected as the foremost university in Spain and received strong royal support.

"That science is called astrology," said Don Quixote.

"I haven't the faintest idea what it's called," retorted Pedro, "but what I do know is that he knew all this and more besides. In the end, not very many months after he came back from Salamanca, he took off his long scholar's gown one day and appeared dressed as a shepherd, with his crook and his sheepskin jacket—and this other man, his great friend Ambrosio, who'd studied with him, he dressed himself up as a shepherd too. I was forgetting to say that Grisóstomo, the dead man, was very good at writing poems—he even used to write the carols for Christmas Eve, and the mystery plays for Corpus Christi[2] that the village lads performed, and everyone said they were brilliant. When the people in the village saw the two scholars suddenly dressed as shepherds they were amazed, and couldn't work out what had led them to make such an odd change. By this time Grisóstomo's father had died and he'd inherited piles of property—royal estate, goods and cattles, cows and horses, sheep and goats, as well as masses of money, and the lad was left the absolute lord of it all, and the truth is he deserved it, because he was a fine companion and very charitable, a good friend to all good men, with a face like an angel. Later it was known that he'd only changed clothes to wander all about these wild places after that shepherdess Marcela the young lad mentioned before, because poor Grisóstomo, God rest his soul, had fallen in love with her. And now I'm going to tell you, because it's something you should know, who that lass is—it's possible, and more than possible, that you won't hear anything like it in all the days of your life, even if you live to be older than noses."

"*Moses* you should have said," interrupted Don Quixote, who couldn't abide the goatherd's word-mangling.

"Noses have been around for quite a while, too," retorted Pedro, "and if you're going to be picking on every other word I use, sir, we shan't be done in a twelvemonth."

"Forgive me, my friend," said Don Quixote. "I only mentioned it because there is such a difference between noses and Moses; but your reply was an excellent one, for noses are indeed older than Moses; and do continue your history, and I will not interrupt you ever again."

"I was about to say, my dear good sir," said the goatherd, "that there was one farmer in our village even richer than Grisóstomo's father, and he was called Guillermo, and God had given him not only vast riches but also a daughter whose mother, the most honourable woman in all these parts, had died giving birth to her. I can see her even now, that lovely face of hers with the sun in one cheek and the moon in the other. And what a fine housewife she was, and so good to the poor—I do believe that at this very moment her soul must be enjoying God in the other world. Guillermo was heartbroken at the death of such an excellent wife and he died, too, leaving his daughter Marcela young and rich and in the care of one of her uncles, a priest in our village. The girl grew up so beautiful that she put us in mind of her mother, such a great beauty herself, although everyone thought that her daughter was going to be even lovelier. And so she was, and by the time she was fourteen or fifteen all who set eyes on her praised God for making her so beautiful, and most fell hopelessly in love. Her uncle kept her shut up indoors, very bashful and demure, but the fame of her great beauty spread far and wide—and this, and her fortune, brought the men not only of our own village but of all the villages for many miles around, the very best of them too, flocking to ask, beg and pester her uncle for her hand in mar-

2. The feast of Corpus Christi, celebrated in early June, was always an occasion for *autos sacramentales*—mystery plays on a religious theme.

riage. But even though he'd have liked to marry her off straight away, since she was of the right age, being a true and good Christian he was unwilling to do so without her consent—and no, he didn't have an eye on the gains to be made from delaying the girl's marriage and keeping control of her property. This, I can promise you, was said in praise of the good priest in more than one circle of commentators in the village. For I should tell you, errant sir, that in these tiny places everything's discussed and everything's gossiped about; and you can be quite certain, just as I am, that a priest has to be a saint to make his flock speak well of him, especially in a village."

"That is quite true," said Don Quixote, "but do continue, for the story is a very good one, and you, my dear Pedro, are telling it with a certain stylish grace."

"It's the grace of Our Lord God that I'm in need of, which is more to the purpose. Anyway, what happened was that although the priest described to his niece, in detail, the qualities of each one of her many suitors, begging her to choose and marry whichever she preferred, all she ever replied was that she didn't want to marry yet because, being so young, she didn't feel strong enough to bear the burden of matrimony. Faced with excuses as good as these appeared to be, her uncle stopped pressing her, and decided to wait until she was older and able to choose a companion to her taste. For as he said, and said rightly, parents shouldn't provide for their children's future against their will. But lo and behold, like a bolt from the blue, meticulous modest Marcela appears one day converted into a shepherdess, and, despite all the efforts of her uncle and the other villagers to dissuade her, off she goes into the fields with the other shepherdesses in the village to mind her own flock. And once she came into the public gaze and her beauty was exposed to all eyes, I couldn't tell you how many rich youths, hidalgos and farmers dressed up just like Grisóstomo, and wandered about the fields wooing her—among them, as I've said, our deceased friend, who people said no longer loved her, but adored her.

"But you mustn't suppose, just because Marcela has given herself over to this free and easy life, with little privacy or rather none at all, that she's done anything to bring the least discredit upon her modesty or chastity; quite the opposite, she watches so closely over her own honour that of all her suitors and pursuers not one has boasted, or could boast without lying, of having been given the slightest hope of fulfilling his desire. Because although she doesn't avoid the company of shepherds, and treats them with courteous friendliness, as soon as any of them reveals his intentions, even if in a proper and holy proposal of marriage, she hurls him from her like a boulder from a catapult. And in this mood she's wreaking more havoc on these lands than if they'd been invaded by the plague, because her affability and beauty encourage those who know her to serve her and to love her, but her disdainful destruction of their hopes drives them to the brink of suicide; and so they don't know what to say, and only cry that she's cruel and an ingrate, and other similar words that describe her character all too accurately. And if you were to stay here awhile, sir, you'd hear these mountains and these valleys echoing with the laments of the broken-hearted wretches who pursue her.

"Not far from here is a place where there are almost two dozen lofty beeches, and there is not one on whose smooth bark is not engraved the name of Marcela, and above some a crown with which a lover affirms that Marcela wears and deserves to wear the crown of all human beauty.[3] Here a shepherd sighs, there another moans; here songs of love are to be heard, there dirges of despair. There's one who spends

---

3. Writing poems to one's beloved on the bark of a tree was common in pastoral romance.

every hour of the night seated at the foot of some oak or crag, and there, never allow-ing his tear-filled eyes a moment's rest, sunk and lost in his thoughts, he's found by the morning sun; there's another who, finding no relief or respite for his sighs, stretched out on the burning sand in the racking noonday heat of summer, sends his complaints up to merciful heaven. And over every single one of them the lovely Marcela triumphs, footloose and fancy-free, and all of us who know her are waiting to see where her arrogance will lead, and who will be the fortunate man to tame such fe-rocity and enjoy such perfect beauty. Since everything I've narrated is the proven truth, I can well believe that what this young lad here said they're saying about the cause of Grisóstomo's death is also true. And so I advise you, sir, not to miss his bur-ial tomorrow—it'll be well worth seeing, because Grisóstomo has lots of friends, and it isn't a couple of miles from here to where he said he wanted to be buried."

"That is indeed what I intend to do," said Don Quixote, "and I thank you for the pleasure you have afforded me by telling me such a delightful story."

"Oh no!" replied the goatherd. "I don't know half the things that have happened to Marcela's suitors, but it could be that tomorrow we come across some shepherd who can tell us about them. And now it'll be a good idea for you to go and sleep under cover, because sleeping in the damp night air could be bad for your wound—though the remedy you've been given is so effective that there's no fear of an infection set-ting in."

Sancho Panza, who was wishing that the goatherd would take his endless talk with him to the devil, also asked his master to go and sleep in Pedro's hut. He did so, and there he spent most of the night remembering his lady Dulcinea, in imitation of Marcela's suitors. Sancho Panza settled down between Rocinante and his donkey, and there he slept the sleep not so much of a star-crossed lover as of a hoof-ham-mered squire.

from *Chapter 13*

WHICH CONCLUDES THE STORY ABOUT THE SHEPHERDESS MARCELA, TOGETHER WITH OTHER EVENTS

But hardly had the day begun to show itself on the balconies of the east when five of the six goatherds got up and went to wake Don Quixote, to ask him if he still in-tended to go and see the famous burial of Grisóstomo, and to tell him that if he did they would keep him company. Don Quixote, who was longing to go, rose and told Sancho to saddle the horse and fit the pack-saddle on to the donkey immediately, which he did with great diligence; and with the same diligence they all set out on their way. And they'd ridden less than a mile when, as they crossed another path, they saw half a dozen shepherds coming towards them clothed in black sheepskin jackets and with wreaths of cypress and bitter oleander crowning their heads. Each had a stout holly stave in his hand. With them came two gentlemen on horseback, splendidly dressed for travelling, accompanied by three servants on foot. When the two parties met they exchanged courteous greetings, and when they asked each other where they were going they discovered that they were all on their way to the burial, so they travelled together.

One of the horsemen said to his companion:

"It seems to me, Señor Vivaldo, that we're going to count however much time we spend on this famous burial as having been time well spent: it is indeed going to be famous, considering the extraordinary things these shepherds have been telling us about the dead shepherd and the death-dealing shepherdess."

"I think so, too," replied Vivaldo, "and I'm not talking about taking just one day over it, either—I'd happily take four days off for the sake of witnessing it."

Don Quixote asked what it was that they had heard about Marcela and Grisóstomo. The horseman replied that they'd joined up with the shepherds earlier that morning and that, seeing them in such mournful attire, they'd asked why they were dressed like that; and that one of the shepherds had told them all about the secluded life and the beauty of a shepherdess called Marcela, and about the love she inspired in the many men who wooed her, and about the death of that Grisóstomo to whose burial they were going. In short, he told them everything that Pedro had told Don Quixote the day before.

So this conversation came to an end, and another one began when the man called Vivaldo asked Don Quixote what it was that prompted him to ride about such a peaceful part of the world armed in that fashion. And Don Quixote replied:

"The profession that I exercise does not allow me to ride in any other way. Easy living, luxury and repose were invented for effete courtiers; toil, disquiet and arms were created solely for those the world calls knights errant, of whom I, unworthy as I am, am the very least."

On hearing this they all concluded that he was mad; and to make quite certain, and to find out what sort of madness he suffered from, Vivaldo went on to ask him what knights errant were.

"Have you not read," replied Don Quixote, "the annals and histories of England, which treat of the famous exploits of King Arthur, commonly known in our Castilian tongue as Artús, who, according to an ancient tradition divulged throughout that kingdom of Great Britain, did not die but was, by sorcerer's art, turned into a raven, and who, in due course, will recover his sceptre and kingdom, and reign again; for which reason no Englishman has ever been known from that day to this to kill a raven? Well, in the days of that good king the famous order of chivalry of the Knights of the Round Table was founded, and the love between Sir Lancelot of the Lake and Queen Guinevere was consummated as is there recorded, the go-between and confidante being that honourable duenna Quintañona, all of which gave rise to the ballad that is so well known and so highly praised in Spain:

> And never sure was any knight
> So served by damsel or by dame
> As Lancelot, that man of might,
> When here from Brittany he came,

with its smooth and gentle unfolding of its deeds of love and war.[1] Well, from that time onwards, handed on down the generations, the order of chivalry gradually extended and spread throughout many different parts of the world, and its members were famous for their exploits: the valiant Amadis of Gaul with all his sons and grandsons to the fifth generation, and the valorous Felixmarte of Hyrcania, and the never sufficiently praised Tirante the White, and the brave and invincible knight Belianis of Greece, whom we have very nearly been able to see and speak with and hear

---

1. Quixote accurately summarizes the famed legends of Arthur, Lancelot, and Guinevere. Quintañona was added in the Spanish versions of Lancelot's and Guinevere's unchaste love.

in our own times.[2] This, then, gentlemen, is what it is to be a knight errant, and this is the order of chivalry, in which I, as I have said, although a sinner, have professed; and I do profess everything professed by the knights of whom I have told you. And so I roam these lonely and deserted places in search of adventures, with the firm intention to employ my arm and indeed my whole person in the most perilous adventures that fortune sends my way, in aid of the weak and needy."

These words showed the travellers that Don Quixote was indeed out of his wits, and they could now see what kind of madness had taken him over, which astonished them as much as it did everybody else who made this discovery. And, to while away the time during the short journey said to remain, Vivaldo, who was a clever man with a cheerful disposition, decided, when they reached the sierra where the burial was to take place, to provide him with the opportunity to expand on his nonsense. So he said:

"It seems to me, sir knight errant, that you profess one of the very strictest professions in the world, and it's my belief that not even being a Carthusian monk is as strict."[3]

"It may be that it is as strict," replied our Don Quixote, "but whether it is as necessary to the world is something that I am within a hair's breadth of doubting. For, if truth is to be told, the soldier who carries out his captain's orders contributes no less than the captain who gives him those orders. What I mean to say is that monks, in peace and tranquillity, pray to heaven for the well-being of the world; but we soldiers and knights put into practice what they pray for, defending the world with the prowess of our arms and the blades of our swords, and not under cover but in the open air, the targets for unbearable sun-rays in the summer and for the piercing frosts of winter. So we are ministers of God on earth, the arms through which his justice is executed here. . . ."

As they continued on their way engrossed in this conversation they saw, coming down a gorge between two great hills, about twenty shepherds, all wearing black sheepskin jackets and crowned with wreaths some of which were later discovered to be of yew and the others of cypress. Six of the shepherds were carrying a bier covered with a great variety of flowers and branches. At this sight one of the goatherds said:

"Those men over there are bringing Grisóstomo's body, and at the foot of that mountain is the spot where he said he was to be buried."

So they hurried there, just in time, because the shepherds had placed the bier on the ground and four of them had begun digging a grave beside a hard rock with their sharp pickaxes.

The two parties exchanged courteous greetings, and then Don Quixote and those who had come with him went to examine the bier, and on it, covered in flowers, they saw the corpse, dressed as a shepherd, of a man who seemed to be about thirty; and even though he was dead, it was plain to see that in life he'd had handsome features and a gallant disposition. Scattered around him on the bier there were some books and many papers, some open and some folded up. The onlookers, the grave-diggers and all the others kept an extraordinary silence, until one of those who'd brought the body said to another:

"You'd better make quite certain, Ambrosio, that this is the place Grisóstomo said, since you're so concerned for everything in his will to be carried out exactly as he instructed."

---

2. Amadis and Tirante have already been mentioned; Felixmarte is also known as Florismarte of Hircania, the hero of a chivalric work bearing his name (1556). Belianis also appears as hero of a Spanish chivalric romance.
3. Carthusian monks were rigorous contemplatives bound by strict orders of fasting.

"Yes, this is the place," replied Ambrosio, "because it was here that my unhappy friend often told me the story of his misadventures. He told me it was here that he first saw that mortal enemy of the human race; here that he first declared his love, as honourable as it was ardent; and here, at their last meeting, that Marcela sealed her scornful rejection, which led him to put an end to the tragedy of his wretched existence. And here, in remembrance of so many misfortunes, he wished to be laid in the bowels of eternal oblivion."

And, turning to Don Quixote and the travellers, Ambrosio continued:

"This body, gentlemen, that you are contemplating with compassionate eyes, was the dwelling-place of a soul in which heaven placed an infinite portion of its riches. This is the body of Grisóstomo, who was unmatched in intelligence, peerless in courtesy, perfect in politeness, a phoenix in friendship, generous beyond measure, grave without presumptuousness, joyful without vulgarity, and, all in all, the first in virtue, and second to none in misfortune. He loved and was hated; he adored and was disdained; he entreated a dragon, pleaded with marble, chased the wind, cried out in the wilderness and served ingratitude, whose reward was to make him the prey of death in the midst of the course of his life, which was ended by a shepherdess whom he wished to make immortal in the memory of mankind, as those papers at which you are looking could demonstrate, if he had not instructed me to commit them to the flames as soon as I have committed his body to the earth."

"If you do that," said Vivaldo, "you'll be treating them with even harsher cruelty than their owner himself, because it's neither just nor proper to carry out the wishes of a man who orders something that no rational arguments can justify. Augustus Caesar would have been out of his mind if he'd agreed to what the divine Mantuan poet ordered in his will.[4] And so, Señor Ambrosio, even though you are committing your friend's body to the earth, don't commit his writings to oblivion; for if he was so aggrieved as to command it, you shouldn't be so foolish as to obey him. Rather let these papers live, and Marcela's cruelty with them, for ever, as an example to the living, in times to come, so that they can avoid such pitfalls; because I and these friends of mine know the history of this enamoured and desperate friend of yours, and we know about your friendship, and what caused his death, and the instructions he left when he died; from all of which lamentable history it is easy to judge how great was Marcela's cruelty, Grisóstomo's love and your faithful friendship, and also to see what happens to people who rush headlong down the path that delirious love places before their eyes. Last night we learned that Grisóstomo had died and was to be buried in this place, and so, moved by curiosity and compassion, we departed from our route and agreed to come and see for ourselves what we'd been so sad to hear about. And in recognition of this compassion, and of our desire to do something about it if we could, we beg you, O Ambrosio,—or at least I for my part beg you—not to burn these papers and to let me have some of them."

And without waiting for the shepherd to reply, Vivaldo stretched out his hand and took some of the papers closest to him. Seeing which Ambrosio said:

"Courtesy obliges me, sir, to let you keep the papers you've just taken, but it would be vain for you to think I shall not burn the rest."

Vivaldo, longing to see what was written on the papers, opened one of them and saw that its title was *Song of Despair*. On hearing this Ambrosio said:

---

4. Virgil asked from his deathbed that his unfinished *Aeneid* be destroyed.

"This is the last thing the unfortunate man wrote. And so that all can hear, sir, to what a pass his misfortune had brought him, please read it aloud: there'll be time enough to do so while the grave is being dug."

"That I shall do with pleasure," said Vivaldo.

And since all the others were equally curious, they gathered around him, and he read the following in a clear and ringing voice:

from *Chapter 14*

IN WHICH THE DEAD SHEPHERD'S VERSES OF DESPAIR ARE GIVEN,
TOGETHER WITH OTHER UNEXPECTED EVENTS

GRISÓSTOMO'S SONG

Since you would have me publish, cruel maid,
From tongue to tongue, in this and every nation,
The news of your implacable disdain,
I'll call on hell itself to come and aid
My grieving breast with howls of lamentation,
And bend and break my voice with grief and pain.
And as I strive and labour to explain
My sorrow and your cold and heartless deed,
Forth shall the terrifying clamour stream,
And in it fragments of my bowels shall teem
To make my torture exquisite indeed.
So give me your attention: listen now
Not to harmonious sounds, but to the row
That from my bosom's depths in desolation,
Stirred up by bitter frenzy without measure,
Flows for my pleasure and for your vexation. . . .

And now the hour has struck: from deepest hell
Come, thirsting Tantalus, to my ordeal;
Rolling your mighty stone along its way
Come, Sisyphus; come, Tityus, come as well,
And bring your vulture; Ixion, bring your wheel;[1]
Come too, you sisters toiling night and day;[2]
And now let all of you as one convey
Your mortal anguish to my breast, and sigh
(If it's allowed to victims of despair)
Your harrowing laments over my bare
Carcass, refused a shroud in which to lie.[3]
Come, three-faced guardian of the dreadful gate[4]
And all hell's brood of fiends, and celebrate
And sing the doleful descant of your grief;

---

1. The four names illustrate vivid punishments in the afterworld from Greek mythology. Tantalus must forever be suspended between a stream and a cluster of fruit; Sisphyus is doomed to roll a stone up a mountain only to watch it roll back down; Tityus has his liver eaten by a vulture each day only to have it grow back by night; Ixion is strapped to a wheel that never stops turning.

2. Probably the Danaids, condemned to Hades for killing their husbands on their wedding night; their punishment is to try to fill leaky jars for all eternity.
3. Suicides were not permitted burial in consecrated ground.
4. Cerberus, the three-headed dog who guards the entrance to the underworld.

No better tribute can, I think, be due
To lovers who have won death's cold relief.

O Song of Desperation, do not grieve
Now that in desolation I must leave;
But rather, since the cause that gave you birth
By my misfortune grows and grows in gladness,
Be free from sadness, even in the earth.

The members of the audience quite liked Grisóstomo's song, even though the reader said he didn't think it accorded with the account he'd heard of Marcela's modesty and virtue, because Grisóstomo complained about jealousy, suspicion and absence, all to the prejudice of Marcela's good name and reputation. To which Ambrosio replied, as one who knew his friend's most hidden thoughts:

"To satisfy that doubt, sir, I should tell you that when this unfortunate man wrote this song he was far from Marcela, having taken himself away to see if absence would have its customary effect; and, since there's nothing that doesn't worry an absent lover and no fear that doesn't assail him, Grisóstomo was worried by imagined jealousies and suspicions that he feared as if they were real. And so everything that fame affirms about Marcela's virtue is true: except for some cruelty, and a little arrogance, and more than a little disdain, there are no faults at all for envy itself to find in her."

"That's true enough," replied Vivaldo.

As he was about to read another of the papers he'd saved from the fire, he was halted by a miraculous vision (that was what it seemed to be) which came before their eyes: on top of the crag by which the grave was being dug the shepherdess Marcela appeared, so beautiful that her beauty was even greater than it was famed to be. Those who had never seen her before gazed at her in silent amazement, and those who were used to seeing her stood in no less awe. But as soon as Ambrosio saw her he said, with indignation in his looks:

"Have you come, perhaps, fierce basilisk of these mountains, to see if your presence will make the wounds of this poor man slain by your cruelty spout blood? Or have you come to gloat over the achievements of your barbarity; or to contemplate from those heights, like another pitiless Nero, the flames of burning Rome; or to ride roughshod in your arrogance over this luckless corpse, as the ungrateful daughter did over her father Tarquin?[5] Tell us now why you've come and what you want; because knowing that Grisóstomo's very thoughts never failed to obey you when he was alive, I shall ensure that, even though he's dead, you'll be obeyed by the thoughts of all those who called themselves his friends."

"I haven't come, Ambrosio, for any of the reasons you've mentioned," replied Marcela, "but to defend myself and to demonstrate how wrong are all those who blame me for Grisóstomo's death and for their grief; and so I beg all of you here to give me your attention, because it won't take me very long nor shall I need many words to bring the truth home to people of good sense.

"You all say that heaven made me beautiful, so much so that this beauty of mine, with a force you can't resist, makes you love me; and you say and even demand that, in return for the love you show me, I must love you. By the natural understanding

---

5. The emperor Nero was rumored to have fiddled while Rome burned. The wicked Tullia persuaded her husband to murder her father, and when he was dead, she drove her chariot over his body. Her husband, however, was named Tarquin, her father Servius Tullius.

which God has granted me I know that whatever is beautiful is lovable; but I can't conceive why, for this reason alone, a woman who's loved for her beauty should be obliged to love whoever loves her. What's more, it could happen that the lover of beauty is ugly, and since that which is ugly is loathsome, it isn't very fitting for him to say: 'I love you because you're beautiful; you must love me even though I'm ugly.' And even if they are well-matched as far as beauty goes, that doesn't mean that the attraction's going to be mutual, because not all beauty inspires love. Some beauties delight the eye but don't captivate the heart; just as well, because if all beauty did inspire love and conquer hearts, people's affections would be forever wandering this way and that without knowing where to come to rest—there's an infinite number of beautiful people, so the affections would be infinite, too. And, according to what I've heard, true love can't be divided, and must be voluntary, not forced on you. If this is so, as I believe it is, why do you think I should be obliged to give in to you, just because you say you love me dearly? Or else tell me this: if heaven had made me ugly instead of beautiful, would I have been right to complain about you for not loving me? What's more, you must remember that I didn't choose this beauty of mine— heaven gave it to me, exactly as you see it, quite freely, without my asking for it or picking it. And just as the viper doesn't deserve to be blamed for her poison, even though she kills with it, because nature gave it to her, so I don't deserve to be blamed for being beautiful; because beauty in a virtuous woman is like a distant fire or sharp sword, which don't burn or cut anyone who doesn't come too close. Honour and virtue are ornaments of the soul, and without them the body, even if it is beautiful, shouldn't seem beautiful. Well then, if chastity is one of the virtues that most embellish the soul and the body, why should the woman who's loved for her beauty lose her chastity by responding to the advances of the man who, merely for his own pleasure, employs all his strength and cunning to make her lose it?

"I was born free, and to live free I chose the solitude of the countryside. The trees on these mountains are my company, the clear waters of these streams are my mirrors; and to the trees and the waters I reveal my thoughts and my beauty. I am the distant fire and the far-off sword. Those who have loved me for my looks I have disabused with my words. And if desires are kept alive on hope, I have never given any hope to Grisóstomo or fulfilled any man's desires, so it can truly be said of all of them that they were killed by their own obstinacy rather than by my cruelty. And if it's objected that his intentions were honourable and that for this reason I should have been more responsive to him, I reply that when, in that very place where his grave is being dug now, he revealed those honourable intentions of his to me, I told him that mine were to live in perpetual solitude and to allow nothing but the earth to enjoy the fruits of my seclusion and the remains of my beauty. If, after I'd spoken as plainly as that, he still chose to persevere against all hope and sail against the wind, is it surprising that he sank in the middle of the gulf of his own folly? If I'd encouraged him, I should have been false; if I'd gratified him, I should have been acting against my own intentions, better than his. He persisted although disabused, he despaired although not hated: and now you tell me whether it's just for me to be blamed for his grief! Let the man I deceive complain, let the victim of broken promises despair, let the man I entice nurse hope, let the man I accept rejoice: but let me not be called cruel or murderous by any man whom I have never deceived, made promises to, enticed or accepted.

"Heaven hasn't yet made it my destiny to love, and it's vain to think I'd ever love out of choice. Let this general warning serve for the individual benefit of each of my pursuers; and let it also be understood from now on that if any man dies because of me, he isn't dying from jealousy or mistreatment, because a woman who doesn't love any man can't make any man jealous, and disabuse must not be confused with disdain. He who calls me fierce and a basilisk can leave me alone, as something evil and dangerous; he who calls me an ingrate can stop courting me; he who calls me distant can keep his distance; he who calls me cruel can stop following me: because this fierce basilisk, this ingrate, this cruel and distant woman is most certainly not going to seek, court, approach or follow any of them. If Grisóstomo was killed by his own impatience and uncontrolled passion, why should anyone blame my modest and circumspect behaviour for that? If I keep my purity in the company of the trees, why should anyone want me to lose it in the company of men? As you all know, I have wealth of my own and I don't covet anyone else's; I live in freedom and I don't like to be constrained; I neither love nor hate anybody. I neither deceive this man nor run after that; I neither toy with one, nor amuse myself with another. The innocent company of the village shepherdesses and the care of my goats keep me happy. These mountains mark the limits of my desires, and if they do extend any further it is only for the contemplation of the beauty of the heavens, the way along which the soul travels back to its first abode."

And as she said this she turned and disappeared into the thick of a nearby forest without waiting for an answer, leaving everyone astonished as much at her intelligence as at her beauty. And some of them, wounded by the powerful arrows of the rays flashing from her lovely eyes, made to follow her, heedless of the clear warning that they'd heard. Don Quixote, seeing this, and thinking it a good moment to make use of his chivalry by succouring a maiden in distress, cried in a ringing voice and with his hand on the hilt of his sword:

"Let no man, of whatever estate or condition, dare to follow the beautiful Marcela, under pain of incurring my furious indignation. She has shown with clear and sufficient reasons that she bears little or no blame for Grisóstomo's death, and that she is far from reciprocating the desires of any of her suitors; for which reason it is right that, instead of being pursued and persecuted, she should be honoured and held in esteem by all good men, for she has shown that she is the only woman in the world who lives such a chaste life."

Whether because of Don Quixote's threats or because Ambrosio told them to finish what they were doing for their dead friend, none of the shepherds left the spot until, with the grave dug and Grisóstomo's papers burned, they placed his body in it, not without shedding many tears. They sealed the grave with a thick slab of rock, to be replaced in due course by a tombstone which Ambrosio said he was going to have made, with the following epitaph engraved on it.

> In here, earth's cold and paltry prize,
> The body of a lover lies,
> A shepherd who was cruelly slain
> By one who paid love with disdain.
> Ungrateful, haughty, cold and fair
> Was she who drove him to despair:
> More triumph for man's deadly foe
> As tyrant Love's dominions grow.

They strewed flowers and branches over the grave, condoled with their friend Ambrosio and took their leave of him. Vivaldo and his companion did the same, and Don Quixote said goodbye to his hosts and to the travellers, who begged him to come with them to Seville, because it's just the place to find adventures—on every street and round every corner they're simply waiting for you, more of them than anywhere else in the world.[6] Don Quixote thanked them for the information and for their disposition to extend such courtesies to him, but said that for the time being he did not wish to go to Seville and indeed could not go there, until he had rid all those sierras of foul robbers, with which they were said to be infested. In view of his firm intentions the travellers decided not to pester him any more and, repeating their farewells, they left him and continued their journey, during which they weren't short of things to talk about, what with Marcela's history and Don Quixote's mad deeds. He resolved to go in search of the shepherdess Marcela and offer her all the services in his power. But events didn't turn out as he expected, according to what is related in the course of this true history, the second part of which ends here.

THIRD PART OF THE INGENIOUS HIDALGO
DON QUIXOTE DE LA MANCHA

Chapter 15

WHICH RELATES THE UNFORTUNATE ADVENTURE THAT CAME DON QUIXOTE'S WAY
WHEN HE CAME THE WAY OF SOME WICKED MEN FROM YANGUAS

The wise Cide Hamete Benengeli says that as soon as Don Quixote had taken his leave of his hosts and of everyone else at Grisóstomo's burial, he and his squire rode off into the forest where Marcela had disappeared; and, after they'd wandered about it searching for her in vain for over two hours, they reached a meadow of fresh grass, with a cool, tranquil stream running alongside, which invited and indeed compelled them to spend the hours of early afternoon there, because the heat was beginning to be excessive.

Don Quixote and Sancho dismounted and, leaving the donkey and Rocinante free to graze as they pleased on the lush grass, they ransacked the saddle-bags; and, without ceremony, in peace and good fellowship, master and servant ate what they found in them.

Sancho hadn't bothered to hobble Rocinante, safe in the knowledge that the nag was so meek and chaste that all the fillies in the pastures of Cordoba wouldn't lead him astray. But as fate—or the devil, who isn't always asleep—would have it, there was also in that valley a herd of Galician pony-mares belonging to some muleteers from Yanguas, whose custom it is to take their siesta with their animals wherever there is grass and water. And that place where Don Quixote happened to find himself suited these men from Yanguas very well.

It happened, then, that Rocinante felt the urge to enjoy some fun and games with their ladyships the pony-mares and, abandoning his natural habits and his normal gait the moment he scented them, without requesting his master's permission, he broke into a lively trot and went to inform them of his needs. But it seems that they must have been feeling more like grazing, because they gave him such a welcome with their hooves and their teeth that his girths soon snapped and he was left saddleless and naked. Yet what must have affected him most was that when the muleteers saw the at-

6. Seville's reputation as a city of adventure may have come from its size; it had over 90,000 inhabitants by 1600, making it the fourth largest city in Europe. Proclaimed the central port for all ships bound for the New World, it grew quickly from a provincial town to a commerical capital.

tack that was being made on their mares, they ran over with their walking-staffs and gave him such a good hiding that they left him sprawling on the grass. At this point Don Quixote and Sancho, having witnessed Rocinante's thrashing, arrived breathless on the scene, and Don Quixote said to Sancho:

"From what I can see, friend Sancho, these are not knights, but base and low-born men. I say this because it means that you can freely help me to take due vengeance for the affront to which Rocinante has been subjected before our very eyes."

"How the devil are we going to take vengeance," replied Sancho, "when there are more than twenty of them and just the two of us—or just the one and a half of us, more like?"

"I am the equal of a hundred men," retorted Don Quixote.

And without further thought he seized his sword and attacked the men from Yanguas, and so did Sancho Panza, encouraged by his master's example. Don Quixote dealt one of them a blow that slashed open both his leather smock and a large part of his shoulder.

The muleteers, seeing so many of themselves so rudely handled by only two men, resorted to their walking-staffs, surrounded the pair and began to lay into them for all they were worth. The truth is that with the second blow they knocked Sancho to the ground, and Don Quixote went the same way in spite of all his eager dexterity. As fate would have it, he fell at the prostrate Rocinante's feet, from which one can judge the furious pounding that walking-staffs can give when wielded by wrathful rustic hands. When the men from Yanguas realized what they'd done, they loaded their animals as fast as they could and hurried on their way, leaving the two adventurers looking a sorry sight and feeling in an even worse temper.

Sancho Panza, lying by his master's side, was the first to start groaning, and he said in a feeble, doleful voice:

"Don Quixote sir! Oh, Don Quixote sir!"

"What do you want, brother Sancho?" replied Don Quixote, in the same weak, languishing tones.

"If it's at all possible," replied Sancho Panza, "I'd like a couple of swigs of that Fairy Brass's drink, if you've got some handy. Maybe it's good for broken bones as well as for sore wounds."

"If I had some here, wretch that I am, what more could we want?" replied Don Quixote. "But I swear to you, Sancho Panza, on my word as a knight errant, that before two days have elapsed, if fortune does not ordain otherwise, I shall have some in my possession; given a modicum of luck I shall manage this in the turning of a hand."

"And how long do you think it'll be before we can move our feet?" replied Sancho Panza.

"For myself," said the battered knight Don Quixote, "I must say that I cannot tell how long. But I am to blame for it all, for I should not have drawn my sword against men who are not knights, as I am; and so I believe that, as a penalty for having broken the laws of chivalry, the god of battles has allowed me to be punished in this way. For this reason, Sancho Panza, you must always bear in mind what I am about to tell you, because it concerns the well-being of us both: whenever you see rabble of this kind offering us some affront, do not wait for me to draw my sword against them, for I shall most certainly not do so, but you draw your sword and punish them to your heart's content; and if any knights come to their aid and defence, I shall then defend you and attack them with all my power. You have already had a thousand signs and demonstrations of how far the powers of this mighty arm of mine extend."

This was how arrogant the poor gentleman had become after his victory over the brave Basque. But his warning didn't impress Sancho Panza enough to prevent him from responding, and he said:

"I'm a peaceful man, sir, meek and mild, and I can overlook any insult, because I've got a wife to support and children to bring up. So even though it isn't up to me to give any orders, you bear this in mind, too—in no way am I going to draw my sword against anyone, peasant or knight, and I hereby, before God my Maker, forgive all affronts that anybody ever has offered me or ever will offer me, whether the person who has offered them, offers them or will offer them is of high or low birth, rich or poor, a gentleman or a commoner, not excepting any estate or condition whatsoever."

On hearing this his master replied:

"If only I had breath enough in my body to speak a few words to you at my ease, and if only this pain in my ribs would abate a little, so that I could make you understand, Panza, how wrong you are. Look here, you rogue: should the winds of fortune, hitherto so adverse, turn in our favour, driving the sails of our desire so that with a constant breeze behind us, and in perfect safety, we reach harbour on one of the islands I have promised you, what would become of you if, after conquering it, I made you its lord? Well, you would render things impossible for yourself, through not being a knight or even wanting to be one, or having the courage or the desire to avenge affronts and defend your dominions. For I would have you know that in freshly conquered provinces and kingdoms, the hearts of the natives are never so subdued or so well disposed towards their new master as to leave no fear that they might play some trick, to reverse the state of affairs once more and, as people say, try their luck again; and so the new master must have understanding to be able to govern, and courage to attack and defend in any crisis."

"In this particular crisis we've just been in," replied Sancho, "I do wish I'd had that understanding and courage you're going on about, but I can swear, on my word as a poor man, that I'm in more of a state for plasters than for chit-chat. You try and see if you can get up, and we'll give Rocinante a hand, though he doesn't deserve it, because he was the main cause of all this battering. I never would have believed it of him, I always took him for a pure-minded character, and as peaceful as me. Still, as they say, you need time to get to know people, and there's nothing certain in this life. Who'd have said that after you'd cut that poor knight errant about like that, the follow-up was going to be this great storm of a thumping that's just rained down on our ribs?"

"Your ribs, Sancho," replied Don Quixote, "must at least be accustomed to such squalls; but it is clear that mine, nurtured as they were between cambric and holland-cloth,[1] feel the pain of this misfortune more keenly. And if it were not that I imagine . . .—no, I do not imagine: I know for a certain fact—that all these discomforts are inseparable from the exercise of arms, I should be ready to die of sheer rage, here and now."

To this his squire replied:

"Sir, seeing as how all these disasters are as you might say the harvest of chivalry, I'd be grateful if you'd tell me whether they happen very often, or just at certain set times, because to my mind after two harvests like this one we're going to be useless for the third, unless God in his infinite mercy helps us."

"Let me tell you, friend Sancho," replied Don Quixote, "that the life of a knight errant is subject to a thousand dangers and misfortunes, and it is equally true that

---

1. Two kinds of fine linen, made in the Netherlands.

knights errant are potential emperors and kings, as is shown by the experience of many different knights, about whose histories I am fully informed. And I could tell you now, if the pain would allow me, about some who by the might of their arms alone have risen to the high estate I have just mentioned; and yet these selfsame knights, both before and afterwards, were engulfed in various calamities and misfortunes. The valiant Amadis of Gaul once found himself in the power of his mortal enemy the enchanter Arcalaus, who, it is attested, had him tied to a column in his courtyard and gave him more than two hundred lashes with the reins of his horse. And there is an anonymous author of no small credit who says that after the Knight of the Sun had been caught in a trap by a door that opened under his feet in a certain castle, and found himself bound hand and foot in a deep pit underground, there he was given what is known as an enema, of snow-water and sand, which was nearly the end of him; and if he had not been succoured in that sore extremity by a sage who was a great friend of his, the poor knight would have fared very ill.[2] So I can well have patience, being as I am in such good company; for they suffered greater affronts than those which we have undergone. And I would have you know, Sancho, that wounds received from weapons that happen accidentally to be in the assailants' hands are not dishonourable, and this is explicitly stated in the law of challenges: if a shoemaker hits a man with the last he is holding, that man cannot be said to have been birched, even if the last is made of this particular wood. I am only telling you this to prevent you from thinking that, just because we have taken a battering in this dispute, we have been dishonoured, for the arms borne by those men, with which they belaboured us, were only their walking-staffs, and none of them, so far as I can remember, was carrying a rapier, a sword or a dagger."

"They didn't give me a chance to look into details like that," replied Sancho. "I'd hardly drawn my own trusty blade when they gave my shoulders such a thrashing with those pine trees of theirs that they knocked the sight out of my eyes and the strength out of my feet and left me where I'm lying now, and where wondering whether the beating was dishonourable or not doesn't bother me in the slightest—all that does bother me is the pain of those staff-blows, and they're going to be as deeply engraved in my memory as they are on my shoulders."

"For all that, brother Panza," replied Don Quixote, "allow me to remind you that there is no memory that time does not efface, no pain that death does not destroy."

"Well, what bigger disaster could there ever be," retorted Panza, "than the one that has to wait for time to efface it and for death to destroy it? If this mishap of ours was one of those that can be cured with a couple of plasters it wouldn't be so bad, but I'm beginning to think that all the bandages in a hospital aren't going to be enough to even begin to sort us two out."

"Stop that talk, Sancho, and attempt to make the best of a bad business," replied Don Quixote, "because that is what I shall do; and now let us see how Rocinante is, because it seems to me that not the least part of this misfortune has fallen to the poor fellow's share."

"There's nothing surprising about that," retorted Sancho, "seeing as how he's such a fine knight errant. But what does surprise me is that my donkey's still in the pink, while we're black and blue all over."

"Fortune always leaves a door open in adversity, to provide a remedy," said Don Quixote. "I say this because that creature of yours can now replace Rocinante, and bear me to some castle where I can be cured of my wounds. Furthermore, I shall not

2. Apparently an episode of Don Quixote's own invention.

count it dishonourable to ride on such a beast, for I remember reading that when good old Silenus, the tutor of the merry god of laughter, rode into the city of the hundred gates, he did so, much to his satisfaction, on a handsome ass."[3]

"I expect it's true he rode on an ass, as you say," replied Sancho, "but there's a big difference between riding an ass and being slung across an ass's back like a sack of rubbish."

To which Don Quixote replied:

"Wounds received in battle do not detract from honour, but bestow it; and so, friend Panza, stop answering me back and do as you are told, get up as best you can and put me on top of your donkey in the posture that most pleases you; and let us be gone from here before night falls and catches us in this wild place."

"Well, well," said Panza, "I have heard you say that it's right and proper for knight errants to sleep on open plains and deserts for most of the year, and that they count themselves lucky to do it."

"All that," said Don Quixote, "is when there is no alternative, or when they are in love; and this is so true that there have been knights who have remained on top of a crag, in sunlight and shadow and all the inclemencies of the heavens, for two whole years, unknown to their ladies. And one of these was Amadis, when he called himself Beltenebros and took up his quarters on the Peña Pobre, for eight years or eight months—I cannot quite remember which, but all that matters is that he was doing penance there for some vexation or other that the lady Oriana had caused him.[4] But let us leave these matters, Sancho, and do make haste, before some misfortune like Rocinante's befalls the donkey."

"Then there'd be the devil and all to do," said Sancho.

And letting out thirty groans and sixty sighs and one hundred and twenty curses on the head of the person who'd brought him there, he hauled himself to his feet, but he was so exhausted that he stopped half way up, bent over in the form of a Turkish bow and incapable of straightening himself any further; yet despite all these troubles he harnessed his donkey, which had also taken advantage of the day's excess of liberty to go a little astray. Then he righted Rocinante, who, if he'd had a tongue to complain with, certainly wouldn't have been matched by Sancho or his master.

from *Chapter 18*

WHICH RELATES THE CONVERSATION THAT SANCHO PANZA HAD WITH HIS MASTER DON QUIXOTE, AND OTHER ADVENTURES WORTH RELATING

* * * As Don Quixote and his squire discussed these matters, Don Quixote saw that a huge, dense cloud of dust was approaching them along the road, and he turned to Sancho and said:

"This is the day, O Sancho, when will be seen the good that fortune has in store for me; this is the day, I say, when the might of my arm will be displayed as never before, and when I shall do deeds that will remain written in the book of fame for the ages to come. Do you see that cloud of dust rising up over there, Sancho? Well,

---

3. The merry god of laughter (and drunkenness) is Bacchus, god of the vine; the elderly satyr Silenus who rode into Thebes astride an ass was his tutor.

4. An episode from the *Amadis de Gaul,* it treats of the penance that Amadis believes he must do for his beloved Oriana. Because of the imprudence of his dwarf, Ardian,

Amadis has been banished from Oriana's sight, and he retreats to the Peña Pobre; she later repents and sends a messenger asking that Amadis come to her at once. Dulcinea is mentioned later in *Don Quixote* as coming from a lesser family than Oriana.

it is being raised by a vast army from countless different nations, marching towards us."

"In that case there must be two armies," said Sancho, "because opposite it, back there behind us, there's another dust cloud just like it."

Don Quixote turned round and saw that Sancho was right; and then he was beside himself with joy, because he knew that these were two armies marching to clash in the middle of that broad plain. Every minute of every hour his imagination was filled with those battles, enchantments, adventures, extravagances, loves and challenges that books of chivalry recount, and everything he said, thought or did was channelled into such affairs. And the dust clouds were being raised by two great droves of sheep approaching from opposite directions along the same road, but the dust prevented the sheep from being seen until they came close. And Don Quixote was so insistent they were armies that Sancho believed him, and said:

"So what are we going to do now, sir?"

"What are we going to do?" said Don Quixote. "Favour and assist the needy and helpless. And you should know, Sancho, that this army approaching from in front of us is led and directed by the great Emperor Alifanfarón, lord of the great island of Taprobana;[1] the other army coming up behind me belongs to his enemy, the King of the Garamantes, known as Pentapolín of the Uprolled Sleeve, because he always goes into battle with his right arm bare."[2]

"But why do these two lords hate each other so much?" asked Sancho.

"They hate each other," replied Don Quixote, "because this Alifanfarón is a wild pagan, and he is in love with Pentapolín's daughter, who is a very beauteous and, moreover, charming lady, and a Christian, and her father will not give her in marriage to the pagan king unless this man first abjures the religion of his false prophet Muhammad and is converted to Christianity."

"My eye!" said Sancho. "Pentapolín's doing just the right thing, and I'm going to help him in every way I can."

"Then you will be doing your duty, Sancho," said Don Quixote, "because to take part in battles of this kind it is not necessary to be knighted."

"I'm very well aware of that," replied Sancho, "but where are we going to put this ass of mine so that we can be sure of finding it again once the fighting's over? Because I don't expect going into battle on something like this is what people usually do."

"That is true," said Don Quixote. "What you can do with the ass is to leave it free to have its own adventures, whether it goes missing or not, because we shall possess so many horses when we emerge victorious that even Rocinante will be in danger of being replaced by another. But now pay attention to me and keep your eyes open, for I am going to inform you about the most important knights in these two armies. And so that you can see and observe them better, let us withdraw to that hill over there, from where both armies must be visible."

This they did, and from the hill they would indeed have had a clear view of the two flocks that were armies for Don Quixote, if the clouds of dust they were raising hadn't interfered with the view. Yet seeing in his imagination what he didn't see and didn't exist, he began to proclaim:

1. Taprobana is Sri Lanka, the emperor a fantasy of Don Quixote's.

2. The Garamantes were a fierce people from Africa; Pentapolín is another invention of Don Quixote.

"That knight you can see over there in yellow armour, with a crowned lion lying submissive at a damsel's feet on his shield, is the valiant Laurcalco, Lord of the Silver Bridge; the other one, with golden flowers on his armour, and on his shield three silver crowns on a blue field, is the much-feared Micocolembo, the Grand Duke of Quirocia; that other one on his right, with gigantic limbs, is the fearless Brandabarbarán de Boliche, Lord of the Three Arabias, wearing that serpent's skin for armour and, instead of a shield, bearing a door which is reputed to be one of the doors of the temple pulled down by Samson when in dying he avenged himself on his enemies.[3] But look in the other direction and you will see at the front of the other army the ever victorious, never vanquished Timonel de Carcajona, the Prince of Nueva Vizcaya, with his armour quartered blue, green, white and yellow, and on his shield he has a golden cat on a tawny field with the word *Miau,* which is the beginning of his lady's name, for it is said that she is the peerless Miulina, the daughter of Duke Alfeñiquén of the Algarve; that other knight who burdens the back of that powerful steed, with armour as white as snow and white arms—that is to say a shield without any device on it—is a novice knight from France, called Pierres Papin, Lord of the Baronies of Utrique; that other one, striking his iron spurs into the flanks of that dazzling, fleet zebra, and with armour of blue vair,[4] is the powerful Duke of Nerbia, Espartafilardo of the Wood, who bears on his shield the device of an asparagus plant, with a motto in Castilian that says: 'Divine my fortune.'"

And he went on naming imaginary knights from one army and the other and, swept along by the fancies of his unique madness, he improvised armour, colours, devices and mottoes for all of them; and without a pause he continued:

"This other army, facing us, is formed of people of many races: here are those who have drunk the sweet waters of famous Xanthus; mountaineers who tread the Massilian fields; those who sift fine gold dust in Arabia Felix; those who enjoy the famous, cool banks of clear Thermodon; those who bleed golden Pactolus along many different channels; and the Numidians, breakers of promises; the Persians, bowmen of great renown; the Parthians and the Medes, who fight as they flee; the Arabs, who move their dwellings; the Scythians, as cruel as they are pale; the Ethiopians, with pierced lips, and other infinite peoples, whose faces I see and recognize, even though I do not remember their names. In this other squadron come those who drink the crystalline waters of olive-bearing Betis; those who wash their faces in the liquor of the ever rich and golden Tagus; those who enjoy the beneficent waters of the divine Genil; those who tread the lush pastures of the Tartesian fields; those who take delight in the Elysian meadows of Jerez; men of La Mancha, rich and crowned with yellow ears of corn; men clad in iron, ancient relics of Gothic blood; those who bathe in the Pisuerga, renowned for the gentleness of its current; those who graze their flocks and herds on the broad meadows of winding Guadiana, famous for its secret course; those who shiver in the cold of the bosky Pyrenees and among the white snowflakes of the lofty Apennines: in short, all those whom Europe contains and encloses within its boundaries."[5]

3. Once again, for most of this paragraph Don Quixote is indulging in his own fictions. Samson was the Hebrew warrior who was blinded by Delilah and pulled down a temple on top of himself and his enemies, the Philistines.
4. Weasel fur.
5. In this paragraph, Don Quixote mentions real places and warlike peoples. In the "first squadron" are found the Trojans, who lived near the river Xanthus, and numerous other races from countries in Africa and Asia, including Turkey (site of the Thermodon River) and Lydia (site of the Pactolus). The "other squadron" includes peoples from Spain and Italy; all the rivers he lists here run through the Iberian peninsula, including the "winding Guadiana," which flows through La Mancha and frequently makes its "secret course" underground. The Pyrenees are the mountains on the border between Spain and France; the Apennines are mountains running down the center of Italy.

Great God, how many provinces he mentioned, how many races he named, giving to each one of them, with wonderful readiness, its own attributes, steeped as he was in everything he'd read in his lying books! Sancho Panza was hanging on his every word, and didn't utter a single one himself, and every so often he'd turn his head to try to spot the knights and giants his master was naming; and since he couldn't see any of them, he said:

"Look sir, the devil can take any of those men or giants or knights you say there are hereabouts—at least I can't see them, perhaps it's all a magic spell, like those ghosts last night."

"How can you say that?" retorted Don Quixote. "Do you not hear the neighing of the horses, the sounding of the bugles, the beating of the drums?"

"All I can hear," replied Sancho, "is lots of sheep bleating."

And he was right, because the two flocks were coming close.

"It is your fear, Sancho," said Don Quixote, "that is preventing you from seeing or hearing properly; because one of the effects of fear is to muddle the senses and make things seem to be what they are not; and if you are so frightened, stand aside and leave me alone, for I am sufficient by myself to give the victory to whichever army I decide to support."

As he said this he put spurs to Rocinante and, with his lance at the ready, he sped down the hill like a thunderbolt. Sancho shouted after him:

"Come back, come back, Don Quixote sir, I swear to God they're sheep you're charging! Come back! By the bones of my poor old father! What madness is this? Look, there aren't any giants or knights, or cats, or armour, or shields quartered or left in one piece, or blue vairs, or the devil. What are you doing? Lord have mercy on us sinners!"

But nothing would make Don Quixote turn back. Instead he galloped on, crying:

"Come, you knights, fighting beneath the banners of the valiant Emperor Pentapolín of the Uprolled Sleeve, follow me, and you shall see with what ease I give him his revenge over his enemy Alifanfarón of Taprobana!"

With this he rode into the army of sheep and began to spear them with as much fury and determination as if he really were attacking mortal enemies. The shepherds and farmers accompanying the flock were screaming at him to stop, but, seeing that this didn't have any effect, they drew their slings from their belts and started to salute him about the ears with stones the size of fists. Don Quixote didn't take any notice of the stones; instead he galloped this way and that, crying:

"Where are you, proud Alifanfarón? Come here: a lone knight am I, who wishes, in single combat, to try your strength and take your life, as punishment for the distress you have caused the valiant Pentapolín the Garamante."

As he said this a large smooth pebble came and struck him in the side and buried two of his ribs in his body. This left him in such a state that he felt certain he was either dead or sore wounded and, remembering his remedy, he took out the oil-bottle, put it to his mouth and began to pour the liquor into his stomach;[6] but before he could swallow what he considered to be a sufficient amount, another of those sugared almonds came and hit his hand and his bottle with such force that it smashed the bottle, taking out three or four teeth as well, and crushing two fingers.

6. This is the holy balsam of Fierebras that cures all ills, which Don Quixote managed to concoct in Chapter 17 after he and Sancho Panza were badly beaten at an inn Don Quixote took for a castle. Sancho drinks the potion as a cure, and undergoes such "seizures and spasms" that not only he but everyone else in the inn "thought that his end had come."

Such was the first blow, and such was the second, that the poor knight couldn't stop himself from sliding off his horse. The shepherds came up to look at him, and thought they'd killed him, so they made haste to round up their flock, pick up the dead sheep, of which there were more than a few, and make themselves scarce, without looking any further into the matter.

All this time Sancho had been on the hill, watching his master's follies, tearing his beard and cursing the moment when fortune had brought them together. When he saw that Don Quixote was lying on the ground and that the shepherds had gone away, he ventured down the hill and approached him, and found him in a terrible state, although still conscious. And Sancho said:

"Didn't I tell you, Don Quixote sir, to turn back, because what you were attacking wasn't armies, it was flocks of sheep?"

"This just shows how my enemy, that scoundrel of an enchanter, can transform things and make them disappear. I would have you know, Sancho, that it is very easy for such people to make us look like whatever they want, and this villain who is persecuting me, envious of the glory he saw I was about to conquer in this battle, turned the armies of enemy forces into flocks of sheep. If you do not believe me, Sancho, I beg you to do something that will correct your mistake and make you see that I am telling you the truth: mount your ass and stalk them, and you will soon see how, once they have gone a little way, they turn back into what they were at first and, ceasing to be sheep, become real men again, just as I described them to you. But do not go yet, because I have need of your assistance: come here and see how many of my teeth are missing, for it seems to me that there is not one left in my mouth."

Sancho came so close that his eyes were nearly inside his master's mouth; and by now the balsam had done its work in Don Quixote's stomach, and, just as Sancho was peering in, he discharged all its contents with the violence of a shotgun and they exploded in the face of the compassionate squire.

"Holy Mother of God!" cried Sancho. "What's up now? The man's dying, he must be—he's spewing blood!"

But when he examined the evidence more closely he could tell from the colour, taste and smell that it wasn't blood but the balsam he'd seen him drinking from the oil-bottle, and this disgusting discovery so turned his stomach that he vomited his guts all over his master, and both of them were left in the same fine mess. Sancho staggered over to his ass to look in the saddle-bags for something with which to clean himself and see to his master's wounds, and when he couldn't find them he almost went insane. He cursed himself again, and decided in his heart to leave his master and go back home, even if that did mean forfeiting what he was owed for services rendered and his hopes of governing the promised island.

Don Quixote now struggled to his feet, with his left hand clapped to his mouth to stop his remaining teeth from falling out, took hold with the other hand of the reins of the faithful Rocinante, who was so loyal and good-natured that he hadn't budged from his master's side, and went over to his squire, who was leaning over his ass with his hand on his cheek, in the posture of a man overwhelmed by thought. And when Don Quixote saw all these signs of deep distress, he said:

"Allow me to remind you, Sancho, that no man is worth more than any other, unless he achieves more than the other. All these storms falling upon us are signs that the weather will soon clear and that things will go well for us; for neither good nor bad can last for ever, and from this we can deduce that since this bad spell has lasted for a long time, a good one cannot be far away. So you must not be distressed about the misfortunes that I undergo, for you have no part in them."

"No part in them?" retorted Sancho. "The bloke who got blanket-tossed yesterday—was he by any chance any other than my own father's son? And the saddle-bags I've lost today, with all my valuables in them—do they belong to any other than the same?"[7]

"You have lost your saddle-bags, Sancho?" said Don Quixote.

"Yes I have," replied Sancho.

"So we have nothing to eat today," replied Don Quixote.

"We wouldn't have," replied Sancho, "if it wasn't for those herbs you say you know all about growing in the fields, the ones that unfortunate knight errants like you go and pick to make up for lack of food in fixes like this."

"For all that," replied Don Quixote, "I would sooner have a two-pound loaf of white bread or indeed an eight-pound loaf of bran bread and a couple of dozen salted pilchards, than all the herbs described by Dioscorides, even in Dr. Laguna's magnificent edition.[8] But anyway, climb on to your donkey, good Sancho, and follow me, because God, who is the provider of all things, will not fail us, especially since we are engaged in his service; because he does not fail the gnats in the air, or the worms in the earth, or the tadpoles in the water. And he is so merciful that he makes his sun rise on the evil and on the good, and sends his rain on the just and on the unjust."

"You'd have done better as a preacher," said Sancho, "than as a knight errant."

"Knights errant have always known and still must know about everything, Sancho," said Don Quixote, "for there were knights errant in centuries past who would stop to preach a sermon or deliver a speech in the middle of a fair just as if they were graduates of the University of Paris; from which we can infer that the sword has never blunted the pen, nor the pen the sword."[9]

"All right, I'll take your word for it," replied Sancho, "and now let's get going and find somewhere to stay the night, and God grant it's a place where there aren't any blankets, or blanket-tossers, or ghosts, or enchanted Moors—because if there are any of those, I'll send this adventuring lark to the devil, lock, stock and barrel."

"You must pray to God for that, my son," said Don Quixote. "And now guide us where you will, for on this occasion I wish to leave the choice of a lodging to you. But first lend me your hand and feel with your finger how many teeth are missing on this upper right side, because that is where I feel the pain."

Sancho put his fingers in and, as he felt around, he asked:

"How many back teeth did you use to have on this side?"

"Four," replied Don Quixote, "apart from the wisdom tooth, all of them whole and sound."

"Are you quite sure of what you're saying, sir?" said Sancho.

"Yes, four, if not five," replied Don Quixote, "because I have never had any teeth extracted, nor have any fallen out or been destroyed by decay or infection."

"Well, down here below," said Sancho, "you've only got two and a half now, and up above not even half a tooth, it's as smooth as the palm of my hand."

---

7. When Don Quixote leaves the inn without paying, others staying at the inn pull Sancho from his ass, throw him into a blanket, and toss the poor squire up and down in the middle of the yard. Unbeknownst to Sancho, the innkeeper seizes his saddle-bags in exchange for the missing payment.

8. Dioscorides was a Greek physician during Nero's reign; his botanical treatise was a crucial source for the science of pharmacy, and was translated from the Greek by the doctor Andrés Laguna in 1555.

9. There were ongoing debates in the Renaissance as to the respective merits of the pen (the privilege of the scholars and clerics) and the sword (that of knights).

"Oh, unhappy me!" said Don Quixote as he heard the sad news his squire was giving him. "I would rather have lost an arm, so long as it was not my sword arm. For I would have you know, Sancho, that a mouth without teeth is like a mill without a millstone, and that a tooth is much more worthy of esteem than a diamond. But those of us who profess the order of chivalry in all its severity are subject to this. Mount your donkey, my friend, and lead the way, and I shall follow at whatever pace you prefer."

Sancho did so, heading towards where he thought they might find a place to stay without leaving the highway, which was uninterrupted in that part.

As they plodded along, because the pain in Don Quixote's jaws didn't give him any respite or any inclination to ride faster, Sancho tried to amuse him and cheer him up by chatting to him, and said, among other things, what is recorded in the next chapter.

* * *

Chapter 20

ABOUT THE UNPRECEDENTED AND UNIQUE ADVENTURE UNDERTAKEN BY THE VALIANT DON QUIXOTE DE LA MANCHA, THE ONE THAT WITH THE LEAST DANGER WAS EVER BROUGHT TO A HAPPY CONCLUSION BY ANY FAMOUS KNIGHT IN THE WORLD

"All this grass, sir, must be a sign that there's a spring or a stream near here watering it, so it'll be a good plan to carry on a little further, and we'll find somewhere we can quench this terrible thirst of ours—I'm sure thirst hurts even more than hunger does."

Don Quixote thought this was good advice, and he took Rocinante by the reins, and Sancho loaded his ass with all the left-overs and took it by the halter, and they began to feel their way up the meadow, because the darkness of the night prevented them from seeing anything; but they hadn't gone a couple of hundred paces when a sound of thundering water reached their ears, as if it were crashing down from some great cliff. They were overjoyed at this but, when they stopped to work out where the sound was coming from, they suddenly heard another noise that diluted the pleasure of the water, especially for Sancho, with his timid, fearful nature. What they heard was a steady pounding and some sort of a clanking of iron and chains that, added to the water's furious roaring, would have struck fear into any other heart than that of Don Quixote.

In this dark night they'd wandered in among some tall trees whose leaves, blown by the breeze, rustled eerily; and the combination of the solitude, the surroundings, the darkness, the noise of the water and the rustling of the leaves filled them with fear and dread, all the more so when they found that the pounding didn't cease, the breeze didn't die down and the morning didn't come; and, on top of all this, they had no idea where they were. But Don Quixote, steeled by his intrepid heart, leapt upon Rocinante, grasped his little round shield, clasped his pike and said:

"Friend Sancho, I would have you know that I was born, by the will of heaven, in this iron age of ours, to revive in it the age of gold, or golden age, as it is often called. I am the man for whom dangers, great exploits, valiant deeds are reserved. I am, I repeat, the man who will revive the Knights of the Round Table, the Twelve Peers of France and the Nine Worthies, and who will consign to oblivion the Platirs, the Tablantes, the Olivantes and Tirantes, the Phoebuses and Belianises, together with the whole crowd of illustrious knights errant of olden times, by performing in this age in which I live such prodigies, such wonders, such feats of arms as to eclipse the most brilliant deeds that they ever accomplished. You are aware, faithful and trusty squire, of the darkness of this night, its unearthly silence, the confused and muffled hubbub of the trees, the fearsome roar of the water that we have come to seek and that seems to crash down from the heights of the Mountains of the Moon,[1] and the incessant pounding that assails and wounds our ears; all of which together, and indeed each by itself, would be enough to infuse fear and terror and dismay into the breast of Mars himself, let alone one unaccustomed to such occurrences and adventures. Now all of this that I depict for you is an incentive and a stimulant for my spirit, making this heart of mine burst in my breast with a desire to launch out on this adventure, however difficult it seems to be. So tighten Rocinante's girths a little, and God be with you, and await me here for just three days, after which, if I should not return, you may go back to our village, and from thence, as a favour and a service to me, you shall go to El Toboso, where you shall inform my incomparable lady Dulcinea that her hapless knight died attempting exploits which would make him worthy to call himself hers."

When Sancho heard his master's words he began to weep tears of infinite tenderness and said:

"Sir, I don't know why you want to take on this fearful adventure—it's night now, nobody can see us here, we can easily ride the other way and avoid the danger, even if we have to go for three days without a drink, and since there's no one to see us, there's no one to think we're cowards, either. What's more, I've heard our village priest, who you know well, saying in a sermon that danger loved is death won, so it isn't a good idea to go tempting God by taking on such a tremendous feat that you can only get out of alive by some miracle—you ought to be content with the ones that heaven worked on you when it stopped you from being tossed in a blanket, as I was, and when it brought you out safe, sound and victorious from among all those enemies that were riding with that corpse. And if all this doesn't move or soften that hard heart of yours, let's see if this does—just think that as soon as you've gone away I'll be ready to give up the ghost to whoever wants to take it, out of pure fear. I left my village and my children and my wife to come and serve you, in the belief that I'd be better for it rather than the opposite, but greed breaks the sack and it's broken all my hopes, because just when they were brightest and I thought I was going to get my hands on that damned island you've promised me so often, I find that instead you want to leave me in a place like this, far from all human company. In the name of the one true God, sir, let not this wrong be done unto me, and if you just can't hold yourself back from doing this daring deed, at least put it off till morning—according to the lore I learned as a shepherd, dawn can't be three hours away, because the Little Bear's mouth is on top of its head, and at midnight it's in line with its left arm."[2]

"But Sancho," asked Don Quixote, "how can you tell where that line goes, or where that mouth or small bear is, when the night is so dark that there is not a star to be seen in the sky?"

"That's true enough," said Sancho, "but fear has many eyes, and it can see things under the ground so it's got even more reason to see them up in the sky, but anyway you only need to use your head to realize that it isn't long till daybreak."

"However long it is," replied Don Quixote, "it shall not be said of me, now or ever, that tears and pleas deflected me from acting as I should, in a true knightly fashion; so I beg you, Sancho, to hold your tongue; for God, who has placed in my heart the desire to undertake this unique and dreadful adventure, will be sure to watch over my well-being and console your grief. What you must do is to make

---

1. The Nile was believed to have its source in the "Mountains of the Moon," in Ethiopia.

2. Sancho is imagining that he sees the constellation Ursa Minor, or "Little Bear."

Rocinante's girths as tight as may be, and wait here, for I shall soon return, alive or dead."

Sancho realized that this was his master's final decision, and that tears, advice and pleas weren't having any effect, so he decided to make use of his cunning to force him to wait until daybreak, if he could: as he was tightening the horse's girths he took his ass's halter and, ever so carefully and quietly so as not to be noticed, he tied Rocinante's hind legs together, so that when Don Quixote tried to set off he couldn't, because the only way in which the horse could move was in fits and starts. When Sancho saw that his trick had worked, he said:

"There you are, sir—the heavens, moved by my tears and my prayers, have ordained that Rocinante can't move, and if you keep on spurring him again and again like that you'll only annoy fortune and, as they say, kick against the pricks."

Don Quixote was close to despair, and the more he gave his horse the spur the less it budged; and, not suspecting the ligature, he resigned himself to calming down and waiting either for dawn to come or for Rocinante to move, ascribing the problem to everything except Sancho's cunning. And so he said:

"Since the fact is, Sancho, that Rocinante cannot move, I am content to wait until dawn smiles on us, even though I weep at her delay."

"No, you mustn't weep," replied Sancho. "I'll keep you amused by telling you stories till daybreak, unless you'd rather get off your horse and lie down for a little nap on the green grass, as knight errants often do, so as to feel nice and fresh when day comes and it's time to go off on that enormous adventure that's in store for you."

"What do you mean, get off my horse and lie down for a little nap?" said Don Quixote. "Am I, perchance, one of those knights who repose in the midst of danger? You can sleep, for you were born to sleep—indeed you can do as you wish—but I shall behave as I consider befits my aspirations."

"Don't be angry, sir," replied Sancho, "I didn't mean it like that."

And coming up to him he held on to the front of his saddle with one hand and on to the back of it with the other, so that he was left embracing his master's left thigh, not daring to stir one inch from it, so scared was he of the pounding, which continued unabated. Don Quixote asked him to tell a story to while the time away, as he had promised, to which Sancho replied that he would, if his fear of what he was hearing let him.

"But in spite of that I will try my hardest to tell you a true story that, if I manage to tell it properly and don't get interrupted, is the best true story there ever was, and now you must pay attention because I'm about to begin. 'Once upon a time and may good befall us all and evil come to him that evil seeks . . .' And you can see, sir, that in those ancient times they didn't start their stories any old way, but with a saying by Cato the Senseless of Rome,[3] who says 'And evil come to him that evil seeks,' which just about fits the bill here, to persuade you to stay put and not wander off seeking evil, and let's go the other way instead, sir, because nobody's forcing us to carry on in this direction, with all these terrors putting the fear of God into us."

"Continue with your story, Sancho," said Don Quixote, "and leave me to worry about the direction in which we are travelling."

"I was saying, then," continued Sancho, "that in a village in Extremadura there once lived a goat-shepherd, in other words a man who looked after goats, and this shepherd or goat-shepherd my story's all about was called Lope Ruiz, and this

---

3. Sancho means Cato the Censor, known for his moral austerity during the days of Rome's republic as well as his many pithy sayings.

Lope Ruiz was in love with a shepherdess called Torralba, and this shepherdess called Torralba was the daughter of a rich stock farmer, and this rich stock farmer . . ."

"If that is the way in which you tell your story, Sancho," said Don Quixote, "repeating everything you say, in two days' time you still will not have finished; either tell it straightforwardly, like a man of good sense, or do not tell it at all."

"The way I'm telling it," retorted Sancho, "is the way tales are always told where I come from, and I don't know any other way to tell it, and it isn't fair to expect me to learn new habits."

"Tell it however you like, then," replied Don Quixote, "and since fate decrees that I cannot avoid listening, you had better continue."

"And so, my dear good sir," continued Sancho, "as I was saying, this herdsman was in love with Torralba the shepherdess, who was a plump lass, unruly and a bit mannish, because she had the beginnings of a moustache—I can almost see her even now."

"So you knew her, did you?" said Don Quixote.

"I didn't know her as such," replied Sancho, "but the person who told me the story said it was so very true that when I told it to anyone else I could swear blind I'd seen it all for myself. So the days came and the days went and the devil, who doesn't sleep and meddles and muddles in everything, made the love that the herdsman felt for the shepherdess turn into deadly hatred, and the cause, so the gossips said, was a dose of jealousy-pangs she gave him, that went well beyond the pale; and the herdsman hated her so much from then on that, so as never to see her again, he decided to leave that land and go where he wouldn't ever clap eyes on her. As soon as Torralba saw that Lope scorned her, she fell in love with him, even though she'd never been at all fond of him before that."

"That is the way with woman," said Don Quixote: "to disdain the man who loves her, and to love the man who disdains her. Continue, Sancho."

"What happened," said Sancho, "was that the herdsman put his plan into action, and he drove his goats in front of him through the fields of Extremadura to cross over into the Kingdom of Portugal. The Torralba woman found out and went after him, and followed him at a distance on her bare feet, with her staff in her hand and her two satchels hanging from her neck and containing, so it's said, a piece of a mirror and a piece of a comb and some sort of jar of face lotion, but whatever it was she was carrying, and I'm not going to start trying to find that out now, all I will say is that it's said that the herdsman and his goats reached the River Guadiana,[4] and it was swollen almost to overflowing, and there wasn't any ferry or any other boat to take him and his animals across, which put him in a tizzy because he could see that the Torralba woman was getting close and she was going to make a nuisance of herself with all her pleading and moaning, but he kept looking so hard that he saw a fisherman with a boat by his side, so small that there was only room in it for one person and one goat, and in spite of this he spoke to him and bargained with him and they agreed that the fisherman would ferry him and his three hundred goats across to the other bank. The fisherman climbed into his boat and took one goat across, and he came back and took another goat across, and he came back again and took another goat across. You've got to keep count of the goats that the fisherman takes across, because if you let just one of them slip from

4. A river that runs through La Mancha and into southern Portugal.

your memory the story will come to an end and I won't be able to tell you another word of it. To continue, then, I ought to say that the landing-stage on the other side was very muddy and slippery, and the fisherman was taking a long time going to and fro. All the same, he came for another goat, and another goat, and another goat . . ."

"Just assume that he has ferried them all across," said Don Quixote. "Don't keep coming and going like that—you won't get them to the other side in a year."

"How many goats has he taken across so far?" asked Sancho.

"How the devil do you expect me to know that?" replied Don Quixote.

"That's just what I told you—to keep good count. Well, by God, the story's over, I'm not going on."

"How can that be?" replied Don Quixote. "Is it so essential to the story to know exactly how many goats have gone across that if we are so much as one out you cannot continue telling it?"

"No, sir, not at all," replied Sancho. "It's just that when I asked you to tell me how many goats had gone and you replied that you didn't know, at that very instant I clean forgot what I had left to say, and it was full of good things, I can tell you that much."

"So your story is finished?" said Don Quixote.

"As sure as my mother is," said Sancho.

"I can honestly say," replied Don Quixote, "that you have just told one of the most original tales, true or false, that anybody could ever have dreamed of, and that your way of telling it and concluding it is something never heard before nor to be heard again, although I did expect no less from your fine mind. But this does not surprise me, because that incessant pounding must have turned your brain."

"That's as may be," replied Sancho, "all I know is, that's the end of my story—it finishes where you start to make mistakes in counting the goats."

"It is welcome to finish wherever it wishes," said Don Quixote. "Now let us see if Rocinante can move."

He set spurs to his horse again, and again the horse jumped and froze, for Sancho's knots were good knots.

It appears that at this moment, either because of the cold of the morning, which was fast approaching, or because Sancho had eaten something loosening for his supper, or because of natural processes (which seems most likely), he felt the urgent need to do the job of work that nobody could do for him; but so great was the fear which had entered his heart that he didn't dare to move as much as a hair's-breadth from his master's side. Yet not doing what he had to do wasn't a possibility, either; and so what he did, for the sake of peace and concord, was to draw his right hand away from the back of Don Quixote's saddle and use it with great stealth to loosen the running knot that was all that held his breeches up, at which they slid down and encircled his ankles like fetters. Then he lifted up his shirt as best he could, and thrust two ample buttocks into the night air. Once he'd done this, which he'd thought was all he needed to do to escape from his harrowing predicament, he found himself in another even worse plight: he thought that he wasn't going to be able to relieve himself in silence, and he began to grit his teeth and hunch his shoulders and hold his breath for as long as he could, but in spite of all these precautions he was unfortunate enough, in the end, to make a small noise, quite different from the noise causing him such great fear. Don Quixote heard it and said:

"What murmuring is that, Sancho?"

"I don't know, sir," he replied. "It must be some new business, because adventures and misadventures never come singly."

He tried his luck again, and such was his success that, with no greater noise than the previous time, he relieved himself of the burden that had been weighing so heavily upon him. But since Don Quixote's sense of smell was as acute as his sense of hearing, and since Sancho was clinging so very close to him, it was inevitable that some of the fumes, rising almost in a straight line, would reach his nostrils, whereupon he went to their rescue by squeezing them between finger and thumb, and said in somewhat nasal tones:

"It seems to me, Sancho, that you are very frightened."

"That I am," replied Sancho, "but what makes you notice it now more than at other times?"

"The fact that now, more than at other times, you smell, and not of ambergris," replied Don Quixote.

"You could well be right," said Sancho, "but I'm not the one to blame—you are, for dragging me into such wild places at these unearthly hours."

"Move three or maybe four places backwards, my friend," said Don Quixote, without taking his hand from his nose, "and from now on be more careful with your person and with what is due to mine; for it is my familiarity with you that has given rise to this contempt."

"I bet you're thinking," said Sancho, "that I've done something with my person that I didn't ought to have done."

"The more you stir it the worse it gets, friend Sancho," replied Don Quixote.

In this and other similar conversations master and servant spent the night; but when Sancho saw that morning was fast approaching, he very quietly united Rocinante and tied his breeches. Once Rocinante found himself free it seems that, although he wasn't a high-spirited animal, the after-effects of his confinement made him begin pawing, because prancing (begging his pardon) was beyond him. And when Don Quixote noticed that Rocinante could move again, he considered it to be a favourable sign indicating, he believed, that it was time for him to undertake that terrible adventure.

And now dawn broke at last, and objects began to be clearly visible, and Don Quixote saw that he was beneath some tall trees, chestnuts, which cast a deep, dark shade. He also noticed that the pounding didn't cease, but he couldn't see what was causing it; and so, without further delay, he let Rocinante feel the spur and, saying goodbye again to Sancho, told him to wait there for three days, at the most, just as he had told him before, and, if by the end of them he hadn't returned, to take it as certain that it had been God's will that he should end his life in that perilous adventure. He repeated his instructions about the message to be taken on his behalf to his lady Dulcinea, and told Sancho not to worry about the matter of the payment for his services, because he had made his will before leaving home and in it he had made full provision for wages covering the time served, *pro rata;*[5] and he added that, if God brought him out of that peril safe and sound and ransomless, Sancho could count with total certainty on receiving the promised island.

Sancho wept again as he heard his good master's doleful words once more, and he resolved not to leave him until the absolute final end of that particular incident. From these tears of Sancho Panza's and from this honourable decision of his the author of this history concludes that he must have been of good family and, at the very

5. At the going rate.

least, of pure old Christian stock. And his master was moved by his feelings, but not so much as to make him waver in the slightest; on the contrary he hid his emotion as best he could and began to ride in the direction from which he thought the noise of the water and the pounding were coming. Sancho followed on foot, leading his donkey— his perpetual companion in prosperous and adverse fortune—by the halter, as he so often did; and after they'd advanced some way under those gloomy chestnut trees, they came to a little meadow at the foot of a high cliff from which a great waterfall came tumbling down. Beneath the cliff there were some roughly constructed build-ings that looked more like ruins than anything else, and the two men realized that the ceaseless pounding din was coming from over there. Rocinante started at the racket of the water and the pounding, and Don Quixote soothed him and then inched his way towards the buildings, commending himself with all his heart to his lady and implor-ing her to favour him in this dreadful enterprise, and while he was about it he also commended himself to God and asked not to be forgotten by him. Sancho never strayed from his side, and he poked his neck out as far as he could and he peered as hard as he could between Rocinante's legs, to try to make out what it was that was filling him with such dread.

They must have advanced another hundred paces when, as they came round the side of a hillock, they saw, starkly exposed to their gaze, without any room for doubt, the cause of that hideous and, for them, horrendous din that had kept them so bewildered and scared throughout the night. And it was (please don't take this amiss, dear reader) six fulling-hammers making all the noise with their alternating blows.[6]

When Don Quixote saw what it was he fell silent and stiffened from top to toe. Sancho looked up at Don Quixote and saw that his head was sunk on his breast in manifest mortification. Don Quixote looked down at Sancho and saw that his cheeks were puffed up and his mouth was filled with mirth, about to explode with it; and the knight's dejection was not so great that it could prevent him from laughing at the sight of Sancho, and when Sancho saw that his master had begun to laugh, he released his own captive so suddenly that he had to press his fists to his sides so as not to explode. Four times he calmed down, and four times he started laughing again, every bit as hard as the first time, and Don Quixote was becoming more and more enraged, partic-ularly when he heard Sancho say by way of mockery:

"'I would have you know, friend Sancho, that I was born, by the will of heaven, in this iron age of ours, to revive in it the age of gold, or golden age. I am the man for whom dangers, great exploits, valiant deeds are reserved . . .'"

And he went on to repeat most of what Don Quixote had said when they'd first heard the dreadful pounding. Seeing Sancho making fun of him, Don Quixote was so furious that he raised his pike and struck him two such blows that if they'd connected with his head instead of his shoulders there wouldn't have been any need to pay any wages, except to his heirs. Now that his jolly jest had turned into ugly earnest, and fearful that his master might give him some more of the same, Sancho grovelled:

"Calm down, do, sir, please—I swear to God I was only joking."

"You may be joking, sir, but I am not," retorted Don Quixote. "Look here, my merry fellow: do you fancy that, if these were not fulling-hammers but some perilous

---

6. "Fulling" is the process by which cloth is thickened and cleaned; in a fulling-mill, cloth is first beaten with heavy wooden mallets or hammers, and then cleansed with soap.

new adventure, I should have failed to display the courage needed to undertake and conclude it? Am I, perchance, sir, obliged—being, as I am, a knight and a gentle-man—to identify and distinguish between sounds, and tell whether they come from fulling-mills or not? And furthermore it could be the case, as indeed it is, that I have never seen such things in my life, just as you must have seen them often, being a mis-erable peasant, born and brought up among them. Or else, sir, you just turn these six hammers into six giants, and set them on me one by one or all together, and if I do not topple each and every one of them, then you can laugh at me as much as you please."

"Enough said, sir," said Sancho, "I will admit I was a bit free with my giggles. But tell me, now we're at peace again, and may God get you out of all your adven-tures to come as safe and sound as out of this one—wasn't it a great joke, and won't it make a fine story, this enormous fear of ours? My fear I mean, because I'm aware you don't even know what fear is, sir, or what it feels like to be afraid."

"I do not deny," replied Don Quixote, "that what has happened to us is worth laughing at; but it is not worth telling, because not all people are intelligent enough to see things in the right perspective."

"At least you got your pike in the right perspective," replied Sancho, "aiming at my head and hitting my shoulders, thanks to God and the care I took to duck. But there we are, it all comes out in the wash, and I've often heard people say 'you've got to be cruel to be kind,' and what's more, when important gentlemen give their ser vants a good talking-to, they normally give them a pair of breeches afterwards, though I don't know what they give them after beatings, but maybe what knight er-rants give after beatings are islands, or kingdoms on dry land."

"The dice could well fall in such a way," said Don Quixote, "that what you say comes true; and forgive me for what has just happened, because you are intelligent and so you understand that man's first impulses are beyond his control; and pay heed from now on to what I am about to say, so that you refrain from talking to me exces-sively: in all the books of chivalry I have read, an infinity of them, I have never come across any squire who talked to his master as much as you do to yours. And in truth I consider it a great fault in both you and me; in you, because you show me scant re-spect; in me, because I do not make you respect me more. Yes, indeed: Gandalin, Amadis of Gaul's squire, was the Count of the Firm Isle, yet we read that he always addressed his master cap in hand, with his head bowed and his body bent double, in the Turkish fashion. And what shall we say of Gasabal, Sir Galaor's squire, who was so quiet that to convey the excellence of his miraculous silence his name is only mentioned once in the whole of that great and true history?[7] From all that I have said you should infer, Sancho, that a distance must be kept between master and man, be tween lord and lackey, between knight and squire. So from now on we must behave with more respect, and not indulge in our little jokes, for in whatever way I become annoyed with you, sir, take note that it is always the pitcher that is broken. The boons and favours that I have promised you will arrive in good time, and if they do not arrive you will not, at least, forfeit your wages, as I have already informed you."

"All you say is very well said," replied Sancho, "but what I'd like to know, just in case the time of the favours never does come round and I have to fall back on wages, is how much knights' squires used to earn in those olden days, and whether they were hired by the month or on a daily basis like builders' labourers."

7. In *Amadis of Gaul,* Don Galaor is Amadis's brother, although ignorant of his legacy; Gasabal is his squire.

"I do not believe," replied Don Quixote, "that such squires were ever paid wages: they depended upon favour. And if I have provided for you to be paid wages, in the sealed will I left in my house, that was only because of what might happen; for I do not yet know how chivalry will fare in these calamitous times of ours, and I should not want my soul to suffer in the other world for the sake of a mere trifle. For I would have you know, Sancho, that there is no profession in this world more hazardous than that of knight adventurer."

"That's true enough," said Sancho, "because it only needed the sound of some hammers in a fulling-mill to strike fear and terror into the heart of a really brave errant adventurer like yourself. But you can take it from me that from this moment on I won't open my mouth to make fun of your doings, but only to honour you as my master and natural lord."

"In that case," replied Don Quixote, "your days will be long on the face of the earth, because next to our parents, our masters should be respected as if they were our parents."

* * *

Chapter 22

ABOUT HOW DON QUIXOTE FREED MANY WRETCHES WHO, MUCH AGAINST THEIR WILL, WERE BEING TAKEN WHERE THEY WOULD HAVE PREFERRED NOT TO GO

Cide Hamete Benengeli, the Arab author from La Mancha, relates in this most grave, grandiloquent, meticulous, delightful and imaginative history that after the conversation between the famous Don Quixote de la Mancha and his squire Sancho Panza recorded at the end of the twenty-first chapter, Don Quixote raised his eyes and saw that some twelve men on foot, strung by the neck, like beads, on a great iron chain, and with shackles on their hands, were plodding towards them along the road. Two men on horseback and two others on foot were escorting them. The mounted men were carrying firelocks and the others swords and spears, and as soon as Sancho Panza saw them he said:

"Here comes a chain-gang of convicts, on their forced march to the King's galleys."

"What do you mean, forced march?" demanded Don Quixote. "Is it possible that the King uses force on anyone?"

"I don't mean that," replied Sancho, "just that they've been sentenced to serve the King in his galleys for their crimes, and they've got a long walk to get there."

"In short," replied Don Quixote, "whatever the details may be, these people, wherever they are going, are being forced to march there, and are not doing it of their own free will."

"That's right," said Sancho.

"In that case," said his master, "this situation is calling out for the exercise of my profession: the redressing of outrages and the succour and relief of the wretched."

"Look, sir," said Sancho. "Justice, and that means the King himself, isn't doing these people any outrages, only punishing them for their crimes."

At this point the chain-gang came up, and Don Quixote, in courteous language, asked the guards to be so kind as to inform him of the reason or reasons why they were bearing those people off in that way. One of the guards on horseback replied that they were all convicts, detained at His Majesty's pleasure and on their way to the galleys, and that there was nothing else to be said and nothing else that he had any business to know.

"All the same," said Don Quixote, "I should like to hear from each one of them individually the cause of his misfortune."

He added other such polite expressions to persuade them to tell him what he wanted to know that the other guard on horseback said:

"We do have here the documents and certificates with the sentences that each of these wretches has been given, but this is no time to stop to take them out and read them; so you'd better come and ask the men yourself, and they'll tell you if they want to—and they will want to, because these are fellows who really enjoy getting up to their evil tricks and bragging about them afterwards."

With this permission, which Don Quixote would have taken for himself if it hadn't been given him, he approached the chain-gang and asked the first convict what sins had put him in that plight. The convict replied that he was there for being in love.

"For no more than that?" replied Don Quixote. "If they send men to the galleys for being in love, I could have been rowing in them for a long time by now."

"It isn't love of the sort you think," said the convict. "Mine was for a washing-basket that was chock-a-block with linen, and I loved it so much, and I hugged it so tight, that if the law hadn't taken it off me by force I still wouldn't have let go of it of my own freewill to this day. I was caught red-handed, there wasn't any need for torture, the trial's over and done with, they gave me a hundred of the best plus three in the tubs and that's that."

"What are tubs?" asked Don Quixote.

"Tubs is galleys," replied the convict.

He was a young man of maybe twenty-four, and he said he was a native of Piedrahita. Don Quixote put the same question to the second convict, who was so overcome by melancholy that he didn't offer a word in reply, but the first one answered for him and said:

"This one, sir, is here for being a canary-bird, that is to say for being a singer and musician."

"What?" said Don Quixote. "Do men go to the galleys for being singers and musicians, too?"

"Yes, sir," replied the convict, "because there's nothing worse than singing in your throes."

"On the contrary," said Don Quixote, "I have often heard it said that one can sing away sorrows and cast away care."

"Here it's the opposite," said the convict. "Sing just that once and you'll weep for the rest of your life."

"I fail to understand," said Don Quixote.

But one of the guards explained:

"Sir knight, among these ungodly people singing in your throes means confessing under torture. This sinner was tortured and he confessed to his crime—he's a prigger of prancers, in other words a horse-thief—and because he confessed he was sentenced to six years in the galleys and two hundred strokes of the lash, and these he's already been given; and he's always sad and lost in his thoughts, because the other criminals back there in prison and here in the chain-gang despise and mock and maltreat him and make his life impossible for confessing and not having the guts to keep saying no. They say, you see, that "nay" has no more letters in it than "aye," and that a delinquent's a lucky man if his life or death depends on his own tongue and not on witnesses or evidence, and it's my belief they aren't far wrong."

"That is my understanding, too," replied Don Quixote.

He moved on to the third convict and put the same question to him; the reply was ready and assured:

"I'm off to our old friends the tubs for five years, for the lack of ten ducats."

"I will most gladly give you twenty," said Don Quixote, "to relieve you of such distress."

"That looks to me," replied the convict, "like having money in the middle of the ocean when you're starving and there isn't anywhere to buy what you need. I'm saying this because if I'd had those twenty ducats you're offering me when I needed them, I'd have used them to grease the clerk's pen and liven up my lawyer's wits, and now I'd be in the middle of Zocodover Square in Toledo instead of in the middle of this road, like a greyhound on a leash. But God is good, and you've just got to be patient."

Don Quixote went on to the fourth convict, a man with a venerable face and a white beard reaching below his chest who, when asked why he was there, began to weep and didn't reply; but the fifth convict acted as interpreter and said:

"This honourable man is going to the galleys for four years, having been paraded in state through the customary streets, all dressed up and on a fine horse."

"That means, I think," said Sancho, "that he was exposed to public shame."[1]

"That's right," said the convict, "and the crime he was given this punishment for was stockbroking, or to be more exact bodybroking. What I mean to say is that this gentleman's here for being a pimp, and also for having a touch of the sorcerer about him."

"If it were not for the touch of the sorcerer," said Don Quixote, "for being a pimp alone he does not deserve to go to row in the galleys, but rather to be the admiral in charge of them. Because the pimp's trade is no ordinary trade; it must be carried out by intelligent people and it is absolutely essential to any well-ordered society, and only the well-born should exercise it; and there should be an official inspector of pimps, as there is of other trades, and a maximum permitted number of them established and published, as is the case with stockbrokers, and this would be the way to forestall many evils that arise from the fact that this trade is in the hands of untrained and unqualified people such as little strumpets, page-boys and other scoundrels of no age or experience who, when at a critical moment some decisive action is called for, make a mess of the whole thing because they cannot tell their right hands from their left. I should like to go on to give the reasons why it would be advisable to make a careful selection of those who do such a necessary job in society, but this is not the place: one day I shall present my ideas to the proper authorities. All I shall say now is that the distress caused me by the sight of these white hairs and this venerable face in such a plight through his being a pimp is dissipated by the addition of his being a sorcerer. I know, of course, that there are no spells in the world that can control a person's will, as some simple people believe; for our free will is sovereign, and there is no herb or enchantment that can control it. What some silly little strumpets and deceitful rogues do is to make certain poisonous mixtures that they use to turn men mad, claiming that they have the power to make them fall in love, whereas it is, as I have just said, impossible to coerce the will."

"Right you are," said the old man, "and honestly, sir, I wasn't guilty of being a sorcerer, though I couldn't deny the charge of being a pimp. But I never thought I was doing any harm, all I wanted was for everyone to be happy and live in peace and

---

1. A common form of punishment in early modern Europe; he would have been flogged and then paraded through the city's main streets with a placard denouncing his crimes.

quiet, without any quarrels or sadness—but these good intentions weren't any use to prevent me from being sent where I don't expect to come back from, what with my advanced age and my bladder trouble, that doesn't give me a moment's peace."

And here he started weeping again, and Sancho felt so sorry for him that he took a real from inside his shirt and handed it over. Don Quixote moved on to the next man and asked what was his crime, and he replied with no less brio than the last, indeed with rather more of it:

"I'm here because I fooled around too much with two girl-cousins of mine, and with two girl-cousins of somebody else's; and, in short, I fooled around so much with the lot of them that as a result the family tree's become so complicated that I don't know who the devil would be able to work it out. It was all proved against me, there weren't any strings for me to pull, I hadn't got any money, I was within an inch of having my neck stretched, I was sentenced to the galleys for six years and I accepted my fate: it's the punishment for my crime, I'm still young, long live life, while there's life there's hope. If, sir knight, you've got anything on you that you could spare for us poor wretches, God will repay you for it in heaven, and here on earth we'll take care to pray to God that your life and your health may be as long and as good as you obviously deserve."

He was wearing a student's gown, and one of the guards said that he was a great talker and a first-rate latiner.

Behind all of these was a man of thirty, very good-looking except that he squinted a little. He was shackled in a different way from the others: he had a chain on his ankle so long that he'd wound it all round his body, and two neck-irons, one linking him to the other convicts and the other, one of the sort called a keep-friend or friend's foot, from which descended two bars to his waist, where his wrists were manacled to them with great padlocks, so that he could neither raise his hands to his mouth nor lower his head to his hands. Don Quixote asked why this man was wearing so many more fetters than the others. The guard replied that it was because he'd committed more crimes than all the others put together, and that he was so reckless and such a villain that, even though he was shackled up like that, they didn't feel at all safe with him, and feared he was going to escape.

"What crimes can he have committed, though," asked Don Quixote, "if he was not given a worse punishment than the galleys?"

"He's going for ten years," replied the guard, "which is civil death, more or less. All you need to know is that this man is the famous Ginés de Pasamonte, also known as Ginesillo de Parapilla."[2]

"Look you here, sergeant," said the convict, "just watch your step, and don't be in such a hurry to fix names and nicknames on to people. I'm called Ginés, not Ginesillo, and my family name is Pasamonte, not the Parapilla you said, and I'd advise you lot to stop poking your noses into other people's business."

"Less impudence, you double-dyed villain," replied the sergeant, "unless you want me to shut your mouth for you."

"It isn't hard to spot," replied the convict, "that at the moment I'm reduced to what God has seen fit to send me; but one day somebody's going to find out whether I'm called Ginesillo de Parapilla or not."

2. Ginesillo is the diminutive for Ginés, and implies a lack of respect.

"Isn't that what people call you, then, you liar?" said the guard.

"Yes, that's what they call me," replied Ginés, "but I'll stop them calling me that, or else I'll pull out every single hair from my I know what. If you've got something to give us, sir knight, let's have it, and then you can clear off, because you're beginning to get on my nerves with all your prying into other people's lives—and if you want to know about mine, let me tell you I'm Ginés de Pasamonte, and my life has been written by these very fingers here."

"Now he's telling the truth," said the sergeant. "He's written his own life-history himself and a good one it is, too, and he pawned the book in prison for two hundred reals."

"And I mean to redeem it," said Ginés. "And I would, even if I'd pawned it for two hundred ducats."

"Is it as good as all that?" said Don Quixote.

"It's so good," replied Ginés, "that I wouldn't give a fig for *Lazarillo de Tormes* and all the others of that kind that have been or ever will be written.[3] What I can tell you is that it deals with facts, and that they're such fine and funny facts no lies could ever match them."

"And what is the title of your book?" asked Don Quixote.

"The Life of Ginés de Pasamonte," replied the man of that name.

"And have you finished it?" asked Don Quixote.

"How can I have finished it," he replied, "if my life hasn't finished yet? What's written so far is from my birth to when I was sentenced to the galleys this last time."

"Have you been to the galleys before, then?" asked Don Quixote.

"I have, serving God and the King for four years, so I know what biscuits taste like and I know what the lash tastes like," replied Ginés. "And I'm not too worried about going back, because it'll give me a chance to finish my book—there are lots of things left for me to say, and in Spanish galleys there's more than enough peace and quiet, not that I need much of that for what I've got left to write, because I know it all by heart."

"You seem to be an able fellow," said Don Quixote.

"And an unfortunate one, too," replied Ginés, "because misfortunes always pursue men of genius."

"They pursue villains," said the sergeant.

"I've already told you, sergeant," replied Pasamonte, "to watch your step—you weren't given that staff to ill-treat us poor wretches, but to guide and take us to where His Majesty commands. Otherwise—by the blood of . . .!—all sorts of things might come out in the wash one day, like those stains that were made at the inn, for example. So everyone keep his mouth shut, and live a good life, and speak even better words, and let's get moving, because this little joke has been going on for far too long."

The sergeant raised his staff to hit Pasamonte in reply to his threats, but Don Quixote thrust himself between them and begged the sergeant not to maltreat the fellow, for it was only to be expected that one whose hands were so tightly bound would loosen his tongue a little. And turning to the chain-gang he said:

"From everything that you have told me, dearly beloved brethren, I have gathered that, although it is for your crimes you have been sentenced, the punishments

---

3. *The Life of Lazarillo of Tormes* was a popular novel in mid-16th-century Spain about a young boy forced to make his way in the world. The anonymous novel, written as an autobiography, launched the genre of the "picaresque," or works about down-and-out rogues (*picaro* means rascal). Ginés is obviously capitalizing on the public's thirst for such works.

you are to suffer give you little pleasure, and that you are on your way to receive them with reluctance and against your will; and it could be that one man's lack of courage under torture, another's lack of money, another's lack of strings to pull and, to be brief, the judge's perverse decisions, were the causes of your downfall and of his failure to recognize the right that was on your side. All of which is now so power-fully present in my mind that it is persuading, telling and even obliging me to demon-strate on you the purpose for which heaven sent me into this world and made me pro-fess in it the order of chivalry that I do profess, and the vow that I made to favour the needy and those oppressed by the powerful. But because I know that one essential part of prudence is never to do by force what can be achieved by consent, I hereby re-quest these guards and this sergeant to be so kind as to release you and allow you to go in peace, for there will be no lack of other men to serve the King in happier cir-cumstances, and it does seem excessively harsh to make slaves of those whom God and nature made free. What is more, guards," added Don Quixote, "these poor men have done nothing to you. Let each answer for his sins in the other world; there is a God in heaven who does not neglect to punish the wicked and reward the virtuous, and it is not right for honourable men to be the executioners of others, if they have no personal concern in the matter. I am making my request in this mild and measured manner so that, if you accede to it, I shall have reason for thanking you; but if you do not accede voluntarily, this lance and this sword and the might of my arm will force you to comply."

"That's a good one that is!" said the sergeant. "That's a fine joke he's come out with at long last! He wants us to hand the King's prisoners over to him, as if we had the authority to let them go or he had the authority to tell us to! You'd better clear off and make tracks, sir, and straighten that chamber-pot you've got on your head, and don't go around trying to put the cat among the pigeons."

"You are the cat, and the rat, and the villain, too!" retorted Don Quixote. He matched his deeds to his words and his attack was such a sudden one that he tumbled the man to the ground with a pike-wound before he had a chance to defend himself; and it was fortunate for Don Quixote that this was the guard with the firelock. The other guards were amazed and disconcerted by this unexpected development, but they rallied, and those on horseback seized their swords, and those on foot their spears, and they all fell upon Don Quixote, who was calmly awaiting them; yet he'd have fared badly if the convicts, seeing their chance to be free, hadn't succeeded by breaking the chain on which they were threaded. The hurly-burly was such that the guards, trying both to control the convicts, who were unshackling themselves, and to attack Don Quixote, who was attacking them, chased around in circles and achieved nothing.

Sancho, for his part, helped with the freeing of Ginés de Pasamonte, who was the first to spring into action as he launched himself at the fallen sergeant, snatched up his sword and his firelock and, pointing this at one man and then at another, without fir-ing it, made all the guards disappear as they fled both from the gun and from the stones being hurled at them by the escaped convicts.

This incident saddened Sancho, because he supposed that the fleeing men would go and inform the Holy Brotherhood, who would sound the alarm and come out in pursuit of the wrongdoers; and Sancho said so to his master, and begged him to agree to a quick getaway to hide in the forests in the nearby sierra.

"That is a good idea," said Don Quixote, "but there is something I must do first."

And he called out to the convicts, who were creating a furor as they stripped the sergeant naked; they gathered around to see what he wanted, and he said:

"It is a mark of well-born people to be grateful for benefits received, and one of the sins most offensive to God is ingratitude. I am saying this because you have seen, gentlemen, manifest before your eyes, the benefit that you have received from me; in payment of which it is my wish and desire that you should set out without delay, bearing that chain that I have taken from your necks, for the city of El Toboso, and present yourselves before the lady Dulcinea del Toboso, and tell her that her knight, the Knight of the Sorry Face,[4] presents his compliments, and relate to her, stage by stage, every detail of this famous adventure up to and including my restoration of the liberty that you so desired; and once you have done this you can go wherever you like, and may good fortune attend you."

Ginés de Pasamonte replied on behalf of them all, and said:

"This that you order us to do, dear lord and liberator, is utterly and totally out of the question, because we can't travel together—we've got to split up and go alone, each along his own road, and try to find a way into the very bowels of the earth so as not to be caught by the Holy Brotherhood, who'll be coming out after us, for certain. What you can do and what it'd be right for you to do is to replace that toll or tax payable to the lady Dulcinea del Toboso by a certain number of Ave Marias and Credos, which we'll say for your kindness, and this is something that can be done by night and by day, running away and resting, in peace and in war; but to think that we're going back to the flesh-pots of Egypt,[5] in other words picking up our chain again and setting off for El Toboso, is like thinking it's night-time already when it isn't yet ten in the morning—it's like trying to get figs from thistles."

"By my faith," cried Don Quixote, by now in a fury, "you little bastard, Don Ginesillo de Paropillo or whatever you're called—now you shall go there alone, with your tail between your legs and the whole chain on your back!"

Pasamonte wasn't a long-suffering sort, and from Don Quixote's absurd desire to set them free he'd realized that the man wasn't very sane, so when he found himself thus addressed, he tipped his companions the wink and they edged away and began to rain so many stones on Don Quixote that, however he ducked and dodged behind his little round shield, he couldn't fend them off; and poor Rocinante paid no more attention to the spurs than if he'd been made of bronze. Sancho sheltered behind his ass from the hailstorm falling on them both. Don Quixote couldn't prevent countless stones from hitting his body with enough force to knock him to the ground, and as soon as he did fall the student leapt on him, snatched the basin from his head and smashed it three or four times on his back and as many more times on the earth, pounding it almost to pieces. Then they stripped him of a surcoat he was wearing over his armour and would have stripped him of his stockings, too, if his leg armour hadn't made this impossible. They took Sancho's topcoat and left him in his shirtsleeves, and they shared the rest of the spoils of battle, and each went his own way, more concerned to escape from the dreaded Holy Brotherhood than to burden himself with the chain and go to present himself before the lady Dulcinea del Toboso.

The ass and Rocinante, Sancho and Don Quixote were left alone: the ass hanging its head, lost in its thoughts, flapping its ears every so often in the belief that the storm of stones wasn't yet over, because it was still raging inside its skull; Rocinante

4. In Chapter 19, Sancho hits upon a fitting epithet for Don Quixote: *Caballero de la Triste Figura*, or Knight of the Sad or Sorry Face. Don Quixote immediately takes a liking to the name, declaring that "the sage whose task it is to write the history of my exploits must have thought it right for me to take some appellation, as all previous knights have done": he therefore magically must have placed the epithet in Sancho's mind.

5. Back to the lap of luxury; the phrase is from Exodus 16.

stretched out by his master's side, because he'd also been brought down by a stone; Sancho in his shirtsleeves and fearful of the Holy Brotherhood; and Don Quixote sulking at being left in such a sorry state by men for whom he had done so much.

* * *

from *Chapter 25*

CONCERNING THE STRANGE THINGS THAT HAPPENED TO THE BRAVE KNIGHT OF LA MANCHA IN THE SIERRA MORENA, AND HIS IMITATION OF THE PENANCE OF BELTENEBROS[1]

* * * "What I say, Sancho," replied Don Quixote, "is that you must do as you please, for your idea does not seem a bad one; and I also say that you shall depart three days from now, because I want you to spend this time witnessing what I do and say for her sake, so that you can tell her about it."

"And what else have I got to see," asked Sancho, "apart from what I've seen already?"

"You are well informed about these matters, I must say!" Don Quixote retorted. "Now I must tear my garments, scatter my armour and dash my head against these rocks, and perform other similar actions that will amaze you."

"For God's sake," said Sancho Panza, "do be careful how you go around dashing your head, because you could pick on such a rock and hit it in such a place that you put paid to the whole penance business with the very first knock you gave it. And if you really think head-dashing's essential and this job can't be done without it, to my mind you ought to be content, since it's all make-believe, a fake and a sham, to dash your head against the water, or something soft like cotton, and leave the rest to me—I'll tell my lady you were knocking it against a jutting crag, harder than diamonds."

"I am grateful to you for meaning well, friend Sancho," replied Don Quixote, "but I would have you know that I am doing all these things not in jest but very much in earnest; for to behave otherwise would be to contravene the commands of chivalry, which instruct one never to tell a lie, on pain of being punished as a recidivist;[2] and to do one thing instead of another is the same as lying. So my blows on the head must be real, firm and effective, with no element of the sophistical or the fantastic about them. And you will have to leave me some lint to cure my wounds, for fate has left us without our balsam."

"Losing the ass was worse," replied Sancho, "because the lint and all was lost with it. And I'd ask you very kindly not to bring that damned potion up again—just hearing it mentioned turns not only my stomach but my very soul inside-out. And I'd also ask you, as regards those three days you allocated for watching the crazy things you're going to do, to make believe they're over and done with, because I'll be happy to take them for granted as if seen and approved, and I'll tell my lady wonders. So you write your letter and then send me packing, because I'm longing to come back and get you out of this purgatory where I'm leaving you."

"Purgatory you call it, Sancho?" said Don Quixote. "You would do better to call it hell, or worse, if there is anything worse."

1. Don Quixote and Sancho have reached the desolate region of the Sierra Morena, where Don Quixote prepares to perform penance in imitation of Amadis de Gaul, who took the name "Beltenebros," or "beautiful shadows."

Sancho is preparing to depart to report to Dulcinea what he has seen of his master's penitence.
2. A backslider or repeat offender.

"In hell," replied Sancho, "*nulla est retentio,* so I've heard say."[3]

"I do not understand what you mean by *retentio,*" said Don Quixote.

"*Retentio* means," replied Sancho, "that people in hell never get out, and can't get out. It'll be the reverse with you, though, so long as I get my heels working, if I'm wearing spurs to make Rocinante move, that is—and you just wait till I reach El Toboso, and come before my lady Dulcinea, and then I'll tell her such stories about the acts of madness and stupidity, which comes to the same thing, that you've done and are doing as will make her as sweet as a nut, even if she's as hard as a cork-oak when I start work on her. And I'll come back through the air like a sorcerer with her honeyed answer, and I'll rescue you from this purgatory that seems like hell but isn't, because there's a hope of getting out of it, which people in hell haven't got, as I've just said, and I don't suppose you'll want to disagree with that."

"True," said the Knight of the Sorry Face, "but how are we going to manage to write that letter?"

"And that donkey-warrant," added Sancho.

"It will all be included," said Don Quixote, "and, since we have no paper, it would be appropriate to write it, as the ancients did, on leaves from the trees, or on tablets of wax; yet it would be as difficult to find these now as paper itself. But I have just thought of a good place, indeed an excellent one, to write it: the notebook that used to belong to Cardenio,[4] and you must take care to have it copied in a clear hand on to a sheet of paper in the first village with a schoolmaster, or else any sexton will copy it for you; but do not ask a clerk to copy it, because they use a corrupt and degenerate hand that Satan himself would not be able to read."

"And what's to be done about your signature?" asked Sancho.

"The letters of Amadis are never signed," replied Don Quixote.

"That's as may be," replied Sancho, "but the warrant must be signed, and if it's copied out they'll say the signature's a fake and I'll be left without my donkeys."

"The warrant will be signed in the notebook, and when my niece sees it she will not raise any objections about complying with it. And as regards the love-letter, you will have it signed: "Yours until death, The Knight of the Sorry Face." It will matter little that it is signed in another hand, because as far as I remember Dulcinea cannot read or write, and she has never seen a letter written by me, because the love between us has always been platonic, never going beyond a modest glance. And even this has been so occasional that I can truly swear that, in the twelve years I have loved her more than the light of these eyes that the earth will one day devour, I have not seen her as many as four times; and it is possible that on those four occasions she has not even once noticed that I was looking at her, such is the reserve and seclusion in which her father Lorenzo Corchuelo and her mother Aldonza Nogales have brought her up."

"Oho!" said Sancho. "So Lorenzo Corchuelo's daughter is the lady Dulcinea del Toboso, also known as Aldonza Lorenzo, is she?"

"She is," said Don Quixote, "and she it is who deserves to be the mistress of the entire universe."

"I know her well," said Sancho, "and let me tell you she pitches a bar as far as the strongest lad in all the village. Good God, she's a lusty lass all right, hale and hearty, strong as an ox, and any knight errant who has her as his lady now or in the future can

---

3. While Sancho's explanation is a canny one, his Latin is mangled; he should have said "in hell, *nulla est redemptio*" (nothing is redeemed) rather than "nothing is retained." The line is from the service for the dead.

4. Sancho and Don Quixote were first alerted to Cardenio's whereabouts when they discovered a satchel with his notebooks in Chapter 23.

count on her to pull him out of the mire! The little baggage, what muscles she's got on her, and what a voice! Let me tell you she climbed up one day to the top of the church belfry to call to some lads of hers who were in a fallow field of her father's, and even though they were a good couple of miles off they could hear her just as if they'd been standing at the foot of the tower. And the best thing about her is she isn't at all priggish, she's a real courtly lass, enjoys a joke with everyone and turns every-thing into a good laugh. And now I can say, Sir Knight of the Sorry Face, that not only is it very right and proper for you to get up to your mad tricks for her sake—you've got every reason to give way to despair and hang yourself, too, and nobody who knows about it will say you weren't justified, even if it does send you to the devil. And I wish I was on my way already, just to take a look at her, because I haven't seen her for days, and she must be changed by now, because women's faces get spoiled by always being out in the fields, in the sun and the wind. And I must be honest with you, Don Quixote sir—until now I've been completely mistaken, because I really and truly believed that the lady Dulcinea must be some princess you were in love with, or at least someone who deserved all those fine gifts you've sent her, that Basque and those convicts, and lots of others that there must have been, too, consider-ing how many victories you must have won before I became your squire. But all things considered, what will the lady Aldonza Lorenzo I mean the lady Dulcinea del Toboso care whether the knights you defeat and send to her get down on their bended knees before her? Because when they turn up she might be combing flax or threshing wheat in the yard, and then they'd be all embarrassed and she'd burst out laughing and turn up her nose at the gift."

"I have often told you before now, Sancho," said Don Quixote, "that you are a chatterbox and that, although you are a dim-witted fellow, you often try to be too clever by half; but, so that you can see how stupid you are and how intelligent I am, I want you to listen to a little story. There was once a widow who was beautiful, young, unattached, rich and, above all, carefree, and who fell in love with a certain lay brother, a well-fleshed, corpulent young man; his superior found out, and said to the good widow one day, by way of friarly reprehension:

"'I am surprised, madam, and not without good reason, that a woman of your quality, as beautiful and as wealthy as you are, should have fallen in love with such a low, vulgar and ignorant fellow, when in this house there are so many bachelors, mas-ters and doctors of divinity among whom you could have chosen as among pears at a fruit-stall, saying: "I'll have this one; no, not that."'

"But she replied to him with wit and dash:

"'You are much mistaken, sir, and very old-fashioned in your ideas, if you think I have made a bad choice, however stupid he may seem to you because for what I want of him he knows as much philosophy as Aristotle, and more.'"

"And so, Sancho, for what I want of Dulcinea del Toboso, she is as good as the most exalted princess in the world. Yes indeed, for not all poets who praise ladies un-der a name that they choose for them really have any such mistresses at all. Do you really believe that the Amaryllises, Phyllises, Sylvias, Dianas, Galateas, Alidas and others that fill books, ballads, barbers' shops and theatre stages were real ladies of flesh and blood, and the mistresses of those that praise and have praised them?[5] No, of course not, the poets themselves invent most of them, to have something to write

5. All names of female characters from the many pastoral romances written in the second half of the 16th century. Cer-vantes' own pastoral romance was called *La Galatea*.

their poetry about, and to make people think that they are in love and that they have it in them to be lovers. And so it is enough for me to be convinced that the good Aldonza Lorenzo is beautiful and virtuous, and the question of lineage is not very important, because nobody is going to be enquiring into it to see whether she is entitled to robes of nobility, and for me she is the greatest princess in the world. For I would have you know, Sancho, if you do not know it already, that there are just two qualities that inspire love more than any others, and these are great beauty and good repute, and these two qualities are to be found in abundance in Dulcinea, because no woman can equal her in beauty, and few can approach her in good repute. And to put it in a nutshell, I imagine that everything I say is precisely as I say it is, and I depict her in my imagination as I wish her to be, both in beauty and in rank, and Helen cannot rival her, nor can Lucretia or any other of the famous women of past ages, whether Greek, Barbarian or Roman, equal her.[6] And people can say what they like, because if I am reproached by the ignorant for this, I shall not be punished by even the most severe judges."

"And I say you're right as right can be," replied Sancho, "and I'm an ass—but I don't know why I'm talking about asses, because you don't mention ropes in the house of the man that hanged himself. Let's have the letter, though, and then I'll be off."

Don Quixote took out the notebook and, drawing a little aside, he began with great deliberation to write the letter; and as he finished he called Sancho and said that he was going to read it aloud, so that Sancho could learn it by heart, in case he lost it on the way, because with his bad luck anything could happen. To which Sancho replied:

"You just write it down two or three times in the book and then let me have it, and I'll take good care of it—it's madness to think I'm going to learn it by heart, because my memory's so bad I often forget my own name. But read it to me all the same, I'll enjoy listening to it, because it must be a beauty."

"Listen, then; it goes like this," said Don Quixote.

Letter from Don Quixote to Dulcinea del Toboso

Sovereign and noble lady,

One sore-wounded by the dart of absence and lacerated to the very fabric of his heart, O sweetest Dulcinea del Toboso, wishes you the good health that he does not enjoy. If your beauteousness scorns me, if your worth does not favour me, if your disdain is my humiliation, I shall ill be able, albeit I am well furnished with longanimity,[7] to suffer a grief that is not merely intense but protracted. My good squire Sancho will render you a full account, O lovely ingrate, O beloved enemy of mine, of the state to which I am reduced for your sake. If it be your wish to succour me, I am yours, and if not, do what you will, for by ending my life I shall satisfy your cruelty and my desire.

Yours until death,
THE KNIGHT OF THE SORRY FACE

"By my dear father's bones!" cried Sancho. "That's the very finest thing I ever did hear! Damn it all, how well you say everything you want to say, and how well it

---

6. Lucretia was the chaste wife of the Roman Collatinus; when raped by Sextus Tarquinius, son of the despot Tarquinius Superbus, she killed herself, after calling on her family to bring down Rome's king. They did so, founding the Roman republic.

7. Long-suffering or forbearance.

all suits the signature 'The Knight of the Sorry Face'! To be sure you're the very devil, there isn't anything you don't know!"

"Everything is needed," replied Don Quixote, "in the profession that I follow."

"Come on, then," said Sancho, "turn over the page and write the warrant for the three donkeys, and sign it clear as clear, so they know your signature as soon as they see it."

"Very well," said Don Quixote.

And once he'd written it he read it out:

> On receipt of this my first donkey-warrant, please order that three of the five that I left at home in your charge be given to my squire Sancho Panza. Which three donkeys I hereby order to be delivered to him and duly paid for, in return for the like number received from him here; and this bill, together with his receipt, will be sufficient for this transaction. Given in the heart of the Sierra Morena on the twenty-second of August of the current year.

"That's good," said Sancho. "Now sign it."

"There is no need for me to sign it," said Don Quixote. "All I have to do is to append my flourish, which counts as a signature, and that is sufficient for three asses, and even for three hundred."

"I'll believe you," replied Sancho. "Now let me go and saddle Rocinante, and you get ready to give me your blessing, because I'm leaving straight away, without waiting to see any of these antics you're going to get up to, though I'll tell her I saw you do so many of them that she'll be more than satisfied."

"At least, Sancho, I want you, because it is essential—what I mean to say is that I want you to see me naked, performing a dozen or two dozen mad deeds, which will only take me half an hour, so that having seen them with your own eyes you can safely swear to any others that you may care to add; and I can assure you that you will not tell her of as many as I intend to perform."

"For the love of God, sir, don't make me see you naked, I'll feel so sorry for you I shan't be able to help crying. And my head's in such a state after crying so much last night for my dun that I'm in no condition for any more tears, so if you want me to see some of your antics, do them with your clothes on—quick antics, just the most relevant ones. What's more, there isn't any need for all this as far as I'm concerned, and, as I said, it would mean I'd come back all the sooner with the news that you want and deserve to hear. If not, the lady Dulcinea had better look out, because if she doesn't reply as she ought to, I take my solemn oath that I'll kick and punch the right answer out of her guts. Because who can put up with a famous knight errant like you going mad, without any reason at all, for a   ? And the lady had better not make me say it, or else by God I'll upset the apple cart, and hang the consequences! And I can! She doesn't know what I'm like! If she did, she'd stand in fear of me, she would!"

"And so, Sancho," said Don Quixote, "it seems that you are no saner than I am."

"No, I'm not as mad as you," said Sancho, "but I am angrier. Leaving all that aside, though, what are you going to eat while I'm away? Are you going to waylay goatherds and steal your food, like Cardenio?"

"You must not worry about that," replied Don Quixote, "for even if I had any food, all I should eat would be whatever herbs and other fruit of the land this meadow and these trees provide; for the beauty of my plan lies precisely in not eating and in other equivalent mortifications. And so goodbye."

"But do you know what I'm scared of? Not finding the way back here where I'm leaving you, because it's so secluded."

"You take good note of the landmarks, and I shall try not to move far off," said Don Quixote, "and I shall even take the precaution of climbing the highest of these crags here to see if I can spot you when you return. In addition, your surest way of not getting lost and missing me will be to cut some of this broom growing so abundantly hereabouts, and to drop a branch every so often until you reach the plain, and they will serve as guide-marks on your return, like the thread in Perseus's labyrinth."[8]

"That's what I'll do," replied Sancho Panza.

He cut some broom, asked his master for his blessing and, not without many tears on both sides, said goodbye. And climbing on to Rocinante, whom Don Quixote warmly entrusted to Sancho's safe-keeping, with the instruction to take as good care of him as of his own person, he headed off towards the plain, scattering broom-branches every so often, as his master had advised. And so he rode away, even though Don Quixote was still insisting that he should watch a couple of his wild deeds, at least. But Sancho hadn't gone a hundred steps when he turned and came back and said:

"I think you were right, sir, and to be able to swear with a clear conscience that I've seen you doing mad deeds, I'd better see one of them at least, although I must say I've seen a big enough one already—you staying here."

"Did I not tell you so?" said Don Quixote. "Just wait a minute, Sancho, I shall perform them in the saying of a creed."

And pulling down his breeches as fast as ever he could, he stood there in his shirt and then did two leaps in the air followed by two somersaults, revealing things that made Sancho turn Rocinante so as not to have to see them again; and he felt fully satisfied that he could swear his master was mad. And we shall allow him to go his way until his return, which was speedy.

* * *

from *Chapter 52*

ABOUT DON QUIXOTE'S FIGHT WITH THE GOATHERD, AND THE SINGULAR ADVENTURE OF THE
PENITENTS, WHICH HE BROUGHT TO A HAPPY CONCLUSION BY THE SWEAT OF HIS BROW[1]

* * * The goatherd[2] looked at Don Quixote, and finding him such a sorry sight he asked the barber—who was sitting next to him—in some bewilderment:

"Who is this man, sir, that cuts such a figure and speaks in such a way?"

"Who should he be," answered the barber, "but the famous Don Quixote de la Mancha, the redresser of injuries, the righter of wrongs, the protector of damsels, the terror of giants and the victor in battles?"

---

8. A reference to the labyrinth in which the Minotaur was housed, and which Theseus (not Perseus) successfully navigated by means of a thread.

1. In the intervening chapters, Don Quixote leaves the Sierra Morena, hears a variety of tales from Cardenio and others, and suffers the effects of an enchantment orchestrated by the barber and the priest, who are trying to bring him back to La Mancha. Don Quixote is bound hand and foot while sleeping in an inn and placed as a captive in an ox-cart, with which the disguised barber and priest will take him home. A canon from Toledo, along with his servants and several "peace-officers" or members of the Holy Brotherhood, have joined the company as well.

2. The goatherd is a young man named Eugenio, who has just finished telling a story about his love for a woman who eloped with a trickster and has been put by her father in a convent. The current discussion is taking place in an inn, after Don Quixote is let temporarily out of his cage and promises not to run away: "I do indeed give my word," he says, "and in any case, a person who is enchanted, as I am, is not at liberty to dispose of his person as he wishes, because the man who enchanted him can prevent him from moving for three centuries on end, and if he flees he will bring him back in the twinkling of an eye."

"That sounds to me," replied the goatherd, "like what you read in books about knights errant, who used to do all those things you said this man does, but it's my opinion that either you're joking or some of the rooms in this character's upper storey are empty."

"You are a villainous wretch," Don Quixote burst out, "and you are the one who is empty and a fool, and I am fuller than the whore of a bitch who bore you ever was."

And with these words he snatched up a loaf and hurled it at the goatherd's face with such furious force that he flattened his nose; and the goatherd, who couldn't take a jest and found himself being assaulted in earnest, disregarded the carpet and the tablecloths and all the people who were eating, and leapt upon Don Quixote, seized him by the throat with both hands and wouldn't have hesitated to throttle him if Sancho Panza hadn't rushed over, grabbed the goatherd by the shoulders and flung him down on the table, breaking plates, smashing cups and overturning and scattering everything else. As soon as Don Quixote found himself free he jumped on top of the goatherd, who, bloody-faced and pounded by Sancho's feet, was crawling over the tablecloths in search of a knife with which to take some gory revenge, but the canon and the priest were making sure this couldn't happen; and then the barber intervened to enable the goatherd to climb on top of Don Quixote, at whom he flailed away until as much blood was pouring from the poor knight's face as from his own. The canon and the priest were laughing fit to burst, the peace-officers were jumping with joy, everyone was cheering the two men on as dogs are cheered on when they're fighting; only Sancho Panza was in despair, because he couldn't wriggle free of the grasp of one of the canon's servants who was preventing him from going to help his master.

In short, just when everyone was enjoying this festival of fun, except the two battered, scratching warriors, they heard a trumpet call, so mournful that it made them all turn towards where it seemed to be coming from; but the man who was most affected by the sound was Don Quixote who, although he was under the goatherd, much against his will and most severely mauled, said to him:

"Brother devil, for that is what you must be, since you have found the resolve and the strength to overpower me: I request that we agree on a truce for just one hour, because the sorrowful sound of that trumpet which we can hear appears to be summoning me to a new adventure."

The goatherd, who by now was tired of thumping and being thumped, climbed off without more ado, and Don Quixote stood up and looked with the others in the direction of the sounds, and as he did so a horde of men dressed as penitents in white suddenly came into sight as they descended one of the sides of the valley. What had happened was that the clouds had withheld their moisture from the earth that year, and processions, public prayers and acts of penitence were being organized in all the villages in the area to entreat God to open the hands of his mercy and send down some rain; and to this end the people from a nearby village were coming in a procession to a holy chapel on one side of the valley.[3] Don Quixote, seeing the processionists' strange dress, and not pausing to remember that he must have seen such penitents many times before, imagined that this was the subject for an adventure, and that it was his task alone, as a knight errant, to undertake it; and he was further confirmed in this belief when he saw a holy image swathed in mourning that they were carrying, and

---

3. Such processions to pray for changes in weather were fairly common, particularly in rural areas. The participants would generally pray and sing while flogging themselves in penitence for sins of the community, and would often carry with them large statues or images of Mary and the saints.

thought it was some eminent lady whom those arrant and insolent knaves were bearing off against her will; and no sooner had this idea found its way into his head than he charged over to where Rocinante was grazing, unhooked both the horse's bit and his own shield from the pommel, put the bit in its place in the twinkling of an eye, told Sancho to give him his sword, mounted Rocinante, took up his shield and cried to all present:

"And now, O doughty company, you shall perceive how important it is that knights who profess the order of knight-errantry should exist in the world; now, I say, you shall perceive, in the freeing of that good lady who is being carried away captive, whether or not knights errant are worthy of esteem."

And as he said this he put thighs to Rocinante, because he wasn't wearing any spurs, and at a canter, because we don't read anywhere in this true history that Rocinante ever ventured on a full gallop, he advanced on the penitents, despite all the efforts of the priest and the canon and the barber to stop him; but it was impossible, and Sancho couldn't do anything to dissuade him, either, by yelling:

"What are you going to do now, Don Quixote sir? What demons have you got inside your breast egging you on against our holy Catholic faith? I'll be damned—look, look, that's a penitents' procession, and that lady they're carrying on the platform is the blessed image of the immaculate Virgin. Be careful, sir, what you're doing—this time I'm really sure it isn't what you think it is."

But Sancho laboured in vain, because his master was so set on confronting the men in white and freeing the lady in black that he didn't hear a word; and even if he had heard one he wouldn't have turned back, not if it had been the King himself ordering him. So on he cantered towards the procession and then he halted Rocinante, who was by now ready to take a rest, and he cried in a hoarse and agitated voice:

"O you who hide your faces, perchance because you are evil: pay attention and listen to what I have to say to you."

The first to stop were the men carrying the image, and one of the four priests chanting the litanies took one look at Don Quixote's strange figure, Rocinante's thinness and other ludicrous aspects of the knight's appearance, and replied with the words:

"If you want to say something to us, my good man, say it quickly, because our brethren here are tearing their flesh to shreds, and we cannot and must not stop to listen to anything unless it's brief enough to be said in a couple of words."

"I shall say it all in one word," replied Don Quixote, "and it is this: you must at this very instant set free that beautiful lady, whose tears and sorrowful face are clear proof that you are bearing her off against her will and that you have done her some very great mischief; and I, who came into this world to redress such injuries, will not permit you to take one step forward unless you give her the liberty that she desires and deserves."

These words made all those who heard them realize that Don Quixote must be some madman, and they burst into hearty laughter, which was like pouring gunpowder on to the fire of Don Quixote's wrath: without another word he drew his sword and charged at the platform. One of the men carrying it left his companions holding it up, came out to meet Don Quixote brandishing the forked prop on which he helped to support it whenever they paused for a rest, used this prop to ward off a mighty sword-stroke that the knight aimed at him and that cut it in two and then, with the part left in his hand, delivered such a blow to the shoulder of his enemy's sword arm, which the shield couldn't protect against brute strength, that poor Don Quixote tumbled to the ground in dire straits. Sancho Panza, who came puffing after his master, saw him fall and cried out to his demolisher not to hit him again, he was only a poor enchanted knight who'd never done anyone any harm in all the days of his born life. But what stopped the peasant wasn't Sancho's shouts but seeing that Don Quixote wasn't stirring, not so much as a hand or a foot; and so, in the belief that he'd killed him, he hoisted his tunic up to his waist and ran away across the fields like a deer.

And now Don Quixote's companions arrived on the scene, as did the other processionists, who saw their opponents come running up with the peace-officers clutching their crossbows, feared the worst and swarmed around the holy image with their hoods raised from their faces, brandishing their scourges while the priests wielded their great processional candle-sticks, awaiting the assault in the determination to defend themselves and even attack their assailants if they could; but fortune treated them better than they'd thought it would, because all Sancho did was to throw himself upon his master's body and pour over him the most piteous and laughable lament ever heard, in the belief that he was dead. Our priest was recognized by one of the priests in the procession, and this calmed the fears that had developed in both squadrons. The first priest gave the second one a brief account of Don Quixote, and then he went with the throng of penitents to see whether the poor knight was dead, and they all heard Sancho Panza saying, with tears in his eyes:

"O flower of chivalry, whose well-spent life just one thump with a cudgel has done for! O pride of your family, honour and glory of all La Mancha and all the world—now that you've gone from it, it'll fill up with evil-doers who won't be frightened of being punished for their wicked ways! O you who were more open-handed than all the Alexanders, because for only eight months' service you said you'd give me the best island that ever had the sea all round it! O you who were humble to the haughty and haughty to the humble, tackler of dangers, taker of insults, in love without a cause, imitator of the good, scourge of the wicked, enemy of villains—in a word, knight errant, and that says it all!"

Sancho's cries and groans revived Don Quixote, and what he first said was:

"He who lives absent from you, sweetest Dulcinea, is subject to even greater calamities than this. Help me, dear Sancho, to climb on to the enchanted cart: I am no longer in any fit state to burden Rocinante's saddle, for this shoulder of mine has been smashed to smithereens."

"I'll do that with a will, sir," replied Sancho, "and let's go back to our village with these gentlemen, who only want what's best for you, and there we'll work out a way to make another sally that'll bring us more profit and renown."

"You are speaking sound sense," replied Don Quixote, "and it will be wise indeed to wait for the presently prevailing malign influence of the stars to dissipate."

The canon and the priest and the barber told him that he would be quite right to do as he'd said; and so, having been most wonderfully entertained by Sancho Panza's absurdities, they put Don Quixote back on the cart. The religious procession formed up again, and went on its way. The goatherd said goodbye to everyone. The peace-officers refused to go any further, and the priest paid them what he owed them. The canon asked the priest to let him know what happened to Don Quixote, whether he recovered from his madness or continued in the same state, and then begged their leave to continue his journey.

And so the party split up and each followed his own road, leaving the priest and the barber, Don Quixote and Panza and the good Rocinante, as patient as his master in the face of everything he'd undergone. The carter yoked his oxen, put Don Quixote on top of a truss of hay, followed with his usual sedateness the route indicated by the priest; and six days later they reached their village, which they entered at noon, and as it happened to be a Sunday everybody was in the square, through the middle of which the cart trundled on its way. Everyone went over to see what was in the cart, and when they recognized their neighbour they were astonished, and a lad ran to tell the housekeeper and the niece that their master and uncle had come back, thin and pale, and lying on top of a pile of hay in an ox-cart. It was pitiful to hear the cries these two good ladies let loose, the slaps they gave themselves, the curses they again directed at those damned books of chivalry; all of which they renewed when they saw Don Quixote coming in through the door.

At the news of Don Quixote's arrival Sancho Panza's wife hurried to his house, because she had discovered that her husband had gone away with him as his squire, and when she saw Sancho the first thing she asked was whether the ass was well. Sancho replied that the ass was better than its master was.[4]

"Thanks be to God for his great goodness to me," she replied. "And now tell me, husband, what have you got out of all this squiring of yours? How many fine skirts have you brought back for me? How many pairs of shoes for your children?"

"I haven't brought any of all that, wife," said Sancho. "But I've got other stuff that's much more special and important."

"I'm very pleased to hear it, too," his wife replied. "Now show me this stuff that's so much more important and special, husband—I'd love to see it to cheer up this heart of mine that's been so sad and out of sorts all these ages that you've been away."

"I'll let you see it when we get home," said Panza, "and meantime you can count yourself lucky, because if it's God's will for us to go off again in search of adventures you'll soon see me made an earl or the governor of an island, and not any old island either but the very best island there is."

"May heaven grant it, husband, we need it badly enough. But tell me, what's all this about islands? I don't understand you."

"Honey wasn't made for the mouths of asses," Sancho retorted. "You'll see in due course, wife, and you'll get a surprise, I can tell you, when you hear all your vassals calling you your ladyship."

"What's this you're saying, Sancho, about ladyships, islands and vassals?" replied Juana Panza, for this was the name of Sancho's wife, not that they were blood relations but because it's the custom in La Mancha for women to take their husbands' surnames.

"Don't you be in such a hurry, Juana, to know about all these things; I'm telling you the truth, and that's enough for you, so shut up. All I will say, since I'm on the subject, is that there's nothing better in life than being an honest man who's the squire of a knight errant who goes in search of adventures. It is true that most of the adventures you find don't turn out as well as what you'd like them to, because out of a hundred you come across ninety-nine usually go skew-whiff. I know that from experience, because I've ended up blanket-tossed in some and beaten black and blue in others. But in spite of all that, it's great to be waiting to see what's going to happen next as you ride across mountains, explore forests, climb crags, visit castles and put up at inns as and when you like, and not the devil a farthing to pay."

While Sancho Panza and his wife Juana Panza chatted away like this, Don Quixote's housekeeper and niece welcomed their master, undressed him and laid him

4. The ass mysteriously returns to Sancho after its theft by Ginés de Pasamonte, an oversight that Cervantes will make fun of in Book 2.

on his ancient bed. He was peering at them through unfocused eyes, and couldn't fathom where on earth he was. The priest told the niece to make sure to pamper her uncle and have him watched so that he didn't escape again, and described what they'd had to do to bring him back home. And then the two women again raised the roof with their outcry; again they renewed their cursing of the books of chivalry; again they implored heaven to cast the authors of all those lies and absurdities into the depths of the bottomless pit. All this left them bewildered and fearful that as soon as their master and uncle felt a little better they'd lose him again; and that was indeed what happened.

But although the author of this history has searched with the most meticulous care for an account of the deeds performed by Don Quixote during his third sally, he hasn't been able to find any information about them, not at least in writings by reputable authors; tradition alone has preserved, in the memory of La Mancha, the belief that the third time Don Quixote left home he went to Saragossa, where he took part in some famous jousts and underwent experiences worthy of his courage and intelligence. But the author could not discover any information about how Don Quixote met his end, nor would he ever have even known about it if good fortune had not sent him an aged doctor who had in his possession a lead casket which, he said, had been found among the foundations of an old, ruined chapel that was being rebuilt. In this casket there were some parchments with texts written in Roman letters but in Castilian verse, describing many of his exploits and giving accounts of Dulcinea del Toboso's beauty, Rocinante's looks, Sancho Panza's loyalty and Don Quixote's grave, in various epitaphs and eulogies about his life and works. And those that could be read and understood have been set down here by the trustworthy author of this original and matchless history, who only asks from his readers, in recompense for the immense trouble that he has taken to scrutinize and explore all the archives in La Mancha so as to be able to bring it to the light of day, that they give it the same credit that people of good sense give to books of chivalry, so highly prized by all; and this will make him feel well rewarded and satisfied, and encourage him to search out other histories, perhaps less authentic than this one but no less ingenious or entertaining.

[*Several verses by local wits praising Don Quixote and Sancho follow, ending with the following poems.*]

HOBGOBLIN, A MEMBER OF THE ARGAMASILLA ACADEMY,[5] ON THE GRAVE OF DON QUIXOTE

EPITAPH

Here lies a knight, a man of pluck,
Rich in thumpings, poor in luck,
Who, perched on Rocinante's back,
Rode up this path and down that track.
And Sancho Panza is the dolt
Who lies beside him in this vault;
The loyallest man in our empire
Who ever earned the name of squire.

---

5. Argamasilla is a village in La Mancha; this may be the "forgotten" town from which Don Quixote hails. Academies were men's clubs that convened on civic and festive occasions, and churned out mediocre verses to honor important events; the academy mentioned here is completely imaginary, as the silly names of its members attest.

DING-DONG, A MEMBER OF THE ARGAMASILLA ACADEMY,
ON THE GRAVE OF DULCINEA DEL TOBOSO

EPITAPH

Fair Dulcinea here is laid
And though she was a meaty maid
Death turned her into dust and clay
In his horrendous, dreadful way.
Of a true breed she surely came,
She was the great Don Quixote's flame,
She wore with style a lady's gown:
The glory of Toboso town.

These were the verses that were legible; since the others were worm-eaten, they were handed to an academician for him to decipher. It is reported that he has done so, after long vigils and much toil, and that he intends to publish them, as we await Don Quixote's third sally.

Forse altri canterà con miglior plectio.[6]

Book 2[1]
Chapter 3

ABOUT THE RIDICULOUS DISCUSSION BETWEEN DON QUIXOTE, SANCHO PANZA
AND SANSÓN CARRASCO, BA

Don Quixote remained deep in thought as he awaited the young graduate Carrasco, from whom he was expecting to hear news about himself published in a book, as Sancho had said; and he couldn't persuade himself that such a history existed—the blood of the enemies that he had killed was not yet dry on the blade of his sword, and people were already claiming that his noble deeds of chivalry had appeared in print! Despite this, though, it did occur to him that some sage, friendly or hostile, must have published his deeds by way of enchantment: if friendly, to exalt them and place them above the most renowned exploits ever performed by any knight errant; if hostile, to dismiss them and present them as being meaner than the wretchedest deeds that the basest squire had ever been described as doing, but then again (he said to himself), squires' exploits had never been recorded; and if it was true that this history did exist, the fact that it concerned a knight errant was a guarantee that it would be grandiloquent, lofty, illustrious, magnificent and true.

This thought offered him some consolation, but then he lost heart again when he remembered that the name Cide suggested that the author was a Moor, and not a word of truth was to be expected from any of those, since the whole lot of them are deceivers, liars and story-tellers. He was afraid that the author might have handled his

---

6. "Perhaps others will sing with better lyre than I." From *Orlando furioso* (canto 30, stanza 16).
1. Book 2 of *Don Quixote* was published in 1615, ten years after Book 1. After an introductory chapter, Chapter 2 has Don Quixote eager to discover what others are saying about him, and he urges Sancho to sally forth to find one Sansón Carrasco. Carrasco has just returned from his studies at Salamanca University and has told Sancho that

his story has been put into a book called *The Ingenious Hidalgo Don Quixote de la Mancha*. As Sancho reports to Don Quixote, "he says I'm named in it with my very own name of Sancho Panza, and the lady Dulcinea del Toboso too, and things are even mentioned when you and I were alone when we did them"—prompting Don Quixote to declare "that the author of our history must be some wise enchanter."

love affair in an indelicate manner that would cause detraction and damage to the chastity of his lady Dulcinea del Toboso; he hoped that he had portrayed his faithfulness and the unswerving correctness of his behaviour towards her, snubbing queens, empresses and damsels of all ranks, and holding in leash the powerful urges of his natural passions; and in this state, engrossed in these and many other thoughts careering about his brain, he was found by Sancho and Carrasco, whom Don Quixote greeted with gracious courtesy.

Despite his name[2] the new graduate wasn't a big man, although he was a great leg-puller; his complexion was dull but his wits were sharp; he'd have been about twenty-four, with a moon face, a snub nose and a large mouth, all signs that he had a waggish disposition and loved joking and jesting, as he showed when he saw Don Quixote by throwing himself on to his knees before him and saying:

"Pray give me your hands, Don Quixote de la Mancha; I swear by this habit of St Peter that I'm wearing, even though I've only taken minor orders,[3] that you are one of the most famous knights errant that have ever existed or indeed ever will exist in the whole wide world. A blessing on Cide Hamete Benengeli for having written the history of your great deeds, and a double blessing on the diligent man who took care to have it translated from Arabic into our Castilian vernacular, for the amusement and entertainment of all."

Don Quixote brought him to his feet and said:

"It is true, then, is it, that a history of me exists, and that it was a Moor and a sage who wrote it?"

"It's so true, sir," said Sansón, "that I'm to understand that more than twelve thousand copies of the history are in print at this moment; and if you don't believe me, just ask Portugal, Barcelona and Valencia, where they were printed; and there's a report that it's being printed now in Antwerp, and all the signs are that there's no language in the world into which it won't be translated."[4]

"One of the things," Don Quixote put in, "that must give the greatest happiness to a virtuous and eminent man is to find himself with a good name on everybody's lips, and in print, while he is still alive. I said "with a good name" because, if the opposite were the case, no death could equal it."

"As far as good names and good reputations are concerned," the young graduate said, "you have gained the palm from all other knights errant, because the Moor in his language, and the Christian in his, took good care to depict most vividly for us your gallantry, your courage in confronting perils, your patience in adversity, your long-suffering in misfortune and when wounded, and your chastity and continence in that most platonic love-affair between you and my lady Doña Dulcinea del Toboso."

"I've never heard anyone," Sancho butted in, "calling my lady Dulcinea Doña, but just the lady Dulcinea del Toboso—so the history's wrong about that, for starters."

"That isn't an important objection," Carrasco replied.

"Certainly not," said Don Quixote, "but tell me, sir, which of my deeds are most highly praised in the history?"

"About that," the young graduate replied, "opinions differ, as tastes do: some prefer the adventure of the windmills, which you thought were Briareuses and giants;

2. Sansón is Spanish for Samson, the Hebrew warrior who possessed great strength as long as he didn't cut his hair.
3. Carrasco would have been wearing a habit of someone who was a minor cleric.

4. By 1615, *Don Quixote* had already been translated into English as well as French; numerous editions in Spanish had been published in Valencia, Barcelona, Lisbon, and Madrid as well as Brussels and Milan.

others, the adventure of the fulling-mill; others, the description of the two armies that turned out to be two flocks of sheep; one man praises the adventure of the corpse being taken to Segovia to be buried; another says that the best one of them all is the freeing of the convicts; yet another that none of them equals the adventure of the two Benedictine giants and the fight with the brave Basque."

"Could you please tell me, sir," Sancho put in, "whether they've included the adventure of the men from Yanguas, when good old Rocinante had the bright idea of reaching for the stars?"

"The sage didn't leave anything out," replied Sansón. "He includes and describes it all, even the capers cut by Sancho in the blanket."

"I didn't cut any capers in the blanket," Sancho retorted. "I cut them in the air, and more of them than I'd have chosen to."

"I suppose," added Don Quixote, "that every history that has ever been written has its ups and its downs, especially those that deal with chivalric exploits, for they cannot recount successful adventures alone."

"For all that," the young graduate replied, "some of those who've read the history say that they'd have been happier if its authors had overlooked some of the countless beatings that Don Quixote received in various confrontations."

"That's where the truth of the history comes in," said Sancho.

"But they could, in all fairness, have kept quiet about them," said Don Quixote, "because there is no need to narrate actions that do not alter or undermine the truth of the history, if they are going to result in the discrediting of the hero. I am sure that Aeneas was not as pious as Virgil depicts him, nor was Ulysses as prudent as Homer says."

"That's true," Sansón replied, "but it's one thing to write as a poet and quite another to write as a historian: the poet can narrate or sing events not as they were but as they should have been, and the historian must record them not as they should have been but as they were, without adding anything to the truth or taking anything away from it."

"Well if this Moorish bloke's after telling the truth," said Sancho, "I bet the thumpings they handed out to me will be in there among the ones my master got, because they never took the measure of his shoulders without taking it of my whole body. But that's no surprise, because as my master says, all the limbs have got to share the headache."

"You are a sly dog, Sancho," replied Don Quixote. "I must say your memory works well enough when you want it to."

"Even if I did want to forget the thrashings I've been given," said Sancho, "the bruises wouldn't let me, still fresh here on my ribs."

"Keep quiet, Sancho," said Don Quixote, "and stop interrupting our friend from the university, whom I entreat to continue telling me what is said about me in this history."

"And about me, too," said Sancho. "They say I'm one of the main caricatures in it, too."

"*Characters*, not *caricatures*, friend Sancho," said Sansón.

"Oh no, not another blunders-expert!" said Sancho. "If you two start up on that again, we'll all be here till the ends of our lives."

"May God give me a bad life, Sancho," replied the young graduate, "if you aren't the second most important character in the history, and there are those who'd rather hear you talk than the finest of the others, even though there are also people who say you were too gullible in believing you could ever become governor of that island offered you by Don Quixote here."

"All is not yet lost," said Don Quixote, "and as Sancho matures he will, with the experience that only the passing years can bring, become more suited and better qualified for the post of governor than he is at present."

"For God's sake, sir," said Sancho, "the island I can't govern at my age. I shan't be able to govern when I'm as old as Moses. The problem is that this island of yours is biding its time God only knows where, not that I haven't got the gumption to govern it."

"Entrust the matter to God's good care, Sancho," said Don Quixote, "for everything will turn out well, better perhaps than you think: not a leaf stirs on a tree unless God wishes it to."

"That's true enough," said Sansón, "and, if it is God's will, there shall be a thousand islands for Sancho to govern, let alone one."

"I've seen governors about the place," said Sancho, "that to my mind can't hold a candle to me, yet, for all that, they get called my lord and they eat off plates of silver."

"Those aren't governors of islands," replied Sansón, "but of other less demanding things; because those who govern islands must at the very least have some knowledge of syntax."

"I could cope with the sin," said Sancho, "but I'll pass on the tax—it's something I haven't ever come to grips with. But to leave me being governor in God's hands, and may he send me where I can be of most service to him—what I say, Sansón Carrasco sir, is that I'm very very glad that the author of this here history has talked about me in such a way that what he says doesn't give offence, because I swear to you as a loyal squire that if he'd said anything that wasn't fit to be said about a pure-bred Christian, which is what I am, the deafest of the deaf would have heard what I'd have had to say to him."

"That would have been a miracle," Sansón replied.

"Miracle or no miracle," said Sancho, "everyone should watch out how he talks or writes about the next man and not just shove down the first thing that comes into his brain-box."

"One of the faults that have been found in this history," said the young graduate, "is that the author included a tale called *Inappropriate Curiosity;* not that it's a bad one or badly told, but it's out of place and has nothing to do with the history of the great Don Quixote."[5]

"I bet," replied Sancho, "that the bastard's gone and made a right old hotchpotch."

"I do now have to say," said Don Quixote, "that the author of my history is no sage but some ignorant prattler, who started writing it in a haphazard and unplanned way and let it turn out however it would, like Orbaneja, the famous artist of Úbeda,[6] who, when asked what he was painting, replied: 'Whatever emerges.' On one occasion he was painting a cockerel so badly and so unlike a real cockerel that he had to write in capital letters by its side: 'This is a cockerel.' My history must be like that, needing a commentary to make it intelligible."

"No, no," replied Sansón, "it's so very intelligible that it doesn't pose any difficulties at all: children leaf through it, adolescents read it, grown men understand it and old men praise it, and, in short, it's so well-thumbed and well-perused and well-known by all kinds of people that as soon as they see a skinny nag pass by they say: 'Look, there goes Rocinante.' And the people who have most taken to it are the pageboys. There's not a lord's antechamber without its *Quixote:* if one person puts it aside, another picks it up; some ask to be lent it, others run up and snatch it away. All in all, this history provides the most delightful and least harmful entertainment ever, because nowhere in it can one find the slightest suspicion of language that isn't wholesome or thoughts that aren't Catholic."

"To write in any other way," said Don Quixote, "would be to write not truths but falsehoods, and historians who have recourse to falsehoods should be burnt, like counterfeiters; and I do not know what could have made the author turn to stories about other people when there was so much to write about me: I suppose he was relying on the saying, 'It's all fish that comes to the net.' Yet the truth of the matter is that just by recording my thoughts, my sighs, my tears, my worthy designs and my missions he could have written a volume bigger than all the works of El Tostado[7] put together, or at any rate as big. Be that as it may, my understanding of the matter, my dear sir, is that to write histories and other books one needs a fine mind and a mature understanding. To tell jokes and write wittily is the work of geniuses; the most intelligent character in a play is the fool, because the actor playing the part of a simpleton must not be one. History is, as it were, sacred, because it must be truthful, and where there is truth there is God, because he is truth; and yet, in spite of all this, there are those who toss off books as if they were pancakes."

"There's no book so bad," said the young graduate, "that there isn't something good in it."

"About that there is no doubt," Don Quixote replied, "but it often happens that men who have deservedly achieved and won fame by their writings lose it completely or find it diminished in part as soon as they publish them."

"The reason for that," said Sansón, "is that printed works are read at leisure and their defects are easily spotted, and the more famous the author the more closely they're scrutinized. Men renowned for their genius—great poets, illustrious historians—are usually envied by those whose pleasure and pastime is to pass judgement on what others have written, without ever having published anything themselves."

"That is not surprising," said Don Quixote, "because there are many theologians who cannot preach, yet are experts at identifying the faults and the excesses of those who can."

"It is exactly as you say, Don Quixote," said Carrasco, "but I do wish that such critics were more forgiving and less censorious, and did not pay such attention to the spots on the brilliant sun of the work they grumble at; for if *aliquando bonus dormitat Homerus,*[8] they should also remember how very long Homer stayed awake to give us the light of his work with the least possible shadow; and it could even be that what they think are faults are in reality beauty spots, which often increase the loveliness of a face; so, you see, anyone publishing a book exposes himself to enormous risk, because it's absolutely impossible to write one in such a way that it satisfies and pleases all those who read it."

"The book that has been written about me," said Don Quixote, "will not have pleased many people."

"Quite the contrary: since *stultorum infinitus est numerus,*[9] innumerable are those who have relished this history. Some have found fault with the author's memory and accused him of deception because he forgets to tell us who was the thief that stole

---

7. Alonso de Madrigal, bishop of Avila in the 15th century who wrote a large number of religious works.
8. "Even the good Homer sometimes nods"; from Horace's

Art of Poetry.
9. "The number of fools is infinite."

Sancho's dun—[1]the incident isn't narrated and we just have to infer that somebody has stolen it, and a little later we find Sancho riding the very same donkey without having recovered it. They also say that the author forgot to state what Sancho did with the hundred escudos he found in the travelling bag in the Sierra Morena, which are never mentioned again; and there are many people who would like to know what happened to them, or what he spent them on, which is one of the essential points omitted from the book."

Sancho replied:

"Right now, Señor Carrasco, I'm in no state to go into any accounts or explanations, because I've just gone all a-flutter in my tummy, and if I don't get a couple of swigs of the old stuff inside me to put it right I'll soon be nothing but skin and bone. I'll have to go home for it, and the wife's waiting for me—as soon as I've done eating I'll come back and answer all the questions you and anyone else want to put to me, both about the loss of the ass and about the spending of the hundred escudos."

And without awaiting a reply or saying another word he went home. Don Quixote insisted that the graduate must share his humble board. The graduate accepted the invitation and stayed for the meal, a couple of squabs were added to the pot, the conversation at table was about deeds of chivalry, Carrasco played along with his host, the banquet came to an end, they had their afternoon nap, Sancho returned and the previous conversation was resumed.

Chapter 4

IN WHICH SANCHO PANZA PROVIDES THE ANSWERS TO THE YOUNG GRADUATE SANSÓN CARRASCO'S DOUBTS AND QUESTIONS; TOGETHER WITH OTHER EVENTS WORTH KNOWING AND TELLING

Sancho Panza returned to Don Quixote's house and to the previous conversation, and he said:

"To what Señor Sansón said about people wanting to know who stole my donkey, and how and when, it is my reply that on the very same night when we went to hide from the Holy Brotherhood in the Sierra Morena, after the adventure or misadventure of the convicts, and the other one of the dead body being taken to Segovia, me and my master rode into a clump of trees where my master leaned on his lance and I sat on my dun, both of us dead beat after the fights we'd had, and we dozed off just as if we were lying on half-a-dozen feather mattresses, and in particular I fell so very fast asleep that whoever it was managed to come and prop up the pack saddle, with me sitting there and all, on top of four poles one in each corner, and get the dun out from underneath without me noticing a thing."

That is easy enough to do, and no new occurrence: it is what happened to Sacripante when he was at the siege of Albracca and that famous thief Brunello removed his horse from between his legs using the same trick.[1]

"Dawn broke," Sancho resumed, "and as soon as I gave myself a good shake the poles caved in and I came down with an almighty thump, and I looked around for my donkey and I couldn't find it, and the tears filled my eyes and I made such a lament that if the author of our history hasn't put it in he can take it from me he hasn't put anything worthwhile in. A few days later, I can't rightly remember how many, I was

---

1. Cervantes actually corrected this oversight in Book 1, reporting on Ginés's theft.

1. In *Orlando furioso*, Brunello is notorious for his thievery; he steals Sacripante's horse in Canto 27.

walking along with Princess Micomicona when I spotted my donkey, and on top of it wearing gipsy clothes was that character Ginés de Pasamonte, that crook, that great villain me and my master set free from the chain."[2]

"That isn't the mistake," Sansón replied. "The mistake is that before the ass has reappeared the author says Sancho's riding it!"

"I don't know what to say to that," said Sancho, "but maybe the historian got it wrong, or it might have been a slip of the printer's."

"I'm sure you're right," said Sansón, "but what happened to the hundred escudos? Did they disappear into thin air?"

Sancho replied:

"I laid them out on the well-being of my person and of my wife and children, and those escudos are the only reason why my wife's putting up with me going off along all those highways and byways serving my master Don Quixote, because if after all that time I'd come back home penniless and donkeyless I'd have been in for it—and if there's anything else you want to know about me here I am, and I'll answer to the King himself in person, and there's no cause for anybody to be poking their noses into whether I brought money back with me or not and whether I spent it or not. Because if the thumpings I was given on my travels had to be paid for in hard cash, even if they were only priced at four maravedís apiece another hundred escudos wouldn't be enough to pay for the half of them, and people can put their hands on their hearts and say what they'd have done, and stop making out that what's white's black and what's black's white—each of us is how God made him and many are much worse."

"I'll take care," said Carrasco, "to warn the author of the history that if he prints it again he mustn't forget what the worthy Sancho has just said—for this will carry it to even greater heights."

"Are there any other features of this book that need correcting, my dear young graduate?" Don Quixote asked.

"Yes, there must be," he replied, "but none of them can be as important as those that I have mentioned."

"And does the author," Don Quixote asked, "by any chance promise a second part?"

"Yes, he does," Sansón replied, "but he says he hasn't found it and doesn't know who's got it, so we can't tell whether it'll come out or not—and both because of this and because some people are saying, 'Second parts are never any good,' and others are saying, 'What's already been written about Don Quixote is quite enough,' there are doubts about the appearance of this second part; although other people who are jovial rather than saturnine say, 'Let's have more quixotry—let Don Quixote charge and Sancho Panza talk, and that'll keep us happy, whatever he writes.'"

"And what is the author's position?"

"He says," Sansón replied, "that as soon as he does find the history, for which he's searching with the utmost diligence, he's going to have it printed immediately, more for the profit he can make out of it than to win anybody's praise."

At which Sancho remarked:

"So the author's hoping to make some money out of it, is he? That'd be a miracle, because it'll be hurry, hurry, hurry, like a tailor on the day before a fiesta, and rushed jobs are never as well done as they ought to be. That Moorish bloke, or what-

---

2. In Chapter 44 of Book 1. Princess Micomicona is really the young Dorotea, an accomplice in the priest's and barber's elaborate plans to lure Don Quixote out of the Sierra Morena. She pretends to be a princess who needs her kingdom restored to her by none other than Don Quixote himself.

ever he is, had better take care to be on his mettle—me and my master are going to hand him such a supply of raw materials in the shape of adventures and all kinds of other doings that he'll be able to write not just one second part but a hundred of them. I suppose that character thinks we're resting on our laurels here—well, if he holds up our feet to be shod he'll soon see if there's anything wrong with our hooves. All I can say is that if my master took my advice we'd be out in the fields by now, redressing grievances and righting wrongs as all the best knight errants do."

Sancho had hardly finished speaking when they heard Rocinante neighing, which Don Quixote took as a most happy omen, so he decided to make another sally in three or four days' time. He informed the young graduate of his decision, and asked his advice about where to start the campaign; and the reply was that they should travel to the kingdom of Aragon and the city of Saragossa, where solemn jousts were soon to be held to celebrate St George's day[3]—and these would give Don Quixote the chance to outshine all the knights in Aragon, which would be the same as outshining all the knights in the world. Sansón commended Don Quixote's decision as a most honourable and courageous one, and warned him to be more cautious when he confronted dangers, because his life was not his own: it belonged to all those who needed his aid and protection in their misfortunes. * * *

Chapter 10

WHICH DESCRIBES SANCHO'S CUNNING ENCHANTMENT OF THE LADY DULCINEA, AND OTHER EVENTS AS RIDICULOUS AS THEY ARE TRUE

As the author of this great history reaches the events that he narrates in this chapter, he says that he'd have preferred to pass over them in silence, fearing he wouldn't be believed, because here Don Quixote's mad deeds approached the limits of the imaginable, and indeed went a couple of bowshots beyond them. But in the end, and in spite of these fears and misgivings, he described those deeds exactly as they happened, without adding or subtracting one atom of truth or concerning himself with any accusations that might be made that he was lying; and he was right to do so, because the truth might be stretched thin but it never breaks, and it always surfaces above lies, as oil floats on water.

And so, continuing his history, he says that as soon as Don Quixote had hidden in the glade, wood or oak-grove close to El Toboso, he ordered Sancho to return to the city and not to appear in his presence again without having spoken on his behalf to his lady and besought her to be so gracious as to grant her hapless knight an audience and deign to bestow her blessing on him, so that he could hope for the greatest success in all his undertakings and difficult enterprises, thanks to her. Sancho agreed to do exactly as he was told, and to bring back as good a reply as he had brought back the first time.[1]

"On your way, then, my friend," replied Don Quixote, "and do not be plunged into confusion when you find yourself in the presence of the light of the sun of beauty that you are now going to seek. Happy are you above all the squires in the world! Stay alert, and make sure that you do not fail to observe the way in which she receives you: whether her colour changes as you deliver my message; whether

---

3. April 23, feast day of the proverbial slayer of dragons.
1. This was in Book 1 when Don Quixote was in the Sierra Morena; Sancho returns to Don Quixote in Chapter 27 with instructions by the priest and barber to tell him that Dulcinea had replied by word of mouth, commanding Don Quixote to come and see her at once.

she seems disturbed or disquieted on hearing my name; whether her cushion seems not to be able to hold her, if perchance you find her seated upon the rich dais proper to her dignity—and if she is standing, watch her to see whether she shifts her weight from one foot to the other; whether she repeats her answer maybe two or three times; whether she changes it from a kind one to a harsh one, or from a cruel one to a loving one; whether she raises her hand to her hair to pat it into place, even though it is not untidy; and in short, my son, watch her every action, her every movement, because if you tell me about them I shall deduce how she feels in the most secret places of her heart about my love for her; for I would have you know, Sancho, if you do not know it already, that the external actions and movements made by lovers while the conversation concerns their love are messengers between them giving totally reliable accounts of what is happening in their souls. So off you go, my friend, and may better fortune than mine guide you and send you a happier outcome than that which I, here in this my bleak solitude, fear and expect."

"Yes, I'm going, and I'll soon be back," said Sancho. "And do try and stop that poor little heart of yours from shrinking so, it must be about the size of a hazel nut by now, and remember what they say, a good heart conquers ill fortune, and where there isn't any bacon there aren't any hooks to hang it from and, as they also say, the hare leaps up where you least expect it to. I'm only mentioning all this because if we didn't find my lady's palace or castle last night, now it's daytime I do intend to find it, when I'm least expecting to, and once I've found it, you just leave her to me."

"This I will say, Sancho," said Don Quixote. "I do hope that God gives me even better fortune in my aspirations than you have in choosing proverbs appropriate to our discussions."

After this, Sancho turned away and gave his dun the stick, and Don Quixote was left sitting on his nag, resting in his stirrups and leaning on his lance, overwhelmed by sorrowful and confused musings, where we shall leave him and go off with Sancho Panza, who was no less pensive and bewildered than his master; so much so, that he was hardly out of the wood when, looking back and seeing that Don Quixote was no longer in sight, he climbed off his donkey, sat down at the foot of a tree, and began to talk to himself and to say:

"Pray be so good as to tell us, brother Sancho, where it is that you're going. To look for some donkey that you've lost? No, most certainly not. So what are you looking for? Oh, I'm just going to look for some princess, that's all, the sun of beauty and the whole of heaven in one person. And where do you expect to find all that, Sancho? Where? In the great city of El Toboso. Very well, and on whose behalf are you going to look for her? On behalf of the famous knight Don Quixote de la Mancha, who rights wrongs and gives food to the thirsty and drink to the hungry. That is all most commendable. And do you know where she lives, Sancho? My master says she must live in a royal palace or a splendid castle. And have you ever seen her by any chance? Neither me nor my master have ever clapped eyes on the woman. And do you think it would be right and proper for the men of El Toboso, if they found out that you're here intending to spirit away their princesses and raise a rumpus among their ladies, to come and give you such a going-over that they didn't leave a bone unbroken in your body? Yes, they'd be in the right, unless they bore in mind that I'm just an errand-boy, and

> You're but a messenger, my friend,
> You don't deserve the blame.[2]

2. From a ballad about the hero Bernardo del Carpio, the Castilian who defeats Roland.

No, you can't rely on that, Sancho, because the people of La Mancha are as hot-tempered as they're honourable, and they won't let anyone play around with them. God Almighty, if they suspect what you're up to, I can promise you a bad time of it! No, you can get lost, Old Nick, you're not catching me in a hurry! Oh yes, I'm going to go stirring up a hornet's nest for the sake of somebody else's pleasure, I am! What's more, looking for Dulcinea in El Toboso would be like looking for a student in Salamanca or a girl called María in Madrid. Yes, yes, it was the devil, the devil and 'nobody else that got me into this mess!'"

The result of Sancho's soliloquy was that he talked to himself again, and said:

"On the other hand, there's a remedy for all things but death, under whose yoke we must all pass, like it or not, at the end of our lives. I've seen a thousand signs that this master of mine is a raving lunatic, and I'm not much better myself, because I'm even stupider than he is, following him and serving him as I do, if there's any truth in the proverb that says a man is known by the company he keeps, and that other one about birds of a feather flocking together. So him being as he is mad, and with a madness that usually makes him take one thing for another and think that white is black and black is white, as anyone could see when he said that those windmills were giants, and those friars' mules were dromedaries, and those flocks of sheep were enemy armies, and all sorts of other stuff like that, it won't be all that difficult to make him believe that some peasant girl, the very first one I come across, is lady Dulcinea—and if he doesn't believe it I'll swear she is, and if he swears she isn't I'll swear she is again, and if he insists I'll insist even more, and so I'll make sure I always have the last word, come what may. Maybe by insisting like this I'll make him stop sending me off on all these errands, seeing what a mess I make of them—or on the other hand maybe he'll think, as I expect he will, that one of those evil enchanters that he says hate him so much has changed her looks to spite him and do him harm."

These thoughts calmed Sancho's breast, and he counted the business as good as settled; and he waited where he was until the afternoon, to leave enough time for Don Quixote to believe that he'd gone to El Toboso and come back; and events fell out so well for him that when he got up to climb on his dun he saw three peasant girls coming towards him from El Toboso on three jackasses, or she-asses, because the author isn't explicit on this point, though it's more likely that they were she-asses, this being what peasant girls usually ride on; but since it doesn't matter much one way or the other, there's no need to stop to elucidate the matter. So, to cut a long story short, as soon as Sancho saw the peasant girls he rode back to his master Don Quixote as fast as he could go, and found him sighing and breathing a thousand amorous laments When Don Quixote saw Sancho he said:

"What news, Sancho my friend? Can I mark this day with a white stone or with a black stone?"[3]

"It'll be best," Sancho replied, "for you to mark it in bright red paint, like new professors' names on college walls, so that everyone who sees it sees it clearly."

"That means," said Don Quixote, "that you bring good news."

"Such good news," Sancho replied, "that all you've got to do to find the lady Dulcinea del Toboso is to clap spurs to Rocinante and ride out of the wood—she's on her way with two of her maids to see you."

3. From the Roman practice of using white stones to mark lucky days, black stones unlucky ones.

"Good God! What are you saying, friend Sancho?" said Don Quixote. "You had better not be deceiving me, or attempting to beguile my real grief with false joy."

"What would I gain from deceiving you?" Sancho replied, "specially now I'm so close to showing you the truth of what I'm saying. Just get your spurs into action, sir, and come with me, and you'll see the princess, our mistress, on her way here, dressed and bedecked just like what she is. She and her maids are all one blaze of flaming gold, all spindlefuls of pearls, they're all diamonds, all rubies, all brocade more than ten levels deep, with their hair flowing over their shoulders like sunbeams playing with the wind, and what's more each of them's riding her piebald poultry, a sight for sore eyes."

"I think you mean *palfrey,* Sancho."

"There isn't that much of a difference," Sancho replied, "between poultry and palfrey, but whatever they're riding they're looking as spruce and ladylike as you could ever wish, specially my lady Princess Dulcinea—she fair takes your breath away, she does."

"Let us go, Sancho my son," Don Quixote said, "and as a reward for this news, as splendid as it is unexpected, I hereby promise you the best spoils I win in the first adventure that I undertake, and if this does not satisfy you I promise you all the foals born this year to my three mares: as you know, they are awaiting the happy event on the village green."

"I'll take the foals," replied Sancho, "because it isn't too clear that the spoils of the first adventure are going to be that brilliant."

As he said this, they emerged from the wood and saw the three peasant girls not far away. Don Quixote surveyed the road to El Toboso, and since all he could see was these three peasants he became alarmed and asked Sancho if the ladies had been outside the city when he'd left them.

"What do you mean, outside the city?" Sancho replied. "Do you keep your eyes in the back of your head or something, to stop you from seeing that they're these ladies here, shining like the very sun at noon?"

"All I can see, Sancho," said Don Quixote, "is three peasant girls on three donkeys."

"God save my soul from damnation!" Sancho replied. "Is it possible for three palfreys or whatever they're called, as white as the driven snow, to seem to you like donkeys? Good Lord, I'd pull out every single hair on my chin if that was true!"

"Well, I am telling you, friend Sancho," said Don Quixote, "that it is as true that they are asses, or maybe she-asses, as it is that I am Don Quixote and you are Sancho Panza; or at least this is how it seems to me."

"Hush, sir," said Sancho, "you mustn't talk like that—open those eyes of yours and come and do homage to the lady of your life, now she's so close at hand."

And as he said this he rode forward to greet the three peasant girls, and, dismounting from his dun, he seized one of their asses by the halter, fell to his knees and said:

"O queen and princess and duchess of beauty, may your highness and your mightiness be pleased to receive into your grace and goodwill this your hapless knight, standing over there like a marble statue, all flustered and flummoxed at finding himself in your magnificent presence. I am his squire Sancho Panza, and he is the harassed knight Don Quixote de la Mancha, also known as the Knight of the Sorry Face."

Don Quixote had by now knelt at Sancho's side and was staring with clouded vision and bulging eyes at the woman whom Sancho called queen and lady; and since all he could see there was a peasant girl, and not a very pretty one at that, because she was moon-faced and flat-nosed, he was dumbstruck and didn't dare open his mouth. The peasant girls were equally astonished, at the sight of such an ill-assorted pair kneeling in front of one of them and impeding her progress. But she broke the silence and spoke with neither goodwill nor grace:

"Get out of the bloody way and let us through, we're in a hurry!"

To which Sancho replied:

"O princess and universal lady of El Toboso! How is it that your magnanimous heart is not melted by the sight of the column and foundation of knight-errantry kneeling here in your sublimated presence?"

When one of the other girls heard this, she said:

"Come to cast pearls before swine, have we? Look at these fine gents trying to make fun of us village girls, as if we didn't know how to take the piss as well! You two go on your way, and let us go on ours, if you want to stay in one piece."

"Arise, Sancho," Don Quixote put in. "I can see that fortune, not content with my sufferings, has blocked all the roads along which some happiness might have come to this wretched soul contained within my flesh. And you, O perfection of all the excellence that the heart can desire, acme of human courtesy, the sole remedy of this afflicted heart that adores you: even though the malicious enchanter is hounding me, and has placed clouds and cataracts over my eyes, and for them alone and not for other eyes has altered and transformed your face of peerless beauty into that of some poor peasant wench, I beg you—so long as he has not also changed my face into that of some monster, to make me abominable in your sight—not to refuse to look on me with gentleness and love, seeing in my position of submission and prostration before your disguised beauty the self-humiliation of my soul's adoration."

"Hark at old grandad!" the village girl replied. "Don't I just love oily eyewash like that! Come on, shift over and let us through, thank you very much."

Sancho shifted over and let her through, delighted to have extricated himself from that particular muddle. As soon as the peasant girl who'd played the part of Dulcinea found herself free she prodded her poultry with a nail on a stick that she was carrying and it broke into a canter across the field. And feeling the nail, which annoyed it more than usual, it started to prance and buck, and dumped Lady Dulcinea among the daisies; Don Quixote rushed to pick her up and Sancho hurried to put the pack-saddle, which had slipped round under the ass's belly, back into place. Once Sancho had done this, Don Quixote went to lift his enchanted lady in his arms and place her on the ass; but the lady saved him the trouble by jumping to her feet, taking a couple of strides backwards, bounding up to the ass, bringing both hands down on to its rump and vaulting, as swift as a falcon, on to the pack-saddle, where she sat astride as if she were a man; and then Sancho said:

"By holy St Roch,[4] our lady and mistress is nimbler than a hobby-hawk, and she could teach the best rider from Cordova or Mexico how to jump on to a horse Arab-style! Over the crupper she went in one leap, and without any spurs she's making her palfrey gallop like a zebra. And her maids aren't being outdone, they're going like the wind, too."

---

4. Saint Roch (or Roque), 14th-century figure from Montpellier who healed plague victims and who is invoked against disease.

And Sancho was right, because once Dulcinea was mounted the other two girls spurred after her, not turning their heads back for more than a mile. Don Quixote pursued them with his gaze, and when they were out of sight he turned to Sancho and said:

"Sancho, what is your opinion about this grudge that the enchanters bear me? You can see how far their malice and hatred extend, for they have deprived me of the joy that I could have experienced on beholding my lady in her true being. I was indeed born to be a mirror of misfortune, the eternal target for the arrows of adversity. And you should also note, Sancho, that those traitors were not content just to transform my Dulcinea, but had to transform her into a figure as wretched and ugly as that peasant wench, and at the same time they took away from her what is so characteristic of fine ladies; the sweet smell that they derive from living among ambergris and flowers. Because I would have you know, Sancho, that when I went to replace Dulcinea on her palfrey (as you call it, although I thought it was a donkey), I was half suffocated by a blast of raw garlic that poisoned my very soul."

"Oh you miserable wretches!" Sancho burst out. "Oh you fateful and spiteful enchanters, I'd like to see you all hanging by your gills like pilchards on a string! Aren't you clever, aren't you powerful and aren't you bloody well active! You ought to have been happy, you villains, with turning those eyes of pearl of my lady's into oak-apples, and her tresses of purest gold into hairs from the tail of a sorrel ox, and, all in all, every one of her features from good to bad, without messing about with her smell, too—from her smell we'd at least have been able to work out what was hidden under that ugly outside although, to tell you the truth, I never did see her ugliness but only her beauty, which was boosted no end by a mole she had on the right side of her lip, a bit like a moustache, with seven or eight blond hairs like threads of gold growing out of it, more than a handsbreadth long."

"According to the rules of correspondence between facial moles and bodily moles," said Don Quixote, "Dulcinea must have another mole on the thick of the thigh on the same side as the one on her face; but hairs of the length that you have indicated are very long indeed for moles."

"Well, I can tell you," Sancho replied, "they were there all right, just as if she'd been born with them."

"I believe you, my friend," replied Don Quixote, "because nature has given Dulcinea nothing that is not complete and perfect; and so, if she had a hundred moles like the one you have described, on her they would not be moles but moons—resplendent moons and shining stars. But tell me, Sancho, the object that seemed to me like a pack-saddle, which you straightened for her—was it an ordinary saddle or a lady's saddle with arms?"

"It was nothing less than a great tall Arab-style saddle," Sancho replied, "with a saddle-cloth so precious it's worth half a kingdom."

"And to think that I could not see any of that, Sancho!" said Don Quixote. "I say it again, and I shall say it a thousand times: I am the most unfortunate of men."

The sly rogue Sancho had his work cut out to hide his laughter as he listened to the nonsense being blurted by his master, whom he had deceived with such finesse. In the end, after the two had talked for a good while longer, they remounted and followed the road that led towards Saragossa, where they planned to arrive in time for the solemn festivities held each year in that famous city. But before they arrived certain things happened to them, so many, so important and so strange, that they deserve to be written and read about, as will be seen in what follows.

* * *

from *Chapter 25*

WHICH BEGINS THE AMUSING ADVENTURE OF THE PUPPETEER, TOGETHER
WITH THE MEMORABLE DIVINATIONS OF THE FORTUNE-TELLING APE

* * * "And that's quite enough of this matter for now; so let us go and see Master
Pedro's puppet show, for I imagine that it might offer a certain novelty," said Don
Quixote.[1]

"What do you mean, a certain novelty?" Master Pedro replied. "This puppet show
of mine offers sixty thousand novelties—I'm telling you, Don Quixote sir, it's one of
the sights most worth seeing in the whole wide world, but *operibus credite, et non ver-
bis,*[2] so let's set to work, because it's getting late and we have a lot to do, and say, and
show."

Don Quixote and Sancho did as they were told, and walked over to where the
puppet theatre had been erected and uncovered, glowing all over with wax tapers that
made it a glittering, resplendent sight. Master Pedro disappeared inside it, because he
was the one who worked the puppets, and in front of it stood a boy, Master Pedro's
servant, to act as announcer and interpreter of the mysteries of the show: he held a
pointer to indicate the puppets as they emerged. With everyone at the inn in front of
the puppet theatre, some of them standing, and with Don Quixote, Sancho, the page
and the cousin in the best seats, the announcer began to say what anyone who reads
the next chapter or has it read to him will see or hear.

Chapter 26

WHICH CONTINUES THE AMUSING ADVENTURE OF THE PUPPETEER,
TOGETHER WITH OTHER REALLY VERY GOOD THINGS

The Tyrians and the Trojans all were silent,[1]

what I mean to say is that everyone in the audience was hanging, as it were, on the
lips of the announcer of the marvels of the puppet show, when the sounds of war-
drums and trumpets and artillery fire rang out from inside the theatre and suddenly
died down again, and the boy proclaimed:

"This true history that is about to be performed before your very eyes has been
taken word for word from the French chronicles and from the Spanish ballads that
people sing, and boys too, in the street. It's about how Don Gaiferos freed his wife
Melisendra, who was a prisoner of the Moors in Spain, in the city of Sansueña, which
is what Saragossa was called then; and here you can see Don Gaiferos playing
backgammon, as that song goes:

> And Don Gaiferos, playing at the tables,
> Has not a thought for Melisendra now.[2]

---

1. Earlier in this chapter, Don Quixote and Sancho encounter in an inn a famous puppeteer named Master Pedro,
accompanied by an ape who can predict the future. Remarkably, he instantly recognizes Don Quixote as the "illustrious reviver of the forgotten order of knight-errantry."
2. "Believe works, not words"; an echo from John 10:38
in which Jesus says that actions are heeded more than
words.
1. From the beginning of *Aeneid* 2, as the Trojans and

Tyrians (Dido's people) fall silent to hear Aeneas's tale of
the fall of Troy and his subsequent travels.
2. Melisendra, daughter of Charlemagne, was captured by
the Moors because of the negligence of her husband, Don
Gaiferos, who then rescued her in a daring mission and
took her to France. Subject of a popular ballad in Spain,
the story had originally derived from the medieval stories
around Charlemagne's court.

And that character coming into view over there with a crown on his head and a sceptre in his hands—he's the Emperor Charlemagne, Melisendra's foster father, who's
angry at his son-in-law's laziness and negligence and is coming to scold him; and see
with what warmth and feeling he does it, it looks as if he's going to bang him on the
head half a dozen times with his sceptre, and some authorities reckon that's exactly
what he did, good and hard; and after telling him all sorts of things about the danger
his honour is in from not trying to free his wife, it's said that he said:

> I've said enough; see to it now.

You can also see how the Emperor turns away and leaves Don Gaiferos fuming, and
now you see him in his rage hurling the backgammon board far from him and calling
for his arms and armour, and he asks his cousin Roland to lend him his sword Duran-
dal, and Roland refuses, offering him instead his company in the difficult task ahead;
but our angry hero will not accept this, and says he's quite capable of rescuing his
wife alone even if she's imprisoned deep in the centre of the earth; and then he goes
away to don his armour and set off. Now look at that tower you can see over there,
which we must imagine is one of the towers of Saragossa Castle, today called the Al-
jafería; and that lady in Moorish clothes on that balcony is the matchless Melisendra,
who often used to come out on to it to gaze at the road to France, and to console herself in her imprisonment by daydreaming about Paris and her husband. And now
watch out for a new incident that's about to happen, maybe never seen before. Can't
you see that Moor sneaking up behind Melisendra with his forefinger over his lips?
Well, now look how he gives her a kiss slap on the mouth, and how soon she spits and
wipes her lips with the white sleeve of her blouse, and how she wails and tears her
lovely hair in grief, as if her hair were to blame for that evil deed. And see that grave
Moor on that balcony, King Marsilio of Sansueña: he spotted the Moor's insolent action and, even though the fellow was a relative and a great favourite of his, ordered
him to be arrested and given two hundred lashes, after being paraded through the city
along the customary streets,

> With squawkers before him
> And truncheons behind,

and now you can see they're coming to carry out the sentence, and the crime's hardly
even been committed yet, because the Moors don't go in for notification of the charge
or detention on remand, as we do."

"Come, boy," exclaimed Don Quixote, "proceed with your story in a straight
line, and don't go wandering round bends or up side-roads; for to reach the truth
about something like that, proof upon proof is needed."

And Master Pedro said from inside the theatre:

"Look here, my lad, I don't want any flourishes, just do as the gentleman says,
that'll be the wisest course—stick to plain chant without any counterpoint,[3] and don't
you go and spin the thread so fine you break it."

"All right," the lad replied, and he continued: "this figure appearing here on
horseback, muffled in a Gascon cape, is Don Gaiferos himself; and here his wife,
avenged for the amorous Moor's effrontery, with a happier and calmer look on her

---

3. Plain chant was sung in unison by monks; counterpoint was the practice of adding one or more melodies to a plainsong.
The accompanying notes (or "points") were set "against" those of the original song.

face, has come out on to the tower balcony and is talking to her husband in the belief that he's some passer-by, and they had that conversation in that ballad that goes:

> Sir knight, if it's to France you go,
> Pray ask for Don Gaiferos.

"But I shan't repeat the conversation now, because long-windedness breeds boredom; it's enough to see how Don Gaiferos reveals who he is, and from Melisendra's gestures of joy we're given to understand that she's recognized him, and even more so now that we see her letting herself down from the balcony to sit on the crupper of her good husband's horse. But oh how unlucky, look, the hem of her skirt's got caught on one of the balcony railings, and she's been left hanging in the air and can't reach the ground. But now you can see that merciful heaven sends aid at times of greatest need, because up comes Don Gaiferos and without worrying about tearing her fine skirt he seizes her and tugs her down whether she likes it or not, and with a leap he puts her on to the crupper of his horse, astride, just like a man, and tells her to hold on tight and put her arms over his shoulders and across his chest so as not to fall off, because madam Melisendra wasn't used to galloping around like that. Observe, too, how the neighing of the horse shows how happy it is with the burden of bravery and beauty it bears in the shape of its master and mistress. Observe how they turn and leave the city, and full of joy and happiness they take the road to Paris. Go in peace, O peerless pair of true lovers! May you arrive safely in your longed-for homeland, and may fortune raise no barrier to hinder your happy journey! May your friends and relations see you enjoying the remainder of your life in peace and tranquillity, and may your days be as many as Nestor's!"[4]

Here Master Pedro shouted out again:

"Keep it simple, boy, none of those flights of yours! Affectation's always bad!"

The announcer didn't reply, but continued:

"Idle eyes see everything, and there they were to see Melisendra getting down and then getting up, and off they went to tell King Marsilio, who ordered the alarm to be sounded, and look how fast—the whole city's shaking with the bells being rung from all the mosque towers!"

"No, no," Don Quixote intervened. "Those bells are a grave blunder by Master Pedro, because Moors do not use bells but kettle drums, and a kind of pipe rather like our shawm;[5] and to have bells ringing in Sansueña is most definitely a gross absurdity."

When Master Pedro heard this he stopped ringing his bells and said:

"Don't worry about trivialities, Don Quixote sir—you can't make anything without making mistakes. Aren't thousands of plays performed all the time full of thousands of blunders and absurdities, and despite that they have a good run and are greeted not only with applause but with admiration too? You carry on, my lad, and let them say what they like—so long as I fill my money bags it doesn't matter if I make more blunders than there are atoms in the sun."

"That is true enough," Don Quixote replied.

And the boy said:

---

4. Elderly Greek statesman and counselor in Homer.

5. Medieval musical instrument with a double reed, like an oboe.

"See all the resplendent cavalry riding out of the city in pursuit of the two Christian lovers; how many trumpets blaring, how many pipes rather like shawms playing, how many kettle drums and other sorts of drums beating. I'm afraid they're going to catch up with them and return with them tied to the tail of their own horse, which would be a horrendous sight."

Seeing such hordes of Moors and hearing such a racket, Don Quixote thought it would be a good idea to help the fugitives, and he sprang to his feet and cried:

"Never while there is still breath in my body will I consent to such an insult being offered in my presence to such a famous knight and bold innamorato[6] as Don Gaiferos. Desist, you low-born rabble; do not follow him, do not pursue him, or you shall do battle with me!"

And acting even as he spoke he drew his sword and with one leap positioned himself in front of the stage, and with speedy and unprecedented fury began to hack at the hordes of puppet Moors, knocking some over, beheading others, wrecking this one, destroying that; and one down-stroke among many others would have lopped Master Pedro's head off as easily as if it had been made of marzipan, if he hadn't ducked and crouched and made himself into a ball. Master Pedro was crying:

"Stop, stop, Don Quixote sir, look, these you're knocking down and smashing and killing aren't real Moors but papier mâché figures. I'll be damned, you're destroying everything I own in the world!"

But this didn't stop Don Quixote from raining down his cuts and thrusts and two-handers and fore-strokes and back-strokes. And in the time it takes to say a couple of creeds he left the whole show in a heap on the floor, with the puppets and the fittings cut into little pieces, King Marsilio critically injured, and the Emperor Charlemagne with his head and his crown split in two. The senate of spectators was in an uproar, the monkey escaped through the window on to the roof, the cousin was frightened, the page was panic-stricken and even Sancho Panza was petrified because, as he swore once the storm was over, he'd never seen his master in such a temper. Once the demolition of the puppet show was complete, Don Quixote grew somewhat calmer and said:

"I should like to have here before me all those who do not and will not believe how beneficial knights errant are to society: for look—if I had not been present, what would have become of the worthy Don Gaiferos and the lovely Melisendra? By now those dogs would most certainly have caught up with them and done them some mischief. Long live knight-errantry, then, above all else on earth!"

"Yes, long live knight-errantry," Master Pedro commented, in feeble tones, "and quick death to me, so wretched that I can well say with King Rodrigo:

> But yesterday the lord of Spain . . .
> Today not one embattlement
> That I can call my own![7]

Not half an hour ago, indeed not half a minute ago, I was the master of kings and emperors, and my stables, my coffers and my bags were full of countless horses and innumerable pieces of finery; and now I'm abject and desolate, poverty-stricken and a beggar and, what's worst of all, monkeyless, for I'll have to sweat blood to get that animal back,

6. Lover (Italian).
7. From a famous ballad about King Rodrigo, the last Visigoth king of Spain; in 713, thanks to his losses in bat-

tle, Spain was completely absorbed within the dominion of the Muslims.

all because of the wrongheaded fury of this knight here, who's said to succour orphans, and right wrongs, and do other charitable works, yet only with me have his good intentions misfired—blessed and praised be heaven above in the highest of the high. I suppose it had to be the Knight of the Sorry Face who came to deface the faces of my puppets."

Sancho was moved by Master Pedro's words, and said:

"Don't cry like that, Master Pedro, don't wail so, you're breaking my heart—and I can tell you my master Don Quixote's such a scrupulous and Catholic Christian that if he realizes he's done you any harm he'll say so and pay you double."

"If Don Quixote paid me for just half the figures of mine he's disfigured I'd be happy enough, and that would clear his conscience—because there's no salvation for the man who's holding on to something against its owner's will and doesn't give it back to him."

"That is true enough," said Don Quixote, "but I am not aware that I am retaining anything of yours, Master Pedro."

"What do you mean?" replied Master Pedro. "And all these relics scattered about this hard and sterile soil—what was it that smashed and scattered them if not the invincible power of that mighty arm of yours? And who did they belong to if not to me? And how did I support myself except with them?"

"Now I am utterly convinced," Don Quixote inserted, "of what I have many times thought might be true: the ploy of these enchanters who pursue me is to place before my eyes things as they are, and then change them into what they want them to be. I can assure you really and truly, all you who hear me, that I did believe that everything happening here happened exactly as it seemed to happen: that Melisendra was Melisendra, Don Gaiferos was Don Gaiferos, Marsilio was Marsilio and Charlemagne was Charlemagne. That is why I lost my temper and, to do what I had to do as a knight errant, I decided to aid and assist the people who were fleeing, and with that worthy aim in mind I did what you have seen me do; if it has all turned out the opposite of how I intended, that is not my fault, but the fault of the wicked ones who pursue me; and despite all this, although my mistake did not proceed from malice aforethought, I hereby award costs against myself: so Master Pedro must assess what he wants for his broken puppets, and I will pay for them in good current Castilian coin."[8]

Master Pedro bowed and said:

"I expected no less from the unprecedented Christian virtue of the brave Don Quixote de la Mancha, true help and support of all needy and distressed vagrants; and the good innkeeper and the worthy Sancho will be assessors and arbiters between you and me of what the broken puppets are worth, or rather were worth."

The innkeeper and Sancho agreed to this, and Master Pedro picked up King Marsilio of Saragossa, minus his head, and said:

"You can see how impossible it is to restore this king to his original state; and so it seems to me, and subject to your better judgement, that for his sad demise and sorry end I should be given four and a half reals."

"Continue!" said Don Quixote.

"And for this crack from top to bottom," Master Pedro continued, picking up the broken Emperor Charlemagne, "I wouldn't be asking very much if I asked for five and a quarter reals."

"That's no small sum," said Sancho.

---

8. When he leaves La Mancha again in Book 2, Don Quixote furnishes himself with money, and his dealings with others are thus different than when he was the penurious knight of Book 1.

"Not a large one either," replied the innkeeper. "Split the difference and give him five reals."

"Give him the full five and a quarter," said Don Quixote, "because this notable misfortune is not to be measured in quarters of a real; and I wish Master Pedro would hurry up, it is time for supper and I am beginning to feel the pangs of hunger."

"For this figure," said Master Pedro, "minus its nose and an eye, the figure of the lovely Melisendra, I want two reals and twelve maravedís, and that's only fair."

"There will be the devil and all to do," said Don Quixote, "if Melisendra and her husband are not on the French border by now, at least, because I thought the horse they were riding was flying rather than galloping; so don't you come trying to sell me a pig in a poke, and presenting me with a noseless Melisendra when she must, if given half a chance, be frolicking in France with her husband to her heart's content. God help each of us to what is rightly his, Master Pedro, and let us all march on with a firm foot and honest intentions. Pray continue."

Master Pedro could see that Don Quixote was beginning to rave again and to return to his earlier fixation, and didn't want to let him off the hook, and so he said:

"This one can't be Melisendra, then, but one of her maidservants, so if I'm given sixty maravedís for her I'll be happy enough."

And in this way he put prices to many other wrecked puppets, which the arbitrators moderated to the satisfaction of the two parties, and it came to a total of forty and three-quarter reals; and on top of this sum, which Sancho paid out immediately, Master Pedro asked for two reals for the trouble of going for his ape.

"Give them to him, Sancho," said Don Quixote, "although what he'll go for with them has more to do with grapes than with apes; and I would give two hundred reals this very moment as a reward to anyone who could tell me for certain that Doña Melisendra and Don Gaiferos are in France among their own people."

"Nobody will be able to tell us that better than my monkey," said Master Pedro, "but the devil himself wouldn't be able to catch him now; though I imagine that his affection for me, and his hunger, will force him to come back to look for me tonight— and God will send us his light, and then we'll see."

So the storm over the puppet show died down and all had supper together in peace and good fellowship, at the expense of Don Quixote, who was an extremely generous man.

The man transporting the lances and halberds left before dawn, and once it was light the cousin and the page came to take their leave of Don Quixote, one to go back home and the other to continue on his way, as a help with which Don Quixote gave him a dozen reals. Master Pedro didn't want any more argy-bargy with Don Quixote, whom he knew all too well,[9] and so he rose before the sun, took his monkey and the remains of his puppet theatre, and went off in search of his own adventures. The innkeeper, who didn't know Don Quixote, was as amazed at his capers as at his generosity. And Sancho paid him well, on his master's orders, and at a little before eight o'clock in the morning they left the inn and took to the road, where we shall leave them to go on their way, as we must in order to provide an opportunity to record other matters that are relevant to the narration of this famous history.

* * *

9. As Cervantes reveals in Chapter 27, Master Pedro is Ginés de Pasamonte, the notorious criminal and writer of autobiography with whom Quixote has had earlier dealings.

Chapter 59

ABOUT THE STRANGEST AND MOST SINGULAR EXPERIENCE UNDERGONE BY DON QUIXOTE
IN THE WHOLE COURSE OF THIS GREAT HISTORY

* * * So suppertime came round, Don Quixote retired to his room and the landlord brought the stew, just as it was, and Don Quixote sat down to eat it with a will.[1] It seems that in a room next to Don Quixote's, divided from it only by a flimsy partition, he heard someone saying:

"I beg you, Don Jerónimo—while dinner's being fetched do let's read another chapter of the second part of *Don Quixote de la Mancha*."[2]

The instant Don Quixote heard his name he started to his feet and pricked up his ears to listen to what these people were saying, and he heard Don Jerónimo's reply:

"Why do you want to us read all that nonsense, Don Juan? Nobody who has read the first part of the history of Don Quixote de la Mancha can possibly derive any pleasure from reading this second part."

"All the same," said Don Juan, "it'll be as well to read it, because there's no book so bad that there isn't something good in it. What I most dislike about this one is that it describes Don Quixote as no longer in love with Dulcinea del Toboso."

When Don Quixote heard this he flared up and cried:

"If anyone claims that Don Quixote de la Mancha has forgotten or can forget Dulcinea del Toboso, I shall, with equal arms, force him to acknowledge that he is very far from the truth, because neither can the peerless Dulcinea del Toboso be forgotten, nor is Don Quixote capable of forgetting. His motto is constancy, and his profession is to observe this principle with ease and without constraint."

"Who is that answering us?" came the reply from the other room.

"Who do you think it is," Sancho replied, "if not the very same Don Quixote de la Mancha? And he'll make good everything he's just said and everything he hasn't said yet, too, because a good payer's a good pledger."

Hardly had Sancho finished speaking when two gentlemen, as they gave every sign of being, walked in through the door, and one of them put his arms round Don Quixote's neck and said:

"Neither can your presence belie your name, nor can your name fail to accredit your presence: there can be no doubt that you, sir, are the real Don Quixote de la Mancha, guide and lodestar of knight-errantry, in spite and in defiance of the one who has attempted to usurp your name and obliterate your deeds, as has the author of this book I have here."

And taking a book from his companion he handed it to Don Quixote, who began to thumb through it in silence, and after a short while he returned it with the words:

"In the little I have seen I have found three aspects of this author's work that are worthy of rebuke. First, certain statements in the prologue;[3] secondly, the fact that the

1. Following numerous adventures—such as Sancho's being rewarded with governorship of a (fake) island by a Duke and Duchess who have enjoyed teasing Don Quixote and his squire—the pair find themselves, finally alone, at an inn en route to Saragossa, where Don Quixote plans to participate in the jousts for St. George's Day.

2. A spurious Book 2 of Don Quixote's story (*Segundo tomo del ingenioso hidalgo don Quixote de la Mancha*) was published in 1614, by one Alonso Fernández de Avellaneda, a pseudonym for an unidentified author. Beginning with this episode, Cervantes has a great deal of fun with the book that spurred him into publishing his own sequel a year later.

3. Most likely attacks made on Cervantes, which Cervantes himself mentions in the prologue to Book 2. Thus he writes, "Avellaneda attacks me for being old and one-handed, as if it had been in my power to halt time and prevent it from ravaging me, or as if I had been maimed in some tavern brawl rather than at the greatest battle that past or present ages have ever seen or that future ages can ever hope to see" (the battle at Lepanto, against the Moors).

language is Aragonese, because he often omits the article;[4] and thirdly, and this is what most confirms his ignorance, he blunders and strays from the truth in the most central feature of the whole history, because he says here that my squire Sancho Panza's wife is called Mari Gutiérrez, when she is called nothing of the sort, but Teresa Panza; and if someone can make a mistake about such an important matter we can well fear that he is mistaken in everything else that he says in his history."[5]

To which Sancho added:

"That's a fine thing in a historian! He must be really clued up on our doings if he calls my wife Teresa Panza Mari Gutiérrez! Take another look at the book, sir, and see if I'm in it, and if he's changed my name too."

"From what I have heard, my friend," said Don Jerónimo, "you must be Sancho Panza, Don Quixote's squire."

"That's me," Sancho replied, "and proud of it."

"Well the fact is," the gentleman said, "that this novice author doesn't treat you with the scrupulosity that you display in your person: he represents you as a glutton, and simple-minded, and not at all funny, very different from the Sancho described in the first part of the history of your master."

"God forgive him," said Sancho. "He should have left me in my corner and forgotten all about me, because you've got to know your strings before you pluck them, and St Peter's all right in Rome."

The two gentlemen asked Don Quixote into their room to share their dinner, as they were well aware that there was no food to be had at that inn fit for him to consume. Don Quixote, courteous as always, acceded to their request and dined with them; Sancho was left with the stew, absolute lord and master of it all, and sat himself at the head of the table, and by his side sat the innkeeper, no less fond than Sancho of his heels and of his feet.

During dinner Don Juan asked Don Quixote what news he had of his lady Dulcinea del Toboso: whether she had married, whether she had given birth or was pregnant, or whether on the contrary she was still intact and still remembered (always preserving her decorum and propriety) Don Quixote's amorous intentions. To which he replied:

"Dulcinea is indeed intact, and my intentions are firmer than ever; our communications are as unsatisfactory as they ever were; her beauty has been transformed into that of a coarse peasant girl."

And he went on to give a detailed account of Dulcinea's enchantment, and what had happened in the Cave of Montesinos, together with the arrangements made by the sage Merlin for her to be disenchanted, in other words Sancho's self-flagellation.[6] It gave the two gentlemen great pleasure to hear Don Quixote narrating the strange events of his own history, and they were as astonished by his mad antics as by the elegant manner in which he described them. One minute they thought him an intelligent

4. The Aragonese dialect is used in the region (at one time the kingdom) of Aragon, in northeast Spain.
5. Cervantes himself had made this "mistake" in Book 1.
6. Shortly before meeting up with Master Pedro, Don Quixote descends into the great cave of Montesinos (Chapters 22 and 23), where he has a vision of the great warrior Montesinos himself, who confirms for him the fact of Dulcinea's enchantment. Upon telling this to Sancho Panza, Sancho breaks out in laughter, "he himself having been the enchanter and the concocter of evidence." In Chapter 35 of Book 2, the sage Merlin, riding in a triumphal cart designed by the Duke and Duchess

who have continued to orchestrate the majority of events in the second half of Book 2, appears before Sancho Panza and Don Quixote. Merlin instructs Sancho that in order for Dulcinea to be transformed from the coarse peasant girl encountered in Chapter 10 to the beautiful lady of El Toboso, he must flog himself "on both his buttocks, big and bold and bare," 3,300 times. Naturally, Sancho wants nothing to do with this act of penitence, but he finally agrees, assuming some conditions are met such as "I'm not to have to make myself bleed, and if some of the lashes turn out to be more like swatting flies they're still valid."

man, the next minute he skidded off into absurdity, and they couldn't decide where to place him between sound sense and madness.

Sancho finished his supper and, leaving the innkeeper pie-eyed and tangle-footed, he went through to the room where his master was, and as he walked in he said:

"I'll be blowed, gents, if the author of that book you've got there doesn't want to get on bad terms with me—and if he calls me a greedy-guts, as you say he does, I only hope he doesn't call me a boozer into the bargain."

"Oh yes he does," said Don Jerónimo, "but I don't remember his exact words, although I do know that they're offensive ones and, what's more, quite untrue, as I can plainly see from the physiognomy of the worthy Sancho who stands before me."

"You mark my words," said Sancho, "the Sancho and the Don Quixote in that there history can't be the same as the ones in the history by Cide Hamete Benengeli, which is us—my master, brave and wise and in love, and me, a down-to-earth funny man, and not a greedy-guts or a boozer either."

"That's what I think, too," said Don Juan, "and if it were possible a law ought to be passed that nobody should presume to write about the doings of the great Don Quixote, except the first author Cide Hamete, just as Alexander ordered that nobody should presume to represent him on canvas except Apelles."[7]

"Anyone who so wishes can represent me," said Don Quixote, "but not misrepresent me; for patience often fails when it is overloaded with insults."

"No insult can be offered to Don Quixote," said Don Juan, "that he cannot avenge, unless he wards it off with the shield of his patience, which, in my belief, is large and strong."

They spent a great part of that night in conversation of this sort, and, although Don Juan would have liked Don Quixote to read some more of the book, to see what other comments he made, they couldn't persuade him to, and he said that he took it as read and assumed that it was absurd through and through; for if by any chance the author discovered that he had held it in his hands, he was unwilling to give that man the pleasure of knowing that he had read it; because our thoughts, and still more our eyes, must be kept aloof from everything lewd and obscene.

They asked Don Quixote where he was intending to go next. He replied that he was on his way to Saragossa, to take part in the jousts for the suit of armour that is held in that city each year. Don Juan told him that the new history related how Don Quixote, or whoever it was, had participated there in the riding at the ring, an episode depicted without imagination, with poor mottoes, even poorer costumes, and rich only in absurdities.

"Well, for that very reason," Don Quixote replied, "I shall not set foot in Saragossa, and thus I shall announce that novice historian's lie to the whole world, and people will be made aware that I am not the Don Quixote about whom he writes."

"That will be an excellent move," said Don Jerónimo, "and they hold other jousts in Barcelona, where Don Quixote will be able to display his prowess."

"And that is what I intend to do," said Don Quixote, "and now, with your permission, it is time for me to retire to bed, and please count me in the number of your firmest friends and most devoted servants."

"Me too," said Sancho, "who knows, I might come in handy sometime."

7. Alexander the Great's favorite painter.

And so they said goodnight, and Don Quixote and Sancho returned to their room, leaving Don Juan and Don Jerónimo lost in amazement at the mixture that the knight had contrived of sound sense and sheer madness; and they felt quite certain that these, and not the pair described by the Aragonese author, were the real Don Quixote and Sancho.

Don Quixote rose early next morning and, knocking on the partition, said good-bye to the men in the other room. Sancho showered wealth upon the innkeeper and advised him that in future he should either be less boastful about the provision at his inn, or keep it better provided.

* * *

Chapter 72

CONCERNING THE ARRIVAL OF DON QUIXOTE AND SANCHO AT THEIR VILLAGE[1]

Don Quixote and Sancho spent all that day at the village inn, waiting for nightfall: one of them to bring his exercise in flagellation to a conclusion in the open air, and the other to witness its completion and with it the accomplishment of his desires. Meanwhile a traveller arrived on horseback with three or four servants, one of whom said to the man who seemed to be their master:

"You can rest here, Don Álvaro Tarfe sir, while the sun is high—the inn seems clean and cool."

When Don Quixote heard this he said to Sancho:

"Look, Sancho, when I thumbed through that book containing the second part of my history, I think I came across the name Don Álvaro Tarfe."

"You could be right," Sancho replied. "Let's wait for him to dismount and then we'll ask him."

The gentleman dismounted, and the innkeeper's wife gave him a ground-floor room opposite Don Quixote's, decorated with painted cloths of the same sort. The recent arrival went to change into more comfortable clothes and, strolling out into the cool, spacious porch, where Don Quixote was pacing up and down, he asked:

"And where might you be bound for, my dear sir?"

And Don Quixote replied:

"To a village near here, where I live. And where are you going?"

"I am on my way to Granada, sir," the gentleman replied, "my home town."

"And a very fine town it is, too!" Don Quixote replied. "But please be so kind as to tell me your name; because I think it is going to be of more interest to me to know it than I can well explain."

"My name is Don Álvaro Tarfe," the guest said.

To which Don Quixote replied:

"I do believe you must be the very same Don Álvaro Tarfe who appears in the second part of the *History of Don Quixote de la Mancha,* recently printed and published by a novice author."

"Indeed I am," the gentleman replied, "and that man Don Quixote, the protagonist of the history, was a very close friend of mine, and I was the one who took him

---

1. In Barcelona, Don Quixote experiences humiliating defeat at the hands of the Knight of the White Moon, who is really the graduate Sansón Carrasco in disguise. Carrasco exacts from him the promise that for one year hence, he will remain in his village. The dejected Quixote starts toward La Mancha, and in Chapter 71 Sancho approaches the end of his "penance," adminstering in the dark such a severe flogging to a nearby tree that Don Quixote, unaware of the trick, fears for his squire's life.

away from home, or at least I persuaded him to travel to Saragossa to take part in jousts held there, where I was going; and the truth of the matter is that I did him many favours and prevented the executioner from tickling his ribs for his recklessness."

"And please tell me, Señor Don Álvaro, am I at all like that Don Quixote to whom you refer?"

"No, certainly not," the guest replied, "not in the slightest."

"And did that Don Quixote," said our one, "have with him a squire called Sancho Panza?"

"Yes, he did," Don Álvaro replied, "and although he had the reputation of being a comical fellow, not one of his attempts to be funny that I heard ever succeeded."

"I can believe that all right," Sancho butted in, "because not everybody's good at being funny, and that Sancho you're talking about, my good sir, must be some great scoundrel, as much a crook as he's unfunny; I'm the real Sancho Panza, and I'm so funny it's as if fun had rained down on me from heaven, and if you don't believe me just give me a try, and follow me around for a year or so, and you'll see how the fun gushes out of me at every turn, so much of it and such high quality that even though most of the time I don't know what I'm saying I make everyone listening to me laugh. And the real Don Quixote de la Mancha, the famous one, the brave and wise one, the lover, the righter of wrongs, the guardian of minors and orphans, the protector of widows and the slaughterer of maidens, the one whose only lady is the peerless Dulcinea del Toboso, is this gentleman here present, who's my master. All other Don Quixotes and all other Sancho Panzas besides us two are so much jiggery-pokery, figures from dreamland."

"And I believe you too, by God!" Don Álvaro Tarfe replied. "Because you've said more funny things, my friend, in the half-a-dozen words you've just spoken than the other Sancho Panza managed in all the words I heard from him. He was better at gorging himself than at talking, and was more foolish than funny, and I consider it a certain fact that the enchanters who pursue Don Quixote the Good have been chasing after me with Don Quixote the Bad. But I don't know what to say—I'd go as far as to swear that I left him in the Toledo madhouse awaiting treatment, and now another Don Quixote pops up here, quite different from mine."

"I do not know," said Don Quixote, "whether I am good, but I do know that I am not the bad Quixote, as proof of which I should like you to know, Don Álvaro Tarfe sir, that I have never in my life set foot in Saragossa; on the contrary, having been told that the fantasy Don Quixote had taken part in the jousts in that city, I refused to go there, to prove to all the world that he is a fraud; and so I went straight on to Barcelona, the storehouse of courtesy, the refuge of strangers, the hospital of the poor, the homeland of the brave, the avenger of the affronted and the appreciative returner of firm friendship, unique in its setting and its beauty. And although what happened to me there was not very pleasant, indeed was most disagreeable, I can bear it all without heaviness of heart, just for the sake of having seen Barcelona. In short, Don Álvaro Tarfe sir, I am the Don Quixote de la Mancha of whom fame speaks—not that wretch who sought to usurp my name and exalt himself with my thoughts. I entreat you, sir, as you are a gentleman, to be so kind as to make a formal declaration before the mayor of this village to the effect that you have never in all the days of your life seen me until now, and that I am not the Don Quixote who appears in the second part, nor is this squire of mine Sancho Panza the man whom you knew."

"I shall be delighted to do so," Don Álvaro replied, "even though it amazes me to see two Don Quixotes and two Sancho Panzas at the same time, as identical in name as they are antithetical in action; and I repeat and confirm that I have not seen what I have seen and that what has happened to me has not happened."

"I'm sure," said Sancho, "that you must be under a spell too, like my lady Dulcinea, and would to God I could get rid of it for you by giving myself another three thousand odd lashes like the ones I'm giving myself for her—and I'd do it without expecting anything for it, either."

"I don't understand this talk of lashes," said Don Álvaro.

And Sancho replied that it was a long story, but he'd tell it if they happened to be going the same way. By now it was time for lunch; Don Quixote and Don Álvaro ate together. The village mayor happened to walk into the inn with a notary, and to the said mayor Don Quixote presented a petition to the effect that it was his wish and right that Don Álvaro Tarfe, the gentleman who was there present, should depose before His Worship that the said deponent did not know Don Quixote de la Mancha, who was also there present, and that the said Don Quixote was not the man who appeared in print in a history entitled *The Second Part of Don Quixote de la Mancha* written by one Avellaneda, from Tordesillas. And the mayor took all the appropriate steps: the deposition was drawn up with all the legal requisites, as is proper in such cases, which delighted Don Quixote and Sancho, as if such a deposition were vital to their welfare, and as if their deeds and their words didn't clearly show the difference between the two Don Quixotes and between the two Sanchos. Many courtesies and offers were exchanged between Don Álvaro and Don Quixote, in the course of which the great man of La Mancha displayed such good sense that he disabused Don Álvaro of his error; and Don Álvaro reached the conclusion that he must indeed have been enchanted, since he'd seen with his own eyes two such contrasting Don Quixotes.

Evening came, they left the village and after a couple of miles the road forked, one way leading to Don Quixote's village and the other to where Don Álvaro was going. In this short interval Don Quixote told him about his calamitous defeat, and about Dulcinea's enchantment and disenchantment, all of which filled Don Álvaro with fresh amazement; and then he embraced Don Quixote and Sancho and went on his way, as did Don Quixote, who spent that night among some more trees, to give Sancho the opportunity to complete his penance, which he did as he had on the previous night, at the expense of the bark of the beeches rather than the skin of his back, of which he took such good care that the lashes wouldn't have brushed a fly off it if there had been one there. The deluded Don Quixote didn't fail to count a single stroke, and found that together with the previous night's score the total was three thousand and twenty-nine. It seems that the sun rose early to witness the sacrifice, and by its light the pair continued on their way, discussing Don Álvaro's delusion and what a good idea it had been to have him make his deposition before the proper authorities in such a correct and formal manner. That day and that night they pressed on, and nothing worth mentioning happened to them, except that during the night Sancho completed his task, to Don Quixote's unutterable joy, and he waited eagerly for daylight, to see if he could find his lady Dulcinea along the way, disenchanted; and as he rode there was not a woman whom he did not approach to examine her and discover whether she was Dulcinea del Toboso, because he was absolutely certain that Merlin's promises could not be false. Full of these thoughts and expectations they climbed a hill, from the top of which they could see their village, and Sancho fell to his knees, exclaiming:

"Open your eyes, my longed-for village, and see your son Sancho Panza returning, not very rich but very well lashed. Open your arms, too, to welcome your son Don Quixote, who has been conquered by another's arm but comes here as the conqueror of himself; and that, he's told me, is the best conquering you can wish for. I've got some money with me, because if I've been given a good lashing I've had a ride on a good horse, as the thief said to the executioner."

"Stop all that nonsense," said Don Quixote, "and let's put our best feet forward as we make our entry into the village, where we'll give free play to our imaginations and settle our plans for the pastoral life that we're going to lead."

And with this they went down the hill towards their village.

Chapter 73

ABOUT THE OMENS THAT DON QUIXOTE ENCOUNTERED AS HE ENTERED HIS VILLAGE,
TOGETHER WITH OTHER EVENTS THAT ADORN AND AUTHENTICATE THIS GREAT HISTORY

As they approached it, according to Cide Hamete Benengeli, Don Quixote saw two boys squabbling on the threshing floor, and one said to the other:

"Don't keep on, Periquillo—that's something that's never ever going to happen."

Don Quixote overheard him, and said to Sancho:

"Didn't you hear, friend Sancho, what that boy said—'that's something that's never ever going to happen'?"

"And who cares," said Sancho, "what the boy said?"

"Who cares?" replied Don Quixote. "Can't you see that if you apply these words to my hopes, they mean that I'll never see Dulcinea again?"

Sancho was about to reply when he was stopped by the sight of a hare dashing across the fields, chased by many greyhounds and huntsmen, and in its terror it sought shelter and squatted between the dun's feet. Sancho picked it up and presented it to Don Quixote, who was saying:

"*Malum signum! Malum signum!*[1] Hare flees, greyhounds chase: Dulcinea appears not!"

"You're a strange one," said Sancho. "Let's suppose that this here hare is Dulcinea del Toboso and those there greyhounds chasing it are the knavish enchanters that turned her into a peasant girl—she runs away, I grab her and put her into your charge, and now she's in your arms and you're caring for her, so how can that be a bad sign, and what bad omen can you see in that?"

The two squabbling boys came to look at the hare, and Sancho asked one of them why they'd been quarrelling. The answer came from the one who'd said "that's something that's never ever going to happen"—he had taken a cricket cage from the other boy and was never ever going to give it back to him. Sancho took four quarter-reals out of his waist-pouch and gave them to the boy for the cage, which he placed in Don Quixote's hands, saying:

"Here you are, sir—your omens foiled and come to nought, and I might be a fool but to my mind they haven't got any more to do with our affairs than last year's clouds. And if I'm not much mistaken, I've heard the village priest saying that sensible Christian persons shouldn't pay any attention to such nonsense, and you yourself told me the same thing a few days back, and showed me that all Christians who heeded omens were idiots. But there's no need for me to keep on about it—let's go into the village."

The huntsmen came up and asked for their hare, and Don Quixote gave it back to them; the pair continued, and in a meadow on the outskirts of the village they found

---

1. "A bad sign, a bad sign!", often uttered by doctors. Hares were bad omens.

the priest and the graduate Carrasco at their devotions. It should be mentioned that Sancho Panza had draped over his dun and the bundle of armour, as a kind of sumpter-cloth, the buckram robe with flames painted all over it that he'd been made to wear in the Duke's castle on the night Altisidora came back to life.[2] And he'd also put the inquisitional cardboard cone on the donkey's head, the most original transformation and adornment ever effected on any ass in the world.[3] The pair were immediately recognized by the priest and the graduate, who ran over to them with open arms. Don Quixote dismounted and embraced them warmly, while the village boys—boys' lynx eyes see everything—spotted the donkey's headgear and came to stare at it, calling to each other:

"Come over here, lads, if you want to see an ass looking as spruce as a sparrow and an old hack as skinny as a skeleton—and then you can have a good giggle at the dun and Rocinante, too."

Finally, surrounded by boys and accompanied by the priest and the graduate, they entered the village and went to Don Quixote's house, and at the door they found the housekeeper and the niece, who'd already been told of his arrival. So too had Teresa Panza, Sancho's wife, who, dishevelled and half naked, clutching her daughter Sanchica by the hand, hurried out to meet her husband; and when she saw that he wasn't as smart as she thought a governor ought to be, she said:

"Why are you looking like that, husband? I'd say you've come here on foot and it hasn't done your feet much good either—you look more unruly, than a ruler."

"Shut up, Teresa," Sancho replied. "Often where there are hooks there isn't any bacon to hang on them, so let's go home, and then you'll hear marvels. I've brought some money back with me, and that's what counts, and I've earned it with my own wiles, without doing any harm to anybody."

"So long as you've brought some money back, good husband," Teresa said, "you can have earned it this way or that for all I care—however you've earned it you won't have started up any new customs in the world."

Sanchica hugged her father and asked him if he'd brought anything for her, she'd been longing to see him like rain in a drought; and with her hanging on to one side of his belt and pulling his dun along behind her, and his wife holding his hand, they made for their house, leaving Don Quixote in his, in the care of his niece and his housekeeper, and in the company of the priest and the graduate.

Without a moment's delay, Don Quixote took the graduate and the priest aside and gave them a brief account of his defeat and of the promise that he'd made not to leave the village for a year,[4] which he intended to keep to the letter, without breaking it in the slightest detail, as became a true knight errant, bound by all the discipline and order of knight-errantry—and he added that his intention was to become a shepherd for the year, and amuse himself in the solitude of the fields, where he could give free rein to his thoughts of love as he practised that virtuous pastoral way of life, and that he entreated them, if they didn't have too much to do and weren't prevented by more important matters, to consent to be his companions; he'd buy sheep enough to qualify

2. Reference to a recent episode (Chapter 69) in which, as part of yet another plan engineered by the Duke and Duchess, Altisidora had feigned to be in love with Don Quixote. In fact, the episode prompts Cide Hamete himself to say in Chapter 70 that he "considers that the perpetrators of the hoax were as mad as the victims, and that the Duke and Duchess, going to such lengths to make fun of two fools, were within a hairsbreadth of looking like fools themselves."
3. Those denounced by the Inquisition and forced to repent publicly had to wear tall white cones on their heads, along with a sign stating their sin.
4. The promise exacted of Don Quixote by the supposed Knight of the White Moon, Carrasco himself.

them as shepherds, and he could tell them that the most essential part of the business was already settled, because he'd provided them with names that would fit like gloves. The priest told him to say what they were. Don Quixote replied that he himself was going to be called the shepherd Quixotiz, the graduate the shepherd Carrascón, the priest the shepherd Curambro and Sancho Panza the shepherd Panzino.[5]

They were both astonished at Don Quixote's latest delusion; but to prevent him from wandering away from the village again on his chivalric exploits, and in the hope that during the year he might be cured, they consented to his new project, acclaimed his folly as sound sense and agreed to join him in his new way of life.

"And what's more," said Sansón Carrasco, "as everybody knows, I'm a famous poet and at every turn I'll write pastoral verse or courtly verse or whatever verse best suits my purpose, to keep us amused in the Godforsaken places where we're going a-wandering; and what's most essential, gentlemen, is for each of us to choose the name of the shepherdess he's going to honour in his verses, and for us not to leave a single tree, however hard the wood, where her name isn't carved, as is the habit and custom among shepherds in love."

"That is most fitting," Don Quixote replied, "even though I have no need to search for the name of a fictitious shepherdess, because I already have the peerless Dulcinea del Toboso, the glory of these riverbanks, the ornament of these meadows, the mainstay of beauty, the cream of all the graces, and, in short, one worthy to receive all praise, however hyperbolical it might appear to be."

"Quite right too," said the priest, "but the rest of us will look for nice obliging shepherdesses who'll be just what the doctor ordered."

To which Sansón Carrasco added:

"And if they haven't got appropriate names, we'll give them the names of the shepherdesses that come printed in all those books—the world's full of them: Phyllises, Amaryllises, Dianas, Fléridas, Galateas, Belisardas; and since they're sold in the market squares, we've got every right to buy them and keep them for ourselves. If my lady or, more accurately, my shepherdess happens to be called Ana, I'll sing her praises under the name of Anarda; if she's Francisca, I'll call her Francenia; if she's Lucía, Lucinda; and so on and so forth. And if Sancho Panza is going to join the club, he can sing his wife's praises with the name Teresaina."

Don Quixote laughed at the invention of the name, and the priest lauded his virtuous and honourable decision, and again offered to accompany them for as long as he could spare from his unavoidable duties. With this they took their leave and advised and begged him to take care of his health, and to indulge in everything that was good for him. As fate would have it, his niece and housekeeper overheard the conversation between the three men, and as soon as Don Quixote was alone they walked in, and the niece said:

"What's all this, uncle? Just when we were thinking you'd come back home to stay, and to live a quiet and honourable life here, you want to go off into yet more labyrinths, turning yourself into a

> Little Shepherd, coming, coming,
> Little Shepherd, going, going?[6]

Well, the plain fact is the straw's a bit old for making whistles."

---

5. All diminutives, reflective of shepherds' lowly status.   6. From a Christmas carol.

To which the housekeeper added:

"And are you going to be able to put up with the heat of the summer afternoons, the damp of the winter nights, the howling of the wolves, out there in the country? Of course not—that's a job for strong men, brought up and hardened to it pretty well since they were babes in arms. And of the two evils it's better to be a knight errant than a shepherd. Look, sir, take my advice, which I'm not giving you on a belly full of bread and wine but on an empty stomach and fifty years of experience—stay at home, look after your property, go often to confession, give alms to the poor, and on my conscience be it if I'm wrong."

"Hush, my daughters," Don Quixote replied, "I know what's good for me. Take me to my bed now, because I don't feel very well, and rest assured that, whether an actual knight errant or a would-be shepherd, I shall never fail to provide for your needs, as you will see for yourselves."

And his good daughters (as the housekeeper and the niece surely were) took him to his bed, where they gave him some food and lavished all possible attentions on him.

Chapter 74

CONCERNING HOW DON QUIXOTE FELL ILL, THE WILL THAT HE MADE, AND HIS DEATH

Since what is human is not eternal, but is in continuous decline from its beginnings to its conclusion, this being particularly true of men's lives, and since Don Quixote's life had not been granted any special privilege by heaven to halt the course of its decline, it reached its end when he was least expecting it to; because, either out of the depression brought on by his defeat or by divine ordination, he was seized by a fever that kept him in bed for six days, during which time he was often visited by his friends the priest, the graduate and the barber, while his good squire Sancho Panza never left his bedside. In the belief that dejection at his defeat and the disappointment of his hopes for Dulcinea's deliverance and disenchantment had brought him to this state, they tried in every way they knew to raise his spirits; and the graduate told him to cheer up and get out of bed to make a start on the pastoral life, for which he'd already written an eclogue that would be bad news for all the eclogues Sannazaro had ever produced[1]—and with his own money he'd bought two splendid dogs to keep watch over the flock, one of them called Barcino and the other Butrón, which a herdsman from Quintanar had sold him. But none of this roused Don Quixote from his melancholy.

His friends called in the doctor, who felt his pulse and wasn't happy with what he found, and said that to be on the safe side he should look to the well-being of his soul, because the well-being of his body was in some danger. Don Quixote listened with great composure, but not so his housekeeper, his niece and his squire, who started to weep tender tears as if he were already lying dead before them. The doctor's opinion was that depression and despondency were killing him. Don Quixote asked to be left alone, because he needed a little sleep. They did as he asked, and he slept for more than six hours at a stretch, as the saying goes: indeed he slept for so long that the housekeeper and the niece thought that he was going to die in his sleep. But he did eventually awake, and he bellowed:

---

1. The Neapolitan Jacopo Sannazaro wrote *Arcadia*, the first pastoral romance; published in 1504, it juxtaposes verse eclogues with a prose sequence that tells the story of a desperate lover's attempts to escape his sorrow and live among the shepherds. It inspired more than a century's worth of pastoral literature.

"Blessed be Almighty God, who has done me such good! Indeed his mercy knows no bounds, and the sins of men do not lessen or obstruct it."

The niece paid careful attention to her uncle's words, and they seemed more rational than usual, during his recent illness at least, and she asked him:

"What are you saying, sir? Has something happened? What's this mercy you're on about, and these sins of men?"

"The mercy, niece," Don Quixote replied, "is that which God has this instant shown me, unobstructed, as I said, by my sins. My mind has been restored to me, and it is now clear and free, without those gloomy shadows of ignorance cast over me by my wretched, obsessive reading of those detestable books of chivalry. Now I can recognize their absurdity and their deceitfulness, and my only regret is that this discovery has come so late that it leaves me no time to make amends by reading other books that might be a light for my soul. It is my belief, niece, that I am at death's door; I should like to make myself ready to die in such a way as to indicate that my life has not been so very wicked as to leave me with a reputation as a madman; for even though this is exactly what I have been, I'd rather not confirm this truth in the way in which I die. Call my good friends, my dear: the priest, the graduate Sansón Carrasco, and Master Nicolás the barber, because I want to confess my sins and make my will."

But she was saved her trouble by the entrance of all three. As soon as Don Quixote saw them he said:

"You must congratulate me, my good sirs, because I am no longer Don Quixote de la Mancha but Alonso Quixano, for whom my way of life earned me the nickname of 'the Good.' I am now the enemy of Amadis of Gaul and the whole infinite horde of his descendants; now all those profane histories of knight-errantry are odious to me; now I acknowledge my folly and the peril in which I was placed by reading them; now, by God's mercy, having at long last learned my lesson, I abominate them all."

When the three heard all this they were certain that he was in the grips of some new madness. And Sansón said:

"Now that we've had news, Don Quixote sir, that the lady Dulcinea has been disenchanted, you come out with all that? Now that we're on the point of becoming shepherds, to spend all our time singing and living like lords, you want to turn yourself into a hermit? Stop it for goodness sake, and come to your senses, and forget all that idle nonsense."

"The nonsense in which I have been involved so far," Don Quixote replied, "has been real enough as regards the harm it has done me, but my death will, with heaven's help, turn it to my benefit. Gentlemen: I can feel that I am dying, and dying quickly; please leave jests aside and bring me a confessor to confess me and a notary to write down my will, because at times like this a man must not trifle with his soul. And so I implore you to send someone for the notary while the priest confesses me."

They looked at each other, amazed at Don Quixote's words, and although they didn't know what to think they ended up by believing him; and one of the signs that led them to conclude that he really was dying was the ease with which he had turned from a madman into a sane man; for to what he had already said he added some more that was so well expressed, so Christian and so coherent that it removed all doubt from their minds and convinced them that he was indeed sane.

The priest ordered everybody out of the room and was left alone with him, and confessed him.

The graduate went to fetch the notary and returned a little later with him and with Sancho Panza, who had been told by the graduate about the state his master was in and who, finding the housekeeper and the niece in tears, began to pucker his lips and shed some of his own. The confession ended and the priest emerged, saying:

"Alonso Quixano the Good really is dying, and he really is sane; we'd better go back in so that he can make his will."

This news was a terrible stimulus for the housekeeper's, the niece's and the good squire Sancho Panza's swollen eyes, so much so that it made the tears burst from them, and a thousand deep sighs burst from their breasts; because the truth is, as has been said before, that while Don Quixote was plain Alonso Quixano the Good—and while he was Don Quixote, too—he was always of gentle disposition and affable behaviour, and well loved not only by his own household but by everybody who knew him. The notary went in with the others and once he had drawn up the heading and Don Quixote had disposed of his soul with all the necessary Christian formalities, they reached the part concerning the disposal of property, and he said:

"Likewise it is my will that with respect to certain monies in the possession of Sancho Panza, whom in my madness I made my squire, inasmuch as between the two of us there has been a certain amount of haggling, of give and take, he should not be held accountable for them, nor should any claim be made against him but that, if anything remains after he has paid himself what I owe him, it should all be his, although there will be little enough of it, and much good may it do him; and if, just as when I was mad I helped to procure for him the governorship of an island, I could now that I am sane make him the ruler of a kingdom, I would do it, because the straightforwardness of his character and the fidelity of his conduct deserve it."

And turning his face towards Sancho, he said:

"Forgive me, my friend, for making you seem mad, like me, and for making you fall into my own error of believing that knights errant ever have existed or do exist."

"Oh no, don't die, master!" Sancho replied, crying. "Take my advice and live for a long long time, because the maddest thing a man can do in this life is to let himself die, just like that, without anybody killing him or any other hands except the hands of depression doing away with him. Come on, don't be lazy, get out of that bed of yours, and let's go off into the countryside dressed up as shepherds as we said we would—and perhaps behind some bush or other we'll find the lady Dulcinea, disenchanted and looking as pretty as a picture. If you're dying from sadness because you were defeated, you just blame me and say you were knocked down because I didn't girth Rocinante properly—and what's more you must have read in your books of chivalry that it's an everyday event for knights to knock each other down, and for the one who's defeated today to be the victor tomorrow."

"Very true," said Sansón, "and the worthy Sancho Panza has hit the nail right on the head."

"Not so fast, gentlemen," said Don Quixote: "you won't find this year's birds in last year's nests. I was mad, and now I am sane: I was Don Quixote de la Mancha and now, as I said, I am Alonso Quixano the Good. May my repentance and my sincerity restore me in your eyes to the esteem in which I used to be held, and let the notary continue taking down my will:

"Likewise I bequeath all my estate in its entirety to my niece Antonia Quixana, here present, once what is needed for my other bequests has been deducted from the most readily disposable part of it; and it is my will that the first of these shall be the payment of the wages that I owe my housekeeper for all the time that she has been serving me, and in addition twenty ducats for a dress. I appoint the priest and the graduate Sansón Carrasco, here present, to be my executors.

"Likewise it is my will that if my niece Antonia Quixana should wish to marry, it must be to a man about whom it has first been formally established that he does not so much as know what books of chivalry are; and if it is discovered that he does, and, despite that, my niece still insists on marrying him, and she does so, she is to forfeit everything that I have left her, and my executors can distribute it in pious works as they see fit.

"Likewise I request the aforementioned gentlemen, my executors, if they are fortunate enough to meet the author who is said to have written a history that is circulating under the title of *The Second Part of the Exploits of Don Quixote de la Mancha,* to beg him on my behalf, as earnestly as they can, to forgive me for unintentionally having provided him with the opportunity to write all the gross absurdities contained in that book; because I am leaving this life with scruples of conscience for having given him an excuse for writing them."

Here he ended his testament, and was overcome by a fainting fit that prostrated him on his bed. The company was thrown into alarm and hurried to help him, and during the three days that he lived after making his will he fainted frequently. The whole house was in turmoil; but still the niece ate, the housekeeper toasted and Sancho Panza enjoyed himself; because inheriting always does something to dispel or temper in the heir the thoughts of the grief that the dead man will, of course, leave behind him.

Eventually Don Quixote's last day on earth arrived, after he had received all the sacraments and had expressed, in many powerful words, his loathing of books of chivalry. The notary was present, and he said that he'd never read in any book of chivalry of any knight errant dying in his bed in such a calm and Christian manner as Don Quixote, who, amidst the tears and lamentations of everybody present, gave up the ghost; by which I mean to say he died.

At which the priest asked the notary to write out a certificate to the effect that Alonso Quixano the Good, commonly known as Don Quixote de la Mancha, had passed on from this life, and died from natural causes. And he said that he was requesting this certificate to deprive any author other than Cide Hamete Benengeli of the opportunity to bring him falsely back to life and write endless histories of his exploits.

This was the end of the Ingenious Hidalgo of La Mancha, the name of whose village Cide Hamete couldn't quite recall, so that all the towns and villages of La Mancha could fight among themselves for the right to adopt him and make him their own son, just as the seven cities of Greece contended for Homer.[2] The lamentations of Sancho, the niece and the housekeeper are omitted from this account, as are the fresh epitaphs that were placed upon his tomb, although Sansón Carrasco did have this one put there.

> This is a doughty knight's repose;
> So high his matchless courage rose
> That, as it's plain enough to see,
> He granted death no victory,
> Not even when in death's last throes.
> This world he didn't ever prize:
> He was a scarecrow in its eyes,
> And yet he was its bugbear, too.
> He had the luck, with much ado,
> To live a madman, yet die wise.

2. The birthplace of the poet called Homer is unknown.

And the sage Cide Hamete said to his pen:

"Here you shall rest, hanging from this rack on this length of brass wire, O quill of mine—whether well trimmed or not I do not know—and here you shall live on for many centuries, unless presumptuous and knavish historians take you down to profane you. But before they touch you, you can warn them and tell them as best you can:

> 'Hands off, hands off, you paltry knaves;
> My noble king, let none
> Attempt this enterprise: you know
> It's kept for me alone.'[3]

For me alone was Don Quixote born, and I for him; it was for him to act, for me to write; we two are as one, in spite of that false writer from Tordesillas who has had and may even again have the effrontery to write with a coarse and clumsy ostrich quill about my valiant knight's deeds, because this is not a burden for his shoulders or a subject for his torpid wit. And you can warn him, if you do happen to meet him, to leave Don Quixote's weary mouldering bones at rest in his tomb, and not to try to take him, in the face of all the prerogatives of death, to Old Castile,[4] making him rise from the grave where he really and truly does lie stretched out at full length, quite incapable of any third sally or fresh campaign; because to make fun of all those campaigns waged by so very many knights errant his two are quite sufficient, such has been the approval and delight of all those who have known of them, both in Spain and in foreign realms. And so you will have carried out your Christian mission, giving good advice to one who wishes you ill, and I shall feel proud and satisfied to have been the first author to enjoy the full fruit of his writings, as I desired, because my only desire has been to make men hate those false, absurd histories in books of chivalry, which thanks to the exploits of my real Don Quixote are even now tottering, and without any doubt will soon tumble to the ground. Farewell."

⤲

RESONANCE

Jorge Luis Borges: Pierre Menard, Author of the "Quixote"[1]

The visible *œuvre*[2] left by this novelist can be easily and briefly enumerated; unpardonable, therefore, are the omissions and additions perpetrated by Mme. Henri Bachelier in a deceitful catalog that a certain newspaper, whose Protestant leanings

---

3. Lines from a popular ballad about the siege of Granada, the last part of the Moorish kingdom to fall into Christian hands (in 1492).

4. A northern region of central Spain, formerly part of the Kingdom of Castile. This may be an ironic gesture on Cervantes' part; almost all of *Don Quixote* takes place in what was once Castile, and almost all of the characters except for the meddling Duke and Duchess are from Castile.

1. Translated by Andrew Hurley. The great Argentinian writer Jorge Luis Borges (1899–1986) was one of many 20th-century writers who saw Cervantes' masterpiece as foreshadowing their own playful confrontations of fiction

and reality. A poet, essayist, and short story writer, Borges wrote "Pierre Menard" while supporting himself in the late thirties as a library administrator. Afflicted by worsening eyesight, which would lead to blindness by the mid-1950s, Borges increasingly focused on writing short, enigmatic fictions, often describing imaginary books and worlds. (See Volume F for more on Borges and a full selection of his work.) The pedantic narrator in this story describes the works of an (imaginary) writer, Pierre Menard, then details Menard's remarkable effort to remake *Don Quixote* as his own book.

2. Body of published work.

are surely no secret, has been so inconsiderate as to inflict upon that newspaper's deplorable readers—few and Calvinist (if not Masonic and circumcised) though they be. Menard's true friends have greeted that catalog with alarm, and even with a degree of sadness. One might note that only yesterday were we gathered before his marmoreal place of rest, among the dreary cypresses, and already Error is attempting to tarnish his bright Memory. . . . Most decidedly, a brief rectification is imperative.

I am aware that it is easy enough to call my own scant authority into question. I hope, nonetheless, that I shall not be prohibited from mentioning two high testimonials. The baroness de Bacourt (at whose unforgettable *vendredis*[3] I had the honor to meet the mourned-for poet) has been so kind as to approve the lines that follow. Likewise, the countess de Bagnoregio, one of the rarest and most cultured spirits of the principality of Monaco (now of Pittsburgh, Pennsylvania, following her recent marriage to the international philanthropist Simon Kautzsch—a man, it grieves me to say, vilified and slandered by the victims of his disinterested operations), has sacrificed "to truth and to death" (as she herself has phrased it) the noble reserve that is the mark of her distinction, and in an open letter, published in the magazine *Luxe,* bestows upon me her blessing. Those commendations are sufficient, I should think.

I have said that the *visible* product of Menard's pen is easily enumerated. Having examined his personal files with the greatest care, I have established that his body of work consists of the following pieces:

a. a symbolist sonnet that appeared twice (with variants) in the review *La Conque* (in the numbers for March and October, 1899);

b. a monograph on the possibility of constructing a poetic vocabulary from concepts that are neither synonyms nor periphrastic locutions for the concepts that inform common speech, "but are, rather, ideal objects created by convention essentially for the needs of poetry" (Nîmes, 1901);

c. a monograph on "certain connections or affinities" between the philosophies of Descartes, Leibniz, and John Wilkins[4] (Nîmes, 1903);

d. a monograph on Leibniz' *Characteristica universalis* (Nîmes, 1904);

e. a technical article on the possibility of enriching the game of chess by eliminating one of the rook's pawns (Menard proposes, recommends, debates, and finally rejects this innovation);

f. a monograph on Ramon Lull's *Ars magna generalis* (Nîmes, 1906);

g. a translation, with introduction and notes, of Ruy López de Segura's *Libro de la invención liberal y arte del juego del axedrez*[5] (Paris, 1907);

h. drafts of a monograph on George Boole's symbolic logic;

i. a study of the essential metrical rules of French prose, illustrated with examples taken from Saint Simon (*Revue des langues romanes,* Montpellier, October 1909);

j. a reply to Luc Durtain (who had countered that no such rules existed), illustrated with examples taken from Luc Durtain (*Revue des langues romanes,* Montpellier, December 1909);

k. a manuscript translation of Quevedo's *Aguja de navegar cultos,*[6] titled *La boussole des précieux;*

---

3. Thursday afternoon gatherings.
4. A contemporary of the Enlightenment philosophers Descartes and Leibniz, bishop and scientist John Wilkins wrote a treatise called *The Discovery of a World in the*
Moon (1638).
5. "Book of the liberal invention and art of chess."
6. "Compass for getting around the cultivated."

l. a foreword to the catalog of an exhibit of lithographs by Carolus Hourcade (Nîmes, 1914);

m. a work entitled *Les problèmes d'un problème* (Paris, 1917), which discusses in chronological order the solutions to the famous problem of Achilles and the tortoise (two editions of this work have so far appeared; the second bears an epigraph consisting of Leibniz' advice "*Ne craignez point, monsieur, la tortue,*"[7] and brings up to date the chapters devoted to Russell and Descartes);

n. a dogged analysis of the "syntactical habits" of Toulet (*N.R.F.*, March 1921) (Menard, I recall, affirmed that censure and praise were sentimental operations that bore not the slightest resemblance to criticism);

o. a transposition into alexandrines of Paul Valéry's *Cimetière marin* (*N.R.F.*, January 1928);

p. a diatribe against Paul Valéry, in Jacques Reboul's *Feuilles pour la suppression de la realité*[8] (which diatribe, I might add parenthetically, states the exact reverse of Menard's true opinion of Valéry; Valéry understood this, and the two men's friendship was never imperiled);

q. a "definition" of the countess de Bagnoregio, in the "triumphant volume" (the phrase is that of another contributor, Gabriele d'Annunzio) published each year by that lady to rectify the inevitable biases of the popular press and to present "to the world and all of Italy" a true picture of her person, which was so exposed (by reason of her beauty and her bearing) to erroneous and/or hasty interpretations;

r. a cycle of admirable sonnets dedicated to the baroness de Bacourt (1934);

s. a handwritten list of lines of poetry that owe their excellence to punctuation.[9]

This is the full extent (save for a few vague sonnets of occasion destined for Mme. Henri Bachelier's hospitable, or greedy, *album des souvenirs*) of the *visible* lifework of Pierre Menard, in proper chronological order. I shall turn now to the other, the subterranean, the interminably heroic production—the *œuvre nonpareil,* the *œuvre* that must remain—for such are our human limitations!—unfinished. This work, perhaps the most significant writing of our time, consists of the ninth and thirty-eighth chapters of Part I of *Don Quixote* and a fragment of Chapter XXII. I know that such a claim is on the face of it absurd; justifying that "absurdity" shall be the primary object of this note.[1]

Two texts, of distinctly unequal value, inspired the undertaking. One was that philological fragment by Novalis—number 2005 in the Dresden edition, to be precise—which outlines the notion of *total identification* with a given author. The other was one of those parasitic books that set Christ on a boulevard, Hamlet on La Cannabière, or don Quixote on Wall Street. Like every man of taste, Menard abominated those pointless travesties, which, Menard would say, were good for nothing but occasioning a plebeian delight in anachronism or (worse yet) captivating us with the elementary notion that all times and places are the same, or are different. It might be

7. "Have no fear, sir, of the tortoise."
8. "Pages for the suppression of reality." The poet and theorist Paul Valéry (1871–1945) was a leader of the Symbolist school that wrote poetry meant to evoke the shifting moods of inner consciousness rather than objective, external reality.
9. Mme Henri Bachelier also lists a literal translation of Quevedo's literal translation of St. Francis de Sales's *Introduction à la vie dévote*. In Pierre Menard's library there is no trace of such a work. This must be an instance of one of our friend's droll jokes, misheard or misunderstood [narrator's note].
1. I did, I might say, have the secondary purpose of drawing a small sketch of the figure of Pierre Menard—but how dare I compete with the gilded pages I am told the baroness de Bacourt is even now preparing, or with the delicate sharp *crayon* of Carolus Hourcade? [narrator's note].

more interesting, he thought, though of contradictory and superficial execution, to attempt what Daudet had so famously suggested: conjoin in a single figure (Tartarin, say) both the Ingenious Gentleman don Quixote and his squire. . . .

Those who have insinuated that Menard devoted his life to writing a contemporary *Quixote* besmirch his illustrious memory. Pierre Menard did not want to compose *another* Quixote, which surely is easy enough—he wanted to compose *the* Quixote. Nor, surely, need one have to say that his goal was never a mechanical transcription of the original; he had no intention of *copying* it. His admirable ambition was to produce a number of pages which coincided—word for word and line for line—with those of Miguel de Cervantes.

"My purpose is merely astonishing," he wrote me on September 30, 1934, from Bayonne. "The final term of a theological or metaphysical proof—the world around us, or God, or chance, or universal Forms—is no more final, no more uncommon, than my revealed novel. The sole difference is that philosophers publish pleasant volumes containing the intermediate stages of their work, while I am resolved to suppress those stages of my own." And indeed there is not a single draft to bear witness to that years-long labor.

Initially, Menard's method was to be relatively simple: Learn Spanish, return to Catholicism, fight against the Moor or Turk, forget the history of Europe from 1602 to 1918—*be* Miguel de Cervantes. Pierre Menard weighed that course (I know he pretty thoroughly mastered seventeenth-century Castilian) but he discarded it as too easy. Too impossible, rather!, the reader will say. Quite so, but the undertaking was impossible from the outset, and of all the impossible ways of bringing it about, this was the least interesting. To be a popular novelist of the seventeenth century in the twentieth seemed to Menard to be a diminution. Being, somehow, Cervantes, and arriving thereby at the Quixote—that looked to Menard less challenging (and therefore less interesting) than continuing to be Pierre Menard and coming to the Quixote *through the experiences of Pierre Menard.* (It was that conviction, by the way, that obliged him to leave out the autobiographical foreword to Part II of the novel. Including the prologue would have meant creating another character—"Cervantes"—and also presenting Quixote through that character's eyes, not Pierre Menard's. Menard, of course, spurned that easy solution.) "The task I have undertaken is not *in essence* difficult," I read at another place in that letter. "If I could just be immortal, I could do it." Shall I confess that I often imagine that he did complete it, and that I read the Quixote—the *entire* Quixote—as if Menard had conceived it? A few nights ago, as I was leafing through Chapter XXVI (never attempted by Menard), I recognized our friend's style, could almost hear his voice in this marvelous phrase: "the nymphs of the rivers, the moist and grieving Echo." That wonderfully effective linking of one adjective of emotion with another of physical description brought to my mind a line from Shakespeare, which I recall we discussed one afternoon:

> Where a malignant and a turban'd Turk . . .

Why the Quixote? my reader may ask. That choice, made by a Spaniard, would not have been incomprehensible, but it no doubt is so when made by a *Symboliste* from Nîmes, a devotee essentially of Poe—who begat Baudelaire, who begat Mallarmé, who begat Valéry, who begat M. Edmond Teste.[2] The letter mentioned above throws some light on this point. "The *Quixote*," explains Menard,

2. Character in essays by Paul Valéry.

deeply interests me, but does not seem to me—*comment dirai-je?*[3]—inevitable. I cannot imagine the universe without Poe's ejaculation "Ah, bear in mind this garden was enchanted!" or the *Bateau ivre* or the *Ancient Mariner,* but I know myself able to imagine it without the *Quixote.* (I am speaking, of course, of my personal ability, not of the historical resonance of those works.) The *Quixote* is a contingent work; the *Quixote* is not necessary. I can premeditate committing it to writing, as it were—I can write it—without falling into a tautology.[4] At the age of twelve or thirteen I read it—perhaps read it cover to cover, I cannot recall. Since then, I have carefully reread certain chapters, those which, at least for the moment, I shall not attempt. I have also glanced at the interludes, the comedies, the *Galatea,* the Exemplary Novels, the no doubt laborious *Travails of Persiles and Sigismunda,* and the poetic *Voyage to Parnassus.* . . . My general recollection of the *Quixote,* simplified by forgetfulness and indifference, might well be the equivalent of the vague foreshadowing of a yet unwritten book. Given that image (which no one can in good conscience deny me), my problem is, without the shadow of a doubt, much more difficult than Cervantes'. My obliging predecessor did not spurn the collaboration of chance; his method of composition for the immortal book was a bit *à la diable,*[5] and he was often swept along by the inertiæ of the language and the imagination. I have assumed the mysterious obligation to reconstruct, word for word, the novel that for him was spontaneous. This game of solitaire I play is governed by two polar rules: the first allows me to try out formal or psychological variants; the second forces me to sacrifice them to the "original" text and to come, by irrefutable arguments, to those eradications. . . . In addition to these first two artificial constraints there is another, inherent to the project. Composing the *Quixote* in the early seventeenth century was a reasonable, necessary, perhaps even inevitable undertaking; in the early twentieth, it is virtually impossible. Not for nothing have three hundred years elapsed, freighted with the most complex events. Among those events, to mention but one, is the *Quixote* itself.

In spite of those three obstacles, Menard's fragmentary Quixote is more subtle than Cervantes'. Cervantes crudely juxtaposes the humble provincial reality of his country against the fantasies of the romance, while Menard chooses as his "reality" the land of Carmen during the century that saw the Battle of Lepanto and the plays of Lope de Vega. What burlesque brush-strokes of local color that choice would have inspired in a Maurice Barrès or a Rodríguez Larreta![6] Yet Menard, with perfect naturalness, avoids them. In his work, there are no gypsy goings-on or conquistadors or mystics or Philip IIs or *autos da fé.* He ignores, overlooks—or banishes—local color. That disdain posits a new meaning for the "historical novel." That disdain condemns *Salammbô,*[7] with no possibility of appeal.

No less amazement visits one when the chapters are considered in isolation. As an example, let us look at Part I, Chapter XXXVIII, "which treats of the curious discourse that Don Quixote made on the subject of arms and letters." It is a matter of common knowledge that in that chapter, don Quixote (like Quevedo[8] in the analogous, and later, passage in *La hora de todos*) comes down against letters and in favor of arms. Cervantes was an old soldier; from him, the verdict is understandable. But that *Pierre Menard*'s don Quixote—a contemporary of *La trahison des clercs* and Bertrand Russell[9]—should repeat those cloudy sophistries! Mme. Bachelier sees in them an ad-

3. "How should I put it?"
4. Needless repetition.
5. "Devil-may-care."
6. The French writer Maurice Barrès wrote colorful accounts of Spain; Enrique Rodriguez Larreta (1875–1961) wrote historical novels in archaic language.

7. A novel in rich poetic style set in ancient Carthage, by Gustave Flaubert (1862).
8. Francisco Gómez de Quevedo (1580–1645), Spanish satirist and poet.
9. British mathematician and rationalist philosopher (1872–1970).

mirable (typical) subordination of the author to the psychology of the hero; others (lacking all perspicacity) see them as a *transcription* of the Quixote; the baroness de Bacourt, as influenced by Nietzsche. To that third interpretation (which I consider irrefutable), I am not certain I dare to add a fourth, though it agrees very well with the almost divine modesty of Pierre Menard: his resigned or ironic habit of putting forth ideas that were the exact opposite of those he actually held. (We should recall that diatribe against Paul Valéry in the ephemeral Surrealist journal edited by Jacques Reboul.) The Cervantes text and the Menard text are verbally identical, but the second is almost infinitely richer. (More *ambiguous,* his detractors will say—but ambiguity is richness.)

It is a revelation to compare the *Don Quixote* of Pierre Menard with that of Miguel de Cervantes. Cervantes, for example, wrote the following (Part I, Chapter IX):

> . . . truth, whose mother is history, rival of time, depository of deeds, witness of the past, exemplar and adviser to the present, and the future's counselor.

This catalog of attributes, written in the seventeenth century, and written by the "ingenious layman" Miguel de Cervantes, is mere rhetorical praise of history. Menard, on the other hand, writes:

> . . . truth, whose mother is history, rival of time, depository of deeds, witness of the past, exemplar and adviser to the present, and the future's counselor.

History, the *mother* of truth!—the idea is staggering. Menard, a contemporary of William James,[1] defines history not as a *delving into* reality but as the very *fount* of reality. Historical truth, for Menard, is not "what happened"; it is what we *believe* happened. The final phrases—*exemplar and adviser to the present, and the future's counselor*—are brazenly pragmatic.

The contrast in styles is equally striking. The archaic style of Menard—who is, in addition, not a native speaker of the language in which he writes—is somewhat affected. Not so the style of his precursor, who employs the Spanish of his time with complete naturalness.

There is no intellectual exercise that is not ultimately pointless. A philosophical doctrine is, at first, a plausible description of the universe; the years go by, and it is a mere chapter—if not a paragraph or proper noun—in the history of philosophy. In literature, that "falling by the wayside," that loss of "relevance," is even better known. The Quixote, Menard remarked, was first and foremost a pleasant book; it is now an occasion for patriotic toasts, grammatical arrogance, obscene *de luxe* editions. Fame is a form—perhaps the worst form—of incomprehension.

Those nihilistic observations were not new; what was remarkable was the decision that Pierre Menard derived from them. He resolved to anticipate the vanity that awaits all the labors of mankind; he undertook a task of infinite complexity, a task futile from the outset. He dedicated his scruples and his nights "lit by midnight oil" to repeating in a foreign tongue a book that already existed. His drafts were endless; he stubbornly corrected, and he ripped up thousands of handwritten pages. He would allow no one to see them, and took care that they not survive him.[2] In vain have I attempted to reconstruct them.

1. American philosopher (1842–1910), a founder of Pragmatism, which assessed the truth of ideas by their practical results.
2. I recall his square-ruled notebooks, his black crossings-out, his peculiar typographical symbols, and his insect-like handwriting. In the evening, he liked to go out for walks on the outskirts of Nîmes; he would often carry along a notebook and make a cheery bonfire [narrator's note].

I have reflected that it is legitimate to see the "final" Quixote as a kind of palimpsest,[3] in which the traces—faint but not undecipherable—of our friend's "previous" text must shine through. Unfortunately, only a second Pierre Menard, reversing the labors of the first, would be able to exhume and revive those Troys. . . .

"Thinking, meditating, imagining," he also wrote me, "are not anomalous acts—they are the normal respiration of the intelligence. To glorify the occasional exercise of that function, to treasure beyond price ancient and foreign thoughts, to recall with incredulous awe what some *doctor universalis* thought, is to confess our own languor, or our own *barbarie*. Every man should be capable of all ideas, and I believe that in the future he shall be."

Menard has (perhaps unwittingly) enriched the slow and rudimentary art of reading by means of a new technique—the technique of deliberate anachronism and fallacious attribution. That technique, requiring infinite patience and concentration, encourages us to read the *Odyssey* as though it came after the *Æneid,* to read Mme. Henri Bachelier's *Le jardin du Centaure* as though it were written by Mme. Henri Bachelier. This technique fills the calmest books with adventure. Attributing the *Imitatio Christi* to Louis Ferdinand Céline or James Joyce[4]—is that not sufficient renovation of those faint spiritual admonitions?

⚬⚬

＋◄◊►＋

Lope Félix de Vega Carpio
1562–1635

Even more than Cervantes, Lope de Vega may be Spain's most beloved literary figure, although he has not achieved Cervantes' renown outside of Spain. Almost single-handedly, Cervantes crafted the modern novel and bequeathed it to a Europe that translated it at once. Lope wrote for his time and for Spain, fashioning a national theater that took Madrid and its entertainment-loving royalty by storm—despite protests by nervous clerics and occasional closings. When Lope died in 1635, thousands attended his funeral, and the decision of the government nine years later to censor his works, "which had caused such great harm to our customs," could not stop Spaniards from using the phrase *Es de Lope* ("It's Lopean") to refer to anything of excellence.

Nor, of course, could it stop them from reading his plays: more than 1,500, according to Lope himself, from a memoir he wrote toward the end of his life. Modern scholarship places the number around a more reliable 340, taking the twenty-five volumes of Lope's *Comedias,* published between 1604 and 1647, as a start. Still, Lope's extant output is more than ten times that of Shakespeare, without taking into consideration his extensive body of poetry and a first-rate autobiographical novel, *La Dorotea.* Lope was a figure utterly consumed by the task of writing, seeking not merely to become Madrid's most popular playwright, but to leave to posterity work of far less ephemeral stature: a pastoral poem, an epic, sacred verse, historical works that would assure him the position of Royal Historian (they didn't). But Lope's tremendous energies were not limited to literature, which in any case rarely paid well, and his modest origins—he was the son of an embroiderer—and large number of offspring demanded that he be ever attentive to

---

3. A reused manuscript, with one text written over an erased earlier one.

4. Céline and Joyce, experimental modernist writers; the *Imitatio Christi* (1426) was a treatise by the theologian Thomas à Kempis.

providing for himself and his family. During his long lifetime he served as soldier (surviving the disastrous 1588 Armada expedition against England), secretary, and priest. Nor did he let his professions, that of priest included, preclude amorous occasion. The early seventeenth century finds him in Toledo supporting two households: one for his second wife, daughter of a wealthy meat merchant, and another for the famous actress Micaela de Luján.

Micaela wasn't the first actress with whom Lope was involved. An earlier passion for Elena Osorio, whose father directed an acting troupe, seems to have introduced Lope to the world of the stage. While not exactly in its infancy, Spanish theater was still a fairly young institution; public theaters (*corrales*) opened in Madrid only in the 1580s, and most of Spain's theaters were run by religious groups called confraternities, which tended to be highly selective about the kinds of plays that could be performed and the times of the performances (only feast days and Sundays). Large structures that were built around open courtyards and lacked roofs, the early Spanish theaters were not the most hospitable places for aspiring playwrights, and crowds could be notoriously hostile and easily bored.

After his affair with Osorio soured, Lope associated with an innovative group of playwrights intent on raising the status of the theater and shaping the influential plays of Italy and Latin antiquity into a distinctively Spanish repertory. This apprenticeship in the early 1590s would help him discover the formulas to successful drama and spark a long season of theatrical activity in which Tirso de Molina, Pedro Calderón de la Barca, and others would eventually take part. Two decades later, in a measured diatribe against Madrid's conservative Royal Academy, Lope argued that the modern era should dispense with the need for classical genres and the ancient norms formulated by Aristotle, which the fussy Academy embraced. The crowds who now gathered breathlessly in Spain's *corrales* to see his plays should be the true arbiters of literary taste, and in very non-Aristotelian fashion, Lope advocated the mixed genre of tragicomedy, encouraged plots where women change costume frequently to disguise themselves as men, and suggested that three, rather than five, acts represented the perfect dramatic structure: "What can I do if I have written, including the one that I have finished this week, four hundred and eighty-three comedies? For all except six of them sin grievously against art. But after all, I defend what I have written and I know that though they might have been better in another manner, they would not have found the favor they have; for sometimes that which is contrary to correctness for that very reason pleases the taste."

To chart a trajectory of Lope's writing career is virtually impossible: not simply because of the sheer number of his works, whatever the final figure, but because of their scope. Lope's *comedias* run the gamut from saints' lives to *autos sacramentales* (one-act Eucharist plays), from revenge tragedies to social comedies and history plays about Columbus discovering the new world. Lope developed for the Spanish stage supple new rhyme schemes that were a far cry from the stilted octaves then in use, and he introduced into the theater the everyday language of the plazas and streets that he frequented. Popular ballads and proverbs fill his plays, and he has a keen sense of the random social exchanges that shape opinions and make or break individuals' reputations; as the peasant Laurencia says to the man who loves her in *Fuenteovejuna*, "the way you were looking at me down by the stream was enough to set the whole village gossiping—not that they aren't already." As Lope instructed the Academy, his was a "new art of writing comedies" for a Spanish public enjoying an era of imperial expansiveness, even as Spain was quickly losing the ability to maintain that empire.

The reign of Ferdinand and Isabella in the late 1400s had marked Spain's consolidation as a nation-state, and it provides the backdrop for *Fuenteovejuna* (the title refers to a village in southwestern Spain, and the word literally means "sheep's well"). Lope went to the chronicles for the story of the town's rebellion against its abusive feudal overlord in 1476. But he felt free to revise the historical record and suggest that the evil lord, Fernando Gómez de Guzmán, fought against Ferdinand's and Isabella's claims to Portugal, and so deserves punishment for more than one crime. Like characters from other Lope plays, Fernando is a nobleman who abuses his power and believes that as lord and Commander of the Order of Calatrava he has rights to any women in the lands over which he has jurisdiction. Such a theme is not unique to Lope. Tirso de Molina's *The Trickster of Seville* (and subsequently Mozart's *Don Giovanni*) features the infamous Don Juan, who interrupts a peasant's wedding to try and satiate his lust and demonstrate his power over his subjects. There was in fact a long-standing tradition, ended by King Ferdinand in 1486, that lords had "first rights" to newly wedded brides; and Lope's sources suggest that the town rebelled for strong economic reasons as well. But Lope limits Fernando's abusiveness in *Fuenteovejuna* to sexual matters, while inventing his defiance of the king and queen. The result is a new definition of honor, the elusive quality with which Spain was as obsessed in the fifteenth century as it was in the seventeenth. In *Fuenteovejuna* honor becomes the product of loyalty to one's monarchs and the defense of one's property and person rather than an accident of birth. This is a theme found in Lope's play *Peribañez,* in which a peasant kills the Commander of Ocaña who threatens to rape his wife, and is subsequently made a captain in King Henry III's army.

The portrait of peasants in *Fuenteovejuna* is not a homogeneous one, despite the collective slogan beneath which the townspeople will eventually take shelter after their heinous act: *Fuenteovejuna lo hizo* ("Fuenteovejuna did it"). For one thing, the masses aren't all virtuous, and some of the peasant women readily succumb to Fernando's charms. For another, there are strong personalities among the peasants: Esteban, the town's grave mayor; the lover Frondoso; the "bachelor" Leonelo, who has studied at the prestigious university of Salamanca; the plump and feisty Mengo: all resist the stereotyping common in other plays featuring (and often disparaging) rustics. Laurencia, the play's heroine, is the most forcefully drawn of Lope's characters. She resembles the Roman Lucretia, whose challenge to her kinsfolk precipitated the overthrow of Rome's tyrannical kings, a parallel that lends the story the weight of classical significance—as do echoes of Aristophanes' *Lysistrata.* Lope's treatment of his rustic actors also makes *Fuenteovejuna* and his other peasant plays very different from the more widespread pastorals with their lovesick shepherds and shepherdesses who are often little more than nobles in disguise. Lope's rustics are noble too, but their nobility consists in their forceful rebellion against feudalism's excesses. At the same time, it is a woman who incites them to violence, after calling the men "sheep" and thus true denizens of the village called "Sheep's well." Lope thus suggests that the peasants are generally reluctant to challenge the status quo and believe themselves worthy of behaving "honorably."

First performed around 1614, *Fuenteovejuna* has been adapted to more recent historical times, most notably in the 1930s, when a production by the poet and playwright García Lorca called attention to the ongoing exploitation of Spain's rural poor by wealthy landowners. Lope, however, seems to have been interested in primarily one thing when it came to his theater— pleasing the crowds who generally adored his action-packed, fast-moving plays. And yet as he laments in a late poem to a friend, Claudio, this finally was only a desperate means of survival: "I should have been lucky enough to have had a Maecenas [rich patron], but my luck was so bad that I had to write five large sheets every single day of my life in order to keep my head above water. . . . and in order not to offend my oppressor—the people—I could never write about anything that had genuine substance to it." Along with a number of other plays that have survived the test of almost four centuries, *Fuenteovejuna* may well prove Lope wrong about his own work.

PRONUNCIATIONS:

Frondoso: fron-DOH-soh

Fuenteovejuna: FWEN-tay-oh-vay-HOO-nah

Jacinta: ya-CHIN-tah

Lope Felix de Vega: LO-pay FAY-leex de VAY-gah

Ortuño: or-TUNE-yo

Pascuala: pass-KWAL-ah

Rodrigo Téllez Girón: ro-DREE-go TELL-eth hee-ROWN

Fuenteovejuna[1]

Characters

KING FERNANDO OF ARAGON

QUEEN ISABEL OF CASTILE

RODRIGO TÉLLEZ GIRÓN, MASTER *of the Order of Calatrava*

FERNANDO GÓMEZ DE GUZMÁN, *Chief* COMMANDER *of the Order*

DON MANRIQUE

A JUDGE

ORTUÑO
FLORES } *Servants to the* COMMANDER

ESTEBAN
ALONSO } *Joint mayors of* FUENTEOVEJUNA

LAURENCIA
PASCUALA } *Peasant girls*
JACINTA

JUAN ROJO
FRONDOSO
MENGO } *Peasants*
BARRILDO

LEONELO, *a Bachelor of Arts*

CIMBRANOS, *a soldier*

A BOY

ALDERMEN, PEASANTS, SOLDIERS, MUSICIANS

The action takes place in and around FUENTEOVEJUNA, *and in* ALMAGRO, MEDINA DEL CAMPO, CIUDAD REAL, TORO, *and* TORDESILLAS, *in 1476.*[2]

ACT 1

A room in the house of the Master of the Order of Calatrava[3] *in Almagro*

[*Enter the Commander and his servants, Flores and Ortuño.*]

COMMANDER: Does he know that I am here?

FLORES: He is informed, sir.

ORTUÑO: He grows a little more serious as his years increase. Time may make him a gentleman.

1. Translated by Jill Booty. Lope wrote almost all of his plays in verse; *Fuenteovejuna* is mostly written in octo-syllabics (eight-syllable lines) characterized by strong as-sonance, and generally obeying an *a-b-b-a* rhyme scheme. Booty describes her prose translation as "an ac-tion version," meant to convey the liveliness of Lope's language.

2. Medina del Campo, Tordesillas, and Toro are towns northwest of Madrid, near the Portuguese border; Ciudad Real and Almagra are south of Madrid. Fuenteovejuna is a village in southern Spain, not far from Córdoba and Seville.

3. A religious-military order founded in the 12th century to reconquer what had once been Christian portions of Spain from the Muslims. In exchange for their services, members of the Order of Calatrava and the other two principal orders in Castile (Alcántara and Santiago) re-ceived extensive holdings of land. The Master of the Or-der had authority over more than a million people and generally had anywhere up to 1,500 knights at his ser-vice. The Master of the Order of Calatrava in 1476 was the 20-year-old Rodrigo Téllez Girón (Lope lowers his age to 17, possibly to make him seem more receptive to the influence of others), while the "Comendador" Fer-nando Gómez de Guzmán is second in command.

COMMANDER: Indeed? And is he also informed that I am Fernando Gómez de Guzmán?

FLORES: He is only a boy, sir.

COMMANDER: Or if my name is nothing to him, is my title also nothing—Chief Commander of the Order?

ORTUÑO: The fault will lie with flattering counselors who have told him that he has no need of common courtesy, now that he is Master of the Order of Calatrava.

COMMANDER: He will earn little love if he continues so. Courtesy is the key to men's good will, discourtesy the surest way to enmity.

ORTUÑO: Indeed, if an arrogant man could see how he is hated, even by those who flatter him, he would rather die than continue in his insolence.

FLORES: Arrogance is the worst form of insult, and makes for bitter feeling. Discourtesy is folly between equals, and sheer tyranny from a superior. But do not take it ill, my lord. He is but a boy and has not yet learned how much he needs the love of those whom he commands.

COMMANDER: The sword of knighthood which he received when the cross of Calatrava first adorned his breast should have sufficed to teach him courtesy.

FLORES: You will soon discover if any has been speaking ill of you.

ORTUÑO: If you have any cause to doubt him, wait no longer, my lord.

COMMANDER: I wish to see what sort of youth he is.

[*Enter the Master of Calatrava, accompanied.*]

MASTER: Pardon me, I beg you, by my life, Fernando Gómez de Guzmán. Only now have I been told of your presence in the town.

COMMANDER: I had good cause to blame you, since faith in your love and knowledge of your virtuous upbringing had led me to expect a fairer welcome, our ranks being as they are: you the Master of Calatrava, I your Commander—and your servant.

MASTER: I was ignorant, Fernando, of your most welcome arrival, but now I bid you welcome with great joy.

COMMANDER: You do well to honor me, for on your behalf I have risked much, disputed much, before his Holiness the Pope was finally persuaded to overlook your age.[4]

MASTER: It is true. And by the holy signs we two bear upon our breasts, I swear I will repay you with respect and honor you as a father.

COMMANDER: I am content.

MASTER: What news of the war?

COMMANDER: Attend closely, my lord, and you will learn soon enough where your duty lies.

MASTER: Proceed, and I will hear you.

COMMANDER: Eight years ago, my lord, your noble father raised you to great estate, resigning into your young hands the Masterhood of our ancient Order. As a surety it was decreed by papal bull that your uncle, Don Juan Pacheco, Grand Master of Santiago, should act as your adviser, which decree was sworn to by kings and knights commander. Now that Don Juan Pacheco is dead, the responsibility is yours alone, and I have come to urge you to win fame and honor in this present

---

4. Pope Pius II had to be persuaded to allow Rodrigo to become Master of the Order in 1464, when he was only eight.

quarrel between Portugal and the united strength of Aragon and Castile.[5] You know well, Rodrigo, that since the death of Enrique IV your kindred have chosen to obey as vassals King Alfonso of Portugal, who, since his marriage to Juana, Enrique's daughter, lays rightful claim to her inheritance—the kingdom of Castile. Fernando, Aragon's great King, makes a similar claim through his wife, Isabel of Castile. But in the eyes of your noble kindred, his claim is not so clear as that of Alfonso, King of Portugal. Ties of blood, my lord, demand that you should aid Alfonso in this strife. And so I have come to counsel you to gather together the knights of Calatrava in Almagro, and to take by storm Ciudad Real, which stands astride the frontier of Andalusia and Castile and commands them both.[6] Little force will be needed, for there will only be a few knights and men from the surrounding villages to uphold the cause of Isabel and Fernando in Ciudad Real. Although you are only a child, Rodrigo, you would do well to surprise those who say that the cross you bear is too grave a weight for your weak shoulders. Consider the Counts of Urueña from whom you are descended and let the laurels they won urge you to equal fame. Remember the lords of Villena, and all the other noble captains, almost too numerous for the wings of fame to bear them. Draw that white blade, which you shall dye in battle as deep a crimson as the cross you wear. Rightful Master of the Cross of Calatrava, both must be the color of blood! And then, Rodrigo Téllez Girón, your youth and valor will truly crown the fame of your immortal ancestors.

MASTER: Fernando Gómez, know at once that in this I will uphold the cause of my family and Portugal, for I see that so to do is right. And if my first step should be to take Ciudad Real, then you shall see me strike its city walls like a bolt from heaven. Let not my people think, or those unknown to me, that because my uncle is dead, my young spirit died with him. I will draw my white sword and its brightness shall be bathed in blood till it is the color of this cross. Where is your lodging? Have you soldiers with you?

COMMANDER: Few, but those my faithful servants. If you will accept their services, my lord, they will fight like lions. In Fuenteovejuna there are only humble folk, not trained, though, for war, but skilled in labor in the fields.[7]

MASTER: And that is where you live?

COMMANDER: It is. I chose, from all my lands, a house to suit me in these changing times. Call to your aid every man you have, my lord, let not a vassal remain.

MASTER: This day you shall see me ride, Fernando, with my lance couched ready for action in the field.

The square in Fuenteovejuna

[*Enter Pascuala and Laurencia.*]

---

5. "This present quarrel" concerns the struggle of Portugal against the recent unification of the kingdoms of Aragon and Castile, brought about in 1469 by the marriage of Ferdinand (heir to the throne of Aragon) and Isabella (heir to the throne of Castile). Both would succeed to their respective thrones in 1479. The competing claims to the order's allegiance center on the destiny of Castile following the death of its king, Henry IV, in 1474: should it become part of Portugal, ruled by Alfonso, who had married Henry's daughter? Or should it belong to Aragon, whose future king had married Henry's half-sister, Isabella?

6. Ciudad Real was an important city, capital of the province of New Castile, and strategically located on the border with Castile.

7. Fuenteovejuna would have numbered fewer than a thousand inhabitants in the late 15th century.

LAURENCIA: I pray God he never comes back!

PASCUALA: And yet I thought you looked just a little disappointed when I told you the news that he was gone.

LAURENCIA: I hope Fuenteovejuna never sets eyes on him again.

PASCUALA: I have seen many girls just as proud, just as determined, as you, some even more so. But when it came to it—their hearts were as soft as butter.

LAURENCIA: I will no more budge than that holm oak.

PASCUALA: How can you be so sure? Nobody can safely say "I will never do a certain thing."

LAURENCIA: Well, I do say it. And I mean it, Pascuala. Though you and the whole world contradict me! Say I were to fall in love with Fernando Gómez de Guzmán, what good would it do me? Would he marry me?

PASCUALA: No.

LAURENCIA: Then there is your answer. I will have nothing to do with him. How many girls have I seen in this village put their trust in the Commander, only to find out how wrong and stupid they were!

PASCUALA: I think it will be a miracle if you escape.

LAURENCIA: He has been following me for a month already, and not a glimmer of hope have I given him. And neither shall I. That Flores, his pander, and that other scoundrel, Ortuño, showed me a jacket, a sash, and a bonnet, and they brought me such messages from their master, Fernando, that I must say that at the time they scared me. But whatever those court caterpillars say will not change my mind.

PASCUALA: Where did they talk to you?

LAURENCIA: Down by the stream, almost a week ago.

PASCUALA: I am afraid they will deceive you in the end, Laurencia.

LAURENCIA: What, me?

PASCUALA: Yes, you, Laurencia. Do you think I meant the priest?

LAURENCIA: The Commander may think I am just a spring chicken, but he will find me tough meat for his table. I do not want his so-called "love," Pascuala. I had rather have a sizzling rasher of bacon for breakfast, with a slice of my own baked bread, and a sly glass of wine from mother's jar. I would sooner watch a lump of veal bobbing about among the cabbage and bubbling its foamy midday music. Or arrange a tasty marriage between an onion and a slice of ham when I come home hungry. Or pass the time while supper cooks with a bunch of grapes from my own vineyard—may God keep the hail away! And when at last the supper is ready, it is a tasty fry of pork and peppers and spice all sizzling in olive oil. Then I go to bed content and say my prayers, and fall asleep when I reach "lead us not into temptation."[8] For all their wiles and tricks, their so-called love serves no other purpose than to get us to bed with pleasure, to wake in the morning with disgust.

PASCUALA: You are right, Laurencia. That is as long as their love lasts. They are no more grateful than the sparrows that flutter around your door in winter when all the fields are frozen, and twitter coaxingly "Sweety-heart, sweety-heart," and coyly accept the crumbs you give them. As soon as the cold weather is past and the flowers come out in the fields, and they see better food to be got elsewhere, they forget the "sweety-heart," and mock you from the roof with "Idiot, idiot!" Men are just the same. When they need us, we are their life, their being, their soul, their every-

---

8. A line from the end of the Lord's Prayer.

thing. But when their lust is spent, they behave worse than the sparrows and we are no longer "Sweety-hearts" or even "idiots," but drabs and whores!

LAURENCIA: You cannot trust one of them.

PASCUALA: Not one, Laurencia.

[*Enter Mengo, Barrildo, and Frondoso.*]

FRONDOSO: Barrildo! Why persist? You will not persuade him.

BARRILDO: Ah, but here I see a judge who will settle the matter fairly.

MENGO: Agreed. But before she makes her judgment you must both promise to honor the wagers that you made, should she decide the matter in my favor.

BARRILDO: Right. We agree. But if you lose, what will you give?

MENGO: I will give my fiddle. It is worth a lot of money, and I value it even higher than its worth.

BARRILDO: Very well, I am satisfied.

FRONDOSO: Come then, let us approach them. God keep you, lovely ladies.

LAURENCIA: Did you call us ladies, Frondoso?

FRONDOSO: I was merely following the fashion. Nowadays the bachelor of arts is called professor, the blind man is said to be myopic, or, if you squint, you have a slight cast in one eye. A man with a wooden leg is a trifle lame, and a careless spendthrift a good chap. An ignorant ass is said to be the silent type, a braggart is known as soldierly. A large mouth is called generous, and a beady eye, shrewd. The quibbler is said to be punctilious, and the gossip, a wit. A chatterbox is called intelligent, and a loud-mouthed bully, brave. The coward is a quiet sort, the pusher, eccentric. A bore is companionable, and a madman easygoing. The grumbler is grave, a bald head is a noble brow, foolishness passes for wit, and large feet are firm foundations. One with the pox has a slight chill, an arrogant man is reserved, a wangler has a quick brain, and a hunchback is the learned type. I might go on for ever, but I think I have said enough for you to see that I go no further than the fashion, when I address you as ladies.

LAURENCIA: That may be the courtesy used in the city, Frondoso, but I am more familiar with the sound of a less flattering vocabulary.

FRONDOSO: How does that go? Give us a sample of it.

LAURENCIA: It is quite the opposite of yours. For here a grave man is a bore, one who tells the truth is rude, a serious man, melancholy, and he who justly reprehends does so out of spite. Anyone who dares to give advice is a busy-body, and if you are generous, you are an interfering nuisance. If you are just, you are called cruel, if merciful, then you are weak. One who is constant is called boorish, the polite man is a flatterer, one who gives alms, a hypocrite, and a true Christian is only doing it in order to get on. Hard-won happiness is called luck, truth is wild speaking; patience, cowardice; misfortune, proof of evil-doing. A virtuous woman is a fool, and a beautiful one is a whore, however chaste she may be. And an honorable woman . . . But that is enough. I have answered you.

MENGO: You are the very devil.

LAURENCIA: There, what did I tell you!

MENGO: I'll bet when you were christened, the priest used something stronger than water.

LAURENCIA: I thought I heard you arguing. What was the dispute?

FRONDOSO: Oh, yes, Laurencia, hear it, please.

LAURENCIA: Tell me then.

FRONDOSO: I trust your understanding completely.

LAURENCIA: I hope I can repay your trust. What was the argument?

FRONDOSO: Barrildo and I were against Mengo.

LAURENCIA: And what does Mengo say?

BARRILDO: He denies a known fact, which is certain and undeniable.

MENGO: I deny it because I know I am right.

LAURENCIA: But what does he deny?

BARRILDO: That there is such a thing as love.

LAURENCIA: I should have said that we could not do without it.

BARRILDO: We could not do without it. Exactly. The world could not go on.

MENGO: I do not know how to philosophize. As for reading, I only wish I could. But if, as I hear, the elements live eternally by discord, and if our bodies receive from them all the sustenance by which they live: choler, melancholy, phlegm and blood, then there you are. That proves it.[9]

BARRILDO: The world both here and yonder is all harmony, Mengo, not discord. And harmony is pure love, for love is concord.

MENGO: I do not deny that there is such a thing as self-love. I know the value of that. It governs and balances all things we see, besides seeking to preserve them. I have never denied that. . . . It defends things as they are—the status quo. My hand will defend my face from the blow that comes toward it, or my feet will protect my body by running away from any danger that threatens it. My eyelids will close at once to guard my eyes. But that is only natural love—self-love.

PASCUALA: Then what is the argument?

MENGO: That no one has any love other than for his own person.

PASCUALA: Forgive me, Mengo, but you lie. Can you deny the power which makes a man love a woman, or an animal its mate?

MENGO: That is still only self-love, I say. What is this love you talk about?

LAURENCIA: It is a desire for what is beautiful.

MENGO: And what does it desire the beautiful for?

LAURENCIA: To enjoy it.

MENGO: There you are. Just as I thought: is not the enjoyment simply selfish?

LAURENCIA: It is.

MENGO: Then does not love seek the thing which will give it pleasure out of sheer self-interest?

LAURENCIA: That is true.

MENGO: That proves my argument. There is no love other than that which says: "I want a thing, and I want it for myself alone, to give me pleasure."

BARRILDO: I remember the priest once saying in a sermon something about a man called Plato. He was supposed to know all about love, and he only loved the soul and the virtue in things.[1]

PASCUALA: Now you are talking right above our heads. That is what the learned professors in schools and academies spend their hours boiling down and sorting out.

---

9. Mengo refers briefly to the theory of the humors, by which the body can only be healthy if the four humors listed here are in balance. The theory dates back to the ancient Greek physician Hippocrates.

1. Plato's *Symposium* explicates the philosopher's theory of true love. Plato's works were translated into Latin and vernacular languages in late 15th-century Europe, and enjoyed vigorous discussion in numerous academies in Spain, Italy, and elsewhere.

LAURENCIA: Pascuala is right. There is nothing for us in this debate but frayed nerves and ragged tempers, so stop arguing and give thanks to Heaven, Mengo, that it has made you free from love.

MENGO: Do you love, Laurencia?

LAURENCIA: Yes—my honor.

FRONDOSO: May your hard heart be punished with the pangs of jealousy.

BARRILDO: Who is the winner of our argument?

PASCUALA: You must take your problem elsewhere. Let the sacristan or the priest resolve it for you. Laurencia says she is not in love, and I have too little experience to tell either way. So how can we give a judgment?

FRONDOSO: Well. That has put us in our place.

[*Enter Flores.*]

FLORES: God be with you.

FRONDOSO: Here comes one of the Commander's servants.

LAURENCIA: His bird of prey. Where do you come from, my friend?

FLORES: From battle. Can you not see from my dress?

LAURENCIA: Has Don Fernando returned as well?

FLORES: The battle is over, though not without costing us both lives and blood.

FRONDOSO: What happened up there?

FLORES: Who can tell you better than I, whose eyes were witness to it all? To storm the city of Ciudad Real, our gallant Master of Calatrava, young Rodrigo, called to arms two thousand proud yeomen from among his vassals, besides three hundred mounted knights, both secular and clerical—for the red cross of Calatrava obliges all who bear it to respond to the call to arms, even though they be of holy orders[2]—but only to war against the impious Moors, you understand. The gallant youth rode out, a figure of dazzling elegance and pride. The green surcoat he wore was bordered with golden ciphers and at the elbow, where the sleeve parted, the silver bracelets of his armor shone, linked with frogs cunningly wrought in gold. A dapple-gray charger bore him, a noble creature, born and bred on the banks of the Guadalquivir,[3] that had drunk its clear waters and cropped its fertile pastures. Tooled leather strips bound his tail, his mane was adorned with bows of white ribbon which glittered in the sun like snowflakes, as if reflecting the brightness of those upon his dappled skin, where they seemed banked to greater depth in smooth, gleaming drifts on flank and shoulder. Your own Commander, Fernando Gómez, rode beside him, his mount a stallion the color of rich honey, shading to black, with a splash of brilliant white upon its nose. Over a coat of mail in the Turkish style he wore a brilliant breastplate and backplate, both edged with a bright orange border, trimmed with pearls set in gold. The helm, crowned with white plumes, seemed as a ripe orange that had spilled forth a spray of snowy blossoms. About his arm was a red and white garter couching a lance that seemed a whole ash tree, such that the fear of him might reach into Granada itself, and strike terror into every Moor that breathes there.[4] The city rose to arms as they approached the walls and their spokesman declared boldly that they would never

2. Even friars were allowed to fight for the order.
3. Important river in southern Spain that runs through Córdoba and Seville.

4. The Moors still occupied the province of Granada in southern Spain at the time of the play's historical setting; they would finally be overthrown in 1492.

desert the royal crown of Fernando and Isabel, and that they were ready to defend their city and their royal masters. Battle was joined, but at length, after mighty resistance, the Master forced his way in—as victor. He ordered all rebels and any who had dared to insult his honor to be beheaded, while those of vulgar blood were to be publicly whipped with gags in their mouths. Now he is so feared and so admired in Ciudad Real that all who witnessed the youth perform such deeds in fighting, winning, and chastising believe that when he grows to maturity he will be the scourge of the African race, and extinguish every blue crescent moon that shines before his scarlet cross. What is more, he showed such liberality to the Commander, and to all who aided him in this enterprise, that the sack of the city looked like the sack of his own fortune, such generous gifts did he give. But I hear music! They are coming! Receive them joyfully, for no victor's laurel is so welcome to the returning hero as the good will of those he left at home.

[*Enter the Commander, Ortuño, Musicians, Juan Rojo, Esteban, and Alonso.*]

MUSICIANS [*singing*]:

> *Welcome the Commander,*
> *Returned from conquering lands and killing men.*
> *Welcome the Commander!*
> *In him great Alexander lives again.*[5]
> *In Ciudad Real, he conquered and showed his might,*
> *But now he returns in peace, a gentle, courteous knight.*
> *He comes to Fuenteovejuna, his banners flying.*
> *Long live our brave Commander,*
> *May his fame be undying.*

COMMANDER: Fuenteovejuna, I give you thanks for the loving welcome you have given me.

ALONSO: Sir, we can only show the meanest tithe of what we feel, for however great our love and loyalty, yet you merit more.

ESTEBAN: Fuenteovejuna and its municipal councilors, whom you honor today, sir, with your presence, beg you to accept this small token of loyalty. We offer it to you not without some shame, sir, for these carts are loaded more with our good will than with rich gifts. First there are two baskets of our potters' best earthenware crocks, then in this cart a flock of geese, all sticking out their heads to praise your martial valor. Ten whole salted hogs, fine prime beasts every one, not to mention other various trifles, such as these sides of hung beef. But best among them, or so we think, are the hides of these ten hogs, which to us are of more worth than amber-scented gloves. One hundred pairs of capons and hens, which have left their widowed cocks in all the villages you can see around. We bring no arms or horses, or trappings adorned with gold—unless you consider the love of your vassals golden—but there is one further thing, which in truth seems to me worthy of mention: twelve skins of wine, such that if it should reinforce your men, they would hold a wall for you even in January weather and feel safer than with arms of steel, and think it better than armor. For wine, they say, makes swords flash brighter and more valiantly. I will not trouble you to tell of the cheeses and other trifles, but let

---

5. Alexander the Great of Macedon, known for his conquest of Egypt, Asia Minor, and Persia in the 4th century B.C.E.

these gifts speak to you in their own voices of the good will which your vassals have for you, and may they bring good cheer to you and to your household.

COMMANDER: I am most grateful to the people and councilors of Fuenteovejuna. May you go in peace.

ALONSO: And may you, sir, have good rest, knowing that you are most welcome back to us, and I would the cattail and the sedge around your threshold were laden with orient pearls, for so would they be if it lay within our power to grant you the impossible.

COMMANDER: I do believe you, good people. May God go with you.

ESTEBAN: Now singers! Give us the chorus once again!

MUSICIANS [*singing*]:

> *Welcome the Commander,*
> *Returned from conquering lands and killing men.*

[*The Peasants and Musicians go.*]

COMMANDER: You there! Stay!

LAURENCIA: Is he speaking to you, Pascuala?

PASCUALA: To me? Not likely. You know whom he means, as well as I do.

LAURENCIA: Do you address me, my lord?

COMMANDER: You, proud virgin, and the other girl: are you not my vassals?

PASCUALA: Yes, sir. Yours to command.

LAURENCIA: Within reason.

COMMANDER: Come, do not be afraid to pass my gates. You will not be alone, my men are there.

LAURENCIA: If the councilors go in—and one of them is my father—then we will enter. If not . . .

COMMANDER: Flores . . .

FLORES: Sir . . .

COMMANDER: You observe how they refuse to obey my will?

FLORES: Go in.

LAURENCIA: Let go of us.

FLORES: Go in.

PASCUALA: Just so that you may lock the door on us?

FLORES: Go in. He desires only to show you the spoils he has brought from the wars.

COMMANDER: When they enter, Flores, see that the gates are closed.

[*Exit the Commander.*]

LAURENCIA: Flores, let us go.

ORTUÑO: Are these presents, like all the other stuff?

PASCUALA: How dare you! Get out of our way. . . .

FLORES: Mind what you say! You are plucky little chicks. . . .

LAURENCIA: Has not your master received enough flesh for one day?

ORTUÑO: But yours is the kind he wants.

LAURENCIA: May it choke him.

[*The two girls break clear and run away.*]

FLORES: Now what are we to do? He will hardly be pleased to hear that they escaped. There will be trouble for us.

ORTUÑO: You must expect that when you enter a great man's service. If you wish to prosper, you have to learn to bear his displeasure with patience. If it irks you, then my advice is, leave his service quickly.

[*They go.*]

A room in the palace of Fernando and Isabel in Medina del Campo.

[*Enter the King, Queen, Don Manrique, and Courtiers.*]

ISABEL: My opinion, sir, is that we should proceed swiftly and diligently, for Alfonso is known to be preparing his army even now, and holds a strong position. If we do not act at once, it may be too late.

KING: We can rely on help from Navarre and from Aragon, and, given time, I hope to have the Castilian forces fully reorganized, so that together we may rout the Portuguese.

ISABEL: Indeed, concerted action is the key to this.

MANRIQUE: Sir, there are two aldermen from Ciudad Real without. They await your pleasure. Shall they be admitted?

KING: Let them come in.

FIRST ALDERMAN: Most Catholic King Fernando, sent from Aragon by Heaven to be the strength and the protector of Castile: we present ourselves humbly in the name of Ciudad Real to crave your royal protection. We hold ourselves most fortunate in being your subjects, but adverse fate has now conspired to snatch that honor from us. Don Rodrigo Téllez Girón, the Master of Calatrava, is now, despite his youth, a knight renowned throughout the land for his reckless courage in battle. He, with intent to increase his noble estate, laid siege to our city. The citizens rose to arms and offered such a brave resistance that soon our streets flowed with streams of blood from the dead and wounded. Finally he gained possession of the town. And yet he would not have done so, had not Fernando Gómez assisted, advised, and controlled the young man's actions. Now he commands our city, and we, your rightful vassals, must become his, unless immediate aid is given us.

KING: Where is Fernando Gómez now?

FIRST ALDERMAN: In Fuenteovejuna, I believe, sir, where he enjoys the title of overlord. He has a house and estates there. It is rumored that he keeps the citizens of that place far from contented with his tyranny.

KING: Is there a captain among you?

SECOND ALDERMAN: None, sir. Not a single nobleman escaped. All were captured, wounded, or killed.

ISABEL: Ciudad Real must be retaken without delay, or the bold attacker will grow in strength and pride. Besides, sir, Portugal may see this as his chance to enter our kingdom without check or hindrance, using this new breach in Extremadura as the means to invade us.

KING: Don Manrique, take two companies at once. Give the youth no respite until he has paid for his foolhardy venture. With you we shall send the Count of Cabra,[6] who has a world-wide reputation as a soldier. That is the most I can spare you at this time.

6. Diego Fernández of Córdoba, who had served in Henry IV's army and was rewarded with the title of Count in 1458 at the age of 20.

MANRIQUE: I shall obey your wise command with willing heart. I will put an end to this boy's bold excesses if my life is spared to me.

ISABEL: With you, Manrique, leading our undertaking, we are already sure of victory.

[*They go.*]

The countryside near Fuenteovejuna

[*Frondoso and Laurencia enter.*]

LAURENCIA: Frondoso! Now do you see what lengths you drive me to? I have had to leave the washing only half wrung out down by the stream simply because the way you were looking at me down there was enough to set the whole village gossiping—not that they aren't already. Oh, I admit I look at you too! Everybody has noticed how smartly you dress—they all say you are quite the most handsome, lively, and amusing boy in the village, and as far as Fuenteovejuna is concerned, we are as good as married already. So no wonder I had to leave the washing. You should be ashamed. . . . They are counting the days till Juan Chamorro, the sacristan, will stop playing his bassoon for a few minutes to write our marriage lines in the vestry. They would be occupying their time more usefully filling their barns with shining grain and their jars with must. Why cannot they stop gossiping? But let them do as they will. Nothing they say can worry me or make me lose my sleep, since I know that it is quite untrue.

FRONDOSO: My lovely Laurencia; why are you so cold toward me? Every time I try to see you or to hear you speak I feel as if I am taking my life in my hands. You never reward me with one word of hope, and yet you know that my desire and my intention is to be your husband.

LAURENCIA: What should I do?

FRONDOSO: Laurencia, how can you see me in such agony, not eating, not drinking, not sleeping, for thinking of you, and still have no pity on me? How can your angel's face be so harsh toward me? I mean it, Laurencia, my love will drive me mad.

LAURENCIA: Then you had best try the apothecary. He might give you a remedy for madness.

FRONDOSO: You are the only apothecary that can cure me, and the remedy would be the two of us cooing happily together. . . .

LAURENCIA: Beak to beak?

FRONDOSO: After the Church has given us its blessing. . . .

LAURENCIA: Then tell my uncle, Juan Rojo. For though I do not say I am in love with you, yet who knows, I might. . . .

FRONDOSO: You might . . . ! Someone is coming.

LAURENCIA: It is the Commander. Hide there in those bushes.

FRONDOSO: Hide?

LAURENCIA: Yes, over there!

[*Enter the Commander.*]

COMMANDER: A happy stroke of fortune! I was hunting deer, but did not think to find such dear game as this!

LAURENCIA: I was resting here a moment, but with your leave, sir, I must now return to the stream and finish wringing out the clothes.

COMMANDER: Sweet Laurencia, such rude behavior mingles strangely with the fair graces that Heaven has bestowed on you. Your actions should suit your looks, otherwise you will seem a monster of nature. But, Laurencia, if on other occasions you have fled from my gentle wooing, this time there is no need, for the countryside is a discreet and silent friend that will not carry tales. Why should you alone be so proud and haughty? Who are you that you can afford to scorn your master? Sebastiana Redondo was not so prim, and she was a married woman, neither was Martín del Pozo's wife, after only two days of marriage.

LAURENCIA: That may be, sir, but if they did give way to you, it was only because many other men had enjoyed their favors first. God be with you, sir, and may you catch your quarry, the deer which you were hunting. But for the cross you wear on your breast, I should take you for the Devil, dogging my footsteps.

COMMANDER: Your manner of speech offends me, but I need no bow to bring this quarry down. I will overcome your peasant prudery barehanded. [*He puts down his crossbow.*]

LAURENCIA: Have you lost your mind?

[*Frondoso enters and takes up the Commander's bow.*]

FRONDOSO: I have his bow! Oh, God, let me not have cause to use it.

COMMANDER: Why resist? No one can hear your cries.

LAURENCIA: Oh, Heaven help me.

COMMANDER: We are alone.

FRONDOSO: Noble Commander, leave the girl, or by my faith, your breast shall be the target for the arrows of my offended anger, though I confess I fear the cross you wear.

COMMANDER: Peasant dog!

FRONDOSO: A peasant, but I see no dog. Now, Laurencia, run.

LAURENCIA: Frondoso, take care!

FRONDOSO: Run, quickly! [*She goes.*]

COMMANDER: My sword! What madness to be parted from one's sword! Yet I left it behind for fear that it might frighten her.

FRONDOSO: Now, sir, I have only to release this trigger and you die.

COMMANDER: She has gone now. Put down that bow, traitor.

FRONDOSO: So that you can kill me with it? Love is deaf and hears no reason. Love brooks no overlord.

COMMANDER: What, shall a knight of Calatrava turn his back before a peasant? Shoot, peasant, shoot, and then beware, for I break the laws of knighthood to dally with you.[7]

FRONDOSO: No. I will not shoot. A peasant cannot kill his overlord. But for the sake of my own life I will keep the bow.

COMMANDER: This peasant shall pay dearly for insulting me. By Heaven, I will have vengeance!

ACT 2

The village square in Fuenteovejuna

[*Enter Esteban and another Alderman.*]

---

7. The "laws of knighthood" as the Commander interprets them suggest that it is below his station to fight a duel with someone who is not a member of the nobility. Frondoso's reply equally respects such "laws," as he invokes obligations of social hierarchy in his refusal to murder Fernando.

ESTEBAN: I consider it wisest that we should draw no more on the stocks in the public granary. It looks like being a bad harvest. We should reserve what we have, even if it proves an unpopular measure.

ALDERMAN: You are in the right. Caution has always been my watchword throughout many years of local government.

ESTEBAN: Let us make an appeal to Fernando Gómez. We do not want any of those astrologers who know nothing of the future or anything else coming here, making their long speeches about things that are nobody's business but God's.[1] They will discourse for hours about the theological implications concerning what has happened and what will happen, but if you ask any of them a straight-forward question about what is happening now, then they do not know the first thing about it. You would think they keep the weather locked up in their top attics to let it out as they think fit. How do they know what goes on in heaven? And who gives them the right to scare us telling us about it? They tell us when and how to sow, where to put the wheat, where the cucumbers, and where the mustard. They foretell that a cow is going to die, and when it doesn't they tell you it happened in Transylvania. Or they tell you that wine will be short, but that there will be a glut of beer in certain parts of Germany. The cherry crop will be frozen in Gascony, and there will be a lot of tigers in Hircania.[2] All of which is no help at all, and whatever we do, the year still ends in December.

[*Enter Barrildo and Leonelo, a bachelor of arts.*]

LEONELO: Ah, we are not the first comers; I see the gossip's corner is already occupied.

BARRILDO: How did you enjoy your time in Salamanca?[3]

LEONELO: Oh, that is a long story.

BARRILDO: You must be a real Bártolo.[4]

LEONELO: No, I am not even the barber. But my faculty has afforded me many moments of amusement.

BARRILDO: You must have studied very hard.

LEONELO: I managed to learn one or two of the more important notions.

BARRILDO: Now they are printing so many books, everyone you meet imagines himself a sage.

LEONELO: And yet I should say that there is more ignorance in the world than ever before. For already an excess of printed matter has come from the presses, which, contrary to the original intentions of spreading knowledge, has only led to confusion, and those who read most become most befuddled with this mass of print. I do not deny that the invention of printing has brought to light the works of many writers whose works might otherwise have gone unnoticed save by a discerning minority, nor do I deny that it has great uses as a means of preserving works for posterity. It was invented, as I am sure you are aware, by a famous German from Mainz, called Gutenberg, whose name will long be remembered for this service.[5] And yet many who passed for sages before have quickly lost their reputations now that their works have appeared in print. Besides, there are those who publish their own

1. Astrology was a disreputable but popular "science" in Lope's time, and Lope wastes no words attacking those who claim to be able to tell the future.

2. A region in Persia, known for its tigers (as Germany was for beer, and Gascony in France was for cherries).

3. Home of one of Spain's most prestigious universities.

4. A jurist whose works were taught in law schools. Leonelo's response to Barrildo plays on "Bártolo" and "barbero."

5. Johannes Gutenberg, renowned as the inventor of movable type in the early 1450s; he spent most of his life in the city of Mainz.

inanities under the name of some respected author and so damage his reputation in order to fill their own pockets, or else to make him they envy appear foolish in the eyes of the world.[6]

BARRILDO: I do not agree, Leonelo.

LEONELO: It has often been said that the ignoramus resents the man of knowledge.

BARRILDO: But printing is important. It is a great step forward.

LEONELO: The writers of the past managed for centuries without it. Can you name one man of genius, a Saint Jerome or Saint Augustine, whom printing has given to the world?

BARRILDO: Come, there is no need to get overheated about it. Let us sit down.

[*Enter Juan Rojo and another peasant.*]

JUAN ROJO: These days you need four farms to make up a dowry, and still they grumble and say it is not enough. That is how the fashion goes, and a ridiculous fashion it is too. I say—

PEASANT: What news of the Commander? If one dare ask that question.

JUAN ROJO: What, after the way he treated Laurencia! . . .

PEASANT: I'd be glad to see him hanged for a whore-master and a tyrant. Hanged from that tree, I say.

[*Enter the Commander, Ortuño, and Flores.*]

COMMANDER: God keep you all, my good people.

ALDERMAN: Sir!

COMMANDER: Remain seated, all of you.

ESTEBAN: Sir, pray you be seated, we are well content to stand.

COMMANDER: I say be seated.

ESTEBAN: It becomes honorable men to give honor where it is due. And only those who have honor can give it.

COMMANDER: Sit down. I wish to talk with you.

ESTEBAN: Did you see the greyhound we sent, sir?

COMMANDER: Yes, Alderman, my servants were delighted with its speed.

ESTEBAN: It is a fine animal. It could outpace a prisoner on the run or the confessions of a coward under torture.

COMMANDER: However, at the moment I am more interested in a certain young rabbit which I have pursued many times in vain. That would be an even more welcome gift.

ESTEBAN: Where is it to be found, sir?

COMMANDER: I think you know better than I where your daughter is to be found.

ESTEBAN: My daughter!

COMMANDER: Your daughter.

ESTEBAN: Sir, is her rank such that she is worthy to be wooed by you?

COMMANDER: She has been troubling me of late. I could name a woman—what is more, a woman of good standing, the wife of one present in this square—who was not above meeting me. She obeyed my wishes at once.

ESTEBAN: Then she did wrong, and you, sir, do not do well to speak of it so freely.

---

6. A complaint more relevant to Lope's time than to Gutenberg's; inferior playwrights would often print one of Lope's plays as their own to make money on his name. The complaint uttered here was one he made frequently.

COMMANDER: What an eloquent peasant we have here. Flores, see that he is presented with a copy of Aristotle. The *Politics* would amuse him, I think.[7]

ESTEBAN: Sir, we of this village would live honorably under your rule. There are people of worth among us, though of peasant blood.

LEONELO: Did you ever hear such brazen speech!

COMMANDER: What, have I said something to offend you, Alderman?

ALDERMAN: You have spoken unjustly, sir. It is not right that you should deprive us of our honor by speaking in such terms.

COMMANDER: A peasant rebukes me, Flores. In the name of honor too. You will soon aspire to join the brotherhood of Calatrava, no doubt?

ALDERMAN: There may be some that proudly boast the cross of knighthood, whose blood is not so pure.[8]

COMMANDER: Whose blood do I sully by joining mine with yours?

ALDERMAN: Evil desires make any blood unclean.

COMMANDER: I honor your wives by giving a thought to them.

ESTEBAN: Your speech dishonors us and you, sir. We cannot believe you mean it.

COMMANDER: Oh, this tedious peasant logic! Give me the city life where no one seeks to hinder the pleasures of a man of quality! There husbands are flattered when their wives receive attentive visitors.

ESTEBAN: There is still God's justice, even in cities, my lord, and, so I understand, an earthly one too, which does not wait on Heaven before it takes revenge. You will not thus persuade us to live without honor or respect.

COMMANDER: Go! Leave this place.

ESTEBAN: Do you wish me to repeat what has passed between us?

COMMANDER: Go, I say! Leave the square empty. Not one of you remain.

ESTEBAN: We go.

COMMANDER: Peasant insolence!

FLORES: Sir, take care what you do.

COMMANDER: These peasants have grown truculent in my absence! They will soon be forming factions.

ORTUÑO: Have a little patience, sir.

COMMANDER: I marvel I have shown so much! Now, each of you, off to your own home directly. I will have none forming groups on the way, do you hear me?

LEONELO: Just Heaven, will you let this pass?

ESTEBAN: I shall take my way home, my friends.

[*The peasants go.*]

COMMANDER: Ortuño, what say you to these peasant manners?

ORTUÑO: Sir, your own thoughts are clear, you have no wish to hear our opinion any more than theirs.

COMMANDER: Do they seek to make themselves my equals?

---

7. The Commander shows off his own learning by giving Estaban a copy of Aristotle's *Politics*, generally acknowledged by the Renaissance as the most important work of political philosophy ever written. At the same time, the *Politics* is a denunciation of tyranny, and the Commander's invocation of the work is ironic.

8. *Que no es de sangre tan limpia:* a reference to the Spanish obsession with "pure blood." The alderman is suggesting that the Commander's blood is "tainted" with that of Jews or Muslims. Unlike many members of the nobility, those of the peasant classes had not intermarried with non-Christians over the generations, and they could boast the "purest" of blood, as does the hero of another Lope peasant play, *Peribañez*, who claims to the King and Queen: "although I am a peasant, I am of pure Spanish blood untainted by any drop of Jew or Moor."

FLORES: That is not their intention, sir, I am certain.

COMMANDER: And is the peasant that stole the bow to go unpunished? A free man?

FLORES: Last night I saw him outside Laurencia's door. At least, I thought that it was he. I laid him out with a blow behind the ear, only to find it was someone else who looked like him.

COMMANDER: And where is this Frondoso now?

FLORES: They say he is about the village still.

COMMANDER: What, does the man who threatened me with death still dare to walk my lands?

FLORES: Yes, like an unwary bird that does not heed the snare, or an innocent fish swimming after the baited hook.

COMMANDER: Córdoba and Granada tremble at the sight of my sword, and now a village lout aims my own bow at my heart! I think the world is coming to an end, Flores.

FLORES: Such is the power of love.

ORTUÑO: You owe him a little gratitude, sir. He did not kill you.

COMMANDER: Ortuño, I have disguised my feeling beyond all bearing. Had I given my anger its head, I tell you that within two hours this whole village would have felt the edge of my sword. Yet let it be. My revenge shall wait until its time is ripe. What news of Pascuala?

FLORES: She replies that she is already betrothed.

COMMANDER: And desires credit until then? . . .

FLORES: Never fear, sir, she will give you payment in full.

COMMANDER: And what of Olalla?

ORTUÑO: She sent back a witty answer, sir.

COMMANDER: She is a lively girl. What did she say?

ORTUÑO: That her husband is very jealous of your attentions, but says that once his back is turned, you may enter as before.

COMMANDER: Good news indeed. But her husband is too watchful.

ORTUÑO: Watchful, sir, and quick to anger.

COMMANDER: And Inés?

FLORES: Which Inés?

COMMANDER: Inés de Antón.

FLORES: She is ready when you are. I spoke to her in her back yard. You may enter there when you will.

COMMANDER: Oh, these easy women. I love them well and pay them ill. If only they valued themselves at their real worth, Flores!

FLORES: When a man is never put in doubt, the delight he gains means nothing to him. A quick surrender denies the exquisite anticipation of pleasure. But has not the philosopher said that there are also those women who as naturally desire a man as form desires its matter?[9] And that it should be so is not surprising, for—

COMMANDER: A man crazed with love is ever delighted to be easily and instantly rewarded, but then as easily and instantly he forgets the object of his desire. Even the most generous man is quick to forget that which cost him little.

[*Enter Cimbranos, a soldier.*]

9. The "philosopher" is Aristotle, who argues for women's inferiority in his *Physics*. The line echoes the most famous Spanish play of the 16th-century, *La Celestina*, in which the servant Sempronio asks his master, "Did you never read the philosopher who tells you that as matter desires form, so woman desires man?"

CIMBRANOS: Is the Commander here?

ORTUÑO: Can you not see you are in his presence?

CIMBRANOS: Oh, gallant Fernando Gómez! Exchange, I beg you, that green cap for a helmet of shining silver, your soft coat for glistening armor. Don Rodrigo calls for aid! He is besieged in Ciudad Real by the armies of Queen Isabel, led by the Master of Santiago[1] and the Count of Cabra. That which was bought with so much blood may soon be lost to us. The light from the beacons on the high battlements of the city reveals the troops of Castile and of León massed together against us, strong as castles, fierce as lions, and reinforced by solid ranks of sturdy Aragonese.[2] And though the King of Portugal should heap every kind of honor and title upon young Rodrigo, yet we, sir, should be thankful beyond all present hope if he returns alive to Almagro. To horse, sir, for the very sight of you will suffice to put the enemy to flight.

COMMANDER: Say no more. Ortuño, have a trumpet sounded in the square immediately. What forces have I here?

ORTUÑO: You have fifty men at your command, sir.

COMMANDER: Bid them all mount at once.

CIMBRANOS: If you do not make haste, Ciudad Real falls to Fernando and Isabel.

COMMANDER: Have no fear. I come at once. [*They go.*]

A field near Fuenteovejuna

[*Enter Mengo, Laurencia, and Pascuala, running.*]

PASCUALA: Do not leave us, Mengo.

MENGO: Why, what are you afraid of?

LAURENCIA: These days we find it safer, Mengo, not to go out alone. We keep together as much as we can for fear of meeting him.

MENGO: We live in Hell fearing that pitiless devil.

LAURENCIA: He plagues us day and night.

MENGO: I would Heaven would send a thunderbolt to strike the madman.

LAURENCIA: And now he lusts for blood as well as flesh. He is a poisonous plague upon our lives.

MENGO: I hear Frondoso aimed an arrow at his heart and threatened to kill him to protect you, Laurencia, down by the stream.

LAURENCIA: I cared for no man, Mengo. But I have changed my mind since then. Frondoso was brave. But I am afraid that it may cost him his life.

MENGO: He would do best to leave the village if he values his skin.

LAURENCIA: I told him to, despite my love for him, or rather because of it. But he scorned my warning, even though the Commander has sworn that he will hang him by one foot.

PASCUALA: May he be strangled!

MENGO: No, stoned, I say, and I would like the stoning of him. All I ask is one shot from my sling, the sling I take when I go to the sheepfold. I would show him with one shot to the head. Old Sabalus or whatever he was called, that Roman, was a saint compared to him.

---

1. The Order of Santiago was another knightly order founded in the 12th century to defeat the Moors; unlike that of Calatrava, this order has fully allied itself with Ferdinand and Isabel.

2. The insignias of the three kingdoms of León, Castile, and Aragon.

LAURENCIA: You mean Heliogabalus, the tyrant. An inhuman beast they called him, too.[3]

MENGO: Yes, that is right, Healy of Gabulous. I never could remember history. An inhuman beast? Is that what they said? Well, his memory will smell sweeter by comparison with this Fernando Gómez. Can there be another man in the world to match him for brutality?

LAURENCIA: No. Nature gave him the savagery of a tiger.

[Enter Jacinta.]

JACINTA: Help me, for the love of God, help me! For friendship's sake, or what you will, only help me.

LAURENCIA: What is it, Jacinta, what is it?

PASCUALA: We will both stand by you.

JACINTA: The Commander's servants—they are setting out for Ciudad Real—armed rather with their own vicious natures than with sharp steel—and they intend to take me with them.

LAURENCIA: Then, Jacinta, may God help you. I cannot. If he will ill-treat you, he will do a thousand times worse to me. I must escape. *[Laurencia goes]*

PASCUALA: Jacinta, I cannot protect you from them. I am not a man, I have no arms.

[She goes.]

MENGO: Well, that leaves me. Come, Jacinta.

JACINTA: Have you weapons?

MENGO: The first and best in the world!

JACINTA: I would you had.

MENGO: Stones, Jacinta, stones. Here, come on.[4]

[Enter Flores and Ortuño with soldiers.]

FLORES: Did you think that you could run away from us?

JACINTA: Mengo, I am dead.

MENGO: Sirs, have pity on—

ORTUÑO: Do you defend the lady?

MENGO: As her close relation, I plead on her behalf. I would—

FLORES: Kill the swine.

MENGO: Now, I warn you, do not push me too far. I will loose my sling at you, then you will buy her dearly.

[Enter the Commander and Cimbranos.]

COMMANDER: What is happening here? Must I dismount to deal with petty matters of this kind?

FLORES: The people of this vile village are making trouble again, my lord. You would be wise to destroy it entirely, since nothing of Fuenteovejuna is pleasing to you. They defy our authority, sir.

---

3. Heliogabalus was a Roman emperor during the early 3rd century, known for his gluttony and cruelty. "Sábalo," like Galván, whom Mengo will refer to with "Healy of Gabulous," were heroes in the Spanish romance tradition. Sancho Panza too will distort famous names in *Don Quixote.*

4. Stones were the "first weapon" insofar as Cain was thought to have killed his brother Abel with stones (Genesis 4); Mengo may also suggest that he is like the humble David, who used only his slingshot to kill the "giant" Goliath in the Old Testament.

MENGO: Sir, if pity can move you, then punish these soldiers for their cruelty. In your name they tried to seize this innocent girl, snatching her from her husband and her family. Give me leave, I beseech you, to take her home.

COMMANDER: I give them leave to chastise your insolence. Put down that sling.

MENGO: Sir . . . !

COMMANDER: Flores, Ortuño, Cimbranos, tie his hands with it.

MENGO: Is this your way to protect her honor?

COMMANDER: What do they say of me in Fuenteovejuna?

MENGO: What have I done, sir, to offend you or the law?

FLORES: Is he to die?

COMMANDER: No! Do not soil your swords. They will be put to more honorable use soon enough.

ORTUÑO: What is your command?

COMMANDER: Beat him. Take him and tie him to that oak. Strip him and beat him with your belts. . . ,

MENGO: Pity, sir, pity, as you are a nobleman!

COMMANDER: Beat him until the buckles come loose from their stitches.

MENGO: Dear God in Heaven, shall such ugly deeds go unpunished? [*They go.*]

COMMANDER: You, girl, why do you flee from me? Is a laborer to be preferred to a man of my birth and valor?

JACINTA: Sir, is this all you will do to protect my honor?

COMMANDER: They robbed you of your honor by trying to take you with them?

JACINTA: Yes, for I have an honored father, who, if he does not equal you in high birth, yet is a man worthy of respect and one who betters you in manners.

COMMANDER: Such foolhardy speech will do little to cool my anger. Come.

JACINTA: Where to?

COMMANDER: Where I take you.

JACINTA: Sir, think what you do.

COMMANDER: I have thought, and it will be the worse for you. I will have none of you. You shall be the army's baggage and go with them, their common property.

JACINTA: No power on earth can force me to such a fate while I yet live.

COMMANDER: Get along there!

JACINTA: Have pity, sir!

COMMANDER: Enough of pity!

JACINTA: Is there justice in Heaven? Oh God, have mercy!

[*She is dragged off.*]

Esteban's house

[*Enter Laurencia and Frondoso.*]

LAURENCIA: You are risking death to come here, Frondoso.

FRONDOSO: Then the more is my love for you proved, Laurencia. From the hilltop, I saw the Commander ride out with his soldiers, and then I thought of you and all my fear flooded away, and I came straight down to the village. God grant he rides to a dishonorable death.

LAURENCIA: No, do not curse him. Those who are cursed most, live longest.

FRONDOSO: Then may he live a thousand years, all happy ones. That should settle his future for him! Laurencia, I came here to discover if my loyalty has opened a door to your affections. Tell me you love me! You yourself said the whole village looks upon us as almost married already, and marvels that we hesitate so long. Come, now, answer me yes or no.

LAURENCIA: Very well, I answer both the village and you, yes, we shall be!

FRONDOSO: Oh, Laurencia, I thank you, I kiss your hands, I cannot speak for joy. . . . Laurencia—

LAURENCIA: Since we are decided, Frondoso, let us waste no time in compliments. You must go and tell my father at once. But here he comes, talking with my uncle. Have no doubt, Frondoso, we shall be married. May good fortune attend you.

FRONDOSO: I shall put my trust in God.

[*Laurencia hides.*]

[*Enter Esteban and the Alderman.*]

ESTEBAN: The man is mad! For a moment I thought there would be a riot in the square, he behaved so abominably. But Jacinta has suffered most at his hands, poor girl.

ALDERMAN: Spain will soon be under the laws of Fernando and Isabel—the Catholic Monarchs as they call them[5]—then we can hope for better things. Even now I hear that the Master of Santiago has been appointed Captain General and has laid siege to Rodrigo Girón in Ciudad Real.[6] But still, my heart bleeds for Jacinta. She was a good girl.

ESTEBAN: And then to flog young Mengo for trying to defend her.

ALDERMAN: I saw him. His back was like a bundle of red flannel and black mourning cloth.

ESTEBAN: I cannot bear to talk about it. Only to think of the way he abuses us makes me burn with anger. Am I mayor of this village for nothing? Is this staff of office worthless?

ALDERMAN: It is no fault of yours, Esteban. You cannot blame yourself for what his servants do.

ESTEBAN: You may not have heard, but they told me that the day he raped Pedro Redondo's wife in the valley he flung her to his servants, once his own foul lust was satisfied.

ALDERMAN: There is someone here! Who is it?

FRONDOSO: It is I. I was waiting to speak to you.

ESTEBAN: Frondoso, you have no need to stand on ceremony in my house. I brought you up and you know I love you as a son.

FRONDOSO: Then sir, trusting in the love you bear me, I wish to ask of you a favor. You know me well and my father too—

ESTEBAN: What is it, boy, have you also been offended by Fernando Gómez?

FRONDOSO: Not a little.

ESTEBAN: I knew it in my heart.

FRONDOSO: But sir, I want to ask, as one more token of your goodness to me, if you will give me permission to marry Laurencia, whom I dearly love. Forgive me if you think this is an impertinence, for I know that some might say that I was forward in asking.

5. An anachronism; Ferdinand and Isabella would be designated "The most Catholic Kings" by the pope only in 1494.
6. The Spanish reference to the Master of Santiago is less

specific: "Santiago comes on his horse as Captain General." The Alderman thus refers both to the Master of Santiago and to St. Santiago (St. James), who appeared on a white horse to help the Spaniards.

ESTEBAN: My heart rejoices at your words, Frondoso. My son, I give thanks to God that you have come to protect Laurencia's honor with your pure and loving zeal. You have relieved me of my greatest fear. But we must not run before we walk. Have you your own father's consent? I happily give mine provided he agrees to the match. If so, then I count myself a fortunate man indeed.

ALDERMAN: You should get the girl's opinion first, before making any promises, Esteban.

ESTEBAN: Why, do you think they will not have got it all settled before coming to me? Now, about the dowry: I have a little put aside that will give you a start.

FRONDOSO: I need no dowry, sir. I beg you, do not trouble yourself about one.

ALDERMAN: He will take her as God made her!

ESTEBAN: I will call her and see what she says.

FRONDOSO: Oh, yes, sir, do. Her wishes must be considered.

ESTEBAN: Laurencia! Daughter!

LAURENCIA: You called, Father?

ESTEBAN: There, what did I tell you? You see how soon she answered! Laurencia, my dear, come here a moment. We have been asked our opinion as to whether your friend Gila would make a good wife for Frondoso. What do you think, is he worthy of her?

LAURENCIA: Is Gila getting married?

ESTEBAN: I should say they will make an ideal match, wouldn't you?

LAURENCIA: Yes, Father, I agree.

ESTEBAN: Yes, but on second thought, she is not as pretty as you, Laurencia. I should have thought a handsome boy like Frondoso would have set his cap for you. But apparently not. . . .

LAURENCIA: Father, your jokes are almost as old as you!

ESTEBAN: Do you love him?

LAURENCIA: I have always been very fond of him, but of course, now he is going to marry Gila. . . .

ESTEBAN: No more nonsense. Shall I tell him you will have him?

LAURENCIA: Yes, Father, tell him.

ESTEBAN: Very well, the keys are in my hands. It shall be done. We will go and seek your father in the square, Frondoso.

ALDERMAN: Come.

ESTEBAN: Now, son, about the dowry, what shall we say? I can give you four thousand maravedis.[7]

FRONDOSO: I told you, I do not ask for a dowry, sir.

ESTEBAN: Come, Frondoso, you have too many scruples. A little help when first married never hurt anyone. Refuse now and you may live to regret it.

[*They go, leaving Frondoso and Laurencia.*]

LAURENCIA: Well, Frondoso, are you happy?

FRONDOSO: Oh, so happy! My heart is brimming over with joy. I am almost mad with happiness, Laurencia, to see you as my own sweet possession.

The countryside near Ciudad Real

[*Enter the Master, the Commander, Flores and Ortuño.*]

7. This is a generous gift, more than a laborer would make in a year.

COMMANDER: Fly, my lord, fly! There is no other remedy.

MASTER: The weakness of the wall was to blame—and the strength of the enemy.

COMMANDER: It cost them blood enough. They must have lost half their army.

MASTER: They can never boast that they took our standard of Calatrava. That is one honor they cannot add to their spoils.

COMMANDER: Your hopes are at an end, Rodrigo, even so.

MASTER: A man can do little to turn back blind Fortune's wheel. Yesterday I rode on high, today she casts me down.

VOICES [off]: Victory! Victory to Isabel and Fernando! Castile wins the day!

MASTER: Already they crown the battlements with the fires of victory, and deck the windows of the high towers with their flags.

COMMANDER: They would do better to paint them with the blood that they have lost, for this day is more a tragedy than a feast, for victor and vanquished alike.

MASTER: I will return to Calatrava, Fernando Gómez.

COMMANDER: And I to Fuenteovejuna. I will await your orders there, sir, while you decide whether you will continue on your kinsmen's side or make your peace with the Catholic Monarchs.

MASTER: I will write to tell you what I intend to do.

COMMANDER: Time will teach you the best path.

MASTER: Perhaps, but I fear my youth is yet an easy victim for the deceits of time.

The countryside near Fuenteovejuna

[*Enter wedding guests, Musicians, Mengo, Frondoso, Laurencia, Pascuala, Barrildo, Esteban, Alderman, and Juan Rojo.*]

MUSICIANS [*singing*]:
> *Long live the bride and bridegroom!*
> *Long may they live!*

MENGO: I'll bet you did not spend much time composing the words to that song.

BARRILDO: And the one you have written? Will it be any better?

FRONDOSO: I reckon you had all the music knocked out of you the other day, Mengo. Am I right?

MENGO: Some of you would not look so handsome yourselves if the Commander had—

BARRILDO: Not now, Mengo. Let us not cast a shadow over the celebrations by naming him.

MENGO: A hundred to one, those were the odds against me, I tell you. . . . And there was I, armed with nothing but my sling. Oh, they administered a leathery, brass-buckled enema to a certain honorable man—whose name I need not mention. You needn't laugh, I did not find it funny.

BARRILDO: No, I am sure you did not.

MENGO: The kind of enema my arse received was no joke. I know they say it is good for you and clears the system but it nearly killed me.

FRONDOSO: Come, Mengo, let us hear the verses you have written, provided they are fit for the ears of this present company.

MENGO:
> *Long live the happy pair,*
> *That is my hope.*
> *May no envy or jealousy*

> *Make them worry or mope.*
> *May their joys be long-lasting,*
> *Their quarrels ephemeral,*
> *And when they get tired of living,*
> *May they have a happy funeral.*

FRONDOSO: Thank you, Mengo, I hope so too. But Heaven did not intend you to be a poet, I fear.

BARRILDO: Remember how quickly he wrote it.

MENGO: Well, if you want my opinion on poetry, it is like a baker making doughnuts. He takes the lumps of dough and throws them into the boiling oil until he has a pan full. They start off all the same, but turn out different. Some puff up, light and fluffy, some go flat and squashy. A few turn out perfectly round, while many of them stick together in a soggy mess. Some get burnt to a cinder, others are brown and crisp. That is how I see a poet making up his verses. His subject matter is like the dough; he makes lumps of it in the form of lines of poetry, and then throws it down onto the paper which is his pan, hoping that the dollop of honey in the middle will make them acceptable. More often than not they are too rich for anybody's palate but his own, and so he has to eat them all himself. That is the tragedy of being a baker.

BARRILDO: Hush, Mengo, eat your doughnuts and be quiet, we are here to give our respects and good wishes to the bride and bridegroom.

LAURENCIA: We both kiss your hands in gratitude.

JUAN ROJO: Mine, child? I have done nothing. Here is your father; it is he that you should thank. Both you and Frondoso have reason to be grateful to him.

ESTEBAN: No, all I want is to see you happy, with Heaven's blessing upon you.

FRONDOSO: But still we thank you, Father.

JUAN ROJO: Come, musicians, let us have a song, now that we seem to have them safely married at last.

MUSICIANS [*singing*]:

> *The maiden walks in the valley,*
> *Her dark hair floats in the breeze.*[8]
> *The knight of Calatrava follows.*
> *She hides, startled, among the trees.*
> *Why do you hide from me, sweet girl?*
> *For my desires, lynx-eyed, can see through walls.*[9]—
> *She draws the boughs across her face*
> *And shrinks deeper into the leafy shade.*
> *If she could, she would weave an iron lattice*
> *To defend her from the approaching lord.*
> *Why do you hide from me, sweet girl?*
> *For my desires, lynx-eyed, can see through walls.*

8. The musicians' composition, far more polished than that of Mengo or Barrildo, uses the well-known genre of the *pastorella* as a haunting, seemingly inappropriate wedding song, but one that clearly takes stock of the dangers confronting the bride. First composed in the medieval period, the *pastorella* takes as its theme the confrontation between a knight and a shepherdess or peasant girl in a verdant landscape, often ending in seduction or rape. Less frequently the young woman consents to become the knight's lover, or successfully escapes with the help of other peasants. Lope wrote a number of these songs independently of his plays.

9. According to the Roman writer Pliny—whose *Natural History* furnished for the Renaissance a treasure trove of information on nature, medicine, and Roman customs—the lynx was said to have the most acute vision of any mammal.

> *Love leaps over mountains and oceans,*
> *Love creeps between the branches of trees.*
> *The knight's shadow falls where the maiden cowers.*
> *She cannot avoid the searching eyes.*
> *Why do you hide from me, sweet girl?*
> *For my desires, lynx-eyed, can see through walls.*

[*Enter the Commander, Flores, Ortuño, and Cimbranos.*]

COMMANDER: Pray do not interrupt the festivities on my account.

JUAN ROJO: On the contrary, sir, we would honor you. Will you be seated? We must give you a conqueror's welcome, now you have returned from the wars.

FRONDOSO: This is my death! Heaven help me!

LAURENCIA: Quickly, Frondoso, run, this way.

COMMANDER: Arrest that man.

JUAN ROJO: Obey, my son.

FRONDOSO: What, would you have them kill me, Father?

JUAN ROJO: No, they have no cause to kill you.

COMMANDER: I do not kill a man without cause. But for me, these soldiers here would have run him through ere now. Take him to the prison where his own father shall try, and punish, his offense.

PASCUALA: But, sir, it is his wedding day.

COMMANDER: The cause of justice heeds not wedding days. I am sure there are others waiting and willing to take his place.

PASCUALA: If he offended you, sir, forgive him, as you are a nobleman.

COMMANDER: This matter does not concern me alone, Pascuala. It was Téllez Girón, the Master of the Order of Calatrava, who suffered insult indirectly at his hands. He who insults the honor of the Order must, I fear, be punished as an example. If he goes free others may be tempted to question its authority. For, lest any here are yet ignorant of this man's crime, know that he aimed a bow at the heart of the High Commander of the Order.

ESTEBAN: I believe, sir, that it may not be out of place for a father-in-law to speak a word in his defense. Is it surprising, sir, that a young man in love should be moved to disloyal anger when you attempted to rob him of his wife? Is it surprising that he should seek to defend her?

COMMANDER: Mayor, you are a bumbling fool.

ESTEBAN: But a well-intentioned one, sir.

COMMANDER: I made no attempt to rob him of his wife —he had none.

ESTEBAN: My lord, you did. Let us hear no more. For there are a king and queen in Castile, who will create new orders of knighthood that shall put down the old dis-orders that have oppressed us. And when their wars are over, they will not tolerate proud, powerful men creating havoc in their towns and villages, bearing great crosses on their breasts. Let the king alone wear such emblems, since he alone is worthy of them.[1]

COMMANDER: Remove that staff from this old fool's hand.[2]

ESTEBAN: Take it, sir, I have no more use for it.

---

1. Esteban's words are prophetic; Ferdinand would in fact bring the orders under his dominion by 1487, as well as legislating against the widespread custom of feudal over-lords "enjoying" the bride before she slept with her new husband.

2. The mace, symbol of the mayor's authority.

COMMANDER: Let him be beaten with it for being a disobedient ass.

ESTEBAN: You are still my master, sir. Do as you will.

PASCUALA: Do you beat an old man?

LAURENCIA: If this is your revenge upon me, how do you profit by it?

COMMANDER: Take that girl, and let ten men guard her with their lives.

[*The Commander and his men go.*]

ESTEBAN: May justice descend from Heaven.

[*He goes.*]

PASCUALA: The wedding has turned to mourning.

BARRILDO: Is there no man here that will speak out?

MENGO: I have already been flogged till I had enough purple about me to fill the Vatican. Let somebody else try crossing him.

JUAN ROJO: We must make a stand together.

MENGO: All keep quiet together, you mean. Unless you want a staff broken across your backs.

ACT 3

Council room in Fuenteovejuna

[*Enter Esteban, Alonso, and Barrildo.*]

ESTEBAN: Are they not coming to the meeting?

BARRILDO: As yet they have not come.

ESTEBAN: Every minute our danger grows greater. . . .

BARRILDO: They will come, have no fear. They all know about the meeting.

ESTEBAN: Frondoso a captive in his tower, and my daughter taken too! If heavenly mercy does not intercede, then—

[*Enter Juan Rojo and the Alderman.*]

JUAN ROJO: Esteban, why are you shouting? For all our sakes this meeting must be secret.

ESTEBAN: The greatest wonder is that I am not shouting any louder.

[*Enter Mengo.*]

MENGO: I thought I would come after all.

ESTEBAN: My honorable friends, a man whose gray beard is bathed in grief asks you what obsequies are to be paid over the corpse of our lost honor. Is there any man among us who still can say he has not suffered some indignity at the hands of this barbarian, Fernando Gómez? Answer me. Can none reply? Then since every one of us feels degraded and dishonored, can we not act together? We are all equally affronted and yet we hesitate to take a just revenge. Could any misery be greater?

JUAN ROJO: None. But already it is published abroad and known for truth that the rightful king and queen hold Castile in peaceful rule, therefore, I say, let two councilors be sent to Córdoba,[1] where they are soon to hold court, and cast themselves at their feet and beg them to redress our wrongs.

1. Fuenteovejuna was in the province of Córdoba, where judicial and legislative decisions for the outlying towns were made. The King and Queen made Córdoba their official residence from 1478–1479.

BARRILDO: King Fernando will never spare the time to deal with our problem. He will be too busy establishing his rule after his recent conquests.

ALDERMAN: Friends, hear me a moment. I vote we evacuate the whole village, man, woman and child.

JUAN ROJO: That would take too much time.

MENGO: Speak lower! If we are overheard, I fear this council will lose a few lives among its members.

ALDERMAN: Now the mast of patience is broken and fear blows the ship wildly from its course. The daughter is violently stolen from a virtuous man who governs this town in which you live, and his staff of office is unjustly broken about his head. If we were slaves we could not be more harshly treated.

JUAN ROJO: What would you have the people do?

ALDERMAN: Die, or bring death to the tyrants, for we are many, they are few.

BARRILDO: What, rise in arms against our master?

ESTEBAN: Only the King is master under heaven, not Fernando Gómez. If God is with us in our zeal for justice, then how can we go wrong?

MENGO: Listen, sirs, we should tread carefully upon such shifting ground. I represent the laborers upon this council, and they are always the ones to get the heavier end of the stick, so I can best put forward their fears——

JUAN ROJO: This misfortune is shared equally, Mengo. By all, whether laborer or farmer. Why do we hesitate to risk our lives? They burn our homes and our vineyards. They are tyrants. Let us have vengeance, I say.

[*Enter Laurencia, disheveled.*[2]]

LAURENCIA: Let me come in. A woman has a right, if not to vote in this council of men, yet to have a voice. Do you know me?

ESTEBAN: Great heaven! My daughter!

JUAN ROJO: Laurencia!

LAURENCIA: Well may you doubt that it is I, seeing me as I am.

ESTEBAN: My daughter!

LAURENCIA: Call me not daughter.

ESTEBAN: Why Laurencia? Why not?

LAURENCIA: Why? I will tell you why! Because you allow tyrants to kidnap me and do not avenge me, traitors to snatch me, and do not rescue me. Oh, do not say it was Frondoso's duty as my husband, and not yours, for until the wedding night a bride is still her father's charge, and the night was not yet come. As when a jewel is bought, so the man who sells must guard it until it is handed over to the buyer. Fernando Gómez carried me off while you looked on. Like coward shepherds, you let the wolf make off with the lamb. You let me be threatened with knives, insulted with their foul language, and brutally maltreated in their attempts to avenge their lewd appetites upon my chastity! Look how my hair has been dragged and torn out! See the cuts and bruises where they tortured me! Do you call yourselves men? Do you? My father? Or you, Uncle? Are your hearts unmoved to see me so full of woe? Well may this village be called Fuenteovejuna— Sheepwell! for its people are nothing but sheep. A flock of bleating sheep who run from curs. Give me a sword! Let me have arms! Oh, you are stone, bronze, jasper! Tigers without——

---

2. Laurencia's "disheveled" appearance would have probably signaled to the audience that she has been violated by the Commander.

No! Not tigers, for tigers hunt and slay any that steal their young before they have had time to lock their gates in their faces. Meek rabbits were you born, not noble Spaniards. Hens! You stand by and cluck while other men enjoy your wives! Why do you wear swords at your belts?—put distaffs there![3] By God, I swear, only the women here shall have the glory of shedding the blood of this tyrant, and when it is done we shall throw stones at you, for the effeminate pimps and cowards that you are. From tomorrow, go dressed in wimples and petticoats and paint your faces with rouge. Even now the Commander may be ordering Frondoso to be hanged, untried, for so he has sworn to do. And he will do the same to all of you. And I shall laugh to see it and be glad that this village has been emptied of you, its old women, and the days of the Amazons shall return in Fuenteovejuna, to be the wonder of the earth![4]

ESTEBAN: Daughter, I will not deserve the names you give us. I will go alone, though all the world should stand against me.

JUAN ROJO: I too, though fearing the greatness of your enemy.

ALDERMAN: Let us all challenge death together.

BARRILDO: Find a cloth and fix it to a pole. We will raise our banner to the winds, and death to these monsters!

JUAN ROJO: What shall be our order?

MENGO: Kill him! Never mind about order! We all agree, the whole village knows what must be done. Down with tyrants!

ESTEBAN: Take any arms you can find!—swords, lances, bows, pikes, sticks of wood.

MENGO: Long live the King and Queen!

ALL: Long live the King and Queen!

MENGO: And down with traitors and tyrants! Let Fernando Gómez bleed!

ALL: Death to the tyrant!

[*They all go.*]

LAURENCIA: May heaven hear your cry! Rise up, women of Fuenteovejuna! Come out and win back your honor.

[*Enter Pascuala, Jacinta, and other women.*]

PASCUALA: What is it, Laurencia? What is happening?

LAURENCIA: Look there! They go to kill Fernando Gómez. Every man in the village, and young boys too, all running furiously with one intent—death! Shall we let them alone reap the honor of this deed? Shall we stay at home when we were the greatest sufferers from his wrongs?

JACINTA: What must we do? Tell us.

LAURENCIA: We shall march in order upon his house, and there take our revenge. Our vengeance shall strike fear into the hearts of men everywhere. Jacinta, you suffered most, you shall be corporal of this band of women.

JACINTA: You suffered no less.

LAURENCIA: Pascuala, you shall be our standard-bearer.

PASCUALA: Give me a banner. I will fix it to a pole. I shall be a fine standard-bearer.

---

3. Reference to the story of Hercules, who as a punishment had to serve Queen Omphale for three years, wearing feminine attire and doing women's work while she assumed his lion's skin and club. More generally, Laurencia predicts an overturning of the "order of things," arguing that women should command and men should stay at home with their distaffs, or staffs used for spinning wool.
4. The Amazons were a mythical group of warrior women who lived in Scythia and were hostile to men.

LAURENCIA: There is no time. We must strike now, our only standards must be the shawls we wear.

PASCUALA: We must name the captain.

LAURENCIA: No. No captain.

PASCUALA: Why not?

LAURENCIA: I for one can show my valor without any title of captain or general.[5]

[*They go.*]

A room in the Commander's house

[*Enter Frondoso with his hands tied, Flores, Ortuño, Cimbranos, and the Commander.*]

COMMANDER: Hang him up by the rope which binds his hands, he will suffer longer.

FRONDOSO: Your lofty titles, sir, conceal the truer names that men might call you.

COMMANDER: Hang him from the nearest tower.

FRONDOSO: When I had the chance to kill you, I spared your life.

FLORES: What is that noise?

COMMANDER: What noise?

FLORES: Now they would interrupt your justice, my lord!

ORTUFIO: They are breaking the doors down.

COMMANDER: The doors of my house! The official residence of our great Order!

FLORES: The entire village is coming.

JUAN ROJO [*off*]: Smash, crush, cast down, burn, and kill!

ORTUÑO: A mass uprising!

COMMANDER: The populace against me!

ORTUÑO: We shall never stop this mob.

FLORES: They are advancing wildly. They have smashed the doors down.

COMMANDER: Untie him. Frondoso, go out and pacify them. Show them you are unharmed.

FRONDOSO: I go. But remember it is love that drives them, sir.

[*He goes.*]

MENGO [*off*]: Long live Fernando and Isabel, and death to the Commander!

FLORES: Sir, for God's sake, do not let them find you here.

COMMANDER: They will not come this far. They dare not. Besides, this room is strong and well defended.

FLORES: When outraged people rise, my lord, there is no quelling them until they have taken their full revenge.

COMMANDER: Come, we will defend that door. Our swords shall be the portcullis[6] to keep them out.

FRONDOSO [*off*]: Long live Fuenteovejuna!

COMMANDER: What a captain! Let us attack these peasant curs, the sharp edge of our swords shall cure their madness.

---

5. In the Spanish, Lope has Laurencia refer specifically to two famous generals of war when she says "You will not need either the Cid or Rodomonte!" The Cid, or Rodrigo Díaz de Bivar, was the great Spanish hero who captured Valencia from the Moors in the 11th century (and whose name is taken from the Arabic word for "Lord").

Rodomonte was a fierce Muslim warrior and king who attacks Charlemagne's Paris in Ariosto's epic romance, *Orlando furioso*, and dies in a final duel with the Christian Ruggiero.

6. The iron gate that protected a castle's entrance.

FLORES: They will cure yours, I fear.

ESTEBAN [*off*]: There they are! There is the tyrant and his servants. Fuenteovejuna! Death to them all!

[*All the peasants rush in.*]

COMMANDER: My people, wait!

ALL: Insults cannot wait. Revenge cannot wait!

COMMANDER: What insults? What wrongs do you complain of? You shall have full redress.

ALL: Fuenteovejuna! Long live King Fernando! Death to the Commander! Death to the traitor! Death to the hypocrite. Kill the foul lecher.

COMMANDER: Hear me. I speak. I am your lord——

ALL: Our lords are the Catholic Monarchs.

COMMANDER: Wait—

ALL: Fuenteovejuna! And death to Fernando Gómez!

[*The peasants go off following the Commander. The women enter armed.*]

LAURENCIA: Stop. Here is the place where our honor shall be avenged. Remember, show yourselves not as women in this deed, but as soldiers without pity.

PASCUALA: Those we called women before have caught him already. They are letting his blood. Let us not wait longer.

JACINTA: We will impale his body on our spears.

PASCUALA: We are all agreed. We will go together.

ESTEBAN [*off*]: Die, treacherous Commander!

COMMANDER: I die. Pity, oh Lord. I trust in your mercy!

BARRILDO [*off*]: Here is Flores.

MENGO [*off*]: Let me get at the swine. He was the one that beat the hide off me.

FRONDOSO [*off*]: I shall not be avenged till I have the soul out of his body.

LAURENCIA: We must go in.

PASCUALA: Be careful! We must guard the door.

BARRILDO [*off*]: Plead with me? Now it is your turn to weep!

LAURENCIA: Pascuala, I go in there. My sword shall not remain imprisoned in its sheath.

[*She goes.*]

BARRILDO [*off*]: Here is Ortuño.

FRONDOSO [*off*]: Slash his face.

[*Enter Flores pursued by Mengo.*]

FLORES: Pity, Mengo. I am not to blame!

MENGO: You were his go-between. I felt your belt on my back.

PASCUALA: Leave him to us, Mengo. Stop! Leave him to us!

MENGO: There you are, he is yours. I have finished with him.

PASCUALA: I will avenge your beating, Mengo.

MENGO: Do, Pascuala!

JACINTA: Death to the pander.

FLORES: Among women!

JACINTA: A fitting death for such as you!

PASCUALA: And do you weep now?

JACINTA: Die, you cringing pimp!
LAURENCIA [*off*]: Death to the traitor!
FLORES: Pity, ladies!

[*Enter Ortuño fleeing from Laurencia.*]

ORTUÑO: Listen, I beg you, I am not the one——

[*Enter Laurencia.*]

LAURENCIA: I know who you are. Go in there, all of you. You will find employment for your conquering arms in there!
PASCUALA: I will die killing.
ALL: God for Fuenteovejuna and King Fernando!

[*They go.*]

The palace of Fernando and Isabel in Toro

[*Enter King and Queen and Don Manrique.[7]*]

MANRIQUE: And so, sir, our timely action achieved the result that you desired, with few losses on our side. Little resistance was shown, and even if there had been more, I think it would have carried little weight against our forces. Cabra is now occupying the town lest by any chance the bold adversary should dare to attack again.
KING: You have both done wisely. But he must be assisted further. Let forces be sent to fortify his position. Thus may we best guard ourselves against Alfonso, who is still gathering men in Portugal. I am well pleased to know that the Count of Cabra is holding Ciudad Real. He is a captain who has proved his skill and courage many times in battle. We can rely on him to be a watchful sentry against those who wish our kingdom harm.

[*Enter Flores, wounded.*]

FLORES: Catholic King, Great Fernando, to whom Heaven has granted the crown of Castile, as a worthy tribute to the greatest knight: hear now a tale of cruel rebellion, the worst ever known in any land between the rising and setting of the sun.
KING: Speak.
FLORES: Great King: my wounds do not permit me to dally in telling my sad story, for death will soon overtake me. I come from Fuenteovejuna, where, with remorseless hatred, the people have conspired together and have killed their rightful master. Fernando Gómez is dead, murdered by his own vassals, a mob inflamed with little cause to senseless fury. They all took up the cry, and, driven to frenzy by their own ever-increasing chant of "Traitor, traitor," they swept through his house, burning and destroying all that stood in their way. They took no heed of his noble promise that all their wrongs should be set right and all debts paid. Not only would they not listen to him, but, in their madness, they hacked his breast and the cross it wore with a thousand cruel strokes. They flung his body from the high windows to the ground where the women of the village impaled it on pikes and swords. Then they took his corpse to a house in the village where they fought among themselves to tear out his hair and beard in handfuls and slash his face. Their lust for blood grew

---

7. Master of the Order of Santiago.

to such a pitch that even when they had torn him into pieces, they were still unsatisfied. They hacked away his coat of arms above the door with their pikes, exclaiming as they did it that they would hang your royal arms there in place of his that had offended them. They sacked his house as if it had been the house of an enemy, and with delight divided his goods among themselves. I saw all this with my own eyes from where I was hiding, for, alas, unkind fate left me living amid the chaos. I lay hidden all day until nightfall when I could escape unseen to tell you of the deed. Sir, since you are known to be a just king, I beg you to revenge my master's noble blood, shed without reason by his barbarous vassals.

KING: You may rest assured that they shall not go unpunished. I confess myself amazed at this tale of horror. We shall send a judge at once to confirm the truth of the matter, and to chastise the guilty as an example to all Spain. A captain shall go with the judge to protect him. Such bold treason shall receive fitting punishment. See that this soldier's wounds are attended to.

[*They go.*]

The village square in Fuenteovejuna

Enter the peasants of Fuenteovejuna with the head of Fernando Gómez on a lance.[8]

MUSICIANS [*singing*]:   *Long live Fernando and Isabel,*
And death to tyrants.

BARRILDO: Give us your verse, Frondoso.

FRONDOSO: Very well, here it is, and if the odd foot is missing here and there,[9] then anyone more skilled in verses than I is welcome to improve it:

> *Long live Isabel the Queen,*
> *And King Fernando too.*
> *Long together may they reign,*
> *And be the happiest couple in Spain*
> *Till Heaven receive the two.*[1]
> *Long live our Catholic King and Queen,*
> *And death to tyrants.*

LAURENCIA: Let us hear yours, Barrildo.

BARRILDO: Listen carefully. It took me hours to write it.

PASCUALA: Be sure you give it a proper rendering and do it justice, then.

BARRILDO:

> *Long live our famous King and Queen,*
> *May they be happy and serene.*
> *God keep them free from woes,*
> *And shield them from their foes,*
> *Whether dwarves or giants.*
> *And death to tyrants!*

8. This gory detail is Lope's innovation on the historical record; it may prompt us to think of the visual imagery of the story of Judith and Holofernes, in which the brave Hebrew woman murdered the Assyrian general Holofernes in his bed, then carried his head back to her town, where the villagers placed it on their walls; see the Book of Judith, ch.13.

9. A reference to Frondoso's amateur talents at verse-making.

1. The translation omits a reference to St. Michael greeting the King and Queen as they enter heaven's gates. Michael is often depicted in Renaissance art as an archangel who is trampling on defeated devils and dragons while also playing a role in deciding where souls should be sent after death.

MUSICIANS [*singing*]:   *Long live Fernando and Isabel,*
                          And death to tyrants.

LAURENCIA: Now for Mengo's verse!
FRONDOSO: Yes, come along, Mengo.
MENGO: As you all know, I am a very gifted poet.
PASCUALA: We all know you are a gifted whipping post.
MENGO:

> *I've got the laugh on the Commander.*
> *He played a tune on my backside:*
> *Now the Commander is asunder,*
> *But I am still inside my hide.*
> *Long live our Catholic King and Queen,*
> *And down with tyrants!*[2]

MUSICIANS [*singing*]:   *Long live Fernando and Isabel,*
                          And death to tyrants.

ESTEBAN: Take down that head, good people.
MENGO: Yes, he does not look very happy up there, does he?

[*Juan Rojo brings on a shield with the royal arms.*]

ALDERMAN: Here is the new coat of arms.
ESTEBAN: Hold it up, Juan, so that we can all see it.
JUAN: Where is it to be placed?
ALDERMAN: Here, on the front of the town hall.
ESTEBAN: It is a fine shield.
BARRILDO: Just what we wanted.
FRONDOSO: It is the sun that rises. Our day begins to dawn.
ESTEBAN: Long live León, Castile, and Aragon, and death to tyranny! Now, my friends, will you hear an old man's advice? The King and Queen will order an inquiry into the death of the Commander, and they will be the more interested since their own route brings them to these parts. So let us be prepared and agree on what we shall say.
FRONDOSO: What would you advise?
ESTEBAN: When we are questioned, we shall name no names, but say only: "Fuenteovejuna did it."[3] Even if we die for it, we will say no more than that.
FRONDOSO: Yes, that is what we must do. Fuenteovejuna did it.
ESTEBAN: Do you all agree to say that?
ALL: We do.
ESTEBAN: Very well, we will have a rehearsal. I will be the judge. Now, Mengo, you are the one to be questioned.
MENGO: Could you not find someone weaker than me? Someone more likely to break down?
ESTEBAN: We are only pretending, Mengo.

---

2. While the final two lines are to be taken seriously—Mengo contrasts the monarchs' just ways with the tyranny of the Commander—for the sake of rhyme, Mengo calls the monarchs *Reyes Cristiánigos* (rather than *cristianos*) and tyrants (*tiránigos*), giving the closing lines the comic, burlesque style of the earlier ones.

3. *Fuenteovejuna lo hizo:* the battle cry that will save the villagers from persecution and that would become a proverbial phrase used to suggest that guilt for some crime was communal, rather than individual.

MENGO: Come along then, ask me.
ESTEBAN: Who killed the Commander?
MENGO: Fuenteovejuna did it.
ESTEBAN: Dog! I will put you on the rack!
MENGO: Nay! Kill me, sir.
ESTEBAN: Confess, scoundrel.
MENGO: Very well, I confess.
ESTEBAN: Who was it?
MENGO: Fuenteovejuna.
ESTEBAN: Give the rack another turn.
MENGO: Give it twenty turns, I care not!
ESTEBAN: That is the way we will treat them at the trial.

[Enter the Alderman.]

ALDERMAN: What in the world are you doing here?
FRONDOSO: What has happened, Cuadrado?
ALDERMAN: The judge has arrived.
ESTEBAN: Now scatter, all of you, to your homes.
ALDERMAN: A captain has come with him.
ESTEBAN: Let the devil come with him. You know what your answer is to be.
ALDERMAN: They are already arresting everyone they see. Not a soul will be left out.
ESTEBAN: Have no fear. Who killed the Commander, Mengo?
MENGO: Fuenteovejuna.

[They go.]

In the Master of Calatrava's house in Almagro

[Enter the Master and a Soldier.]

MASTER: What an unlooked-for misfortune! To murder the Commander of our Order!
I have a mind to kill you for the news you bring.
SOLDIER: Sir, I am only a messenger. I have no wish to offend you.
MASTER: To think that a whole village should have dared to rise up and commit so
terrible a crime. I will swoop down upon them with five hundred men and raze the
village to the ground. Not so much as a memory of their names shall be left.
SOLDIER: Sir, stay your anger, for they have gone over to King Fernando. You were
best not to incur his displeasure any further.
MASTER: How can they have gone over to the King? Their village belongs to my Order. It is part of my estates!
SOLDIER: The King himself can best answer that.
MASTER: No lawyer would support my claim if the King now rules in Fuenteovejuna.
Whether I will or no, I must recognize him as my sovereign. Therefore do I stay
my anger. My best course now is to crave audience of His Majesty. For though I
have been guilty of offending him, my youth may excuse me in his eyes and incline him to pardon me. I go to him with shame, and yet I must, if I am to protect
my honor, as my father bade me.

[They go.]

The square at Fuenteovejuna

[*Enter Laurencia, alone.*]

LAURENCIA: Unhappy Laurencia, what will you do if unkind Fate snatches Frondoso from you? Fear is the rack on which my love is tormented. My mind, which I thought so steadfast, now quails in horror to think of our present plight. Oh, you Heavens, guard my husband from danger, for Laurencia becomes as nothing if she loses him. Oh, Frondoso, Frondoso, when you are here, I am terrified for your safety, and when you are gone, I can scarce live without you.

[*Enter Frondoso.*]

FRONDOSO: Laurencia!

LAURENCIA: Dear husband! How can you dare to show yourself here?

FRONDOSO: Laurencia, is this all the thanks you give me for my love in coming to you?

LAURENCIA: Frondoso, my love, take care. Think of the danger. . . .

FRONDOSO: Laurencia. Heaven would never be so cruel as to hurt you in anything.

LAURENCIA: But you see how ruthlessly the others are being treated, and they are not so deeply involved as you, Frondoso. If the judge is harsh with them, what will he not do to you? Save your life. Flee, my love. Do not wait here for evil to overwhelm you.

FRONDOSO: How can I, Laurencia? How can you ask? I could not leave the others in danger. And you, could I leave you when I cannot bear to be out of your sight? Do not tell me to flee. I will not leave Fuenteovejuna in agony to save my own skin. [*Voices off.*] Hark! It sounds as if the judge is using the rack![4] Listen. Perhaps we can hear what they say.

JUDGE [*off*]: Now tell the truth, old man.

FRONDOSO: Laurencia! They are torturing an old man.

LAURENCIA: They will stop at nothing.

ESTEBAN [*off*]: Let loose a little.

JUDGE [*off*]: Let it go. Now tell me. Who killed the Commander?

ESTEBAN [*off*]: Fuenteovejuna did it.

LAURENCIA: Father, may you live forever.

FRONDOSO: He kept his word.

JUDGE [*off*]: That boy! We will take him next. You know who did it, child. Come, tell me. What, will you be silent, dog? Turn the wheel, you drunken oaf.

BOY [*off*]: Fuenteovejuna, sir.

JUDGE [*off*]: Now, by the King's life, do you want me to hang you all with my own hands? Who killed the Commander?

FRONDOSO: It is beyond belief. That they could torture a child, and he answer like that.

LAURENCIA: The village is showing great courage.

FRONDOSO: Courage and determination.

JUDGE [*off*]: Now stretch that woman on the rack. Good. Give it another turn.

LAURENCIA: He is growing wild with rage.

---

4. One of the favored instruments of torture used by the Inquisition as well as by the Spanish government for forcing confession. This scene of torture is based closely on the account Lope found in the *Chronicles:* "The Judge commanded that many women and children of young age be put to torture."

JUDGE [*off*]: Believe me, I will kill every one of you on this rack. I will find out the truth. Who killed the Commander?

PASCUALA [*off*]: Fuenteovejuna, my lord.

JUDGE [*off*]: Go on. Tighter.

FRONDOSO: It is no good.

LAURENCIA: Pascuala is not giving in.

FRONDOSO: When the children will not confess, how could the rest?

JUDGE [*off*]: It seems they enjoy it. Give it another turn!

PASCUALA [*off*]: Merciful heaven!

JUDGE [*off*]: Another turn, you fool, are you deaf?

PASCUALA [*off*]: Fuenteovejuna killed him.

JUDGE [*off*]: Bring me that fat fellow, the one with the paunch and no shirt on.

LAURENCIA: Poor Mengo.

FRONDOSO: I am afraid Mengo will confess.

MENGO [*off*]: Oh! Oh!

JUDGE [*off*]: Now, begin.

MENGO [*off*]: Oh!

JUDGE [*off*]: Do you need help?

MENGO [*off*]: Oh! Oh!

JUDGE [*off*]: Now, slave, who killed your Master?

MENGO [*off*]: Oh, I will tell you, sir!

JUDGE [*off*]: Let loose a little.

FRONDOSO: He is giving way.

JUDGE [*off*]: No answer? Right, put your back into it.

MENGO [*off*]: No, no, I will confess.

JUDGE [*off*]: Who killed him?

MENGO [*off*]: Little old Fuenteovejuna did it.

JUDGE [*off*]: Was there ever seen such stubborn knavery as this? They mock at pain; even those in whom I placed most hope say nothing. Let them go. I am weary.

FRONDOSO: Oh, Mengo, Heaven bless you. You have banished all my fears.

[*The other peasants come out.*]

BARRILDO: Bravo, Mengo!

ALDERMAN: You did splendidly.

BARRILDO: Mengo, well done.

FRONDOSO: Well done indeed.

BARRILDO: Here, my friend, here is a drink for you. Have some of this too.

MENGO: Oh! Oh! What is it?

BARRILDO: Candied fruit.

MENGO: Mm! Oh! Oh!

FRONDOSO: Give him another drink.

BARRILDO: Here, Mengo.

LAURENCIA: Have another fruit.

MENGO: Oh! Oh!

BARRILDO: Here, drink this, Mengo, it is on me.

LAURENCIA: Come, Mengo, there is no need to look so serious about it.

FRONDOSO: If he can mock at the rack, he has a right to take his drinking seriously.

ALDERMAN: Have another, Mengo.

MENGO: Oh. Oh! Yes.

FRONDOSO: You drink your fill, Mengo, you have earned it.

LAURENCIA: Give him a chance, he is downing them as fast as he can already.

FRONDOSO: Put something round him. He is freezing.

BARRILDO: Would you like any more, Mengo?

MENGO: Any amount. Oh, oh!

FRONDOSO: Is there any more wine?

BARRILDO: Yes, drink as much as you can, Mengo. What is the matter?

MENGO: I think I have a cold coming on.

BARRILDO: What you need is a drink.

MENGO: I think this is a little rough to the palate.

FRONDOSO: Have some of this. It is better. Who killed the Commander, Mengo?

MENGO: Little old Fuenteovejuna!

[*They go. Frondoso and Laurencia are left.*]

FRONDOSO: Mengo deserves all the honors they can give him. But tell me, my love, who killed the Commander?

LAURENCIA: Fuenteovejuna, my dear.

FRONDOSO: Who killed him?

LAURENCIA: Oh, you terrify me. Fuenteovejuna did it.

FRONDOSO: And how did I kill you?

LAURENCIA: How? By making me love you so much.

[*They go.*]

In the royal palace at Tordesillas

[*Enter the King and Queen.*]

ISABEL: Sir, I count myself most fortunate to meet you here thus unexpectedly.

KING: I am overjoyed to look upon you again, my queen. Of necessity I had to halt here before resuming the expedition against Portugal.

ISABEL: Perhaps Your Majesty turned a little out of your way because you wished to come here, as now you turn your words to tell me it was "of necessity."

KING: In what state did you leave Castile?

ISABEL: Content and at peace.

KING: How could it be otherwise, when it is you that keeps it so?

[*Enter Don Manrique.*]

MANRIQUE: Your Majesties, the Master of Calatrava has just arrived. He begs that you may grant him audience.

ISABEL: He arrives at a good time. I wished to speak with him.

MANRIQUE: Madam, I would urge you to do so, for despite his youth, he is a valiant soldier.

[*Manrique goes, and returns with the Master.*]

MASTER: Rodrigo Téllez Girón, Master of Calatrava, who never ceases to praise Your Majesties, humbly craves your pardon and forgiveness. I confess that I was deceived, and that I far exceeded the bounds of what was just and pleasing to you. I was misled by Fernando Gómez's advice and my own desire for personal glory. I was faithful to the wrong cause, and now I beg for pardon. And should I be worthy of such mercy at your hands, then from this moment I offer myself as your faithful knight and will prove to you the valor of my sword in your campaign against the Moors of Granada.[5] There shall you see me spread dismay among the heathen, when I raise my red crosses upon their highest towers. Furthermore, I will bring with me five hundred soldiers to serve under your command, and give you my word as a true knight never in my life to offend you more.

KING: Rise up, Master, from the ground. Now you have come to us, you shall evermore be welcome.

MASTER: Your Majesties, my heart finds consolation to hear you pardon me.

ISABEL: We find you a perfect knight, and of rare valor.

MASTER: Most fair Esther, and divine Xerxes.[6]

[Enter Manrique.]

MANRIQUE: Sir, the judge has returned from Fuenteovejuna, and would present himself before Your Majesty.

KING: Be judge of these aggressors, Lady.

MASTER: Sir, if I had not seen your clemency, have no doubt that I would teach them to kill a Commander of our Order.

KING: The matter no longer concerns you, Master.

QUEEN: I confess, I would prefer to leave this judgment to you alone, my lord.

[Enter the Judge.]

JUDGE: Your Majesties, I went to Fuenteovejuna as you commanded, and conducted the inquiry with particular care and diligence. But not one page of evidence was forthcoming with regard to the crime in question, for they all, as one man, and, I must confess, most courageously, replied when questioned: "Fuenteovejuna did it." Three hundred were rigorously questioned upon the rack, and yet, sir, I could extract no further information. All, from children of ten years of age upwards, were tried, but neither coaxing, nor threatening, nor the most cunning questioning would avail. Since I have had no success in revealing any proof of guilt, I submit to Your Majesties, that either you must pardon them or execute the entire population. They are all present here, ready to be brought before you if you wish for more information from them.

KING: Let them come in.

[Enter the Alderman, Frondoso, Esteban, Mengo, Laurencia, and other villagers of Fuenteovejuna.]

LAURENCIA: Are those the King and Queen?

FRONDOSO: Yes, the rulers of all Castile.

LAURENCIA: My word, how beautiful they are! May Saint Anthony bless them.[7]

ISABEL: Are these the murderers?

5. The historical Téllez Girón would die fighting the Moors, in 1482; Granada was one of the Moors' last strongholds in the late 15th century, and they finally left the city in Ferdinand's and Isabella's hands in 1492.
6. As Lope relates in his play *The Beautiful Esther* (drawn from the biblical book), Esther was the Jewish wife of the Persian king Ahasuerus, who appealed with him for the safety of her people when one of Ahasuerus's trusted courtiers commanded their slaughter; Ahasuerus listened to his wife, and saved the Hebrews from death. Xerxes was a king of Persia as well, from the 5th century B.C.E.; he did much to consolidate his kingdom, crushing revolts in Egypt and Babylon. In at least one version of the Book of Esther, Xerxes is listed as Esther's spouse.
7. St. Anthony of Padua, known for his struggle against corrupt clergy and oppressors of the poor.

ESTEBAN: Madam, Fuenteovejuna presents itself in all humbleness before Your Majesties, ready to serve you. The cruel tyranny of the late Commander, and the thousand insults which he heaped upon us, were the cause of the trouble. He robbed us of our property, raped our wives and daughters, and was a stranger to all pity.

FRONDOSO: Indeed, Your Majesties, even on our wedding day, he stole this girl whom Heaven blessed me with, and for whom I count myself the luckiest man alive. . . . On our wedding night, I say, he took her to his house as if she had been his own. If this virtuous girl had not shown the spirit she did in the defense of her honor, then the outcome could have been much worse.[8]

MENGO: Now it is my turn to speak. If you will give me leave, then I will make you marvel at the way he abused me. Because I tried to protect a girl whom his men, with bestial arrogance, had tried to rape, that brutal Nero[9] treated me in such a manner that the reverse side of my person was the color of smoked salmon. Three men flogged me and I can show Your Majesties, if you wish, the scars which I carry with me to this day. But suffice it to say that I have spent more than my land is worth in myrtle powders[1] and liniments to heal the skin. . . .

ESTEBAN: Sir, we would be your vassals. You are our rightful king, and therefore have we already presumed to set up your royal arms on our town hall. We hope for your clemency, and that you will accept the pledge of our innocence that we offer you.

KING: Since there is no written evidence forthcoming, although the crime is great, it must be pardoned. And since its people have shown such loyalty to me, this village shall come under my direct jurisdiction.[2] So it shall remain until such time as a Commander worthy of its charge shall emerge to inherit it.

FRONDOSO: Your Majesty has spoken the words that most delight our hearts. And so this tale of Fuenteovejuna ends in happiness.[3]

————— ⊷ ⊠⊹⊠ ⊶ —————

William Shakespeare
1564–1616

Like his contemporary Montaigne, whose remarkable essay "On Cannibals" informs *The Tempest,* William Shakespeare was an armchair traveler. And like Montaigne, he seldom took anything at face value. For his plays, he devoured novellas by Italians, chapbooks by Englishmen, snatches of songs by Spaniards, and tourist propaganda by the New Virginians, who in 1610 were boasting that "after some planting and husbanding the Americas could supply not only England's needs but those of other nations as well." Virginia, that is to say, could be Carthage to England's Rome: the breadbasket for a Europe that still perenially suffered from plague and bad harvests. First performed in 1611, *The Tempest* is a recasting and rigorous questioning of pamphlets such as these, as it explores the anxieties that accompanied England's belated foray

---

8. While Frondoso clearly defends Laurencia's virginity, such a defense seems to go against the logic of the play itself.

9. A reference to the decadent Roman emperor of the 1st century.

1. Ground up, myrtle was said to have healing properties.

2. Formerly tied to Córdoba, Fuenteovejuna was wrested from state control by the Commander in 1467; it will now be placed directly under the monarchs' jurisdiction. While he clearly doesn't justify what the peasants did, the King suggests that he will deal far more justly with the villagers than had the Commander.

3. In the Spanish, Frondoso directly addresses the audience as *discreto senado* or "discreet assembly" as he and the other actors take their leave.

into a New World already occupied by Spanish plantations to the south and French missionaries to the north, not to mention by the native peoples themselves. Shipwreck and drowning, drunken brawls, seditious murder, tense confrontations between natives and Europeans, tender romance, and all within three hours: *The Tempest* is one of only two of Shakespeare's plays that respect the unities of time and place. And all of it is orchestrated by an exiled duke named Prospero, whose exceptional skills at magic and theatrical arts have resulted in many an audience seeing him as a self-portrait of his notoriously elusive creator.

Traditionally read as the culmination of Shakespeare's career, *The Tempest* is a retrospective of earlier plays, and thus of a long and successful theatrical career. It was a career marked by shrewd business practice and shrewd relationships with figures in authority, and one for which the young Will Shakespeare (or Shaxpeare, or Shakyspere, or Shakspere, or Shackspeare—there are over two dozen different spellings of his name) seemed well-prepared. The oldest of five siblings, Shakespeare enjoyed a relatively comfortable bourgeois childhood in Stratford-on-Avon. His mother, Mary Arden, was the daughter of an affluent farmer; his father was a wool-dealer and glover who went into local politics. Stratford-on-Avon was a booming country town on a river that brought in a great deal of traffic, and the town's general prosperity enabled it to hire first-class teachers for the grammar school, where its most famous citizen became well-read in classics, history, and rhetoric.

Little is known of the period between Shakespeare's departure from Stratford Grammar School in 1578 and his marriage in 1582 to Anne Hathaway—he may have apprenticed as a glover for his father—and there are again no records of him until 1587, when he shows up in London, acting and possibly already writing plays. His extraordinarily rapid rise to the top of the competitive theater industry is attested by his success in purchasing a coat-of-arms in 1596 and, a year later, the biggest house in Stratford. In 1599, he was one of five actors in the Lord Chamberlain's Men to hold half the lease for the new Globe Theatre, built by the acting company after their lease at James Burbage's Theatre had expired. By then not only was he listed as "principal comedian" for the company, but he had already written and produced his great history plays and his comedies, one of them—*The Merry Wives of Windsor,* with the burly Falstaff as its protagonist and a town not unlike his native Stratford as its setting—at the specific request of his Queen, Elizabeth I. It may have been Elizabeth's formidable presence that inspired Shakespeare to create for his other comedies some of the classiest heroines in dramatic literature, albeit ones played by boys: notably, the self-possessed Rosalynde, who commandeers the events that transpire in Arden in *As You Like It,* and Viola, in *Twelfth Night,* who wins for herself a duke.

The season of Shakespeare's great tragedies followed, and with it, a change of monarchs and a corresponding change in Shakespeare's status. King James I, formerly James VI of Scotland, ruled England after Elizabeth's death in 1603, and promptly elevated Shakespeare's troupe to the King's Men, authorizing the actors to wear livery and inviting them to play some thirteen times a year at court. *Julius Caesar* and *Hamlet* predate James's succession, while *Othello, Macbeth,* and *King Lear* were written shortly after James became king. They were followed by works that do not fit nicely into distinct categories. *Antony and Cleopatra,* with its flirtatious Egyptian queen, lacks the momentum and drive of the earlier tragedies, and *Measure for Measure* ends too uneasily to be confused with the earlier comedies. Shakespeare's increasing interest in experimenting with dramatic structure is evident in the final plays of his career: *Winter's Tale, Cymbeline, Pericles,* and *The Tempest.* With their exotic settings and fantastic plots, their mixture of deaths and comic rebirths, they represent yet again a sharp departure from what had come before, while returning to themes that had always sparked Shakespeare's interest—jealousy, the trials of kingship, the possibilities afforded by escape to a pastoral world. Shakespeare officially retired from the stage in 1613, the year the capacious Globe Theatre burned down while *Henry VIII,* which Shakespeare wrote in collaboration with John Fletcher, was being performed. In April of 1616 he died in Stratford, having bequeathed to the

English-speaking world several long narrative poems, over a hundred and fifty sonnets, and thirty-seven plays (see page 235 for a selection of the sonnets).

The Tempest opened the voluminous collection overseen and published by Shakespeare's fellow actors in 1623. The First Folio, as it has been traditionally called, groups Shakespeare's works by genre. The fact that *The Tempest* is followed by *Two Gentlemen of Verona* and *Merry Wives of Windsor* suggests that the actors perceived it as a comedy. And so, in many respects, it is. It celebrates the magician's powers and those of the theater in which Shakespeare spent his adult life. It effects reconciliations undreamed of and lures us and its characters into brave new worlds; written on the edge of the baroque, it remarks throughout on theater's capacity to use illusion for peaceful resolutions—the most resounding of which is the love affair between Prospero's daughter Miranda and the dashing Ferdinand. An island spirit named Ariel is Prospero's Puckish servant, who does his master's bidding by transforming himself into (mostly female) roles and controlling characters as though they were puppets, first befuddling them, then bringing them together on the stage for revelations of life and death. Yet Shakespeare is also conscious of art's limitations, especially when confronted by the messiness of politics and family affairs. *The Tempest* is relentlessly realistic with respect to the extent to which "human nature" resists even the most artful Machiavellian tactics. Indeed, Prospero, the play's reigning Machiavellian, while provoking sympathy for his plight at his brother Antonio's hands, was a bad ruler who ignored office of state to pursue his magical arts; and it is only on the island that Prospero finds a means of bringing statecraft and witchcraft together for manipulative, at times, sadistic effect. The doubleness of Prospero's achievement is highlighted at the play's end, when Prospero must address the gaping Europeans' wonder not over a beautiful Miranda but over his "deformed" slave: "the thing of darkness" that he acknowledges, in a perplexing moment, as his own. Indeed, Caliban, whose name may be an anagram for "cannibal," represents a terrain which Machiavelli, in his cynical portrait of the ideal Renaissance ruler of a century earlier, had barely imagined: colonial encounters abroad with defiant indigenous peoples. The tumultuous relationship between Prospero and Caliban would inspire the later meditations of Caribbean and Latin American writers, especially Aimé Césaire, whose own twentieth-century *Tempest* is excerpted in the Resonance that follows.

Yet Caliban is no "cannibal," and some of his lines—as when he reminds Prospero that once he "lov'd thee, / And show'd thee all the qualities o'th'isle, / The fresh springs, brine-pits, barren place and fertile"—are some of the most poetic in the play. At the same time, he is versatile enough to speak in bantering prose with the "jester" Trinculo and with Stephano, a "drunken butler," who contemplate taking the island over as theirs. Shakespeare's own ability to move back and forth between stunning poetry and prosaic wit distinguishes almost his entire dramatic canon, as he draws for his characters on extremely diverse segments of society and convincingly creates a world through their language; Elizabethans said they would go to *hear,* not *see,* a play, and this emphasis on the ear suggests for us the power that the dramatic word could have. But Shakespeare also derives his fast-paced dialogues and moving verse from a wealth of literary and dramatic traditions, both ancient and contemporary. The vibrant practices of the Italian professional theater or the *commedia dell'arte*—literally, the actor's guild, although the expression has come to designate the improvised scenarios of masked actors such as the hunchbacked merchant, the bumbling doctor, the wily servant—have long been considered an influence particularly on *The Tempest,* with its slapstick scenes of low life. On the other hand, Rome's most accomplished poet, Virgil, furnished not only the source of the wondering lines spoken by Ferdinand when he imagines Miranda to be a goddess, but the chaotic storm with which both the *Aeneid* and *The Tempest* open. And Ovid's *Metamorphoses* gave Shakespeare the powerful verses recited by Prospero when he abjures his "rough magic" and promises to drown his book: they are the words of Medea, the vengeful sorceress of Greek and Roman myth. If Shakespeare on the one hand lends to his characters' language the cadences of everyday life, on the other he infuses it with the resonant poetry of earlier literary geniuses, and thereby participates in the broader cultural project of the English Renaissance, making the legacy of Roman empire and the European Renaissance alike England's own.

And yet not entirely its own. The haunting poetry of the waif Ariel—"Full fathom five thy father lies, / Of his bones are coral made"—would have been sung to an uncomprehending Ferdinand and audience alike, as though Shakespeare was making us and Ferdinand experience the unsettling feeling of what it is like to be in a place where we have lost our normal bearings. But this may in fact be what all of Shakespeare's theater tries to accomplish. The geography of London was such that the public theaters were on the other side—the wrong side—of the Thames River from the city's official neighborhoods, and the entertainment district was in some sense discontinuous with the real London. Similarly, *The Tempest* takes place like so many of Shakespeare's plays not at "home" but somewhere else: in this case, on an unnamed island in the Mediterranean that vanishes off the surface of the map as soon as the play is done. In remarking again and again on the insubstantialities of a play that has given us a narrative about marriage between old world and new, between the seasoned colonist Ferdinand and the innocent Miranda, Shakespeare points to the strange insubstantialities of stories about love and conquest alike. At the same time, in calling attention to the extent to which the problematic figure of Prospero is behind those stories, Shakespeare takes care to insinuate that he, like his audience, bears responsibility for what can happen to narratives once they are set in motion.

PRONUNCIATIONS:

Prospero: PROS-pe-ro
Trinculo: TRIN-coo-lo

The Tempest

The Names of the Actors

ALONSO, *King of Naples*
SEBASTIAN, *his brother*
PROSPERO, *the right Duke of Milan*
ANTONIO, *his brother, the usurping*
    Duke of Milan
FERDINAND, *son to the King of Naples*
GONZALO, *an honest old councillor*
ADRIAN *and* ⎱ *lords*
FRANCISCO, ⎰
CALIBAN, *a savage and deformed slave*
TRINCULO, *a jester*

STEPHANO, *a drunken butler*
MASTER *of a ship*
BOATSWAIN
MARINERS
MIRANDA, *daughter to Prospero*
ARIEL, *an airy spirit*
IRIS
CERES
JUNO   ⎱ (*presented by*) *spirits*
NYMPHS
REAPERS

[*Other Spirits attending on Prospero*]

Scene: An uninhabited island

ACT 1

Scene 1

[*A tempestuous noise of thunder and lightning heard. Enter a Shipmaster and a Boatswain.*][1]

MASTER: Boatswain!
BOATSWAIN: Here, Master. What cheer?

1. Location: On board ship.

MASTER: Good, speak to the mariners. Fall to 't yarely,[2] or we run ourselves aground. Bestir, bestir!

[Exit.]

[Enter Mariners.]

BOATSWAIN: Heigh, my hearts! Cheerly, cheerly, my hearts! Yare, yare! Take in the topsail. Tend[3] to the Master's whistle.—Blow[4] till thou burst thy wind, if room enough![5]

[Enter Alonso, Sebastian, Antonio, Ferdinand, Gonzalo, and others.]

ALONSO: Good Boatswain, have care. Where's the Master? Play[6] the men.

BOATSWAIN: I pray now, keep below.

ANTONIO: Where is the Master, Boatswain?

BOATSWAIN: Do you not hear him? You mar our labor. Keep your cabins! You do assist the storm.

GONZALO: Nay, good, be patient.

BOATSWAIN: When the sea is. Hence! What cares these roarers[7] for the name of king?
15   To cabin! Silence! Trouble us not.

GONZALO: Good, yet remember whom thou hast aboard.

BOATSWAIN: None that I more love than myself. You are a councillor; if you can command these elements to silence and work the peace of the present, we will not hand[8] a rope more. Use your authority. If you cannot, give thanks
20   you have lived so long and make yourself ready in your cabin for the mischance of the hour, if it so hap.—Cheerly, good hearts!—Out of our way, I say.

[Exit.]

GONZALO: I have great comfort from this fellow. Methinks he hath no drowning mark upon him; his complexion is perfect gallows.[9] Stand fast, good Fate, to
25   his hanging! Make the rope of his destiny our cable, for our own doth little advantage.[1] If he be not born to be hanged, our case is miserable.

[Exeunt (courtiers).]

[Enter Boatswain.]

BOATSWAIN: Down with the topmast! Yare! Lower, lower! Bring her to try wi' the main course.[2] *[A cry within.]* A plague upon this howling! They are louder than the weather or our office.[3]

[Enter Sebastian, Antonio, and Gonzalo.]

30   Yet again? What do you here? Shall we give o'er and drown? Have you a mind to sink?

SEBASTIAN: A pox o'your throat, you bawling, blasphemous, incharitable dog!

BOATSWAIN: Work you, then.

---

2. Quickly.
3. Attend.
4. Addressed to the wind.
5. As long as we have sea room enough.
6. Ply? Urge the men to exert themselves.
7. Waves or wind.

8. Handle.
9. Alludes to the proverb "He that's born to be hanged need fear no drowning."
1. Doesn't do much good.
2. Sail her close to the wind.
3. The noise we make at our work.

ANTONIO: Hang, cur! Hang, you whoreson, insolent noisemaker! We are less afraid
35   to be drowned than thou art.
GONZALO: I'll warrant him for drowning,[4] though the ship were no stronger than a
     nutshell and as leaky as an unstanched[5] wench.
BOATSWAIN: Lay her ahold,[6] ahold! Set her two courses.[7]
     Off to sea again! Lay her off!

[Enter Mariners, wet]

MARINERS: All lost! To prayers, to prayers! All lost!

[The Mariners run about in confusion, exiting at random.]

BOATSWAIN: What, must our mouths be cold?[8]
GONZALO: The King and Prince at prayers! Let's assist them,
     For our case is as theirs.
SEBASTIAN: I am out of patience.
ANTONIO: We are merely° cheated of our lives by drunkards.   *utterly*
45   This wide-chapped° rascal! Would thou mightst lie drowning   *wide-jawed*
     The washing of ten tides![9]
GONZALO: He'll be hanged yet,
     Though every drop of water swear against it
     And gape at wid'st to glut° him.   *gobble*
     [A confused noise within.]   "Mercy on us!"—
     "We split, we split!"—"Farewell my wife and children!" —
50   "Farewell, brother!"—"We split, we split, we split!"

                                        [Exit Boatswain.]

ANTONIO: Let's all sink wi' the King.
SEBASTIAN: Let's take leave of him.

                                        [Exit (with Antonio).]

GONZALO: Now would I give a thousand furlongs of sea for an acre of barren ground:
     long heath, brown furze; anything. The wills above be done! But I would
55   fain die a dry death.

                                        [Exit.]

Scene 2[1]

[Enter Prospero (in his magic cloak) and Miranda]

MIRANDA: If by your art, my dearest father, you have
     Put the wild waters in this roar, allay them.
     The sky, it seems, would pour down stinking pitch,
     But that the sea, mounting to th' welkin's cheek,°   *the sky's face*
5   Dashes the fire out. O, I have suffered

---

4. Guarantee against.
5. Loose (suggesting also "menstrual").
6. Close to the wind.
7. Sets of sails.
8. Must we drown in the cold sea; or, let us heat up our

mouths with liquor.
9. Pirates were hanged on the shore and left until three
tides had come in.
1. Location: The island, near Prospero's cell.

With those that I saw suffer! A brave° vessel,   *splendid*
Who had, no doubt, some noble creature in her,
Dashed all to pieces. O, the cry did knock
Against my very heart! Poor souls, they perished.
10   Had I been any god of power, I would
Have sunk the sea within the earth or ere°   *before*
It should the good ship so have swallowed and
The freighting° souls within her.   *forming the cargo*
PROSPERO: Be collected.°   *composed*
No more amazement.° Tell your piteous° heart   *consternation / pitying*
There's no harm done.
MIRANDA: O, woe the day!
PROSPERO: No harm.
I have done nothing but in care of thee,
Of thee, my dear one, thee, my daughter, who
Art ignorant of what thou art, naught knowing
Of whence I am, nor that I am more better
20   Than Prospero, master of a full° poor cell,   *very*
And thy no greater father.
MIRANDA: More to know
Did never meddle° with my thoughts.   *mingle*
PROSPERO: 'Tis time
I should inform thee farther. Lend thy hand
And pluck my magic garment from me. So,

[laying down his magic cloak and staff]

25   Lie there, my art.—Wipe thou thine eyes. Have comfort.
The direful spectacle of the wreck,° which touched   *shipwreck*
The very virtue° of compassion in thee,   *essence*
I have with such provision° in mine art   *foresight*
So safely ordered that there is no soul—
30   No, not so much perdition° as an hair   *loss*
Betid° to any creature in the vessel   *happened*
Which thou heard'st cry, which thou saw'st sink. Sit down.
For thou must now know farther.
MIRANDA *[sitting]*:   You have often
Begun to tell me what I am, but stopped
35   And left me to a bootless inquisition,°   *fruitless inquiry*
Concluding, "Stay, not yet."
PROSPERO: The hour's now come;
The very minute bids thee ope thine ear.
Obey, and be attentive. Canst thou remember
A time before we came unto this cell?
40   I do not think thou canst, for then thou wast not
Out° three years old.   *fully*
MIRANDA: Certainly, sir, I can.
PROSPERO: By what? By any other house or person?
Of anything the image, tell me, that
Hath kept with thy remembrance.

MIRANDA: 'Tis far off,
45   And rather like a dream than an assurance
         That my remembrance warrants.[2] Had I not
         Four or five women once that tended me?
PROSPERO: Thou hadst, and more, Miranda. But how is it
         That this lives in thy mind? What seest thou else
50   In the dark backward and abysm of time?[3]
         If thou rememberest aught ere thou cam'st here,
         How thou cam'st here thou mayst.
MIRANDA: But that I do not.
PROSPERO: Twelve year since, Miranda, twelve year since,
         Thy father was the Duke of Milan and
         A prince of power.
MIRANDA: Sir, are not you my father?
PROSPERO: Thy mother was a piece° of virtue, and   *masterpiece*
         She said thou wast my daughter; and thy father
         Was Duke of Milan, and his only heir
         And princess no worse issued.°   *no less nobly born*
MIRANDA: O the heavens!
60   What foul play had we, that we came from thence?
         Or blessèd was 't we did?
PROSPERO: Both, both, my girl.
         By foul play, as thou sayst, were we heaved thence,
         But blessedly holp° hither.   *helped*
MIRANDA: O, my heart bleeds
         To think o' the teen° that I have turned you to,[4]   *trouble*
65   Which is from° my remembrance! Please you, farther.   *out of*
PROSPERO: My brother and thy uncle, called Antonio—
         I pray thee mark me—that a brother should
         Be so perfidious!—he whom next° thyself   *next to*
         Of all the world I loved, and to him put
70   The manage° of my state, as at that time   *management*
         Through all the seigniories[5] it was the first,
         And Prospero the prime duke, being so reputed
         In dignity, and for the liberal arts
         Without a parallel; those being all my study,
75   The government I cast upon my brother
         And to my state grew stranger,[6] being transported°   *carried away*
         And rapt in secret studies. Thy false uncle—
         Dost thou attend me?
MIRANDA: Sir, most heedfully.
PROSPERO: Being once perfected° how to grant suits,   *grown skillful*
80   How to deny them, who t' advance and who
         To trash for overtopping,[7] new created
         The creatures that were mine, I say, or° changed 'em,   *either*

---

2. A certainty that my memory guarantees.
3. Abyss of the past.
4. I've caused you to remember.

5. City-states of northern Italy.
6. Withdrew from my responsibilities as a duke.
7. To check for going too fast, like hounds.

Or else new formed 'em; having both the key[8]
Of officer and office, set all hearts i' the state
85   To what tune pleased his ear, that° now he was   *so that*
The ivy which had hid my princely trunk
And sucked my verdure out on 't. Thou attend'st not.

MIRANDA: O, good sir, I do.

PROSPERO: I pray thee, mark me.
I, thus neglecting worldly ends, all dedicated
90   To closeness° and the bettering of my mind   *seclusion*
With that which, but by being so retired,
O'erprized° all popular rate,° in my false brother   *outvalued / estimation*
Awaked an evil nature; and my trust,
Like a good parent,[9] did beget of° him   *in*
95   A falsehood in its contrary as great
As my trust was, which had indeed no limit,
A confidence sans° bound. He being thus lorded°   *without / made a lord*
Not only with what my revenue yielded
But what my power might else exact, like one
100 Who, having into° truth by telling of it,   *unto*
Made such a sinner of his memory
To° credit his own lie,[1] he did believe   *as to*
He was indeed the Duke, out° o' the substitution   *as a result*
And executing th' outward face of royalty
105 With all prerogative. Hence his ambition growing—
Dost thou hear?

MIRANDA: Your tale, sir, would cure deafness.

PROSPERO: To have no screen between this part he played
And him he played it for, he needs will be°   *insisted on becoming*
Absolute Milan.[2] Me, poor man, my library
110 Was dukedom large enough. Of temporal royalties
He thinks me now incapable; confederates—°   *allies himself*
So dry° he was for sway—wi' the King of Naples   *thirsty*
To give him annual tribute, do him homage,
Subject his coronet to his crown, and bend
115 The dukedom yet° unbowed—alas, poor Milan!—   *previously*
To most ignoble stooping.

MIRANDA: O the heavens!

PROSPERO: Mark his condition° and th' event,° then tell me   *pact / outcome*
If this might be a brother.

MIRANDA: I should sin
To think but nobly of my grandmother.
120 Good wombs have borne bad sons.

PROSPERO: Now the condition.
This King of Naples, being an enemy
To me inveterate, hearkens° my brother's suit,   *listens to*

---

8. Key for unlocking; tool for tuning stringed instruments.
9. Alludes to the proverb that good parents often bear bad
children; see line 120.

1. Who starts to believe his own lie.
2. Duke of Milan in fact.

Which was that he, in lieu o' the premises[3]
Of homage and I know not how much tribute,
125   Should presently° extirpate° me and mine   *immediately / remove*
Out of the dukedom and confer fair Milan,
With all the honors, on my brother. Whereon,
A treacherous army levied, one midnight
Fated° to th' purpose did Antonio open   *devoted*
130   The gates of Milan, and, i' the dead of darkness,
The ministers° for the purpose hurried thence   *agents*
Me and thy crying self.

MIRANDA: Alack, for pity!
I, not remembering how I cried out then,
Will cry it o'er again. It is a hint°   *occasion*
That wrings[4] mine eyes to 't.

PROSPERO: Hear a little further,
And then I'll bring thee to the present business
Which now's upon 's, without the which this story
Were most impertinent.°   *irrelevant*

MIRANDA: Wherefore° did they not   *why*
That hour destroy us?

PROSPERO: Well demanded,° wench.   *asked*
140   My tale provokes that question. Dear, they durst not,
So dear the love my people bore me, nor set
A mark so bloody on the business, but
With colors fairer painted their foul ends.
In few,° they hurried us aboard a bark,°   *few words / ship*
145   Bore us some leagues to sea, where they prepared
A rotten carcass of a butt,° not rigged,   *tub*
Nor tackle, sail, nor mast; the very rats
Instinctively have quit it. There they hoist us,
To cry to th' sea that roared to us, to sigh
150   To th' winds whose pity, sighing back again,
Did us but loving wrong.

MIRANDA: Alack, what trouble
Was I then to you!

PROSPERO: O, a cherubin
Thou wast that did preserve me. Thou didst smile,
Infused with a fortitude from heaven,
155   When I have decked° the sea with drops full salt,   *adorned*
Under my burden groaned, which raised in me
An undergoing stomach,° to bear up   *courage to endure*
Against what should ensue.

MIRANDA: How came we ashore?

PROSPERO: By Providence divine.
160   Some food we had, and some fresh water, that
A noble Neapolitan, Gonzalo,

---

3. In exchange for the guarantee.   4. Constrains; wrings tears from.

Out of his charity, who being then appointed
Master of this design, did give us, with
Rich garments, linens, stuffs,° and necessaries,   *supplies*
165   Which since have steaded much.° So, of his gentleness,   *been of much use*
Knowing I loved my books, he furnished me
From mine own library with volumes that
I prize above my dukedom.

MIRANDA: Would I might
But ever see that man!

PROSPERO: Now I arise. [*He puts on his magic cloak.*]
170   Sit still, and hear the last of our sea sorrow.
Here in this island we arrived; and here
Have I, thy schoolmaster, made thee more profit°   *profit more*
Than other princes'° can, that have more time   *princesses*
For vainer hours and tutors not so careful.

MIRANDA: Heavens thank you for 't! And now, I pray you, sir—
For still 'tis beating in my mind—your reason
For raising this sea storm?

PROSPERO: Know thus far forth:
By accident most strange, bountiful Fortune,
Now my dear lady, hath mine enemies
180   Brought to this shore; and by my prescience
I find my zenith° doth depend upon   *apex of fortune*
A most auspicious star, whose influence
If now I court not, but omit,° my fortunes   *neglect*
Will ever after droop. Here cease more questions.
185   Thou art inclined to sleep. 'Tis a good dullness,°   *drowsiness*
And give it way. I know thou canst not choose.

[*Miranda sleeps.*]

Come away,° servant, come! I am ready now.   *come here*
Approach, my Ariel, come.

[*Enter Ariel.*]

ARIEL: All hail, great master, grave sir, hail! I come
190   To answer thy best pleasure; be 't to fly,
To swim, to dive into the fire, to ride
On the curled clouds, to thy strong bidding task°   *make demands upon*
Ariel and all his quality.°   *cohorts or abilities*

PROSPERO: Hast thou, spirit,
Performed to point° the tempest that I bade thee?   *in detail*

ARIEL: To every article.
I boarded the King's ship. Now on the beak,°   *prow*
Now in the waist,° the deck,° in every cabin,   *midships / poop*
I flamed amazement.[5] Sometimes I'd divide
And burn in many places; on the topmast,

---

5. Struck terror by appearing as St. Elmo's fire, an electric discharge seen at the prominent parts of ships in stormy weather.

200   The yards, and bowsprit would I flame distinctly,°   *in different places*
         Then meet and join. Jove's lightning, the precursors
         O' the dreadful thunderclaps, more momentary
         And sight-outrunning° were not. The fire and cracks   *swifter than sight*
         Of sulfurous roaring the most mighty Neptune
205   Seem to besiege and make his bold waves tremble,
         Yea, his dread trident shake.

PROSPERO: My brave spirit!
         Who was so firm, so constant, that this coil°   *uproar*
         Would not infect his reason?

ARIEL: Not a soul
         But felt a fever of the mad and played
210   Some tricks of desperation. All but mariners
         Plunged in the foaming brine and quit the vessel,
         Then all afire with me. The King's son, Ferdinand,
         With hair up-staring°—then like reeds, not hair—   *standing on end*
         Was the first man that leapt; cried, "Hell is empty,
         And all the devils are here!"

PROSPERO: Why, that's my spirit!
         But was not this nigh shore?

ARIEL: Close by, my master.

PROSPERO: But are they, Ariel, safe?

ARIEL: Not a hair perished.
         On their sustaining garments[6] not a blemish,
         But fresher than before; and, as thou bad'st me,
220   In troops I have dispersed them 'bout the isle.
         The King's son have I landed by himself,
         Whom I left cooling of the air with sighs
         In an odd angle° of the isle, and sitting,   *corner*
         His arms in this sad knot. [*He folds his arms.*]

PROSPERO: Of the King's ship,
225   The mariners, say how thou hast disposed,
         And all the rest o' the fleet.

ARIEL: Safely in harbor
         Is the King's ship; in the deep nook,° where once   *bay*
         Thou called'st me up at midnight to fetch dew[7]
         From the still-vexed° Bermudas,[8] there she's hid;   *ever stormy*
230   The mariners all under hatches stowed,
         Who, with a charm joined to their suffered° labor,   *undergone*
         I have left asleep. And for the rest o' the fleet,
         Which I dispersed, they all have met again
         And are upon the Mediterranean float°   *sea*
235   Bound sadly home for Naples,
         Supposing that they saw the King's ship wrecked

---

6. Garments that buoyed them up in the sea.
7. For magical purposes; see line 322.
8. Perhaps refers to the then-recent Bermuda shipwreck of 1609, when one of nine ships sailing from England to

Virginia was driven onto the Bermuda coast in a severe storm. As in *The Tempest*, all on board survived, although the news took a while to reach those in England, who had presumed the crew lost.

And his great person perish.

PROSPERO: Ariel, thy charge
Exactly is performed. But there's more work.
What is the time o' the day?

ARIEL: Past the mid season.°   *noon*

PROSPERO: At least two glasses.° The time twixt six and now   *hourglasses*
Must by us both be spent most preciously.

ARIEL: Is there more toil? Since thou dost give me pains,°   *labors*
Let me remember° thee what thou hast promised,   *remind*
Which is not yet performed me.

PROSPERO: How now? Moody?
What is't thou canst demand?

ARIEL: My liberty.

PROSPERO: Before the time be out? No more!

ARIEL: I prithee,
Remember I have done thee worthy service,
Told thee no lies, made thee no mistakings, served
Without or grudge or grumblings. Thou did promise
To bate° me a full year.   *remit*

PROSPERO: Dost thou forget
From what a torment I did free thee?

ARIEL: No.

PROSPERO: Thou dost, and think'st it much to tread the ooze
Of the salt deep,
To run upon the sharp wind of the north,
255   To do me° business in the veins⁹ o' the earth   *do for me*
When it is baked° with frost.   *hardened*

ARIEL: I do not, sir.

PROSPERO: Thou liest, malignant thing! Hast thou forgot
The foul witch Sycorax, who with age and envy°   *malice*
Was grown into a hoop?¹ Hast thou forgot her?

ARIEL: No, sir.

PROSPERO: Thou hast. Where was she born? Speak. Tell me.

ARIEL: Sir, in Argier.°   *Algiers*

PROSPERO: O, was she so? I must
Once in a month recount what thou hast been,
Which thou forget'st. This damned witch Sycorax,
265   For mischiefs manifold and sorceries terrible
To enter human hearing, from Argier,
Thou know'st, was banished. For one thing she did°   *becoming pregnant*
They would not take her life. Is not this true?

ARIEL: Ay, sir.

PROSPERO: This blue-eyed² hag was hither brought with child°   *pregnant*
And here was left by the sailors. Thou, my slave,
As thou report'st thyself, was then her servant;
And, for° thou wast a spirit too delicate   *because*

9. Of minerals, or underground streams.   2. With dark circles under her eyes, implying pregnancy.
1. So bent with age as to resemble a hoop.

	To act her earthy and abhorred commands,	
275	Refusing her grand hests,° she did confine thee,	*orders*
	By help of her more potent ministers	
	And in her most unmitigable rage,	
	Into a cloven pine, within which rift	
	Imprisoned thou didst painfully remain	
280	A dozen years; within which space she died	
	And left thee there, where thou didst vent thy groans	
	As fast as mill wheels strike.³ Then was this island—	
	Save° for the son that she did litter° here,	*except / give birth to*
	A freckled whelp,° hag-born—not honored with	*animal offspring*
	A human shape.	

ARIEL: Yes, Caliban her son.

PROSPERO: Dull thing, I say so:⁴ he, that Caliban
Whom now I keep in service. Thou best know'st
What torment I did find thee in. Thy groans
Did make wolves howl, and penetrate the breasts

290	Of ever-angry bears. It was a torment	
	To lay upon the damned, which Sycorax	
	Could not again undo. It was mine art,	
	When I arrived and heard thee, that made gape°	*open wide*
	The pine and let thee out.	

ARIEL: I thank thee, master.

PROSPERO: If thou more murmur'st, I will rend an oak
And peg thee in his° knotty entrails till   *its*
Thou hast howled away twelve winters.

ARIEL: Pardon, master.
I will be correspondent° to command   *obedient*
And do my spriting⁵ gently.°   *graciously*

PROSPERO: Do so, and after two days
I will discharge thee.

ARIEL: That's my noble master!
What shall I do? Say what? What shall I do?

PROSPERO: Go make thyself like a nymph o' the sea. Be subject
To no sight but thine and mine, invisible
To every eyeball else. Go take this shape

| 305 | And hither come in 't. Go, hence with diligence! | |

                                                        [*Exit (Ariel).*]

Awake, dear heart, awake! Thou hast slept well.
Awake!

MIRANDA: The strangeness of your story put
Heaviness° in me.   *drowsiness*

PROSPERO: Shake it off. Come on,
We'll visit Caliban, my slave, who never
Yields us kind answer.

---

3. As the blades of a mill wheel strike water.   5. Duties as a spirit.
4. Exactly, that's what I said, you dimwit.

MIRANDA: 'Tis a villain, sir,
        I do not love to look on.
PROSPERO: But, as 'tis,
        We cannot miss° him. He does make our fire,   *do without*
        Fetch in our wood, and serves in offices°   *functions*
        That profit us.—What ho! Slave! Caliban!
        Thou earth, thou! Speak.
CALIBAN [*within*]:   There's wood enough within.
PROSPERO: Come forth, I say! There's other business for thee.
        Come, thou tortoise! When?[6]

        [*Enter Ariel like a water nymph.*]

        Fine apparition! My quaint° Ariel,   *ingenious*
        Hark in thine ear. [*He whispers.*]
ARIEL: My lord, it shall be done.

                                                                       [*Exit.*]

PROSPERO: Thou poisonous slave, got° by the devil himself   *begotten*
        Upon thy wicked dam,° come forth!   *mother*

        [*Enter Caliban.*]

CALIBAN: As wicked dew as e'er my mother brushed
        With raven's feather from unwholesome fen°   *marsh*
        Drop on you both! A southwest° blow on ye   *diseased wind*
325   And blister you all o'er!
PROSPERO: For this, be sure, tonight thou shalt have cramps,
        Side-stitches that shall pen thy breath up. Urchins[7]
        Shall forth at vast° of night that they may work[8]   *desolate time*
        All exercise on thee. Thou shalt be pinched
330   As thick as honeycomb, each pinch more stinging
        Than bees that made 'em.
CALIBAN: I must eat my dinner.
        This island's mine, by Sycorax my mother,
        Which thou tak'st from me. When thou cam'st first,
        Thou strok'st me and made much of me, wouldst give me
335   Water with berries in 't, and teach me how
        To name the bigger light, and how the less,
        That burn by day and night. And then I loved thee
        And showed thee all the qualities° o' th' isle,   *resources*
        The fresh springs, brine pits, barren place and fertile.
340   Cursed be I that did so! All the charms°   *spells*
        Of Sycorax, toads, beetles, bats, light on you!
        For I am all the subjects that you have,
        Which first was mine own king; and here you, sty° me   *put me in a sty*
        In this hard rock, whiles you do keep from me
        The rest o' th' island.

6. Expression of impatience.   8. Malignant spirits were thought to prowl at night.
7. Hedgehogs (here, goblins in the shape of hedgehogs).

PROSPERO: Thou most lying slave,
         Whom stripes° may move, not kindness! I have used thee,   *lashes*
         Filth as thou art, with humane care, and lodged thee
         In mine own cell, till thou didst seek to violate
         The honor of my child.
CALIBAN: O ho, O ho! Would't had been done!
         Thou didst prevent me; I had peopled else°   *otherwise populated*
         This isle with Calibans.
MIRANDA:⁹   Abhorrèd slave,
         Which any print° of goodness wilt not take,   *imprint*
         Being capable of all ill! I pitied thee,
355   Took pains to make thee speak, taught thee each hour
         One thing or other. When thou didst not, savage,
         Know thine own meaning, but wouldst gabble like
         A thing most brutish, I endowed thy purposes°   *meanings*
         With words that made them known. But thy vile race,°   *nature*
360   Though thou didst learn, had that in 't which good natures
         Could not abide to be with; therefore wast thou
         Deservedly confined into this rock,
         Who hadst deserved more than a prison.
CALIBAN: You taught me language, and my profit on 't
365   Is I know how to curse. The red° plague rid° you   *bubonic / destroy*
         For learning me your language!
PROSPERO: Hagseed, hence!
         Fetch us in fuel, and be quick, thou'rt best,¹
         To answer other business²: Shrugg'st thou, malice?
         If thou neglect'st or dost unwillingly
370   What I command, I'll rack thee with old³ cramps,
         Fill all thy bones with aches,⁴ make thee roar
         That beasts shall tremble at thy din.
CALIBAN: No, pray thee.
         [*Aside.*] I must obey. His art is of such power
         It would control my dam's god, Setebos,⁵
         And make a vassal of him.
PROSPERO: So, slave, hence!

                                              [*Exit Caliban.*]

    [*Enter Ferdinand; and Ariel, invisible,⁶ playing and singing. (Ferdinand does
not see Prospero and Miranda.)*]

                         [*Ariel's Song.*]

ARIEL: *Come unto these yellow sands,*
                              And then take hands;
                         Curtsied when you have, and kissed

---

9. This speech is sometimes assigned by editors to Prospero.
1. You'd be well advised.
2. Perform other tasks.
3. Such as old people have.

4. Pronounced "aitches."
5. A god of the Patagonians, at the tip of South America,
named in Richard Eden's *History of Travel*, 1577.
6. To the other characters.

     The wild waves whist⁷;
380   *Foot it featly° here and there,*   *dance nimbly*
     And, sweet sprites, bear
     The burden. Hark, hark!
     [*Burden,° dispersedly (within): Bow-wow.*]   *Refrain*
     The watchdogs bark.
385   [*Burden, dispersedly within: Bow-wow.*]
     Hark, hark! I hear
     The strain of strutting chanticleer
     Cry Cock-a-diddle-dow.

FERDINAND: Where should this music be? I' th' air or th' earth?
390 It sounds no more; and sure it waits upon
    Some god o' th' island. Sitting on a bank,
    Weeping again the King my father's wreck,
    This music crept by me upon the waters,
    Allaying both their fury and my passion°   *lamentation*
395 With its sweet air. Thence I have followed it,
    Or it hath drawn me rather. But 'tis gone.
    No, it begins again.

       [Ariel's Song.]

ARIEL: *Full fathom five thy father lies.*
      Of his bones are coral made.
400   *Those are pearls that were his eyes.*
      Nothing of him that doth fade
     But doth suffer a sea change
      Into something rich and strange.
     Sea nymphs hourly ring his knell.
     [*Burden (within): Ding dong.*]
405   *Hark, now I hear them, ding dong bell.*

FERDINAND: The ditty does remember° my drowned father. *allude to*
    This is no mortal business, nor no sound
    That the earth owes.° I hear it now above me.   *owns*
PROSPERO [*to Miranda*]: The fringèd curtains of thine eye advance° *raise*
    And say what thou seest yond.
MIRANDA: What is 't? A spirit?
    Lord, how it looks about! Believe me, sir,
    It carries a brave° form. But 'tis a spirit.   *excellent*
PROSPERO: No, wench, it eats and sleeps and hath such senses
    As we have, such. This gallant which thou seest
415 Was in the wreck; and, but he's something stained° *disfigured*
    With grief, that's beauty's canker,° thou mightst call him *cankerworm*
    A goodly person. He hath lost his fellows
    And strays about to find 'em.
MIRANDA: I might call him
    A thing divine, for nothing natural

---

7. Kissed the waves into silence.

I ever saw so noble.

PROSPERO [*aside*]:   It goes on, I see,
As my soul prompts° it.—Spirit, fine spirit, I'll free thee   *would like*
Within two days for this.

FERDINAND [*seeing Miranda*]:   Most sure,° the goddess   *this is certainly*
On whom these airs° attend!—Vouchsafe° my prayer   *songs / grant*
May know if you remain° upon this island,   *dwell*
425   And that you will some good instruction give
How I may bear me° here. My prime request,   *conduct myself*
Which I do last pronounce, is—O you wonder!⁸—
If you be maid⁹ or no?

MIRANDA: No wonder, sir,
But certainly a maid.

FERDINAND: My language? Heavens!
430   I am the best° of them that speak this speech,   *in birth*
Were I but where 'tis spoken.

PROSPERO [*coming forward*]:   How? The best?
What wert thou if the King of Naples heard thee?

FERDINAND: A single¹ thing, as I am now, that wonders
To hear thee speak of Naples.° He does hear me,   *King of Naples*
435   And that he does I weep. Myself am Naples,
Who with mine eyes, never since at ebb,° beheld   *dry*
The King my father wrecked.

MIRANDA: Alack, for mercy!

FERDINAND: Yes, faith, and all his lords, the Duke of Milan
And his brave son² being twain.

PROSPERO [*aside*]:   The Duke of Milan
440   And his more braver° daughter could control° thee,   *splendid / refute*
If now 'twere fit to do 't. At the first sight
They have changed eyes.°—Delicate Ariel,   *exchanged love looks*
I'll set thee free for this. [*To Ferdinand.*] A word, good sir.
I fear you have done yourself some wrong.° A word!   *told a lie*

MIRANDA [*aside*]: Why speaks my father so ungently? This
Is the third man that e'er I saw, the first
That e'er I sighed for. Pity move my father
To be inclined my way!

FERDINAND: O, if a virgin,
And your affection not gone forth, I'll make you
The Queen of Naples.

PROSPERO: Soft, sir! One word more.
[*Aside.*] They are both in either's power's; but this swift business
I must uneasy° make, lest too light winning   *difficult*
Make the prize light. [*To Ferdinand.*] One word more: I charge thee
That thou attend° me. Thou dost here usurp   *listen to*
455   The name thou ow'st° not, and hast put thyself   *ownest*

8. Miranda's name means "to be wondered at."   feeble.
9. As opposed to either a goddess or a married woman.   2. Antonio's son is not mentioned elsewhere.
1. Solitary, being at once King of Naples and myself;

Upon this island as a spy, to win it
From me, the lord on 't.

FERDINAND: No, as I am a man.

MIRANDA: There's nothing ill can dwell in such a temple.
If the ill spirit have so fair a house,
Good things will strive to dwell with 't.

PROSPERO: Follow me.—
Speak not you for him; he's a traitor.—Come,
I'll manacle thy neck and feet together.
Seawater shalt thou drink; thy food shall be
The fresh-brook mussels, withered roots, and husks
Wherein the acorn cradled. Follow.

FERDINAND: No!
I will resist such entertainment° till   *treatment*
Mine enemy has more power. [*He draws, and is charmed from moving.*]

MIRANDA: O dear father,
Make not too rash° a trial° of him, for   *harsh / judgment*
He's gentle,° and not fearful.³   *noble*

PROSPERO: What, I say,
470   My foot° my tutor?—Put thy sword up, traitor,   *subordinate*
Who mak'st a show but dar'st not strike, thy conscience
Is so possessed with guilt. Come, from thy ward,°   *defensive posture*
For I can here disarm thee with this stick
And make thy weapon drop. [*He brandishes his staff.*]

MIRANDA [*trying to hinder him*]:   Beseech you, father!

PROSPERO: Hence! Hang not on my garments.

MIRANDA: Sir, have pity!
I'll be his surety.°   *guarantee*

PROSPERO: Silence! One word more
Shall make me chide thee, if not hate thee. What,
An advocate for an impostor? Hush!
Thou think'st there is no more such shapes as he,
480   Having seen but him and Caliban. Foolish wench,
To° the most of men this is a Caliban,   *compared to*
And they to him are angels.

MIRANDA: My affections
Are then most humble; I have no ambition
To see a goodlier man.

PROSPERO [*to Ferdinand*]:   Come on, obey.
485   Thy nerves° are in their infancy again   *sinews*
And have no vigor in them.

FERDINAND: So they are.
My spirits,° as in a dream, are all bound up.   *vital powers*
My father's loss, the weakness which I feel,
The wreck of all my friends, nor this man's threats
490   To whom I am subdued, are but light° to me,   *unimportant*

3. Frightening; cowardly.

Might I but through my prison once a day
Behold this maid. All corners else° o' th' earth   *other regions*
Let liberty make use of; space enough
Have I in such a prison.
PROSPERO [*aside*]:   It works. [*To Ferdinand.*] Come on.—
495   Thou hast done well, fine Ariel! [*To Ferdinand.*] Follow me.
          [*To Ariel.*] Hark what thou else shalt do me.°   *for me*
MIRANDA [*to Ferdinand*].   Be of comfort.
          My father's of a better nature, sir,
          Than he appears by speech. This is unwonted°   *unusual*
          Which now came from him.
PROSPERO [*to Ariel*]:   Thou shalt be as free
500   As mountain winds; but then° exactly do   *until then*
          All points of my command.
ARIEL: To th' syllable.
PROSPERO [*to Ferdinand*]: Come, follow. [*To Miranda.*] Speak not for him.

                                                                        [*Exeunt.*]

                              A C T   2

                              Scene 1[1]

[*Enter Alonso, Sebastian, Antonio, Gonzalo, Adrian, Francisco, and others.*]

GONZALO [*to Alonso*]: Beseech you, sir, be merry. You have cause,
          So have we all, of joy, for our escape
          Is much beyond our loss. Our hint° of woe   *occasion*
          Is common; every day some sailor's wife,
5   The masters of some merchant, and the merchant,[2]
          Have just our theme of woe. But for the miracle,
          I mean our preservation, few in millions
          Can speak like us. Then wisely, good sir, weigh
          Our sorrow with our comfort.
ALONSO: Prithee, peace.
SEBASTIAN [*aside to Antonio*]: He receives comfort like cold porridge.[3]
ANTONIO [*aside to Sebastian*]: The visitor[4] will not give him o'er[5] so.
SEBASTIAN: Look, he's winding up the watch of his wit; by and by it will strike.
GONZALO [*to Alonso*]: Sir—
SEBASTIAN [*aside to Antonio*]: One. Tell °   *keep count*
GONZALO: When every grief is entertained
          That's offered, comes to th' entertainer—
SEBASTIAN: A dollar.[6]
GONZALO: Dolor comes to him, indeed. You have spoken truer than you purposed.
SEBASTIAN: You have taken it wiselier than I meant you should.
GONZALO [*to Alonso*]: Therefore, my lord—

---

1. Location: Another part of the island.
2. Officers of some merchant vessel and the owner himself.
3. Broth, with a pun on *peace* (peas), often used in porridge.
4. One taking comfort to the sick, as Gonzalo is doing.

5. Let him alone.
6. Widely circulated coin. (Sebastian puns on *entertainer* in the sense of inn-keeper; to Gonzalo, *dollar* suggests "dolor," or grief.)

ANTONIO: Fie, what a spendthrift is he of his tongue!

ALONSO [*to Gonzalo*]: I prithee, spare.°   *forbear*

GONZALO: Well, I have done. But yet—

SEBASTIAN [*aside to Antonio*]: He will be talking.

ANTONIO [*aside to Sebastian*]: Which, of he or Adrian, for a good wager, first begins
to crow?[7]

SEBASTIAN: The old cock.°   *Gonzalo*

ANTONIO: The cockerel.°   *Adrian*

SEBASTIAN: Done. The wager?

ANTONIO: A laughter.[8]

SEBASTIAN: A match!°   *agreed*

ADRIAN: Though this island seem to be desert—°   *uninhabited*

ANTONIO: Ha, ha, ha!

SEBASTIAN: So, you're paid.

ADRIAN: Uninhabitable and almost inaccessible—

SEBASTIAN: Yet—

ADRIAN: Yet—

ANTONIO: He could not miss 't.

ADRIAN: It must needs be of subtle, tender, and delicate temperance.°   *climate*

ANTONIO: Temperance° was a delicate wench.[9]   *girl's name*

SEBASTIAN: Ay, and a subtle,° as he most learnedly delivered.[1]   *sexually tricky*

ADRIAN: The air breathes upon us here most sweetly.

SEBASTIAN: As if it had lungs, and rotten ones.

ANTONIO: Or as 'twere perfumed by a fen.

GONZALO: Here is everything advantageous to life.

ANTONIO: True, save° means to live.   *except*

SEBASTIAN: Of that there's none, or little.

GONZALO: How lush and lusty° the grass looks! How green!   *healthy*

ANTONIO: The ground indeed is tawny.°   *dull brown*

SEBASTIAN: With an eye° of green in 't.   *spot*

ANTONIO: He misses not much.

SEBASTIAN: No. He doth but° mistake the truth totally.   *merely*

GONZALO: But the rarity of it is—which is indeed almost beyond credit—

SEBASTIAN: As many vouched rarities[2] are.

GONZALO: That our garments, being, as they were, drenched in the sea, hold notwithstanding their freshness and glosses, being rather new-dyed than stained with
salt water.

ANTONIO: If but one of his pockets[3] could speak, would it not say he lies?

SEBASTIAN: Ay, or very falsely pocket up[4] his report.

GONZALO: Methinks our garments are now as fresh as when we put them on first in
Afric, at the marriage of the King's fair daughter Claribel to the King of
Tunis.

SEBASTIAN: 'Twas a sweet marriage, and we prosper well in our return.

---

7. Speak.
8. Whoever laughs, wins.
9. Antonio is mocking Adrian's Puritan phrase, *tender, and delicate temperance,* by applying it to a young woman.

1. Puritan cant for "well-phrased." (Sebastian joins Antonio in baiting the Puritans.)
2. Wonders guaranteed to be true.
3. I.e., because they are muddy.
4. Suppress.

ADRIAN: Tunis was never graced before with such a paragon to[5] their queen.

GONZALO: Not since widow Dido's[6] time.

ANTONIO [*aside to Sebastian*]: Widow? A pox o' that! How came that "widow" in? Widow Dido!

SEBASTIAN: What if he had said "widower Aeneas" too? Good Lord, how you take it!

ADRIAN [*to Gonzalo*]: "Widow Dido" said you? You make me study of that. She was
70   of Carthage, not of Tunis.

GONZALO: This Tunis, sir, was Carthage.

ADRIAN: Carthage?

GONZALO: I assure you, Carthage.

ANTONIO: His word is more than the miraculous harp.[7]

SEBASTIAN: He hath raised the wall, and houses too.

ANTONIO: What impossible matter will he make easy next?

SEBASTIAN: I think he will carry this island home in his pocket and give it his son for an apple.

ANTONIO: And, sowing the kernels of it in the sea, bring forth more islands.

GONZALO: Ay.[8]

ANTONIO: Why, in good time.

GONZALO [*to Alonso*]: Sir, we were talking that our garments seem now as fresh as when we were at Tunis at the marriage of your daughter, who is now queen.

ANTONIO: And the rarest that e'er came there.

SEBASTIAN: Bate,° I beseech you, widow Dido.   *except*

ANTONIO: O, widow Dido? Ay, widow Dido.

GONZALO: Is not, sir, my doublet as fresh as the first day I wore it? I mean, in a sort.[9]

ANTONIO: That "sort"[1] was well fished for.

GONZALO: When I wore it at your daughter's marriage.

ALONSO: You cram these words into mine ears against
          The stomach of my sense.[2] Would I had never
          Married° my daughter there! For, coming thence,   *married off*
          My son is lost and, in my rate,° she too,   *estimation*
          Who is so far from Italy removed
95   I ne'er again shall see her. O thou mine heir
          Of Naples and of Milan, what strange fish
          Hath made his meal on thee?

FRANCISCO: Sir, he may live.
          I saw him beat the surges° under him   *waves*
          And ride upon their backs. He trod the water,
100   Whose enmity he flung aside, and breasted
          The surge most swoll'n that met him. His bold head
          'Bove the contentious waves he kept, and oared
          Himself with his good arms in lusty stroke

5. For.
6. Queen of Carthage, deserted by Aeneas. (She was, in fact, a widow when Aeneas, a widower, met her, but Antonio may be amused at Gonzalo's prudish use of "widow" for a woman deserted by her lover.)
7. The harp of Amphion, which raised the walls of Thebes; Gonzalo has exceeded that deed by recreating ancient Carthage mistakenly on the site of modern-day Tunis.
8. This and Antonio's rejoinder have not been satisfactorily explained.
9. Comparatively.
1. Play on the idea of drawing lots, or else fishing for something to say.
2. My appetite to hear them.

	To th' shore, that o'er his° wave-worn basis° bowed,	*its / base*
105	As° stooping to relieve him. I not doubt	*as if*
	He came alive to land.	

ALONSO: No, no, he's gone.

SEBASTIAN [*to Alonso*]: Sir, you may thank yourself for this great loss,

	That° would not bless our Europe with your daughter,	*you who*
	But rather loose° her to an African,	*release; lose*
110	Where she at least is banished from your eye,	
	Who hath cause to wet the grief on 't.	

ALONSO: Prithee, peace.

SEBASTIAN: You were kneeled to and importuned otherwise

By all of us, and the fair soul herself

Weighed between loathness and obedience at

| 115 | Which end o' the beam should bow.[3] We have lost your son, | |

I fear, forever. Milan and Naples have

More widows in them of this business' making

Than we bring men to comfort them.

The fault's your own.

| ALONSO: So is the dear'st° o' the loss. | *heaviest* |

GONZALO: My lord Sebastian,

The truth you speak doth lack some gentleness

And time to speak it in. You rub the sore

| When you should bring the plaster.° | *bandage* |

SEBASTIAN: Very well.

| ANTONIO: And most chirurgeonly.° | *like a surgeon* |

GONZALO [*to Alonso*]: It is foul weather in us all, good sir,

When you are cloudy.

SEBASTIAN [*to Antonio*]:   Fowl weather?

ANTONIO [*to Sebastian*]:   Very foul.

GONZALO: Had I plantation[4] of this isle, my lord—

ANTONIO [*to Sebastian*]: He'd sow 't with nettle seed.

SEBASTIAN: Or docks, or mallows.[5]

GONZALO: And were the king on 't, what would I do?

| SEBASTIAN: Scape° being drunk for want° of wine. | *escape / only for lack* |

GONZALO: I' the commonwealth I would by contraries[6]

| Execute all things; for no kind of traffic° | *trade* |

Would I admit; no name of magistrate;

Letters° should not be known; riches, poverty,	*learning*
135	And use of service,° none; contract, succession,°	*servants / inheritance*
	Bourn,° bound of land, tilth,° vineyard, none;	*borders / tilled soil*
	No use of metal, corn,° or wine, or oil;	*grain*

No occupation; all men idle, all,

And women too, but innocent and pure;

No sovereignty—

SEBASTIAN: Yet he would be king on 't.

ANTONIO: The latter end of his commonwealth forgets the beginning.

---

3. Which side of the moral scale was heavier.   5. Antidotes to nettle stings.
4. Colonization; planting.   6. In contrast to custom.

GONZALO: All things in common nature should produce
Without sweat or endeavor. Treason, felony,
Sword, pike,° knife, gun, or need of any engine°   *lance / weapon*
145   Would I not have; but nature should bring forth,
Of its own kind, all foison,° all abundance,   *plenty*
To feed my innocent people.

SEBASTIAN: No marrying 'mong his subjects?

ANTONIO: None, man, all idle—whores and knaves.

GONZALO: I would with such perfection govern, sir,
T' excel the Golden Age.[7]

SEBASTIAN: 'Save° His Majesty!   *God save*

ANTONIO: Long live Gonzalo!

GONZALO: And—do you mark me, sir?

ALONSO: Prithee, no more. Thou dost talk nothing to me.

GONZALO: I do well believe Your Highness, and did it to minister occasion[8] to these
155   gentlemen, who are of such sensible[9] and nimble lungs that they always use
to laugh at nothing.

ANTONIO: 'Twas you we laughed at.

GONZALO: Who in this kind of merry fooling am nothing to you; so you may continue, and laugh at nothing still.

ANTONIO: What a blow was there given!

SEBASTIAN: An[1] it had not fallen flat-long.[2]

GONZALO: You are gentlemen of brave mettle; you would lift the moon out of her
sphere if she would continue in it five weeks without changing.

[*Enter Ariel (invisible) playing solemn music.*]

SEBASTIAN: We would so, and then go a-batfowling.[3]

ANTONIO: Nay, good my lord, be not angry.

GONZALO: No, I warrant you, I will not adventure my discretion[4] so weakly. Will you
laugh me asleep? For I am very heavy.[5]

ANTONIO: Go sleep, and hear us.

[*All sleep except Alonso, Sebastian, and Antonio.*]

ALONSO: What, all so soon asleep? I wish mine eyes
Would, with themselves, shut up my thoughts. I find
They are inclined to do so.

SEBASTIAN: Please you, sir,
Do not omit° the heavy offer of it.   *neglect*
It seldom visits sorrow; when it doth,
It is a comforter.

ANTONIO: We two, my lord,
Will guard your person while you take your rest,
And watch your safety.

---

7. In Hesiod, an age of innocence and abundance.
8. Provide opportunity.
9. Sensitive.
1. If.
2. Fallen flat.

3. Hunting birds at night with sticks (bats); duping a fool
(Gonzalo).
4. Risk my reputation for discretion.
5. Sleepy.

ALONSO: Thank you. Wondrous heavy.

[*Alonso sleeps. Exit Ariel.*]

SEBASTIAN: What a strange drowsiness possesses them!
ANTONIO: It is the quality o' the climate.
SEBASTIAN: Why
180   Doth it not then our eyelids sink? I find not
         Myself disposed to sleep.
ANTONIO: Nor I. My spirits are nimble.
         They fell together all, as by consent;°   *agreement*
         They dropped, as by a thunderstroke. What might,
         Worthy Sebastian, O, what might—? No more.
185   And yet methinks I see it in thy face,
         What thou shouldst be. Th' occasion speaks° thee, and   *summons*
         My strong imagination sees a crown
         Dropping upon thy head.
SEBASTIAN: What, art thou waking?
ANTONIO: Do you not hear me speak?
SEBASTIAN: I do, and surely
190   It is a sleepy language, and thou speak'st
         Out of thy sleep. What is it thou didst say?
         This is a strange repose, to be asleep
         With eyes wide open—standing, speaking, moving—
         And yet so fast asleep.
ANTONIO: Noble Sebastian,
195   Thou lett'st thy fortune sleep—die, rather; wink'st°   *shut your eyes*
         Whiles thou art waking.
SEBASTIAN: Thou dost snore distinctly;°   *articulately*
         There's meaning in thy snores.
ANTONIO: I am more serious than my custom. You
         Must be so too if heed° me, which to do   *you heed*
         Trebles thee o'er.[6]
SEBASTIAN: Well, I am standing water.
ANTONIO: I'll teach you how to flow.
SEBASTIAN: Do so. To ebb
         Hereditary sloth[7] instructs me.
ANTONIO: O,
         If you but knew how you the purpose cherish°   *enrich*
         Whiles thus you mock it! How, in stripping it,
205   You more invest° it! Ebbing men, indeed,   *clothe*
         Most often do so near the bottom run
         By their own fear or sloth.
SEBASTIAN: Prithee, say on:
         The setting° of thine eye and cheek proclaim   *expression*
         A matter from thee, and a birth indeed
210   Which throes° thee much to yield.   *pains*

6. Will make you three times as powerful.   7. Natural laziness; the position of younger son.

ANTONIO: Thus, sir:
    Although this lord of weak remembrance,° this   *memory*
    Who shall be of as little memory°   *as little remembered*
    When he is earthed,° hath here almost persuaded—   *buried*
    For he's a spirit of persuasion, only
215 Professes° to persuade—the King his son's alive,   *functions*
    'Tis as impossible that he's undrowned
    As he that sleeps here swims.
SEBASTIAN: I have no hope
    That he's undrowned.
ANTONIO: O, out of that "no hope"
    What great hope have you! No hope that way is
220 Another way so high a hope that even
    Ambition cannot pierce a wink° beyond,   *glimpse*
    But doubt discovery there. Will you grant with me
    That Ferdinand is drowned?
SEBASTIAN: He's gone.
ANTONIO: Then tell me,
    Who's the next heir of Naples?
SEBASTIAN: Claribel.
ANTONIO: She that is Queen of Tunis; she that dwells
    Ten leagues beyond man's life; she that from Naples
    Can have no note,° unless the sun were post°—   *news / messenger*
    The Man i' the Moon's too slow—till newborn chins
    Be rough and razorable; she that from° whom   *leaving*
230 We all were sea-swallowed, though some cast[8] again,
    And by that destiny to perform an act
    Whereof what's past is prologue, what to come
    In yours and my discharge.°   *business*
SEBASTIAN: What stuff is this? How say you?
    'Tis true my brother's daughter's Queen of Tunis,
235 So is she heir of Naples, twixt which regions
    There is some space.
ANTONIO: A space whose every cubit°   *unit of length*
    Seems to cry out, "How shall that Claribel
    Measure us° back to Naples? Keep in Tunis,   *the cubits*
    And let Sebastian wake." Say this were death
240 That now hath seized them, why, they were no worse
    Than now they are. There be that can rule Naples
    As well as he that sleeps, lords that can prate°   *prattle*
    As amply and unnecessarily
    As this Gonzalo. I myself could make
245 A chough° of as deep chat. O, that you bore   *jackdaw*
    The mind that I do! What a sleep were this
    For your advancement! Do you understand me?
SEBASTIAN: Methinks I do.

---

8. Thrown up; cast, as in a play.

ANTONIO: And how does your content°   *desire*
                Tender° your own good fortune?   *regard*
SEBASTIAN: I remember
250   You did supplant your brother Prospero.
ANTONIO: True.
                And look how well my garments sit upon me,
                Much feater° than before. My brother's servants   *more suitably*
                Were then my fellows.° Now they are my men.°   *equals / servants*
SEBASTIAN: But, for your conscience?
ANTONIO: Ay, sir, where lies that? If 'twere a kibe,°   *sore on the heel*
                'Twould put me to° my slipper; but I feel not   *make me wear*
                This deity in my bosom. Twenty consciences
                That stand twixt me and Milan, candied° be they   *sugared*
                And melt ere they molest!° Here lies your brother,   *interfere*
260   No better than the earth he lies upon,
                If he were that which now he's like—that's dead,
                Whom I, with this obedient steel, three inches of it,
                Can lay to bed forever; whiles you, doing thus,
                To the perpetual wink° for aye° might put   *sleep / ever*
265   This ancient morsel, this Sir Prudence, who
                Should not° upbraid our course. For all the rest,   *would not be able to*
                They'll take° suggestion as a cat laps milk;   *respond to*
                They'll tell the clock° to any business that   *chime in*
                We say befits the hour.
SEBASTIAN: Thy case, dear friend,
270   Shall be my precedent. As thou gott'st Milan,
                I'll come by Naples. Draw thy sword. One stroke
                Shall free thee from the tribute which thou payest,
                And I the king shall love thee.
ANTONIO: Draw together;
                And when I rear my hand, do you the like
                To fall it° on Gonzalo. [*They draw.*]   *let it fall*
SEBASTIAN: O, but one word. [*They talk apart.*]

        [*Enter Ariel (invisible), with music and song.*]

ARIEL [*to Gonzalo*]: My master through his art foresees the danger
                That you, his friend, are in, and sends me forth—
                For else his project dies—to keep them living.

        [*Sings in Gonzalo's ear.*]

                                        While you here do snoring lie,
280   *Open-eyed conspiracy*
                                                His time° doth take.   *opportunity*
                                        If of life you keep a care,
                                        Shake off slumber, and beware.
                                        Awake, awake!

ANTONIO: Then let us both be sudden.°   *quick*
GONZALO [*waking*]: Now, good angels preserve the King!

[*The others wake.*]

ALONSO: Why, how now, ho, awake? Why are you drawn?
      Wherefore this ghastly looking?
GONZALO: What's the matter?
SEBASTIAN: Whiles we stood here securing° your repose,   *guarding*
290   Even now, we heard a hollow burst of bellowing
      Like bulls, or rather lions. Did 't not wake you?
      It struck mine ear most terribly.
ALONSO: I heard nothing.
ANTONIO: O, 'twas a din to fright a monster's ear,
      To make an earthquake! Sure it was the roar
      Of a whole herd of lions.
ALONSO: Heard you this, Gonzalo?
GONZALO: Upon mine honor, sir, I heard a humming,
      And that a strange one too, which did awake me.
      I shaked you, sir, and cried. As mine eyes opened,
      I saw their weapons drawn. There was a noise,
300   That's verily.° 'Tis best we stand upon our guard,   *true*
      Or that we quit this place. Let's draw our weapons.
ALONSO: Lead off this ground, and let's make further search
      For my poor son.
GONZALO: Heavens keep him from these beasts!
      For he is, sure, i' th' island.
ALONSO: Lead away.
ARIEL [*aside*]: Prospero my lord shall know what I have done.
      So, King, go safely on to seek thy son.

                                [*Exeunt (separately).*]

S C E N E 2°

[*Enter Caliban with a burden of wood. A noise of thunder heard.*]

CALIBAN: All the infections that the sun sucks up
      From bogs, fens, flats,° on Prosper fall, and make him   *swamps*
      By inchmeal° a disease! His spirits hear me,   *inch by inch*
      And yet I needs must° curse. But they'll nor° pinch, *have to / neither*
5   Fright me with urchin shows,° pitch me i' the mire, *hedgehog goblins*
      Nor lead me, like a firebrand,[1] in the dark
      Out of my way, unless he bid 'em. But
      For every trifle are they set upon me,
      Sometimes like apes, that mow° and chatter at me   *make faces*
10   And after bite me; then like hedgehogs, which
      Lie tumbling in my barefoot way and mount
      Their pricks at my footfall. Sometimes am I
      All wound with adders, who with cloven tongues

---

9. Location: another part of the island.
1. In the form of a will-'o-th'-wisp, a light that appears at

night over marshy ground, often a metaphor for false
hope.

Do hiss me into madness.

[*Enter Trinculo.*]

15   Lo, now, lo!
Here comes a spirit of his, and to torment me
For bringing wood in slowly. I'll fall flat.
Perchance he will not mind° me. [*He lies down.*]   notice
TRINCULO: Here's neither bush nor shrub to bear off[2] any weather at all. And another
20   storm brewing; I hear it sing i' the wind. Yond same black cloud, yond huge
one, looks like a foul bombard[3] that would shed his[4] liquor. If it should
thunder as it did before, I know not where to hide my head. Yond same
cloud cannot choose but fall by pailfuls. [*Seeing Caliban.*] What have we
here, a man or a fish? Dead or alive? A fish, he smells like a fish; a very
25   ancient and fishlike smell; a kind of not-of-the-newest poor-John.[5] A
strange fish! Were I in England now, as once I was, and had but this fish
painted,[6] not a holiday fool there but would give a piece of silver. There
would this monster make a man.[7] Any strange beast there makes a man.
When they will not give a doit[8] to relieve a lame beggar, they will lay out
30   ten to see a dead Indian. Legged like a man, and his fins like arms! Warm, o'
my troth! I do now let loose my opinion, hold it no longer: this is no fish, but
an islander, that hath lately suffered[9] by a thunderbolt. [*Thunder.*] Alas, the
storm is come again! My best way is to creep under his gaberdine.[1] There is
no other shelter hereabout. Misery acquaints a man with strange bedfel-
35   lows. I will here shroud[2] till the dregs of the storm be past. [*He creeps under
Caliban's garment.*]

[*Enter Stephano, singing, (a bottle in his hand).*]

STEPHANO: "I shall no more to sea, to sea,
Here shall I die ashore—"
This is a very scurvy tune to sing at a man's funeral.
Well, here's my comfort. [*Drinks.*]

[*Sings.*]

40   *"The master, the swabber, the boatswain, and I,*
The gunner and his mate,
Loved Mall, Meg, and Marian, and Margery,
But none of us cared for Kate.
For she had a tongue with a tang,
45   *Would cry to a sailor, 'Go hang!'*
She loved not the savor of tar nor of pitch,
Yet a tailor might scratch her where'er she did itch.
Then to sea, boys, and let her go hang!"

This is a scurvy tune too. But here's my comfort. [*Drinks.*]

2. Ward off.
3. Leather bottle.
4. Its.
5. Salted fish.
6. Painted on a sign outside a booth at a fair.
7. Make a man's fortune; be indistinguishible from an

Englishman.
8. Small coin.
9. Died.
1. Cloak.
2. Take shelter.

CALIBAN: Do not torment me! O!

STEPHANO: What's the matter?[3] Have we devils here? Do you put tricks upon 's with savages and men of Ind,[4] ha? I have not scaped drowning to be afeard now of your four legs. For it hath been said, "As proper[5] a man as ever went on four[6] legs cannot make him give ground"; and it shall be said so again
55   while Stephano breathes at' nostrils.

CALIBAN: This spirit torments me! O!

STEPHANO: This is some monster of the isle with four legs, who hath got, as I take it, an ague. Where the devil should he learn[7] our language? I will give him some relief, if it be but for that.[8] If I can recover[9] him and keep him tame
60   and get to Naples with him, he's a present for any emperor that ever trod on neat's leather.[1]

CALIBAN: Do not torment me, prithee. I'll bring my wood home faster.

STEPHANO: He's in his fit now and does not talk after the wisest. He shall taste of my bottle. If he have never drunk wine afore, it will go near to remove his
65   fit. If I can recover him and keep him tame, I will not take too much[2] for him. He shall pay for him that hath him, and that soundly.

CALIBAN: Thou dost me yet but little hurt; thou wilt anon,[3] I know it by thy trembling. Now Prosper works upon thee.

STEPHANO: Come on your ways. Open your mouth. Here is that which will give
70   language to you, cat.[4] Open your mouth. This will shake your shaking, I can tell you, and that soundly. [*Giving Caliban a drink.*] You cannot tell who's your friend. Open your chaps[5] again.

TRINCULO: I should know that voice. It should be—but he is drowned, and these are devils. O, defend me!

STEPHANO: Four legs and two voices—a most delicate[6] monster! His forward voice now is to speak well of his friend; his backward voice is to utter foul speeches and to detract. If all the wine in my bottle will recover him, I will help[7] his ague. Come. [*Giving a drink.*] Amen! I will pour some in thy other mouth.

TRINCULO: Stephano!

STEPHANO: Doth thy other mouth call me?[8] Mercy, mercy! This is a devil, and no monster. I will leave him. I have no long spoon.[9]

TRINCULO: Stephano! If thou beest Stephano, touch me and speak to me, for I am Trinculo—be not afeard—thy good friend Trinculo.

STEPHANO: If thou beest Trinculo, come forth. I'll pull thee by the lesser legs. If
85   any be Trinculo's legs, these are they. [*Pulling him out.*] Thou art very Trinculo indeed! How cam'st thou to be the siege[1] of this mooncalf?[2] Can he vent[3] Trinculos?

TRINCULO. I took him to be killed with a thunderstroke. But art thou not drowned, Stephano? I hope now thou art not drowned. Is the storm overblown?[4]

---

3. What's going on here?
4. India.
5. Handsome.
6. The expression supplies *two* legs, but Stephano thinks he sees a creature with four.
7. Could he have learned.
8. His speaking our language.
9. Restore.
1. Cowhide.
2. No price will be too much.
3. Presently.

4. Allusion to the proverb "Liquor will make a cat talk."
5. Jaws.
6. Ingenious.
7. Cure.
8. Call my name (know who I am).
9. Allusion to the proverb "He who sups with the devil must have a long spoon."
1. Excrement.
2. Monster.
3. Excrete.
4. Blown over.

90   I hid me under the dead mooncalf's gaberdine for fear of the storm. And art
thou living, Stephano? O Stephano, two Neapolitans scaped! [*He capers
with Stephano.*]

STEPHANO: Prithee, do not turn me about. My stomach is not constant.[5]

CALIBAN: These be fine things, an if[6] they be not spirits.

95   That's a brave[7] god, and bears celestial liquor.
I will kneel to him.

STEPHANO: How didst thou scape? How cam'st thou hither? Swear by this bottle
how thou cam'st hither. I escaped upon a butt of sack[8] which the sailors
heaved o'erboard—by this bottle, which I made of the bark of a tree with

100   mine own hands since I was cast ashore.

CALIBAN [*kneeling*]: I'll swear upon that bottle to be thy true subject, for the liquor is
not earthly.

STEPHANO: Here. Swear then how thou escapedst.

TRINCULO: Swum ashore, man, like a duck. I can swim like a duck, I'll be sworn.

STEPHANO: Here, kiss the book.[9] Though thou canst swim like a duck, thou art made
like a goose.[1] [*Giving him a drink.*]

TRINCULO: O Stephano, hast any more of this?

STEPHANO: The whole butt, man. My cellar is in a rock by the seaside, where my wine
is hid.—How now, mooncalf? How does thine ague?

CALIBAN: Hast thou not dropped from heaven?

STEPHANO: Out o' the moon, I do assure thee. I was the Man i' the Moon when
time was.[2]

CALIBAN: I have seen thee in her, and I do adore thee.
My mistress showed me thee, and thy dog, and thy bush.[3]

STEPHANO: Come, swear to that. Kiss the book. I will furnish it anon with new contents. Swear. [*Giving him a drink.*]

TRINCULO: By this good light, this is a very shallow monster! I afeard of him? A very
weak monster! The Man i' the Moon? A most poor credulous monster! Well
drawn,[4] monster, in good sooth!

CALIBAN [*to Stephano*]: I'll show thee every fertile inch o' th' island,
And I will kiss thy foot. I prithee, be my god.

TRINCULO: By this light, a most perfidious and drunken monster! When 's god's
asleep, he'll rob his bottle.

CALIBAN: I'll kiss thy foot. I'll swear myself thy subject.

STEPHANO: Come on then. Down, and swear.

[*Caliban kneels.*]

TRINCULO: I shall laugh myself to death at this puppy-headed monster. A most scurvy
monster! I could find in my heart to beat him—

STEPHANO: Come, kiss.

TRINCULO: But that the poor monster's in drink.[5] An abominable monster!

CALIBAN: I'll show thee the best springs. I'll pluck thee berries.

---

5. Unsteady.
6. If.
7. Magnificent.
8. Barrel of Canary wine.
9. I.e., the bottle (ironic allusion to swearing on the Bible).

1. With a long neck.
2. Once upon a time.
3. The Man in the Moon was popularly imagined to have with him a dog and a thorn-bush.
4. Drawn from the bottle.
5. Drunk.

I'll fish for thee and get thee wood enough.
A plague upon the tyrant that I serve!
I'll bear him no more sticks, but follow thee,
Thou wondrous man.

TRINCULO: A most ridiculous monster, to make a wonder of a poor drunkard!

CALIBAN: I prithee, let me bring thee where crabs° grow,   *crab apples*
And I with my long nails will dig thee pignuts,°   *peanuts*
Show thee a jay's nest, and instruct thee how
To snare the nimble marmoset.° I'll bring thee   *small monkey*
140   To clustering filberts, and sometimes I'll get thee
Young scamels[6] from the rock. Wilt thou go with me?

STEPHANO: I prithee now, lead the way without any more talking.—Trinculo, the King and all our company else being drowned, we will inherit[7] here.—Here, bear my bottle.—Fellow Trinculo, we'll fill him by and by[8] again.

CALIBAN [*sings drunkenly*]: Farewell, master, farewell, farewell!

TRINCULO: A howling monster; a drunken monster!

CALIBAN: *No more dams I'll make for fish,*
           Nor fetch in firing°   *firewood*
           At requiring,
150   *Nor scrape trenchering,° nor wash dish.*   *wooden plates*
           'Ban, 'Ban, Ca-Caliban
           Has a new master. Get a new man!°   *servant*

Freedom, high-day![9] High-day, freedom! Freedom, high-day, freedom!

STEPHANO: O brave monster! Lead the way. [*Exeunt.*]

ACT 3

Scene 1[1]

[*Enter Ferdinand, bearing a log.*]

FERDINAND: There be some sports are painful,° and their labor   *strenuous*
      Delight in them sets off.° Some kinds of baseness   *compensates*
      Are nobly undergone, and most poor matters°   *poorest affairs*
      Point to rich ends. This my mean° task   *lowly*
5   Would be as heavy to me as odious, but°   *but that*
      The mistress which I serve quickens° what's dead   *brings to life*
      And makes my labors pleasures. O, she is
      Ten times more gentle than her father's crabbed,
      And he's composed of harshness. I must remove
10   Some thousands of these logs and pile them up,
      Upon a sore injunction.° My sweet mistress   *severe command*
      Weeps when she sees me work and says such baseness
      Had never like executor. I forget;
      But these sweet thoughts do even refresh my labors,
      Most busy lest[2] when I do it.

---

6. Unexplained, but either a shellfish or a rock-nesting bird.
7. Take possession.
8. Soon.

9. Holiday.
1. Location: Before Prospero's cell.
2. Busy, but with my mind on other things.

[*Enter Miranda; and Prospero (at a distance, unseen).*]

MIRANDA: Alas now, pray you,
    Work not so hard. I would the lightning had
    Burnt up those logs that you are enjoined° to pile!   *commanded*
    Pray, set it down and rest you. When this burns,
    'Twill weep° for having wearied you. My father   *exude resin*
20   Is hard at study. Pray now, rest yourself.
    He's safe for these three hours.
FERDINAND: O most dear mistress,
    The sun will set before I shall discharge
    What I must strive to do.
MIRANDA: If you'll sit down,
    I'll bear your logs the while. Pray, give me that.
    I'll carry it to the pile.
FERDINAND: No, precious creature,
    I had rather crack my sinews, break my back,
    Than you should such dishonor undergo
    While I sit lazy by.
MIRANDA: It would become me
    As well as it does you; and I should do it
30   With much more ease, for my good will is to it,
    And yours it is against.
PROSPERO [*aside*]:   Poor worm, thou art infected!
    This visitation[3] shows it.
MIRANDA: You look wearily.
FERDINAND: No, noble mistress, 'tis fresh morning with me
    When you are by° at night. I do beseech you—   *nearby*
35   Chiefly that I might set it in my prayers—
    What is your name?
MIRANDA: Miranda.—O my father,
    I have broke your hest° to say so.   *command*
FERDINAND: Admired Miranda![4]
    Indeed the top of admiration, worth
    What's dearest to the world! Full many a lady
40   I have eyed with best regard, and many a time
    The harmony of their tongues hath into bondage
    Brought my too diligent° ear. For several° virtues   *attentive / different*
    Have I liked several women, never any
    With so full soul° but some defect in her   *so wholeheartedly*
45   Did quarrel with the noblest grace she owed°   *owned*
    And put it to the foil.[5] But you, O you,
    So perfect and so peerless, are created
    Of every creature's best!
MIRANDA: I do not know
    One of my sex; no woman's face remember,

---

3. Visit; attack of plague (in the metaphor of *infected*).   5. Overthrow; contrast.
4. Her name means "to be admired or wondered at."

50   Save, from my glass, mine own. Nor have I seen
    More that I may call men than you, good friend,
    And my dear father. How features are abroad°   *elsewhere*
    I am skilless° of; but, by my modesty,°   *ignorant / virginity*
    The jewel in my dower, I would not wish
55   Any companion in the world but you;
    Nor can imagination form a shape,
    Besides yourself, to like of.° But I prattle   *care for*
    Something° too wildly, and my father's precepts   *somewhat*
    I therein do forget.

FERDINAND: I am in my condition°   *rank*
60   A prince, Miranda; I do think, a king—
    I would,° not so!—and would no more endure   *wish*
    This wooden slavery than to suffer
    The flesh-fly[6] blow° my mouth. Hear my soul speak: *lay eggs*
    The very instant that I saw you did
65   My heart fly to your service, there resides
    To make me slave to it, and for your sake
    Am I this patient log-man.

MIRANDA: Do you love me?

FERDINAND: O heaven, O earth, bear witness to this sound,
    And crown what I profess with kind event°   *favorable outcome*
70   If I speak true! If hollowly,° invert°   *falsely / turn*
    What best is boded° me to mischief!° I   *in store for / harm*
    Beyond all limit of what else i' the world
    Do love, prize, honor you.

MIRANDA [*weeping*]:   I am a fool
    To weep at what I am glad of.

PROSPERO [*aside*]:   Fair encounter
75   Of two most rare affections! Heavens rain grace
    On that which breeds between 'em!

FERDINAND: Wherefore weep you?

MIRANDA: At mine unworthiness, that dare not offer
    What I desire to give, and much less take
    What I shall die[7] to want.° But this is trifling,   *lack*
80   And all the more it seeks to hide itself
    The bigger bulk it shows. Hence, bashful cunning,°   *coyness*
    And prompt me, plain and holy innocence!
    I am your wife, if you will marry me;
    If not, I'll die your maid.[8] To be your fellow°   *equal*
85   You may deny me, but I'll be your servant
    Whether you will° or no.   *desire it*

FERDINAND: My mistress, dearest,
    And I thus humble ever.

MIRANDA: My husband, then?

FERDINAND: Ay, with a heart as willing

---

6. Insect that lays eggs in dead flesh.   8. Servant; virgin.
7. Probably with unconscious sexual meaning.

90   As bondage e'er of freedom.° Here's my hand.   *to win freedom*

MIRANDA [*clasping his hand*]:
     And mine, with my heart in 't. And now farewell
     Till half an hour hence.

FERDINAND: A thousand thousand!°   *farewells*

[*Exeunt (Ferdinand and Miranda, separately).*]

PROSPERO: So glad of this as they I cannot be,
     Who are surprised with all; but my rejoicing
95   At nothing can be more. I'll to my book,
     For yet ere suppertime must I perform
     Much business appertaining.°   *relevant*

[*Exit.*]

SCENE 2[9]

[*Enter Caliban, Stephano, and Trinculo.*]

STEPHANO: Tell not me. When the butt is out,[1] we will drink water, not a drop before. Therefore bear up and board 'em.[2] Servant monster, drink to me.

TRINCULO: Servant monster? The folly of this island! They say there's but five upon this isle. We are three of them; if th' other two be brained[3] like us, the state
5   totters.

STEPHANO: Drink, servant monster, when I bid thee. Thy eyes are almost set[4] in thy head. [*Giving a drink.*]

TRINCULO: Where should they be set[5] else? He were a brave[6] monster indeed if they were set in his tail.

STEPHANO: My man-monster hath drowned his tongue in sack. For my part, the sea cannot drown me. I swam, ere I could recover[7] the shore, five and thirty leagues off and on. By this light, thou shalt be my lieutenant, monster, or my standard.[8]

TRINCULO: Your lieutenant, if you list;[9] he's no standard.[1]

STEPHANO: We'll not run,[2] Monsieur Monster.

TRINCULO: Nor go[3] neither, but you'll lie[4] like dogs and yet say nothing neither.

STEPHANO: Mooncalf, speak once in thy life, if thou beest a good mooncalf.

CALIBAN: How does thy honor? Let me lick thy shoe.
     I'll not serve him. He is not valiant.

TRINCULO: Thou liest, most ignorant monster, I am in case[5] to jostle a constable. Why, thou debauched fish, thou, was there ever man a coward that hath drunk so much sack[6] as I today? Wilt thou tell a monstrous lie, being but half a fish and half a monster?

CALIBAN: Lo, how he mocks me! Wilt thou let him, my lord?

9. Location: Another part of the island.
1. Empty.
2. Drink up (using the language of a nautical assault).
3. Have brains.
4. Sunk, like the sun.
5. Placed.
6. Fine.
7. Reach.

8. Standard-bearer.
9. Prefer.
1. Not able to stand up.
2. Retreat; urinate.
3. Walk.
4. Tell lies; lie down; excrete.
5. Fit condition.
6. Spanish white wine.

TRINCULO: "Lord," quoth he? That a monster should be such a natural![7]

CALIBAN: Lo, lo, again! Bite him to death, I prithee.

STEPHANO: Trinculo, keep a good tongue in your head. If you prove a mutineer—
the next tree![8] The poor monster's my subject, and he shall not suffer
indignity.

CALIBAN: I thank my noble lord. Wilt thou be pleased
To hearken once again to the suit I made to thee?

STEPHANO: Marry, will I. Kneel and repeat it. I will stand, and so shall Trinculo.

[*Caliban kneels.*]

[*Enter Ariel, invisible.*]

CALIBAN: As I told thee before, I am subject to a tyrant,
A sorcerer, that by his cunning hath
35   Cheated me of the island.

ARIEL [*mimicking Trinculo*]: Thou liest.

CALIBAN: Thou liest, thou jesting monkey, thou!
I would my valiant master would destroy thee.
I do not lie.

STEPHANO: Trinculo, if you trouble him any more in 's tale, by this hand, I will supplant[9] some of your teeth.

TRINCULO: Why, I said nothing.

STEPHANO: Mum, then, and no more.– Proceed.

CALIBAN: I say by sorcery he got this isle;
45   From me he got it. If thy greatness will
Revenge it on him—for I know thou dar'st,
But this thing° dare not—   *Trinculo*

STEPHANO: That's most certain.

CALIBAN: Thou shalt be lord of it, and I'll serve thee.

STEPHANO: How now shall this be compassed? Canst thou bring me to the party?[1]

CALIBAN: Yea, yea, my lord. I'll yield him thee asleep,
Where thou mayst knock a nail into his head.

ARIEL: Thou liest; thou canst not.

CALIBAN: What a pied ninny's° this! Thou scurvy patch!°—   *motley fool / clown*
55   I do beseech thy greatness, give him blows
And take his bottle from him. When that's gone
He shall drink naught but brine, for I'll not show him
Where the quick freshes° arc.   *freshwater springs*

STEPHANO: Trinculo, run into no further danger. Interrupt the monster one word
60   further and, by this hand, I'll turn my mercy out o' doors and make a stock-
fish[2] of thee.

TRINCULO: Why, what did I? I did nothing. I'll go farther off.

STEPHANO: Didst thou not say he lied?

ARIEL: Thou liest.

STEPHANO: Do I so? Take thou that. [*He beats Trinculo.*] As you like this, give me the
lie[3] another time.

---

7. Fool; as opposed to "unnatural."
8. I.e., you'll hang.
9. Remove.

1. Person.
2. Dried cod, prepared by beating.
3. Call me a liar.

TRINCULO: I did not give the lie. Out o' your wits and hearing too? A pox o' your bottle! This can sack and drinking do. A murrain[4] on your monster, and the
devil take your fingers!

CALIBAN: Ha, ha, ha!

STEPHANO: Now, forward with your tale. [*To Trinculo.*] Prithee, stand further off.

CALIBAN: Beat him enough. After a little time
I'll beat him too.

STEPHANO: Stand farther.—Come, proceed.

CALIBAN: Why, as I told thee, 'tis a custom with him
I' th' afternoon to sleep. There thou mayst brain him,
Having first seized his books; or with a log
Batter his skull, or paunch° him with a stake,   *stab in the belly*
Or cut his weasand° with thy knife. Remember   *windpipe*
80   First to possess his books, for without them
He's but a sot,° as I am, nor hath not   *fool*
One spirit to command. They all do hate him
As rootedly as I. Burn but his books.
He has brave utensils°—for so he calls them—   *furnishings*
85   Which, when he has a house, he'll deck withal.°   *furnish with them*
And that most deeply to consider is
The beauty of his daughter. He himself
Calls her a nonpareil. I never saw a woman
But only Sycorax my dam and she;
90   But she as far surpasseth Sycorax
As great'st does least.

STEPHANO: Is it so brave° a lass?   *splendid*

CALIBAN: Ay, lord. She will become° thy bed, I warrant,   *suit (sexually)*
And bring thee forth brave brood.

STEPHANO: Monster, I will kill this man. His daughter and I will be king and
95   queen—save Our Graces!—and Trinculo and thyself shall be viceroys. Dost
thou like the plot, Trinculo?

TRINCULO: Excellent.

STEPHANO: Give me thy hand. I am sorry I beat thee; but, while thou liv'st, keep a
good tongue in thy head.

CALIBAN: Within this half hour will he be asleep.
Wilt thou destroy him then?

STEPHANO: Ay, on mine honor.

ARIEL [*aside*]: This will I tell my master.

CALIBAN: Thou mak'st me merry; I am full of pleasure.
Let us be jocund. Will you troll the catch°   *sing the song*
105   You taught me but whilere?°   *just now*

STEPHANO: At thy request, monster, I will do reason, any reason.[5]—
Come on, Trinculo, let us sing. [*Sings.*]

            "*Flout° 'em and scout° 'em*   *scoff at / deride*
            And scout 'em and flout 'em!
110   *Thought is free.*"

4. Cattle disease.   5. Anything reasonable.

CALIBAN: That's not the tune.

> [*Ariel plays the tune on a tabor° and pipe.*]   *small drum*

STEPHANO: What is this same?

TRINCULO: This is the tune of our catch, played by the picture of Nobody.[6]

STEPHANO: If thou beest a man, show thyself in thy likeness. If thou beest a devil,
115   take 't as thou list.[7]

TRINCULO: O, forgive me my sins!

STEPHANO: He that dies pays all debts. I defy thee. Mercy upon us!

CALIBAN: Art thou afeard?

STEPHANO: No, monster, not I.

CALIBAN: Be not afeard. The isle is full of noises,
>   Sounds, and sweet airs, that give delight and hurt not.
>   Sometimes a thousand twangling instruments
>   Will hum about mine ears, and sometimes voices
>   That, if I then had waked after long sleep,
125   Will make me sleep again; and then, in dreaming,
>   The clouds methought would open and show riches
>   Ready to drop upon me, that when I waked
>   I cried to dream again.

STEPHANO: This will prove a brave kingdom to me, where I shall have my music
130   for nothing.

CALIBAN: When Prospero is destroyed.

STEPHANO: That shall be by and by.° I remember the story.   *right away*

TRINCULO: The sound is going away. Let's follow it, and after do our work.

STEPHANO: Lead, monster; we'll follow. I would I could see this taborer! He lays
135   it on.[8]

TRINCULO: Wilt come? I'll follow, Stephano.

> [*Exeunt (following Ariel's music).*]

SCENE 3[9]

[*Enter Alonso, Sebastian, Antonio, Gonzalo, Adrian, Francisco, etc.*]

GONZALO: By'r lakin,[1] I can go no further, sir.
>   My old bones aches. Here's a maze trod indeed
>   Through forthrights° and meanders! By your patience,   *straight paths*
>   I needs must rest me.

ALONSO: Old lord, I cannot blame thee,
5   Who am myself attached° with weariness,   *seized*
>   To th' dulling of my spirits. Sit down and rest.
>   Even here I will put off my hope, and keep it
>   No longer for° my flatterer. He is drowned   *as*
>   Whom thus we stray to find, and the sea mocks
10   Our frustrate° search on land. Well, let him go.   *frustrated*

[*Alonso and Gonzalo sit.*]

---

6. Familiar image with head, arms, legs, but no trunk.
7. Suit yourself.
8. I.e., plays the drum vigorously.

9. Location: Another part of the island.
1. By our Ladykin (Virgin Mary).

ANTONIO [*aside to Sebastian*]: I am right glad that he's so out of hope.
　　　Do not, for° one repulse, forgo the purpose　　　　　　　*because of*
　　　That you resolved t' effect.
SEBASTIAN [*to Antonio*]:　　　　　　The next advantage
　　　Will we take throughly.°　　　　　　　　　　　　　　　*thoroughly*
ANTONIO [*to Sebastian*]:　　　　　Let it be tonight,
15　　For, now they are oppressed with travel, they
　　　Will not, nor cannot, use such vigilance
　　　As when they are fresh.
SEBASTIAN [*to Antonio*]:　　　　I say tonight. No more.

[*Solemn and strange music; and Prospero on the top,*[2] *invisible.*]

ALONSO: What harmony is this? My good friends, hark!
GONZALO: Marvelous sweet music!

[*Enter several strange shapes, bringing in a banquet, and dance about it with gentle actions of salutations; and, inviting the King, etc., to eat, they depart.*]

ALONSO: Give us kind keepers,° heavens! What were these?　　*guardian angels*
SEBASTIAN: A living drollery.[3] Now I will believe
　　　That there are unicorns; that in Arabia
　　　There is one tree, the phoenix' throne, one phoenix
　　　At this hour reigning there.
ANTONIO:　　　　　　　　　　I'll believe both;
25　　And what does else want credit,° come to me　　　　*lack credibility*
　　　And I'll be sworn 'tis true. Travelers ne'er did lie,
　　　Though fools at home condemn 'em.
GONZALO:　　　　　　　　　　　　　If in Naples
　　　I should report this now, would they believe me
　　　If I should say I saw such islanders?
30　　For, certes,° these are people of the island,　　　　　　　*certainly*
　　　Who, though they are of monstrous shape, yet note,
　　　Their manners are more gentle, kind, than of
　　　Our human generation you shall find
　　　Many, nay, almost any.
PROSPERO [*aside*]:　　　　　　Honest lord,
35　　Thou hast said well, for some of you there present
　　　Are worse than devils.
ALONSO:　　　　　　　　　I cannot too much muse
　　　Such shapes, such gesture, and such sound, expressing—
　　　Although they want° the use of tongue—a kind　　　　　　*lack*
　　　Of excellent dumb discourse.
PROSPERO [*aside*]:　　　　　　Praise in departing.[4]
FRANCISCO: They vanished strangely.
SEBASTIAN:　　　　　　　　No matter, since
　　　They have left their viands° behind, for we have stomachs.°　*food / appetites*
　　　Will't please you taste of what is here?

2. An upper level of the theater.
3. Puppet show with live actors.

4. Save your praise for the end of the performance (proverbial).

ALONSO: Not I.

GONZALO: Faith, sir, you need not fear. When we were boys,
         Who would believe that there were mountaineers
45   Dewlapped[5] like bulls, whose throats had hanging at 'em
         Wallets° of flesh? Or that there were such men   *wattles*
         Whose heads stood in their breasts?[6] Which now we find
         Each putter-out of five for one[7] will bring us
         Good warrant of.

ALONSO: I will stand to° and feed,   *take the risk*
50   Although my last[8]—no matter, since I feel
         The best is past. Brother, my lord the Duke,
         Stand to, and do as we. [*They approach the table.*]

      [*Thunder and lightning. Enter Ariel, like a harpy,[9] claps his wings upon the
table, and with a quaint[1] device the banquet[2] vanishes.*]

ARIEL: You are three men of sin, whom Destiny—
         That hath to° instrument this lower world   *as its*
55   And what is in 't—the never-surfeited sea
         Hath caused to belch up you, and on this island
         Where man doth not inhabit, you 'mongst men
         Being most unfit to live. I have made you mad;
         And even with suchlike valor men hang and drown
         Their proper° selves.   *own*

      [*Alonso, Sebastian, and Antonio draw their swords.*]

60   You fools! I and my fellows
         Are ministers of Fate. The elements
         Of whom° your swords are tempered° may as well   *which / composed*
         Wound the loud winds, or with bemocked-at° stabs   *scorned*
         Kill the still-closing° waters, as diminish   *ever-closing*
65   One dowl° that's in my plume. My fellow ministers   *feather*
         Are like° invulnerable. If you could hurt,   *likewise*
         Your swords are now too massy° for your strengths   *massive*
         And will not be uplifted. But remember—
         For that's my business to you—that you three
70   From Milan did supplant good Prospero;
         Exposed unto the sea, which hath requit° it,   *avenged*
         Him and his innocent child; for which foul deed
         The powers, delaying, not forgetting, have
         Incensed the seas and shores, yea, all the creatures,
75   Against your peace. Thee of thy son, Alonso,
         They have bereft; and do pronounce by me
         Ling'ring perdition,° worse than any death   *ruin*
         Can be at once, shall step by step attend

---

5. With folds of flesh at the neck.
6. Like the Anthropophagi described in *Othello* 1.3.146.
7. Traveler whose insurance policy guarantees five to one repayment on his return.
8. Even if this were my last meal.

9. Monster with a woman's face and breasts and a vulture's body, supposed to bring divine vengeance.
1. Ingenious.
2. The food only.

You and your ways; whose wraths to guard you from—
80 Which here, in this most desolate isle, else° falls   *or else*
    Upon your heads—is nothing° but heart's sorrow   *there is no way*
    And a clear° life ensuing.   *innocent*

[*He vanishes in thunder; then, to soft music, enter the shapes again, and dance,
with mocks and mows,*[3] *and carrying out the table.*]

PROSPERO: Bravely the figure of this harpy hast thou
            Performed, my Ariel; a grace it had devouring.[4]
85   Of my instruction hast thou nothing bated°   *omitted*
            In what thou hadst to say. So,° with good life°   *similarly / acting*
            And observation strange,° my meaner ministers   *close attention*
            Their several kinds° have done. My high charms work,   *separate parts*
            And these mine enemies are all knit up
90   In their distractions.° They now are in my power;   *trances*
            And in these fits I leave them, while I visit
            Young Ferdinand, whom they suppose is drowned,
            And his and mine loved darling.

                                                                     [*Exit above.*]

GONZALO: I' the name of something holy, sir, why stand you
            In this strange stare?
ALONSO: O, it is monstrous, monstrous!
            Methought the billows° spoke and told me of it;°   *waves / my sin*
            The winds did sing it to me, and the thunder,
            That deep and dreadful organ pipe, pronounced
            The name of Prosper; it did bass° my trespass.   *boom*
100   Therefore my son i' th' ooze is bedded; and
            I'll seek him deeper than e'er plummet sounded,°   *probed*
            And with him there lie mudded.

                                                                          [*Exit.*]

SEBASTIAN: But one fiend at a time,
            I'll fight their legions o'er.°   *one by one*
ANTONIO: I'll be thy second.

                                              [*Exeunt (Sebastian and Antonio).*]

GONZALO: All three of them are desperate. Their great guilt,
105   Like poison given to work a great time after,
            Now 'gins to bite the spirits. I do beseech you,
            That are of suppler joints, follow them swiftly
            And hinder them from what this ecstasy°   *madness*
            May now provoke them to.
ADRIAN: Follow, I pray you.

                                                                  [*Exeunt omnes.*]

---

3. Grimaces and gestures.   as the blessing at meals and "devouring" as in "ravishing
4. Causing the banquet to disappear, with puns on "grace"   grace."

ACT 4

Scene 1[1]

[Enter Prospero, Ferdinand, and Miranda.]

PROSPERO: If I have too austerely punished you,
    Your compensation makes amends, for I
    Have given you here a third[2] of mine own life,
    Or that for which I live; who once again
5   I tender° to thy hand. All thy vexations   *offer*
    Were but my trials of thy love, and thou
    Hast strangely° stood the test. Here, afore heaven,   *extraordinarily*
    I ratify this my rich gift. O Ferdinand,
    Do not smile at me that I boast her off;°   *boast of her*
10   For thou shalt find she will outstrip all praise
    And make it halt° behind her.   *limp*
FERDINAND: I do believe it
    Against an oracle.[3]
PROSPERO: Then, as my gift and thine own acquisition
    Worthily purchased, take my daughter. But
15   If thou dost break her virgin-knot before
    All sanctimonious° ceremonies may   *sacred*
    With full and holy rite be ministered,
    No sweet aspersion° shall the heavens let fall   *blessing*
    To make this contract grow; but barren hate,
20   Sour-eyed disdain, and discord shall bestrew
    The union of your bed with weeds[4] so loathly
    That you shall hate it both. Therefore take heed,
    As Hymen's lamps shall light you.[5]
FERDINAND: As I hope
    For quiet days, fair issue,° and long life,   *offspring*
25   With such love as 'tis now, the murkiest den,
    The most opportune place, the strong'st suggestion°   *temptation*
    Our worser genius can,° shall never melt   *bad angel can make*
    Mine honor into lust, to take away
    The edge of that day's celebration
30   When I shall think or Phoebus' steeds are foundered[6]
    Or Night kept chained below
PROSPERO.   Fairly spoke.
    Sit then and talk with her. She is thine own.

[Ferdinand and Miranda sit and talk together.]

    What, Ariel! My industrious servant, Ariel!

[Enter Ariel.]

---

1. Location: Before Prospero's cell.
2. The other two thirds being his knowledge and his power?
3. Even if an oracle should deny it.
4. As opposed to flowers.

5. Hymen was the Greek and Roman god of marriage, whose torches burned brightly for a happy marriage and smokily for a troubled one.
6. Either the sun-god's horses are lame.

ARIEL: What would my potent master? Here I am.

PROSPERO: Thou and thy meaner fellows° your last service   *subordinates*
        Did worthily perform, and I must use you
        In such another trick. Go bring the rabble,
        O'er whom I give thee power, here to this place.
        Incite them to quick motion, for I must
40   Bestow upon the eyes of this young couple
        Some vanity° of mine art. It is my promise,   *show*
        And they expect it from me.

ARIEL: Presently?°   *now*

PROSPERO: Ay, with a twink.°   *now*

ARIEL: Before you can say "Come" and "Go,"
45   And breathe twice, and cry "So, so,"
        Each one, tripping on his toe,
        Will be here with mop and mow.°   *antics and gestures*
        Do you love me, master? No?

PROSPERO: Dearly, my delicate Ariel. Do not approach
50   Till thou dost hear me call.

ARIEL: Well; I conceive.°   *understand*

                                          [Exit.]

PROSPERO: Look thou be true;° do not give dalliance   *true to your word*
        Too much the rein. The strongest oaths are straw
        To the fire i' the blood. Be more abstemious,
        Or else good night your vow!

FERDINAND: I warrant you, sir,
55   The white cold virgin snow upon my heart
        Abates the ardor of my liver.[7]

PROSPERO: Well.
        Now come, my Ariel! Bring a corollary,°   *surplus*
        Rather than want° a spirit. Appear, and pertly!°—   *lack / briskly*
        No tongue! All eyes! Be silent. *[Soft music.]*

     [Enter Iris.[8]]

IRIS: Ceres,[9] most bounteous lady, thy rich leas°   *meadows*
        Of wheat, rye, barley, vetches,° oats, and peas;   *fodder*
        Thy turfy mountains, where live nibbling sheep,
        And flat meads° thatched with stover,° them to keep; *meadows / fodder*
        Thy banks with pionèd and twillèd brims,[1]
65   Which spongy° April at thy hest° betrims   *wet / command*
        To make cold nymphs chaste crowns; and thy broom groves,° *clumps of gorse*
        Whose shadow the dismissèd° bachelor loves,   *rejected*
        Being lass-lorn; thy poll-clipped° vineyard;   *pruned*
        And thy sea marge,° sterile and rocky hard,   *shore*
70   Where thou thyself dost air: the queen o' the sky,°   *Juno*

---

7. Supposed seat of the passions.
8. Goddess of the rainbow and Juno's messenger.
9. Goddess of fertility.

1. Dug under by the current and protected by woven layers of branches.

Whose watery arch° and messenger am I,   *rainbow*
Bids thee leave these, and with her sovereign grace,

[*Juno descends (slowly in her car).*]

Here on this grass plot, in this very place,
To come and sport. Her peacocks[2] fly amain.°   *at full speed*
75   Approach, rich Ceres, her to entertain.°   *receive*

[*Enter Ceres.*]

CERES: Hail, many-colored messenger, that ne'er
Dost disobey the wife of Jupiter,
Who with thy saffron° wings upon my flowers   *yellow*
Diffusest honeydrops, refreshing showers,
80   And with each end of thy blue bow° dost crown   *rainbow*
My bosky° acres and my unshrubbed down,   *wooded*
Rich scarf to my proud earth. Why hath thy queen
Summoned me hither to this short-grassed green?
IRIS: A contract of true love to celebrate,
85   And some donation freely to estate°   *bestow*
On the blest lovers.
CERES: Tell me, heavenly bow,
If Venus or her son,[3] as thou dost know,
Do now attend the Queen? Since they did plot
The means that dusky Dis my daughter got,[4]
90   Her and her blind boy's scandaled° company   *disgraceful*
I have forsworn.
IRIS: Of her society
Be not afraid. I met her deity°   *her Divine Majesty*
Cutting the clouds towards Paphos,[5] and her son
Dove-drawn with her. Here thought they to have done°   *placed*
95   Some wanton charm upon this man and maid,
Whose vows are that no bed-right shall be paid
Till Hymen's torch be lighted; but in vain.
Mars's hot minion° is returned again;   *Venus*
Her waspish-headed° son has broke his arrows,   *spiteful*
100   Swears he will shoot no more, but play with sparrows[6]
And be a boy right out.°   *outright*

[*Juno alights.*]

CERES: Highest Queen of state,
Great Juno, comes; I know her by her gait.
JUNO: How does my bounteous sister?° Go with me   *fellow goddess*
To bless this twain, that they may prosperous be,
105   And honored in their issue.°   *offspring*

[*They sing.*]

---

2. Birds sacred to Juno, that drew her chariot.
3. Cupid, often portrayed as blind-folded.
4. Pluto (Dis), god of the underworld, kidnapped Ceres's

daughter Proserpina.
5. In Cyprus, center of Venus's cult.
6. Thought to be lustful, sparrows were sacred to Venus.

JUNO: *Honor, riches, marriage blessing,*
                             Long continuance, and increasing,
                             Hourly joys be still° upon you!   constantly
                             Juno sings her blessings on you.

CERES: *Earth's increase, foison° plenty,*   abundance
                             Barns and garners° never empty,   granaries
                             Vines with clustering bunches growing,
                             Plants with goodly burden bowing;
                             Spring come to you at the farthest
115   *In the very end of harvest!*[7]
                             Scarcity and want shall shun you;
                             Ceres' blessing so is on you.

FERDINAND: This is a most majestic vision, and
        Harmonious charmingly. May I be bold
120   To think these spirits?
PROSPERO: Spirits, which by mine art
        I have from their confines called to enact
        My present fancies.
FERDINAND: Let me live here ever!
        So rare a wondered° father and a wife   wonderful
        Makes this place Paradise.

        [*Juno and Ceres whisper, and send Iris on employment.*]

PROSPERO: Sweet now, silence!
125   Juno and Ceres whisper seriously;
        There's something else to do. Hush and be mute,
        Or else our spell is marred.
IRIS [*calling offstage*]:
        You nymphs, called naiads, of the windring° brooks,   winding
        With your sedged° crowns and ever-harmless looks,   made of reeds
130   Leave your crisp° channels, and on this green land   rippling
        Answer your summons; Juno does command.
        Come, temperate° nymphs, and help to celebrate   chaste
        A contract of true love. Be not too late.

        [*Enter certain nymphs.*]

        You sunburned sicklemen, of August° weary,   the harvest
135   Come hither from the furrow and be merry.
        Make holiday; your rye-straw hats put on,
        And these fresh nymphs encounter every one
        In country footing.°   dancing

        [*Enter certain reapers, properly habited. They join with the nymphs in a graceful
        dance, towards the end whereof Prospero starts suddenly, and speaks; after which, to
        a strange, hollow, and confused noise, they heavily vanish.*]

PROSPERO [*aside*]: I had forgot that foul conspiracy

---

7. I.e., with no winter in between.

140   Of the beast Caliban and his confederates
        Against my life. The minute of their plot
        Is almost come. [*To the Spirits.*] Well done! Avoid;° no more!   *be off*
FERDINAND [*to Miranda*]: This is strange. Your father's in some passion
        That works° him strongly.   *affects*
MIRANDA: Never till this day
145   Saw I him touched with anger so distempered.
PROSPERO: You do look, my son, in a moved sort,°   *troubled state*
        As if you were dismayed. Be cheerful, sir.
        Our revels now are ended. These our actors,
        As I foretold you, were all spirits and
150   Are melted into air, into thin air;
        And, like the baseless° fabric of this vision,   *insubstantial*
        The cloud-capped towers, the gorgeous palaces,
        The solemn temples, the great globe itself,°   *(glances at theater)*
        Yea, all which it inherit,° shall dissolve,   *occupy it*
155   And, like this insubstantial pageant faded,
        Leave not a rack° behind. We are such stuff   *cloud*
        As dreams are made on,° and our little life   *of*
        Is rounded° with a sleep. Sir, I am vexed.   *surrounded*
        Bear with my weakness. My old brain is troubled.
160   Be not disturbed with my infirmity.
        If you be pleased, retire into my cell
        And there repose. A turn or two I'll walk
        To still my beating° mind.   *agitated*
FERDINAND, MIRANDA: We wish your peace.

                                   [*Exeunt (Ferdinand and Miranda).*]

PROSPERO: Come with a thought!° I thank thee, Ariel. Come.   *right now*

        [*Enter Ariel.*]

ARIEL: Thy thoughts I cleave to. What's thy pleasure?
PROSPERO: Spirit,
        We must prepare to meet with Caliban.
ARIEL: Ay, my commander. When I presented° Ceres,   *played; introduced*
        I thought to have told thee of it, but I feared
        Lest I might anger thee.
PROSPERO: Say again, where didst thou leave these varlets?
ARIEL: I told you, sir, they were red-hot with drinking;
        So full of valor that they smote the air
        For breathing in their faces, beat the ground
        For kissing of their feet; yet always bending
175   Towards their project. Then I beat my tabor,
        At which, like unbacked° colts, they pricked their ears,   *unbroken*
        Advanced° their eyelids, lifted up their noses   *raised*
        As they smelt music. So I charmed their ears
        That calflike they my lowing followed through
180   Toothed briers, sharp furzes, pricking gorse, and thorns,
        Which entered their frail shins. At last I left them

I' the filthy-mantled° pool beyond your cell,   *scummed*
There dancing up to the chins, that the foul lake
O'erstunk their feet.

PROSPERO: This was well done, my bird.
185   Thy shape invisible retain thou still.
The trumpery° in my house, go bring it hither,   *cheap goods*
For stale° to catch these thieves.   *decoy*

ARIEL: I go, I go.

                                                                              [*Exit.*]

PROSPERO: A devil, a born devil, on whose nature
Nurture can never stick; on whom my pains,
190   Humanely taken, all, all lost, quite lost!
And as with age his body uglier grows,
So his mind cankers.° I will plague them all,   *festers*
Even to roaring.

[*Enter Ariel, loaden with glistering apparel, etc.*]

                    Come, hang them on this line.°   *lime tree*

[*(Ariel hangs up the showy finery; Prospero and Ariel remain, invisible.) Enter Caliban, Stephano, and Trinculo, all wet.*]

CALIBAN: Pray you, tread softly, that the blind mole may
195   Not hear a foot fall. We now are near his cell.
STEPHANO: Monster, your fairy, which you say is a harmless fairy, has done little better than played the jack[8] with us.
TRINCULO: Monster, I do smell all horse piss, at which my nose is in great indignation.
STEPHANO: So is mine. Do you hear, monster? If I should take a displeasure against you, look you—
TRINCULO: Thou wert but a lost monster.
CALIBAN: Good my lord, give me thy favor still.
Be patient, for the prize I'll bring thee to
205   Shall hoodwink° this mischance. Therefore speak softly.   *cover over*
All's hushed as midnight yet.
TRINCULO: Ay, but to lose our bottles in the pool—
STEPHANO: There is not only disgrace and dishonor in that, monster, but an infinite loss.
TRINCULO: That's more to me than my wetting. Yet this is your harmless fairy, monster!
STEPHANO: I will fetch off my bottle, though I be o'er ears[9] for my labor.
CALIBAN: Prithee, my king, be quiet. Seest thou here,
This is the mouth o' the cell. No noise, and enter.
215   Do that good mischief which may make this island
Thine own forever, and I thy Caliban
For aye thy footlicker.

---

8. Knave; jack o' lantern, will o' th' wisp.   9. Submerged or drowned.

STEPHANO: Give me thy hand. I do begin to have bloody thoughts.

TRINCULO [*seeing the finery*]: O King Stephano! O peer![1]

220   O worthy Stephano! Look what a wardrobe here is for thee!

CALIBAN: Let it alone, thou fool, it is but trash.

TRINCULO: O ho, monster! We know what belongs to a frippery.[2] O King Stephano! [*He puts on a gown.*]

STEPHANO: Put off that gown, Trinculo. By this hand, I'll have that gown.

TRINCULO: Thy Grace shall have it.

CALIBAN: The dropsy[3] drown this fool! What do you mean
        To dote thus on such luggage? Let 't alone
        And do the murder first. If he awake,
        From toe to crown he'll fill our skins with pinches,
230   Make us strange stuff.

STEPHANO: Be you quiet, monster.—Mistress line, is not this my jerkin?[4] [*He takes it down.*] Now is the jerkin under the line.[5] Now, jerkin, you are like to lose your hair and prove a bald jerkin.

TRINCULO: Do, do! We steal by line and level,[6] an 't like[7] your Grace.

STEPHANO: I thank thee for that jest. Here's a garment for 't. [*He gives a garment.*] Wit shall not go unrewarded while I am king of this country. "Steal by line and level" is an excellent pass of pate.[8] There's another garment for 't.

TRINCULO: Monster, come, put some lime[9] upon your fingers, and away with the rest.

CALIBAN: I will have none on 't. We shall lose our time,
        And all be turned to barnacles,[1] or to apes
        With foreheads villainous low.

STEPHANO: Monster, lay to[2] your fingers. Help to bear this away where my hogshead of wine is, or I'll turn you out of my kingdom. Go to, carry this.

TRINCULO: And this.

STEPHANO: Ay, and this.

    [*They loud Caliban with more and more garments.*]

    [*A noise of hunters heard. Enter divers spirits, in shape of dogs and hounds, hunting them about, Prospero and Ariel setting them on.*]

PROSPERO: Hey, Mountain, hey!

ARIEL: Silver! There it goes, Silver!

PROSPERO: Fury, Fury! There, Tyrant, there! Hark! Hark! [*Caliban, Stephano, and Trinculo are driven out.*]

250   Go, charge my goblins that they grind their joints
        With dry[3] convulsions, shorten up their sinews
        With agèd cramps, and more pinch-spotted make them
        Than pard or cat o'mountain.[4]

---

1. Alludes to the ballad beginning "King Stephen was a worthy peer . . ."
2. Old-clothes shop.
3. Disease in which joints fill with fluid.
4. Leather jacket.
5. Lime tree; pun on the equator, south of which sailors supposedly caught scurvy and lost their hair.
6. Methodically (pun on *line*).

7. If it please.
8. Witticism.
9. Bird-lime (sticky and good for stealing).
1. Geese.
2. Start using.
3. Aged.
4. Leopard or wildcat.

ARIEL: Hark, they roar!
PROSPERO: Let them be hunted soundly. At this hour
255   Lies at my mercy all mine enemies.
           Shortly shall all my labors end, and thou
           Shalt have the air at freedom. For a little
           Follow, and do me service.

                                              [*Exeunt.*]

                    A C T 5

                    Scene 1[1]

[*Enter Prospero in his magic robes, (with his staff,) and Ariel.*]

PROSPERO: Now does my project gather to a head.
           My charms crack° not, my spirits obey, and Time   *fail*
           Goes upright with his carriage.[2] How's the day?
ARIEL: On the sixth hour, at which time, my lord,
5   You said our work should cease.
PROSPERO: I did say so,
           When first I raised the tempest. Say, my spirit,
           How fares the King and 's followers?
ARIEL: Confined together
           In the same fashion as you gave in charge,
           Just as you left them; all prisoners, sir,
10   In the line grove which weather-fends° your cell.   *protects from weather*
           They cannot budge till your release.° The King,   *you release them*
           His brother, and yours abide all three distracted,°   *mad*
           And the remainder mourning over them,
           Brim full of sorrow and dismay; but chiefly
15   Him that you termed, sir, the good old lord, Gonzalo.
           His tears runs down his beard like winter's drops
           From eaves of reeds.° Your charm so strongly works 'em   *thatched roof*
           That if you now beheld them your affections°   *feelings*
           Would become tender.
PROSPERO: Dost thou think so, spirit?
ARIEL: Mine would, sir, were I human.
PROSPERO: And mine shall.
           Hast thou, which art but air, a touch,° a feeling   *a sense*
           Of their afflictions, and shall not myself,
           One of their kind, that relish° all° as sharply   *feel / quite*
           Passion as they, be kindlier moved than thou art?
25   Though with their high wrongs I am struck to the quick,
           Yet with my nobler reason 'gainst my fury
           Do I take part. The rarer° action is   *nobler*
           In virtue than in vengeance. They being penitent,
           The sole drift of my purpose doth extend
30   Not a frown further. Go release them, Ariel.

---

1. Location: Before Prospero's cell.   2. Time's burden is light.

My charms I'll break, their senses I'll restore,
And they shall be themselves.

ARIEL: I'll fetch them, sir.

[*Exit.*]

[*Prospero traces a charmed circle with his staff.*]

PROSPERO:[3] Ye elves of hills, brooks, standing lakes, and groves,
And ye that on the sands with printless foot
35   Do chase the ebbing Neptune, and do fly him
When he comes back; you demi-puppets° that   *fairies*
By moonshine do the green sour ringlets° make,   *circles in grass*
Whereof the ewe not bites; and you whose pastime
Is to make midnight mushrooms, that rejoice
40   To hear the solemn curfew;° by whose aid,   *evening bell*
Weak masters° though ye be, I have bedimmed   *forces*
The noontide sun, called forth the mutinous winds,
And twixt the green sea and the azured vault°   *the sky*
Set roaring war; to the dread rattling thunder
45   Have I given fire, and rifted° Jove's stout oak[4]   *split*
With his own bolt; the strong-based promontory
Have I made shake, and by the spurs° plucked up   *roots*
The pine and cedar; graves at my command
Have waked their sleepers, oped, and let 'em forth
50   By my so potent art. But this rough magic
I here abjure, and when I have required°   *requested*
Some heavenly music—which even now I do—
To work mine end upon their senses that[5]
This airy charm° is for, I'll break my staff,   *music*
55   Bury it certain fathoms in the earth,
And deeper than did ever plummet sound
I'll drown my book. [*Solemn music.*]

[*Here enters Ariel before; then Alonso, with a frantic gesture, attended by Gonzalo; Sebastian and Antonio in like manner, attended by Adrian and Francisco. They
all enter the circle which Prospero had made, and there stand charmed; which Prospero observing, speaks:*]

[*To Alonso.*] A solemn air,° and° the best comforter   *song / which is*
To an unsettled fancy, cure thy brains,
60   Now useless, boiled within thy skull! [*To Sebastian and Antonio.*] There stand,
For you are spell-stopped.—
Holy Gonzalo, honorable man,
Mine eyes, e'en sociable° to the show° of thine,   *sympathetic / sight*
Fall° fellowly drops. [*Aside.*] The charm dissolves apace,   *let fall*
65   And as the morning steals upon the night,

---

3. This famous passage, lines 33–50, is an embellished
paraphrase of Golding's translation of Ovid's *Metamorphoses* 7.197–219.

4. Tree sacred to Jove.
5. The senses of those whom.

Melting the darkness, so their rising senses
Begin to chase the ignorant fumes that mantle°   *envelop*
Their clearer reason.—O good Gonzalo,
My true preserver, and a loyal sir
70   To him thou follow'st! I will pay thy graces°   *favors*
Home° both in word and deed.—Most cruelly   *fully*
Didst thou, Alonso, use me and my daughter.
Thy brother was a furtherer° in the act.—   *accomplice*
Thou art pinched for 't now, Sebastian. [*To Antonio.*] Flesh and blood,
75   You, brother mine, that entertained ambition,
Expelled remorse° and nature,° whom, with Sebastian,   *pity / natural feeling*
Whose inward pinches therefore are most strong,
Would here have killed your king, I do forgive thee,
Unnatural though thou art.—Their understanding
80   Begins to swell, and the approaching tide
Will shortly fill the reasonable shore°   *shore of the mind*
That now lies foul and muddy. Not one of them
That yet looks on me, or would know me.—Ariel,
Fetch me the hat and rapier in my cell.

[*Ariel goes to the cell and returns immediately.*]

85   I will discase° me and myself present   *disrobe*
As I was sometime Milan.⁶ Quickly, spirit!
Thou shalt ere long be free.

[*Ariel sings and helps to attire him.*]

ARIEL: *Where the bee sucks, there suck I.*
                            In a cowslip's bell I lie;
90   *There I couch° when owls do cry.*   *lie*
                            On the bat's back I do fly
                            After° summer merrily.   *pursuing*
                            Merrily, merrily shall I live now
                            Under the blossom that hangs on the bough.

PROSPERO: Why, that's my dainty Ariel! I shall miss thee,
           But yet thou shalt have freedom. So, so, so.
           To the King's ship, invisible as thou art!
           There shalt thou find the mariners asleep
           Under the hatches. The Master and the Boatswain
100   Being awake, enforce them to this place,
           And presently,° I prithee.   *right away*
ARIEL: I drink the air° before me and return   *consume space*
           Or ere° your pulse twice beat.   *before*

                                                                   [*Exit.*]

GONZALO: All torment, trouble, wonder, and amazement
105   Inhabits here. Some heavenly power guide us

---

6. As I looked when I was Duke of Milan.

Out of this fearful° country!   *frightening*
PROSPERO: Behold, sir King,
 The wrongèd Duke of Milan, Prospero.
 For more assurance that a living prince
 Does now speak to thee, I embrace thy body;
110 And to thee and thy company I bid
 A hearty welcome. [*Embracing him.*]
ALONSO: Whe'er thou be'st he or no,
 Or some enchanted trifle° to abuse° me,   *trick / deceive*
 As late° I have been, I not know. Thy pulse   *lately*
 Beats as of flesh and blood; and, since I saw thee,
115 Th' affliction of my mind amends, with which
 I fear a madness held me. This must crave°—   *require*
 An if this be° at all—a most strange story.   *is happening*
 Thy dukedom I resign, and do entreat
 Thou pardon me my wrongs. But how should Prospero
 Be living, and be here?
PROSPERO [*to Gonzalo*]:   First, noble friend,
 Let me embrace thine age,° whose honor cannot   *yourself*
 Be measured or confined. [*Embracing him.*]
GONZALO: Whether this be
 Or be not, I'll not swear.
PROSPERO: You do yet taste
 Some subtleties° o' th' isle, that will not let you   *illusions*
125 Believe things certain. Welcome, my friends all!

 [*Aside to Sebastian and Antonio.*]

 But you, my brace° of lords, were I so minded,   *pair*
 I here could pluck° his Highness' frown upon you   *pull down*
 And justify° you traitors. At this time   *prove*
 I will tell no tales.
SEBASTIAN: The devil speaks in him.
PROSPERO: No.
130 [*To Antonio.*] For you, most wicked sir, whom to call brother
 Would even infect my mouth, I do forgive
 Thy rankest fault—all of them; and require
 My dukedom of thee, which perforce° I know   *necessarily*
 Thou must restore.
ALONSO: If thou be'st Prospero,
135 Give us particulars of thy preservation,
 How thou hast met us here, whom three hours since
 Were wrecked upon this shore; where I have lost—
 How sharp the point of this remembrance is!—
 My dear son Ferdinand.
PROSPERO: I am woe° for 't, sir.   *sorry*
ALONSO: Irreparable is the loss, and patience
 Says it is past her cure.
PROSPERO: I rather think
 You have not sought her help, of whose soft grace

PROSPERO: For the like loss I have her sovereign° aid   *effective*
And rest myself content.

ALONSO: You the like loss?

PROSPERO: As great to me as late,° and supportable   *recent*
To make the dear° loss, have I means much weaker   *grievous*
Than you may call to comfort you; for I
Have lost my daughter.

ALONSO: A daughter?
O heavens, that they were living both in Naples,
150   The king and queen there! That° they were, I wish   *so that*
Myself were mudded° in that oozy bed   *buried in mud*
Where my son lies. When did you lose your daughter?

PROSPERO: In this last tempest. I perceive these lords
At this encounter do so much admire°   *wonder*
155   That they devour their reason° and scarce think   *are open-mouthed*
Their eyes do offices° of truth, their words   *perform services*
Are natural breath. But, howsoever you have
Been jostled from your senses, know for certain
That I am Prospero and that very duke
160   Which was thrust forth of Milan, who most strangely
Upon this shore, where you were wrecked, was landed
To be the lord on 't. No more yet of this,
For 'tis a chronicle of day by day,°   *many days' telling*
Not a relation for a breakfast nor
165   Befitting this first meeting. Welcome, sir.
This cell's my court. Here have I few attendants,
And subjects none abroad.° Pray you, look in.   *elsewhere*
My dukedom since you have given me again,
I will requite° you with as good a thing,   *repay*
170   At least bring forth a wonder to content ye
As much as me my dukedom.

[*Here Prospero discovers° Ferdinand and Miranda, playing at chess.*]   *discloses*

MIRANDA: Sweet lord, you play me false.

FERDINAND: No, my dearest love,
I would not for the world.

MIRANDA: Yes, for a score of kingdoms you should wrangle,
And I would call it fair play.[7]

ALONSO: If this prove
A vision° of the island, one dear son   *illusion*
Shall I twice lose.

SEBASTIAN: A most high miracle!

FERDINAND [*approaching his father*]: Though the seas threaten, they are merciful;
I have cursed them without cause. [*He kneels.*]

ALONSO: Now all the blessings
180   Of a glad father compass° thee about!   *encompass*
Arise, and say how thou cam'st here.

---

7. Miranda would still love Ferdinand, even if he did not play fair.

[*Ferdinand rises.*]

MIRANDA: O, wonder!
　　　How many goodly creatures are there here!
　　　How beauteous mankind is! O brave° new world   *splendid*
　　　That has such people in 't!
PROSPERO: 'Tis new to thee.
ALONSO: What is this maid with whom thou wast at play?
　　　Your eld'st° acquaintance cannot be three hours.   *longest*
　　　Is she the goddess that hath severed us,
　　　And brought us thus together?
FERDINAND: Sir, she is mortal;
　　　But by immortal Providence she's mine.
190　　I chose her when I could not ask my father
　　　For his advice, nor thought I had one. She
　　　Is daughter to this famous Duke of Milan,
　　　Of whom so often I have heard renown,
　　　But never saw before; of whom I have
195　　Received a second life; and second father
　　　This lady makes him to me.
ALONSO: I am hers.
　　　But O, how oddly will it sound that I
　　　Must ask my child forgiveness!
PROSPERO: There, sir, stop.
　　　Let us not burden our remembrances with
　　　A heaviness° that's gone.   *sadness*
GONZALO: I have inly° wept,   *inwardly*
　　　Or should have spoke ere this. Look down, you gods,
　　　And on this couple drop a blessèd crown!
　　　For it is you that have chalked forth the way
　　　Which brought us hither.
ALONSO: I say amen, Gonzalo!
GONZALO: Was Milan° thrust from Milan, that his issue   *the Duke of Milan*
　　　Should become kings of Naples? O, rejoice
　　　Beyond a common joy, and set it down
　　　With gold on lasting pillars: In one voyage
　　　Did Claribel her husband find at Tunis,
210　　And Ferdinand, her brother, found a wife
　　　Where he himself was lost; Prospero his dukedom
　　　In a poor isle; and all of us ourselves°   *our senses*
　　　When no man was his own.°   *sane*
ALONSO [*to Ferdinand and Miranda*]: Give me your hands.
　　　Let grief and sorrow still° embrace his heart   *always*
　　　That doth not wish you joy!
GONZALO: Be it so! Amen!

[*Enter Ariel, with the Master and Boatswain amazedly following.*]

　　　O, look, sir, look, sir! Here is more of us.
　　　I prophesied, if a gallows were on land,
　　　This fellow could not drown.—Now, blasphemy,°   *blasphemer*

That swear'st grace o'erboard, not an oath on shore?
220   Hast thou no mouth by land? What is the news?
BOATSWAIN: The best news is that we have safely found
Our King and company; the next, our ship—
Which, but three glasses° since, we gave out° split—   *hours / reported*
Is tight and yare° and bravely rigged as when   *shipshape*
We first put out to sea.
ARIEL [*aside to Prospero*]:   Sir, all this service
Have I done since I went.
PROSPERO [*aside to Ariel*]:   My tricksy° spirit!   *ingenious*
ALONSO: These are not natural events; they strengthen
From strange to stranger. Say, how came you hither?
BOATSWAIN: If I did think, sir, I were well awake,
230   I'd strive to tell you. We were dead of sleep,
And—how we know not—all clapped under hatches,
Where but even now, with strange and several° noises   *various*
Of roaring, shrieking, howling, jingling chains,
And more diversity of sounds, all horrible,
235   We were awaked; straightway at liberty;
Where we, in all her trim,° freshly beheld   *sail*
Our royal, good, and gallant ship, our Master
Cap'ring° to eye° her. On a trice, so please you,   *dancing / see*
Even in a dream, were we divided from them
And were brought moping° hither.   *in a daze*
ARIEL [*aside to Prospero*]:   Was't well done?
PROSPERO [*aside to Ariel*]: Bravely, my diligence. Thou shalt be free.
ALONSO: This is as strange a maze as e'er men trod,
And there is in this business more than nature
Was ever conduct° of. Some oracle   *conductor*
Must rectify our knowledge.
PROSPERO: Sir, my liege,
Do not infest° your mind with beating on   *bother*
The strangeness of this business. At picked° leisure,   *chosen*
Which shall be shortly, single° I'll resolve° you,   *privately / explain*
Which to you shall seem probable, of every°   *every one of*
250   These happened accidents;° till when, be cheerfull   *incidents*
And think of each thing well. [*Aside to Ariel.*] Come hither, spirit.
Set Caliban and his companions free.
Untie the spell. [*Exit Ariel.*] How fares my gracious sir?
There are yet missing of your company
255   Some few odd lads that you remember not.

[*Enter Ariel, driving in Caliban, Stephano, and Trinculo, in their stolen apparel.*]

STEPHANO: Every man shift[8] for all the rest,[9] and let no man take care for himself; for
all is but fortune. Coragio,[1] bully monster,[2] coragio!

8. Provide.   1. Courage.
9. Stephano drunkenly gets wrong the saying "Every man   2. Gallant monster (ironical).
for himself."

TRINCULO: If these be true spies³ which I wear in my head, here's a goodly sight.

CALIBAN: O Setebos, these be brave° spirits indeed!   *handsome*

260   How fine° my master is! I am afraid   *well-dressed*

     He will chastise me.

SEBASTIAN: Ha, ha!

     What things are these, my lord Antonio?

     Will money buy 'em?

ANTONIO;   Very like. One of them

     Is a plain fish, and no doubt marketable.

PROSPERO: Mark but the badges of these men,° my lords,   *servants*

     Then say if they be true.° This misshapen knave,   *honest*

     His mother was a witch, and one so strong

     That could control the moon, make flows and ebbs,

     And deal in her° command without° her power.   *the moon's / beyond*

270   These three have robbed me, and this demidevil—

     For he's a bastard° one—had plotted with them   *counterfeit*

     To take my life. Two of these fellows you

     Must know and own.° This thing of darkness I   *acknowledge*

     Acknowledge mine.

CALIBAN: I shall be pinched to death.

ALONSO: Is not this Stephano, my drunken butler?

SEBASTIAN: He is drunk now. Where had he wine?

ALONSO: And Trinculo is reeling ripe.° Where should they   *stumbling drunk*

     Find this grand liquor that hath gilded⁴ 'em?

     [*To Trinculo.*] How cam'st thou in this pickle?⁵

TRINCULO: I have been in such a pickle since I saw you last that, I fear me, will never out of my bones. I shall not fear flyblowing.⁶

SEBASTIAN: Why, how now, Stephano?

STEPHANO; O, touch me not! I am not Stephano, but a cramp.

PROSPERO: You'd be king o' the isle, sirrah?⁷

STEPHANO: I should have been a sore⁸ one, then.

ALONSO [*pointing to Caliban*]: This is a strange thing as e'er I looked on.

PROSPERO: He is as disproportioned in his manners

     As in his shape.—Go, sirrah, to my cell.

     Take with you your companions. As you look

290   To have my pardon, trim° it handsomely.   *decorate*

CALIBAN: Ay, that I will; and I'll be wise hereafter

     And seek for grace.° What a thrice-double ass   *favor*

     Was I to take this drunkard for a god

     And worship this dull fool!

PROSPERO: Go to. Away!

ALONSO: Hence, and bestow your luggage where you found it.

SEBASTIAN: Or stole it, rather.

                   [*Exeunt Caliban, Stephano, and Trinculo.*]

3. Sharp eyes.
4. Intoxicated; covered with gold (suggesting horse urine).
5. Predicament; pickling brine (here, horse urine).
6. Being soiled by fly eggs (he is protected by being

pickled).
7. Address to an inferior (here, a reprimand).
8. Tyrannical; sorry; aching.

PROSPERO: Sir, I invite Your Highness and your train
        To my poor cell, where you shall take your rest
        For this one night; which, part of it, I'll waste°   *spend*
300   With such discourse as, I not doubt, shall make it
        Go quick away: the story of my life,
        And the particular accidents° gone by   *events*
        Since I came to this isle. And in the morn
        I'll bring you to your ship, and so to Naples,
305   Where I have hope to see the nuptial
        Of these our dear-belovèd solemnized;
        And thence retire me to my Milan, where
        Every third thought shall be my grave.
ALONSO: I long
        To hear the story of your life, which must
        Take° the ear strangely.   *captivate*
PROSPERO: I'll deliver° all;   *tell*
        And promise you calm seas, auspicious gales,
        And sail so expeditious that shall catch
        Your royal fleet far off. [*Aside to Ariel.*] My Ariel, chick,
        That is thy charge. Then to the elements
315   Be free, and fare thou well!—Please you, draw near.

                       [*Exeunt omnes (except Prospero).*]

EPILOGUE

[*Spoken by Prospero.*]

        Now my charms are all o'erthrown,
        And what strength I have's mine own,
        Which is most faint. Now, 'tis true,
        I must be here confined by you
5   Or sent to Naples. Let me not,
        Since I have my dukedom got
        And pardoned the deceiver, dwell
        In this bare island by your spell,°   *silence*
        But release me from my bands°   *bonds*
10   With the help of your good hands.°   *applause*
        Gentle breath of yours my sails
        Must fill, or else my project fails,
        Which was to please. Now I want°   *lack*
        Spirits to enforce,° art to enchant,   *control*
15   And my ending is despair,
        Unless I be relieved by prayer,°   *this very speech*
        Which pierces so that it assaults°   *gains the attention of*
        Mercy itself, and frees° all faults.   *earns pardon for*
        As you from crimes° would pardoned be,   *sins*
20   Let your indulgence° set me free.   *humoring; pardon*

                                  [*Exit.*]

❧

RESONANCE

Aimé Césaire: from *A Tempest*[1]

Characters as in Shakespeare

Two alterations: Ariel, a mulatto slave
Caliban, a black slave[2]

ACT I, SCENE 2

Prospero with Ariel and Caliban[3]

[*Enter Caliban.*]

CALIBAN: Uhuru![4]

PROSPERO: What did you say?

CALIBAN: I said, Uhuru!

PROSPERO: Back to your native language again. I've already told you, I don't like it. You could be polite, at least; a simple "hello" wouldn't kill you.

CALIBAN: Oh, I forgot. . . . But as froggy, waspish, pustular and dung-filled a "hello" as possible. May today hasten by a decade the day when all the birds of the sky and beasts of the earth will feast upon your corpse!

PROSPERO: Gracious as always, you ugly ape! How can anyone *be* so ugly?

CALIBAN: You think I'm ugly . . . well, I don't think you're handsome either. With that big hooked nose, you look just like some old vulture. [*Laughing.*] An old vulture with a scrawny neck!

PROSPERO: Since you're so fond of invective, you could at least thank me for having taught you to speak at all. You savage . . . a dumb animal, a beast I educated, trained, dragged up from the bestiality that still sticks out all over you!

CALIBAN: In the first place, that's not true. You didn't teach me a thing! Except to jabber in your own language so that I could understand your orders—chop the wood, wash the dishes, fish for food, plant vegetables, all because you're too lazy to do it yourself.[5] And as for your learning, did you ever impart any of *that* to me? No, you

1. Translated by Emile Snyder and Sanford Upson. The full title is *A Tempest Based on Shakespeare's "The Tempest": Adaptation for a Black Theatre*. Aimé Césaire was born to an impoverished black family in Martinique in 1913. Along with the Senegalese poet Léopold Senghor, he established the influential movement of "négritude," which encouraged a return to African roots and a reaction against European values. While Césaire writes in French, he often infuses his language with words of African origin and distorts original meanings and syntax. *A Tempest*, written in 1969, takes Shakespeare's late romance as a model to be subverted, although Césaire was also arguably influenced by an 1878 play entitled *Caliban* by the French intellectual Ernest Renan. Additional selections from Césaire's work can be found in Volume F.

2. Césaire maintains the list of characters in Shakespeare's play, but specifies that Ariel is a mulatto (of mixed ancestry) and Caliban is black or African. The set-

ting is unspecified; in his notes to the "Characters," Césaire suggests that the atmosphere is one of a "psychodrama" in which the actors enter "one after the other and each chooses a mask of his liking."

3. The play opens with a flashback to Prospero's exile from Milan, and a discussion of the storm produced by Prospero, with Ariel's assistance, in which the Neapolitans—portrayed by Césaire as ruthless conquerors—are tempest-tossed and in danger of death. At the beginning of Act I, Scene 2, Ariel asks Prospero to be released from having to do such work in the future, and after Prospero sternly rebukes his slave ("Ingrate!. . . . As for your freedom, you'll have it when I'm good and ready") he summons Caliban to the cave: "I've been keeping my eye on him and he's getting a little too emancipated."

4. Swahili word for freedom.

5. Césaire bases the exchange on *The Tempest*, 1.2.322–75 in which Caliban argues with both Prospero and Miranda.

took care not to. All your science and know-how you keep for yourself alone, shut up in big books like those.

PROSPERO: What would you be without me?

CALIBAN: Without you? I'd be the king, that's what I'd be, the King of the Island. The king of the island I inherited from my mother, Sycorax.

PROSPERO: There are some family trees it's better not to climb! She's a ghoul! A witch from whom—and may God be praised—death has delivered us.

CALIBAN: Dead or alive, she was my mother, and I won't deny her! Anyhow, you only think she's dead because you think the earth itself is dead. . . . It's so much simpler that way! Dead, you can walk on it, pollute it, you can tread upon it with the steps of a conqueror. I respect the earth, because I know that it is alive, and I know that Sycorax is alive. Sycorax. Mother.

> Serpent, rain, lightning.
> And I see thee everywhere!
> In the eye of the stagnant pool into which I gaze
> unflinching,
> through the rushes,
> in the gesture made by twisted root and its awaiting thrust.
> In the night, the all-seeing blinded night,
> the nostril-less all-smelling night!

. . . Often, in my dreams, she speaks to me and warns me. . . . Yesterday, even, when I was lying by the stream on my belly lapping at the muddy water, when the Beast was about to spring upon me with that huge stone in his hand. . . .

PROSPERO: If you keep on like that even your sorcery won't save you from punishment!

CALIBAN: That's right, that's right! In the beginning, he was all sweet talk: dear Caliban here, my little Caliban there! And what do you think you'd have done without me in this strange land? Ingrate! I taught you the trees, fruits, birds, the seasons, and now you don't give a damn. . . . Caliban the animal, Caliban the slave! I know that story! Once you've squeezed the juice from the orange, you toss the rind away!

PROSPERO: Oh!

CALIBAN: Do I lie? Isn't it true that you threw me out of your house and made me live in a filthy cave, a hovel, a slum, a ghetto?

PROSPERO: It's easy to say "ghetto"! It wouldn't be such a ghetto if you took the trouble to keep it clean! And there's something you forgot, which is that what forced me to get rid of you was your lust. Good God, you tried to rape my daughter!

CALIBAN: Rape! Rape! Listen, you old goat, you're the one that puts those sexy thoughts in my head. Let me tell you something: I couldn't care less about your daughter, or about your cave, for that matter. If I complain, it's on principle, because I didn't like living with you at all, as a matter of fact. Your feet stink!

PROSPERO: I did not summon you here to argue. Away with you! Back to work! Wood, water, and lots of both! I'm expecting company today.

CALIBAN: I've had just about enough. There's already a pile of wood that high. . . .

PROSPERO: Enough! Take care, Caliban! If you keep grumbling you will be thrashed. And if you don't step lively, if you try to go on strike or to sabotage things, I'll beat you. Beating is the only language you really understand. So much the worse for you: I'll speak it, loud and clear. Off with you, and hurry!

CALIBAN: All right, I'm going . . . but this is the last time. It's the last time, do you hear me? Oh . . . I forgot: I've got something important to tell you.

PROSPERO: Important? Well, out with it.

CALIBAN: It's this: I've decided I don't want to be called Caliban any longer.

PROSPERO: What kind of rot is that? I don't understand.

CALIBAN: Put it this way: I'm *telling* you that from now on I won't answer to the name Caliban.

PROSPERO: What put that notion into your head?

CALIBAN: Well, because Caliban isn't my name. It's as simple as that.

PROSPERO: It's mine, I suppose!

CALIBAN: It's the name given me by hatred, and every time it's spoken it's an insult.

PROSPERO: My, how sensitive we're getting to be! All right, suggest something else. . . . I've got to call you something. What will it be? Cannibal would suit you, but I'm sure you wouldn't like that, would you? Let's see . . . what about Hannibal?[6] That fits. And why not . . . they all seem to like historical names.

CALIBAN: Call me X.[7] That would be best. Like a man without a name. Or, to be more precise, a man whose name has been *stolen.* You talk about history . . . well, that's history, and everyone knows it! Every time you call me it reminds me of a basic fact, the fact that you've stolen everything from me, even my identity! Uhuru! [*He exits.*]

[*Enter Ariel as a sea-nymph.*]

PROSPERO: My dear Ariel, did you see how he looked at me, that glint in his eye? That's something new. Well, let me tell you, Caliban is the enemy. As for those people on the boat, I've changed my mind about them. Give them a scare, but for God's sake don't touch a hair of their heads! You'll answer to me if you do!

ARIEL: I've suffered too much myself from having had to be the agent of their sufferings not to be pleased at your mercy. You can count on me, Master.

PROSPERO: Yes, however great their crimes, if they repent you can assure them of my forgiveness. They are men of my race, and of high rank. As for me, at my age one must rise above disputes and quarrels and think about the future. I have a daughter. Alonso has a son. If they were to love each other, I would give my consent. Let Ferdinand marry Miranda, and may their marriage bring us harmony and peace. That is my plan. I wish to see it carried out. As for Caliban, does it matter what that villain plots against me? All the nobility of Italy, Naples and Milan henceforth combined, will protect my person. Go!

ARIEL: Yes, Master. Your orders will be fully carried out.

[*Ariel sings.*][8]

> Sandy seashore, deep blue sky,
> Surf is rising, sea birds fly
> Here the lover finds delight,
> Sun at noontime, moon at night.
> Join hands lovers, join the dance,
> Find contentment, find romance.
>
> Sandy seashore, deep blue sky,
> Cares will vanish . . . so can I . . .

---

6. Famous general from Carthage in North Africa and a bitter enemy of Rome in the Punic Wars.

7. A possible allusion to Malcolm X, who rejected his name Malcom Little as a relic of slavery; he converted to the Nation of Islam while in prison and was assassinated in 1965.

8. Ariel's song and Ferdinand's subsequent appearance are also from Act 1, Scene 2, of *The Tempest.*

FERDINAND: What is this music? It has led me here and now it stops. . . . No, there it is
again. . . .

ARIEL [*singing*]:

> *Waters move, the ocean flows,*
> *Nothing comes and nothing goes . . .*
> *Strange days are upon us . . .*
>
> *Oysters stare through pearly eyes*
> *Heart-shaped corals gently beat*
> *In the crystal undersea*
> *Here the journey ends—oh see:*
>
> *Waters move and ocean flows,*
> *Nothing comes and nothing goes . . .*
> *Strange days are upon us . . .*

FERDINAND: What do I see before me? A goddess? A mortal?

MIRANDA: I know what *I'm* seeing: a flatterer. Young man, your ability to pay compliments in the situation in which you find yourself at least proves your courage.
Who are you?

FERDINAND: As you see, a poor shipwrecked soul.

MIRANDA: But one of high degree!

FERDINAND: In other surroundings I might be called "Prince," "son of the King". . . .
But, no, I was forgetting . . . not "Prince" but "King," alas. . . . "King" because my
father has just perished in the disaster.

MIRANDA: Poor young man! Here, you'll be received with hospitality and we'll support you in your misfortune.

FERDINAND: Alas, my father. . . . Can it be that I am an unnatural son? Your pity
would make the greatest of sorrows seem sweet.

MIRANDA: I hope you'll like it here with us. The island is pretty. I'll show you the
beaches and the forests, I'll tell you the names of fruits and flowers, I'll introduce
you to a whole world of insects, of lizards of every hue, of birds. . . . Oh, you cannot imagine! The birds! . . .

PROSPERO: That's enough, daughter! I find your chatter irritating . . . and let me assure you, it's not at all fitting. You are doing too much honor to an imposter.
Young man, you are a traitor, a spy, and a woman-chaser to boot! No sooner has
he escaped the perils of the sea than he's sweet-talking the first girl he meets! You
won't get round me that way. Your arrival is convenient, because I need more
manpower: you shall be my house servant.

FERDINAND: Seeing the young lady, more beautiful than any wood-nymph, I thought I
was Ulysses on Nausicaa's isle.[9] But hearing you, Sir, I now understand my fate a
little better—I see I have come ashore on the Barbary Coast and am in the hands of
a cruel pirate.[1] [*Drawing his sword.*] However, a gentleman prefers death to dishonor! I shall defend my life with my freedom!

PROSPERO: Poor fool: your arm is growing weak, your knees are trembling! Traitor! I
could kill you now . . . but I need help. Follow me.

---

9. In the *Odyssey*, Ulysses was shipwrecked on the island
of the Phaiakians; naked and hungry, he appeals to Nausicaa, daughter of the king, for help.
1. The Barbary Coast is in North Africa.

ARIEL: It's no use trying to resist, young man. My master is a sorcerer: neither your passion nor your youth can prevail against him. Your best course would be to follow and obey him.

FERDINAND: Oh God! What sorcery is this? Vanquished, a captive—yet far from rebelling against my fate, I am finding my servitude sweet. Oh, I would be imprisoned for life if only heaven will grant me a glimpse of my sun each day, the face of my own sun. Farewell, Nausicaa.

[*They exit.*]

from ACT 2, SCENE 1

Caliban's cave. Caliban is singing as he works when Ariel enters. He listens to him for a moment.

CALIBAN [*singing*]:

> *May he who eats his corn heedless of Shango[2]*
> *Be accursed! May Shango creep beneath*
> *His nails and into his every pore!*
> *Shango, Shango ho!*
>
> *Forget to give him room if you dare!*
> *He will make himself at home on your nose!*
>
> *Refuse to have him under your roof at your own risk!*
> *He'll tear off your roof and wear it as a hat!*
> *Whoever tries to mislead Shango*
> *Will suffer for it!*
> *Shango, Shango ho!*

* * *

from ACT 3, SCENE 5[3]

* * *

PROSPERO: Enough! Today is a day to be benevolent, and it will do no good to try to talk sense to you in the state you're in. . . . Leave us. Go sleep it off, drunkards. We raise sail tomorrow.

TRINCULO: Raise sail! But that's what we do all the time, Sire, raise things, Stephano and I . . . at least, we raise our glasses, from dawn till dusk till dawn. . . . The hard part is putting them down, decking, as you might say.

PROSPERO: Scoundrels, would that in your voyage through life you might one day put in at the harbor of Temperance and Sobriety!

ALONSO [*indicating Caliban*]: That is the strangest creature I've ever seen!

PROSPERO: And the most devilish too!

GONZALO: What's that? Devilish! You've reprimanded him, preached at him, you've given orders and made him obey, and you say he is still indomitable!

PROSPERO: Honest Gonzalo, it is as I have said.

---

2. Shango is a Yoruba god of thunder and war, worshipped in the Antilles, Africa, and Brazil.
3. The final scene brings to a culmination the various threads of the play, much as in *The Tempest*. As the scene opens, Ferdinand and Miranda are playing chess, and Prospero tells the entire group, assembled in his grotto, that they will all set sail for Italy on the following day; with that, he sets Ariel free.

GONZALO: Well—and forgive me, Counsellor, if I give counsel—on the basis of my long experience the only thing left is exorcism. "Begone, unclean spirit, in the name of the Father, of the Son and of the Holy Ghost." That's all there is to it!

[*Caliban bursts out laughing.*]

GONZALO: You were absolutely right! And more so than you thought. . . . He's not just a rebel, he's a hardened criminal! [*To Caliban.*] So much the worse for you, my friend. I have tried to save you. I give up. I leave you to the secular arm![4]

PROSPERO: Draw near, Caliban. What say you in your own defense? Take advantage of my good humor. Today, I feel in a forgiving mood.

CALIBAN: I'm not interested in defending myself. My only regret is that I've failed.

PROSPERO: What were you hoping for?

CALIBAN: To get back my island and regain my freedom.

PROSPERO: And what would you do all alone here on this island, haunted by the devil, tempest tossed?

CALIBAN: First of all, I'd get rid of you! I'd spew you out, all your works and pomps! Your "white" magic!

PROSPERO: That is a fairly negative program. . . .

CALIBAN: You don't understand it. . . . I say I'm going to spew you out, and that's very positive. . . .

PROSPERO: Well, the world is really upside down. . . . We've seen everything now: Caliban as a dialectician! However, in spite of everything I'm fond of you, Caliban. Come, let's make peace. We've lived together for ten years and worked side by side! Ten years count for something, after all! We've ended up by becoming compatriots!

CALIBAN: You know very well that I'm not interested in peace. I'm interested in being free! Free, you hear?

PROSPERO: It's odd . . . no matter what you do, you won't succeed in making me believe that I'm a tyrant!

CALIBAN: Understand what I say, Prospero:

> For years I bowed my head
> for years I took it, all of it—
> your insults, your ingratitude . . .
> and worst of all, more degrading than all the rest,
> your condescension,
> But now, it's over!
> Over, do you hear?
> Of course, at the moment
> You're still stronger than I am.
> But I don't give a damn for your power
> or for your dogs or your police or your inventions!
> And do you know why?
> It's because I know I'll get you!
> I'll impale you! And on a stake that you've
> sharpened yourself!

4. Having played at being the exorcist, Gonzalo "releases" Caliban to the "state."

You'll have impaled yourself!
Prospero, you're a great magician:
you're an old hand at deception.
And you lied to me so much,
about the world, about yourself,
that you ended up by imposing on me
an image of myself:
underdeveloped, in your words, incompetent,
that's how you made me see myself!
And I loathe that image . . . and it's false!
But now I know you, you old cancer,
And I also know myself!

And I know that one day my bare fist, just that, will be enough to crush your
world. The old world is falling apart!

Isn't it true? Just look. It even bores *you* to death.
And by the way . . . you have a chance to get
it over with: you can fuck off.
You can go back to Europe. But in a pig's eye you will!
I'm sure you won't leave. You make me laugh
with your "mission"!
Your "vocation"!
Your vocation is to give me shit.
And that's why you'll stay . . . just like those
guys who founded the colonies
and who now can't live anywhere else.
You're just an old colonial addict, that's what you are!

PROSPERO: Poor Caliban! You know that you're headed toward your own ruin.
You're sliding toward suicide! You know I will be the stronger, and stronger all
the time. I pity you!

CALIBAN: And I hate you!

PROSPERO: Beware! My generosity has its limits.

CALIBAN [*shouting*]:

> *Shango marches with strength*
> *along his path, the sky!*
> *Shango is a fire-bearer,*
> *his arms shake the heavens*
> *and the earth*
> *Oh, Shango! Shango!*

PROSPERO: I have uprooted the oak and raised the sea,
I have caused the mountain to tremble and have bared my chest to adversity.
With Jove I have traded thunderbolt for thunderbolt.
Better yet—from a brutish monster I have made man!
But ah! To have failed to find the path to man's heart . . .
if that be where man is.
[*To Caliban.*] Well, I hate you as well!
For it is you who have made me doubt myself for the first time.

[*To the Nobles.*] My friends, draw near. I take my leave of you . . . I shall not
be going. My fate is here: I shall not run from it.

ANTONIO: What, Sire?

PROSPERO: Hear me well. I am not in any ordinary sense a master,
as this savage thinks,
but rather the conductor of a boundless score—
this isle,
summoning voices—I alone—
and mingling them at my pleasure,
arranging out of confusion
one intelligible line.
Without me, who would be able to draw music from all that?
This isle is mute without me.
My duty, thus, is here, and here I shall stay.

GONZALO: Oh day full rich in miracles!

PROSPERO: Do not be distressed. Antonio, be you the lieutenant of my goods and
make use of them as procurator until that time when Ferdinand and Miranda may
take effective possession of them, joining them with the Kingdom of Naples.
Nothing of that which has been set for them must be postponed: let their marriage
be celebrated at Naples with all royal splendor. Honest Gonzalo, I place my trust in
your word. You shall stand as father to our Princess at this ceremony.

GONZALO: Count on me, Sire.

PROSPERO: Gentlemen, farewell.

[*They exit.*]

And now Caliban, it's you and me!
What I have to tell you will be brief:
Ten times, a hundred times, I've tried to save you,
above all from yourself.
But you have always answered me with wrath and venom,
like the opossum that pulls itself up by its own tail
the better to bite the hand that tears it from the darkness.
Well, my boy, I shall set aside my indulgent nature
and henceforth I will answer your violence
with violence!

[*Time passes, symbolized by the curtain's being lowered halfway and reraised.
In semi-darkness Prospero appears, aged and weary. His gestures are jerky and au-
tomatic, his speech weak, toneless.*]

PROSPERO: Odd, but for some time now we seem to be overrun with opossums. Pec-
carys,[5] wild boar, all of the unpleasant animals! But mainly opossums. With those
eyes! And the vile grin they have! It's as though the jungle was laying siege to the
cave. . . . But I shall stand firm . . . I shall not let my work perish! [*Shouting.*] I
shall protect civilization! [*He fires in all directions.*] They're done for! Now, this

---

5. A piglike, hoofed mammal with long dark bristles, found in the Americas; from the Carib word *pekira*.

way I'll be able to have some peace and calm for a while. But it's cold. Odd how the climate's changed. Cold on this island. . . . Have to think about making a fire. . . . Well, Caliban, old fellow, it's just us two now, here on the island . . . only you and me. You and me. You-me . . . me-you! What in the hell is he up to? [*Shouting.*] Caliban!

[*In the distance, above the sound of the surf and the chirping of birds, we hear snatches of Caliban's song.*]

FREEDOM HI-DAY, FREEDOM HI-DAY!!

John Donne
1572–1631

"Life is shrunke, / Dead and enterr'd." John Donne's arresting phrase probably responded to the death of his wife in 1617—a sudden death, after a difficult childbirth, that ended the intense love affair that is the subject of many of Donne's secular poems. But the love affair had also derailed the career of an aspiring courtier and diplomat who had succeeded to the enviable position of secretary for Sir Thomas Egerton, one of the most powerful men in Elizabethan England. Donne made the mistake of falling in love with Anne More, Egerton's niece and Donne's social superior. Their elopement led to her disownment and his unemployment and imprisonment; as his first biographer, Izak Walton, would write, "though he endured not a hard service for her, yet he lost a good one." Before his marriage in 1601, Donne had a promising career ahead of him. Educated at Cambridge, Oxford, and Lincoln's Inn, he had participated in several expeditions in the company of Lord Essex and had been a member of Parliament. For many years thereafter, however, he and his ever-growing family were forced to move frequently about as he searched for new "service," and it was only in 1615 that he took holy orders to become an Anglican priest and embark on a stabler career. It was a career very different from the one he had once imagined for himself, and a far cry too from the ardent Catholicism embraced by his mother, brother, and great-great-uncle, Sir Thomas More.

Indeed, it is common to separate Donne's Anglican phase from his earlier life as would-be courtier, lover, and occasional cad, his deeply religious writings from his erotic and satirical ones. On the one hand, after 1615, he did turn his pen largely to sermons—over 150 of which survive—and biblical commentaries. He was appointed Dean of Saint Paul's Cathedral in 1621, and preached a number of sermons to James I and his son Charles I and members of their courts. Other religious writings from the last decade of his life include a series of devotions inspired by the Psalms, written when he was ill with fever in 1624. Yet the opening line from one of his holy sonnets—"Inconstancy unnaturally hath begot / A constant habit"—should warn us against finding in Donne's work the signs of definitive conversion, a project rendered difficult in any case by the uncertain dates of so much of his poetry. It is telling that two of his favorite writers were Augustine, whose sinful youth was the subject of much of the *Confessions,* and David, supposed author of the Psalms and miserable penitent for his own crime of passion: the murder of his lover's husband. Like both of these figures, the one a father of the Church, the other king of Judea, Donne found that writing could serve as a vehicle for his ongoing spiritual crises, no matter what form it took: poetry or prose, public sermons or intimate meditations.

Intriguing continuities run through Donne's writing, which sometimes violently distorts conventional notions of space and time, as the sun is crammed into the lovers' narrow room, the veins of the body become rivers, an hour away from one's beloved is computed as a century. God is courted in the Holy Sonnets in "prayers and flattering speaches" just as Donne's nude mistress is praised in the famous elegy, "Going to Bed," banned from the earliest published collection of Donne's poems. And in one sermon Heaven is compared to America—the America that in the same titillating elegy is compared to the mistress, a kingdom "safeliest when with one man manned."

All of Donne's writing is exacting and syntactically and metrically complex, demanding our willingness to be engaged and enter fully into what one scholar has called the creation of a vision, whether it be of his difficulties after his wife's death, lovers parting, or God's inexplicable mercy and his command to love: "Wilt thou love God, as he thee?" he asks insistently of his reader in one of the holy sonnets. Above all, there is the presence of a strong personal voice enmeshed in self-doubt even as it exudes stylistic self-confidence. This is the man who wrote, when still young, a treatise on suicide, and who as an established preacher twenty years later would reflect painfully on his limitations:

> I throw my selfe downe in my Chamber, and I call in, and invite God, and his Angels thither, and when they are there, I neglect God and his Angels, for the noise of a Flie, for the ratling of a Coach, for the whining of a doore . . . A memory of yesterdays pleasures, a feare of to morrows dangers, a straw under my knee, a noise in mine eare, a light in mine eye, an any thing, a nothing, a fancy, a Chimera in my braine, troubles me in my prayer. So certainly is there nothing, nothing in spirituall things, perfect in this world.

Never strong in health, he died before turning sixty; the last sermon he preached before the King, a month before his death, was entitled "Death's Duell."

The Sun Rising

Busy old fool, unruly Sun,
　Why dost thou thus,
Through windows and through curtains call on us?
Must to thy motions lovers' seasons run?
5　　　Saucy pedantic wretch, go chide
　　Late school boys, and sour prentices,°　　　　　　*apprentices*
Go tell court-huntsmen, that the King will ride,
　　Call country ants to harvest offices;
Love, all alike,° no season knows, nor clime,　　　*when reciprocated*
10　　Nor hours, days, months, which are the rags of time.

　　Thy beams, so reverend and strong
　　Why shouldst thou think?
I could eclipse and cloud them with a wink,
But that I would not lose her sight so long:
15　　　If her eyes have not blinded thine,
　　Look, and tomorrow late, tell me,
Whether both th' India's of spice and mine[1]
　　Be where thou leftst them, or lie here with me.
Ask for those Kings whom thou saw'st yesterday,
20　　And thou shalt hear, All here in one bed lay.

---

1. Both the East Indies, origin of spices, and the West Indies, known for its gold mines.

She is all States, and all Princes, I,
Nothing else is.
Princes do but play us; compar'd to this,
All honor's mimic;° All wealth alchemy;°   *fake / counterfeit*
25   Thou sun art half as happy as we,
In that the world's contracted thus.[2]
Thine age asks ease, and since thy duties be
To warm the world, that's done in warming us.
Shine here to us, and thou art everywhere;
30   This bed thy center is, these walls, thy sphere.

Elegy 19: To His Mistress Going to Bed[1]

Come, Madam, come, all rest my powers defy,
Until I labour, I in labour lie.
The foe oft-times having the foe in sight,
Is tir'd with standing though he never fight.
5   Off with that girdle, like heaven's Zone° glittering,   *the zodiac*
But a far fairer world encompassing.
Unpin that spangled breastplate° which you wear,   *bodice*
That th'eyes of busy fools may be stopt there.
Unlace yourself, for that harmonious chime
10   Tells me from you, that now it is bed time.
Off with that happy busk,° which I envy,   *corset*
That still can be, and still can stand so nigh.
Your gown going off, such beauteous state reveals,
As when from flowery meads th'hill's shadow steals.
15   Off with that wiry coronet° and show   *crown*
The hairy diadem which on you doth grow:
Now off with those shoes, and then softly tread
In this love's hallow'd temple, this soft bed.
In such white robes, heaven's angels us'd to be
20   Receiv'd by men: thou angel bring'st with thee
A heaven like Mahomet's Paradise,[2] and though
Ill spirits walk in white, we easily know,
By this these angels from an evil sprite,
Those set our hairs, but these our flesh upright.
25   License my roving hands, and let them go,
Behind, before, above, between, below.
O my America! my new-found-land,
My kingdom, safeliest when with one man man'd,
My mine of precious stones: My empery,°   *empire*
30   How blest am I in this discovering thee!
To enter in these bonds, is to be free;
Then where my hand is set, my seal[3] shall be.

2. Into the small space of the bedroom.
1. Refused a license for publication in 1633, the poem was
first published more than 20 years after Donne's death.
Elegies were used for a variety of purposes, among them

the celebration of love and lust.
2. The Islamic paradise described by Muhammad was said
to be populated by virgins who would tend to the elect.
3. Wax impression; also a seal or sign of ownership.

Full nakedness! All joys are due to thee,
As souls unbodied, bodies uncloth'd must be,
35   To taste whole joys. Gems which you women use
Are like Atlanta's balls, cast in men's views,[4]
That when a fool's eye lighteth on a Gem,
His earthly soul may covet theirs, not them:
Like pictures or like books gay coverings made
40   For laymen,° are all women thus array'd.   *ordinary readers*
Themselves are mystic books, which only we
(Whom their imputed grace will dignify)
Must see reveal'd. Then since that I may know,
As liberally, as to a midwife show
45   Thyself: cast all, yea, this white linen hence,
There is no penance due to innocence:[5]
     To teach thee I am naked first; why then
What needst thou have more covering then a man?

Air and Angels

Twice or thrice had I loved thee,
Before I knew thy face or name;
So in a voice, so in a shapeless flame,
Angels affect us oft, and worship'd be;[1]
5   Still when, to where thou wert, I came,
Some lovely glorious nothing I did see,
     But since, my soul, whose child love is,
Takes limbs of flesh, and else could nothing do,
     More subtle° than the parent is,   *airy*
10   Love must not be, but take a body too,
     And therefore what thou wert, and who
          I bid Love ask, and now
That it assume thy body, I allow,
And fix itself in thy lip, eye, and brow.

15   Whilst thus to ballast° love, I thought,   *weigh down*
And so more steadily to have gone,
With wars which would sink admiration,
I saw, I had love's pinnace° overfraught,   *light sailing vessel*
     Ev'ry thy hair for love to worke upon
20   Is much too much, some fitter must be sought;
          For, nor in nothing, nor in things
Extreme, and scatt'ring bright, can love inhere;[2]

4. The swift Atalanta was outwitted by her would-be lover Hippomenes when he cast three golden apples into her path; she stooped to pick them up, and when she lost the race, she was forced to marry. Donne would make men the ones distracted by the gems cast in their way.
5. Innocence does not require penance. An alternate manuscript tradition has instead "Here is no penance much less innocence."
1. Scholastic doctrine had suggested that angels could take on bodies of air; or as Donne himself would write in a sermon from November 1627: "we say that they are creatures that have not so much of a body as flesh is, as froth is, as a vapour is, as a sigh is, and yet with a touch they shall moulder a rock into less atoms, than the sand that it stands upon."
2. Love cannot exist in nothing; nor can it inhere in the "extreme" brightness that is angelic fire.

Then as an angel, face and wings
Of air, not pure as it, yet pure doth wear,
So thy love may be my love's sphere;[3]
Just such disparity
As is 'twixt air and angels purity,
'Twixt women's love, and men's will ever be.

A Valediction: Forbidding Mourning[1]

As virtuous men pass mildly away,
And whisper to their souls, to go,
Whilst some of their sad friends do say,
The breath goes now, and some say, no:

So let us melt,° and make no noise, *part*
No tear-floods, nor sigh-tempests move,
'Twere profanation of our joys
To tell the layety our love.

Moving of th'earth brings harms and fears,
Men reckon what it did and meant,
But trepidation of the spheres,
Though greater far, is innocent.[2]

Dull sublunary[3] lovers' love
(Whose soul is sense) cannot admit
Absence, because it doth remove
Those things which elemented° it. *composed*

But we by a love, so much refin'd,
That ourselves know not what it is,
Inter-assured of the mind,
Care less, eyes, lips, and hands to miss.

Our two souls therefore, which are one,
Though I must go, endure not yet
A breach, but an expansion,
Like gold to airy thinness beat.

If they be two, they are two so
As stiff twin compasses are two,[4]
Thy soul the fix'd foot, makes no show
To move, but doth, if th'other do.

And though it in the center sit,
Yet when the other far doth roam,

3. Her love will be the "ballast" or weighty sphere for his.
1. Izak Walton, Donne's earliest biographer, suggests that Donne wrote the poem to his wife in 1611 on the occasion of his journey to France. A "valediction" is a leave-taking.
2. Donne compares earthquakes, thought of as God's punishment to sinful man, to the tremulous and occasional movement of the spheres constituting the Ptolemaic universe; their movements, while greater than that of earthquakes, were not the products of man's sin.
3. Under the moon's influence; hence, earthly and sensual.
4. The two legs of a compass, often used as an emblem for constancy.

It leans and hearkens after it,
    And grows erect, as that comes home.

Such wilt thou be to me, who must
    Like th'other foot obliquely run.[5]
35 Thy firmness makes my circle just,°   *accurate*
    And makes me end, where I begun.

The Relic

When my grave is broke up again
Some second guest to entertain,[1]
(For graves have learn'd that woman-head°   *womanhood*
To be to more than one a bed)
5   And he that digs it, spies
A bracelet of bright hair about the bone,
    Will he not let us alone,
And think that there a loving couple lies,
Who thought that this device might be some way
10 To make their souls, at the last busy day,°   *Judgment Day*
Meet at this grave, and make a little stay?

    If this fall in a time, or land,
    Where mis-devotion doth command,
    Then, he that digs us up, will bring
15   Us to the Bishop, and the King,
      To make us reliques; then
Thou shalt be a Mary Magdalen, and I
    A something else thereby;[2]
All women shall adore us, and some men;
20 And since at such time, miracles are sought,
I would have that age by this paper taught
What miracles we harmless lovers wrought.

    First, we lov'd well and faithfully,
    Yet knew not what we lov'd, nor why,
25   Difference of sex no more we knew,
    Then our guardian angels do;[3]
      Coming and going, we
Perchance might kiss, but not between those meals;°   *kisses*
    Our hands ne'er touch'd the seals
30 Which nature, injur'd by late law, sets free:[4]
These miracles we did; but now alas,
All measure, and all language, I should pass,
Should I tell what a miracle she was.

---

5. The errant foot will at last circle round to its starting-point.
1. Grave sites were often reused for later burials.
2. Mary Magdalen was a follower of Jesus, often thought (erroneously) to have been a reformed prostitute; the

"something else" would presumably be Christ.
3. Their love was not sensual, but spiritual.
4. The "seal" is probably the hymen; the "late law" would be men's attempts to curb sexual desire.

The Computation

For the first twenty years, since yesterday,[1]
  I scarce believ'd thou could'st be gone away,
For forty more, I fed on favours past,
  And forty on hopes that thou would'st, they might last.
5   Tears drown'd one hundred, and sighs blew out two,
  A thousand, I did neither think, nor do,
Or not divide, all being one thought of you;
  Or in a thousand more, forgot that too.
Yet call not this long life; but think that I
10   Am, by being dead, immortal; can ghosts die?[2]

from HOLY SONNETS[1]

Oh my black soul! now thou art summoned

Oh my black soul! now thou art summoned
By sickness, death's herald and champion;
Thou art like a pilgrim, which abroad hath done
Treason, and durst not turn to whence he's fled,
5   Or like a thief, which till death's doom be read,
Wisheth himself deliverd from prison;
But damn'd and hal'd° to execution,   *dragged*
Wisheth that still he might be imprisoned;
Yet grace, if thou repent, thou canst not lack;
10   But who shall give thee that grace to begin?
Oh make thyself with holy mourning black,
And red with blushing, as thou art with sin;
Or wash thee in Christ's blood, which hath this might
That being red, it dyes red souls to white.[2]

Death be not proud, though some have called thee

Death be not proud, though some have called thee
Mighty and dreadful, for thou art not so,
For those whom thou think'st thou dost overthrow,
Die not, poor death, nor yet canst thou kill me;
5   From rest and sleep, which but thy pictures be,
Much pleasure, then from thee much more must flow,
And soonest our best men with thee do go,
Rest of their bones, and souls' delivery.
Thou'art slave to Fate, chance, kings, and desperate men,
10   And dost with poison, war, and sickness dwell,
And poppy,°or charms can make us sleep as well,   *used to induce sleep*
And better then thy stroke; why swell'st thou then?

---

1. Each hour is a hundred years in the poem's "computation."
2. With a possible pun on "dying" as slang for "orgasm."
1. Donne wrote a total of 19 holy sonnets, 16 of which also bear the subtitle of "Divine Meditations" in the manuscripts. Most of the sonnets seem to have been written around the period of 1609–1610, although like the rest of Donne's poetry, they were not published until after his death.
2. See 1 John 1:7: "If we walk in the light, as he is in the light, we have fellowship one with another, and the blood of Jesus Christ his Son cleanseth us from all sin."

One short sleep past, we wake eternally,
And death shall be no more: Death, thou shalt die.

Batter my heart, three-person'd God

Batter my heart, three-person'd God;³ for, you
As yet but knock, breath, shine, and seek to mend;
That I may rise, and stand, o'erthrow me, and bend
Your force, to break, blow, burn and make me new.
5   I, like an usurpt town, to another° due,   *Satan*
Labour to admit you, but oh, to no end,
Reason your viceroy in me, me should defend,
But is captiv'd, and proves weak or untrue,
Yet dearly I love you, and would be lov'd fain,°   *willingly*
10   But am betroth'd unto your enemy,
Divorce me, untie, or break that knot again,
Take me to you, imprison me, for I
Except you enthrall me, never shall be free,
Nor ever chaste, except you ravish me.

I am a little world made cunningly

I am a little world made cunningly
Of elements, and an angelike spright,°   *spirit*
But black sin hath betray'd to endless night
My world's both parts and (oh) both parts⁴ must die.
5   You° which beyond that heaven which was most high   *Christ*
Have found new spheres, and of new lands can write,⁵
Pour new seas in mine eyes, that so I might
Drown my world with my weeping earnestly,
Or wash it if it must be drown'd no more:⁶
10   But oh it must be burnt;⁷ alas the fire
Of lust and envy have burnt it heretofore,
And made it fouler: Let their flames retire,
And burne me, oh Lord, with a fiery zeal
Of thee and thy house, which doth in eating heal.⁸

Oh, to vex me, contraries meet in one

Oh, to vex me, contraries meet in one:
Inconstancy unnaturally hath begot
A constant habit; that when I would not
I change in vows, and in devotion.
5   As humorous° is my contrition   *changeable*
As my prophane love, and as soon forgot:

---

3. The Trinity: the Father, Son, and Holy Spirit.
4. His body and his soul.
5. Donne may be referring here to Galileo's discovery of the "new lands" of the moon; it is equally possible that he is simply calling attention to the recent explorations in general.

6. God promises Noah in Genesis 9 that he will not send a second flood.
7. Revelation 20 speaks of the "pool of fire" as the "second death" at the end of the world.
8. Eating Christ's "house" (his body) will bring the sinner life.

As ridlingly distemper'd, cold and hot,
As praying, as mute; as infinite, as none.
I durst not view heaven yesterday; and today
10   In prayers and flattering speeches I court God:
Tomorrow I quake with true fear of his rod.
So my devout fits come and go away
Like a fantastic ague:° save that here   *imaginary fever*
Those are my best days, when I shake with fear.

from Devotions Upon Emergent Occasions[1]
10: They find the disease to steal on insensibly,
and endeavour to meet with it so.[2]

MEDITATION

This is nature's nest of boxes: the heavens contain the earth; the earth, cities; cities, men. And all these are concentric; the common centre to them all is decay, ruin; only that is eccentric which was never made; only that place, or garment rather, which we can imagine but not demonstrate.[3] That light, which is the very emanation of the light of God, in which the saints shall dwell, with which the saints shall be apparelled, only that bends not to this centre, to ruin; that which was not made of nothing is not threatened with this annihilation. All other things are; even angels, even our souls; they move upon the same poles, they bend to the same centre; and if they were not made immortal by preservation, their nature could not keep them from sinking to this centre, annihilation. In all these (the frame of the heavens, the states upon earth, and men in them, comprehend all), those are the greatest mischiefs which are least discerned; the most insensible in their ways come to be the most sensible in their ends. The heavens have had their dropsy, they drowned the world; and they shall have their fever, and burn the world.[4] Of the dropsy, the flood, the world had a foreknowledge one hundred and twenty years before it came;[5] and so some made provision against it, and were saved; the fever shall break out in an instant and consume all; the dropsy did no harm to the heavens from whence it fell, it did not put out those lights, it did not quench those heats; but the fever, the fire, shall burn the furnace itself, annihilate those heavens that breathe it out. Though the dogstar have a pestilent breath, an infectious exhalation, yet, because we know when it will rise, we clothe ourselves, and we diet ourselves, and we shadow ourselves to a sufficient prevention;[6] but comets and blazing stars, whose effects or significations no man can interrupt or frustrate, no man foresaw: no almanack tells us when a blazing star will break out, the matter is carried up in secret; no astrologer tells us when the effects will be accomplished, for that is a

---

1. The *Devotions Upon Emergent Occasions* were written in 1624 while Donne was recovering from severe illness. There are 23 devotions in all, each one focusing on a different stage of the disease, and each one divided into three parts: "Meditations upon our Humane Condition"; "Expostulations, and Debatements with God"; and "Prayers, upon the severall Occasions, to him."
2. The opening phrase is written in Latin; "they" refer to the physicians who have been presiding over the patient.
3. The "common centre" is the earth's center; anything "eccentric" lacked a fixed center for its orbit.

4. A reference to Revelation 8:5.
5. Genesis 6:3 has God setting the span of a man's life, sometimes seen as a warning of the flood that would soon ensue: "My spirit shall not remain in man forever . . . His lifetime shall be one hundred and twenty years." Donne is contrasting the salvational language of Genesis with the apocalyptic furor of the Bible's final book.
6. The Dog-star, or Sirius, is associated with the dog days of late summer, when Sirius was said to spread disease and tremendous heat, as noted by the Greek physician Hippocrates and others.

secret of a higher sphere than the other; and that which is most secret is most dangerous. It is so also here in the societies of men, in states and commonwealths. Twenty rebellious drums make not so dangerous a noise as a few whisperers and secret plotters in corners. The cannon doth not so much hurt against a wall, as a mine under the wall; nor a thousand enemies that threaten, so much as a few that take an oath to say nothing. God knew many heavy sins of the people, in the wilderness and after, but still he charges them with that one, with murmuring, murmuring in their hearts, secret disobediences, secret repugnances against his declared will;[7] and these are the most deadly, the most pernicious. And it is so too with the diseases of the body; and that is my case. The pulse, the urine, the sweat, all have sworn to say nothing, to give no indication of any dangerous sickness. My forces are not enfeebled, I find no decay in my strength; my provisions are not cut off, I find no abhorring in mine appetite; my counsels are not corrupted nor infatuated, I find no false apprehensions to work upon mine understanding; and yet they see that invisibly, and I feel that insensibly, the disease prevails. The disease hath established a kingdom, an empire in me, and will have certain *arcana imperii,* secrets of state,[8] by which it will proceed and not be bound to declare them. But yet against those secret conspiracies in the state, the magistrate hath the rack; and against these insensible diseases physicians have their examiners; and those these employ now.

EXPOSTULATION

My God, my God, I have been told, and told by relation, by her own brother that did it, by thy servant Nazianzen, that his sister in the vehemency of her prayer, did use to threaten thee with a holy importunity, with a pious impudency.[9] I dare not do so, O God; but as thy servant Augustine wished that Adam had not sinned, therefore that Christ might not have died,[1] may I not to this one purpose wish that if the serpent, before the temptation of Eve, did go upright and speak, that he did so still, because I should the sooner hear him if he spoke, the sooner see him if he went upright? In his curse I am cursed too; his creeping undoes me; for howsoever he begin at the heel, and do but bruise that, yet he, and *death* in him, *is come into our windows;* into our eyes and ears, the entrances and inlets of our soul. He works upon us in secret and we do not discern him; and one great work of his upon us is to make us so like himself as to sin in secret, that others may not see us; but his masterpiece is to make us sin in secret, so as that we may not see ourselves sin. For the first, the hiding of our sins from other men, he hath induced that which was his offspring from the beginning, a lie; for man is, in nature, yet in possession of some such sparks of ingenuity and nobleness, as that, but to disguise evil, he would not lie. The body, the sin, is the serpent's; and the garment that covers it, the lie, is his too. These are his, but the hiding of sin from ourselves is he himself: when we have the sting of the serpent in us, and do not sting ourselves, the venom of sin, and no remorse for sin, then, as thy blessed Son said of Judas, *He is a devil;*[2] not that he had one, but was one; so we are become devils to ourselves, and we have not only a serpent in our bosom, but we ourselves are to ourselves that serpent. How far did thy servant David press upon thy pardon in that petition, *Cleanse thou me from secret sins?* Can any sin be secret? for a great part of our

---

7. While they are in the desert, the Hebrews "murmur" against God, provoking his wrath; Numbers 14:26.
8. Used to describe the king's prerogative to act without the advice of his ministers.
9. Gregory of Nazianzus reports in his elegy for his sister

Gorgonia that she put her head on the altar and refused to move it until God cured her.
1. From the treatise entitled *Against Two Letters of the Pelagians,* 4.6, by Augustine, 4th-century church father.
2. John 6:70.

sins, though, says thy prophet, we conceive them in the dark, upon our bed, yet, says he, we do them in the light; there are many sins which we glory in doing, and would not do if nobody should know them.[3] Thy blessed servant Augustine confesses that he was ashamed of his shamefacedness and tenderness of conscience, and that he often belied himself with sins which he never did, lest he should be unacceptable to his sinful companions.[4] But if we would conceal them (thy prophet found such a desire, and such a practice in some, when he said, *Thou hast trusted in thy wickedness, and thou hast said, None shall see me*)[5], yet can we conceal them? Thou, O God, canst hear of them by others: the voice of Abel's blood will tell thee of Cain's murder; the heavens themselves will tell thee. Heaven shall reveal his iniquity; a small creature alone shall do it, *A bird of the air shall carry the voice, and tell the matter;* thou wilt trouble no informer, thou thyself revealedst Adam's sin to thyself;[6] and the manifestation of sin is so full to thee, as that thou shalt reveal all to all; *Thou shalt bring every work to judgment, with every secret thing; and there is nothing covered that shall not be revealed.*[7] But, O my God, there is another way of knowing my sins, which thou lovest better than any of these; to know them by my confession. As physic works, so it draws the peccant humour to itself, that, when it is gathered together, the weight of itself may carry that humour away;[8] so thy Spirit returns to my memory my former sins, that, being so recollected, they may pour out themselves by confession. *When I kept silence,* says thy servant David, *day and night thy hand was heavy upon me;* but when I said, *I will confess my transgressions unto the Lord, thou forgavest the iniquity of my sin.*[9] Thou interpretest the very purpose of confession so well, as that thou scarce leavest any new mercy for the action itself. This mercy thou leavest, that thou armest us thereupon against relapses into the sins which we have confessed. And that mercy which thy servant Augustine apprehends when he says to thee, "Thou hast forgiven me those sins which I have done, and those sins which only by thy grace I have not done":[1] they were done in our inclination to them, and even that inclination needs thy mercy, and that mercy he calls a pardon. And these are most truly secret sins, because they were never done, and because no other man, nor I myself, but only thou knowest, how many and how great sins I have escaped by thy grace, which, without that, I should have multiplied against thee.

PRAYER

O eternal and most gracious God, who as thy Son Christ Jesus, though he knew all things, yet said he knew not the day of judgment, because he knew it not so as that he might tell us; so though thou knowest all my sins, yet thou knowest them not to my comfort, except thou know them by my telling them to thee. How shall I bring to thy knowledge, by that way, those sins which I myself know not? If I accuse myself of original sin, wilt thou ask me if I know what original sin is? I know not enough of it to

3. From Psalm 19:12; David is "thy prophet." The Psalms are often seen as penitential vehicles for David, whose sins of passion are recounted in the second book of Samuel.
4. One of Augustine's admissions of his youthful sins from the *Confessions,* 2. 3. 7.
5. Isaiah 47:10, in which Isaiah is addressing the kingdom of Babylon.
6. Donne combines several biblical passages here, including Genesis 3 and 4, which tell, respectively, of Adam's sin and that of his son, Cain, who slew Abel, and a pas-

sage in Ecclesiastes 10:20 that warns against criticizing the powerful: "Even in your thoughts do not make light of the king . . . because the birds of the air may carry your voice, a winged creature may tell what you say."
7. From Christ's directives to his disciples in Matthew 10:26.
8. Donne is drawing on humoural theory, which involved purging from the body only the humor that was in excess.
9. Psalms 32:3–4.
1. Augustine's *Confessions* 10.30. 41–42.

satisfy others, but I know enough to condemn myself, and to solicit thee. If I confess to thee the sins of my youth, wilt thou ask me if I know what those sins were? I know them not so well as to name them all, nor am sure to live hours enough to name them all (for I did them then faster than I can speak them now, when every thing that I did conduced to some sin), but I know them so well as to know that nothing but thy mercy is so infinite as they. If the naming of sins of thought, word and deed, of sins of omission and of action, of sins against thee, against my neighbour and against myself, of sins unrepented and sins relapsed into after repentance, of sins of ignorance and sins against the testimony of my conscience, of sins against thy commandments, sins against thy Son's Prayer, and sins against our own creed, of sins against the laws of that church, and sins against the laws of that state in which thou hast given me my station; if the naming of these sins reach not home to all mine, I know what will.[2] O Lord, pardon me all those sins which thy Son Christ Jesus suffered for, who suffered for all the sins of all the world; for there is no sin amongst all those which had not been my sin, if thou hadst not been my God, and antedated me a pardon in thy preventing grace.[3] And since sin, in the nature of it, retains still so much of the author of it that it is a serpent, insensibly insinuating itself into my soul, let thy brazen serpent (the contemplation of thy Son crucified for me) be evermore present to me, for my recovery against the sting of the first serpent; that so, as I have a Lion against a lion, the Lion of the tribe of Judah against that lion that seeks whom he may devour, so I may have a serpent against a serpent, the wisdom of the serpent against the malice of the serpent, and both against that lion and serpent, forcible and subtle temptations, thy dove with thy olive in thy ark, humility and peace and reconciliation to thee, by the ordinances of thy church.[4] Amen.

from _17: Now, this bell tolling softly for another, says to me:_ _Thou must die._[1]

And when [the church] buries a man, that action concerns me: all mankind is of one author, and is one volume; when one man dies, one chapter is not torn out of the book, but translated into a better language; and every chapter must be so translated; God employs several translators; some pieces are translated by age, some by sickness, some by war, some by justice; but God's hand is in every translation, and his hand shall bind up all our scattered leaves again for that library where every book shall lie open to one another. As therefore the bell that rings to a sermon calls not upon the preacher only, but upon the congregation to come, so this bell calls us all; but how much more me, who am brought so near the door by this sickness. There was a contention as far as a suit (in which both piety and dignity, religion and estimation, were mingled), which of the religious orders should ring to prayers first in the morning; and it was determined, that they should ring first that rose earliest. If we understand aright the dignity of this bell that tolls for our evening prayer, we would be glad to make it ours by rising early, in that application, that it might be ours as well as his, whose indeed it is. The bell doth toll for him that thinks it doth; and though it intermit[2] again, yet from that minute that that occasion wrought upon him, he is united to

2. A semisatirical list of sins as catalogued by medieval theologians.
3. The grace that God gives man before he has sought it.
4. A series of images from the Book of Revelation (the Lion of the tribe of Judah and the malicious serpent),

Matthew (the wise serpent), and Genesis (the dove and olive branch that God sends as promises against another flood).
1. Church bells rang when a person was dying.
2. Ceases momentarily.

God. Who casts not up his eye to the sun when it rises? but who takes off his eye from a comet when that breaks out? Who bends not his ear to any bell which upon any occasion rings? but who can remove it from that bell which is passing a piece of himself out of this world? No man is an island, entire of itself; every man is a piece of the continent, a part of the main. If a clod be washed away by the sea, Europe is the less, as well as if a promontory were, as well as if a manor of thy friend's or of thine own were: any man's death diminishes me, because I am involved in mankind, and therefore never send to know for whom the bells tolls; it tolls for thee. Neither can we call this a begging of misery, or a borrowing of misery, as though we were not miserable enough of ourselves, but must fetch in more from the next house, in taking upon us the misery of our neighbours. Truly it were an excusable covetousness if we did, for affliction is a treasure, and scarce any man hath enough of it. No man hath affliction enough that is not matured and ripened by it, and made fit for God by that affliction. If a man carry treasure in bullion, or in a wedge of gold, and have none coined into current money, his treasure will not defray him as he travels. Tribulation is treasure in the nature of it, but it is not current money in the use of it, except we get nearer and nearer our home, heaven, by it. Another man may be sick too, and sick to death, and this affliction may lie in his bowels, as gold in a mine, and be of no use to him; but this bell, that tells me of his affliction, digs out and applies that gold to me: if by this consideration of another's danger I take mine own into contemplation, and so secure myself, by making my recourse to my God, who is our only security.

from The Second Prebend Sermon, on Psalm 63:7[1]
Because thou hast been my help,
therefore in the shadow of thy wings will I rejoice

Let me wither and wear out mine age in a discomfortable, in an unwholesome, in a penurious prison, and so pay my debts with my bones, and recompense the wastefulness of my youth, with the beggery of mine age; let me wither in a spittle under sharp and foul and infamous diseases, and so recompense the wantonness of my youth, with that loathsomeness in mine age; yet, if God withdraw not his spiritual blessings, his Grace, his Patience, if I can call my suffering his doing, my passion his action, all this that is temporal, is but a caterpiller got into one corner of my garden, but a mildew fallen upon one acre of my corn; the body of all, the substance of all is safe, as long as the soul is safe. But when I shall trust to that, which we call a good spirit, and God shall deject, and empoverish, and evacuate that spirit, when I shall rely upon a moral constancy, and God shall shake, and enfeeble, and enervate, destroy and demolish that constancy; when I shall think to refresh myself in the serenity and sweet air of a good conscience, and God shall call up the damps and vapours of hell itself, and spread a cloud of diffidence, and an impenetrable crust of desperation upon my conscience; when health shall fly from me, and I shall lay hold upon riches to succour me

---

1. Following the lengthy fever that inspired his *Devotions,* Donne returned to the pulpit of St. Paul's Cathedral in the spring of 1624, and the period of his greatest sermons followed. "Prebend" derives from the medieval word for pension, and was the stipend derived from the revenues of a cathedral and given to the canons or members of the church. Donne had one of 30 "prebendaries" associated with St. Paul's Cathedral. Having been told while he was sick with fever that additional money would be committed to his prebendary, he resolved to give a series of five Prebend sermons, each of them based on one of the Psalms (62 through 66). The second sermon was given at St. Paul's on 29 January 1625.

and comfort me in my sickness, and riches shall fly from me, and I shall snatch after favour and good opinion to comfort me in my poverty; when even this good opinion shall leave me, and calumnies and misinformations shall prevail against me; when I shall need peace, because there is none but thou, O Lord, that should stand for me, and then shall find that all the wounds that I have come from thy hand, all the arrows that stick in me, from thy quiver; when I shall see, that because I have given myself to my corrupt nature, thou hast changed thine; and because I am all evil towards thee, therefore thou hast given over being good towards me: When it comes to this height, that the fever is not in the humors but in the spirits, that mine enemy is not an imaginary enemy, fortune, nor a transitory enemy, malice in great persons, but a real, and an irresistible, and an inexorable, and an everlasting enemy, the Lord of Hosts himself, the Almighty God himself, the Almighty God himself only knows the weight of this affliction, and except he put in that *pondus gloriae,* that exceeding weight of an eternal glory, with his own hand, into the other scale, we are weighed down, we are swallowed up, irreparably, irrevocably, irrecoverably, irremediably.

This is the feareful depth, this is spiritual misery, to be thus fallen from God. * * * [2]

If you look upon this world in a map, you find two hemispheres, two half worlds. If you crush heaven into a map, you may find two hemispheres too, two half heavens: Half will be joy, and half will be glory; for in these two, the joy of heaven and the glory of heaven, is all heaven often represented unto us. And as of those two Hemispheres of the world, the first hath been known long before, but the other (that of America, which is the richer in treasure) God reserved for later discoveries; so though he reserve that hemisphere of heaven, which is the glory thereof, to the Resurrection, yet the other hemisphere, the joy of heaven, God opens to our discovery, and delivers for our habitation even whilst we dwell in this world. As God hath cast upon the unrepentant sinner two deaths, a temporal, and a spiritual death, so hath he breathed into us two lives; for so, as the word for death is doubled, *Morte morieris, Thou shalt die the death,* so is the word for life expressed in the plural, *Chaiim, vitarum, God breathed into his nostrils the breath of lives,* of divers lives.[3] Though our natural life were no life, but rather a continual dying, yet we have two lives besides that, an eternal life reserved for heaven, but yet a heavenly life too, a spiritual life, even in this world. And as God doth thus inflict two deaths, and infuse two lives, so doth he also pass two judgements upon man, or rather repeats the same judgement twice. For, that which Christ shall say to thy soul then at the last Judgement, *Enter into thy Master's joy,* He says to thy conscience now, *Enter into thy Master's joy.*[4] The everlastingness of the joy is the blessedness of the next life, but the entering, the inchoation is afforded here. For that which Christ shall say then to us, *Venite benedicti, Come ye blessed,* are words intended to persons that are coming, that are upon the way, though not at home; here in this world he bids us *Come,* there in the next, he shall bid us *Welcome.* The angels of heaven have joy in thy conversion, and canst thou be without that joy in thyself? If thou desire revenge upon thine enemies, as they are God's enemies, that God would be pleased to remove, and root out all such as oppose him, that

---

2. Donne turns to a consideration of David's plight when he was in the wilderness repenting for his sins and "his danger of falling into spiritual miseries," after which he moves to the "second part": to "resolve upon" a "course for the future."

3. From Genesis 2:7 and the creation of man. "Life" in Hebrew (*chaiim*) is plural in form.

4. Matthew 25:23, from the parable of the talents, when the master rewards his faithful servant.

affection appertains to Glory; let that alone till thou come to the Hemisphere of Glory; there join with those martyrs under the altar, *usquequo Domine,* How long, O Lord, dost thou defer judgement?[5] and thou shalt have thine answer there for that. Whilst thou art here, here join with David and the other Saints of God, in that holy increpation[6] of a dangerous sadness, *Why art thou cast down O my soul? why art thou disquieted in me?*[7] That soul that is dissected and anatomized to God in a sincere confession, washed in the tears of true contrition, embalmed in the blood of reconciliation, the blood of Christ Jesus, can assign no reason, can give no just answer to that interrogatory, *Why art thou cast down O my soul? why art thou disquieted in me?* No man is so little as that he can be lost under these wings, no man so great as that they cannot reach to him; *Semper ille major est, quantumcumque creverimus,*[8] To what temporal, to what spiritual greatness soever we grow, still pray we him to shadow us under his wings; for the poor need those wings against oppression, and the rich against envy. The Holy Ghost, who is a dove, shadowed the whole world under his wings; *Incubabat aquis,* He hovered over the waters, he sat upon the waters, and he hatched all that was produced, and all that was produced so, was good.[9] Be thou a Mother where the Holy Ghost would be a Father; conceive by him; and be content that he produce joy in thy heart here. First think, that as a man must have some land, or else he cannot be in wardship,[1] so a man must have some of the love of God, or else he could not fall under God's correction; God would not give him his physic, God would not study his cure, if he cared not for him. And then think also, that if God afford thee the shadow of his wings, that is, consolation, respiration, refreshing, though not a present and plenary deliverance, in thy afflictions, not to thank God is a murmuring, and not to rejoice in God's ways, is an unthankfulness. Howling is the noise of hell, singing the voice of heaven; sadnesse the damp of hell, rejoicing the serenity of heaven. And he that hath not this joy here, lacks one of the best pieces of his evidence for the joys of heaven; and hath neglected or refused that earnest, by which God uses to bind his bargain, that true joy in this world shall flow into the joy of heaven, as a river flowes into the sea.

⊷ ⚹ ⊶

Anne Bradstreet
1612–1672

Anne Bradstreet, whose heart rose at "a new World and new manners," was anything but the stereotypically dour Puritan, although she had ample reason to be so. Torn from a comfortable life in England at eighteen to journey with her husband and parents to the unseasonable climate of uncivilized Massachusetts; childless until the advanced age of twenty-one following five years of marriage (she would eventually have eight children, seven of whom would survive

---

5. In Revelation 6:10 the martyrs greet the Lamb as he opens the fifth seal and cry, "How long, O Lord . . . doest thou refrain from judging and from avenging our blood on those who dwell on the earth?"
6. Reproof or rebuke.
7. Psalm 42:5.
8. From Augustine's commentary on the Psalms: "That

one is always greater [than us], no matter how much we will bring forth."
9. Donne continues to develop the bird imagery by making the God who "stirs above the waters" in Genesis 1:2 a bird.
1. A ward was a minor whose inheritance was entrusted to a guardian until he or she came of age.

her); wracked throughout her life by illness: these were inauspicious conditions for the woman who would become the first published north American poet—without her knowledge. An admiring audience in England would praise her as the "tenth muse" in 1650 after her brother-in-law smuggled her manuscript to London, refusing to entrust it to Boston's single printing house.

To be sure, there are passages in her poetry that seem to convey a dispiriting anti-Renaissance vision of man as "at the best a creature frail and vain, / In knowledge ignorant, in strength but weak, / Subject to sorrows, losses, sickness, pain, / Each storm his state, his mind, his body break." But Bradstreet balanced her recognition of man's—and woman's—limitations with her perceptions of the world's beauty, the "autumnal Tide's . . . trees all richly clad" that ravish her view in "Contemplations," New England's first nature poem, and that finally prevent her from groaning "deeply . . . for that divine Translation" to a God whose design she usually found everywhere. Not, always, however, with ease. Bradstreet willingly admited how difficult it is to perceive divine presence, and she acknowledged her attachment to things earthly and pleasurable—such as her love for her husband, Simon, who would live to the ripe age of ninety-four and become, like his father-in-law, governor of Massachusetts. As a result, she is far more the engaging writer than an apologist either for the stringent Puritanism that had encouraged her family to leave decadent England and settle in a "Cittie on a Hill" or for the venture itself, which resulted in the creation of Harvard University and the founding of Cambridge (where her house stood in what is now Harvard Square). Bradstreet has the keen and occasionally unforgiving eye of her later Massachusetts compatriot, Emily Dickinson—a line such as "If what I do prove well, it won't advance. / They'll say it's stol'n, or else it was by chance" exhibits a characteristic Dickinsonian terseness. Yet Bradstreet avails herself of daily joys and not-so-common tribulations: her husband's absence, a raging fever, and the burning of her house ("Farewell my pelf, farewell my store").

Educated in England, Bradstreet had read broadly in European letters. Milton's contemporary, she shared his vast knowledge of biblical writings and political history, as exemplified in her lengthy poem, entitled "The Four Monarchies," published by her brother-in-law in *The Tenth Muse*. Scholars have argued that her face was turned ever toward England and the Continent, despite the forty-two years she lived in "Nov-anglia." Yet the vivid New England "autumnal tide" that greeted her on the "pathless paths" she strolled around her house looms large in her writing. Moreover, her break with the comforts of "home" in all its connotations forced her to fashion new habits of life and thought in the absence of old ones, no doubt making her the original writer she could not have been in England: an England that during her lifetime knew unsettling times with the overthrow and beheading of a king and the ushering in—and out—of a Puritan commonwealth. Too, the relative starkness of colonial life and her husband's frequent traveling must have given her time to work seriously as a poet and perfect her craft. "The Author to Her Book," her embarrassed reaction to seeing her earliest poems in print, records her laborious corrections, and she clearly planned on a revision and amplification of her first collection. *Several Poems Compiled with Great Variety of Wit and Learning. . . . by a Gentle-woman in New-England* was published in Boston by her nephew-in-law, John Rogers, future president of Harvard, six years after her death.

Still, Bradstreet's finest poems were never meant for publication. Rogers included intimate poems such as "To My Dear and Loving Husband" in the posthumous 1678 volume, even though he knew they weren't intended for "publick view." Bradstreet's revealing autobiography, which shows her to be as elegant a writer in prose as in poetry, was written a few years before her death and was dedicated only to her children. In this "book by any yet unread" she writes not to "to show my skill" as a poet, but to reflect on her life as a Christian, hoping that her children "may find / What was your living mother's mind." She also offers herself to them as an example, not so much in spite of, but because of her many struggles and doubts: "that when I am no more with you, yet I may be daily in your remembrance . . . [and] that you may gain some spiritual advantage by my experience."

The Author to Her Book[1]

Thou ill-formed offspring of my feeble brain,
Who after birth didst by my side remain,
Till snatched from thence by friends, less wise than true,
Who thee abroad, exposed to public view,

5   Made thee in rags, halting to th' press to trudge,
Where errors were not lessened (all may judge).
At thy return my blushing was not small,
My rambling brat (in print) should mother call,
I cast thee by as one unfit for light,

10   Thy visage° was so irksome in my sight;   *face*
Yet being mine own, at length affection would
Thy blemishes amend, if so I could:
I washed thy face, but more defects I saw,
And rubbing off a spot still made a flaw.[2]

15   I stretched thy joints to make thee even feet,[3]
Yet still thou run'st more hobbling than is meet;
In better dress to trim thee was my mind,
But nought save homespun cloth i' th' house I find.
In this array 'mongst vulgars° may'st thou roam.   *common people*

20   In critic's hands beware thou dost not come,
And take thy way where yet thou art not known;
If for thy father asked, say thou hadst none;
And for thy mother, she alas is poor,
Which caused her thus to send thee out of door.

To My Dear and Loving Husband[1]

If ever two were one, then surely we.
If ever man were loved by wife, then thee;
If ever wife was happy in a man,
Compare with me, ye women, if you can.

5   I prize thy love more than whole mines of gold
Or all the riches that the East doth hold.
My love is such that rivers cannot quench,
Nor ought but love from thee, give recompense.
Thy love is such I can no way repay,

10   The heavens reward thee manifold, I pray.
Then while we live, in love let's so persevere
That when we live no more, we may live ever.

---

1. *The Tenth Muse;* the book was published in London in 1650 without Bradstreet's consent. This poem appeared as the first poem in the second and revised edition of *The Tenth Muse,* published in Boston in 1678 after the poet's death.
2. A reference to Bradstreet's revisions of the 1650 edition.
3. To even out the metrical units of the poems.
1. This and the following poems were clearly not intended for publication. The editor of the 1678 edition prefaces them with the statement "Several other Poems made by the Author upon Diverse Occasions, were found among her Papers after her Death, which she never meant should come to publick view; amongst which, these following (at the desire of some friends that knew her well) are here inserted."

A Letter to Her Husband, Absent upon Public Employment[1]

My head, my heart, mine eyes, my life, nay, more,
My joy, my magazine° of earthly store,   *container*
If two be one, as surely thou and I,
How stayest thou there, whilst I at Ipswich lie?[2]
5   So many steps, head from the heart to sever.
If but a neck, soon should we be together.
I, like the Earth this season, mourn in black,
My Sun is gone so far in's zodiac,
Whom whilst I 'joyed, nor storms, nor frost I felt,
10   His warmth such frigid colds did cause to melt.
My chilled limbs now numbed lie forlorn;
Return, return, sweet Sol, from Capricorn;[3]
In this dead time, alas, what can I more
Than view those fruits° which through thy heat I bore?   *their children*
15   Which sweet contentment yield me for a space,
True living pictures of their father's face.
O strange effect! now thou art southward gone,
I weary grow the tedious day so long;
But when thou northward to me shalt return,
20   I wish my Sun may never set, but burn
Within the Cancer[4] of my glowing breast,
The welcome house of him my dearest guest.
Where ever, ever stay, and go not thence,
Till nature's sad decree shall call thee hence;
25   Flesh of thy flesh, bone of thy bone,[5]
I here, thou there, yet both but one.

Before the Birth of One of Her Children

All things within this fading world hath end,
Adversity doth still our joys attend;
No ties so strong, no friends so dear and sweet,
But with death's parting blow is sure to meet.
5   The sentence past is most irrevocable,
A common thing, yet oh inevitable;
How soon, my Dear, death may my steps attend,[1]
How soon't may be thy lot to lose thy friend,
We both are ignorant, yet love bids me
10   These farewell lines to recommend to thee,
That when that knot's untied that made us one,
I may seem thine, who in effect am none.

1. Simon Bradstreet traveled frequently in New England; he also journeyed to London on occasion.
2. A village near Andover where the Bradstreets lived in the 1640s.
3. Bradstreet invokes the signs of the zodiac to refer to the season: Capricorn, the goat, signifies winter. "Sol" is Bradstreet's "Sun," i.e. her husband, whose rays are less efficacious during the colder seasons.
4. Zodiacal sign for summer.
5. From the wedding service, based on Genesis 2:23: "Then the man said, 'She is now bone of my bone, and flesh of my flesh; she shall be called Woman, for from man she has been taken.'"
1. Death in childbirth was frequent in the 17th century; the lifetime risk for Englishwomen has been calculated at between 5 and 7 percent.

And if I see not half my days that's due,
What nature would, God grant to yours and you;
15   The many faults that well you know I have,
Let be interr'd in my oblivious grave;
If any worth or virtue were in me,
Let that live freshly in thy memory
And when thou feel'st no grief, as I no harms,
20   Yet love thy dead, who long lay in thine arms:
And when thy loss shall be repaid with gains
Look to my little babes, my dear remains.
And if thou love thyself, or loved'st me
These O protect from step-dam's° injury.   *stepmother's*
25   And if chance to thine eyes shall bring this verse,
With some sad sighs honour my absent hearse;°   *corpse*
And kiss this paper for thy love's dear sake,
Who with salt tears this last farewell did take.

Upon the Burning of Our House, July 10th, 1666[1]

In silent night when rest I took,
For sorrow ne'er I did not look,
I waken'd was with thund'ring noise
And piteous shreiks of dreadful voice.
5   That fearful sound of fire and fire,
Let no man know is my desire.

I, starting up, the light did spy,
And to my God my heart did cry
To strengthen me in my Distress
10   And not to leave me succourless.°   *helpless*
Then coming out beheld apace
The flame consume my dwelling place.

And, when I could no longer look,
I blest his Name that gave and took,[2]
15   That lay'd my goods now in the dust:
Yea so it was, and so 'twas just.
It was his own: it was not mine;
Far be it that I should repine

He might of all justly bereft,
20   But yet sufficient for us left.
When by the ruins oft I past,
My sorrowing eyes aside did cast,
And here and there the places spy
Where oft I sat, and long did lie.

1. The tragic fire burned down the Bradstreet house in Merrimack, what is today North Andover, after a maid apparently placed hot ashes above the porch. Among other things, the fire destroyed the Bradstreets' collection of over 800 books, one of the largest libraries in New England at the time.
2. From Job 1:21: "The Lord gave, and the Lord hath taken away; blessed be the name of the Lord."

25   Here stood that trunk, and there that chest;
      There lay that store I counted best:
      My pleasant things in ashes lie,
      And them behold no more shall I.
      Under thy roof no guest shall sit,
30   Nor at thy table eat a bit.

      No pleasant tale shall e'er be told,
      Nor things recounted done of old.
      No candle e'er shall shine in thee,
      Nor bridegroom's voice e'er heard shall be.
35   In silence ever shalt thou lie;
      Adeiu, Adeiu; all's vanity.[3]

      Then straight I 'gin my heart to chide,
      And did thy wealth on earth abide?
      Didst fix thy hope on mould'ring dust,
40   The arm of flesh didst make thy trust?
      Raise up thy thoughts above the sky
      That dunghill mists away may fly.

      Thou hast an house on high erect
      Fram'd by that mighty Architect,
45   With glory richly furnishéd,
      Stands permanent tho' this be fled.
      It's purchaséd, and paid for too
      By him who hath enough to do.

      A price so vast as is unknown,
50   Yet, by his gift, is made thine own.
      There's wealth enough, I need no more;
      Farewell my pelf,° farewell my store.   riches
      The world no longer let me love,
      My hope and treasure lies above.

On My Dear Grand-child Simon Bradstreet,
Who died on 16. Novemb. 1669. being but a month, and one day old[1]

      No sooner come, but gone, and fal'n asleep,
      Acquaintance short, yet parting caus'd us weep,
      Three flow'rs, two scarcely blown, the last i'th' bud,[2]
      Cropt by th' Almighty's hand; yet is he good,
5   With dreadful awe before him let's be mute,
      Such was his will, but why, let's not dispute,
      With humble hearts and mouths put in the dust,
      Let's say he's merciful as well as just.

---

3. An echo of the opening of Ecclesiastes: "Vanity of vanities, says Coheleth, vanity of vanities! All things are vanity! What profit has man from all the labor which he toils at under the sun?"
1. Bradstreet wrote elegies for three of her deceased

grandchildren, as well as for one of her daughters-in-law.
2. The other two "flowers" were Elizabeth, who died at a year and a half, and Anne, named for her grandmother, and deceased at "three years and seven months old."

He will return, and make up all our losses,
10   And smile again, after our bitter crosses.
Go pretty babe, go rest with sisters twain
Among the blest in endless joys remain.

To My Dear Children[1]

This book by any yet unread,
I leave for you when I am dead,
That being gone, here you may find
What was your living mother's mind.
Make use of what I leave in love,
And God shall bless you from above.
                                                    A. B.

My dear children,

I, knowing by experience that the exhortations of parents take most effect when the speakers leave to speak, and those especially sink deepest which are spoke latest, and being ignorant whether on my death bed I shall have opportunity to speak to any of you, much less to all, thought it the best, whilst I was able, to compose some short matters (for what else to call them I know not) and bequeath to you, that when I am no more with you, yet I may be daily in your remembrance (although that is the least in my aim in what I now do), but that you may gain some spiritual advantage by my experience. I have not studied in this you read to show my skill, but to declare the truth, not to set forth myself, but the glory of God. If I had minded the former, it had been perhaps better pleasing to you, but seeing the last is the best, let it be best pleasing to you.

The method I will observe shall be this: I will begin with God's dealing with me from my childhood to this day.

In my young years, about 6 or 7 as I take it, I began to make conscience of my ways, and what I knew was sinful, as lying, disobedience to parents, etc., I avoided it. If at any time I was overtaken with the like evils, it was as a great trouble, and I could not be at rest 'till by prayer I had confessed it unto God. I was also troubled at the neglect of private duties though too often tardy that way. I also found much comfort in reading the Scriptures, especially those places I thought most concerned my condition, and as I grew to have more understanding, so the more solace I took in them.

In a long fit of sickness which I had on my bed I often communed with my heart and made my supplication to the most High who set me free from that affliction.

But as I grew up to be about 14 or 15, I found my heart more carnal, and sitting loose from God, vanity and the follies of youth take hold of me.

About 16, the Lord laid His hand sore upon me and smote me with the smallpox. When I was in my affliction, I besought the Lord and confessed my pride and vanity, and He was entreated of me and again restored me. But I rendered not to Him according to the benefit received.

---

1. Included among the papers left by Bradstreet at her death was this autobiography, addressed to her children.

After a short time I changed my condition and was married, and came into this country, where I found a new world and new manners, at which my heart rose. But after I was convinced it was the way of God, I submitted to it and joined to the church at Boston.[2]

After some time I fell into a lingering sickness like a consumption together with a lameness, which correction I saw the Lord sent to humble and try me and do me good, and it was not altogether ineffectual.

It pleased God to keep me a long time without a child, which was a great grief to me and cost me many prayers and tears before I obtained one, and after him gave me many more of whom I now take the care, that as I have brought you into the world, and with great pains, weakness, cares, and fears brought you to this, I now travail in birth again of you till Christ be formed in you.

Among all my experiences of God's gracious dealings with me, I have constantly observed this, that He hath never suffered me long to sit loose from Him, but by one affliction or other hath made me look home, and search what was amiss; so usually thus it hath been with me that I have no sooner felt my heart out of order, but I have expected correction for it, which most commonly hath been upon my own person in sickness, weakness, pains, sometimes on my soul, in doubts and fears of God's displeasure and my sincerity towards Him; sometimes He hath smote a child with a sickness, sometimes chastened by losses in estate, and these times (through His great mercy) have been the times of my greatest getting and advantage; yea, I have found them the times when the Lord hath manifested the most love to me. Then have I gone to searching and have said with David, "Lord, search me and try me, see what ways of wickedness are in me, and lead me in the way everlasting,"[3] and seldom or never but I have found either some sin I lay under which God would have reformed, or some duty neglected which He would have performed, and by His help I have laid vows and bonds upon my soul to perform His righteous commands.

If at any time you are chastened of God,[4] take it as thankfully and joyfully as in greatest mercies, for if ye be His, ye shall reap the greatest benefit by it. It hath been no small support to me in times of darkness when the Almighty hath hid His face from me that yet I have had abundance of sweetness and refreshment after affliction and more circumspection in my walking after I have been afflicted. I have been with God like an untoward child, that no longer than the rod has been on my back (or at least in sight) but I have been apt to forget Him and myself, too. Before I was afflicted, I went astray, but now I keep Thy statutes.

I have had great experience of God's hearing my prayers and returning comfortable answers to me, either in granting the thing I prayed for, or else in satisfying my mind without it, and I have been confident it hath been from Him, because I have found my heart through His goodness enlarged in thankfulness to Him.

I have often been perplexed that I have not found that constant joy in my pilgrimage and refreshing which I supposed most of the servants of God have, although He hath not left me altogether without the witness of His holy spirit, who hath oft given me His word and set to His seal that it shall be well with me. I have sometimes tasted

---

2. The Massachusetts Bay Company had established under John Winthrop a church that would eventually be called Congregational; for the original founders, however, it had no such precise denomination, but reflected the settlers' ideas about Christian community and their "covenant" with God.
3. From the final lines of Psalm 139.
4. Chastised by God.

of that hidden manna that the world knows not, and have set up my Ebenezer,[5] and have resolved with myself that against such a promise, such tastes of sweetness, the gates of hell shall never prevail; yet have I many times sinkings and droopings, and not enjoyed that felicity that sometimes I have done. But when I have been in darkness and seen no light, yet have I desired to stay myself upon the Lord, and when I have been in sickness and pain, I have thought if the Lord would but lift up the light of His countenance upon me, although He ground me to powder, it would be but light to me; yea, oft have I thought were I in hell itself and could there find the love of God toward me, it would be a heaven. And could I have been in heaven without the love of God, it would have been a hell to me, for in truth it is the absence and presence of God that makes heaven or hell.[6]

Many times hath Satan troubled me concerning the verity of the Scriptures, many times by atheism how I could know whether there was a God; I never saw any miracles to confirm me, and those which I read of, how did I know but they were feigned? That there is a God my reason would soon tell me by the wondrous works that I see, the vast frame of the heaven and the earth, the order of all things, night and day, summer and winter, spring and autumn, the daily providing for this great household upon the earth, the preserving and directing of all to its proper end. The consideration of these things would with amazement certainly resolve me that there is an Eternal Being. But how should I know He is such a God as I worship in Trinity, and such a Saviour as I rely upon? Though this hath thousands of times been suggested to me, yet God hath helped me over. I have argued thus with myself. That there is a God, I see. If ever this God hath revealed himself, it must be in His word, and this must be it or none. Have I not found that operation by it that no human invention can work upon the soul, hath not judgments befallen diverse who have scorned and contemned it, hath it not been preserved through all ages maugre[7] all the heathen tyrants and all of the enemies who have opposed it? Is there any story but that which shows the beginnings of times, and how the world came to be as we see? Do we not know the prophecies in it fulfilled which could not have been so long foretold by any but God Himself?

When I have got over this block, then have I another put in my way, that admit this be the true God whom we worship, and that be his word, yet why may not the Popish religion be the right?[8] They have the same God, the same Christ, the same word. They only enterpret it one way, we another.

This hath sometimes stuck with me, and more it would, but the vain fooleries that are in their religion together with their lying miracles and cruel persecutions of the saints, which admit were they as they term them, yet not so to be dealt withal.

The consideration of these things and many the like would soon turn me to my own religion again.

But some new troubles I have had since the world has been filled with blasphemy and sectaries[9] and some who have been accounted sincere Christians have been carried away with them, that sometimes I have said, "Is there faith upon the earth?" and I

---

5. Manna was given to the Hebrews in the desert by God as sustenance; Ebenezer means "stone of help," called as such by Samuel in 1 Samuel 7 when the Lord enables him to withstand an attack by the Philistines.
6. While Bradstreet would not have known Milton's *Paradise Lost,* the language is very close to that used by Satan: "Which way I fly is Hell; myself am Hell; / And in

the lowest deep a lower deep / Still threat'ning to devour me opens wide, / To which the Hell I suffer seems a Heav'n" (4:75–78).
7. Notwithstanding.
8. Catholicism.
9. Sects.

have not known what to think; but then I have remembered the works of Christ that so it must be, and if it were possible, the very elect should be deceived. "Behold," saith our Saviour, "I have told you before."[1] That hath stayed my heart, and I can now say, "Return, O my Soul, to thy rest, upon this rock Christ Jesus will I build my faith, and if I perish, I perish"; but I know all the Powers of Hell shall never prevail against it. I know whom I have trusted, and whom I have believed, and that He is able to keep that I have committed to His charge.

Now to the King, immortal, eternal and invisible, the only wise God, be honour, and glory for ever and ever, Amen.

This was written in much sickness and weakness, and is very weakly and imperfectly done, but if you can pick any benefit out of it, it is the mark which I aimed at.

⊷ ⋈ ⊷

John Milton
1608–1674

What will betide the few
His faithful, left among the unfaithful herd,
The enemies of truth . . .? (*Paradise Lost* 12.480–482)

John Milton wrote against the backdrop of the most violent period in English history: a civil war that dominated the decade of the 1640s. King was turned against Parliament, Anglican against Puritan, and too often—as in Milton's own family—brother against brother. The war ended in 1649 with the triumph of the anti-Royalists and the public execution of both King Charles I and his Archbishop, William Laud. Milton himself, whose reputation rested at this point on a series of fiery prose tracts advocating reformation, liberty of conscience, and divorce, was called in to write a treatise defending regicide. He willingly complied with *Eikonoklastes*, in which he likens Charles to the wicked Pharaoh: beseiged by the plagues sent by God, Pharaoh "soon found that evil which before slept, came suddenly upon him, by the preposterous way he took to shun it. Passing by examples between, and not shutting willfully our eyes, we may see the like story brought to pass in our own land."

A Protectorate was established—a Puritan Republic under Oliver Cromwell, whom Milton would serve as Secretary from an office in Scotland Yard—but it was short-lived. Within ten years, a new Pharaoh, Charles's son, returned from France (where he had become acquainted with Parisian culture, including its many actresses), and Milton, calling still for a republic, was imprisoned. In light of what must have seemed to him the permanent victory of the Royalists, he has Adam plaintively ask the archangel Michael, sent below to admonish and console the sinners with a vision of the future, what will happen to the chosen "few" once Christ reascends to heaven. In the difficult years after Charles' restoration, Milton may well have imagined himself to be one of those few: opposed to monarchy, an intolerant state religion too close to the Catholicism England had forsworn long ago, and any regulation that would prevent him from following his conscience in the pursuit of "truth"—always "strong," Milton had written, "next to the Almighty." Burdened moreover by blindness, he no doubt felt that his many efforts to allow for truth's pursuit had borne little fruit. Like the Florentine Machiavelli,

---

1. Matthew 24:25, when Christ is speaking to his disciples to warn them against believing in false prophets in the last days.

in many ways his antithesis, Milton turned from active political engagement after 1659 to writing poetry, cast into figurative if not physical exile.

Yet this image of Milton is not wholly accurate. *Paradise Lost,* probably completed in 1664 and published in 1667, had been in Milton's thoughts for decades, as had his desire to excel as a poet. While still studying at Christ's College, Cambridge, Milton published a poem for Shakespeare's Fourth Folio; his first major literary "event" was the performance of *Comus, A Masque,* in 1634, for the aging patroness of Edmund Spenser. Four years later he published his moving pastoral poem "Lycidas," in honor of a drowned fellow-student. Refusing upon graduation to enter the corrupt Anglican clergy, Milton took a seminal voyage to Italy, where he met, among others, Galileo. But plans to continue to Sicily and Greece were abandoned when he heard of the death of his close friend Charles Diodati as well as of growing turmoil in England. In 1645 he published his collected poems, among them "Lycidas" and a number of sonnets. But if Milton had not perservered in his plans to write on the theme of "Adam Unparadiz'd," first conceived as a tragedy in the early 1640s, his reputation would be primarily that of the polemical prose-writer who criticized his king and the Anglican church and tirelessly defended the Puritan cause throughout twenty years of turmoil. It was only toward the end of those two decades that Milton returned to more youthful plans to compose a poem that would, as he forthrightly declared in the opening lines, "justify the ways of God to man."

Such a line suggests much about *Paradise Lost* and Milton's intentions for it. For one thing, it cannot simply be read as a commentary on recent events, as much as those events may have stirred Milton to write about the bitterness of loss and hope for redemption. (It is hard not to imaging an aging, dour Milton, married by 1663 to his third wife, reciting to his amanuensis the despairing lines in Book 7 as though they were pure autobiography: "On evil days though fallen, and evil tongues.") The poem's subject matter far exceeds any narrowly conceived nationalistic lore such as "the fables of knights" with which Milton had once flirted, or the defeat of the Puritan republic. Instead, it reaches back to the epic par excellence of the European Renaissance: the Bible, Old Testament as well as New, retold in Milton's translation, as bold as that of Wycliff or Tyndale before him. Moreover, in taking the Bible as his primary model, Milton forces a reconsideration of both the classical epics and the medieval romances that had inspired his contemporaries.

Milton, in fact, is at pains to underscore how anti-epic his poem truly is. There is indeed a battle (the war in heaven), a great journey (Satan's flight out of hell), rousing speeches (Satan's plea to the devils in Book 1) and acts of heroism (Raphael's challenge to Satan). But the poem's main action takes place in a garden, and its primary characters are a naked man and woman whose goal is relatively dull: to "stand fast." Milton opposes this Christian inheritance to the bloodthirsty wrath of an Achilles or the deceptiveness of an Odysseus. (A suffering Aeneas was more to Milton's liking—and Virgil's Latinity is everywhere evident in Milton's sonorous English—but even Aeneas ultimately yields to bloodthirsty revenge, and the empire his acts presage is altogether too worldly.) It is Satan to whom Milton entrusts the overreaching of epic and tragic characters—hence Satan's reassuring familiarity and his charm that has infected many listeners beside Eve. Yet his slinking away from Eden after Eve's fall is symptomatic of the banality of evil and the limitations, for Milton, of classical epic. Something more must, and does, come following Satan's triumph over man, and that is a different kind of heroics. When Adam learns from Michael that Christ will ultimately defeat Satan, he demands breathlessly, "Say where and when the fight," and Michael can only instruct him—and us— "Dream not of their fight / As of a duel." Christ's birth in a stable and ensuing sacrifice forecast a very different kind of epic poetry, the kind that Dante had crafted in his *Divine Comedy* and to which Milton himself would turn in *Paradise Regained,* a poem, as critics have frequently commented, in which "nothing happens," as Satan unsuccessfully tries to tempt Jesus to sin.

Paradise Lost would also, ideally, have been a poem in which "nothing happens," had it not been for Eve's yielding to her desire to be equal to God and Adam's yielding to "female charms." All of the poem is, in some sense, preparatory to the "tragic notes" that mark Book 9, the book of the fall; and therein the reader is forced to wrestle with questions that were fundamental to the era itself—among them, at what point man first sinned, and whether Adam should have divorced Eve after she ate the apple. But few questions are more central than the one Milton had asked twenty years earlier in his classic defense of freedom from censorship, *Areopagitica:* "what were vertue but a name" unless it is put through trial? (*Areopagitica,* it should be added, didn't defend freedom for everyone; Milton excludes protection for Catholicism, "which, as it extirpates all religious and civil supremacies, so itself should be extirpate.") This question about "vertue" is one Eve herself asks, as she fearlessly abandons Adam in the protective shade of the bower to labor on her own, despite the imminent threat of an escapee from hell: "And what is faith, love, virtue unassayed / Alone, without exterior help sustained"? (9:335–36). How, in short, is one to know if one is virtuous unless faced by the "assays" or "trials" to which Eve—and, of course, Milton and his contemporaries—are put? Moved by Eve's and Adam's plight, Christ provides one answer: it would have been far, far better if man had known "good by itself / evil not at all" (11.85). Yet Milton and his readers, unlike Adam and Eve, have no choice. Thus if the poem on one level indicts its once-innocent protagonists, on another it vindicates the active component of a faith tried and made resilient in the rough and tumble of public life.

At the same time, *Paradise Lost* looks toward the necessary inwardness of faith set apart from any physical or worldly manifestation, as well as from bondage to creeds and external restrictions of any kind. Milton claims in his 1668 Preface that in abandoning rhyme, his poem "is to be esteemed an example set, the first in English, of ancient liberty recovered to heroic poem from the troublesome and modern bondage of rhyming." "God attributes to place no sanctity," Michael informs Adam; and while his lines attack the idolatry that pervaded Catholicism and Anglicanism alike, they also free Adam and Eve to live where they wish, to carry within them even in exile their own paradise in the same way that Satan, lamenting his distance from the beauties of earth, must always bring with him his murky home: "myself am Hell" (4:75). This separation from the world was even more manifest in Milton's last two poems: Christ in *Paradise Regained* is ethereal next to the increasingly frustrated Satan, and in Milton's tragedy, *Samson Agonistes,* Samson's blindness becomes metaphorical for his indifference to place. The political freedoms that Milton had not succeeded in bringing about for the English people, the religious freedoms he could not experience for himself under a monarchy, are finally inconsequential compared to the radical freedom of the individual will. As Raphael tells Adam minutes before the "tragic notes" begin, "To stand or fall / Free in thine own arbitrement it lies" (8.640).

All of Milton's writings, in some sense, are an attempt to cultivate the sharpened awareness one must have in order to be responsive to Raphael's dictum: the belief that one can—and must—choose "to stand." The necessary exercising of the will is hardly novel in a period that includes a multitude of Machiavellis. Yet rarely had it been framed within such a tense and accessible human drama. Such accessibility derives from both the stance of the narrator—confiding, as no epic narrator before him, his weaknesses, his limitations, his despair—and the characters of Adam and Eve: immediate in their coyness, their blandishments, their quarrels, their misery and tearful repentance, too late. This particular couple, of course, is a trifle unusual insofar as they dwell for a time in the world's most beautiful garden, and have angels as dinner guests; nor will the modern reader find Eve's apparent inferiority to Adam the poem's most attractive feature. Yet the compelling poetry of *Paradise Lost* is not only that of Satan awakening his fellow fallen, or of Michael as he patiently explains to Adam the future of Christ's sacrifice while God grants Eve the same vision through a dream. Equally it is in the ordinary exchanges between husband and wife as they trim bushes, discuss breakfast, and revel in the beauties of the bower and each other—as well as in their wrestling together as they try to comprehend the wonder and mystery of the universe they have lost.

On the Late Massacre in Piedmont[1]

Avenge O Lord thy slaughtered saints, whose bones
Lie scattered on the Alpine mountains cold,
Even them who kept thy truth so pure of old
When all our Fathers worshiped stocks and stones,
5   Forget not: in thy book record their groans
Who were thy sheep and in their ancient fold
Slain by the bloody Piemontese that rolled
Mother with infant down the rocks. Their moans
The vales redoubled to the hills, and they
10   To Heaven. Their martyred blood and ashes sow
O'er all th' Italian fields where still doth sway
The triple tyrant:° that from these may grow   *the Pope*
A hundred-fold, who having learnt thy way
Early may fly the Babylonian woe.[2]

When I Consider How My Light Is Spent[1]

When I consider how my light is spent,
Ere half my days,[2] in this dark world and wide,
And that one talent which is death to hide,
Lodged with me useless, though my soul more bent
5   To serve therewith my Maker, and present
My true account, lest he returning chide,
Doth God exact day-labor, light denied,
I fondly° ask; but Patience to prevent   *foolishly*
That murmur, soon replies, "God doth not need
10   Either man's work or his own gifts,[3] who best
Bear his mild yoke, they serve him best, his state
Is kingly. Thousands at his bidding speed
And post o'er land and ocean without rest:
They also serve who only stand and wait."

from PARADISE LOST[1]

from Book 1
The Argument

This first Book proposes, first in brief, the whole Subject, *Man's disobedience, and the loss thereupon of Paradise wherein he was plac't:* Then touches *the prime cause*

---

1. Written in 1655, this sonnet refers to a bloodbath suffered by villagers in the lower Alps who professed to a Protestant sect founded long before the Reformation by Peter Valdes. In April 1655, the Duke of Savoy sent an army to remove them from their homes; when the villagers fled, the army pursued, and killed over a thousand men, women, and children. As Secretary of Cromwell's government, Milton was in charge of writing letters to European dignitaries protesting the violence enacted on the French-Italian border.
2. The Roman Catholic Church.

1. Milton was totally blind by the early 1650s, and the poem is probably from the first part of that decade.
2. May refer to Milton's age, which was 42 in 1651; his father had lived to be 84.
3. The phrase may be a reference to Job 22:2; it is in any case a forceful declaration of a Protestant doctrine that God's grace is all that is necessary to salvation.
1. Our text is taken, and the notes are adapted, from John Carey and Alastair Fowler, eds., *The Poems of John Milton*.

of his fall, the Serpent, or rather Satan *in the Serpent; who revolting from God, and drawing to his side many Legions of Angels, was by the command of God driven out of Heaven with all his Crew into the great Deep.* Which action past over, the Poem hastes into the midst of things,[2] presenting *Satan with his Angels now fallen into Hell,* describ'd here, *not in the Centre* (for Heaven and Earth may be suppos'd as yet not made, certainly not yet accurst) *but in a place of utter darkness, fitliest call'd* Chaos: *Here Satan with his Angels lying on the burning Lake, thunder-struck and astonisht, after a certain space recovers, as from confusion, calls up him who next in Order and Dignity lay by him; they confer of thir miserable fall.* Satan *awakens all his Legions, who lay till then in the same manner confounded; They rise, thir Numbers, array of Battle, thir chief Leaders nam'd, according to the Idols known afterwards in* Canaan *and the Countries adjoining. To these* Satan *directs his Speech, comforts them with hope yet of regaining Heaven, but tells them lastly of a new World and new kind of Creature to be created, according to an ancient Prophecy or report in Heaven;* for that Angels were long before this visible Creation, was the opinion of many ancient Fathers. *To find out the truth of this Prophecy, and what to determine thereon he refers to a full Council. What his Associates thence attempt.* Pandemonium *the Palace of* Satan *rises, suddenly built out of the Deep: The infernal Peers there sit in Council.*

>   Of Man's First Disobedience, and the Fruit
> Of that Forbidden Tree, whose mortal[3] taste
> Brought Death into the World, and all our woe,[4]
> With loss of *Eden*, till one greater Man[5]
> 5   Restore us, and regain the blissful Seat,
> Sing Heav'nly Muse,[6] that on the secret top
> Of *Oreb*, or of *Sinai*, didst inspire
> That Shepherd, who first taught the chosen Seed,[7]
> In the Beginning how the Heav'ns and Earth
> 10   Rose out of *Chaos:* Or if *Sion* Hill[8]
> Delight thee more, and *Siloa's* Brook[9] that flow'd
> Fast° by the Oracle of God; I thence   *close*
> Invoke thy aid to my advent'rous Song,
> That with no middle flight intends to soar
> 15   Above th' *Aonian* Mount,[1] while it pursues
> Things unattempted yet in Prose or Rhyme.[2]
> And chiefly Thou O Spirit, that dost prefer

2. Following Horace's rule that the epic should plunge *in medias res.*
3. "Death-bringing" (Latin *mortalis*) but also "to mortals."
4. This definition of the first sin follows Calvin's Catechism.
5. Christ, in Pauline theology the second Adam (see Romans 5:19). The people and events referred to in these lines have a typological connection, i.e., the Christian interpretation of the Old Testament as a prefiguration of the New.
6. Rhetorically, lines 1–49 are the *invocatio,* consisting of an address to the Muse, and the *principium* that states the whole scope of the poem's action. The "Heavenly Muse," later addressed as the muse of astronomy Urania (7.1), is here identified with the Holy Spirit of the Bible, which inspires Moses.

7. The "Shepherd" is Moses, who was granted the vision of the burning bush on Mount Oreb (Exodus 3) and received the Law, either on Mount Oreb (Deuteronomy 4:10) or on its lower part, Mount Sinai (Exodus 19:20). Moses, the first Jewish writer, taught "the chosen seed," the children of Israel, about the beginning of the world in Genesis.
8. The sanctuary, a place of ceremonial song but also (Isaiah 2:3) of oracular pronouncements.
9. A spring immediately west of Mount Zion and beside Calvary, often used as a symbol of the operation of the Holy Ghost.
1. Helicon, sacred to the Muses.
2. Ironically translating Ariosto's boast in the invocation to *Orlando furioso.*

Before all Temples th' upright heart and pure,[3]
Instruct me, for Thou know'st; Thou from the first
20   Wast present, and with mighty wings outspread
Dove-like satst brooding on the vast Abyss
And mad'st it pregnant:[4] What in me is dark
Illumine, what is low raise and support;
That to the highth of this great Argument°   *theme*
25   I may assert Eternal Providence,
And justify[5] the ways of God to men.
      Say first, for Heav'n hides nothing from thy view
Nor the deep Tract of Hell, say first what cause
Mov'd our Grand[6] Parents in that happy State,
30   Favor'd of Heav'n so highly, to fall off
From thir Creator, and transgress his Will
For° one restraint, Lords of the World besides?°   *because of / otherwise*
Who first seduc'd them to that foul revolt?
Th' infernal Serpent;[7] hee it was, whose guile
35   Stirr'd up with Envy and Revenge, deceiv'd
The Mother of Mankind; what time his Pride
Had cast him out from Heav'n, with all his Host
Of Rebel Angels, by whose aid aspiring
To set himself in Glory above his Peers,
40   He trusted to have equall'd the most High,[8]
If he oppos'd; and with ambitious aim
Against the Throne and Monarchy of God
Rais'd impious War in Heav'n and Battle proud
With vain attempt. Him the Almighty Power
45   Hurl'd headlong flaming from th' Ethereal Sky[9]
With hideous ruin and combustion down
To bottomless perdition, there to dwell
In Adamantine Chains[1] and penal Fire,
Who durst defy th' Omnipotent to Arms.
50   Nine times the Space that measures Day and Night[2]
To mortal men, hee with his horrid crew
Lay vanquisht, rolling in the fiery Gulf
Confounded though immortal: But his doom

3. The Spirit is the voice of God, which inspired the Hebrew prophets.
4. Identifying the Spirit present at the creation (Genesis 1:2) with the Spirit in the form of a dove that descended on Jesus at the beginning of his ministry (John 1:32). Vast: large; deserted (Latin *vastus*).
5. Does not mean merely "demonstrate logically" but has its biblical meaning and implies spiritual rather than rational understanding.
6. Implies not only greatness, but also inclusiveness of generality or parentage.
7. "That old serpent, called the Devil, and Satan" (Revelation 12:9) both because Satan entered the body of a serpent to tempt Eve and because his nature is guileful and dangerous to humans.
8. Satan's crime was not his aspiring "above his peers"

but aspiring "To set himself in [divine] Glory." Numerous verbal echoes relate lines 40–48 to the biblical accounts of the fall and binding of Lucifer, in 2 Peter 2:4, Revelation 20:1–2, and Isaiah 14:12–15: "Thou hast said . . . I will exalt my throne above the stars of God . . . I will be like the most High. Yet thou shalt be brought down to hell."
9. Mingling an allusion to Luke 10:18, "I beheld Satan as lightning fall from heaven," with one to Homer, *Iliad* 1.591, Hephaistos "hurled from the ethereal threshold."
1. 2 Peter 2:4; "God spared not the angels that sinned, but . . . delivered them into chains of darkness."
2. The devils fall for the same number of days that the Titans fall from heaven when overthrown by the Olympian gods (see Hesiod, *Theogony* 664–735).

Reserv'd him to more wrath; for now the thought
Both of lost happiness and lasting pain
Torments him; round he throws his baleful° eyes   *evil, suffering*
That witness'd huge affliction and dismay
Mixt with obdúrate° pride and steadfast hate: *unyielding*
At once as far as Angels' ken° he views   *power of vision*
The dismal° Situation waste and wild,   *dreadful, sinister*
A Dungeon horrible, on all sides round
As one great Furnace flam'd, yet from those flames
No light, but rather darkness visible
Serv'd only to discover sights of woe,[3]
Regions of sorrow, doleful shades, where peace
And rest can never dwell, hope never comes
That comes to all;[4] but torture without end
Still urges,° and a fiery Deluge, fed   *presses*
With ever-burning Sulphur unconsum'd:
Such place Eternal Justice had prepar'd
For those rebellious, here thir Prison ordained
In utter° darkness, and thir portion set   *complete; outer*
As far remov'd from God and light of Heav'n
As from the Center thrice to th' utmost Pole.[5]
O how unlike the place from whence they fell!
There the companions of his fall, o'erwhelm'd
With Floods and Whirlwinds of tempestuous fire,
He soon discerns, and welt'ring by his side
One next himself in power, and next in crime,
Long after known in *Palestine,* and nam'd
Beëlzebub.[6] To whom th' Arch-Enemy,
And thence in Heav'n call'd Satan,[7] with bold words
Breaking the horrid silence thus began.[8]
    If thou beest hee; But O how fall'n! how chang'd
From him, who in the happy Realms of Light
Cloth'd with transcendent brightness didst outshine
Myriads though bright:[9] If he whom mutual league,
United thoughts and counsels, equal hope,
And hazard in the Glorious Enterprise,
Join'd with me once, now misery hath join'd
In equal ruin: into what Pit thou seest
From what highth fall'n, so much the stronger prov'd

Line numbers: 55, 60, 65, 70, 75, 80, 85, 90

3. See the account of the land of the dead in Job 10:22: "the light is as darkness."
4. The phrase echoes Dante's *Inferno,* Canto 3: "All hope abandon, ye who enter here."
5. Milton refers to the Ptolemaic universe in which the earth is at the center of ten concentric spheres. Milton draws attention to the numerical proportion, heaven-earth:earth-hell—i.e., earth divides the interval between heaven and hell in the proportion that Neoplatonists believed should be maintained between reason and concupiscence.
6. Lord of the flies (Hebrew); Matthew 12:24, "the prince of the devils."
7. Enemy (Hebrew). After his rebellion, Satan's "former name" (Lucifer) was no longer used (5.658).
8. Rhetorically, the opening of the action proper. The 41-line speech beginning here, the first speech in the book, exactly balances the last, which also is spoken by Satan and also consists of 41 lines (12.622–62).
9. The break in grammatical concord (between "him" and "didst") reflects Satan's doubt whether Beelzebub is present and so whether second-person forms are appropriate.

He with his Thunder: and till then who knew
The force of those dire Arms? yet not for those,
95   Nor what the Potent Victor in his rage
Can else inflict, do I repent or change,
Though chang'd in outward luster; that fixt mind
And high disdain, from sense of injur'd merit,
That with the mightiest rais'd me to contend,
100   And to the fierce contention brought along
Innumerable force of Spirits arm'd
That durst dislike his reign, and mee preferring,
His utmost power with adverse power oppos'd
In dubious Battle on the Plains of Heav'n,
105   And shook his throne.[1] What though the field be lost?
All is not lost; the unconquerable Will,
And study° of revenge, immortal hate,   *pursuit*
And courage never to submit or yield:
And what is else not to be overcome?
110   That Glory[2] never shall his wrath or might
Extort from me. To bow and sue for grace
With suppliant knee, and deify his power
Who from the terror of this Arm so late
Doubted° his Empire, that were low indeed,   *feared for*
115   That were an ignominy and shame beneath
This downfall; since by Fate the strength of Gods
And this Empyreal substance cannot fail,[3]
Since through experience of this great event
In Arms not worse, in foresight much advanc't,
120   We may with more successful hope resolve
To wage by force or guile eternal War
Irreconcilable to our grand Foe,
Who now triúmphs, and in th' excess of joy
Sole reigning holds the Tyranny of Heav'n.[4]
125   So spake th' Apostate Angel, though in pain,
Vaunting aloud, but rackt with deep despair:
And him thus answer'd soon his bold Compeer.°   *comrade*
      O Prince, O Chief of many Throned Powers,
That led th' imbattl'd Seraphim[5] to War
130   Under thy conduct, and in dreadful deeds
Fearless, endanger'd Heav'n's perpetual King;
And put to proof his high Supremacy,
Whether upheld by strength, or Chance, or Fate;[6]

1. The Son's chariot, not Satan's armies, shakes heaven to its foundations, as we learn in Book 6. Throughout the present passage, Satan sees himself as the hero of a pagan epic.
2. Either "the glory of overcoming me" or "my glory of will."
3. Implying not only that as angels they are immortal, but also that the continuance of their strength is assured by fate.

4. An obvious instance of the devil's bias.
5. The traditional nine orders of angels are seraphim, cherubim, thrones, dominions, virtues, powers, principalities, archangels, and angels, but Milton does not use these terms systematically.
6. The main powers recognized in the devils' ideology. God's power rests on a quality that does not occur to Beelzebub: goodness.

Too well I see and rue the dire event,
135   That with sad overthrow and foul defeat
Hath lost us Heav'n, and all this mighty Host
In horrible destruction laid thus low,
As far as Gods and Heav'nly Essences
Can perish: for the mind and spirit remains
140   Invincible, and vigor soon returns,
Though all our Glory extinct, and happy state
Here swallow'd up in endless misery.
But what if he our Conqueror (whom I now
Of force° believe Almighty, since no less   *necessarily*
145   Than such could have o'erpow'rd such force as ours)
Have left us this our spirit and strength entire
Strongly to suffer and support our pains,
That we may so suffice° his vengeful ire,   *satisfy*
Or do him mightier service as his thralls
150   By right of War, whate'er his business be
Here in the heart of Hell to work in Fire,
Or do his Errands in the gloomy Deep;
What can it then avail though yet we feel
Strength undiminisht, or eternal being
155   To undergo eternal punishment?[7]
Whereto with speedy words th' Arch-fiend repli'd.
        Fall'n Cherub, to be weak is miserable
Doing or Suffering: but of this be sure,
To do aught good never will be our task,
160   But ever to do ill our sole delight,
As being the contrary to his high will
Whom we resist.[8] If then his Providence
Out of our evil seek to bring forth good,
Our labor must be to pervert that end,
165   And out of good still to find means of evil;
Which oft-times may succeed, so as perhaps
Shall grieve him, if I fail not, and disturb
His inmost counsels from thir destin'd aim.
But see the angry Victor hath recall'd
170   His Ministers of vengeance and pursuit
Back to the Gates of Heav'n: the Sulphurous Hail
Shot after us in storm, o'erblown hath laid°   *subdued*
The fiery Surge, that from the Precipice
Of Heav'n receiv'd us falling, and the Thunder,
175   Wing'd with red Lightning and impetuous rage,
Perhaps hath spent his shafts, and ceases now
To bellow through the vast and boundless Deep.

7. Being that is eternal, merely so that our punishment
may also be eternal.
8. This fundamental disobedience and disorientation
make Satan's heroic virtue into the corresponding excess
of vice. Lines 163–65 look forward to 12.470–78 and
Adam's wonder at the astonishing reversal whereby God
will turn the Fall into an occasion for good.

Let us not slip° th' occasion, whether scorn,   *lose*
Or satiate fury yield it from our Foe.
180 Seest thou yon dreary Plain, forlorn and wild,
The seat of desolation, void of light,
Save what the glimmering of these livid flames
Casts pale and dreadful? Thither let us tend
From off the tossing of these fiery waves,
185 There rest, if any rest can harbor there,
And reassembling our afflicted° Powers,   *downcast*
Consult how we may henceforth most offend°   *harm*
Our Enemy, our own loss how repair,
How overcome this dire Calamity,
190 What reinforcement we may gain from Hope,
If not what resolution from despair.
      Thus Satan talking to his nearest Mate
With Head up-lift above the wave, and Eyes
That sparkling blaz'd, his other Parts besides
195 Prone on the Flood, extended long and large
Lay floating many a rood,° in bulk as huge   *six to eight yards*
As whom the Fables name of monstrous size,
Titanian, or *Earth-born,* that warr'd on *Jove,*
Briareos or *Typhon,*[9] whom the Den
200 By ancient *Tarsus*[1] held, or that Sea-beast
Leviathan,[2] which God of all his works
Created hugest that swim th' Ocean stream:
Him haply slumb'ring on the *Norway* foam
The Pilot of some small night-founder'd° Skiff,   *sunk in night*
205 Deeming some Island, oft, as Seamen tell,
With fixed Anchor in his scaly rind
Moors by his side under the Lee, while Night
Invests° the Sea, and wished Morn delays: *wraps*
So stretcht out huge in length the Arch-fiend lay
210 Chain'd on the burning Lake, nor ever thence
Had ris'n or heav'd his head, but that the will
And high permission of all-ruling Heaven
Left him at large to his own dark designs,
That with reiterated crimes he might
215 Heap on himself damnation, while he sought
Evil to others, and enrag'd might see
How all his malice serv'd but to bring forth
Infinite goodness, grace and mercy shown
On Man by him seduc't, but on himself

---

9. The serpent-legged Briareos was a Titan, the serpent-headed Typhon (Typhoeus) a Giant. Each was a son of Earth; each fought against Jupiter; and each was eventually confined beneath Aetna (see lines 232–37). Typhon was so powerful that when he first made war on the Olympians, they had to resort to metamorphoses to escape (Ovid, *Metamorphoses* 5.325–31 and 346–58).

1. The biblical Tarsus was the capital of Cilicia, and both Pindar and Aeschylus describe Typhon's habitat as a Cilician cave or "den."
2. The monster of Job 41, identified in Isaiah's prophecy of judgement as "the crooked serpent" (Isaiah 27:1) but also sometimes thought of as a whale.

220   Treble confusion, wrath and vengeance pour'd.
        Forthwith upright he rears from off the Pool
        His mighty Stature; on each hand the flames
        Driv'n backward slope thir pointing spires, and roll'd
        In billows, leave i' th' midst a horrid° Vale.   *bristling*
225   Then with expanded wings he steers his flight
        Aloft, incumbent[3] on the dusky Air
        That felt unusual weight, till on dry Land
        He lights, if it were Land that ever burn'd
        With solid, as the Lake with liquid fire
230   And such appear'd in hue;[4] as when the force
        Of subterranean wind transports a Hill
        Torn from *Pelorus,*[5] or the shatter'd side
        Of thund'ring *Aetna,* whose combustible
        And fuell'd entrails thence conceiving Fire,
235   Sublim'd[6] with Mineral fury,[7] aid the Winds,
        And leave a singed bottom all involv'd°   *wreathed*
        With stench and smoke: Such resting found the sole
        Of unblest feet. Him follow'd his next Mate,
        Both glorying to have scap't the *Stygian*[8] flood
240   As Gods, and by thir own recover'd strength,
        Not by the sufferance of supernal Power.
            Is this the Region, this the Soil, the Clime,
        Said then the lost Arch-Angel, this the seat
        That we must change° for Heav'n, this mournful gloom   *exchange*
245   For that celestial light? Be it so, since he
        Who now is Sovran can dispose and bid
        What shall be right: fardest° from him is best   *farthest*
        Whom reason hath equall'd, force hath made supreme
        Above his equals. Farewell happy Fields
250   Where Joy for ever dwells: Hail horrors, hail
        Infernal world, and thou profoundest Hell
        Receive thy new Possessor: One who brings
        A mind not to be chang'd by Place or Time.
        The mind is its own place, and in itself
255   Can make a Heav'n of Hell, a Hell of Heav'n.[9]
        What matter where, if I be still the same,
        And what I should be, all but less than hee
        Whom Thunder hath made greater? Here at least
        We shall be free; th' Almighty hath not built
260   Here for his envy, will not drive us hence:
        Here we may reign secure, and in my choice

3. Pressing with his weight.
4. In the 17th century, "hue" referred to surface appearance and texture as well as color.
5. Pelorus and Aetna are volcanic mountains in Sicily.
6. Converted directly from solid to vapor by volcanic heat in such a way as to resolidify on cooling.

7. Disorder of minerals, or subterranean disorder.
8. Of the river Styx—i.e., hellish.
9. The view that heaven and hell are states of mind was held by Amaury de Bene, a medieval heretic often cited in 17th-century accounts of atheism.

To reign is worth ambition[1] though in Hell:
Better to reign in Hell, than serve in Heav'n.
But wherefore let we then our faithful friends,
265 Th' associates and copartners of our loss
Lie thus astonisht on th' oblivious Pool,[2]
And call them not to share with us their part
In this unhappy Mansion: or once more
With rallied Arms to try what may be yet
270 Regain'd in Heav'n, or what more lost in Hell?
     So *Satan* spake, and him *Beëlzebub*
Thus answer'd. Leader of those Armies bright,
Which but th' Omnipotent none could have foiled,
If once they hear that voice, thir liveliest pledge
275 Of hope in fears and dangers, heard so oft
In worst extremes, and on the perilous edge°   *front line*
Of battle when it rag'd, in all assaults
Thir surest signal, they will soon resume
New courage and revive, though now they lie
280 Groveling and prostrate on yon Lake of Fire,
As we erewhile, astounded and amaz'd;
No wonder, fall'n such a pernicious highth.
     He scarce had ceas't when the superior Fiend
Was moving toward the shore; his ponderous shield
285 Ethereal temper,[3] massy, large and round,
Behind him cast; the broad circumference
Hung on his shoulders like the Moon, whose Orb
Through Optic Glass the *Tuscan* Artist[4] views
At Ev'ning from the top of *Fesole,*
290 Or in *Valdarno,* to descry new Lands,
Rivers or Mountains in her spotty Globe.
His Spear, to equal which the tallest Pine
Hewn on *Norwegian* hills, to be the Mast
Of some great Ammiral,° were but a wand,   *flagship*
295 He walkt with to support uneasy steps
Over the burning Marl,° not like those steps   *ground*
On Heaven's Azure, and the torrid Clime
Smote on him sore besides, vaulted with Fire;
Nathless° he so endur'd, till on the Beach   *not*
300 Of that inflamed Sea, he stood and call'd
His Legions, Angel Forms, who lay intrans't
Thick as Autumnal Leaves that strow the Brooks
In *Vallombrosa,* where th' *Etrurian* shades

1. Worth striving for (Latin *ambitio*). Satan refers not
merely to a mental state but also to an active effort that is
the price of power.
2. The pool attended by forgetfulness.
3. Tempered in celestial fire.

4. Galileo, w[...]
had been [...]
Flore[...]
A[...]

ptic glass"),
quisition near
e Valley of the
or Fiesole.

High overarch't imbow'r;[5] or scatter'd sedge
305   Afloat, when with fierce Winds *Orion* arm'd
Hath vext the Red-Sea Coast,[6] whose waves o'erthrew
Busiris and his *Memphian* Chivalry,
While with perfidious hatred they pursu'd
The Sojourners of *Goshen,* who beheld
310   From the safe shore thir floating Carcasses
And broken Chariot Wheels;[7] so thick bestrown
Abject and lost lay these, covering the Flood,
Under amazement of thir hideous change.
He call'd so loud, that all the hollow Deep
315   Of Hell resounded. Princes, Potentates,
Warriors, the Flow'r of Heav'n, once yours, now lost,
If such astonishment as this can seize
Eternal spirits; or have ye chos'n this place
After the toil of Battle to repose
320   Your wearied virtue,° for the ease you find   *strength*
To slumber here, as in the Vales of Heav'n?
Or in this abject posture have ye sworn
To adore the Conqueror? who now beholds
Cherub and Seraph rolling in the Flood
325   With scatter'd Arms and Ensigns,° till anon   *battle flags*
His swift pursuers from Heav'n Gates discern
Th' advantage, and descending tread us down
Thus drooping, or with linked Thunderbolts
Transfix us to the bottom of this Gulf.
330   Awake, arise, or be for ever fall'n. * * *[8]

from Book 4
The Argument

Satan *now in prospect of* Eden, *and nigh the place where he must now attempt the bold enterprise which he undertook alone against God and Man, falls into many doubts with himself, and many passions, fear, envy, and despair; but at length confirms himself in evil, journeys on to Paradise, whose outward prospect and situation is described, overleaps the bounds, sits in the shape of a Cormorant on the Tree of Life, as highest in the Garden to look about him. The Garden describ'd;* Satan's *first ʾight of* Adam *and* Eve; *his wonder at thir excellent form and happy state, but with ʾlution to work thir fall; overhears thir discourse, thence gathers that the Tree of*

34:4: "and all their host shall fall down, as
ʾf from the vine, and as a falling fig from
leaves were an enduring simile for the
Homer, *Iliad* 6.146; Virgil, *Aeneid*
ʾ12. Milton adds an actual local-
ʾ Florence.
ʾd Amos 5:8 interpreted the
ʾf God's power to raise
ʾdgments. Thus Mil-
ʾhelmed by God's
ʾ one. The Hebrew
ʾe."

7. Contrary to his promise, the Pharaoh with his Memphian (i.e., Egyptian) charioteers pursued the Israelites—who had been in captivity in Goshen—across the Red Sea. The Israelites passed over safely; but the Egyptians' chariot wheels were broken (Exodus 14:25), and the rising sea engulfed them and cast their corpses on the shore.
8. After much debate, the "Councel" of hell agrees to send Satan to search out the "new World" and its inhabitants. Following a difficult journey, during which he changes himself into a "Fair Angel" in order to receive directions from the guardian angel Uriel, Satan arrives on Earth, alighting on the top of Mount Niphates.

Knowledge was forbidden them to eat of, under penalty of death; and thereon intends to found his Temptation, by seducing them to transgress: then leaves them a while, to know further of thir state by some other means. Meanwhile Uriel *descending on a Sun-beam warns* Gabriel, *who had in charge the Gate of Paradise, that some evil spirit had escap'd the Deep, and past at Noon by his Sphere in the shape of a good Angel down to Paradise, discovered after by his furious gestures in the Mount.* Gabriel *promises to find him ere morning. Night coming on,* Adam *and* Eve *discourse of going to thir rest: thir Bower describ'd; thir Evening worship.* Gabriel *drawing forth his Bands of Night-watch to walk the round of Paradise, appoints two strong Angels to* Adam's *Bower, lest the evil spirit should be there doing some harm to* Adam *or* Eve *sleeping; there they find him at the ear of* Eve, *tempting her in a dream, and bring him, though unwilling, to* Gabriel; *by whom question'd, he scornfully answers, prepares resistance, but hinder'd by a Sign from Heaven, flies out of Paradise.*

        O for that warning voice, which he who saw
    Th' *Apocalypse,* heard cry in Heav'n aloud,
    Then when the Dragon, put to second rout,
    Came furious down to be reveng'd on men,
5   *Woe to the inhabitants on Earth!*[1] that now,
    While time was, our first Parents had been warn'd
    The coming of thir secret foe, and scap'd
    Haply so scap'd his mortal snare; for now
    Satan, now first inflam'd with rage, came down,
10   The Tempter ere th' Accuser of man-kind,
    To wreck° on innocent frail man his loss   *avenge*
    Of that first Battle, and his flight to Hell:
    Yet not rejoicing in his speed, though bold,
    Far off and fearless, nor with cause to boast,
15   Begins his dire attempt, which nigh the birth
    Now rolling, boils in his tumultuous breast,
    And like a devilish Engine back recoils
    Upon himself; horror and doubt distract
    His troubl'd thoughts, and from the bottom stir
20   The Hell within him, for within him Hell
    He brings, and round about him, nor from Hell
    One step no more than from himself can fly
    By change of place: Now conscience wakes despair
    That slumber'd, wakes the bitter memory
25   Of what he was, what is, and what must be
    Worse; of worse deeds worse sufferings must ensue.
    Sometimes towards *Eden* which now in his view
    Lay pleasant,[2] his griev'd look he fixes sad,
    Sometimes towards Heav'n and the full-blazing Sun,
30   Which now sat high in his Meridian Tow'r:
    Then much revolving, thus in sighs began.

1. The Apocalypse of St. John relates a vision of a second battle in heaven between Michael and "the Dragon," Satan.

2. The etymological meaning of "Eden" is "pleasure, delight."

O thou that with surpassing Glory crown'd,
Look'st from thy sole Dominion like the God
Of this new World; at whose sight all the Stars
35   Hide thir diminisht heads; to thee I call,
But with no friendly voice, and add thy name
O Sun, to tell thee how I hate thy beams
That bring to my remembrance from what state
I fell, how glorious once above thy Sphere;
40   Till Pride and worse Ambition threw me down
Warring in Heav'n against Heav'n's matchless King:[3]
Ah wherefore! he deserv'd no such return
From me, whom he created what I was
In that bright eminence, and with his good
45   Upbraided none;[4] nor was his service hard.
What could be less than to afford him praise,
The easiest recompense, and pay him thanks,
How due! yet all his good prov'd ill in me,
And wrought but malice; lifted up so high
50   I sdein'd° subjection, and thought one step higher   *disdained*
Would set me highest, and in a moment quit°   *pay off*
The debt immense of endless gratitude,
So burdensome, still paying, still to owe;
Forgetful what from him I still receiv'd,
55   And understood not that a grateful mind
By owing owes not, but still pays, at once
Indebted and discharg'd; what burden then?[5]
O had his powerful Destiny ordain'd
Me some inferior Angel, I had stood
60   Then happy; no unbounded hope had rais'd
Ambition. Yet why not? some other Power
As great might have aspir'd, and me though mean
Drawn to his part; but other Powers as great
Fell not, but stand unshak'n, from within
65   Or from without, to all temptations arm'd.
Hadst thou the same free Will and Power to stand?
Thou hadst: whom hast thou then or what to accuse,
But Heav'n's free Love dealt equally to all?
Be then his Love accurst, since love or hate,
70   To me alike, it deals eternal woe.
Nay curs'd be thou; since against his thy will
Chose freely what it now so justly rues.
Me miserable! which way shall I fly
Infinite wrath, and infinite despair?
75   Which way I fly is Hell; myself am Hell;
And in the lowest deep a lower deep

:cording to Edward Phillips, lines 32–41 were shown
a and some others "before the Poem was begun,"
filton intended to write a tragedy on the Fall.

4. Demanded no return for his benefits; see James 1:5.
5. Simply by owning an obligation gratefully, one ceases
to owe it.

Still threat'ning to devour me opens wide,
To which the Hell I suffer seems a Heav'n.
O then at last relent: is there no place
80 Left for Repentance, none for Pardon left?
None left but by submission; and that word
Disdain forbids me, and my dread of shame
Among the Spirits beneath, whom I seduc'd
With other promises and other vaunts
85 Than to submit, boasting I could subdue
Th' Omnipotent. Ay me, they little know
How dearly I abide that boast so vain,
Under what torments inwardly I groan:
While they adore me on the Throne of Hell,
90 With Diadem and Sceptre high advanc'd
The lower still I fall, only Supreme
In misery; such joy Ambition finds.
But say I could repent and could obtain
By Act of Grace[6] my former state; how soon
95 Would highth recall high thoughts, how soon unsay
What feign'd submission swore: ease would recant
Vows made in pain, as violent and void.
For never can true reconcilement grow
Where wounds of deadly hate have pierc'd so deep:
100 Which would but lead me to a worse relapse,
And heavier fall: so should I purchase dear
Short intermission bought with double smart.
This knows my punisher; therefore as far
From granting hee, as I from begging peace:
105 All hope excluded thus, behold instead
Of us out-cast, exil'd, his new delight,
Mankind created, and for him this World.
So farewell Hope, and with Hope farewell Fear,
Farewell Remorse: all Good to me is lost;
110 Evil be thou my Good; by thee at least
Divided Empire with Heav'n's King I hold
By thee, and more than half perhaps will reign;
As Man ere long, and this new World shall know.
    Thus while he spake, each passion dimm'd his face,
115 Thrice chang'd with pale, ire, envy and despair,
Which marr'd his borrow'd visage, and betray'd
Him counterfeit, if any eye beheld.
For heav'nly minds from such distempers foul
Are ever clear. Whereof hee soon aware,
120 Each perturbation smooth'd with outward calm,
Artificer° of fraud; and was the first   *inventor*
That practis'd falsehood under saintly show,

6. By concession of favor, not of right; often used for a formal pardon by Parliament.

Deep malice to conceal, couch't° with revenge: *hidden*
Yet not anough had practis'd to deceive
125   *Uriel* once warn'd; whose eye pursu'd him down
The way he went, and on th' *Assyrian* mount°   *Niphates*
Saw him disfigur'd, more than could befall
Spirit of happy sort: his gestures fierce
He mark'd and mad demeanor, then alone,
130   As he suppos'd, all unobserv'd, unseen.
So on he fares, and to the border comes
Of *Eden,* where delicious Paradise,
Now nearer, Crowns with her enclosure green,
As with a rural mound the champaign° head   *unenclosed, level*
135   Of a steep wilderness, whose hairy sides
With thicket overgrown, grotesque and wild,
Access deni'd; and over head up grew
Insuperable highth of loftiest shade,
Cedar, and Pine, and Fir, and branching Palm,
140   A Silvan Scene, and as the ranks ascend
Shade above shade, a woody Theatre
Of stateliest view. Yet higher than thir tops
The verdurous wall of Paradise up sprung:
Which to our general Sire° gave prospect large   *Adam*
145   Into his nether Empire neighboring round.
And higher than that Wall a circling row
Of goodliest Trees loaden with fairest Fruit,
Blossoms and Fruits at once of golden hue
Appear'd, with gay enamell'd° colors mixt: *lustrous*
150   On which the Sun more glad impress'd his beams
Than in fair Evening Cloud, or humid Bow,°   *rainbow*
When God hath show'r'd the earth; so lovely seem'd
That Lantskip:° And of pure now purer air   *landscape*
Meets his approach, and to the heart inspires
155   Vernal delight and joy, able to drive
All sadness but despair: now gentle gales
Fanning thir odoriferous wings dispense
Native perfúmes, and whisper whence they stole
Those balmy spoils. As when to them who sail
160   Beyond the *Cape* of *Hope,* and now are past
Mozambic,[7] off at Sea North-East winds blow
Sabean[8] Odors from the spicy shore
Of *Araby* the blest, with such delay
Well pleas'd they slack thir course, and many a League
165   Cheer'd with the grateful smell old Ocean smiles.
So entertain'd those odorous sweets the Fiend
Who came thir bane, though with them better pleas'd

7. Mozambique, a Portuguese colony on the east coast of Africa; the trade route lay between Mozambique and Madagascar.

8. Of Saba or Sheba (now Yemen). Milton draws on the description of "Araby the blest"—"Arabia felix"—in Diodorus Siculus 3.46.

Than *Asmodeus* with the fishy fume,
That drove him, though enamor'd, from the Spouse
170   Of *Tobit's* Son, and with a vengeance sent
From *Media* post to *Egypt,* there fast bound.[9]
     Now to th' ascent of that steep savage° Hill   *wild*
Satan had journey'd on, pensive and slow;
But further way found none, so thick entwin'd,
175   As one continu'd brake, the undergrowth
Of shrubs and tangling bushes had perplext
All path of Man or Beast that pass'd that way:
One Gate there only was, and that look'd East
On th' other side: which when th' arch-felon saw
180   Due entrance he disdain'd, and in contempt,
At one slight bound high overleap'd all bound
Of Hill or highest Wall, and sheer within
Lights on his feet. As when a prowling Wolf,
Whom hunger drives to seek new haunt for prey,
185   Watching where Shepherds pen thir Flocks at eve
In hurdl'd Cotes° amid the field secure,   *shelters*
Leaps o'er the fence with ease into the Fold:
Or as a Thief bent to unhoard the cash
Of some rich Burgher, whose substantial doors,
190   Cross-barr'd and bolted fast, fear no assault,
In at the window climbs, or o'er the tiles:
So clomb° this first grand Thief into God's Fold: *climbed*
So since into his Church lewd Hirelings[1] climb.
Thence up he flew, and on the Tree of Life,
195   The middle Tree and highest there that grew,
Sat like a Cormorant;[2] yet not true Life
Thereby regain'd, but sat devising Death
To them who liv'd; nor on the virtue thought
Of that life-giving Plant, but only us'd
200   For prospect,° what well us'd had been the pledge   *lookout*
Of immortality. So little knows
Any, but God alone, to value right
The good before him, but perverts best things
To worst abuse, or to thir meanest use.
205   Beneath him with new wonder now he views
To all delight of human sense expos'd
In narrow room Nature's whole wealth, yea more,
A Heaven on Earth: for blissful Paradise
Of God the Garden was, by him in the East
210   Of *Eden* planted; *Eden* stretch'd her Line
From *Auran* Eastward to the Royal Tow'rs

9. The apocryphal book Tobit relates the story of Tobit's son Tobias, who was sent into Media on an errand and there married Sara. Sara had previously been given to seven men, but all were killed by the jealous spirit Asmodeus before their marriages could be consummated. By the advice of Raphael, however, Tobias succeeded by creating a fishy smoke to drive away the devil Asmodeus.
1. Wicked men motivated only by material gain.
2. A voracious sea bird, often used to describe greedy clergy.

Of Great *Seleucia,* built by *Grecian* Kings,
Or where the Sons of *Eden* long before
Dwelt in *Telassar:*[3] in this pleasant soil
215 His far more pleasant Garden God ordain'd;
Out of the fertile ground he caus'd to grow
All Trees of noblest kind for sight, smell, taste;
And all amid them stood the Tree of Life,
High eminent, blooming Ambrosial Fruit
220 Of vegetable Gold; and next to Life
Our Death the Tree of Knowledge grew fast by,
Knowledge of Good bought dear by knowing ill.[4]
Southward through *Eden* went a River large,
Nor chang'd his course, but through the shaggy hill
225 Pass'd underneath ingulft, for God had thrown
That Mountain as his Garden mould high rais'd
Upon the rapid current, which through veins
Of porous Earth with kindly° thirst up-drawn,   natural
Rose a fresh Fountain, and with many a rill
230 Water'd the Garden;[5] thence united fell
Down the steep glade, and met the nether Flood,
Which from his darksome passage now appears,
And now divided into four main Streams,
Runs diverse, wand'ring many a famous Realm
235 And Country whereof here needs no account,
But rather to tell how, if Art could tell,
How from that Sapphire Fount the crisped° Brooks,   wavy
Rolling on Orient Pearl and sands of Gold,
With mazy error° under pendant shades   wandering
240 Ran Nectar, visiting each plant, and fed
Flow'rs worthy of Paradise which not nice° Art   careful
In Beds and curious Knots, but Nature boon°   bounteous
Pour'd forth profuse on Hill and Dale and Plain,
Both where the morning Sun first warmly smote
245 The open field, and where the unpierc't shade
Imbrown'd° the noontide Bow'rs: Thus was this place,   darkened
A happy rural seat of various view:
Groves whose rich Trees wept odorous Gums and Balm,
Others whose fruit burnisht with Golden Rind
250 Hung amiable,° *Hesperian* Fables true,[6]   lovely
If true, here only, and of delicious taste:
Betwixt them Lawns, or level Downs, and Flocks
Grazing the tender herb, were interpos'd,
Or palmy hillock, or the flow'ry lap
255 Of some irriguous° Valley spread her store,   well-watered

---

3. Auran was an eastern boundary of the land of Israel. Great Seleucia was built by Alexander's general Seleucus Nicator as a seat of government for his Syrian empire. The mention of Telassar prophesies war in Eden; see 2 Kings 14:11ff., where Telassar is an instance of lands de-stroyed utterly.
4. See Genesis 2:9.
5. See Genesis 2:10.
6. Golden fruit like the legendary apples of the western islands, the Hesperides.

Flow'rs of all hue, and without Thorn the Rose:[7]
Another side, umbrageous° Grots and Caves   *shady*
Of cool recess, o'er which the mantling Vine
Lays forth her purple Grape, and gently creeps
260 Luxuriant; meanwhile murmuring waters fall
Down the slope hills, disperst, or in a Lake,
That to the fringed Bank with Myrtle crown'd,
Her crystal mirror holds, unite thir streams.
The Birds thir choir apply;° airs, vernal airs,[8]   *practice*
265 Breathing the smell of field and grove, attune
The trembling leaves, while Universal *Pan*[9]
Knit with the *Graces* and the *Hours* in dance
Led on th' Eternal Spring.[1] Not that fair field
Of *Enna*, where *Proserpin* gath'ring flow'rs
270 Herself a fairer Flow'r by gloomy *Dis*
Was gather'd, which cost *Ceres* all that pain
To seek her through the world;[2] nor that sweet Grove
Of *Daphne* by *Orontes*, and th' inspir'd
Castalian Spring[3] might with this Paradise
275 Of *Eden* strive; nor that *Nyseian* Isle
Girt with the River *Triton*, where old *Cham*,
Whom Gentiles *Ammon* call and *Lybian Jove*,
Hid *Amalthea* and her Florid° Son,   *ruddy-complexioned*
Young *Bacchus*, from his Stepdame *Rhea's* eye;[4]
280 Nor where *Abassin* Kings thir issue Guard,
Mount *Amara*, though this by some suppos'd
True Paradise under the *Ethiop* Line
By *Nilus* head, enclos'd with shining Rock,
A whole day's journey high,[5] but wide remote
285 From this *Assyrian* Garden, where the Fiend
Saw undelighted all delight, all kind
Of living Creatures new to sight and strange:
Two of far nobler shape erect and tall,
Godlike erect, with native Honor clad
290 In naked Majesty seem'd Lords of all,
And worthy seem'd, for in thir looks Divine
The image of thir glorious Maker shone,[6]
Truth, Wisdom, Sanctitude severe and pure,

---

7. The thornless rose was used to symbolize the sinless state of humanity before the Fall; or the state of grace.
8. Breezes and melodies.
9. Pan (Greek for "all") was a symbol of universal nature.
1. Neoplatonists thought the triadic pattern of their dance expressed the movement underlying all natural generation.
2. The rape of Proserpina by Dis, the king of hell, was located in Enna by Ovid (*Fasti* 4.420ff.). The search for her made the world barren, and even when she was found, she was restored to Ceres—and fruitfulness to the world— only for half the year.
3. The grove called "Daphne" beside the River Orontes,

near Antioch, had an Apolline oracle and a stream named after the famous Castalian spring of Parnassus.
4. Ammon, King of Libya, had an illicit affair with a maiden Amaltheia, who gave birth to a marvelous son Dionysus (Bacchus). To protect mother and child from the jealousy of his wife Rhea, Ammon hid them on Nysa, an island near modern Tunis. The identifications of Ammon with the Libyan Jupiter and with Noah's son Ham were widely accepted.
5. Milton takes his description of Mount Amara from Peter Heylyn's *Cosmographie* 4.64.
6. See Genesis 1:27: "God created man in his own image."

Severe, but in true filial freedom plac't;
295   Whence true autority in men; though both
Not equal, as thir sex not equal seem'd;
For contemplation hee and valor form'd,
For softness shee and sweet attractive Grace,
Hee for God only, shee for God in him:[7]
300   His fair large Front° and Eye sublime° declar'd   *forehead / uplifted*
Absolute rule; and Hyacinthine Locks
Round from his parted forelock manly hung
Clust'ring, but not beneath his shoulders broad:
Shee as a veil down to the slender waist
305   Her unadorned golden tresses wore
Dishevell'd, but in wanton ringlets wav'd
As the Vine curls her tendrils, which impli'd
Subjection, but requir'd with gentle sway,
And by her yielded, by him best receiv'd,
310   Yielded with coy° submission, modest pride,   *modest*
And sweet reluctant amorous delay.
Nor those mysterious parts were then conceal'd,
Then was not guilty shame: dishonest shame
Of Nature's works, honor dishonorable,
315   Sin-bred, how have ye troubl'd all mankind
With shows instead, mere shows of seeming pure,
And banisht from man's life his happiest life,
Simplicity and spotless innocence.
So pass'd they naked on, nor shunn'd the sight
320   Of God or Angel, for they thought no ill:
So hand in hand they pass'd, the loveliest pair
That ever since in love's imbraces met,
Adam the goodliest man of men since born
His Sons, the fairest of her Daughters *Eve*.
325   Under a tuft of shade that on a green
Stood whispering soft, by a fresh Fountain side
They sat them down, and after no more toil
Of thir sweet Gard'ning labor than suffic'd
To recommend cool *Zephyr*,[8] and made ease
330   More easy, wholesome thirst and appetite
More grateful, to thir Supper Fruits they fell,
Nectarine Fruits which the compliant boughs
Yielded them, side-long as they sat recline°   *lying down*
On the soft downy Bank damaskt with flow'rs:
335   The savory pulp they chew, and in the rind
Still as they thirsted scoop the brimming stream;
Nor gentle purpose,° nor endearing smiles   *conversation*
Wanted,° nor youthful dalliance as beseems   *lacked*
Fair couple, linkt in happy nuptial League,

---

7. See 1 Corinthians 11:3: "The head of every man is   head of Christ is God."
Christ; and the head of the woman is the man; and the   8. The west wind.

340 Alone as they. About them frisking play'd
   All Beasts of th' Earth, since wild, and of all chase
   In Wood or Wilderness, Forest or Den;
   Sporting the Lion ramp'd,° and in his paw   *reared up*
   Dandl'd the Kid; Bears, Tigers, Ounces,° Pards°   *lynxes / leopards*
345 Gamboll'd before them, th' unwieldy Elephant
   To make them mirth us'd all his might, and wreath'd
   His Lithe Proboscis; close the Serpent sly
   Insinuating,[9] wove with Gordian twine[1]
   His braided train, and of his fatal guile
350 Gave proof unheeded; others on the grass
   Coucht, and now fill'd with pasture gazing sat,
   Or Bedward ruminating;[2] for the Sun
   Declin'd was hasting now with prone career
   To th' Ocean Isles,[3] and in th' ascending Scale
355 Of Heav'n the Stars that usher Evening rose:
   When *Satan* still in gaze, as first he stood,
   Scarce thus at length fail'd speech recover'd sad.
    O Hell! what do mine eyes with grief behold,
   Into our room of bliss thus high advanc't
360 Creatures of other mould, earth-born perhaps,
   Not Spirits, yet to heav'nly Spirits bright
   Little inferior; whom my thoughts pursue
   With wonder, and could love, so lively shines
   In them Divine resemblance, and such grace
365 The hand that form'd them on thir shape hath pour'd.
   Ah gentle pair, yee little think how nigh
   Your change approaches, when all these delights
   Will vanish and deliver ye to woe,
   More woe, the more your taste is now of joy;
370 Happy, but for so happy ill secur'd
   Long to continue, and this high seat your Heav'n
   Ill fenc't for Heav'n to keep out such a foe
   As now is enter'd; yet no purpos'd foe
   To you whom I could pity thus forlorn
375 Though I unpitied: League with you I seek,
   And mutual amity so strait,° so close,   *intimate*
   That I with you must dwell, or you with me
   Henceforth; my dwelling haply may not please
   Like this fair Paradise, your sense, yet such
380 Accept your Maker's work; he gave it me,
   Which I as freely give; Hell shall unfold,[4]
   To entertain you two, her widest Gates,
   And send forth all her Kings; there will be room,

---

9. Penetrating by sinuous ways.
1. Coil, convolution, as difficult to undo as the Gordian knot, which it took the hero Alexander to cut.
2. Chewing the cud before going to rest.

3. The Azores.
4. A blasphemous echo of Matthew 10:8 ("freely ye have received, freely give").

Not like these narrow limits, to receive
385   Your numerous offspring; if no better place,
Thank him who puts me loath to this revenge
On you who wrong me not for him who wrong'd.
And should I at your harmless innocence
Melt, as I do, yet public reason[5] just,
390   Honor and Empire with revenge enlarg'd,
By conquering this new World, compels me now
To do what else though damn'd I should abhor.
    So spake the Fiend, and with necessity,
The Tyrant's plea, excus'd his devilish deeds.
395   Then from his lofty stand on that high Tree
Down he alights among the sportful Herd
Of those fourfooted kinds, himself now one,
Now other, as thir shape serv'd best his end
Nearer to view his prey, and unespi'd
400   To mark what of thir state he more might learn
By word or action markt: about them round
A Lion now he stalks with fiery glare,
Then as a Tiger, who by chance hath spi'd
In some Purlieu° two gentle Fawns at play,   *edge of a forest*
405   Straight couches close, then rising changes oft
His couchant watch, as one who chose his ground
Whence rushing he might surest seize them both
Gript in each paw: when *Adam* first of men
To first of women *Eve* thus moving speech,
410   Turn'd him° all ear to hear new utterance flow.   *Satan*
    Sole partner and sole part of all these joys,[6]
Dearer thyself than all; needs must the Power
That made us, and for us this ample World
Be infinitely good, and of his good
415   As liberal and free as infinite,
That rais'd us from the dust and plac't us here
In all this happiness, who at his hand
Have nothing merited, nor can perform
Aught whereof hee hath need, hee who requires
420   From us no other service than to keep
This one, this easy charge, of all the Trees
In Paradise that bear delicious fruit
So various, not to taste that only Tree
Of Knowledge, planted by the Tree of Life,[7]
425   So near grows Death to Life, whate'er Death is,
Some dreadful thing no doubt; for well thou know'st
God hath pronounc't it death to taste that Tree,
The only sign of our obedience left

5. Reason of state, a perversion of the Ciceronian principle (*Laws* 3.3.8) that the good of the people is the supreme law.

6. The first "sole" means "only"; the second, "unrivalled."
7. See Genesis 2:16ff.

Among so many signs of power and rule
430   Conferr'd upon us, and Dominion giv'n
Over all other Creatures that possess
Earth, Air, and Sea.[8] Then let us not think hard
One easy prohibition, who enjoy
Free leave so large to all things else, and choice
435   Unlimited of manifold delights:
But let us ever praise him, and extol
His bounty, following our delightful task
To prune these growing Plants, and tend these Flow'rs,
Which were it toilsome, yet with thee were sweet.
440   To whom thus Eve repli'd. O thou for whom
And from whom I was form'd flesh of thy flesh,[9]
And without whom am to no end, my Guide
And Head, what thou hast said is just and right.[1]
For wee to him indeed all praises owe,
445   And daily thanks, I chiefly who enjoy
So far the happier Lot, enjoying thee
Preëminent by so much odds,°while thou   *advantage*
Like consort to thyself canst nowhere find.
That day I oft remember, when from sleep
450   I first awak't, and found myself repos'd
Under a shade on flow'rs, much wond'ring where
And what I was, whence thither brought, and how.
Not distant far from thence a murmuring sound
Of waters issu'd from a Cave and spread
455   Into a liquid Plain, then stood unmov'd
Pure as th' expanse of Heav'n; I thither went
With unexperienc't thought, and laid me down
On the green bank, to look into the clear
Smooth Lake, that to me seem'd another Sky.
460   As I bent down to look, just opposite,
A Shape within the wat'ry gleam appear'd
Bending to look on me, I started back,
It started back, but pleas'd I soon return'd,
Pleas'd it return'd as soon with answering looks
465   Of sympathy and love; there I had fixt
Mine eyes till now, and pin'd with vain desire,[2]
Had not a voice thus warn'd me, What thou seest,
What there thou seest fair Creature is thyself,
With thee it came and goes: but follow me,
470   And I will bring thee where no shadow stays°   *awaits*

---

8. See Genesis 1:28: "God said unto them . . . have dominion over the fish of the sea, and over the fowl of the
air, and over every living thing that moveth upon the
earth."
9. See 1 Corinthians 11:9: "Neither was the man created
for the woman; but the woman for the man." See Genesis
2:23.

1. See 1 Corinthians 11:3: "The head of every man is
Christ; and the head of the woman is the man; and the
head of Christ is God."
2. Alluding to Ovid's story of the proud youth Narcissus,
who was punished for his scornfulness by being made to
fall in love with his own reflection in a pool.

Thy coming, and thy soft imbraces, hee
Whose image thou art, him thou shalt enjoy
Inseparably thine, to him shalt bear
Multitudes like thyself, and thence be call'd
475   Mother of human Race: what could I do,
But follow straight, invisibly thus led?
Till I espi'd thee, fair indeed and tall,
Under a Platan, yet methought less fair,
Less winning soft, less amiably mild,
480   Than that smooth wat'ry image; back I turn'd,
Thou following cri'd'st aloud, Return fair *Eve,*
Whom fli'st thou? whom thou fli'st, of him thou art,
His flesh, his bone; to give thee being I lent
Out of my side to thee, nearest my heart
485   Substantial Life, to have thee by my side
Henceforth an individual° solace dear;   *inseparable*
Part of my Soul I seek thee, and thee claim
My other half: with that thy gentle hand
Seiz'd mine, I yielded, and from that time see
490   How beauty is excell'd by manly grace
And wisdom, which alone is truly fair.
     So spake our general Mother, and with eyes
Of conjugal attraction unreprov'd,°   *innocent*
And meek surrender, half imbracing lean'd
495   On our first Father, half her swelling Breast
Naked met his under the flowing Gold
Of her loose tresses hid: hee in delight
Both of her Beauty and submissive Charms
Smil'd with superior Love, as *Jupiter*
500   On *Juno* smiles, when he impregns° the Clouds   *impregnates*
That shed *May* Flowers; and press'd her Matron lip
With kisses pure: aside the Devil turn'd
For envy, yet with jealous leer malign
Ey'd them askance, and to himself thus plain'd.°   *complained*
505   Sight hateful, sight tormenting! thus these two
Imparadis't in one another's arms
The happier *Eden,* shall enjoy thir fill
Of bliss on bliss, while I to Hell am thrust,
Where neither joy nor love, but fierce desire,
510   Among our other torments not the least,
Still unfulfill'd with pain of longing pines;°   *troubles*
Yet let me not forget what I have gain'd
From thir own mouths; all is not theirs it seems:
One fatal Tree there stands of Knowledge call'd,
515   Forbidden them to taste: Knowledge forbidd'n?
Suspicious, reasonless. Why should thir Lord
Envy them that? can it be sin to know,
Can it be death? and do they only stand
By Ignorance, is that thir happy state,

520 The proof of thir obedience and thir faith?
 O fair foundation laid whereon to build
 Thir ruin! Hence I will excite thir minds
 With more desire to know, and to reject
 Envious commands, invented with design
525 To keep them low whom Knowledge might exalt
 Equal with Gods; aspiring to be such,
 They taste and die: what likelier can ensue?
 But first with narrow search I must walk round
 This Garden, and no corner leave unspi'd;
530 A chance but chance[3] may lead where I may met
 Some wand'ring Spirit of Heav'n, by Fountain side,
 Or in thick shade retir'd, from him to draw
 What further would be learnt. Live while ye may,
 Yet happy pair; enjoy, till I return,
535 Short pleasures, for long woes are to succeed.
  So saying, his proud step he scornful turn'd,
 But with sly circumspection, and began
 Through wood, through waste, o'er hill, o'er dale his roam.
 Meanwhile in utmost Longitude,[4] where Heav'n
540 With Earth and Ocean meets, the setting Sun
 Slowly descended, and with right aspect
 Against the eastern Gate of Paradise
 Levell'd his ev'ning Rays: it was a Rock
 Of Alablaster,° pil'd up to the Clouds,   *alabaster*
545 Conspicuous far, winding with one ascent
 Accessible from Earth, one entrance high;
 The rest was craggy cliff, that overhung
 Still as it rose, impossible to climb.[5]
 Betwixt these rocky Pillars *Gabriel*° sat
550 Chief of th' Angelic Guards, awaiting night;
 About him exercis'd Heroic Games
 Th' unarmed Youth of Heav'n, but nigh at hand
 Celestial Armory, Shields, Helms, and Spears
 Hung high with Diamond flaming, and with Gold.
555 Thither came *Uriel,* gliding through the Even
 On a Sun-beam, swift as a shooting Star
 In *Autumn* thwarts° the night, when vapors fir'd *crosses*
 Impress the Air, and shows the Mariner
 From what point of his Compass to beware
560 Impetuous winds:[7] he thus began in haste.
  Gabriel, to thee thy course by Lot hath giv'n
 Charge and strict watch that to this happy place
 No evil thing approach or enter in;

3. An accident and an opportunity.
4. The farthest west.
5. A possible source is the paradise of Mt. Amara in Heylyn's *Cosmographie.*

6. "Strength of God," one of the four archangels ruling the corners of the world.
7. Shooting stars were thought to be a sign of storm because in falling they were thrust down by winds.

This day at highth of Noon came to my Sphere

565   A Spirit, zealous, as he seem'd, to know

More of th' Almighty's works, and chiefly Man

God's latest Image: I describ'd° his way   *observed*

Bent all on speed, and markt his Aery Gait;

But in the Mount that lies from *Eden* North,

570   Where he first lighted, soon discern'd his looks

Alien from Heav'n, with passions foul obscur'd:

Mine eye pursu'd him still, but under shade

Lost sight of him; one of the banisht crew

I fear, hath ventur'd from the Deep, to raise

575   New troubles; him thy care must be to find.

      To whom the winged Warrior thus return'd:

Uriel,[8] no wonder if thy perfect sight,

Amid the Sun's bright circle where thou sitst,

See far and wide: in at this Gate none pass

580   The vigilance here plac't, but such as come

Well known from Heav'n; and since Meridian hour

No Creature thence: if Spirit of other sort,

So minded, have o'erleapt these earthy bounds

On purpose, hard thou know'st it to exclude

585   Spiritual substance with corporeal bar.

But if within the circuit of these walks

In whatsoever shape he lurk, of whom

Thou tell'st, by morrow dawning I shall know.

      So promis'd hee, and *Uriel* to his charge

590   Return'd on that bright beam, whose point now rais'd

Bore him slope downward to the Sun now fall'n

Beneath th' *Azores;* whither the prime Orb,

Incredible how swift, had thither roll'd

Diurnal,° or this less volúbil[9] Earth   *in one day*

595   By shorter flight to th' East, had left him there

Arraying with reflected Purple and Gold

The Clouds that on his Western Throne attend:[1]

Now came still Ev'ning on, and Twilight gray

Had in her sober Livery all things clad;

600   Silence accompanied, for Beast and Bird,

They to thir grassy Couch, these to thir Nests

Were slunk, all but the wakeful Nightingale;

She all night long her amorous descant sung;

Silence was pleas'd: now glow'd the Firmament

605   With living Sapphires: *Hesperus*[2] that led

The starry Host, rode brightest, till the Moon

Rising in clouded Majesty, at length

Apparent Queen unveil'd her peerless light,

---

8. "Light of God."

9. Capable of ready rotation on its axis.

1. The appearance of sunset can be regarded as caused ei-

ther by orbital motion of the sun about the earth or by the earth's rotation (a lesser movement).

2. The evening star.

And o'er the dark her Silver Mantle threw.
610   When *Adam* thus to *Eve:* Fair Consort, th' hour
Of night, and all things now retir'd to rest
Mind us of like repose, since God hath set
Labor and rest, as day and night to men
Successive, and the timely dew of sleep
615 Now falling with soft slumbrous weight inclines
Our eye-lids; other Creatures all day long
Rove idle unimploy'd, and less need rest;
Man hath his daily work of body or mind
Appointed, which declares his Dignity,
620 And the regard of Heav'n on all his ways;
While other Animals unactive range,
And of thir doings God takes no account.
Tomorrow ere fresh Morning streak the East
With first approach of light, we must be ris'n,
625 And at our pleasant labor, to reform
Yon flow'ry Arbors, yonder Alleys green,
Our walk at noon, with branches overgrown,
That mock our scant manuring,° and require   *cultivating*
More hands than ours to lop thir wanton growth:
630 Those Blossoms also, and those dropping Gums,
That lie bestrown unsightly and unsmooth,
Ask riddance, if we mean to tread with ease;
Meanwhile, as Nature wills, Night bids us rest.
To whom thus *Eve* with perfect beauty adorn'd.
635 My Author° and Disposer, what thou bidd'st   *origin*
Unargu'd I obey; so God ordains,
God is thy Law, thou mine: to know no more
Is woman's happiest knowledge and her praise.
With thee conversing I forget all time,
640 All seasons³ and thir change, all please alike.
Sweet is the breath of morn, her rising sweet,
With charm° of earliest Birds; pleasant the Sun   *song*
When first on this delightful Land he spreads
His orient Beams, on herb, tree, fruit, and flow'r,
645 Glist'ring with dew; fragrant the fertile earth
After soft showers; and sweet the coming on
Of grateful Ev'ning mild, then silent Night
With this her solemn Bird and this fair Moon,
And these the Gems of Heav'n, her starry train:
650 But neither breath of Morn when she ascends
With charm of earliest Birds, nor rising Sun
On this delightful land, nor herb, fruit, flow'r,
Glist'ring with dew, nor fragrance after showers,
Nor grateful Ev'ning mild, nor silent Night

3. Time of day; not "seasons of the year," since it is still eternal spring.

655 With this her solemn Bird, nor walk by Moon,
Or glittering Star-light without thee is sweet.
But wherefore all night long shine these, for whom
This glorious sight, when sleep hath shut all eyes?
    To whom our general Ancestor repli'd.
660 Daughter of God and Man, accomplisht *Eve,*
Those have thir course to finish, round the Earth,
By morrow Ev'ning, and from Land to Land
In order, though to Nations yet unborn,
Minist'ring light prepar'd, they set and rise;
665 Lest total darkness should by Night regain
Her old possession, and extinguish life
In Nature and all things, which these soft fires
Not only enlighten, but with kindly heat
Of various influence foment and warm,
670 Temper or nourish, or in part shed down
Thir stellar virtue on all kinds that grow
On Earth, made hereby apter to receive
Perfection from the Sun's more potent Ray.⁴
These then, though unbeheld in deep of night,
675 Shine not in vain, nor think, though men were none,
That Heav'n would want spectators, God want praise;
Millions of spiritual Creatures walk the Earth
Unseen, both when we wake, and when we sleep:
All these with ceaseless praise his works behold
680 Both day and night: how often from the steep
Of echoing Hill or Thicket have we heard
Celestial voices to the midnight air,
Sole, or responsive each to other's note
Singing thir great Creator: oft in bands
685 While they keep watch, or nightly rounding walk,
With Heav'nly touch of instrumental sounds
In full harmonic number join'd, thir songs
Divide the night, and lift our thoughts to Heaven.
    Thus talking hand in hand alone they pass'd
690 On to thir blissful Bower; it was a place
Chos'n by the sovran Planter, when he fram'd
All things to man's delightful use; the roof
Of thickest covert was inwoven shade
Laurel and Myrtle, and what higher grew
695 Of firm and fragrant leaf; on either side
Acanthus, and each odorous bushy shrub
Fenc'd up the verdant wall; each beauteous flow'r,
Iris all hues, Roses, and Jessamin°   *jasmine*
Rear'd high thir flourisht heads between, and wrought

---

4. In Neoplatonic astrology, Sol was said to accomplish the generation of new life by acting through each of the other planets in turn; their function was only to modulate his influence or to select from his complete spectrum of virtues. After the Fall, the influence of the stars becomes less "kindly" (benign; natural).

700   Mosaic; underfoot the Violet,
      Crocus, and Hyacinth with rich inlay
      Broider'd the ground, more color'd than with stone
      Of costliest Emblem:[5] other Creature here
      Beast, Bird, Insect, or Worm durst enter none;
705   Such was thir awe of Man. In shadier Bower
      More sacred and sequester'd, though but feign'd,
      Pan or *Silvanus* never slept, nor Nymph,
      Nor *Faunus* haunted.[6] Here in close recess
      With Flowers, Garlands, and sweet-smelling Herbs
710   Espoused *Eve* deckt first her Nuptial Bed,
      And heav'nly Choirs the Hymenaean° sung,   *wedding hymn*
      What day the genial° Angel to our Sire   *nuptial, generative*
      Brought her in naked beauty more adorn'd,
      More lovely than *Pandora,* whom the Gods
715   Endow'd with all thir gifts, and O too like
      In sad event, when to the unwiser Son
      Of *Japhet* brought by *Hermes,* she ensnar'd
      Mankind with her fair looks, to be aveng'd
      On him who had stole *Jove's* authentic fire.[7]
720   Thus at thir shady Lodge arriv'd, both stood,
      Both turn'd, and under op'n Sky ador'd
      The God that made both Sky, Air, Earth and Heav'n
      Which they beheld, the Moon's resplendent Globe
      And starry Pole:° Thou also mad'st the Night,   *sky*
725   Maker Omnipotent, and thou the Day,
      Which we in our appointed work imploy'd
      Have finisht happy in our mutual help
      And mutual love, the Crown of all our bliss
      Ordain'd by thee, and this delicious place
730   For us too large, where thy abundance wants
      Partakers, and uncropt falls to the ground.
      But thou hast promis'd from us two a Race
      To fill the Earth, who shall with us extol
      Thy goodness infinite, both when we wake,
735   And when we seek, as now, thy gift of sleep.
          This said unanimous, and other Rites
      Observing none, but adoration pure

5. Any ornament of inlaid work; the other sense of "emblem" (pictorial symbol) also operates here, to draw attention to the emblematic properties of the flowers (the humility of the violet, prudence of the hyacinth, amiability of the jasmine, etc.). The bower as a whole is an emblem of true married love.

6. Pan, Silvanus, and Faunus were confused, for all were represented as half man, half goat. Pan was a symbol of fecundity; Silvanus, god of woods, symbolized gardens and limits; Faunus, the Roman Pan, a wood god, and the father of satyrs, was an emblem of concupiscence.

7. Milton has followed Charles Estienne's version of the myth: "Pandora . . . is feigned by Hesiod the first woman—made by Vulcan at Jupiter's command— . . . she was called Pandora, either because she was 'endowed with all [the gods'] gifts,' or because she was endowed with gifts by all." She was "sent with a closed casket to Epimetheus, since Jupiter wanted revenge on the human race for the boldness of Prometheus, who had stolen fire from heaven and taken it . . . down to earth; and that Epimetheus received her and opened the casket, which contained every kind of evil, so that it filled the world with diseases and calamities." Prometheus and Epimetheus were sons of Iapetus, the Titan son of Coelus and Terra. Milton identifies Iapetus with Iaphet (Noah's son).

Which God likes best, into thir inmost bower
Handed they went; and eas'd the putting off
740   These troublesome disguises which wee wear,
Straight side by side were laid, nor turn'd I ween
Adam from his fair Spouse, nor *Eve* the Rites
Mysterious of connubial Love refus'd:
Whatever Hypocrites austerely talk
745   Of purity and place and innocence,
Defaming as impure what God declares
Pure, and commands to some, leaves free to all.
Our Maker bids increase,[8] who bids abstain
But our Destroyer, foe to God and Man?
750   Hail wedded Love, mysterious Law, true source
Of human offspring, sole propriety
In Paradise of all things common else.
By thee adulterous lust was driv'n from men
Among the bestial herds to range, by thee
755   Founded in Reason, Loyal, Just, and Pure,
Relations dear, and all the Charities°   *affections*
Of Father, Son, and Brother first were known.
Far be it, that I should write thee sin or blame,
Or think thee unbefitting holiest place,
760   Perpetual Fountain of Domestic sweets,
Whose bed is undefil'd and chaste pronounc't,[9]
Present, or past, as Saints and Patriarchs us'd.
Here Love his golden shafts imploys,[1] here lights
His constant Lamp, and waves his purple wings,
765   Reigns here and revels; not in the bought smile
Of Harlots, loveless, joyless, unindear'd,
Casual fruition, nor in Court Amours,
Mixt Dance, or wanton Mask, or Midnight Ball,
Or Serenate, which the starv'd Lover sings
770   To his proud fair, best quitted with disdain.
These lull'd by Nightingales imbracing slept,
And on thir naked limbs the flow'ry roof
Show'r'd Roses, which the Morn repair'd.° Sleep on,   *made up for*
Blest pair; and O yet happiest if ye seek
775   No happier state, and know to know no more.[2]
         Now had night measur'd with her shadowy Cone
Half way up Hill this vast Sublunar Vault,[3]
And from thir Ivory Port the Cherubim
Forth issuing at th' accustom'd hour stood arm'd

---

8. See Genesis 1:28.
9. See Hebrews 13:4: "Marriage is honourable in all, and
the bed undefiled."
1. Cupid's "golden shafts" were sharp and gleaming and
kindled love, while those of lead were blunt and put love
to flight (Ovid, *Metamorphoses* 1.468–41).
2. Either "know that it is best not to seek new knowledge

(by eating the forbidden fruit)" or "know how to limit
your experience to the state of innocence."
3. The earth's shadow is a cone that appears to circle
around it in diametrical opposition to the sun. When the
axis of the cone reaches the meridian, it is midnight; but
here it is only "Half way up," so the time is nine o'clock.

780   To thir night watches in warlike Parade,
         When *Gabriel* to his next in power thus spake.
              Uzziel,[4] half these draw off, and coast the South
         With strictest watch; these other wheel the North;
         Our circuit meets full West. As flame they part
785   Half wheeling to the Shield, half to the Spear.[5]
         From these, two strong and subtle Spirits he call'd
         That near him stood, and gave them thus in charge.
              Ithuriel and *Zephon,* with wing'd speed
         Search through this Garden, leave unsearcht no nook,
790   But chiefly where those two fair Creatures Lodge,
         Now laid perhaps asleep secure° of harm.   *careless*
         This Ev'ning from the Sun's decline arriv'd
         Who tells of some infernal Spirit seen
         Hitherward bent (who could have thought?) escap'd
795   The bars of Hell, on errand bad no doubt:
         Such where ye find, seize fast, and hither bring.
              So saying, on he led his radiant Files,
         Dazzling the Moon; these to the Bower direct
         In search of whom they sought: him there they found
800   Squat like a Toad, close at the ear of *Eve;*
         Assaying by his Devilish art to reach
         The Organs of her Fancy, and with them forge
         Illusions as he list, Phantasms° and Dreams,   *illusions*
         Or if, inspiring venom, he might taint
805   Th' animal spirits[6] that from pure blood arise
         Like gentle breaths from Rivers pure, thence raise
         At least distemper'd,° discontented thoughts,   *vexed*
         Vain hopes, vain aims, inordinate desires
         Blown up with high conceits ingend'ring pride.
810   Him thus intent *Ithuriel* with his Spear
         Touch'd lightly; for no falsehood can endure
         Touch of Celestial temper, but returns
         Of force to its own likeness: up he starts
         Discover'd and surpris'd. As when a spark
815   Lights on a heap of nitrous[7] Powder, laid
         Fit for the Tun[8] some Magazin to store
         Against° a rumor'd War, the Smutty grain   *preparing for*
         With sudden blaze diffus'd inflames the Air:
         So started up in his own shape the Fiend.
820   Back stepp'd those two fair Angels half amaz'd

---

4. "Uzziel" (Strength of God) occurs in the Bible as an ordinary human name (e.g., Exodus 6:18), and so does "Zephon" (Searcher of Secrets· Numbers 26:15). "Ithuriel" (Discovery of God) is not from the Bible.
5. "Shield" for "left" and "spear" for "right" were ancient military terms.
6. Spirits in this sense were fine vapors, regarded by some as a medium between body and soul, by others as a separate soul. Animal spirits (Latin *anima,* soul) ascended to the brain and issued through the nerves to impart motion to the body. Local movement of the animal spirits could also produce imaginative apparitions, by which angels were thought to affect the human mind.
7. Mixed with niter (potassium nitrate or saltpeter, an ingredient in gunpowder) to form an explosive.
8. In proper condition for casking, ready for use.

So sudden to behold the grisly King;
Yet thus, unmov'd with fear, accost him soon.
   Which of those rebel Spirits adjudg'd to Hell
Com'st thou, escap'd thy prison, and transform'd,
825   Why satst thou like an enemy in wait
Here watching at the head of these that sleep?
   Know ye not then said *Satan*, fill'd with scorn,
Know ye not mee?[9] * * *

Book 9
The Argument

Satan *having compast the Earth, with meditated guile returns as a mist by Night into Paradise, enters into the Serpent sleeping.* Adam *and* Eve *in the Morning go forth to thir labors, which* Eve *proposes to divide in several places, each laboring apart:* Adam *consents not, alleging the danger, lest that Enemy, of whom they were forewarn'd, should attempt her found alone:* Eve *loath to be thought not circumspect or firm enough, urges her going apart, the rather desirous to make trial of her strength;* Adam *at last yields: The Serpent finds her alone; his subtle approach, first gazing, then speaking, with much flattery extolling* Eve *above all other Creatures.* Eve *wond'ring to hear the Serpent speak, asks how he attain'd to human speech and such understanding not till now; the Serpent answers, that by tasting of a certain Tree in the Garden he attain'd both to Speech and Reason, till then void of both:* Eve *requires him to bring her to that Tree, and finds it to be the Tree of Knowledge forbidden: The Serpent now grown bolder, with many wiles and arguments induces her at length to eat; she pleas'd with the taste deliberates awhile whether to impart thereof to* Adam *or not, at last brings him of the Fruit, relates what persuaded her to eat thereof:* Adam *at first amaz'd, but perceiving her lost, resolves through vehemence[1] of love to perish with her; and extenuating[2] the trespass, eats also of the Fruit: The effects thereof in them both; they seek to cover thir nakedness; then fall to variance and accusation of one another.*

    No more of talk where God or Angel Guest
With Man, as with his Friend, familiar us'd
To sit indulgent, and with him partake
Rural repast, permitting him the while
5   Venial° discourse unblam'd: I now must change   *permissible*
Those Notes to Tragic; foul distrust, and breach
Disloyal on the part of Man, revolt,
And disobedience: On the part of Heav'n
Now alienated, distance and distaste,

9. Ithuriel and Zephon take Satan to Gabriel, who orders him to return to Hell. Satan rises up to fight the assembled angels—"His Stature reacht the Sky, and on his Crest / Sat horror Plum'd"—but then God displays scales in heaven, showing victory tilting to Gabriel, and Satan flees.
    Books 5 through 8 largely relate the visit of the angel Raphael to Adam and Eve to warn them of Satan's arrival. He also tells them of the great battle that took place when Satan and his angels challenged God (Book 6), the creation of Earth (Book 7) and the movements of the celestial bodies (Book 8). He then departs, admonishing Adam to "stand fast" and "all temptation to transgress repel."
1. The root meaning of Latin "vehementia" is mindlessness.
2. Carrying further, drawing out.

10   Anger and just rebuke, and judgment giv'n,
        That brought into this World a world of woe,
        Sin and her shadow Death, and Misery
        Death's Harbinger: Sad task, yet argument
        Not less but more Heroic than the wrath
15   Of stern *Achilles* on his Foe pursu'd
        Thrice Fugitive about *Troy* Wall; or rage
        Of *Turnus* for *Lavinia* disespous'd,
        Or *Neptune's* ire or *Juno's,* that so long
        Perplex'd the *Greek* and *Cytherea's* Son;[3]
20   If answerable° style I can obtain   *equal, accountable*
        Of my Celestial Patroness,[4] who deigns
        Her nightly visitation unimplor'd,
        And dictates to me slumb'ring, or inspires
        Easy my unpremeditated Verse:
25   Since first this Subject for Heroic Song
        Pleas'd me long choosing, and beginning late;
        Not sedulous by Nature to indite
        Wars, hitherto the only Argument
        Heroic deem'd, chief maistry to dissect
30   With long and tedious havoc fabl'd Knights
        In Battles feign'd; the better fortitude
        Of Patience and Heroic Martyrdom
        Unsung; or to describe Races and Games,
        Or tilting Furniture, emblazon'd Shields,
35   Impreses[5] quaint, Caparisons[6] and Steeds;
        Bases and tinsel Trappings, gorgeous Knights
        At Joust and Tournament; then marshall'd Feast
        Serv'd up in Hall with Sewers,° and Seneschals;°   *waiters / stewards*
        The skill of Artifice or Office mean,
40   Not that which justly gives Heroic name
        To Person or to Poem.[7] Mee of these
        Nor skill'd nor studious, higher Argument
        Remains, sufficient of itself to raise
        That name,[8] unless an age too late, or cold
45   Climate, or Years damp my intended wing
        Deprest; and much they may, if all be mine,
          Not Hers who brings it nightly to my Ear.
        The Sun was sunk, and after him the Star

---

3. Achilles is "stern" in his "wrath" because he refused any covenant with Hector, and Turnus dies fighting Aeneas for the hand of Lavinia, whereas Messiah, more heroically, is not implacable in his anger. He issued his sole commandment "sternly" (8.333); but when it is disobeyed, he works for reconciliation. Similarly, God's anger is distinguished from "Neptune's ire" and "Juno's" (which merely "perplexed" Odysseus and Aeneas) in that it is expressed in justice rather than in victimization.

4. The heavenly Muse, Urania. Both ancient and modern epics had always had war, or at least fighting, as a princi-

pal ingredient. (So has *Paradise Lost,* in the first half of the poem; but in the second half this subject is transcended.) Milton now glances unfavorably at the typical matter of the romantic epic.

5. Heraldic devices, often with accompanying mottos.

6. Ornamented coverings spread over the saddle of a horse.

7. Artifice implies mechanic or applied art. It is beneath the dignity of epic to teach etiquette and social ceremony and heraldry.

8. The name of epic.

	Of *Hesperus,*° whose Office is to bring	*the planet Venus*
50	Twilight upon the Earth, short Arbiter	
	Twixt Day and Night, and now from end to end	
	Night's Hemisphere had veil'd the Horizon round:	
	When *Satan* who late fled before the threats	
	Of *Gabriel* out of *Eden,*[9] now improv'd°	*intensified*
55	In meditated fraud and malice, bent	
	On Man's destruction, maugre what might hap	
	Of heavier on himself,[1] fearless return'd.	
	By Night he fled, and at Midnight return'd	
	From compassing the Earth, cautious of day,	
60	Since *Uriel* Regent of the Sun descri'd	
	His entrance, and forewarn'd the Cherubim	
	That kept thir watch; thence full of anguish driv'n,	
	The space of seven continu'd Nights he rode	
	With darkness, thrice the Equinoctial Line	
65	He circl'd, four times cross'd the Car of Night	
	From Pole to Pole, traversing each Colure;[2]	
	On th'eighth return'd, and on the Coast averse	
	From entrance or Cherubic Watch, by stealth	
	Found unsuspected way. There was a place,	
70	Now not, though Sin, not Time, first wrought the change,	
	Where *Tigris* at the foot of Paradise	
	Into a Gulf shot under ground, till part	
	Rose up a Fountain by the Tree of Life;	
	In with the River sunk, and with it rose	
75	*Satan* involv'd in rising Mist, then sought	
	Where to lie hid; Sea he had searcht and Land	
	From *Eden* over *Pontus,* and the Pool	
	Maeotis, up beyond the River *Ob;*[3]	
	Downward as far Antarctic; and in length	
80	West from *Orontes* to the Ocean barr'd	
	At *Darien,* thence to the Land where flows	
	Ganges and *Indus:*[4] thus the Orb he roam'd	
	With narrow search; and with inspection deep	
	Consider'd every Creature, which of all	
85	Most opportune might serve his Wiles, and found	
	The Serpent subtlest Beast of all the Field.[5]	
	Him after long debate, irresolute°	*undecided*
	Of thoughts revolv'd, his final sentence° chose	*judgment*
	Fit Vessel, fittest Imp° of fraud, in whom	*offshoot*

9. At the end of Book 4, a week earlier.

1. Despite the danger of heavier punishment.

2. By keeping to earth's shadow, Satan contrives to experience a whole week of darkness. The two colures were great circles, intersecting at right angels at the poles and dividing the equinoctial circle (the equator) into four equal parts.

3. In his north-south circles, Satan passed Pontus (the Black Sea), the "pool / Maeotis" (the Sea of Azov), and the Siberian River Ob, which flows north into the Gulf of Ob and from there into the Arctic Ocean.

4. In his westward circling of the equinoctial line, he crossed the Syrian River Orontes, then the Pacific ("peaceful") "Ocean barred" by the Isthmus of Darien (Panama) and India.

5. See Genesis 3:1.

90   To enter, and his dark suggestions hide
      From sharpest sight: for in the wily Snake,
      Whatever sleights none would suspicious mark,
      As from his wit and native subtlety
      Proceeding, which in other Beasts observ'd
95   Doubt° might beget of Diabolic pow'r   *suspicion*
      Active within beyond the sense of brute.
      Thus he resolv'd, but first from inward grief
      His bursting passion into plaints thus pour'd:
         O Earth, how like to Heav'n, if not preferr'd
100   More justly, Seat worthier of Gods, as built
      With second thoughts, reforming what was old!
      For what God after better worse would build?
      Terrestrial Heav'n, danc't round by other Heav'ns
      That shine, yet bear thir bright officious Lamps,
105   Light above Light, for thee alone, as seems,
      In thee concentring all thir precious beams
      Of sacred influence:[6] As God in Heav'n
      Is Centre, yet extends to all, so thou
      Centring receiv'st from all those Orbs; in thee,
110   Not in themselves, all thir known virtue appears
      Productive in Herb, Plant, and nobler birth
      Of Creatures animate with gradual life
      Of Growth, Sense, Reason, all summ'd up in Man.[7]
      With what delight could I have walkt thee round,
115   If I could joy in aught, sweet interchange
      Of Hill and Valley, Rivers, Woods and Plains,
      Now Land, now Sea, and Shores with Forest crown'd,
      Rocks, Dens, and Caves; but I in none of these
      Find place or refuge; and the more I see
120   Pleasures about me, so much more I feel
      Torment within me, as from the hateful siege°   *conflict*
      Of contraries; all good to me becomes
      Bane,° and in Heav'n much worse would be my state.   *poison*
      But neither here seek I, no nor in Heav'n
125   To dwell, unless by maistring Heav'n's Supreme;
      Nor hope to be myself less miserable
      By what I seek, but others to make such
      As I, though thereby worse to me redound:
      For only in destroying I find ease
130   To my relentless thoughts; and him destroy'd,
      Or won to what may work his utter loss,
      For whom all this was made, all this will soon
      Follow, as to him linkt in weal or woe,
      In woe then: that destruction wide may range:[8]

6. The case for an earth-centered universe, put at 8.86–114 by Raphael, is now put by Satan.
7. "Growth, sense, reason" are the activities of the veg-etable, animal, and rational souls, respectively, in humans.
8. The created cosmos will follow humans to destruction.

135 To mee shall be the glory sole among
     Th'infernal Powers, in one day to have marr'd
     What he *Almight* styl'd, six Nights and Days
     Continu'd making, and who knows how long
     Before had been contriving, though perhaps
140 Not longer than since I in one Night freed
     From servitude inglorious well nigh half
     Th' Angelic Name, and thinner left the throng
     Of his adorers: hee to be aveng'd,
     And to repair his numbers thus impair'd,
145 Whether such virtue° spent of old now fail'd   *power*
     More Angels to Create, if they at least
     Are his Created, or to spite us more,
     Determin'd to advance into our room
     A Creature form'd of Earth, and him endow,
150 Exalted from so base original,
     With Heav'nly spoils, our spoils; What he decreed
     He effected; Man he made, and for him built
     Magnificent this World, and Earth his seat,
     Him Lord pronounc'd, and, O indignity!
155 Subjected to his service Angel wings,
     And flaming Ministers to watch and tend
     Thir earthy Charge: Of these the vigilance
     I dread, and to elude, thus wrapt in mist
     Of midnight vapor glide obscure, and pry
160 In every Bush and Brake, where hap may find
     The Serpent sleeping, in whose mazy folds
     To hide me, and the dark intent I bring.
     O foul descent! that I who erst contended
     With Gods to sit the highest, am now constrain'd
165 Into a Beast, and mixt with bestial slime,
     This essence to incarnate and imbrute,
     That to the highth of Deity aspir'd;
     But what will not Ambition and Revenge
     Descend to? who aspires must down as low
170 As high he soar'd, obnoxious° first or last   *exposed*
     To basest things. Revenge, at first though sweet,
     Bitter ere long back on itself recoils;
     Let it, I reck not, so it light well aim'd,
     Since higher I fall short, on him who next
175 Provokes my envy, this new Favorite
     Of Heav'n, this Man of Clay, Son of despite,
     Whom us the more to spite his Maker rais'd
     From dust: spite then with spite is best repaid.
         So saying, through each Thicket Dank or Dry,
180 Like a black mist low creeping, he held on
     His midnight search, where soonest he might find
     The Serpent: him fast sleeping soon he found
     In Labyrinth of many a round self-roll'd,

His head the midst, well stor'd with subtle wiles:
185 Not yet in horrid Shade or dismal Den,
Nor nocent° yet, but on the grassy Herb   *harmful, guilty*
Fearless unfear'd he slept: in at his Mouth
The Devil enter'd, and his brutal sense,
In heart or head, possessing soon inspir'd
190 With act intelligential; but his sleep
Disturb'd not, waiting close° th' approach of Morn.   *concealed*
Now whenas sacred Light began to dawn
In *Eden* on the humid Flow'rs, that breath'd
Thir morning incense, when all things that breathe,
195 From th' Earth's great Altar send up silent praise
To the Creator, and his Nostrils fill
With grateful Smell, forth came the human pair
And join'd thir vocal Worship to the Choir
Of Creatures wanting voice; that done, partake
200 The season, prime for sweetest Scents and Airs:
Then cómmune how that day they best may ply
Thir growing work: for much thir work outgrew
The hands' dispatch of two Gard'ning so wide.
And *Eve* first to her Husband thus began.
205   *Adam,* well may we labor still to dress
This Garden, still to tend Plant, Herb and Flow'r,
Our pleasant task enjoin'd, but till more hands
Aid us, the work under our labor grows,
Luxurious by restraint; what we by day
210 Lop overgrown, or prune, or prop, or bind,
One night or two with wanton growth derides
Tending to wild. Thou therefore now advise
Or hear what to my mind first thoughts present,
Let us divide our labors, thou where choice
215 Leads thee, or where most needs, whether to wind
The Woodbine round this Arbor, or direct
The clasping Ivy where to climb, while I
In yonder Spring of Roses intermixt
With Myrtle, find what to redress till Noon:
220 For while so near each other thus all day
Our task we choose, what wonder if so near
Looks intervene and smiles, or object new
Casual discourse draw on, which intermits
Our day's work brought to little, though begun
225 Early, and th' hour of Supper comes unearn'd.
To whom mild answer *Adam* thus return'd.
Sole *Eve,* Associate sole, to me beyond
Compare above all living Creatures dear,
Well hast thou motion'd,° well thy thoughts imploy'd   *proposed*
230 How we might best fulfil the work which here
God hath assign'd us, nor of me shalt pass
Unprais'd: for nothing lovelier can be found

In Woman, than to study household good,
And good works in her Husband to promote.
235   Yet not so strictly hath our Lord impos'd
Labor, as to debar us when we need
Refreshment, whether food, or talk between,
Food of the mind, or this sweet intercourse
Of looks and smiles, for smiles from Reason flow,
240   To brute deni'd, and are of Love the food,
Love not the lowest end of human life.
For not to irksome toil, but to delight
He made us, and delight to Reason join'd.
These paths and Bowers doubt not but our joint hands
245   Will keep from Wilderness with ease, as wide
As we need walk, till younger hands ere long
Assist us: But if much converse perhaps
Thee satiate, to short absence I could yield.
For solitude sometimes is best society,
250   And short retirement urges sweet return.
But other doubt possesses me, lest harm
Befall thee sever'd from me; for thou know'st
What hath been warn'd us, what malicious Foe
Envying our happiness, and of his own
255   Despairing, seeks to work us woe and shame
By sly assault; and somewhere nigh at hand
Watches, no doubt, with greedy hope to find
His wish and best advantage, us asunder,
Hopeless to circumvent us join'd, where each
260   To other speedy aid might lend at need;
Whether his first design be to withdraw
Our fealty from God, or to disturb
Conjugal Love, than which perhaps no bliss
Enjoy'd by us excites his envy more;
265   Or this, or worse,⁹ leave not the faithful side
That gave thee being, still shades thee and protects.
The Wife, where danger or dishonor lurks,
Safest and seemliest by her Husband stays,
Who guards her, or with her the worst endures.
270   To whom the Virgin° Majesty of *Eve*,   *chaste, innocent*
As one who loves, and some unkindness meets,
With sweet austere composure thus repli'd.
        Offspring of Heav'n and Earth, and all Earth's Lord,
That such an Enemy we have, who seeks
275   Our ruin, both by thee inform'd I learn,
And from the parting Angel over-heard
As in a shady nook I stood behind,
Just then return'd at shut of Ev'ning Flow'rs.

9. Whether this or worse (be his first design).

But that thou shouldst my firmness therefore doubt
280   To God or thee, because we have a foe
May tempt it, I expected not to hear.
His violence thou fear'st not, being such,
As wee, not capable of death or pain,
Can either not receive, or can repel.
285   His fraud is then thy fear, which plain infers
Thy equal fear that my firm Faith and Love
Can by his fraud be shak'n or seduc't;
Thoughts, which how found they harbor in thy breast,
Adam, misthought of her to thee so dear?
290   To whom with healing words *Adam* repli'd.
Daughter of God and Man, immortal *Eve,*
For such thou art, from sin and blame entire:°   *free*
Not diffident° of thee do I dissuade   *mistrustful*
Thy absence from my sight, but to avoid
295   Th' attempt itself, intended by our Foe.
For hee who tempts, though in vain, at least asperses°   *falsely charges*
The tempted with dishonor foul, suppos'd
Not incorruptible of Faith, not proof
Against temptation: thou thyself with scorn
300   And anger wouldst resent the offer'd wrong,
Though ineffectual found: misdeem not then,
If such affront I labor to avert
From thee alone, which on us both at once
The Enemy, though bold, will hardly dare,
305   Or daring, first on mee th' assault shall light.
Nor thou his malice and false guile contemn;
Subtle he needs must be, who could seduce
Angels, nor think superfluous others' aid.
I from the influence of thy looks receive
310   Access° in every Virtue, in thy sight   *increase*
More wise, more watchful, stronger, if need were
Of outward strength; while shame, thou looking on,
Shame to be overcome or over-reacht
Would utmost vigor raise, and rais'd unite.
315   Why shouldst not thou like sense within thee feel
When I am present, and thy trial choose
With me, best witness of thy Virtue tri'd.
      So spake domestic *Adam* in his care
And Matrimonial Love; but *Eve,* who thought
320   Less° attribúted to her Faith sincere,   *too little*
Thus her reply with accent sweet renew'd.
      If this be our condition, thus to dwell
In narrow circuit strait'n'd by a Foe,
Subtle or violent, we not endu'd
325   Single with like defense, wherever met,
How are we happy, still in fear of harm?
But harm precedes not sin: only our Foe

Tempting affronts us with his foul esteem
Of our integrity: his foul esteem
330   Sticks no dishonor on our Front,° but turns   *face*
Foul on himself; then wherefore shunn'd or fear'd
By us? who rather double honor gain
From his surmise prov'd false, find peace within,
Favor from Heav'n, our witness from th' event.
335   And what is Faith, Love, Virtue unassay'd
Alone, without exterior help sustain'd?
Let us not then suspect our happy State
Left so imperfet by the Maker wise,
As not secure to single or combin'd.
340   Frail is our happiness, if this be so,
And *Eden* were no Eden[1] thus expos'd.
        To whom thus Adam fervently repli'd.
O Woman, best are all things as the will
Of God ordain'd them, his creating hand
345   Nothing imperfet or deficient left
Of all that he Created, much less Man,
Or aught that might his happy State secure,
Secure from outward force; within himself
The danger lies, yet lies within his power:
350   Against his will he can receive no harm.
But God left free the Will, for what obeys
Reason, is free, and Reason he made right,
But bid her well beware, and still erect,[2]
Lest by some fair appearing good surpris'd
355   She dictate false, and misinform the Will
To do what God expressly hath forbid.
Not then mistrust, but tender love enjoins,
That I should mind thee oft, and mind thou me.
Firm we subsist, yet possible to swerve,
360   Since Reason not impossibly may meet
Some specious object by the Foe suborn'd,
And fall into deception unaware,
Not keeping strictest watch, as she was warn'd.
Seek not temptation then, which to avoid
365   Were better, and most likely if from mee
Thou sever not: Trial will come unsought.
Wouldst thou approve° thy constancy, approve   *demonstrate*
First thy obedience; th' other who can know,
Not seeing thee attempted, who attest?
370   But if thou think, trial unsought may find
Us both securer° than thus warn'd thou seem'st,   *more careless*
Go; for thy stay, not free, absents thee more;
Go in thy native innocence, rely

1. No pleasure, the literal Hebrew meaning of "Eden."   2. Always attentive, but also with a glance at upright.

On what thou hast of virtue, summon all,
375   For God towards thee hath done his part, do thine.
            So spake the Patriarch of Mankind, but *Eve*
        Persisted, yet submiss, though last, repli'd.
            With thy permission then, and thus forewarn'd
        Chiefly by what thy own last reasoning words
380   Touch'd only, that our trial, when least sought,
        May find us both perhaps far less prepar'd,
        The willinger I go, nor much expect
        A Foe so proud will first the weaker seek;
        So bent, the more shall shame him his repulse.
385   Thus saying, from her Husband's hand her hand
        Soft she withdrew, and like a Wood-Nymph light,
        Oread or *Dryad,* or of *Delia's* Train,[3]
        Betook her to the Groves, but *Delia's* self
        In gait surpass'd and Goddess like deport,
390   Though not as shee with Bow and Quiver arm'd,
        But with such Gard'ning Tools as Art yet rude,
        Guiltless° of fire had form'd, or Angels brought.[4]   innocent, ignorant
        To Pales, or Pomona, thus adorn'd,
        Likest she seem'd, Pomona when she fled
395   *Vertumnus,* or to *Ceres* in her Prime,
        Yet Virgin of *Proserpina* from *Jove.*[5]
        Her long and ardent look his Eye pursu'd
        Delighted, but desiring more her stay.
        Oft he to her his charge of quick return
400   Repeated, shee to him as oft engag'd
        To be return'd by Noon amid the Bow'r,
        And all things in best order to invite
        Noontide repast, or Afternoon's repose.
        O much deceiv'd, much failing, hapless *Eve,*
405   Of thy presum'd return! event perverse!
        Thou never from that hour in Paradise
        Found'st either sweet repast, or sound repose;
        Such ambush hid among sweet Flow'rs and Shades
        Waited with hellish rancor imminent
410   To intercept thy way, or send thee back
        Despoil'd of Innocence, of Faith, of Bliss.
        For now, and since first break of dawn the Fiend,
        Mere° Serpent in appearance, forth was come,   plain
        And on his Quest, where likeliest he might find
415   The only two of Mankind, but in them
        The whole included Race, his purpos'd prey.

---

3. Oreads, were mountain nymphs, such as attended on Diana; dryads were wood nymphs. Neither class of nymphs were immortal.
4. Only as a result of the Fall did it become necessary for humans to have some means of warming themselves. There may also be an allusion to the fire stolen from heaven by Prometheus.
5. Pales was the Roman goddess of pastures; Pomona was the nymph or goddess of fruit trees, seduced by the disguised Vertumnus; Ceres was the goddess of corn and agriculture who bore Proserpina to Jove.

In Bow'r and Field he sought, where any tuft
Of Grove or Garden-Plot more pleasant lay,
Thir tendance° or Plantation for delight,   *object of care*
420   By Fountain or by shady Rivulet,
He sought them both, but wish'd his hap° might find   *chance*
Eve separate, he wish'd, but not with hope
Of what so seldom chanc'd, when to his wish,
Beyond his hope, *Eve* separate he spies,
425   Veil'd in a Cloud of Fragrance, where she stood,
Half spi'd, so thick the Roses bushing round
About her glow'd, oft stooping to support
Each Flow'r of slender stalk, whose head though gay
Carnation, Purple, Azure, or speckt with Gold,
430   Hung drooping unsustain'd, them she upstays
Gently with Myrtle band, mindless the while,
Herself, though fairest unsupported Flow'r,
From her best prop so far, and storm so nigh.[6]
Nearer he drew, and many a walk travers'd
435   Of stateliest Covert, Cedar, Pine, or Palm,
Then voluble and bold, now hid, now seen
Among thick-wov'n Arborets and Flow'rs
Imborder'd on each Bank, the hand° of *Eve:*   *handiwork*
Spot more delicious than those Gardens feign'd
440   Or of reviv'd *Adonis,* or renown'd
Alcinoüs, host of old *Laertes'* Son,
Or that, not Mystic, where the Sapient King
Held dalliance with his fair *Egyptian* Spouse.[7]
Much hee the Place admir'd, the Person more.
445   As one who long in populous City pent,
Where Houses thick and Sewers annoy the Air,
Forth issuing on a Summer's Morn to breathe
Among the pleasant Villages and Farms
Adjoin'd, from each thing met conceives delight,
450   The smell of Grain, or tedded° Grass, or Kine,°   *mown / cows*
Or Dairy, each rural sight, each rural sound;
If chance with Nymphlike step fair Virgin pass,
What pleasing seem'd, for her now pleases more,
She most, and in her look sums all Delight.
455   Such Pleasure took the Serpent to behold
This Flow'ry Plat,° the sweet recess of *Eve*   *piece of ground*
Thus early, thus alone; her Heav'nly form
Angelic, but more soft, and Feminine,
Her graceful Innocence, her every Air
460   Of gesture or least action overaw'd

6. See 4.270, page 717, where Proserpina (and by impli-
cation Eve) was "Herself a fairer flower" when she was
carried off by the king of hell.
7. "The sapient king" was Solomon (Song of Songs 6:2).
Milton alludes to Spenser's addition to the myth of Adonis, that Venus keeps Adonis hidden in a secret garden
(*The Faerie Queene* 3.6). "Laertes' son" was Odysseus;
much-traveled as he was, he marveled when he saw the
Garden of Alcinoüs (Homer, *Odyssey* 7).

His Malice, and with rapine sweet bereav'd
His fierceness of the fierce intent it brought:
That space the Evil one abstracted stood
From his own evil, and for the time remain'd
465   Stupidly good, of enmity disarm'd,
Of guile, of hate, of envy, of revenge;
But the hot Hell that always in him burns,
Though in mid Heav'n, soon ended his delight,
And tortures him now more, the more he sees
470   Of pleasure not for him ordain'd: then soon
Fierce hate he recollects, and all his thoughts
Of mischief, gratulating,° thus excites.   *rejoicing*
    Thoughts, whither have ye led me, with what sweet
Compulsion thus transported to forget
475   What hither brought us, hate, not love, nor hope
Of Paradise for Hell, hope here to taste
Of pleasure, but all pleasure to destroy,
Save what is in destroying, other joy
To me is lost. Then let me not let pass
480   Occasion which now smiles, behold alone
The Woman, opportune° to all attempts,   *exposed*
Her Husband, for I view far round, not nigh,
Whose higher intellectual more I shun,
And strength, of courage haughty, and of limb
485   Heroic built, though of terrestrial mould,°   *formed of earth*
Foe not informidable, exempt from wound,
I not; so much hath Hell debas'd, and pain
Infeebl'd me, to what I was in Heav'n.
Shee fair, divinely fair, fit Love for Gods,
490   Not terrible, though terror be in Love
And beauty, not approacht by stronger hate,
Hate stronger, under show of Love well feign'd,
The way which to her ruin now I tend.
    So spake the Enemy of Mankind, enclos'd
495   In Serpent, Inmate bad, and toward *Eve*
Address'd his way, not with indented wave,
Prone on the ground, as since, but on his rear,
Circular base of rising folds, that tow'r'd
Fold above fold a surging Maze, his Head
500   Crested aloft, and Carbuncle his Eyes;[8]
With burnisht Neck of verdant Gold, erect
Amidst his circling Spires,° that on the grass   *coils*
Floated redundant:° pleasing was his shape,   *abundant to excess*
And lovely, never since of Serpent kind
505   Lovelier, not those that in *Illyria* chang'd
Hermione and *Cadmus,* or the God

8. "Carbuncle" or reddish eyes denoted rage.

In *Epidaurus;*[9] nor to which transform'd
Ammonian Jove, or *Capitoline* was seen,
Hee with *Olympias,* this with her who bore
510   *Scipio* the highth of Rome.[1] With tract oblique
At first, as one who sought access, but fear'd
To interrupt, side-long he works his way.
As when a Ship by skilful Steersman wrought
Nigh River's mouth or Foreland, where the Wind
515   Veers oft, as oft so steers, and shifts her Sail;
So varied hee, and of his tortuous Train
Curl'd many a wanton wreath in sight of *Eve,*
To lure her Eye; shee busied heard the sound
Of rustling Leaves, but minded not, as us'd
520   To such disport before her through the Field,
From every Beast, more duteous at her call,
Than at *Circean* call the Herd disguis'd.[2]
Hee bolder now, uncall'd before her stood;
But as in gaze admiring: Oft he bow'd
525   His turret Crest, and sleek enamell'd Neck,
Fawning, and lick'd the ground whereon she trod.
His gentle dumb expression turn'd at length
The Eye of *Eve* to mark his play; he glad
Of her attention gain'd, with Serpent Tongue
530   Organic, or impulse of vocal Air,
His fraudulent temptation thus began.
     Wonder not, sovran Mistress, if perhaps
Thou canst, who are sole Wonder, much less arm
Thy looks, the Heav'n of mildness, with disdain,
535   Displeas'd that I approach thee thus, and gaze
Insatiate, I thus single, nor have fear'd
Thy awful brow, more awful thus retir'd.
Fairest resemblance of thy Maker fair,
Thee all things living gaze on, all things thine
540   By gift, and thy Celestial Beauty adore
With ravishment beheld, there best beheld
Where universally admir'd: but here
In this enclosure wild, these Beasts among,
Beholders rude, and shallow to discern
545   Half what in thee is fair, one man except,
Who sees thee? (and what is one?) who shouldst be seen
A Goddess among Gods, ador'd and serv'd
By Angels numberless, thy daily Train.

---

9. Cadmus was turned into a serpent first; only after he had embraced his wife Hermione (Harmonia) in his new form did she too change (Ovid, *Metamorphoses* 4.572–603). Aesculapius, the god of healing, once changed into a serpent to help the Romans in that form (Ovid, *Metamorphoses* 15.626–744).
1. Jupiter Ammon, the "Lybian Jove," as a serpent mated with Olympias to father Alexander the Great, just as the Roman Jupiter, Capitolinus, took the form of a snake to father the great general Scipio.
2. Homer's Circe changed men into beasts who surprised Odysseus's company by fawning on them like dogs (*Odyssey* 10.212–19).

So gloz'd° the Tempter, and his Proem° tun'd;   *flattered / prelude*
550   Into the Heart of *Eve* his words made way,
        Though at the voice much marvelling; at length
        Not unamaz'd she thus in answer spake.
            What may this mean? Language of Man pronounc't
        By Tongue of Brute, and human sense exprest?[3]
555   The first at least of these I thought deni'd
        To Beasts, whom God on thir Creation-Day
        Created mute to all articulate sound;
        The latter I demur,° for in thir looks   *hesitate about*
        Much reason, and in thir actions oft appears.
560   Thee, Serpent, subtlest beast of all the field
        I knew, but not with human voice endu'd;
        Redouble then this miracle, and say,
        How cam'st thou speakable of mute,[4] and how
        To me so friendly grown above the rest
565   Of brutal kind, that daily are in sight?
        Say, for such wonder claims attention due.
            To whom the guileful Tempter thus repli'd.
        Empress of this fair World, resplendent *Eve*,
        Easy to mee it is to tell thee all
570   What thou command'st and right thou should'st be obey'd:
        I was at first as other Beasts that graze
        The trodden Herb, of abject° thoughts and low,   *mean-spirited*
        As was my food, nor aught but food discern'd
        Or Sex, and apprehended nothing high:
575   Till on a day roving the field, I chanc'd
        A goodly Tree far distant to behold
        Loaden with fruit of fairest colors mixt,
        Ruddy and Gold: I nearer drew to gaze;
        When from the boughs a savory odor blown,
580   Grateful to appetite, more pleas'd my sense
        Than smell of sweetest Fennel, or the Teats
        Of Ewe or Goat dropping with Milk at Ev'n,
        Unsuckt of Lamb or Kid, that tend thir play.
        To satisfy the sharp desire I had
585   Of tasting those fair Apples, I resolv'd
        Not to defer; hunger and thirst at once,
        Powerful persuaders, quick'n'd at the scent
        Of that alluring fruit, urg'd me so keen.
        About the mossy Trunk I wound me soon,
590   For high from ground the branches would require
        Thy utmost reach or *Adam's:* Round the Tree
        All other Beasts that saw, with like desire
        Longing and envying stood, but could not reach.

---

3. Milton is unusually favorable to Eve in making her ask the serpent how it came by its voice. The Eve of Scriptural exegesis, by contrast, is carried away by the words and makes no inquiry into their source.
4. How did you become capable of speech from being dumb?

Amid the Tree now got, where plenty hung
595 Tempting so nigh, to pluck and eat my fill
I spar'd not, for such pleasure till that hour
At Feed or Fountain never had I found.
Sated at length, ere long I might perceive
Strange alteration in me, to degree
600 Of Reason in my inward Powers, and Speech
Wanted not long, though to this shape retain'd.
Thenceforth to Speculations high or deep
I turn'd my thoughts, and with capacious mind
Consider'd all things visible in Heav'n,
605 Or Earth, or Middle, all things fair and good;
But all that fair and good in thy Divine
Semblance, and in thy Beauty's heav'nly Ray
United I beheld; no Fair° to thine   *beauty*
Equivalent or second, which compell'd
610 Mee thus, though importune perhaps, to come
And gaze, and worship thee of right declar'd
Sovran of Creatures, universal Dame.
     So talk'd the spirited[5] sly Snake; and *Eve,*
Yet more amaz'd unwary thus repli'd.
615   Serpent, thy overpraising leaves in doubt
The virtue° of that Fruit, in thee first prov'd: *power*
But say, where grows the Tree, from hence how far?
For many are the Trees of God that grow
In Paradise, and various, yet unknown
620 To us, in such abundance lies our choice,
As leaves a greater store of Fruit untoucht,
Still hanging incorruptible, till men
Grow up to thir provision, and more hands
Help to disburden Nature of her Birth.
625   To whom the wily Adder, blithe and glad.
Empress, the way is ready, and not long,
Beyond a row of Myrtles, on a Flat,
Fast by a Fountain, one small Thicket past
Of blowing° Myrrh and Balm; if thou accept   *blooming*
630 My conduct,° I can bring thee thither soon.   *guidance*
     Lead then, said Eve. Hee leading swiftly roll'd
In tangles, and made intricate seem straight,
To mischief swift. Hope elevates, and joy
     Bright'ns his Crest, as when a wand'ring Fire,
635 Compact° of unctuous vapor, which the Night   *made up*
Condenses, and the cold invirons round,
Kindl'd through agitation to a Flame,
Which oft, they say, some evil Spirit attends,
Hovering and blazing with delusive Light,

5. Endowed with an animating spirit, stirred up; also energetic, enterprising, possessed by a spirit.

640   Misleads th' amaz'd Night-wanderer from his way
    To Bogs and Mires, and oft through Pond or Pool,
    There swallow'd up and lost, from succor far.
    So glister'd the dire Snake, and into fraud
    Led *Eve* our credulous Mother, to the Tree
645   Of prohibition, root of all our woe;
    Which when she saw, thus to her guide she spake.
      Serpent, we might have spar'd our coming hither,
    Fruitless to mee, though Fruit be here to excess,
    The credit of whose virtue rest with thee,
650   Wondrous indeed, if cause of such effects.
    But of this Tree we may not taste nor touch;
    God so commanded, and left that Command
    Sole Daughter of his voice;[6] the rest, we live
    Law to ourselves, our Reason is our Law.
655   To whom the Tempter guilefully repli'd.
    Indeed? hath God then said that of the Fruit
    Of all these Garden Trees ye shall not eat,
    Yet Lords declar'd of all in Earth or Air?[7]
      To whom thus *Eve* yet sinless. Of the Fruit
660   Of each Tree in the Garden we may eat,
    But of the Fruit of this fair Tree amidst
    The Garden, God hath said, Ye shall not eat
    Thereof, nor shall ye touch it, lest ye die.
      She scarce had said, though brief, when now more bold
665   The Tempter, but with show of Zeal and Love
    To Man, and indignation at his wrong,
    New part puts on, and as to passion mov'd,
    Fluctuates disturb'd, yet comely, and in act
    Rais'd, as of some great matter to begin.
670   As when of old some Orator renown'd
    In *Athens* or free *Rome,* where Eloquence
    Flourish'd, since mute, to some great cause addrest,
    Stood in himself collected, while each part,
    Motion, each act won audience ere the tongue,
675   Sometimes in highth began, as no delay
    Of Preface brooking through his Zeal of Right.[8]
    So standing, moving, or to highth upgrown
    The Tempter all impassion'd thus began.
      O Sacred, Wise, and Wisdom-giving Plant,
680   Mother of Science,° now I feel thy Power   *knowledge*
    Within me clear, not only to discern
    Things in thir Causes, but to trace the ways
    Of highest Agents, deem'd however wise.

6. A Hebraism for "voice sent from heaven."
7. Lines 655–58 closely follow Genesis 3:1.
8. This simile blends oratorical, theatrical, and theological meanings. Thus "part" means "part of the body," "dra-matic role," and "moral act"; "motion" means "gesture," "mime" (or "puppet-show"), and "instigation, persuasive force, inclination"; "act" means "action," "performance of a play," and "the accomplished deed itself."

Queen of this Universe, do not believe
685   Those rigid threats of Death; ye shall not Die:
How should ye? by the Fruit? it gives you Life
To° Knowledge: By the Threat'ner? look on mee,   *in addition to*
Mee who have touch'd and tasted, yet both live,
And life more perfet have attain'd than Fate
690   Meant mee, by vent'ring higher than my Lot.
Shall that be shut to Man, which to the Beast
Is open? or will God incense his ire
For such a petty Trespass, and not praise
Rather your dauntless virtue, whom the pain
695   Of Death denounc't, whatever thing Death be,
Deterr'd not from achieving what might lead
To happier life, knowledge of Good and Evil;
Of good, how just? of evil, if what is evil
Be real, why not known, since easier shunn'd?[9]
700   God therefore cannot hurt ye, and be just;
Not just, not God; not fear'd then, nor obey'd:
Your fear itself of Death removes the fear.
Why then was this forbid? Why but to awe,
Why but to keep ye low and ignorant,
705   His worshippers; he knows that in the day
Ye Eat thereof, your Eyes that seem so clear,
Yet are but dim, shall perfetly be then
Op'n'd and clear'd, and ye shall be as Gods,
Knowing both Good and Evil as they know.[1]
710   That ye should be as Gods, since I as Man,
Internal Man,[2] is but proportion meet,
I of brute human, thee of human Gods.
So ye shall die perhaps, by putting off
Human, to put on Gods, death to be wisht,
715   Though threat'n'd, which no worse than this can bring.[3]
And what are Gods that Man may not become
As they, participating° God-like food?   *sharing*
The Gods are first, and that advantage use
On our belief, that all from them proceeds;
720   I question it, for this fair Earth I see,
Warm'd by the Sun, producing every kind,
Them nothing: If they° all things, who enclos'd   *if they produce*
Knowledge of Good and Evil in this Tree,
That who so eats thereof, forthwith attains
725   Wisdom without their leave? and wherein lies
Th' offense, that Man should thus attain to know?

9. If the knowledge is good, how is it just to prohibit it?
Here occurs the most egregious logical fallacy in speech.
(For evil to be "shunned," it is not at all necessary that it
should be "known" in the sense of being experienced.)
1. See Genesis 3:5.
2. The serpent's pretence is that his "inward powers" are

human.
3. Satan offers a travesty of Christian mortification and
death to sin; see Colossians 3:1–15: "ye have put off the
old man with his deeds; And have put on the new man,
which is renewed in knowledge after the image of him
that created him."

What can your knowledge hurt him, or this Tree
Impart against his will if all be his?
Or is it envy, and can envy dwell

730   In heav'nly breasts?[4] these, these and many more
Causes import° your need of this fair Fruit.   *suggest*
Goddess humane, reach then, and freely taste.
    He ended, and his words replete with guile
Into her heart too easy entrance won:

735   Fixt on the Fruit she gaz'd, which to behold
Might tempt alone, and in her ears the sound
Yet rung of his persuasive words, impregn'd°   *impregnated*
With Reason, to her seeming, and with Truth;
Meanwhile the hour of Noon drew on, and wak'd

740   An eager appetite, rais'd by the smell
So savory of that Fruit, which with desire,
Inclinable now grown to touch or taste,
Solicited her longing eye;[5] yet first
Pausing a while, thus to herself she mus'd.

745   Great are thy Virtues, doubtless, best of Fruits,
Though kept from Man, and worthy to be admir'd,
Whose taste, too long forborne, at first assay
Gave elocution to the mute, and taught
The Tongue not made for Speech to speak thy praise:[6]

750   Thy praise hee also who forbids thy use,
Conceals not from us, naming thee the Tree
Of Knowledge, knowledge both of good and evil;
Forbids us then to taste, but his forbidding
Commends thee more, while it infers the good

755   By thee communicated, and our want·
For good unknown, sure is not had, or had
And yet unknown, is as not had at all.
In plain° then, what forbids he but to know,   *plainly*
Forbids us good, forbids us to be wise?

760   Such prohibitions bind not. But if Death
Bind us with after-bands, what profits then
Our inward freedom? In the day we eat
Of this fair Fruit, our doom is, we shall die.
How dies the Serpent? hee hath eat'n and lives,

765   And knows, and speaks, and reasons, and discerns,
Irrational till then. For us alone
Was death invented? or to us deni'd
This intellectual food, for beasts reserv'd?
For Beasts it seems: yet that one Beast which first

770   Hath tasted, envies not, but brings with joy

---

4. See Virgil, *Aeneid* 1.11; Satan is inviting Eve to participate in a pagan epic, complete with machinery of jealous
gods.
5. For lines 735–43, see Genesis 3:6.

6. Eve has trusted Satan's account of the fruit and consequently argues from false premises, such as its magical
power.

The good befall'n him, Author unsuspect,[7]
Friendly to man, far from deceit or guile.
What fear I then, rather what know to fear[8]
Under this ignorance of Good and Evil,

775   Of God or Death, of Law or Penalty?
Here grows the Cure of all, this Fruit Divine,
Fair to the Eye, inviting to the Taste,
Of virtue° to make wise: what hinders then   *power*
To reach, and feed at once both Body and Mind?

780   So saying, her rash hand in evil hour
Forth reaching to the Fruit, she pluck'd, she eat:°   *ate*
Earth felt the wound, and Nature from her seat
Sighing through all her Works gave signs of woe,
That all was lost. Back to the Thicket slunk

785   The guilty Serpent, and well might, for *Eve*,
Intent now wholly on her taste, naught else
Regarded, such delight till then, as seem'd,
In Fruit she never tasted, whether true
Or fancied so, through expectation high

790   Of knowledge, nor was God-head from her thought.[9]
Greedily she ingorg'd without restraint,
And knew not eating Death:[1] Satiate at length,
And hight'n'd as with Wine, jocund and boon,°   *jolly*
Thus to herself she pleasingly began.

795   O Sovran, virtuous, precious of all Trees
In Paradise, of operation blest
To Sapience,[2] hitherto obscur'd, infam'd,°   *defamed*
And thy fair Fruit let hang, as to no end
Created; but henceforth my early care,

800   Not without Song, each Morning, and due praise
Shall tend thee, and the fertile burden ease
Of thy full branches offer'd free to all;
Till dieted by thee I grow mature
In knowledge, as the Gods who all things know;

805   Though others[3] envy what they cannot give;
For had the gift been theirs, it had not here
Thus grown. Experience, next to thee I owe,
Best guide; not following thee, I had remain'd
In ignorance, thou op'n'st Wisdom's way,

810   And giv'st access, though secret she retire.
And I perhaps am secret; Heav'n is high,
High and remote to see from thence distinct
Each thing on Earth; and other care perhaps

---

7. Eve means "informant not subject to suspicion."
8. What fear I, then—or rather (since I'm not allowed to
know anything) what do I know that is to be feared?
9. She expected to achieve godhead.
1. She knew not that she was eating death; "she was unaware, while she ate death" or even "she 'knew'"; not eating (immediate) death."
2. "Sapience" is derived from Latin *sapientia* (discernment,
taste) and ultimately from *sapere* (to taste).
3. I.e., God. Eve's language is now full of lapses in logic
and evasions in theology.

May have diverted from continual watch
815   Our great Forbidder, safe with all his Spies
About him. But to *Adam* in what sort
Shall I appear? shall I to him make known
As yet my change, and give him to partake
Full happiness with mee, or rather not.
820   But keep the odds of Knowledge in my power
Without Copartner? so to add what wants
In Female Sex, the more to draw his Love,
And render me more equal, and perhaps,
A thing not undesirable, sometime
825   Superior: for inferior who is free?
This may be well: but what if God have seen,
And Death ensue? then I shall be no more,
And *Adam* wedded to another *Eve*,
Shall live with her enjoying, I extinct;
830   A death to think. Confirm'd then I resolve,
Adam shall share with me in bliss or woe:
So dear I love him, that with him all deaths
I could endure, without him live no life.
      So saying, from the Tree her step she turn'd,
835   But first low Reverence done, as to the power
That dwelt within, whose presence had infus'd
Into the plant sciential⁴ sap, deriv'd
From Nectar, drink of Gods. *Adam* the while
Waiting desirous her return, had wove
840   Of choicest Flow'rs a Garland to adorn
Her Tresses, and her rural labors crown,
As Reapers oft are wont thir Harvest Queen.
Great joy he promis'd to his thoughts, and new
Solace in her return, so long delay'd;
845   Yet oft his heart, divine° of something ill,   *prophet*
Misgave him; hee the falt'ring measure⁵ felt;
And forth to meet her went, the way she took
That Morn when first they parted; by the Tree
Of Knowledge he must pass; there he her met,
850   Scarce from the Tree returning; in her hand
A bough of fairest fruit that downy smil'd,
New gather'd, and ambrosial smell diffus'd.
To him she hasted, in her face excuse
Came Prologue, and Apology to prompt,⁶
855   Which with bland words at will she thus addrest.
      Hast thou not wonder'd, *Adam,* at my stay?
Thee I have misst, and thought it long, depriv'd

4. Endowed with knowledge.
5. The rhythm of his own heart.
6. The expression on Eve's face is visible in advance as she approaches and so is like the prologue-speaker of a play. But it also remains on her face as she speaks, to help out her words, and so is like the prompter of the play. The actor prompted is Apology, i.e., justification or defense personified.

Thy presence, agony of love till now
Not felt, nor shall be twice, for never more
860   Mean I to try, what rash untri'd I sought,
The pain of absence from thy sight. But strange
Hath been the cause, and wonderful to hear:
This Tree is not as we are told, a Tree
Of danger tasted,° nor to evil unknown   *if tasted*
865   Op'ning the way, but of Divine effect
To open Eyes, and make them Gods who taste;
And hath been tasted such: the Serpent wise,
Or not restrain'd as wee, or not obeying,
Hath eat'n of the fruit, and is become,
870   Not dead, as we are threat'n'd, but thenceforth
Endu'd with human voice and human sense,
Reasoning to admiration, and with mee
Persuasively hath so prevail'd, that I
Have also tasted, and have also found
875   Th' effects to correspond, opener mine Eyes,
Dim erst, dilated Spirits, ampler Heart,
And growing up to Godhead; which for thee
Chiefly I sought, without thee can despise.
For bliss, as thou hast part, to me is bliss,
880   Tedious, unshar'd with thee, and odious soon.
Thou therefore also taste, that equal Lot
May join us, equal Joy, as equal Love;
Lest thou not tasting, different degree[7]
Disjoin us, and I then too late renounce
885   Deity for thee, when Fate will not permit.
         Thus *Eve* with Count'nance blithe her story told;
But in her Cheek distemper[8] flushing glow'd.
On th' other side, *Adam,* soon as he heard
The fatal Trespass done by *Eve,* amaz'd,
890   Astonied° stood and Blank, while horror chill   *stunned*
Ran through his veins, and all his joints relax'd;
From his slack hand the Garland wreath'd for *Eve,*
Down dropp'd, and all the faded Roses shed:
Speechless he stood and pale, till thus at length
895   First to himself he inward silence broke.
         O fairest of Creation, last and best
Of all God's Works, Creature in whom excell'd
Whatever can to sight or thought be form'd,
Holy, divine, good, amiable, or sweet!
900   How art thou lost, how on a sudden lost,
Defac't, deflow'r'd, and now to death devote?°   *given over*
Rather how hast thou yielded to transgress
The strict forbiddance, how to violate

---

7. Differing position in the scale of creatures.   8. A disordered condition due to disturbance of the temperament of the bodily humors.

The sacred Fruit forbidd'n! some cursed fraud
905   Of Enemy hath beguil'd thee, yet unknown,
And mee with thee hath ruin'd, for with thee
Certain my resolution is to Die;
How can I live without thee, how forgo
Thy sweet Converse and Love so dearly join'd,
910   To live again in these wild Woods forlorn?
Should God create another *Eve,* and I
Another Rib afford, yet loss of thee
Would never from my heart; no no, I feel
The Link of Nature draw me: Flesh of Flesh,
915   Bone of my Bone thou art, and from thy State
Mine never shall be parted, bliss or woe.
    So having said, as one from sad dismay
Recomforted, and after thoughts disturb'd
Submitting to what seem'd remediless,
920   Thus in calm mood his Words to *Eve* he turn'd.
    Bold deed thou hast presum'd, advent'rous *Eve,*
And peril great provok't, who thus hath dar'd
Had it been only coveting to Eye
That sacred Fruit, sacred° to abstinence,   *devoted*
925   Much more to taste it under ban to touch.
But past who can recall, or done undo?
Not God Omnipotent, nor Fate; yet so
Perhaps thou shalt not Die, perhaps the Fact°   *crime, deed*
Is not so heinous now, foretasted Fruit,
930   Profan'd first by the Serpent, by him first
Made common and unhallow'd ere our taste;
Nor yet on him found deadly, he yet lives,
Lives, as thou said'st, and gains to live as Man
Higher degree of Life, inducement strong
935   To us, as likely tasting to attain
Proportional ascent, which cannot be
But to be Gods, or Angels Demi-gods.
Nor can I think that God, Creator wise,
Though threat'ning, will in earnest so destroy
940   Us his prime Creatures, dignifi'd so high,
Set over all his Works, which in our Fall,
For us created, needs with us must fail,
Dependent made; so God shall uncreate,
Be frustrate, do, undo, and labor lose,
945   Not well conceiv'd of God, who though his Power
Creation could repeat, yet would be loath
Us to abolish, lest the Adversary
Triumph and say; Fickle their State whom God
Most Favors, who can please him long? Mee first
950   He ruin'd, now Mankind; whom will he next?
Matter of scorn, not to be given the Foe.
However I with thee have fixt my Lot,

Certain to undergo like doom;[9] if Death
Consort with thee, Death is to mee as Life;
955   So forcible within my heart I feel
The Bond of Nature draw me to my own,
My own in thee, for what thou art is mine;
Our State cannot be sever'd, we are one,
One Flesh; to lose thee were to lose myself.
960   So *Adam,* and thus *Eve* to him repli'd.
O glorious trial of exceeding Love,
Illustrious evidence, example high!
Ingaging me to emulate, but short
     Of thy perfection, how shall I attain,
965   *Adam,* from whose dear side I boast me sprung,
And gladly of our Union hear thee speak,
One Heart, one Soul in both; whereof good proof
This day affords, declaring thee resolv'd,
Rather than Death or aught than Death more dread
970   Shall separate us, linkt in Love so dear,
To undergo with mee one Guilt, one Crime,
If any be, of tasting this fair Fruit,
Whose virtue, for of good still good proceeds,
Direct, or by occasion[1] hath presented
975   This happy trial of thy Love, which else
So eminently never had been known.
Were it I thought Death menac't would ensue
This my attempt, I would sustain alone
The worst, and not persuade thee, rather die
980   Deserted, than oblige° thee with a fact   *make liable*
Pernicious to thy Peace, chiefly assur'd
Remarkably so late of thy so true,
So faithful Love unequall'd; but I feel
Far otherwise th' event,° nor Death, but Life   *result*
985   Augmented, op'n'd Eyes, new Hopes, new Joys,
Taste so Divine, that what of sweet before
Hath toucht my sense, flat seems to this, and harsh.
On my experience, *Adam,* freely taste,
And fear of Death deliver to the Winds.
990   So saying, she embrac'd him, and for joy
Tenderly wept, much won that he his Love
Had so ennobl'd, as of choice to incur
Divine displeasure for her sake, or Death.
In recompense (for such compliance bad
995   Such recompense best merits) from the bough
She gave him of that fair enticing Fruit
With liberal hand: he scrupl'd not to eat
Against his better knowledge, not deceiv'd,

---

9. Three separate meanings are possible: judgment, irrevocable destiny, and death.

1. I.e., directly or indirectly.

	But fondly overcome with Female charm.[2]
1000	Earth trembl'd from her entrails, as again
	In pangs, and Nature gave a second groan,
	Sky low'r'd, and muttering Thunder, some sad drops
	Wept at completing of the mortal Sin
	Original;[3] while *Adam* took no thought,
1005	Eating his fill, nor *Eve* to iterate
	Her former trespass fear'd, the more to soothe
	Him with her lov'd society, that now
	As with new Wine intoxicated both
	They swim in mirth, and fancy that they feel
1010	Divinity within them breeding wings
	Wherewith to scorn the Earth: but that false Fruit
	Far other operation first display'd,
	Carnal desire inflaming, hee on *Eve*
	Began to cast lascivious Eyes, she him
1015	As wantonly repaid; in Lust they burn:
	Till *Adam* thus 'gan *Eve* to dalliance move.

> *Eve,* now I see thou are exact of taste,
> And elegant, of Sapience[4] no small part,
> Since to each meaning savor[5] we apply,
> 1020 And Palate call judicious; I the praise
> Yield thee, so well this day thou hast purvey'd.°   *provided*
> Much pleasure we have lost, while we abstain'd
> From this delightful Fruit, nor known till now
> True relish, tasting; if such pleasure be
> 1025 In things to us forbidden, it might be wish'd,
> For this one Tree had been forbidden ten.
> But come, so well refresh't, now let us play,
> As meet is, after such delicious Fare;
> For never did thy Beauty since the day
> 1030 I saw thee first and wedded thee, adorn'd
> With all perfections, so inflame my sense
> With ardor to enjoy thee, fairer now
> Than ever, bounty of this virtuous Tree.[6]

	So said he, and forbore not glance or toy° *caress*
1035	Of amorous intent, well understood
	Of° *Eve,* whose Eye darted contagious Fire. *by*
	Her hand he seiz'd, and to a shady bank,
	Thick overhead with verdant roof imbowr'd
	He led her nothing loath; Flow'rs were the Couch,
1040	Pansies, and Violets, and Asphodel,

2. See 1 Timothy 2:14: "And Adam was not deceived, but the woman being deceived was in the transgression."
3. The only occurrence in *Paradise Lost* of the term "Original Sin." In his *De doctrina* (1.11), Milton defines Original Sin as "the sin which is common to all men, that which our first parents, and in them all their posterity committed, when, casting off their obedience to God, they tasted the fruit of the forbidden tree."
4. Wisdom, from Latin *sapere,* to taste.
5. Tastiness, understanding.
6. See Homer, *Iliad* 14, where Hera, bent on deceiving Zeus, comes to him wearing Aphrodite's belt and seems more charming to him than ever before.

And Hyacinth, Earth's freshest softest lap.
There they thir fill of Love and Love's disport
Took largely, of thir mutual guilt the Seal,
The solace of thir sin, till dewy sleep
1045   Oppress'd them, wearied with thir amorous play.
Soon as the force of that fallacious Fruit,
That with exhilarating vapor bland°   *pleasing*
About thir spirits had play'd, and inmost powers
Made err, was now exhal'd, and grosser sleep
1050   Bred of unkindly fumes,[7] with conscious dreams
Encumber'd, now had left them, up they rose
As from unrest, and each the other viewing,
Soon found thir Eyes how op'n'd, and thir minds
How dark'n'd;[8] innocence, that as a veil
1055   Had shadow'd them from knowing ill, was gone,
Just confidence, and native righteousness,
And honor from about them, naked left
To guilty shame: hee cover'd, but his Robe
Uncover'd more. So rose the *Danite* strong
1060   *Herculean Samson* from the Harlot-lap
Of *Philistean Dalilah,* and wak'd
Shorn of his strength, They destitute and bare
Of all thir virtue:[9] silent, and in face
Confounded long they sat, as struck'n mute,
1065   Till *Adam,* though not less than *Eve* abasht,
At length gave utterance to these words constrain'd.
     O *Eve,* in evil hour thou didst give ear
To that false Worm, of whomsoever taught
To counterfeit Man's voice, true in our Fall,
1070   False in our promis'd Rising; since our Eyes
Op'n'd we find indeed, and find we know
Both Good and Evil, Good lost, and Evil got,
Bad Fruit of Knowledge, if this be to know,
Which leaves us naked thus, of Honor void,
1075   Of Innocence, of Faith, of Purity,
Our wonted Ornaments now soil'd and stain'd,
And in our Faces evident the signs
Of foul concupiscence; whence evil store;
Even shame, the last of evils; of the first
1080   Be sure then. How shall I behold the face
Henceforth of God or Angel, erst with joy
And rapture so oft beheld? those heav'nly shapes
Will dazzle now this earthly, with thir blaze
Insufferably bright. O might I here
1085   In solitude live savage, in some glade

---

7. Unnatural vapors or exhalations rising from the stomach to the brain.
8. See Genesis 3:7: "The eyes of them both were opened, and they knew that they were naked."
9. See Judges 16 for the story of Samson's betrayal by Delilah.

Obscur'd, where highest Woods impenetrable
To Star or Sun-light, spread thir umbrage broad,
And brown as Evening: Cover me ye Pines,
Ye Cedars, with innumerable boughs
1090   Hide me, where I may never see them more.
But let us now, as in bad plight, devise
What best may for the present serve to hide
The Parts of each from other, that seem most
To shame obnoxious,° and unseemliest seen,   *exposed*
1095   Some Tree whose broad smooth Leaves together sew'd,
And girded on our loins, may cover round
Those middle parts, that this new comer, Shame,
There sit not, and reproach us as unclean.[1]
        So counsell'd hee, and both together went
1100   Into the thickest Wood, there soon they chose
The Figtree,[2] not that kind for Fruit renown'd,
But such as at this day to *Indians* known
In *Malabar* or *Decan* spreads her Arms
Branching so broad and long, that in the ground
1105   The bended Twigs take root, and Daughters grow
About the Mother Tree, a Pillar'd shade
High overarch't, and echoing Walks between;
There oft the *Indian* Herdsman shunning heat
Shelters in cool, and tends his pasturing Herds
1110   At Loopholes cut through thickest shade: Those Leaves
They gather'd, broad as Amazonian Targe,°   *shield*
And with what skill they had, together sew'd,
To gird thir waist, vain Covering if to hide
Thir guilt and dreaded shame; O how unlike
1115   To that first naked Glory. Such of late
Columbus found th' *American* so girt
With feather'd Cincture,° naked else and wild   *belt*
Among the Trees on Isles and woody Shores.
Thus fenc't, and as they thought, thir shame in part
1120   Cover'd, but not at rest or ease of Mind,
They sat them down to weep, nor only Tears
Rain'd at thir Eyes, but high Winds worse within
Began to rise, high Passions, Anger, Hate,
Mistrust, Suspicion, Discord, and shook sore
1125   Thir inward State of Mind, calm Region once
And full of Peace, now toss't and turbulent:
For Understanding rul'd not, and the Will
Heard not her lore, both in subjection now
To sensual Appetite, who from beneath
1130   Usurping over sovran Reason claim'd
Superior sway: From thus distemper'd breast,

---

1. See Genesis 3:7.   2. Milton's description of the banyan or Indian fig comes
                                       from Gerard's *Herball* (1597).

Adam, estrang'd in look and alter'd style,
Speech intermitted thus to *Eve* renew'd.
    Would thou hadst heark'n'd to my words, and stay'd
1135   With me, as I besought thee, when that strange
Desire of wand'ring this unhappy Morn,
I know not whence possess'd thee; we had then
Remain'd still happy, not as now, despoil'd
Of all our good, sham'd, naked, miserable.
1140   Let none henceforth seek needless cause to approve°   *give proof of*
The Faith they owe;[3] when earnestly they seek
Such proof, conclude, they then begin to fail.
    To whom soon mov'd with touch of blame thus *Eve.*
What words have past thy Lips,[4] *Adam* severe,
1145   Imput'st thou that to my default, or will
Of wand'ring, as thou call'st it, which who knows
But might as ill have happ'n'd thou being by,
Or to thyself perhaps: hadst thou been there,
Or here th' attempt, thou couldst not have discern'd
1150   Fraud in the Serpent, speaking as he spake;
No ground of enmity between us known,
Why hee should mean me ill, or seek to harm.
Was I to have never parted from thy side?
As good have grown there still a lifeless Rib.
1155   Being as I am, why didst not thou the Head[5]
Command me absolutely not to go,
Going into such danger as thou said'st?
Too facile° then thou didst not much gainsay,   *permissive*
Nay, didst permit, approve, and fair dismiss.
1160   Hadst thou been firm and fixt in thy dissent,
Neither had I transgress'd, nor thou with mee.
    To whom then first incenst Adam repli'd.
Is this the Love, is this the recompense
Of mine to thee, ingrateful *Eve,* express't
1165   Immutable° when thou wert lost, not I,   *unchangeable*
Who might have liv'd and joy'd immortal bliss,
Yet willingly chose rather Death with thee:
And am I now upbraided, as the cause
Of thy transgressing? not enough severe,
1170   It seems, in thy restraint: what could I more?
I warn'd thee, I admonish'd thee, foretold
The danger, and the lurking Enemy
That lay in wait; beyond this had been force,
And force upon free Will hath here no place.
1175   But confidence then bore thee on, secure
Either to meet no danger, or to find

---

3. Be under obligation to render or possess.
4. Echoes Odysseus's disapproval of a speech of Agamem-
non's (*Iliad* 14.83).

5. Alludes to 1 Corinthians 11:3: "The head of every man
is Christ; and the head of the woman is the man; and the
head of Christ is God."

Matter of glorious trial; and perhaps
I also err'd in overmuch admiring
What seem'd in thee so perfet, that I thought
1180   No evil durst attempt thee, but I rue
That error now, which is become my crime,
And thou th' accuser. Thus it shall befall
Him who to worth in Woman overtrusting
Lets her Will rule; restraint she will not brook,
1185   And left to herself, if evil thence ensue,
Shee first his weak indulgence will accuse.
        Thus they in mutual accusation spent
The fruitless hours, but neither self-condemning,
And of thir vain contést appear'd no end.[6]

from Book 12

        He° ended; and thus *Adam* last repli'd.   *Michael*
How soon hath thy prediction, Seer blest,
Measur'd this transient World, the Race of time,
555   Till time stand fixt: beyond is all abyss,
Eternity, whose end no eye can reach.
Greatly instructed I shall hence depart,
Greatly in peace of thought, and have my fill
Of knowledge, what this Vessel can contain;
560   Beyond which was my folly to aspire.
Henceforth I learn, that to obey is best,
And love with fear the only God, to walk
As in his presence, ever to observe
His providence, and on him sole depend,
565   Merciful over all his works, with good
Still overcoming evil, and by small
Accomplishing great things, by things deem'd weak
Subverting worldly strong, and worldly wise
By simply meek; that suffering for Truth's sake
570   Is fortitude to highest victory,
And to the faithful Death the Gate of Life;
Taught this by his example whom I now
Acknowledge my Redeemer ever blest.
        To whom thus also th' Angel last repli'd;
575   This having learnt, thou hast attain'd the sum
Of wisdom; hope no higher, though all the Stars
Thou knew'st by name, and all th' ethereal Powers,
All secrets of the deep, all Nature's works,
Or works of God in Heav'n, Air, Earth, or Sea,
580   And all the riches of this World enjoy'dst,

6. God visits his judgment on Adam and Eve, as well as on Satan and his followers, who are turned into serpents. Adam and Eve languish in despair, turning to God in "sorrow unfeign'd," and at Christ's request, God sends Michael to show Adam what will happen before the flood (Book 11) and then to tell him of Christ and man's redemption in Book 12.

And all the rule, one Empire; only add
Deeds to thy knowledge answerable, add Faith,
Add Virtue, Patience, Temperance, add Love,
By name to come call'd Charity, the soul

585 Of all the rest:[1] then wilt thou not be loath
To leave this Paradise, but shalt possess
A paradise within thee, happier far.
Let us descend now therefore from this top
Of Speculation;[2] for the hour precise

590 Exacts our parting hence; and see the Guards,
By mee encampt on yonder Hill, expect
Thir motion,[3] at whose Front a flaming Sword,
In signal of remove, waves fiercely round;
We may no longer stay: go, waken *Eve;*

595 Her also I with gentle Dreams have calm'd
Portending good, and all her spirits compos'd
To meek submission: thou at season fit
Let her with thee partake what thou hast heard,
Chiefly what may concern her Faith to know,

600 The great deliverance by her Seed to come
(For by the Woman's Seed)[4] on all Mankind,
That ye may live, which will be many days,[5]
Both in one Faith unanimous though sad,
With cause for evils past, yet much more cheer'd

605 With meditation on the happy end.
He ended, and they both descend the Hill;
Descended, *Adam* to the Bow'r where *Eve*
Lay sleeping ran before, but found her wak't;
And thus with words not sad she him receiv'd.

610 Whence thou return'st, and whither went'st, I know;
For God is also in sleep, and Dreams advise,
Which he hath sent propitious, some great good
Presaging, since with sorrow and heart's distress
Wearied I fell asleep: but now lead on;

615 In mee is no delay; with thee to go,
Is to stay here; without thee here to stay,
Is to go hence unwilling; thou to mee
Art all things under Heav'n, all places thou,
Who for my wilful crime art banisht hence.[6]

620 This further consolation yet secure
I carry hence; though all by mee is lost,

---

1. Compare 2 Peter 1:5–7: "Add to your faith virtue; and
to virtue knowledge; and to knowledge temperance; and
to temperance patience; and to patience godliness; and to
godliness brotherly kindness; and to brotherly kindness
charity."
2. Vantage point but also height of theological speculation.
3. Await deployment, marching orders.

4. Alluding to the birth of Jesus.
5. Adam lived to be 930 years of age (Genesis 5:5).
6. Eve has assimilated Michael's exhortation at 11.292:
"where [Adam] abides, think there thy native soil." There
is also a resonance with Eve's song at 4.635–56 (every
time of day is pleasing with Adam, none is pleasing without him).

Such favor I unworthy am voutsaf't,
By mee the Promis'd Seed shall all restore.
    So spake our Mother *Eve,* and *Adam* heard
625 Well pleas'd, but answer'd not; for now too nigh
Th' Arch-Angel stood, and from the other Hill
To thir fixt Station, all in bright array
The Cherubim descended; on the ground
Gliding meteorous,° as Ev'ning Mist   *meteoric*
630 Ris'n from a River o'er the marish° glides,   *marsh*
And gathers ground fast at the Laborer's heel
Homeward returning. High in Front advanc't,
The brandisht Sword of God before them blaz'd
Fierce as a Comet; which with torrid heat,
635 And vapor as the *Libyan* Air adust,°   *scorched*
Began to parch that temperate Clime; whereat
In either hand the hast'ning Angel caught
Our ling'ring Parents, and to th' Eastern Gate
Led them direct, and down the Cliff as fast
640 To the subjected° Plain; then disappear'd.   *underlying*
They looking back, all th' Eastern side beheld
Of Paradise, so late thir happy seat,
Wav'd over by that flaming Brand,[7] the Gate
With dreadful Faces throng'd and fiery Arms:
645 Some natural tears they dropp'd, but wip'd them soon;
The World was all before them, where to choose
Thir place of rest, and Providence thir guide:[8]
They hand in hand with wand'ring steps and slow,
Through *Eden* took thir solitary way.

The End

7. See Genesis. 3:24: "a flaming sword which turned
every way."

8. Note that "Providence" can be the object of "choose":
decisions of faith lie ahead.

Mayan relief of Lady Xoc, c. 700 C.E. Queen of the city of Yaxchilán in southern Mexico in the early 700s, Lady Xoc is shown in several beautifully carved frescos in her city's major temple. Here she makes an offering to the fire serpent god Xiuhcoatl, who curves upward from her brazier, disgorging an armed warrior from his mouth. The serpent is framed in hieroglyphs that function as integral parts of the sculpture.

Mesoamerica:
Before Columbus and After Cortés

New worlds are constantly being discovered in early modern literature. In 1516, Sir Thomas More claimed that one of Amerigo Vespucci's sailors had gone on from Brazil to find the ideal island republic of *Utopia*. At the close of the early modern period, Milton's Satan voyages from Hell to the "boundless Continent" of Earth, where he hopes to increase his "Honor and Empire . . . / By conquering this new World" (*Paradise Lost* 4.390–91). The rapid expansion of European exploration and settlement involved discoveries in both directions. In one Aztec poem from around 1550, the poet describes traveling to Rome to meet Pope Clement VII:

> The pope is on God's mat and seat and speaks for him.
> Who is this reclining on a golden chair? Look! It's the pope.
> He has his turquoise blowgun and he's shooting in the world.
> It seems it's true, he has his cross and golden staff,
> and these are shining in the world.

European as well as native writers soon began to give their works a double perspective. In Shakespeare's *Tempest,* when Miranda exclaims "O brave new world / That has such people in't!," she is expressing the astonishment of an inhabitant of a distant island on first encountering the *Europeans* who have been shipwrecked on her shore. "'Tis new to thee," her father curtly replies: one person's "new" can be another person's "old" world, and their comparative merits may lie in the eye of the beholder as well.

ORIGINS AND EARLY HISTORY

The New World could be a paradise of innocence and natural harmony, free from the corruption and decay of the European world; or it could be a region of primitive savagery, ripe for conversion, settlement, and economic exploitation. The Europeans who encountered the natives of the Americas wondered what to make of them and where they could have come from. Were they "aborigines," present in these lands from the first creation of the world—a wholly separate human race—or had they somehow migrated from the "old" world? Particularly surprising were the populous and sophisticated cultures of the Aztecs in Mexico, the Maya in Guatemala and the Yucatan Peninsula, and the Inca in Peru: perhaps, the explorers speculated, they were the descendants of the Lost Tribes of Israel? Mistaken in their attempt to connect the native populations to sacred biblical history, the early explorers were right in suspecting that these Americans had, in fact, migrated from the Eurasian landmass. They had come, though, not from Palestine but from east Asia, and they had arrived not in biblical times but between ten and twenty thousand years ago, in waves of migration across the Bering Straits to Alaska and then gradually southward.

Settled agriculture had begun by 6500 B.C.E. in the region scholars call Meso-america: central and southern Mexico, the Yucatan Peninsula, and the northern portion of Central America. Corn became the most fundamental crop, together with beans and squashes, tomatoes, and also chilies and chocolate: *tomatl, chilli,* and *chocolatl* are the original names for these last three foods in the Aztecs' language of Nahuatl. The region's fertile soil and favorable climate supported the growth of the largest population in the Americas; at the time of the Conquest, some twenty million people lived in Mesoamerica. Cities began to form in the first millennium B.C.E., dominated by pyramid temples, and two groups built regional empires: the Maya in the south and east and a group in central Mexico who built the great city known as Teotihuacán, later associated with a shadowy group called the Toltecs.

These early empires collapsed by around 900 C.E., apparently as a result of some combination of climatic change, overpopulation, and warfare. The Maya continued to be the major presence in their region, chiefly in the form of small groups speaking many different dialects and languages, practicing subsistence farming in the Guatemalan highlands and along the Yucatan coast; Chichén Itzá and other ancient lowland cities were abandoned. Teotihuacán too was largely deserted; even its name as we know it today was given by the later-arriving Aztecs: they thought its stupendous monuments must be divine work and named it "City of the Gods."

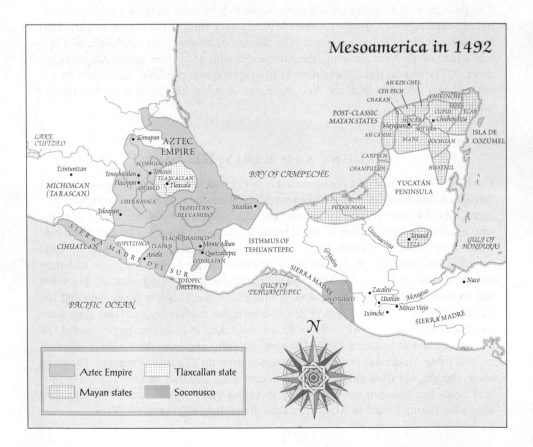

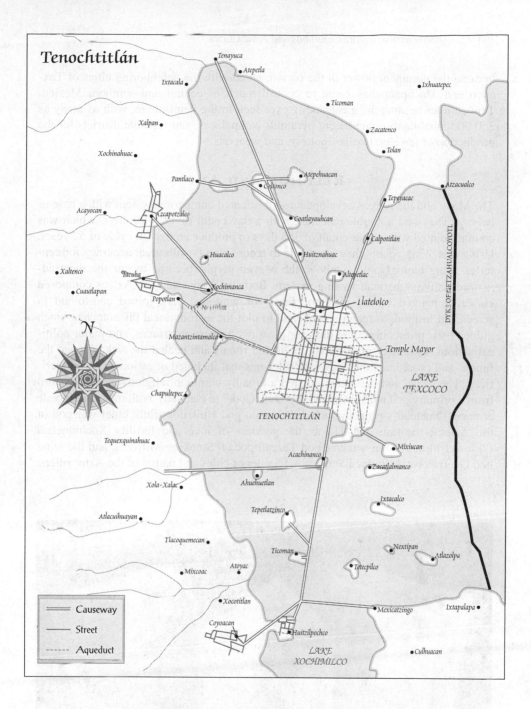

Tenochtitlán

Tenayuca
Atepetla
Ixtacala
Ixhuatepec
Ticoman
Xalpan
Zacatenco
Xochinahuac
Tolan
Atepehuacan
Pantlaco
Coltonco
Acayocan
Coatlayauhcan
Tepeyacac
Azcapotzalco
Calpotitlan
Huacalco
Huitznahuac
Xaltenco
Altepetlac
Tacuba
Cuautlapan
Xochimanca
Tlatelolco
Popotlan
Nextlalpan
Mazantzintamalco
Temple Mayor
LAKE
TEXCOCO
Chapultepec
TENOCHTITLÁN
Tequexquinahuac
Míxiucan
Acachinanco
Zacatlalmanco
Xola-Xalac
Ahuehuetlan
Ixtacalco
Atlacuihuayan
Tepetlatzinco
Tlacoquemecan
Ticoman
Nextipan
Atlazolpa
Míxcoac
Atoyac
Tetecpilco
Xocotitlan
Mexicatzingo
Ixtapalapa
Coyacan
Huitzilpochco
Culhuacan
LAKE
XOCHIMILCO

DYKE OF NETZAHUALCOYOTL

N

- ── Causeway
- ── Street
- ----- Aqueduct

When the Aztecs had migrated into central Mexico from the arid north in the thirteenth century, they were forced to settle in undesirable marshlands around the large lake in the Valley of Mexico. There, they took advantage of their strategic position to trade around the lake and to build extensive *chimalpas,* "floating gardens" extending into the lake. They gradually expanded a pair of islands into their double capital city, Tenochtitlán-Tlatelolco. During the reign of a king named Itzcoatl (1428–1440) they became the dominant power in the region; allied with the neighboring cities of Texcoco and Tlacopan, they came to control much of central and southern Mexico. Tenochtitlán became the greatest city ever seen in the hemisphere, with as many as 350,000 inhabitants, magnificent pyramids and palaces, and separate districts for the production of jewelry, textiles, pottery, and weapons.

Religion and Art

The Maya and the Aztecs developed a sophisticated numbering system with a base of twenty. They had a double calendar, with a day count of 13×20 days, which was counterpointed with a year count of 365 days to produce an overall cycle of 52 years. Using this "long count" they were able to record events with great accuracy for centuries using hieroglyphic symbols; the Mayan glyphs became by far the most advanced native American writing system. Both the Maya and the Aztecs composed elaborate painted books, made of sheets of whitened bark joined end-to-end in screenfold fashion, to record events and to plot the astronomical phenomena, which guided their priests in setting days for planting, harvest, marriages, and major political actions. Extensive priesthoods conducted rituals and healed the sick, divined the future, and propitiated the gods with offerings that included occasional human sacrifices. The Maya and the Aztecs shared a broadly common religious pantheon, born from a primary god named Ometeotl ("Dual God," in Nahuatl), both male and female at once. Ometeotl's progeny included the sun god Huitzilopochtli, chief war god of the Aztecs; the rain god Tlaloc; the goddess of love and fertility Xochiquetzal ("Flower Plume"); the sorcerer god Tezcatlipoca ("Smoking Mirror"); and the wind god Quetzalcoatl ("Plumed Serpent"), founder of cities and patron of the Aztec rulers.

Aztec screenfold book c. 1500.

At the time of the Conquest, the divine Quetzalcoatl was often merged with a legendary Toltec king named Ce Acatl Quetzalcoatl, who was said to have sailed east across the Caribbean to found the Yucatecan ritual center of Chichén Itzá or Tulan, a city whose surviving structures do in fact show affinities with the monuments of Teotihuacán and the Toltec capital of Tollan. Both the Maya and the Aztecs believed that Quetzalcoatl (Kulkulcan in Mayan) would one day return across the Caribbean Sea to resume his rule—a legend that Hernán Cortés would later exploit to his advantage. Conversely, in colonial times the Maya didn't hesitate to adapt Christian legends to their own purposes. In 1554, the lords of the Mayan city of Totonicapán bolstered their rights to the land by identifying their culture hero, Balam-Qitzé, with Moses. Claiming that their ancestors had come from across the sea, they declared that when their ancestors arrived at the edge of the ocean, "Balam-Qitzé touched it with his staff and at once a path opened, which then closed up again, for thus the great God wished it to be done, because they were sons of Abraham and Jacob."

Whether founded by individuals or the product of slow growth, the major Mesoamerican cities became both religious and political centers, with temple and court establishments centered on magnificent temple pyramids and lavish palaces, filled with frescoes and elaborate furnishings, and surrounded by pleasure gardens. The cities also had extensive playing grounds for the ball games to which the Mesoamericans were addicted, in which two teams would attempt to get a rubber ball through the opposing side's goal, using their upper arms and thighs but not their hands. Often played purely for sport, these games came also to be played for ritual purposes, with the losing team providing human sacrifices to the gods.

There was much literary activity, more in oral than written form, as hieroglyphics were used as prompts to memory rather than to compose freestanding texts. Mythological and historical tales were told and retold, most memorably recorded in the Mayan *Popol Vuh* or Council Book, and hymns and songs were sung to the accompaniment of flutes, drums, and rattles. Among the Aztecs in particular, court poetry became a highly developed art, with cadres of talented young singers trained in *cuicacalli* or "houses of song." Songs would be written by a lyricist (*cuicapiqui*) collaborating with a composer (*cuicacano*), their productions carefully checked for content by a "conservator" or censor.

Often performed for entertainment at court, poems could also be turned to military as well as religious use: adolescent warriors were taught inspiring songs and dances in the group houses where they lived while in training. The large output of poetry led to an increasingly rich and aesthetically self-aware body of poems, some three hundred of which survive, chiefly in two manuscripts of the early colonial period, the *Cantares Mexicanos* and the *Romances de los Señores de la Nueva España* (Ballads of the Lords of New Spain), which together preserve the largest body of early Amerindian poetry ever recorded.

The region's cultures were not at all advanced technologically—most tools were of stone or wood; goods had to be carried by people, as the Mesoamericans didn't use beasts of burden or even the wheel. Yet the Mayan and Aztec artisans developed remarkably delicate artworks. They were especially adept in mosaic work using semiprecious stones like turquoise, and they made pottery figures of a charming and often humorous realism. They made jewelry of silver and gold, but they placed highest

Mayan ballplayers. These lively ceramic figures boldly await the ball; they are protected with heavy padding and wear yokes around their waists to deflect blows.

value on two materials: durable jade and delicate bird plumes, especially the turquoise feathers of the quetzal bird, which decorated many objects and could be made into entire robes.

Widely distributed across Mesoamerica, during the century before the Conquest these skills became increasingly concentrated in the Aztec capital of Tenochtitlán and in the major cities of their allies. As the Aztecs built their empire, the difficulties of transportation and supply made it hard to carry on sustained warfare at any distance from home; instead, the Aztecs extended their sway by complex negotiations and a policy of selective, exemplary violence. According to later native chronicles, this policy was developed by the emperor Itzcoatl's chief adviser, Tlacaelel, beginning in the late 1420s. Tlacaelel vastly expanded the scope of human sacrifice, elaborating a politically useful theology according to which the life of the gods, and the present age of the world itself, could only be sustained by the frequent offering of human hearts. Where human sacrifice had formerly been a regular but small-scale practice among both the Maya and the Aztecs, under Tlacaelel it became widespread, with thousands of foreign captives being sacrificed on major festivals, in a theater of terror to which neighboring rulers were pointedly invited.

The Aztecs even appear to have left at least one nearby people unconquered so as to provide a ready supply of victims and to keep their own allies in line. According to Diego Durán's *History of the Indies of New Spain* (1581), Tlacaelel once justified this reign of terror by asserting that the war god Huitzilopochtli wouldn't accept sacrifices from distant regions: "Those places are too remote," Tlacaelel says, "and, furthermore, our god does not like the flesh of those barbarous people. They are like hard, yellowish, tasteless tortillas in his mouth." Sacrificial victims from nearby cities, on the other hand, "will come to our god like warm tortillas, soft, tasty, straight from the fire." By the early 1500s, the Aztecs' enemies and even most of their allies were bitterly resentful of the Aztecs' sacrifices, heavy taxation, and conscription of youths to serve as warriors and build temples and palaces. They were more than ready for things to change.

THE EUROPEANS ARRIVE

The traditional Amerindian cultures are often called "pre-Columbian," literally referring to the era before Columbus's voyage of 1492, and more generally including the period before a given culture's first substantial European contact, which for much of Mesoamerica meant the invasion of Hernán Cortés between 1519 and 1521. In letters to Queen Isabella of Spain, Columbus himself was the first European to write about his wonder at the scattered native populations he found on the Caribbean islands he discovered on his voyages. He never found the Asian cities he was sure he would find, nor did he go far enough west to discover the great cities of the Aztecs and their allies on the mainland. To the end of his life, in fact, Columbus continued to insist that he hadn't discovered a new world at all but a new route to Asia; hence the native inhabitants came to be called "Indians," as though their lands were outposts of India.

It was an Italian explorer, Amerigo Vespucci, who sailed south along the coast of South America in 1499 and 1501 and who insisted that the extensive lands he was seeing must represent an entirely unknown continent. In honor of his discoveries, an early mapmaker named his newly found land "America." For twenty-five years after Columbus's first voyage, a steadily increasing trickle of European adventurers came to the region, settling many of the Caribbean islands and driving off or enslaving the natives who survived the diseases they brought with them. In the early 1500s the Spanish began tentatively exploring the coasts of the Yucatan and northern South America. They heard rumors of wealthy cities far inland, but the first efforts to penetrate the mainland were repelled by hostile natives who had learned of the fate of the native islanders.

The decisive breakthrough came in 1519 when Hernán Cortés, then only the mayor of a town in Cuba, assembled a pick-up army of five hundred men and sixteen horses and determined to march directly into the heart of Mexico and conquer it for his monarch, Emperor Charles V. As he and his men proceeded inland, they learned of the vast wealth of the Aztec empire—and of the resentment felt by many of the Aztecs' neighbors at their treatment by their overlords. Cortés boldly marched into the Aztec capital Tenochtitlán, settled into lodgings offered him by the king, Moctezuma, and began plotting. Over the course of the next two and a half years, Cortés gradually created alliances with the Aztecs' enemies—and their restless allies—and after a series of conflicts he succeeded in overthrowing the Aztecs and destroying Tenochtitlán in a protracted battle. (See Perspectives: The Conquest and Its Aftermath, page 810, for more about these events.) By August of 1521, Cortés was in effective control of Mexico. Before long, however, bitter opposition from enemies in Cuba and back in Spain left Cortés on the sidelines of colonial rule, but he retained vast estates and the grand title of "Marquis of the Valley of Oaxaca."

Frustrated in his ambition to rule Mexico, in 1524 Cortés mounted a new expedition of exploration and conquest into the jungles of Honduras, but this expedition was a disaster. He barely emerged alive, to find that his enemies had seized much of his property and had seriously damaged his reputation with the Spanish court. He spent the rest of his life trying unsuccessfully to restore his fortunes and his credit. His example, however, had already inspired other adventurers. His lieutenant, Pedro de Alvarado, conquered the highland Mayan center of Guatemala in 1523, and in 1532 another Spaniard, Francisco Pizarro, took a small force to Peru, home of the other greatest New World empire, that of the Inca. Taking a page from Cortés's widely read letters to King Charles on his conquest, Pizarro professed friendship for the Incan emperor Atahualpa, then seized him, extracted ransom, and executed him. Peru was soon another Spanish colony, famed especially for the vast amounts of silver extracted from its mines by the forced labor of native workers. With the region's great empires defeated, the New World was open to piecemeal conquest and settlement by Europe, with Portuguese settlers gaining control over Brazil, the Spanish dominating the rest of South and Central America, and Spanish, French, and English colonizers vying for control over North America.

THE COLONIAL PERIOD, AND BEYOND

The colonial period lasted in the Mesoamerican region until Mexico and Guatemala achieved independence from Spain in 1821. At that time, Mexico's territory included Texas, California, and much of the American southwest; in a series of conflicts with the growing United States, the present borders were eventually established in 1848. During the early colonial period, the Spanish settlers sharply debated the terms of their responsibility toward the native inhabitants. Some Europeans believed that the Indians weren't fully human, and slavery was the best they could expect; others, like the missionary friar Bartolomé de Las Casas, argued passionately that the Indians—or at least those who converted to Christianity—deserved to be treated as citizens and should have the full protection of the law.

Conversion of the natives to Christianity was a major emphasis. Cortés brought several Franciscan friars with him, and constantly tried to have his native hosts tear down their "idols" and replace them with images of Christ and the Virgin Mary. Soon after the conquest, the Pope sent a dozen missionaries, their number symbolically matching Jesus's twelve apostles, and conversion efforts began in earnest. The friars soon realized that preaching alone was not going to suffice, and they developed an elaborate body of dramatic literature, in Spanish and in native languages, to convey the gospel message and its meaning. The great seventeenth-century poet Sor Juana Inés de la Cruz (Color Plate 8) wrote several of these plays, prior to her death while aiding victims of plague; one play explicitly makes allowance for the Aztec *dios de las semillas* ("god of the seeds") within the new Christian order.

As it evolved, Catholicism in Mexico took on elements of traditional forms of worship, such as the use of sacred dances with masked figures. Stories of death and resurrection had been central to native American religions as well as to Christianity, and an attachment to ancestral gods could be adapted to making offerings and prayers to saints. Such similarities could become unsettling for missionaries; as one Jesuit in Peru complained in the early seventeenth century, the Inca were becoming far too skilled at "carrying water on both shoulders." A shrine to the Virgin Mary was estab-

The Virgin of Guadalupe on a cactus, from Miguel Sánchez, *Images of the Virgin Mary, Mother of God of Guadalupe* (1648). The Creole priest Miguel Sánchez was the first to collect the varied oral traditions circulating about the appearance of the Virgin Mary to young Juan Diego and turn them into a celebration of Mexican pride. His reading of the Book of Revelation, the last book in the New Testament, led him to associate the "woman clothed with the sun" and possessed of eagle's wings, with the Virgin of Guadalupe. This image from Sánchez's popular book turns the humble lady seen by the Juan Diego into this apocalyptic figure, while the author also has recourse to the coat of arms of the ancient Aztec capital, Tenochtitlán, for further details: the "device" of the city had been "a royal eagle on a cactus." In placing the Virgin herself on the prickly-pear cactus, Sánchez achieves a fascinating mix of biblical prophecy and native Mexican lore.

lished in the provincial city of Guadalupe, after the Virgin appeared in a vision to a native peasant on a hill that had been the site of a temple to Tonantzin, the mother of the gods. Images of the Virgin circulated that associated her with old fertility symbols, and Guadalupe became a national center of syncretistic or mixed religious practices, as it remains to this day.

The control of much of Mexico by Spanish grandees holding fiefdoms or *encomiendas* left most native inhabitants in positions of virtual slavery, though the colonial government showed more respect for Indian land claims and property rights than did most American governments, including those of the North American colonies and the subsequent young United States. Even so, Indians were often forced to work as slave labor on farms or in dangerous mines; mortality rates were high, and communities were regularly left without schools or other services. Indians were commonly excluded from participation in the political process, with governments run by people of purely Spanish descent, and to a lesser extent by the mestizos, or people of mixed heritage, who made up a growing proportion of the population. Only in the twentieth century have people of purely native descent begun to have an active voice in public affairs, as is notably the case today, in Mexico with figures like the popular mayor of Mexico City, Cuauhtemoc Cárdenas—named after the prince who led the defense of Tenochtitlán against Cortés—and the Mayan activist and writer Rigoberta Menchú, winner of the 1992 Nobel Peace Prize.

Over the centuries, a rich and varied culture has evolved in Mexico and Central America among the increasingly mixed populations of the descendants of the Spanish settlers and the native Amerindians. A major element in this evolution has been a powerful literary heritage, from the rhetorically charged writings of the conquistadors and the haunting poetry of their adversaries, to the dramas and lyrics of Sor Juana in the seventeenth century, to such contemporary writers as Octavio Paz, Carlos Fuentes, and the Guatemalan Miguel Ángel Asturias, winner of the 1967 Nobel Prize for Literature, who translated the *Popol Vuh* into Spanish and incorporated many of its themes into his novels. Today, hundreds of thousands of people in Mexico and Central America still speak native languages as their first or even sole language, and poetry is being composed in Mayan and in Nahuatl, as members of the indigenous cultures seek to assess and adapt their heritage in the contemporary world. In her 1998 book *Crossing Borders,* Rigoberta Menchú compared her ancestral culture to the *nagual* or spirit double that protects each child from birth onward:

> I am not a woman who idealizes my identity. I am simply proud of having been born a Mayan. The Mayans are much greater than one generation. We are merely bridges from one generation to another. . . . Identity passes through the community, it passes along pavements, it passes down veins, and it exists in thoughts. . . . It is like the *nagual,* the shadow that accompanies you. It is the other, the one beside you. . . . The *nagual* can be an animal, a sheep, a deer, or a coyote. It can also be a hill or a tree. Or it can be a mere shadow carried on the wind or scurrying along paths. It is important to understand that a hill and a tree live longer than a person. So your identity lives longer than you do.

The identities of the "old" and "new" worlds have become increasingly intertwined over the years. The native and Spanish writings of the sixteenth and seventeenth centuries eloquently preserve the fullest record we have of the early contacts of these worlds, setting the terms of cultural connection and contestation that continue to play out today.

PRONUNCIATIONS:

Hernán Cortés: air-NAHN core-TEZ
Huitzilopochtli: weets-ill-oh-POTCH-tlee
Itzcoatl: eats-COH-at'l
Moctezuma: mock-tay-ZOO-mah
Nahuatl: NAH-waht'l
Ometeotl: oh-may-TAY-ought'l
Quetzalcoatl: kayt-zahl-COH-aht'l
Quiché: kee-CHAY

Sor Juana: soar HWA-nah
Tenochtitlán: tay-notch-tee-TLAN
Teotihuacán: tay-oh-tee-wa-CAHN
Texcoco: tesh-COH-co
Tezcatlipoca: taytz-caht-lee-POH-ca
Tlacaelel: tlah-cah-EY-lel
Xochiquetzal: show-chee-KET-zal

⊶ ⚹⚹⚹ ⊷

The Legend of the Suns
Recorded 1558

Among the oldest of all surviving Mesoamerican literary works are versions of "The Legend of the Suns," mythic accounts of the origins of the universe. Peoples across Mesoamerica believed that the world had been created, destroyed, and re-created several times (four times by the Mayan count, five times according to the Aztecs). The version of this legend given here was included in a historical survey known as *The Annals of Cuauhtitlan* (a major Aztec city). As is typical in Nahuatl accounts, four failed early creations precede the present era. The great god Quetzalcoatl first tries making the human race of ashes, but they are washed away when the world's first age ends—as in Genesis—in a vast flood. No Noah figure survives this flood, and the gods determine that next time they will need to make a stronger form of humans, and so they create giants, but these great creatures have trouble moving and are caught and eaten by tigers. Two more ages come and go, until finally the world enters its fifth age, the age of the present.

"The Legend of the Suns" presents a severe view of the world's five ages, including the modern "Age of Movement." The world is inherently unstable and violent, and human survival remains precarious. "The Legend of the Suns" can be compared to the creation/flood stories in Genesis and in the Babylonian *Enuma Elish* (see Volume A), as well as to the Norse myths of creation and ultimate destruction in *The Prose Edda* (Volume B). Nearer at hand, the Mayan *Popol Vuh*, which follows, gives a lively and often comic account of the world's several ages and of the underworld adventures of its trickster heroes.

The Legend of the Suns[1]

Thus it is told, it is said:
there have already been four manifestations
and this one is the fifth age.

So the old ones knew this,
5   that in the year 1-Rabbit[2]
heaven and earth were founded.
And they knew this,
that when heaven and earth were founded
there had already been four kinds of men,
10   four kinds of manifestations.
Also they knew that each of these
had existed in a Sun, an age.

And they said of the first men,
their god made them, fashioned them of ashes.
15   This they attributed to the god Quetzalcóatl,
whose sign is 7-Wind,
he made them, he invented them.
The first Sun or age which was founded,

---

1. Translated by Miguel León-Portilla and Grace Lobanov.
2. In the Mesoamerican reckoning, each year had a name that combined a sequence of 13 numbers and a series of 20 day names of animals or natural forces.

its sign was 4-Water,

20   it was called the Sun of Water.
Then it happened
that water carried away everything.
The people were changed into fish.

Then the second Sun or age was founded.
25   Its sign was 4-Tiger.
It was called the Sun of Tiger.
Then it happened
that the sky was crushed,
the Sun did not follow its course.
30   When the Sun arrived at midday,
immediately it was night
and when it became dark,
tigers ate the people.
In this Sun giants lived.
35   The old ones said
the giants greeted each other thus:
"Do not fall down," for whoever falls,
he falls forever.

Then the third Sun was founded.
40   Its sign was 4-Rain-of-Fire.
It happened then that fire rained down,
those who lived there were burned.
And then sand rained down.
And they say that then
45   it rained down the little stones we see,
that the *tezontle* stone boiled
and the big rocks became red.

Its sign was 4-Wind,
when the fourth Sun was founded.
50   It was called the Sun of Wind.
Then everything was carried away by the wind.
People were turned into monkeys.
They were scattered over the mountains,
and the monkey-men lived there.

55   The fifth Sun,
4-Movement its sign.
It is called the Sun of Movement
because it moves, follows its course.
And the old ones go about saying,
60   now there will be earthquakes,
there will be hunger
and thus we will perish.
In the year 13-Reed,
they say it came into existence,
65   the sun which now exists was born.

That was when there was light,
when dawn came,
the Sun of Movement which now exists.
4-Movement is its sign.
70   This is the fifth Sun which was founded,
in it there will be earthquakes,
in it there will be hunger.

This Sun, its name 4-Movement,
this is our Sun,
75   in which we now live,
and this is its sign,
where the Sun fell in fire
on the divine hearth,
there in Teotihuacán.[3]
80   Also this was the Sun
of our prince of Tula,
of Quetzalcóatl.

—•—=◊=—•—

Popol Vuh
Recorded mid-1550s

The greatest known compilation of ancient Mayan myths and legends, the *Popol Vuh* presents
an epic account of the origins of the world and the creation of humanity. As in the Book of
Genesis, this global history leads into the story of the authors' own people, the Quiché Maya of
highland Guatemala. The unnamed authors bring their history down to the time of writing in
the 1550s—like the first ages of the world, a time of destruction and recreation, as the Quiché
confronted the rapidly growing influence of their European conquerors. Most directly, the authors adapted to the European presence by using the newly imported Roman alphabet to record
the *Popol Vuh* itself as we now have it. Originally the *Popol Vuh* would have been the kind of
screenfold book shown on page 764, written on jointed sheets of bark, in a mixture of pictures
and hieroglyphs. This version, however, has not come down to us; the *Popol Vuh* we have is
the version written down in early colonial times, still in the Quiché language but in the Roman
alphabet. This most wide-ranging record of ancient myths is thus itself the product of the mixing of cultures already underway throughout Mesoamerica.

In pre-Conquest times, the *Popol Vuh* had a threefold purpose, embracing past, present,
and future: it was a record of history, a guide to ritual practice, and an aid to divination. As in
the Bible and the Qur'an, legendary accounts were included above all to ground and underwrite
its religious purposes. The original pictorial version of the book would have contained extensive records of astronomical phenomena, such as the phases of the moon and the times for the
rising and setting of Venus. Priests would use this information in foretelling the future and setting auspicious dates for important events, with clusters of hieroglyphs serving as captions to
the illustrations and as aids to memory for oral recitation. "Popol Vuh" means "Council Book"

3. This account sees the present age as having been established at the future site of the Temple of the Sun at the ancient city
of Teotihuacán, northeast of Mexico City.

in Mayan; the council of Mayan rulers would consult it to plot the future along the twin trajectories of the heavens and of the past.

The conquistadors systematically sought to destroy the old books that recorded the accumulated traditional lore and astronomical knowledge. Only vaguely aware at best of the books' contents and purposes, they could see that they were filled with depictions of idols and demons and ought to be burned. The *Popol Vuh* we have was written without illustrations, in the evident hope that the old stories might survive even if the remaining pictorial books were destroyed. The anonymous authors of this version claim, in fact, that the pictorial *Popol Vuh* no longer exists: "there is the original book and ancient writing owned by the lords, now lost," as they assert at the book's end, though at the beginning of the book they describe it more ambiguously as "hidden." We can't be sure whether the pictorial *Popol Vuh* had really been destroyed, perhaps when Cortés's lieutenant Pedro de Alvarado sacked and burned the important Mayan city of Utatlán in 1524. It may be instead that our authors have hidden it away for secret consultation; several passages in the alphabetic version seem to be commenting on a picture the authors have before their eyes. In either event, the new version written in Roman script could be used in public as a record of early history and support for Mayan claims to rights to retain their lands.

In time, at any rate, the pictorial *Popol Vuh* was in fact lost. Even the alphabetic version barely survived, in a single copy made a century and a half later by a friar named Francisco Ximénez, who borrowed it from his parishioners in the town of Chichicastenango and made a careful copy with a facing translation into Spanish. Padre Ximénez then returned the original to his parishioners, and it was eventually lost in turn. His copy was preserved first in a monastery and eventually in the library of the University of San Carlos in Guatemala City. There it was seen and copied in the 1850s by two visiting European scholars, each of whom translated it after returning home. Three hundred years after it was composed, the alphabetic *Popol Vuh* was first published in Vienna and in Paris, worlds away from its point of origin. Despite the intervening centuries, however, many of the stories and rituals it records have continued to be known up to the present time. Dennis Tedlock produced the luminous translation used here by working collaboratively in the late 1970s with Andrés Xiloj, a Mayan diviner or "daykeeper" in the Guatemalan town of Momostenango. Xiloj had never seen the *Popol Vuh* before, but he could identify and explain ritual practices he still carried on himself. Tedlock's translation is thus also a product of complex and fruitful cultural interactions.

The selections given here present both the book's ancient history and its modern framing. The opening section recounts the creation of the world, in terms directly reminiscent of the opening chapter of Genesis. Here the *Popol Vuh* can be seen at its most "syncretistic" (from Greek for "mixing together"): it combines Christian and native accounts, fitting old polytheistic traditions into the general structure of the biblical creation story. Even within its loosely biblical form, the Mayan account of creation is distinctive in many ways: in the variety of heavenly beings working with Sovereign Plumed Serpent to create the world; in the importance given to the four sacred directions; and in the fourfold attempts to create humanity. Unlike in the Aztec "Legend of the Suns," the entire world isn't repeatedly destroyed in the process, but the gods have to make four attempts before they finally find the perfect material to form human beings: not clay, as in Genesis, but corn. Throughout Mayan culture, corn was one of the most basic of foods, and the kernels were (and still are) used as important aids to divination.

Before describing this culminating act of creation, the book details the adventures of two sets of divine twins, whose heroic activities on earth and in the underworld make earth a safer place for humanity. Pure folktales on their surface, these stories all have astronomical significance as well: the characters' movements and fates set the pattern for the rising and setting of Mars, Venus, and other heavenly bodies. The episodes move back and forth in time and space between the two sets of twins as they outwit and defeat a series of evil figures such as Seven

Macaw and his two sons, a crocodile-like monster named Zipacna and a second son named Earthquake. The older set of twins is supposed to have died before the younger set is born, but the book freely alternates their adventures, first describing earthly events and then moving to underworld locales. The older twins rashly descend to the underworld kingdom, Xibalba, but the underworld deities repeatedly outwit them and finally kill them. By then, however, an underworld goddess has become pregnant from the blood of one of the twins, and she gives birth to the second set of twins, Hunahpu and Xbalanque. Given here are the climactic adventures of these twins when they in turn descend into the underworld to avenge the deaths of their father and uncle. Cleverly avoiding the traps that had undone their predecessors, Hunahpu and Xbalanque use trickery of their own, plus exceptional skill at the sacred Mayan ball game, to defeat the underworld's rulers, One Death and Seven Death. Henceforth the underworld gods will only have power over evildoers, and now the story goes on to detail the final creation, from corn, of the first eight humans—an Adam and Eve for each of the four sacred directions.

The final sections of the book describe the growth of the human race and the establishment of the great early city of Tulan, also known as "Seven Caves, Seven Canyons." The number of tribes grows and they migrate away from Tulan. As they spread through the region, the tribes' speech begins to diverge, and different languages are born. In (perhaps deliberate) contrast to the Tower of Babel story in Genesis, the division of languages comes about not through human sin but through the tribes' error in forsaking the unity of their sacred homeland:

> "Alas! We left our language behind. How did we do it? We're lost! Where were we deceived? We had only one language when we came to Tulan, and we had only one place of emergence and origin. We haven't done well," said all the tribes beneath the trees.

These final episodes of the book are filled with a haunting sense of loss and dispersal, together with a determination to hold together despite everything. The ancestors of the Quiché people preserve their tribe by retrieving sacred writings from the East, and by using these writings their rulers are able to establish the Mayan kingdom: "They were great lords, they were people of genius. . . . Whether there would be death, or whether there would be famine, or whether quarrels would occur, they knew it for certain, since there was a place to see it, there was a book, Council Book"—*Popol Vuh*—"was their name for it." The *Popol Vuh* thus includes itself within the story of the universe and of the Mayan people, and it closes with genealogies that trace the Quiché rulership down to the present day, "amid the preaching of God, in Christendom now."

The authors of the alphabetic *Popol Vuh* created a work of extraordinary sweep and ambition, tying together heaven, earth, and underworld, mythic past and colonial present, oral tradition and written records, folding in biblical elements and countering them with radically divergent stories of their own. The greatest compilation of pre-Conquest Mayan tales and beliefs, the *Popol Vuh* is also one of the most resolute responses to the challenge of the Conquest itself.

PRONUNCIATIONS
Hunahpu: who-nah-PU
Popol Vuh: po-pull VOOH
Quiché: kee-CHAY
Tonatiuh: toe-nah-TEE-you
Xbalanque: shball-anh-KAY
Xibalba: she-ball-BAH
Xiloj: she-LOWSH
Xmucane: shmoo-cah-NAY
Xpiyacoc: shpee-yah-COCK

from Popol Vuh: The Mayan Council Book[1]

[CREATION]

This is the beginning of the Ancient Word, here in this place called Quiché. Here we shall inscribe, we shall implant the Ancient Word, the potential and source for everything done in the citadel of Quiché, in the nation of Quiché people.

And here we shall take up the demonstration, revelation, and account of how things were put in shadow and brought to light

> by the Maker, Modeler, named Bearer, Begetter,
> Hunahpu Possum, Hunahpu Coyote,[2]
> Great White Peccary, Tapir,
> Sovereign Plumed Serpent,
> Heart of the Lake, Heart of the Sea,
> Maker of the Blue-Green Plate,
> Maker of the Blue-Green Bowl,

as they are called, also named, also described as

> the midwife, matchmaker
> named Xpiyacoc, Xmucane,
> defender, protector,
> twice a midwife, twice a matchmaker,

as is said in the words of Quiché. They accounted for everything—and did it, too—as enlightened beings, in enlightened words. We shall write about this now amid the preaching of God, in Christendom now. We shall bring it out because there is no longer a place to see it, a Council Book,

> a place to see "The Light That Came from Across the Sea,"
> the account of "Our Place in the Shadows,"
> a place to see "The Dawn of Life,"

as it is called. There is the original book and ancient writing, but he who reads and ponders it hides his face. It takes a long performance and account to complete the emergence of all the sky-earth:

> the fourfold siding, fourfold cornering,
> measuring, fourfold staking,
> halving the cord, stretching the cord
> in the sky, on the earth,[3]
> the four sides, the four corners,

as it is said,

> by the Maker, Modeler,
> mother-father of life, of humankind,
> giver of breath, giver of heart,
> bearer, upbringer in the light that lasts
> of those born in the light, begotten in the light;

---

1. Translated by Dennis Tedlock.
2. Epithets of the twins Hunahpu and Xbalanque as wandering dancers and magicians. These names link them to

the trickster figures of many Native American traditions; see the Coyote Tales in Volume E.
3. The world is being measured out like a cornfield.

worrier, knower of everything, whatever there is:
sky-earth, lake-sea.

This is the account, here it is:

Now it still ripples, now it still murmurs, ripples, it still sighs, still hums, and it is empty under the sky.

Here follow the first words, the first eloquence:

There is not yet one person, one animal, bird, fish, crab, tree, rock, hollow, canyon, meadow, forest. Only the sky alone is there; the face of the earth is not clear. Only the sea alone is pooled under all the sky; there is nothing whatever gathered together. It is at rest; not a single thing stirs. It is held back, kept at rest under the sky.

Whatever there is that might be is simply not there: only the pooled water, only the calm sea, only it alone is pooled.

Whatever might be is simply not there: only murmurs, ripples, in the dark, in the night. Only the Maker, Modeler alone, Sovereign Plumed Serpent, the Bearers, Begetters are in the water, a glittering light. They are there, they are enclosed in quetzal feathers, in blue-green.

Thus the name, "Plumed Serpent." They are great knowers, great thinkers in their very being.

And of course there is the sky, and there is also the Heart of Sky. This is the name of the god, as it is spoken.

And then came his word, he came here to the Sovereign Plumed Serpent, here in the blackness, in the early dawn. He spoke with the Sovereign Plumed Serpent, and they talked, then they thought, then they worried. They agreed with each other, they joined their words, their thoughts. Then it was clear, then they reached accord in the light, and then humanity was clear, when they conceived the growth, the generation of trees, of bushes, and the growth of life, of humankind, in the blackness, in the early dawn, all because of the Heart of Sky, named Hurricane. Thunderbolt Hurricane comes first, the second is Newborn Thunderbolt, and the third is Raw Thunderbolt.

So there were three of them, as Heart of Sky, who came to the Sovereign Plumed Serpent, when the dawn of life was conceived:

"How should it be sown, how should it dawn? Who is to be the provider, nurturer?"

"Let it be this way, think about it: this water should be removed, emptied out for the formation of the earth's own plate and platform, then comes the sowing, the dawning of the sky-earth. But there will be no high days and no bright praise for our work, our design, until the rise of the human work, the human design," they said.

And then the earth arose because of them, it was simply their word that brought it forth. For the forming of the earth they said "Earth." It arose suddenly, just like a cloud, like a mist, now forming, unfolding. Then the mountains were separated from the water, all at once the great mountains came forth. By their genius alone, by their cutting edge alone they carried out the conception of the mountain-plain, whose face grew instant groves of cypress and pine.

And the Plumed Serpent was pleased with this:

"It was good that you came, Heart of Sky, Hurricane, and Newborn Thunderbolt, Raw Thunderbolt. Our work, our design will turn out well," they said.

And the earth was formed first, the mountain-plain. The channels of water were separated; their branches wound their ways among the mountains. The waters were divided when the great mountains appeared.

Such was the formation of the earth when it was brought forth by the Heart of Sky, Heart of Earth, as they are called, since they were the first to think of it. The sky was set apart, and the earth was set apart in the midst of the waters.

Such was their plan when they thought, when they worried about the completion of their work.

Now they planned the animals of the mountains, all the guardians of the forests, creatures of the mountains: the deer, birds, pumas, jaguars, serpents, rattlesnakes, yellowbites, guardians of the bushes.

A Bearer, Begetter speaks:

"Why this pointless humming? Why should there merely be rustling beneath the trees and bushes?"

"Indeed—they had better have guardians," the others replied. As soon as they thought it and said it, deer and birds came forth.

And then they gave out homes to the deer and birds:

"You, the deer; sleep along the rivers, in the canyons. Be here in the meadows, in the thickets, in the forests, multiply yourselves. You will stand and walk on all fours," they were told.

So then they established the nests of the birds, small and great:

"You, precious birds: your nests, your houses are in the trees, in the bushes. Multiply there, scatter there, in the branches of trees, the branches of bushes," the deer and birds were told.

When this deed had been done, all of them had received a place to sleep and a place to stay. So it is that the nests of the animals are on the earth, given by the Bearer, Begetter. Now the arrangement of the deer and birds was complete.

And then the deer and birds were told by the Maker, Modeler, Bearer, Begetter:

"Talk, speak out. Don't moan, don't cry out. Please talk, each to each, within each kind, within each group," they were told—the deer, birds, puma, jaguar, serpent.

"Name now our names, praise us. We are your mother, we are your father. Speak now:

> 'Hurricane,
> Newborn Thunderbolt, Raw Thunderbolt,
> Heart of Sky, Heart of Earth,
> Maker, Modeler,
> Bearer, Begetter,'

speak, pray to us, keep our days," they were told. But it didn't turn out that they spoke like people: they just squawked, they just chattered, they just howled. It wasn't apparent what language they spoke; each one gave a different cry. When the Maker, Modeler heard this:

"It hasn't turned out well, they haven't spoken," they said among themselves. "It hasn't turned out that our names have been named. Since we are their mason and sculptor, this will not do," the Bearers and Begetters said among themselves. So they told them:

"You will simply have to be transformed. Since it hasn't turned out well and you haven't spoken, we have changed our word:

"What you feed on, what you eat, the places where you sleep, the places where you stay, whatever is yours will remain in the canyons, the forests. Although it turned out that our days were not kept, nor did you pray to us, there may yet be strength in the keeper of days, the giver of praise whom we have yet to make. Just accept your service, just let your flesh be eaten.

"So be it, this must be your service," they were told when they were instructed—the animals, small and great, on the face of the earth.

And then they wanted to test their timing again, they wanted to experiment again, and they wanted to prepare for the keeping of days again. They had not heard their speech among the animals; it did not come to fruition and it was not complete.

And so their flesh was brought low: they served, they were eaten, they were killed—the animals on the face of the earth.

Again there comes an experiment with the human work, the human design, by the Maker, Modeler, Bearer, Begetter:

"It must simply be tried again. The time for the planting and dawning is nearing. For this we must make a provider and nurturer. How else can we be invoked and remembered on the face of the earth? We have already made our first try at our work and design, but it turned out that they didn't keep our days, nor did they glorify us.

"So now let's try to make a giver of praise, giver of respect, provider, nurturer," they said.

So then comes the building and working with earth and mud. They made a body, but it didn't look good to them. It was just separating, just crumbling, just loosening, just softening, just disintegrating, and just dissolving. Its head wouldn't turn, either. Its face was just lopsided, its face was just twisted. It couldn't look around. It talked at first, but senselessly. It was quickly dissolving in the water.

"It won't last," the mason and sculptor said then. "It seems to be dwindling away, so let it just dwindle. It can't walk and it can't multiply, so let it be merely a thought," they said.

So then they dismantled, again they brought down their work and design. Again they talked:

"What is there for us to make that would turn out well, that would succeed in keeping our days and praying to us?" they said. Then they planned again:

"We'll just tell Xpiyacoc, Xmucane, Hunahpu Possum, Hunahpu Coyote, to try a counting of days, a counting of lots," the mason and sculptor said to themselves. Then they invoked Xpiyacoc, Xmucane.

Then comes the naming of those who are the midmost seers: the "Grandmother of Day, Grandmother of Light," as the Maker, Modeler called them. These are names of Xpiyacoc and Xmucane.

When Hurricane had spoken with the Sovereign Plumed Serpent, they invoked the daykeepers, diviners, the midmost seers:

"There is yet to find, yet to discover how we are to model a person, construct a person again, a provider, nurturer, so that we are called upon and we are recognized: our recompense is in words.

> Midwife, matchmaker,
> our grandmother, our grandfather,
> Xpiyacoc, Xmucane,
> let there be planting, let there be the dawning
> of our invocation, our sustenance, our recognition

by the human work, the human design,
the human figure, the human mass.

So be it, fulfill your names:

> Hunahpu Possum, Hunahpu Coyote,
> Bearer twice over, Begetter twice over,
> Great Peccary, Great Tapir,
> lapidary, jeweler,
> sawyer, carpenter,
>
> Maker of the Blue-Green Plate,
> Maker of the Blue-Green Bowl,
> incense maker, master craftsman,
> Grandmother of Day, Grandmother of Light.

You have been called upon because of our work, our design. Run your hands over the kernels of corn, over the seeds of the coral tree, just get it done, just let it come out whether we should carve and gouge a mouth, a face in wood," they told the daykeepers.

And then comes the borrowing, the counting of days; the hand is moved over the corn kernels, over the coral seeds, the days, the lots.[4]

Then they spoke to them, one of them a grandmother, the other a grandfather.

This is the grandfather, this is the master of the coral seeds: Xpiyacoc is his name.

And this is the grandmother, the daykeeper, diviner who stands behind others: Xmucane is her name.

And they said, as they set out the days:

> "Just let it be found, just let it be discovered,
> say it, our ear is listening,
> may you talk, may you speak,
> just find the wood for the carving and sculpting
> by the builder, sculptor.
> Is this to be the provider, the nurturer
> when it comes to the planting, the dawning?
> You corn kernels, you coral seeds,
> you days, you lots:
> may you succeed, may you be accurate,"

they said to the corn kernels, coral seeds, days, lots. "Have shame, you up there, Heart of Sky: attempt no deception before the mouth and face of Sovereign Plumed Serpent," they said. Then they spoke straight to the point:

"It is well that there be your manikins, woodcarvings, talking, speaking, there on the face of the earth."

"So be it," they replied. The moment they spoke it was done: the manikins, woodcarvings, human in looks and human in speech.

This was the peopling of the face of the earth:

They came into being, they multiplied, they had daughters, they had sons, these manikins, woodcarvings. But there was nothing in their hearts and nothing in their

---

4. Mayan diviners today still make predictions by taking a handful of corn, grouping the kernels into fours, then counting along the groups as if they were the days of the 260-day calendar. The character of the day they reach at the end of the row will indicate the prospects for whatever is being considered.

minds, no memory of their mason and builder. They just went and walked wherever they wanted. Now they did not remember the Heart of Sky.

And so they fell, just an experiment and just a cutout for humankind. They were talking at first but their faces were dry. They were not yet developed in the legs and arms. They had no blood, no lymph. They had no sweat, no fat. Their complexions were dry, their faces were crusty. They flailed their legs and arms, their bodies were deformed.

And so they accomplished nothing before the Maker, Modeler who gave them birth, gave them heart. They became the first numerous people here on the face of the earth.

Again there comes a humiliation, destruction, and demolition. The manikins, wood-carvings were killed when the Heart of Sky devised a flood for them. A great flood was made; it came down on the heads of the manikins, woodcarvings.

The man's body was carved from the wood of the coral tree by the Maker, Modeler. And as for the woman, the Maker, Modeler needed the pith of reeds for the woman's body. They were not competent, nor did they speak before the builder and sculptor who made them and brought them forth, and so they were killed, done in by a flood:

There came a rain of resin from the sky.

There came the one named Gouger of Faces: he gouged out their eyeballs.

There came Sudden Bloodletter: he snapped off their heads.

There came Crunching Jaguar: he ate their flesh.

There came Tearing Jaguar: he tore them open.

They were pounded down to the bones and tendons, smashed and pulverized even to the bones. Their faces were smashed because they were incompetent before their mother and their father, the Heart of Sky, named Hurricane. The earth was blackened because of this; the black rainstorm began, rain all day and rain all night. Into their houses came the animals, small and great. Their faces were crushed by things of wood and stone. Everything spoke: their water jars, their tortilla griddles, their plates, their cooking pots, their grinding stones, each and every thing crushed their faces. Their dogs and turkeys told them:

"You caused us pain, you ate us, but now it is *you* whom *we* shall eat." And this is the grinding stone:

"We were undone because of you.

> Every day, every day,
> in the dark, in the dawn, forever,
> r-r-rip, r-r-rip,
> r-r-rub, r-r-rub
> right in our faces, because of you.

This was the service we gave you at first, when you were still people, but today you will learn of our power. We shall pound and we shall grind your flesh," their grinding stones told them.

And this is what their dogs said, when they spoke in their turn:

"Why is it you can't seem to give us our food? We just watch and you just keep us down, and you throw us around. You keep a stick ready when you eat, just so you can hit us. We don't talk, so we've received nothing from you. How could you not have known? You *did* know that we were wasting away there, behind you.

"So, this very day you will taste the teeth in our mouths. We shall eat you," their dogs told them, and their faces were crushed.

And then their tortilla griddles and cooking pots spoke to them in turn:

"Pain! That's all you've done for us. Our mouths are sooty, our faces are sooty. By setting us on the fire all the time, you burn us. Since *we* felt no pain, *you* try it. We shall burn you," all their cooking pots said, crushing their faces.

The stones, their hearthstones were shooting out, coming right out of the fire, going for their heads, causing them pain. Now they run for it, helter-skelter.

They want to climb up on the houses, but they fall as the houses collapse.

They want to climb the trees; they're thrown off by the trees.

They want to get inside caves, but the caves slam shut in their faces.

Such was the scattering of the human work, the human design. The people were ground down, overthrown. The mouths and faces of all of them were destroyed and crushed. And it used to be said that the monkeys in the forests today are a sign of this. They were left as a sign because wood alone was used for their flesh by the builder and sculptor.

So this is why monkeys look like people: they are a sign of a previous human work, human design—mere manikins, mere woodcarvings.

[HUNAHPU AND XBALANQUE IN THE UNDERWORLD][5]

Happy now, they went to play ball at the court. So they played ball at a distance, all by themselves. They swept out the court of their fathers.

And then it came into the hearing of the lords of Xibalba:

"Who's begun a game again up there, over our heads? Don't they have any shame, stomping around this way? Didn't One and Seven Hunahpu die trying to magnify themselves in front of us? So, you must deliver another summons," they said as before, One and Seven Death, all the lords.

"They are hereby summoned," they told their messengers. "You are to say, on reaching them:

"'They must come,' say the lords. 'We would play ball with them here. In seven days we'll have a game,' say the lords,' you will say when you arrive," the messengers were told.

* * *

First they entered Dark House.

And after that, the messenger of One Death brought their torch, burning when it arrived, along with one cigar apiece.

"'Here is their torch,' says the lord. 'They must return the torch in the morning, along with the cigars. They must return them intact,' say the lords," the messenger said when he arrived.

"Very well," they said, but they didn't burn the torch—instead, something that looked like fire was substituted. This was the tail of the macaw, which looked like a torch to the sentries. And as for the cigars, they just put fireflies at the tips of those cigars, which they kept lit all night.

"We've defeated them," said the sentries, but the torch was not consumed—it just looked that way. And as for the cigars, there wasn't anything burning there—it just looked that way. When these things were taken back to the lords:

---

5. The younger pair of twins is now playing the same noisy ball game that had annoyed the underworld lords when One Hunahpu and Seven Hunahpu played it above their heads before.

"What's happening? Where did they come from? Who begot them and bore them? Our hearts are really hurting, because what they're doing to us is no good. They're different in looks and different in their very being," they said among themselves. And when they had summoned all the lords:

"Let's play ball, boys," the boys were told. And then they were asked by One and Seven Death:

"Where might you have come from? Please name it," Xibalba said to them.

"Well, wherever did we come from? We don't know," was all they said. They didn't name it.

"Very well then, we'll just go play ball, boys," Xibalba told them.

"Good," they said.

"Well, this is the one we should put in play, here's our rubber ball," said the Xibalbans.

"No thanks. This is the one to put in, here's ours," said the boys.

"No it's not. This is the one we should put in," the Xibalbans said again.

"Very well," said the boys.

"After all, it's just a decorated one," said the Xibalbans.

"Oh no it's not, it's just a skull! We've said enough," said the boys.

"No it's not," said the Xibalbans.

"Very well," said Hunahpu. When it was sent off by Xibalba, the ball was stopped by Hunahpu's yoke.

And then, while Xibalba watched, the White Dagger came out from inside the ball. It went clattering, twisting all over the floor of the court.

"What's that!" said Hunahpu and Xbalanque. "Death is the only thing you want for us! Wasn't it *you* who sent a summons to us, and wasn't it *your* messenger who went? Truly, take pity on us, or else we'll just leave," the boys told them.

And this is what had been ordained for the boys: that they should have died right away, right there, defeated by that knife. But it wasn't like that. Instead, Xibalba was again defeated by the boys.

"Well, don't go, boys. We can still play ball, but we'll put yours into play," the boys were told. * * *

Now after that, when the ball was dropped in, they just played to a tie. When they finished the game they made an arrangement with each other:

"At dawn again," said Xibalba.

"Very well," said the boys, then they were finished.

And now they entered Cold House. There are countless drafts, thick-falling hail inside the house, the home of cold. They diminished the cold right away by shutting it out. The cold dissipated because of the boys. They did not die, but were alive when it dawned.

So, although Xibalba had wanted them to die there, they did not, but were alive when it dawned. They came out when the pages arrived and the guards left.

"Why haven't they died?" said the rulers of Xibalba. Again they were amazed at the feats of the boys, Hunahpu and Xbalanque.

So next they entered Jaguar House, the jaguar-packed home of jaguars:

"Don't eat *us*. There *is* something that should be yours," the jaguars were told.

With that, they scattered bones before the animals.

After that, the jaguars were wrestling around there, over the bones.

"So they've made good work of them, they've eaten their very hearts. Now that the boys have given themselves up, they've already been transformed into skeletons," said the sentries, all of them finding it sweet. But they hadn't died; they were well. They came out of Jaguar House.

"What sort of people are they? Where did they come from?" said all the Xibalbans.

So next they entered the midst of the fire, a house of fire with only fire alone inside. They weren't burned by it, just toasted, just simmered, so they were well when it dawned. Although it had been ordained that they be quickly killed in there, overcome, they weren't, and instead it was the Xibalbans who lost heart over this.

Now they were put inside Bat House, with bats alone inside the house, a house of snatch-bats, monstrous beasts, their snouts like knives, the instruments of death. To come before these is to be finished off at once.

When they were inside they just slept in their blowgun;[6] they were not bitten by the members of the household. But this is where they gave one of themselves up because of a snatch-bat that came down, he came along just as one of them showed himself. They did it because it was actually what they were asking for, what they had in mind.

And all night the bats are making noise:

"Squeak! Squeak!"

they say, and they say it all night.

Then it let up a little. The bats were no longer moving around. So there, one of the boys crawled to the end of the blowgun, since Xbalanque said:

"Hunahpu? Can you see how long it is till dawn?"

"Well, perhaps I should look to see how long it is," he replied. So he kept trying to look out the muzzle of the blowgun, he tried to see the dawn.

And then his head was taken off by a snatch-bat, leaving Hunahpu's body still stuffed inside.

"What's going on? Hasn't it dawned?" said Xbalanque. No longer is there any movement from Hunahpu. "What's this? Hunahpu hasn't left, has he? What have you done?" He no longer moves; now there is only heavy breathing.

After that, Xbalanque despaired:

"Alas! We've given it all up!" he said. And elsewhere, the head meanwhile went rolling onto the court, in accordance with the word of One and Seven Death, and all the Xibalbans were happy over the head of Hunahpu.

After that, Xbalanque summoned all the animals: coati,[7] peccary, all the animals, small and great. It was at night, still nighttime when he asked them for their food:

"Whatever your foods are, each one of you: that's what I summoned you for, to bring your food here," Xbalanque told them.

"Very well," they replied, then they went to get what's theirs, then indeed they all came back.

There's the one who only brought his rotten wood.

6. Apparently they can shrink themselves to fit inside their blowgun.   7. A raccoon-like animal with a long snout.

There's the one who only brought leaves.

There's the one who only brought stones.

There's the one who only brought earth, on through the varied foods of the animals, small and great, until the very last one remained: the coati. He brought a squash, bumping it along with his snout as he came.

And this became a simulated head for Hunahpu. His eyes were carved right away, then brains came from the thinker, from the sky. This was the Heart of Sky, Hurricane, who came down, came on down into Bat House. The face wasn't finished any too quickly; it came out well. His strength was just the same, he looked handsome, he spoke just the same.

And this is when it was trying to dawn, reddening along the horizon:

"Now make the streaks, man," the possum was told.

"Yes," said the old man. When he made the streaks he made it dark again; the old man made four streaks.

"Possum is making streaks," people say today, ever since he made the early dawn red and blue, establishing its very being.

"Isn't it good?" Hunahpu was asked.

"Good indeed," he replied. His head was as if it had every bone; it had become like his real head.

After that, they had a talk, they made arrangements with each other:

"How about not playing ball yourself? You should just make lots of threats, while I should be the one to take all the action," Xbalanque told him. After that, he gave instructions to a rabbit:

"Your place is there above the court, on top. Stay there in the oaks," the rabbit was told by Xbalanque, "until the ball comes to you, then take off while I get to work," the rabbit was told. He got his instructions while it was still dark.

After that, when it dawned, both of them were just as well as ever.

And when the ball was dropped in again, it was the head of Hunahpu that rolled over the court:

> "We've won! You're done!
> Give up! You lost!"

they were told. But even so Hunahpu was shouting:

"Punt the head as a ball!" he told them.

"Well, we're not going to do them any more harm with threats," and with this the lords of Xibalba sent off the ball and Xbalanque received it, the ball was stopped by his yoke, then he hit it hard and it took off, the ball passed straight out of the court, bouncing just once, just twice, and stopping among the oaks. Then the rabbit took off hopping, then they went off in pursuit, then all the Xibalbans went off, shouting, shrieking, they went after the rabbit, off went the whole of Xibalba.

After that, the boys got Hunahpu's head back. Then Xbalanque planted the squash; this is when he went to set the squash above the court.

So the head of Hunahpu was really a head again, and the two of them were happy again. And the others, those Xibalbans, were still going on in search of the ball.

After that, having recovered the ball from among the oaks, the boys cried out to them:

"Come back! Here's the ball! We've found it!" they said, so they stopped. When the Xibalbans got back:

"Have we been seeing things?" they said. Then they began their ball game again, and they made equal plays on both sides again.

After that, the squash was punted by Xbalanque. The squash was wearing out; it fell on the court, bringing to light its light-colored seeds, as plain as day right in front of them.

"How did you get ahold of that? Where did it come from?" said Xibalba.

With this, the masters of Xibalba were defeated by Hunahpu and Xbalanque. There was great danger there, but they did not die from all the things that were done to them.

[*The boys decide to trick the underworld gods into allowing themselves to be killed. They entertain the gods by destroying things and then magically restoring them, prompting the gods to ask for more.*]

"You have yet to kill a person! Make a sacrifice without death!" they were told.

"Very well," they said.

And then they took hold of a human sacrifice.

And they held up a human heart on high.

And they showed its roundness to the lords.

And now One and Seven Death admired it, and now that person was brought right back to life. His heart was overjoyed when he came back to life, and the lords were amazed:

"Sacrifice yet again, even do it to yourselves! Let's see it! At heart, that's the dance we really want from you," the lords said now.

"Very well, lord," they replied, and then they sacrificed themselves.

And this is the sacrifice of Hunahpu by Xbalanque. One by one his legs, his arms were spread wide. His head came off, rolled far away outside. His heart, dug out, was smothered in a leaf, and all the Xibalbans went crazy at the sight.

So now, only one of them was dancing there: Xbalanque.

"Get up!" he said, and Hunahpu came back to life. The two of them were over-joyed at this—and likewise the lords rejoiced, as if they were doing it themselves. One and Seven Death were as glad at heart as if they themselves were actually doing the dance.

And then the hearts of the lords were filled with longing, with yearning for the dance of Hunahpu and Xbalanque, so then came these words from One and Seven Death:

"Do it to us! Sacrifice us!" they said. "Sacrifice both of us!" said One and Seven Death to Hunahpu and Xbalanque.

"Very well. You ought to come back to life. After all, aren't you Death? And aren't we making you happy, along with the vassals of your domain?" they told the lords.

And this one was the first to be sacrificed: the lord at the very top, the one whose name is One Death, the ruler of Xibalba.

And with One Death dead, the next to be taken was Seven Death. They did not come back to life.

And then the Xibalbans were getting up to leave, those who had seen the lords die. They underwent heart sacrifice there, and the heart sacrifice was performed on the two lords only for the purpose of destroying them.

As soon as they had killed the one lord without bringing him back to life, the other lord had been meek and tearful before the dancers. He didn't consent, he didn't accept it:

"Take pity on me!" he said when he realized. All their vassals took the road to the great canyon, in one single mass they filled up the deep abyss. So they piled up there and gathered together, countless ants, tumbling down into the canyon, as if they were being herded there. And when they arrived, they all bent low in surrender, they arrived meek and tearful.

Such was the defeat of the rulers of Xibalba. The boys accomplished it only through wonders, only through self-transformation.

[THE FINAL CREATION OF HUMANS]

And here is the beginning of the conception of humans, and of the search for the ingredients of the human body. So they spoke, the Bearer, Begetter, the Makers, Modelers named Sovereign Plumed Serpent:

"The dawn has approached, preparations have been made, and morning has come for the provider, nurturer, born in the light, begotten in the light. Morning has come for humankind, for the people of the face of the earth," they said. It all came together as they went on thinking in the darkness, in the night, as they searched and they sifted, they thought and they wondered.

And here their thoughts came out in clear light. They sought and discovered what was needed for human flesh. It was only a short while before the sun, moon, and stars were to appear above the Makers and Modelers. Broken Place, Bitter Water Place is the name: the yellow corn, white corn came from there.[8]

And these are the names of the animals who brought the food: fox, coyote, parrot, crow. There were four animals who brought the news of the ears of yellow corn and white corn. They were coming from over there at Broken Place, they showed the way to the break.

And this was when they found the staple foods.

And these were the ingredients for the flesh of the human work, the human design, and the water was for the blood. It became human blood, and corn was also used by the Bearer, Begetter.

And so they were happy over the provisions of the good mountain, filled with sweet things, thick with yellow corn, white corn, and thick with pataxte and cacao, countless zapotes, anonas, jocotes, nances, matasanos, sweets—the rich foods filling up the citadel named Broken Place, Bitter Water Place. All the edible fruits were there: small staples, great staples, small plants, great plants. The way was shown by the animals.

And then the yellow corn and white corn were ground, and Xmucane did the grinding nine times. Corn was used, along with the water she rinsed her hands with, for the creation of grease; it became human fat when it was worked by the Bearer, Begetter, Sovereign Plumed Serpent, as they are called.

After that, they put it into words:

> the making, the modeling of our first mother-father,
> with yellow corn, white corn alone for the flesh,
> food alone for the human legs and arms,
> for our first fathers, the four human works.

It was staples alone that made up their flesh.

---

8. In the Navajo creation stories recorded in the 19th century, the first women and men are similarly made from yellow and white corn (see "The Story of the Emergence" in Volume E.).

These are the names of the first people who were made and modeled.

> This is the first person: Jaguar Quitze.
> And now the second: Jaguar Night.
> And now the third: Mahucutah.
> And the fourth: True Jaguar.

And these are the names of our first mother-fathers. They were simply made and modeled, it is said; they had no mother and no father. We have named the men by themselves. No woman gave birth to them, nor were they begotten by the builder, sculptor, Bearer, Begetter. By sacrifice alone, by genius alone they were made, they were modeled by the Maker, Modeler, Bearer, Begetter, Sovereign Plumed Serpent. And when they came to fruition, they came out human:

They talked and they made words.

They looked and they listened.

They walked, they worked.

They were good people, handsome, with looks of the male kind. Thoughts came into existence and they gazed; their vision came all at once. Perfectly they saw, perfectly they knew everything under the sky, whenever they looked. The moment they turned around and looked around in the sky, on the earth, everything was seen without any obstruction. They didn't have to walk around before they could see what was under the sky; they just stayed where they were.

As they looked, their knowledge became intense. Their sight passed through trees, through rocks, through lakes, through seas, through mountains, through plains. Jaguar Quitze, Jaguar Night, Mahucutah, and True Jaguar were truly gifted people.

And then they were asked by the builder and mason:

"What do you know about your being? Don't you look, don't you listen? Isn't your speech good, and your walk? So you must look, to see out under the sky. Don't you see the mountain-plain clearly? So try it," they were told.

And then they saw everything under the sky perfectly. After that, they thanked the Maker, Modeler:

> "Truly now,
> double thanks, triple thanks
> that we've been formed, we've been given
> our mouths, our faces,
> we speak, we listen,
> we wonder, we move,
> our knowledge is good, we've understood
> what is far and near,
> and we've seen what is great and small
> under the sky, on the earth.
> Thanks to you we've been formed,
> we've come to be made and modeled,
> our grandmother, our grandfather,"

they said when they gave thanks for having been made and modeled. They understood everything perfectly, they sighted the four sides, the four corners in the sky, on the earth, and this didn't sound good to the builder and sculptor:

"What our works and designs have said is no good:

'We have understood everything, great and small,' they say." And so the Bearer, Begetter took back their knowledge:

"What should we do with them now? Their vision should at least reach nearby, they should see at least a small part of the face of the earth, but what they're saying isn't good. Aren't they merely 'works' and 'designs' in their very names? Yet they'll become as great as gods, unless they procreate, proliferate at the sowing, the dawning, unless they increase."

"Let it be this way: now we'll take them apart just a little, that's what we need. What we've found out isn't good. Their deeds would become equal to ours, just because their knowledge reaches so far. They see everything," so said

> the Heart of Sky, Hurricane,
> Newborn Thunderbolt, Raw Thunderbolt,
> Sovereign Plumed Serpent,
> Bearer, Begetter,
> Xpiyacoc, Xmucane,
> Maker, Modeler,

as they are called. And when they changed the nature of their works, their designs, it was enough that the eyes be marred by the Heart of Sky. They were blinded as the face of a mirror is breathed upon. Their eyes were weakened. Now it was only when they looked nearby that things were clear.

And such was the loss of the means of understanding, along with the means of knowing everything, by the four humans. The root was implanted.

And such was the making, modeling of our first grandfather, our father, by the Heart of Sky, Heart of Earth.

And then their wives and women came into being. Again, the same gods thought of it. It was as if they were asleep when they received them, truly beautiful women were there with Jaguar Quitze, Jaguar Night, Mahucutah, and True Jaguar. With their women there they became wider awake. Right away they were happy at heart again, because of their wives.

Celebrated Seahouse is the name of the wife of Jaguar Quitze.

Prawn House is the name of the wife of Jaguar Night.

Hummingbird House is the name of the wife of Mahucutah.

Macaw House is the name of the wife of True Jaguar.

So these are the names of their wives, who became ladies of rank, giving birth to the people of the tribes, small and great.

And this is our root, we who are the Quiché people.

[MIGRATION AND THE DIVISION OF LANGUAGES][9]

And this is the name of the mountain where they went, Jaguar Quitze, Jaguar Night, Mahucutah, True Jaguar, and the Tams and Ilocs: Tulan Zuyua, Seven Caves, Seven Canyons is the name of the citadel. Those who were to receive the gods arrived there.

And they arrived there at Tulan, all of them, countless people arrived, walking in crowds, and their gods were given out in order, the first being those of Jaguar Quitze, Jaguar Night, Mahucutah, and True Jaguar. They were happy:

---

9. The first parents produce three lineages and a total of thirteen tribes, including the Tum and the Ilocs, who were allied with the Quiché. The tribes start to wander in search of a home.

"We have found what we were looking for," they said. And this one was the first to come out:

Tohil is the name of the god loaded in the backpack borne by Jaguar Quitze. And the others came out in turn:

Auilix is the name of the god that Jaguar Night carried.

Hacauitz, in turn, is the name of the god received by Mahucutah.

Middle of the Plain is the name of the god received by True Jaguar.

And there were still other Quiché people, since the Tams also received theirs, but it was the same Tohil for the Tams, that's the name received by the grandfather and father of the Tam lords, as they are known today.

And third were the Ilocs: again, Tohil is the name of the god received by the grandfather and father of those lords, the same ones known today.

And such was the naming of the three Quichés. They have never let go of each other because the god has just one name: Tohil for the Quiché proper, and Tohil for the Tams and Ilocs. There is just one name for their god, and so the Quiché threesome has not come apart, those three. Tohil, Auilix, and Hacauitz are truly great in their very being.

And then all the tribes came in: Rabinals, Cakchiquels, those of the Bird House, along with the Yaqui people, as the names are today. And the languages of the tribes changed there; their languages became differentiated. They could no longer understand one another clearly when they came away from Tulan.

And there they broke apart. There were those who went eastward and many who came here, but they were all alike in dressing with hides. There were no clothes of the better kinds. They were in patches, they were adorned with mere animal hides. They were poor. They had nothing of their own. But they were people of genius in their very being when they came away from Tulan Zuyua, Seven Caves, Seven Canyons, so says the Ancient Word.

They walked in crowds when they arrived at Tulan, and there was no fire. Only those with Tohil had it: this was the tribe whose god was first to generate fire. How it was generated is not clear. Their fire was already burning when Jaguar Quitze and Jaguar Night first saw it:

"Alas! Fire has not yet become ours. We'll die from the cold," they said. And then Tohil spoke:

"Do not grieve. You will have your own even when the fire you're talking about has been lost," Tohil told them.

> "Aren't you a true god!
> Our sustenance and our support!
> Our god!"

they said when they gave thanks for what Tohil had said.

> "Very well, in truth,
> I am your god: so be it.
> I am your lord: so be it,"

the penitents and sacrificers were told by Tohil.

And this was the warming of the tribes. They were pleased by their fire.

After that a great downpour began, which cut short the fire of the tribes. And hail fell thickly on all the tribes, and their fires were put out by the hail. Their fires didn't start up again. So then Jaguar Quitze and Jaguar Night asked for their fire again:

"Tohil, we'll be finished off by the cold," they told Tohil.

"Well, do not grieve," said Tohil. Then he started a fire. He pivoted inside his sandal.

After that, Jaguar Quitze, Jaguar Night, Mahucutah, and True Jaguar were pleased.

After they had been warmed, the fires of the other tribes were still out. Now they were being finished off by the cold, so they came back to ask for their fire from Jaguar Quitze, Jaguar Night, Mahucutah, and True Jaguar. They could bear the cold and hail no longer. By now they were chattering and shivering. There was no life left in them. Their legs and arms kept shaking. Their hands were stiff when they arrived.

"Perhaps we wouldn't make ourselves ashamed in front of you if we asked to remove a little something from your fire?" they said when they arrived, but they got no response. And then the tribes cursed in their thoughts. Already their language had become different from that of Jaguar Quitze, Jaguar Night, Mahucutah, and True Jaguar.

"Alas! We left our language behind. How did we do it? We're lost! Where were we deceived? We had only one language when we came to Tulan, and we had only one place of emergence and origin. We haven't done well," said all the tribes beneath the trees and bushes.

* * *

And there, always, they were facing the east, when they were there in the place named Tulan Zuyua. Their gods came from there. It wasn't really here that they received their fiery splendor and their dominion, but rather there that the tribes, great and small, were subjugated and humiliated. When they were cut open before Tohil, all the peoples gave their blood, their gore, their sides, their underarms. Fiery splendor came to them all at once at Tulan, along with great knowledge, and they achieved this in the darkness, in the night.

And now they came away, they tore themselves away from there. Now they left the east:

"Our home is not here. Let's go on until we see where we belong," said Tohil. He actually spoke to them, to Jaguar Quitze, Jaguar Night, Mahucutah, and True Jaguar.

"It remains for you to give thanks, since you have yet to take care of bleeding your ears and passing a cord through your elbows. You must worship. This is your way of giving thanks before your god."

"Very well," they replied, then they bled their ears. They cried in their song about coming from Tulan. They cried in their hearts when they came away, when they made their departure from Tulan:

> "Alas! We won't be here when we see the dawn,
> when the sun is born, when the face of the earth is lit,"

they said.

And then they came away, just camping on the road. People were just camping there, each tribe slept and then got up again. And they were always watching for the star, the sign of the day. They kept this sign of the dawn in their hearts when they came away from the east. In unity they passed beyond the place named Great Abyss today.

And then they arrived on top of a mountain there. All the Quiché people got together there, along with the other tribes, and all of them held council there. The name the mountain has today is from when they took counsel together: Place of Advice is the name of the mountain. They got together and identified themselves there:

"Here am I: I am a Quiché person, and you there, you are Tams, this will be your name," the Tams were told. And then the Ilocs were told:

"You are the Ilocs, this will be your name. The three Quichés must not be lost. We are united in our word," they said when they fixed their names.

And then the Cakchiquels were named: their name became Cakchiquels. So, too, with the Rabinals; this became their name. It hasn't been lost today.

And then there are those of the Bird House, as they are named today.

These are the names they named for each other. When they held council there, they were still waiting for the dawning, watching for the appearance of the rising star, the one that came before the sun when it was born.

"When we came away from Tulan, we broke ourselves apart," they told each other.

This is what kept weighing on their hearts, the great pain they went through: there was nothing to eat, nothing to feed on. They were just smelling the tips of their staffs as if they were thinking of eating them, but they weren't eating at all as they came.

And it isn't clear how they crossed over the sea. They crossed over as if there were no sea. They just crossed over on some stones, stones piled up in the sand. And they gave it a name: Rock Rows, Furrowed Sands was their name for the place where they crossed through the midst of the sea. Where the waters divided, they crossed over.

[THE DEATH OF THE QUICHÉ FOREFATHERS]

Now this is where we shall tell about the death of Jaguar Quitze, Jaguar Night, Mahucutah, and True Jaguar, as they are named. Since they knew about their death and disappearance, they left instructions with their sons. They weren't sickly yet, they weren't gasping for breath when they left their word with their sons.

These are the names of their sons:

Jaguar Quitze begot these two: Cocaib was the name of the firstborn and Cocauib was the name of the second of the sons of Jaguar Quitze, the grandfather and father of the Cauecs.

And again, Jaguar Night begot two. These are their names: Coacul was the name of his first son, and the other was called Coacutec, the second son of Jaguar Night, of the Greathouses.

And Mahucutah begot just one son, named Coahau.

These three had sons, but True Jaguar had no son. They were all true penitents and sacrificers, and these are the names of their sons, with whom they left instructions. They were united, the four of them together. They sang of the pain in their hearts, they cried their hearts out in their singing. "The Blame Is Ours" is the name of the song they sang.

And then they advised their sons:

"Our dear sons: we are leaving. We are going back. We have enlightened words, enlightened advice to leave with you—and with you who have come from faraway mountains, our dear wives," they told their wives. They advised each one of them:

"We are going back to our own tribal place. Again it is the time of our Lord Deer, as is reflected in the sky. We have only to make our return. Our work has been done, our day has been completed. Since you know this, neither forget us nor put us aside. You have yet to see your own home and mountain, the place of your beginning.

"Let it be this way: you must go. Go see the place where we came from," were the words they spoke when they gave their advice.

And then Jaguar Quitze left a sign of his being:

"This is for making requests of me. I shall leave it with you. Here is your fiery splendor. I have completed my instructions, my counsel," he said when he left the sign of his being, the Bundle of Flames, as it is called. It wasn't clear just what it was; it was wound about with coverings. It was never unwrapped. Its sewing wasn't clear because no one looked on while it was being wrapped.

In this way they left instructions, and then they disappeared from there on the mountain of Hacauitz. Their wives and children never saw them again. The nature of their disappearance was not clear. But whatever the case with their disappearance, their instructions were clear, and the bundle became precious to those who remained. It was a memorial to their fathers. Immediately they burned offerings before this memorial to their fathers.

[RETRIEVING WRITINGS FROM THE EAST]

And then they remembered what had been said about the east. This is when they remembered the instructions of their fathers. The ancient things received from their fathers were not lost. The tribes gave them their wives, becoming their fathers-in-law as they took wives. And there were three of them who said, as they were about to go away:

"We are going to the east, where our fathers came from," they said, then they followed their road. The three of them were representative sons:

Cocaib was the name of the son of Jaguar Quitze who represented all the Cauecs.

Coacutec was the name of the son of Jaguar Night who served as the sole representative of the Greathouses.

Coahau was the name of the only son of Mahucutah, representing the Lord Quichés.

So these are the names of those who went across the sea. There were only three who went, but they had skill and knowledge. Their being was not quite that of mere humans. They advised all their brothers, elder and younger, who were left behind. They were glad to go:

"We're not dying. We're coming back," they said when they went, yet it was these same three who went clear across the sea.

And then they arrived in the east; they went there to receive lordship. Next comes the name of the lord with dominion over those of the east, where they arrived.

And then they came before the lord named Nacxit,[1] the great lord and sole judge over a populous domain. And he was the one who gave out the signs of lordship, all the emblems; the signs of the Keeper of the Mat and the Keeper of the Reception House Mat were set forth.

And when the signs of the splendor and lordship of the Keeper of the Mat and Keeper of the Reception House Mat were set forth, Nacxit gave a complete set of the emblems of lordship. Here are their names:

> Canopy, throne.
> Bone flute, bird whistle.
> Paint of powdered yellow stone.
> Puma's paw, jaguar's paw.

---

1. "Four feet," a title of the king (or god) Quetzalcoatl.

Head and hoof of deer.
Bracelet of rattling snail shells.
Gourd of tobacco.
Nosepiece.
Parrot feathers, heron feathers.

They brought all of these when they came away. From across the sea, they brought back the writings about Tulan. In the writings, in their words, they spoke of having cried.

And then, when they got back up in their citadel, named Hacauitz, all the Tams and Ilocs gathered there. All the tribes gathered themselves together: they were happy. When Cocaib, Coacutec, and Coahau came back, they resumed their lordship over the tribes. The Rabinals, the Cakchiquels, and those of the Bird House were happy. Only the signs of the greatness of lordship were revealed before them. Now the lords became great in their very being; when they had displayed their lordship previously, it was incomplete.

This was when they were at Hacauitz. The only ones with them were all those who had originally come from the east. And they spent a long time there on that mountain. * * * Then splendor and majesty grew among the Quiché. The greatness and weight of the Quiché reached its full splendor and majesty with the surfacing and plastering of the canyon and citadel. The tribes came, whether small or great and whatever the titles of their lords, adding to the greatness of the Quiché. As splendor and majesty grew, so grew the houses of gods and the houses of lords.

But the lords could not have accomplished it, they could not have done the work of building their houses or the houses of the gods, were it not for the fact that their vassals had become numerous. They neither had to lure them nor did they kidnap them or take them away by force, because each one of them rightfully belonged to the lords. And the elder and younger brothers of the lords also became populous.

Each lord led a crowded life, crowded with petitions. The lords were truly valued and had truly great respect. The birthdays of the lords were made great and held high by their vassals. Those who lived in the canyons and those who lived in the citadels multiplied then. Even so they would not have been numerous, had not all the tribes arrived to give themselves up.

And when war befell their canyons and citadels, it was by means of their genius that the Lord Plumed Serpent and the Lord Cotuha blazed with power. Plumed Serpent became a true lord of genius:

On one occasion he would climb up to the sky; on another he would go down the road to Xibalba.

On another occasion he would be serpentine, becoming an actual serpent.

On yet another occasion he would make himself aquiline, and on another feline; he would become like an actual eagle or a jaguar in his appearance.

On another occasion it would be a pool of blood; he would become nothing but a pool of blood.

Truly his being was that of a lord of genius. All the other lords were fearful before him. The news spread; all the tribal lords heard about the existence of this lord of genius.

And this was the beginning and growth of the Quiché, when the Lord Plumed Serpent made the signs of greatness. His face was not forgotten by his grandsons and sons. He didn't do these things just so there would be one single lord, a being of genius, but they had the effect of humbling all the tribes when he did them. It was just his way of revealing himself, but because of it he became the sole head of the tribes.

This lord of genius named Plumed Serpent was in the fourth generation of lords; he was both Keeper of the Mat and Keeper of the Reception House Mat.

And so he left signs and sayings for the next generation. They achieved splendor and majesty, and they, too, begot sons, making the sons still more populous. Tepepul and Iztayul were begotten; they merely served out their reign, becoming the fifth generation of lords. They begot another generation of lords. * * * They were great lords, they were people of genius. Plumed Serpent and Cotuha were lords of genius, and Quicab and Cauizimah were lords of genius. They knew whether war would occur; everything they saw was clear to them. Whether there would be death, or whether there would be famine, or whether quarrels would occur, they knew it for certain, since there was a place to see it, there was a book. Council Book was their name for it.

[CONCLUSION]

And here shall appear the faces, one by one, of each of the Quiché lords:

Jaguar Quitze, origin of the Cauecs.

Cocauib, in the second generation after Jaguar Quitze.

Jaguar Conache, who began the office of Keeper of the Mat, was in the third generation.

Cotuha and Iztayul, in the fourth generation.

Plumed Serpent and Cotuha, at the root of the lords of genius, were in the fifth generation.

Tepepul and Iztayul next, sixth in the sequence.

Quicab and Cauizimah, in the seventh change of lordship, were the culmination of genius.

Tepepul and Xtayub, in the eighth generation.

Tecum and Tepepul, in the ninth generation.

Eight Cords, with Quicab, in the tenth generation of lords.

Seven Thought and Cauatepech next, eleventh in the sequence of lords.

Three Deer and Nine Dog, in the twelfth generation of lords. And they were ruling when Tonatiuh[2] arrived. They were hanged by the Castilian people.

Tecum and Tepepul were tributary to the Castilian people. They had already been begotten as the thirteenth generation of lords.

Don Juan de Rojas and don Juan Cortés, in the fourteenth generation of lords. They are the sons of Tecum and Tepepul.

So these are the generations, the sequences of lordships for the Keeper of the Mat and Keeper of the Reception House Mat, the lords who have led the Cauecs of Quiché. * * * This is enough about the being of Quiché, given that there is no longer a place to see it. There is the original book and ancient writing owned by the lords, now lost, but even so, everything has been completed here concerning Quiché, which is now named Santa Cruz.

---

2. "The Sun," the native name for Pedro de Alvarado.

⊶ ⊷

Songs of the Aztec Nobility

15th–16th century

The court poets of the Aztecs and their allies created the most extensive and exquisite body of poetry ever known to have existed in Mesoamerica. Many of these lyrics are marked by a gentle melancholy and a delicate aestheticism, with poems often taking poetry itself as their subject. Poetry was commonly described metaphorically in Nahuatl as *in xochitl in cuicatl,* "flowers and birdsong," emblems of beauty in a transient world. The poets delighted in creating beautiful images and in elegant plays on words, and often intertwined friendship and poetry together as the greatest human values. As one poem puts it in the collection known as *Cantares Mexicanos:*

> We lift our songs, our flowers,
> these songs of the Only Spirit.
> Then friends embrace,
> the companions in each others' arms.
> So it has been said by Tochihuitzin,
> so it has been said by Coyolchiuqui:
> We come here only to sleep,
> we come here only to dream.

The same images and methods came to be used for very different purposes as the Aztec empire grew over the course of the century before the Spanish conquest. Court poets began to celebrate the beauties of conquest, and death in battle became an act of almost poetic virtue: "Jaguar flowers are opening," one poem declares; "knife-death flowers are becoming delicious upon the field." As another poem puts it, "We'll dare to go where fame, where glory, is gotten, where nobility is gotten, where flower death is won."

Aztec poetry underwent a further revolution with the coming of Cortés and the fall of the Aztec empire. Now the surviving poets had to consider the brevity of human life in a new way, involving not only individual mortality but the swift defeat of the greatest empire the region had ever known. Both the traditional themes and the unsettling colonial context are apparent in the poems as they have come down to us, chiefly in two manuscripts compiled between 1550 and 1585: the *Cantares Mexicanos* ("Songs of the Mexicans") and the *Romances de los Señores de la Nueva España* ("Ballads of the Lords of New Spain"). Written in the Roman alphabet but in the Aztecs' language, Nahuatl, these collections of close to two hundred poems record songs that likely come from a range of times. Some appear to be purely pre-Conquest poems, showing no trace of later events; others seem to be traditional poems revised in light of the Conquest; others (like the "Fish Song" and the "Water-Pouring Song" below) were clearly composed as direct responses to the Conquest itself.

The poems interweave the natural imagery of brightly colored tropical birds and flowers with a social landscape of great nobles, such as the Aztec king Moctezuma and the pre-Conquest ruler Nezahualcoyotl (1402–1472), king of the allied city of Texcoco. Often the poet sings in the name of these rulers or other nobles, and traditionally many poems were ascribed to Nezahualcoyotl himself, much as the Hebrew psalms were ascribed to King David. In post-Conquest times, the poems at times refer to still living figures, at other times recall great heroes of the past, invoking their aid in the ongoing struggle for life and liberty. Even the most pressing historical events are seen through the prism of metaphor, as in the "Fish Song," whose speaker presents the Aztecs as fish, hoping the new bishop will stop eating them now that Lent is over and Easter has come. The long, haunting "Water-Pouring Song" shows the nobles pressed into service hauling water, and the poet turns their water jugs into images of Aztec culture and finally of the poem itself.

The "Water-Pouring Song" extends its range abroad, recounting a trip across the ocean by the Mexican leader Martín Ecatl in 1525 to meet Spain's emperor Charles V, and it includes a surreal encounter with Pope Clement VII, sitting on his mat with his turquoise blowgun. The post-Conquest poems often speak directly to the new God whom the Spaniards have brought, Dios (or Tios, or Tiox, as they call him) and his companions Jesus, Mary, and the Holy Spirit (*spilitu xanto* in the manuscript). Often God is addressed as Ipalnemoani, "Giver of Life," or as Tloque Nahuaque, "The Ever Present, Ever Near," traditional names for the great god Tezcatlipoca. Never named outright or seen directly, the old gods often seem still to be in the wings in these poems.

As it is set down in the manuscripts, Aztec poetry is written not in verse form but in paragraphs of varying lengths, sometimes prefaced with syllables that indicate rhythms to be used (*titico titico titico, toco toco toti*). A modern translator has a choice: to break these paragraphs into shorter lines corresponding to verses, usually guided by repetitions and variations in phrasing; or to retain the paragraphing of the manuscripts, presenting the poems as chants rather than as lyric utterances. The first selection here is set in verse form, which is how the poems have usually been published by Mexican scholars; the rest of the selections are given in paragraph form, in the eloquent contemporary translations of John Bierhorst.

The largest compilation of Aztec poetry, the *Cantares* manuscript, was apparently assembled by native informants under the direction of the Spanish friar Bernardino de Sahagún, compiler of the great historical and cultural survey called the *General History of the Affairs of New Spain* (see page 846). Sahagún was evidently seeking to collect the poems to serve as a sort of sourcebook he could use in composing hymns and psalms in Nahuatl for his parishioners to use; see page 122 for selections from these psalms. Fascinated by the native cultures and deeply learned in Nahuatl, Sahagún had no interest in preserving the poems for their own sake; on the contrary, in his preface to his book of psalms he wrote that his parishioners' "persistence in singing their old songs arouses a good deal of suspicion as to the sincerity of their Christian Faith." It is a fitting poetic irony that these poems have been preserved for us today thanks to Sahagún's effort to study and then replace them so that "the praises of idols and idolatry be buried as they deserve."

PRONUNCIATIONS:

Dozens of names of people and places appear in the following poems; only a few of the most common are listed here. Generally Nahuatl names are pronounced as they are spelled, following Spanish usage at the time; *x* is pronounced *sh; h* is silent (*hua* has the sound *wa*); and *que* has the sound *kay*. Names are usually accented on the next to last syllable.

cuicatl: KWEE-cahtl
Cantares Mexicanos: cahn TAH-race muy-hi-CAH-nohs
Huexotzinco: way-show-TZEEN-coh
Moctezuma: mock-tay-ZOOM-ah
Nahuatl: NAH-waht'l
Nezahualcoyotl: nets-ah-wahl-COY-yaht'l
Tezozomoc: tet-zoh-TZOH-mock
xochitl: SHOW-cheet'l
Sahagún: sah-ah-GOUN

Songs of the Aztec Nobility

Make your beginning, you who sing[1]

Xi huel om pehua
ti cuicanitl.
Ma oc xocon tzotzona
moxochihuehueuh.
Ma ic xi quimahuiltia
in tepilhuan
in cuauhtin in ocelo.
Cuel achic tiquitotlanehuia.

Make your beginning,
you who sing.
May you beat again
your flowered drum,
may you give joy
to my lords,
the eagles, the jaguars.[2]
Briefly are we here together.

In zan iyollo ya quinequi
in ipal nemohuani
in cozcatli in quetzalli
in quipuztequiz oncan.
in quimmonequiz
quimontepehuatiuh
in cuauhtin in ocelo.
Cuel achic tiquitotlanehuia.

The one heart's desire
of the Giver of Life
is jewels, is quetzal plumes—
to tear them apart.
This is his desire:
to scatter apart
the eagles, the jaguars.
Briefly are we here together.

Quexquich cozcatli
quexquich quetzalli
tlatilo. Oo
ac a chalchiuhitli
ac a teocuitlatl.
In ma ye ica on xon ahuiyacan
ma ye ica on popolihui
a in totlaocol antepilhuan.

How many jewels,
how many quetzal plumes,
have been destroyed? Ah,
though it was jade,
though it was gold.
So may you now be happy:
for surely too will perish
our sorrow, my lords.

Auh in tocuic
auh in toxochiuh
ya in tonequimilol
xon ahuiyacan
ic malinticac
cuauhyotl ocelyotl
ica tiyazque
in canon ye yuhcan.

And these our songs,
these our flowers,
they are our shrouds.
So be happy:
woven into them
is the eagle, the jaguar;
we will go with them
there where it is all the same.

Zaniyo ye nican
titocnihua in tlalticpac.
Zan cuel achica tontiximati
zan titotlanehuico ye nican.
Ohua zan cuel achic
in inahuac in ipal nemoani
zan tocontlanehuico
ichimalxochiuh
a ixtlahuacateca.

It is only here
we have friends, on earth.
Only briefly do we know one another,
only here are we together
Ah, only briefly here
do we share with the Giver of Life;
we are only given a loan
of his flowered shield—
soon it must be returned.

1. Translated by David Damrosch.

2. Orders of warriors.

In ma oc ompa papaqui in toyollo	So let us rejoice within our hearts,
yeehuaya in tlalticpac	all who are on earth;
zan cuel achica tontiximati	only briefly do we know one another,
45 zan titotlanehuico ye nican.	only here are we together.
Maca xi tlaocoyacan antepilhuan	So do not be saddened, my lords:
ayac ayac	no one, no one
mocauhtiaz in tlalticpac.	is left behind on earth.

Burnishing them as sunshot jades[1]

Burnishing them as sunshot jades, mounting them as trogon feathers, I recall the root songs, I, the singer, composing good songs as troupials:[2] I've scattered them as precious jades, producing a flower brilliance to entertain the Ever Present, the Ever Near.

As precious troupial feathers, as trogons, as roseate swans, I design my songs. Gold jingles are my songs. I, a parrot corn-tassel bird, I sing, and they resound. In this place of scattering flowers I lift them up before the Ever Present, the Ever Near.

Delicious are the root songs, as I, the parrot corn-tassel bird, lift them through a conch of gold, the sky songs passing through my lips: like sunshot jades I make the good songs glow, lifting fumes of flower fire, a singer making fragrance before the Ever Present, the Ever Near.

The spirit swans are echoing me as I sing, shrilling like bells from the Place of Good Song. As jewel mats, shot with jade and emerald sunray, the Green Place flower songs are radiating green. A flower incense, flaming all around, spreads sky aroma, filled with sunshot mist, as I, the singer, in this gentle rain of flowers sing before the Ever Present, the Ever Near.

As colors I devise them. I strew them as flowers in the Place of Good Song. As jewel mats, shot with jade and emerald sunray, the Green Place flower songs are radiating green. A flower incense, flaming all around, spreads sky aroma, filled with sunshot mist, as I, the singer, in this gentle rain of flowers sing before the Ever Present, the Ever Near.

I exalt him, rejoice him with heart-pleasing flowers in this place of song. With narcotic fumes my heart is pleasured. I soften my heart, inhaling them. My soul grows dizzy with the fragrance, inhaling good flowers in this place of enjoyment. My soul is drunk with flowers.

Flowers are our only adornment

Flowers are our only adornment. Only through songs does our pain subside—within your home, O God.

Will companions be lost to me, comrades lost to me, when also I, Yoyontzin,[1] have gone to the Singing Place, to Life Giver's home?

Let's have these turquoise-swanlike flowers! These are trogons, and they're spinning—these dead, dry flowers. You enshroud yourself with these, O king, O Nezahualcoyotl!

---

1. This and the remaining poems are translated by John Bierhorst.
2. Tropical orioles whose orange and black feathers were

highly valued.
1. A name for Nezahualcoyotl.

Let your hearts know this, O princes, O eagles, O jaguars: not forever are we comrades! Only for a moment here, and all will be departing for His home.

Your fame will never be destroyed, O prince, O Tezozomoc. This would seem to be
your song. Ah! Indeed, I'm weeping here, I'm suffering. You've gone to His home.

It seems I suffer, I grieve. Nevermore, never again will I come to earth and find you.
You've gone to His home.

I cry, I grieve, knowing we're to go away

I cry, I grieve, knowing we're to go away and leave these good flowers, these good
songs. Let's be pleasured, let's sing. We're off to be destroyed in His home.

Our friends are ill at ease? Sick, my hearts are vexed! We're not born twice, we're not
engendered twice. Rather we must leave this earth.

Near and in the presence of this company a moment! It can never be. I can never be
pleasured, never be content.

Where does my heart live? Where is my home? Where does my city lie? I am poor
on earth.

You give a gift of jadestones, You unfold them spun as plumes: You give a flower
crown of troupial to the princes.

And when these sundry flowers have clothed my heart, making it drunk, then I cry
and go before our mother, Santa María.

I say to Life Giver, "Do not frown, do not be reluctant here on earth. Let us—us!—
live beside you in your home within the sky."

But can what I say be real, O Life Giver? We merely sleep, we were merely born to
dream, and though I say it here on earth it falls on no one's ears.

Though it be jade, though it be jewels, directed to Life Giver, even so it falls on no
one's ears.

Your hearts are shaken down as paintings, O Moctezuma[1]

Your hearts are shaken down as paintings, O Moctezuma. I come bringing forth,
come shaking down, these laughing ones. The quetzal-butterfly flowers come
winging like plumes: I cause them to dance, making skillful music with a jade-
water conch horn, blowing jade flutes as though gold.

I crave your flowers, O Life Giver, O God. Shaking them down, I'm provided with
songs.

These flowers, these hearts of mine are stirring as parrots. These flowers, these log
drums of mine are stirring as parrots. As flowers, as pictures, as parrots I spread
out His words.

Be joyful. Be pleasured. These are not forever here: we must go to His home, my
brave, my lord, O Moctezuma. On earth they are loaned: the delicious flowers
are loaned.

In blaze land, fragrantly, you come filled with sunray and as flowers, O God. Ah, He
that shines among the jaguar blades, He, the eagle, screams. Ah, He is in His place.

---

1. A note in the margin of the manuscript says: "A Heuxotzincan piece, those of Huexotzinco coming to ask Moctezuma
for aid against Tlaxcala." Huexotzinco was an allied city south of the Valley of Mexico, which appealed to Moctezuma in
1515 for support against their mutual enemy Tlaxcala.

I soar along, winging, in God's presence. And the roseate swans, the troupials, the plumelike captive butterflies, are shaken down as noble lords in the presence of all. By means of a flower-water conch horn my songs are marching forth.

I arrive, come from where the green Great Water lies. Most definitely does it stir, seethe: it roars. I fly, a quetzal. I become a turquoise swan and go to be amid the flood in Huexotzinco.

I'll follow along and get to know these braves, these jade swans, turquoise swans, these golden butterflies, jewel-like birds that stand guard amid the flood in Huexotzinco.

Amid flower water, where water of gold and water of jades are pouring, sings the Plume Duck: plume and tail are whirling.

I, the singer, stand aloft. Where the Troupial shines, where the rushes are, I'm unfurling these songs, I who provide Him with flowers.

I strike it up—here!—I, the singer

I strike it up—here!—I, the singer. Flowers, good songs, are blooming in my heart. With these I fan Life Giver.

I'm dancing—here!—I, the singer. Flowers, good songs, are blooming in my heart. With these I fan Life Giver.

Nobles and kings are sprouting as eagles, greening as jaguars, in Mexico: Lord Ahuitzotl is singing arrows, singing shields.

Life Giver, let your flowers not be gathered! Dust and lords are smoking on the field. You've given necklaces to Totoquihuaztli and Acolhuacan's Nezahualpilli. You've adorned them in blaze flowers, shield flowers. Lord Ahuitzotl is singing arrows, singing shields.

I grieve, I weep. What good is this? The shield flowers are carried away, they're sent aloft. Ah, where can I find what my heart desires?

Incomparable war death! Incomparable flower death![1] Life Giver has blessed it. Ah, where can I find what my heart desires?

I seek the good songs whence they come—and I am poor. Let me not sing.

Where am I to find your flowers, Life Giver? Alas, I am poor. Let me not sing.

Where are you? You're entertained, O Life Giver! Yonder you're served at your turquoise-swan throne! You're regaled with flowers: these songs that I, the singer, lift for you beside the drum are painted as flowers.

It's here that you're pleasured, O Life Giver. These songs that I, the singer, lift for you beside the drum are painted as flowers.

God! Life Giver! Where are you? You're in the sky. You cradle the earth: the world lies in your arms.

You're served everywhere. People cry out to you all over the world. You're asked, you're petitioned, for your splendor, your glory. You're in the sky: and the world lies in your arms.

Perhaps these glorious jades and bracelets are your hearts and loved ones, O father. God! Life Giver! So many do I utter near you and in your presence—I that am Totoquihuaztli.[2] How could you run weary? How could you run slack?

---

1. The Aztecs and certain neighbors engaged in "flower wars," tournaments whose losers would become human sacrifices in the other city's temples.

2. King of the city of Tlacopan, who died during the Conquest in 1519.

Easily, in a moment might you slacken, O father. God! Life Giver! So many do I utter
near you and in your presence!—I that am Totoquihuaztli. How could you run
weary? How could you run slack?

They make my heart drunk: they flower, they intoxicate me here on earth: I am drunk
with war flowers.

He shows mercy to everyone. Thus people are alive on earth. Heaven comes here!
And I am drunk with war flowers.

from Fish Song: It was composed when we were conquered
1

Rise, O all you golden fishes! For forty days there's been a fast. Today it seems that
Jesucristo Ipaltinemi is risen up, is resurrected. Hail, nephew!

It seems he's really arrived—he who went to sit on the right hand of his father, God.
Hail, nephew!

By all means be careful, you golden fish! We're poor, we have no songs in the water
here, and we crave the reed-thrush plume who sings like a precious bell, who
sings for the Only Spirit. Hail, nephew!

And so I weep. What have we done to deserve this, we sandfish, we mudfish? The
bishop celebrates a feast at our expense. Yet don't we become God's creatures
that way? Hail, nephew!

I sigh, dear cob. O elder brother, O Axolohua, we crave our comrades—even Axayacatl[1] the boat bug—who shrill, whose songs are good. It seems that he reverber-
ates, a chili-red locust on high, he, the green frog. Ah!

Woe to us, friend water beetle, dear water bug! We've offended God: we're not good
to eat. Lucky the parrot fish, the little shrimp, and the jade amaranth! They're all
in heaven.

We poor little Chichimec fish are miserable. Our comrades surround us here in these
waters, this Mexico. Where can we go, we that are conquered here?

Take heart! All the princes are fleeing to Coyonacazco—the roseate-swan fish
Oquiztzin, the eagle mudfish Tlacotzin, the jaguar fish Motelchiuh. Would they
roast him? Would God in Coyohuacan have a feast at their expense?[2]

4

Over the dry land he scatters us fishes, us Mexicans, over the turf. Ah yes, we reed
frogs are hopping. A blaze, a flower flood! He spreads it upon us, and houses are
smoking. He does it! In Santiago!

The parrot fish and all the teosintes have returned. O comrades, let it be done with!
Let us Mexicans be plunged in water-weed. A blaze, a flower flood! He spreads
it upon us, and houses are smoking. He does it! In Santiago!

O Tápia Motelchiuh, the Only Spirit has caused you to see things in this picture place
of yours, amid your paintings. And he causes weeping, causes sadness here: the

---

1. A pun: "Axayacatl" is a proper name but also the name
of a water beetle.
2. The final battle of the conquest of the capital took place
at Coyonazco at the northern end of the island. After their
surrender, Cuauhtemoc and other surviving Aztec nobles
were held in Cortés's encampment at Coyohuacan on the
mainland.

Mexican nation is passing away. He scatters us fishes in Santiago, each and every one, and all are passing away.

Hail, nephew, O younger brother, Tápia, and you, Don Juan! Let's carry him down, a cotinga, him, the tlatoani Guzmán! Ah!

I'm a plume fish, running through the waters, passing among jade reed flowers, seeking the songs of God.

And trogons are coming, appearing: they all have music. There! Where flowers lie, the reed frogs itch: they sing.

Let us poor green frogs go sadly singing among these turquoise-swan rushes. O Tápia!

With these, his songs, we wait upon our lord, the Only Spirit. O whitefishes! On Saturdays there's a tribute![3]

5

Our songs are twirling as new-minted golden flowers. And ah! the little fishes are dancing with these. O plume-water whirler, O turquoise cricket, sing in Mexico! Hail, nephew, comrade!

It seems that corn-blossom plumes are strewn on earth: you flower as squash-blossom jades, and within them you sip, O turquoise pollen bee.

I, a little jade marsh crab, say, "Where shall we go—tomorrow, the next day? Let us be trapped in the bulrush net! Not so, my friend? Let us be cheered!"

Indeed I recall him. It's quite as though I were a precious shrimp, come out among water-weed, reaching the forebears, I, a Mexican fish. Not so, my friend? Let us be cheered!

Ah! Come forth! Let's all dance—all us fishes—in this, God's place of rain! We're off to be born in the Bishop Lord's presence.

Let every man sing. We fishes have stood up our drums. Dance, Fray Pedro! What would our father, the Bishop Lord, think of you now?

8

The bishop begins, he strikes up a song, and Your glory now lives in the world. You're stirring as plumes: Your words are scattered, Your reed-flower jades, Your reed-flower pearl shells. Let us be pleasured with these!

Hail, lords! Now we fishes will die content, for we will have seen the World Owner, God. Be pleasured!

You're little fishes, whose souls are strewn as countless paintings, as pictures, as jades, as beads. Because of these we too are singing. These shall pray to God. Hail, nephew! O fish in the world! O Tápia!

Come, your home is in the waters, O all you little fish plumes. Now God has music. Hail, nephew! O fish in the world! O Tápia!

God's water-dwelling creatures, indeed, the mud-puppy fish and the dace, have no songs at all. They use the green frog, the reed frog, as their song, and it sings and becomes glorious. The Axayacatls are pleasured!

No one sees them! How do their songs, their flowers, exist?—these water chilis, these crimson reed flowers, these flowers of the sun that make Jade-Water paintings

---

3. Spanish Catholics at this time abstained from meat on Saturdays, eating fish instead.

dance? They use the green frog, the reed frog, as their song, and it sings and becomes glorious! The Axayacatls are pleasured!

9

Via jade waters you pass among picture plumes here in Mexico, you cotinga fish, you, Don Juan, you, Itztlolinqui, in God's home. Hear it, you Huexotzincans!—the jade-gong pealing of San Francisco's church-bell flowers!

"I, a Mexican, grieve, as I wander among the jade reeds, I, Mud-Puppy Soldier, awaiting God's words in this home of his. Truly, take heart!"

Hail, nephews! Yes, Life Giver has dried us out, us little fishes, there in Coyonacazco. And so the end has come. Where might we go, alas? Truly, take heart!

Ah! Whoever is His friend, it seems, has been ensnared. Forsake Him—and hail!—O friends. O friends, we little fishes are gathered together in Axomolco, and one of us—one of these days—will fall into the net, and just in this way we will bloody ourselves. Rejoice! And hail!

A singer am I, and here in the water I strike it up, I beat my flower drum. O Mud-Puppy Soldier! Be pleasured with these, your flower banners!

O you that dwell among many-hued water lilies! Mud-Puppy Soldier! Be pleasured with these, your flower banners!

My hearts are grieving where waters and the navel lie: "Ah, we Mexicans are little fishes!" But there! Where waters part, you've come to life. There! You're born, Don Juan, and you, Tápia! Golden sedges glisten where the waters lie, among the plumelike willows.

Let us Mexicans, us little fish, be pleasured where the waters part within the lake. Golden sedges glisten where the waters lie, among the plumelike willows.

When our Lord spoke out a third time, He made two fish: a male and then a female. He charged them: "You, you are the ones who shall live in the waters.

"Oh, they never shall rest. All the fishes shall serve. Yet no matter how many shall catch you, you are my charges, you, you shall dwell in the waters."

from Water-Pouring Song
1

There were plume willows at the turquoise-green waters in Chapolco. We Mexicans had reached jade water's flowing-out place. Ah! And the waters are His, and He drinks them, it's true. Drinks them, it's true. And ah, this Mexico arrives in that Chapolco yonder. Aya!

It resembles that time of our utmost eagerness when we Mexicans set out from Acocolco[1] to reach this place that is here. And ah, the waters are His, and He drinks them, it's true.

When the Captain arrived in Mexico and Moctezuma went out to meet him, then he got down from his horse; and he adorned him with a gold necklace, spoke to him, and embraced him. And the waters are His, and He drinks them, it's true.

And right away he says to him, "You've wearied yourself in reaching your city, this Mexico. You've come to govern your mat and your seat. For but a moment and a

---

1. As the Aztecs' ancestors migrated south into the Valley of Mexico, they lived for a time at Acocolco.

day I've tended things for you. Poor is your vassal." He speaks to him, embraces him. And the waters are His, and He drinks them, it's true.

Now woe! He gives off smoke! This is how he enters, this conquistador, this Captain. Now all the lords are yet alive: Commander Atlixcatzin and the troop chief Tepehuatzin. And as these princes come forth pouring water, Mexico is handed over. Oh! the waters are His, and He drinks them, it's true.

"We who've come to Water's Midst to marvel are Tlaxcalans: Mexican princes are pouring out their waters!" Lord Moctezuma's hauling vats of water. And the city passes on, ensconced in water-whorl flowers. Thus Mexico is handed over. Oh! the waters are His, and He drinks them, it's true.

Iye! The lady María[2] comes shouting. María comes saying, "O Mexicans, your water jars go here! Let all the lords come carrying." And Acolhuacan's Quetzalacxoyatl arrives. And Cuauhpopoca. Oh! the waters are His, and He drinks them, it's true.

O Life Giver, these urgently required ones have been broken, these, our water jars, and we are Mexicans. A cry goes up. They're picking them off at Eagle Gate, where recognition is achieved. Oh! the waters are His, and He drinks them, it's true.

They've been ruined with water hauling, and they're smoking—Nezahualquentzin and the troop chief Tepehuatzin. It's because we Mexicans are hauling water. And the waters are His, and He drinks them, it's true.

And so they're flowing. Indeed the ruler Moctezuma himself comes forth to pour one out. As roseate-swan flowers, as flower shoots, as trogons, as pine flowers, would he go off whirling his garlands: thus he glorifies Tenochcans. Oh! the waters are His, and He drinks them, it's true.

Oh never would our water pitchers be destroyed. These broad ones, these turquoise gems, are strewn as gold. Ensconced in roseate-swan hand-flowers, he's moved on to You. Shattered, he's moved on to Water's Midst, where waters and the navel lie: and so he glorifies Tenochcans. Oh! the waters are His, and He drinks them, it's true.

3

O nephews, hail! And hear a work assignment: we've come to do our water pouring. Now who will go and fetch the jadestone jars that we must carry? And yonder we're assembled, at Shore of the Bells, at the Place of Green Waters.

Oh none with us shall work for tribute. We're to pass away. Our guardian Don Diego Tehuetzquiti is to lead us. And yonder we're assembled, at Shore of the Bells, at the Place of Green Waters.

Our cups are born. It seems they're twirling—and as maize flowers—at the water's edge. These jade-water drums! At Chapultepec's side! Let all our brothers pour. Clean waters, then, will flow in beauty.

But I wonder, am I blessed? And so I grieve. O friends, where am I to go that I might pour these? For my heart desires them. Let Yonder be the church![3]

I weep, I sorrow, and I sing: I've broken these, my turquoise gems, my pearls, these water jars.

And merely in this manner let it be that I return them. Chirping for these flowers, let me head for home. At Flower Waters let me weep, composing them: I've broken these, my turquoise gems, my pearls, these water jars.

---

2. Cortés's interpreter and common-law wife Doña María or Malinche.

3. *Iquelexia* in the manuscript, from the Spanish *iglesia*, "church."

Indeed I seek those lords who drew the water. Nezahualtecolotl and Lord Coaihuitl.
In serenity I come to pour these waters at the emperor's. And may you all take
heart. Hey Don Pedrotli![4]
Nobility will flow in beauty here. Could our carried waters perish then? Take heart.
Hey Don Pedrotli!

4

God and Only Spirit, you and you alone lay down the mirror and the flame that stands
here in the world,[5]
Where there used to be the black and color of your creatures who were carried-water
masters, who were lords.
I pass, I pass away, I pass beyond, that I might reach the plume-shore turquoise lode.
There I'll fetch my limpid green one. Ah!
"O Ixtlilxochitl! O Mexicans!" So it is that they who were swallowed are painted as
shields—these hidden ones.
O charges of the flood-and-blaze! And so it is that they shall pour them. And it's in this
manner that Tenochcans are to labor. Oh it seems that they themselves are done
for, they, Cuauhtemoc, Coanacoch, ah! and Tetlepanquetzatzin: they've heard the
multitude.
So it is that they who were swallowed are painted as spears. Indeed, the lord Captain[6]
has said it: "Paint them as turquoise pictures: the Mexicans' labor's in pictures!"
And oh it would seem that this labor's been taken from everywhere into the city.
Now they who've wept in sadness are the lords and rulers. It's our destiny and circumstance: they've painted them as turquoise pictures!
We must go to hear them. Ho, Cuauhtemoc! Oquiztzin! Huanitl! He's handed down
His judgment: our carried waters will never be destroyed. Take heart. And where
in time are we to go? To the emperor![7]
Take heart, nephews. Cuauhtemoc! Let's go have these captured ones, our pitchers,
be a raining mist of trogons. Off they go to fall as dew. Let our garlands flow pro-
fusely and as gold. Let us make our entry side by side with these, our carried wa-
ters. Off to the emperor!
Indeed I seek those lords who drew the water: Nezahualtecolotl and Lord Coaihuitl.
In serenity I come to pour these waters at the emperor's. May you all take heart.
Thus nobility will flow in beauty. Could our babes then perish? May you all take heart.

5

I, Lord Xicotencatl, am the one who's saying, "Pass away, and not in vain! Fetch your
shields, flowers, water jars. They're your pitchers—that is, your well-wrought
blade-jar urns!" With these we'll carry water: we'll go get water there in Mexico—Chapolco! Yes, in Water's Midst.
"Pass away, and not in vain, O nephew." Brothers! Nephews! Princes of the flood!
I'm pouring water, Lord Cuauhtencoz. Let's all go and carry water. Yes, we'll get the
water. Hey!

---

4. Don Pedro Temilotzin, a leader of resistance after the
Conquest.
5. God ("Tiox") has taken over the power of Tezcatlipoca,
"Smoking Mirror."
6. Cortés, who had illustrated reports prepared to send

home to Spain.
7. In 1525 Cortés brought a group of Aztec nobles to
Spain; some went on to Rome, where they met Pope
Clement VII.

Now brother Motelchiuh must shout. O friends, it's said that we're to fetch him in the dawn, him, our carried water, this very limpid one, this limpid green one, gleaming like an emerald. And yonder we arrive. O cup!

Pass away, and not in vain! Must Nanahuatl have a craving? O brother, O Commander Cuitlachihuitl! Truly he's well wrought, like gold, this painted one, our water jar—and he's gone painting Lord Axayacatl. Scattered, we're to pass beyond. And yonder we arrive. O cup!

Jade water sprinkles. My adornments fall in a raining mist. My Tlaxcalan uncles have come to give me Huanitl, my flower-water charge. O Chichimecs, pass away, and not in vain.

Blaze flowers, shield flowers, are blossoming in quantity: these flower shoots are bursting: they're scattered plentifully, because it seems they've come to take them, these, these golden ones, as captives. And yes, in bearing off these precious water jars of mine, I fetch those painted green ones. O my great ones!

O Acolhuacan's Don Antonio! Let me take you away! Hail, nephew! O Tehuetzquiti! And they pass away reviving as reed flowers, as colored banners, pass away as captives. This is how I carry off these painted green ones, these precious water jars of mine. See me, O great ones!

And I who recall these painted ones, these precious water jars—am Fray Pedro! Before he went away, the bishop Don Fray Juan purified this city with a golden balm and sprinkled it with water.

Yes, it seems that our beloved father, the bishop, has gone away. And before he went, he purified this city with a golden balm and sprinkled it with water.

Let's be off to Plume-Shore Chapultepec! And these handflowers? They pass away as turquoise swans reviving, for they've been captured, they, our pitcher jades. Hail, brothers! But be cautious. Beware of being broken, for Our Lord would scold us.

So let them follow onward. Go carefully! And yonder we're assembled. To Mexico, where tunas[8] lie, they're off to be revived as turquoise swans.

Friends, willow men, behold the pope, who's representing God, who speaks for him.

The pope is on God's mat and seat and speaks for him.

Who is this reclining on a golden chair? Look! It's the pope. He has his turquoise blowgun and he's shooting in the world.

It seems it's true: it seems he has his cross and golden staff, and these are shining in the world.

I grieve in Rome and see his flesh, and he's San Pedro, San Pablo![9]

It seems that from the four directions they've been captured: you've made them enter the golden refuge, and it's shining.

It seems the pope's home lies painted in golden butterflies. It's beaming.

6

Wind arises, roaring, hissing. The ocean seethes, and the boat goes creaking along.

We see great waves flowing over us, wonderful things of God. It's raining flowers, and the boat goes creaking along.

Friends, rejoice in these waters. You're splitting it open, O Don Martín! It's broken to pieces here on the ocean.

---

8. Prickly pears, grown for their fruit.

9. The Pope was regarded as the successor of the apostles Peter and Paul.

O Life Giver, you're alive in this place of fear. The waves are rolling over us. Let's go
 perish at the navel, at the roundel.

"No one in this boat is precious, friends. Can we return?" Let's go be counted at the
 navel, at the roundel!

Alas, I grieve. The emerald dew is on us. And where are we to go?

Life Giver causes grief. If only He were my friend, if only He were a kinsman. No
 one cares anymore about anyone here in the boat.

Inside this boat, this place of fear, jade waters are flowing over us, seething. Ah, these
 garlands roar, these fish are flying. See them!

Ah, and yonder stands the tree of sustenance, stands our palace. And these garlands
 roar, these fish are flying. See them!

9

We've been required right here, and this would seem to be the emperor's home. Would
 that His waters might make an appearance. They're being recited! Would God
 agree?

Let's call to the Only Spirit. It may be that in this manner we, the vassals, are allowed
 to spend a day near him and in his presence.

We, mere Mexicans, are off to marvel on the sea, the emperor commanding us: he's
 told us, "Go and see the holy father."

He's said: What do I need? Gold! Everybody bow down! Call out to God in excelsis![1]

And it's just for this that he sends us to Rome. He's told us, "Go and see the holy father."

Our hearts will be content, for he sends us on to Rome. He's told us, "Go and see the
 holy father."

It would seem that at the pope's, where the cavern house of colors stands, are golden
 words that give us life.

On account of trumpets there's a stirring. Aya! And they're honored where it stands:
 God's words, these trogons! They're ensconced in war capes. Ah, they give us life.

Bring them in, you princes. They're our comrades. Where? With God in Rome! Aya,
 there the pope is paying honor.

There in Rome she dwells, she the mother called Santa Cecelia! Aya, there the pope is
 paying honor.

Your flowers, it would seem, are budding, greening, in Willow Place, O Axayacatl.
 Indeed, you went away deserving. It's where the tunas lie!

White feather flowers are sifting down at Water Face. And it would seem that they're
 your flowers, Lord Axayacatl. Indeed, you went away deserving. It's where the
 tunas lie!

In the Place Unknown, where all are shorn, in heaven and as jades, perhaps, or
 turquoises, they're marshaled, they, the princes. They're with God.

Lord Oquiztzin flies along, perhaps, as a roscate swan. Perhaps Tlacotzin is an eagle
 plume. Yes, all are alive, and they're with God.

Take a look at the Only Spirit's flower field. There's a freshening in that place of
 heart pleasers: there's a plume dew raining all around.

Yonder dwells the turquoise swan-bird Don Martín. An egret bird is pleasured, and
 it's Coaihuitl. There's Don Juan!

---

1. In the highest (Latin).

Red feather trees are blossoming in God's home, and princes are inhaling them. Lord
   Anahuacatl and perhaps Commander Cuitlachihuitl are rejoicing in heaven.
They've been broken as plume jades or perhaps as turquoise gems: they're princes,
   and they're Mexicans, these Huexotzincans. Lord Anahuacatl and perhaps Commander Cuitlachihuitl are rejoicing in heaven.

In the flower house of sapodilla you remain a flower

In the flower house of sapodilla you remain a flower, a water whorl—at the flower
   throne of sapodilla—gone beyond to our father, God, the Only Spirit.
And You're the tinctured popcorn tree blooming here in Mexico: within You quetzal
   butterflies imbibe, here on earth: within You eagle birds imbibe: they're flying.
Gold is shining in your sapodilla house of trogons. Your home abounds in jade water
   whorls, O prince, O Jesucristo. You're singing in Anahuac.
Flowers are scattered. Your drums are shrilling with the sound of jingles. O prince, O
   Jesucristo, you're singing in Anahuac.
You're the red feather tree, blooming here in Mexico, diffusing fragrance, spreading
   over us throughout Anahuac.
Jades are scattered: flowers—your songs—are born. You lift them here in Mexico,
   your flowers: they're shining.
Jingles shrill in the midst of the field. Beyond is Tlacahuepan, carried off, diffusing
   the fragrance of yellow flowers, moving on to the Place Unknown.
You're hidden away at Seven Caves, where the mesquite grows.[1] The eagle cries, the
   jaguar whines: you, in the midst of the field—a roseate swan—fly onward, in the
   Place Unknown.

Moctezuma, you creature of heaven, you sing in Mexico

Moctezuma, you creature of heaven, you sing in Mexico, in Tenochtitlan.
Here where eagle multitudes were ruined, your bracelet house stands shining—there
   in the home of God our father.
There and in that place they come alive, ah! on the field! For a moment they come
   whirling, they the eagles, ah! the nobles Ixtlilcuechahuac and Matlaccuiatzin.
And in that place these nobles gain renown and honor: bells are scattered, dust and
   lords grow golden.
Onward, friends! We'll dare to go where fame, where glory's, gotten, where nobility
   is gotten, where flower death is won.
Your name and honor live, O prince. Prince Tlacahuepan! Ixtlilcuechahuac! You've
   gone and won war death.
Sky dawn is rising up. The multitude, the birds, are shrilling. Precious swans are being created. Turquoise troupials are being created.
Lucky you, arrayed in chalk and plumes. O flower-drunk Moctezuma! Precious
   swans are being created. Turquoise troupials are being created.

---

1. A suggestion of ongoing resistance: the departed warriors are gathering in the northern desert region from which they
originally came to conquer the Valley of Mexico.

➾ PERSPECTIVES ➾

The Conquest and Its Aftermath

When Hernán Cortés sailed from Cuba in 1519 to invade Mexico with his little army, he went in defiance of his superior Diego Velázquez, the governor of the recently established Spanish colony at Cuba. Velázquez was well aware of the precariousness of his foothold in the area and was not yet ready to attempt a major invasion on the mainland; at most, Cortés was authorized simply to establish an outlying base colony. Any sensible person, in fact, would never have thought of doing more with so small a force, but Cortés was convinced that God would enable him to succeed against all odds. To recruit men for his expedition, he had banners made that proclaimed, "Brothers and comrades, let us follow the sign of the Holy Cross in true faith, for under this sign we shall conquer." Having assembled his forces, he sailed first to the Yucatan coast, where his ships were attacked by hostile natives and he could only stay briefly on shore. There, however, he had the good fortune to come upon a sailor, Jerónimo de Aguilar, who had been shipwrecked on the coast several years before; he had settled in and learned the local Mayan language in the process.

Cortés could now communicate with the natives, and he soon had a second stroke of good fortune: he took on board a young Mexican noblewoman who was fluent in Mayan as well as in her native Nahuatl. Now Cortés could communicate with the Aztecs, through a double process of translation: Jerónimo de Aguilar could translate from Spanish into Mayan, and she could translate from Mayan into Nahuatl. Having her baptized as Doña Maria, Cortés made her his common-law wife, interpreter, and confidante; she became known to the Indians as "La Malinche."

Cortés next made a successful landing on the gulf coast of Mexico, at a swampy site he grandly dubbed La Villa Rica de la Vera Cruz, "The Rich Town of the True Cross." Though by all rights his mission should have ended there, he burned his boats so as to keep his troops from leaving. In letters to Charles V, Cortés claimed that his men had threatened to desert the new colony, but probably he was really preventing anyone from returning to Cuba to help his great rival, Diego Velázquez, establish authority on the mainland. The ships destroyed, Cortés and some four hundred men began the march into the interior. As they made their way toward the Aztec capital of Tenochtitlán, Cortés began to hear of the natives' widespread anger against their Aztec overlords. He also soon received ambassadors from the Aztec king, Moctezuma II, who was concerned to learn whether Cortés might possibly be the returning god Quetzalcoatl, as rumored, or whether he was an impostor.

Later accounts both by Spanish historians and by native chroniclers probed the enigma of Moctezuma's shifting responses to the news of Cortés's approach, which he alternately welcomed and rebuffed. Once Cortés reached the capital, he succeeded in placing Moctezuma under house arrest, a development that fatally damaged Moctezuma's prestige among his allies. Some sources describe the Aztec king as gullibly convinced that Cortés was indeed the returning Quetzalcoatl, yet a different picture emerges from close reading of accounts such as those given here by Bernal Díaz del Castillo and by Bernardino de Sahagún's native informants. Even as he appears to welcome Cortés with open arms, Moctezuma tries a variety of strategies to put him off from approaching the capital. As the historian Davíd Carrasco has argued in a book called *Quetzalcoatl and the Irony of Empire,* the Aztec ruling house had shorn up its political power by claiming to be ruling on behalf of the absent divine Toltec king. Moctezuma could hardly refuse to welcome him outright, particularly after Cortés got wind of the old legend and began to intimate that he was indeed the returned monarch, or at least his ambassador (with the Spanish king Charles V in place of Quetzalcoatl). Further, even though it soon became clear that Cortés and his rough-and-ready troops were no divinities, it appears likely that Moctezuma hoped to use the newcomers to reinforce his fragile position at home among his

Cortés accepting the Aztecs' surrender, from a native chronicle called the *Lienzo de Tlaxcala,* (1550). Wearing an improbable feathered headdress, Cortés is shown with La Malinche standing behind him as translator, as he accepts the surrender of the Aztec leader Cuauhtemoc. The Tlaxcalans, who had sided with the Spanish, are shown with a Spanish soldier in the lower right. The Nahuatl caption says *Yc poliuhque mexica,* "Here perished the Mexica."

restive allies. He was unaware that Cortés—who protested friendship and admiration for him—was actively negotiating with his neighbors to destroy his empire.

After several months of a sort of standoff in Tenochtitlán, Cortés was forced to return to the coast to defeat a Spanish force sent from Cuba to bring him to heel. He left behind his hotheaded captain Pedro de Alvarado to keep watch over Moctezuma; while Cortés was away, however, Alvarado rightly or wrongly concluded that the natives were about to rise against him, and he engineered a massacre of many of the nobility in the midst of a religious festival. The enraged Aztecs retaliated in full force. During a bloody night known as the *noche triste* ("night of sorrows"), they succeeded in driving the Spaniards from the city. As they regrouped onshore, the would-be conquistadors could see captured comrades, high on the summit of Huitzilopochtli's temple, made to dance in the war god's honor before having their hearts cut out.

Undeterred by this disaster, Cortés soon returned to the Valley of Mexico with more men, and began campaigning among the Aztecs' neighbors to make a decisive strike against the capital. Aided by a combined force of 200,000 native warriors, Cortés mounted a long siege of Tenochtitlán, whose position out in Lake Texcoco, ordinarily very secure, became a trap once the inhabitants lost control of the causeways linking the city to the mainland. Starvation began to set in, and the situation became still more grave when plague broke out in the crowded city. By August of 1521, after weeks of street-to-street fighting, Cortés had destroyed the Aztecs' capital and was master of their empire. As an anonymous account from Tlatelolco recalled in 1528,

> Broken spears lie in the roads;
> we have torn our hair in our grief.
> The houses are roofless now,
> and their walls are red with blood.
>
> . . . . . .
>
> We have pounded our hands in despair
> against the adobe walls,
> for our inheritance, our city, is lost and dead.
> The shields of our warriors were its defense,
> but they could not save it.

In his *True History of the Conquest of New Spain,* Cortés's solider Bernal Díaz del Castillo describes with real regret the destruction of the capital and the neighboring cities, cities so magnificent that when they first saw them, he and his comrades thought they must be dreaming. "Today," he wrote in 1564, "everything is torn down, lost, so there is nothing left." He was right that much had been destroyed: palaces and temples were pulled down, their stones used to build churches; "idolatrous" native books were burned en masse; over the course of the century as much as ninety percent of the native population perished from warfare, brutal mistreatment, and imported diseases like smallpox and plague. Yet more of the culture survived than either Bernal Díaz or the Tlatelolcan chronicler believed: religious and medical practices carried on out of Spanish view or recast into Spanish forms; historical traditions preserved in native languages with the convenient technology of the Roman alphabet; poems old and new, sung in memory of past greatness and in response to present struggles. The later readings in this section show how vital native culture remained in the colonial period. Even amid the destruction of Tenochtitlán, one post-Conquest poem says, poetry sustained the Aztec nobles as the Spaniards tortured them in search of gold:

> Yet peacefully were Motelchiuh and Tlacotzin taken away.
> They fortified themselves with song in Acachinanco
> when they went to be delivered to the fire in Coyohuacan.

PRONUNCIATIONS:
Hernán Cortés: air-NAHN core-TEZ
Malinche: mah-LEAN-chay
Moctezuma: mock-tay-ZOO-mah
Tenochtitlán: tay-nokh-tea-TLAN
Tlatelolco: tlah-tell-OLE-co

Christopher Columbus
1451–1506

The credit for the lasting European "discovery" of the New World continues to rest with Christopher Columbus, even if he didn't recognize the world he stumbled upon as new. That insight was left to Columbus's countryman, Amerigo Vespucci, who in a letter to Lorenzo de' Medici of 1502 speaks of the coast of Guinea as a *terra nuova* ("new land"). And it was also the letter by Vespucci that circulated under the title of *Mundus Novus* which caught the attention of the German mapmaker Martin Waldseemüller, who promptly christened the new continent with Vespucci's name: "Inasmuch as both Europe and Asia received their names from women, I see no reason why anyone should object to calling this part Amerige, i.e., the land of Amerigo, or America, after Amerigo, its discoverer, a man of great ability." The name, needless to say, stuck. Yet Columbus continues to occupy a far more vibrant place in the historical imagination.

By the time Vespucci penned his famous letter, Columbus had already completed three of his voyages and was seeking funds for what would be his fourth and final trip—one marked by hurricanes, mutinous sailors, and an ignominious episode spent in chains. Such disasters had become virtually predictable events for a man whose life resembles the contours of a picaresque novel. Born in 1451 in the maritime republic of Genoa, whose possessions included islands off the coast of Turkey, Cristóbal Colón took to the sea at age fourteen. By 1484 Columbus was in Portugal, married to a woman from a noble family, and attempting to persuade King John II to finance his plan to find a shortcut to India—a rich source of trade but a very long voyage by the only known sea route, down and around the southern tip of Africa. Failing to find support in Libson, he moved on to a newly unified Spain. Over the next seven years, when Columbus wasn't navigating the coast of Africa, he was doggedly trying to convince Spain's rulers, Isabella and Ferdinand, to support his voyage. He promised to bring back enough gold from the Indies to finance the Crusade they hoped to wage to recover the Holy Land from Muslim rule. The victory over the Moors of Granada and the expulsion of the Jews from Spain in 1492 provided the monarchs with the capital necessary to send Columbus's three ships across the Atlantic Ocean, equipped with provisions and some eighty-two men, including a converted Jew who could speak Arabic, which the Chinese were believed to understand. It was a journey that landed them not among the Chinese, but among the gentle Arawak Indians who dwelled on the Caribbean island Columbus christened San Salvador on October 12.

This successful first voyage resulted in a hero's welcome for Columbus when he returned to Spain in March 1493, accompanied by several "Indios" (Indians), green parrots, and samples of native gold work. But Columbus's moment in the sun would be brief. His subsequent three voyages to the Indies failed to produce the massive quantities of gold he had promised, and the men he brought with him to the new lands in order to extend Spain's empire—no fewer than 1200 for his second voyage—frequently rebelled under his hand. Even though Columbus eventually did establish a colony on the island of Hispaniola, a number of men died of starvation and disease or were killed by the natives, who were not as docile as Columbus had first imagined. Accused of treating his "subjects" tyrannically, Columbus returned from his third venture to the new world in chains; the fourth trip, in which he reached the coast of Panama, was beseiged by hurricanes that marooned the expedition on Jamaica for a year. Queen Isabella, his strongest supporter, died less than a month after he finally returned to Spain, and Columbus himself died, in near poverty, in 1506.

Columbus's original log has long been lost; what has survived is a manuscript extensively revised by Bartolomé de Las Casas (for more on Las Casas, see page 874). Columbus's letters offer a more direct portrait of a man who combined the seemingly contradictory roles of accomplished navigator, shrewd businessman, and mystic. Written in Spanish with a smattering of nautical terms in Portuguese (Columbus probably never learned to write in Italian and would have spoken a Genoese dialect in any case), the letters from his first, third, and fourth voyages re-create both the highlights and the discouragements of his transatlantic crossings. At the same time, they create for us—as in a picaresque novel—an authorial voice that dazzles in its sheer verve, as Columbus describes himself surpassing all expectations and guided by God, who "grants to all those who walk in his way victory over apparent impossibilities."

Despite considerable setbacks over the next ten years, Columbus remained convinced that he had discovered not Cuba but Japan, not a new world but the original garden of Eden, and that he alone had been chosen by God to fulfill a divine mission. In the midst of the shipwreck on Jamaica during his final voyage, wracked by fever and exhaustion, Columbus hears "a compassionate voice" say to him: "O fool, slow to believe and serve thy God, the God of all! What more did he do for Moses or David his servant than he has done for thee? . . . He gave thee the Indies, which are so rich a part of the world, for thine own. . . . " Such faith in his unquestionable abilities as a sailor and in the righteousness of claiming the Indies as his "own" goes far toward explaining how and why Christopher Columbus succeeded in accomplishing the impossible—even if he never fully admitted to himself or to others that the world he coined an *otra mundo* ("other world") was a new world very different from the one he thought he would encounter.

Letter to the Sovereigns[1]

[4 March 1493]

Most Christian and lofty and powerful sovereigns:

That eternal God who has given Your Highnesses so many victories now gave you the greatest one that to this day He has ever given any prince. I come from the Indies with the armada[2] Your Highnesses gave me, to which [place] I traveled in thirty-three days after departing from your kingdoms;[3] after fourteen of the thirty-three there were light winds in which I covered very little ground. I found innumerable people and very many islands, of which I took possession in Your Highnesses' name, by royal crier and with Your Highnesses' royal banner unfurled, and it was not contradicted. To the first [island] I gave the name of San Salvador, in memory of His Supreme Majesty [Jesus Christ], to the second Santa María de la Concepción, to the third Fernandina, to the fourth Isabela, to the fifth Juana, and to the others almost a new name.[4] After I arrived at Juana I followed its coast to the west and found it to be so large that I thought it was probably not an island, but rather a mainland, and most likely the province of Cathay;[5] but I could not verify this because everywhere I arrived the people fled and I could not speak with them. And because I was unable to find a notable settlement, I thought that by hugging the coast I could not fail to find some town or great city, like those who have gone to that province overland tell it. And after following this land for a long while, I found that I was veering away from the west and it was leading me to the north and I found the wind that came from that direction, with which I tried to contend until it passed and a different one arrived, because it was already winter and I had no other intention but to avoid the south [wind], and so I turned back. In the meantime I already understood something of the speech and signs of certain Indians I had taken on the island of San Salvador, and I understood [from them] that this was still an island. And thus I came to a very good harbor, from which I sent two men inland, three days' journey, with one of the Indians I brought, who had become friendly with me, so that they could see and determine if there were any cities or large settlements, and which land it was, and what there was in it. They found many settlements and innumerable people, but no government of any importance. And so they returned,

1. Translated by Margarita Zamora. The sovereigns are Ferdinand and Isabella, the "most Catholic kings of Spain," who had agreed to finance Columbus's voyage. Written several months after the initial discovery when Columbus was just off the Portuguese coast, the letter is the earliest that has been found that reports directly to the King and Queen of Columbus's experiences. Another letter addressed to Luis de Santángel, an official of the Aragonese court and very similar in its details, was written during the month of February, 1493, although finalized on the same date as this letter, March 4.

2. Fleet.
3. Columbus set sail from the port of Palos in southern Spain on 3 August 1492.
4. The cluster of islands Columbus encountered were situated around Cuba (the "fifth" island Columbus names here, which he rechristens Juana, and which he thought to be part of the Asiatic mainland). Cuba was known by the Indians as Guanahani, where Columbus landed on October 12; the other islands were North Caico, Little Inagua, and Great Inagua.
5. China.

and I departed and took certain Indians at the said harbor so that I could also hear or learn from them about said lands. And thus I followed the seacoast of this island toward the east one hundred and seven leagues to where it ended. And before leaving it, I saw another island to the east, eighteen leagues out from this one, which I later named Española.[6] And then I went to it and followed its coast on the north side, just like in the case of La Juana, due east for one hundred and eighty-eight very long leagues. And I continued to enter very many harbors, in each of which I placed a very large cross in the most appropriate spot, as I had done in all the other [harbors] of the other islands, and in many places I found promontories sufficient [for this purpose]. So I went on in this fashion until the sixteenth of January, when I determined to return to Your Highnesses, as much because I had already found most of what I sought as because I had only one caravel left, because the nao[7] that I brought I had left in Your Highnesses' village of La Navidad,[8] with the men who were using it for fortification. There was another caravel, but a man from Palos whom I had put in charge of her, expecting good service, made off with her, with the intention of taking much [damaged section of manuscript] . . . and it is the sweetest [thing] to navigate and with the least danger for ships of all sorts. However, for discovering, small caravels are better suited, because going close to land or rivers, in order to discover much, [vessels] must require but little depth and be capable of being assisted with oars. Neither is there ever stormy weather, since in every place I have been I see the grass and trees growing into the sea.

Besides the above-mentioned islands, I have found many others in the Indies, of which I have not been able to tell in this letter. They, like these others, are so extremely fertile, that even if I were able to express it, it would not be a marvel were it to be disbelieved. The breezes [are] most temperate, the trees and fruits and grasses are extremely beautiful and very different from ours; the rivers and harbors are so abundant and of such extreme excellence when compared to those of Christian lands that it is a marvel. All these islands are densely populated with the best people under the sun; they have neither ill-will nor treachery. All of them, women and men alike, go about naked like their mothers bore them, although some of the women wear a small piece of cotton or a patch of grass with which they cover themselves. They have neither iron nor weapons, except for canes on the end of which they place a thin sharp stick. Everything they make is done with stones [stone tools]. And I have not learned that any one of them has private property, because while I was spending a few days with this king in the village of La Navidad, I saw that all of the people, and the women in particular, would bring him agís,[9] which is the food they eat, and he would order them to be distributed; a very singular sustenance.

Nowhere in these islands have I known the inhabitants to have a religion, or idolatry, or much diversity of language among them, but rather they all understand each other. I learned that they know that all powers reside in heaven. And, generally, in whatever lands I traveled, they believed and believe that I, together with these ships

---

6. "La Isla Española" or Hispaniola, which Columbus thought might be Japan and which today is divided into two nations, Haiti and the Dominican Republic.

7. A boat larger than a caravel; Santa María is the nao to which Columbus is referring, which had run aground on December 25.

8. A site on Hispaniola where Columbus orders a fortress to be built, seeing as how, as he says in another letter, it is

"situated in a remarkably favorable spot, and in every way convenient for the purposes of gain and commerce." Quarrels over women would lead to the Indians' massacre of the first settlers at La Navidad, as Columbus discovered on his second voyage, and as was reported by the physician who traveled with him, one Doctor Chanca.

9. Hot red peppers.

and people, came from heaven, and they greeted me with such veneration. And today, this very day, they are of the same mind, nor have they strayed from it, despite all the contact they [the Spaniards at La Navidad] may have had with them. And then, upon arriving at whatever settlement, the men, women, and children go from house to house calling out, "Come, come and see the people from heaven!" Everything they have or had they gave for whatever one gave them in exchange, even taking a piece of glass or broken crockery or some such thing, for gold or some other thing of whatever value. One sailor got more than two and a half castellanos[1] for the ends of leather latchets. There are ten thousand like occurrences to tell.

The islands are all very flat and low-lying, except for La Juana and La Española. These two are very high lands, and there are mountain chains and very high peaks, much higher than those of the island of Tenerife.[2] The mountains are of a thousand different shapes and all [are] most beautiful, and fertile and walkable and full of trees; it seems they touch the sky. And both the one and the other of the said islands are very large, such that, as I have said, I traveled in a straight line . . . [the next three lines are damaged; not enough context to translate] . . . is much larger than England and Scotland together;[3] this other one [stained] is certainly larger than the whole of La Española such that, as I said above, I traveled in a straight line, from west to east, one hundred and eighty-eight large leagues which comprise that side [of the island]. La Juana has many rivers, and great mountains, and very large valleys and meadows and fields, and it is all full of trees and huge palms of a thousand varieties, such as to make one marvel. La Spañola has the advantage in every respect; the trees are not so tall or of the same kind, but rather very fruitful and broad; and [they are] delectable lands for all things, and for sowing and planting and raising livestock, of which I have not seen any kind on any of these islands. This island has marvelously temperate breezes, and marvelous meadows and fields incomparable to those of Castile;[4] and the same can be said of the rivers of great and good waters, most of which are gold-bearing. There are so many and such good sea harbors that it has to be seen to be believed. I have not tarried in these islands or the others for many reasons, as I said above, but especially because it was winter when I sailed these coasts, which did not allow me to go south because I was on their north side and the [winds] were almost always easterly, which were contrary to continuing my navigation. Then I did not understand those people nor they me, except for what common sense dictated, although they were saddened and I much more so, because I wanted to have good information concerning everything. And what I did to remedy this was the Indians I had with me, for they learned our language and we theirs, and the next voyage will tell. So, there was no reason for me to tarry at any harbor wasting time when the opportunity came to set sail. Moreover, as I have said, these vessels I brought with me were too large and heavy for such a purpose, especially the *nao* I brought over, about which I was quite troubled before leaving Castile. I would much have preferred taking small caravels, but since this was the first voyage and the people I brought were afraid of running into high seas and uncertain about the voyage, and there was and has been so much opposition, and anybody dared to contradict this route and ascribe to it a thousand dangers without being able to give me any reasons, they caused me to act against my own judgment and do everything that those who were to go with me wanted, in

---

1. Gold coins.
2. One of the Canary Islands.

3. A gross exaggeration.
4. The kingdom of Castile, in Spain.

order to get the voyage finally under way and find the land. But Our Lord, who is the light and strength of all those who seek to do good and makes them victorious in deeds that seem impossible, wished to ordain that I should find and was to find gold and mincs and spicery and innumerable peoples . . . . [the next four lines are damaged; not enough context to translate] I left in it [La Española], in possession of the village of La Navidad, the people I brought on the *nao* and some from the caravels, stocked with provisions to last over a year, [with] much artillery and quite without danger from anyone, but rather with much friendship from the king of that place, who prided himself in calling me and having me for a brother; who [also] appeared to accept everything as the greatest boon in the world, as I said. And the others [feel] just like the king, so that the people I left there suffice to subjugate the entire island without danger.[5] This island is in a place, as I have said, signaled by the hand of Our Lord, where I hope His Majesty will give Your Highnesses as much gold as you need, spicery of a certain pepper [to fill] as many ships as Your Highnesses may order to be loaded, and as much mastic[6] as you may order to load, which today can only be found on the island of Chios, in Greece, and the government sells it as they see fit, and I believe they get more than 45,000 ducats for it each year. And as much lignum aloe as you may order to be loaded,[7] and as much cotton as you may order to be loaded, and so many slaves that they are innumerable; and they will come from the idolaters.[8] And I believe there is rhubarb and cinnamon. All this I found on this hasty trip, but I have faith in God that upon my return the people I left there will have found a thousand other things of importance, because that is the charge I left them with. And I left them a boat and its equipment and [the tools] to make boats and *fustas,*[9] and masters in all the nautical arts. And above all I consider all the above-mentioned islands as belonging to Your Highnesses and you may command them as you do the kingdoms of Castile, and even more completely, especially this one of Española.

I conclude here: that through the divine grace of He who is the origin of all good and virtuous things, who favors and gives victory to all those who walk in His path, that in seven years from today I will be able to pay Your Highnesses for five thousand cavalry and fifty thousand foot soldiers for the war and conquest of Jerusalem, for which purpose this enterprise was undertaken.[1] And in another five years another five thousand cavalry and fifty thousand foot soldiers, which will total ten thousand cavalry and one hundred thousand foot soldiers; and all of this with very little investment now on Your Highnesses' part in this beginning of the taking of the Indies and all that they contain, as I will tell Your Highnesses in person later. And I have reason for this [claim] and do not speak uncertainly, and one should not delay in it, as was the case with the execution of this enterprise, may God forgive whoever has been the cause of it.

---

5. About 40 men.
6. An aromatic resin used for treating rheumatism and, among other things, loose teeth, as observed by the Roman author Pliny in his *Natural History,* a font of information about medicinal remedies and with which Columbus would have been familiar. Unfortunately, however, Columbus confused his plants, and the New World turned out not to be a source of mastic. Chios, just off the coast of Turkey, was part of the Genoese empire until 1566, and a place to which Columbus had frequently traveled.
7. The European Aloe vera, used as a laxative, was also misidentified by Columbus.

8. By 1492, the slave trade was already well underway, thanks to the Portuguese ventures into Africa in the 1470s. The "idolaters" of whom Columbus speaks are probably the Caribs. Ferdinand and Isabella would prohibit enslaving the natives, whom they believed should be converted; the Spanish would argue, however, that Caribs or "cannibals" were less than human and therefore deserving of enslavement.
9. Small sailing vessels, probably of Turkish origin.
1. One impetus for the journey was to amass enough gold to launch another Crusade, so that Jerusalem could be reclaimed by the Christians.

Most powerful sovereigns: all of Christendom should hold great celebrations, and especially God's Church, for the finding of such a multitude of such friendly peoples, which with very little effort will be converted to our Holy Faith, and so many lands filled with so many goods very necessary to us in which all Christians will have comfort and profits, all of which was unknown nor did anyone speak of it except in fables. Great rejoicing and celebrations in the churches [damaged] . . . Your Highnesses should order that [many] praises should be given to the Holy Trinity [damaged] your kingdoms and domains, because of the great love [the Holy Trinity?] has shown you, more than to any other prince.

Now, most serene sovereigns, remember that I left my wife and children behind and came from my homeland to serve you, in which [service] I spent what I had. And I spent seven years of my time and put up with a thousand indignities and disgrace and I suffered much hardship.[2] I did not wish to deal with other princes who solicited me, although Your Highnesses' giving of your protection to this voyage has been due more to my importuning [you] than to anything else. And not only has no favor been shown to me, but moreover nothing of what was promised me has been fulfilled. I do not ask favors of Your Highnesses in order to amass treasure, for I have no purpose other than to serve God and Your Highnesses and to bring this business of the Indies to perfection, as time will be my witness. And therefore I beseech you that honor be bestowed upon me according to [the quality of] my service.

The Church of God should also work for this: providing prelates and devout and wise religious; and because the matter is so great and of such a character, there is reason for the Holy Father to provide prelates who are very free of greed for temporal possessions and very true to the service of God and of Your Highnesses. And therefore I beseech you to ask the Church, in the letter you write regarding this victory, for a cardinalate for my son, and that it be granted him although he may not yet be of sufficient age, for there is little difference in his age and that of the son of the Medici of Florence, to whom a cardinal's hat was granted without him having served or had a purpose so honorable to Christianity, and that you give me the letter pertaining to this matter so that I [myself] may solicit it.[3]

Furthermore, most serene sovereigns, because the sin of ungratefulness was the first one to be punished, I realize that since I am not guilty of it I must at all times try to gain from Your Highnesses the following [favor], because, without a doubt, were it not for Villacorta,[4] who every time it was necessary persuaded and worked on [the enterprise's] behalf, because I was already sick of it and everyone who had been and was involved in the matter was tired [and the enterprise would not have succeeded]. Therefore, I beseech Your Highnesses that you do me the favor of making him paymaster of the Indies, for I vouch that he will do it well.

Wherefore Your Highnesses should know that the first island of the Indies, closest to Spain,[5] is populated entirely by women, without a single man, and their comportment is not feminine, but rather they use weapons and other masculine practices. They carry bows and arrows and take their adornments from the copper mines, which

---

2. It took Columbus seven years to persuade the monarchs to finance his voyage.

3. Columbus's son was Diego; the Medici son who received a cardinal's hat (at age 13) was Giovanni, son of Lorenzo the Magnificent, and who would go on to become Pope Leo X.

4. Pedro de Villacorta was one of Columbus's trusted companions on the first voyage. In a return letter dated March 30, the King and Queen promise Columbus that he will receive "many favors" for his contributions, but they don't specify what they will be.

5. The island of Matenino, one of the Virgin Islands.

metal they have in very large quantity. They call this island Matenino, the second Caribo,[6] [blank] leagues out from this one. Here are found those people which all of the other islands of the Indies fear; they eat human flesh, are great bowmen, have many canoes almost as big as oar-powered *fustas,* in which they travel all over the islands of the Indies, and they are so feared that they have no equal. They go about naked like the others, except that they wear their hair very full, like women. I think the great cowardice . . . [damaged] peoples of the other islands, for which there is no remedy, makes them say that these of Caribe are brave, but I think the same of them as of the rest. And when Your Highnesses give the order for me to send slaves, I hope to bring or send [you] these for the most part; these are the ones who have intercourse with the women of Matenino, who if they bear a female child they keep her with them, and if it is a male child, they raise him until he can feed himself and then they send him to Cardo. Between the islands of Cardo and Española there is another island they call Borinque,[7] and all of it is a short distance from the other region of the island of Juana which they call Cuba. In the westernmost part [of Cuba], in one of the two provinces I did not cover, which is called Faba, everyone is born with a tail. Beyond this island of Juana, still within sight, there is another that these Indians assured me was larger than Juana, which they call Jamaica, where all the people are bald. On this one there is gold in immeasurable quantities;[8] and now I have Indians with me who have been on these [islands] as well as the others and they know the language and customs. Nothing further, except that may the Holy Trinity guard and make Your Highnesses' royal estate prosper in Its service. Written in the sea of Spain, on the fourth day of March of the year fourteen ninety-three. At sea.

from Letter to Ferdinand and Isabella[1]

[7 July 1503]

Most serene, and very high and mighty Princes, the King and Queen, our Sovereigns: My passage from Cadiz to the Canaries occupied four days, and thence to the Indies, from which I wrote, sixteen days.[2] My intention was to expedite my voyage as much as possible while I had good vessels, good crews and stores, and because Jamaica was the place to which I was bound. I wrote this in Dominica; and until now my time has been occupied in gaining information.

Up to the period of my reaching these shores I experienced most excellent weather, but the night of my arrival came on with a dreadful tempest, and the same bad weather has continued ever since. On reaching the island of Española I dispatched a packet of letters, by which I begged as a favor that a ship should be supplied me at my own cost in lieu of one of those that I had brought with me, which had become unseaworthy, and could no longer carry sail. The letters were taken, and your Highnesses will know if a reply has been given to them. For my part I was forbidden

6. Query Carib, or Puerto Rico. The Caribs were the fierce enemies of the peoples whom Columbus had encountered, the Arawaks, who clearly hoped that the Spaniards would help protect them from the Caribs.
7. Borinque would be renamed San Juan de Puerto Rico by Columbus.
8. An unfounded myth, as are so many of the "facts" that Columbus mentions in this paragraph.

1. Translated by R. H. Major, with occasional revisions. This letter, written in Spanish, is from Columbus's fourth and final voyage to the New World, and represents a situation far different from the optimistic one Columbus portrayed to the sovereigns a decade earlier.
2. Columbus had left Cadiz, in southern Spain, on 3 April 1502, with four ships. The Canary Islands are off the coast of Africa.

to go on shore;[3] the hearts of my people failed them lest I should take them further, and they said that if any danger were to befall them, they should receive no succor, but, on the contrary, in all probability have some great affront offered them. Moreover every man had it in his power to tell me that the new Governor[4] would have the superintendence of the countries that I might acquire.

The tempest was terrible throughout the night, all the ships were separated, and each one driven to the last extremity, without hope of anything but death; each of them also looked upon the loss of the rest as a matter of certainty. What man was ever born, not even excepting Job, who would not have been ready to die of despair at finding himself as I then was, in anxious fear for my own safety, and that of my son, my brother and my friends, and yet refused permission either to land or to put into harbor on the shores which by God's mercy I had gained for Spain with so much toil and danger?[5]

But to return to the ships: although the tempest had so completely separated them from me as to leave me single, yet the Lord restored them to me in His own good time. The ship which we had the greatest fear for, had put out to sea for safety, and near the island the *Gallega* lost her boat and a great part of her provisions, which latter loss, indeed, all the ships suffered. The vessel in which I was, though dreadfully buffeted, was saved by our Lord's mercy from any injury whatever; my brother went in the ship that was unsound, and he under God was the cause of its being saved. With this tempest I struggled on till I reached Jamaica, and there the sea became calm, but there was a strong current which carried me as far as the Queen's Garden[6] without seeing land. Hence as opportunity offered I pushed on for terra firma, in spite of the wind and a fearful contrary current, against which I contended for sixty days, and during that time only made seventy leagues. All this time I was unable to get into harbor, nor was there any cessation of the tempest, which was one continuation of rain, thunder and lightning; indeed it seemed as if it were the end of the world. I at length reached Cape of Gracias a Dios,[7] and after that the Lord granted me fair wind and tide; this was on the twelfth of September. Eighty-eight days did this fearful tempest continue, during which I was at sea, and saw neither sun nor stars; my ships lay exposed, with sails torn, and anchors, rigging, cables, boats and a great quantity of provisions lost; my people were very weak and humbled in spirit, many of them promising to lead a religious life, and all making vows and promising to perform pilgrimages, while some of them would frequently go to their messmates to make confession. Other tempests have been experienced, but never of so long duration or so fearful as this: many whom we look upon as brave men, on several occasions showed considerable trepidation; but the distress of my son who was with me grieved me to the soul, and the more when I considered his tender age, for he was but thirteen years old, and he enduring so much toil for so long a time. Our Lord, however, gave him strength even to enable him to encourage the rest, and he worked as if he had been eighty years at sea, and all this was a consolation to me. I myself had fallen sick, and

3. Columbus had encountered considerable problems with the settlers of Hispaniola during his third voyage; a rebellion among the men impatient with the slow progress Columbus had made in finding them gold wound up with the Admiral being sent back to Spain in chains. Ferdinand and Isabella thus commanded that for Columbus's safety he not put in at Hispaniola during his fourth voyage, but continue heading westward.

4. Nicolas de Ovando was the governor or *comendador* of Hispaniola.

5. Columbus's brother Bartolomé and illegitimate son Ferdinand, who would later write a biography of his father, accompanied him on this journey. Job is noted in the Bible for his suffering.

6. Jardin de la Reina, to the west of Cuba.

7. On the Mosquito Coast, in what is now Nicaragua.

was many times at the point of death, but from a little cabin that I had caused to be constructed on deck, I directed our course. My brother was in the ship that was in the worst condition and the most exposed to danger; and my grief on this account was the greater that I brought him with me against his will.

Such is my fate, that the twenty years of service through which I have passed with so much toil and danger have profited me nothing, and at this very day I do not possess a roof in Spain that I can call my own; if I wish to eat or sleep, I have nowhere to go but to the inn or tavern, and most times lack wherewith to pay the bill. Another anxiety wrung my very heart-strings, which was the thought of my son Diego, whom I had left an orphan, in Spain, and stripped of the honor and property which were due to him, on my account, although I had looked upon it as a certainty, that your Majesties, as just and grateful Princes, would restore it to him in all respects with increase. * * *

In the month of January the mouth of the river[8] was entirely closed up, and in April the vessels were so eaten with the teredo,[9] that they could scarcely be kept above water. At this time the river forced a channel for itself, by which I managed, with great difficulty, to extricate three of them after I had unloaded them. The boats were then sent back into the river for water and salt, but the sea became so high and furious, that it afforded them no chance of exit; upon which the Indians collected themselves together in great numbers, and made an attack upon the boats, and at length massacred the men. My brother, and all the rest of our people, were in a ship which remained inside; I was alone, outside, upon that dangerous coast, suffering from a severe fever and worn with fatigue. All hope of escape was gone. I toiled up to the highest part of the ship, and, with a quivering voice and fast-falling tears, I called upon your Highnesses' war-captains from each point of the compass to come to my succor, but there was no reply. At length, groaning with exhaustion, I fell asleep, and heard a compassionate voice address me thus: "O fool, and slow to believe and to serve thy God, the God of all; what did He do more for Moses, or for David his servant, than He has done for thee?[1] From thine infancy He has kept thee under His constant and watchful care. When He saw thee arrived at an age which suited His designs respecting thee, He brought wonderful renown to thy name throughout all the land. He gave thee for thine own the Indies, which form so rich a portion of the world, and thou hast divided them as it pleased thee, for He gave thee power to do so. He gave thee the keys of those barriers of the ocean sea which were closed with such mighty chains; and thou wast obeyed through many lands, and gained an honorable fame throughout Christendom. What more did the Most High do for the people of Israel, when He brought them out of Egypt? or for David, whom from a shepherd He made to be a king in Judea? Turn to Him, and acknowledge thine error—His mercy is infinite. Thine old age shall not prevent thee from accomplishing any great undertaking. He holds under His sway the greatest possessions. Abraham had exceeded a hundred years of age when he begat Isaac; nor was Sarah young.[2] Thou criest out for uncertain help; answer, who has afflicted thee so much and so often, God or the world? The privileges promised by God He never fails in bestowing; nor does He ever declare, after a service has been rendered Him, that such was not agreeable with His intention,

8. A river in Veragua (now Panama), in Central America. Columbus had landed there on January 6, but constant rains had prevented him from doing extensive exploration for several months.
9. The worm.

1. As Columbus indicates below, God led Moses and the Hebrews out of slavery in Egypt, while he raised David up from a lowly shepherd to king of Judea.
2. Abraham and Sarah become the parents of Isaac only when they are elderly (Genesis 18).

or that He had regarded the matter in another light; nor does He inflict suffering, in order to give effect to the manifestation of His power. His acts answer to His words; and it is His custom to perform all His promises with interest. Thus I have told you what the Creator has done for thee, and what He does for all men. Even now He partially shows thee the reward of so many toils and dangers incurred by thee in the service of others."

I heard all this, as it were, in a trance; but I had no answer to give in definite words, and could but weep for my errors. He who spoke to me, whoever it was, concluded by saying, "Fear not, trust; all these tribulations are recorded on marble, and not without cause." I rose as soon as I could; and at the end of nine days there came fine weather, but not sufficiently so as to allow of drawing the vessels out of the river. I collected the men who were on land, and, in fact, all of them that I could, because there were not enough to admit of one party remaining on shore while another stayed on board to work the vessel. I myself should have remained with my men to defend the buildings I had constructed, had your Highnesses been cognizant of all the facts; but the doubt whether any ships would ever reach the spot where we were, as well as the thought, that while I was asking for succor I might bring succor to myself, made me decide upon leaving. I departed, in the name of the Holy Trinity, on Easter night, with the ships rotten, worn out, and eaten into holes. One of them I left at Belen, with a supply of necessaries; I did the same at Belpuerto.[3] I then had only two left, and they in the same state as the others. I was without boats or provisions, and in this condition I had to cross seven thousand miles of sea; or, as an alternative, to die on the passage with my son, my brother, and so many of my people. Let those who are accustomed to slander and aspersion, ask, while they sit in security at home, "Why didst thou not do so and so under such circumstances?" I wish that they were now embarked in this voyage. I verily believe that another journey of another kind awaits them, if there is any reliance to be placed upon our holy faith. * * *[4]

I do not state as certain, nor do I confirm even the sixth part of all that I have said or written, nor do I pretend to be at the fountain-head of the information. The Genoese, Venetians, and all other nations that possess pearls, precious stones, and other articles of value, take them to the ends of the world to exchange them for gold. Gold is the most precious of all commodities; gold constitutes treasure, and he who possesses it has all he needs in this world, as also the means of rescuing souls from purgatory, and restoring them to the enjoyment of paradise.[5] They say that when one of the lords of the country of Veragua dies, they bury all the gold he possessed with his body. There were brought to Solomon at one journey six hundred and sixty-six quintals of gold, besides what the merchants and sailors brought, and that which was paid in Arabia.[6] Of this gold he made 200 lances and 300 shields, and the entablature which was above them was also of gold, and ornamented with precious stones: many

3. Both on the coast of Veragua.
4. Columbus continues on in this pessimistic vein, correcting his earlier assessment that at one point he had believed that the Indies were "the richest domain in the whole world." Because he had not instantly produced gold, pearls, and spices, he was subject to considerable abuse: "This punishment causes me to refrain from relating anything but what the natives tell me." Nonetheless, hope springs eternal, for Columbus has it on good report that "in this land of Veragua I saw more signs of gold in the first two days than I saw in Hispaniola in four years, and that there is not a more fertile or better cultivated country in all the world."
5. The Church was in the practice of selling indulgences, which allowed Catholics to buy their way—as well as the way of those already dead—out of purgatory.
6. Solomon was the builder of the great temple in Jerusalem, for which he commanded his slaves to bring back gold and other materials such as pinewood from "Ophir," or India. He also sent "vessels" to Tharsis in the Orient, which brought back gold, silver and ivory; Columbus clearly hopes that his trip to the East will make of Ferdinand and Isabella new Solomons. See 2 Chronicles 9.

other things he made likewise of gold, and a great number of vessels of great size, which he enriched with precious stones. This is related by Josephus in his chronicle *De Antiquitatibus;*[7] mention is also made of it in the Chronicles and in the Book of Kings. Josephus thinks that this gold was found in the Aurea;[8] if it were so, I contend that these mines of the Aurea are identical with those of Veragua, which, as I have said before, extends westward twenty days' journey, at an equal distance from the Pole and the Line. Solomon bought all of it—gold, precious stones and silver—but your Majesties need only to send to seek them to have them at your pleasure. David, in his will, left three thousand quintals of Indian gold to Solomon, to assist in building the Temple; and, according to Josephus, it came from these lands. Jerusalem and Mount Zion are to be rebuilt by the hands of Christians, as God has declared by the mouth of His prophet in the Fourteenth Psalm.[9] The Abbe Joaquim said that he who should do this was to come from Spain; Saint Jerome showed the holy woman the way to accomplish it; and the Emperor of China has, some time since, sent for wise men to instruct him in the faith of Christ.[1] Who will offer himself for this work? Should any one do so, I pledge myself, in the name of God, to convey him safely thither, provided the Lord permits me to return to Spain. The people who have sailed with me have passed through incredible toil and danger, and I beseech your Highnesses, since they are poor, to pay them promptly, and to be gracious to each of them according to their respective merits; for I can safely assert, that to my belief they are the bearers of the best news that ever were carried to Spain. With respect to the gold which belongs to Quibian, the cacique[2] of Veragua, and other chiefs in the neighboring country, although it appears by the accounts we have received of it to be very abundant, I do not think it would be well or desirable, on the part of your Highnesses, to take possession of it in the way of plunder; by fair dealing, scandal and disrepute will be avoided, and all the gold will thus reach your Highnesses' treasury without the loss of a grain. With one month of fair weather I shall complete my voyage. As I was deficient in ships, I did not persist in delaying my course; but in everything that concerns your Highnesses' service, I trust in Him who made me, and I hope also that my health will be reëstablished. I think your Highnesses will remember that I had intended to build some ships in a new manner, but the shortness of the time did not permit it. I had certainly foreseen how things would be. I think more of this opening for commerce, and of the lordship over such extensive mines, than of all that has been done in the Indies. This is not a child to be left to the care of a stepmother.

I never think of Española, and Paria,[3] and other countries, without shedding tears. I thought that what had occurred there would have been an example for others; on the contrary, these settlements are now in a languid state, although not dead, and the malady is incurable, or at least very extensive: let him who brought the evil come now and cure it, if he knows the remedy, or how to apply it; but when a disturbance is on

7. Flavius Josephus was a first-century Jewish statesman and author of *A History of the Jewish Wars.*

8. Aurea Chersonese, or the modern Malay Peninsula.

9. A creative interpretation of Psalm 14:7: "Oh, that out of Sion would come the salvation of Israel! When the Lord restores the well-being of his people, then shall Jacob exult and Israel be glad."

1. The Abbot Joachim de Fiore (1132–1202) prophesied the end of the world in his numerous works, but nothing he says indicates that Spain would have a part in the final days. The reference to Jerome's "holy woman" probably concerns Marcella, to whom he showed the way to Jerusalem (see *Epistle* 46), while the Grand Khan of Cathay (China) had sent an ambassador to Pope Eugenius IV requesting that scholars visit him so he could learn of Christianity. Columbus apparently had great faith in the supposedly Christian sympathies of the Great Khan, which Marco Polo had emphasized in his widely read *Travels* (see Volume B).

2. Leader.

3. On the coast of what is now Venezuela.

foot, every one is ready to take the lead. It used to be the custom to give thanks and promotion to him who placed his person in jeopardy; but there is no justice in allowing the man who opposed this undertaking to enjoy the fruits of it with his children. Those who left the Indies, avoiding the toils consequent upon the enterprise, and speaking evil of it and me, have since returned with official appointments: such is the case now in Veragua: it is an evil example, and profitless both as regards the business in which we are embarked and as respects the general maintenance of justice. The fear of this, with other sufficient considerations which I clearly foresaw, caused me to beg your Highnesses, previously to my coming to discover these islands and terra firma, to grant me permission to govern in your royal name. Your Highnesses granted my request; and it was a privilege and treaty granted under the royal seal and oath, by which I was nominated Viceroy, and Admiral, and Governor-General of all: and your Highnesses limited the extent of my government to a hundred leagues beyond the Azores and Cape Verde Islands, by a line passing from one pole to the other, and gave me ample power over all that I might discover beyond this line; all which is more fully described in the official document.[4]

But the most important affair of all, and that which cries most loudly for redress, remains inexplicable to this moment. For seven years was I at your royal court, where every one to whom the enterprise was mentioned treated it as ridiculous; but now there is not a man, down to the very tailors, who does not beg to be allowed to become a discoverer. There is reason to believe that they make the voyage only for plunder, and that they are permitted to do so, to the great disparagement of my honor, and the detriment of the undertaking itself. It is right to give God his due, and to receive that which belongs to one's self. This is a just sentiment and proceeds from just feelings. The lands in this part of the world which are now under your Highnesses' sway, are richer and more extensive than those of any other Christian power, and yet, after that I had, by the Divine will, placed them under your high and royal sovereignty and was on the point of bringing your Majesties into the receipt of a very great and unexpected revenue; and while I was waiting for ships to convey me in safety, and with a heart full of joy, to your royal presence, victoriously to announce the news of the gold that I had discovered, I was arrested and thrown, with my two brothers, loaded with irons, into a ship, stripped, and very ill-treated, without being allowed any appeal to justice. Who could believe that a poor foreigner would have risen against your Highnesses, in such a place, without any motive or argument on his side; without even the assistance of any other prince upon which to rely; but on the contrary, amongst your own vassals and natural subjects, and with my sons staying at your royal court? I was twenty-eight years old when I came into your Highnesses' service, and now I have not a hair upon me that is not grey; my body is infirm, and all that was left to me, as well as to my brothers, has been taken away and sold, even to the frock that I wore, to my great dishonor. I cannot but believe that this was done without your royal permission. The restitution of my honor, the reparation of my losses, and the punishment of those who have inflicted them, will redound to the honor of your royal character; a similar punishment also is due to those who plundered me of my pearls, and who have brought a disparagement upon the privileges of

---

4. Before he left for his first voyage, Columbus had been promised the governorship of any islands he would discover between Spain and China. In 1494, John II of Portugal and Ferdinand and Isabella signed the Treaty of Tordesillas, which declared that all land 370 leagues west of the Cape Verde Islands belonged to Spain; land east of the line would belong to Portugal.

my Admiralty. Great and unexampled will be the glory and fame of your Highnesses, if you do this; and the memory of your Highnesses, as just and grateful sovereigns, will survive as a bright example to Spain in future ages. The honest devotedness I have always shown to your Majesties' service, and the so unmerited outrage with which it has been repaid, will not allow my soul to keep silence, however much I may wish it: I implore your Highnesses to forgive my complaints. I am indeed in as ruined a condition as I have related; hitherto I have wept over others; may Heaven now have mercy upon me, and may the earth weep for me. With regard to temporal things, I have not even a blanca for an offering;[5] and in spiritual things, I have ceased here in the Indies from observing the prescribed forms of religion. Solitary in my trouble, sick, and in daily expectation of death, surrounded by millions of hostile savages full of cruelty, and thus separated from the blessed sacraments of our holy Church, how will my soul be forgotten if it be separated from the body in this foreign land? Weep for me, whoever has charity, truth, and justice! I did not come out on this voyage to gain to myself honor or wealth; this is a certain fact, for at that time all hope of such a thing was dead. I do not lie when I say that I went to your Highnesses with honest purpose of heart and sincere zeal in your cause. I humbly beseech your Highnesses, that if it please God to rescue me from this place, you will graciously sanction my pilgrimage to Rome and other holy places.[6] May the Holy Trinity protect your Highnesses' lives, and add to the prosperity of your exalted position.

Done in the Indies, in the island of Jamaica, on the seventh of July, in the year one thousand five hundred and three.[7]

Bernal Díaz del Castillo
1492–1584

Born in the very year in which Christopher Columbus made his momentous first voyage across the Atlantic, Bernal Díaz grew up to become a soldier, adventurer, and the most vivid chronicler of the conquest of Mexico. Son of a magistrate in a provincial city in Spain, he received enough education to develop a fluent prose style and an enduring love of adventure stories and knightly romances, including the tales of Amadis of Gaul whose fictional exploits would later inspire Cervantes's hero Don Quixote. In his early twenties he sailed for the newly discovered New World, taking part in an unsuccessful quest for gold in Panama in 1514 and then attempting to establish himself in Cuba. There he signed on as a soldier serving Hernán Cortés, becoming part of the force with which Cortés invaded Mexico in 1519. After the two and a half years of struggle and hardship that culminated in the fall of Tenochtitlán, Bernal Díaz sought to achieve fame and fortune in Spain's new empire, but with only moderate success. The major political offices and land grants went to others with closer links to Cortés or with higher social standing and better connections at the royal court in Madrid.

Eventually, Bernal Díaz had to content himself with a modest position in Guatemala, where he served as a magistrate, carrying on his father's profession in a very different world. In the 1560s—irritated by an early history of the Conquest that gave credit largely to Cortés

---

5. A farthing; he has no money to pay for masses to be said in his name.
6. Pilgrimages to Rome were performed as penance for past sins; often pilgrims needed official "sponsors" to provide for their trip.
7. Columbus would return to Spain, on 7 November 1504.

alone—Bernal Díaz decided to record his own reminiscences and set the record straight. His account didn't arouse the interest he had hoped; it remained unpublished until 1632, long after his death in Guatemala in 1584 at the age of ninety-two. As he wrote in a preface to his manuscript, "as luck would have it, I have gained nothing of value to leave to my children and descendants but this true story, and they will presently find out what a wonderful story it is."

Writing with lively directness and with remarkably clear recall of events forty years before, Bernal Díaz didn't hesitate to reconstruct or even invent speeches, but comparison with other sources shows that he rarely seems to have misremembered events. He gives unforgettable portraits of Cortés and of Moctezuma ("Montezuma," as he calls him). He details Cortés's bold moves and shrewd negotiations while also criticizing his high-handedness and greed, and he gives us the fullest contemporary account of Doña Marina, also known as "La Malinche," the Aztec noblewoman who became Cortés's interpreter and wife. He records as well both Moctezuma's ambivalent, shifting responses and the heroic valor of the Aztec warriors in the face of the Spanish invasion. Altogether, *The True History of the Conquest of New Spain* is an unparalleled, soldier's-eye view of the Conquest, and a prime testimony to the wonder and mystery of the first European encounters with the great civilizations of Mesoamerica.

PRONUNCIATIONS:

Coyoacan: coy-oh-AH-cahn
Huexotzingo: way-shot-ZINC-go
Huichilobos: we-chill-LOW-bose
Iztapalapa: eats-tah-pah-LAH-pah
Malinche: mah-LEAN-chay
Montezuma: mon-tay-ZOU-mah
Narvaez: nar-VAH-yez
Texcoco: tesh-COH-coh
Tezcatepuca: tez-cat-eh-POU-cah
Tlaxcala: tlash-CAH-la

from The True History of the Conquest of New Spain[1]

[PREFACE]

I have observed that the most celebrated chroniclers, before they begin to write their histories, first set forth a Prologue and Preface with the argument expressed in lofty rhetoric in order to give lustre and repute to their statements, so that the studious readers who peruse them may partake of their melody and flavour. But I, being no Latin scholar, dare not venture on such a preamble or prologue, for in order properly to extol the adventures which we met with and the heroic deeds we accomplished during the Conquest of New Spain and its provinces in the company of that valiant and doughty Captain, Don Hernando Cortés (who later on, on account of his heroic deeds, was made Marqués del Valle) there would be needed an eloquence and rhetoric far beyond my powers. That which I have myself seen and the fighting I have gone through, with the help of God, I will describe quite simply, as a fair eye witness without twisting events one way or another. I am now an old man, over eighty-four years of age, and I have lost my sight and hearing, and, as luck would have it, I have gained nothing of value to leave to my children and descendants but this my true story, and they will presently find out what a wonderful story it is.

1. Translated by Alfred Percival Maudslay.

[CORTÉS PREPARES HIS EXPEDITION]

As soon as Hernando Cortés had been appointed General he began to search for all sorts of arms, guns, powder and crossbows, and every kind of warlike stores which he could get together, and all sorts of articles to be used for barter, and other things necessary for the expedition.

Moreover he began to adorn himself and be more careful of his appearance than before, and he wore a plume of feathers with a medal, and a gold chain, and a velvet cloak trimmed with knots of gold, in fact he looked like a gallant and courageous Captain. However, he had no money to defray the expenses I have spoken about, for at that time he was very poor and much in debt, although he had a good *encomienda*[2] of Indians who were getting him a return from his gold mines, but he spent all of it on his person and on finery for his wife, whom he had recently married, and on entertaining some guests who had come to visit him. For he was affable in his manner and a good talker, and he had twice been chosen mayor of the town of Santiago Baracoa where he had settled, and in that country it is esteemed a great honour to be chosen as mayor.

When some merchant friends of his saw that he had obtained this command as Captain General, they lent him four thousand gold dollars in coin and gave him merchandise worth another four thousand dollars secured on his Indians and estates. Then he ordered two standards and banners to be made, worked in gold with the royal arms and a cross on each side with a legend which said, "Comrades, let us follow the sign of the holy Cross with true faith, and through it we shall conquer." And he ordered a proclamation to be made with the sound of drums and trumpets in the name of His Majesty and by Diego Velásquez in the King's name, and in his own as Captain General, to the effect that whatsoever person might wish to go in his company to the newly discovered lands to conquer them and to settle there, should receive his share of the gold, silver and riches which might be gained, and an *encomienda* of Indians after the country had been pacified, and that to do these things Diego Velásquez held authority from His Majesty. ˄ ˄ ˄

We continued to enlist soldiers and to buy horses, which at that time were both scarce and costly, and as Alonzo Hernández Puertocarrero neither possessed a horse nor the wherewithal to buy one, Hernando Cortés bought him a gray mare, and paid for it with some of the golden knots off the velvet cloak which as I have said he had made at Santiago de Cuba.

[*Cortés's expedition sails along the Yucatan coast. They are driven off from some places, but find Jerónimo de Aguilar and take him on board as interpreter. They land further along the coast and fight a major battle, killing eight hundred natives. Their chiefs ("Caciques") then come to make peace.*]

Early the next morning many Caciques and chiefs of Tabasco and the neighbouring towns arrived and paid great respect to us all, and they brought a present of gold, consisting of four diadems and some gold lizards, and two ornaments like little dogs, and earrings and five ducks, and two masks with Indian faces and two gold soles for sandals, and some other things of little value. I do not remember how much the things were worth; and they brought cloth, such as they make and wear, which was quilted stuff.

---

2. A royal grant of peasants and land.

This present, however, was worth nothing in comparison with the twenty women that were given us, among them one very excellent woman called Doña Marina, for so she was named when she became a Christian. Cortés received this present with pleasure. * * * Cortés allotted one of the women to each of his captains and Doña Marina, as she was good looking and intelligent and without embarrassment, he gave to Alonzo Hernández Puertocarrero. When Puertocarrero went to Spain, Doña Marina lived with Cortés, and bore him a son named Don Martin Cortés. * * *

Before telling about the great Montezuma and his famous City of Mexico and the Mexicans, I wish to give some account of Doña Marina, who from her childhood had been the mistress and Cacica of towns and vassals. It happened in this way:

Her father and mother were chiefs and Caciques of a town called Paynala, which had other towns subject to it, and stood about eight leagues from the town of Coatzacoalcos.[3] Her father died while she was still a little child, and her mother married another Cacique, a young man, and bore him a son. It seems that the father and mother had a great affection for this son and it was agreed between them that he should succeed to their honours when their days were done. So that there should be no impediment to this, they gave the little girl, Doña Marina, to some Indians from Xicalango, and this they did by night so as to escape observation, and they then spread the report that she had died, and as it happened at this time that a child of one of their Indian slaves died they gave out that it was their daughter and the heiress who was dead.

The Indians of Xicalango gave the child to the people of Tabasco and the Tabasco people gave her to Cortés. I myself knew her mother, and the old woman's son and her halfbrother, when he was already grown up and ruled the town jointly with his mother, for the second husband of the old lady was dead. When they became Christians, the old lady was called Marta and the son Lázaro. I knew all this very well because in the year 1523 after the conquest of Mexico and the other provinces, when Cristóbal de Olid revolted in Honduras, and Cortés was on his way there, he passed through Coatzacoalcos and I and the greater number of the settlers of that town accompanied him on that expedition as I shall relate in the proper time and place. As Doña Marina proved herself such an excellent woman and good interpreter throughout the wars in New Spain, Tlaxcala, and Mexico (as I shall show later on) Cortés always took her with him, and during that expedition she was married to a gentleman named Juan Jaramillo at the town of Orizaba.

Doña Marina was a person of the greatest importance and was obeyed without question by the Indians throughout New Spain. * * * Doña Marina knew the language of Coatzacoalcos, which is that common to Mexico, and she knew the language of Tabasco, as did also Jerónimo de Aguilar, who spoke the language of Yucatan and Tabasco, which is one and the same. So that these two could understand one another clearly, and Aguilar translated into Castilian for Cortés.

This was the great beginning of our conquests and thus, thanks be to God, things prospered with us. I have made a point of explaining this matter, because without the help of Doña Marina we could not have understood the language of New Spain and Mexico.

[*Cortés is met by emissaries from Montezuma, lead by a noble named Teuhtlilli ("Tendile" as Díaz recalls him). They exchange gifts and Cortés describes his intention to go and meet Montezuma. Tendile sends on Corté's gifts and awaits instructions.*]

---

3. A Nahuatl-speaking coastal city near the beginning of the Mayan-speaking Yucatan Peninsula.

Then one morning, Tendile arrived with more than one hundred laden Indians, accompanied by a great Mexican Cacique, who in his face, features and appearance bore a strong likeness to our Captain Cortés and the great Montezuma had sent him purposely, for it is said that when Tendile brought the portrait of Cortés all the chiefs who were in Montezuma's company said that a great chief named Quintalbor looked exactly like Cortés and that was the name of the Cacique, who now arrived with Tendile; and as he was so like Cortés, we called them in camp "our Cortés" and "the other Cortés." To go back to my story, when these people arrived and came before our Captain they first of all kissed the earth and then fumigated him and all the soldiers who were standing around him, with incense which they brought in braziers of pottery. Cortés received them affectionately and seated them near himself, and that chief who came with the present had been appointed spokesman together with Tendile. After welcoming us to the country and after many courteous speeches had passed he ordered the presents which he had brought to be displayed, and they were placed on mats over which were spread cotton cloths. The first article presented was a wheel like a sun, as big as a cartwheel, with many sorts of pictures on it, the whole of fine gold, and a wonderful thing to behold, which those who afterwards weighed it said was worth more than ten thousand dollars. Then another wheel was presented of greater size made of silver of great brilliancy in imitation of the moon with other figures shown on it, and this was of great value as it was very heavy—and the chief brought back the helmet full of fine grains of gold, just as they are got out of the mines, and this was worth three thousand dollars. This gold in the helmet was worth more to us than if it had contained twenty thousand dollars, because it showed us that there were good mines there.

Then were brought twenty golden ducks, beautifully worked and very natural looking, and some ornaments like dogs, and many articles of gold worked in the shape of tigers and lions and monkeys, and ten collars beautifully worked and other necklaces; and twelve arrows and a bow with its string, and two rods like staffs of justice, five palms long, all in beautiful hollow work of fine gold. Then there were presented crests of gold and plumes of rich green feathers, and others of silver, and fans of the same materials, and deer copied in hollow gold and many other things that I cannot remember for it all happened so many years ago. And then over thirty loads of beautiful cotton cloth were brought worked with many patterns and decorated with many coloured feathers, and so many other things were there that it is useless my trying to describe them for I know not how to do it. When all these things had been presented, this great Cacique Quintalbor and Tendile asked Cortés to accept this present with the same willingness with which his prince had sent it, and divide it among the *teules*[4] and men who accompanied him. Cortés received the present with delight and then the ambassadors told Cortés that they wished to repeat what their prince, Montezuma, had sent them to say. First of all they told him that he was pleased that such valiant men, as he had heard that we were, should come to his country, for he knew all about what we had done at Tabasco, and that he would much like to see our great emperor who was such a mighty prince and whose fame was spread over so many lands, and that he would send him a present of precious stones; and that meanwhile we should stay in that port; that if he could assist us in any way he would do so with the greatest pleasure; but as to the interview, they should not worry about it; that there was no need for it and they (the ambassadors) urged many objections. * * *

---

4. Lords.

I will go on to relate how, one morning, we woke up to find not a single Indian in any of their huts, neither those who used to bring the food, nor those who came to trade, nor Pitalpitoque himself; they had all fled without saying a word. The cause of this, as we afterwards learned, was that Montezuma had sent orders to avoid further conversation with Cortés and those in his company; for it appears that Montezuma was very much devoted to his idols, named Tezcatepuca, and Huichilobos,[5] the latter the god of war, and Tezcatepuca the god of hell; and daily he sacrificed youths to them so as to get an answer from the gods as to what he should do about us; for Montezuma had already formed a plan, if we did not go off in the ships, to get us all into his power, and to raise a breed of us and also to keep us for sacrifice. As we afterwards found out, the reply given by the gods was that he should not listen to Cortés, nor to the message which he sent about setting up a cross and an image of Our Lady, and that such things should not be brought to the city. This was the reason why the Indians left our camp without warning.

[*Cortés and his men sail to the east coast of central Mexico and establish the settlement of Vera Cruz. At the coastal city of Cempoala they find the natives bitterly resentful of Aztec taxes and oppression, and promise to free them from Aztec rule.*]

We slept the night in those huts, and all the caciques bore us company all the way to our quarters in their town. They were really anxious that we should not leave their country, as they were fearful that Montezuma would send his warriors against them, and they said to Cortés that as we were already their friends, they would like to have us for brothers, and that it would be well that we should take from their daughters, so as to have children by them; and to cement our friendship, they brought eight damsels, all of them daughters of caciques, and gave one of these cacicas, who was the niece of the fat cacique, to Cortés; and one who was the daughter of another great cacique was given to Alonzo Hernández Puertocarrero. All eight of them were clothed in the rich garments of the country, beautifully ornamented as is their custom. Each one of them had a golden collar around her neck and golden earrings in her ears, and they came accompanied by other Indian girls who were to serve as their maids. When the fat cacique presented them, he said to Cortés: "Tecle (which in their language means Lord)—these seven women are for your captains, and this one, who is my niece, is for you, and she is the señora of towns and vassals."

Cortés received them with a cheerful countenance, and thanked the caciques for the gifts, but he said that before we could accept them and become brothers, they must get rid of those idols which they believed in and worshipped, and which kept them in darkness, and must no longer offer sacrifices to them, and that when he could see those cursed things thrown to the ground and an end put to sacrifices that then our bonds of brotherhood would be most firmly tied. He added that these damsels must become Christians before we could receive them. Every day we saw sacrificed before us three, four or five Indians whose hearts were offered to the idols and their blood plastered on the walls, and the feet, arms and legs of the victims were cut off and eaten, just as in our country we eat beef brought from the butchers. I even believe that they sell it by retail in the *tianguez* as they call their markets. Cortés told them that if they gave up these evil deeds and no longer practised them, not only would we be their friends, but we would make them lords over other provinces. All the caciques,

---

5. Tezcatlipoca and Huitzilopochtli.

priests and chiefs replied that it did not seem to them good to give up their idols and sacrifices and that these gods of theirs gave them health and good harvests and everything of which they had need.

[THE APPROACH TO TENOCHTITLAN]

Just as we were starting on our march to Mexico there came before Cortés four Mexican chiefs sent by Montezuma who brought a present of gold and cloths. After they had made obeisance according to their custom, they said: "Malinche,[6] our Lord the Great Montezuma sends you this present and says that he is greatly concerned for the hardships you have endured in coming from such a distant land in order to see him, and that he has already sent to tell you that he will give you much gold and silver and chalchihuites[7] as tribute for your Emperor and for yourself and the other Teules in your company, provided you do not come to Mexico, and now again he begs as a favour, that you will not advance any further but return whence you have come, and he promises to send you to the port a great quantity of gold and silver and rich stones for that King of yours, and, as for you, he will give you four loads of gold and for each of your brothers one load, but as for going on to Mexico your entrance into it is forbidden, for all his vassals have risen in arms to prevent your entry, and besides this there is no road thither, only a very narrow one, and there is no food for you to eat." And he used many other arguments about the difficulties to the end that we should advance no further.

Cortés with much show of affection embraced the Ambassadors, although the message grieved him, and he accepted the present, and said that he marvelled how the Lord Montezuma, having given himself out as our friend, and being such a great Prince, should be so inconstant; that one time he says one thing and another time sends to order the contrary, and regarding what he says about giving gold to our Lord the Emperor and to ourselves, he is grateful to him for it, and what he sends him now he will pay for in good works as time goes on. * * * As for what he said about there being little or no food, not enough to support us, we were men who could get along even if we have but little to eat, and we were already on the way to his city, so let him take our coming in good part.

As soon as the messengers had been despatched, we set out for Mexico, and as the people of Huexotzingo and Chalco had told us that Montezuma had held consultations with his Idols and priests, who had said he was to allow us to enter and that then he could kill us, and as we are but human and feared death, we never ceased thinking about it. As that country is very thickly peopled we made short marches, and commended ourselves to God and to Our Lady his blessed Mother, and talked about how and by what means we could enter the City, and it put courage into our hearts to think that as our Lord Jesus Christ had vouchsafed us protection through past dangers, he would likewise guard us from the power of the Mexicans. * * *

During the morning, we arrived at a broad Causeway and continued our march towards Iztapalapa,[8] and when we saw so many cities and villages built in the water and other great towns on dry land and that straight and level Causeway going towards Mexico, we were amazed and said that it was like the enchantments they tell of in the legend of Amadis, on account of the great towers and cues and buildings rising from

---

6. The name used either for Doña María or for Cortés himself (as here).

7. Pieces of carved jade (Nahuatl *chalchiuhitli*).

8. City on the southern shore of Lake Texcoco; endpoint of one of the three main causeways linking Tenochtitlán to the mainland.

the water, and all built of masonry. And some of our soldiers even asked whether the things that we saw were not a dream. It is not to be wondered at that I here write it down in this manner, for there is so much to think over that I do not know how to describe it, seeing things as we did that had never been heard of or seen before, not even dreamed about.

Thus, we arrived near Iztapalapa, to behold the splendour of the other Caciques who came out to meet us, who were the Lord of the town named Cuitlahuac, and the Lord of Culuacan, both of them near relations of Montezuma. And then when we entered the city of Iztapalapa, the appearance of the palaces in which they lodged us! How spacious and well built they were, of beautiful stone work and cedar wood, and the wood of other sweet-scented trees, with great rooms and courts, wonderful to behold, covered with awnings of cotton cloth.

When we had looked well at all of this, we went to the orchard and garden, which was such a wonderful thing to see and walk in, that I was never tired of looking at the diversity of the trees, and noting the scent which each one had, and the paths full of roses and flowers, and the many fruit trees and native roses, and the pond of fresh water. There was another thing to observe, that great canoes were able to pass into the garden from the lake through an opening that had been made so that there was no need for their occupants to land. And all was cemented and very splendid with many kinds of stone monuments with pictures on them, which gave much to think about. Then the birds of many kinds and breeds which came into the pond. I say again that I stood looking at it and thought that never in the world would there be discovered other lands such as these, for at that time there was no Peru, nor any thought of it. Of all these wonders that I then beheld to-day all is overthrown and lost, nothing left standing.

Let us go on, and I will relate that the Caciques of that town and of Coyoacan brought us a present of gold, worth more than two thousand pesos.

Early next day we left Iztapalapa with a large escort of those great Caciques whom I have already mentioned. We proceeded along the Causeway which is here eight paces in width and runs so straight to the City of Mexico that it does not seem to me to turn either much or little, but, broad as it is, it was so crowded with people that there was hardly room for them all, some of them going to and others returning from Mexico, besides those who had come out to see us, so that we were hardly able to pass by the crowds of them that came; and the towers and cues[9] were full of people as well as the canoes from all parts of the lake. It was not to be wondered at, for they had never before seen horses or men such as we are.

Gazing on such wonderful sights, we did not know what to say, or whether what appeared before us was real, for on one side, on the land, there were great cities, and in the lake ever so many more, and the lake itself was crowded with canoes, and in the Causeway were many bridges at intervals, and in front of us stood the great City of Mexico, and we—we did not even number four hundred soldiers! and we well remembered the words and warnings given us by the people of Huexotzingo and Tlaxcala, and the many other warnings that had been given that we should beware of entering Mexico, where they would kill us, as soon as they had us inside.

9. Pyramids.

Let the curious readers consider whether there is not much to ponder over in this that I am writing. What men have there been in the world who have shown such daring? But let us get on, and march along the Causeway. When we arrived where another small causeway branches off (leading to Coyoacan, which is another city) where there were some buildings like towers, which are their oratories, many more chieftains and Caciques approached clad in very rich mantles, the brilliant liveries of one chieftain differing from those of another, and the causeways were crowded with them. The Great Montezuma had sent these great Caciques in advance to receive us, and when they came before Cortés they bade us welcome in their language, and as a sign of peace, they touched their hands against the ground, and kissed the ground with the hand.

There we halted for a good while, and Cacamatzin, the Lord of Texcoco, and the Lord of Iztapalapa and the Lord of Tacuba and the Lord of Coyoacan went on in advance to meet the Great Montezuma, who was approaching in a rich litter accompanied by other great Lords and Caciques, who owned vassals. When we arrived near to Mexico, where there were some other small towers, the Great Montezuma got down from his litter, and those great Caciques supported him with their arms beneath a marvellously rich canopy of green coloured feathers with much gold and silver embroidery and with pearls and chalchihuites suspended from a sort of bordering, which was wonderful to look at. The Great Montezuma was richly attired according to his usage, and he was shod with sandals, the soles were of gold and the upper part adorned with precious stones. The four Chieftains who supported his arms were also richly clothed according to their usage, in garments which were apparently held ready for them on the road to enable them to accompany their prince, for they did not appear in such attire when they came to receive us. Besides these four Chieftains, there were four other great Caciques who supported the canopy over their heads, and many other Lords who walked before the Great Montezuma, sweeping the ground where he would tread and spreading cloths on it, so that he should not tread on the earth. Not one of these Chieftains dared even to think of looking him in the face, but kept their eyes lowered with great reverence, except those four relations, his nephews, who supported him with their arms.

When Cortés was told that the Great Montezuma was approaching, and he saw him coming, he dismounted from his horse, and when he was near Montezuma, they simultaneously paid great reverence to one another. Montezuma bade him welcome and our Cortés replied through Doña Marina wishing him very good health. And it seems to me that Cortés, through Doña Marina, offered him his right hand, and Montezuma did not wish to take it, but he did give his hand to Cortés and then Cortés brought out a necklace which he had ready at hand, made of glass stones, which I have already said are called Margaritas, which have within them many patterns of diverse colours, these were strung on a cord of gold and with musk so that it should have a sweet scent, and he placed it round the neck of the Great Montezuma and when he had so placed it he was going to embrace him, and those great Princes who accompanied Montezuma held back Cortés by the arm so that he should not embrace him, for they considered it an indignity.

Then Cortés through the mouth of Doña Marina told him that now his heart rejoiced at having seen such a great Prince, and that he took it as a great honour that he had come in person to meet him and had frequently shown him such favour.

Then Montezuma spoke other words of politeness to him, and told two of his nephews who supported his arms, the Lord of Texcoco and the Lord of Coyoacan, to go with us and show us to our quarters, and Montezuma with his other two relations, the Lord of Cuitlahuac and the Lord of Tacuba who accompanied him, returned to the city, and all those grand companies of Caciques and chieftains who had come with him returned in his train. As they turned back after their Prince we stood watching them and observed how they all marched with their eyes fixed on the ground without looking at him, keeping close to the wall, following him with great reverence. Thus space was made for us to enter the streets of Mexico, without being so much crowded. But who could now count the multitude of men and women and boys who were in the streets and on the azoteas,[1] and in canoes on the canals, who had come out to see us. It was indeed wonderful, and, now that I am writing about it, it all comes before my eyes as though it had happened but yesterday. Coming to think it over it seems to be a great mercy that our Lord Jesus Christ was pleased to give us grace and courage to dare to enter into such a city; and for the many times He has saved me from danger of death, as will be seen later on, I give Him sincere thanks, and in that He has preserved me to write about it, although I cannot do it as fully as is fitting or the subject needs. Let us make no words about it, for deeds are the best witnesses to what I say here and elsewhere.

[AVIARIES AND TEMPLES]

Let us leave this and proceed to the Aviary, and I am forced to abstain from enumerating every kind of bird that was there and its peculiarity, for there was everything from the Royal Eagle and other smaller eagles, and many other birds of great size, down to tiny birds of many-coloured plumage, also the birds from which they take the rich plumage which they use in their green feather work. The birds which have these feathers are about the size of the magpies in Spain, they are called in this country *Quezales,* and there are other birds which have feathers of five colours—green, red, white, yellow and blue; I don't remember what they are called; then there were parrots of many different colours, and there are so many of them that I forget their names, not to mention the beautifully marked ducks and other larger ones like them. From all these birds they plucked the feathers when the time was right to do so, and the feathers grew again. All the birds that I have spoken about breed in these houses, and in the setting season certain Indian men and women who look after the birds place the eggs under them and clean the nests and feed them, so that each kind of bird has its proper food. In this house that I have spoken of there is a great tank of fresh water and in it there are other sorts of birds with long stilted legs, with body, wings and tail all red; I don't know their names, but in the Island of Cuba they are called *Ypiris,* and there are others something like them, and there are also in that tank many other kinds of birds which always live in the water.

Let us leave this and go on to another great house, where they keep many Idols, and they say that they are their fierce gods, and with them many kinds of carnivorous beasts of prey, tigers and two kinds of lions, and animals something like wolves and foxes, and other smaller carnivorous animals, and all these carnivores they feed with flesh, and the greater number of them breed in the house. They give them as food deer and fowls, dogs and other things which they hunt, and I have heard it said that they feed them on the bodies of the Indians who have been sacrificed. It is in this way: you

---

1. Roof terraces.

have already heard me say that when they sacrifice a wretched Indian they saw open the chest with stone knives and hasten to tear out the palpitating heart and blood, and offer it to their Idols, in whose name the sacrifice is made. Then they cut off the thighs, arms and head and eat the former at feasts and banquets, and the head they hang up on some beams, and the body of the man sacrificed is not eaten but given to these fierce animals. They also have in that cursed house many vipers and poisonous snakes which carry on their tails things that sound like bells. These are the worst vipers of all, and they keep them in jars and great pottery vessels with many feathers, and there they lay their eggs and rear their young, and they give them to eat the bodies of the Indians who have been sacrificed, and the flesh of dogs which they are in the habit of breeding.

Let me speak now of the infernal noise when the lions and tigers roared and the jackals and foxes howled and the serpents hissed, it was horrible to listen to and it seemed like a hell. * * *

[THE VIEW FROM THE TEMPLE MAYOR]

When we arrived there Montezuma came out of an oratory where his cursed idols were, at the summit of the great Cue, and two priests came with him, and after paying great reverence to Cortés and to all of us he said: "You must be tired, Señor Malinche, from ascending this our great Cue," and Cortés replied through our interpreters who were with us that he and his companions were never tired by anything. Then Montezuma took him by the hand and told him to look at his great city and all the other cities that were standing in the water, and the many other towns on the land round the lake, and that if he had not seen the great market place well, that from where they were they could see it better.

So we stood looking about us, for that huge and cursed temple stood so high that from it one could see over everything very well, and we saw the three causeways which led into Mexico, that is the causeway of Iztapalapa by which we had entered four days before, and that of Tacuba, and that of Tepeaquilla, and we saw the fresh water that comes from Chapultepec which supplies the city, and we saw the bridges on the three causeways which were built at certain distances apart through which the water of the lake flowed in and out from one side to the other, and we beheld on that great lake a great multitude of canoes, some coming with supplies of food and others returning loaded with cargoes of merchandise; and we saw that from every house of that great city and of all the other cities that were built in the water it was impossible to pass from house to house, except by drawbridges which were made of wood or in canoes; and we saw in those cities Cues and oratories like towers and fortresses and all gleaming white, and it was a wonderful thing to behold; then the houses with flat roofs and on the causeways other small towers and oratories which were like fortresses.

After having examined and considered all that we had seen we turned to look at the great market place and the crowds of people that were in it, some buying and others selling, so that the murmur and hum of their voices and words that they used could be heard more than a league off. Some of the soldiers among us who had been in many parts of the world, in Constantinople, and all over Italy, and in Rome, said that so large a market place and so full of people, and so well regulated and arranged, they had never beheld before.

Let us leave this, and return to our Captain, who said to Fray Bartolomé de Olmedo, who happened to be near by him: "It seems to me, Señor Padre, that it would be a good thing to throw out a feeler to Montezuma, as to whether he would allow us to build our church here"; and the Padre replied that it would be a good thing if it were successful, but it seemed to him that it was not quite a suitable time to speak about it, for Montezuma did not appear to be inclined to do such a thing.

Then our Cortés said to Montezuma: "Your Highness is indeed a very great prince and worthy of even greater things. We are rejoiced to see your cities, and as we are here in your temple, what I now beg as a favour is that you will show us your gods and Teules." Montezuma replied that he must first speak with his high priests, and when he had spoken to them he said that we might enter into a small tower and apartment, a sort of hall, where there were two altars, with very richly carved boardings on the top of the roof. On each altar were two figures, like giants with very tall bodies and very fat, and the first which stood on the right hand they said was the figure of Huichilobos their god of War; it had a very broad face and monstrous and terrible eyes, and the whole of his body was covered with precious stones, and gold and pearls, and with seed pearls stuck on with a paste that they make in this country out of a sort of root, and all the body and head was covered with it, and the body was girdled by great snakes made of gold and precious stones, and in one hand he held a bow and in the other some arrows. And another small idol that stood by him, they said was his page, and he held a short lance and a shield richly decorated with gold and stones. Huichilobos had round his neck some Indians' faces and other things like hearts of Indians, the former made of gold and the latter of silver, with many precious blue stones.

There were some braziers with incense which they call copal, and in them they were burning the hearts of the three Indians whom they had sacrificed that day, and they had made the sacrifice with smoke and copal. All the walls of the oratory were so splashed and encrusted with blood that they were black, the floor was the same and the whole place stank vilely. Then we saw on the other side on the left hand there stood the other great image the same height as Huichilobos, and it had a face like a bear and eyes that shone, made of their mirrors which they call *Tezcat,* and the body plastered with precious stones like that of Huichilobos, for they say that the two are brothers; and this Tezcatepuca was the god of Hell and had charge of the souls of the Mexicans, and his body was girt with figures like little devils with snakes' tails. The walls were so clotted with blood and the soil so bathed with it that in the slaughter houses of Spain there is not such another stench. * * *

Our Captain said to Montezuma through our interpreter, half laughing: "Señor Montezuma, I do not understand how such a great Prince and wise man as you are has not come to the conclusion, in your mind, that these idols of yours are not gods, but evil things that are called devils, and so that you may know it and all your priests may see it clearly, do me the favour to approve of my placing a cross here on the top of this tower, and that in one part of these oratories where your Huichilobos and Tezcatepuca stand we may divide off a space where we can set up an image of Our Lady (an image which Montezuma had already seen) and you will see by the fear in which these Idols hold it that they are deceiving you."

Montezuma replied half angrily (and the two priests who were with him showed great annoyance), and said: "Señor Malinche, if I had known that you would have said such defamatory things I would not have shown you my gods, we consider them to be very good, for they give us health and rains and good seed times and seasons and as many victories as we desire, and we are obliged to worship them and make sacrifices, and I pray you not to say another word to their dishonour."

When our Captain heard that and noted the angry looks he did not refer again to the subject, but said with a cheerful manner: "It is time for your Excellency and for us to return," and Montezuma replied that it was well, but that he had to pray and offer certain sacrifices on account of the great *tatacul,* that is to say sin, which he had committed in allowing us to ascend his great Cue, and being the cause of our being permitted to see his gods, and of our dishonouring them by speaking evil of them, so that before he left he must pray and worship.

Then Cortés said: "I ask your pardon if it be so," and then we went down the steps, and as they numbered one hundred and fourteen, and as some of our soldiers were suffering from tumours and abscesses, their legs were tired by the descent.

[*Hearing of a skirmish between native warriors and the men he had left behind at Vera Curz, Cortés decides to use the excuse to take Montezuma prisoner.*]

When Cortés entered, after having made his usual salutations, he said to him through our interpreters: "Señor Montezuma, I am very much astonished that you, who are such a valiant Prince, after having declared that you are our friend, should order your Captains, whom you have stationed on the coast near to Tuxpan, to take arms against my Spaniards, and that they should dare to rob the towns which are in the keeping and under the protection of our King and master and to demand of them Indian men and women for sacrifice, and should kill a Spaniard, one of my brothers, and a horse." (He did not wish to speak of the Captain nor of the six soldiers who died as soon as they arrived at Villa Rica, for Montezuma did not know about it, nor did the Indian Captains who had attacked them.) Cortés went on to say: "Being such a friend of yours I ordered my Captains to do all that was possible to help and serve you, and you have done exactly the contrary to us. Also in the affair at Cholula your Captains and a large force of warriors had received your own commands to kill us. I forgave it at the time out of my great regard for you, but now again your vassals and Captains have become insolent, and hold secret consultations stating that you wish us to be killed. I do not wish to begin a war on this account nor to destroy this city, I am willing to forgive it all, if silently and without raising any disturbance you will come with us to our quarters, where you will be as well served and attended to as though you were in your own house, but if you cry out or make any disturbance you will immediately be killed by these my Captains, whom I brought solely for this purpose."

When Montezuma heard this he was terrified and dumbfounded, and replied that he had never ordered his people to take arms against us, and that he would at once send to summon his Captains so that the truth should be known, and he would chastise them, and at that very moment he took from his arm and wrist the sign and seal of Huichilobos, which was only done when he gave an important and weighty command which was to be carried out at once. With regard to being taken prisoner and leaving his Palace against his will, he said that he was not the person to whom such an order could be given, and that he would not go. Cortés replied to him with very good arguments and Montezuma answered him with even better, showing that he ought not to leave his house. In this way more than half an hour was spent over talk, and when Juan Velásquez de Leon and the other Captains saw that they were wasting time over it and could not longer await the moment when they should remove him from his house and hold him a prisoner, they spoke to Cortés somewhat angrily and said: "What is the good of your making so many words, let us either take him prisoner, or stab him, tell him once more that if he cries out or makes an uproar we will kill him, for it is better at once to save our lives or to lose them," and as Juan Velásquez said this with a loud and rather terrifying voice, for such was his way of speaking, Montezuma, who saw that our Captains were angered, asked Doña Marina what they were saying in such loud tones.

As Doña Marina was very clever, she said: "Señor Montezuma, what I counsel you is to go at once to their quarters without any disturbance at all, for I know that they will pay you much honour as a great Prince such as you are, otherwise you will remain here a dead man, but in their quarters you will learn the truth." Then Montezuma said to Cortés: "Señor Malinche, if this is what you desire, I have a son and two legitimate daughters, take them as hostages, and do not put this affront on me, what will my chieftains say if they see me taken off as a prisoner?" Cortés replied to him that he must come with them himself and there was no alternative. At the end of much more discussion that took place, Montezuma said that he would go willingly, and then Cortés and our Captains bestowed many caresses on him and told him that they begged him not to be annoyed, and to tell his captains and the men of his guard that he was going of his own free will, because he had spoken to his Idol Huichilobos and the priests who attended him, and that it was beneficial for his health and the safety of his life that he should be with us. His rich litter, in which he was used to go out with all the Captains who accompanied him, was promptly brought, and he went to our quarters where we placed guards and watchmen over him.

All the attentions and amusements which it was possible for him to have, both Cortés and all of us did our best to afford him, and he was not put under any personal restraint, and soon all the principal Mexican Chieftains and his nephews came to talk with him, and to learn the reason of his seizure, and whether he wished them to attack us. Montezuma answered them that he was delighted to be here some days with us of his own free will and not by force, and that when he wished for anything he would tell them so, and that they must not excite themselves nor the City, nor were they to take it to heart, for what had happened about his being there was agreeable to his Huichilobos, and certain priests who knew had told him so, for they had spoken to the Idol about it. In this way which I have now related the capture of the Great Montezuma was effected.

There, where he remained, he had his service and his women and his baths in which he bathed himself, and twenty great chiefs always stayed in his company holding their ancient offices, as well as his councillors and captains, and he stayed there a prisoner without showing any anger at it, and Ambassadors from distant lands came there with their suites, and brought him his tribute, and he carried on his important business.

I will not say anything more at present about this imprisonment, and will relate how the messengers whom Montezuma sent with his sign and seal to summon the Captains who had killed our soldiers, brought them before him as prisoners and what he said to them I do not know, but he sent them on to Cortés, so that he might do justice to them, and their confession was taken when Montezuma was not present and they confessed that what I have already stated was true, that their Prince had ordered them to wage war and to extract tribute, and that if any Teules should appear in defence of the towns, they too should be attacked or killed. When Cortés heard this confession he sent to inform Montezuma how it implicated him in the affair, and Montezuma made all the excuses he could, and our captain sent him word that he believed the confession himself, but that although Montezuma deserved punishment in conformity with the ordinances of our King, to the effect that any person causing others, whether guilty or innocent, to be killed, shall die for it, yet he was so fond of him and wished him so well, that even if that crime lay at his door, he, Cortés, would pay the penalty with his own life sooner than allow Montezuma's to pass away. With all this that Cortés sent to tell him, Montezuma felt anxious, and without any further discussion Cortés sentenced those captains to death and to be burned in front of Montezuma's palace. This sentence was promptly carried out, and, so that there could be no obstruction while they were being burned, Cortés ordered shackles to be put on Montezuma himself, and when this was done Montezuma roared with rage, and if before this he was scared, he was then much more so.

After the burning was over our Cortés with five of our captains went to Montezuma's apartment and Cortés himself took off the fetters, and he spoke such loving words to him that his anger soon passed off, for our Cortés told him that he not only regarded him as a brother, but much more, and that, as he was already Lord and King of so many towns and provinces, if it were possible he would make him Lord of many more countries as time went on, such as he had not been able to subdue, and which did not now obey him, and he told him that if he now wished to go to his Palace, that he would give him leave to go. Cortés told him this through our interpreters and while Cortés was saying it the tears apparently sprang to Montezuma's eyes. He answered with great courtesy, that he thanked him for it (but he well knew that Cortés' speech was mere words), and that now at present it was better for him to stay there a prisoner, for there was danger, as his chieftains were numerous, and his nephews and relations came every day to him to say that it would be a good thing to attack us and free him from prison, that as soon as they saw him outside they might drive him to it. He did not wish to see revolutions in his city, but if he did not comply with their wishes possibly they would want to set up another Prince in his place. And so he was putting those thoughts out of their heads by saying that Huichilobos had sent him word that he should remain a prisoner.

[*As Cortés solidified his position in Mexico, he sent letters and gold directly to the king in Spain, ignoring his superior, Diego Velázquez, governor of Cuba. Angered, Velázquez sent a force of four hundred men, commanded by his lieutenant Pánfilo de Narvaez, to Vera Cruz to supplant Cortés. Cortés hurried to the coast with most of his men, leaving Pedro de Alvarado and a small force to keep Montezuma under house arrest. Cortés defeated Narvaez, and enlisted most of Narvaez's men in his own service.*]

Let us return now to Narvaez and a black man whom he brought covered with smallpox, and a very black affair it was for New Spain, for it was owing to him that the whole country was stricken and filled with it, from which there was great mortality, for according to what the Indians said they had never had such a disease, and, as they did not understand it, they bathed very often, and on that account a great number of them died; so that dark as was the lot of Narvaez, still blacker was the death of so many persons who were not Christians.

Let me say how ill luck suddenly turns the wheel, and after great good fortune and pleasure follows sadness; it so happened that at this moment came the news that Mexico was in revolt, and that Pedro de Alvarado was besieged in his fortress and quarters, and that they had set fire to this same fortress in two places, and had killed seven of his soldiers and wounded many others, and he sent to demand assistance with great urgency and haste. This news was brought by two Tlaxcalans without any letter, but a letter soon arrived by two other Tlaxcalans sent by Pedro de Alvarado in which he told the same story. When we heard this bad news, God knows how greatly it depressed us.

By forced marches we began our journey to Mexico, Narvaez and Salvatierra remaining as prisoners in Villa Rica.

Just at this moment, as we were ready to start, there arrived four great chieftains sent to Cortés by the great Montezuma to complain to him of Pedro de Alvarado, and what they said, with tears streaming from their eyes, was that Pedro de Alvarado sallied out from his quarters with all the soldiers that Cortés had left with him, and, for no reason at all, fell on their chieftains and Caciques who were dancing and celebrating a feast in honour of their Idols Huichilobos and Tezcatepuca, Pedro de Alvarado having given them leave to do so. He killed and wounded many of them and in defending themselves they had killed six of his soldiers. Thus they made many complaints against Pedro de Alvarado, and Cortés, somewhat disgusted, replied to the messengers that he would go to Mexico and put it all to rights. So they went off with that reply to their great Montezuma, who it is said, resented it as a very bad one and was enraged at it.

[THE BATTLE FOR THE CITY BEGINS]

Diego de Ordás set out in the way that he was ordered with his four hundred soldiers, but he had hardly reached the middle of the street along which he was to march, when so many squadrons of Mexican warriors fell on him and so many more were on the roofs of the houses, and they made such fierce attacks that on the first assault they killed eight soldiers and wounded all the rest, and Diego de Ordás himself was wounded in three places, and in this manner he could not advance one step further but had to return little by little to his quarters. During the retreat they killed another good soldier named Lyscano who, with a broadsword, had done the work of a very valiant man.

At that moment, while many squadrons came out against Ordás, many more approached our quarters and shot off so many javelins and stones from slings, and arrows, that they wounded on that occasion alone over forty-six of our men, and twelve of them died of their wounds; and such a number of warriors fell upon us that Diego de Ordás, who was coming in retreat, could not reach our quarters on account of the fierce assaults they made on him, some from the rear and others in front and others from the roofs.

Little availed our cannon, or our muskets, crossbows and lances, or the thrusts we gave them, or our good fighting, for although we killed and wounded many of them, yet they managed to reach us by pushing forward over the points of our swords and lances, and closing up their squadrons never desisted from their brave attack, nor could we push them away from us. * * *

We passed the night in dressing wounds and in mending the breaches in the walls that the enemy had made, and in getting ready for the next day. Then, as soon as it was dawn, our Captain decided that all of us and Narvaez' men should sally out to fight with them and that we should take the cannon and muskets and crossbows and endeavour to defeat them, or at least to make them feel our strength and valour better than the day before. I may state that when we came to this decision, the Mexicans were arranging the very same thing. We fought very well, but they were so strong, and had so many squadrons which relieved each other from time to time, that even if ten thousand Trojan Hectors and as many more Roldans[2] had been there, they would not have been able to break through them.

2. Rolando, a great hero of medieval romance.

We noted their tenacity in fighting, but I declare that I do not know how to describe it, for neither cannon nor muskets nor crossbows availed, nor hand-to-hand fighting, nor killing thirty or forty of them every time we charged, for they still fought on in as close ranks and with more energy than in the beginning. Sometimes when we were gaining a little ground or a part of the street, they pretended to retreat, but it was merely to induce us to follow them and cut us off from our fortress and quarters, so as to fall on us in greater safety to themselves, believing that we could not return to our quarters alive, for they did us much damage when we were retreating.

Then, as to going out to burn their houses, I have already said that between one house and another they have wooden drawbridges, and these they raised so that we could only pass through deep water. Then we could not endure the rocks and stones hurled from the roofs, in such a way that they damaged and wounded many of our men. I do not know why I write thus so lukewarmly, for some three or four soldiers who were there with us and who had served in Italy, swore to God many times that they had never seen such fierce fights, not even when they had taken part in such between Christians and against the artillery of the King of France, or of the Great Turk, nor had they seen men like those Indians with such courage in closing up their ranks.

[THE NOCHE TRISTE]

Let us go back to our story. It was decided to sue for peace so that we could leave Mexico, and as soon as it was dawn many more squadrons of Mexicans arrived and very effectually surrounded our quarters on all sides, and if they had discharged many stones and arrows before, they came much thicker and with louder howls and whistles on this day, and other squadrons endeavoured to force an entrance in other parts, and cannon and muskets availed nothing, although we did them damage enough.

When Cortés saw all this, he decided that the great Montezuma should speak to them from the roof and tell them that the war must cease, and that we wished to leave his city. When they went to give this message from Cortés to the great Montezuma, it is reported that he said with great grief: "What more does Malinche want from me? I neither wish to live nor to listen to him, to such a pass has my fate brought me because of him." And he did not wish to come, and it is even reported that he said he neither wished to see nor hear him, nor listen to his false words, promises or lies. Then the Padre de la Merced and Cristóbal de Olid went and spoke to him with much reverence and in very affectionate terms, and Montezuma said: "I believe that I shall not obtain any result towards ending this war, for they have already raised up another Lord and have made up their minds not to let you leave this place alive, therefore I believe that all of you will have to die."

Montezuma was placed by a battlement of the roof with many of us soldiers guarding him, and he began to speak to his people, with very affectionate expressions telling them to desist from the war, and that we would leave Mexico. Many of the Mexican Chieftains and Captains knew him well and at once ordered their people to be silent and not to discharge darts, stones or arrows, and four of them reached a spot where Montezuma could speak to them, and they to him, and with tears they said to him: "Oh! Señor, and our great Lord, how all your misfortune and injury and that of your children and relations afflicts us, we make known to you that we have already raised one of your kinsmen to be our Lord," and there he stated his name, that he was called Cuitlahuac, the Lord of Ixtapalapa, and moreover they said that the war must be carried through, and that they had vowed to their Idols not to relax it until we were all dead, and that they prayed every day to their Huichilobos and Texcatepuca to guard him free and safe from our power, and that should it end as they desired, they would not fail to hold him in higher regard as their Lord than they did before, and they begged him to forgive them.

They had hardly finished this speech when suddenly such a shower of stones and darts were discharged that (our men who were shielding him having neglected for a moment their duty, because they saw how the attack ceased while he spoke to them) he was hit by three stones, one on the head, another on the arm and another on the leg, and although they begged him to have the wounds dressed and to take food, and spoke kind words to him about it, he would not. Indeed, when we least expected it, they came to say that he was dead. Cortés wept for him, and all of us Captains and soldiers, and there was no man among us who knew him and was intimate with him, who did not bemoan him as though he were our father, and it is not to be wondered at, considering how good he was. It was stated that he had reigned for seventeen years and that he was the best king there had ever been in Mexico, and that he had conquered in person, in three wars which he had carried on in the countries he had subjugated.

* * *

Now we saw our forces diminishing every day and those of the Mexicans increasing, and many of our men were dead and all the rest wounded, and although we fought like brave men we could not drive back nor even get free from the many squadrons which attacked us both by day and night, and the powder was giving out, and the same was happening with the food and water, and the great Montezuma being dead, they were unwilling to grant the peace and truce which we had sent to demand of them. In fact we were staring death in the face, and the bridges had been raised. It was therefore decided by Cortés and all of us captains and soldiers that we should set out during the night. * * *

When they heard this many of the soldiers of Narvaez and some of our people loaded themselves with gold. I declare that I had no other desire but the desire to save my life, but I did not fail to carry off from some small boxes that were there, four chalchihuites, which are stones very highly prized among the Indians, and I quickly placed them in my bosom under my armour, and, later on, the price of them served me well in healing my wounds and getting me food.

After we had learnt the plans that Cortés had made about the way in which we were to escape that night and get to the bridges, as it was somewhat dark and cloudy and rainy, we began before midnight to bring along the baggage, and the horses and mare began their march, and the Tlaxcalans who were laden with the gold. Then the bridge was quickly put in place, and Cortés and the others whom he took with him in the first detachment and many of the horsemen, crossed over it. While this was happening, the voices, trumpets, cries and whistles of the Mexicans began to sound and they called out in their language to the people of Tlatelolco, "Come out at once with your canoes for the Teules are leaving; cut them off so that not one of them may be left alive."

When I least expected it, we saw so many squadrons of warriors bearing down on us, and the lake so crowded with canoes that we could not defend ourselves. Many of our soldiers had already crossed the bridge, and while we were in this position, a great multitude of Mexicans charged down on us with the intention of removing the bridge and wounding and killing our men who were unable to assist each other; and as fortune is perverse at such times, one mischance followed another, and as it was raining, two of the horses slipped and fell into the lake. When I and others of Cortés' Company saw that, we got safely to the other side of the bridge, and so many warriors charged on us, that despite all our good fighting, no further use could be made of the bridge, so that the passage or water opening was soon filled up with dead horses, Indian men and women, servants, baggage and boxes.

Fearing that they would not fail to kill us, we thrust ourselves ahead along the causeway, and we met many squadrons armed with long lances waiting for us, and they used abusive words to us, and among them they cried: "Oh! villains, are you still alive?"—and with the cuts and thrusts we gave them, we got through, although they then wounded six of those who were going along with me. Then if there was some sort of plan such as we had agreed upon it was an accursed one; for Cortés and the captains and soldiers who passed first on horseback, so as to save themselves and reach dry land and make sure of their lives, spurred on along the causeway, and they did not fail to attain their object, and the horses with the gold and the Tlaxcalans also got out in safety. I assert that if we had waited (the horsemen and the soldiers one for the other) at the bridges, we should all have been put an end to, and not one of us would have been left alive; the reason was this, that as we went along the causeway, charging the Mexican squadrons, on one side of us was water and on the other azoteas, and the lake was full of canoes so that we could do nothing. Moreover the muskets and crossbows were all left behind at the bridge, and as it was night time, what could we do beyond what we accomplished? which was to charge and give some sword-thrusts to those who tried to lay hands on us, and to march and get on ahead so as to get off the causeway.

Had it been in the day-time, it would have been far worse, and we who escaped did so only by the Grace of God. To one who saw the hosts of warriors who fell on us that night and the canoes full of them coming along to carry off our soldiers, it was terrifying.

[*Two-thirds of the Spaniards having been killed, the four hundred survivors reach the territory of Tlaxcala, enemies of the Aztecs. Over a period of months, Cortés gets reinforcements from Cuba, rallies native support against the Aztecs, and builds boats to aid in a new attack on Tenochtitlán. In May of 1521 they begin the assault.*]

After hearing Mass, which was said by Father Juan Díaz, and commending ourselves to God, we agreed that with the two Divisions together, we should go out and cut off the water of Chapultepec by which the city was supplied which was about half a league distant from Tacuba.

As we were marching to break the pipes, we came on many warriors who were waiting for us on the road, for they fully understood that would be the first thing by which we could do them damage, and so when they met us near some bad ground, they began to shoot arrows at us and hurl javelins and stones from slings, and they wounded three of our soldiers, but we quickly made them turn their backs and our friends the Tlaxcalans followed them so that they killed twenty and we captured eighteen of them.

As soon as these squadrons had been put to flight we broke the conduits through which the water flowed to the city, and from that time onwards it never flowed into Mexico so long as the war lasted. * * *

From time to time the Mexicans changed about and relieved their squadrons as we could tell by the devices and distinguishing marks on their armour. Whenever we left a bridge or barricade unguarded after having captured it with much labour, the enemy would retake and deepen it that same night, and construct stronger defences and even make hidden pits in the waters, so that the next day when we were fighting, and it was time for us to retire, we should get entangled among the defences. To prevent the launches from coming to our assistance, they had fixed many stakes hidden in the water so that they should get impaled on them.

When we drew off in the night we treated our wounds by searing them with oil, and a soldier named Juan Catalan blessed them for us and made charms, and truly we found that our Lord Jesus Christ was pleased to give us strength in addition to the many mercies he vouchsafed us every day, for the wounds healed rapidly. Wounded and tied up in rags as we were we had to fight from morning until night, for if the wounded had remained in camp without coming out to fight, there would not have been twenty men in each company well enough to go out. * * *

We made attacks on the Mexicans every day and succeeded in capturing many idol towers, houses, canals, and other openings and bridges which they had constructed from house to house, and we filled them all up with adobes and the timbers from the houses that we pulled down and destroyed and we kept guard over them, but notwithstanding all this trouble that we took, the enemy came back and deepened them and widened the openings and erected more barricades. * * *

I well understand that interested readers will be surfeited with seeing so many fights every day but one cannot do less, for during the ninety and three days that we besieged this strong and great City we had war and combats every day and every night as well. However, when it seemed to us that we were victorious, great disasters were really coming upon us, and we were in the greatest danger of perishing in all three camps, as will be seen later on. * * *

When we had retreated near to our quarters and had already crossed a great opening where there was much water the arrows, javelins and stones could no longer reach us. Sandoval, Francisco de Lugo and Andrés de Tápia were standing with Pedro de Alvarado each one relating what had happened to him and what Cortés had ordered, when again there was sounded the dismal drum of Huichilobos and many other shells and horns and things like trumpets and the sound of them all was terrifying, and we all looked towards the lofty Cue where they were being sounded, and saw that our comrades whom they had captured when they defeated Cortés were being carried by force up the steps, and they were taking them to be sacrificed. When they got them up to a small square in front of the oratory, where their accursed idols are kept, we saw them place plumes on the heads of many of them and with things like fans in their hands they forced them to dance before Huichilobos, and after they had danced they immediately placed them on their backs on some rather narrow stones which had been prepared as places for sacrifice, and with stone knives they sawed open their chests and drew out their palpitating hearts and offered them to the idols that were there, and they kicked the bodies down the steps, and Indian butchers who were waiting below cut off the arms and feet and flayed the skin off the faces, and prepared it afterwards like glove leather with the beards on, and kept those for the festivals when they celebrated drunken orgies, and the flesh they ate in *chilmole*.[3] In the same way they sacrificed all the others and ate the legs and arms and offered the hearts and blood to their idols, as I have said, and the bodies, that is their entrails and feet, they threw to the tigers and lions which they kept in the house of the carnivores which I have spoken about in an earlier chapter.

When we saw those cruelties all of us in our camp said the one to the other: "Thank God that they are not carrying me off to-day to be sacrificed."

3. Chili sauce.

It should also be noted that we were not far away from them, yet we could render them no help, and could only pray God to guard us from such a death.

* * *

From all three camps we were now advancing into the City, Cortés on his side, Sandoval on his and Pedro de Alvarado on our side, and we reached the spot where the spring was, that I have already spoken about, where the Mexicans drank the brackish water, and we broke it up and destroyed it so that they might not make use of it. Some Mexicans were guarding it and we had a good skirmish with them. We could already move freely through all parts of the streets we had captured, for they were already levelled and free from water and openings and the horses could move very easily.

Thus the ten Companies of Pedro de Alvarado advanced fighting and reached Tlatelolco, and there were so many Mexicans guarding their Idols and lofty cues, and they had raised so many barricades that we were fully two hours before we were able to capture them and get inside. Now that the horses had space to gallop, although most of them were wounded, they helped us very much, and the horsemen speared many Mexicans.

[*Day after day, the Spanish penetrate further into the city, systematically levelling blocks of houses as they proceed. As they take the last districts of the city, the new ruler Cuauhtemoc ("Guatemoc") tries to flee by canoe. He is caught and brought to Cortés.*]

While they were bringing him, Cortés ordered a guest chamber to be prepared as well as could be done at the time, with mats and cloths and seats, and a good supply of the food which Cortés had reserved for himself. Sandoval and Holguin soon arrived with Guatemoc, and the two captains between them led him up to Cortés, and when he came in front of him he paid him great respect, and Cortés embraced Guatemoc with delight, and was very affectionate to him and his captains. Then Guatemoc said to Cortés: "Señor Malinche, I have surely done my duty in defence of my City, and I can do no more and I come by force and a prisoner into your presence and into your power. Take that dagger that you have in your belt and kill me at once with it," and when he said this he wept tears and sobbed and other great Lords whom he had brought with him also wept. Cortés answered him through Doña Marina and Aguilar very affectionately, that he esteemed him all the more for having been so brave as to defend the City, and he was deserving of no blame, on the contrary it was more in his favour than otherwise.

What he wished was that Guatemoc had made peace of his own free will before the city had been so far destroyed, and so many of his Mexicans had died, but now that both had happened there was no help for it and it could not be mended, let his spirit and the spirit of his Captains take rest, and he should rule in Mexico and over his provinces as he did before. Then Guatemoc and his Captains said that they accepted his favour, and Cortés asked after his wife and other great ladies, the wives of other Captains who, he had been told, had come with Guatemoc. Guatemoc himself answered and said that he had begged Gonzalo de Sandoval and García Holguin that they might remain in the canoes while he came to see what orders Malinche gave them. Cortés at once sent for them and ordered them all to be given of the best that at that time there was in the camp to eat, and as it was late and was beginning to rain, Cortés arranged for them to go to Coyoacan, and took Guatemoc and all his family and household and many chieftains with him, and he ordered Pedro de Alvarado, Gonzalo de Sandoval and the other captains each to go to his own quarters and camp, and we went to Tacuba, Sandoval to Tepeaquilla and Cortés to Coyoacan. Guatemoc and his captains were captured on the thirteenth day of August at the time of vespers on the day of Señor San Hipólito in the year one thousand five hundred and twenty-one, thanks to our Lord Jesus Christ and our Lady the Virgin Santa Maria, His Blessed Mother. Amen.

Bernardino de Sahagún
c. 1499–1590

Born and raised in Spain, where he took holy orders and became a Franciscan friar, Bernardino de Sahagún came to Mexico in 1529; he stayed until his death at the age of ninety-one. He helped establish the first seminary in the new colony, where he and his colleagues began to train native converts to serve as priests. Like other Franciscans, Sahagún believed that the native languages and cultures needed to be understood if the population was to be genuinely converted to Christianity, and not merely make a perfunctory show of adhering to the new faith. Having become fully fluent in Nahuatl, he composed a book of hymns and psalms in Nahuatl (see page 122 for excerpts), and most ambitiously he began to work with native seminarians and other informants to assemble a vast archive of information on Aztec culture.

Sahagún drew up inquiries on a wide range of topics, chiefly concerned with native rituals and beliefs and with the region's history. He then had his native assistants go to surviving nobles and record their responses, setting them down directly in Nahuatl, using the Roman alphabet. In responding to Sahagún's queries, the Aztec nobles were able to give a remarkably detailed account of their history and culture. Sahagún then edited and assembled these responses, in a project that occupied him intermittently for two decades, from around 1547 to 1568, by which time it had grown to twelve large volumes collectively called the *General History of the Affairs of New Spain* (*Historia General de las Cosas de la Nueva España*). Never published in Sahagún's lifetime, and long ignored by successors who had far less interest in understanding the old customs of idolatrous days, the *General History* ended up in a library in Florence, Italy; it is often called *The Florentine Codex* as a result.

The following selections come from the twelfth and final book of the *General History*, which centered on the Conquest itself. Starting with the evil omens that figure prominently at the outset, this native narrative differs markedly from that of a conquistador like Bernal Díaz del Castillo. While the omens suggest that the Spanish arrival is in some sense fated, the native historians also probe Moctezuma's vacillating character to try and understand why he didn't repel the Spaniards when it might still have been possible to do so. Cultural uncertainty runs in both directions: Moctezuma sends ambassadors bearing symbolic regalia to determine whether Cortés truly is a god, as is rumored, but Cortés assumes the gifts are mere trinkets. Where Bernal Díaz struggles to come to terms with Aztec customs like human sacrifice, the native account tells of the surprises of first encountering such Spanish accoutrements as guns and horses. Finally, the text's moving accounts of plague, warfare, and the fall of Tenochtitlán give a dramatic view of these pivotal events from a native perspective.

from General History of the Affairs of New Spain[1]

[OMENS]

When the Spaniards had not arrived, by ten years, an omen first appeared in the heavens. It was like a tongue of fire, like a flame, as if showering the light of the dawn. It

---

1. Translated by Arthur J. O. Anderson and Charles E. Dibble.

looked as if it were piercing the heavens. It was wide at the base and pointed at the head. To the very midst of the sky, to the very heart of the heavens it extended; to the very midpoint of the skies stood stretched that which was seen off to the east. When it arose and thus came forth, when it appeared at midnight, it looked as if day had dawned. When day broke, later, the sun destroyed it when he arose. For a full year the sign came forth. (It was in the year Twelve House that it began.) And when it appeared, there was shouting; all cried out striking the palm of the hand against the mouth. All were frightened and waited with dread. * * *

A seventh omen: at one time the fisher folk who hunted or snared with nets took captive an ashen hued bird like a crane. Then they went to show it to Moctezuma, who was in the Black Palace. It was past noon, and still daytime. On its head was as it were a mirror, round, circular, and as if pierced in the middle, where were to be seen the heavens, the stars—the Fire Drill constellation. And Moctezuma took it as an omen of great evil when he saw the stars and the Fire Drill. And when he looked at the bird's head a second time, a little beyond the stars he saw people who came as though massed, who came as conquerors, girt in war array. Deer bore them upon their backs. And then he summoned the soothsayers and the sages. He said to them: "Do you not know what I have seen there, which was as if people came massed?" And when they would answer him, what they looked at vanished. They could tell him nothing more.

An eighth omen: often were discovered men of monstrous form, having two heads but only one body. They took them there to the Black Palace, where Moctezuma beheld them; but when he looked at them, they then vanished.

[THE SPANIARDS MARCH TOWARD TENOCHTITLAN]

Fourth Chapter. Here is told what Moctezuma then commanded when he knew that the Spaniards had come back: the second time that they came, they did so under Don Hernando Cortés.

He said to them: "Come, my jaguar warriors; come! It is said that our lord has at last arrived. Receive him. Listen sharply; lend your ears well to what he will say. You will bring back what is well heard. Behold wherewith you will arrive before our lord."

First was the array of Quetzalcoatl: a serpent mask made of turquoise mosaic; a quetzal feather head fan; a plaited neckband of precious green stone beads, in the midst of which lay a golden disc; and a shield with bands of gold crossing each other, or with bands of gold crossing other bands of sea shells, with spread quetzal feathers about the lower edge and with a quetzal feather flag; and a mirror upon the small of the back, with quetzal feathers, and this mirror for the small of the back was like a turquoise shield, of turquoise mosaic—encrusted with turquoise, glued with turquoise; and green stone neck bands, on which were golden shells; and then the turquoise spear thrower, which had on it only turquoise with a sort of serpent's head; it had the head of a serpent; and obsidian sandals.

The second gift which they went offering him was the array of Tezcatlipoca[2]—the headpiece of feathers, with stars of gold; and his golden shell earplugs; and a necklace of sea shells; and the breast ornament decorated and fringed with small shells; and the sleeveless jacket painted with a design, with eyelets on its border, and fringed with feathers; and a mantle with blue knots, which was called *tzitzilli*, grasped

2. Moctezuma wants to see whether Cortés is actually divine and will want the regalia of either Quetzalcoatl or Tezcatlipoca.

by the corners in order to tie it across the back; also, over it, a mosaic mirror lying on the small of the back; and, as another thing, golden shells bound on the calves of the legs; and one more thing, white sandals. * * *

Thereupon were baskets filled; wooden frames for carrying burdens on the back were loaded. And the five messengers named, Moctezuma then commanded; he said to them: "Go! Linger nowhere! Pray to our lord the god; say to him: 'Your servant Moctezuma has sent us; behold what he offers you, for the god has come to reach his wretched home in Mexico.'"

And when they had gone to reach the coast, they ferried them across, they took them by boat across to Xicalanco. * * *

When they had proceeded to go up into the boat, each in his turn disposed himself to kiss the earth before the Captain. Having done so, they said to him:

"May the god deign to hear: for his vassal, Moctezuma, who guards over Mexico for him, prays to him. For so he says: 'The god has suffered, he is weary from travel.'"

Upon this, they adorned the Captain himself; they put on him the turquoise mosaic serpent mask; with it went the quetzal feather head fan; and with it went—in it they had set and with it went hanging—the green stone ear plugs in the form of serpents. And they clad him in the sleeveless jacket; they put the sleeveless jacket upon him. And they put the necklace upon him: the plaited green stone neck band in the midst of which lay the golden disc. With this they bound, on the small of his back, the mirror for the small of the back. Also with it they laid upon his back the cape named *tzitzilli*. And about the calf of his leg they placed the green stone band with the golden shells. And they gave him, and placed upon his arm, the shield with lines of gold and shells crossing, on whose lower rim went spread quetzal feathers and a quetzal feather flag. And before him they set the obsidian sandals.

And the other three sets of adornment, the array of the gods, they only laid in rows and placed in order before him.

And when this had been done, the Captain said to them: "Are these all your gifts, all your greetings?"

They answered: "This is all we brought, O our lord."

* * *

Then they speedily departed from there and soon came to reach Mexico. It was deep night when they went reaching the city; they came in here quite by night.

And when this was happening, Moctezuma could enjoy no sleep, no good. Never could one speak to him. What he did was only as if it were in vain. He often sighed; he was spent, downcast. He felt delight in no savory morsel, joy, or pleasure.

For he said: "What will now become of us? Who, now, is in command? Alas, until now, I. In great torment is my heart, as if run through with chili water, so that it burns and stings. Where, in truth, may we turn, O our lord?"

Then the messengers commanded those watched; they said to those at the head of the guard: "Even if he is sleeping, tell him: 'Lo, they whom you sent over the water have come!'"

And when they went to tell him, then he replied: "I shall not hear it here; I shall hear it in the Coacalli.[3] There let them go." And he commanded and said: "Let two captives be covered with chalk."

---

3. "Serpent House," a temple of Quetzalcoatl.

And then the messengers went to the Coacalli, and also the noble Moctezuma himself.

There before them were slain the captives; they slashed open their breasts; they sprinkled the messengers with their blood. For this reason did they so do: that they had traveled into very perilous places; that they had gone to see—had looked into the faces and at the heads of, and had even spoken to—the gods.

And after this, they then informed Moctezuma; they told him how they had gone in astonishment; and they showed him what their food was like.

And when he had heard how the messengers reported, he was exceeding fearful and terror-struck. And much did he marvel at their food.

Yet more was he frightened when he heard how the shot discharged, at the Spaniards' command, from the gun; how it resounded like thunder when it went off. Indeed, it overpowered one; it deafened our ears. And when it discharged something like a round pellet came forth from within. Fire went scattered forth; sparks showered forth. And its smoke smelled very foul; it had a fetid odor which truly, wounded the head. And when the pellet struck a mountain, it was as if it fell apart and crumbled. And when it struck a tree, it splintered, seeming to vanish as if someone blew it away.

All iron was their war array. They clothed themselves in iron. They covered their heads with iron. Iron were their swords. Iron were their crossbows. Iron were their shields. Iron were their lances.

And their deer, which bore them upon their backs, were as high as roof-tops.

And they covered all parts of their bodies. Alone to be seen were their faces—very white. They had eyes like chalk; they had yellow hair, although the hair of some was black. Long were their beards, and also yellow; they were yellow-bearded. The hair of the Negroes was kinky and curly.

And their food was like lords' food—very large, and white; not heavy like tortillas, but like the stalks of maize plants—as if of ground maize stalks; it tasted a little sweet, a little honeyed—it tasted honeyed, it tasted sweet.

And their dogs were very large. They had ears doubled over; great, hanging jowls; blazing eyes—flaming yellow, fiery yellow eyes; thin flanks, with ribs showing; and gaunt stomachs. They were very tall and fierce. They went about panting, with tongues hanging. They were spotted like ocelots; they had spots.

And when Moctezuma heard this, he was filled with a great dread, as if he were swooning. His soul was sickened, his heart was anguished.

Then Moctezuma sent emissaries. He dispatched his most gifted men—soothsayers and magicians. And he sent the constables, hardy warriors, chieftains, to provide the Spaniards all they might need of food: turkeys, eggs, white tortillas, and all they might ask for as well as whatsoever might satisfy their hearts' desire. They were to watch them well. He sent captives, so that they might be prepared if perchance the Spaniards would drink their blood. And just so did the messengers do.

And when the Spaniards beheld this, their stomachs turned. They spat; they blinked; they shut their eyes and shook their heads. For the food, which they had sprinkled and spattered with blood, sickened and revolted them. For it reeked of blood.

And thus had Moctezuma provided, for he thought them gods; he took them for gods; he paid them reverence as gods. For they were called and named "gods come from the heavens." And the black ones were said to be black gods.

Later they ate white tortillas, grains of maize, eggs, turkeys, and all manner of fruit—sapotas, red sapotas, yellow sapotas, black sapotas, sweet potatoes, manihot, white and yellow sweet potatoes, colored sweet potatoes, *jícamas,* plums, *jobos,* guavas, *guajilotes,* avocadoes, carob fruit, *tejocotes,* cherries, tuna cactus fruit, mulberries, white, yellow, and whitish-red cactus fruit, *pitahayas,* water *pitahayas.* And the food for the deer was *pipillo* and *tlachicaztli.*

And it is told why Moctezuma sent magicians and soothsayers—that they might see what kind of men they were, and that perchance they might bewitch and cast a spell over them. Perhaps they might blow them away, or enchant them. Perhaps they might cast something at them, or they might, with some words of the Evil One, utter an incantation over them, so that they might sicken and die, or else because of it turn back.

But these, when they performed their charge and commission upon the Spaniards, were at once powerless. They could do nothing.

Then they quickly returned and came to tell Moctezuma what they were like and how strong they were: "We cannot contend against them; we are as nothing."

Then Moctezuma commanded sternly, charged, enjoined, and ordered on pain of death, that the stewards and all the noblemen and constables should see to it that the Spaniards be cared for in all that they might need.

And when the Spaniards had crossed over to the land, when finally they came, when already they moved, proceeded, and marched ahead, they were well cared for; they were honored. They passed from hand to hand as they took their way. Much was done for them.

* * *

And Moctezuma thereupon sent and charged the noblemen, whom Tziuacpopocatzin led, and many others besides of his henchmen, to go to meet Cortés between Iztactepetl and Popocatepetl,[4] there in Quauhtechcac. They laid before them golden streamers, quetzal feather streamers, and golden necklaces.

And when they had given them the gift, they appeared to smile, to rejoice exceedingly, and to take great pleasure. Like monkeys they seized upon the gold. It was as if then they were satisfied, sated, and gladdened. For in truth they thirsted mightily for gold; they stuffed themselves with it, and starved and lusted for it like pigs.

And they went about moving the golden streamer back and forth, and showed it to one another, all the while babbling; what they said was gibberish.

* * *

And when the Spaniards had been satisfied, then they moved on and settled themselves at Itztapalapan. Thereupon they called for and sought the rulers known as the Four Lords—those of Itztapalapan, Mexicatzinco, Colhuacan, and Uitzilopochco. In the same manner they spoke to and addressed them (as it has been told). And just so they peacefully and quietly submitted to the Spaniards.

And Moctezuma commanded that none make war upon them nor contend against and meet them in battle. He ordered only that they not neglect the Spaniards' needs; that great care be taken of them.

And upon this, here in Mexico, all lay quiet; the people did not go out or venture forth. Mothers did not let children go out. The roads were empty, and clear; the roads were clean, as in early morning. None crossed others' paths—they did not dare; they retired to their houses only to know that there was woe. The common folk said: "Pay no heed. Let the hour be accursed. What will you do? For now we shall die; we shall perish. Now we await our death."

---

4. Two tall volcanos marking the southeastern entrance to the Valley of Mexico.

[Moctezuma Meets Cortés]

And after this, when the Spaniards reached Xoloco, when affairs had thus far developed, and had reached this point, thereupon Moctezuma arrayed and adorned himself in order to meet them. And with him were a number of great lords and princes, his chief men and nobles. Upon this, they went to meet them. In shining gourds they set out fine flowers—sun flowers and magnolias, and, lying in the midst of them, popcorn flowers, yellow magnolias, and cacao blossoms; and there were wreaths for the head and garlands. And they bore golden neck bands, neck bands with pendants, and plaited neck bands.

And when, there at Uitzillan, Moctezuma met them, he then offered gifts to the war leaders, to the leaders of the warriors; he gave them flowers; he bejeweled them with neck bands; he hung garlands about them; he placed chains of flowers on them and wreaths upon their heads. Thereupon he spread out before Cortés the golden neck bands—all the greeting gifts with which the welcome closed. Some he hung with neck bands.

Then Cortés said to Moctezuma: "Is this not, is this not you? Are you Moctezuma?"

Moctezuma replied: "It is so; I am he."

At this he arose to meet him face to face, did a great reverence to him, drew close to him, and stood firm.

Thus did he pray and speak to Cortés: "O our lord, you have suffered fatigue; you have spent yourself. You have arrived on earth; you have come to your noble city of Mexico. You have come to occupy your noble mat and seat, which for a little time I have guarded and watched for you. For your former governors have gone—the rulers Itzcoatl, Moctezuma the Elder, Axayacatl, Tizoc, Auitzotl—who, not very long ago, came to guard your mat and seat for you and to govern the city of Mexico. Under their protection the common folk came here. Could they, perchance, now find their descendants, those left behind? If only one of them could see, could marvel at what has come about, what I see, who am the only descendant of our lords. For I am not dreaming, I am not sleepwalking, nor see this as in a trance. I do not dream that I see you and look into your face. Lo, I have been troubled for a long time. I have gazed into the unknown whence you have come—the place of mystery. For the rulers of old have gone, saying that you would come to instruct your city, that you would descend to your mat and seat; that you would return. And now it is fulfilled: you have returned; you have suffered fatigue; you have spent yourself. Arrive now in your land. Rest, lord; visit your palace that you may rest your body. Let our lords arrive in the land."

And when Moctezuma had ended his address, which he had directed to the Marquis, Marina explained and interpreted for him. And when the Marquis had heard Moctezuma's words, then he spoke to Marina. He addressed them in a barbarous tongue; he said in his strange language:

"May Moctezuma quiet his heart and not be frightened. We love him much. Now our hearts are satisfied, because we have known and heard him. For a long time we have wished to see him and to look upon his face. And now that we have seen him and have come to his home in Mexico, at leisure he may hear our words."

Thereupon they took him by the hand and went leading him by it. They clapped him on the back in order to make known to him their love.

And the Spaniards beheld and examined him. They walked about on foot, and mounted or dismounted in order to look at him.

And the nobles, as many as accompanied him, were, first, Cacamatzin, ruler of Texcoco; second, Tetlepanquetzatzin, ruler of Tlacopan; third Itzquauhtzin, a general, ruler of Tlatilolco; and fourth, Topantemoctzin, of Tlatilolco, who was Moctezuma's store keeper. These accompanied him. And still other noblemen of Tenochtitlan were Atlixcatzin, a commanding general; Tepeuatzin, a general; Totomotzin, the army commander; Ecatenpatiltzin, and Quappiatzin. When Moctezuma was taken, they only hid themselves and took refuge. They abandoned him in desperation.

[THE MASSACRE AT THE TEMPLE][5]

And when the Feast of Toxcatl had arrived, toward sundown they began to give man's form to the body of the amaranth seed dough image of Huitzilopochtli. They formed it, and gave it the look and appearance of a man. And of this one they fashioned the body only of a dough of amaranth seed and of fish amaranth seed. They formed him on a framework of twigs—the framework of Huitzilopochtli; one laid in angles.

And when he had already taken shape, then they pasted his head with feather down and made his diagonally-striped face painting, and gave him his serpent ear plug of glued turquoise mosaic. And from the serpent ear plugs hung the circlet of thorns, made of gold, with toes—cut in the form of toes. And his nose rod was arrow-shaped; of beaten gold was it wrought and set with stones. It was shaped of metal plate painted as if with stones. Likewise from it hung what was called the thorn circlet, painted with diagonal stripes. Thus was it diagonally striped: on it were alternating blue and yellow bands. And upon his head stood his humming bird disguise. Then there was, besides, what was named *anecuyotl,* his headdress of featherwork, round, a little narrow and pointed at its base. After that they placed upon the back of his head the ball of yellow parrot feathers, from which hung his child's lock of hair. And he had his cape of stinging nettles, colored black, in five places ornamented with feathers—with eagle down. It was wrapped about him. And below, he was wrapped in his cape with severed heads and bones; and above, he was wrapped, also, in his jerkin painted with the limbs and members of men—all painted there with severed heads, ears, hearts, entrails, livers, lungs, and prints of the hand and the foot. And he was given a breech clout. Only the breech clout was very finely wrought. And its design was also the limbs and members of men; it was so woven. But his large breech clout was only of paper; it was of white paper, one fathom wide and twenty long, with a design painted on it in blue. And as for the blood banner with the flint knife at the point: his blood banner was only of paper, painted red, as if striped with blood. And the flint knife at the point was likewise only of paperwork, and also similarly painted—colored as if with blood. And his shield, which he carried, was of reedwork; it was a shield of coarse reeds decorated in four places with feathers—with eagle down—with tufts of feathers. It was called *teueuelli.* And the shield banner was painted like the blood banner. And his four arrows he held together with his shield. And his left arm band was hanging from his arm; it was composed of strips of coyote fur, and from it hung paper cut in strips.

And when dawn broke, when it was now the feast day, early in the morning, then those who had made vows before him unwrapped him. Before him they stood in one

---

5. Here follows the native account of the festival in honor of the war god Huitzilopochtli that caused Pedro de Alvarado to panic and order a massacre; compare Bernal Díaz del Castillo's account on page 840.

row and offered him incense; before him they laid all manner of gifts—feast foods, rolls of amaranth seed dough. And this was when they had not yet taken him up and elevated him to Itepeyoc. And all the men, the young, seasoned warriors, were as if determined and eager to proceed with and observe the feast, and thus show, exhibit proudly, and demonstrate it to the Spaniards. * * *

And after this, when already the feast was taking place, all were dancing and singing, and there was song with dance. The song roared.

When now it was time, and the moment was opportune for the Spaniards to slay them, then they issued forth girt for battle; they came to block everywhere the ways leading out and in, called Quauhquiauac, Tecpantzinco, Acatl Yiacapan, and Tezcacoac. And when they had closed them off and also various other places, the people were contained, so that nowhere could they get out.

And this having been done, they then entered the temple courtyard to slay them. They whose task it was to kill them went only afoot, each with his leather shield, some with their iron-studded shields, and each with iron sword. Then they surrounded those who danced whereupon they went among the drums. Then they struck the arms of the one who beat the drums; they severed both his hands, and afterwards struck his neck, so that his neck and head flew off, falling far away. Then they pierced them all with iron lances, and they struck each with the iron swords. Of some they slashed open the back, and then their entrails gushed out. Of some, they split the head; they hacked their heads to pieces; their heads were completely cut up. And of some they hit the shoulder; they split open and cut their bodies to pieces. Some they struck in the shank; some on the thigh. Of some, they struck the belly, and then their entrails streamed forth. And when one in vain would run, he would only drag his entrails like something raw, as he tried to flee. Nowhere could he go. And one who tried to go out, there they struck and pierced him.

But some climbed the wall, and so succeeded in taking flight. Some entered the various tribal temples, and there escaped. And some eluded the Spaniards among the dead; they went in among those who had died, only feigning death, and were able to escape. But one who stirred, when they saw him, they pierced.

And the blood of the chieftains ran like water; it spread out slippery, and a foul odor rose from the blood. And the entrails lay as if dragged out. And the Spaniards walked everywhere, searching in the tribal temples; they went making thrusts everywhere in case someone were hidden there. Everywhere they went, ransacking every tribal temple as they hunted.

And when all this became known, there then was a shout: "O chieftains! O Mexicans! Hasten here! Let all prepare the devices, shields, and arrows! Come! Hasten here! Already the chieftains have died; they have been put to death, destroyed, shattered, O Mexicans, O chieftains!" Thereupon arose an outcry, a shouting, a shrieking with hands striking the lips. Quickly the chieftains marshaled themselves; as if working with one will they brought the arrows and shields. Then the fray joined. They shot at them with barbed arrows, spears, and tridents, and they loosed darts with broad, obsidian points at them. It was as if a mass of deep yellow reeds spread over the Spaniards.

And the Spaniards fortified themselves. And the Spaniards also shot at the Mexicans with iron arrows, and fired the guns at them. And then they put Moctezuma in irons.

And all the chieftains who had died in the temple courtyard were thereupon taken out and brought forth, and identified. And the mothers and fathers raised a cry of weeping; all wept over them; there was wailing. First they took them to their homes. Later they carried them to the temple courtyard, brought them together there, and burned them together there at the place called Quauhxicalco.

[PLAGUE AND WARFARE]

And even before the Spaniards had risen against us, a pestilence first came to be prevalent: the smallpox. It was the month of Tepeilhuitl when it began, and it spread over the people as great destruction. Some it quite covered with sores on all parts— their faces, their heads, their breasts, etc. There was great havoc. Very many died of it. They could not walk; they only lay in their resting places and beds. They could not move; they could not stir; they could not change position, nor lie on one side, nor face down, nor on their backs. And if they stirred, much did they cry out. Great was its destruction. Covered, mantled with sores, very many people died of them. And very many starved; there was death from hunger, for none could take care of the sick; nothing could be done for them.

And on some the sores were widely separated; they did not suffer greatly, neither did many of them die. Yet many people were marred by them on their faces; one's face or nose was pitted. Some lost their eyes; they were blinded.

At this time, this pestilence prevailed sixty days, sixty day signs. When it left, when it abated, when there was recovery and the return of life, the plague had already moved toward Chalco, whereby many were disabled—not, however, completely crippled. When it came to be prevalent, it was the month of Teotl-eco. And when it went, weakened, it was Panquetzaliztli. Then the Mexicans, the chieftains, could revive.

And after this, then the Spaniards came; they marched from Texcoco. By way of Quauhtitlan they set out, and quartered themselves at Tlacopan. There then the task was divided; their routes were there separated. Pedro de Alvarado's charge became the road leading into Tlatilolco. And the Marquis went to and established quarters at Coyoacan, and it became the Marquis' charge—as well as the road from Acachinanco which led into Tenochtitlan; for the Marquis knew that those of Tenochtitlan were great warriors, great chieftains.

And at Nextlatilco, or Iliacac, there in truth first came the fighting, when they quickly came and reached Nonoalco. The chieftains came pursuing them. None of the Mexicans died. Then the Spaniards turned back. The chieftains, who fought valiantly by boat, the warboatmen, shot darts at them. Their darts rained upon the Spaniards. They then entered Nonoalco. And the Marquis thereupon threw himself upon those of Tenochtitlan; he proceeded along the Acachinanco road. Many times, in truth, there was battle, and the Mexicans contended against him.

* * *

And some days thereafter the Spaniards once again resolved to war upon us. Then they came, and chose the Quauecatitlan road which led direct to the salt market. But there on the Quauecatitlan road, they could not spread out. So all those of Tlaxcalla, Acolhuacan, and Chalco thereupon filled in the canals. And on the road where they could not spread out, they cast adobes and roof beams; door lintels, pillars, and round logs were set in; they threw bundles of reeds into the water. And when it was filled in, then the Spaniards, disposed in battle order, very slowly proceeded: a cotton banner led them; they went blowing trumpets and beating drums. And behind them went in position all the Tlaxcallans, and indeed all those of other allied cities. Those of Tlaxcalla became very brave; they shook their heads, beat their chests, and sang.

The Mexicans also sang. There was chanting on both sides. They intoned whatever they remembered. Thus they were able to animate themselves.

And as they reached Tlalhuacan, all the chieftains were crouched; they stretched themselves out very flat, and were well hidden. They hid their heads. They waited until the time that the command to charge would be given, the time that they would hear the battle cry, and the order to advance. And when the cry was given, it was: "O Mexicans, onward against them!" Then the Tlapaneca Ecatzin, an Otomí warrior, came to engage them and to hurl himself at them. He said: "O chieftains of Tlatilolco, onward! Who are these barbarians? Move forward!" Then he proceeded to throw himself against a Spaniard and struck him to the ground. This Ecatzin came first to cast him to the ground. He did it to him first. And when he had gone to overthrow him, then they went dragging the Spaniard off.

And when this had come to pass, then the chieftains who had been crouched, together fell upon them; they fell upon them from their ambush in the spaces among houses. And the Spaniards, when they saw this, were as if drunk. Thereupon were captives made. Many men of Tlaxcalla, Acolhuacan, Chalco, Xochimilco, etc., were taken. Truly, myriads of captives were made and men slain. Truly, they forced the Spaniards into the water, and indeed all the allied people.

And the road became very slippery. It could no longer be traveled; each one could only slip and slide. And the captives were dragged along. Here in this place the Spaniards' standard was taken. Here it was seized. Those of Tlatilolco took it. It was captured there where now is the church named San Martín. But the Spaniards showed no concern over it; they were not troubled over it. And others escaped the Mexicans' hands. They went leaving them exhausted at Colhuacatonco, at the edge of the canal. There they retired to establish themselves.

And after this they took the captives there to Yacacolco. They were urged forward; they went surrounding their captives. One went weeping; one singing; one crying war cries while striking the mouth with the palm of the hand. And when they had been brought to Yacacolco, thereupon they were placed in rows, in files. One by one they proceeded to the small pyramid, where they were slain. First went the Spaniards. They took the lead. But all those of the allied cities came only last, following. And when they had been slain, then they strung the severed heads of the Spaniards, each one, on the horizontal staves of the skull rack. They also strung up the heads of the horses, arranging them below, while the heads of the Spaniards were above. It appeared as if they were strung facing the rising sun. But as for all the various allied people, they did not string up the heads of the people of distant provinces. And fifty-three Spaniards were captured, and four horses.

Nevertheless, in all places watch was kept. There was fighting. Not because of this success did posting of watchmen cease. Everywhere those of Xochimilco went hemming us in, in their boats. On both sides were captives taken; on both sides there was killing.

And all the common folk suffered torments of famine. Many died of hunger. No more did they drink pure, clean water—only brackish water did they drink. Of it many people died, and many people therefore suffered from a bloody flux, of which they died. And all was eaten—lizards and swallows; and maize straw, and salt-grass. And they ate *colorin* wood, and they ate the glue orchid, and the frilled flower; and tanned hides, and buckskin, which they roasted, baked, toasted, or burned, so that they could eat them; and they gnawed weeds and mud bricks. Never had there been such suffering. It was terrifying how they were besieged; truly, in great numbers they starved. And quite calmly the enemy hemmed us in and contained us.

[SURRENDER BY CUAUHTEMOC]

Here is told how the men of Tlatilolco and Tenochtitlan and their leaders yielded to the Spaniards, and what befell when they were among them.

And when they had betaken themselves to bring him and disembark him, thereupon all the Spaniards came to see. They drew him along; the Spaniards took him by the hand. After that they took him up to the roof-top, where they went to stand him before the Captain, the war leader. And when they had proceeded to stand him before Cortés, they looked at Cuauhtemoc, made much of him, and stroked his hair. Then they seated him with Cortés and fired the guns. They hit no one with them, but only made them go off above, so that they passed over the heads of the common folk. Then some Mexicans took and got into a boat and guided it there to the house of Coyoueuetzin. And when they arrived, then they climbed up to the roof-top, whereupon once again they slew men and many died there. But the Mexicans only fled. With this the war reached its end.

Then there was shouting; they said: "Enough! Let it end! Eat greens!" When they heard this, the common folk thereupon issued forth. On this, they went, even into the lagoon.

And as they departed, leaving by the great road, once more they there slew some, and so the Spaniards were angry that still some again had taken up their obsidian-bladed swords and their shields. Those who dwelt in house clusters went straightway to Amaxac; they went direct to where the ways divide. There the common folk separated. So many went toward Tepeyacac, so many toward Xoxouiltitlan, so many toward Nonoalco. But toward Xolloco and toward Mazatzintamalco no one went.

And all who lived in boats and in houses on poles, and those at Tolmayecan, went into the water. On some, the water reached to the stomach; some, to the chest; and on some it reached to the neck. And some were all submerged, there in the deeps. Little children were carried on the backs of their elders; some cried and wept, but some were laughing, happy at being carried along the crowded road. And those who owned boats, all the boatmen, left by night, and even continued to leave all day. It was as if they pushed and crowded one another as they set out.

And everywhere the Spaniards were seizing and robbing the people. They sought gold; as nothing did they value the green stone, quetzal feathers, and turquoise. The gold was everywhere in the bosoms or in the skirts of the wretched women. And as for the men, it was everywhere in their breech clouts and in their mouths.

And the Spaniards seized and set apart the pretty women—those of light bodies, the fair-skinned ones. And some women, when they were to be assaulted, covered their faces with mud and put on old, mended skirts and rags for their shifts. They put all rags on themselves.

And also some men were singled out—those who were strong, grown to manhood, and next the young boys, of whom they would make messengers, who would be their servants, and who were known as their runners. And on some they burned brand marks on their cheeks; on some they put paint on their cheeks; on some they put paint on their lips.

And when the shield was laid down, when we gave way, it was the year count Three House and the day count was One Serpent.

The Aztec-Spanish Dialogues of 1524

Following the military conquest of Mexico, it soon became clear that the spiritual conquest of the population was going to involve a much longer struggle. In 1524 the Pope authorized the Spanish emperor Charles V to send a select band of "twelve Apostles" to Mexico to oversee this process. Not long after their arrival, the twelve staged a public disputation with a group of Aztec priests and nobles; this extraordinary text is the result of those debates. Over several days, the Spanish friars and the Aztec spokesmen took turns in making the case for and against conversion. Hoping for a decisive and exemplary success, the friars arranged for extensive notes to be taken in Nahuatl, to provide a written record that could be used to persuade groups elsewhere. Forty years later, the tireless Bernardino de Sahagún organized the transcript and enlisted the aid of several of his native seminarians and four native elders "to transcribe it into suitably polished Nahuatl," as he wrote in a preface to the compilation. This revised manuscript was never published, perhaps because it proved to give such eloquent expression to the Aztec priests' reasons for remaining loyal to their gods even after their spectacular defeat by the Europeans. Preserved in secret archives at the Vatican and long forgotten, it was rediscovered and published only in 1924.

According to a Spanish summary that Sahagún wrote at the beginning of the manuscript, the dialogues did conclude with the conversion of the native speakers, but the second half of the manuscript has been lost. In the fourteen surviving chapters, the friars argue that the native gods are really devils who have rightly been overthrown by God, while the native elders defend their loyalty to the gods who have sustained their culture over many centuries. Jorge Klor de Alva's sensitive translation divides the elevated rhetoric of the speeches into units of sense, approximating the effect that oral delivery might have had, as the Aztec nobles attempt to negotiate a space for traditional beliefs and values in a radically changed world.

from The Aztec-Spanish Dialogues of 1524[1]

[THE FRIARS' OPENING SPEECH]

      Listen well, our beloved,
      you who caused yourselves to bear witness here,
20   you who came out together here,
      you Mexicas, you Tenochcas, you lords, you speakers,
      please approach hither and consider well.
      If only it be able to settle where your heart makes a home,
      (when we set it forth, when we say it)
25   the word of the message.

      Let us not disconcert you as to something,
      take care lest you see us as something superior,
      indeed, we are only your peers, we are only common people,
      we are men such as you are, we are surely not gods.
30   We are also inhabitants on the earth, we also drink, we also eat,
      we also die of cold, we are also overwhelmed by heat,
      we are also mortal, we are also destructible.
      Indeed, we are only messengers, we were only sent here,

1. Translated by Jorge Klor de Alva.

to the place of your homeland, to your water, to your mountain.
35   We came bearing it, his honorable breath, his honorable word,
of this one who everywhere in the world, on the earth,
is the great speaker of divine things,
his name is Holy Father Pope.

* * *

And it is not something else for which we came,
for which we were sent hither;
125   only on account of spiritual compassion for you,
for your salvation.
Then, nothing earthly does he desire,
the great speaker of divine things,
hence, neither jade, nor gold,
130   nor quetzal plumes, nor anything precious.
Now, only your completely total salvation he desires.

* * *

But, perhaps, you ask, now, perhaps, you say,
this one, the divine word you mention with reverence,
where did it come from? Where did it appear?
Who gave it to you? Who showed it to you?
Where did the great speaker of divine things acquire it?
275   Be so kind as to raise your ears, so you will be able to hear,
from where came the divine word we come to give you,
we come to make you comprehend.
Understand and pursue earnestly the truth of it,
that your heart may be properly filled.
280   Indeed, already it has been a long time,
since He, the True God, Speaker,[2]
Possessor of the Near, Possessor of the Surrounding,[3]
He by Whom All Live, showed it to His most beloved,
to His servants, these whose heart was very good, upright,
285   His great knowledge, His choices,
their name is patriarchs, prophets.
And, indeed, here on the earth a man He came to make Himself,
He was able, as a man, to appeal to them,
the apostles, the evangelists.
290   And they are those to whom He gave
His venerable breath, His venerable word, the divine word.
And He commanded them so they will paint it,
so that it will be preserved on the earth,
so that the men on the earth will be instructed by the divine word.
295   And the Holy Father guards all the divine words they left,
these formerly mentioned, His beloved of Our Lord, God.
All is in the divine book, it lies blackened, it lies colored.
All is there, everything is conserved,

---

2. *Tlatoani* in Nahuatl, the traditional term for "ruler."   3. Epithets of the god Tezcatlipoca, now transferred to the Christian God.

300
these which now are the very marvelous divine words.
And likewise, he made us bear it hither now, he, the Holy Father,
so that we will give it to you, we will notify you of it.
Indeed, this one, the divine word,
does not resemble the speech of the common people on the earth.
Indeed, very marvelous, true is His venerable breath, His venerable word,

305
the Creator of Men's and this one of the Savior of Men,
the One Sole God, the Speaker,
Possessor of the Near, Possessor of the Surrounding,
On account of that it is properly named divine word;
very truly the one followed.

310
Absolutely no one will be able to contradict it,
even though he is a great knower of things on earth.

* * *

There it is told, indeed, how on the earth,

580
there, is His precious dominion as a man, Our Lord Jesus Christ.
He, the Only True God, Speaker,
Creator of Men, and Savior of Men, Jesus Christ,
here on the earth He founded His precious dominion,
His honorable mat, His honorable seat, He set down,

585
and it is this whose name is dominion of heaven,
moreover, its name is Holy Catholic Church.[4]
Because of that, it is called the dominion of heaven,
indeed, absolutely no one will enter heaven
if he will not belong to it, the Holy Church.

* * *

640
There where He resides, He by Whom All Live, Jesus Christ,
it is very necessary for you that you detest them,
you despise them, you hate them, and you spit on them,
these whom you have always regarded as gods.
These gods which you esteemed, indeed, are truly not gods,

645
indeed, they only make a mockery of anyone.
Furthermore, moreover, it is very necessary that you avoid them,
that you abandon them, all these various transgressions,
these injuries to the heart of the Possessor of the Near,
    Possessor of the Surrounding,
He by Whom All Live, which you have continually caused.

[THE AZTECS' REPLY]

After it ended, it terminated,
this the venerable speech of the twelve Fathers,
at once one of those lords, speakers,

695
stood up, he greeted the divine guardians,
and a little bit, one lip, two lips,
by this he returned their venerable breath, their venerable words.

---

4. *Sancta yglesia catholica* in the Nahuatl text.

He said: Our lords, you have endured much,
indeed, when you came to approach us on this land,
700   indeed, when you came to govern it
from your honorable water, your honorable mountain.
From where? What kind of place is it, the place of our lords,
there, from where you came?
Indeed, from among the clouds, from among the mist, you have come out.
705   Indeed, before you, about you we carefully observe, admire,
the possessors of the water, the possessors of the mountain.
Here we acquire it, we seize it, the new word,
as if it were something celestial, that which you say.
And here it is shown to us, it is opened for us,
710   His precious coffer, His precious hamper,
that of the Man, Our Lord, Possessor of Heaven, Possessor of Earth.
And, thus, he sends you hither, the man, the great speaker,
from where his breath is made known,
from the place of our lords, the Holy Father, and the Emperor.
715   Indeed, here before us you place the turquoise, the bracelet,
here we marvel at it as if it were a round jade
able to shine without its shade, without its defect,
and as if it were a large precious quetzal plume, extremely green.
Indeed, they left, He destroyed them,
720   He burnt them, the Man, Our Lord,
the speakers, these who came to be,
these who came to live on the earth,
and who came to guard it, who came to govern it,
your honorable mat, your honorable seat,
725   for a brief day, for a moment,
here in Mexico, in Tenochtitlan,
and here in Aculhuacan, Tetzcoco, here in Tlacopan:
Motecuhzomatzin,[5]
Ahuitzotzin, Axayacatzin, Tizocicatzin, and Itzcoatzin,
the elder Motecuhzoma and Nezahualcoyotzin,
730   Nezahualpilli, Totoquihuaztli, and the elder Tezozomoctli.
If it had occurred during their time,
indeed, they would have returned
your precious breath, your precious word.
Likewise, they would have entreated you
735   by reason of your precious love for people,
which we admire here.
But, we, what now, immediately, will we say?
Supposing that we, we are those who shelter the people,
we are mothers to the people, we are fathers to the people,
740   perchance, then, are we, here before you, to destroy it, the ancient law;
the one which was greatly esteemed by our grandparents, our women;

---

5. A list follows of ten earlier kings.

the one which they would go speaking of favorably,
the one which they would go admiring, the lords, the speakers?

And these, oh our lords,
745   indeed, they are there, they still guide us,
these who carry us, these who govern us,
in relation to these being served,
indeed, these who are our gods, these who have their merit,
that of the tail, of the wing,
750   the ones who offer things, the ones who offer incense,
and those named the feathered serpents.
These are knowers of the word,
and their charge with which they trouble themselves,
by night, by day, is the act of burning *copal,*
755   the act of offering incense, thorns, *acxoyatl,*[6] the act of blood letting.
These see, these trouble themselves,
with the journey, the orderly course of the heavens,
according to how the night is divided.
And these continually look at it, these continually relate it,
760   these continually cause the book to cackle.
The black, the color, is in the paintings they continually carry.
Indeed, they are the ones who continually carry us,
they guide us, they cause the path to speak to us.
They are the ones who put it in order,
765   such as how a year falls,
such as how the count of the destinies-feasts follows its path,
and each one of the complete counts.
They trouble themselves with it,
they have their charge, their commission,
770   their duty which is the divine word,
And we are those, indeed, who but have as our sole task
(what is called) divine water, fire. And only we speak on it,
we trouble ourselves with the tribute, of the tail, the wing;
so that it seizes its headdress of heron feathers, its jacket of cords,
775   and its digging stick, its tumpline;[7]
that which is placed in front of the hearth;
in this way people are made "slaves."
Let us, for now, assemble them,
the ones who offer things, the feathered serpents.
780   Let us give them His precious breath, His precious word,
this one of the Man, Our Lord.
So that they, perhaps, will restore it, will return it,
this which we have seized, this which we have grasped,
from your honorable breasts, your honorable heads,
785   we will elevate it, our lords.

---

6. Needles used for ritual bloodletting.   7. A band running across the forehead and back behind
the shoulders to support a pack.

If only you would calm your precious hearts, your precious flesh;
remain on your honorable mat, your honorable seat.

[THE AZTECS' SECOND SPEECH][8]

And now, what, in what manner, what sort of thing will we say,
915   which we will raise to your honorable ears?

*   *   *

Have we, perhaps, been negligent in doing things?
Oh, where, by chance, are we truly to go?
Indeed, we are common people, we are destructible, we are mortal.
935   Oh, indeed, let us die, oh, indeed, let us perish,
since, indeed, the gods have been defeated!
If only it would settle itself,
your honorable heart, your honorable flesh (Oh, our lords).
Indeed, on account of this, we divide something very little,
940   now, on account of this, we open it very little,
his coffer, his hamper, this one of the man, our lord.

You tell them, indeed, that we do not know Him,
the Possessor of the Near, Possessor of the Surrounding,
the Possessor of Heaven, Possessor of Earth.
945   You tell them, indeed, that our gods are not real gods.
It is a new word, this one you tell them,
and because of it we are distressed,
because of it we are extremely frightened.
Indeed, these our makers,
950   these who came to be, these who came to live on the earth,
did not speak in this way.
Verily, they gave us their law.
They followed them as true, they served them,
they honored them, the gods.
955   They taught us all their forms of serving, their modes of honoring.
Thus, before them we eat earth, thus, we bleed ourselves,
thus, we discharge the debt ourselves, thus, we burn *copal*,
and, thus, we cause something to be killed.
They used to say that, verily, they, the gods, by whose grace one lives,
960   they merited us.
When? Where? While it was still night.
And they used to say, indeed, they give us our supper, our breakfast,
and all that is drinkable, edible,
this our meat, the corn, the bean,
965   the wild amaranth, the lime-leaved sage.
They are those from whom we request the water, the rain,
by which the things of the earth are made.
Furthermore, they are rich themselves, they are happy themselves,

---

8. After hearing renewed Spanish arguments that their gods are really devils, the Aztecs take time to consult and then return to speak further.

they are possessors of goods, they are owners of goods,
970 by which always, forever, it germinates there, it grows green in their house.
Where? What kind of place is it, the place of Tlaloc?[9]
Hunger never occurs there, nothing is diseased, nothing is poor.
And also, they give to the people prowess, courage, the chase, and the
    lip-grass,
the instrument by which something is bound, the loincloth, the mantle,
975 the flowers, the tobacco,
the jade, the quetzal plumes, the gold.

And when, where were these thus summoned,
when implored, when held as gods, when honored?
It is already a very long time.
980 When? At another time it was in Tula.
When? At another time it was in Huapalcalco.
When? At another time it was in Xochitlalpan.
When? At another time it was in Tamoanchan.
At another time it was in Yoallichan.
985 When? At another time it was in Teotihuacan.
Indeed, they, everywhere in the world,
they caused the people to construct with stones their mat, their seat.
They gave to the people the lordship, the dominion, the fame, the glory.

And, perchance, now, are we those who will destroy it, the ancient law?
990 The law of the Chichimecs? The law of the Toltecs?
The law of the Colhuaque? The law of the Tepanecs?
Already our heart is this way:
through him one is made to live,
through him one is given birth,
995 on account of him one is made to grow,
on account of him one is made to mature,
by means of this one, who is summoned,
by means of this one, who is implored.
Hear, our lords, beware of doing something to them,
1000 this your precious tail, your precious wing,
so much the more so that it will be abandoned,
so much the more so that it will be destroyed.
In this way also the old man,
in this way also the old woman had her growth, had her increase in age.
1005 Oh, that the gods be not angry with us.
Oh, that their anger, their wrath, not come.
And let us beware that on account of that
it not rise before us, on us, the tail, the wing.
Let us beware that on account of that we not stir it up,
1010 let us beware that on account of that we not provoke it,
by saying to it: no longer will it summon them,
no longer will it implore them.

9. The heavenly realm of Tlaloc, god of rain.

In the meantime, calmly, peacefully,
consider it, our lords, whatever is necessary.

1015 Indeed, our heart is not able to be full.
And, indeed, absolutely we do not yet agree to it ourselves,
we do not yet make it true for ourselves.
We ourselves will cause you injury to the heart.
Indeed, here they lie, the possessors of water, the possessors of mountains,

1020 the lords, the speakers, these who carry it, these who bear it, the world.
It is enough that we have already left it alone,
we have lost it, we have had it taken away,
we have had it prohibited, the mat, the seat.
Indeed, if we will only remain there,

1025 we will only cause them to be restricted.
Do it to us, whatever it is you will desire.
Indeed, we return it all by this, by this we respond to it,
your precious breath, your precious word, our lords.

[THE FRIARS REPLY]

Indeed, we will tell you everything,
we will cause you to hear it, if you desire it.

1115 And we will be able to cause you to have a full heart,
because we guard it, the divine book, the divine word,
there where it lies visible, it lies painted,
it lies arranged, all that which is His precious word,
this one of the Possessor of the Near, Possessor of the Surrounding.

* * *

You did not guard it, the divine book, the divine word.

1145 It never came to reach you,
His precious breath, His precious word,
this one of the Possessor of Heaven, the Possessor of Earth.
And, then, you are blind, you are deaf,
as if in darkness, in gloom, you live.

1150 On account of this your faults are, furthermore, not very great.
But now, if you do not desire to hear it,
the precious breath, the precious word of God
(this one He gives to you), you will be in much danger.
And God, Who has commenced your destruction,

1155 will conclude it, you will be completely lost.

Our beloved, so that you may hear it rightly, that which you desire,
likewise, so that your heart will be able to be full,
it is necessary that first we will cause you to hear,
we will manifest to you, of what precious sort is Our Lord God,

1160 He by Whom All Live, This One we came to show you.
And, indeed, already it is late, now, already, the time to eat is distant.
Tomorrow at dawn, when the sun comes out,
everybody will come hither,
here one will be assembled, something will be heard.

1165 For now all may depart, please go, eat something.
For now rest, let your heart be settled.

Hernando Ruiz de Alarcón
c. 1587–c. 1645

Born and raised in Mexico, Hernando Ruiz de Alarcón followed his older brother Juan in studying at the fledgling University of Mexico, from which he received a degree in 1606. Chafing at the limited opportunities of life in the colonial capital, Juan went to Spain to make his fortune, becoming one of the leading playwrights of his age. Hernando took a very different route away from home: he became a priest and went to serve parishes in the mountainous countryside of Guerrero, several days' ride south of Mexico City. Twenty years later, he unexpectedly fell into literary activity of his own. His bishop appointed him as an ecclesiastical judge, charged to root out and punish heresy among the natives of his region—chiefly their persistence in pre-Christian religious practices and beliefs. Ruiz de Alarcón decided to write up an account of the "sorceries" widely being practiced by his parishioners, as a guide to fellow pastors. The result was the fullest surviving compendium of seventeenth-century native beliefs and ritual and medical practices, including the powerful incantations that accompanied them. At once fascinated and horrified by what he was hearing, Ruiz de Alarcón faithfully transcribed these incantations in Nahuatl, adding a Spanish translation and commentary.

Ruiz de Alarcón's treatise eventually reached several hundred pages in length, and in 1629 he presented a fair copy to his bishop. Few colonial settlers at the time, however, shared his interest in understanding what the natives were really thinking and saying as they carried on their idolatrous practices, and the treatise remained unpublished until the end of the nineteenth century. Read today, the incantations give a unique window into popular piety and the poetry of daily life, in language and rhythms very different from the elaborate lyrics of the old Aztec nobility.

PRONUNCIATIONS:
    nahualli: na-WALL-ee
    Hernando Ruiz de Alarcón: air-NAN-doh rue-EASE day al-are-CONE

from Treatise on the Superstitions of the Natives of this New Spain[1]

[OPENING DISCUSSION OF SORCERY]

So great is the ignorance or simplemindedness of almost all the Indians—I do not say *all,* since I have not traveled through the entire land, but there must be little variation—that, as is well known, they are all extremely easy to persuade of whatever one would have them believe. Thus, through their ignorance they had and still have so many kinds of gods and so many different forms of worship that in ascertaining what they are based on and what they all are, we find as little to get hold of as if we wished to grasp smoke or wind in the fist.

What is certain is that most or almost all present-day forms of worship or idolatrous actions which we now come across, and on which we can pass judgement, are the same ones to which their ancestors were accustomed. These have their roots and formal basis in their belief that the clouds are angels and gods, capable of being worshipped. Likewise do they judge the winds, which they believe live in all parts of the land—in the hills, mountains, valleys, and ravines. They believe the same of the rivers, lakes, and springs, since they offer wax and incense to all of the above. That to which they pay more veneration and which almost all take for a god is fire, as will be seen in the tract on idolatry.

---

1. Translated by Michael D. Coe and Gordon Whittaker.

One should point out that almost every time they are moved to offer sacrifice to their imagined gods, there springs up from the other Indians some satrap, doctor, sorcerer, or diviner to so order and arrange it; most of these ground themselves in their spells, or else are made foolish by the drink which they call *ololiuhqui*,[2] or by peyote or tobacco, as will be made clear in its proper place.

For greater clarity, I shall begin this tract with what they did to a person from the moment he was born, proceeding to his end and death. So excessive is the veneration and honor which all Indians pay to fire, that from the moment they are born they are entangled in this superstition. They place it in the parturient's room, and continue encouraging it there, without removing an ember, until the dawn watch; they believe that if they remove any ember from the fire before this, some clouds will appear in the eyes of the newborn. The ancient Indians used to remove the newborn from the room at the dawn watch, together with the fire, and give four blows to the head with it. I have not succeeded in finding out if this is done today.

When they gave the four blows to the head—two on one side and two on the other—they gave him the name that he was to have, pertaining to the god under which he was born, just as the Devil seeks that his followers imitate in his service the manner of Christians in that of Our Lord God. They would take this name from some calendars: I have found out that this kind are divided into days by animal names, such as *ocēlotl*, jaguar; *quauhtli*, eagle; *cuetzpalli*, cayman; *coatl*, snake; and inanimate things like *átl, calli*, water, house. From this I have concluded that they were dedicated to the animal that the Devil revealed to them, which was to be what they call *náhualli*, as I shall tell below. In this manner the child remained baptized after their fashion, having that for a name. Others acted differently, in that they performed this imitation of baptism with water, washing the child's head at the dawn watch and giving it its name.

They entrusted all of this business of fire and water to the wise man whose occupation it was; among them are those with the name and profession of doctors, the which are usually liars, full of ceremony and aspiring to persuade one that they are consummate in knowledge, since they give one to understand that they know what happens elsewhere and that they foresee what is to come—which might be, if the Devil, who is able by science and conjecture to foresee many future happenings, reveals it.

Because I have spoken of the *náhualli*, I shall next say what I feel, according to what I infer from what I have seen and experienced.

Trustworthy persons have told me that an Indian they were with began to shout, saying, "Ay, they are killing me, they are chasing me, they are killing me!" On asking him what he was saying, he responded, "The cowhands of such and such a ranch are killing me." Leaving for the countryside, they went to the field of the above-mentioned ranch and found that its cowhands had run down and killed a fox or vixen; when they returned to see the Indian, they found him dead, and, if memory serves me well, from the same blows and wounds which the fox had.

The same, they assured me, had happened to another Indian and a cayman. The Indian, without anyone attacking him, began to complain that they were killing him in the river. On going to the river, they discovered a dead cayman in it, and afterwards the Indian died in the same way.

How this might happen, I shall tell below. But since these two cases do not strike us with much force, the persons who related them not being exceptional in every respect, I shall recount others with witnesses who are faultless.

---

2. A hallucinogenic drink made from morning-glory seeds.

Father Andrés Ximénez of the Dominican Order told me that when two fathers of his faith were in a cell towards nightfall, a bat—much larger than usual—came in through a window. The two monks followed the bat, throwing their hats and other things at it, until it escaped them and departed. The next day, an old Indian woman came to the porter's lodge of the monastery; summoning one of the two monks, she asked why he had mistreated her so, and had he wanted to kill her. The monk in turn asked her if she was crazy, for where and how could that be. She replied by asking if it were true that on the previous night he and the other monk had mistreated and many times struck a bat that had entered a cell by a window. On the monk saying, "Can this be so?", the Indian woman said, "For the bat was I, and I am still very tired." Hearing this in wonder, the monk wished to summon his companion to meet the Indian woman, and, to detain her, he asked her to wait, that he would go inside to get some alms. He went in, and returning with his companion, he discovered neither the Indian woman, nor where she had gone. * * *

I have heard of many cases of the sort described above. Assuming them to be true, although curious and outside of what is known of other nations and peoples accustomed to having a pact with the Devil, we shall examine how this can be. I first call attention to the cunning which Satan employs with this kind of people, so that once they are captives to this sin, correction appears impossible, since they wickedly deny it, even though they might be prosecuted and convinced until they die impenitent. It is the same with the sorcerers whom they call *tēxòxanî, téyollòquāni,* or *tétlàchihuani,* which are almost the same thing, they never confess, even though there be information against them, as the one sort or the other have been before me in different provinces, but I have never been able to make them confess so as to bring it completely to light. * * *

In all cases on which I have information, this kind of *nahualli* wizard differs from the witches of Spain. Firstly, I infer that when a child is born, the Devil, by the expressed or implied pact which the parents make with him, dedicates or subjects him to the animal that the said child has to consider as a *nahual,* which is to say as the owner of his birth and master of his actions, or what the pagans used to call "fate." In virtue of this pact, the child remains subject to all of the dangers and travails which the animal suffers, until death. In return, the Devil brings it about that the animal always obeys the command of the child, or rather the Devil himself carries it out, using the animal as his instrument. In this way the inconceivable transformations and other difficulties are accounted for. This I infer from many cases of this sort, as I have said above, in which one of these Indians, considered to be a *nahualli,* threatens another Indian or Spaniard. The threatened Indian or Spaniard then happens to have a fight in the river with a cayman, or in the countryside with some other animal, the animal coming out wounded or hurt; afterwards they discover the Indian who made the threat with the same wounds that the cayman or animal got out of the dispute, the said Indian being absent at the time and occupied in other activities.

This is what I have been able to ascertain in this kind of matter. I have not found a minister or other person who might provide me a further explanation or a better resolution of these cases, and so I leave it here.

I point out firstly that I take it as doubtless that such a child, for whom the parents made the pact with the Devil, after arriving at the use of reason, reiterates the pact or ratifies it tacitly or expressly, because without this condition it is unbelievable that the Devil would have such power, especially against a baptized person. The other thing that I point out is the denomination and significance of the name *nahualli,* which can be derived from one of three roots. These signify: the first, "to command," the second, "to speak with command," the third, "to hide oneself" or "to muffle oneself up." Although there are advantages to which the first two meanings accommodate themselves, that which suits me better is the third, which is from the verb *nahualtia,* which is "to muffle oneself up"; thus *nahualli* would mean "muffled up" or "disguised" in the form of such an animal, as they commonly believe.

[A SPELL FOR ATTRACTING LOVE]

The superstition of attracting the affection of another's will is of the kind referred to before, and is used by those in love to see if it will be of benefit to them, and so it begins here in its proper place. This superstition is based on words alone, to which they attribute the power of making whomever one fancies yield to one's will. They say, then, the words of the spell:

tezcatepec	On the mountain of mirrors,[3]
nenamicoyā	In the place of encounters,
niçihuanotza	I call to women,
niçihuacuica	I sing to women.
nonnentlamati	I am unhappy there,
nihualnentlamati	I am unhappy here.
ye nocōhuica	Already I am carrying off
in nohueltiuh in xochiquetzal	My elder sister Flower Plume;[4]
ce coatl ica	With 1 Serpent
apantiuitz	She comes bedecked,
ce coatl ica	With 1 Serpent
cuitlalpitihuitz	She comes girded,
tzonilpitiuitz	She comes braided.
ye yalhua	Yesterday,
ye huiptla	The day before,
ica nichoca	I wept over it,
ica ninentlamati	I was unhappy about it.
ca mach nelli teotl	For indeed she is truly a goddess,
ca mach nelli mahuiztic	For indeed she is truly marvellous.
cuix quin moztla	Is it tomorrow?
cuix quin huiptla	Is it the day after?
niman aman	Right now!
nòmatca nehuatl	I myself,
nitelpochtli	I am the Youth,

3. Ruiz de Alarcón's translation of "the mountain of mirrors" probably misses a veiled appeal to the god Tezcatlipoca, "Smoking Mirror."

4. Xochiquetzal, "Flower Plume," goddess of love, was Tezcatlipoca's consort.

niyaotl	I am the Adversary,[5]
nonitonac	I have shone forth,
nonitlathuic	I have dawned.
cuix çan cana onihualla	Have I come forth just anywhere?
cuix çan cana onihualquiz	Have I set forth just anywhere?
ompa onihualla	Over there I have come forth,
ompa onihualquiz	Over there I have set forth.

The rest of the words, even though somewhat disguised, are such that they are not put here for reasons of modesty and chaste ears. Finally they conclude, saying:

ca mach nelli teotl	For indeed she is truly a goddess,
ca mach nelli mahuiztic	For indeed she is truly marvellous.
cuix quin moztla	Is it tomorrow,
cuix quin huiptla	Is it the day after
niquitaz	That I shall see her?
nyman aman	Right now!
tomatla nehual	I myself,
nitelpochtli	I am the Youth,
niyaotl	I am the Adversary.
cuix nelli niyaotl	Am I truly the Adversary?
ahmo nelli niyaotl	I am not truly the Adversary,
çan nicihuayotl	I am just the Adversary of Women.

[Cures for Love-induced Illness]

Among the pagan superstitions that have persisted among the Indians, not the least harmful is the fiction that there are sicknesses caused by illicit love affairs and prohibited desires, the subject matter of which is contained in this chapter. * * *

The stratagem of the Enemy is such that, to profit by the opportunities given for our harm, he has introduced and established the idea that many sicknesses proceed from illicit love affairs and desires; for example, when some third party has fallen sick, and for that reason has to draw himself away from the opinion that the best thing is for everybody to live well. The Devil, converting everything into evil and working and compounding poison even from Holy Doctrine, has extracted two kinds of harm from this. The first is that because of the profit that those charlatans who claim to be doctors, expert soothsayers, and curers of these sicknesses and maladies gain in the course of their imagined cure, there are many who hunger for this profession. The second and more serious harm is that with this opportunity he introduces the idea, and persuades them, that it is good to sin; the reason being that it is quite visible if, on the exterior and skin of this superstition, the sicknesses and maladies caused by sins advertise themselves. Attention is carefully drawn to its interior, and to the vicious intention of the Enemy, who only feigns this corporal and temporal harm through his

---

5. An epithet of Tezcatlipoca.

participation in what happens and occurs, paying no attention to matters eternal and spiritual among the offenders. For he wishes to establish as something not to be doubted that such sicknesses and harms can be cured and remedied by committing other similar or greater crimes, sins through which their pretended cause is leveled or overcome. * * *

Let us now go on to the fraudulent cure for these sicknesses, which is the second part of this chapter. They apply to all these sicknesses the same remedy, which they call *tetlacolaltiloni,* meaning "bath for the sicknesses caused by loves and by affection." But even though they have this as the sole remedy, they do not exclude in this fashion the one which they introduce for excess of transgressions, which is to match them and exceed them—a purely pagan blindness.

The baths (a fraud and general cure for these illnesses) are customarily as follows. The imposter prepares himself with fire, copal, and water, and, stretching out a clean cloth on a mat, he places the patient on foot near it. Then he speaks to the fire, then to the water, saying:

tla xihualhuia	Please come forth,
ayauhtli ytzon	Hair of Mist,
pctli tzon	Hair of Smoke,
nonã chalchicueye	My mother Jade-skirted One,
istac cihuatl	White Woman.
tla xihualhuiã	Please come forth,
in antlaçolteteo	You who are Goddesses of Filth,
in tiquato	You, Quato,
in ticaxoch	You, Caxoch,
in titlahui	You, Tlahui,
in tixapel	You, Xapel.

While naming them, he gathers up the fire and throws the copal on it, and censes the patient as if offering him those goddesses that he has named. Next he bathes him with the prepared water and transfers him to the cloth which is on the mat, so that he may be cleansed of the illness which he had, or at least be in a better state. While he is committing all these frauds and fictions, he does not stop his spell, but continues the above, saying:

xinechitztimamaniqui	Look to me,
yayauhqui tlaçolli	Dark Filth,
iztac tlaçolli	White Filth,
xoxouhqui tlaçolli	Blue-green Filth.
onihualla	I have come,
nitlamacazqui	I the Priest,
ninahualtecutli	I the Lord of Enchantments.
xoxouhqui tlaloc	Blue-green Tlaloc,
iztac tlaloc	White Tlaloc:
ma noca techuat	May you not rise against me,

ma noca timilacatzoti	May you not turn against me.
nomatca nehuatl	I myself,
nitlamacazqui	I am the Priest,
ninahualtecutli	I am the Lord of Enchantments.

* * *

This is the general cure that these wretches use for all of those illnesses which they entitle "from love affairs, or from superfluity and transgressions in the partner," although, as has been pointed out, for these minor ailments and misfortunes which they pretend come about from an excess of transgressions in the partner (whether licit or illicit), they prescribe as a remedy, in addition to this bath, that one should equal and surpass the partner's transgressions with others much greater and more numerous—a remedy which could only have come from Hell and its denizens, whence originate all these fabrications and idolatrous superstitions.

Finally, it has occurred to me that in this bath our Enemy tries to imitate the Holy Sacrament of baptism; since just as we, as Christians, believe that by this means we attain purity of the soul and the remedy against all the harms wrought by our faults and their results, so does the ancient and astute Enemy seek that these unfortunates, blind in their pagan errors, believe and be persuaded that these supposed baths can accomplish the cleansing of the body and their liberation from misfortunes and wordly harms. May God by His mercy undeceive them and bring them to a true understanding, inspiring in His ministers new fervor for the instruction of such a barbarous and blind people, so that all may be converted for His greater honor and glory. Amen.

RESONANCE

Julio Cortázar: Axolotl[1]

There was a time when I thought a great deal about the axolotls. I went to see them in the aquarium at the Jardin des Plantes and stayed for hours watching them, observing their immobility, their faint movements. Now I am an axolotl.

I got to them by chance one spring morning when Paris was spreading its peacock tail after a wintry Lent. I was heading down the boulevard Port-Royal, then I took Saint-Marcel and L'Hôpital and saw green among all that grey and remembered the lions. I was friend of the lions and panthers, but had never gone into the dark, humid building that was the aquarium. I left my bike against the gratings and went to look at the tulips. The lions were sad and ugly and my panther was asleep. I decided on the

1. Translated by Paul Blackburn. One of the major Latin American writers of the 20th century, Julio Cortázar (1914–1984) was born in Brussels to Argentinian parents who relocated to Buenos Aires when he was six years old; in adulthood he worked as a translator, while also writing poetry and playing jazz. Opposed to the authoritarian government of Juan Perón, he moved to Paris in 1952 and lived there until his death. Starting in the sixties, Cortázar became widely known for his fiction, in which he explored the ambiguities of human interactions in such works as his short story "Blow-Up" (memorably filmed in 1966 by Michelangelo Antonioni) and his experimental novel *Hopscotch*, written in numbered sections that can be read in various orders. His fiction often involves the dislocations of European and Latin American cultural encounters, as in the story presented here, set in the botanical garden in Paris. In this unlikely setting, Ruiz de Alarcón's uneasy account of human/animal transformations finds a modern analog, in an enigmatic parable about the persisting power of Aztec culture in metropolitan Paris.

aquarium, looked obliquely at banal fish until, unexpectedly, I hit it off with the axolotls. I stayed watching them for an hour and left, unable to think of anything else.

In the library at Sainte-Geneviève, I consulted a dictionary and learned that axolotls are the larval stage (provided with gills) of a species of salamander of the genus
Ambystoma. That they were Mexican I knew already by looking at them and their little pink Aztec faces and the placard at the top of the tank. I read that specimens of
them had been found in Africa capable of living on dry land during the periods of
drought, and continuing their life under water when the rainy season came. I found
their Spanish name, *ajolote,* and the mention that they were edible, and that their oil
was used (no longer used, it said) like cod-liver oil.

I didn't care to look up any of the specialized works, but the next day I went back
to the Jardin des Plantes. I began to go every morning, morning and afternoon some
days. The aquarium guard smiled perplexedly taking my ticket. I would lean up
against the iron bar in front of the tanks and set to watching them. There's nothing
strange in this, because after the first minute I knew that we were linked, that something infinitely lost and distant kept pulling us together. It had been enough to detain
me that first morning in front of the sheet of glass where some bubbles rose through
the water. The axolotls huddled on the wretched narrow (only I can know how narrow
and wretched) floor of moss and stone in the tank. There were nine specimens, and
the majority pressed their heads against the glass, looking with their eyes of gold at
whoever came near them. Disconcerted, almost ashamed, I felt it a lewdness to be
peering at these silent and immobile figures heaped at the bottom of the tank. Men-
tally I isolated one, situated on the right and somewhat apart from the others, to study
it better. I saw a rosy little body, translucent (I thought of those Chinese figurines of
milky glass), looking like a small lizard about six inches long, ending in a fish's tail
of extraordinary delicacy, the most sensitive part of our body. Along the back ran a
transparent fin which joined with the tail, but what obsessed me was the feet, of the
slenderest nicety, ending in tiny fingers with minutely human nails. And then I discovered its eyes, its face. Inexpressive features, with no other trait save the eyes, two
orifices, like brooches, wholly of transparent gold, lacking any life but looking, letting themselves be penetrated by my look, which seemed to travel past the golden
level and lose itself in a diaphanous interior mystery. A very slender black halo ringed
the eye and etched it onto the pink flesh, onto the rosy stone of the head, vaguely triangular, but with curved and irregular sides which gave it a total likeness to a statuette
corroded by time. The mouth was masked by the triangular plane of the face, its considerable size would be guessed only in profile; in front a delicate crevice barely slit
the lifeless stone. On both sides of the head where the ears should have been, there
grew three tiny sprigs red as coral, a vegetal outgrowth, the gills, I suppose. And they
were the only thing quick about it; every ten or fifteen seconds the sprigs pricked up
stiffly and again subsided. Once in a while a foot would barely move, I saw the
diminutive toes poise mildly on the moss. It's that we don't enjoy moving a lot, and
the tank is so cramped—we barely move in any direction and we're hitting one of the
others with our tail or our head—difficulties arise, fights, tiredness. The time feels
like it's less if we stay quietly.

It was their quietness that made me lean toward them fascinated the first time I
saw the axolotls. Obscurely I seemed to understand their secret will, to abolish space
and time with an indifferent immobility. I knew better later; the gill contraction, the
tentative reckoning of the delicate feet on the stones, the abrupt swimming (some of
them swim with a simple undulation of the body) proved to me that they were capable

of escaping that mineral lethargy in which they spent whole hours. Above all else, their eyes obsessed me. In the standing tanks on either side of them, different fishes showed me the simple stupidity of their handsome eyes so similar to our own. The eyes of the axolotls spoke to me of the presence of a different life, of another way of seeing. Glueing my face to the glass (the guard would cough fussily once in a while), I tried to see better those diminutive golden points, that entrance to the infinitely slow and remote world of these rosy creatures. It was useless to tap with one finger on the glass directly in front of their faces; they never gave the least reaction. The golden eyes continued burning with their soft, terrible light; they continued looking at me from an unfathomable depth which made me dizzy.

And nevertheless they were close. I knew it before this, before being an axolotl. I learned it the day I came near them for the first time. The anthropomorphic features of a monkey reveal the reverse of what most people believe, the distance that is traveled from them to us. The absolute lack of similarity between axolotls and human beings proved to me that my recognition was valid, that I was not propping myself up with easy analogies. Only the little hands . . . But an eft, the common newt, has such hands also, and we are not at all alike. I think it was the axolotls' heads, that triangular pink shape with the tiny eyes of gold. That looked and knew. That laid the claim. They were not *animals*.

It would seem easy, almost obvious, to fall into mythology. I began seeing in the axolotls a metamorphosis which did not succeed in revoking a mysterious humanity. I imagined them aware, slaves of their bodies, condemned infinitely to the silence of the abyss, to a hopeless meditation. Their blind gaze, the diminutive gold disc without expression and nonetheless terribly shining, went through me like a message: "Save us, save us." I caught myself mumbling words of advice, conveying childish hopes. They continued to look at me, immobile; from time to time the rosy branches of the gills stiffened. In that instant I felt a muted pain; perhaps they were seeing me, attracting my strength to penetrate into the impenetrable thing of their lives. They were not human beings, but I had found in no animal such a profound relation with myself. The axolotls were like witnesses of something, and at times like horrible judges. I felt ignoble in front of them; there was such a terrifying purity in those transparent eyes. They were larvas, but larva means disguise and also phantom. Behind those Aztec faces, without expression but of an implacable cruelty, what semblance was awaiting its hour?

I was afraid of them. I think that had it not been for feeling the proximity of other visitors and the guard, I would not have been bold enough to remain alone with them. "You eat them alive with your eyes, hey," the guard said, laughing; he likely thought I was a little cracked. What he didn't notice was that it was they devouring me slowly with their eyes, in a cannibalism of gold. At any distance from the aquarium, I had only to think of them, it was as though I were being affected from a distance. It got to the point that I was going every day, and at night I thought of them immobile in the darkness, slowly putting a hand out which immediately encountered another. Perhaps their eyes could see in the dead of night, and for them the day continued indefinitely. The eyes of axolotls have no lids.

I know now that there was nothing strange, that that had to occur. Leaning over in front of the tank each morning, the recognition was greater. They were suffering, every fiber of my body reached toward that stifled pain, that stiff torment at the bottom of the tank. They were lying in wait for something, a remote dominion destroyed, an age of liberty when the world had been that of the axolotls. Not possible that such a terrible expression which was attaining the overthrow of that forced blankness on their stone faces should carry any message other than one of pain, proof of that eternal sentence, of that liquid hell they were undergoing. Hopelessly, I wanted to prove to myself that my own sensibility was projecting a nonexistent consciousness upon the axolotls. They and I knew. So there was nothing strange in what happened. My face was pressed against the glass of the aquarium, my eyes were attempting once more to penetrate the mystery of those eyes of gold without iris, without pupil. I saw from very close up the face of an axolotl immobile next to the glass. No transition and no surprise, I saw my face against the glass, I saw it on the outside of the tank, I saw it on the other side of the glass. Then my face drew back and I understood.

Only one thing was strange: to go on thinking as usual, to know. To realize that was, for the first moment, like the horror of a man buried alive awaking to his fate. Outside, my face came close to the glass again, I saw my mouth, the lips compressed with the effort of understanding the axolotls. I was an axolotl and now I knew instantly that no understanding was possible. He was outside the aquarium, his thinking was a thinking outside the tank. Recognizing him, being him himself, I was an axolotl and in my world. The horror began—I learned in the same moment—of believing myself prisoner in the body of an axolotl, metamorphosed into him with my human mind intact, buried alive in an axolotl, condemned to move lucidly among unconscious creatures. But that stopped when a foot just grazed my face, when I moved just a little to one side and saw an axolotl next to me who was looking at me, and understood that he knew also, no communication possible, but very clearly. Or I was also in him, or all of us were thinking humanlike, incapable of expression, limited to the golden splendor of our eyes looking at the face of the man pressed against the aquarium.

He returned many times, but he comes less often now. Weeks pass without his showing up. I saw him yesterday, he looked at me for a long time and left briskly. It seemed to me that he was not so much interested in us any more, that he was coming out of habit. Since the only thing I do is think, I could think about him a lot. It occurs to me that at the beginning we continued to communicate, that he felt more than ever one with the mystery which was claiming him. But the bridges were broken between him and me, because what was his obsession is now an axolotl, alien to his human life. I think that at the beginning I was capable of returning to him in a certain way— ah, only in a certain way—and of keeping awake his desire to know us better. I am an axolotl for good now, and if I think like a man it's only because every axolotl thinks like a man inside his rosy stone semblance. I believe that all this succeeded in communicating something to him in those first days, when I was still he. And in this final solitude to which he no longer comes, I console myself by thinking that perhaps he is going to write a story about us, that, believing he's making up a story, he's going to write all this about axolotls.

❦

─+ ❧❀❧ +─

Bartolomé de Las Casas
1474–1566

Scourge of the *conquistadors,* excoriated by land-holding Spaniards and generations of Spanish historians, the Dominican friar Bartolomé de Las Casas was the sixteenth century's most ardent spokesman for human rights. A one-time plantation owner in Hispaniola (so named because the island, today divided between the Dominican Republic and Haiti, reminded Columbus of

Spain), Las Casas experienced firsthand the injustices of a system that made Spain the wealthiest country in Europe. In exchange for forcibly saving the native Americans' souls, Spaniards reaped the fruits of the natives' backbreaking labor in America's gold and silver mines and vast agricultural empires. After liberating his own slaves in 1512, Las Casas spent the next thirty-five years traveling between the Americas and Europe to convince kings and popes that the *encomienda* system of indentured servitude as it was called was unchristian. He argued that the Indians were a rational people who in Tenochtitlán and elsewhere had constructed a highly developed civilization. While Las Casas's efforts clearly influenced the papal bull "Sublimus Deus" of 1537 stating that Indians had the right to exercise their free will, as well as the "New Laws" of 1542 abolishing *encomiendas,* these proclamations from across the Atlantic were difficult to put into practice—as Las Casas, who had attempted to create a utopian community in Venezuela and who would weather a series of Indian rebellions and Spanish mutinies while Bishop of Chiapas, knew only too well. In his last years he wrote a number of polemical treatises and finished his lengthy *History of the Indies,* composed, he said, for the honor and glory of God and "for the common benefit, both spiritual and temporal, of the innumerable Indians—if there are any left when I finish my history." He died in Madrid, convinced that the Spanish should have left the Indians alone.

from Apologetic History[1]

[INDIAN HOUSES, FEATHERWORK, AND SILVERWORK]

The first thing [Aristotle] says is incumbent upon men, in order that philosophers may be kings, is that they construct their own houses.[2] These people built these houses in accord with the region they inhabited and their experience of their needs; they made them strong, suitable, and also attractive—very well fabricated. The inhabitants of this island of Hispaniola, of these neighboring islands, of the part of Tierra Firme near the shores of Paria,[3] and elsewhere made their houses of wood and thatch in the shape of a bell. These were quite high and roomy, so that ten or more citizens with their families dwelt in each one.

They drove posts as a thick as a man's leg or thigh almost three feet deep into the ground, close together. All met overhead and were tied by lashings of woody vines. . . . Above this frame they placed many other thin pieces of wood crosswise, closely fastened with those vines. For the inside they made designs and symbols and patterns from wood and bark dyed black, and from other wood peeled so as to remain white so that they seemed to be made from some other beautiful painted materials.

They adorned other houses with reeds, peeled and very white—a kind of thin, delicate cane. They made very graceful ornaments and designs from these so that the interiors of the houses seemed to have been painted. Outside, they covered the houses with beautiful, fragrant grass. * * * I saw one of these Indian houses that a Spaniard sold to another for 600 castellanos or gold pesos, each one worth 450 maravedis.[4]

In New Spain and for more than 500 leagues around Mexico City, they made houses of adobe or sun-baked brick, of wood, and many hewn stones—also in Florida and Cibola. In Peru, they made them of great hewn stones, almost like strong forts.

---

1. Translated by George Sanderlin. The *Apologetic History* was originally part of Las Casas's massive *History of the Indies,* finished in 1559; Las Casas then integrated material largely anthropological in nature into the separate, shorter book. The material excerpted below on Indian houses is from Chapters 43, 62, and 63 of the *Apologetic History,* while the section on the marketplace is from Chapter 70.

2. *Economics* 1. 1–5; Aristotle also talks about the necessity of houses for civilized societies in the first book of his *Politics.* Las Casas goes on to demonstrate the existence of such houses in Mexico and elsewhere.
3. The coast of Venezuela.
4. A considerable amount for the time; a copper maravedi was worth the equivalent of roughly 13 cents at today's prices.

But what appears without double to exceed all human genius * * * is the art which those Mexican peoples have so perfectly mastered, of making from natural feathers, fixed in position with their own natural colors, anything that they or any other first-class painters can paint with brushes. They were accustomed to make many things out of feathers, such as animals, birds, men, capes or blankets to cover themselves, vestments for their priests, crowns or mitres, shields, flies, and a thousand other sorts of objects which they fancy.

These feathers were green, red or gold, purple, bright red, yellow, blue or pale green, black, white, and all the other colors, blended and pure, not dyed by human ingenuity but all natural, taken from various birds. Therefore they placed a high value on every species of birds, because they made use of all. They preserved the color hues of even the smallest birds that could be found on land or in the air, so that certain hues would harmonize with others, and they might adorn their work as much as, and more fittingly than, any painter in the world.

They would seat this feather on cotton cloth, or on a board, and on that would add little feathers of all colors, which they kept in small individual boxes or vessels, just as they would have taken prepared paints from shells or small saucers with paint brushes. If they wished to make a man's face, the form of an animal, or some other object which they had decided on and for which a white feather was needed, they selected one from the whites; if a green was required, they took one from the greens; if a red, from the reds; and they attached it very delicately, with a certain paste. Thus for the eyes in the face of a man or animal, requiring black and white and the pupil, they made, and continue to make, the different parts of feathers, with the delicacy of a great painter using a very fine brush—and surely this is a marvel.

And granted that before we Christians entered there they made perfect and wonderful things by this art, such as a tree, a rose, grass, a flower, an animal, a man, a bird, a dainty butterfly, a forest and a stone or rock, so skillfully that the object appeared alive or natural * * * yet after the Spaniards went there and they saw our statues and other things, they had, beyond comparison, abundant material and an excellent opportunity to show the liveliness of their intellects, the integrity and disengagement of their powers or interior and exterior senses, and their great talent. For since our statues and altar-pieces are large and painted in divers colors, they had occasion to branch out, to practice, and to distinguish themselves in that new and delicate art of theirs, seeking to imitate our objects.

One of the great beauties they achieve in what they make—a canopy, cloak, vestment, or anything else especially large—is to place the feather in such a way that seen from one direction it appears gilded, although it lacks gold; from another, it seems iridescent; from another, it has a green luster, without being chiefly green; from another, viewed crossways, it has still another beautiful tint * * * and similarly from many other angles, all lustrous colors of marvelous attractiveness. Hence it is that one of their craftsmen is accustomed to go without food and drink for a whole day, arranging and removing feathers according to how in his view the hues best harmonize, and so that the work will produce greater diversity of colors and more beauty. He observes it, as I said, from one direction and then from another; one time in sunlight, other times in shade, at night, during the day or when it is almost night, under much or little light, cross-ways or from the opposite side.

To sum up, out of feathers they have made and still make, every day, statues, altar-pieces, and many other things of ours; they also interpose bits of gold at suitable places, making the work more beautiful and charming so that the whole world may wonder at it. They have made trimming for chasubles and mantles,[5] covers or silk cases for crosses, for processions and for divine service, and mitres for bishops. And certainly, with no exaggeration, if these had been of gold or silver brocade, three thicknesses on rich crimson, or embroidered richly with gold or silver thread, with rubies, emeralds, and other precious stones, they would not have been more beautiful or more pleasing to look on. The craftsmen who surpass everyone in New Spain in this art are those of the province of Mechuacán.[6]

Although the featherwork craftsmen are unquestionably excellent and demonstrate their great talent, the silversmiths of New Spain are not unworthy of our admiration for their delicate, outstanding work. They have made, and still make, unusual pieces, of a fineness very different from that of silverwork in any part of our Europe. What makes the pieces more admirable is that the silversmiths form and shape them only by means of fire, and with stone or flint, without any iron tool or anything that can help them produce that nicety and beauty. They made birds, animals, men, idols, vessels of various shapes, arms for war, beads or rosaries, necklaces, bracelets, earrings, and many other jewels worn by men and women. They make all this by pouring the molten metal into a cast. After casting it, they take out a vessel like a pitcher, or one like a kettle with its handle cast like a bell, not fastened but free to move from side to side. They take out a bird, such as a parrot, whose head, tongue, and wings move as if alive; the beak of an eagle does likewise. They take out a frog, and a fish with many scales, the gold scales alternating with silver ones, all having been cast, which astonishes our craftsmen.

They cast a gold she-monkey which plays with its hands and feet, and holds a spindle and seems to spin, or with an apple that it appears to eat—and other equally laughable objects. They may pour a plate divided into quarters, or more; one quarter is of gold, another of silver, and the secret of this is also hidden from our craftsmen. They made other excellent things, thousands more, while they were pagan, but now they make many more of our things, such as crosses, chalices, monstrances,[7] wine vessels for Mass, vessels for the altar, and many other delicate things.

In the beginning, there would be an Indian, all wrapped up in a blanket, in their fashion, with only his eyes showing; he would be at some distance from the shop of one of our silver-smiths, dissembling and pretending to observe nothing. The silversmith would be shaping some gold or silver article, very delicate and of great craftsmanship. And the Indian, simply from seeing him make some part of the article, would go off to his house, make it himself as well or better, and soon carry it from there in his hand to sell to whoever would buy it.

They have made and copied thousands of our objects in these arts, faultlessly; therefore, all our craftsmen avoid making things in front of them. * * * As soon as the Indians saw flutes, oboes, sackbuts,[8] and other musical instruments, they made them perfectly, without anyone teaching them. They make a sackbut out of a candlestick. I don't know whether they have made organs, but I don't doubt that they could make them, and make them well, without difficulty.

In the square of Mexico City, I myself saw an Indian with fetters on his feet, a slave, who had three or four large, excellent guitars. The ornaments, especially, were very neat and delicate, so artfully made that I stopped to look at them and also at the

---

5. Ecclesiastical vestments.
6. A province in central Mexico.
7. Vessels, often made of silver or gold, in which the Eu-

charist was exposed.
8. A trumpetlike instrument with a slide for changing pitch.

fetters he wore as a slave. Near him was a Spaniard, his master; I asked the Spaniard if they had brought those guitars from Castile, and I started to praise the ornaments. He replied that the maker of the guitars was the one who held them in his hand.

"And the ornaments?" I asked.

"Yes, also of the ornaments," he answered.

I remained admiring, and could not have believed him if he had not strongly affirmed his statement.

[THE MARKETPLACE OF MEXICO CITY]

A sight which can scarcely be exaggerated is that of the markets of Mexico City. This city has two districts, and in each one there is a most impressive market, in a very large square. One is called the market square or marketplace of Mexico, and the other that of Tlatelulco; the Franciscans have been located here, so we all call it Santiago.[1] In each square there is room for over 200,000 souls; every day, especially the five week days, there are more than 100,000 souls in each square.

All the crafts and products there can be, throughout New Spain, are found there. There is no lack of goods to supply the natural needs, nor of things for unusual tastes. Each craft and kind of merchandise has its separate place, which no one else dares disturb or occupy. But the people who come to the markets are so numerous that the squares, even though they are large, lack space for all the merchandise; therefore, goods which cause an obstruction and take up much room, such as stone, brick, adobe or sun-baked brick, lime, sand, lumber, firewood, charcoal, and other cumbersome things are placed at the entrances of the nearest streets.

All the foodstuffs, raw and cooked, are found there. One essential product is salt, made from the water of the salt lake there and from there distributed through much of New Spain. There are fabrics for cotton blankets and white woolen blankets, coarse pieces of cloth lightly or deeply colored, with rich colors, for shirts, for tablecloths, for handkerchiefs * * * and for many other things. There is an abundance of clothing and footwear of many kinds.

Various fine colors are sold to those who practice the craft of painting. There are admirable featherwork goods; there are feathers of all colors, not artificially dyed, but natural. There are all the birds which go through the air or breed on land, dead or live, for whoever wishes to buy them; also animals, dead or live.

Hares, rabbits, and little dogs which do not bark but grunt and, as they say, are good to eat, are sold there. They sell deer, quartered or whole, and other animals which they hunt. There are meat and fish, boiled and roasted, the fish consisting of what they catch in the lake; also baked bread, loaves kneaded with kidney beans which are like the lupines of Castile, although not exactly the same color, for these are black and tawny and other shades. There are many other vegetables, an infinite amount of maize. A great variety of fruits are sold, and there is no counting the edible roots and greens brought here for good or for medicinal purposes.

There are many taverns one may enter in order to eat and drink their wines made from maize. * * * They sell honey and must, the honey from bees and the must from agaves which * * * are called *metl*.[2] They sell wax, usually yellow and, much of it, nearly black, and this is from bees which live underground.

---

1. The shrine of Santiago de Compostela in Spain, where the body of St. James (Santiago in Spanish) was believed to have been buried, was a great pilgrimage center in the Middle Ages; numerous sites in the New World were named after him.

2. Agaves were a distinctive type of aloe; must is the pulp or juice of the plant.

There are many jewels set in gold and silver, also pearls and stones like turquoise, and others. However, there are few precious stones, either because there are none naturally in that land or because the Indians do not show them. Montezuma and his lords did possess them, but they were consumed after we hastily entered.[3] There are silk weavers who make and sell many delicate laces and other things of silk.

They sell the hides of animals, wonderfully dressed, as we say, and they also prepare the skins of birds, keeping all the feathers. They sell many kinds of snails, large and small, as well as shells, bones, and other things of this sort which they prize; also different kinds of very pretty crockery, made of painted clay; and vessels which * * * they make from gourds called *hibueros* in this island of Hispaniola,[4] so beautifully that the king will drink from them. Numberless are the products, which I do not now recall, sold in those markets of Mexico City.

Because of all the goods brought from outside * * * and on account of the people coming from many places to buy them, it is thought that 50,000 or 100,000 canoes go on the lake. Canoes are small boats made from dugout logs, the prow narrower than the poop; each holds twenty, thirty, fifty and more persons. In this island of Hispaniola and in Cuba, there were very large canoes which held eighty persons. * * * The word *canoe* comes from this island of Hispaniola; its name in the Mexican language was *atcale,* from *at,* meaning "water," and *cale,* meaning "house"—as if to say, "house upon water." * * *

And these products are bought in exchange for others, for the most part by a barter system, according to their valuation of the merchandise. Inequalities between goods exchanged are made up by money consisting of the beans * * * called cacao. It usually suffices to pay for less valuable goods with cacao.

And with this, we conclude the fourth part of our description of the self-sufficient republic,[5] provisioned and well governed.

Sor Juana Inés de la Cruz
c. 1651–1695

Cortés's venture in Mexico was primarily military, but not exclusively so. Accompanying Cortés on his entrance into Mexico City in 1520 were several Franciscan friars, whose presence marked a secondary reason for Spanish intervention in the New World: the spreading of Catholicism. For those Indians who survived death by disease or guns, there was another kind of subjection: to the missions, comprised of colleges and "seminaries" where the native peoples were instructed through catechism, preaching, and perhaps surprisingly, theater, often presented on feast days such as Corpus Christi.

In the hands of Sor Juana, the Mexican nun who would write over 150 years after Cortés, such theater drew on not one but two vibrant traditions: that of seventeenth-century Spain, particularly the *auto sacramental* or religious drama, and the rituals of the indigenous Aztecs,

---

3. Montezuma (Moctezuma II), emperor at the time of the Spanish conquest, and other Aztecs reputedly swallowed gold nuggets after Tenochtitlán was invaded.
4. Las Casas had originally settled in Hispaniola; in 1523, he joined the Dominican monastery there, where he began work on his history.
5. *Apologetic History* had opened with a description of the island and a general study of the Indians, who were said by Las Casas to be temperate and intelligent. With

Chapter 59, Las Casas, following Aristotle, lists the six classes of a "good and well-ordered republic" and argues that the Indians have shown themselves to be capable of establishing such a republic, insofar as their society has workers, artisans, warriors, citizens involved in commerce (from which the section on the marketplace is excerpted), priests (the longest section of the work, in which he discusses, among other things, idolatry, magic, and demonology), and judges.

marked by considerable pageantry and dance. Written in 1688, *The Divine Narcissus,* if it was performed at all, was shown only in Madrid, not Mexico. Part of the *loa* or prefatory act (excerpted below) explicitly debates its propriety for the Spanish stage, since it was written in the "backward" colonies. But the *loa* is also strikingly anticolonial. Like so many Mexican works, it commemorates the conquest of New World by Old (represented by the figures of Zeal and Religion). Yet the new-world characters of Occident and America are dignified in their resistance to these European figures revealed, by turns, as unnecessarily violent and hypocritical. Perhaps most intriguing is Sor Juana's grasp of Aztec customs and her occasional use of Nahuatl words in the play, as well as the final triumph of the *dios de las Semillas* whom America praises at the beginning of the *loa* as the Aztec fertility god. As much as he can be seen as a hybrid of Christ and an Aztec deity, his name—"the god of seeds"—persists at the end of the *loa,* despite the fact that the Europeans have obviously emerged victorious. For a selection of sonnets by Sor Juana, see page 241; her "Response to Sor Filotea" is on page 138.

from The Loa for the Auto Sacramental of the Divine Narcissus[1]

An Allegory[2]

Speaking Characters

Occident	Religion
America	Musician
Zeal	Soldiers

SCENE 1

[*Enter Occident, a gallant-looking Aztec, wearing a crown. By his side is America, an Aztec woman of poised self-possession. They are dressed in the* mantas *and* huipiles *worn for singing a* tocotín.[3] *They seat themselves on two chairs. On each side, Aztec men and women dance with feathers and rattles in their hands, as is customary for those doing this dance. While they dance, Music sings.*]

MUSIC: O, Noble Mexicans,
             whose ancient ancestry
             comes forth from the clear light
             and brilliance of the Sun,[4]
5   since this, of all the year,
             is your most happy feast
             in which you venerate
             your greatest deity,
             come and adorn yourselves
10   with vestments of your rank;
             let your holy fervor be
             made one with jubilation;

---

1. Translated by Patricia A. Peters and Renée Domeier, O.S.B. The *loa* was the often lengthy preamble to a play, in this case an *auto sacramental* or one-act sacramental or Eucharist play performed for a religious feast day.
2. *Por alegorías* suggests that the play should be read allegorically—that is, using the characters to represent something else.
3. *Manta* is the Spanish word for a blanket or poncho,

while *huipile* is a blouse. A *tocotín* was a traditional Nahuatl ballad, of which Sor Juana wrote at least two.
4. The Mexicans believed that the Sun was their original "father": "The Sun cast down an arrow and made a hole, from which a man emerged . . . and following, a woman," a story Sor Juana could have read about in the writings of Franciscans such as Father Juan de Torquemada, published in Spain in the early 17th century.

and celebrate in festive pomp
the great God of the Seeds!⁵

15 Since the abundance of
our native fields and farms
is owed to him alone
who gives fertility,
then offer him your thanks,
20 for it is right and just
to give from what has grown,
the first of the new fruits.
From your own veins, draw out
and give, without reserve,
25 the best blood, mixed with seed,
so that his cult be served,
and celebrate in festive pomp,
the great God of the Seeds!

[*Occident and America sit, and Music ceases.*]

OCCIDENT: Of all the deities to whom
30 our rites demand I bend my knee—
among two thousand gods or more
who dwell within this royal city
and who require the sacrifice
of human victims still entreating
35 for life until their blood is drawn
and gushes forth from hearts still beating
and bowels still pulsing—I declare,
among all these, (it bears repeating),
whose ceremonies we observe,
40 the greatest is, surpassing all
this pantheon's immensity
the great God of the Seeds.
AMERICA: And you are right, since he alone
daily sustains our monarchy
45 because our lives depend on his
providing crops abundantly;
and since he gives us graciously
the gift from which all gifts proceed,
our fields rich with golden maize,
50 the source of life through daily bread,
we render him our highest praise.
Then how will it improve our lives
if rich America abounds

5. There were several Aztec fertility gods, among them, Centéotl, god of corn; Xiuhteuctli, god of the grass; and Tláloc, god of water and the fecundity of the earth. However, in the context of the *loa,* it seems that Sor Juana is referring to Huitzilopochtli, who was the god of war and the most powerful deity of Tenochtitlán, the Aztecs' capital and what is now Mexico City. Identified with the sun, he was the one who demanded the blood sacrifices that will be referred to by Music.

in gold from mines whose smoke deprives
55 the fields of their fertility
and with their clouds of filthy soot
will not allow the crops to grow
which blossom now so fruitfully
from seeded earth?[6] Moreover, his
60 protection of our people far
exceeds our daily food and drink,
the body's sustenance. Indeed,
he feeds us with his very flesh
(first purified of every stain).
65 We eat his body, drink his blood,
and by this sacred meal are freed
and cleansed from all that is profane,
and thus, he purifies our soul.[7]
And now, attentive to his rites,
70 together let us all proclaim:

THEY [*OCCIDENT, AMERICA, DANCERS*] AND MUSIC: We celebrate in festive pomp,
  the great God of the Seeds!

Scene 2

[*They exit dancing. Enter Christian Religion as a Spanish lady, Zeal as a Captain General in armor, and Spanish soldiers.*][8]

RELIGION: How, being Zeal, can you suppress
  the flames of righteous Christian wrath
75 when here before your very eyes
idolatry, so blind with pride,
adores, with superstitious rites
an idol, leaving your own bride,
the holy faith of Christ disgraced?

ZEAL: Religion, trouble not your mind
  or grieve my failure to attack,
complaining that my love is slack,
for now the sword I wear is bared,
its hilt in hand, clasped ready and
85 my arm raised high to take revenge.
Please stand aside and deign to wait
till I requite your grievances.

[*Enter Occident and America dancing, and accompanied by Music, who enters from the other side.*]

MUSIC: And celebrate in festive pomp,
  the great God of the Seeds!

---

6. An allusion to the extensive mining being practiced by the Spaniards throughout Mexico.
7. Sor Juana may be referring to the Aztec ritual of sacrifice in which those who had imbibed the "god" were slaughtered on the altar.
8. "Religion" represents the missionaries and the spiritual conquest of the Mexicans; "Zeal" the military wing of the conquest.

ZEAL: Here they come! I will confront them.

RELIGION: And I, in peace, will also go
        (before your fury lays them low)
        for justice must with mercy kiss;
        I shall invite them to arise
95   from superstitious depths to faith.

ZEAL: Let us approach while they are still
        absorbed in their lewd rituals.

MUSIC: And celebrate in festive pomp,
        the great God of the Seeds!

    [Zeal and Religion cross the stage.]

RELIGION: Great Occident, most powerful;
        America, so beautiful
        and rich; you live in poverty
        amid the treasures of your land.
        Abandon this irreverent cult
105   with which the demon has waylaid you.
        Open your eyes! Follow the path
        that leads straightforwardly to truth,
        to which my love yearns to persuade you.

OCCIDENT: Who are these unknown people, so
110   intrusive in my sight, who dare
        to stop us in our ecstasy?
        Heaven forbid such infamy!

AMERICA: Who are these nations, never seen,
        that wish, by force, to pit themselves
115   against my ancient power supreme?

OCCIDENT: Oh, you alien beauty fair;
        oh, pilgrim woman from afar,
        who comes to interrupt my prayer,
        please speak and tell me who you are.

RELIGION: Christian Religion is my name,
        and I intend that all this realm
        will make obeisance unto me.

OCCIDENT: An impossible concession!

AMERICA: Yours is but a mad obsession!

OCCIDENT: You will meet with swift repression.

AMERICA: Pay no attention; she is mad!
        Let us go on with our procession.

MUSIC AND ALL *[Aztecs on stage]*: And celebrate in festive pomp,
        the great God of the Seeds!

ZEAL: How is this, barbarous Occident?
        Can it be, sightless Idolatry,
        that you insult Religion,
        the spouse I cherish tenderly?
        Abomination fills your cup
135   and overruns the brim, but see

that God will not permit you to
continue drinking down delight,
and I am sent to deal your doom.

OCCIDENT: And who are you who frightens all
140   who only look upon your face?

ZEAL: I am Zeal. Does that surprise you?
Take heed! for when your excesses
bring disgrace to fair Religion,
then will Zeal arise to vengeance;
145   for insolence I will chastise you.
I am the minister of God,
Who growing weary with the sight
of overreaching tyrannies
so sinful that they reach the height
150   of error, practiced many years,
has sent me forth to penalize you.
And thus, these military hosts
with flashing thunderbolts of steel,
the ministers of His great wrath
155   are sent, His anger to reveal.

OCCIDENT: What god? What sin? What tyranny?
What punishment do you foresee?
Your reasons make no sense to me,
nor can I make the slightest guess
160   who you might be with your insistence
on tolerating no resistance,
impeding us with rash persistence
from lawful worship as we sing.

MUSIC: And celebrate with festive pomp,
165   the great God of the Seeds!

AMERICA: Madman, blind, and barbarous,
with mystifying messages
you try to mar our calm and peace,
destroying the tranquility
170   that we enjoy. Your plots must cease,
unless, of course, you wish to be
reduced to ashes, whose existence
even the winds will never sense.

[*to Occident*]

And you, my spouse, and your cohort,
175   close off your hearing and your sight
to all their words; refuse to heed
their fantasies of zealous might;
proceed to carry out your rite.
Do not concede to insolence
180   from foreigners intent to dull
our ritual's magnificence.

MUSIC: And celebrate with festive pomp,
        the great God of the Seeds!
ZEAL: Since our initial offering
185   of peaceful terms, you held so cheap,
        the dire alternative of war,
        I guarantee you'll count more dear.
        Take up your arms! To war! To war!

[*Drums and trumpets sound.*]

OCCIDENT: What miscarriages of justice
190   has heaven sent against me?
        What are these weapons, blazing fire,
        before my unbelieving eyes?
        Get ready, guards! Aim well, my troops,
        Your arrows at this enemy!
AMERICA: What lightening bolts does heaven send
        to lay me low? What molten balls
        of burning lead so fiercely rain?
        What centaurs crush with monstrous force
        and cause my people such great pain?

[*within*]

200   To arms! To arms! War! War!

[(*Drums and trumpets*) *sound.*]

        Long life to Spain! Long live her king!

[*The battle begins. Indians enter through one door and flee through another with the Spanish pursuing at their heels. From back stage, Occident backs away from Religion and America retreats before Zeal's onslaught.*]

* * *

SCENE 4 [9]

AMERICA: There is much more I want to see,
        and my desire to know is now
        by holy inspiration led.
OCCIDENT: And I desire more keenly still
        to know about the life and death
400   of the God you say is in the bread.
RELIGION. Then come along with me, and I
        shall make for you a metaphor,
        a concept clothed in rhetoric

---

9. In the ensuing scene, America and the Occident are defeated. Zeal is ready to annihilate them, but Religion protests that they be kept alive, insisting that they can be converted. Claiming that she will speak like St. Paul, Religion suggests to Occident and America that the many miracles they recount of fertility and growth are the work not of their "mendacious deities" but of "the One True God" who gave his life for theirs. Particularly striking are the numerous similarities Religion elucidates between the Aztecs' religion and Christianity.

so colorful that what I show
405 to you, your eyes will clearly see;
for now I know that you require
objects of sight instead of words,
by which faith whispers in your ears
too deaf to hear; I understand,
410 for you necessity demands
that through the eyes, faith find her way
to her reception in your hearts.[1]
OCCIDENT: Exactly so. I do prefer
to see the things you would impart.

SCENE 5

RELIGION: Then come.
ZEAL: Religion, answer me:
what metaphor will you employ
to represent these mysteries?
RELIGION: An *auto*[2] will make visible
through allegory images
420 of what America must learn
and Occident implores to know
about the questions that now burn
within him so.
ZEAL: What will you call
this play in allegory cast?
RELIGION: *Divine Narcissus*, let it be,
because if that unhappy maid
adored an idol which disguised
in such strange symbols the attempt
the demon made to counterfeit
430 the great and lofty mystery
of the most Blessed Eucharist,[3]
then there were also, I surmise,
among more ancient pagans hints
of such high marvels symbolized.
ZEAL: Where will your drama be performed?
RELIGION: In the crown city of Madrid,
which is the center of the Faith,
the seat of Catholic majesty,
to whom the Indies owe their best
440 beneficence, the blessed gift

---

1. Illustrations were often used by the missionaries to teach the indigenous Mexicans, as made clear in a work such as *Rhetorica Christiana* by the missionary Diego Valadés. Theater too, particularly the *autos sacramentales* of which Sor Juana's work is an example, was thought to be a highly effective teaching tool.
2. An *auto sacramental* or "Mystery Play."
3. Possibly an allusion to the one-act play that will follow

the *loa*, for which Sor Juana drew on the myth of Narcissus. In her rendition, Narcissus is Christ, in love with the semblance of himself that is humanity, while the figure of Echo is the demonic fallen Angel who tries to tempt him from his love for *naturaleza Humana* or humankind. The work ends with Narcissus's death and resurrection and a hymn celebrating the eucharist.

of Holy Writ, the Gospel light
illuminating all the West.[4]

ZEAL: That you should write in Mexico
for royal patrons don't you see
445   to be an impropriety?[5]

RELIGION: Is it beyond imagination
that something made in one location
can in another be of use?
Furthermore, my writing it
450   comes, not of whimsical caprice,
but from my vowed obedience
to do what seems beyond my reach.[6]
Well, then, this work, however rough
and little polished it might be,
455   results from my obedience,
and not from any arrogance.

ZEAL: Then answer me, Religion, how
(before you leave the matter now),
will you respond when you are chid
460   for loading the whole Indies on
a stage to transport to Madrid?

RELIGION: The purpose of my play can be
none other than to glorify
the Eucharistic Mystery;
465   and since the cast of characters
are no more than abstractions which
depict the theme with clarity,
then surely no one should object
if they are taken to Madrid;
470   distance can never hinder thought
with persons of intelligence,
nor seas impede exchange of sense.

ZEAL: Then, prostrate at his royal feet,
beneath whose strength two worlds are joined
475   we beg for pardon of the King;

RELIGION: and from her eminence, the Queen;[7]

AMERICA: whose sovereign and anointed feet
the humble Indies bow to kiss;

ZEAL: and from the Royal High Council;

RELIGION: and from the ladies, who bring light
into their hemisphere;

---

4. The performance history of *The Divine Narcissus* is unclear, although it was published in a separate edition in
1690. Madrid is called "center of the faith" because it was
the religious and publishing center for the evangelization
of the Indies.
5. Probably because the Mexicans were deemed inferior
to the Spaniards.
6. Sor Juana was asked to write the *loa* by her close friend
María Luisa Manrique de Lara y Gonzaga, the Condesa de

Paredes. Sor Juana addresses her as "Phyllis" in several
poems, and the countess in turn would take Sor Juana's
poems to Spain and arrange for their first publication in
1689. The words spoken by Religion echo sentiments
found in the "Response to Sor Filotea," page 138.
7. Many *loas* close with such a request for pardon directed to the king, queen, the Royal Council, and the
women and poets of the court.

AMERICA: and from
              their poets, I most humbly beg
              forgiveness for my crude attempt,
              desiring with these awkward lines
485   to represent the Mystery.[8]
OCCIDENT: Let's go, for anxiously I long to see
              exactly how this God of yours
              will give Himself as food to me.

     [*America, Occident, and Zeal sing:*]

              The Indies know
490   and do concede
              who is the true
              God of the Seeds.
              In loving tears
              which joy prolongs
495   we gladly sing
              our happy songs.
ALL: Blest be the day
              when I could see
              and worship the
500   great God of Seeds.

     [*They all exit, dancing and singing.*]

          ➤ END OF PERSPECTIVES: THE CONQUEST AND ITS AFTERMATH ➤

---

8. Note America's use of the first person in speaking of the "crude attempt" of the *loa;* perhaps a personal allusion to Sor Juana, who is herself, of course, "American."

BIBLIOGRAPHY

The Early Modern Period

Crosscurrents: The Vernacular Revolution
Vernacular Writing in South Asia • Dilip Chitre, trans., *Says Tuka: Selected Poetry of Tukaram,* 1991. • John Stratton Hawley and Mark Jurgensmeyer, trans., *Songs of the Saints of India,* 1988. • Linda Hess and Shukdev Singh, trans., *The Bijak of Kabir,* 1983. • Stuart McGregor, "The Progress of Hindi, Part 1: The Development of a Transregional Idiom," in *Literary Cultures in History,* ed. S. Pollock, 2003. • D. R. Nagaraj, "Critical Tensions in the History of Kannada Literary Culture." In S. Pollock, ed., *Literary Cultures in History,* 2003. • V. Narayana Rao. "Multiple Literary Cultures in Telugu: Court, Temple, and Village," in *Literary Cultures in History,* ed. S. Pollock, 2003. • Velcheru Narayana Rao and David Shulman, trans., *Classical Telugu Poetry,* 2002. • A. K. Ramanujan, Velcheru Narayana Rao, and David Shulman, trans., *When God is a Customer: Telugu Courtesan Songs by Ksetrayya and Others,* 1994. • Charlotte Vaudeville, *A Weaver Named Kabir: Selected Verses with a Detailed Biographical and Historical Introduction,* 1993. • Charlotte Vaudeville, *Myths, Saints, and Legends in Medieval India,* 1996.

Wu Cheng-en • Glen Dudbridge, *The Hsi-yu Chi. A Study of Antecedents to the Sixteenth-century Chinese Novel,* 1970. • C. T. Hsia, *The Classic Chinese Novel: A Critical Introduction,* 1968. • W. J. F. Jenner, trans., *Journey to the West: An Abridged Version,* 1994. • Lu Xun, *A Brief History of Chinese Fiction,* trans. Yang Hsien-yi and Gladys Yang, 1964. • Victor Mair, ed., *The Columbia History of Chinese Literature,* 2000. • Andrew Plaks, ed., *Chinese Narrative: Critical and Theoretical Essays,* 1977. • Andrew Plaks, *The Four Masterworks of the Ming Novel,* 1987. • David Rolston, ed., *How To Read the Chinese Novel,* 1990. • David Rolston, *Traditional Chinese Fiction and Fiction Commentary: Reading and Writing Between the Lines,* 1997. • Winston L. Y. Yang, *Classical Chinese Fiction: A Guide to Its Study and Appreciation, Essays and Bibliographies,* 1978. • Anthony C. Yu, trans. and ed., *The Journey to the West,* 1977–1983.

The Rise of the Vernacular in Europe • Roger Chartier, *The Cultural Uses of Print in Early Modern France,* 1987. • David Cressy, *Literacy and the Social Order: Reading and Writing in Tudor and Stuart England,* 1980. • Elizabeth L. Eisenstein, *The Printing Press as an Agent of Change,* 2 vols., 1979. • Paul Grendler, *Schooling in Renaissance Italy: Literacy and Learning, 1300–1600,* 1989. • Sandra Hindman, ed., *Printing the Written Word: The Social History of the Book, c. 1450–1520,* 1991. • R. A. Houston, *Literacy in Early Modern Europe: Culture and Education 1500–1800,* 1988. • Martin Lowry, *The World of Aldus Manutius: Business and Scholarship in Renaissance Venice,* 1979.

Biblical Translations • Betty Thomas Chambers, *Bibliography of French Bibles,* 2 vols., 1983–1994. • David Daniell, *William Tyndale: A Biography,* 2001. • T. H. Darlow and H. F. Moule, *Historical Catalogue of the Printed Editions of Holy Scripture in the Library of the British and Foreign Bible Society,* 4 vols., 1963. • Stephen Greenblatt, *Renaissance Self-Fashioning,* 1980. • F. W. Kent, "Sainted Mother, Magnificent Son: Lucrezia Tornabuoni and Lorenzo de'Medici," *Italian History and Culture* 3 (1997): 3–34. • T. H. L. Parker, *Calvin's Old Testament Commentaries,* 1993. • Eugene Rice, *Saint Jerome in the Renaissance,* 1985. • Bernardino de Sahagún, *Psalmodia Christiana,* trans. Arthur J. O. Anderson, 1993. • M. A. Screech, *Clément Marot: A Renaissance Poet Discovers the Gospel,* 1994. • Norman Shapiro, *Lyrics of the French Renaissance: Marot, Du Bellay, Ronsard,* 2002. • *Tyndale's New Testament,* ed. David Daniell, 1989.

Attacking and Defending the Vernacular Bible • Jerry Bentley, *Humanists and Holy Writ: New Testament Scholarship in the Renaissance,* 1983. • S. L. Greenslade, ed., *The West from the Reformation to the Present Day,* vol. 3, *The Cambridge History of the Bible,* 1963–1970. • Gerald Hammond, *The Making of the English Bible,* 1982. • G. W. H. Lampe, ed., *The West from the Fathers to the Reformation,* vol. 2, *The Cambridge History of the*

Bible, 1963–1970. • Jaroslav Pelikan, with Valerie R. Hotchkiss and David Priss, *The Reformation of the Bible/The Bible of the Reformation,* 1996.
Women and the Vernacular • Margaret Ferguson et al., eds., *Rewriting the Renaissance,* 1986. • Constance Jordan, *Renaissance Feminism: Literary Texts and Political Models,* 1990. • Joan Kelly, "Did Women Have a Renaissance?" in *Women, History, and Theory,* 1984. • Margaret King, *Women of the Renaissance,*

1991. • Margaret King and Albert Rabil Jr., eds., *Her Immaculate Hand: Selected Works by and About the Women Humanists of Quattrocento Italy,* 1983. • E. Ann Matter and John Coakley, eds., *Creative Women in Medieval and Early Modern Italy: A Religious and Artistic Renaissance,* 1994. • Suzanne Noffke, *Catherine of Siena: Vision Through a Distant Eye,* 1996. • Erika Rummel, ed., *Erasmus on Women,* 1996.

Early Modern Europe

General • Erich Auerbch, *Mimesis: The Representation of Reality in Western Literature,* 1953. • Leonard Barkan, *Unearthing the Past: Archaeology and Aesthetics in the Making of Renaissance Culture,* 2000. • Hans Baron, *The Crisis of the Early Italian Renaissance,* 1966. • Harry Berger, Jr., *Second World and Green World: Studies in Renaissance Fiction-Making,* 1988. • John Bossy, *Christianity in the West, 1400–1700,* 1985. • Karl Brandi. *The Emperor Charles V,* 1980. • Fernand Braudel, *The Mediterranean and the Mediterranean World in the Age of Philip II,* 2 vols., 1972. • Jerry Brotton, *Trading Territories: Mapping the Early Modern World,* 1997. • Peter Burke, *Popular Culture in Early Modern Europe,* 1978. • Douglas Bush, *Classical Influences in Renaissance Literature,* 1952. • Stanley Chojnacki, *Women and Men in Renaissance Venice,* 2000. • Louise Clubb, *Italian Drama in Shakespeare's Time,* 1989. • Marcia L. Colish, *Medieval Foundations of the Western Intellectual Tradition,* 1998. • Natalie Davis, *Society and Culture in Early Modern France,* 1976. • Robert M. Durling, *The Figure of the Poet in Renaissance Epic,* 1965. • J. H. Elliott, *The Old World and the New, 1492–1650,* 1970. • Eugenio Garin, *Italian Humanism: Philosophy and Civic Life in the Renaissance,* 1965. • Deno Geanakoplos, *Greek Scholars in Venice,* 1962. • Richard Goldthwaite, *The Building of Renaissance Florence,* 1981. • Thomas Greene, *The Light in Troy: Imitation and Discovery in Renaissance Poetry,* 1982. • Thomas Greene, *The Descent from Heaven: A Study in Epic Continuity,* 1963. • Timothy Hampton, *Writing from History: The Rhetoric of Exemplarity in Renaissance Literature,* 1990. • Francis Haskell, *Patrons and Painters,* 1963. • Henry Kamen, *Philip of Spain,* 1997. • Dale Kent, *The Rise of the Medici,* 1978. • Nannerl O. Keohane, *Philosophy and the State in France,* 1980. • Christiane Klapisch-Züber, *Women, Religion and Ritual in Early Modern Italy,* trans. Lydia G. Cochrane, 1985. • Jill Kraye, *The Cambridge Companion to Renaissance Humanism,* 1989. • Paul Oskar Kristeller,

Renaissance Thought and its Sources, 1979. • Frederic C. Lane, *Venice: A Maritime Republic,* 1973. • Frank Lestringant, *Mapping the Renaissance World: The Geographical Imagination in the Age of Discovery,* 1994. • Garrett Mattingly, *The Armada,* 1959. • Samuel Eliot Morison, *The European Discovery of America,* 1974. • Edward Muir, *Ritual in Early Modern Europe,* 1997. • David Norbrook, *Poetry and Politics in the English Renaissance,* 1984. • Erwin Panofsky, *Renaissance and Renascences in Western Art,* 1969. • Patricia Parker, *Inescapable Romance,* 1979. • Boies Penrose, *Travel and Discovery in the Renaissance, 1420–1620,* 1952. • Mary Elizabeth Perry, *Gender and Disorder in Early Modern Seville,* 1990. • J. G. A. Pocock, *The Machiavellian Moment,* 1975. • David Quint, *Epic and Empire,* 1993. • Albert Rabil, Jr., ed., *Renaissance Humanism: Foundations, Forms, and Legacy,* 3 vols., 1988. • Edward Rosen, *Copernicus and the Scientific Revolution,* 1984. • David B. Ruderman, *Jewish Thought and Scientific Discovery in Early Modern Europe,* 1995. • Londa Schiebinger, *The Mind Has No Sex? Women in the Origins of Modern Science,* 1989. • Charles B. Schmitt, *Studies in Renaissance Philosophy and Science,* 1981. • Robert Schwoebel, *The Shadow of the Crescent: The Renaissance Image of the Turks, 1453–1517,* 1973. • Robert W. Scribner, *Popular Culture and Popular Movements in Reformation Germany,* 1987. • Nancy Siraisi, *Medieval and Early Renaissance Medicine,* 1990. • Dava Sobel, *Galileo's Daughter,* 2000. • Jonathan D. Spence, *The Memory Palace of Matteo Ricci,* 1985. • Dora Thornton, *The Scholar in his Study: Ownership and Experience in Renaissance Italy,* 1998. • Richard Trexler, *Public Life in Renaissance Florence,* 1980. • Charles Trinkaus, *In Our Image and Likeness,* 1970. • Jane Tylus, *Writing and Vulnerablity in the Late Renaissance,* 1993. • William Wallace, *Galileo and His Sources,* 1984. • Merry Wiesner-Hanks, *Women and Gender in Early Modern Europe,* 1993. • Edgar Wind, *Pagan Myster-*

ies in the Renaissance, 1968. • Frances Yates, *The French Academies of the Sixteenth Century,* 1947.

Perspectives: Literature of Religious Crisis • Roland H. Bainton, *Erasmus of Christendom,* 1969. • Roland H. Bainton, *Here I Stand: A Life of Martin Luther,* 1950. • Jodi Bilinkoff, *The Avila of Saint Teresa,* 1989. • Marjorie O'Rourke Boyle, *Erasmus on Language and Method in Theology,* 1977. • Patrick Collinson, *The Elizabethan Puritan Movement,* 1967. • Carlos Eire, *War Against the Idols: The Reformation of Worship from Erasmus to Calvin,* 1986. • H. Outram Evennett, *The Spirit of the Counter-Reformation,* 1968. • Carlo Ginzburg, *The Cheese and the Worms: The Cosmos of a Sixteenth-Century Miller,* 1982. • Henry Kamen, *The Spanish Inquisition: An Historical Revision,* 1997. • Anthony Levi, *Renaissance and Reformation,* 2002. • Michael A. Mullett, *The Catholic Reformation,* 1999. • John O'Malley, *The First Jesuits,* 1993. • Steven Ozment, *The Age of Reform: 1250–1550,* 1989. • E. Allison Peers, *Studies of the Spanish Mystics,* vol. I, 1927. • Lewis W. Spitz, *The Protestant Reformation, 1517–1559,* 1985. • Lewis W. Spitz, *Luther and German Humanism,* 1996. • Tom Scott, *Thomas Muntzer: Theology and Revolution in the German Reformation,* 1989. • R. W. Swanson, *Religion and Devotion in Europe, c. 1215–c.1515,* 1995. • Lee Palmer Wandel, *Voracious Idols and Violent Hands,* 1995. • Alison Weber, *Teresa of Avila and the Rhetoric of Femininity,* 1990.

Perspectives: Lyric Sequences and Self-Definition • Glauco Cambon, *Michelangelo's Poetry: Fury of Form,* 1985. • Heather Dubrow, *Echoes of Desire: English Petrarchism and Its Counterdiscourses,* 1995. • Anne Ferry, *The Inward Language: Sonnets of Wyatt, Sidney, Shakespeare, and Donne,* 1983. • Samuel Fiszman, ed., *The Polish Renaissance in Its European Context,* 1988. • Joseph Gibaldi, "Vittoria Colonna: Child, Woman, and Poet," in *Women Writers of the Renaissance and Reformation,* ed. Katharina Wilson, 1987. • Roland Greene, *Post-Petrarchism: Origins and Innovations of the Western Lyric Sequence,* 1991. • Ann Rosalind Jones, *The Currency of Eros: Women's Love Lyric in Europe, 1540–1620,* 1990. • William Kennedy, *Authorizing Petrarch,* 1994. • Stephen Minta, ed., *Petrarch and Petrarchism: The English and French Traditions,* 1980. • Anne Lake Prescott, *French Poets and the English Renaissance,* 1978. • Ernest Hatch Wilkins, *The In-*

vention of the Sonnet and Other Studies in Italian Literature, 1959.

Giovanni Boccaccio • Thomas Bergin, *Boccaccio,* 1982. • Vittore Branca, *Boccaccio: The Man and His Works,* 1976. • Pier Massimo Forni, *Adventures in Speech: Rhetoric and Narration in Boccaccio's Decameron,* 1996. • Victoria Kirkham, *The Sign of Reason in Boccaccio's Fiction,* 1993. • Millicent Marcus, *An Allegory of Form: Literary Self-Consciousness in the Decameron,* 1979. • Giuseppe Mazzotta, *The World at Play in Boccaccio's "Decameron,"* 1986. • Aldo Scaglione, *Nature and Love in the Middle Ages,* 1963. • Daniel Williman, ed., *The Black Death: The Impact of the Fourteenth-Century Plague,* 1982.

Anne Bradstreet • Patricia Caldwell, "Why our First Poet was a Woman: Bradstreet and the Birth of an American Poetic Voice," *Prospects* 13, 1988. • Pattie Cowell and Ann Stanford, *Critical Essays on Anne Bradstreet,* 1983. • David S. Reynolds, *Faith in Fiction: The Emergence of Religious Literature in America,* 1981.

Luis Vaz de Camões • C. M. Bowra, "Camões and the Epic of Portugal," in *From Virgil to Milton,* 1945. • Henry Hart, *Luis de Camões and the Epic of the Lusiads,* 1962. • Alfred Hower and Richard A. Preto-Rodas, eds., *Empire in Transition: The Portuguese World in the Time of Camões,* 1985. • *Journal of the First Voyage of Vasco da Gama,* trans. E. G. Ravenstein, 1898. • David Quint, *Epic and Empire,* 1993. • Peter Russell, *Prince Henry "the Navigator": A Life,* 2000. • A. J. R. Russell-Wood, *A World on the Move: The Portuguese in Africa, Asia, and America, 1415–1808,* 1992. • Sanjay Subrahmanyam, *The Career and Legend of Vasco da Gama,* 1997.

Miguel de Cervantes • Jean Canavaggio, *Cervantes,* 1990. • Anne J. Cruz, *Discourses of Poverty: Social Reform and the Picaresque Novel in Early Modern Spain,* 1999. • Ruth El Saffar, *Critical Essays on Cervantes,* 1986. • Alban Forcione, *Cervantes and the Humanist Vision,* 1982. • Maria Antonia Garcés, *Cervantes in Algiers: A Captive's Tale,* 2002. • Timothy Hampton, *Writing from History,* 1990. • Steven D. Hutchinson, *Cervantine Journeys,* 1992. • Carroll B. Johnson, *Don Quixote: The Quest for Modern Fiction,* 1990. • Carroll B. Johnson, *Cervantes and the Material World,* 2000. • Walter Kaiser, *Praisers of Folly,* 1963. • Georg Lukács, *Theory of the Novel,* 1971. • Melveena McKendrick, *Cervantes,* 1980. • Lowry Nelson, Jr., *Cervantes: A Collection* *of Critical Essays*, 1969. ● Edwin Williamson, *The Half-Way House of Fiction: Don Quixote and Arthurian Romance*, 1984.

John Donne ● R. C. Bald, *John Donne: A Life*, 1970. ● John Carey, *John Donne: Life, Mind, and Art*, 1981. ● T. S. Eliot, "The Metaphysical Poets," in *Selected Essays of T.S. Eliot*, 1964. ● Barbara Keifer Lewalski, *Protestant Poetics and the Seventeenth-Century Religious Lyric*, 1979. ● Arthur F. Marotti, *John Donne, Coterie Poet*, 1986. ● Louis L. Martz, *The Poetry of Meditation*, 1962. ● Earl Miner, *The Metaphysical Mode from Donne to Cowley*, 1969. ● John R. Roberts, ed., *Essential Articles for the Study of John Donne's Poetry*, 1975. ● Peter Desa Wiggins, *Donne, Castiglione, and the Poetry of Courtliness*, 2000.

Lope de Vega ● Anthony Cascardi, *Ideologies of History in the Spanish Golden Age*, 1997. ● Walter Cohen, *Drama of a Nation: Public Theatre in Renaissance England and Spain*, 1985. ● Melveena McKendrick, *Women and Society in the Spanish Drama of the Golden Age*, 1974. ● Melveena McKendrick, *Playing the King: Lope de Vega and the Limits of Conformity*, 2000. ● Dian Fox, *Refiguring the Hero: From Peasant to Noble in Lope de Vega and Calderón de la Barca*, 1991. ● Catherine Swietlicki, "Speech and Writing in *Fuenteovejuna*," *Hispanic Review* 60, 1992.

Marguerite de Navarre ● P. A. Chilton, trans., *The Heptameron*, 1984. ● Samuel Putnam, *Marguerite de Navarre*, 1935. ● Patricia Cholakian, *Rape and Writing in the Heptameron of Marguerite de Navarre*, 1991. ● Barry Collett, *A Long and Troubled Pilgrimage*, 2000. ● John D. Lyons and Mary B. McKinley, eds., *Critical Tales: New Studies of the Heptameron and Early Modern Culture*, 1993. ● Dora Polachek, ed., *Heroic Virtue, Comic Infidelity*, 1993. ● Marcel Tetel, *Marguerite de Navarre's Heptameron: Themes, Language, and Structure*, 1973.

Niccolò Machiavelli ● Albert Ascoli and Victoria Kahn, eds., *Machiavelli and the Discourse of Literature*, 1993. ● Sebastian de Grazia, *Machiavelli in Hell*, 1989. ● Felix Gilbert, *Machiavelli and Guicciardini: Politics and History in Sixteenth-Century Florence*, 1965. ● Thomas Greene, "The End of Discourse in Machiavelli's *Prince*," in *Literary Theory/Renaissance Texts*, eds. Patricia Parker and David Quint, 1986. ● J. R. Hale, *Machiavelli and Renaissance Italy*, 1972. ● John Najemy, "Machiavelli and the Medici," *Renaissance Quarterly*, 1982: 551–76. ● Hannah Pitkin, *Fortune Is a Woman: Gender and Politics in the Thought of Niccolò Machiavelli*, 1984. ● J. G. A. Pocock, *The Machiavellian Moment*, 1975. ● Wayne Rebhorn, *Foxes and Lions: Machiavelli's Confidence Men*, 1988. ● Roberto Ridolfi, *The Life of Niccolò Machiavelli*, trans. Cecil Grayson, 1963. ● Quentin Skinner, *Machiavelli*, 1981.

John Milton ● Arthur Barker, *Milton and the Puritan Dilemma, 1641–1660*, 1942. ● Cedric C. Brown, *John Milton: A Literary Life*, 1995. ● Dennis Danielson, ed., *The Cambridge Companion to Milton*, 1989. ● William Empson, *Milton's God*, 1961. ● Stanley Fish, *Surprised by Sin: The Reader in Paradise Lost*, 1967. ● Christopher Hill, *Milton and the English Revolution*, 1977. ● C. S. Lewis, *A Preface to Paradise Lost*, 1942. ● Mary Nyquist and Margaret Ferguson, eds., *Re-membering Milton: Essays on the Texts and Traditions*, 1988. ● William Riley Parker, *Milton: A Biography*, 2 vols., 1968. ● C. A. Patrides, *Milton and the Christian Tradition*, 1966. ● B. Rajan, *Paradise Lost and the Seventeenth-Century Reader*, 1962. ● Stella Revard, *The War in Heaven*, 1980. ● James Turner, *One Flesh: Paradisal Marriage and Sexual Relations in the Age of Milton*, 1987. ● Joan Webber, *Milton and his Epic Tradition*, 1979.

Michel de Montaigne ● Harold Bloom, ed., *Montaigne's "Essays,"* 1987. ● Donald Frame, *Montaigne: A Biography*, 1965. ● Hugo Friedrich, *Montaigne*, 1968. ● Fredi Chiappelli, ed., *First Images of America: The Impact of the New World on the Old*, 2 vols., 1976. ● George Hoffmann, *Montaigne's Career*, 1998. ● Glyn Norton, *Montaigne and the Introspective Mind*, 1975. ● David Quint, *Montaigne and the Quality of Mercy*, 1998. ● R. A. Sayce, *Essays of Montaigne*, 1972. ● Jean Starobinski, *Montaigne in Motion*, 1985.

Thomas More ● Harry Berger, Jr., *Second World and Green World: Studies in Renaissance Fiction-Making*, 1988. ● John Guy, *Thomas More*, 2000. ● J. H. Hexter, *The Vision of Politics on the Eve of the Reformation*, 1973. ● J. H. Hexter, *More's "Utopia": The Biography of an Idea*, 1952. ● George M. Logan, *The Meaning of More's Utopia*, 1983. ● Richard Marius, *Thomas More: A Biography*, 1984. ● Louis L. Martz, *Thomas More: The Search for the Inner Man*, 1992. ● J. B. Trapp, *Erasmus, Colet and More: The Early Tudor Humanists and their Books*, 1991.

Francis Petrarch • Hans Baron, *From Petrarch to Leonardo Bruni,* 1968. • Thomas Bergin, *Petrarch,* 1970. • Morris Bishop, *Petrarch and his World,* 1963. • Robert M. Durling, "The Ascent of Mount Ventoux and the Crisis of Allegory," *Italian Quarterly* 18, 1974: 7–28. • John Freccero, "The Fig Tree and the Laurel," *Diacritics* 5, 1975: 34–40. • Giuseppe Mazzotta, *The Worlds of Petrarch,* 1993. • Sara Sturm-Maddox, *Petrarch's Laurels,* 1992. • Charles Trinkaus, *The Poet as Philosopher,* 1979. • Marguerite Waller, *Petrarch's Poetics and Literary History,* 1980. • E. H. Wilkins, *Life of Petrarch,* 1961. • E. H. Wilkins, *The Making of the "Canzoniere,"* 1951.

François Rabelais • Mikhail Bakhtin, *Rabelais and his World,* 1968. • Terence Cave, *The Cornucopian Text: Problems of Writing in The French Renaissance,* 1979. • Barbara Bowen, *Enter Rabelais, Laughing,* 1998. • Edwin Duval, *The Design of Rabelais's "Pantagruel,"* 1991. • Thomas Greene, *Rabelais: A Study in Comic Courage,* 1970. • Florence Weinberg, *The Wine and the Will: Rabelais's Bacchic Christianity,* 1972.

William Shakespeare • Jean Wilson, *The Shakespeare Legacy,* 1995. • Leslie Fiedler, *The Stranger in Shakespeare,* 1972. • Charles Frey, "The Tempest and the New World," *Shakespeare Quarterly* 30, 1979. • Northrop Frye, *A Natural Perspective,* 1965. • Stephen Greenblatt, *Marvellous Possessions: The Wonder of the New World,* 1991. • Stephen Greenblatt, "Learning to Curse," in *First Images of America,* ed. Fredi Chiappelli, 1976. • Donna Hamilton, *Virgil and The Tempest: The Politics of Imitation,* 1990. • D. G. James, *The Dream of Prospero,* 1967. • Jeffrey Knapp, *An Empire Nowhere: England, America, and Literature from "Utopia" to "The Tempest,"* 1994. • James Schiffer, ed., *Shakespeare's Sonnets: Critical Essays,* 1999. • Murray M. Schwartz and Coppélia Kahn, eds., *Representing Shakespeare,* 1980. • Bruce Smith, *Homosexual Desire in Shakespeare's England,* 1991. • Stephen Orgel, "Prospero's Wife," in *Representing the English Renaissance,* ed. Stephen Greenblatt, 1988. • Alden T. and Virginia Vaughan, *Shakespeare's Caliban: A Cultural History,* 1991. • Helen Vendler, *The Art of Shakespeare's Sonnets,* 1997.

Mesoamerica: Before Columbus and After Cortés

General • Joan D. Barghusen, *The Aztecs,* 2000. • Robert Carmack, *The Legacy of Mesoamerica,* 1996. • Davíd Carrasco, *Quetzalcoatl and the Irony of Empire,* 1982. • Inga Clendinen, *Aztecs: An Interpretation,* 1991. • Michael D. Coe, *The Maya,* 1987. • Michael D. Coe, *The Maya Scribe and His World,* 1973. • David Damrosch. "The Pope's Blowgun," in *What Is World Literature?,* 2003. • Nancy M. Farriss, *Maya Society Under Colonial Rule: The Collective Enterprise of Survival,* 1984. • Enrique Florescano, *Memory, Myth, and Time in Mexico,* 1994. • Gary H. Gossen and Miguel León-Portilla, eds., *South and Meso-American Native Spirituality,* 1993. • Ross Hassig, *Time, History, and Belief in Aztec and Colonial Mexico,* 2001. • Alvin M. Josephy, ed., *America in 1492: The World of the Indian Peoples Before the Arrival of Columbus,* 1993. • Charles A. F. P. Maza, *Pre-Columbian Socio-Political Structure in the Valley of Mexico,* 1997. • Anthony Pagden, *European Encounters with the New World,* 1994. • Miguel León-Portilla, *The Aztec Image of Self and Society,* 1992. • Miguel León-Portilla, *The Broken Spears: The Aztec Account of the Conquest of Mexico,* 1992. • Miguel León-Portilla, ed., *Native Mesoamerican Spirituality,* 1980. • Bernardino de Sahagún, *The Florentine Codex: General History of the Things of New Spain,* Arthur J.O. Anderson and C.E. Dibble, eds., 1950–1982. • Mary Miller and Karl Taube, *The Gods and Symbols of Ancient Mexico and the Maya,* 1993.

Perspectives: The Conquest and Its Aftermath • Marvin Lunenfield, ed., *1492, Discovery, Invasion, Encounter: Sources and Interpretation,* 1991. • Stuart B. Schwartz, ed., *Victors and Vanquished: Spanish and Nahua Views of the Conquest of Mexico,* 2000. • Patricia Seed, *Ceremonies of Possession in Europe's Conquest of the New World, 1492–1640,* 1995. • Tzvetan Todorov, *The Conquest of America,* 1983. • David M. Traboulay, *Columbus and Las Casas: The Conquest and Christianization of America, 1492–1566,* 1994. • Michael Wood, *Conquistadors,* 2000.

Christopher Columbus • Paula Gunn Allen, *Columbus and Beyond: Views from Native Americans,* 1992. • Miles H. Davidson, *Columbus Then and Now: A Life Reexamined,* 1997. • Anthony Disney, ed., *Columbus and the*

Consequences of 1492, 1994. ● Zvi Dor-Ner, *Columbus and the Age of Discovery*, 1991. ● Roland Greene, *Unrequited Conquests: Love and Empire in the Colonial Americas*, 1999. ● Peter Hulme, *Colonial Encounters: Europe and the Native Caribbean, 1492–1797*, 1986. ● Robert Hume, *Christopher Columbus and the European Discovery of America*, 1992. ● Djelal Kadir, *Columbus at the Ends of the Earth*, 1992. ● Franklin W. Knight, *Christopher Columbus: Myth, Metaphor and Metamorphosis in the Atlantic World, 1492–1992*, 1991. ● Ilaria Caraci Luzzana, *The Puzzling Hero: Studies on Christopher Columbus and the Culture of His Age*, 2002. ● James R. McGovern, ed., *The World of Columbus*, 1992. ● William L. H. Moon, *Columbus in the Americas*, 2002. ● Samuel Eliot Morrison, *Admiral of the Ocean Sea*, 2 vols., 1942. ● John Yewell, Chris Dodge and Jan DeSirey, eds., *Confronting Columbus*, 1992. ● Marguerita Zamora, *Reading Columbus*, 1993.

Hernando Ruíz de Alarcón ● J. Richard Andrews and Ross Hassig, eds., *Treatise on the Heathen Superstitions that Today Live Among the Indians Native to this New Spain, 1692*, 1984. ● Michael Coe and Gordon Whitaker, *Aztec Sorcerers in Seventeenth-Century Mexico: The Treatise on Superstitions of Hernando Ruíz de Alarcón*, 1982.

Sor Juana Inéz de la Cruz ● Electa Arenal and Stacey Schlau, eds., *Untold Sisters: Hispanic Nuns in their Own Works*, 1989. ● Jean Franco, *Plotting Women: Gender and Representation in Mexico*, 1989. ● James Henderson, *Ten Notable Women of Latin America*, 1978. ● Juana Inéz de la Cruz, *A Woman of Genius: The Intellectual Autobiography of Sor Juana Inés de la Cruz*, 1982. ● Pamela Kirk, *Sor Juana Inéz de la Cruz: Religion, Art, and Feminism*, 1998. ● Irving Leonard, *Baroque Times in Old Mexico*, 1966. ● Stephanie Merrim, ed., *Feminist Perspectives on Sor Juana Inéz de la Cruz*, 1999. ● Stephanie Merrim, *Early Modern Women's Writing and Sor Juana Inéz de la Cruz*, 1999. ● Octavio Paz, *Sor Juana, or, The Traps of Faith*, 1988. ● Ruth S. El Saffar, *Rapture Encaged: The Suppression of the Feminine in Western Culture*, 1994. ● George Tavard, *Juana Inés de la Cruz and the Theology of Beauty*, 1991.

Bartolomé de las Casas ● Juan Friede and Benjamin Keen, eds., *Bartolomé de las Casas in History: Toward an Understanding of the Man and His Work*, 1971. ● Lewis Hanke, *All Mankind Is One: A Study of the Disputation Between Bartolomé de Las Casas and Juan Ginés de Sepúlveda in 1550*, 1994. ● Lewis Hanke, *Bartolomé de las Casas*, 1951. ● Benjamin Keen, *Essays in the Intellectual History of Colonial Latin America*, 1998. ● Henry Raup Wagner and Helen Rand Parish, *The Life and Writings of Bartolomé de las Casas*, 1967.

Bernal Díaz del Castillo ● Herbert Cerwin, *Bernal Díaz: Historian of the Conquest*, 1963. ● Charles Gibson, *The Black Legend: Anti-Spanish Attitudes in the Old World and the New*, 1971. ● Lewis Hanke, *All Mankind is One*, 1970. ● Bernal Díaz del Castillo, *The Discovery and Conquest of Mexico*, 1956.

Bernardino de Sahagún ● Lawrence Walden Browne, *Sahagún and the Modern Age*, 1995. ● Munro S. Edmonson, ed., *Sixteenth-Century Mexico: The Work of Sahagún*, 1974. ● J. Jorge Klor de Alva, et al., eds., *The Work of Bernardino de Sahagún, Pioneer Ethnographer of Sixteenth-Century Aztec Mexico*, 1988. ● Miguel León-Portilla, *Bernardino de Sahagún, First Anthropologist*, 2002. ● Bernardino de Sahagún, *The Florentine Codex: General History of the Things of New Spain*, 1950–1982. ● Bernardino de Sahagún, *Psalmodia Christiana*, 1993. ● Luis Villoro, *Sahagún, or, The Limits of the Discovery of the Other*, 1989.

Popul Vuh: The Mayan Council Book ● Michael D. Coe, *Lords of the Underworld*, 1978. ● Jack J. Himelblau, *Quiché Worlds in Creation: The Popol Vuh as a Narrative Work of Art*, 1989. ● Laurel Ann Sherwood, *Maize as Mediator: A Structural Analysis of the Popol Vuh*, 1989. ● Dennis Tedlock, ed., *Popol Vuh: The Mayan Book of the Dawn of Life*, 1988. ● Dennis Tedlock, *Writing and Reflection Among the Maya*, 1989.

Songs of the Aztec Nobility ● John Bierhorst, ed., *Cantares Mexicanos, Songs of the Aztecs*, 1985. ● David Damrosch, "The Aesthetics of Conquest: Aztec Poetry Before and After Cortés," *Representations* 33, 1991. ● T. J. Knab, ed., *Scattering of Jades: Stories, Poems, and Prayers of the Aztecs*, 1994. ● Miguel León-Portilla, *Fifteen Poets of the Aztec World*, 1992. ● Irene Nicholson, *Firefly in the Night: A Study of Ancient Mexican Poetry and Symbolism*, 1959.

CREDITS

ILLUSTRATION CREDITS

FONTS CREDIT